SOUTHERN CROSS

Southern Cross

Civil Law and Common Law
in South Africa

REINHARD ZIMMERMANN

and

DANIEL VISSER

CLARENDON PRESS · OXFORD
1996

Oxford University Press, Great Clarendon Street, Oxford OX2 6DP

Oxford New York
Athens Auckland Bangkok Bogata Bombay
Buenos Aires Calcutta Cape Town Dar es Salaam
Delhi Florence Hong Kong Istanbul Karachi
Kuala Lumpur Madras Madrid Melbourne
Mexico City Nairobi Paris Singapore
Taipei Tokyo Toronto
and associated companies in
Berlin Ibadan

Oxford is a trade mark of Oxford University Press

Published in the United States
by Oxford University Press Inc., New York

British Library Cataloguing in Publication Data
Data available

Library of Congress Cataloging in Publication Data
Zimmermann, Reinhard.
Southern cross : civil law and common law in South Africa /
Reinhard Zimmermann and Daniel Visser.
p.   cm.
Includes bibliographical references.
1. Roman–Dutch law—South Africa—History.   2. Common law—South
Africa—History.   I. Zimmermann, Reinhard, 1952–   .   II. Title.
KTL469.V57   1996
340.5'7'0968—dc20   96–8698
ISBN 0–19–826087–3

1 3 5 7 9 10 8 6 4 2

Typeset by Hope Services (Abingdon) Ltd.
Printed in Great Britain
on acid-free paper by
Biddles Ltd., Guildford and King's Lynn

Preface

'Of all the constellations that stud the sky of the Southern hemisphere, there is none that more strikes a stranger than the Southern Cross' (Philip Henry Gosse, *The Oceans*, London, 1849, p. 178). Equally striking for the stranger is the cross between civil law and common law as it exists today in Southern Africa. The Dutch settlers of the 17th century brought with them the European *ius commune* to the Cape of Good Hope; and the British judges, originally sent out to the 19th century Colony to 'measure out a scanty justice to squalid savages' (cf. (1992) 109 *SALJ* 301) eventually managed to graft English concepts, rules and precedents upon the law of Voet and Vinnius. South African private law has thus been shaped by the vicissitudes of European colonial ambitions and their local aftermath; but, in the process, it has acquired a composite character—an identity as striking and distinctive as the constellation on the Southern sky.

The intellectual objectives of the present attempt to describe the emergence of South Africa's mixed legal system are set out in the Introduction. All that remains here is to thank those who have assisted with the production of the book. In Cape Town, Lisa Duminy and Dale Hutchison gave valuable advice on matters of style. In Regensburg, Coenie de Villiers and Philip Sutherland carefully went through all manuscripts in order to implement the editorial conventions and to prepare the indices. In Oxford, Richard Hart and his team lent their whole-hearted support to the project. To all of them we are very grateful. We are equally grateful to our secretaries, Gabriele Schmitt and Pat Richardson, for their superb professional commitment and their unfailing personal loyalty.

Reinhard Zimmermann and Daniel Visser,
Regensburg/Cape Town, May 1996

Summary of Contents

Part VI

Property Law

Part VII

Fiduciary Transactions

Table of Contents

INTRODUCTION—SOUTH AFRICAN LAW AS A MIXED
LEGAL SYSTEM

by Reinhard Zimmermann and Daniel Visser

CHAPTER 1—ROMAN-DUTCH LAW IN ITS SOUTH AFRICAN HISTORICAL CONTEXT

by Eduard Fagan

CHAPTER 2—AFRICAN LAND—A HISTORY OF DISPOSSESSION

by T.W. Bennett

CHAPTER 3—THE ARCHITECTS OF THE MIXED LEGAL SYSTEM

by Stephen D. Girvin

CHAPTER 4—THE INTERACTION OF SUBSTANTIVE LAW AND PROCEDURE

by H.J. Erasmus

CHAPTER 8—VOIDABLE CONTRACTS

by Gerhard Lubbe

CHAPTER 11—PURCHASE AND SALE

by Jan Lotz

CHAPTER 12—EMPLOYMENT RELATIONS

by Barney Jordaan

CHAPTER 15—NEGOTIABLE INSTRUMENTS

by Charl Hugo

CHAPTER 16—UNJUSTIFIED ENRICHMENT

by Daniel Visser

CHAPTER 17—AQUILIAN LIABILITY I (NINETEENTH-CENTURY)

by Annél van Aswegen

CHAPTER 18—AQUILIAN LIABILITY II (TWENTIETH-CENTURY)

by Dale Hutchison

CHAPTER 19—THE PROTECTION OF PERSONALITY RIGHTS

by Jonathan M. Burchell

CHAPTER 20—OWNERSHIP

by J.R.L. Milton

CHAPTER 21—ORIGINAL ACQUISITION OF OWNERSHIP

by C.G. van der Merwe

CHAPTER 22—TRANSFER OF OWNERSHIP

by David L. Carey Miller

CHAPTER 25—POSSESSION

by Duard Kleyn

CHAPTER 26—TRUST

by Tony Honoré

List of Contributors

T.W. Bennett, BA, LL B, Ph.D., is Professor of Public Law in the University of Cape Town.

Jonathan M. Burchell, BA, LL B, LL M, Ph.D., is Professor of Law in the University of Natal, Pietermaritzburg.

David L. Carey Miller, BA, LL B, LL M, Ph.D., is Professor of Law in the University of Aberdeen.

Alfred Cockrell, BA, LL B, MA, is Professor of Law in the University of the Witwatersrand, Johannesburg.

M.J. de Waal, B.Comm., LL B, LL M, LL D, is Professor of Private Law in the University of Stellenbosch.

H.J. Erasmus, MA, LL B, D.Litt. et Phil., is Emeritus Professor of Law in the University of Stellenbosch.

Eduard Fagan, BA Hons., LL B, Ph.D., is Senior Lecturer in Public Law in the University of Cape Town.

C.F. Forsyth, B.Sc., LL B, Ph.D., is Lecturer in Law in the University of Cambridge and Fellow and Director of Studics in Law at Robinson College.

Stephen D. Girvin, BA, LL B, LL M, Ph.D., is Lecturer in Law in the University of Nottingham.

Tony Honoré, QC, DCL, Hon. LL D, FBA, was formerly Regius Professor of Civil Law in the University of Oxford.

Charl Hugo, BA, LL B, LL M, is Senior Lecturer in Mercantile Law in the University of Stellenbosch.

Dale Hutchison, B.Comm., LL B, Ph.D., is Professor of Private Law in the University of Cape Town.

David J. Joubert, BA, LL B, LL D, is Professor of Roman-Dutch Law in the University of Pretoria and Dean of the Faculty of Law.

Barney Jordaan, BA, LL B, LL D, is Professor of Mercantile Law in the University of Stellenbosch.

Duard Kleyn, BA, LL B, LL D, is Professor of Roman Law in the University of Pretoria.

Carole Lewis, BA, LL B, LL M, is Professor of Law in the University of the Witwatersrand, Johannesburg, and Dean of the Faculty of Law.

Jan Lotz, BA, LL B is Emeritus Professor of Private Law in the University of South Africa, Pretoria.

Gerhard Lubbe, BA, LL B, LL M, is Professor of Private Law in the University of Stellenbosch.

J.R.L. Milton, BA, LL M, Ph.D., is James Scott Wylie Professor of Law in the University of Natal, Pietermaritzburg.

Annél van Aswegen, BA, LL B, LL D, is Professor of Private Law in the University of South Africa, Pretoria.

C.G. van der Merwe, BA, LL B, BA Hons., BCL, LL D, is Professor of Private Law in the University of Stellenbosch.

Derek van der Merwe, BA, LL B, LL D, is Professor of Law in the Rand Afrikaans University, Johannesburg, and Dean of the Faculty of Law.

JP van Niekerk, BA, LL B, LL M, LL M, is Professor of Mercantile Law in the University of South Africa, Pretoria.

Daniel Visser, B.Iur., LL B, LL D, Dr Iur., is Professor of Private Law in the University of Cape Town and Dean of the Faculty of Law.

Reinhard Zimmermann, Dr Iur., LL D, is Professor of Private Law, Roman Law and Comparative Law in the University of Regensburg and Dean of the Faculty of Law.

List of Abbreviations

A	Appellate Division	SA
AC	Law Reports, Appeal cases; Appeal Court	Eng
ACJ	Acting Chief Justice	SA
AD	Law Reports, Appellate Division	SA
Ad & El	Adolphus and Ellis's Reports, King's and Queen's Bench	Eng
A^{i}A^i	*Auli Agerii*	Roman
AJ	Acting Judge	SA
AJA	Acting Judge of Appeal	SA
AJP	Acting Judge President	SA
All ER	All England Law Reports	Eng
ALR	American Law Reports Annotated	US
A°A°	*Aulo Agerio*	Roman
Art.	Article	
Atk	Atkyn's Reports, Chancery	Eng
Aus	Australia	
B & Ald	Barnewall and Alderson's Reports, King's Bench	Eng
B & C	Barnewall and Cresswell's Reports, King's Bench	Eng
BA	Boputatswana Appeal Court	SA
BCLR	Butterworths Constitutional Law Reports	SA
Beav	Beavan's Reports, Rolls Court	Eng
BGB	*Bürgerliches Gesetzbuch*	Ger
Bing NC	Bingham's New Cases, Common Pleas	Eng
Bpk	Beperk (= Limited)	SA
Bro CC	W. Brown's Chancery Reports	Eng
Bro PC	J. Brown's Cases in Parliament	Eng
Buch	Buchanan's Reports, Cape Supreme Court	SA
Buch AC	Buchanan's Appeal Cases, Cape Appeal Court	SA
Burr	Burrow's Reports, King's Bench	Eng
C	Cape Provincial Division	SA
CA	Court of Appeal	Eng
CB	Common Bench Reports	Eng
CBNS	Common Bench Reports (New Series)	Eng
CC	Close Corporation	SA
Can	Canada	
Cases T Talbot	Cases in Equity Temp Talbot	Eng
Ch	Law Reports, Chancery Division	Eng
Ch App	Law Reports, Chancery Appeals	Eng
Chan Cas	Cases in Chancery	Eng

ChD	Law Reports, Chancery Division	Eng
CILSA	*The Comparative and International Law Journal of Southern Africa*	SA
CIR	Commissioner for Inland Revenue	
CJ	Chief Justice	SA
Cl & Fin	Clark and Finnely's Reports, House of Lords	Eng
CLR	Commonwealth Law Reports	Aus
Co	Company	
Co Rep	Coke's Reports	Eng
Co-op	Co-operative	
Coll	Collyer's Reports, Chancery	SA
Comyns	Comyns' Reports, King's Bench, Commmon Pleas, and Exchequer	Eng
Coop G	G. Cooper's Reports, Chancery	Eng
Corp	Corporation	
Cowp	Cowper's Reports, King's Bench	Eng
Cox	Cox's Equity Cases	Eng
CP	Common Pleas Division	Eng
CPD	Law Reports, Common Pleas Division	Eng
CPD	Reports of the Cape Provincial Division	SA
CTR	Cape Times Reports	SA
D	Durban and Coast Local Division	SA
D.	*Digesta*	
DC	Divisional Court	
De G & J	De Gex and Jones's Reports, Chancery Division	Eng
De G & Sm	De Gex and Smale's Reports, Chancery	Eng
De G F & J	De Gex, Fisher and Jones's Reports	Eng
De G J & S	De Gex, Jones and Smith's Chancery Reports	Eng
De G M & G	De Gex, Macnaghten and Gordon's Reports, Chancery	Eng
DLR	Dominion Law Reports	Can
DM	Diamond Mining	
E	Eastern Cape (Local) Division	SA
E & B	Ellis and Blackburn's Reports, Queen's Bench	Eng
E & E	Ellis and Ellis's Reports, Queen's Bench	Eng
E B & E	Ellis, Blackburn and Ellis's Reports, Queen's Bench	Eng
East	East's Reports, King's Bench	Eng
EDC	Reports of the Eastern Districts Courts	SA
Eden	Eden's Reports, Chancery	Eng
EDL	Reports of the Eastern Districts Local Division	SA
Edms	Eiendoms (= Proprietary)	SA
Eins	Eiendoms (= Proprietary)	SA
El & Bl	Ellis and Blackburn's Reports, Queens' Bench	SA

Eng	English	
Eq	Equity Cases	Eng
Eq Cas Abr	Abridgement of Cases in Equity	Eng
ER	English Reports	Eng
Ex D	Law Reports, Exchequer Division	Eng
Exch	Exchequer; Law Reports Exchequer	Eng
FC	Federal Supreme Court of Southern Rhodesia	ZB
Foord	Foord's Reports, Cape Supreme Court	SA
F 2d	Federal Reporter Second Series	US
Ger	German	
GH	Government House Records	SA
Giff	Giffard's Reports, Chancery	Eng
Gov	Government	
Gregorowski	Gregorowski's Reports, Orange Free State High Court	SA
GW	Griqualand West Local Division	SA
GWL	Reports of the Griqualand West Local Division	SA
Hagg	Haggard's Reports, Admiralty	Eng
HC SR	High Court of Southern Rhodesia	ZB
HCG	Reports of the High Court of Griqualand	SA
HL	House of Lords	Eng
HL Cas	Clark's Reports, House of Lords	Eng
Hy Bl	Henry Blackstone's Reports, Common Pleas	Eng
ICJ	International Court of Justice	
Inc	Incorporated	
J	Judge	
J & H	Johnson and Hemming's Reports, Chancery	Eng
JA	Judge of Appeal	
Jac	Jacob's Reports, Chancery	Eng
Jac & W	Jacob and Walker's Reports, Chancery	Eng
JLS	*Journal of Legal Studies*	
JP	Judge President	SA
KB	King's Bench; Law Reports King's Bench	Eng
Ko-op	Ko-operatiewe (= Co-operative)	
Kotzé	Kotzé's Reports, Transvaal High Court	SA
LC	Lord Chancellor	Eng
LJ	*Law Journal*	
LJ	Lord Justice	Eng
LJ (NS) CP	Law Journal (New Series) Common Pleas	Eng
LJ Ch	Law Journal, Chancery	Eng
LJ CP	Law Journal, Common Pleas	
LJ Exch	Law Journal, Exchequer	Eng
LJ QB	Law Journal, Queen's Bench	Eng

Lloyd's Reports	Lloyd's List Reports	Eng
LQR	*Law Quarterly Review*	*Eng*
LR	Law Report	
LR	*Law Review*	
LT	Law Times Reports	Eng
Ltd	Limited	
M & W	Meeson & Welsby's Reports, Exchequer	Eng
Madd	Maddock's Reports, Chancery	Eng
Menz	Menzie's Reports, Cape Supreme Court	SA
MLR	*Modern Law Review*	Eng
Mod	Modern Reports	Eng
Moo PCC	Moore's Privy Council Cases	Eng
Moo PCCNS	Moore's Privy Council Cases, New Series	Eng
MR	Master of the Rolls	Eng
My & Cr	Mylne and Craig's Reports, Chancery	Eng
My & K	Mylne and Keen's Reports, Chancery	Eng
N	Natal Provincial Division	SA
NC	Northern Cape Division	SA
NE	North Eastern Reporter	US
New LR	New Law Reports	Sri Lanka
NLR	Natal Law Reports	SA
N^mN^m	*Numerium Negidium*	Roman
NPD	Reports of the Natal Provincial Division	SA
NY	Reports of the Court of Appeals of the State of New York	US
O	Orange Free State Provincial Division	SA
OFS	Reports of the High Court of the Orange Free State	SA
OPD	Reports of the Orange Free State Provincial Division	SA
OR	Official Reports, High Court of the South African Republic	SA
ORC	Orange River Colony Reports	SA
P Wms	Peere Williams' Reports	Eng
PC	Judicial Committee of the Privy Council	
PH	Prentice Hall Weekly Reports	SA
Phipson	Phipson's Reports, Natal Supreme Court	
Plc	Public limited company	
Prec Ch	Precedents in Chancery	Eng
Pty	Proprietary	
Pvt	Private (Company)	
QB	Queen's Bench Division; Queen's Bench Reports	Eng
QBD	Law Reports Queen's Bench Division	Eng
R	High Court of Rhodesia	ZB
R & N	Rhodesia and Nyasaland Law Reports	ZB

RA	High Court of Rhodesia, Appellate Division	ZB
RabelsZ	*Rabels Zeitschrift für ausländisches und internationales Privatrecht*	Ger
Roscoe	Roscoe's Reports, Cape Supreme Court	SA
SA	South Africa, South African Law Reports	
SAJHR	*South African Journal of Human Rights*	SA
SALJ	*South African Law Journal*	SA
Salkeld	Salkeld's Reports, King's Bench	Eng
SALT	*South African Law Times*	SA
SAR	Reports of the High Court of the South African Republic	SA
SC	Reports of the Cape Supreme Court	SA
Searle	Searle's Reports, Cape Supreme Court	SA
SEC	South Eastern Cape Local Division	SA
s.	section	
SR	High Court of Southern Rhodesia	ZB
Swan	Swanston's Reports, Chancery	Eng
T	Transvaal Provincial Division	SA
Term Rep	Term Reports	Eng
TH	Reports of the Witwatersrand High Court	SA
THRHR	*Tydskrif vir Heedendaagse Romeins-Hollandse Reg*	SA
TLR	Times Law Reports	Eng
Tothill	Tothill's Transactions in Chancery	Eng
TPA	Transvaal Provincial Administration	SA
TPD	Reports of the Transvaal Provincial Division	SA
TS	Reports of the Transvaal Supreme Court	SA
TSAR	*Tydskrif vir die Suid-Afrikaanse Reg*	SA
Tvl	Transvaal	SA
US	United States of America, United States Supreme Court Reports	US
Vern	Vernon's Reports, Chancery	Eng
Ves	Vesey Junior's Reports, Chancery	Eng
Ves Sen	Vesey Senior's Reports, Chancery	Eng
W	Witwatersrand Local Division	SA
Willes	Willes' Reports, Common Pleas	Eng
WLD	Reports of the Witwatersrand Local Division	SA
WLR	Weekly Law Reports	Eng
WR	Weekly Reports	Eng
Y & C Ch Cas	Younge and Collyer's Reports, Chancery Cases	Eng
YB	Year Books	Eng
ZB	Zimbabwe	
ZH	Zimbabwe High Court	ZB
ZS	Zimbabwe Supreme Court	ZB

Table of Cases: South Africa

Table of Cases: England and other Jurisdictions

Introduction
South African Law as a Mixed Legal System

REINHARD ZIMMERMANN and DANIEL VISSER

I. EXPERIENCES AT THE INTERSECTION BETWEEN CIVIL LAW AND
COMMON LAW

1. The civil law–common law divide in Europe

Contrary to nearly all the other disciplines taught in a modern university, legal science in Europe has, at least for the last hundred years, been predominantly national in substance, outlook, and approach. Since the continental legal systems have been codified there have, in principle, been as many legal systems as there are national states. This national isolation of law and legal science has been described as 'humiliating' and 'undignified'.[1] Above all, however, it is entirely anachronistic. For in recent years there has been within the framework of the European Community, a process of legal co-ordination, harmonization, and unification of private law that is likely to gain ever greater momentum.[2] It will have to be supported by a legal scholarship that trandscends both national boundaries and disciplinary divides (like those between legal history, comparative law, and modern legal doctrine). This kind of scholarship should foster an awareness that a common legal tradition informs the modern national legal systems in Europe; it will enable us to perceive similarities, and to understand and evaluate divergences of historical development; and it may provide us with a perspective which reduces existing legal systems to national variations of a common theme. It will turn away the attention of legal scholars and practitioners from purely national concerns and pave the way towards re-establishing a fundamental intellectual unity on a European level.[3]

---

[1] Rudolf von Jhering, *Geist des römischen Rechts auf den verschiedenen Stufen seiner Entwicklung*, vol. I (8th edn., 1924), 15.
[2] On the Europeanization of Private Law within the EC and the problematic features thereof see Reinhard Zimmermann, 'Civil Code and Civil Law' (1994/95) 1 *Columbia Journal of European Law* 63 sqq.
[3] For further elaboration of the approach required see Reinhard Zimmermann, 'Savigny's Legacy: Legal History, Comparative Law and the Emergence of a European Legal Science' (1996) 112 *LQR* forthcoming.

One of the major obstacles to the emergence of a European legal science appears to lie in the civil law–common law divide separating England, Wales, and Ireland from the other continental legal systems. The English common law has traditionally been perceived as flourishing in splendid isolation from (continental) Europe. It has neither experienced a reception of Roman law, nor been subjected to codification. Today, however, it is becoming increasingly clear that England was never entirely isolated from the rest of Europe. Over the centuries there has been ongoing intellectual contact, which has left a definitive and characteristic mark on the English law. Common law and civil law can therefore be regarded as emanations of one and the same, of a 'Western' legal tradition.[4] Of course, the common law has developed certain distinctive features. So have the continental legal systems; but it is obvious today that these peculiarities and jagged edges, on both sides of the Channel, are in the process of being worn away. Basil Markesinis refers to a 'gradual convergence',[5] James Gordley to a 'vanishing distinction' between common law and civil law.[6] This applies to both to the substance of the law and to its institutional and methodological framework.

2. Mixed legal systems

Against this background the historical experiences of a number of so-called 'mixed legal systems' are of specific interest. To some extent of course, all the major legal systems of the Western world are mixed. They have grown together from various roots, and, over the centuries, they have been subject to many different influences. The history of a system of law, in the words of Roscoe Pound,[7] can largely be described as a history of borrowings of legal materials from other legal systems. Or, as Knut Wolfgang Nörr[8] remarks, the law has always shared in that 'most fascinating aspect of relations between peoples, [namely] that not only material goods, but also knowledge and experience, opinions and ideas' may be carried between countries and continents. Nevertheless, the terms 'mixed legal system' or 'mixed jurisdiction' are usually reserved for a number of legal systems at the intersection, so to speak, of civil law and common law.[9] They include

---

[4] For details supporting this assertion see Reinhard Zimmermann, 'Der europäische Charakter des englischen Rechts: Historische Verbindungen zwischen civil law und common law' (1993) 1 *Zeitschrift für Europäisches Privatrecht* 4 sqq.

[5] Basil Markesinis (ed.), *The gradual Convergence: Foreign Ideas, Foreign Influences, and English Law on the Eve of the 21st Century* (1994).

[6] James Gordley,'Common Law und civil law: eine überholte Unterscheidung' (1993) 1 *Zeitschrift für Europäisches Privatrecht* 613 sqq.

[7] As quoted by Alan Watson, *Legal Transplants: An Approach to Comparative Law* (1974), 22.

[8] 'The Problem of Legal Transplants and the Reception of Continental Law in China before 1930', in: *Wege zum japanischen Recht: Festschrift für Zentaro Kitagawa* (1992), 231.

[9] Cf. e.g. T. B. Smith, *Studies Critical and Comparative* (1962); Joseph Dainow (ed.), *The Role of Judicial Decisions and Doctrine in Civil Law and in Mixed Jurisdictions* (1974).

Scotland, Quebec, Louisiana, Sri Lanka, South Africa, Botswana, Lesotho, Swaziland, Namibia, and Zimbabwe. Due largely to historical accident, civilian jurisprudence has, in all these territories, survived within a common law environment. In some of them the civilian heritage has been preserved by way of codification. Thus, in Louisiana a Civil Code was promulgated in 1825,[10] in Quebec in 1866.[11] These codes have tended to shield the substantive civil law against common law influence,[12] but they have also put an end to the use of Roman law as a living source of law. The private law of all the other jurisdictions mentioned has never been codified, and the Roman sources have therefore retained a different status.[13] This book will focus on South African law which, Scotland apart,[14] must be regarded as the leading one among the mixed legal systems still based on common (in the sense of uncodified) law. For Botswana, Lesotho, and Swaziland have all inherited so much of their private law from the Cape of Good Hope as to be part and parcel of a 'Southern African Law Association'.[15] The same can be said of Namibia (which was administered by South Africa until independence in 1990)[16] and

[10] On the history of codification in Louisiana, and on Louisiana's mixed legal system generally, see Joachim Zekoll, 'Zwischen den Welten: Das Privatrecht von Louisiana als europäisch-amerikanische Mischrechtsordnung', in: Reinhard Zimmermann (ed.), *Amerikanische Rechtskultur und europäisches Privatrecht: Impressionen aus der Neuen Welt* (1995), 11 sqq.

[11] On the history of codification in Quebec, and on the latest Civil Code of Quebec (1994), see Pierre Legrand, 'Civil Law Codification in Quebec: A Case of Decivilianization' (1993) 1 *Zeitschrift für Europäisches Privatrecht* 574 sqq.

[12] For this very reason, codification was once also mooted in South Africa: cf. Sir John Wessels, 'The Future of Roman-Dutch Law in South Africa' (1920) 37 *SALJ* 284. Contra, e.g. R. H. Hahlo, '. . . And Save Us From Codification' (1960) 77 *SALJ* 432 sqq.; H. R. hahlo, Ellison Kahn, *The South African Legal System and its Background* (1968), 72 sqq. Most recently, cf. the 'reconsideration' by W. J. Hosten, 'Kodifikasie in Suid-Afrika: 'n Heroorweging?', in: *Huldigingsbundel vir W. A. Joubert* (1988), 59 sqq.

[13] For details see Reinhard Zimmermann, 'Roman Law in a Mixed Legal System: The South African Experience', in: Robin Evans-Jones (ed.), *The Civil Law Tradition in Scotland* (1995), 41 sqq.

[14] For Scotland cf., most recently, the essays in Robin Evans-Jones (ed.), *The Civil Law Tradition in Scotland* (1995) and the overview by Reinhard Zimmermann and Johann A. Dieckmann, 'Das schottische Privatrecht im Spiegel seiner Literatur' (1995) 3 *Zeitschrift für Europäisches Privatrecht* 898 sqq. On the historical relation between Scots law and Roman-Dutch law see T. B. Smith, 'Scots Law and Roman-Dutch Law: A Shared Tradition', in: *Studies Critical and Comparative* (1962), 46 sqq.

[15] A term used by Schreiner JA in: *Annah Lokudzinga Mathenjwa v. R* (1970–76) Swaziland Law Reports 25, 29H. For general comment cf. the entries under the various countries in the *International Encyclopedia of Comparative Law*, vol. I; J. H. Pain, 'The Reception of English and Roman-Dutch Law in Africa with Reference to Botswana, Lesotho and Swaziland' (1978) 11 *Comparative and International Law Journal of Southern Africa* (sic!) 137 sqq.; A. J. G. M. Saunders, 'The Characteristic Features of Southern African Law' (1981) 14 *Comparative and International Law Journal of Southern Africa* 328 sqq. Cf. Peter B. Kutner, *Common Law in Southern Africa* (1990).

[16] When, after the First World War, South Africa was entrusted with the power to administer the then South West, the Roman-Dutch law as applied in the province of the Cape of Good Hope on 1 Jan. 1920 was introduced as the common law of the territory. Roman-Dutch law continues to apply after independence (20 Mar. 1990) in terms of art. 140 I of the Constitution of the Republic of Namibia.

Zimbabwe (which eventually retained the private law of its predecessor, Southern Rhodesia).[17] Sri Lanka also shares a common legal heritage with South Africa. Decisions of South African courts regarding core areas of private law are 'though not absolutely binding . . . treated with great respect'.[18]

By collecting here a number of essays of some of the most important and characteristic institutions of the South African law of obligations and of property, an attempt is made to demonstrate how civil law and common law have been accommodated within one legal system. Thus, we hope to contribute to the understanding of the inherent compatibility (or otherwise) of these two branches of the European legal tradition. At the same time, the essays in this volume document a chapter in the history of the reception of English law throughout the world, a process not unlike that of the earlier reception of Roman law in Europe. The starting point for each essay is the 'pure' Roman-Dutch law which was transplanted to the Cape of Good Hope in the years following 1652, and which has been examined in another volume published in 1992.[19] The analysis focuses on how the Roman-Dutch law has been preserved, changed, modified, or replaced in the course of the nineteenth century when the Cape became a British colony; and on what has happened since the creation of the Union of South Africa in 1910. Each essay therefore attempts, for the field of law with which it deals, to answer questions such as: what was the level of interaction between the civil law and the common law? What were the mechanisms that brought about the particular forms of competition, co-existence, or fusion which exist in that area of the law? Is the process complete or is it still continuing? Can we observe the emergence, from these two roots, of a genuinely South African private law? How is the result to be evaluated?

3. The doctrinal history of South African private law and its context

The intention of this book, however, is not only to contribute to the understanding of the Western legal tradition generally. By allowing a number of prominent scholars in the field of South African private law to reflect on the history of their subject, it constitutes the first attempt to write a doctrinal history of South African law. For whilst the relationship between the civil law and the common law elements of South Africa's legal system has

---

[17] For details see Reinhard Zimmermann, 'Das römisch-holländische Recht in Zimbabwe' (1991) 51 *RabelsZ* 505 sqq.

[18] I. Jennings and H. W. Tambiah, *The Dominion of Ceylon: The Development of its Laws and Constitution* (1970), 188. Cf. T. Nadaraja, *The Legal System of Ceylon in its Historical Setting* (1977); M. H. J. van den Horst, *The Roman-Dutch Law in Sri Lanka* (1985).

[19] Robert Feenstra, Reinhard Zimmermann (eds.), *Das römisch-holländische Recht: Fortschritte des Zivilrechts im 17. und 18. Jahrhundert* (1992). Cf. Reinhard Zimmermann, 'Roman-Dutch Jurisdprudence and its Contribution to European Private Law' (1992) 66 *Tulane LR* 1685 sqq.

received extensive attention,[20] no comprehensive attempt has yet been made to analyse the effect of this interaction on the various branches of private law. As far as general discussions of the history of South African law are concerned,[21] they focus mainly on what one may call the 'external history' rather than the history of the specific legal institutions.

Anyone who wishes to describe the history of South African private law is inevitably confronted with the dilemma that this development occurred within a context of discrimination and oppression. For there can be no doubt that private law was a structural part of the system of domination in South Africa. Understandably, perhaps, South African lawyers often emphasized the 'relative isolation of the development of the common law from the brutal realities of the statutory regime'.[22] Much in the way of a mechanic who carefully tends a well preserved Bugatti motor car, a lawyer who works with a finely tuned legal system is liable to develop a somewhat irrational passion for the object of his attention. That is, of course, because his intimate knowledge of how it is put together reveals it is as more than the sum of its parts: as a work of art; and naturally the lawyer, like the mechanic, will want to overlook the weaknesses that the machine might have. Indeed, in South Africa it was all too often overlooked that most of those who saw the magnificent old vehicle drive past could not afford it and would have been better served had it been not a Bugatti but an omnibus. Thus, it may appear bizarre that the southern tip of Africa should have become one of the last strongholds in the modern world of European jurisprudence in its original uncodified form. Access to law is certainly not facilitated by the multiplicity of legal sources, some of them in ancient, some in modern, but none in indigenous languages.

In putting together this book, we realized that the internal development of the law of obligations and property would reveal very little of the societal forces surrounding it, simply because South African lawyers, like their

---

[20] Cf e.g. H. R. Hahlo, Ellison Kahn, *The Union of South Africa: The Development of its Laws and Constitution* (1960), 17 sqq.; Ben Beinart, 'The English Legal Contribution in South Africa: The Interaction of Civil Law and Common Law' 1981 *Acta Juridica* 7 sqq.; Reinhard Zimmermann, 'Die Rechtsprechung des Supreme Court of the Cape of Good Hope am Ende der sechziger Jahre des 19. Jahrhunderts', in: *Huldigingsbundel Paul van Warmelo* (1984), 286 sq.; *idem*, 'Synthesis in South African Private Law: Civil Law, Common Law and *Usus Hodiernus Pandectarum*' (1986) 103 *SALJ* 259 sqq.; D. P. Visser, 'Daedalus in the Supreme Court: The Common Law Today' (1986) 49 *THRHR* 127 sqq.; H. J. Erasmus, 'Thoughts on Private Law in a Future South Africa' 1994 *Stellenbosch LR* 107 sqq. For Natal see P. R. Spiller, 'The "Romodutchyafricanderenglander" law of nineteenth-century Natal' (1985) 48 *THRHR* 170 sqq.

[21] Hahlo/Kahn (n. 20), 1 sqq.; *idem* (n. 12), 566 sqq.; D. H. van Zyl, *Geskiedenis van die Romeins-Hollandse Reg* (1979), 420 sqq.; Reinhard Zimmermann, *Das römisch-holländische Recht in Südafrika* (1983), 1 sqq.; Wouter de Vos, *Regsgeskiedenis* (1992), 226 sqq. Cf. J. C. de Wet, *Die Ou Skrywers in Perspektief* (1988), 1 sqq.

[22] Martin Chanock, 'Writing South African Legal History: A Prospectus' (1989) 30 *Journal of African History*, 265, 282.

counterparts all over the world tend to create law primarily with reference to the intellectual concerns raised in statutory documents, authoritative court decisions, and learned treatises. However, we wanted to reveal something of the broader socio-political forces that have shaped the legal system over the last two centuries. We also wanted to indicate the effect on society when lawyers act without carefully considering the consequences of their actions; even if lawyers have lost sight of those consequences, they nevertheless exist.[23] We have therefore regarded it as indispensable, even in a book devoted to private law legal doctrine, to commission the first two papers; for they provide the specifically South African context within which the remaining studies in our book must be assessed.[24]

Before we consider some of the essential characteristics of the South African legal system, it is important to note that a general re-orientation is under way, and that the book thus appears at the dawn of a new era. Section 35(3) of the Interim Constitution[25] directs the courts to 'have due regard to the spirit, purport and objects' of the Bill of Rights contained in the Constitution when applying and developing the common law. The working draft of the final Constitution contains a similar provision.[26] South African private law will therefore in future be shaped in the image of the Constitution and the courts are authorized specifically to 'have regard to comparable foreign case law'.[27] This will not mean, as Mr Justice Kentridge put it in the first decision handed down by the Constitutional Court,[28] 'that all the principles of law which have hitherto governed our courts are to be ignored', since they 'obviously contain much of lasting value'.[29] But there will undoubtedly be a major shift in emphasis towards giving recognition to societal considerations reflected in the Bill of Rights.[30] This is also emphasized in the contributions of a number of authors to the present volume.

---

[23] Knut Wolfgang Nörr, (1990) 38 *American Journal of Comparative Law* 403 (review of Alan Watson, *The Evolution of Law* (1990)).

[24] Important studies of the South African legal order in the last 20 years include: John Dugard, *Human Rights and the South African Legal Order* (1978); Hugh Corder, *Judges at Work: The Role of the Appellate Judiciary 1910–1950* (1984); Christopher Forsyth, *In Danger for their Talents: A Study of the Appellate Division of the Supreme Court of South Africa 1950–1980* (1985); A. S. Mathews, *Freedom, State Security and the Rule of Law* (1986); Adrienne van Blerk, *Judge and Be Judged* (1988); David Dyzenhaus, *Hard Cases in Wicked Legal Systems* (1991); and Stephen Ellmann, *In a Time of Trouble* (1992).

[25] Act 200 of 1993.   [26] S. 38(1).

[27] S. 35(1) Interim Constitution and s. 39(1) of the working draft of the final Constitution.

[28] *S v. Zuma* 1995 (4) BCLR 401 (SA).   [29] 412 E–G.

[30] On the drafting of the Bill of Rights in the interim Constitution see Hugh Corder, 'Towards a South African Constitution' (1994) 57 *Modern LR* 491 sqq.

II. A PAN-AFRICAN VIEW: IMPERIAL LAW WITHOUT THE IMPERIALISTS

One of the lasting legacies of Western colonialism is that the legal systems of the European powers have become entrenched in their former colonies. Thus, variants of Spanish, French, Italian, Portuguese, Dutch, and English law determine the daily affairs of people in vast areas of Africa, America, Asia, and Australia. The reasons for the continued influence of the imperial law differ, of course, from country to country. Where the colonizers and their descendants came to outnumber the autochthonous peoples these reasons are obvious; in countries where independence saw the former overlords leave, or remain as a minority, they are more complex. The hidden forces of neo-colonialism, the natural inertia inherent in the law, and the resistance to change brought about by the vested interests of the legal profession have all played a role. Also, European law was bound to appear, to newly independent governments, as the most convenient and useful mechanism for conflict resolution in a modern, largely westernized society.

If we narrow our focus to sub-Saharan Africa, we see that the law imposed by the colonial rulers was almost invariably retained as the general law after the end of the colonial regime. It is true that indigenous customary law was usually given a new status at independence, but mostly without undermining the authority of the colonial law. A number of different patterns of development may be discerned. They are strongly linked to the particular colonial 'mother' country and its manner of administration of justice.

In the British colonies the common law was established as the general law of the land, while the indigenous law was recognized as a separate body of law applicable only to indigenous inhabitants. For example, in Ghana, s. 14 of the Supreme Court Ordinance 1876 introduced English law to the former Gold Coast colony in the following way:

The common law, the doctrines of equity, and the statues of general application which were in force in England at the date when the Colony obtained a local legislature, that is to say, on the 24th day of July, 1874, shall be in force within the jurisdiction of this Court.

After independence the position remained the same, except that s. 66 of the Courts Act 1960 (later replaced by s. 49(1) of the Courts Act 1971), gave customary law a more prominent position by laying down an extensive set of internal conflict of law rules in which common law and customary law were accorded the same status. The story is much the same in Nigeria and in the other British colonies in Central Africa.[31]

---

[31] For a contemporary account of the role of colonial law in the then newly independent African states see e.g. W. C. Daniels, 'The Interaction of English Law with Customary Law in

The position in the French colonies was somewhat different. French law was introduced as the general law of the land and everyone was encouraged to subject himself to this general law. Customary law was recognized, but the policy was eventually to create a composite legal system in which French and indigenous elements were to be fused. This enterprise, which achieved a certain measure of success, also managed to secure the perpetuation of French law as part and parcel of present-day law in the sub-Saharan countries formerly under the control of Paris.

In the countries colonized by Portugal the pattern initially approximated that of the French colonies. After independence, however, the emphasis on socialist values led to a more pronounced transformation of the legal system. Nevertheless, in Mozambique the old civil law (apart from the law of marriage) as well as the law of civil procedure remained in force.[32]

South Africa and the other countries which inherited their law from the Cape of Good Hope fall into yet another category.[33] They conform to the pattern in the former British colonies to the north of them in that they too, while giving greater recognition to indigenous customary law after independence, have retained the colonial law as the basic law of the land. They differ from those countries in that the colonial law itself was, and is, a mixed rather than a purely English legal system.

Whether the common law of South Africa would be retained after the advent of democracy was a question which remained for a long time uncertain. After all, the *leitmotiv* of the freedom struggle was *mayibuye Afrika* (come back Africa) and thus, by virtue of its eurocentric basis, the law inevitably became a target for complete transformation. In the end, however, a view prevailed which was formulated by Mr Justice Albie Sachs (as he now is) in the following words:

In the case of South Africa, the rules that govern purchase and sale and insurance and companies and cheques, that deal with self-defence and dishonesty and with when people should be held responsible for injuries to others, happened to have come from Europe. Like the railways and trousers and dresses and Bibles and the English language, they came in the context of dispossession and domination, but like

West Africa' (1964) 13 *International and Comparative Law Quarterly* 574 sqq.; see generally also A. N. Allott, *New Essays in African Law* (1970), 1 sqq.; F. A. R. Bennion, *The Constitutional Law of Ghana* (1962), 404 sqq.; E. Cotran, 'Tanzania', in: A. N. Allott (ed.), *Judicial and Legal Systems in Africa* (1970), 162 sqq.; T. O. Elias, *Ghana and Sierra Leone: the Development of their Laws and Constitutions* (1962), 131 sqq.; *idem, Nigeria: The Development of its Law and Constitution* (1967), 1 sqq. See now also Chuma N. Himonga, *Family Law and Succession Laws in Zambia* (1995), 55 sqq.

[32] In regard to the colonial situation in the former French colonies see J. W. Salacuse, *An Introduction to French-Speaking Africa*, vol. 1: *Africa South of the Sahara* (1969), 1 sqq. In regard to the position in Mozambique see Albie Sachs, *The Future of Roman-Dutch Law in a Non-Racial Democratic South Africa: Some Preliminary Observations* (1989), 6.

[33] See generally T. W. Bennett, *Application of Customary Law in Southern Africa* (1985), 65 sqq.; Allott (n. 31), 1–27.

the railways and trousers and dresses and the Bible and the English language, they have been taken over in varying degrees by the whole population and have now become South Africanised. Thus, after two hundred years, English has become a South African language: where else in the world can one say—he slipped on his guava? Shorn of their associations with domination, there is no reason why these institutions should not be taken over and infused with a new spirit so as to serve the people as a whole rather than just a minority.[34]

Following in the footsteps of its neighbours, South Africa will therefore retain the common law bequeathed to it by its colonial history. The degree to which the specifically Roman-Dutch heritage of South African private law will be retained is, however, an open question.

III. THE THREE GRACES OF SOUTH AFRICAN LAW

1. Characterizing the general South African law

The genesis of the South African legal system is contextualized by Eduard Fagan in Chapter 1, above. The process that he describes is one in which the narrow concerns of nationalism and other sectional interests played an important role in the shaping of a legal system which is a unique blend of common law and civil law. Ironically, therefore, the very fact that both the common law and the civil law had such dedicated, and sometimes even chauvinistic, supporters among judges, legislators, and professors[35] contributed to modern South African private law becoming a legal system with such a distinctly international flavour.

But how should South African law be categorized? Most often it is described as being a Roman-Dutch (i.e. civilian) system[36] onto which an appreciable amount of English law has been grafted. Others have maintained that South African law is fundamentally and characteristically British: when the Union of South Africa was created in 1910, it was in essence 'a British state created by Britain for British imperial purposes'.[37] Yet it is also obvious that Roman-Dutch law emerged as a dominant source

---

[34] Sachs (n. 32), 3 sq.

[35] On the policy of anglicization of the institutions of the Cape of Good Hope after 1806 see generally H. B. Fine, *The Administration of Criminal Justice at the Cape of Good Hope 1795–1828* (unpublished Ph.D. thesis, University of Cape Town, 1991), 1–104; James Sturgis, 'Anglicization at the Cape of Good Hope in the Early Nineteenth Century' (1982) 11 *Journal of Imperial and Commonwealth History*, 1 sqq.; cf. most recently J. van der Merwe, 'Die reg aan die Kaap tydens die inwerkingtreding van die Regsoktrooie' (1995) 58 *THRHR* 234 sqq. On Afrikaaner nationalism since the 1930s see e.g. Forsyth (n. 24), 1 sqq.; Edwin Cameron, 'Legal Chauvinism, Executive-Mindedness and Justice: L. C. Steyn's Impact on South African Law' (1982) 99 *SALJ* 38 sqq.

[36] See e.g. Dale Hutchison (ed.), *Wille's Principles of South African Law* (8th edn., 1991), 1.

[37] Chanock, (1989) 30 *Journal of African History*, 265, 270.

in many fields—particularly those with which this volume is concerned. Thus, it has been argued that both Roman-Dutch and English law fulfil the role of 'common law' in South Africa.[38] We will not pursue this rather theoretical question. Suffice it to say that in practice today a pragmatic approach prevails. South African legislation and precedents are accorded prime authority; if one has to venture beyond these formal sources, English and Roman-Dutch law carry about equal weight. Instead, we prefer to emphasize two specific features which contribute to the distinctive character of South African private law and which appear to be relevant to all the contributions in the present volume.

2. A characteristic common law feature: the roles of judges and of law reports

One of the crucial aspects in which South African law differs from most modern civil law systems is that it continues to exist as *ius commune*, or common law. Codification has had a considerable impact on the ideology of private lawyers in Europe[39] with ramifications for the nature of legal reasoning and the role of judges. The apparent certainty of the highly systematized civil codes tends to encourage deductive reasoning, which in turn has the effect of reducing the judge to the role of a functionary who merely has to find the one right answer which 'proper' application of the law to the facts is thought to produce:

Traditionally the civil-law judge is a fungible person, one of a group of anonymous, almost colourless, individuals who hide their personality behind the collegiate responsibility of the court. Their duty is to apply the written law, and the meaning of that law is to be discovered from the writings of its academic exponents.[40]

Common law judges are not like that at all. They, rather than the professors, take the lead in shaping the law, and consequently the law in common law countries tends to be, as Zweigert and Kötz have put it, 'forensic and pragmatic' rather than 'academic and theoretical'.[41] An important key to understanding South African private law lies in appreciating the fact that, whilst it is largely civilian in substance, it is also shaped by the traditional conviction of its judges to be the true custodians of the law. Peter Stein has remarked with reference to Quebec and South Africa that 'the visitor cannot help to be aware that the civil law in these countries looks different from elsewhere',[42] and in his contribution

---

[38] Visser, (1986) 49 *THRHR* 127 sqq.

[39] For details see Reinhard Zimmermann, 'Codification: History and Present Significance of an Idea' (1995) 3 *European Review of Private Law* 95 sqq.

[40] Peter Stein, 'Relationships Among Roman Law, Common Law and Modern Civil Law' (1993) 66 *Tulane LR* 1587, 1597.

[41] Konrad Zweigert, Hein Kötz, *Introduction to Comparative Law*, vol. I (2nd edn., reprint 1992, trans. Tony Weir), 266.

to this volume Hennie Erasmus spells out the profound impact of the 'severance of the Roman-Dutch law from its own procedural tradition and the substitution thereof by a procedural system with a different history, methodology and intellectual tradition'. For this reason Chapter 3 by Stephen Girvin provides biographical details of some of the main actors on the judicial stage. South African judges have not been neutral conduits, channelling the law from the books into their judgements, but prime agents in determining the direction of the law. For the same reason, the importance of law reporting to the development of South African law has to be stressed. For whilst the doctrine of *stare decisis* does not distinguish English law from continental law as much as was once thought,[43] it still remains true that the basic common law method of reasoning 'from case to case'[44] requires the relevant case-law to be available, if possible in print. The first Editors' Note appended to this Introduction thus provides an overview of the history of law reporting in South Africa.

3. A characteristic civil law feature: the role of legal writers

In the second place, it should be noted that we are not dealing in South Africa merely with a legal system in which substantive rules of civilian origin are applied within an exclusively English framework. For just as English law has had considerable impact on the level of substantive law, so the civilian approach has also contributed to shape the manner in which the law is perceived, practised, and developed. Thus, South African law is like a *patois* with a mixed vocabulary operating within a strongly adapted grammar, not a legal language consisting of a vocabulary to be used within the context of an alien grammar. The most important factor in the transformation of the common law grammar, the way of 'doing the law job', has been the role of authoritative jurists. Since the days when South African law began to acquire the attributes of a developed legal system, the writings of learned jurists have, in the continental way, been accorded considerable respect by the courts. Until the middle of the twentieth century only the traditional institutional writers of classical Roman-Dutch law were admitted to the Pantheon, but more recently the courts have increasingly taken note of the exposition of the law by contemporary academic writers.[45] This means, in the first place, that the law professors have become important partners in

[42] Stein, (1992) 66 *Tulane LR* 1603; cf. Erasmus, 1994 *Stellenbosch LR* 111.

[43] Cf., as far as Germany is concerned, Reinhard Zimmermann, 'An Introduction to German Legal Culture', in: Werner F. Ebke, Matthew W. Finkin (eds.), *Introduction to German Law* (1996), 14 sqq.

[44] See Zweigert/Kötz/Weir (n. 41), 271; Hahlo/Kahn (n. 12), 591 sqq.

[45] Cf. Alan Watson, *The Making of the Civil Law* (1981), 41 (South African courts have traditionally given 'a place of honour to the legal scholar'); Zimmermann (n. 21), 70 sqq.; cf. Ellison Kahn, 'The Role of Doctrine and Judicial Decision in South African Law', in: Dainow (n. 9), 245 sqq.; Hosten, *Huldigingsbundel Joubert*, 67 sq. But see Susan Scott, 'To burden or not to burden?' (1991) 54 *THRHR* 264 sqq.

the task of developing and further refining the law. Secondly, and more importantly, these authors have often brought civilian legal substance, patterns of argument, and systematic orientation to bear upon the judgments of the courts.[46] The second Editors' Note therefore sketches the growth of legal literature in South Africa.

4. The role of the third Grace: African customary law

What of the third component of South African law, apart from civil law and common law, mentioned above? In keeping with the English colonial approach elsewhere in Africa, the legislature has held indigenous or 'customary' law at arm's length. Since the 1830s official policy has fluctuated from time to time and from area to area. Thus we find examples of both complete recognition of and complete rejection of indigenous law, with, of course, a number of intermediate positions.[47] Nevertheless, certain general trends can be identified: (i) in each of the later provinces of South Africa *some* form of recognition of indigenous law was eventually given; (ii) the recognition was limited to members of the autochthonous peoples, and (iii) in almost all cases the recognition was subject to a 'repugnancy clause', by which customary law which was held to be contrary to the principles of 'fairness', 'justice', or 'equity' could not be enforced.[48] In 1927 a uniform approach was implemented by the Native Administration Act. Section 11(1) relegated the application of customary law to special courts: the Commissioner's Courts. The Act determined, furthermore, that these courts had a discretion to apply African customary law in instances 'involving questions of custom followed by blacks', as long as such law was not 'opposed to the principles of public policy or natural justice'. The colonial disdain for indigenous African law was thus entrenched for the whole Union of South Africa. It was further underlined when the Supreme Court determined that it could not take judicial notice of customary law unless it was proved as 'local custom'.[49] (It was only in 1988 that legislation was

---

[46] On the influence of modern European legal thinking on South African legal writers see generally Hugh Corder, Dennis Davis, 'Law and Social Practice: An Introduction', in: Hugh Corder (ed.), *Essays on Law and Social Practice in South Africa* (1980), 9 sq.

[47] See T. W. Bennett, *A Sourcebook of African Customary Law for Southern Africa* (1991), 110 sqq.

[48] See Bennett (n. 33), 129 sqq. On 'repugnancy' clauses in the rest of Africa see generally Allott (n. 31), 159.

[49] See e.g. *Ex parte Minister of Native Affairs in re: Yako v. Beyi* 1948 (1) SA 388 (A). Cf. generally Allott (n. 31), 257–8 who states: 'That in England any local custom at variance with the law of the land should be proved by the party alleging it is fair and reasonable, and similar considerations might seem relevant in Africa, since customary law derogates from he general law as applied by the courts. It is true that customary law is in a sense local or personal, since it attaches to a given ethnic group or the members of that community or to the area within which they are dominant. Nevertheless, as far as the Africans who are members of that community are concerned, their customary law is not an occasional variant from the law

introduced to make it possible for any court to take judicial notice of African customary law.)

Throughout the apartheid era, therefore, indigenous law had a separate existence. It is true that the general law applied to everyone, but customary law could never apply to whites and the legislative measures described above effectively removed many black people from the operation of the common law. In certain instances, however, it proved impossible to keep the two systems wholly separate. The situation where a widow of customary marriage wishes to institute a delictual claim on the basis of the wrongful, culpable killing of her spouse may serve as an illustration of the limited, and inevitable, extent of interpenetration between the general law and customary law. It also provides a small glimpse of the intricate web apartheid wove around the lives of ordinary South Africans. Before 1960 it was accepted that the widow of a customary union could institute an action in the Commissioner's Court if the defendant happened to be a black person and the matter was dealt with according to the general law. If the defendant was not a black person, the action had to be instituted in the Supreme Court. Then in *Santam v. Fondo*[50] the Appellate Division of the Supreme Court established that, according to Roman-Dutch law, the delictual claim was available only to the deceased's spouse and those other family members whom he had a duty to (and did indeed) support. However, since a customary union does not constitute a valid marriage according to the general law, neither widow nor children could institute an action. This decision probably did not accurately reflect (classical) Roman-Dutch law, but since it constituted a binding precedent which clearly placed thousands of widows in a position of grave disadvantage the legislature had to intervene. Section 31 of Act 76 of 1963 made it possible, once again, for the widow of a customary marriage to sue the person who wrongfully caused the death of her breadwinner for loss of support. (Special provision was made for those instances in which the claimant was one of two or more spouses in a polygamous union.)

However, such legislation (which adapted the general law so as to take account of the fact that the majority of South Africans lived, at least to some extent, according to customary law) was a rarity. Generally, customary law developed quite separately from the general law. This did not mean, however, that it could not be skilfully used as part of the grand strategy of domination. As Bennett put it:

State courts were supposed to be applying 'the law of the people', a law inherited from the founding fathers of the African tribes. A critical examination of this

applicable to them; it is their general law *prima facie* applicable in civil (and formerly in criminal) matters. The tests for their application, and the method by which its rules are ascertained, should not have been blindly borrowed from the English law relating to local custom.'

[50] 1960 (2) SA 467 (A).

assumption revealed that much customary law was in fact the creation of the colonial courts. Although this law had no authentic ancestry, it functioned to legitimate state control of the people. The notion of tradition offered a sense of continuity with the past to a people whose lives had been disrupted by colonial conquest. This was a past that could be moulded and interpreted in ways consonant with state policies. For both colonial, and for many modern African governments, tradition is vital for the preservation of a compliant population and existing social structures.[51]

In South Africa's interim Constitution one of the principles for the drafting of the final Constitution[52] determines that 'indigenous law, like common law, shall be recognized and applied by the Courts'. Indeed the working draft of the final Constitution provides in s. 169(3) that '[t]he courts must apply indigenous law when that law is applicable, subject to the Constitution and any relevant legislation'.

Indigenous law thus continues to be recognized, but it is not certain what that will mean for the legal system as a whole. Clearly, the formal impediments that prevented the use of the general law of the land by so many black South Africans no longer exist. Nobody will therefore be artificially subjected to its operation. Furthermore, the Bill of Rights will enable the courts to remove the distortions that have developed within customary law during the colonial era. The problem is that indigenous law is customary in nature and that its application by the general courts of the land is inevitably bound to distort it. In other words, the danger exists that, even though the judges will (increasingly) be representative of the majority of the people of South Africa, the customary law applied by them will remain an artificial judicial construct. Customary law will also, at least for the time being, continue to function separately, although certain indigenous procedural approaches to law may be introduced by legislation. In the course of time a gradual incorporation of customary law into the main body of law may possibly be effected.[53] However, the problem remains that such incorporation will concern some kind of 'official' customary law while real customary law continues to evolve outside the courtroom.

A seventeenth-century commentator[54] remarked of the civil law, the canon law, and the common law that it seemed strange 'that these three lawes, should not as the three Graces have their hands linked together and

---

[51] Bennett (n. 47), 46. See further Chanock, (1989) 30 *Journal of African History* 283: 'The constituting of the state's version of "customary law", based upon chiefs and headmen, subjecting women to men, and effectively insulating blacks from the common law regime, had implications for the way black lives could be lived.'

[52] Act 200 of 1993; see sched. 4, Principle XIII.

[53] Cf. Sachs (n. 32): 'Thus Roman-Dutch Law, which survived in the past by incorporating transplants of English law, will survive in the future by receiving transfusions of African law and [by thus turning into a truly] South African law.' Cf. Zimmermann, *Gedächtnisschrift Geck* (below, n. 152), 1016 sqq. and the remarks by Erasmus, (1989) 106 SALJ 670 sqq.

[54] William Fulbecke, *A Parallele or Conference on the Civill Law, the Canon Law and the Common Law of this Realme of England* (1601), Introduction.

their lookes directly fixed the one upon the other, but like the two faces of Janus, the one should be turned from the other'. The three Graces of the South African legal system are civil law, common law, and customary law. The free spirit of the third Grace makes it difficult for her to join in the circle. To enable her to do so may be one of the great challenges of the new South African legal order. Someone may then, perhaps, be able to tell the story of the africanization of Roman-Dutch law in twenty-first century South Africa.

EDITORS' NOTES I: LAW REPORTING IN SOUTH AFRICA[55]

1. The colonial period (1857–1910)

The establishment by the Charter of Justice in 1828 of a Supreme Court staffed by British-trained judges was one of the first important steps in the Anglicization of the law at the Cape of Good Hope. As was to be expected, the judges of the Supreme Court soon began to invoke the doctrine of precedent (or *stare decisis*). Thus even as early as the 1830 case of *In re Taute* the Cape Court relied on its own previous decision.[56] Sooner or later, therefore, it inevitably became desirable, in order to allow counsel to refer to previous case-law, to establish some form of law reporting. Yet not until 1857 did this begin, with the single volume of Watermeyer's Reports on cases heard in the Cape Supreme Court in the course of that year. The reporter was the learned and industrious Mr Justice E. B. Watermeyer.[57] Nine years were to pass before the first two volumes of Buchanan's Reports appeared; they were published by James (later Mr Justice) Buchanan[58] and covered the years 1868 and 1869. Perhaps even more importantly, in 1870 Menzies' Reports of Cape decisions between 1828 and 1849 appeared; they were

---

[55] For a general discussion of law reporting in South Africa see Adrienne van Blerk, 'Law Reporting and Law Reports' 1995 *Consultus* 12 sqq. A detailed table of all South African law reports and of the relevant abbreviations can be found in Hahlo/Kahn (n. 12), 293 sqq. Cf. the discussion by Hahlo/Kahn ibid. 282 sqq. For another very useful overview see Ellison Kahn, *Contracts and Mercantile Law* (vol. I, 2nd edn., 1988), XXIII sqq.

[56] (1830) 1 Menz 497; see Hahlo/Kahn (n. 12), 240; and most recently Stephen Girvin, 'Law Reporting: Menzies' Reports, Precedent and Legal Sources at the Cape Colony in the Nineteenth Century' (1995) 43 *Tijdschrift voor rechtsgeschiedenis* 107 sqq. Generally on the doctrine of precedent (the most pernicious one for South African law, according to J. C. de Wet, 'Gemene Reg of wetgewing' (1948) 11 *THRHR* 15), see Hahlo/Kahn (n. 12), 240 sqq.; Gero R. Dolezalek, *'Stare decisis': Persuasive Force of Precedent and Old Authority (12th–20th Century)* (unpublished inaugural lecture, University of Cape Town, 1989); H. J. Erasmus, 'The Interaction of Substantive and Procedural Law: The Southern African Experience in Historical and Comparative Perspective' 1990 *Stellenbosch LR* 348 sqq.

[57] On whom see Stephen Girvin, Chapter 3 below, Section II. 1. (c).

[58] On whom see Stephen Girvin, ibid. Section II. 1. (d). The decisions collected in these 2 volumes have been analysed in *Huldigingsbundel Paul van Warmelo* (1984), 286 sqq.

edited by James Buchanan from the manuscripts of the late Mr Justice William Menzies.[59] There were a variety of other individual volumes or series, published sporadically and at the private initiative of legal practitioners or judges: Searle's Reports covered the period from 1850 to 1867 (and were compiled, *inter alia*, from the notebooks of John Wylde, the first Chief Justice[60]); Foord's Reports were on nine months of a single year (1880); Mr Justice E. J. Buchanan[61] started another series of Buchanan's reports (1873–9); and so on.[62] Some regularity was established only in 1882 when the Cape Supreme Court Reports (SC) began to appear (1880–1910, 27 volumes). To these must be added the Cape Times Reports (CTR) which contain many decisions not reported elsewhere.[63] Cases from the Eastern Districts Court of the Cape of Good Hope (established in 1864) and from the High Court of Griqualand (established in 1871) only began to be reported in 1880 (EDC, with another gap from 1887 to 1891) and 1882 (HCG) respectively.[64]

As the influence of the Empire spread across the subcontinent courts operating on the British model were established in other areas that today form part of South Africa. Natal was annexed in 1845 and became a separate colony in 1856. The Natal Supreme Court was set up in the following year.[65] Phipson's Reports introduced law reporting to the new colony (1858–9); they were followed by Finnemore's Notes and Digest of Decisions of the Natal Supreme Court (covering the period 1860–7, but only published in 1880/81). Since 1867 three series of Natal Law Reports (NLR) have been published.[66]

In the Free State law reporting started in 1874, exactly twenty years after the signing of the Bloemfontein Convention by the British Government and *Voortrekker* leaders, which had made the establishment of the Republic of the Orange Free State possible.[67] Between 1879 and 1887 the decisions were reported in Dutch as *Zaken beslist in het Hooge Gerechtshof van den Oranjevrijstaat*, the last five volumes under the aegis of Mr Justice R. Gregorowski. No reports appeared between 1888 and 1902.[68] Some cases of the late nineties were, however, reported in the *Cape Law Journal*.[69] The

---

[59] On whom see Stephen Girvin, Chapter 3 below, Section II. 1. (b). On Menzies Reports see now the detailed evaluation by Girvin (1995) 43 *Tijdschrift voor rechtsgeschiedenis* 103 sqq.

[60] On whom see Stephen Girvin, Ch. 3 below, Section II. 1. (b).

[61] On whom see Ellison Kahn, *Law, Life and Laughter: Legal Anecdotes and Portraits* (1991), 15.

[62] For details see Van Blerk, 1995 *Consultus* 15; Hahlo/Kahn (n. 12), 282, 293 sq.

[63] Hahlo/Kahn (n. 12), 294.   [64] Ibid. 282.

[65] For all details see Peter Spiller, *A History of the District and Supreme Courts of Natal 1846–1910* (1986).

[66] For details see Hahlo/Kahn (n. 12), 295.

[67] For details on the constitutional history of the Free State see Hahlo/Kahn (n. 20), 72 sqq., 240 sqq.; Van Zyl (n. 21), 466 sqq.; De Vos (n. 21), 253 sqq.

[68] Cf. Van Blerk, 1995 *Consultus* 15.   [69] Hahlo/Kahn (n. 12), 296.

Orange River Colony Reports (ORC) cover the years from 1903 until 1909. On the whole the judgments of the Orange Free State courts have left little mark on the jurisprudence in South Africa;[70] this may be due, *inter alia*, to the fact that the last twenty years of the Free State's life were so uneventful 'that it has been said to have reached the blissful condition of having no history'.[71]

The *trekker* state that had been established beyond the Vaal river was propelled into the limelight of world attention in 1877 when it was annexed by Great Britain.[72] Earlier in the same year it had been decided by the government of the *Zuid-Afrikaansche Republiek* (South African Republic), as the Transvaal had hitherto officially been known, to replace the lay bench (established by the 1858 Constitution) with a professionally staffed High Court. Advocate J. G. Kotzé of Grahamstown was, at the tender age of 28,[73] appointed Chief Justice; as he was travelling to Pretoria to take up his appointment the annexation took place.[74] The British nevertheless retained his services as a judge, though not as Chief Justice. Kotzé initiated law reporting in the Transvaal with a series known as Kotzé's Reports for the period 1877 to 1881, the year of the retrocession following the ignominious British defeat at Majuba. In the same year Kotzé became Chief Justice and served until 1898, when he was dismissed after a celebrated battle with President Paul Kruger on the right of the Court to test legislation passed by the National Assembly.[75] During his time as Chief Justice he continued his law-reporting activities with a series known as the Reports of the High Court of the South African Republic (SAR, 1881–92). Thereafter others mounted a number of different law-reporting efforts: Herzog's Reports appeared for the year 1893;[76] Duxbury's Reports for 1895; and the so-called 'Official Reports' (OR) for 1894–9.[77]

---

[70] Hahlo/Kahn (n. 20), 243.   [71] Ibid. 73.

[72] For details on the constitutional history of the Transvaal see Hahlo/Kahn (n. 20), 21 sqq., 84 sqq., 228 sqq.; Van Zyl (n. 21), 460 sqq.; De Vos (n. 21), 251 sq.

[73] The English writer Anthony Trollope spoke in amazement of a 'boy judge': *South Africa* (vol. II, 1978), 121. On Kotzé, see Stephen Girvin, Ch. 3 below, Section III. 3.

[74] See De Vos (n. 21), 252.

[75] On this crisis see 'What the Position of the Judges of the High Court of the South African Republic should be' (1894) 11 *Cape Law Journal* 176–85; 'Chief Justice Kotzé' (1898) 15 *Cape Law Journal* 28–30; 'The Transvaal Judiciary' (1898) 15 *Cape Law Journal* 58–64; 'Chief Justice Kotzé' (1898) 15 *Cape Law Journal* 90–3; 'The Judiciary and the Legislature' (1889) 15 *Cape Law Journal* 109–15; 'The Judicial Deadlock in the Transvaal' (1898) 15 *Cape Law Journal* 116 sq.; J. W. Gordon, 'The Judicial Crisis in the Transvaal' (1898) 14 *LQR* 343–66; J. G. Kotzé, *Documents and Correspondence Relating to the Judicial Crisis in the South African Republic (Transvaal)* (1898); idem, *An Appeal to the Inhabitants of the South African Republic (Transvaal)* (1898); E. A. Walker, *Lord de Villiers and his Times: South Africa 1842–1914* (1925), 287–320; J. V. van der Westhuizen and D. van der Merwe, 'Die Geskiedenis van die Regspleging in Transvaal (1835–1852)' (1977) 10 *De Jure* 237–60.

[76] The reporter was Mr Justice J. B. M. Hertzog; on whom see Kahn (n. 61), 87 sq. Hertzog was to become Prime Minister of the Union of South Africa, 1924–39.

[77] For details see Hahlo/Kahn (n. 12), 296 sq.; Van Blerk, 1995 *Consultus* 15 sq.

In 1899 the machinations of the Colonial Secretary, Joseph Chamberlain, and the British High Commissioner in South Africa, Sir Alfred Milner, to remove Kruger and his government resulted in war. No law reports were therefore published for 1900 and 1901. After the war the Transvaal became a Crown Colony and both the Transvaal Supreme Court and the Witwatersrand High Court were created. The decisions of these courts were reported until Union in the Reports of the Transvaal Supreme Court (TS), the Reports of the Witwatersrand High Court (TH), and the Leader Law Reports (LLR, 1909–10).

2. After the creation of the Union of South Africa (since 1910)

On 31 May 1910 the Union of South Africa came into being as a self-governing British Colony by virtue of the South Africa Act.[78] Sections 95–116 of this Act established a Supreme Court, with an Appellate Division and four Provincial Divisions, to which a number of Local Divisions were attached. The decisions of these courts were reported in a number of different series devoted to each division until 1947, when the reports of all divisions of the Supreme Court were consolidated in the South African Law Reports, published until today in monthly instalments by South Africa's leading legal publishing house, Juta & Co.[79] Over the years a number of further reports were introduced to complement the general series. Thus, from 1923 until 1995 the Prentice Hall Weekly Legal Service attempted to provide a faster service than could be given by the South African Law Reports.[80] Butterworths, the other big South African law publisher, have just announced the establishment of the All South African Law Reports, to be published weekly from the beginning of 1996. Finally, there are a number of specialized law reports; they include the South African Tax Cases, the Patent Journal, Burrels Patent Law Reports, the Industrial Law Reports, the South African Labour Law Reports, the Commercial Law Digest, Current Commercial Cases, the South African Constitutional Law Reports, the Butterworths Constitutional Law Reports, and the South African Criminal Law Reports.

Unlike in England, there is no official or semi-official body in South Africa charged with the supervision of law reporting.[81] Whether or not a decision is published depends, in the first place, on whether it has been

---

[78] 9 Edw. 7, c. 9.

[79] Apart from the decisions of the Supreme Court of South Africa, this comprehensive series covers the decisions of the Constitutional Court of South Africa (which started operating in 1995), the High Court and Supreme Court of Namibia, and the High Court and Supreme Court of Zimbabwe. The Supreme Courts of Bophutatswana, Ciskei, Transkei, and Venda have now become part of the Supreme Court of South Africa.

[80] Hahlo/Kahn (n. 12), 284 sq.

[81] For discussion of this matter see Van Blerk, 1995 *Consultus* 17.

marked 'reportable' by the judge or judges concerned. The South African Law Reports are then compiled by a number of advocates who act as reporters for the various courts covered by this series. Unreported cases may be quoted in Court and have, in principle, the same precedential value as reported cases.[82]

EDITORS' NOTES II: THE GROWTH OF LEGAL LITERATURE IN SOUTH AFRICA

1. Early days

The fact that academic jurists have come to play an increasingly important role in the shaping of South African law makes the growth of legal literature an integral part of its history.[83] The term 'academic jurists' is here used in a wide sense to include all those who produced legal literature, whether or not they also taught law; for, although of late the greater part of law books have been written by professional academics, this has not always been the case. Indeed the first textbook about South African law, *Observations on the Insolvent Law of the Colony*, was written by Mr Justice William Burton[84] and published in Cape Town in 1829. As might be expected, the rather unsophisticated legal environment at the Cape did not produce much of note until the turn of the century. Apart from the occasional practical manual[85] one might mention the 1859 work on *Community of Property* and the *Law of Inheritance* by Mr Justice E. B. Watermeyer[86] and a flurry of translations of Roman-Dutch works in the last two decades of the nineteenth century.[87] It was only in 1893 that C. H. van Zyl published the first broadly based work on South African law entitled *The Theory of the Judicial Practice of the Colony of the Cape of Good Hope and of South*

---

[82] For all details see Hahlo/Kahn (n. 12), 284 sqq.; Van Blerk, 1995 *Consultus* 16 sq.

[83] On the development of legal literature in South Africa see esp. Adrienne van Blerk, 'The Growth of South African Legal Literature', 1977 *De Rebus Procuratoriis* 561 sqq. See further Corder/Davis (n. 46), 8 sqq.; Van Zyl (n. 21), 495 sqq.; Zimmermann (n. 21), 44 sq.; De Vos (n. 21), 264.

[84] On whom see Stephen Girvin, Ch. 3 below, Section II. 1. (b).

[85] For details see Van Blerk, 1977 *De Rebus Procuratoriis* 561.

[86] On whom see n. 57, below.

[87] For details see Van Blerk, 1977 *De Rebus Procuratoriis* 562 sq. Thus a great number of translations of different parts of Johannes Voet's *Commentarius ad Pandectas* appeared in print. Particularly influential among them was *The Roman and Roman-Dutch Law of Injuries* (1899) by Melius de Villiers. This annotated translation of book 47, title 10 served as a textbook for many years. Other works to be translated included Van der Keessel's *Theses selectae juris Hollandici et Zelandici, ad supplendam Hugonis Grotii Introductionem ad jurisprudentiam Hollandicam* (by C. A. Lorenz, 1868); Hugo Grotius' *Inleiding tot de Hollandsche Rechtsgeleertheyd* (by A. F. S. Maasdorp, 1878), and Van der Linden's *Regtsgeleerd, Practicaal, en Koopmans Handboek* (by H. Juta, 1884).

Africa Generally. It made its author the country's first academic lawyer,[88] for it appeared during Van Zyl's tenure as Professor of Law in the South African College from 1890 to 1896.

The history of the teaching of law in this institution[89] goes back to 1859 when the Council of the South African College decided to establish a Chair in law and to appoint Johannes (Hendricus) Brand as its first incumbent. He was charged with preparing his students for the law examination of the newly established Board of Public Examinations in Literature and Science, which qualified those who passed to be admitted to the Cape Bar.[90] Brand taught for only four years, after which he became President of the Orange Free State.[91] Like his successors, F. S. Watermeyer (the brother of Mr Justice E. B. Watermeyer) and Advocate (later Mr Justice) A. W. Cole,[92] he was first and foremost a practitioner. After Watermeyer's and Cole's brief tenures, the chair remained vacant for twenty-five years until ultimately C. H. van Zyl was appointed. He had by that time already established his name as the principal mentor of those preparing for practice. His book on the *Theory of Judicial Practice* was based on his lecture notes. In the meantime the *Cape Law Journal* had been established, today (under the title *South African Law Journal*) one of the oldest, still existing English-medium law journals in the world.[93]

In the first two decades of the twentieth century a number of books appeared that were to have a significant influence on the development of South African law; they were not, however, written by academic lawyers. First of all, a comparative study, *English and Roman-Dutch Law* (1903) by (Mr Justice) G. T. Morice (who, like the other judges that had served under the Kruger Government, was not re-appointed to the Transvaal bench after the Anglo–Boer War) deserves mention. Much more importantly, in the same year the first two volumes of the *Institutes of Cape Law* were published by Sir Andries Maasdorp, the first Chief Justice of the Orange River Colony

---

[88] A. A. Roberts, *A South African Legal Bibliography* (1942), 346, refers to a 'distinct landmark in the study of Roman-Dutch law in South Africa'.

[89] On which see D. V. Cowen, 'The History of the Faculty of Law, University of Cape Town: A Chapter in the Growth of Roman-Dutch Law in South Africa' 1959 *Acta Juridica* 1 sqq.; for the period after 1910 see D. V. Cowen, 'Taught Law is Tough Law: The Evolution of a South African Law School' (1988) 51 *THRHR* 4 sqq.; and, generally, D. P. Visser, 'As Durable as the Mountain: The Story of the Cape Town Law School since 1859' 1992 *Consultus* 32 sqq.

[90] Admission had hitherto, in terms of the First Charter of Justice, only been granted to those who had 'been admitted as Barristers in England or Ireland or Advocates in the Court of Session of Scotland, or to the degree of Doctor of Laws at the Universities of Oxford, Cambridge or Dublin'.

[91] For further details see Trafford B. Barlow, *The Life and Times of President Brand* (1972).

[92] He left an entertaining and informative booklet entitled *Reminiscences of my Life and of the Cape Bench and Bar* (1896).

[93] See Ellison Kahn, 'Volume 100' (1983) 100 *SALJ* 1 sq.; *idem*, 'The Birth and Life of the South African Law Journal' (1983) 100 *SALJ* 594 sqq.

after the War.[94] This work was to see partly nine and partly ten editions, the last (under the title *Institutes of South African Law*) in the late 1960s and 1970s by Mr Justice C. G. Hall. Maasdorp's *Institutes* were followed in 1904 by the first two volumes of Advocate Manfred Nathan's comprehensive work, *The Common Law of South Africa*,[95] which is described on the title page as 'a treatise based on Voet's Commentaries on the Pandects, with references to the leading Roman-Dutch authorities, South African decisions and statutory enactments in South Africa' and was, like Maasdorp's work, to grow into a four-volume set providing a comprehensive treatment of South African law. In 1908 Johannes Wessels, then a judge in the Transvaal, later Chief Justice of the Union of South African,[96] published his *History of the Roman-Dutch Law*, which added an important dimension to the understanding of South African law, and remains to this day a classic of South African legal literature. Other landmarks were the publication of *Landlord and Tenant in South Africa* in 1910 by George Wille (then practising at the Johannesburg Bar) and of *An Introduction to Roman-Dutch Law in South Africa* in 1915 by R. W. Lee. In Lee we have a transitional figure; he was an academic lawyer, though not one teaching in South Africa for he was Dean of the Law Faculty at McGill University in Montreal, and then, from 1921 to 1956, Professor of Roman-Dutch law at the University of Oxford.[97]

Soon thereafter, however, South African law professors entered the stage. Acts 13 and 14 of 1916 made possible the transformation of the Victoria College into the University of Stellenbosch and of the South African College into the University of Cape Town. In the same year Adv. (later Mr Justice) R. R. Howes was elected as the first Dean of the Law Faculty at Cape Town and actively lobbied for the establishment of full-time chairs in law. In December 1919 the Minister of Education gave permission for one such chair at the University of Cape Town to be advertised and filled. The same was done for Stellenbosch University and in 1920 George Wille and Henry Fagan (subsequently to become Chief Justice of South Africa)[98] took up their positions as the first full-time Professors of Law in the Union of

---

[94] On whom see Stephen Girvin, Ch. 3 below, Section II. 3. *The Institutes of Cape Law* eventually became a work consisting of 4 vols.: vol. I (The Law of Persons), 1903; vol. II (The Law of Things), 1903; vol. III (The Law of Obligations), 1907; vol. V (The Law of Actionable Wrongs), 1909.

[95] Reviewed in (1904) 21 *SALJ* 305 sqq. by J. C. Smuts.

[96] On whom see Stephen Girvin, Ch. 3 below, Section III. 2.

[97] On R. W. Lee, see Kahn (n. 61), 134 sqq. The 5th and last edition of his *Introduction* dates from 1953. Lee also translated Hugo Grotius' *Inleiding tot de Hollandsche Rechtsgeleertheyd*, vol. I (Text and Translation), 1926; vol. II (Commentary), 1936. Another important contribution to South African legal literature was R. W. Lee and A. M. Honoré, *The South African Law of Obligations* (1950; 2nd edn. by E. Newman and D. J. McQuoid Mason, 1978) and R. W. Lee and A. M. Honoré, *The South African Law of Property, Family Relations and Succession* (1954; 2nd edn. by H. J. Erasmus, C. G. van der Merwe, and A. H. van Wyk, 1983).

[98] On whom see Stephen Girvin, Ch. 3 below, Section III. 2.

South Africa. Wille[99] came to the University of Cape Town with three publications to his credit: apart from the work on the law of landlord and tenant mentioned above, he had co-authored with Advocate (later Mr Justice) Philip Millin[100] a treatise on *Mercantile Law in South Africa* (first published in 1917; it has become a classic and is available today in its eighteenth edition[101]), and his *Mortgage and Pledge in South Africa* was in the press.[102] In 1937 he produced *The Principles of South African Law*, which is today in its eighth edition[103] and remains the leading textbook covering the whole of South African private law in one volume.[104]

Practitioners also continued to write. 1917 saw the publication of *The Law of Insolvency in South Africa* by W. H. Mars and of the influential *South African Criminal Law and Procedure* by F. G. Gardiner and C. W. H. Lansdown. *The Civil Practice of the Magistrate's Court in South Africa* by P. S. T. Jones and H. O. Buckle appeared in 1918. G. T. Morice's *Sale in Roman-Dutch Law* as well as R. Norman's *Purchase and Sale*[105] followed in 1919, while two years later yet another book devoted to the law of sale, H. G. Mackeurtan's *Sale of Goods in South Africa*,[106] appeared in print. Academic writing on South African law was now firmly established, but it was still some time before it could be claimed to have come of age.

2. Of purists and pollutionists

Even these early works reflected what would become an abiding concern in South African legal literature: the tension between the English and the civilian legal heritage. Thus, already at this early stage, we find all the various shades of opinion that were to determine the debate for the greater part of the twentieth century. There were the extremists, exemplified by a contributor to the first volume of the *Cape Law Journal* who objected to the 'promiscuous introduction of foreign legal doctrines' into South African law,[107] and by an author writing under the name of *Vindex*, who promoted the 'Repeal of Roman-Dutch Law in South Africa'.[108] However, there were

[99] On whom see Cowen, (1988) 51 *THRHR* 9 sqq.; Kahn (n. 61), 348 sqq.; Reinhard Zimmermann, 'The Contribution of Jewish Lawyers to the Administration of Justice in South Africa', (1995) 29 *Israel LR* 282 sq.

[100] On whom see Kahn (n. 61), 171 sqq.; Zimmermann, (1995) 29 *Israel LR* 275 Wille himself claimed to have contributed the 'solid and accurate law', whereas the 'poetical flourishes' were attributable to Judge Millin.

[101] Ed. J. F. Coaker and D. T. Zeffertt, 1984.

[102] It came out in 1921; today the 3rd edn., 1987, by T. J. and S. Scott is used.

[103] Dale Hutchison (ed.), *Wille's Principles of South African Law* (8th edn., 1991).

[104] Wille played an integral part in building up the Faculty of Law at the University of Cape Town. On this period in the life of the Faculty see, apart from the sources mentioned in n. 89 above, Howard Phillips, *The University of Cape Town 1918–1948: The Formative Years* (1993), 66 sqq.   [105] Today in its 4th edn. 1972, by C. I. Belcher.

[106] Today in its 5th edn., 1984, by G. R. J. Hackwill.

[107] See Hahlo/Kahn (n. 12), 589.   [108] (1901) 18 *SALJ* 153–62.

also moderates like Robert Warden Lee, who predicted in 1906 that South African law 'will be a system in which the best elements of the Roman and the English law will be welded together in an harmonious and indissoluble union'.[109] Even among those who could be expected to be well disposed towards the civilian sources one finds what Hahlo and Kahn have called 'moderate defenders of the faith'.[110] Thus, the inaugural addresses of both Melius de Villiers[111] (who was appointed after the Anglo–Boer War to the Chair of South African Law at the University of Leiden, a chair especially created to help prevent the decline of Roman-Dutch law in South Africa) and H. D. J. Bodenstein[112] (a founding father, with W. M. R. 'Mortie' Malherbe,[113] of the Stellenbosch Law Faculty) adopted a very balanced approach in the early debate as to the 'true' sources of South African law. Certainly George Wille must be reckoned among the moderates, and the teaching programme at the University of Cape Town's Law Faculty has always reflected an even-handed approach, as evidenced for example by the 1917 syllabus:

LL B
1st Year   Latin, English, Dutch, Constitutional History.
2nd Year   1. Roman Law and its History (Sander's Justinian, Sohm & Muirhead).
           2. Elements of Roman Dutch Law and its history (Van der Linden & Wessels).
           3. Jurisprudence (Austin & Salmond).
3rd Year   1. The Roman-Dutch Law of Holland (Grotius, Van der Keessel, Van Leeuwen).
           2. Public International Law (Lawrence and Hall).
           3. Private International Law (Dicey).
4th Year   1. English Law (Anson's Contracts, Pollock's Torts, Kenny's Criminal Law, Phipson's Evidence).
           2. The Roman-Dutch Law as in force in the Union of South Africa (Maasdorp & Case Law).
           3. Statute Law; Insolvency, Company Law, Magistrate's Courts, Criminal Procedure, Bills of Exchange, Prescription, Administration of Estates, Irrigation.[114]

Soon, however, the academic scene was dominated by more partisan voices. The influence of English law on South African law, in the words of Hahlo

---

[109] Cf. Van Blerk, 1977 *De Rebus Procuratoriis* 564.
[110] Hahlo/Kahn (n. 127), 589.
[111] *Het Oud-Hollandsch Recht in Zuid-Afrika* (1905); see also Melius de Villiers, 'On Fundamentalism and Law' (1932) 49 *SALJ* 199 sqq. On Melius de Villiers, brother of Lord de Villiers, see Kahn (n. 61), 45 sq.; Roberts (n. 88), 357.
[112] *Engelse invloeden op het gemeen recht van Zuid-Afrika* (1912); an English translation of this text was published in (1915) 32 *SALJ* 337.
[113] On whom see Kahn (n. 61), 153 sqq.; Zimmermann/Hugo, (1992) 60 *Tijdschrift voor rechtsgeschiedenis* 163.
[114] Visser, 1992 *Consultus* 34.

and Kahn, 'reached its height during the half-century from 1860 to 1910, when the sun of the British Empire stood at its zenith and Britannia, firmly and indisputably, ruled the waves'.[115] Then, however, the tide began to turn. The establishment of Afrikaans-medium law faculties at Stellenbosch[116] and, some years later, in Pretoria[117] created an opportunity for the civilian basis of South African law to be reassessed. Under the aegis of Professor Daan Pont of the University of Pretoria[118] the *Tydskrif vir Hedendaagse Romeins-Hollandse Reg* (Journal for Contemporary Roman-Dutch Law) provided a vehicle for the recivilianization of the law. Much of the legal literature from the late 1930s onwards reflected the growing *bellum juridicum*[119] in one way or another. This battle saw its fiercest skirmishes on the field of the law of delict—as shown below in Chapter 18 by Dale Hutchison[120]—and it was fuelled by a complex and volatile blend of political and intellectual issues. Here it is necessary only to mention the main combatants and their principal weapons.

3. Delict, contract, enrichment, property

In 1933 Robin McKerron, then Professor of Law in the University of the Witwatersrand, Johannesburg,[121] published his textbook on *The Law of Delicts in South Africa*.[122] He found fierce opponents in Daan Pont and Tom Price,[123] Wille's successor as Professor of Roman-Dutch law at the University of Cape Town. Another champion of legal purism was N. J. J. van der Merwe of the University of Pretoria, whose *Die Onregmatige Daad in die Suid-Afrikaanse Reg*, co-authored by P. J. J. Olivier, then Professor of Law in the University of Bloemfontein, now a Judge of Appeal, appeared

---

[115] Hahlo/Kahn (n. 12), 578.

[116] On the Stellenbosch Law Faculty see A. H. van Wyk, 'Die Stellenbosse Regsfakulteit 1920–1989', 1989 *Consultus* 42 sqq.

[117] The University of Pretoria was established in 1930 as a successor to the Transvaal University College. On the history of its law faculty see Kobus van Rooyen, 'Die Regsfakulteit, Universiteit van Pretoria: Meer as Tagtig Jaar Regsonderrig' 1991 *Consultus* 49 sqq.

[118] On whom see Daan van Rensburg (1987) 50 *THRHR* 253 sqq. He died in 1991 at the age of 96.

[119] On which see esp. *Proculus*, '*Bellum Juridicum*: Two Approaches to South African Law' (1951) 68 *SALJ* 306 sqq.; G. A. Mulligan, '*Bellum Juridicum*: Purists, Pollutionists and Pragmatists' (1952) 69 *SALJ* 25 sqq.; A. S. Mathews, J. R. L. Milton, 'An English Backlash', (1965) 82 *SALJ* 31 sqq.; *Proculus Redivivus*, 'South African Law at the Crossroads or: What is Our Common Law?' (1965) 82 *SALJ* 17 sqq.; P. Q. R. Boberg, 'Oak Tree or Acorn?: Conflicting Approaches to our Law of Delict' (1966) 83 *SALJ* 150 sqq.; Cameron, (1982) 99 *SALJ* 38 sqq.; Adrienne van Blerk, 'The Genesis of the "Modernist–Purist" Debate: A Historical Bird's-eye View' (1984) *THRHR* 255 sqq.; Forsyth (n. 24), 182 sqq.

[120] Aquilian Liability II (20th Century).

[121] Founded in 1922. On its history see Ellison Kahn, 'The Wits Faculty of Law 1922–1989: A Story with a Personal Touch' 1989 *Consultus* 103 sqq.

[122] Changed in the 2nd edn. to *The Law of Delict*.

[123] On Price, see Visser, 1992 *Consultus* 35.

in 1966,[124] whilst Professor P. Q. R. Boberg of the University of the Witwatersrand stood up to the excesses of the purist movement and in the end gave the country a brilliant exposition of the fusion of the English and civilian approach in *The Law of Delict* (vol. I, *Aquilian Liability*, 1984). Indeed, his tribute to N. J. J. van der Merwe in the Foreword of that book symbolizes the equilibrium eventually achieved:

Van der Merwe: the talented *enfant terrible*, the brilliant inconoclast who, though a little older than he was when he first made grey heads turn disapprovingly, still retains the power to make us think about the law and marvel at his trenchantly humorous prose. We have crossed swords many times: little did I know how many of his views I would come to share as I wrote this book.[125]

The fact that one of the leading modern textbooks in the field, J. Neethling, J. M. Potgieter, and P. J. J. Visser, *The Law of Delict* appears in both Afrikaans and English versions is further testimony of the maturity reached in this most contested area of South African law.[126] There is today an *embarras de richesse* of general and specialized textbooks on the law of delict.[127]

In the law of contract the struggle for the soul of South African law was not quite so fierce. English law did not threaten to remould this part of the law as comprehensively as it did the law of delict, and the leading figure of the 'purist' movement in this field, Professor J. C. de Wet of the University of Stellenbosch, had a healthy streak of pragmatism: he did not disdain English law *per se*.[128] There can be no doubt that the work of J. C. de Wet and J. P. Yeats, *Die Suid-Afrikaanse Kontraktereg en Handelsreg*, first

---

[124] On Price, see Visser, 1992 *Consultus* 35. [124] Currently in its 6th edn. (1989).
[125] At ix–x.
[126] First Afrikaans edn. 1989, 2nd edn. 1992; 1st English edn. 1990, 2nd edn. 1994.
[127] Apart from the works already mentioned, there are Jonathan Burchell, *Principles of Delict* (1993); D. P. Visser, 'Delict', in: Dale Hutchison (ed.), *Wille's Principles of South African Law* (8th edn., 1991), 645 sqq.; J. Neethling, J. M. Potgieter, T. J. Scott, *Case Book on the Law of Delict* (1991); J. C. van der Walt, *Delict: Principles and Cases* (1979) (somewhat dated, but still often cited); W. E. Cooper, *Motor Law*, vol. 2: *Principles of Liability for Patrimonial Loss* (1987) (a treatment of the general principles of delict in the setting of motor vehicle accidents); out of date are now: R. G. McKerron, *The Law of Delict* (7th edn., 1971) and J. C. Macintosh, C. Norman-Scoble, *Negligence in Delict* (5th edn., 1970). More specialized works include Jonathan Burchell, *The Law of Defamation in South Africa* (1983); H. J. O. van Heerden, J. Neethling, *Unlawful Competition* (1995) (a translated and updated version of *Die Reg aangaande Onregmatige Mededinging* (1983)); J. Neethling, *Persoonlikheidsreg* (3rd edn., 1991); D. J. McQuoid-Mason, *The Law of Privacy in South Africa* (1978); P. J. Visser, J. M. Potgieter, *The Law of Damages* (1993) (also in Afrikaans: *Skadevergoedingsreg* (1993)).
[128] On J. C. de Wet, see Reinhard Zimmermann, Charl Hugo, 'Fortschritte der südafrikanischen Rechtswissenschaft im 20. Jahrhundert: Der Beitrag von J. C. de Wet (1912–1990)' (1992) 60 *Tijdschrift voor rechtsgeschiedenis* 157 sqq.; Edwin Cameron, 'Lawyers, Language and Politics: In Memory of J. C. de Wet and W. A. Joubert' (1993) 110 *SALJ* 51 sqq.; Reinhard Zimmermann, 'De Wet, Johannes Christiaan', in: Michael Stolleis (ed.), *Juristen: Ein biographisches Lexikon* (1995), 161 sqq.

published in 1949,[129] was the central force that kept South African law essentially on a civilian track in the second half of this century. Written in the characteristically abrasive style of its principal author,[130] this work raised hackles, but was destined in the end to dominate the scene. Something of the flavour of the purist–pragmatist debate is revealed in the review of the third edition of De Wet and Yeats by P. M. A. Hunt.[131] After praising the book as 'one of the most valuable and influential of South African legal publications', Hunt lists a number of criticisms, including a charge that the book is unbalanced:

The chapters on General Principles of Contract altogether omit such important topics as: restraint of trade agreements, severance, wagers, the 'ticket cases' and 'standard form' contracts (admittedly the old authorities had not heard of them) . . . [The] text and footnotes, though liberally peppered with references to various German and Dutch (but not modern French) writers, contain very few references to English decisions and none (that I could find) to Williston, Corbin or the *American Restatement*.

He concludes by stating that 'the views propounded in *De Wet and Yeats* are too often influenced by inflexible logic and too seldom by considerations of equity and social policy'.[132]

More often than not, however, the 'inflexible logic' prevailed. De Wet transformed the South African law of contract, in that he set out to design, on the basis of the historical development, a coherent set of concepts and principles rather than to regard judicial precedents as the fixed stars in the legal firmament. Thus, it was the approach even more than the doctrinal substance that De Wet adopted from continental European legal science and which was to have a lasting impact on legal science in South Africa.

Of course, J. C. de Wet was not the only South African writer to have made a significant contribution to the law of contract. Sir Johannes Wessels went before him with his treatise in two volumes, entitled *The Law of Contract* (1937/8),[133] and he was followed by A. J. Kerr,[134] Ellison Kahn,[135] Van Rensburg, Lotz, and Van Rhijn,[136] R. H. Christie,[137] David

---

[129] The last edition to contain both the part on the general principles of contract law and the part on mercantile law was the 4th (1978, by J. C. de Wet and A. H. van Wyk). See now: J. C. de Wet, A. H. van Wyk, *De Wet en Yeats, Die Suid-Afrikaanse Kontraktereg en Handelsreg*, vol. I (ed. G. F. Lubbe, 5th edn., 1991).

[130] 'In differing from the view of the judges the writers have, with respect, too often used the bludgeon. The field is bloody with the mangled remains of slaughtered leading cases': Ellison Kahn (1954) 71 *SALJ* 185, 187.

[131] (1965) 82 *SALJ* 412.   [132] Ibid. 413.

[133] Ed. A. A. Roberts. A second edition (also by A. A. Roberts) appeared in 1951.

[134] *The Principles of the Law of Contract* (1st edn., 1967; 4th edn., 1989).

[135] *Contract and Mercantile Law through the Cases* (1971). See now the 2nd edn.: vol. I (1988), ed. Ellison Kahn, Carole Lewis, and Coenraad Visser; vol. II (1985), ed. Ellison Kahn, David Zeffertt, J. T. Pretorius, and Coenraad Visser.

[136] 'Contract', in: W. A. Joubert (ed.), *The Law of South Africa*, vol. 5 (1978); cf. now the revised version by R. H. Christie in vol. 5, pt. 1 of the First Reissue (1994).

[137] *The Law of Contract in South Africa* (1st edn., 1981; 2nd edn., 1991).

Joubert,[138] Gerhard Lubbe and Christina Murray,[139] Dale Hutchison,[140] and most recently by a team of five authors.[141] Apart from Wessels, De Wet, Kahn, and Hutchison, all these authors deal only with the general principles of contractual liability. However, the specific contracts discussed in the present volume are also well served in modern South African literature.[142]

Turning to unjustified enrichment we find a very solid civilian base, although even here English law has crept in.[143] Since the House of Lords has only recently acknowledged unjust enrichment as a cause of action *eo nomine*, it is not surprising that this area of the law did not see an overt challenge from English law. The standard text today is that of Wouter de Vos, *Verrykingsaanspreeklikheid in die Suid-Afrikaanse Reg*.[144] An excellent short statement is provided by J. G. Lotz in the standard encyclopaedia of South African law.[145] Recently a casebook on the subject has been

---

[138] *General Principles of the Law of Contract* (1987).

[139] *Farlam and Hathaway, Contract: Cases, Materials, Commentary* (3rd edn., 1988). The original edition of this work by I. G. (now Mr Justice) Farlam and E. W. Hathaway appeared in 1968.

[140] 'Contracts', in: Dale Hutchison (ed.), *Wille's Principles of South African Law* (8th edn., 1991), 409–629.

[141] Schalk van der Merwe, L. F. van Huyssteen, M. F. B. Reinecke, G. F. Lubbe, J. G. Lotz, *Contract: General Principles* (1993).

[142] On the contract of sale see *Norman's Purchase and Sale in South Africa* (4th edn. by C. I. Belcher, 1972); D. F. Mostert, D. J. Joubert, G. Viljoen, *Die Koopkontrak* (1972); *Mackeurtan's Sale of Goods in South Africa* (5th edn. by G. R. J. Hackwill, 1984); A. J. Kerr, *The Law of Sale and Lease* (1984); A. J. Kerr and J. M. Otto, 'Sale and Consumer Credit', in: W. A. Joubert (ed.), *The Law of South Africa*, vol. 24 (1986). On agency (usually treated as a specific contract) see D. J. Joubert, *Die Suid-Afrikaanse Verteenwoordigingsreg* (1979); *De Villiers and Macintosh, The Law of Agency in South Africa* (3rd edn. by J. M. Silke, 1981); A. J. Kerr, *The Law of Agency* (3rd edn., 1991); J. C. de Wet (revised by A. G. du Plessis), 'Agency and Representation', in: W. A. Joubert (ed.), *The Law of South Africa*, vol. 1 (First Reissue, 1993). On the employment contract, see A. Rycroft, B. Jordaan, *The Contract of Employment* (1994). On labour law generally see C. Thompson, B. Benjamin, *South African Labour Law* (1995, loose-leaf). As a result of the adoption of the Labour Relations Act 1995 all existing texts on labour law are out of date in major respects. On the law of insurance see D. M. Davis, *Gordon and Getz on the South African Law of Insurance* (4th edn., 1993). On suretyship see C. F. Forsyth, J. T. Pretorius, *Caney's The Law of Suretyship* (4th edn., 1994); J. G. Lotz, 'Suretyship', in: W. A. Joubert (ed.), *The Law of South Africa*, vol. 26 (1986). Concerning the law of negotiable instruments see Dennis V. Cowen, Leonard Gering, *Cowen, The Law of Negotiable Instruments in South Africa*, vol. I: *General Principles* (5th edn., 1985); Leonard Gering, *Handbook on the Law of Negotiable Instruments* (1993, with a 1995 supplement); F. R. Malan, J. T. Pretorius, C. R. de Beer, *Malan on Bills of Exchange, Cheques and Promissory Notes in South African Law* (2nd edn., 1994); Robert Sharrock, Michael Kidd, *Understanding Cheque Law* (1993).

[143] For details see Ch. 16 below by D. P. Visser.

[144] The 1st edn., based on the author's doctoral thesis at the University of Cape Town, was published in 1958. The 3rd edn. dates from 1987.

[145] 'Enrichment', in: W. A. Jourbert (ed.), *The Law of South Africa*, vol. 9 (1979). Cf. D. P. Visser, 'Enrichment', in: Dale Hutchison (ed.), *Wille's Principles of South African Law* (8th edn., 1991), 630 sqq. The first general work on the law of unjustified enrichment published in South Africa was D. G. John, *'n Oorsig van Ongeregverdigde Verryking as Gedingsoorsaak in die Suid-Afrikaanse Reg* (1951).

published[146] whose extensive commentary goes a long way towards allevi-
ating the difficulties that exist as a result of the only full-length textbook
being in Afrikaans.[147]

The law of property has remained the most unassailable stronghold of
civilian jurisprudence, as the contributions to this volume by Milton, C. G.
van der Merwe, De Waal, and Kleyn make abundantly clear. Yet the *bellum juridicum* did rage around certain of its more exposed turrets. Thus,
where the law of property intersects with delict (i.e. in the area of neighbour
disputes) English law has made important advances, as appears from Derek
van der Merwe's discussion of this topic in Chapter 21 below. And of course
the English trust law has managed to infiltrate the citadel. In the process,
however, it had to adapt to the new environment. The story is told in
Chapter 26 below by Tony Honoré. The result is one of the most fascinating instances of a genuine amalgamation of civil law and common law elements. The leading modern text on South African trust law is by Honoré
and Cameron.[148] The most influential author in the field of property law
generally is C. G. van der Merwe of the University of Stellenbosch who
brought out the first edition of his *Sakereg* in 1979.[149] Another general book
of note is D. G. Kleyn and A. Boraine, *Silberberg and Schoeman's The Law
of Property*.[150] An important specialized text is that by D. L. Carey Miller,
The Acquisition and Protection of Ownership (1986).

4. More books (and journals)

The purpose of this Note is not to provide an exhaustive bibliography. It is
merely intended (i) to provide an impression of the extent to which South
African legal literature has in recent years grown to maturity and (ii) to indi-

---

[146] Sieg Eiselen, Gerrit Pienaar, *Unjustified Enrichment: A Casebook* (1993).

[147] *Negotiorum gestio* (i.e. the management of someone else's affairs without authority) is
usually discussed by way of an appendix to unjustified enrichment. It is squarely based on
Roman law. The standard work today is D. H. (now Mr Justice) Van Zyl, *Negotiorum Gestio
in South African Law: An Historical and Comparative Analysis* (1985); cf. *idem, Die saak-
waarnemingsaksie as verrykingsaksie in die Suid-Afrikaanse reg* (unpublished Dr. iur. thesis,
University of Leiden, 1970).

[148] Tony Honoré, Edwin Cameron, *Honoré's South African Law of Trusts* (4th edn., 1992).
The 1st edn. (by Tony Honoré) appeared in 1966. It produced a violent reaction by C. P. (now
Mr Justice) Joubert: 'Honoré se Opvatting oor die Trustreg' (1969) 31 *THRHR* 124 sqq.
Joubert himself had previously, at the University of Leiden, written a doctoral thesis on the
continental 'foundation': *Die Stigting in die Romeins-Hollandse Reg en die Suid-Afrikaanse Reg*
(1951); on which see Robert Feenstra, 'L'histoire des fondations', (1956) 24 *Tijdschrift voor
rechtsgeschiedenis* 381 sqq.

[149] The 2nd edn. appeared in 1989. Cf. *idem*, 'Things', in: W. A. Joubert (ed.), *The Law of
South Africa*, vol. 27 (1987); *idem*, 'Things', in: Lee and Honoré, *Family, Things and Succession*
(2nd edn., 1983); and 'Property', in: Dale Hutchison (ed.), *Wille's Principles of South African
Law* (8th edn., 1991).

[150] This is the 3rd edn. of a work originally written by Silberberg (1975). Cf. H. J. Delport,
N. J. J. Olivier, *Sakereg: Vonnisbundel* (2nd edn., 1985).

cate to the reader the leading texts on the fields of law covered in this book. Much has had to be left out. We cannot, however, conclude our overview without paying tribute to the two best known names in English South African legal literature: Herbert Robert Hahlo (1905–84) and Ellison Kahn.[151]They co-operated very closely on a variety of major scholarly projects. Of particular importance is volume V of the 'Commonwealth Series', *The Union of South Africa: The Development of its Laws and Constitution* which they produced in 1960. It is a monumental work covering the entire spectrum of South African law and has not yet been replaced by any other work of similar sweep or ambition. Eight years later, Hahlo and Kahn published what is still the leading textbook on the jurisprudential, methodological, systematic, and historical 'framework within which the technical law of South Africa must be seen': *The South African Legal System and its Background.*

The serious student of present-day South African law will find a wealth of further material in the ever-increasing number of (mainly) unpublished doctoral theses produced in South Africa's twenty-one law faculties,[152] in a number of prestigious *Festschriften* and *Gedenkschriften*,[153] in a legal encyclopaedia in thirty-two volumes, dedicated to the memory of Johannes Voet and inspired by Halsbury's Laws of England,[154] in the *Annual Survey of South African Law*, in a variety of translations of old authorities,[155] and of

---

[151] For details and further references see Zimmermann, (1995) 29 *Israel LR* 284 sqq.

[152] At the Universities of Cape Town, Stellenbosch, Western Cape, Port Elizabeth, Fort Hare, Rhodes, Transkei, Natal (Pietermaritzburg), Natal (Durban), Durban-Westville, Zululand, Bloemfontein, Potchefstroom, Witwatersrand, Rand Afrikaans University, Vista, Pretoria, South Africa (a correspondence University based in Pretoria), the North, the North-West (formerly Bophuthatswana), and Venda. On the law faculties in South Africa and the problem of legal training in the last 10 years of the apartheid era see Reinhard Zimmermann, ' "Turning and Turning in the Widening Gyre ...": Gegenwartsprobleme der Juristenausbildung in Südafrika', in: *Gedächtnisschrift für W. K. Geck* (1989), 985 sqq.; Johann van der Westhuizen, *On Equality, Justice, the Future of South African Law Schools and Other Dreams*, Occasional Paper No. 1, Centre for Human Rights, University of Pretoria (1993).

[153] They include, in recent years, *Essays in Honour of Ben Beinart* (3 vols., 1978/79); *Fiat Iustitia: Essays in Memory of Oliver Deneys Schreiner* (1983); *Huldigingsbundel Paul van Warmelo* (1984); *Huldigingsbundel vir W. A. Joubert* (1988); *Essays in Honour of Ellison Kahn* (1989); *The Quest for Justice: Essays in Honour of Michael McGregor Corbett* (1995).

[154] W. A. Joubert (Founding Editor), *The Law of South Africa*. The first vol. appeared in 1976, the last in 1995. In the meantime, the first volumes of a 'First Reissue' have begun to appear (since 1993).

[155] Cf. e.g. Simon van Leeuwen, *Het Rooms-Hollands-Regt*: trans. (Mr Justice) J. G. Kotzé, *Commentaries on the Roman-Dutch Law* (2 vols., 1882–6; 2nd edn., 1921–3); Ulrich Huber, *Heedendaegse Rechtsgeleertheyt*: trans. (Mr Justice) Percival Gane, *Jurisprudence of my Time* (2 vols., 1939); Johannes Voet, *Commentarius ad Pandectas*: trans. (Mr Justice) Percival Gane, *The Selective Voet, being the Commentary of the Pandects* (7 vols., 1955–8); for further translations by South African authors of parts of this work see A. A. Roberts, *A Guide to Voet* (1933, 18 sqq.); Ben Beinart, Paul van Warmelo (ed.), *Praelectiones in libros XLVII et XLIII Digestorum, exhibentes jurisprudentiam criminalem ad usum fori Batavi applicatam (duce Cornelio van Eck) et in Novum Codicem Criminalem* 1809 (with translation into English, 6 vols., 1969–81); Ben Beinart, Margaret Hewett (eds.), *Simon van Groenewegen van der Made*,

course in the contributions to scholarly journals. The number of journals existing today may give some indication of the sheer volume of literature produced every year. The *South African Law Journal*, of course, remains the country's leading legal periodical,[156] and the *Tydskrif vir Hedendaagse Romeins-Hollandse Reg* remains its primary competitor. Other general law reviews include *Tydskrif vir die Suid-Afrikaanse Reg, Stellenbosch Law Review, De Jure, Tydskrif vir Regswetenskap, Comparative and International Law Journal of Southern Africa*, and *Acta Juridica*.[157] Among the specialized periodicals some of the leading titles are *South African Journal of Criminal Justice, South African Yearbook of International Law, South African Journal on Human Rights, South African Mercantile Law Journal*, and *South African Public Law*. *Responsa Meridiana* is edited by the law students o the Universities of Cape Town and Stellenbosch. The professions are served by *De Rebus* (formerly *De Rebus Procuratoriis*) and *Consultus*.

Tractatus de legibus abrogatis et inusitatis in Hollandia vicinisque regionibus (with translation into English, 4 vols., 1974–87); Margaret Hewett, Ben Stoop (eds.), *Antonius Matthaeus, De Criminibus* (with transation into English, vol. I, 1987; vol. II, 1993; vol. III, 1994; vol. IV, 1996 (only by M. Hewett).

[156] In its more recent history it has been inseparably linked to the names of H. R. Hahlo and Ellison Kahn who have served as editors from 1950 to 1968 and from 1958 to the present day respectively.

[157] It is published once a year; since 1983 each issue is devoted to a common theme.

PART I

Setting the Scene

1: *Roman-Dutch Law in its South African Historical Context*

EDUARD FAGAN*

I. INTRODUCTION

Lawyers are trained to respect tradition, and Roman-Dutch law, with its roots firmly embedded in Roman law, boasts a lengthy tradition. It is therefore almost inevitable that lawyers writing about the history of the legal system in South Africa should often regard that tradition as almost transcendental, rising above the narrow and time-bound social and political world which is the concern of other historians. What might be termed the immanent approach has resulted in some fine academic work on its own terms. The typical description of the growth of a European system of law in Southern Africa as a somewhat smooth and seamless process has, however, tended to obscure the extent to which that growth paralleled the establishment of a more general European hegemony. Of course, the complexity of the relationship between legal tradition and societal events precludes any simple conclusions. The overview which follows seeks merely to place the development of the Roman-Dutch law within a broader South African historical context, making liberal use of some of the detailed recent work of specialists in South African history. It raises the question of why the legal system is virtually exclusively European. It also seeks to suggest that Roman-Dutch law, with its powerful tradition of legal principle, need be neither narrowly defined nor artificially protected against the enriching influence of other systems.

II. BEFORE EUROPEAN COLONIZATION

Research into the dating and grouping of the early inhabitants of Southern Africa, and into the determination of their links with those peoples reflected in early documented history, has made great strides over the past few decades. No longer based on vague and perhaps predetermined categories of race, research has concentrated on breeding populations, emphasizing

* I wish to thank Reinhard Zimmermann and Daniel Visser for their helpful comments on drafts of this essay.

common gene pools. The complexity of genetic structures has (re-)introduced uncertainty with regard to physical origins.[1]

It can be said with a fair degree of certainty that for many millennia prior to European encroachment upon Southern Africa, including the area later to be known as the Cape of Good Hope, had been populated by groups of gatherer-hunters,[2] some of whom (generally known as the Khoikhoi[3]) in time turned to the herding of sheep and cattle.[4] Not being cultivators, Khoikhoi society 'was based not on the possession of land, but on small kin groups whose members were related to each other through the male line'.[5] It was a society constantly in flux: 'Together the Khoikhoi-hunter cycle and the political weaknesses of pastoralism led to a fluid situation in which people and livestock flowed rapidly from tribe to tribe, and from herding to hunting communities and back again'.[6] It was probably at least partly as a result of this fluidity that the Khoikhoi were in due course almost wholly subsumed by colonial culture.[7]

As early as AD 200 Bantu-speaking Iron Age communities had settled in the more northerly parts of what is now called South Africa; they moved gradually southwards,[8] presumably under the pressure of population growth. Since their mixed economies included widespread cultivation of land and a need for pasturage,[9] their lineages 'were rooted in territo-

---

[1] Martin Hall, *The Changing Past: Farmers, Kings and Traders in Southern Africa, 200–1860* (1987), pp. 18 sq.

[2] R. R. Inskeep, *The Peopling of Southern Africa* (1978), 61 sqq., 84 sqq., 152. Gathering and hunting 'had been established in one form or another in southern Africa for perhaps several million years': Hall (n. 1), 144.

[3] This is the term generally used for the early pastoralists at the Cape, in contradistinction to the term *San* (in itself, like 'bushman', pejorative), referring to the gatherer-hunters of the Holocene. The terminology, and the distinctions, are perforce inexact. See R. R. Inskeep, 'The Archaeological Background', in: Monica Wilson, Leonard Thompson (eds.), *The Oxford History of South Africa*, vol. I, *South Africa to 1870* (1969), 21 sqq.; Monica Wilson, 'The Hunters and Herders', in: Wilson/Thompson, 40 sqq.; Richard Elphick, *Kraal and Castle: Khoikhoi and the Founding of White South Africa* (1977), xxi sqq., 3 sqq., 28; Richard Elphick, V. C. Malherbe, 'The Khoisan to 1828', in: Richard Elphick, Hermann Giliomee (eds.), *The Shaping of South African Society, 1652–1840* (2nd edn., 1988), 4 sq.

[4] Inskeep (n. 3), 22 sqq.; T. R. H. Davenport, *South Africa: A Modern History* (4th edn., 1991), 6, 9, suggests that cattle were first acquired by the Khoikhoi some 2,000 years ago, and introduced to the Western Cape some 1,000 years ago. See also Hall (n. 1), 34.

[5] Elphick/Malherbe (n. 3), 6. Patrilineal clans could, however, at times exceed 2,500 people: Wilson (n. 3), 58; Davenport (n. 4), 6.

[6] Elphick (n. 3), 68.

[7] The possible causes of the collapse of the Western Cape Khoikhoi society are examined fully by Elphick (n. 3), *passim* and in some detail by Elphick/Malherbe (n. 3), 18 sqq.

[8] Hall (n. 1), 13.

[9] Although 'it is probable that the harvest provided most of the food consumed', political power was to be had through the ownership of cattle: Hall (n. 1), 58, 73. See also Monica Wilson, 'The Nguni People', in: Wilson/Thompson (n. 3), 107 sqq. Cattle also constituted the only form of wealth, in any event for the Cape Nguni: Colin Bundy, *The Rise and Fall of the South African Peasantry* (1979), 17.

ries'.[10] The similarity of their social and economic structures to those of the later European colonizers,[11] particularly their organization into large states developed around a tributary mode of production,[12] was an important factor in the continual clashes between these groups.

III. DUTCH SETTLEMENT AT THE CAPE

Although European explorers had been landing on the shores of Southern Africa since the late fifteenth century, the first European settlement of any permanence was established in the mid-seventeenth century. This took the form of a Dutch refreshment station at Table Bay—including a vegetable garden and a hospital—for ships plying the lucrative trade route between the Netherlands and the East Indies.

It has often been said, and bears repetition here, that Jan van Riebeeck, the first commander of the Cape settlement, did not stake his claim in a vacant land.[13] Indeed, the necessity for trade with the inhabitants of the Cape, the Khoikhoi, was recognized by Janssen and Proot, whose *Remonstrantie* of 1649 had strongly influenced the decision of the Dutch East India Company (Vereenigde Geoctroyeerde Oost-Indische Compagnie, abbreviated VOC) to establish a refreshment station.[14] The authors went even further in their aspirations for the local population: 'Wel ende in goede correspondentie met haer levende sal men metter tijd eenige van haer kinderen tot jongens ende dienaers gebruijcken ende in Christelijcke religie optrecken'.[15]

The nature of the Cape project was such that the VOC—a trading company acting at all times under charter of the Netherlands Estates-General— had only very limited territorial ambitions there.[16] Nor could this

[10] Wilson (n. 9), 116. The quote refers specifically to the Nguni, but the principle is also true of other Bantu-speaking societies: Monica Wilson, 'The Sotho, Venda, and Tsonga', in: Wilson/Thompson (n. 3), 159, 175, 177 sq.; Davenport (n. 4), 63. Whilst land vested in the chief, it would be allocated to individual members for usage: Bundy (n. 9), 21.

[11] Hermann Giliomee, 'The Eastern Frontier, 1770–1812', in: Elphick/Giliomee (n. 3), 425 sq.

[12] Hall (n. 1), 74 sqq., 125 sq., 146.

[13] See e.g. Elphick/Malherbe (n. 3), 3.

[14] George McCall Theal, *History of South Africa under the Administration of the Dutch East India Company (1652 to 1795)* (1969), vol. I, 4; Elphick (n. 3), 87 sq.; Leonard Guelke, 'Freehold Farmers and Frontier Settlers, 1657–1780', in: Elphick/Giliomee (n. 3), 69.

[15] (Having established a good relationship with them, one will in time be able to use certain of their children as labourers and servants, and to raise them in the Christian religion.) H. C. V. Leibbrandt, *Précis of the Archives of the Cape of Good Hope: Letters Received and Documents Received 1649–1662*, vol. I, (1898), 15.

[16] This is symbolized by the hedge of wild almond which was planted for reasons, amongst others, of defence, but which also demarcated the original limits of the Commander's jurisdictional interests; see Gerrit Schutte, 'Company and Colonists at the Cape, 1652–1795', in: Elphick/Giliomee (n. 3), 292 sq.

windswept peninsula pretend to offer anything of great value to the high-
flying Dutch during their golden age,[17] other than fresh victuals en route to
and from their more exotic oriental ports of call.[18] One might argue, therefore, that an event of greater importance than that first settlement occurred
some five years later, when a number of *freeburghers* were permitted to farm
for their own profit, albeit still obliged to sell their produce to the VOC at
controlled prices.[19] With this event European settlement began to acquire
the feature of permanence, which was to lead in time to great expansion into
the hinterland, and finally to control over the entire area of present-day
South Africa. The expansion followed the northerly and easterly routes of
migration of the *trekboers*, the semi-nomadic European pastoralists who let
their herds graze over vast areas of the interior.

As the settlement's official frontier consequently shifted—to Stellenbosch
(1682), Swellendam (1743), Graaff-Reinet (1785), and Uitenhage (1803)[20]—
so the area of white domination was extended.[21] It would be unduly simplistic, however, to state that the Dutch regarded the Cape as *res nullius*,[22]
and therefore arrogated to themselves the right to lay claim to such parts
of it as they from time to time desired. The Khoikhoi were, at least initially,
regarded as a foreign people with whom one could trade, do battle, and
treat. Their claims to the land were not dismissed out of hand,[23] but were

[17] The general state of the Seven Provinces of the Netherlands during the 17th C. is neatly
encapsulated in the title of Simon Schama's superb cultural history of the period, *The
Embarrassment of Riches* (1987).

[18] There has been some debate as to whether, on a strict interpretation of the terms of their
respective charters, the Cape fell within the domain of the Dutch West India Company rather
than the Dutch East India Company. See H. R. Hahlo, Ellison Kahn, *The Union of South
Africa: The Development of its Laws and Constitution* (1960), 2, n. 2; *idem, The South African
Legal System and its Background* (1968), 534. The debate is interesting only in that it demonstrates how little value the Cape in itself had for the VOC. Had it been of any real importance,
a clearer determination would no doubt have been forthcoming (as was indeed done some
70 years after the initial charter, in 1674, by the limitation of the Dutch West India Company's
charter to 30 degrees South: see J. C. de Wet, *Die Ou Skrywers in Perspektief* (1988), 18,
n. 87).

[19] Robert Ross, 'The Cape of Good Hope and the World Economy, 1652–1835', in:
Elphick/Giliomee (n. 3), 245 sqq.; Davenport (n. 4), 25.

[20] M. F. Katzen, 'White Settlers and the Origin of a New Society, 1652–1778', in:
Wilson/Thompson (n. 3), 212; Davenport (n. 4), 27. For a useful summary of the extension of
the frontier see Theal, vol. II (n. 14), 410.

[21] Although the first Dutch settlers were in time joined by other Europeans, in particular
Germans and French Huguenots, the latter were subsumed by the prevailing Cape-Dutch culture. Theal, vol. II (n. 14), 324 sqq.; Davenport (n. 4), 20.

[22] De Wet (n. 18), 19. See *contra* Albie Sachs, *Justice in South Africa* (1973), 28 sq. *Res nullius* was first proposed as a political justification for white ownership of land at the Cape in
the 1830s: André du Toit, Hermann Giliomee, *Afrikaner Political Thought: Analysis and
Documents*, vol. I, *1780–1850* (1983), 214.

[23] The Khoikhoi, having initially assumed that the Dutch would, as in the past, be moving
on, soon realized that the Cape settlement was an infringement of their territorial rights, and
accordingly 'hadden sij [the Khoikhoi] wederom te verstaen gegeven dat wij [the Dutch] op
haer landt saten ende sagen dat wij vast lustigh aen bouden om nimmermeer te vertrecken,
ende ons daerom geen beesten meer verruijlen wilden, alsoo wij de beste wijde voor ons beesten

by implication countered by the official, legitimating, argument that the Dutch had both cultivated and fortified the area which fell under their sway.[24] Indeed, the terms of peace treaties concluded in 1660 between the Dutch on one hand and the two most important Peninsular tribes, the Goringhaiqua and the Gorachouqua, on the other included the recognition by the tribes of the VOC's sovereignty over the land settled by the *free-burghers*.[25] Negotiation of this kind was of course quite consistent with the commercial character of the VOC.[26] Legitimating reliance has even been placed on a 'contract of sale' allegedly concluded between the Dutch Government at the Cape and a Khoikhoi chief, Schacher, under whose terms the Cape district was purchased by the former from the latter for a sum payable in goods.[27]

IV. THE INTRODUCTION OF ROMAN-DUTCH LAW AT THE CAPE

The extension of the white frontier led to a gradual—albeit never clearly expressed—change in the relationship between the Dutch and the Khoikhoi. 'The Company's impact on Khoikhoi was gradual and cumulative rather than cataclysmic. Nonetheless, there was a decisive turning point in the mid-1670s when its determination to recognise Khoikhoi independence waned and when it began to impinge on Khoikhoi sovereignty in many ways—military, diplomatic, economic and judicial'.[28] In particular, the Khoikhoi

innamen' (they let us understand that we were in occupation of their land and said that we were building apace, never again to depart, and that they accordingly had no wish to exchange further livestock with us, since we had taken the best grazing for our stock). Also, the *Caepmans* (the collective term used by the Dutch for the Goringhaiqua and the Gorachouqua: Elphick (n. 3), 45) expressly asserted their prior claim to ''t landt van de Caap' (the land of the Cape), although this claim was referred to in the official journal as no more than 'preten-tie van eygendom over dese Caep' (a pretence of ownership over this Cape): D. B. Bosman (ed.), *Daghregister Gehouden by den Opperkoopman Jan Anthonisz van Riebeeck* (1952), vol. I, 287; vol. II, 37 sq.

[24] Carli Coetzee, 'Visions of Disorder and Profit: The Khoi and the First Years of the Dutch East India Company at the Cape', (1994) 20 *Social Dynamics* 45 sq.

[25] Elphick (n. 3), 114; Elphick/Malherbe (n. 3), 12. The point, of course, is that such recog-nition would probably not have been sought had the Cape truly been regarded as *res nullius* (although it is essential to distinguish between the relationship of Dutch to Khoikhoi on the ground and the view of the Cape as it might have been set out in official documentation; Coetzee, (1994) 20 *Social Dynamics* 39, 42).

[26] As Schutte (n. 16), 292 puts it: '[E]mpire-building was contrary to the mentality of the Dutch merchant-regents.'

[27] Hahlo/Kahn, *System* (n. 18), 568, n. 8. See also Peter Kolb, *Unter Hottentotten: 1705–1713* (1979), 48; Du Toit/Giliomee (n. 22), 207. Since the European sense of ownership of land was not a concept shared by the Khoikhoi, the 'contract' was in all probability a legal nonsense. In any event, Schacher (or Osinghkhimma/Mauckkagau) received only a fraction of the agreed purchase price of 10,000 guilders: Elphick (n. 3), 91, 124. For a critical discussion of the 'contract', see Theal, vol. I (n. 14), 196 sqq.

[28] Elphick/Malherbe (n. 3), 12 sq.

became subject to the law and legal procedure introduced at the Cape by the Dutch.

Although the VOC had the authority, in terms of its charter from the Estates-General, to appoint *officiers van justitie*, it did not specifically exercise this power at the Cape.[29] Nevertheless, Van Riebeeck established a rudimentary judicial system, initially manned by himself and his administrative personnel. In 1656 a *Justitie ende Chrijghsraet* was brought into being to deal specifically with legal questions. There was still no separation of powers, however, since the committee included all the members of the administrative *Dagelijcxen Raet*.[30] Save for the introduction of civil courts, called the courts of *landdrosten* and *heemraden*, in territories remote from Cape Town,[31] and some further, relatively superficial changes,[32] the basic structure of the administration of justice was unchanged until the end of the initial period of Dutch occupation in 1795. Although it was at first limited to servants of the VOC, the jurisdiction of the *Justitie ende Chrijghsraet* (and subsequently of the *Raad van Justitie*) was extended,[33] in due course, to *freeburghers*, slaves, manumitted slaves, and Khoikhoi.[34] Nothing better illustrates the changing nature of the Dutch settlement than the fact that the Khoikhoi, initially an alien people, now began to fall under Dutch jurisdiction.[35]

According to a famous letter from the directorate of the VOC, the *Heeren XVII*, to the Governor-General and Council of India[36] dated 4 March 1621, the law to be applied within the territories governed by the latter was that

---

[29] De Wet (n. 18), 1, 19.

[30] Katzen (n. 20), 219; D. H. van Zyl, *Geskiedenis van die Romeins-Hollandse Reg* (1979), 429.

[31] These officials acted at the same time as local government, court, and executive officers for decisions made in Cape Town; see Schutte (n. 16), 290 sq. This serves to underline the fact that there was no separation of powers. The division between civil and criminal jurisdiction was loose, since these local courts also imposed fines and awarded compensation in more minor criminal matters. They also had extensive powers in respect of the punishment of slaves: Katzen (n. 20), 223 sq.

[32] These included the replacement of the *Justitie ende Chrijghsraet* by a *Raad van Justitie* in 1685 and the appointment of *freeburghers*, equal in number to officials, to this latter *Raad* towards the end of the Dutch period of occupation; Katzen (n. 20), 219 sq.; Van Zyl (n. 30), 429 sqq.

[33] Or perhaps *became* extended, there being some vagueness about how the administration of justice was regulated at this time.

[34] Sachs (n. 22), 18.

[35] The first judgments in cases involving Khoikhoi were handed down in 1672; Elphick (n. 3), 127, 183 sq.; Elphick/Malherbe (n. 3), 17. Although the sketchy nature of the court records of the time might make this point incapable of final determination, one strongly suspects that issues such as the area of jurisdiction within which a crime had allegedly been committed or the place where a contract had been concluded were niceties which would not have been regarded as pertinent by the Cape courts.

[36] Subsequently applicable also to the Cape in its capacity as a *buitencomptoir* of the Batavian *hoofdcomptoir*; Hahlo/Kahn, *Union* (n. 18), 12; De Wet (n. 18), 1; Katzen (n. 20), 186, 214; Davenport (n. 4), 25.

of the Province of Holland. Despite its far-reaching consequences the letter in itself carried little weight since the VOC had no legislative authority.[37] The overseas possessions of the Republic of the Seven Provinces at all times remained the common property of the provinces and fell under the control of the Estates-General.[38] However, since the Seven Provinces did not share a legal system it was important to introduce a measure of certainty in the colonies through fixing on a single system which might be applied there. Holland being easily the most influential member province of the VOC,[39] its legal system was adopted.[40]

It is necessary to clarify what is meant, in the statutory context, by the law of Holland. The only body authorized to pass legislation in respect of overseas territories held by the Netherlands was the Estates-General. It appears to have exercised this authority only once with regard to the substantive private law: the *Octrooi* of 1661 sought to regulate part of the law of intestate succession.[41] Clearly any legislation passed by the Estates-General is more than merely the law of the Province of Holland. The statutes of the Estates of that Province had no binding force at the Cape. The confusion which reigned in this regard in South African law should have been brought to an end by the following *dictum* of Van den Heever JA:

If one considers the constitution of the Netherlands at the time of the settlement of the Cape and during all relevant times thereafter, it must be obvious that enactments of the Estates of the province of Holland could have had no application *proprio vigore* to other provinces of the Netherlands or to the Dutch possessions beyond the seas. It was always the conscious policy of the East India Company to avoid all suggestion that any particular province of the Netherlands or its laws enjoyed a kind of hegemony in the overseas possessions . . .[42]

The confusion has continued, however, following the assertion that statutes of the Province of Holland which had become embodied in its common law

[37] In *Spies v. Lombard* 1950 (3) SA 469 (A) Van den Heever JA said (at 482) that 'the "Heeren Zeventien" . . . as is well known had legislative powers conferred by the Generality'. This view was adopted by Hahlo/Kahn, *Union* (n. 18), 14. The better view seems to be that of De Wet (n. 18), 7, who states, unequivocally as ever, that the letter did not constitute a legislative act, nor even a binding instruction from a sovereign power, but (merely) a communication of the views of the *Heeren XVII*. To the extent that the letter might have been intended to be binding in some way, Van Zyl (n. 30), 434 correctly describes it as *ultra vires*.
[38] Hahlo/Kahn, *System* (n. 18), 531. Generally on the political institutions in the 17th C. northern Netherlands see the references in Reinhard Zimmermann, 'Römisch-holländisches Recht: ein Überblick', in: Robert Feenstra, Reinhard Zimmermann (eds.), *Das römisch-holländische Recht: Fortschritte des Zivilrechts im 17. und 18. Jahrhundert* (1992), 18 sq.
[39] For details see Zimmermann (n. 38), 19 sqq.
[40] Hahlo/Kahn, *System* (n. 18), 572.
[41] Hahlo/Kahn, *Union* (n. 18), 13 sq.; De Wet (n. 18), 14 sq. Intestate succession in South Africa is now regulated by the Intestate Succession Act 81 of 1987.
[42] *Spies v. Lombard* 1950 (3) SA 469 (A) 481 sq.

became part of the law of South Africa through such embodiment[43]—by the back door, as it were. This puts the cart before the horse. To the extent that the institutional writers are authoritative in South Africa, it is not of great importance whether they rely on the Digest, on other writers, on judgments,[44] or on statutes for the formulation of their principles.[45]

The local government at the Cape during the years of Dutch occupation issued a large number of *placaaten*, the authority of which appears to have been recognized by the Batavian *hoofdcomptoir*, by the VOC, and presumably by the Estates-General. They were essentially administrative in character.[46] All these local statutes have now been repealed, either expressly or by necessary implication.[47] Taken as a whole, it is true to say that '[b]y the time the Cape was taken over by the British at the end of the eighteenth century the law showed few marks of its prolonged sojourn in South Africa. Such changes as there were (not many or very important ones) had been made in the Netherlands, not in South Africa or Batavia'.[48]

This is just one of the many factors contributing to the complete exclusion of Khoikhoi law[49]—even in areas such as family law and succession, where assimilation of a foreign system is more readily conceivable—from the South African law then commencing its development at the Cape. The nomadic nature of Khoikhoi society, as well as the Khoikhoi's illiteracy, would have rendered their legal process both fragmentary and inaccessible. The nature of the relationship between the Dutch and the Khoikhoi, the latter only gradually becoming incorporated within a cultivating economy as the former extended their frontiers, meant that for a long time—during which their own social institutions collapsed—the Khoikhoi remained for the Dutch at least to some extent a foreign people.[50] The Dutch legal system was better suited to the type of society which was developing at the Cape, where permanent settlement began slowly to predominate over seasonal migration, trade profit over subsistence. Most important, however, was the general Dutch view of the Khoikhoi as inferior. Examples of this abound, from the early description of them as *wilden*[51] to restrictions on

---

[43] Hahlo/Kahn, *Union* (n. 18), 14, and the authorities cited in n. 17; Hahlo/Kahn, *System* (n. 18), 572; Van Zyl (n. 30), 439.

[44] Judgments of the province of Holland are not binding precedents in South Africa: *Wille's Principles of South African Law* (8th edn., 1991), 23, n. 20.

[45] The confusion is merely increased by the distinction drawn between statutes passed pre- and post–1652; cf. Hahlo/Kahn, *Union* (n. 18), 14; Hahlo/Kahn, *System* (n. 18), 572; *Estate Heinamann v. Heinamann* 1919 AD 99, 114.

[46] Hahlo/Kahn, *System* (n. 18), 573.   [47] Hahlo/Kahn, *Union* (n. 18), 16.

[48] Hahlo/Kahn, *System* (n. 18), 575.

[49] On which see Wilson (n. 3), 60 sq.; Elphick (n. 3), 198.

[50] Martin Legassick, 'The Northern Frontier to c. 1840: The Rise and Decline of the Griqua People', in: Elphick/Giliomee (n. 3), 360 makes the point that the Cape Colony was unusual in that settlers were not permitted to integrate themselves into roles in the indigenous society, but that the *freeburghers* were instead left 'clinging to the lifeline' offered by the VOC and the Netherlands.   [51] Bosman, vol. I (n. 23), 21, 99.

interracial concubinage and marriage.[52] The international law which would have made it possible to regard the Cape area as *res nullius*, where *imperium* could be established by *occupatio*,[53] is of course premissed on a sharp division between 'primitive' and 'civilized' societies.

V. THE MEANING OF ROMAN-DUTCH LAW

Although, following the initial period of Dutch occupation, Roman-Dutch law is generally held to be the common law of South Africa,[54] the term Roman-Dutch law is not easily defined. As indicated above, Dutch statutes (by and large) and judgments (exclusively) obtain their authority in South African law through their incorporation into the works of the institutional writers. The usual hierarchy of authority which obtains in South African law, and which rests on the dual principles of parliamentary sovereignty and *stare decisis*, therefore does not apply to Roman-Dutch law. With regard to the institutional writers, there has been some vagueness about their treatment as authoritative sources of the law by the South African courts. I shall attempt to show that, rather than being a weakness, the strength of genuine enrichment inures in such treatment.

Legal custom, which alone determines the ambit of Roman-Dutch law, has by and large left the boundaries undefined with regard to both time and space. There is a continuing debate in South African legal scholarship between those who favour a narrow view—that only the works of the seventeenth and eighteenth-century writers of the province of Holland are to be regarded as authoritative—and those who take a broader view,

---

[52] Although there is some lack of clarity in this regard; e.g. Elphick (n. 3), 205. Certainly, it would appear that the prohibition did not apply to marriages between Europeans and persons of mixed blood: Mary Louise Pratt, *Imperial Eyes: Travel Writing and Transculturation* (1992), 40. In any event—possibly demonstrating the gap between official views and the realities of life at the Cape—it would seem that mixed marriages were tolerated by the authorities; see Richard Shell, Robert Shell, 'Intergroup Relations: Khoikhoi, Settlers, Slaves and Free Blacks, 1652–1795', in: Elphick/Giliomee (n. 3), 197 sqq. It is possible that slavery also played a role in forming the Dutch view; Richard Elphick, Hermann Giliomee, 'The Origins of European Dominance at the Cape, 1652–1840', in: Elphick/Giliomee (n. 3), 529 sq. While the Khoikhoi were never enslaved, there was very widespread importation of slaves from Madagascar, Mozambique, East Africa, and the East Indies; James C. Armstrong, Nigel A. Worden, 'The Slaves, 1652–1834', in: Elphick/Giliomee (n. 3), 111 sqq. On an analysis based on either class or race, the Khoikhoi were thus placed in a position nearer to that of slaves than owners, since as they lost their land and cattle they were increasingly absorbed into the colonial economy in servile positions; see Katzen (n. 20), 184; Elphick (n. 3), 178 sqq.; Elphick/Shell (n. 52), 226; Giliomee (n. 11), 458 sq.; Clifton C. Crais, *White Supremacy and Black Resistance in Pre-Industrial South Africa: The Making of the Colonial Order in the Eastern Cape, 1770–1865* (1992), 28 sq.

[53] De Wet (n. 18), 19, relying on Grotius, *De jure belli ac pacis*, 2–4.

[54] Hahlo/Kahn, *System* (n. 18) 578; Wouter de Vos, *Regsgeskiedenis* (1992), 3 sqq.; *Wille's Principles* (n. 44), 1, 36.

regarding Roman-Dutch law as part of the Roman-Canon *ius commune*, and accordingly not granting certain writers a higher status (on other than meritorious grounds) than others. The narrower view is supported by express *dicta* of the Appellate Division, while the broader view finds sustenance in the more egalitarian approach to the institutional writers generally adopted in practice by the South African courts.[55]

The judgment on which reliance has almost invariably been placed in support of the narrow view is that of Van den Heever JA in *Tjollo Ateljees (Eins) Bpk v. Small*,[56] and more particularly the following *dictum* from that judgment: 'Since we observe the law of Holland we must exclude the Romanists of other countries as well as the pragmatists from neighbouring regions'.[57] The judgment goes on to exclude expressly Flemish and Frisian authorities.[58] No grounds are provided for the conclusion that the South African courts observe the law of the province of Holland.[59] In *Gerber v. Wolson*[60] the same judge appears again to endorse the narrower view:[61]

Pothier is of course a great authority on the Civil law, but his authority is merely suasive, his works having weight only as *ratio scripta*. As an interpreter of the Roman law, our law *in subsidio*, on questions on which the Dutch jurists are silent, his opinions naturally carry much weight. On questions in regard to which the Dutch commentators are in irreconcilable conflict and a Court is bound to apply one or the other of the conflicting doctrines, his authority may be considerable. But it cannot prevail against the opinions of the accepted Dutch authorities.[62]

[55] "[The courts] limit the term Roman-Dutch law to the Province of Holland only when expressly dealing with the subject and even then they do not always limit it in this way. Tacitly they often extend the meaning of the term to include writers from all the phases of development of the *ius commune* . . .': D. P. Visser, *Daedalus in the Supreme Court: The Common Law Today* (1985), 6. For a general discussion of the use of Roman and Roman-Dutch law in South African legal practice see Reinhard Zimmermann, 'Roman Law in a Mixed Legal System: The South African Experience', in: Robin Evans-Jones (ed.), *The Civil Law Tradition in Scotland* (1995), 41 sqq., 62 sqq. (on the two views concerning Roman-Dutch law).
[56] 1949 (1) SA 856 (A).   [57] At 865.   [58] At 865 sq.
[59] Reference is made (at 865) to the case of *Master v. African Mines Corp. Ltd* 1907 TS 925, where Wessels J refers to the need for the court to follow the interpretation by the courts of Holland (at 928). It is clear, though—and this is also the context in which Van den Heever JA applies that *dictum*—that Wessels J was concerned with the distinction between Roman-Dutch law and the Roman law of Justinian, not between writers of the Province of Holland and their contemporaries. It is interesting to note, on the question of the origin of the narrow view, the early criticism of Lord de Villiers, first Chief Justice of the Union of South Africa, because his approach towards the authorities was too narrow: 'Good authorities say . . . that [de Villiers] did not sufficiently allow for the fact that the law of Holland was only one special branch of the Roman Law which was still being developed all over Western Europe': Eric A. Walker, *Lord de Villiers and His Times: South Africa 1842–1914* (1925), 81.
[60] 1955 (1) SA 158 (A).   [61] At 170 sq.
[62] This, despite the oft-stated fact that His Lordship, in a different capacity, wrote: 'Were we bound to follow Dutch writers and them alone, there would be no point in consulting French, Italian, German, Spanish and Belgian authorities; these are constantly quoted in our courts and rightly, for "Roman-Dutch" Law is really a misnomer; that system was for centuries the common law of Western Europe': F. P. van den Heever, *The Partiarian Agricultural Lease in South African Law* (1943), 7. Apparently adopting a similar view, Van Zyl J has used the

It has been contended[63] that the matter has now finally been resolved by the Appellate Division in favour of the narrow view in the case of *Du Plessis v. Strauss*.[64] Reliance for this contention is placed primarily on Van Heerden JA's statement that the relevant question is not whether a particular interpretation of texts from the Digest is the correct one, but rather *'[wat] die stand van die Romeins-Hollandse reg teen die einde van sy ontwikkeling in sy land van herkoms [was]'*.[65] The phrases *'teen die einde van sy ontwikkeling'* and *'land van herkoms'* appear to have been used loosely, since in the very next sentence Van Heerden JA refers to *'die Nederlandse skrywers van die sewentiende en agtiende eeu'* (the Netherlandish writers of the seventeenth and eighteenth centuries). He goes on to canvas writers from Holland, Frisia, the Southern Netherlands, and Utrecht. It is in respect of the writers from Frisia, where the reception of Roman law was most extensive,[66] that 'the famous *dictum* from the *Tjollo Ateljees* case'[67] is quoted. The propagators of the broad view do not, however, seek to rely on the Roman law texts alone,[68] with the result that the matter does not turn on the distinction between Roman law and Roman-Dutch law so much as on an acceptable working definition of the latter term. The real force of the case lies in the concurring judgment of Corbett JA:

To the extent that the law and practice of other countries having cognate legal systems, such as, for example, Friesland, France and the principalities of Germany, may have differed from that in Holland, preference must be given to the latter since Holland is from where our common law derives.

Despite expressing reservations about the application of the law of Holland to the case in question, he concludes 'that the South African case law should not be permitted to override the law of Holland'.[69]

It seems that the narrow approach, apparently based on a misconception about the nature of law in Europe at the relevant time, results in grave difficulties in practice. This is perhaps best illustrated by the fact that the South African courts, despite the isolated strictures to the contrary, have by and

term Roman-European law in referring to the Digest, Grotius, Vinnius, Van Leeuwen, Huber, Voet, and Pothier: *Blesbok Eiendomsagentskap v. Cantamessa* 1991 (2) SA 712 (T) 716.

[63] D. P. Visser, D. B. Hutchison, 'Legislation from the Elysian Fields: The Roman-Dutch Authorities Settle an Old Dispute', (1988) 105 *SALJ* 619 sqq.

[64] 1988 (2) SA 105 (A); see also Zimmermann (n. 55), 68 sq.

[65] ([What] the position of the Roman-Dutch law [was] at the end of its development in its country of origin.) At 133: Visser/Hutchison, (1988) 105 *SALJ* 630.

[66] De Vos (n. 54), 152.　　　　　[67] Visser/Hutchison, (1988) 105 *SALJ* 630.

[68] To suggest that this is the case is to commit an error similar to that of the misreading of Wessels J's *dictum* in *Master v. African Mines Corp. Ltd* 1907 TS 925 (n. 59). That the South African courts adopt a Roman-Dutch perspective on Roman law has been confirmed several times; see *LTA Engineering Co Ltd v. Seacat Investments (Pty) Ltd* 1974 (1) SA 747 (A) 769; *Bisschop v. Stafford* 1974 (3) SA 1 (A) 7 sq.; De Vos (n. 54), 161; and cf. the detailed examination by Zimmermann (n. 55), 58 sqq.

[69] *Du Plessis v. Strauss* (n. 64), 149 sq.

large adopted a broad approach to the use of authorities.[70] Furthermore, the courts have often accepted that an established practice in South African law overrides the Roman-Dutch law.[71] To take the opposite view, as Corbett JA appears to have done, is to raise the Roman-Dutch law to a status analogous to legislation.[72] The antiquarian nature of such an approach contributes neither certainty nor richness to the law.[73] Any attempt to treat the institutional writers as quasi-legislators causes many more problems than it resolves.[74]

One might turn, then, to the misconception in respect of the Roman-Dutch law which seems to underlie the narrow approach. To the extent that during the Middle Ages 'the whole of educated Europe formed a single and undifferentiated cultural unit',[75] the same cohesion would have applied to

[70] Van Zyl (n. 30), 491 sq. points out that Van den Heever JA in the *Tjollo Ateljees* case himself refers to Damhouder, Savigny, and Goudsmit, all of whom fall outside the narrow description of 17th- and 18th-C. writers from the Province of Holland. One might further illustrate the broad view that has been taken by reference to the widespread reliance by the courts on Pothier: Reinhard Zimmermann, 'Der Einfluss Pothiers auf das römisch-holländische Recht in Südafrika', (1985) 102 *Zeitschrift der Savigny-Stiftung für Rechtsgeschichte (Germanistische Abteilung)* 176 sqq.; *idem*, 'Synthesis in South African Private Law: Civil Law, Common Law and *Usus Hodiernus Pandectarum*', (1986) 103 *SALJ* 271 sqq.

[71] So, in *Tjollo Ateljees (Eins) Bpk v. Small* 1949 (1) SA 856 (A) 880 (*per* Hoexter AJA): 'In view of the fact that our practice has been established for more than a century, it is hardly necessary to consider whether *restitutio in integrum* was cognizable by the courts of Holland.' Visser/Hutchison, (1988) 105 *SALJ* 633 sq. point out that in the very volume of the law reports in which the *Du Plessis* case appears, there is another decision of the Appellate Division— *Horowitz v. Brock* 1988 (2) SA 160 (A)—in which the court held that a consistent practice in the South African courts meant that a possibly false perception of the Roman-Dutch law should not be corrected (at 187); see further Zimmermann (n. 55); Hahlo/Kahn, *System* (n. 18), 249 sq., and the Appellate Division authorities to this effect there collected under fn. 15; and *contra* 589.

[72] Visser/Hutchison, (1988) 105 *SALJ* 635 use the term subordinate legislation in quotation marks. Interestingly, the most purist of Appellate Division judges, Steyn CJ, 'never averred in theory or practice that the Roman-Dutch pedigree of a source was enough to constitute it an imperative source alongside statute and binding precedent': Edwin Cameron, 'Legal Chauvinism, Executive-Mindedness and Justice: L. C. Steyn's Impact on South African Law', (1982) 99 *SALJ* 48 sq.

[73] One can do no better than quote the mixed metaphors of Holmes J in *Ex parte De Winnaar* 1959 (1) SA 837 (N) 839: 'Our country has reached a stage in its national development when its existing law can better be described as South African than Roman Dutch. . . . No doubt its roots are Roman Dutch, and splendid roots they are. But continuous development has come through adaptation to modern conditions, through case law, through statutes, and through the adoption of certain principles and features of English law. . . . The original sources of the Roman Dutch law are important, but exclusive preoccupation with them is like trying to return an oak tree to its acorn. It is looking ever backwards. Lot's wife looked back. Our national jurisprudence moves forward where necessary, laying aside its swaddling clothes.'

[74] Where the authorities from Holland are in conflict, does one rely on a ranking list: Grotius first, Voet second . . . ? Or does one, in seeking to establish the law 'teen die einde van sy ontwikkeling', rank Van der Linden first and Grotius near to last (cf. *S. v. Bernardus* 1965 (3) SA 287 (A) 294)? What relevance remains for writers not specifically enhancing our knowledge of the law of Holland? *Et cetera.*

[75] David Knowles, *The Evolution of Medieval Thought* (1962), 80, quoted by Zimmermann, (1986) 103 *SALJ* 268. Although the point is probably overstated, it nevertheless finds

the development of the *ius commune* right up to (and including) the time of the *usus modernus*.[76] It follows from this that the legal tradition which was transplanted to South Africa was a supra- or pre-national tradition.[77] For this reason, too, it has been amply illustrated that attempts at categorizing writers (who were not, of course, self-consciously legislating for a particular territory) according to area are largely artificial.[78] In the circumstances, attempts at narrowing the focus of the South African common law to the law of Holland only are historically insupportable. They are also impoverishing of the South African law, which has the advantage over European continental legal systems of retaining ready access to the manifold sources of the *ius commune*. Contrary to its intention, 'restricting the Roman-Dutch law *as a formal source* to the law of Holland at a particular time'[79] leads to great uncertainty in legal practice, where a new reading of the relevant texts can at a stroke abolish eighty years of judicial precedent.[80] Narrowing the focus and holding oneself bound in this way are two sides of the same coin. Much better is the approach, so often adopted by the South African courts, which gives full recognition to the civilian tradition of the law by having regard to the whole spectrum of the European *ius commune*,[81] and then determines the matter on the basis of 'those opinions which appear to [the court] to be more conformable to reason'.[82]

powerful support in the general agreement which exists among the leading writers on the subject that the nation-state first arose at approximately the time of the French Revolution; Elie Kedourie, *Nationalism* (2nd edn., 1961); Ernest Gellner, *Thought and Change* (1964); *idem*, *Nations and Nationalism* (1983); Eric J. Hobsbawm, *Nations and Nationalism since 1780: Programme, Myth, Reality* (1990).

[76] Zimmermann, (1986) 103 *SALJ* 268 sqq.; *idem*, 'Civil Code and Civil Law: The Europeanization of Private Law within the European Community and the Re-emergence of a European Legal Science', (1994/95) 1 *Columbia Journal of European Law* 63 sqq., 82 sqq. See also Hahlo/Kahn, *System* (n. 18), 562 sq.

[77] Pieter Pauw, 'Die Romeins-Hollandse Reg in Oënskou', 1980 *TSAR* 32 sqq.; Zimmermann (n. 55), 62 sqq.

[78] As De Wet (n. 18), 125 states, it would be wrong to overemphasize regional groupings, for the great jurists such as Grotius, Sande, Matthaeus, Huber, and Voet not only influenced the law of their own provinces but also enjoyed great authority in other regions; further difficulties are that a jurist might have been born in one region but have spent his working life in another, or he might have changed his location in the course of his professional life. See also Zimmermann, (1986) 103 *SALJ* 268 sq.; *idem*, 'Roman-Dutch Jurisprudence and Its Contribution to European Private Law', (1992) 66 *Tulane LR* 1715 (specifically on the Dutch professors of the 17th C.).

[79] Visser/Hutchison, (1988) 105 *SALJ* 630, emphasis in original. It is unclear what is meant by the italicized term, if not something closely akin to legislation.

[80] Also, the certainty sought through a narrower focus will at best be one of degree, since authors from the province of Holland can, and often do, differ from one another.

[81] Even subject to a useful kind of informal hierarchy which appears to have been established among the authorities by the courts; Van Zyl (n. 30), 492.

[82] *Tjollo Ateljees (Eins) Bpk v. Small* 1949 (1) SA 856 (A) 874. See also Hahlo/Kahn, *System* (n. 18), 580.

VI. THE PERIODS OF BRITISH OCCUPATION

In 1795 the Cape was occupied by Britain, albeit in the name of the Prince of Orange as the lawful ruler of the Netherlands,[83] this being the time of the Revolutionary and Napoleonic wars. In 1806, following a three-year intervening period of Batavian rule, the Cape was reoccupied by the British; in 1815 it became a British colony, and remained so until 1910.

During the last quarter of the eighteenth century white hunters, traders, raiders, and pastoralists, moving rapidly eastwards, met their Xhosa counterparts in the Eastern Cape,[84] where the latter had been settled, east of the Great Fish river, for a thousand years.[85] The eastern frontier was open. It was to see a century of battles for domination between white and black, coupled with a process aptly described as the closing of the frontier,[86] the hardening of a fluid frontier into a more rigid border.[87] A similar process occurred, rather less sanguinarily, on the northern Cape frontier. In the eighteenth century a group known as the *Bastaards* emerged at the Cape: primarily persons of mixed birth (both white and Khoikhoi, and slave—or emancipated slave—and Khoikhoi), but also including non-Europeans falling within a higher economic status group.[88] In the late eighteenth and early nineteenth centuries members of this group settled the areas of southern Namibia, the Cape north of the Orange river, the Orange river valley, and Transorangia. Dubbing themselves (predominantly) Griquas,[89] they established stable chiefdoms, essentially independent states accorded a measure of recognition by the Cape Government in 1809, which were eventually to succumb to economic pressure from the white-dominated south in the 1870s.[90] For just as the frontiers hardened into boundaries, so too did the blurred colour line of the eighteenth century become the entrenched ideology of race[91] which was to dominate the following two centuries of South African history.

[83] Hahlo/Kahn, *Union* (n. 18), 4.

[84] Giliomee (n. 11), 421. Of course, this was not the first contact. In 1702 already a raiding party from the Cape settlement had fought a number of Xhosa in the area of the present Somerset East: Monica Wilson, 'Co-Operation and Conflict: The Eastern Cape Frontier', in: Wilson/Thompson (n. 3), 234.

[85] T. Maggs, 'The Early History of the Black People in Southern Africa', in: Trewhella Cameron (genl. ed.), *A New Illustrated History of South Africa* (2nd edn., 1991), 39, 43.

[86] Giliomee (n. 11), 449.

[87] A frontier has been usefully defined as 'a territory or zone of interpenetration between two previously distinct societies', which closes 'when a single political authority has established hegemony over the zone': Howard Lamar, Leonard Thompson, 'Comparative Frontier History', in: *idem* (eds.), *The Frontier in History: North America and Southern Africa Compared* (1981), 7.

[88] Legassick (n. 50), 369 sq.

[89] Wilson (n. 3) 70; Legassick (n. 50), 382.

[90] Legassick (ibid.) 381 sqq.; Davenport (n. 4), 29, 130 sqq.

[91] Legassick (ibid.) 363 sq. See also Martin Legassick, 'The Frontier Tradition in South African Historiography', in: Shula Marks, Anthony Atmore (eds.), *Economy and Society in*

It is worth recalling that until 1795 the Cape had been ruled by a trading company. Almost inevitably, the VOC demonstrated a certain lack of interest in societal regulation or improvement. At the turn of the eighteenth century, therefore, the Cape of colonial settlement was not an orderly place. Where the hunters and *trekboers* went, the Government at the distant Table Bay could exercise no control.[92] The fractiousness is most apparent from the various revolts and declarations of independence which marked the period[93] and constituted 'a boundary between an epoch of uneventful maturation and one of turmoil'.[94] Lack of central control is indeed a characteristic feature of a frontier zone, where the authorities are 'often too weak to prevent challenges which [range] from unauthorised action to rebellion',[95] and where the major institution might well be the commando.[96]

However, the size and complexity of the Cape settlement had increased over the decades to such extent that continuation of the somewhat haphazard form of government there became impracticable. This is best shown by the very different attitude adopted during the period of Batavian rule (the VOC, in the meantime, having slipped into insolvency). In his important memorandum to the Batavian Government,[97] Commissioner-General de Mist emphasized the need for greater professionalism (which included the introduction of qualified Dutch lawyers into the *Raad van Justitie*).[98] Other emblematic changes introduced during the first half of the nineteenth century, reflecting at once a developing economic society,[99] a changing perception by the administrators from Europe of that society,[100] and the influence

Pre-Industrial South Africa (1980), 52 sqq.; Giliomee (n. 11), 456 sqq.; Elphick/Giliomee (n. 52), 554 sqq. By the close of the 19th C. 'scientific racism' was firmly entrenched in England: Saul Dubow, 'Race, Civilisation and Culture: The Elaboration of Segregationist Discourse in the Inter-War Years', in: Shula Marks, Stanley Trapido (eds.), *The Politics of Race, Class and Nationalism in Twentieth-Century South Africa* (1987), 71 sqq.

[92] For a discussion see Hermann Giliomee, 'Processes in Development of the Southern African Frontier', in: Lamar/Thompson (n. 87), 88 sq.

[93] Hermann Giliomee, 'The Burgher Rebellions on the Eastern Frontier, 1795–1815', in: Richard Elphick, Hermann Giliomee (eds.), *The Shaping of South African Society, 1652–1820* (1979), 338 sqq.

[94] Katzen (n. 20), 183. [95] Giliomee (n. 11), 428.

[96] Legassick (n. 50), 361.

[97] J. A. de Mist, *The Memorandum of Commissary J. A. de Mist Containing Recommendations for the Form and Administration of Government at the Cape of Good Hope* (trans. 1920).

[98] William M. Freund, 'The Cape under the Transitional Governments, 1795–1814', in: Elphick/Giliomee (n. 3), 345. Freund points out, at 325, that the lofty aims expressed in the memorandum more often than not—given, amongst other factors, the very brief duration of Batavian rule—remained just that; see also Van Zyl (n. 30), 446.

[99] The Cape was gradually moving away from 'its marginal role in the Europe-Asia trade', towards 'a colonial export economy': Freund (n. 98), 333. Also, the population of the colony increased enormously, from 77,075 in 1806 to 566,158 in 1865 (both figures including the Khoikhoi): T. R. H. Davenport, 'The Consolidation of a New Society: The Cape Colony', in: Wilson/Thompson (n. 3), 273.

[100] Although it should be noted that Britain's interest in hanging on to the Cape was as lukewarm as that of the Batavian Republic: Freund (n. 98), 325 sqq.

of Enlightenment thought on those administrators, were: improvement of the education system; the extension of religious toleration beyond the narrow recognition of the Reformed church only; and the publication of a local newspaper.[101]

A stronger government at the Cape had as its necessary counterparts changes in land policy, in frontier policy, and in the administration of justice.[102] The combination of virtually uncontrolled loan farms and occupation of land on a vast scale without any formal entitlement meant that the government was unable to limit the spread of settlement; accordingly perpetual quitrent title at *ad valorem* rentals was introduced in 1813.[103] The new land policy was aimed, *inter alia*, at firming up the borders of the colony. The same aim was pursued, on the eastern frontier, by means of battle and controlled settlement.[104] At the frontier two fairly powerful groups[105], each resistant to absorption by the other and both pursuing similar economic interests (in particular relating to the keeping of cattle[106]) were brought into close contact with one another. Following a series of skirmishes and battles dating from 1779 (including the so-called First, Second, and Third Frontier Wars), which the Xhosas probably had the better of overall,[107] the British in 1811–12 gathered a military force of a quite different order against the Xhosa, drove perhaps 8,000 of them across the Fish river, and established twenty-seven military posts in the area to prevent their return.[108] The border was further strengthened by the settlement in 1820 of some 4,000 British immigrants in the Eastern Cape.[109] Although this by no

---

[101] Freund (ibid.) 347 sqq.; Davenport (n. 99), 275 sqq., 314 sqq. The role of the 1820 settlers in introducing Enlightenment values should not be underestimated. In particular, their battles with Lord Charles Somerset resulted in the freeing of the Cape press from executive control, by Ordinance 60 of 1829; J. B. Peires, 'The British and the Cape 1814–1834', in: Elphick/Giliomee (n. 3), 477 sqq.

[102] For a discussion linking these three aspects see Crais (n. 52), 58 sqq.

[103] Davenport (n. 99), 291 sq.; *idem* (n. 4), 38. The initial effectiveness of the new system is open to doubt.

[104] In the north, the relative stability of the Griqua chiefdoms, coupled with the 'legitimacy' accorded them by the colonial government, the leading role played in those chiefdoms by members of the London Missionary Society, and the desire of the *Bastaards*/Griquas 'to retain, and even strengthen, certain kinds of links with the colony at the same time that they were separating themselves from it geographically' (Legassick (n. 50), 377), probably all resulted in a lesser need for the colonial government forthwith to seek a further closing of that frontier.

[105] Although the dichotomy amounts to a simplification: see Christopher Saunders, 'Political Processes in the Southern African Frontier Zones', in: Lamar/Thompson (n. 87), 150. For a brief description of the complexity of frontier interaction see Crais (n. 52), 28 sq.

[106] Giliomee (n. 11), 434 has even argued that the inability of either side to drive out the other might have led to the control of cattle becoming a more important consideration than the control of land.

[107] See Giliomee (ibid.) 434 sqq.   [108] Giliomee (ibid.) 448.

[109] See Davenport (n. 4), 38 sqq. There is some dispute as to whether the proximate cause of the settlement was the need for stability along the frontier or the need for a Tory government publicly to demonstrate concern for unemployment in Britain: Peires (n. 101), 474; Crais (n. 52), 87.

means represented the end of conflict in the region, the balance of power had begun its inexorable swing in the settlers' favour.

VII. CHANGES TO THE ADMINISTRATION OF JUSTICE

The practice of justice at the Cape prior to the changes wrought during the first three decades of the second British occupation was described by one of South Africa's pre-eminent liberal historians, who stated simply that the rule of law did not exist there.[110] The vast discretionary authority of the governor and his Council of Policy included unlimited powers of search, detention, and banishment; the *fiscal* both prosecuted and co-judged criminal trials; the *Raad van Justitie*, having conducted a trial behind closed doors, gave no reasons for its decisions; it was openly admitted by the authorities that the legal status of the complainant and accused greatly influenced the severity of sentences;[111] there was no automatic right to legal representation; accused persons did not have the right either to call witnesses or to cross-examine witnesses for the prosecution; confessions were frequently obtained by torture; the judges were untrained and often corrupt.[112] Most importantly: whilst '[f]reemen and Company servants had access to the Court, . . . those whose status was servile *de facto* or *de jure* had not'. The Khoikhoi could be sued, but could not sue.[113]

[110] Davenport (n. 99), 297. For a qualification of this statement see Robert Ross, 'The Rule of Law at the Cape of Good Hope in the 18th Century', (1980) 9 *Journal of Imperial and Commonwealth History* 5; Du Toit/Giliomee (n. 22), 82 sqq.

[111] A Stellenbosch *landdrost* in 1685 relied on Exodus xxi: 20–1 (distinguishing freemen from slaves and servants) in support of this attitude towards punishment: Katzen (n. 20), 224. A letter of 1796 from the *Raad van Justitie* stated that 'the distinction of persons is one of the essential points by which the degree of punishment is measured in most civilized Nations, and this distinction is especially founded upon the Imperial Laws or the Roman Law': Du Toit/Giliomee (n. 22), 91. See also Ross, (1980) 9 *Journal of Imperial and Commonwealth History* 5 sq.

[112] Sir John Truter, President of the *Raad van Justitie* and of the Orphan Chamber, in the latter capacity 'lent' himself and his family some 51,000 rixdollars, which were never repaid: Peires (n. 101), 491. On the legal situation which existed at the turn of the 18th C. and persisted into the autocratic regime of Lord Charles Somerset see Davenport (n. 99), 297; Katzen (n. 20) 220 sqq.; Peires (n. 101), 478.

[113] Davenport (n. 99), 297, 300. See also Katzen (n. 20), 224 sq. At first glance this view appears to be contradicted by Elphick/Malherbe (n. 3), 17, who write that the Khoikhoi were permitted to initiate proceedings in the 17th C. But the inference seems to be drawn from criminal trials, with a Khoikhoi as complainant, rather than from civil trials; Elphick/Malherbe (n. 3), 29 sq. In any event, it is known that the status of the Khoikhoi changed over time from foreigners to servants. In a letter to the Governor written as late as 1797, dealing with the question 'of whether or not a Hottentot has the right to summon a burgher before the College', the *heemraden* of Stellenbosch wrote 'that, as such practices have never before obtained here, they are of the opinion that, if it should be established that a Hottentot is free to cite any inhabitant before the courts, this College would increasingly be obstructed and hindered with trivial matters': Du Toit/Giliomee (n. 22), 94. Slaves, too, could complain to the *fiscal* or local magistrate about ill-treatment, setting in motion possible legal proceedings against their

With the closing of the frontiers, the area of colonial jurisdiction became more surely circumscribed. Within that area, were categories of persons who either had never had or no longer enjoyed a right of access to the courts. The ramifications of this are immediately apparent from a breakdown of the population of the Cape in 1795, where slaves numbered some 26,000 persons, *freeburghers* 17,000, Khoikhoi 14,000, and free blacks 1,000,[114] and it is accordingly no exaggeration to describe the society at the time as slave-owning. The most important changes in legal procedure introduced by the British formed part of a more general movement towards the emancipation of slaves and subject peoples.[115] The measures clarifying the legal status of such peoples have been described as 'undermining the essential structures of the earlier political order'.[116] Slaves, who had been 'considered in the civil law as not existing',[117] were emancipated throughout the British Empire, and from 1838 in the Cape Colony.[118] This placed them on a footing within the colony equivalent to that of the Khoikhoi in a grouping designated 'Coloured'.[119] The position of Coloured persons before the law had already been ameliorated by a number of changes to the legal system introduced by the British. These included the establishment of circuit courts, accessible to all, in 1811; the opening of the court doors to public audiences in 1813; and the introduction of aspects of English criminal procedure in 1819.[120]

In 1822 a Commission of Eastern Inquiry (the Colebrooke-Bigge Commission) was appointed for the purpose of recommending ways in which the Cape administration could be improved. The Commissioners initiated 'one of the biggest upheavals which Cape society ever experienced'.[121] Feeling that the question of slavery had to be settled prior to the establishment of representative institutions, the Commissioners placed their hopes in an independent judiciary which could guard against administrative abuses of power and corruption.[122] Accordingly, following the publication of a

---

owners: Ross, (1980) 9 *Journal of Imperial and Commonwealth History* 7 sqq.; Du Toit/ Giliomee (n. 22), 57; Daniel Visser, 'The Role of Roman Law in the Punishment of Slaves at the Cape of Good Hope under Dutch Rule', in: *Mélanges Felix Wubbe: Offerts par ses collègues et ses amis à l'occasion de son soixante-dixième anniversaire* (1993), 532.

[114] Philip Curtin, Steven Feierman, Leonard Thompson, Jan Vonsina, *African History* (1978), 298.

[115] Davenport (n. 99), 300 sqq., on whom reliance is placed for this contextualization of changes in legal procedure, states that the new humanitarianism was equally influential in the Netherlands, and that only its brief duration prevented the implementation of similar policies during the period of Batavian rule.

[116] Du Toit/Giliomee (n. 22), 78.

[117] Fiscal David Denyssen, (1813), quoted by Davenport (n. 99), 300.

[118] Armstrong/Worden (n. 52), 167.

[119] On the semantic variations this term has undergone see Ian Goldin, 'The Reconstitution of Coloured Identity in the Western Cape', in: Marks/Trapido (n. 91), 156 sqq. On the vague origins of the designation see Wilson (n. 84), 248 sq.

[120] Davenport (n. 99), 302.

[121] Peires (n. 101), 495.

[122] Peires (n. 101), 495 sq.

First Charter of Justice in 1827, the *Raad van Justitie* was from the beginning of 1828 replaced by the new Cape Supreme Court. It was manned by four (reduced in 1834 to three) legally qualified and full-time judges imported from Britain.[123] Further changes recommended and instituted were the confirmation of the division between advocates and attorneys, the substitution of the *fiscal* by an Attorney-General, and the appointment of a Master and a Registrar of Deeds. The existing courts of *landdrost* and *heemraden*, tainted by local bias and patronage, were replaced by resident magistrates, in accordance with the English system. Criminal procedure was brought into even closer accord with that applied in England. So too was civil procedure. The English law of evidence was introduced in 1830, followed by the jury system the following year. The Second Charter of Justice was published in 1832.[124] One further promulgation of great importance resulted from the Commission's recommendations: Ordinance 50 of 1828 sought to embody the principle of uniform liberties for all persons (although in its continued usage of racial terminology it probably fell short of that aim) by, *inter alia*, limiting the powers of employers, abolishing the obligation on Coloured persons to carry passes, and clarifying their right to ownership of land.[125]

Through all of this Roman-Dutch law remained, officially, the common law of the Cape Colony. Before examining what this meant in practice, it is necessary to see what was happening beyond the colony's borders.

VIII. MIGRATIONS

Two great migrations mark the first half of the Southern African nineteenth century. One was the *Mfecane*[126] (or *Lifaqane*), traditionally described as a domino-effect tragedy, of vast proportions, which left few of the

---

[123] Stephen D. Girvin, 'The Establishment of the Supreme Court of the Cape of Good Hope and Its History under the Chief Justiceship of Sir John Wylde: I', (1992) 109 *SALJ* 293 sqq. It is clear from this article, and from the second part thereof in (1992) 109 *SALJ* 652 sqq., that professionalization was somewhat hampered at first by the obvious difficulties involved in getting lawyers of quality to emigrate to the colony. The one shining exception was also the only Scot appointed in the 19th C., William Menzies. On his racist attitude to judicial practice, however, see Leslie Clement Duly, 'A Revisit with the Cape's Hottentot Ordinance of 1828', in: Marcelle Kooy (ed.), *Studies in Economics and Economic History: Essays in Honour of Professor H. M. Robertson* (1972), 41 sqq.

[124] Hahlo/Kahn, *Union* (n. 18), 18 sq.; Van Zyl (n. 30), 451 sq.

[125] Davenport (n. 99), 304 sq.; Duly (n. 123), 29 sqq.; Elphick/Malherbe (n. 3), 47 sq. It should be noted, however, that the legislation according protection to Coloured persons was premissed on the continuation of their position as employees on white farms, and accordingly formed part of a pattern of state intervention aimed at ensuring an adequate labour supply; Susan Newton-King, 'The Labour Market of the Cape Colony, 1807–28', in: Marks/Atmore (n. 91), 196 sqq.

[126] On the origin of the term see Julian Cobbing, 'The Mfecane as Alibi: Thoughts on Dithakong and Mbolompo', (1988) 29 *Journal of African History* 487.

Bantu-speaking peoples of Southern Africa unscathed. The other, of much lesser scale but with similarly tremendous implications for the future history of the subcontinent, was the *Great Trek*.

Very briefly, the standard story of the *Mfecane* commences in 1817 in what became Natal, when Zwide, king of the Ndwandwe, attacked the Mabudu and the Mthethwa. The death of the latter's king, Dingiswayo, permitted the genius of war, Shaka of the Zulu, to take command of the area. His defeated enemies radiated outward to the north, west, and south, triggering further wars and involving such varied other groups as Mosheshwe's Sotho, the Griquas, and the Cape colonials.[127] While the precise causes of the *Mfecane* remain uncertain, it has generally been ascribed to Zulu expansionism, much aided by the natural disaster of two lengthy droughts.[128] A recent challenge to the standard view has questioned both the primacy of Zulu agency and the chain reaction supposedly resulting from it, and argues rather that the leading role was taken by European traders and settlers penetrating ever deeper into the interior and extending their endless demands for cheap or slave labour.[129]

On this argument, to say that the *Mfecane* greatly facilitated white expansion[130] is to say also that the whites made their own luck. In any event, the suggestion that it left the Southern African interior open to white settlement[131] is a restatement of the legitimating myth of the vacant land which seems to inform so much of Afrikaner historiography. Another myth relates to the nobility of purpose of the *voortrekkers*,[132] the small and fractious groups of disaffected Dutch-speakers who left the colony in the 1830s to continue their *trekboer* tradition of the easy life elsewhere, taking their servants along for this purpose. Between 1834 and 1840 some 15,000 persons,[133] perhaps half of them Coloured dependants,[134] left the Eastern Cape, crossed the Orange river, and from there travelled variously north, west, and east as far as Port Natal, Delagoa Bay, and beyond the Limpopo.

[127] Leonard Thompson, 'Co-operation and Conflict: The High Veld', in: Wilson/Thompson (n. 3), pp. 391 sqq.; Curtin/ Feierman/Thompson/Vansina (n. 114), 304 sqq.; Davenport (n. 4), 16 sqq.

[128] For an argument based on an imbalance between population density and available resources see Jeff Guy, 'Ecological Factors in the Rise of Shaka and the Zulu Kingdom', in: Marks/Atmore (n. 91), 102 sqq.

[129] Cobbing, (1988) 29 *Journal of African History* 487 sqq.

[130] Du Toit/Giliomee (n. 22), 19.

[131] See Cobbing, (1988) 29 *Journal of African History* 488, 515, 518 sq.

[132] For discussions of Afrikaner trek mythology see T. Dunbar Moodie, *The Rise of Afrikanerdom: Power, Apartheid, and the Afrikaner Civil Religion* (1975), 197 sqq.; Irving Hexham, *The Irony of Apartheid: The Struggle for National Independence of Afrikaner Calvinism against British Imperialism* (1981), 31 sqq.; André du Toit, 'No Chosen People: The Myth of the Calvinist Origins of Afrikaner Nationalism and Racial Ideology', (1983) 88 *The American Historical Review* 920 sqq.; Isabel Hofmeyr, 'Popularizing History: The Case of Gustav Preller', (1988) 29 *Journal of African History* 521 sqq.

[133] Although the figure could be as low as 6,000: Davenport (n. 4), 46.

[134] Thompson (n. 127), 408.

Although Britain annexed the regions of Natal and British Kaffraria (between the Keiskamma and Kei rivers) in the 1840s, it demonstrated— until the discovery of diamonds and the rediscovery of gold—no sustained interest in the northern interior; this is most apparent from the Conventions at Sandriver and Bloemfontein concluded with the *voortrekkers* in the 1850s.[135] Its absence left the manifold peoples of the interior to continue their assertions of power. For example, the area between the Orange and the Vaal has been described as a 'scene of anarchy' at this time,[136] with a number of rival Sotho states, Griquas, Koras, San, *trekboers*, and *voortrekkers* all fighting for space in the sun. There was a tendency, though, resulting from the dual pressures of the *Mfecane* and the *trek*, for the Bantu-speaking chiefdoms[137] to aggregate into fewer and more powerful hands,[138] most typically those of the skilful South Sotho leader, Mosheshwe. However, sufficient co-operation did not exist[139] to prevent the gradual attainment of dominance by the whites. The rest of the century is marked by the piecemeal annexation of territory forming part of African chiefdoms, both by the British government at the Cape and by the *Trekker* Republics to the north.[140] The process tended to continue the schizophrenic attitude which had commenced on the eastern frontier, where whites regarded blacks as 'native foreigners'[141] and at the same time sought to administer their affairs for them.[142]

The limitation of much South African legal history becomes particularly apparent here, for Roman-Dutch law is described, typically, as advancing easily, together with the *voortrekkers*, towards its destination as the accepted common law of the four provinces of South Africa. The description obscures the political complexity of the nineteenth-century map of

---

[135] See Thompson (n. 127), 420 sqq.

[136] Thompson (ibid.) 415. See also D. Hobart Houghton, 'Economic Development 1865–1965', in: Monica Wilson, Leonard Thompson (eds.), *The Oxford History of South Africa*, vol. II, *South Africa 1870–1966* (1971), 6 sq.

[137] The term is not used in any technical sense: see Hall (n. 1), 63 sq., 146. It seems, however, to encompass more variables than 'kingdoms'.

[138] Davenport (n. 4), 66.

[139] This might be ascribable on one hand to the absence of a race-based sense of identity among the African peoples, and on the other to geographical divisions brought about by white settlement: Leonard Thompson, 'The Subjection of the African Chiefdoms, 1870–1898', in: Wilson/Thompson (n. 136), 246.

[140] See Curtin/Feierman/Thompson/Vansina (n. 114), 312 sqq.; Davenport (n. 4), 113 sqq.

[141] Davenport (n. 99), 310 sq.

[142] Davenport (n. 4), 118. Having described a judicial execution of a black man (for the murder of a British woman), Crais (n. 52), 126 writes: 'The killing simultaneously proclaimed the African a member of a common society with a shared system of meaning as it branded him a pariah. The black became the Other, a constant stranger and perpetual outsider.' At another level: 'The very same Afrikaners who developed a racial ideology to legitimate the coercive labour system were quite prepared to concede equality to the independent African nations living in their vicinity': Peires (n. 101), 508. For considered discussion: Legassick (n. 91), 64 sqq.

Southern Africa, contributing to the assumption of cultural superiority which underpins the unquestioning adoption of a European legal system there. It also gives a false impression of the nature of *voortrekker* society. The trek was partly motivated by the desire to escape the restrictions placed on individual actions by higher authority. It is therefore no surprise that the history of the *voortrekkers* was marked by continual friction and division, religious schism, various declarations of independence, and even civil war (1860–4).[143] The lack of a united front against them obviously assisted African chiefs to maintain their power bases, so that it required, all told, some sixty years and the discovery of mineral wealth for the Transvaal to be conquered by the white settlers, and a similar period for the subjection of the Orange Free State.[144]

IX. ROMAN-DUTCH LAW IN THE NINETEENTH CENTURY

Prior to his departure from the Cape Colony, one of the better educated *voortrekkers*, Piet Retief, published a manifesto in the *Graham's Town Journal* in which he complained 'of the severe losses which we have been forced to sustain by the emancipation of our slaves, and the vexatious laws which have been enacted respecting them', and undertook, 'wherever we go', to 'preserve proper relations between master and servant'.[145] There is little doubt that the publication of Ordinance 50 of 1828, with its potential profoundly to affect those relations, played a leading—if not the leading— role in the determination of the *voortrekkers* to leave.[146] In the circumstances, the *voortrekkers* of course showed a preference for the system of law that had prevailed prior to the British occupation. Although it might be far-fetched to suggest that Roman-Dutch law is substantively either more or less egalitarian than English law, the markedly greater liberalism introduced at the Cape by English adjectival law cannot be doubted. That the preference was politically motivated appears most clearly from article 57 of the 1854 Orange Free State Constitution, read with an 1856 clarification, which provided that the Roman-Dutch law would be applicable as *grondwet* (basic law) 'only in so far as it was found in force in the Cape Colony at the time of the appointment of the English judges in the place of the previously existing Council of Justice'.[147] In the Transvaal the *United Volksraad*

---

[143] Davenport (n. 4), 68 sqq.
[145] Du Toit/Giliomee (n. 22), 214.
[146] See Peires (n. 101), 499 sqq. The Transvaal Constitutions of 1849 and 1858 expressly rejected equality between different peoples: Du Toit/Giliomee (n. 22), 88.
[147] Translation from Hahlo/Kahn, *Union* (n. 18), 22. See also Van Zyl (n. 30), 468; De Wet (n. 18), 38.

[144] Davenport (n. 4), 76, 134 sqq.

(united in name, if not in fact[148]) adopted in 1849 the Thirty-three Articles drawn up five years previously, and which provided somewhat vaguely in article 31 that the '*Hollandsche Wet*' should be the basis of the law, 'but only in a modified way, and in conformity with the customs of South Africa and for the benefit and welfare of the community'.[149] This was confirmed by an Addendum to the 1858 Constitution, which further circumscribed the *Hollandsche Wet* as consisting, *primus inter pares*, of Van der Linden's *Koopmans Handboek*, followed by Van Leeuwen's *Rooms-Hollands-Regt* and Grotius's *Inleiding tot de Hollandsche Rechts-geleertheyd*.[150]

As regards the application of the law, the situation in the *Trekker* Republics attained some respectability in the 1870s with the creation of Supreme Courts having both original and appeal jurisdiction. The Cape policy requiring advocates with British training paid handsome dividends also to the Republics, which were able to import their legal expertise and often appointed persons of outstanding legal ability to the Bench. In the result, judgments handed down by James Buchanan, Melius de Villiers, J. G. Kotzé, Johannes Wessels, James Rose Innes, and others demonstrate a sophistication which ill matches the unsophisticated Orange Free State and (especially) Transvaal communities to which they were addressed. Furthermore, as also in Natal (annexed by Britain in 1843, and a separate colony with its own Supreme Court from 1857[151]), the courts in the Republics inevitably moved beyond the narrow confines of their constitutions, and were much influenced by the decisions of the Cape Supreme Court.[152]

One must look primarily to the Cape Supreme Court therefore to obtain a view of the development of Roman-Dutch law during the nineteenth century. In explaining the persistence of Roman-Dutch law after 1795 and again after 1806, reference is often made to the principle enunciated in the English case of *Campbell v. Hall*,[153] that 'the laws of a conquered country continue in force until they are altered by the conqueror. [T]he King ... has

---

[148] De Wet (n. 18), 39: '*Waar en vir wie die Drie en dertig Artikels gegeld het, is vrae waarop mens geen besliste antwoorde kan gee nie, want voor 1858 het daar in die gebied oorkant die Vaal eintlik geen georganiseerde staat met vaste bestuursinstellings bestaan nie*'. (Where and to whom the Thirty-three Articles were applicable are questions to which no one can give definite answers, for before 1858 no organized state with established administrative institutions really existed on the other side of the [river] Vaal).

[149] Translation from Hahlo/Kahn, *Union* (n. 18), 21. See also Van Zyl (n. 30), 461.

[150] Hahlo/Kahn, (n. 18), 21; Van Zyl (n. 30), 462 sq. That these are indeed the relevant textbooks is a supposition: the addendum refers merely to the *Wetboek* of Van der Linden and Van Leeuwen: De Wet (n. 18), 40.

[151] De Wet (n. 18), 36. For details see Peter Spiller, *A History of the District and Supreme Courts of Natal 1846–1910* (1986); idem, 'The "Romodutchyafricanderenglander" Law of Nineteenth-century Natal', (1985) 48 *THRHR* 164 sqq.

[152] Walker (n. 59), 77 quotes a letter to this effect written by (Lord) de Villiers in 1877.

[153] (1774) 1 Cowp 204 (98 ER 1045, at 1046, 1048).

a power to alter the old and to introduce new laws in a conquered country'.[154] Since this begs the question in South Africa, one does well to add the *dictum* from the earlier case of *Calvin*,[155] 'for if a King come to a Christian Kingdom by conquest, seeing that he hath *vitae et necis potestatem*, he may at his pleasure alter and change the laws of that kingdom: but until he doth make an alteration of those laws the ancient laws of that kingdom remain'[156] and to emphasize all that the epithet 'Christian' would have implied in the century which witnessed the scramble for Africa.

The King (and later the Queen) did not alter the system of law in the Cape which remained officially Roman-Dutch. This is to be inferred, it has been argued, from the Charters of Justice, which enjoined the court to exercise jurisdiction 'according to the laws now in force within our said Colony, and all such other laws as shall at any time hereafter be made'.[157] It was always the intention, however, gradually to introduce the English law.[158] Indeed, the Roman-Dutch authorities held but a tenuous position in the early years of the Supreme Court, as is apparent from an extraordinary judgment which emanated from the Cape's extraordinary first Chief Justice:[159]

Quote what Dutch or Roman books you please—musty or otherwise—and they must be musty if they lay down such doctrines. I belong to a higher court than they refer to—a court not to be broken up or paralysed by their authorities, much less by the maxims of philosophers dozing over the midnight lamp in their solitary chambers. My Queen has sent me here to administer justice under the Royal Charter . . . . [W]hen you speak of the Institutions of Holland, and of binding myself down by the practice of Dutch courts—I absolve myself from that bondage, I look to my Charter, to my oath and to my duty.[160]

There was an almost wholesale importation by statute of substantive English law in some areas, particularly in succession (where freedom of testation was preferred to the legitimate portion) and in the broadly commercial fields of mercantile, company, insurance and insolvency law, the law of negotiable instruments, and the law relating to immaterial property rights.[161] Furthermore, constitutional and administrative law is largely

---

[154] Hahlo/Kahn, *System* (n. 18), 575; Reinhard Zimmermann, *Das römisch-holländische Recht in Südafrika* (1983), 9; De Wet (n. 18), 30. On the absurdity of the purported reliance on this doctrine see Cameron, (1982) 99 *SALJ* 44 sq.

[155] (1608) 7 Coke's Reports 1 (77 ER 377, at 398).   [156] De Wet (n. 18), 29 sq.

[157] Ibid. 33.

[158] Hahlo/Kahn, *Union* (n. 18), 17. This was also the recommendation of the Colebrooke-Bigge Commission; De Wet (n. 18) 32.

[159] Described by his younger brother, who became Lord Chancellor in 1850, as better fitted for the stage than the Bench: Duly (n. 123), 43.

[160] Wylde CJ in *Letterstedt v. Morgan* (1849) 5 Searle 373, at 381. The background to the judgment is described by Girvin, (1992) 109 *SALJ* 656 sq.

[161] Hahlo/Kahn, *Union* (n. 18), 19 sq.; Hahlo/Kahn, *System* (n. 18), 577 sq.; Zimmermann (n. 154), 12.

derived from English law, which also had a noticeable impact on criminal law and on the law of contract and delict.[162]

The tendency towards an admixture of English and Roman-Dutch law was strengthened by various factors, additional to the procedural and substantive changes already mentioned, relating to legal practice at the Cape. These included the exclusive use of English in the courts, the requirement that barristers be trained in Britain, the importation of judges from Britain,[163] and the adoption of the Privy Council as final court of appeal.[164] More generally, there was a need for the law to keep pace with the rapid economic developments of the second half of the nineteenth century. Since legal links with the Netherlands had been severed by the codification of that country's legal system in the early nineteenth century, and since Britain was reaching its imperial zenith, it is not surprising that the local courts looked to English law to complement Roman-Dutch law in those areas—such as commercial law—where the latter was found wanting.[165]

X. INDUSTRIALIZATION

In the last three decades of the nineteenth century the area of South Africa was transformed from a miscellany of chiefdoms and kingdoms, republics, colonies, and independent communities into a unitary state. Above all else, the transformation should be ascribed to the industrial revolution wrought through the mining of diamonds and gold.

As long as Southern Africa remained a loss-making proposition there was little incentive for the British to adopt expansionism.[166] The discovery of diamonds, most importantly the dry diggings at the present Kimberley in 1870, led to the annexation by Britain of Griqualand West, effectively putting an end to the complex political situation in the area. Of even greater moment was the gold rush to the Witwatersrand which began in 1886, transforming in the space of three decades 'a republic founded on a modest

---

[162] Hahlo/Kahn, *Union* (n. 18), 42.

[163] However, Menzies J, the importation from Scotland, did not assist the process through his 'scant regard for English law': Girvin, (1992) 109 *SALJ* 658.

[164] Hahlo/Kahn, *Union* (n. 18), 20 sq.; Hahlo/Kahn, *System* (n. 18), 578; Zimmermann (n. 154), 13 sqq.

[165] All this has led one commentator to state that 'the South African legal system is fundamentally and characteristically British': Martin Chanock, 'Writing South African Legal History: A Prospectus', (1989) 30 *Journal of African History* 269. Generally on the reception of English law in South Africa see Hahlo/Kahn, *Union* (n. 18), 17 sqq.; Ben Beinart, 'The English Legal Contribution in South Africa: The Interaction of Civil Law and Common Law', 1981 *Acta Juridica* 7 sqq.; Reinhard Zimmermann, 'Die Rechtsprechung des Supreme Court of the Cape of Good Hope am Ende der Sechziger Jahre des 19. Jahrhunderts', in: *Huldigingsbundel Paul van Warmelo* (1984), 286 sqq.; De Vos (n. 54), 259 sqq.; Zimmermann (n. 55), 47 sqq.

[166] Thompson (n. 139), 248.

agricultural economy ... into a colony boasting the world's largest and most technically sophisticated gold-mining industry'.[167] The transformation was helped rather than hindered by the Kruger government.[168] Again, the British interest which this stimulated was sufficient to induce first a raid, then a war, and finally the colonial incorporation of the Transvaal and its war-time ally, the Orange Free State.

Towards the end of 1895 Cecil John Rhodes, mining magnate and Cape Prime Minister, sent his loyal minion, Dr. Jameson, on an abortive mission to seize control of the Transvaal by force. It was a scheme in which Joseph Chamberlain, Britain's colonial secretary, was possibly complicitous.[169] Its failure was followed by a period of sustained pressure on the Transvaal government by Lord Milner, Governor-General of the Cape, aimed principally at provoking a declaration of war.[170] His dealings culminated in the Boer War of 1899–1902 which, although won by Britain, resulted in a bitterness which was to be successfully manipulated by Afrikaner politicians for many years to come.

Hand-in-hand with the extension of British supremacy was the process of subjugation of African chiefdoms.[171] The reasons for the decline of African independence are many and complex. Of importance for present purposes is the demand among whites for a constant source of cheap labour. Shortage of labour was a fact of the agricultural economy, where farmers tended to rely on compulsion to obtain the labour necessary.[172] The shortage was both exacerbated by and duplicated in the mining industry, and tended to be blamed on 'the conditions of native life in Africa'.[173] In order, *inter alia*, to render those conditions less amenable, various legislative steps—notably the Cape's Glen Grey Act[174] and the Union's Natives Land Act[175]—were taken. At the same time, and apparently ignoring the obvious correspondences between Afrikaner and black urbanization, various strate-

---

[167] Charles van Onselen, *Studies in the Social and Economic History of the Witwatersrand 1886–1914*, vol. I (1982), xv.

[168] Van Onselen (n. 167), 23.

[169] Thomas Pakenham, *The Boer War* (1982), 27 sqq.; *idem*, *The Scramble for Africa 1876–1912* (1991) 487 sqq., 502 sq. Robert I. Rotberg, *The Founder: Cecil Rhodes and the Pursuit of Power* (1988), 515 sqq.

[170] Pakenham *Boer War* (n. 169), 63 sqq.

[171] See Thompson (n. 139), 257 sqq.

[172] Monica Wilson, 'Farming, 1866–1966', in: Wilson/Thompson (n. 136), 120 sqq.; Curtin/Feierman/Thompson/Vansina (n. 114), 321; Newton-King (n. 125), 176 sqq.

[173] *Report of the Transvaal Labour Commission* (1904), (n. 70), quoted by David Welsh, 'The Growth of Towns', in: Wilson/Thompson (n. 136), 177.

[174] 25 of 1894. In addressing Parliament during the second reading of the Glen Grey Bill, Rhodes, '[w]ith a rapt expression, reminded the House of our duty "to remove these poor children out of their state of sloth and laziness, and give them some gentle stimulant to go forth and find out some of the dignity of labour" ': James Rose Innes, *Autobiography* (ed. B. A. Tindall, 1949), 105.

[175] 27 of 1913; see Bundy (n. 9), 213 sq.

gies were employed to restrict blacks to the position of migrant labourers.[176] In particular, the long history of pass laws reflects '[t]he desire of whites both to absorb non-white labourers into the economy, and to treat them as subordinate aliens in "white" areas'.[177]

This ambivalence was to be perceived also in the exclusion of African law from the prevailing South African legal system, save in such rural areas as were reserved for black occupation.[178] The paternalism of the pre-Union governments, most clearly visible in the Natal[179] and Transvaal[180] legislation which appointed, respectively, the Lieutenant-Governor and the State President as paramount chief of all 'Natives', was perpetuated by the Union's Native Administration Act.[181] The Governor-General 'was made Supreme Chief over all Africans, with authority to appoint native commissioners, chiefs and headmen, define boundaries of chiefdoms, alter their composition, and move chiefdoms or individuals at will "from any place to any other place within the Union upon such conditions as he may determine" '.[182] A hierarchy of special courts was established for dealing with criminal offences committed by 'Natives', as well as 'civil causes and matters between Native and Native only'.[183] Perversely, the Act also granted the Governor-General authority both to make rules with regard to the carrying of passes and to punish words or acts promoting 'any feeling of hostility between Natives and Europeans'.[184] The Act very directly echoes the politico-economic movement towards segregation rather than assimilation, for the Native Affairs Commission of 1903–5 had preferred as ultimate goal the assimilation of African with colonial law.[185]

The continuation of African law within areas of former African sovereignty was a principle established in 1848 by Sir Harry Smith, Governor and High Commissioner at the Cape, following on his dramatic extension of the colonial boundaries.[186] The approach became an article of faith to British administrators in colonial Africa from the turn of the twentieth century, in

---

[176] Rhodes' Glen Grey Act has been described as 'a key moment in the replacement of the assimilationist strategy by one of segregation'. Dubow (n. 91), 74, relying on R. Parry, ' "In a Sense Citizens, but not Altogether Citizens . . .". Rhodes, Race and the Ideology of Segregation at the Cape in the Late Nineteenth Century', (1983) 17 *Canadian Journal of African Studies* 384 sqq.

[177] Welsh (n. 173), 196. See also Charles van Onselen, *Studies in the Social and Economic History of the Witwatersrand 1886–1914*, vol. II (1982), 35 sq.

[178] For a brief history of customary law in colonial Southern Africa see T. W. Bennett, *The Application of Customary Law in Southern Africa: The Conflict of Personal Laws* (1985), 39 sqq.

[179] Ord. 3 of 1849.   [180] Law 4 of 1885.   [181] 38 of 1927.

[182] Davenport (n. 4), 266 sq.   [183] S. 10(1).

[184] S. 29. For a discussion of the technical aspects of the Act, see Hahlo/Kahn, *Union* (n. 18) 327 sqq.

[185] Chanock, (1989) 30 *Journal of African History* 277. For brief discussions of the consequences of this legal segregation see Sachs (n. 22), 115 sqq.; T. W. Bennett, *A Sourcebook of African Customary Law for Southern Africa* (1991), v sqq.

[186] Thompson (n. 139), 418; Noël Mostert, *Frontiers: The Epic of South Africa's Creation and the Tragedy of the Xhosa People* (1992), 952 sq.

imitation of the system of administration introduced by Lugard in northern Nigeria.[187] Inevitably, given the resultant ambivalences pertaining to political power, the so-called 'customary' law applied was a product of the interaction of African societies with the requirements of European colonization.[188]

XI. PURISM

The conclusion of the Boer War in 1902 resulted in the coexistence of four British colonies. Six years later delegates from those colonies met in a national convention aimed at creating a Union. The Convention led to the promulgation by the Imperial Parliament of the South Africa Act,[189] and in 1910 the Union of South Africa was proclaimed. Symbolizing unification, the Act provided for a single Supreme Court, consisting of a number of provincial and local divisions with original and appeal jurisdiction and an Appellate Division.[190] The first Chief Justice was Sir Henry (later Lord) de Villiers, the long-serving Chief Justice of the Cape Colony.

The Union was based on a concept of a united white South Africa.[191] As J. C. Smuts wrote at the time: 'The whole meaning of Union in South Africa is this: We are going to create a nation—a nation which will be of a composite character, including Dutch, German, English and Jew, and whatever white nationality seeks refuge in this land—all can combine. All will be welcome'.[192] The question of black enfranchisement, despite the efforts of Tengo Jabavu, W. P. Schreiner, and others[193] and despite the entrenched section of the South Africa Act relating to Cape voters,[194] was in the circumstances essentially fudged.[195] At least two options were readily available to the Convention delegates. One was the extension of the 'colour-blind' Cape approach to enfranchisement to the rest of the Union. The other was the adoption of a constitution on the Orange Free State model, which had

---

[187] Kristin Mann, Richard Roberts, 'Law in Colonial Africa', in: *idem* (eds.), *Law in Colonial Africa* (1991), 19 sqq.

[188] Ibid. 4 sqq.; Martin Chanock, 'Paradigms, Policies and Property: A Review of the Customary Law of Land Tenure', in: ibid. 61 sqq.

[189] 9 Edw. 7, c. 9, of 1909.

[190] Embodied in ss. 95, 96, and 103 of the South Africa Act. The possibility of an appeal to the Privy Council continued to exist until 1950, however; on the national convention's proposals in respect of superior courts see L. M. Thompson, *The Unification of South Africa 1902–1910* (1960), 260 sqq.

[191] Belinda Bozzoli, *The Political Nature of a Ruling Class: Capital and Ideology in South Africa 1890–1933* (1981), 138 sqq.

[192] Quoted by W. K. Hancock, *Smuts*, vol. I, *The Sanguine Years 1870–1919* (1962), 361.

[193] See Thompson (n. 190), 385 sqq., 402 sqq.   [194] S. 35.

[195] See Walker (n. 59), 445 sqq.; Rose Innes (n. 174), 231 sq.; Thompson (n. 190), 212 sqq.; Hancock (n. 192), 256 sqq., 265 sqq.; John Dugard, *Human Rights and the South African Legal Order* (1978), 26 sq.

borrowed from the United States the principle of a bill of rights together with a judicial power of review[196] (even though it expressly excluded blacks from the vote[197]).

Nothing concentrates the nationalist mind better than war.[198] The Boer War was no exception, and played a most important part in consolidating and strengthening incipient Afrikaner nationalism.[199] The result was that the Union's relationship with Britain—which could also be exploited at another level, that of English- to Afrikaans-speaking white South Africans—came to dominate much of the country's post-Union political debate.[200] The debate, which served to obscure the more pressing issue of the political role to be played by the country's black majority, developed a legal parallel in the contest between English law and Roman-Dutch law. This latter contest, however, also operated at another, more insidious level: it would be naïve to suggest that the racial 'purity' so ardently espoused by (predominantly) Afrikaner politicians[201] did not have its corollary in the movement in favour of 'purity' in South African law—by which is meant the exclusion of what are perceived to be English additions to the pre-existing Roman-Dutch system.[202]

As shown above, Roman-Dutch law's claim to pre-eminence rests, historically, on a fragile base. The South African courts have furthermore over

---

[196] Thompson (n. 139), 430; Michael M. Corbett, 'Political Influences in the Legal Process: Law and Politics in South Africa', 1993 *Consultus* 107. Corbett suggests two reasons for the rejection of the latter option: the English legal training of a substantial number of the delegates; and the review power which had been claimed by Kotzé CJ some years previously in the Transvaal, leading to his dismissal by President Kruger. Indeed, the fear expressed by Smuts of politicization of the courts was generally concurred in by the judges: Chanock (1989) 30 *Journal of African History* 279, fn. 37.

[197] Saunders (n. 105), 169.

[198] On the role of war in creating and sustaining ethnic identities see Anthony D. Smith, *The Ethnic Revival* (1981), 74 sqq.

[199] See Hermann Giliomee, 'The Beginnings of Afrikaner Nationalism, 1870–1915', (1987) 19 *South African Historical Journal* 137 sqq.

[200] See W. K. Hancock, *Smuts*, vol. II, *The Fields of Force 1919–1950* (1968), 21 sqq.; Moodie (n. 132), 73 sqq.

[201] The theme of purity increasingly dominated the language of Afrikaner nationalism, the objective of which 'came to be the capture of the state through ethnic mobilisation': Shula Marks, Stanley Trapido, 'The Politics of Race, Class and Nationalism', in: *idem* (n. 91), 3. Economy and ethnicity are interestingly linked by Isabel Hofmeyr, 'Building a Nation from Words: Afrikaans Language, Literature and Ethnic Identity, 1902–1924', in: Marks/Trapido (ibid.), 116: 'in the very moment that these educated Afrikaners were beginning to explore the category of "their nation" through which they hoped to wrest some of capitalism's benefits for themselves, they were discovering the support which could give their nationalist vision some substance and clout. The process then of becoming a worker . . . was, for some, the process of being made into an Afrikaner. Class formation was, in other words, deeply inscribed with the fabrication or restructuring of ethnicity.' See also Van Onselen (n. 177), 138 sqq.; Dan O'Meara, *Volkskapitalisme: Class, Capital and Ideology in the Development of Afrikaner Nationalism, 1934–1948* (1983), 152 sq., 238 sqq.

[202] On the relationship between legal and racial purism see Cameron, (1982) 99 *SALJ* 50 sq.; David Dyzenhaus, 'L. C. Steyn in Perspective', (1982) 99 *SALJ* 387 sq.

the years often referred to and greatly relied on the decisions of their English counterparts,[203] thereby accepting the need to adapt the principles expressed by the Roman-Dutch lawyers 'to the changing and complicated conditions of modern society'.[204] Roman-Dutch and English law have generally been in a relationship of complementarity rather than opposition. Indeed, it has been said that it was Lord de Villiers's 'supreme achievement . . . to fuse into a single system most of what was good in the Roman-Dutch law with much of what was good in the English'.[205] There has been much support, both judicial and academic, for the view that South African law is a legal system in its own right. Even in those cases where the dominant position of the Roman-Dutch law is assumed, this has not by and large precluded an open-minded approach to the English law.[206]

Running against this legal tide—but not against the prevailing political current—the Appellate Division, under the lengthy chief justiceship of L. C. Steyn (1959–71) and afterwards, sought as far as was practicable to eradicate from South African law all that was regarded as impure accretions emanating from perfidious Albion.[207] It was a calling already pronounced worthy by Van den Heever JA.[208] Its origins might be traced to the

---

[203] For examples see Stephen D. Girvin, 'Perceval Maitland Laurence, Scholar, Writer and Colonial Judge and the High Court of Griqualand in the Late Nineteenth Century', (1994) 111 *SALJ* 121; *idem*, 'John Dove Wilson as Judge President of the Natal Provincial Division 1911–30: His Approach to Legal Authorities and Their Influence in Cases Involving Black Litigants', (1988) 105 *SALJ* 481 sqq.; Cameron, (1982) 99 *SALJ* 51.

[204] Innes (n. 174), 329, paying tribute to Lord de Villiers. Also: *Henderson v. Hanekom* (1903) 20 SC 513, at 519 (*per* De Villiers CJ); *Blower v. Van Noorden* 1909 TS 890, at 905 (*per* Innes CJ); *Daniels v. Daniels* 1958 (1) SA 513 (A) 523 (*per* Schreiner JA); and for a discussion of Schreiner's approach to the question: Ellison Kahn, 'Oliver Deneys Schreiner: The Man and His Judicial World', (1980) 97 *SALJ* 590 sqq.

[205] Walker (n. 59), 74. Generally on Lord de Villiers, apart from Walker's magisterial biography, Reinhard Zimmermann, 'De Villiers, John Henry', in: Michael Stolleis (ed.), *Juristen: Ein biographisches Lexikon* (1995), 160 sq. Lord de Villiers was certainly the most influential judge in South African legal history; he was for 41 years Chief Justice, first of the Cape Colony and later of the Union of South Africa. His work was carried on by James Rose Innes, the longest serving Chief Justice (1914–27) since Union and one of the most highly and most widely respected South African judges (see Zimmermann, in: Stolleis, 312 sq.).

[206] See the discussions in Hahlo/Kahn, *Union* (n. 18), 41 sqq.; Hahlo/Kahn, *System* (n. 18), 582 sqq.; Van Zyl (n. 30), 478 sqq.; Zimmermann, (1986) 103 *SALJ* 274 sqq.

[207] Before his appointment as a judge Steyn had in his *Uitleg van Wette* of 1946 indicated his hostility towards what he regarded as the intrusion of English law; Cameron, (1982) 99 *SALJ* 40 sq.; David Dyzenhaus, *Hard Cases in Wicked Legal Systems: South African Law in the Perspective of Legal Philosophy* (1991), 50. As Chief Justice, Steyn famously set out a similar approach to the authorities in the context of estoppel in *Trust Bank van Afrika Bpk v. Eksteen* 1964 (3) SA 402 (A) 410 sq. For criticism of the judgment see Cameron, (1982) 99 *SALJ* 46 sqq.; Visser (n. 55), 2 sqq. On the *bellum juridicum* of the 1950s and '60s about the true sources of South African law see Zimmermann (n. 55), 50 sqq. and the literature quoted there.

[208] In *Baines Motors v. Piek* 1955 (1) SA 434 (A) 543 (which directly contradicts the tribute of Innes CJ referred to above, n. 204), and *Preller v. Jordaan* 1956 (1) SA 483 (A) 504. Despite the fact that Van den Heever, like Steyn, was originally elevated to the Bench from the civil

development of an indigenous legal scholarship, manifested in the growth of university law faculties (particularly Afrikaans-language faculties) and the publication of a South African legal literature (including, again, many leading Afrikaans textbooks).[209] The positive side of purism is personified in the formidable academic figure of J. C. de Wet, whom no one could accuse of being motivated by the concerns of Afrikaner nationalism. His work is informed, above all else, by the maintenance of a very clear understanding of the principles of Roman-Dutch law, and by the logical systematization of large areas of South African law through the application of those principles. At the same time, it has rightly been written that he concerned himself 'with a wider historical and comparative approach to our law' than that permitted, often, by the opponents of purism[210] (who might well demonstrate a tendency towards facile reliance on English law).

The relationship between purism and politics is not simple. It is, though, correct to say that the high point of the judicial application of the doctrine coincided with a period when relationships between the Appellate Division and the executive were a great deal more harmonious than for some time previously. It is also remarkable that this was a time when people were looking to the courts to protect rights which were being eroded by the government, while 'the true concern that underlies the movement to purism has been logic and principle, not policy', with the consequence that there was an absence of judicial discussion 'of the justice of any particular rule or result'.[211] Also, despite the brilliance of at least one of its proponents, due attention should be given to the historical and political matrix from which the purists' claim to Roman-Dutch law's right of pre-eminence arose.[212] In tacit rebuttal it has been argued, usefully, that a distinction should be

service, and that his best-known poem, *In die Hoëveld*, is thematically related to *Trekkerswee*, the important epic work on the perceived tragedy of urbanization by that arch-Afrikaner nationalist, Totius, he cannot be tarred with the same pro-executive brush as Steyn. For a brief comparison: C. F. Forsyth, *In Danger for Their Talents: A Study of the Appellate Division of the Supreme Court of South Africa from 1950–80* (1985), 38 sq.

[209] Cf. Zimmermann (n. 55), 50, with further references.

[210] John Dugard, 'The "Purist" Legal Method, International Law and Sovereign Immunity', in: J. J. Gauntlett (ed.), *J. C. Noster. 'n Feesbundel* (1979), 39. For an appraisal of De Wet see Reinhard Zimmermann, Charl Hugo, 'Fortschritte der südafrikanischen Rechtswissenschaft im 20. Jahrhundert: Der Beitrag von J. C. de Wet (1912–1990)', (1992) 60 *Tijdschrift voor rechtsgeschiedenis* 157 sqq., who refer specifically (at 164 sq.) to his scathing critique of Lord de Villiers's 'false doctrines'.

[211] Forsyth (n. 208), 192 sq.

[212] In other words: 'It was a breed of men with considerably narrower intellectual vision who used the kind of learning and approach that J. C. [de Wet] pioneered for more nationalistic and chauvinistic aims and directed it against the English-law threads in our legal fabric': Barend van Niekerk, 'J. C. Noster: A Review and a Tribute to Professor J. C. de Wet', (1980) 97 *SALJ* 187. Indeed, the repudiation of English law by the courts has been shown not to have had a greater reference to Continental systems as concomitant: Cameron, (1982) 99 *SALJ* 51.

maintained between imperative and persuasive sources of law, with both the Roman-Dutch and English law falling into the latter category.[213]

Purism has been described as the 'enlightened half brother' of antiquarianism,[214] and much that has been said about the advantages of a broad approach to the Roman-Dutch authorities might also be applied in arguing against a rigid rejection of English law.[215] Indeed, it is altogether logical, in seeking to explain why it was even possible to consider a composite South African legal system, and why that aim has generally resulted in no uneasy fit, to look to the strong historical links and the underlying legal principles which tie the English common law to the European civil law.[216] Since reports of the end of purism so far appear exaggerated, it is worth emphasizing that the doctrine has its origin not in any deep understanding of the process of legal development, but in a political *Zeitgeist* which was concerned, above all else, with the separation of cultures.

XII. CONCLUSION

Due to the length of its tradition and the strength of its principles Roman-Dutch law is able comfortably to accommodate, and indeed adapt itself to, extensive influences from other legal systems. There is much value in the view that Roman-Dutch law 'must be purified of its purifications', and much advantage in accepting that what has developed in South Africa is properly called South African law.[217] In this essay it has been argued that the better approach towards the old authorities is a broad one; it has also been argued that there are no good reasons, either historical or legal, for seeking the exclusion of principles derived from English law; and it has been suggested, as a recurrent theme, that the exclusion of African law requires reconsideration.

[213] Cameron, (1982) 99 *SALJ* 48 sq. For a contrary view see Adrienne van Blerk, 'The Irony of Labels', (1982) 99 *SALJ* 365 sq.

[214] Forsyth (n. 208), 221.

[215] It certainly seems true that for Steyn CJ the two -isms represented the sides of one coin; see the detailed discussion by Forsyth (n. 208), 182 sqq., who concludes that while antiquarianism appears to have failed the same does not hold true for purism, particularly in the field of criminal law. For the view that purism has lapsed into antiquarianism see D. P. Visser, 'The Legal Historian as Subversive or: Killing the Capitoline Geese', in: *idem* (ed.), *Essays on the History of Law* (1989), 21.

[216] For a discussion see Zimmermann, (1986) 103 *SALJ* 274 sqq.; *idem*, 'Der europäische Charakter des englischen Rechts: Historische Verbindungen zwischen civil law and common law', (1993) 1 *Zeitschrift für Europäisches Privatrecht* 4 sqq.

[217] Albie Sachs, *The Future of Roman Dutch Law in a Non-Racial Democratic South Africa: Some Preliminary Observations* (1989), 7.

2: *African Land—A History of Dispossession*

T. W. BENNETT

Property holding is a direct index of power and wealth. A telling indication of the poverty and powerlessness of Africans in South Africa is that they have title to only 13 per cent of the country's total land area, of which only one-third is subject to indigenous tenures. The history of South African land law is therefore an account of how African lands were appropriated by white settlers and how the local systems of landholding were replaced with European tenures.

I. COLONIZATION

1. The Cape Colony

Colonization of Southern Africa began when the Dutch East India Company established a station at Cape Town to provision passing ships.[1] Under the rules of international law prevailing at the time[2] native peoples had only ill-defined rights *vis-à-vis* colonial powers. While Roman law (the chief source of rules on the acquisition of colonial territory) deemed colonized peoples rightless[3] a new principle, formulated by Spanish jurists on the basis of natural law, was gaining currency:[4] native communities retained

---

[1] The Cape settlement was not intended to be a colonial venture. Its status was determined by the charter given to the Company in 1602 by the States-General of the United Provinces of the Netherlands, which licensed the Company to trade. Thus the Company's powers to enter treaties and acquire territory by conquest would have been limited by this general purpose. See H. R. Hahlo, Ellison Kahn, *The South African Legal System and its Background* (1968), 531 sqq.

[2] Which regime determines state power to acquire and dispose of land. Once lawfully in occupation, of course, a state is free to dispose of property as it wishes. Sovereignty comprises the power of government (*imperium*) and title to land (*dominium*): Sir Kenneth Roberts-Wray, *Commonwealth and Colonial Law* (1966), 635.

[3] Their movable property became *res nullius* and their land was forfeited to the conquering state: Gaius, *Institutiones* II, 7; Hugo Grotius, *De Jure Belli ac Pacis*, 4, 1. See M. F. Lindley, *The Acquisition and Government of Backward Territory in International Law* (1926), 337.

[4] De Las Casas and Victoria are the best known: De Victoria *De Indis et de Jure Belli Relectiones*, vol. I, § 334. See further J. Crawford, *The Creation of States in International Law* (1979), 173, 175; Lindley (n. 3), 12 sqq.

various fundamental rights, which were unaffected by colonization.[5] Grotius seems to have accepted this principle as international customary law.[6]

If native rights were to be recognized and enforced, however, the community concerned had to have a recognizable legal system, a requirement which presupposed the community's recognition as a sovereign nation. Colonies with no sovereign government were deemed *terrae nullius*.[7] In consequence they had no legal system or land rights. According to the international law of the seventeenth century,[8] a *terra nullius* could be acquired by mere occupation.[9] Territories subject to sovereign powers had to be won by conquest[10] or cession.[11]

The Cape had no fixed international status as *terra nullius* or otherwise, nor had the Dutch East India Company a firm policy towards the local people.[12] Sometimes the Company bought land from the Khoi, implying that they were a sovereign nation; sometimes it simply appropriated land.[13] As it happened, the Khoi could offer no lasting resistance to Company rule.[14] Dwindling resources, epidemic diseases, and repeated conflicts with the immigrants resulted in their subjection to labour on settler farms or flight into the interior. Once the Cape's native population ceased to exist as a viable community, claims to sovereignty and land rights ceased too.

The Dutch East India Company was in any event less interested in rel-

---

[5] See generally P. G. McHugh, *The Maori Magna Carta: New Zealand Law and the Treaty of Waitangi* (1991), ch. 5.

[6] *Mare Liberum*, ch. 2.

[7] The concept is now arguably obsolete, since *The Western Sahara Case* (Advisory Opinion) (1975) ICJ Reports 12, § 80 held that any territory inhabited by peoples with a social and political organization could not be regarded *terra nullius*. See M. Shaw, *Title to Territory in Africa: International Legal Issues* (1986), 31 sqq. and *Mabo v. Queensland* (1992) 175 CLR 1, 40 sqq.

[8] See I. Brownlie, *Principles of Public International Law* (4th edn., 1990), 131 sqq. for the rules regulating acquisition of territory.

[9] Occupation flowed from symbolic apprehension of the land, such as planting a flag, together with public proclamation of an intention to become sovereign, and later an effective and peaceful display of sovereignty.

[10] Title by conquest was obtained when territory had been effectively (usually forcibly) occupied with a clear intention to annex.

[11] Cession, whether for value or from defeat of a state by war, took the form of a treaty or informal agreement with an acknowledged sovereign.

[12] Its policy was determined by its character as a commercial enterprise. Thus where possible the Company sought good relations, which involved negotiating treaties with local leaders, rather than a show of force. See G. Schutte, 'Company and Colonists at the Cape, 1652–1795', in: R. Elphick, H. Giliomee (eds.), *The Shaping of South African Society 1652–1840* (2nd edn., 1989), 292.

[13] See T. R. H. Davenport, K. S. Hunt, *The Right to the Land* (1974), Docs. 18–21.

[14] Notwithstanding sporadic revolts, such as the 4-year rebellion that broke out in 1799 when Khoi and San servants deserted farms with the aim of reclaiming 'the country of which our fathers have been despoiled': R. Elphick, V. C. Malherbe, 'The Khoisan to 1828', in: Elphick/Giliomee (n. 12) 33.

ations with the Khoi than in controlling its own unruly subjects. Dutch farmers were continually on the move, appropriating new land as and when they could. By extending its jurisdiction over them, the Company was constantly forced to expand its rule.[15] By the mid-eighteenth century immigrant farmers were established far to the east of Cape Town at Graaf Reinet.[16]

Britain occupied the Cape in 1806, and eight years later the Netherlands formally ceded its rights to the territory.[17] Under the feudal theory on which English land law was based, when a new colony was acquired, radical title to all land within it vested in the Crown.[18] Yet for various reasons, moral and pragmatic, Britain's policy was to respect indigenous law, including extant land titles,[19] provided only that it was a 'civilized' system.[20] This self-denying ordinance, in conjunction with the Crown's general dominion over land, meant that only the Crown had power to extinguish aboriginal land rights, with the corollary that only titles granted by the Crown would be enforced.[21]

In the case of the Cape, Britain ignored whatever rights the Khoi and San people might have had. Sedentary agriculture and urbanization were the most reliable tests of a 'civilized' proprietary regime, and these peoples had neither farms nor towns.[22] It followed that they had no recognizable land

---

[15] The commando system was largely responsible for the continual extension of the frontier. Instead of maintaining a standing army the Company used farmers to subdue local uprisings. The cheapest form of compensation was to allow them to take cattle and land as booty.

[16] In 1780, in a vain attempt to restrict further extension of the frontier, the Company prohibited any advance east of the Fish River.

[17] Title to the territory was originally acquired by conquest, first in 1795 and again in 1806.

[18] *Campbell v. Hall* (1774) 1 Cowper 204. This rule was aimed at preventing settlers from independently founding their own colonies and at protecting native peoples from land speculators: *R v. Symonds* (1847) New Zealand Privy Council Cases 387, 391.

[19] *Calvin's Case* (1608) 7 Co Rep 1a, 77 ER 377, 398, a decision occasioned by union with Scotland, had established the rule of recognition. See G. M. Fredrickson, *White Supremacy* (1981), 7 sqq. '[T]he absurd exception as to pagans' in *Calvin's Case* was later overruled by *Campbell v. Hall* (1774) 1 Cowp 204, 209. See too *Omychund v. Barker* (1744) Willes 538 (Ch), 26 ER 15; *Freeman v. Fairlie* (1828) 1 Moore Indian Appeals 305, 324 sq., 18 ER 117, 127 sqq.

[20] 'Civilized' was too political and subjective a requirement to mediate determination of a territory as *terra nullius*. By the 19th C. a more objective criterion was sought in political structures capable of maintaining order. See J. Westlake, *The Collected Papers* (ed. L. Oppenheim, 1914), 143 sqq. Yet even this was a subjective standard, for if a native polity lacked the familiar trappings of European statehood the colonizer would be tempted to regard it as *terra nullius* with no legal system. Australia was a notorious case in point. See *Coe v. Commonwealth* (1979) 53 Australian Law Journal Reports 403, 408.

[21] See e.g. *R v. Symonds* (1847) New Zealand Privy Council Cases 387 and: *Johnson v. M'Intosh* 21 US (8 Wheaton) 543, 594 sq. (1823), *Northwestern Bands of Shoshone Indians v. US* 324 US 335, 337 sq. (1945), *Wi Parata v. Bishop of Wellington* (1878) 3 New Zealand Jurist 72, 77 and *Williams v. A-G for New South Wales* (1913) 16 CLR 404, 439.

[22] According to Locke the only interests worthy of legal protection were those that had been generated by labour. See De Vattel, *Droit des Gens* 1, 18, 208 sq.; A. Ryan, *Property and Political Theory* (1984), chs. 1, 3, 5.

titles.[23] In 1828 an 'equal rights' ordinance was passed giving persons 'of colour' in the Cape the same rights to acquire and dispose of land as the settlers.[24] The Crown could then claim that it had no further responsibility towards its native subjects.[25] The fact that most of them were now landless, and few had the means to buy land, was disregarded.[26]

In the eyes of the new colonial power Roman-Dutch law was native to the Cape. It was deemed a suitably 'civilized' system.[27] Hence only the land titles granted by the Dutch East India Company—*eigendom*,[28] *erfpacht*,[29] and *leeningsplaats*[30]—continued to be recognized by the British administration.[31] However, the legacy of Dutch titles and tenures concerned the authorities less than the problem of how to control the issue of new titles and the collection of rents. Various attempts at tightening up on land administration had little success.[32] Like their Dutch predecessors, British officials in Cape Town were powerless to enforce regulations in outlying areas.[33]

[23] A hundred years later the Privy Council decision in *In Re Southern Rhodesia* [1919] AC 211, 233 would dismiss Ndebele land rights in Southern Rhodesia as irreconcilable with 'the legal ideas of civilized society'. Cf. *Sobhuza II v. Miller* [1926] AC 518 (PC), 525 where, although the Privy Council felt that the idea of individual ownership was foreign to African ideas, it conceded that the native community had at least a type of usufructuary right which was a burden on the radical title of the sovereign.

[24] Art. 3, Ordinance 50 of 1828.

[25] The 1829 settlement of a community of Khoi on land in the Kat River valley was an exceptional measure, prompted partly by considerations of security. See Davenport/Hunt (n. 13), Doc. 24.

[26] Apart from certain remote areas reserved for 'coloured' farmers, most of the indigenous peoples left in the Cape had no option but to seek refuge at the mission stations established by churches of various denominations from the 18th C. onwards: Davenport/Hunt (n. 13), 9. These were areas that later came to be classified as 'coloured reserves' under the Mission Stations and Communal Reserves Act 29 of 1909 (Cape).

[27] *Wi Parata v. Bishop of Wellington* (1878) 3 New Zealand Jurist 72, 78.

[28] A type of freehold but subject to conditions foreign to English law: Davenport/Hunt (n. 13), Doc. 1; L. Guelke, 'Land Tenure and Settlement at the Cape', in: C. G. C. Martin, K. J. Friedlaender (eds.), *History of Surveying and Land Tenure in the Cape 1652–1812* (1984), 8 sqq.

[29] Fifteen-year quitrent leases: Davenport/Hunt (n. 13), Doc. 4; Guelke (n. 28), 13 sqq.

[30] 'Loan farms', i.e., land lent by the Company on condition that an annual 'recognition' fee was paid: Davenport/Hunt (n. 13) Docs. 2 and 3; Guelke (n. 28), 18 sqq.

[31] Existing titles were in any case specifically guaranteed under art. 8 of the Act of Capitulation. Britain's reluctance to uphold Khoisan rights was prompted by other, more pragmatic reasons. Before commercial farming was developed and minerals were discovered, land was the most valuable commodity in the colony: A. J. Christopher, *The Crown Lands of British South Africa 1853–1914* (1984), 1.

[32] The value of land could be only realized, however, if rent was regularly paid and the issuing of new titles controlled. See L. C. Duly, *British Land Policy at the Cape, 1795–1844* (1968), 24 sq., 39, 41.

[33] Where farmers were free to do what they chose: Duly (n. 32), 16 sqq. At the time that British rule was being brought to bear on the Cape, a decision was taken to introduce the Wakefield method of disposing of newly acquired land on the basis of its success in facilitating expansion of the United States. Thus from 1839 onwards Crown land was no longer granted free to the settlers; it was generally sold by public auction at a minimum upset price: Christopher (n. 31), 11; Duly (n. 32), 116 sqq. The Cape nonetheless escaped the full rigours of imperial land policies: Duly (n. 32), 188.

2. Extension of the eastern Cape frontier

Although Britain confirmed the Fish River as the eastern boundary of the Cape in 1812, the settlers' unquenchable desire for more land kept pushing the frontier further east.[34] Here they met more resolute opposition from a group of peoples who have come to be called the Southern Nguni.[35] Power relations amongst the loosely related polities of this group were constantly changing,[36] and to add to an already volatile situation bands of refugees from the north—the Mfengu—had begun migrating into the region.[37]

Rivalries amongst the Southern Nguni gave Britain a pretext for intervention. As early as 1812 it became involved in a power struggle between two factions of the Xhosa.[38] For politically strategic reasons Britain did not treat any of its Southern African colonies as *terrae nullius*; rather, the Crown extended its influence by treaty.[39] Many of these agreements were of doubtful validity. Apart from elements of duress,[40] the parties were often of different minds.[41] African rulers did not always mean to alienate their land, for the idea of selling land was foreign to African customary law.[42] Besides, given persistent succession disputes and the consequent division and regrouping of local polities, the leaders negotiating these treaties may well have lacked the authority to represent their people[43].

To challenge the validity of these agreements, however, would have been an academic exercise. Aside from being powerless to defy the colonial

[34] Assisted again by the commando system: T. R. H. Davenport, 'Some Reflections on the History of Land Tenure in South Africa, seen in the Light of Attempts by the State to Impose Political and Economic Control', 1985 *Acta Juridica* 53, 57.

[35] Consisting of Xhosa, Bomvana, Thembu, Bhaca, Pondomise, Pondo, and Xesibe polities.

[36] A notable instance being the division of the Xhosa (c. 1740) into rival Rharhabe and Gcaleka factions.

[37] The Mfengu were victims of the *mfecane* (a social and political upheaval discussed below) with diverse origins in Bhele, Hlubi, Zizi, and Ngwane polities far from the eastern Cape: P. Maylam, *A History of the African People of South Africa* (1986), 96.

[38] Although one of the leaders, Ngqika, was recognized as paramount leader of the Xhosa, his collaboration brought him no guarantee of British protection. In 1819 his domain was annexed and the border was extended to the Keiskamma river. See generally François Venter, *Die Suid-Afrikaanse Bantoestaatsreg* (unpublished LL. D. thesis, Potchefstroom University, 1978), 38 and Maylam (n. 37), 38.

[39] E. H. Brookes, *The History of Native Policy in South Africa from 1830 to the Present Day* (1924), 15 sqq.

[40] When Pondoland finally surrendered its sovereignty to the Crown in 1894, for instance, its act could hardly be called voluntary, for British troops had been mobilized on the border and the British agent threatened dire consequences if the Pondo did not submit: C. Saunders, 'The Annexation of the Transkei', in: C. Saunders, R. Derricourt (eds.), *Beyond the Cape Frontier* (1974), 185 sqq.; Shaw (n. 7), 42 sqq.

[41] See e.g. the 1845 treaty between the Pedi and eastern Transvaal *trekkers*: P. Delius, *The Land Belongs to Us* (1983), 30 sqq.

[42] M. Wilson, 'Co-operation and Conflict: The Eastern Cape Frontier', in: M. Wilson, L. Thompson (eds.), *The Oxford History of South Africa*, vol. 1 (1969), 268 sq.

[43] Shaw (n. 7) 40. E.g. in *Cook v. Sprigg* [1899] AC 572 it was argued that chief Sigcau was in fact not paramount of all Pondoland.

forces, Africans had no legal means to question the lawfulness of their subjugation.[44] Even if they got as far as bringing suit in a British court, the action would be met by the act of state doctrine,[45] a defence which renders the validity of the Crown's acts in the international sphere non-justiciable.[46] As far as domestic tribunals were concerned, individuals could only question a treaty if it had been incorporated into municipal law by statute.[47]

After the War of the Axe in 1846–7 the policy of negotiating treaties with African rulers was abandoned in favour of annexation. Territory between the Fish and Keiskamma rivers was incorporated into the Cape as the district of Victoria East, and in 1847 the tract between the Keiskamma and Kei was annexed and constituted the dependency of Kaffraria.[48] The land was confiscated to the Crown. Portions were reserved for Mfengu and other local peoples and white colonists were settled in remaining areas.[49]

The next region to fall under the shadow of British rule was the Transkei, the region between the Kei and the Umzimkulu rivers. While the thinly populated zone along the base of the Drakensberg was deemed no man's land (the equivalent of a *terra nullius*), nearer the coast Britain had to contend with three long-established polities: the Pondo, the Gcaleka, and the

[44] Without the assistance of a foreign power or officials in the British government. Moreover, if no objections were raised to a treaty, any later complaint in an international tribunal would be defeated by arguments of acquiescence and estoppel. See Lindley (n. 3), 175.

[45] *Vajesingji Joravarsingji v. Secretary of State for India* (1924) LR 51 Indian Appeals 357, 360. Although the act of state doctrine was usually argued in the context of treaties of cession, it was equally applicable to cases of conquest: *Ex-Rajah of Coorg v. East India Co* (1860) 24 Beav 300, 54 ER 642.

[46] E.g. in New Zealand, by the 1840 Treaty of Waitangi Maori chiefs ceded to the Crown all their 'rights and powers and Sovereignty' in return for which the Crown guaranteed the 'full exclusive and undisturbed possession' of their lands. However, *Wi Parata v. Bishop of Wellington* (1878) 3 New Zealand Jurist 72, 78, held that the treaty as an act of state was not enforceable by municipal courts. See too *Heuheu Tukino v. Aotea District Maori Land Board* [1941] AC 308, 324.

[47] Thus an action could be successfully pursued by a native community only in the rare case where suit occurred in an international tribunal, e.g. in the *Cayuga Indians Claim* vol. 6 (1926) *United Nations, Reports of International Arbitral Awards*, 173. Even here, however, the claimant's lack of *locus standi* might result in defeat. Any litigant claiming rights under a treaty of cession had to show a legal interest flowing from the agreement. According to international law, a treaty between 2 sovereigns can be enforced only by one state against the other through the usual diplomatic means: *Cook v. Sprigg* [1899] AC 572; comments by K. McNeil, *Common Law Aboriginal Title* (1989), 167 sqq. Generally, individuals have no *locus standi* in international law, and the former treaty partner, as a sovereign body that had surrendered its legal personality, would technically have ceased to exist: *Ol le Njogo v. AG* (1913) Kenya LR 70. In e.g. *Cook v. Sprig*, although the Court conceded that a change of sovereignty by cession should not affect private property, the grantee of a concession by the paramount chief of the Pondo was powerless to enforce his rights against the Crown after annexation of Pondoland.

[48] In 1860. The territory was too poor to support itself as an autonomous unit, however, and 6 years later Kaffraria was annexed to the Cape Colony by Act 3 of 1865 (Cape).

[49] Land on the Kaffrarian coast was auctioned off to settlers at a minimum upset price in accordance with the Wakefield system, and military settlements were established in the interior: Christopher (n. 31), 20.

Thembu. For purely financial reasons there was no question of engaging these people in all-out war. Instead, annexation was preceded by the introduction of limited administrative ('magisterial') control until the subject polity was suitably weakened; then it was annexed.[50] However, settlement of the region was tempered by a decision taken in 1864 not to open the Transkei to white immigration.[51] The new territories were to be governed separately and differently from the Cape,[52] which implied recognition of the local customary law.[53]

3. Experiments with individual tenure

Central to the administration of customary land tenure were the political leaders of the community concerned.[54] Chiefs and headmen were seen as providers for their people, a responsibility that entailed allotment of sufficient land to all familyheads for the support of their dependants. Such land included a residential site, a number of arable fields, and access to common resources, notably grazing and water. Rights were precarious in the sense that if the family left the area or died out the land reverted to the authorities for reallocation.[55]

Soon after annexation Britain began experimenting with new forms of tenure in Kaffraria and the Transkei in the hope that the population would be persuaded to abandon their customary regimes. Foremost amongst the reasons for this decision was the need to legitimate the colonial enterprise: African peoples were to be uplifted to British notions of civilization and

[50] The Great Cattle Killing (1856–7) provided another opportunity for intervention. Sir George Grey ordered that the territory between the Kei and Mbashe rivers was to be 'cleared' to ensure that it would not be used as a springboard for attacks into Kaffraria, and in 1860 a 'special Transkeian magistrate' was placed at Idutywa.

[51] More precisely, white settlement was restricted to a few prescribed areas. See H. Rogers, *Native Administration in the Union of South Africa* (2nd edn., 1949), 100 sqq.; Lord Hailey, *An African Survey: A Study of Problems Arising in Africa South of the Sahara* (2nd edn., 1945), 719.

[52] Saunders (n. 40), 193.

[53] Provided it was 'compatible with the general principles of humanity observed throughout the civilized world': s. 23 of Proclamations 110 and 112 of 1879.

[54] See T. W. Bennett, 'Administrative-law Controls over Chiefs' Customary Powers of Removal', (1993) 110 *SALJ* 276, 278 sq.

[55] The following include detailed ethnographic accounts of customary systems of land tenure in Southern Africa: H. Ashton, *The Basuto* (1952), 144 sqq.; I. Hamnett, *Chieftainship and Legitimacy: An Anthropological Study of Executive Law in Lesotho* (1975), 63 sqq.; A. J. B. Hughes, *Land Tenure, Land Rights and Land Communities on Swazi National Land in Swaziland* (1972); M. Hunter, *Reaction to Conquest*, (2nd edn., 1961), 112 sqq.; W. J. O. Jeppe, *Bophuthatswana: Land Tenure and Development* (1980), ch. 2; M. Wilson, M. E. E. Mills, *Keiskammahoek Rural Survey* vol. 4 (1952), ch. 2; M. W. Prinsloo, *Inheemse Publiekreg in Lebowa* (1983), 130 sqq.; I. Schapera, *Native Land Tenure in the Bechuanaland Protectorate* (1943) and *A Handbook of Tswana Law and Custom* (2nd edn., 1955), 195 sqq.; V. G. J. Sheddick, *Land Tenure in Basutoland* (1954). For a legal text see A. J. Kerr, *The Customary Law of Immovable Property and of Succession* (3rd edn., 1990).

converted to Christianity.[56] A less high-minded, but nevertheless vital objective was to undermine chiefly authority by removing their powers over land.[57]

Colonial policy towards African tenure was informed by two tenacious beliefs: that individual ownership of property was the hallmark of civilization and that customary law knew only communal ownership.[58] The first belief was attributable to evolutionist theory.[59] The second followed as an apparently self-evident corollary. Thus the Privy Council's judgment in *Amodu Tijani v. Secretary, Southern Nigeria*[60] (although given eighty years later) was typical of thinking in the nineteenth century.

Land belongs to the community, the village or the family, never to the individual. All members of the community, village or family have an equal right to the land, but in every case the Chief or Headman of the community or village, or head of the family, has charge of the land, and in loose mode of speech is sometimes called the owner. He is to some extent in the position of a trustee, and as such holds the lands for the use of the community or family.[61]

In spite of clear evidence to the contrary, the belief that African society is organized on a communistic or collectivist basis has persisted.[62] Admittedly, many aspects of African life were, and are, inspired by a communitarian spirit: the ethic of mutual support owed to all members of the extended family; the emphasis on the duty to uphold family honour, to promote its prosperity, and to secure the future generations;[63] and the work parties called to tackle large agricultural projects.[64] However, it does not follow that cus-

[56] See S. B. Burman, 'Cape Policies towards African Law in Cape Tribal Territories, 1872–1883' (unpublished Ph. D. thesis, University of Cape Town, 1973), ch. 2.

[57] Other methods of subverting traditional rule were to replace chiefs with white magistrates and, more subtly, to convert chiefs into government stipendiaries: Brookes (n. 39) 90 sqq.; T. W. Bennett, *The Application of Customary Law in Southern Africa* (1985), 41.

[58] This idea persisted throughout the century to dominate the thinking of 2 highly influential commissions: the Cape Commission on Native Laws and Customs (1883) § 108, 40 and the Native Affairs Commission vol. 1 (1905) § 147. See M. Chanock, 'Paradigms, Policies and Property: A Review of the Customary Law of Land Tenure', in: K. Mann, R. Roberts (eds.), *Law in Colonial Africa* (1991), 66 sqq. Even today land subject to customary law is still described as 'communal' land. See e.g. the 1991 White Paper on Land Reform D 5.5.2.

[59] See Sir Henry Maine, *Ancient Law* (1917 Everyman), 152 sqq.; L. H. Morgan, *Systems of Consanguinty and Affinity of the Human Family* (1871), 492. See, too, M. Chanock, 'A Peculiar Sharpness: An Essay on Property in the History of Customary Law in Colonial Africa', (1991) 32 *Journal of African History* 65, 70.

[60] [1921] 2 AC 399, 404.

[61] Also in *Sobhuza II v. Miller* [1926] AC 518, 525 the Council reiterated that individual ownership was foreign to all systems of customary law, including those of Southern Africa; land belonged to the community.

[62] See e.g. A. P. Cheater, 'The Ideology of "Communal" Land Tenure in Zimbabwe: Mythogenesis Enacted?', (1990) 60 *Africa* 188 sqq., who analyses use of the term 'communal' to describe Zimbabwean land tenure in both the colonial and post-independence periods.

[63] See S. K. B. Asante, *Property Law and Social Goals in Ghana* (1975), 18 sqq.

[64] M. F. C. Bourdillon, *The Shona Peoples* (1976), 91; Schapera, *Native Land Tenure* (n. 55), 195; Sheddick (n. 55), 83 sqq.; Jeppe (n. 55), 34; Hamnett (n. 55), 73.

tomary land tenure was (or is) communal.[65] Anthropological fieldwork has shown that landholders do not share their residential sites or arable plots with non-family members. What is more, with the exception of occasional work parties, farming and herding had little to do with mutual co-operation.[66] 'Communal' would be a fair description only of rights to pastureland and natural resources;[67] and the word is unobjectionable where it suggests that an individual's entitlement to land derives from membership of a political community.

At the time, however, western individualism was regarded as not only the polar opposite of African communalism but also pre-ordained to supersede it. Quitrent was chosen as the tenure best suited to facilitate a social transformation.[68] It was a system peculiarly suited to new colonial settlements. Relatively secure rights to defined allotments would encourage farmers to invest in agricultural production, while the Crown's retention of radical title gave it control over land use and guaranteed a constant source of revenue from rent.[69]

The first people to benefit from the quitrent scheme were the Mfengu of the Victoria East district in 1854.[70] Individuals were given title to surveyed plots subject to a set of conditions that was to become more or less standard. An annual rent was set well below the market value of the land. Titleholders were prevented from speculating in land by a prohibition on alienation, subdivision, and subletting. (Rights were, however, heritable.) Tenure was conditional on good behaviour. The Crown as owner could evict holders for breach of any of the conditions attached to the lease, notably failure to pay rent, to occupy beneficially, or commission of an act of disloyalty. On termination of the lease the land reverted to the Crown for reallocation.[71]

[65] In strictly legal terms the word 'communal' is ambiguous. It can mean either that a right is held by a group of people jointly (i.e. by a single inseparable title), or by a group in common (i.e. each person having a separate but identical title).

[66] Based on his fieldwork in Lesotho, Hamnett (n. 55), 73 said that the reverse was true: people worked for their own benefit, regarding one person's gain as another's loss.

[67] Kerr (n. 55) 53.

[68] See Davenport/Hunt (n. 13), Doc. 57; Brookes (n. 39), 360 sqq. Freehold tenure was also available to those who had the means to buy land, but quitrent was a more affordable option.

[69] The Dutch East India Company had introduced quitrent tenure to the Cape in 1732: Davenport, 1985 *Acta Juridica* 54; Davenport/Hunt (n. 13) Doc. 4. In 1813 the British initiated a 'perpetual' variant by giving holders permanent and heritable rights. See Davenport/Hunt (n. 13) Docs. 11 and 13; Duly (n. 32), 46 sqq.

[70] Individual titles were granted only to a few communities outside the Cape: Thaba 'Nchu in the Free State, the Umtwalumi Mission Reserve, and Amanzimtoti and Ifafa in Natal: see B. M. Jones, *Land Tenure in South Africa: Past, Present and Future* (1964), 27, 32.

[71] The experiment was pronounced a success, at least in so far as rents were paid: Brookes (n. 39), 360. No restrictions were imposed on mortgage, however, and in consequence many plots passed into the hands of settlers: Jones (n. 70), 25. For the history of this settlement see Wilson/Mills (n. 55), 69. Quitrent tenure was also introduced to various mission stations in the Cape and it was included in the Native Locations Act 1879, which prefigured the Glen Grey Act. See Brookes (n. 39), 361 sqq.

In 1894 an elaboration of quitrent tenure was introduced in the Glen Grey district.[72] This Act, which became a byword for the Cape's African policy, was concerned principally to establish a new system of local self-government in competition with chiefly rule,[73] but it included provisions on individual title and labour tax. The idea was to create a stable peasantry, who would subsist on surveyed lots to which they had secure title.[74] Those who did not qualify for land would become a permanently landless proletariat, foreshadowing the *apartheid* era.[75]

In bonding holders to their land by the promise of profit from improved agriculture, these enactments were supposed to ease the transition from tribalism to progressive individualism.[76] Economic success was, however, elusive.[77] No doubt more affluent peasants welcomed their relatively secure tenure and their freedom from chiefly rule, but the size of the holdings was too small to allow for competitive commercial farming (and, of course, land accumulation was prohibited).[78] The 1883 Cape Commission on Native

[72] Act 25. See R. T. Ally, 'The Development of the System of Individual Tenure for Africans with Special Reference to the Glen Grey Act, 1894–1922' (unpublished M. A. thesis, Rhodes University, 1985), 12.

[73] Traditional leaders were to be deprived of their control over land distribution and local councils were to usurp their political functions. See Rogers (n. 51), 34 sqq.

[74] The plots could be alienated and they could be inherited according to an order of succession contained in a schedule to Act 25 of 1894, supposed to imitate customary law. Testate succession, however, was forbidden. Mortgaging too was prohibited, a rule that Brookes (n. 39), 366 claims was the finest feature of the system. The problems associated with mortgaging in Thaba 'Nchu are explored by C. Murray, *Black Mountain: Land, Class and Power in the Eastern Orange Free State 1880s–1980s* (1992), 98 sq., 136 sqq.

[75] The whole Act was only applied in Glen Grey. While the local government provisions were applied to most of the Transkei, the land tenure provisions were introduced only to areas considered amenable to Britain's civilizing mission. See W. Beinart, C. Bundy 'State Intervention and Rural Resistance: The Transkei, 1900–1965', in: M. A. Klein (ed.), *Peasants in Africa: Historical and Contemporary Perspectives* (1980), 276; C. Bundy, *The Rise and Fall of the South African Peasantry* (1979), 134 sqq.

[76] In fact the Glen Grey Act provoked considerable opposition, mainly because of the unpopular labour tax (eventually abandoned in 1905). The individual tenure provisions were then introduced only with the consent of the districts concerned: Beinart/Bundy (n. 75), 277.

[77] See Brookes (n. 39), 368 sqq.; W. Beinart, *Political Economy of Pondoland* (1982), 42 for the arguments for and against. C. Bundy, 'The Transkei Peasantry, 1890–1914: "Passing through a Period of Stress" ', in R. Palmer, N. Parsons (eds.), *The Roots of Rural Poverty in Central and Southern Africa* (1977), 201 sqq. says that while some Transkeian peasants were able to benefit from the economic upswing following the discovery of gold they were subject to acute social and economic pressures caused by land shortage, debt, and competition from white farmers. He concludes that by 1914 the peasant community was less economically resilient and self-sufficient than it had been 50 years before. See too Beinart/Bundy (n. 75), 293–8. They conclude (275) that: 'As merchant capital was shouldered aside by industrial capital, it was increasingly labour rather than agricultural produce that was required from the African reserve areas like the Transkei.'

[78] One man, one lot was then (and continued to be) a cardinal principle of all statutory tenures for Africans. The Union Government, *Report on Native Location Surveys* (1922), UG 42 (the 'Vos Report', for which see Davenport/Hunt (n. 13) Doc. 80) listed other complaints against the system: being tied down to prescribed dwelling and garden sites; having to pay the costs of survey and title; the surveyors' failure to take into account the needs of future

Laws and Customs could reach no firm conclusion on the results of the scheme. It still favoured individual tenure, but felt that this should be introduced only on request.[79]

4. Natal: reserves and trusteeship

Colonization of Natal commenced with three treaties by which the King of the Zulus ceded land to white settlers. Since the same area was involved in each cession, the two later agreements were probably invalid,[80] but any dispute was eclipsed by the Battle of Blood River when Dutch *trekkers* in loose alliance with disaffected elements of the local population defeated the Zulu army. In 1838 a Republic of Natalia, bounded by the Tugela and Umzimkulu rivers, was declared. It lasted only five years. In 1843 Natalia was annexed by Britain.[81]

The Zulu kingdom continued to maintain a precarious independence.[82] Inevitably war broke out in 1879, and the Zulu army was defeated at the Battle of Ulundi. Annexation did not immediately follow conquest; Cetshwayo was restored to the throne, albeit with substantially reduced powers. When Britain eventually annexed Zululand in 1887,[83] the decree did not include 'Amatongaland', a territory to the northeast. At first Britain had no interest in the area, but when it became apparent that the Transvaal or Germany might acquire a harbour there the Crown started to assume authority. The legal basis for its action was the somewhat dubious claim that the territory devolved on Britain as successor state to Zululand, for Tongaland had been treated as a Zulu tributary. In 1885 Tongaland was proclaimed a British protectorate,[84] and two years later incorporated into Zululand.[85]

Because Natal was believed to be well suited to commercial farming,[86] Britain encouraged immigration in order to exploit the colony's agricultural

landholders. Rogers (n. 51) 116 adds that the expense of transferring allotments caused additional problems. Transfers were made informally without registration, which led to growing confusion.

[79] *Report*, § 110(9), 41.
[80] In 1824 Shaka granted British settlers full rights to Port Natal (the future city of Durban): Davenport/Hunt (n. 13), Doc. 34. 4 years later a similar grant was made to J. S. King: Davenport/Hunt (n. 13), Doc. 35. Dingane then ceded Port Natal to parties of Dutch *trekkers* from the eastern Cape, who had arrived in the territory in 1838: Davenport/Hunt (n. 13), Doc. 37.
[81] Many of the *trekkers* then left in spite of Sir Harry Smith's offer to respect all 'fair and reasonable' land claims: Christopher (n. 31), 22.
[82] A treaty was concluded with the reigning Zulu king, Mpande, to fix a border between the new colony and the Zulu domain.
[83] Proclamation 33 of 1887 (Natal).   [84] Proclamation 9 of 1895 (Zululand).
[85] Proclamation 10 of 1897 (Zululand).
[86] Christopher (n. 31), 5. Settlers were offered land in accordance with the Wakefield scheme: ibid. 23.

potential.[87] African land rights would probably have been completely extinguished in the scramble for land were it not for Sir Theophilus Shepstone's influence with the Natal Native Commission of 1846–7. Following the recommendations of the Commission ten reserves were created to accommodate the estimated 80,000 people who had returned to Natal from Zululand and areas in the south.[88] Reduction or alienation of this land was prohibited.[89]

Reserves—ostensibly to protect the indigenous population from encroachment by settlers—were a regular feature of the British colonization of Africa.[90] Initially those in Natal were deemed to be Crown land, on which Africans were to have only permissive rights of occupancy. Lieutenant Governor Scott, however, proposed a trust to manage the land on behalf of the occupants and thereby to secure its extent and proper administration.[91] In 1864 his scheme was translated into legislation by the creation of the Natal Native Trust.[92] The Governor and executive council were constituted the board, which held all interests in the land, with power to 'grant, sell, lease, or otherwise dispose of the same . . . for the support, advancement or well being' of the African population.[93] (When Zululand was annexed, reserves were established there too, later to be vested in a Zululand Native Trust[94].) What precisely was intended by trust tenure has never been clear. While the trustee was obviously bound by the beneficial incidents of its tenure, there has been no intimation that the Crown (or state) could be held to account for its administration.[95]

[87] Two waves of settlers arrived in 1849 and 1852. Although the settler population in the colony was never large, immigrants acquired extensive commercial farms, which carried many African 'squatter' cultivators. See Christopher (ibid.), 69 sqq. regarding the disposal of Crown lands in Natal.

[88] D. Welsh, *The Roots of Segregation: Native Policy in Colonial Natal 1845–1910* (2nd edn., 1973), 12 sqq.

[89] Although the amount of land recommended was considered excessive by subsequent commissions in 1848 and 1852–53, the size of the reserves was maintained.

[90] In East, Central, and Southern Africa: Hailey (n. 51), 803 sqq. In West Africa, because only a small amount of land was appropriated by settlers or declared Crown property, the indigenous people retained most of their lands, and so no reserves were created.

[91] Although trusts had been introduced as early as 1854 for various mission stations in the Cape, Davenport/Hunt (n. 13), Doc. 56, so-called trust tenure was developed more fully in Natal.

[92] By Letters Patent issued on 27 Apr. 1864. Davenport/Hunt (n. 13), Doc. 63.

[93] Various deeds of grant were then issued in terms of which most of the Natal reserves were conveyed to the Trust. There were also 19 mission reserves in Natal, for which missionary societies held land in trust for African beneficiaries. The Natal Mission Reserves Act 49 of 1903 incorporated these into the Natal Trust.

[94] Reserves were created by Proclamation 2 of 1887 (Zululand). The Trust was established by deed of grant by the Governor of Natal on 6 Apr. 1909. The trustees were prohibited from alienating any of the lands without the consent of the Secretary of State for the Colonies or the authority of a special act of parliament: Rogers (n. 51), 80.

[95] In the manner of a private-law trustee. See Kerr (n. 55), 38 sqq. citing *Civilian War Claimant's Association Ltd v. The King* [1932] AC 14; *Tito v. Waddell* [1977] Ch 106. Cf. *Guerin v. The Queen* (1985) 13 DLR (4th) 321.

Shepstone continued to shape Natal's policy towards its African subjects. In contradistinction to the Cape, few attempts were made to interfere with traditional customary tenure, which was tolerated in terms of a policy that prefigured Britain's later doctrine of indirect rule. Natal's apparent liberalism was dictated by the most prosaic of reasons: a shortage of funds and personnel. Thus, instead of employing colonial officials to manage the new reserves, Shepstone proposed using African rulers.[96] Once indigenous leaders had been co-opted to the colonial service, it was a short step to recognizing chiefly courts and customary law.[97] This policy was repeated in the Transvaal (both during and after British occupation) and in British Bechuanaland.

5. The Orange Free State

Neither the Orange Free State nor the Transvaal can be said to have been colonized in the strict sense of the term, since the people who were to create new states in the interior came not as agents of a colonial power but as private groups seeking escape from British rule in the Cape.[98] The first Dutch-speaking *trekkers* to arrive in the Free State, for instance, were clearly not conquerors. They negotiated the purchase of land from a local Taung chieftaincy and forged an alliance with Moroka, leader of the Rolong of Thaba 'Nchu. Britain remained in pursuit, however, and in 1848 annexed the Free State.[99] Six years later it withdrew and under the Bloemfontein Convention recognized the Orange Free State as an independent nation.[100]

The Free State's relations with the people living within its borders were unique to South African history. The two territories, later to become reserves, were at first allowed virtual autonomy.[101] Outside these areas ownership of land was restricted to *burghers* of the Republic, a status not permitted to persons of colour.[102] The Rolong kept their special position until

[96] Against stiff opposition from the settlers: Welsh (n. 88), 25.

[97] Ordinance 3 of 1849 confirmed the application of customary law 'so far as it was not repugnant to the general principles of humanity observed throughout the civilized world'. This was an exception to the general law of the colony, which according to Ordinance 12 of 1845 was Roman-Dutch law.

[98] If they were not technically colonists they could qualify as aborigines, and thus (paradoxically) they would be entitled to assert their own aboriginal title (for which see below) to whatever lands they acquired.

[99] Which it named the Orange River Sovereignty. During this period Moroka's domain at Thaba 'Nchu was declared a reserve.

[100] The Republic then extended its territory eastwards at the expense of Moshoeshoe's kingdom in Lesotho. See C. C. Eloff, 'Lesotho Claims to Part of the Orange Free State', (1978) 4 *South African Yearbook of International Law* 109 sqq.

[101] As evidenced by treaties of alliance and friendship concluded with the Free State in 1865 and 1883: Venter (n. 38), 184.

[102] Ch. XXXIV, Wetboek. Arts. 11 and 12 specially exempted the Moroka district from the purview of the law, however: Davenport/Hunt (n. 13), Doc. 61.

1884, when the Free State intervened after a succession dispute to annex the territory. It was then constituted a reserve.[103]

6. The Transvaal

It took more than fifty years for effective control to be established over the whole territory of the South African Republic.[104] Appropriation of land was legally far from straightforward. The basic title of the South African Republic (SAR) rested on a claim that has since become one of the most controversial issues in South African history: the *trekkers'* contention that the interior of Southern Africa was 'empty' when they arrived.[105] By implication it was *terra nullius*, and so open to occupation.[106]

The truth or otherwise of this claim depends on the historicity of events that occurred shortly before the arrival of the trekkers: the *mfecane* (or *difaqane*). According to conventional historical sources, the peoples of the interior had been thrown into turmoil by successive waves of invasion set in motion by the birth of the Zulu kingdom. Between 1822 and 1837 the Tlokwa, Kololo, and Ndebele had overrun the Free State and Transvaal destroying or putting to flight all in their path.[107] Until recently then, the accepted view was that much of the Transvaal had been depopulated and dominated by Mzilikazi's Ndebele.[108]

In 1836 *trekkers* defeated Mzilikazi and forced him to withdraw to what is now Zimbabwe. In November 1837 Hendrik Potgieter proclaimed annexation by conquest of the territory previously controlled by the Ndebele and

---

[103] See Rogers (n. 51), 102 sq. The other reserve, located on the northeastern border, was originally occupied by an independent ruler, Witsi. Law 9 of 1898 constituted his successor, Mopeli, and the population of Witzieshoek subjects of the Republic.

[104] Venter (n. 38), 218 sqq.

[105] G. M. Theal, *A History of South Africa, 1795–1834* (1891), 328, cited by Davenport/Hunt (n. 13), Doc. 31.

[106] African colonies were seldom treated as *terrae nullius*. See C. H. Alexandrowicz, *The European-African Confrontation* (1973), 12 sq., 185; Lindley (n. 3), 339.

[107] J. D. Omer-Cooper, *The Zulu Aftermath* (1966), 115 sqq. The reasons for and the circumstances of this event were originally documented by the missionary-author A. T. Bryant, *The Zulu People* (1949), who pieced together his account from Zulu oral traditions in the 50 years after 1883. Now, however, it is thought that his work is flawed both in detail and in its larger conception. See J. Wright, C. Hamilton, 'The Phongolo-Mzimkhulu Region in the Late Eighteenth and Early Nineteenth Centuries', in: A. H. Duminy, B. Guest (eds.), *Natal and Zululand: From Earliest Times to 1910* (1989), 68 sqq.; E. A. Eldredge, 'Sources of Conflict in Southern Africa, ca 1820–30: The "Mfecane" Reconsidered', (1992) 33 *Journal of African History* 1 sqq.; C. Saunders, *Writing History: South Africa's Urban Past and Other Essays* (1992), 81 sqq. Saunders concludes: 'those who want simple truths will have to learn to live with complexities.'

[108] Who had settled in the western area of the Transvaal. See Omer-Cooper (n. 107), 134; W. D. Hammond-Tooke (ed.), *The Bantu-speaking Peoples of Southern Africa* (2nd edn., 1974), 385; W. A. Stals 'Die Kwessie van Naturelle-eieondomsreg op Grond in Transvaal, 1838–1884', (unpublished M. A. thesis, University of Pretoria, 1970), 1.

formally declared the South African Republic.[109] The extent of the new state was obviously vague, but it included at least the western portion of the Transvaal.[110] Appropriation of the northern areas was *ad hoc* and informal. Within the confines of a generally accepted border on the Limpopo[111] farmers either took land at will or occasionally were given farms by the state.[112] Whether the SAR's title to land rested on succession to the undefined Ndebele realm, conquest, cession, or occupation, however, was never clear.[113]

In the eastern Transvaal title to territory was derived from the exploits of splinter groups of *trekkers* who moved east after 1837. A band under the leadership of Hendrik Potgieter, for instance, negotiated a grant of land in the region of Andries-Ohrigstad from the Pedi leader, Sekwati, in 1845.[114] Yet whether Sekwati had rights to give is questionable, for the Swazi considered this area part of their domain. Another group of *trekkers* entered a separate agreement with the Swazi king by which he sold them a generous expanse of territory that partially overlapped Potgieter's grant.[115] Initially cordial, relations between the immigrants and the Pedi soon deteriorated. The *trekkers* regarded the Pedi as subjects, although they had no legal basis for doing so since the Pedi had not been defeated in battle nor had they ceded their sovereignty.[116] Disputes were settled by the British who, after annexing the Transvaal, went on to defeat the Pedi in 1879.[117]

Treatment of the Pedi was symptomatic of the European powers' attitude to many African nations during the scramble for Africa. All too often subject status was simply presumed. Hence, despite a proposal at the Berlin Conference of 1885 that African polities should be treated as states deserving legal recognition,[118] the final Declaration glossed over the issue.[119]

---

[109] Venter (n. 38), 220 sqq. The sovereignty of this entity was subsequently confirmed by Britain at the Sand River Convention 1852, when Britain recognized the right of 'the emigrant farmers beyond the Vaal River ... to manage their own affairs and to govern themselves according to their own laws'.

[110] Venter (n. 38), 222.   [111] Ibid. 235

[112] J. D. Fage, R. Oliver, in: *The Cambridge History of Africa* vol. 5 (1976), 388.

[113] See Venter (n. 38), 224 sq.

[114] There is no documentary evidence of this agreement aside from a note in the *Volksraad* minutes of 20 Aug. 1845: Venter (n. 38), 227.

[115] The grant was made in 1846 and included land between the Crocodile and Oliphants rivers. Of course, it is again doubtful whether the Swazi had rights to dispose, for this region included Pedi territory, not to mention Ndebele and Sotho domains. See Delius (n. 41), 30 sqq.

[116] Sekhukhune did, however, negotiate a peace with the Republic in 1877 after serious military defeat in 1876.

[117] Relations with the dominant people of the north, the Venda, soured after the death of their ruler, Ramabulana, in 1864. In 1898 Republican forces defeated Ramabulana's heir, thereby subjugating the last of South Africa's indigenous peoples the year before the Anglo-Boer War broke out.

[118] Which would follow if prospective colonies were not regarded as *terrae nullius*. See Crawford (n. 4), 178 sq.

[119] Instead the Berlin Declaration stressed the conditions of effective occupation for African territory, i.e. public notification and an obligation to assure sufficient control of the territory to protect acquired rights and freedom of trade. See Lindley (n. 3), 324 sqq.

Questions of African sovereignty tended to be submerged in international politics. Once the borders of the Transvaal had been recognized by Britain, for example, it was taken for granted that everyone within the Republic was a subject; and unless a European power was prepared to argue their case native peoples had no voice in the international sphere.[120]

Unlike Natal and the Cape, the Transvaal Government paid little attention to the governance of the African population or to their land requirements.[121] The first evidence of any land policy is a *Volksraad* resolution of 1853 providing that Africans could be granted land conditional upon their good behaviour;[122] but two years later another resolution declared that non-*burghers* were forbidden to own land.[123] Indigenous land rights were eventually secured by Britain. The Pretoria Convention of 1881 expressly stipulated that Africans had the right to acquire land in the Republic[124] and art. 21 obliged the SAR to appoint a standing 'Locations Commission' to delimit such reserves as the peoples of the territory 'may be fairly and equitably entitled to'. In accordance with the Commission's recommendations reserves were created in the Rustenberg, Lichtenburg, Marico, and Sekhukuneland districts.[125]

However, it was not clear whether the trusteeship principle applied to reserves in the Transvaal, since the Pretoria Convention, the charter for their creation, made no provision in this regard.[126] Land purchased by Africans, on the other hand, was held in trust, for art. 13 of the Convention provided that whatever land they bought was to be transferred to the Locations Commission in trust.[127]

[120] When the Transvaal was given its independence from Britain in 1881 the boundaries of the Republic were fixed, and so far as Britain was concerned the Transvaal had more or less full powers over all the peoples within its borders. However, because the 1884 London Convention stipulated that the SAR could conclude no treaty with any state other than the Free State unless approved by Britain, it was questionable whether the Transvaal could be regarded as a sovereign state: *R v. Christian* 1924 AD 101, 108, 125 sq. See, too, J. Dugard, *International Law: A South African Perspective* (1994), 15 sq.

[121] A firm policy regarding African law and government dates from Law 4 of 1885. The main object of this enactment was to establish control over the African population, but at the same time customary law was recognized, unless inconsistent with general principles of civilization recognized throughout the world.   [122] Of 28 Nov.: Rogers (n. 51), 103.

[123] Resolution 159 of 18 June 1855: Davenport/Hunt (n. 13), Doc. 65.

[124] Although transfer was to be registered on the buyer's behalf in the name of the Locations Commission, a rule that prevailed until *Tsewu v. Registrar of Deeds* 1905 TS 130. See Davenport/Hunt (n. 13), Doc. 65.

[125] The Commission's work, still far from complete, was interrupted by the outbreak of the Anglo-Boer in 1899. In 1905, during the post-war period of reconstruction, another Locations Commission was appointed to deal with the remaining areas. It reported in 1907, and except for a few minor changes its recommendations were accepted: Jones (n. 70), 11.

[126] Stals (n. 108), 129 sq. concludes that before 1877 the trusteeship concept was not applied in the Transvaal.

[127] See Venter (n. 38), 245. It was uncertain exactly who owned these properties: Brookes (n. 39), 359; Stals (n. 108), 206. After *Tsweu v. Registrar of Deeds* 1905 TS 130 Africans could receive transfer of land directly and could own their lands personally, but the decision took effect only prospectively: Brookes, *ibidem*.

II. SEGREGATION

1. The Lagden Report and the 1913 Land Act

In 1903, after the Anglo-Boer War, Lord Milner convened a Commission under the chairmanship of Sir Godfrey Lagden to report on 'native' affairs in the four Southern African colonies that were soon to become the Union of South Africa. The Commission's almost unanimous conclusion, 'conceived to be in the interests of the Europeans', was that the country should be segregated: land owned by Africans, held in trust for them or subject to customary law, was to be kept strictly separate from land in 'white' South Africa.[128]

The Lagden Report and the legislation it spawned have traditionally been interpreted as the racist response of a threatened white minority, but the decision to divide South Africa had far more complex origins, as the economic implications of this policy were to demonstrate. Segregation put an immediate brake on the development of African agriculture by limiting the amount of land available for expansion. Land shortage, together with an increase in the African population, meant that the inhabitants of the reserves became dependent for subsistence upon work on white farms and in the mining industry. In other words, the effect of segregation was to transform the reserves into labour pools.[129]

The Natives Land Act[130]—the first 'pillar of apartheid—was originally intended to be an interim measure to halt the acquisition of land by Africans outside 'scheduled' areas.[131] In 1916 a commission was appointed according to the terms of the Act (the Beaumont Commission) to determine which lands were to be demarcated as African. When interest groups objected to what they considered to be overly generous proposals, the Government instructed local committees to re-examine the recommendations. The Beaumont proposals were then drastically reduced: Africans were given only 7.3 per cent of the South African land area.[132]

---

[128] Para. 193 of the Report vol. 1, cited by Davenport/Hunt (n. 13), Doc. 66. In § 207 the Commission said that the time had arrived when land reserved for Africans should be legislatively defined and 'that this should be done with a view to finality in the provision of land for the Native population and that thereafter no more land should be reserved for Native occupation'.

[129] T. J. Keegan, *Rural Transformations in Industrializing South Africa* (1986). See, however, H. M. Feinberg, 'The 1913 Natives Land Act in South Africa: Politics, Race and Segregation in the Early 20th Century', (1993) 26 *International Journal of African Historical Studies* 65 sqq.

[130] No. 27.

[131] A term that comes from the schedule to the Act in which they were listed. Conversely, of course, whites were prohibited from acquiring land within those areas.

[132] According to the 1911 census whites numbered 1,250,000, coloureds and Indians 600,000, and Africans approximately three million. Hence 67.3% of the population were allowed ownership in only 7.3% of the country's land.

So far as tenure in the scheduled areas was concerned, the Lagden Commission was torn between the Cape and Natal models: pursuing individual tenure or allowing customary, communal tenure. It finally recommended that although 'sub-division and individual holding' were to be encouraged, the 'communal or tribal system' should be retained. Where individual tenure was introduced the Commission felt that it should continue to be subject to quitrent-like conditions.[133]

The tenure proposals in the Lagden Report marked a departure from Britain's mission to 'civilize' its colonial territories in favour of a decision to 'retribalize' the African population. The new policy came into effect in the 1920s, a time when traditional leaders, who in the nineteenth century had constantly threatened the colonial venture, were debilitated and losing popular support. Former subjects of chiefly rule now formed a sizeable urban proletariat. Through political and labour associations they had begun to challenge the government on their own terms. The decade was marked in urban areas by labour unrest and in rural areas by stiffening resistance to state interference in land tenure. By reviving African institutions it was hoped that confrontation might be deflected.[134]

2. The 1936 Trust and Land Act

In urban centres the process of segregation was carried forward by the 1922 Transvaal Local Government (Stallard) Commission. Its report laid down the broad principle that towns were a creation of the white man and that Africans should be allowed there only as temporary sojourners. From this understanding flowed the second pillar of apartheid: the Natives (Urban Areas) Act.[135] This Act mandated local authorities, assisted by 'native advisory councils', to establish African locations and single-sex hostels in urban areas. Africans were not allowed to live outside these areas—and, of course, non-Africans were barred from acquiring land rights in them.[136]

In 1927 the Native Administration Act[137] was passed. This, the third and in many respects the most formidable pillar of apartheid created an entirely new legislative, administrative, and judicial infrastructure for controlling the African people. From now on ultimate powers vested in the Governor-

[133] Vol. 1, §§ 147 and 157 respectively. Cited by Davenport/Hunt (n. 13), Doc. 66.
[134] S. Dubow, *Racial Segregation and the Origins of Apartheid in South Africa* (1989), 71; N. Worden, *The Making of Modern South Africa* (1994), 76 sq.
[135] 20 of 1923. Although frequently amended and once consolidated (by Act 25 of 1945), it remained the main statutory instrument controlling Africans in urban areas until 1986.
[136] In 1937 an amendment to the Act (Act 46 of 1937) prohibited Africans from entering urban areas to look for work. Only those who had approved employment were entitled to stay in the towns. Under s. 17 (later s. 29 of the 1945 consolidation Act) persons deemed 'idle, dissolute or disorderly' could be repatriated to the reserves or sent to work colonies.
[137] No. 38.

General, who was accorded the title of 'Supreme Chief'[138] with authority to create tribes and to move either tribes or individuals as he saw fit.[139] His position, however, was titular. In practice the Governor-General's powers were exercised by the Native Affairs Department, which soon had an all-embracing jurisdiction over the lives of Africans.[140] Unchecked by other branches of government, it took on the quality of a state within a state.[141] Henceforth the Department prepared all legislation regarding Africans (which was now passed by simple proclamation) and controlled the separate system of courts set up to hear African civil suits.[142]

During the depression of the 1930s the effects of segregation became distressingly apparent. The 1932 Native Economic Commission revealed that erosion, overstocking, and over-population had already seriously damaged land in reserves and that food production was declining.[143] Urgent remedial action was recommended. The proposed solutions to these problems were the Native Trust and Land Act of 1936[144] and 'betterment' regulations.

The primary purpose of the Act was to increase the size of the reserves. The Government set a target of buying an additional seven million *morgen* of land,[145] which would increase the size of the reserves from 7 to 13 per cent of the country's area. A statutory authority, the South African Native Trust,[146] was established on the model of the Natal Trust to acquire land and supervise tenure 'for the settlement, support, benefit, and material and moral welfare' of Africans.[147] (Although the Governor-General was sole trustee, he could delegate his powers to the Minister of Native

---

[138] This constitutional curiosity originated in Natal under Ordinance 3 of 1849. See D. Welsh, 'The State President's Powers under the Bantu Administration Act', 1968 *Acta Juridica* 81, 89 sq. The position was inherited by the State President when South Africa became a Republic in 1961.

[139] Under s. 5 of the Native Administration Act.

[140] See S. Dubow, 'Holding "A Just Balance between White and Black": The Native Affairs Department in South Africa c. 1920–33', (1986) 12 *Journal of Southern African Studies* 217 sqq.

[141] J. F. Holleman, *Chief, Council and Commissioner* (1969), 15 sqq. documents the same development in the Department of Native Affairs in Southern Rhodesia.

[142] Consisting of chiefs' and headmen's courts, native commissioners and a Native Appeal Court. See Bennett (n. 57), 47 sq.

[143] UG 22 of 1932. Thus rural farming could no longer provide subsistence, and the earnings of migrant labourers became a vital source of income for entire families. See P. B. Rich, 'Administrative Ideology, Urban Social Control and the Origins of Apartheid Theory 1930–1939', (1980) 7 *Journal of African Studies* 70 sqq.

[144] No. 18. The Minister outlined the objectives that the Act was supposed to achieve in the House of Assembly Debates, 30 Apr. 1936, cols. 2746 sqq., cited by Davenport/Hunt (n. 13), Doc. 71.

[145] 'Released' land in the language of the Act, to be distinguished from land 'scheduled' under the 1913 Act.

[146] Later to be known as the South African Development Trust (SADT).

[147] Because the Trust's most important function was to acquire land in private ownership that had been identified for release (s. 10), it had the power of expropriation (s. 13). It also had power under s. 18(2) to grant, sell, lease, or otherwise dispose of land, but according to s. 18(1) only to Africans.

Affairs.[148]) Earlier trusts were merged into this body, which became nominal owner of all Crown land in the reserves.[149]

Land vested in the SADT was progressively subjected to a special statutory tenure,[150] which had antecedents in the quitrent and Glen Grey tenures.[151] Officers of the Department of Native Affairs, 'native commissioners', supervised the control and allotment of all SADT lands.[152] Without their written permission no person was permitted a right of occupancy,[153] and without their approval transfer, leasing, sub-letting, hypothecation or sub-division was prohibited.[154] The principle of one man, one lot still prevailed,[155] and rights were still precarious.[156] Despite the origins of this system in the colonial drive to promote individualism, rights of occupancy were not consciously intended to break with customary tenure. Far from it: the legitimacy of this tenure lay in its similarity to customary law.[157] Individuals had no absolute rights to their land: tenancy was granted by political authorities, and was contingent on good behaviour and observance of the regulations.

All SADT land was subject to 'betterment planning'. While occasioned by the best of intentions, betterment provoked more ill-feeling in rural areas than any other government intervention, including even the implementation of segregation. The invasiveness of betterment was a major cause of resentment: long-established patterns of tenure were totally disrupted by an increasingly authoritarian bureaucracy.[158]

[148] Under s. 48(1)(c) and (g) of the Act, the Department of Native Affairs (via the Governor-General and the Trust) could prescribe conditions upon which Africans might purchase or occupy Trust land.

[149] Ss. 5 and 6.

[150] Over the years a disparate collection of regulations had come to govern tenures in various different reserves in the country, notably Proclamations 302 of 1928 (Cape), 123 of 1931 (Natal), 186 of 1941 (OFS), 12 of 1945 (Cape and Natal), and 13 of 1945 (Transvaal and Thaba 'Nchu). In 1969 they were all repealed and consolidated by the Black Areas Land Regulations Proclamation 188 of 1969. Further references to regulations over SADT land will be to this enactment.

[151] The principal difference between quitrent and the SADT rights of occupancy lay in the fact that land subject to the former was surveyed.

[152] S. 5 of the Regs.   [153] Ss. 6 and 47(1) *ibid.*   [154] S. 56(1) *ibid.*

[155] Married men and single women with dependants were the main beneficiaries: Jones (n. 70), 38. See M. K. Robertson, 'Black Land Tenure: Disabilities and Some Rights', in: A. Rycroft (ed.), *Race and the Law* (1987), 127.

[156] Proclamation 236 of 1957 provided that the Minister of Native Affairs might, whenever he deemed it expedient, cancel the right of any African to occupy land owned by the Trust and order him and his family to depart. Proclamation 236 of 1957 was repealed by s. 4 of Proclamation 188 of 1969. A maximum size of half a *morgen* for residential sites and 4 *morgen* for arable sites was prescribed (s. 49(2)), but in practice scarcity of land dictated much smaller allotments.   [157] Kerr (n. 55), 71 sq.

[158] The first instance of opposition to such state intervention was provoked by the Diseases of Stock Act 14 of 1911, which introduced various measures to avert East Coast fever. Although local farmers were experiencing severe economic hardship at the time, they were expected to meet most of the costs of quarantine, dipping, fencing, and branding. Not surprisingly, they refused to co-operate: Beinart/Bundy (n. 75), 280 sqq.

Overstocking was the official explanation for degradation of land in the reserves.[159] In 1937, therefore, the Government introduced a proclamation aimed at upgrading the pedigree of livestock.[160] No improvement was discernible, however, mainly because the quality of pasturage remained poor, and so a more comprehensive enactment was passed two years later.[161] While the 1939 Proclamation applied automatically to SADT land, the Minister could declare other 'betterment areas' after consulting the communities to be affected.[162] Once a betterment area had been declared, the Department began culling livestock and gathering scattered homesteads into what were called 'betterment villages',[163] a process that involved strict separation between residential, arable, and grazing lands.[164]

The culling provisions took immediate effect, and they provoked fierce opposition. Cattle were vital to the rural economy. Their economic value aside, cattle were a form of savings, an essential item of religious ceremony, and vital for cementing social relationships.[165] Popular reaction is summed up in the following:

[159] Report of the Native Economic Commission UG of 1932, 4. Aside from the deleterious effect cattle had on the land, they were of poor quality, vulnerable to disease, and unsuitable for draught purposes. See J. Yawitch, *Betterment: The Myth of Homeland Agriculture* (1981), 10 sqq. for the thinking of this period.

[160] Proclamation 180 of 1937.

[161] Proclamation 31 of 1939.

[162] Efforts were made to persuade rural farmers of the wisdom of betterment planning, but once they realized that it entailed reduction of stock they resisted: M. Horrell, *The African Reserves of South Africa* (1969), 34.

[163] The carrying capacity of the land would first be estimated, followed by an official count of the livestock in the area. Any surplus had to be slaughtered or removed. Murray (n. 74), 161 sqq. describes the implementation of betterment at Thaba 'Nchu: although the area was considered overstocked in the sense that the badly denuded land could not support the number of cattle, it was understocked in the sense that people did not have enough livestock to plough to produce their own food supplies. What is more, when livestock were unequally distributed among households it became impossible to administer culling fairly. See too C. J. de Wet, P. A. McAllister, 'Betterment Planning and its Consequences in Rural Ciskei and Transkei', (1985) 81 *SA Tydskrif vir Wetenskap* 555 sqq.

[164] Which disrupted existing settlement patterns. People preferred establishing their homesteads close to arable fields and water sources so that they could keep an eye on crops and minimize walking distances. See Yawitch (n. 159), 48 sq. The Department of Native Affairs maintained the orthodox rule, that 4 *morgen* of arable land per family-head was sufficient for subsistence, but at the same time it proposed a 3-season fallow period: Murray (n. 74) 162. Restricting landholding to 4 *morgen* spelt disaster for larger farmers, who had more than 2 spans of oxen. They 'must be obliged to sell their oxen and plows and be ruined instead of having their praiseworthy industry encouraged by the Government': Murray (n. 74), 163 quoting the Secretary of the Thaba 'Nchu African Farmers' Association.

[165] See Yawitch (n. 159) 11 sq. Small stockholders with only 2 or 3 cattle were particularly threatened, since the culling of 1 beast would drastically affect their ability to plough and to meet bridewealth obligations: Beinart/Bundy (n. 75), 300 sqq. The landless and the wealthy, who were less seriously affected, tended to comply with the new regulations.

The scheme seems to be another Cattle Killing Episode modernised. The scheme is designed to impoverish, to suppress the economic and social growth of the African in the native reserves. It is a means of preserving white superiority.[166]

Countrywide revolts occurred in the 1930s and '40s. Fences were cut, beacons removed, and people refused to move into the betterment villages.[167]

None the less, in 1945, after the Second World War, the Secretary for Native Affairs pressed on with an even more comprehensive 'New Era of Reclamation', when 'man's reason is to be employed in the place of blind custom, where such custom stands in the way of a better and fuller life'.[168] The general principles of betterment were to be pursued, but the Department now decided to concentrate on promoting a small group of commercially viable farmers. The rest of the population (then estimated at over 50 per cent of the reserve inhabitants) would have to leave the land.[169]

III. APARTHEID

1. The Tomlinson Commission and its aftermath

In 1948 the Nationalist Party came to power. Segregation had already been achieved, but at a ruinous cost. Problems of over-population and under-development in the reserves were even worse than before the War.[170] The new Government appointed the Tomlinson Commission to devise a scheme to promote the social and economic regeneration of the reserves, but this time with reference to the ethnic composition of the African population. The Commission's report, the most comprehensive ever published on the subject, appeared in 1955.[171]

---

[166] B. Hirson, 'Rural Revolt in South Africa, 1937–1951', in: Institute of Commonwealth Studies (ed.), *The Societies of Southern Africa in the Nineteenth and Twentieth Centuries* (1977), 115, 126. As Yawitch (n. 159), 12 says, people saw the stock sales following culling operations as opportunities for white speculators to buy at artificially low prices.

[167] See further Murray (n. 74), 172 sqq. and Hirson (n. 166), 115 sqq.

[168] Cited by Yawitch (n. 159), 25. See Rogers (n. 51), 156 sqq. for the betterment programme.

[169] Because the resources to implement a full rehabilitation programme were not available, the Department decided to concentrate on preventing further deterioration of the land. See Beinart/Bundy (n. 75), 299; Yawitch (n. 159), 18 sq., 25.

[170] Problems for which African farmers were held solely accountable. They were regarded as backward (because they were hostile to betterment planning) and wasteful (because they caused soil erosion): Yawitch (n. 159), 14. Hence unproductive use of land was ascribed to the conservatism of African tradition. Cf. A. Fischer, 'Land Tenure in Mhala: Official Wisdom "Locked Up" in Tradition and People "Locked Up" in Development', (1987) 4 *Development Southern Africa* 502 sqq.

[171] *Report of the Commission for the Socio-Economic Development of the Bantu Areas within the Union of South Africa* (1955) UG 61. A more manageable version of the Report was prepared by D. Hobart Houghton *The Tomlinson Report: A Summary of the Findings and Recommendations in the Tomlinson Commission Report* (1956).

A premise basic to the Commission's calculations was the income necessary to support a family on the land. At first Tomlinson assumed that each African family required a gross income of £120 *per annum*. On this estimate it appeared that only 20 per cent of the families then living in the reserves could be adequately provided for, a number considered too low. Accordingly the average subsistence income was halved to arrive at a figure of £60, although even on this amount the reserves were reckoned to contain enough land to support only half the African population.[172] While more land was obviously needed,[173] the Commission expected a large proportion of the rural population to abandon agriculture in order to earn their livelihoods in industry and mining.[174]

With hindsight it is clear that the Tomlinson Commission figures were gross underestimates. However, the Government had no intention of implementing its recommendations, which it regarded as too radical, too expensive, and unsuited to its broader racial policies.[175] H. F. Verwoerd (who had never supported Tomlinson) became Minister of Native Affairs in 1950.[176] He immediately set about realizing his own vision of the apartheid regime. Official thinking assumed that existing reserves were the traditional homelands of their occupants. Inaccurate though this was, given the long history of questionable treaties, uncertain borders, and vague claims to occupation of *terra nullius*, the *bantustans* (in the language of apartheid) were the natural places of abode for Africans.

The Bantu are only temporarily resident in the European areas of the Republic, for as long as they offer their labour there. As soon as they become, for some reason or another, no longer fit for work or superfluous in the labour market, they are expected to return to their country of origin or the territory of the national unit where they fit ethnically.[177]

In particular, cities were to be reserved for whites. Thus, under the notorious s. 10 of the Native (Urban Areas) Consolidation Act,[178] only those Africans born in a city, who had lived there continuously for fifteen years,

[172] At the 1951 census.

[173] The 3 million *morgen* set aside at the time of the 1936 Act had still to be acquired.

[174] To rehabilitate the reserve economy in the first 10-year programme the Commission called for £104m. to be spent, for 50,000 jobs to be created each year, and for private white investment. It claimed that if this tempo of development were maintained the reserves could support a population of 9 million by 1981. Two million of this number were expected to live on the earnings of migrant workers, which would leave 6 million people living in white South Africa.

[175] T. R. H. Davenport, 'Can Sacred Cows be Culled? An Historical Review of Land Policy in South Africa, with Some Questions About the Future', (1987) 4 *Development Southern Africa* 388, 395. The Government's objections to the Report were set out in White Paper 'F' (1956).

[176] H. Kenney, *Architect of Apartheid: H. F. Verwoerd: An Appraisal* (1980), 86 sq., 104.

[177] Department of Bantu Administration and Development, General Circular No. 25, 1967, cited by E. M. Letsoalo, *Land Reform in South Africa: A Black Perspective* (1987), 50.

[178] 25 of 1945.

or who had worked continuously for the same employer for ten years had a right to live permanently in an urban area.[179]

Traditional political structures and cultural differences were fully exploited to give legitimacy to the *bantustan* system. Under the Bantu Authorities Act of 1951[180] governance of the reserves was handed over to chiefs and headmen. '[W]ith due regard to Native law and custom',[181] provision was made for the creation of a three-tiered system of 'traditional' rule.[182] Responsibility for administering betterment planning[183] was now transferred to chiefs appointed under the Act.[184]

2. From *bantustans* to homelands

In 1959 apartheid took a new turn. To placate growing international criticism, Verwoerd (now Prime Minister) announced a policy of 'separate development'. Under the Promotion of Bantu Self-Government Act[185] *bantustans* could seek self-government and ultimately complete independence from South Africa. The African people were said not to constitute a homogeneous people but rather individual nations, each with their own languages and cultures.[186] The Tomlinson Commission had isolated seven such units. For the purposes of the Promotion of Bantu Self-Government Act, the Government identified eight (with the appropriate homelands): North-Sotho (Lebowa), South-Sotho (QwaQwa), Tswana (Bophuthatswana), Zulu (KwaZulu), Swazi (KaNgwane), Tsonga (Gazankulu), Venda (Venda), and

[179] An amendment to the main Act inserted by Act 54 of 1952.

[180] 68 of 1951. J. L. Comaroff, 'Chiefship in a South African Homeland', (1974) 1 *Journal of Southern African Studies* 36, 42 sqq.; D. Hammond-Tooke, 'Chieftainship in Transkeian Political Development', (1964) 2 *Journal of Modern African Studies* 513, 518 sqq. give brief accounts of the problems and contradictions generated by this Act.

[181] Section 2(1)(a) of the Act.

[182] Leaders who were not amenable to Government directives, no matter what traditional legitimacy they might have enjoyed, were ousted from office or passed over in matters of succession: J. C. Bekker, 'Tribal Government at the Crossroads', (1991) 21 *Africa Insight* 126, 128.

[183] Now via a Limitation, Control and Improvement of Livestock and of Pastoral and Agricultural Resources Proclamation 116 of 1949 (which repealed Proclamation 31 of 1939).

[184] Which served only to increase opposition to the system by tainting it with apartheid: Murray (n. 74), 174 sqq. On this basis Yawitch (n. 159), 11, 20 divides protest against betterment into 2 periods: the 1930s and the 1950s.

[185] 46 of 1959.

[186] Hence Helgaard Muller could say in his *Address to the General Assembly of the UN* (1964) that 'South Africa is in fact and in the first place a multi-national country, rather than a multi-racial country. Apart from the South African nation of European stock, the country comprises the homelands of a number of other nations. These have their own separate identities, each with its own undeniable right to separate nationhood in a land which, too, has been its own. I am, of course, referring to the various Bantu nations, differing from one another in language, culture, tradition, and in everything else that determines national identities, rights and aspirations. . .' See D. Posel, *The Making of Apartheid 1948–1961: Conflict and Compromise* (1991), 231 sq.

Xhosa (Transkei and Ciskei). Later an Ndebele unit (KwaNdebele) was added to the list.[187]

The Bantu Homelands Citizenship Act of 1970[188] had the effect of de-nationalizing Africans living in South Africa by deeming them to be citizens of one or other of the homelands.[189] The following year the Bantu Homelands Constitution Act[190] empowered the State President to confer self-government on any of the eight territorial authorities by proclamation. Transkei was granted independence in 1976,[191] soon to be followed by Bophuthatswana, Venda, and Ciskei.[192] After this any charge that the majority of South Africa's citizens had been denied political rights could be countered by pointing to the right of self-determination (in the traditional homelands) that had been given to the ethnic minorities constituting the South African population.

While South Africa was being politically dismembered, approximately three and a half million people were being forced out of white farms and cities into the reserves.[193] This process (in government parlance 'resettlement') had three principal grounds. First, 'black spots' had to be eliminated because they offended the racial uniformity of predominantly white areas.[194] Secondly, the government started consolidating the homelands in an attempt to make some geographic sense out of fragmented political units. Thirdly, a concerted effort was made to abolish squatting. Earlier, although not fully enforced until 1954,[195] ch. 4 of the 1936 Trust and Land Act had sanctioned a general attack on squatters, especially farm labourers.[196]

[187] See M. West, 'Confusing Categories: Population Groups, National States and Citizenship', in: E. Boonzaier, J. Sharp (eds.), *South African Keywords* (1988), 100, 106 sqq.

[188] No. 26.

[189] South African authorities were then afforded a new measure of controlling migration to white areas: the deportation of unwanted aliens. See J. Dugard, 'South Africa's "Independent" Homelands: An Exercise in Denationalization', (1980) 10 *Denver Journal of International Law & Policy* 11 sqq.

[190] 21 of 1971. Under s. 36 (as read with s. 4 *bis* of the 1936 Native Trust and Land Act) the President could by proclamation vest in the homelands any land that had been the property of the South African government, provincial administration, or SADT.

[191] Status of the Transkei Act 100 of 1976. Transkei's constitutional development did not follow the same course as that of the other homelands, however, for it had already gained partial autonomy under the Transkei Constitution Act 48 of 1963.

[192] In 1977, 1979, and 1981, respectively.

[193] Surplus People Project (L. Platzky, C. Walker eds.), *Forced Removals in South Africa* vols. 1–5 (1983), carefully document the forced removals, most of which occurred between 1960 and 1982.

[194] In the jargon of the day 'black spot' meant land that Africans had bought freehold before the 1913 Land Act lying outside the scheduled or released areas.

[195] By Act 18 of 1954.

[196] Surplus People Project vol. 1 (n. 193), 3, 6. Section 26 of the Trust and Land Act 18 of 1936 prohibited landowners from allowing Africans to congregate or reside on their land unless registered as full-time employees (or wives and dependants of such employees), *bona fide* visitors to lawful residents, or registered squatters. The Act was supplemented by other laws aimed at restricting African occupation of rural land, notably the Prevention of Illegal Squatting Act 52 of 1951 and the Trespass Act 6 of 1959, but these laws were on the face of it racially neutral.

Squatting was the cause of perpetual complaints by whites, partly because it undermined the segregationist ideal and partly because it enabled Africans to evade the pressures of working on white farms and mines.[197] Both labour tenancy and squatting had become widespread phenomena, an inevitable consequence of dispossession and land shortage.

3. Reforms of the 1980s: 'orderly urbanization'

By the late 1970s the Government was forced to contemplate major political reform[198]. Its solution, the Republic of South Africa Constitution Act,[199] sought to co-opt 'coloureds' and Indians into Government. Constitutional adjustments notwithstanding, it was evident that the costly and elaborate experiment in apartheid was not working. Within the country resistance, especially from labour, had intensified; international opinion had grown more hostile; and a new, less overt challenge to the Government's policies was being posed by the economy. Instead of mining and agriculture, a highly capitalized manufacturing industry which required permanently available semi-skilled workers had come to dominate the South African economy. Segregation and apartheid, which had been critical to the success of mining and farming, no longer met this demand.[200]

The Government's cautious reaction was to recognize the right of Africans to remain permanently in the cities.[201] In 1984 the Black Communities Development Act[202] allowed Africans to acquire ninety-nine year leases over land outside the reserves. At the same time the imminent collapse of influx control regulations prompted a new demographic policy,[203] which entered

---

[197] Robertson (n. 155), 121. To secure a right to remain on white farms Africans might negotiate formal or informal leases involving the regular payment of rent in cash or portion of an annual crop. Alternatively, Africans might find employment as full-time labourers or they might render services to the farmers. (Labour tenancy, however, was formally abolished by *GN* 2089 of Sept. 1980.) Although provincial enactments had sought to limit the number of families on any one farm (by requiring Africans to be in full-time employment or by requiring special permits/licences to be issued), they had limited success. See C. O'Regan, 'No More Forced Removals? An Historical Analysis of the Prevention of Illegal Squatting Act', (1989) 5 *SAJHR* 361, 363, fn. 13.

[198] The *Report of the Commission of Inquiry into Matters Relating to the Coloured Population Group*, R. P. 38/1976 (the Theron Commission) was important in this respect, for it condemned many aspects of the apartheid regime.

[199] 110 of 1983.

[200] See A. M. D. Humphrey, 'The Changing Role of the Reserves', (1977) 6 *Africa Perspective* 32 sqq. for a succinct account of the role of reserves in relation to demands of the South African economy.

[201] Also to halt forced removals. See O'Regan, (1989) 5 *SAJHR* 361 sqq. Critical to its change of direction was the *Report of the Commission of Inquiry into Legislation Affecting the Utilisation of Manpower*, R. P. 32/1979 (the Riekert Commission), which had been charged to investigate the position of Africans in the urban labour market.   [202] 4 of 1984.

[203] Recommended by the Constitutional Committee of the President's Council, *Report of the Committee for Constitutional Affairs of the President's Council on an Urbanization Strategy for the RSA*, P. C. 3/1985.

South African law under the title of 'orderly urbanization'. In 1986 the Stallard doctrine was rescinded: influx control laws were abolished together with s. 10 of the Urban Areas Act.[204]

At last it seemed that freedom of movement was recognized and the aim of restricting urban growth had been abandoned in favour of urban planning. Whatever the Government's liberal rhetoric, however, commentators were sceptical of its true intentions.[205] Anti-squatting legislation in particular remained a powerful tool for restricting the movement of job-seekers into the cities.[206] As it happened, neither tentative reform nor squatter laws could hope to stem the flood of people to urban areas or to reverse the economic recession.

Political resistance grew simultaneously in town and in country. The crisis culminated the mid-1980s with the declaration of a state of emergency. By 1987 an impasse was reached. Dissidents could not overthrow the state; the state was unable to eliminate the opposition.[207]

IV. THE 1990S AND THE INTERIM CONSTITUTION

1. Nationalist Party reforms

In 1990 the Government was finally driven to lift its ban on the ANC, the PAC, and the South African Communist Party. Political prisoners were released. The next year, in order to maintain its political initiative, and to pre-empt the ANC, the Government issued a White Paper on Land Reform. This was soon followed by two statutes which radically changed South African land law. The Abolition of Racially Based Land Measures Act[208] repealed key acts of the segregation/apartheid era, notably the 1913 and 1936 Land Acts and the Group Areas Act.[209] The old Department of Native

---

[204] Abolition of Influx Control Act 68 of 1986. At the same time the courts responsible for enforcing influx control, the commissioners' courts (established under the 1927 Native Administration Act), were abolished by Act 34 of 1986, and pass laws were repealed by the Identification Act 72 of 1986.

[205] D. C. Hindson, 'Orderly Urbanization and Influx Control', (1985) 25 *Cahiers d'Études Africaines* 401 sqq.; Robertson (n. 155), 107 sqq.

[206] Namely, the Prevention of Illegal Squatting Act 52 of 1951. See Robertson (n. 155), 112 sqq.; O'Regan (n. 197), 393. Following the repeal of ch. 4 of the Trust and Land Act 1936, the Squatting Act was amended by Act 104 of 1988 to introduce new and sweeping measures to control rural squatting. Any black person living but not employed on a white farm became liable to eviction. See O'Regan (1989) 5 *SAJHR* 383 sqq.

[207] P. Frankel, 'Beyond Apartheid: Pathways for Transition', in: P. Frankel, N. Pines, M. Swilling (eds.), *State, Resistance and Change in South Africa* (1988), 280.

[208] 108 of 1991.

[209] 36 of 1966. In fact this Act had had little effect on African landholding: J. T. Schoombee, 'Group Areas Legislation: The Political Control of Ownership and Occupation of Land', 1985 *Acta Juridica* 77, 78.

Affairs (now the Department of Development Aid) was disbanded amidst allegations of corruption and inefficiency.

The Government not only eliminated segregation but also upgraded the precarious statutory rights that Africans had formerly held in land: quitrent leaseholds, permissions to occupy, short-term and ninety-nine year leases. In order to stimulate economic growth, and more specifically the property market,[210] the Upgrading of Land Tenure Rights Act[211] was passed. With the exception of customary interests,[212] this enactment elevated a broad spectrum of rural and urban land rights to full ownership.

The new political climate served also to heighten awareness of the illegitimacy of many land titles in South Africa.[213] Yet on this issue the Government was less than enthusiastic about restoring land lost through colonization and apartheid.[214] Admittedly a Commission on Land Allocation was set up to investigate claims for return of land, but its progress was negligible.[215] In this regard, the ANC's proposals for land reform were more far-reaching. Not only did they address the question of restoring land to those who had been dispossessed but they also announced their intention of redistributing land to those in need.[216]

2. The Interim Constitution: regaining lost titles

While the Interim Constitution was being drafted, repeated demands were made for inclusion of a right to restitution of land in the chapter on fundamental rights.[217] The result was s. 8(3)(b) of the Constitution. It provided that 'every person or community dispossessed of rights in land' under racially discriminatory laws was entitled to claim restitution. Section 121(1) of the Constitution obliged Parliament to pass legislation to facilitate these claims, and the remainer of s. 121 laid down the general terms of the future Act: individuals or communities could claim restitution from the state,[218]

---

[210] White Paper on Land Reform (1991) B 2.9.   [211] 112 of 1991.

[212] An individual's customary interests did not fall within the purview of s. 3(1) of the Act: T. W. Bennett, J. W. Roos, 'The 1991 Land Reform Acts and the Future of African Customary Law', (1992) 109 *SALJ* 477, 452. Instead, land subject to customary law was governed by s. 20(1) of the Act, which provided that tribes could request the Minister of Public Works 'to transfer tribal land the control of which vests in the tribe to the tribe in ownership'.

[213] A. Sachs, *Protecting Human Rights in a New South Africa* (1990), 112; T. Marcus, 'Land Reform: Considering National, Class and Gender Issues', (1990) 6 *SAJHR* 178 sqq.; Z. Skweyiya, 'Towards a Solution to the Land Question in Post-apartheid South Africa: Problems and Models', (1990) 6 *SAJHR* 195, 197 sqq.

[214] White Paper (n. 210), A 2.11(f).

[215] Under s. 89 of the Abolition Act, as amended by Act 110 of 1993.

[216] See A. N. C., *Policy Guidelines for a Democratic South Africa* (as adopted at a National Conference 28–31 May 1992), E 2.2.4, E 2.5.1.

[217] H. Corder, 'Towards a South African Constitution', (1994) 57 *Modern LR* 491, 519 sqq.

[218] S. 121(2)(a).

provided that they were dispossessed after 19 June 1913,[219] and provided that the purpose of their dispossession was racial discrimination.[220]

In November 1994 the Restitution of Land Rights Act was promulgated.[221] This provided that persons and communities dispossessed[222] could apply for return of land by lodging claims with a Commission on Restitution of Land Rights.[223] The state's commitment to restore land was limited in two ways: the land must have been lost as a result of a racist law and the dispossession must have occurred after 19 June 1913.[224] These conditions exclude many potential claims arising out of dispossession during the colonial period. Nevertheless, people who do not fall within the purview of the Act are not left without remedy. They may take action on the basis of aboriginal title, the primordial right devised in 16th century customary international law to protect the rights of indigenous peoples from colonial immigrants. Although aboriginal title is judicially untested in South Africa, it may well become a common-law ground for revising colonial acts of appropriation.[225]

A problem which the new South African government will find more difficult to resolve is the question of what tenure to apply in rural areas. Current debate has a ring of the nineteenth century: customary tenure is still believed to be inimical to economic development, due principally to its communal nature.[226] Thus African forms of landholding are said to be uncertain and insecure; to discourage conservation of natural resources, credit, and investment; to hinder sound farming practices; to result in unequal distribution of land, shortages, and the fragmentation of land units; and to perpetuate family rivalries and ethnic divisions.[227] Given this abundance of prejudices, it is not surprising that development programmes usually prefer individual, registered titles over customary law.

Notwithstanding these views, few would now advocate interference with established local customs.[228] When the International Commission of Jurists

---

[219] S. 121(3). [220] Namely, was inconsistent with s 8(2) of the Constitution.

[221] 22 of 1994. [222] Or their direct descendants.

[223] Established under ch. 2 of the Act.

[224] The principal beneficiaries will therefore be victims of forced removals under the 1913 and 1936 Land Acts and later apartheid legislation.

[225] T. W. Bennett, 'Redistribution of Land and the Doctrine of Aboriginal Title in South Africa', (1993) 9 *SAJHR* 443 sqq.

[226] Cf D. E. Ault, G. L. Rutman, 'The Development of Individual Rights to Property in Tribal Africa', (1979) 22 *Journal of Law & Economics* 163 sqq., who note how customary law has adapted to changing economic imperatives.

[227] See F. M. Mifsud, *Customary Land Law in Africa* (1967), 2; and A. J. van der Walt, 'Towards the Development of Post Apartheid Land Law: An Exploratory Survey', (1990) 23 *De Jure* 1, 12 sq.

[228] C. Cross, 'An Alternative Legality: The Property Rights Question in Relation to South African Land Reform', (1992) 8 *SAJHR* 305, 324 sq. Similarly, a Workshop on Land Tenure and Rural Development (reported in (1987) 4 *Development Southern Africa* 377 sqq.) concluded that reform of tenure was not a priority, since there was no proof that tenure systems had a clear influence on agricultural productivity.

launched a project in 1993 to investigate land in economic and social development,[229] for instance, one of its main concerns was to counter the tendency to replace customary tenures with western forms of ownership. The social effects of abolishing indigenous tenures may be unpredictable and unwanted,[230] and research has shown that giving people individual title does not always result in a more equitable pattern of landholding.[231] Positive values are now being discovered in customary law. The principle underlying land allocation—that all members of a community must have enough land to support themselves—helps to preserve the integrity of family units.[232] Also, the customary bar on alienation prevents impoverished families from cashing in on their most valuable asset for what may prove to be only short-term financial relief.[233] Above all, it is now appreciated that '[t]he land represents the link between the past and the future; ancestors lie buried there, children will be born there. Farming is more than just a productive activity, it is an act of culture, the centre of social existence, and the place where personal identity is forged'.[234]

[229] The project is entitled 'On Land Rights in Human Rights and Development'. See R. Plant, 'Land Rights in Human Rights and Development: Introducing a New ICJ Initiative', (1993) 51 *International Commission of Jurists Review* 10, 14 sqq.

[230] Even during the colonial period, Hailey (n. 51), 875 sq. and (1952) 4 *Special Supplement to Journal of African Administration* 3 cautioned against allowing rural farmers to acquire individual rights.

[231] Women are particularly disadvantaged. See R. E. Downs, S. P. Reyna (eds.), *Land and Society in Contemporary Africa* (1988) 13, S. F. R. Coldham, 'Effect of Registration of Title upon Customary Land Rights in Kenya', (1978) 22 *Journal of African Law* 91 sqq.; Plant (n. 229), 29.

[232] Evidence in South Africa, for instance, shows that customary tenure is functioning to preserve family stability. See A. J. van der Walt, 'The Fragmentation of Land Rights', (1992) 8 *SAJHR* 431, 439; C. R. Cross, 'The Land Question in KwaZulu: Is Land Reform Necessary?', (1987) 4 *Development Southern Africa* 428 sqq.

[233] Plant (n. 229), 26 sq.   [234] Sachs (n. 213), 115.

3: *The Architects of the Mixed Legal System*

STEPHEN D. GIRVIN

I. INTRODUCTION

The mixed system of law in South Africa owes a great deal to the judges appointed to administer justice, both in the pre-Union territories and colonies, and to those who have served on the bench since Union in 1910. The names of the most important judges appear throughout the contributions in this book, as do the courts to which they were appointed. For those not familiar with the South African legal system, the references to the courts and the judges in the pages that follow may be mystifying. This chapter therefore provides an outline of the structure of the courts, both in the period before Union in 1910 and afterwards. The major part of the chapter is, however, devoted to a biographical introduction to the most important judges, placed in the context of the court(s) in which they served. The emphasis is on introducing those judges who served in the period up to 1961, but brief reference will also be made to those judges who have served on the Appellate Division since then.

II. COLONIAL COURTS AND JUDGES (1827–1910)

1. Cape Colony[1]

(a) The courts

Following the occupation of the Cape by Britain, first in 1795 and again in 1806, certain important changes in the administration of justice were introduced, all of which gave evidence of an intention to anglicize the system at the Cape.[2] Indeed the arrival of 5,000 British settlers in 1820 provided the

---

[1] For a detailed consideration see H. R. Hahlo, Ellison Kahn, *The Union of South Africa: The Development of its Laws and Constitution* (1960), ch. 5. On the administration of justice at the Cape of Good Hope in the late 1860s, and for an analysis of the decisions of the Cape Supreme Court as published in Buchanan's Reports (1869–70), see Reinhard Zimmermann, 'Die Rechtsprechung des Supreme Court of the Cape of Good Hope am Ende der sechziger Jahre des 19. Jahrhunderts', in: *Huldigingsbundel Paul van Warmelo* (1984), 286 sqq.

[2] E.g. the creation of circuit courts in 1811, the opening of the doors of the courts to the public in 1813, and the replacement of Dutch with English as the official language of the courts. See Hahlo/Kahn (n. 1), 204, fn. 41; George Denoon, 'The introduction of English as the official language at the Cape', (1953) 70 *SALJ* 90 sqq.

impetus for moves to reorder the unsophisticated system of justice then prevailing.

The First Charter of Justice was promulgated in the Government Gazette on Tuesday, 11 December 1827.[3] It established a new Supreme Court headed by a Chief Justice and three puisne judges who had to be members of the English, Scots, Irish, or Cape bars. Similarly, advocates were to be members of the English, Scots, or Irish bars, or alternatively doctors of law of Oxford, Cambridge, or Dublin. The Court was granted full original and review jurisdiction. Further appeal as of right was enabled to the Privy Council in cases involving claims of stlg. 500 or more, and otherwise with special leave of the Privy Council. A Second Charter of Justice of 4 May 1832 extended the terms of the earlier Charter by providing that the Supreme Court was to exercise its jurisdiction according to 'the laws now in force within our said colony, and all such other laws as shall at any time hereafter be made'.[4]

The expansion of the boundaries of the Colony, especially in the Eastern Cape, soon led to demands for a supreme court separate from that at Cape Town. In 1864, therefore, the Eastern Districts Court (EDC) was established at Grahamstown. It was to serve as a local division of the Cape Supreme Court and to have concurrent jurisdiction. Appeal lay to the Supreme Court in Cape Town and thereafter to the Privy Council in London. Following the incorporation of the adjacent territory of British Kaffraria into the Cape Colony in 1866, its Supreme Court was absorbed by the Eastern Districts Court. The Eastern Districts Court was eventually enlarged to three judges, headed by a Judge President.

A further territory annexed by the Crown, Griqualand West, was given a High Court with its seat at Kimberley in 1871. Initially the judicial officer was a recorder but, following the annexation of the territory by the Cape in 1880, the recorder was upgraded to a full judge. The Supreme Court (the High Court of Griqualand or HCG) had concurrent jurisdiction with the Supreme Court in Cape Town. It was enlarged to three judges, headed by a Judge President in 1882.

A separate Court of Appeal was established in 1879 to hear civil appeals from circuit courts and also from the Eastern Districts Court and High Court of Griqualand. This court consisted of the Chief Justice, two puisne judges sitting at Cape Town, and the Judge President of the Eastern Districts Court. The Judge President of the HCG joined the Court of Appeal in 1882. However, the Court of Appeal was abolished in 1886 and its powers were remitted to the Supreme Court at Cape Town.

---

[3] See CO 380/127 (Draft Letters Patent, Commissions, Royal Instructions, Warrants—Cape of Good Hope 1796–1831). All CO references in this paper are to the Colonial Office archive, Public Record Office, London.

[4] Hahlo/Kahn (n. 1) 17.

(b) The early Cape judges (1827–50)

JOHN WYLDE[5] (1781–1859), first Chief Justice at the Cape from 1827 to 1858, was educated at St Paul's School and Trinity College, Cambridge, where he graduated in law (LL B) in 1805. He was called to the bar by the Middle Temple on 8 November 1805 and practised for the next ten years as a special pleader.[6] In 1816 Wylde took the position of Judge Advocate of New South Wales but, following the dissolution of that Court in 1824,[7] he returned to practice in England. In 1827 he took the Cambridge degree of LL D[8] and was appointed Chief Justice and judge of the Vice-Admiralty court of the Cape Colony. A knighthood was conferred on him in recognition of his new status.[9]

Wylde was a controversial Chief Justice. In 1828, on taking the oaths as a member of the Council of Advice, he objected to having to take an oath of secrecy and his services were terminated.[10] The taint of scandal was present on at least two occasions: in 1831 Wylde was accused of incest with his daughter but was officially exonerated,[11] and in 1835 his wife arrived in Cape Town with a daughter born three years after he had last seen her, in New South Wales.[12] As a judge, Wylde was no great defender of Roman-Dutch law:

Quote what Dutch or Roman books you please—musty or otherwise—and they must be musty if they lay down such doctrines. I belong to a higher court than they refer to—a court not to be broken up or paralysed by their authority, much less by the maxims of philosophers dozing over the midnight lamp in their solitary chambers. My Queen has sent me here to administer justice under the Royal Charter . . . But when you speak of the Institutions of Holland, and of binding myself down by the practice of the Dutch courts—I absolve myself from that bondage, I look to my Charter, to my oath and to my duty.[13]

Wylde CJ was completely overshadowed throughout his tenure by his senior puisne judge, Menzies J. The former's domestic difficulties during the early part of his career at the Cape suggest, if anything, a somewhat pompous and overbearing personality.

[5] See S. D. Girvin, 'The Establishment of the Supreme Court of the Cape of Good Hope and its History under the Chief Justiceship of Sir John Wylde', (1992) 109 *SALJ* 291 sqq., 652 sqq.; idem, *The influence of a British legal education and practice at the Bar on the judges appointed to the Supreme Courts of Southern Africa 1827–1910* (unpublished Ph.D. thesis, University of Aberdeen, 1990).

[6] Girvin, (1992) 109 *SALJ* 296.

[7] On this period of his life see *Australian Dictionary of Biography*, vol. 2 (1967), 627 sqq.

[8] The requirements for that degree were not excessively demanding. A candidate for the LL D was required to perform two 'acts' (or public disputations) and an opponency. For a description of the process see H. E. Malden, *Trinity Hall* (1896), 231 sqq.

[9] Girvin, (1992) 109 *SALJ* 299.

[10] Ralph Kilpin, *The Romance of a Colonial Parliament* (1930), 45 sqq.

[11] Girvin, (1992) 109 *SALJ* 305.   [12] Ibid. 655.

[13] *Letterstedt v. Morgan* (1849) 5 Searle 373, 381.

WILLIAM MENZIES (1795–1850),[14] senior puisne judge from 1827 to 1850, was born in Edinburgh and educated at the High School there and at Edinburgh University, where he attended lectures in law. He was admitted by the Faculty of Advocates on 6 June 1816 following successful examination on Justinian's *Digest* 28.7.8, *De Conditionibus Institutionum*, and he commenced practice at the Edinburgh bar.[15] On his arrival at the Cape in 1827, Menzies J soon revealed himself to be outstanding amongst the four initial appointments to the Cape bench. In the early years of its existence the new court had to grapple with the whole gamut of intricate legal problems and in many cases gave effect to the Roman-Dutch common law, but also, and to a marked extent, to English law, especially in the areas of commercial and procedural law. The Court was referred to all the important Roman-Dutch authorities and, at Menzies J's prompting, the judges were generally in agreement as to how it should approach these authorities. Several reported judgments testify to the scope of Menzies J's wide-ranging and scholarly analyses of the Roman-Dutch authorities.[16] More importantly, Menzies J revealed a tendency against English law, particularly when this was in conflict with Roman-Dutch law. In an unreported libel case he stated:

The gentleman who is advocating the cause of the defendant states 'That according to the Laws of England' and he quotes Blackstone 'where there is no injury, no damages can be claimed'. If this be English law, I am happy we are not governed by English law in this Colony; but it is not English law, neither is it Dutch law.[17]

Menzies J's contribution to early South African law was substantial. Apart from his function in drafting early procedural ordinances and generally setting the Court on a firm foundation, he toiled throughout his career to produce reports of the cases heard by the Court—the only reports available of the cases of this period. The manuscript reports were recognized as precedents by the Supreme Court and were frequently referred to in important arguments by bench and bar. After his death they were edited from his manuscripts by James Buchanan and published in 1870 as *Menzies' Reports*, the contents arranged according to subject matter.[18]

WILLIAM WESTBROOKE BURTON (1794–1888),[19] second puisne

[14] S. D. Girvin, 'William Menzies of Edinburgh: Judge at the Cape 1827–1850', 1993 *Juridical Review* 279 sqq.
[15] On this period of his career see Girvin, 1993 *Juridical Review* 279 sqq.
[16] See e.g. *Caffin et uxor v. Heurtley's Executors* (1832) 1 Menz 178; *Reeves v. Reeves* (1832) 1 Menz 244; *Breda v. Muller* (1829) 1 Menz 425. See also Girvin, 1993 *Juridical Review* 286 sq.
[17] Reported in the *South African Commercial Advertiser*, Sat. 6 Dec. 1828.
[18] S. D. Girvin, 'Law Reporting: Menzies Reports, Precedent and Legal Authority at the Cape Colony in the Nineteenth Century', (1995) 63 *Tijdschrift voor rechtsgeschiedenis* 103 sqq.
[19] *Australian Dictionary of Biography*, vol. 1 (1966), 184; *Dictionary of South African Biography*, vol. 1 (1968), 139; A. A. Roberts, *A South African Legal Bibliography* (1942), 352; W. A. Shaw, *The Knights of England* (1906), 345; J. Whishaw, *A Synopsis of Members of the*

judge from 1827 to 1832, was a native of Daventry, Northamptonshire who initially followed a career in the Royal Navy until 1819 when he decided to study law. He was called to the bar by the Inner Temple on 26 November 1824 and commenced practice at the common law bar. In 1826 he was appointed to the minor recordership of Daventry and, almost exactly a year later, he was appointed puisne judge at the Cape. Prior to his departure for the Cape he made a visit to Holland 'for the purpose of acquiring the Dutch language'.[20] He served at the Cape for five years and played an important part in setting the newly established Supreme Court at the Cape firmly on its feet. Soon after his arrival Burton J was largely responsible for drafting the rules of civil and criminal procedure, the latter in conjunction with Menzies J. Also with Menzies J he drafted much other legislation at the Cape and continually expressed opinions on legislative measures. His joint work with Menzies J in drafting Insolvency Ordinance 64 of 1829 led him to publish the first legal textbook in South Africa, *Observations on the Insolvent Law of the Colony of the Cape of Good Hope*, described later by Innes CJ as 'a work of high standing'.[21]

Although overshadowed in court by Wylde CJ and by the scholarship of Menzies J, it is nevertheless evident that Burton J was no passive onlooker; he contributed to the work of the Court with alacrity and was seldom found wanting in contributing his opinions. His dissenting judgments reveal that he had an independent mind and was unafraid to express his differences of opinion. He drafted Ordinance 50 of 1828 for the improvement 'of the conditions of the Hottentots and other free persons of colour' and gave them civil and political equality with the settlers. His role in the case of *Mackay v. Philip*,[22] in which he accused the *landdrost* of Somerset East of wanton cruelty and oppression of Hottentots, is testimony to his sense of duty and social conscience.

Following the reduction of the judicial establishment at the Cape to three in 1832 Burton took up an appointment to the Supreme Court of New South Wales. Here he published two books, *The State of Religion and Education in New South Wales* and *The Insolvent law of New South Wales*. In 1844 he was appointed puisne judge of Madras and was knighted (KCB). He remained at Madras until 1857 and then returned to Sydney where he was President of the Legislative Council from 1858 to 1861. He retired finally to Bayswater in London where he lived until his ninety-fourth year.[23]

English Bar (1835), 23; (1888) 85 *Law Times* 308; *Times*, 13 Aug. 1888; *Law List* (1825), 20; Ibid. (1826), 20, 323; F. St L. Searle, 'Honourable Sir W. W. Burton', (1935) 52 *SALJ* 257 sqq.; Ellison Kahn, 'What happened to Mr Justice Burton?', (1981) 98 *SALJ* 557 sqq.

[20] See CO 48/114 (Cape of Good Hope: Original Correspondence: Individuals 1827).
[21] *Webster v. Ellison* 1911 AD 73, 91.
[22] (1830) 1 Menz 455. On the legal significance of this case see the contribution by Jonathan Burchell to the present volume.
[23] See obituary, (1888) 85 *Law Times* 308.

GEORGE KEKEWICH (1778–1862),[24] third puisne judge at the Cape from 1827 to 1843, was born in London. He was awarded a foundation scholarship to Emmanuel College, Cambridge in 1795 and attained his BA in 1800 and an MA in 1803. He was called to the bar by Lincoln's Inn on 25 November 1803.[25] In 1804 he published *A Digested Index to the earlier Chancery Reports*. In 1809 he emigrated to the Cape Colony and on 7 June 1810 he was appointed Assessor in Civil and Criminal cases in the Appeals Court.[26] This was followed by his appointment by letters patent as judge of the Vice-Admiralty Court, although it is unlikely that any particular experience was required for such a post. A despatch of 28 July 1827 confirmed his appointment as the third puisne judge at the Cape.[27] His was a weak appointment, however; he contributed almost nothing in contrast to the learned judgments of Menzies J, or the more pedestrian and sometimes long-winded ones of Wylde CJ, and was not noted for his knowledge of the Roman-Dutch authorities. He was left to attend to criminal cases which turned on fact, rather than law, and even in these he had a reputation for leniency.[28] He retired to Exeter in England on grounds of ill-health on 12 October 1843.

(c) Cape Judges 1850–73

WILLIAM MUSGRAVE (1792–1854),[29] a Londoner, succeeded Kekewich as third puisne judge in 1843. After his call to the bar by the Inner Temple on 14 June 1814 he had secured an appointment as Solicitor-General (later Attorney-General) for Antigua, Barbuda, and Montserrat. On 30 December 1836 he was admitted as an advocate at the Cape and acquired a sound reputation, appearing in most of the important cases during his seven years at the bar.[30] Musgrave J was sworn in on 12 October 1843[31] and held the distinction of being the first English-born advocate admitted to practice at the Cape bar and the first advocate of the Cape bar to be elevated to the bench. As to his knowledge of the authorities, it is evident that he was influenced by the practice of the rest of the Court[32] and did not reveal a notable com-

---

[24] *Dictionary of South African Biography*, vol. 2 (1972), 359; W. P. Baildon (ed.), *Lincoln's Inn Black Books 1422–1845*, vol. 4 (1902), 243; A. F. Hattersley, *A Victorian Lady at the Cape* (1950), 122; Philip, *British Residents at the Cape 1785–1819* (1981), 216; Roberts (n. 19) 367; J. & J.A. Venn, *Alumni Cantabrigienses 1752–1900* (Part 2, 1940), 8; Whishaw (n. 19) 79; (1863) 38 *Law Times* 397.

[25] *Lincoln's Inn Black Book*, vol. 19 (1807–15), 20.

[26] His duties were to 'examine and report his opinion upon all appeals from Sentences of the Court of Justice, referring to and stating the law which bears upon the respective points to the Governor as Judge'. See *Cape of Good Hope Blue Book* (1827), 62 sqq.: CO 53/64.

[27] Despatch no. 19 of 1827. See *Cape of Good Hope Blue Book* (1827), 54 sqq.: CO 53/64.

[28] C. G. Botha, 'The Honourable William Menzies 1795–1850', (1916) 33 *SALJ* 385 sqq.

[29] Girvin, (1992) 109 *SALJ* 655 sqq.

[30] *Moodie v. Fairbairn* (1837) 3 Menz 14; *Harris v. Trustees of Buisinne* (1840) 2 Menz 105; *Keyter v. Le Roux* (1841) 3 Menz 23.

[31] *Cape Town Mail*, Sat. 14 Oct. 1843.   [32] *Twentyman v. Green* (1845) 3 Menz 161.

mitment to Roman-Dutch law in any of his judgments, preferring to rely on his knowledge of English law. Nevertheless, he succeeded Menzies J as the senior puisne judge in 1851. Three years later he succumbed to illness caused by a combination of fatigue and exposure during the course of the previous circuit.[33] Though not generally regarded as a learned man he was apparently friendly and likeable, and according to Lucy Gray was 'almost the only [judge] who bears a good character'.[34] It was later noted that 'as a judge, he stood deservedly high with the colonists for his integrity, his uprightness, and his impartiality . . . and was a model in many respects to all who may hold the judicial office'.[35]

HENDRIK CLOETE (1792–1870),[36] Recorder (judge) of Natal from 1846 to 1855[37] and then judge of the Cape Supreme Court until 1865, was a Capetonian. He was educated in the Netherlands where he took his LL D at Leiden under Van der Keessel in 1811. He then studied with the special pleader, Sir Samuel Toller, at Lincoln's Inn, was called to the bar by Lincoln's Inn on 24 April 1812, and returned to the Cape where he began his professional career as an advocate. As the sole judge at Natal for nearly ten years, Cloete was highly regarded. Indeed he frequently showed a comprehensive knowledge of both the Dutch and Latin texts of the Roman-Dutch authorities and also of the most important sources of English law. Cloete's period on the Natal bench was marred by the dispute between himself and a magistrate, in the case of *Meller v. Buchanan*,[38] which led to his suspension in 1853. Although this was overturned by the Privy Council in 1854, in August 1855 Cloete accepted the position of third puisne judge at Cape Town and left Natal. It is unfortunate that none of Cloete's judgments from Natal were reported, although they were quoted by those who had served under him. However he seems to have left an indelible mark on the legal scene there. The leading historian of this period in Natal has remarked that

[O]verall one is left with a deep admiration for Cloete J and his legal abilities. His talent, learning, high ideals, desire to educate and adjudicate well, his love of the law and devotion to duty, shone as splendid lights in the otherwise grey setting of the Natal legal system of the nineteenth century. [H]is enthusiastic and erudite application of Roman-Dutch law played an important role in keeping alive this legal system in Natal, in the face of concerted efforts to dislodge it.[39]

[33] *South African Commercial Advertiser*, Sat. 7 Oct. 1854.   [34] Hattersley (n. 24), 27.

[35] *South African Commercial Advertiser and Cape Town Mail*, Sat. 2 June 1855.

[36] See J. H. De V. Cloete, 'Mr Justice Cloete', (1934) 51 *SALJ* 1 sqq.; A. W. Cole, *Reminiscences of my Life* (1896), 34 sqq.

[37] On the Natal period see Peter Spiller, 'Hendrik Cloete, Recorder of Natal: as Revealed in his Judgments', (1982) 45 *THRHR* 148 sqq.

[38] Peter Spiller, *A History of the District and Supreme Courts of Natal 1846–1910* (1986), 24 sq.

[39] Ibid. 10, 36.

Cloete served the Cape Supreme Court well during his ten years on the bench and, although not regarded as an outstandingly brilliant judge, his mastery of the Roman-Dutch authorities earned him considerable recognition. A commentator of his Cape Town period noted that he was 'distinguished, not alone for his deep research and his extensive knowledge of the law he administers, but also for the readiness with which he brings his learning to bear on the case before him. ... [A]n elaborate judgment of Mr Justice Cloete, on an important question, is in itself an excellent lesson in Roman-Dutch law'.[40] He was indeed a most worthy successor to William Menzies.

EGIDIUS BENEDICTUS WATERMEYER (1824–67),[41] judge at the Cape from 1857 to 1867, was another able judge who had been educated at Leiden, graduating LL D *cum laude* for his thesis *Dissertatio de jure patronatus* in 1843. After graduating he moved to London where he read for the English bar in the chambers of Samuel Warren. He was called to the bar by the Inner Temple in 1847. On his return to the Cape in the same year he commenced practice as an advocate. During his period of ten years on the bench Watermeyer established a solid reputation as a judge. Sir John Kotzé was later to describe him as 'a man of solid as well as brilliant parts, of fine literary taste, high character and dignity, and a great judge'.[42] Alfred Whaley Cole, himself eventually a judge on the Eastern Districts Court and High Court of Griqualand,[43] referred to him as 'the ablest and most learned judge who has occupied the Cape Bench in my time'.[44] Another commentator remarked that 'his power of reasoning was very strong; nothing was too subtle, nothing too large for his intellectual grasp: he detected sophistry almost instinctively, and the clear and easy sentences in which he used to brush away its webs were the delight of those who listened to him'.[45] Watermeyer was also noted for having greatly promoted legal education at the Cape, being responsible for the setting up of the Board of Public Examiners in Literature and Science in 1858, constituted by Act 4 of 1858.[46] He also gave lectures on various topics, including 'The Government of the Dutch East India Company', 'Roman law', 'Community of Property', and 'The Law of Inheritance'.[47] Finally, Watermeyer is remembered for *Watermeyer's Reports*, his reports of the cases in the Cape Supreme Court for 1857.[48]

[40] *Cape Monthly Magazine*, Nov. 1859, cited in (1934) 51 *SALJ* 9.
[41] Cole (n. 36), 34; F. St L. Searle, 'Mr Justice E. B. Watermeyer', (1935) 52 *SALJ* 135 sqq.; Kotzé (n. 173), vol. II, 89; *Dictionary of South African Biography*, vol. 2 (1972), 832 sq.
[42] See Roberts (n. 19), 382.
[43] S. D. Girvin, 'Alfred Whaley Cole', (1992) 109 *SALJ* 726 sqq.
[44] Cole (n. 36), 34.   [45] Cited in (1935) 52 *SALJ* 138.
[46] See D. V. Cowen, 'The History of the Faculty of Law in the University of Cape Town, 1859–1959', 1959 *Acta Juridica* 8 sqq.
[47] Published in *Selections from his Writings* (1877): see Cowen, 1959 *Acta Juridica* 8.
[48] See H. R. Hahlo, Ellison Kahn, *The South African Legal System and its Background* (1968), 293.

Wylde's successor as Chief Justice in 1858 was Sir WILLIAM HODGES (1808–68).[49] He was born at Melcombe Regis in England and educated in Salisbury and was then one of the first students to be admitted in 1826 at University College, London. Here he studied law and jurisprudence under John Austin, although at this stage no degrees in law were offered by the University. Hodges was called to the bar by the Inner Temple on 3 May 1833 and practised common law. His ambition was to establish himself in the Court of Common Pleas and in 1835 he commenced reporting cases in the Court; the reports were published as *Reported Cases in the Courts of Common Pleas and King's Bench* and appeared from 1836 to 1838. Hodges also published (with G. Lumsdaine) *A Report of the Case of Queen v. Lumsdaine, with Observations on the Parochial Assessment Act* in 1839, and in collaboration with G. Willmore and F. L. Wollaston *Reports of Cases Argued and Determined in the Court of Queen's Bench from Hilary Term to Michaelmas Term 1840*. Other publications during this period include *The Law Relating to the Assessment of Railways to the Relief of the Poor* and *The Statute Law relating to Railways in England and Ireland*.

Hodges was appointed Recorder of Poole, Dorset in 1846 and soon afterwards published *The Law Relating to Railways and Railway Companies*. He gained experience as a parliamentary draftsman and this led to him being commissioned by Sir Robert Peel's government to prepare and draft what became the Public Health Act of 1848.[50]

A Royal Warrant was issued appointing Hodges Chief Justice of the Cape on 2 February 1858 and shortly thereafter he was knighted by the Queen. In considering his contribution, it cannot be said that he ever had any pretensions to being a profound lawyer. It is clear that he did have a quick and logical intellect and when placed alongside his predecessor, Wylde CJ, his manner was unostentatious. Hodges CJ did most of the circuit and criminal work and had a reputation for leniency in stocktheft cases. He was conscientious and 'anything oppressive and tyrannical was utterly foreign to his nature'.[51] He died in office in 1868.

SYDNEY SMITH BELL (1805–79),[52] second puisne judge at the Cape

---

[49] *Dictionary of South African Biography*, vol. 3 (1977), 396; *Dictionary of National Biography*, vol. 26 (1917), 62; Girvin, *Influence* (n. 5), 136 sqq.; Roberts (n. 19), 364; A. W. Cole, 'Reminiscences of the Cape Bar and Bench', (1888) 5 *Cape LJ* 9; idem (n. 36), 14; F. St L. Searle, 'Sir William Hodges', (1934) 51 *SALJ* 303 sqq.; J.G. Kotzé, *Biographical Memoirs and Reminiscences* (1949), 88; (1868) 45 *Law Times* 394.

[50] 11 & 12 Vict. c. 63.

[51] *Commercial Advertiser and Mail*, 18 Aug. 1868, cited in Searle, (1934) 51 *SALJ* 307. His appointment to the Chief Justiceship at the Cape had caused considerable surprise: '. . . on his arrival in the Colony his ignorance of Roman-Dutch law was complete. In endeavouring to make himself acquainted with it, his defective scholarship offered an impediment, as he could not read the Latin authorities with much facility': Cole, (n. 36) 16.

[52] *Dictionary of South African Biography*, vol. 2 (1972), 51; W. I. Addison, *The Matriculation Albums of the University of Glasgow 1728–1858* (1913); F. Boase, *Modern English Biography* vol. 1 (1892), 231; Cole (n. 36), 7, 11, 41; Roberts (n. 19), 348; F. St L. Searle, 'The Honourable

from 1851 to 1868 and then Hodges' successor as Chief Justice from 1868 until 1873, was a Londoner by birth. He was apprenticed to a solicitor in Edinburgh and attended classes at Edinburgh with a view to becoming a member of the Scots bar. However, he became seriously ill in 1829 and this confined him to his room for almost ten years.[53] During his illness Bell provided the profession with *Morrison's Dictionary, Dictionary of Decisions of the Court of Session 1808 to 1833.* On 3 May 1839 he was called to the bar by the Inner Temple and commenced practice as an equity draftsman. During the early part of his career he published his *Answer to the Opium Question by Samuel Warren* and in 1843 was appointed a judicial reporter to the House of Lords in Scots appeals.[54] Bell published *The Law of Property as Arising from the Relation of Husband and Wife* in London in 1849. As a judge at the Cape, Bell J shouldered the burden of delivering judgments with considerable force of character and acquired a reputation as something of a dissenter during the early period of his career on the bench.[55]

As Chief Justice, Bell was erudite and his judgments were based on sound principles. He quickly revealed his competence with the old authorities and with English and Scots law, valuable skills in the developing law of the colony. In *Louw v. JH Hofmeyr*, an action to set aside a sale and transfer by executors to their co-executor, Bell CJ noted that though the sale was a good one, the Roman-Dutch law was different to English Law in this respect. He thought English Law rested on a 'good and wholesome ground' but observed that Roman-Dutch law allowed an executor to purchase from his co-executor in the manner performed by the defendant. He therefore concluded that though the Roman-Dutch rule 'may by some be regarded as a vicious law . . .; we cannot help [that], being here to administer the law as we find it, and not to make it'.[56]

After being affected by paralysis during the course of 1873, Bell was forced to resign as Chief Justice.[57] The advocates at the Cape sent him an address referring to

your learning and industry, your independence and your zeal for truth and justice [that] have been acknowledged by the whole colony. . . . The soundness and ability

Sir Sydney Smith Bell', (1933) 50 *SALJ* 437 sqq.; (1910) 1 *Union Law Review* 254 sqq.; 'Sir S. S. Bell', (1879) 67 *Law Times* 364; *Times,* 17 Sept. 1879; *Law List* (1841), 19; Ibid. (1843), 19.

[53] Searle, (1933) 50 *SALJ* 438.

[54] Seven volumes of reports were edited by him: *Cases decided in the House of Lords on appeal from the Courts of Scotland* (1843–52).

[55] See *Haupt's Trustees v. P J Haupt & Co* (1852) 1 Searle 287; *Le Roes v. Le Roes* (1853) 2 Searle 13; *Muller v. Whitehouse* (1854) 2 Searle 38; *Weeber v. Van der Spuy* (1854) 2 Searle 40; *Van Vuuren v. Van Vuuren* (1854) 2 Searle 116.

[56] (1869) 2 Buch 290, 294.

[57] See CO 48/466 (Cape of Good Hope: Original correspondence: Despatches 26 July 1873–24 Dec. 1873).

of your judgments and the keen penetration which enabled you alike to unravel complicated facts and to discriminate between apparently conflicting cases will long remain among the traditions of the Court over which you presided.[58]

PETRUS JOHANNES DENYSSEN (1811–83)[59] was a judge of the Eastern Districts Court from 1865 to 1868 and thereafter a judge of the Cape Supreme Court until 1877. He was born in Cape Town and educated briefly at the South African College. He then attended Leiden University, where he graduated LL D *cum laude*, after which he read in the chambers of Serjeant Wylde[60] and was called to the bar by the Inner Temple on 18 November 1836. On his return to the Cape he was admitted to practice on 12 July 1837. He practised from 1837 to 1840 and from 1856 to 1865. In the intervening period he was Secretary to the Cape Town Municipality. It is said that he 'was a man of determined character but of very generous and affectionate disposition. His manner on the Bench was always most courteous and dignified. . . . [H]e also manifested great common sense and ability as a judge'.[61] He died in Bonn, Germany, where he went after his retirement from the Cape bench.

CHARLES THOMAS SMITH (1823–1901),[62] judge of the Eastern Districts Court from 1867 to 1880 and then of the Cape Supreme Court until 1892, was educated at the Western Grammar School, Brompton, and at Wiesbaden in Germany. He then studied at Gonville and Caius College, Cambridge, from where he graduated BA in 1847, fifth Senior Optime in the Mathematics Tripos of his year. Smith was awarded an MA in 1850 and an LL D in 1875. After the award of his degree, Smith remained at Caius as tutor in mathematics until 1857. He then called to the bar by the Inner Temple on 30 April 1857 and practised common law. During this time he collaborated with David Keane QC in editing the thirteenth edition of *Selwyn's Abridgement of the Law of Nisi Prius* (1869); he also edited the *Lawyers Companion* for 1869.

Smith was appointed to a vacancy in the Eastern Districts Court with effect from 10 February 1869.[63] On 1 May 1880 he was transferred to Cape Town. He took considerable efforts to become conversant with the Roman-Dutch authorities. He also campaigned tirelessly for an improvement in the condition of the country's gaols. In an address to the Grand Jury at the

---

[58] The address was signed by Brand, Reitz, Dreyer, Cole, Hodges, Maasdorp, M. de Villiers and Buchanan. See CO 48/469 (Cape of Good Hope: Original Correspondence: Despatches May–July 1874). For another positive evaluation see Kotzé (n. 173), 88. But see Cole (n. 36), 11: '. . . the most wonderful combination of learning and ignorance I ever knew.'

[59] Roberts (n. 19), 355; 'The late Hon. Petrus J. Denyssen', (1903) 20 *SALJ* 221 sqq.

[60] The brother of Sir John Wylde, later Baron Truro. See J. B. Atlay, *The Victorian Chancellors* (1906), vol. I, 417 sqq.

[61] (1903) 20 *SALJ* 223.

[62] See S. D. Girvin, 'Charles Thomas Smith', (1992) 109 *SALJ* 319 sqq.; 'Death of the Hon. Mr Justice Smith', (1901) 18 *SALJ* 100 sq.; Roberts (n. 19), 376.

[63] *Cape of Good Hope Blue Book* (1869), Q 96 sq.

Criminal Sessions held in Cape Town in January 1884 he drew special attention to the want of classification of prisoners in the colony.[64]

Smith J retired from the Cape Bench on 12 April 1892, when the Chief Justice paid tribute to him, stating that during his time at the Cape 'not a whisper had ever been heard affecting his integrity, his independence, and all those high qualities which were required of an honest and upright judge'.[65]

(d) Judges of the Eastern Districts Court and High Court of Griqualand

Sir JACOB DIRK BARRY (1832–1905),[66] a native of Swellendam (though of Irish parentage on his father's side) was Recorder of Griqualand West from 1871 to 1878 and then judge (later Judge President) of the Eastern Districts Court from 1878 to 1901. He was educated at Swellendam and then at Cheltenham College (1848 to 1851) before proceeding to Trinity College, Cambridge. He was awarded a BA in 1855 with a First in the Moral Sciences Tripos, and a distinction in Moral Philosophy. He studied for the bar and was called by the Inner Temple on 17 November 1858. On his return to the Cape in 1859 he was admitted as advocate and commenced practice at Cape Town. By 1865 he was in practice at the then new Grahamstown bar. During this period he was also a member of the Cape Legislative Assembly and was Attorney-General of the Cape during 1867 and 1868. He was knighted on 16 August 1878, on his appointment to the Eastern Districts Court. One commentator remarked that 'Sir Jacob Barry's main characteristic, whether off the bench or on it, is an untiring activity, physical and intellectual'.[67] Another considered that he 'was deservedly one of the most respected judges of his time in South Africa'.[68]

Sir SIDNEY GODOLPHIN ALEXANDER SHIPPARD (1837–1902),[69] a contemporary of Barry, was a judge of the Eastern Districts Court from 1880 to 1885, a mere five years, before taking up the position of Administrator of Bechuanaland (Botswana). Nevertheless, his time on the bench established his reputation as an outstanding judge: 'He was not merely a sound and painstaking scholar; he was a practical lawyer who has added much to the great fabric of our South African Common Law'.[70]

---

[64] (1901) 18 *SALJ* 229 sq.   [65] "Judicial Changes', (1892) 9 *Cape LJ* 101.
[66] *Dictionary of South African Biography*, vol. 4 (1981), 19 sqq.; George Randell, *Bench and Bar* (1982), 11 sq.; Roberts (n. 19) 348; W. W. Rouse Ball, J. A. Venn, *Admissions to Trinity College, Cambridge* (1913), vol. 5 (1851–1900), 11; 'Sir Jacob D. Barry', (1900) 17 *Cape LJ* 213 sqq.; 'The Late Sir Jacob Barry', (1905) 22 *SALJ* 417 sq.
[67] (1900) 17 *Cape LJ* 217.   [68] (1905) 22 *SALJ* 417.
[69] *Dictionary of South African Biography*, vol. 2 (1972), 662 sqq.; *Dictionary of National Biography*, vol. 3 (1912), 307; *Who was Who 1897–1915*, 475; Ellison Kahn, *Law, Life & Laughter* (1991), 231 sq.; Randell (n. 66), 12 sq.; Roberts (n. 19), 375; C. L. Shadwell, *Registrum Orielense*, vol. 2, 1701–1900 (1902), 508; 'Sir G. A. Shippard at the Royal Colonial Institute', (1897) *Cape LJ* 120 sqq.; 'Sir Sydney Shippard', (1902) 19 *SALJ* 323.
[70] (1902) 19 *SALJ* 323.

Furthermore, 'his knowledge of Roman-Dutch law was profound'.[71] He was born in Brussels and educated in England, first at King's College School in London and then at Oriel and Hertford Colleges, Oxford,[72] where he graduated BA in the honour school of Law and Modern History in 1863.[73] He was awarded the Oxford degrees of MA and BCL in 1864 and DCL in 1878.[74] He was called to the bar by the Inner Temple on 26 January 1867. In 1870 he emigrated to the Cape where he was admitted to practice on 18 August 1870. He was Attorney-General of Griqualand West from 1873 to 1877 before returning to practice at the Grahamstown bar. He resigned his judgeship in September 1885 on being appointed Administrator of British Bechuanaland. He was created CMG in 1886 and KCMG in 1887.

JAMES BUCHANAN (1841–1893),[75] a Capetonian who later became Recorder of Griqualand West, and eventually the Judge President of its High Court from 1882 to 1887, was educated in Cape Town at the South African College. Here he obtained the Certificate in Science and Literature and a First Class Certificate in Law and these entitled him to gain admission as an advocate.[76] Buchanan was admitted at the Cape bar on 1 February 1865. After a period of successful practice, he took an appointment as *Staats Prokureur* of the South African Republic in 1872 'with a view to the federation of my country'.[77] In 1876 he was appointed a judge of the Orange Free State as colleague of F. W. Reitz (Chief Justice) and Melius de Villiers, but he resigned in order to take up the recordership of Griqualand West at Kimberley. He was Judge President from 1882 to 1887, when he resigned on account of ill health. Buchanan has the distinction of being one of the few nineteenth century Cape judges who received his entire education in South Africa. He is widely regarded as 'belonging to that band of pioneer judges who did so much to elucidate the Roman-Dutch law and lay the foundation of our Common law'.[78]

Buchanan's reputation, however, was not founded solely on his work as an advocate and judge. He was also known as a writer and provided translations of the first three books of Voet's *Commentarius ad Pandectas*, in 1880, 1881, and 1883. He was the editor of *Menzies' Reports,* which were published for the first time in 1870.

---

[71] Ibid. 326.

[72] He was elected Ireland exhibitioner at Oriel College in 1856 and, a year later, Lushby Scholar at Hertford College.

[73] There was no separate honour school of Jurisprudence until 1872. See F. H. Lawson, *The Oxford Law School 1850–1965* (1968), 34 sqq.

[74] The title of his thesis was *Dissertatio de vindicatione rei emptae et traditione.*

[75] See F. St L. Searle, 'The Hon. Mr Justice James Buchanan', (1932) 49 *SALJ* 137 sqq.

[76] Act 12 of 1858, s. 2.　　　　　　　　　　　　　[77] Searle, (1932) 49 *SALJ* 140.

[78] Ibid. 142.

Sir PERCEVAL MAITLAND LAURENCE (1854–1930),[79] a native of Lincolnshire who eventually became second puisne judge and then Judge President of the High Court of Griqualand, was educated privately. In 1872 he was admitted a pensioner and scholar of Corpus Christi College, Cambridge. In 1874, like his father before him, Laurence was President of the Cambridge Union. He was awarded the Members' Prize for English Essay in 1876, the year in which he graduated with a BA, being placed joint eighth in the first class of the Classical Tripos. In 1877 he was awarded the Yorke Prize and Whewell Scholarship in International Law. He became LL M in 1879 and was awarded the Chancellor's Gold Medal for Legal Studies. The Cambridge LL D followed in 1885. Laurence was elected a Fellow of Corpus Christi in 1876 (Honorary Fellow, 1914) and was tutor in Classics at Lucy Cavendish College.

Laurence was awarded a Tancred Studentship in common law by Lincoln's Inn.[80] He was called to the bar by Lincoln's Inn on 18 November 1878[81] and commenced practice as a special pleader and conveyancer. During these years at the English bar Laurence published frequently in the prominent journals of the day. Following a deterioration in his health, his medical advisers recommended emigration to the Cape Colony, where the climate was known to have a healing effect on sufferers of consumption.[82] On 29 November 1880 he was admitted to practice at the Cape bar but soon departed for the diamond mining centre of Kimberley in the Northern Cape in 1881, possibly because of the drier climate there. He was in practice in Kimberley for a year before his appointment as second puisne judge of the High Court of Griqualand on 7 September 1882. Six years later, on 16 March 1888, he succeeded James Buchanan as Judge President.

The main characteristic of Laurence JP's judgments is his scholarly approach and meticulous attention to detail. In *Preston & Dixon v. Trustee of Biden*, in a judgment running to nearly sixty pages in the reports, Laurence J (as he then was) concluded:

I think I have clearly shown that according to the principles of the ancient civil law, of the Roman-Dutch law, as stated in Grotius, Van der Keessel, and Voet, of the modern Dutch law, of the modern Indian law, as codified in the Contract Act, of the English law when carefully examined and rightly appreciated, and therefore, I have no hesitation in adding, of the law of this colony as well, an agent for an undisclosed principal . . . is as a rule personally liable on the contract.[83]

In *Jacobson v. Nitch*, Laurence JP cautioned against an uncritical use of the Roman-Dutch authorities:

[79] See S. D. Girvin, 'Perceval Maitland Laurence, Scholar, Writer and Colonial Judge and the High Court of Griqualand in the Late Nineteenth Century', (1994) 111 *SALJ* 112 sqq. Cf. P. M. Laurence, *On Circuit in Kafirland* (1903).

[80] *Lincoln's Inn Black Book*, vol. 34 (1875–9), 61 sqq.   [81] Ibid. 405 sqq.

[82] *Colonial Office List* (1862), 50 sqq.   [83] (1883) 1 HCG 248, 294.

There is no doubt a danger against which English or Scotch judges administering the law of this colony have to be constantly on their guard; the danger, I mean, of adopting decisions or statements of the text-writers as laying down general principles of the Roman-Dutch law, which on a closer examination may prove to be merely decisions or statements as to the customs of particular districts or as to the law merchant as interpreted by particular courts, and to constitute deviations from, rather than illustrations of, the general law of the Netherlands.[84]

Laurence JP left Kimberley for Cape Town in February 1905, following a reduction in the judicial establishment brought about by a decline in the volume of work in Kimberley. He served as Chairman of the War Losses Compensation and the Transvaal Delimitation Commissions and was knighted for this work in 1906. Following his role on the first Union Delimitation Committee which sat 1909–10 he was made KCMG in 1911. After Union he sat in the Cape Provincial Division (the successor to the Cape Supreme Court) until March 1911. He also held various appointments as Acting Ordinary and Acting Additional Judge of Appeal in the Appellate Division (in 1911 and 1912 respectively) and was Acting Judge President of the Natal Provincial Division. He retired on pension in 1913[85] and returned to England where he served on the Royal Commission on Fire Brigades and Fire Prevention (1921–3).

Laurence was the most academic judge to grace the bench of the colonial courts in Southern Africa during the later nineteenth and early twentieth centuries. His detailed knowledge of a wealth of law of different jurisdictions sometimes aided his research into difficult points on unsettled areas of law. He was conscious of the need for caution concerning the adoption of principles from individual Roman-Dutch writers when these reflected merely local custom and in this respect he took an important lead from the judgments of his contemporary, De Villiers CJ. Nevertheless, little remains of his legacy to modern South African law and he does not rank as one of the foremost judges of his time.

2. Natal[86]

Following the annexation of Natal by Britain on 31 May 1844, the Cape Parliament passed legislation establishing a District Court of Natal in 1845. This Court, which commenced hearings in January 1846, had its seat at Pietermaritzburg and was presided over by a Recorder, administering Roman-Dutch law as applied at the Cape. Appeal lay to the Supreme Court in Cape Town and thence to the Privy Council. After Natal achieved representative government on 15 July 1856 the District Court was abolished and replaced by a Supreme Court, composed of a Chief Justice and two

---

[84] (1889) 5 HCG 449, 453. [85] "Sir Perceval Laurence', (1913) 30 *SALJ* 204 sqq.
[86] For a comprehensive account see the work by Spiller cited in n. 38.

puisne judges. This court commenced sittings on 15 April 1858. Appeal to the Cape Supreme Court ended.[87] Nevertheless, within the context of nineteenth century South Africa the Cape Supreme Court was regarded as the pre-eminent legal tribunal. There were strong links between the two colonies, promoted by the appointment of judges who had served at the Cape. Henry Cloete, before his appointment to the recordership of Natal, was for thirty years in practice at the Cape bar. Thus he saw had Cape and Natal courts as being 'subject to the same system of laws ... and their mutual co-operation and assistance is essential to the well-being of, and to a proper administration of justice throughout South Africa'.[88] The practice of treating precedents in *Menzies Reports* as conclusive authority was widespread among the Natal judges (who tended towards mediocrity) but there was a notable difference between most of them and Natal's most brilliant judge, Henry Connor,[89] especially when one looks at the later decisions of the Cape Supreme Court.

Sir HENRY CONNOR (1817–90),[90] first puisne judge at Natal from 1858 to 1874 and Chief Justice from 1874 to 1890, was born in Dublin. He was awarded a BA at Trinity College, Dublin in 1837, and during the final two years of his degree he kept terms at King's Inns, Dublin. After completing his Dublin degree Connor kept terms, as was the practice at this time,[91] at the Inner Temple in London. On his return to Ireland in 1839 he was called to the bar by King's Inns and commenced study for the LL B, which he obtained from Trinity College, Dublin in 1841. He practised as a barrister in Dublin between 1841 and 1854 and then accepted the preferment as Chief Justice and Judicial Assessor at the Gold Coast. In 1857, however, he was appointed the first puisne judge of Natal. He served on the Eastern Districts Courts bench in 1865 and 1866 and was on the Cape bench during 1867 and 1868. In 1877, his old university, Trinity College, Dublin awarded him its LL D (*honoris causa*). He was knighted in November 1879.

Initially, Connor's knowledge of Roman-Dutch law was derived from English translations of the standard works, such as they were at the time. However, especially after his period on the Cape bench, he began to acquire an extensive library of Roman-Dutch authorities which he took delight in analyzing. Indeed he repeatedly asserted the superior claims of Roman-

---

[87] For a comprehensive account see the work by Spiller cited in n. 1.   [88] Ibid. 100.

[89] Roberts describes him as 'undoubtedly one of the outstanding South African judges ...': (n. 19), 354. On other Irish judges see S. D. Girvin, 'Three Irish-Born Judges at the Cape 1861–1896', (1989) 34 *Irish Jurist* 99 sqq. (published 1993). On James Coleman Fitzpatrick cf. Zimmermann (n. 1), 290.

[90] See Spiller (n. 38), 31 sqq., 119. Connor is described by Kahn and Bamford as 'unwordly, shy [and] erudite' ((1966) 83 *SALJ* 210); cf. Roberts (n. 19), 354: '... he was a bachelor recluse who knew little about men and less about women.'

[91] A statute of 1542 specified that a student for the Irish bar had to spend a certain proportion of his time studying at one of the English Inns. This requirement was abolished in 1885. See Daire Hogan, *The Legal Profession in Ireland 1789–1922* (1986), 14, 32 sqq.

Dutch law over English law and not infrequently he pressed counsel with the question: 'It was so in the English law, but was it so under the Roman-Dutch law?'[92] He was known to preface his analysis of the legal issues with an analysis of relevant Roman law texts which in his view 'anticipated everything in human affairs'. So far as his use of the Roman-Dutch authorities is concerned, Connor's thorough knowledge of Latin enabled him to master the contents of works written in this language. However his lack of competence in Dutch required him to make use of available English translations, especially of Grotius and Van der Linden. His preference was for the works of the later Roman-Dutch writers. Thus in *Natal Fire Assurance and Trust Co. v. Loveday*, Connor J noted his 'considerable difficulty' in adopting Voet's view because it was 'opposed to what the more recent jurist of authority, Van der Keessel, lays down, and unsupported, also, as it is, by the still more recent writer Van der Linden; and therefore, we may suppose, not borne out by decisions of the Courts of Holland after Voet's time'.[93] Thus, largely thanks to Connor CJ and his earlier predecessor, Recorder Hendrik Cloete, the otherwise widespread recourse to English authorities by those practising at the bar and by Connor's less astute colleagues was not able to dislodge the Roman-Dutch foundations of the legal system at Natal. A measure of Connor CJ's reputation may be seen in De Villiers CJ's comment that Connor CJ was one of the 'clearest exponents of the Dutch law that have ever occupied a seat on the judicial bench of South Africa'.[94] On another occasion De Villiers CJ expressly adopted Connor CJ's view that the revenue was not liable to compensate for the alleged delicts of government officials, noting that 'the remarks of Chief Justice Connor, just referred to, were not disapproved of [by the Privy Council]'.[95]

Sir Henry Connor was succeeded as Chief Justice by Sir MICHAEL HENRY GALLWEY (1826–1912),[96] a native of County Cork, Ireland who, like Connor before him, was a graduate of Trinity College, Dublin and a Barrister of King's Inns. There, however, the resemblance ended, for Gallwey was appointed to the post in recognition of his long and efficient service in Natal. His judgments were no match for the erudition of Connor CJ. In place of Connor CJ's fully researched and careful judgments came decisions based on 'it seems to me' and 'under what I consider the Roman-Dutch law'.[97]

On his retirement in 1901, Sir Henry Gallwey was succeeded by the Pietermaritzburg-born Sir HENRY BALE (1854–1910),[98] who was chief justice until Union in 1910. Unlike both his predecessors, Bale was completely devoid of university education or other legal training and this

---

[92] See Spiller (n. 38), 86.   [93] 1869 NLR 81 and 93.
[94] Ibid. 113. Cf. the analysis of his decisions in 1869/70 by Zimmermann (n. 1), 291 sqq.
[95] *Binda v. Colonial Government* (1887) 5 SC 284 at 291 (cited by Spiller (n. 38) 113).
[96] Spiller (n. 38), 37 sqq.   [97] Ibid.   [98] Ibid. 39 sqq.

manifested itself in the 'prolonged and anxious time' he needed to find legal sources and the fact that he had to call upon the advocates appearing before him to produce translations of the texts. His judgments had a tendency to be based upon his personal philosophy of an 'ordinary man possessed of an average sense of decency'.[99]

Sir JOHN CARNEGIE DOVE WILSON (1865–1935),[100] puisne judge of Natal from 1904 and then Judge President (of what had become the Natal Provincial Division) from 1910 to 1930, was the only other judge of note at Natal in the colonial period. He was born in Stonehaven, Aberdeenshire, the son of the Professor of Scots and Roman Law in Aberdeen University from 1891 to 1901.[101] The younger Dove Wilson was educated at the University of Aberdeen where he gained an MA in Moral Philosophy and Natural History in 1885.[102] He earned his LL B (with honours) at Edinburgh University in 1888 and in the same year was admitted a member of the Faculty of Advocates.[103] In his early years in practice, Dove Wilson acted as Sheriff-Substitute of the Lothians and Peebles in Edinburgh, and occasionally of Aberdeen, Banff, and Kincardine at Aberdeen. He was also a reporter for the Authorised Reports of the Court of Session for five years, and the editor of the fourth edition of his father's book, *The Practice of the Sheriff Courts of Scotland in Civil Causes*. However, he soon acquired a good practice and was briefed to appear before both the Privy Council and the House of Lords. In 1904 he took silk and was offered a puisne judgeship in the Supreme Court of Natal. Just prior to his arrival, the Bench in Natal was made up entirely of acting appointments, consisting of Finnemore ACJ, Broome AJ, and Bird AJ; little wonder that the bench was described as 'lamentably weak' and of 'amateur status'.[104] Recognition of Dove Wilson's success at Natal came in the form of a knighthood in 1918.[105]

Dove Wilson's judgments were characterized by features such as his notable facility in delivering *ex tempore* judgments.[106] More important was

[99] Spiller (n. 38), 39 sqq.

[100] See S. D. Girvin, 'John Dove Wilson as Judge President of the Natal Provincial Division 1911–30: His Approach to Legal Authorities and their Influence in Cases Involving Black Litigants', (1988) 105 *SALJ* 479 sqq.; *idem*, 'An Evaluation of the Career of a Scots Colonial Judge: John Dove Wilson of Natal', 1990 *Juridical Review* 35 sqq.

[101] See S. D. Girvin, 'Professor John Dove Wilson of Aberdeen', 1992 *Juridical Review* 60 sqq.

[102] See Girvin, 1990 *Juridical Review* 35 (n. 4).

[103] He was admitted on 9 Nov. 1888. See F. J. Grant (ed.), *The Faculty of Advocates in Scotland 1532–1943* (1944), 221.

[104] Spiller (n. 38), 51.

[105] *Natal Mercury*, 3 Jan. 1918. He was President of the Special Treason Court, established in response to the Witwatersrand miners' riots in 1922, and was appointed Acting Additional Judge of Appeal in Bloemfontein 1911–14, 1917–18, 1920, and 1923.

[106] Frank Broome in his autobiography, *Not the Whole Truth* (1962), 115, comments that 'Dove Wilson was a fluent and eloquent speaker . . . [and] delivered many *extempore* judgments which were a joy to listen to . . .'. See also Mr. Justice A. A. R. Hathorn's funeral address, *The Natal Witness*, 25 Apr. 1935, cited by Girvin, 1990 *Juridical Review* 50.

Dove Wilson JP's independent mode of reasoning and expression. On occasion, he boldly distinguished judgments which had been given by Connor CJ.[107] Unlike Connor CJ, however, Dove Wilson was no Roman-Dutch scholar; it seems likely that he referred to those translations which were available. In *Coll v. Murray*,[108] construing a passage from Justinian, he referred to the translation by A. F. S. Maasdorp.

Throughout his Judge Presidency, Dove Wilson frequently had recourse to English authorities.[109] However, unlike his less competent predecessors who had referred exclusively to English law to the detriment of South African law, his was a more balanced approach. Indeed his surveys of South African law were both generous and far-reaching and showed an intelligent grasp of contemporary developments. These judgments have played a small but significant role in the development of South African law and some of them have been cited by later judges as correct and authoritative statements of South African law.[110]

3. Orange Free State

In this territory a *Grondwet* of 1854 established a High Court comprising three *landdrosten*, untrained legal officials required to administer Roman-Dutch law. In 1875 a High Court of Justice was established at Bloemfontein, with a Chief Justice and two puisne judges. This court had little substantial influence on South African jurisprudence, probably because there was minimal litigation and very few law reports. Following annexation by Britain in 1902, a new High Court was established, consisting of a Chief Justice and two puisne judges. Appeal lay from this court to the Privy Council.

FRANCIS WILLIAM REITZ (1844–1934),[111] Chief Justice from 1874 to 1888, was born at Swellendam and educated at the South African College. He obtained the Second Class Certificate in Literature and Science in 1863 and was called to the English bar by the Inner Temple on 11 June 1867. On 23 January 1868 he was admitted an advocate at the Cape. He is probably better known for having been President of the Orange Free State from 1888 to 1895, when he was forced to resign for reasons of ill health. He recovered sufficiently to resume practice as an advocate at Pretoria and was a judge in the Transvaal for six months during 1898, after Kotzé's dismissal by President Kruger.

[107] *Union Share Agency & Investment Ltd v. Madsen* (1927) 48 NLR.
[108] (1917) 38 NLR.
[109] S. D. Girvin, *An Evaluation of the Judge Presidency of John Dove Wilson of Natal 1910–1930* (unpublished LL M thesis, University of Natal, 1987), 152 sqq.
[110] Girvin, 1990 *Juridical Review* 46.
[111] *Dictionary of South African Biography*, vol. 2 (1972), 577 sqq.; Roberts (n. 19), 370; S. B. Kitchin, 'The Honourable F. W. Reitz', (1916) *SALJ* 239 sqq.

Reitz's judicial colleagues were James Buchanan (on whom see *supra*, 1(d)) and MELIUS DE VILLIERS (1849–1938), younger brother of Henry de Villiers, the first Chief Justice of the Union. Melius de Villiers was Reitz's successor as Chief Justice. After the Boer War he was Professor of Roman-Dutch law at Leiden from 1905 to 1909.[112] The judges of the Orange River Colony (as it had now become) in 1902 were Sir Andries Maasdorp (Chief Justice until 1919), Archibald Walter Fawkes, and Daniel Ward.[113]

Sir ANDRIES FERDINAND STOCKENSTROOM MAASDORP (1847–1931)[114] was educated at Graaff-Reinet Grammar School and the Government School, and then at University College, London where he was awarded a BA in 1869. He was called to the bar by the Inner Temple on 17 November 1871 and practised at the Cape from March 1872. He was appointed Solicitor-General at Grahamstown in 1878 and held this post until 1896 while continuing to practise at the bar. He took silk in 1890. After leaving Grahamstown Maasdorp practised in Pretoria but returned to Grahamstown shortly before the start of the Boer War. It is probably true to say that he is best known for the publications which flowed from his pen, including *The Introduction to Dutch Jurisprudence* (1878), a translation of Grotius' *Inleiding*, and his magisterial *Institutes of Cape Law* which were published in four volumes in 1903. He was knighted in 1904. It has been said of him that 'his career . . . was distinguished by a profound knowledge and insight into the principles of Roman-Dutch law'.[115]

ALEXANDER JOHN McGREGOR (1864–1946),[116] was a judge of the Orange Free State High Court from 1892 to 1895, of the Eastern Cape Local Division from 1892 to 1895, and judge of the Orange Free State Provincial Division from 1915 to 1929. He was born at Robertson, Cape and educated at the South African College School, where he won a Queen's Scholarship. He then proceed to the South African College (now separate from the School) and graduated with a first-class BA from the University of the Cape of Good Hope in 1883. He was awarded the Maynard and University Scholarships and armed with these he went up to Oriel College, Oxford where he gained a First in Modern History (BA, 1887). He was the first South African to be President of the Oxford Union (1888). McGregor

---

[112] See Roberts (n. 19), 357.

[113] See S. D. Girvin, 'The Influence of an English Background on Four Judges Appointed to the Supreme Courts of the Transvaal and Orange River Colony 1902–1910', (1994) 62 *Tijdschrift voor rechtsgeschiedenis* 145 sqq.

[114] *Dictionary of South African Biography*, vol. I (1968), 482 sq.; Roberts (n. 19), 370; 'The Chief Justice, Orange River Colony', (1901) 18 *SALJ* 223 sq.; 'The Hon. A. F. S. Maasdorp KC, Chief Justice Orange River Colony', (1902) 19 *SALJ* 225 sqq.

[115] (1902) 19 *SALJ* 227.

[116] Roberts (n. 19), 370; Kahn (n. 69), 138 sq.; Randell (n. 66), 32 sq.; Ellison Kahn (ed.), *The Quest for Justice: Essays in Honour of Michael McGregor Corbett* (1995), 66 sqq.; 'Mr Justice McGregor', (1919) 36 *SALJ* 125 sqq.; 'The Late Mr Justice A. J. McGregor', (1947) 64 *SALJ* 3 sqq.

was called to the English bar by the Inner Temple on 28 January 1889 and on his return to the Cape that year was admitted to practice at the Cape bar. He was State Attorney of the Orange Free State from 1889 to 1892. After relinquishing his judgeship in Bloemfontein in 1895 he returned once again to practice at the Cape bar until 1913. At the same time he held the part-time position of Professor of Law at the South African College. In 1897, his translation of Book 36, Titles 1 and 2 of Voet's *Commentarius ad Pandectas* was published. Next was a *Comparative Digest of Laws Affecting Natives in British South Africa* (1904). McGregor took silk in 1907 and a year later relinquished his position at the College.

4. South African Republic[117]

The 1858 *Grondwet* of the Transvaal vested judicial power in lay judges. The High Court of Justice was staffed by three *landdrosten* who had to be over thirty years of age, in possession of immoveable property, enfranchised for two years, members of the Dutch Reformed congregation, and also free of any sentence. Small wonder that following the British annexation of the Transvaal in 1877 a new High Court of Justice was established. Initially with one judge, within a very short time this number was increased to three, one of whom was appointed as Chief Justice. This structure remained in place following the Pretoria Convention of 3 August 1881, which marked the end of this first period of British rule. In 1900, after the British annexation, the judicial structure changed. The superior courts were now the Supreme Court of the Transvaal sitting at Pretoria and presided over either by a Full Bench of three judges or by two judges. In addition there was a local division, the Witwatersrand High Court, which sat at Johannesburg, presided over by one judge.[118] Further appeal lay to the Privy Council. The Pretoria court heard important cases and appeals and was presided over by the Chief Justice. The puisne judges served in rotation in Johannesburg.

With the exception of the brilliant JOHN GILBERT KOTZÉ (later a Judge of Appeal of the Supreme Court of South Africa; cf. *infra* III. 3) the bench of the Transvaal prior to the Boer War was rather undistinguished. However, one or two appointments are worth highlighting. REINHOLD GREGOROWSKI (1856–1922),[119] a native of Somerset East in the Cape, held judicial appointments in the Orange Free State and then at the Transvaal both before and after the Boer War. He was educated at Gill College, Somerset East and was awarded a BA in 1875 by the University of

---

[117] See esp. Ellison Kahn, 'The History of the Administration of Justice in the South African Republic', (1958) 75 *SALJ* 294 sqq., 397 sqq; (1959) 76 *SALJ* 46 sqq. See also Manfred Nathan, 'The Republican Bench and Bar', (1932) 1 *SALT* 13 sqq.

[118] See the Establishment of the Supreme Court and High Court Ordinance, No. 2 of 1902, s. 2; the Administration of Justice Proclamation of 1902.

[119] See *Dictionary of South African Biography*, vol. 2 (1972), 274 sq.; Roberts (n. 19), 362.

the Cape of Good Hope. This University, established in 1873, replaced the old Board of Public Examiners and was purely a degree-conferring body. The first degree examinations were instituted in 1874, including examinations for the LL B degree.[120]

Gregorowski was awarded a Porter Scholarship and entered Gray's Inn, where he also was awarded a studentship. He was called to the bar on 18 November 1878 and returned to Cape Town where he commenced practice. After only three years, aged 25, he was appointed a judge at the Orange Free State. He resigned from this post in 1892 and became State Attorney, with the right to private practice, until 1894. He was a judge of the Transvaal High Court in 1896 and 1897 and was appointed Chief Justice on 31 March 1898. After the Boer War he resumed practice at the Transvaal bar until his appointment in 1913 to the bench of what was now the Transvaal Provincial Division.

Gregorowski was in the public eye during the period when he presided as a special criminal judge in the trial of those involved in the infamous Jameson Raid. Four were found guilty of high treason and sentenced to death, but this sentence was later commuted by the President of the Republic. His judgment met with sharp and bitter criticism, although the better view is that it displayed his independence and clear insight. One commentator has remarked that he 'made an important contribution to a South African tradition, the integrity and independence of the bench'.[121]

GEORGE THOMAS MORICE (1858–1930),[122] judge of the Transvaal High Court from 1890 to 1899, was born in Aberdeen, Scotland and educated there at Aberdeen University (MA). He then attended Lincoln College, Oxford and was awarded a BA in Classics. He was called to the bar by the Middle Temple on 17 November 1883. After this he went to Holland to study Dutch. He was admitted to practice in Pretoria in 1884. After the Boer War he commenced practice in Pretoria and published *English and Roman-Dutch Law* (1903) and *Sale in Roman-Dutch Law* (1919).

Following the Boer War the then Governor-General, Lord Milner, assembled an extremely strong bench: James Rose Innes, the former Attorney-General of the Cape, was appointed Chief Justice; the puisne judges were: William Henry Solomon, previously of the Eastern Districts Court; John William Wessels, previously in practice at the Transvaal bar; William Smith, Chief Justice of British Guyana; Arthur Weir Mason, previously a judge at Natal; and Leonard Syer Bristowe, a chancery barrister. Each of the first three eventually became Chief Justices of the Appellate

---

[120] See Cowen, 1959 *Acta Juridica* 13.
[121] *Dictionary of South African Biography* (n. 119), 275.
[122] Ibid. vol. 4 (1981), 375 sqq.; J. Foster, *Alumni Oxonienses 1715–1886*, vol. 3 (1888), 989; C. L. Shadwell, *Oxford Honours 1220–1894* (1894), 176; Roberts (n. 19) 372; 'Mr G. T. Morice KC', (1929) 46 *SALJ* 137 sqq.; Nathan (1932) 1 *SALT* 63.

Division of the Supreme Court of South Africa after Union (see *infra*, III. 2).

Sir WILLIAM JAMES SMITH (1853–1912)[123] was educated at Taunton School and Trinity Hall, Cambridge. He graduated BA (1875), MA, and LL M (1878). The Inner Temple admitted him as a student on 16 January 1872 and Lincoln's Inn did likewise, on 19 July 1873.[124] He read in the chambers of Archibald Levin Smith, one of the leading and most brilliant junior barristers of his day (he was to become Master of the Rolls). Smith was called to the bar by Lincoln's Inn on 7 June 1875[125] and commenced practice. In December 1880 he was appointed puisne judge to the Gold Coast Colony but resigned in July 1881 because of the inclement climate and returned to practice in London. In 1882 he was appointed a judge of the Supreme Court of Cyprus and became Chief Justice in 1892. On 23 January 1896 a knighthood was conferred on him, and in 1897 he became Chief Justice of Guyana.

In 1901 Smith represented the Crown Colonies at the Colonial Conference held in London, almost a year after he had presided over a special treason court in Natal. This court had been created specifically to try the 'Natal Rebels'—Afrikaners who had responded to the Anglo-Boer War by joining the Republican forces.[126] Smith was much praised for the 'unprejudiced, fair and sympathetic manner' in which the trials were conducted.[127] At the conclusion of the Colonial Conference in London he was approached to become the third puisne judge in the High Court of the Transvaal and took up his appointment in February 1902. In Innes's view Smith's 'legal experience and knowledge of human nature made him a helpful and instructive colleague; his judicial manner was a model to us all'.[128] Smith had a competent knowledge of the Roman-Dutch writers, perhaps acquired when he was Chief Justice of British Guyana. At the same time, he was cautious about the unquestioning adoption of English principles. Smith remained on the Transvaal bench until 21 October 1912 when he retired. He was described by Sir John Wessels as 'in reality . . . with Sir James Rose Innes and Sir William Solomon, . . . one of the three great pillars of the court prior to Union'.[129]

---

[123] *Who was who 1897–1915*, 486; Roberts (n. 19), 376; Venn (n. 24), 574; 'Sir William Smith Kt.', (1911) 28 *SALJ* 465 sqq.; (1912) 134 *Law Times* 99 sq.; 'The late Sir William Smith', (1912) 29 *SALJ* 368 sqq.; *Times*, 15 Nov., 18 Nov. and 21 Nov. 1912; *Law List* (1876), 171.

[124] *Lincoln's Inn Black Book*, vol. 33 (1872–1875), 243 sq.

[125] Ibid. 521; vol. 34 (1875–1879), 3.

[126] See E. H. Brookes, C. de B. Webb, *A History of Natal* (1965), 210.

[127] (1911) 28 *SALJ* 468.

[128] James Rose Innes, *Autobiography* (ed. B. A. Tindall, 1949), 200.

[129] Leslie Blackwell, who began practice at the Transvaal bar during Smith's time, described him as a 'very handsome man who looked the very embodiment of British justice'. See 'Fifty years at the Bar', (1959) 76 *SALJ* 79.

Sir ARTHUR WEIR MASON (1860–1924),[130] judge of Natal from 1896 to 1902 and thereafter on the Transvaal bench from 1902 to 1924, was born at Palmerton in Pondoland, then educated at Bath College and London University, where he obtained a BA with Honours in Classics and German in 1879. He was admitted as an attorney at Natal in 1881 and thereafter for a period of three years acted as a reporter for the Natal Law Reports. He was admitted as an advocate in 1884 and from 1888 to 1895 was a partner in the firm of Hathorn and Mason in Pietermaritzburg. During his time as an advocate he appeared often before Connor CJ, who undoubtedly remained an inspiration to him during his career. During his six years on the Natal bench he was noted for approaching legal disputes with an independent mind; in particular, he distinguished those aspects of English law which were inapplicable. In determining Roman-Dutch principles he canvassed precedents from all the colonial jurisdictions in South Africa.[131] He was knighted in 1922.

LEONARD SYER BRISTOWE (1857–1935)[132], judge at the Transvaal from 1903 to 1922, was educated at Westminster School and Christ Church, Oxford, where he was an exhibitioner. He obtained his BA in 1880 with first class honours in *Literae Humaniores*. He obtained an MA in 1883.

The Inner Temple awarded him a pupil scholarship in equity in 1882 and he read first in the chambers of a leading chancery junior, Cornelius Warmington of Lincoln's Inn, and then with Robert MacSwinney. He was called to the bar by the Inner Temple on 17 November 1882 and practised at the Chancery bar as an equity draftsman and conveyancer. During the early years of his practice Bristowe published several books, beginning in 1888 with *The Coal Mines Regulation Act 1887* in collaboration with MacSwinney. This was followed by the third edition of Tudor's *The Law of Charities and Mortmain* in 1889, *A Treatise on the Mortmain and Charitable Uses Act 1891*, *The Legal Restrictions on Gifts to Charity* in 1891, and *A Legal Handbook for the Use of Hospital Authorities* in 1894. He assisted MacSwinney in the preparation of a second edition of *The Law of Mines, Quarries and Minerals* in 1897. Bristowe also reported law cases for the *Weekly Reporter* and later the *Law Times*.

Bristowe accepted a position on the Transvaal bench in January 1903.[133] Innes later described him as 'our philosopher. As an equity pleader, he was familiar with civil law doctrine. He had a keen intellect and was a master

---

[130] See Roberts (n. 19), 371; Kahn (n. 69), 162; Spiller (n. 38), 49, 124; 'The Hon. A. W. Mason', (1916) 33 *SALJ* 1 sqq.

[131] Spiller (n. 38), 49.

[132] J. Foster (n. 122), 56; Kahn (n. 69), 14; Roberts (n. 19), 350; G. F. Russell Barker, A. H. Stenning, *The Record of Old Westminsters*, vol. 1 (1928), 122; C. L. Shadwell, *The Historical Register of the University of Oxford 1220–1900* (1900), 31; *Idem* (n. 122), 338, 471; 'The Late Mr Justice Bristowe', (1935) 4 *SALT* 66; *Times*, 8 Apr. 1935, 13 June 1935.

[133] CO 291/54 (Transvaal: Original Correspondence: Despatches Jan–Mar. 1903).

of felicitous exposition.'[134] Bristowe sat at the High Court in Johannesburg as the fifth puisne judge, but later sat more regularly in Pretoria. He acquired a reputation for being careful, patient, and lucid. On his death in 1935 it was said that he generally formed an opinion quickly and firmly 'and was not to be easily moved'.[135] An obituary in the *South African Law Times* similarly stated that 'when he took a certain view it was almost impossible to shake his opinion, and he was accused of obstinacy'.[136]

III. UNION (1910–1961)

1. Courts

The South Africa Act of 1909[137] united the four former British colonies, Cape, Natal, Orange River, and Transvaal, into the Union of South Africa. A new Supreme Court of South Africa was created with an Appellate Division (AD) at Bloemfontein as the highest court of appeal in the country (although until 1950[138] it was still possible to appeal to the Privy Council). The Supreme Courts of the former colonies now became provincial divisions of the Supreme Court of South Africa: the Cape Provincial Division (CPD), the Transvaal Provincial Division (TPD), the Orange Free State Provincial Division (OPD), and the Natal Provincial Division (NPD). The old Eastern Districts Court became the Eastern Cape Local Division (ECLD) and the High Court of Griqualand became the Griqualand West Local Division (GWLD). Both these local divisions were attached to the Cape Provincial Division but became separate courts in their own right, known as the Eastern Cape Division (EPD, from 1957) and the Northern Cape Division (NC, from 1969). A South West Africa Division was added in 1959. In addition, there were two other important local divisions: the Witwatersrand Local Division at Johannesburg (WLD), attached to the Transvaal Provincial Division, and the Durban and Coast Local Division (D & CLD) at Durban, attached to the Natal Provincial Division.

2. The Chief Justices

The first Chief Justice, JOHN HENRY DE VILLIERS (1842–1914),[139] had previously been a highly distinguished Chief Justice of the Cape Supreme

---

[134] Innes (n. 128), 200.
[135] See obituary in *Times*, 8 Apr. 1935.
[136] (1935) 4 *SALT* 66.
[137] 9 Edw 7, c. 9.
[138] Privy Council Appeals Act 16 of 1950. See C. F. Forsyth, *In Danger for Their Talents* (1985), 3 sqq.
[139] *Dictionary of South African Biography*, vol. 1 (1968), 224 sqq.; Hugh Corder, *Judges at Work* (1984), 34 sq.; Kahn (n. 69), 41 sqq.; Roberts (n. 19), 356 sq.; E. A. Walker, *Lord De Villiers and his Times* (1925), 72 sqq.; 'Sir J. H. de Villiers', (1901) 18 *SALJ* 1 sqq.; 'Lord de

Court from 1873 until Union. He was born in Paarl and received his schooling at the South African College in Cape Town where he was awarded the
Second Class Certificate in Literature and Science in 1861.[140] He proceeded
to Utrecht, where he intended to study for the ministry, and then Berlin
where he intended to study medicine. However he decided to qualify in law
and was called to the bar by the Middle Temple on 17 November 1865. On
his return to the Cape he was admitted as advocate on 18 January 1866, one
of the four advocates in practice at the time. In 1872 he became the
Attorney-General and, remarkably, was offered the Chief Justiceship in succession to Sir Sydney Bell in 1873. During his time as Chief Justice of the
Cape he received many honours, being knighted in 1877. In 1881 he became
KCMG. He was made Privy Counsellor in 1897 and became Baron de
Villiers of Wynberg in 1910. In the same year he was appointed South
Africa's first Chief Justice and served in that capacity until 1914 when he
died in office. Since 1908 he had presided over the National Convention that
eventually led to the creation of the Union of South Africa. In the course
of his tenure as Chief Justice of the Union he acted on several occasions as
Governor General. Though sometimes accused of too pronounced an incli-
nation to borrow from English law at the expense of Roman-Dutch rules,[141]
his primary aim was to entrench and modernize the specifically Southern
African branch of Roman-Dutch law in the interests of fair and speedy dispute settlement. Although well versed in the Roman-Dutch authorities,
notably Voet, he was not so great a scholar as some of his contemporaries.
On his death, James Rose Innes (his brilliant successor) said:

[H]is position among South African jurists was, and is, and will remain unique. To
this many factors contributed; his intellectual qualities, his force of character and his
length of service. His keen and logical mind, his grasp of legal principle and his
remarkable capacity for going to the root of a tangled matter . . . [H]e possessed in
a rare degree the gift of lucid and precise exposition. He was a man of firm decision
and yet . . . he was always ready to entertain and to weigh fresh argument. He was
fearless in the execution of his office, and gave effect to his view of the law regardless of the consequences. He was the foremost of that band of judicial workers . . .
who, taking the magnificent body of jurisprudence bequeathed to us by the lawyers
of Holland, adapted and applied its living principles to the changing and complicated conditions of modern society.[142]

Villiers, CJ: An Appreciation', (1921) 37 *LQR* 473 sqq.; 'The Late Chief Justice: Baron de
Villiers', (1922) *SALJ* 52 sqq.; M. M. Corbett, 'Lord de Villiers of Wynberg', (1994) 111 *SALJ*
373 sqq.; Reinhard Zimmermann, 'De Villiers, John Henry', in: Michael Stolleis (ed.), *Juristen:
Ein biographisches Lexikon* (1995), 160 sq.

[140] In 1902 he was awarded an LL D (*honoris causa*) by the University of the Cape of Good
Hope. See 'Cape University Degrees', (1901) 18 *SALJ* 320.

[141] He was responsible for drafting the General Law Amendment Act 8 of 1879.

[142] 'The late Chief Justice of South Africa', (1914) 31 *SALJ* 422 sq. Cf. the balanced evaluation by Zimmermann (n. 139), 160 sq.

Another commentator has remarked that 'he left the judiciary with a *cachet* for excellence that was to spread over all South Africa and to remain'.[143]

Sir JAMES ROSE INNES (1855–1942),[144] the second Chief Justice of South Africa from 1914 to 1927 (previously a Judge of Appeal), was born at Grahamstown and educated at schools in Uitenhage, Bedford, and finally Gill College, Somerset East. He obtained a BA from the University of the Cape of Good Hope in 1874 and, by private study, an LL B in 1877. He was admitted to practice at the Cape Bar on 12 February 1878. He served as Attorney-General of the Cape from 1890 to 1893 and again from 1900 to 1902. In between he was in practice at Cape Town. He was appointed QC in 1890 and in 1901 was made KCMG. In 1902 he was appointed as the Chief Justice of the Transvaal, and in 1910 a Judge of Appeal. At this time, it was said that

[b]y his lucid and learned judgments [as Chief Justice of the Transvaal] he has contributed extensively to the stores of legal lore. He has at all times maintained Roman-Dutch principles in their integrity, and with such profound scholars and expounders as Sir J. W. Wessels and Sir William Solomon on either side of him, there has never been any danger of specious arguments becoming the means of mischievous infractions upon a system of jurisprudence which has justly been described as 'replete with wisdom and equity'.[145]

On his appointment as Chief Justice in 1914, an office he held until 1927, he became a Privy Counsellor. He is famed by many as South Africa's greatest judge. On his appointment as Chief Justice a commentator noted that 'his knowledge of Roman-Dutch law and of its practice in South Africa is deep and thorough'.[146] C. G. Hall, editor of the *South African Law Journal*, noted in his review of Innes' autobiography (edited by B. A. Tindall) that 'so far as the law was concerned [Innes] . . . was a master builder. He was one of the great lawyers whom South Africa has produced, and we do well to be proud of him'.[147] N. J. de Wet, Chief Justice at the time of Innes' death, noted that he was an 'indefatigable champion of the principles of Roman-Dutch law'.[148]

On Innes' retirement in 1927 he was succeeded as Chief Justice by his lifelong friend, Sir WILLIAM HENRY SOLOMON (1852–1930).[149] Born at

[143] *Dictionary of South African Biography* (n. 139), 229.

[144] Ibid. vol. 2 (1972), 328 sqq.; Corder (n. 139), 35 sq. and *passim*; Innes (n. 128); Kahn (n. 69), 96 sqq.; Roberts (n. 19), 374; 'Sir James Rose Innes', (1902) 19 *SALJ* 1 sqq.; 'Sir James Rose Innes', (1910) 27 *SALJ* 503; 'Sir James Rose Innes', (1914) 31 *SALJ* 426; 'The Late Sir James Rose Innes', (1942) 59 *SALJ* 30 sq.; Reinhard Zimmermann, 'Innes, James Rose', in: Michael Stolleis (ed.) (n. 139), 312 sq.

[145] (1910) 27 *SALJ* 503.   [146] (1914) 31 *SALJ* 426.

[147] (1949) 66 *SALJ* 458.

[148] (1942) 59 *SALJ* 30. Cf. the evaluation by Zimmermann (n. 144), 312 sq. who draws attention to Innes' remarkable commitment to social justices and political equality.

[149] *Dictionary of South African Biography*, vol. I (1968), 683 sqq.; Corder (n. 139), 36; Kahn (n. 69), 245 sqq.; Roberts (n. 19), 376 sq.; Venn (n. 24), 590; T. A. Walker, *Admissions to*

Philippolis, Orange Free State, Solomon was educated at Lovedale and at Bedford Public School, where he was a contemporary of Innes. He then went to the South African College and obtained a BA from the University of the Cape of Good Hope in 1872. He was awarded a Porter Scholarship which took him to Peterhouse, Cambridge.[150] Here he was awarded a BA in Mathematics in 1876. He received an MA in 1880, and in 1915 was elected an Honorary Fellow of his old college. He was called to the bar by the Inner Temple on 17 November 1877, having read in the chambers of Mr Justice Jelf. He was admitted to the Cape Bar on 12 April 1878 and practised first in Cape Town and then at Kimberley. On 1 October 1883 he was appointed Assistant Legal Adviser to the Crown at Griqualand West and in 1887 was elevated to the bench as first puisne judge. In 1896 he went to the Eastern Districts Court, and in 1902 was transferred to the Transvaal bench after a period as president of the special indemnity court.[151] At Union in 1910 he was made a Judge of Appeal. He was knighted in 1907, becoming KCMG in 1913 and KCSI in 1914. He was appointed a Privy Counsellor in 1928 on assuming the position of Chief Justice. A year later the University of Cape Town conferred on him the degree of LL D (*honoris causa*). He served as Chief Justice, retiring in October 1929 after only two years in office. Throughout his career he was noted for his 'clear perception, logical mind, rejection of the irrelevant and ruthless application of hard principle to the facts before him ... qualities as admirable as they are rare'.[152]

JACOB ABRAHAM JEREMY DE VILLIERS (1868–1932)[153] succeeded Sir William as Chief Justice in 1929. He was born at Fauresmith, Orange Free State and educated at Grey College, Bloemfontein. He proceeded to Victoria College, Stellenbosch and graduated with a BA (Classics) from the University of the Cape of Good Hope; he was awarded a Porter Scholarship. This took him first to the University of Amsterdam and then to the Middle Temple following the award of a Senior Studentship in 1891. He was called to the bar by the Middle Temple on 26 January 1893. On his return to South Africa in 1894 he joined the Johannesburg bar and practised there until 1896, again during 1898 and 1899, and finally from 1903 to 1907. He was State Attorney of the Orange Free State from 1896 to 1898

Peterhouse or St. Peter's College (1912), 541; W. H. Somerset Bell, 'The Hon. W. H. Solomon', (1904) 21 *SALJ* 189 sqq.; 'Opening of the New Appeal Court: Retirement of Sir William Solomon', (1930) 47 *SALJ* 44 sq.; Reinhard Zimmermann, 'The Contribution of Jewish Lawyers to the Administration of Justice in South Africa', (1995) 29 Israel Law Review 276.

[150] At this College he was elected Parke Scholar in 1873 and North & Woodward Scholar in 1874.

[151] Under the Indemnity and Special Tribunals Act 6 of 1900.

[152] Bell, (1904) 21 *SALJ* 193.

[153] Corder (n. 139), 26, 36; Kahn (n. 69), 39 sqq.; Roberts (n. 19), 355 sq.; 'The Hon. Jacob de Villiers', (1907) 24 *SALJ* 237; (1932) 1 *SALT* 31.

and Minister of Mines and Attorney-General of the Transvaal from 1907
to 1910. In 1910 he became Judge President of the Transvaal Provincial
Division, a position he occupied until 1920 when he became a Judge of
Appeal. He was made Privy Counsellor in 1931 and died at Ruthven Castle,
Wales, while on sick leave on 16 September 1932.

Sir JOHN (JOHANNES) WILHELMUS WESSELS (1862–1936),[154]
appointed Chief Justice in 1932 in the place of De Villiers, had a highly distinguished career. Born in Cape Town, he was educated at the South
African College where he was awarded a Queen's Scholarship in 1875. He
obtained a BA (Hons.) from the University of the Cape of Good Hope in
1882 and was awarded a University Scholarship in Literature and
Philosophy as well as a Jamison Scholarship. These took him to Downing
College, Cambridge where he was awarded a college law scholarship in
1883. He came second in the first class of the Law Tripos and graduated
with the degrees of BA and LL B in 1885. He was also awarded the George
Long Scholarship in Roman Law and Jurisprudence. In 1923 his college
elected him to an Honorary Fellowship. After graduating at Cambridge,
Wessels read in the chambers of Pollard and was awarded a Middle Temple
Scholarship in International Law and Jurisprudence. He was called to the
bar by the Middle Temple on 26 January 1886, and on 29 June 1886 was
admitted as an advocate of the Cape bar.

In 1887 Wessels commenced practice in Pretoria where he remained until
the Boer War. After the war he was appointed a judge of the Transvaal
Supreme Court (1902) and Judge President of the Transvaal Provincial
Division from 1920 to 1923. He was knighted in 1909. In 1923 he was raised
to the Appellate Division as a Judge of Appeal and served as Chief Justice
from 1932 to 1936. In 1933 he became a Privy Counsellor and in 1934 the
University of South Africa awarded him the degree of LL D (*honoris causa*).

Superlatives abound in assessments of his career; for Roberts, 'Wessels
was probably the most dynamic personality in the legal history of South
Africa . . . he was a man of extremely high principles, outstanding intellect,
amazing industry, profound scholarship and great moral courage'.[155] Some
of these characteristics may be found in his *History of Roman-Dutch Law*,
published in 1908, which initially appeared as thirty-nine articles in the
South African Law Journal between 1903 and 1907, and *The Law of*

---

[154] *Dictionary of South African Biography*, vol. I (1968), 874 sqq.; Corder (n. 139), 37 sq.;
Kahn (n. 69), 337 sqq.; Roberts (n. 19), 382 sq.; 'The Hon. J. W. Wessels', (1905) 22 *SALJ* 241
sqq.; 'Chief Justice Wessels', (1932) 1 *SALT* 166 sqq.; (1934) 3 *SALT* 98; (1936) 5 *SALT* 166;
'Sir John Wessels', (1937) 54 *SALJ* 451 sqq.

[155] Roberts (n. 19), 383. Cf. H. H. Morris, as quoted by Kahn (n. 69), 338: '. . . a man of
strong character, forceful, blunt and pugnacious. . . . To him a spade was a spade, and not an
agricultural instrument. And yet, with all this, he was an exceedingly kind-hearted man.' Oliver
Deneys Schreiner in a letter to his wife (printed in Kahn (n. 69), 337 sq.) refers to Wessels as
'cantankerous as usual—he really is a poisonous chap on a trial bench'.

Contract in South Africa, which he did not 'think would ever see the deep water of publication',[156] was published posthumously in 1937, revised by Alfred Adrian Roberts.[157] Wessels' *History* has frequently been criticized for being unreliable and incomplete, but this has to be seen in the context of its being the first work of its kind in South Africa.[158] His work on *Contract* was the product of his profound scepticism about the future of Roman-Dutch law in South Africa; he was for many years an ardent advocate of codification. J. S. Curlewis, in a funeral oration, considered that Wessels' 'profound knowledge of our common law entitles him, in my view, to rank among the three greatest Roman-Dutch lawyers of our time'.[159]

JOHN STEPHEN CURLEWIS (1863–1940),[160] Wessels' successor as Chief Justice from 1936 to 1938, was (like Lord de Villiers, the first Chief Justice) born at Paarl. He was educated at the Diocesan College School and the University of the Cape of Good Hope. After attaining his BA (1881) he became a schoolmaster and then joined the Cape Civil Service, eventually holding a position in the Registrar's Office, Kimberley. Meanwhile he studied law and obtained the LL B in 1887. He was admitted an advocate on 12 October 1887 and commenced practice at the Pretoria Bar in 1888. He was appointed a judge of the Transvaal High Court in 1903, later becoming Judge President of the Transvaal Provincial Division in 1924. Curlewis was made a Judge of Appeal in 1927.

JAMES STRATFORD (1869–1952)[161] succeeded Curlewis as Chief Justice for a brief period in 1938, retiring in 1939 on reaching the age of seventy. He was born at Port Elizabeth and educated at St Aiden's College in Grahamstown. He qualified as a surveyor before proceeding to Exeter College, Oxford, where he graduated with a BA (Jurisprudence) in 1897 and a BCL in 1898. After being called to the bar by the Inner Temple on 22 June 1898 he read in the chambers of Lord Cave for a period of three years. On his return to the Cape he was admitted to the bar on 6 September 1901 but transferred his practice to Johannesburg in 1902. He took silk in 1912 and was appointed a judge of the Transvaal Provincial Division in 1921. He was raised to the Appellate Division in 1927. The University of the

---

156 Cited in Kahn, *Essays Corbett* (n. 116), 90.

157 See '*In memoriam*: A. A. Roberts QC', (1964) 81 *SALJ* 141 sqq.

158 Wessels was himself not an admirer of the work: 'Believe me I am no great admirer of my book. It was meant as a kind of *vade mecum* for English students who know neither Dutch nor Latin.' Cited in Kahn, *Essays Corbett* (n. 116), 90.

159 (1937) 54 *SALJ* 452.

160 Corder (n. 139), 38; Kahn (n. 69), 33 sq.; Roberts (n. 19), 354; 'The Hon. John S. Curlewis', (1903) 20 *SALJ* 387 sqq.; 'The Honourable John Stephen Curlewis', (1925) 42 *SALJ* 121 sqq.

161 Corder (n. 139), 38; Kahn (n. 69), 259 sq.; Roberts (n. 19), 378; 'The Hon. Mr Justice Stratford', (1921) 38 *SALJ* 248 sqq.; G. A. Mulligan, 'The Hon. James Stratford', (1952) 69 *SALJ* 1.

Witwatersrand awarded him an LL D *honoris causa* in 1944.[162] Assessments of his ability as a judge indicate that

he did not pretend to be a profound Roman-Dutch scholar, but he was an outstanding judge, strong, clear-headed, with a high sense of duty, an extremely acute mind and a gift of clear exposition. In spite of his reputed contempt for the 'musty manuals of the middle ages' his judgments contain many a valuable contribution to the interpretation of our common law.[163]

NICOLAAS JACOBUS DE WET (1873–1960),[164] Chief Justice from 1939 to 1943, was born at Aliwal North, where he received his schooling at the Public School. He then attended Victoria College, Stellenbosch and graduated with a BA from the University of the Cape of Good Hope in 1893. He was admitted to Downing College, Cambridge as a pensioner in 1893 and subsequently became a non-collegiate student. He gained the LL B First Class in 1895, winning the Chancellor's Gold Medal for English Law. On his return to South Africa he was admitted advocate both at the Cape and subsequently in the Transvaal. He took silk in 1912 and was Minister of Justice from 1913 to 1924. He was a Senator from 1924 to 1929 and then resumed practise at the Transvaal bar. He was appointed to the Transvaal Provincial Division as a judge in 1932 and became a Judge of Appeal in 1937. Of his judicial qualities it was said:

When a question of common law was in issue, the result of Mr Justice de Wet's early training in Courts presided over by jurists such as Kotzé, Innes and Wessels was that he naturally turned to Roman-Dutch law for the answer. He avoided excursions among the more recondite commentators but he was familiar with the works of the Roman-Dutch writers and the Dutch consultations and he did much during his ten years on the Bench to secure adherence to the principles of our own law.[165]

ERNEST FREDERICK WATERMEYER (1880–1958),[166] Chief Justice from 1943 to 1950, was born at Graaff-Reinet and educated at Stellenbosch Gymnasium and then at Bath College in England. He obtained an entrance scholarship to Gonville and Caius College, Cambridge in 1899 and was awarded a BA in Mathematics in 1902. A year later he took Part II of the Law Tripos and was awarded an LL B. He was called to the bar by the Inner Temple on 27 April 1904 and admitted to practice at the Cape on 23 February 1905. He was Chairman of the Income Tax Court from 1920 to 1922 and took silk in 1921. He was a judge of the Cape Provincial Division

---

[162] (1944) 61 *SALJ* 258.   [163] Roberts (n. 19), 378.
[164] Corder (n. 139), 30, 41; Roberts (n. 19), 358; 'The Hon. N. J. de Wet, KC, Minister of Justice', (1914) 31 *SALJ* 369 sqq.; (1932) 1 *SALT* 2; B. A. Tindall, 'The Chief Justice', (1943) 60 *SALJ* 275 sqq.
[165] Tindall, (1943) 60 *SALJ* 278.
[166] Corder (n. 139), 41; Kahn (n. 69), 336; Roberts (n. 19), 382; 'Mr Justice Watermeyer', (1923) 40 *SALJ* 99 sqq.; (1933) 2 *SALT* 48; 'The New Chief Justice', (1943) 60 *SALJ* 429; *Alpha*, 'The Rt. Honourable E. F. Watermeyer', (1950) 67 *SALJ* 332 sqq.

from 1922 to 1937, and then became a Judge of Appeal. It is said that 'he at once proceeded to justify his appointment [as a judge] and showed himself to be an erudite Roman-Dutch lawyer'.[167] Another commentator noted that

he was an indefatigable champion of Roman-Dutch law, and the numerous important judgments delivered by him during his long judicial career show his infinite care and painstaking research into the authorities in unravelling the many intricate legal problems which he was called upon to solve. Authority for a supposed proposition of law never satisfied him unless that authority was of the highest and even then his keen intellect would enquire whether the highest authority did not perchance err.[168]

ALBERT VAN DER SANDT CENTLIVRES (1887–1966),[169] Chief Justice from 1950 to 1957, was born at Cape Town and educated at the South African College. He was awarded a BA (Hons.) in Classics in 1906 and then, on obtaining a Rhodes Scholarship, went to New College, Oxford. Here he obtained a BA (Jurisprudence) in 1909 (Second Class) and a BCL in 1910 (Third Class). He was called to the bar by the Middle Temple on 17 November 1910 and commenced practice at the Cape bar in 1911. From 1920 to 1935 he was a Parliamentary draftsman, and in 1927 took silk. In 1935 he became a judge of the Cape Provincial Division and was raised to the Appellate Division in 1939. Oxford awarded him its DCL (*honoris causa*) in 1953. He was Chancellor of the University of Cape Town from 1951 to 1966. In the opinion of a later Chief Justice, L. C. Steyn, Centlivres was 'well versed in the old authorities [but] his strength lay in the realm of statute law and case law'.[170]

HENRY ALLAN FAGAN (1889–1963),[171] Chief Justice from 1957 to 1959, was born at Tulbagh and educated at Victoria College, Stellenbosch, where he obtained a BA in Literature at the University of the Cape of Good Hope. He went to London University and was awarded an LL B in 1913. He was called to the bar by the Inner Temple in 1914. After a brief spell as the first professor of law at the University of Stellenbosch from 1919 to 1920, he practised at the Cape bar from 1920 to 1938 and took silk in 1927. He was a Member of Parliament from 1933 to 1943 and Minister of Native

---

[167] (1923) 40 *SALJ* 104. See his contribution 'The Roman-Dutch law in South Africa', in: *The Cambridge History of the British Empire*, vol. 8 (1963), 858 sqq.

[168] *Alpha*, (1950) 67 *SALJ* 333.

[169] Corder (n. 139), 41 sq.; Forsyth (n. 138), 8; Kahn (n. 69), 25; Roberts (n. 19), 353; F. St L. Searle, 'Hon. Mr Justice A. v. d. S. Centlivres', (1935) 52 *SALJ* 409 sqq.; 'Retirement of Mr J. Centlivres, Chief Justice of South Africa', (1957) 74 *SALJ* 1 sqq.; Ellison Kahn, '*In memoriam*: The Hon. A. van der S. Centlivres', (1966) 83 *SALJ* 387 sqq.; L. C. Steyn, 'The late Hon. A. van der S. Centlivres', (1967) 84 *SALJ* 87 sq.

[170] Steyn, (1967) 84 *SALJ* 87.

[171] Corder (n. 139), 44 sq.; Kahn (n. 69), 54 sqq.; C. G. Hall, 'The Hon. Mr Justice H. A. Fagan', (1943) 60 *SALJ* 1 sqq.; 'The New Chief Justice: Mr Justice Fagan', (1957) 74 *SALJ* 6; 'Retirement of Mr Justice Fagan', (1959) 76 *SALJ* 117 sq.; 'Senator The Hon. H. A. Fagan', (1964) 81 *SALJ* 127 sq.

Affairs from 1933 to 1939. Thereafter he returned to practice, and in 1943 was raised to the bench of the Cape Provincial Division. He was made a Judge of Appeal in 1950. He was 'a notable exponent of *petere fontes*—he is said to be one of the very few judges who went to the original *Digest* and Voet before looking at the translations'.[172] His judicial work apart, Fagan also made a notable contribution to the development of Afrikaans literature.

3. Notable Judges of Appeal to 1961

During the Union, the Appellate Division was served by several Judges of Appeal who, although not elevated to the position of Chief Justice, in certain instances outshone the incumbents of that office. Here one thinks in particular of Sir JOHN GILBERT KOTZÉ (1849–1940),[173] Judge of Appeal from 1922 to 1927, who had served as a judge since 1877 (apart from a period of five years). Kotzé was born in Cape Town and educated at the South African College. He read law at London University, obtaining an LL B in 1873. The Council of Legal Education awarded him a Senior Exhibition in the Common Law in 1872 and he read in the chambers of Dr David Lyell of 11 King's Bench Walk, and then with William Willis QC. He was called to the bar by the Inner Temple on 30 April 1874 and, on admission to the Cape bar on 18 August 1874, he practised at Cape Town until 1876 before moving to Grahamstown.

In 1877 he was appointed a judge of the High Court of the Transvaal and, four years later, following the retrocession, became the Chief Justice.[174] During this period he completed his translation and annotation of Simon van Leeuwen's *Rooms-Hollands-Regt,* under the title *Commentaries on the Roman Dutch Law.*[175]

Following a serious difference of opinion between Kotzé and President Kruger concerning the case of *Brown v. Leyds* in 1898, in a highly publicized episode the President dismissed his Chief Justice.[176] Kotzé returned (briefly) to practice at the Cape bar until his appointment in 1900 as Attorney-General of Rhodesia. He took silk in 1902, and in 1903 was

---

[172] (1959) 76 *SALJ* 117.

[173] *Dictionary of South African Biography*, vol. I (1968), 438 sqq.; Corder (n. 139), 37; Kahn (n. 69), 115 sqq.; Randell (n. 66), 18 sqq.; Roberts (n. 19), 367 sq.; W. A. Shaw, *University of London, The Historical Record 1836–1912* (1912), 247; W. H. Somerset Bell, *Bygone Days* (1933), 139 sqq.; Anthony Trollope, *South Africa*, vol. 2 (1878), 121; 'The Hon. J. G. Kotzé', (1903) 20 *SALJ* 101 sqq.; 1934 3 *SALT* 178; 'Extracts from letters written by Sir John Kotzé to Professor R. W. Lee, 1911 to 1936', (1950) 67 *SALJ* 174 sqq., 265 sqq. See also Kotzé's *Biographical Memoirs and Reminiscences*, vol. I (1934), vol. II (1949).

[174] For details see (1903) 20 *SALJ* 103.

[175] Published in 2 vols. in London, 1882–6. See Hahlo/Kahn (n. 48), 555, fn. 53.

[176] (1897) 4 OR 17; see (1903) 20 *SALJ* 108 sq.; and see Kahn, (1958) 75 *SALJ* 411 sqq.; Nathan, (1932) 1 *SALT* 156.

appointed a judge at the Eastern Districts Court at Grahamstown. At this time a commentator noted:

As a Roman-Dutch lawyer he is one of the most able in South Africa. It may be said that he and Sir Henry de Villiers have done more than any other living lawyer to expound and settle the principles and more obscure points of the Roman-Dutch system of law, although it may be added, they have not always seen eye to eye.[177]

Another commentator remarked that he 'wedded to his accurate knowledge of the Dutch authorities a more scientific conception of jurisprudence [than Sir Henry de Villiers]'.[178]

Kotzé was Judge President of the Eastern Districts Court from 1903 until 1913. He then took up a position on the bench of the Cape Provincial Division. He became Judge President of that court in 1920 and occupied this post until his elevation to the Appellate Division in 1922. Many honours came his way. In 1917 he was knighted. The University of the Cape of Good Hope awarded him an LL D *honoris causa* in 1912, as also did the University of Cape Town in 1927 and the University of the Witwatersrand in 1939.

Another notable appointment was that of CHRISTIAN GEORGE MAASDORP (1848–1926),[179] Judge of Appeal from 1910 to 1922. Born at Malmesbury in the Cape Colony, he went to school in Graaff-Reinet and obtained a Second Class Certificate in Literature and Science of the Cape Board of Examiners in 1867. A year later he achieved the First Class Certificate. Following the University Incorporation Amendment Act 1896, Maasdorp took the Cape degree of MA, his entitlement as the holder of the First and Second Class Certificates. He was called to the bar by the Inner Temple on 6 June 1871 and admitted to the Cape bar on 3 August 1871. He subsequently practised at Griqualand West and in Grahamstown. He was Attorney-General of the Transvaal from 1877 to 1880, then returned to the Cape bar. From 1885 to 1896 he was a judge of the Eastern Districts Court at Grahamstown, and from 1896 to 1910 a judge of the Cape Supreme Court[180].

Sir HENRY HUBERT JUTA (1857–1930),[181] Judge of Appeal from 1920 to 1923, was born in Cape Town where he attended the South African College. He then went up to the University of London, where he obtained an LL B, before being called to the bar by the Inner Temple on 17 September 1880. He was admitted to the Cape bar on 14 September 1880 and practised there from 1880 to 1914. Juta took silk in 1893. In political

---

[177] (1903) 20 *SALJ* 110.   [178] Nathan, (1932) 1 *SALT* 14.

[179] Corder (n. 139), 26, 36; Roberts (n. 19), 370; 'The Hon. C. G. Maasdorp', (1907) 24 *SALJ* 129 sqq.; 'The Hon. C. G. Maasdorp', (1914) 31 *SALJ* 426.

[180] 'As Euclid viewed geometry, so does Mr Justice Maasdorp deal with his cases': (1907) 24 *SALJ* 131.

[181] Corder (n. 139), 36 sq.; Kahn (n. 69), 106 sqq.; Roberts (n. 19), 366; R. P. B. Davis, 'The Honourable Sir Henry Hubert Juta, Kt.', (1915) 32 *SALJ* 1 sqq.

life he was Speaker of the House of Assembly from 1896 to 1898. He was knighted in 1897. He was appointed Judge President of the Cape Provincial Division in 1914 and held this position until his elevation to the Appellate Division. Of his judicial abilities it is said that he had a sound knowledge of the law coupled with 'a robust common sense and, above all, an admirable "court manner" '.[182] He is probably best known, today, for reporting the cases of the Cape Supreme Court in the period from 1880 to 1893. Juta was a nephew of Karl Marx.

FREDERICK WILLIAM BEYERS (1867–1938),[183] a native of Paarl, was educated at the South African College and was awarded a BA (1900) and an LL B (1901) by the University of the Cape of Good Hope, the latter with distinction. After a period as attorney with the Johannesburg firm of Tredgold, Steytler, and Beyers he was admitted to the Johannesburg bar on 1 March 1905. Much of his life thereafter was spent in politics. Nevertheless, he was a Judge of Appeal from 1932 to 1937. He is notable for being appointed straight to the Appellate Division without first holding an appointment in one of the provincial divisions. He was the first to write judgments of the Court in Afrikaans.

BENJAMIN ARTHUR TINDALL (1879–1963),[184] Judge of Appeal from 1938 to 1949, was born at Leliefontein (Namaqualand) and educated at Victoria College, Stellenbosch. Here he obtained a first-class BA in Literature. An LL B followed in 1901. After a brief period in the Cape Civil Service Innes, Chief Justice of the Transvaal, appointed him as his private secretary in March 1902. He was admitted to the Cape bar on 5 February 1903, and one month later to the Pretoria bar. From 1902 to 1910 he was an official reporter for the Transvaal Supreme Court. Tindall practised at Pretoria until 1922, taking silk in 1919. In 1922 he was appointed a judge of the Transvaal Provincial Division. It was noted that 'the new judge is a quick, conscientious and indefatigable worker, and he will bring a thorough knowledge of Roman-Dutch law and a highly developed legal mind to bear on the many difficult and intricate legal problems which call for decision by the Transvaal judiciary'.[185] He was Judge President from 1937 to 1938.[186]

REGINALD PERCY BASIL DAVIS (1881–1948)[187] was never

---

[182] Davis, (1915) 32 *SALJ* 6.

[183] Corder (n. 139), 39 sq.; Kahn (n. 69), 6 sqq.; Roberts (n. 19), 349; 'Die weledele F. W. Beyers, KC', (1924) 41 *SALJ* 417 sq.

[184] Corder (n. 139), 41; Kahn (n. 69), 265 sqq.; Roberts (n. 19), 378 sq.; 'The Hon. Mr Justice Tindall', (1923) 40 *SALJ* 245 sq.; L. C. Steyn, '*In memoriam*: The Hon. B. A. Tindall', (1963) 80 *SALJ* 164 sq.

[185] (1923) 40 *SALJ* 246.

[186] At the time of his death Steyn CJ noted that 'his expositions of our law command respect and are not lightly to be departed from': (1963) 80 *SALJ* 165.

[187] Kahn (n. 69), 35; Roberts (n. 19) 354 sq.; F. St L. Searle, 'The Hon. Mr Justice R. P. B. Davis', (1936) 53 *SALJ* 147 sqq.; E. F. Watermeyer, 'Tribute to the late Mr Justice R. P. B. Davis', (1949) 66 *SALJ* 1 sqq.

appointed to a permanent position on the Appellate Division, but served with considerable success as an Acting Judge of Appeal from 1944 to 1947. He was born in London and educated at the South African College School and the Diocesan College School (Bishops) in Cape Town, followed by a period at Harrow. On his return to South Africa in 1900 he was an articled clerk with Van Zyl and Buissinné. He took a BA (Hons.) in Classics from the University of the Cape of Good Hope in 1903. Armed with the Porter Scholarship he proceeded to New College, Oxford where he graduated with a BA (Jurisprudence), Second Class, in 1907. On 15 January 1908 he was called to the bar by the Inner Temple but returned immediately to Cape Town, where he was admitted to practice on 27 February 1908. During this period he was assistant editor of the *South African Law Journal* from 1913 to 1922[188] and General Editor of the South African Law Reports from 1924. He was also a part-time Lecturer in Law at the University of Cape Town from 1914 to 1923.

Davis took silk in 1924. He was a judge of the Cape Provincial Division from 1935 to 1948 and Judge President in 1948. On his death Mr Justice Watermeyer, the Chief Justice, noted:

he has been a stout upholder of our Roman-Dutch legal system and his scholarship and familiarity with old authorities as well as his readiness to discuss and throw light upon its obscurities have been invaluable; his reported judgments contain many useful expositions of the law.[189]

LEOPOLD GREENBERG (1885–1964)[190] was a Judge of Appeal from 1943 to 1955. He was born at Calvinia, Orange Free State, educated at Grey College, Bloemfontein, and obtained a BA (Hons.) from the University of the Cape of Good Hope in 1904. He obtained the LL B by private study in 1907 while working in an attorney's office in Johannesburg. He practised as attorney from 1909 to 1911 but was then admitted as an advocate and practised at Johannesburg until 1924. Although he only took silk in 1924, he was appointed almost immediately to the Transvaal bench, serving as Judge President from 1938 to 1943. G. A. Mulligan noted at this time: 'it is no limited opinion which considers that South Africa's youngest members of the judiciary will emerge as one of South Africa's greatest judges'.[191] He was

---

[188] See Ellison Kahn, 'The Birth and Life of the South African Law Journal', (1983) 100 *SALJ* 605 sq.

[189] Watermeyer (1949) 66 *SALJ* 2.

[190] Corder (n. 139), 32, 43; Forsyth (n. 138), 9; Kahn (n. 69), 70 sqq.; Roberts (n. 19), 32; 'Mr Justice Greenberg', (1926) 43 *SALJ* 1 sq.; (1932) 1 *SALT* 169; G. A. Mulligan, 'Retirement of the Hon. Mr Justice Greenberg', (1955) 72 *SALJ* 1 sqq.; '*In memoriam*: The Hon. L. Greenberg', (1964) 81 *SALJ* 405 sqq.; Zimmermann (1995) 29 Israel Law Review 274 sq.

[191] Mulligan, (1955) 72 *SALJ* 43. Ellison Kahn, 'Jews who have risen to eminence in South African Law', in: Leon Feldberg (ed.), *South African Jewry* (1965), cols. 80 sqq. describes Greenberg as one of the giants of the South African judiciary, though not 'absolutely at home in the black letter law' of the old Roman and Roman-Dutch authorities.

awarded an LL D *honoris causa* by both the University of the Witwatersrand and the University of Cape Town, and the Hebrew University, Jerusalem named its Institute for Forensic Medicine after him. In his funeral oration Steyn CJ stated:

In the thirty-one years during which he served on the Bench, his name came to be a name of eminence, associated with many decisions which have gone into the exposition and shaping of our law. He is one of those who has left a large and beneficial heritage of legal learning. His judgments are characterized by thoroughness and clarity of language, and bear the imprint of a fair and vigorous mind acutely responsive to the merits and demerits of contentions advanced. His ready perception of essential issues, the swiftness with which he detected and laid bare flaws in an argument, and his power of orderly exposition, conferred upon him a remarkable proficiency in giving impromptu judgments. Some of them are known to be among his best.[192]

OSCAR HENDRIK HOEXTER (1893–1970)[193] was a Judge of Appeal from 1949 to 1963.[194] He was born and educated in Rouxville, Orange Free State. On matriculating, he was awarded the Thomas Robertson Bursary to Grey University College, and graduated with a BA (Hons.) in Classics (First Class) from the University of the Cape of Good Hope. He went to Emmanuel College, Cambridge in 1911 and took a double First in the Economics Tripos under Keynes. In 1915 he held a research scholarship in banking and currency. During his time in Cambridge he was President of the Union. He was offered, but declined, a Fellowship at Columbia University in 1916 and returned to South Africa to become a clerk to Jacob de Villiers, then Judge President of the Transvaal Provincial Division. By private study he obtained an LL B from the University of the Cape of Good Hope in 1917. He practised at the Bloemfontein bar from 1918 to 1938 and took silk in 1929. From 1938 to 1944 he was a judge on the bench of South West Africa. He was then transferred to the Eastern Cape where he was Judge President from 1948 to 1949. On his retirement in 1963 a commentator noted:

To [the bare bones of his career] must be added the flesh that gives the picture of the man at work: the sharp intellect, the ability to read and absorb essentials with uncanny speed, the keen sense of humour, the wit, the friendliness. He has the reputation of being able to tear the guts out of an appeal record so devastatingly that appearance before him is, if not an ordeal, at least an experience. If his decisions are perhaps more renowned for their incisive analysis of complex facts and statutes than for their exposition and development of legal principle, there are still many that are memorable.[195]

[192] (1964) 81 *SALJ* 406.
[193] Corder (n. 139), 44; Kahn (n. 69), 90 sq.; Randell (n. 66), 62 sqq.; Roberts (n. 19), 364; 'Hon. Mr Justice O. H. Hoexter', (1940) 57 *SALJ* 241 sq.; 'Retirement of Mr Justice O. H. Hoexter', (1963) 80 *SALJ* 165 sqq.
[194] His son, G. G. Hoexter, was until recently also a Judge of Appeal.
[195] (1963) 80 *SALJ* 167.

Perhaps more famous than any of the above is OLIVER DENEYS
SCHREINER (1890–1980),[196] Judge of Appeal from 1945 to 1960. Born in
Cape Town he was educated at Rondebosch High School and the South
African College School. In 1910 he was awarded a BA (Hons.) by the
University of the Cape of Good Hope with a First in Classics. He was
awarded a Jamison Scholarship which enabled him to go to Trinity College,
Cambridge to read law. He came top in Part I of the Law Tripos in 1912
and was awarded the George Long Prize in Roman Law and Jurisprudence
and a Trinity College Senior Scholarship. In 1915, while on active service,[197]
he was granted the Cambridge degree of BA and in 1916 he was elected a
Fellow of Trinity College. He was called to the bar by the Inner Temple on
17 November 1919, following the award of a Yerburgh-Anderson
Scholarship. He then read in chambers with Wilfrid Greene (later Greene
MR) and with Geoffrey Lawrence (later Lord Oaksey).

On his return to South Africa in 1920, Schreiner practised at the
Johannesburg bar until 1937. In the early years of practice he taught part-
time at the University of the Witwatersrand. He took silk in 1935 and was
appointed a judge of the Transvaal Provincial Division in 1937. Following
his elevation to the Appellate Division in 1945 he might in the ordinary
course have become the Chief Justice, the practice until then being that the
senior judge of appeal was appointed to the post. He was, however, twice
passed over, first on the retirement of Centlivres in 1957 and then on that
of Fagan in 1959.[198] He was clearly regarded as politically unsafe by the
Nationalist government of the day, a reputation he had earned during the
great constitutional crisis of the fifties. With some justification, Schreiner JA
has therefore been described as 'the greatest Chief Justice South Africa
never had'.[199]

In a speech many years later, Mr Justice H. C. Nicholas of the Transvaal
Provincial Division remarked:

The whole legal profession was disappointed and dismayed when Schreiner was
passed over for the Chief Justiceship in 1957. He was the most senior of the judges
of appeal. His judicial stature placed him among the giants of the past: Lord de
Villiers, Sir James Rose Innes and Sir William Solomon. No other judge of appeal
had a higher claim to the office. . . . [W]e can see that it is unimportant to his pres-
tige that Schreiner JA did not become Schreiner CJ. What is important is that the
authority of his judgments remains undisturbed, and that the esteem, the respect,
the reverence in which he was universally held remain unimpaired.[200]

---

[196] Ellison Kahn (ed.), *Fiat Iustitia: Essays in Memory of Oliver Deneys Schreiner* (1983);
Kahn (n. 69), 218 sqq.; Roberts (n. 19), 374 sq.; 'Hon. Mr Justice O. D. Schreiner', (1938) 55
SALJ 1 sqq.; Ellison Kahn, 'Oliver Deneys Schreiner: the Man and his Judicial World', (1980)
97 *SALJ* 566 sqq.; *idem*, 'A Find of Oliver Schreiner Papers', (1993) 110 *SALJ* 801 sqq.
[197] He was later awarded the Military Cross for his conduct at the Battle of the Somme.
[198] See Kahn, (1980) 97 *SALJ* 574 sq.; *idem* (n. 196), 49 sqq.
[199] Kahn (n. 196), 1.   [200] Kahn, (1980) 97 *SALJ* 579.

On his retirement from the bench in 1960, a commentator noted:

Oliver Schreiner will take his place as one of South Africa's greatest judges, of the company of men like Henry de Villiers, James Rose Innes and William Solomon. His decisions have not only cleansed many dusty corners of our legal system, clarified what for so long had been opaque, simplified what for many had been complex: but have actively promoted that orderly and equitable advancement of the common law through judicial decision that is the hall-mark of a progressive society. His judgments are distinguished by their lucidity, their carefully marshalled, cogent and incisive reasons and their compelling persuasiveness.[201]

Schreiner was awarded three LL D degrees *honoris causa*: by the Universities of Cape Town (1958), Witwatersrand (1961), and Rhodes (1963). His recognition outside South Africa was such that in 1967 he was invited to deliver the Hamlyn Lectures at Cambridge on the subject 'The contribution of English law to South African law; and the Rule of Law in South Africa'.

FRANÇOIS PETRUS (TOON) VAN DEN HEEVER (1894–1956),[202] Judge of Appeal from 1948 to 1956 and a contemporary of Schreiner JA, was born at Heidelberg, Transvaal and educated at Ermelo. He read for a BA (Hons.) in Modern Languages (1916) at the Transvaal University College in Pretoria. After teaching for a few years, he was awarded an LL B after part-time study, in 1919. On graduating he became a clerk to Gregorowski J and then Gutsche J in South West Africa. He was at the bar at Windhoek from 1921 to 1926. Thereafter he was a Law Adviser to the Union Government from 1926 to 1928 and State Attorney from 1931 to 1933. He was raised to the bench in South West Africa in 1933 and served in that capacity until 1938 when he was transferred to the Orange Free State Provincial Division. He was Judge President of that Court in 1948 when he was raised to the Appellate Division. Centlivres CJ expressed the widely-shared view that:

Toon will always be remembered in legal history as an ardent exponent of the principles of Roman-Dutch law. He had an uncanny knowledge of those principles and the sources from which they sprang. Being an accomplished linguist, he was able to refer with ease to all the great writers on Roman-Dutch and Roman law.[203]

Van den Heever wrote two academic treatises: *Aquilian Damages in South African Law* appeared in 1945 and *Breach of Promise and Seduction in South African Law* in 1954. His work as a jurist aside, Van den Heever was also renowned as a man of letters, especially as an Afrikaans poet.

[201] (1961) 78 *SALJ* 12. See also Rumpff CJ's appreciation, cited in Kahn, (n. 200), 578 sq.
[202] Corder (n. 139), 44; Kahn (n. 69), 274 sqq.; 'The Hon. Mr Justice F. P. van den Heever', (1949) 66 *SALJ* 135 sqq. And see the 'Van den Heeveriana' collected by Kahn/Bamford, (1966) 83 *SALJ* 213 sq.
[203] A. S. van der S. Centlivres, 'In memoriam: Mr Justice F. P. Van den Heever', (1956) 73 *SALJ* 119.

IV. REPUBLIC (SINCE 1961)

1. Courts

On the establishment of the Republic of South Africa in 1961 there were no substantive changes to the structure of the courts, apart from the addition of Supreme Courts in the so-called 'Independent Homelands' (Transkei, Bophutatswana, Ciskei, and Venda) of the apartheid era. Since the momentous political changes of the early 1990s, a notable innovation was the establishment of a Constitutional Court, which is not subject to the jurisdiction of the Appellate Division of the Supreme Court.[204]

2. Chief Justices

The appointment of LUCAS CORNELIUS STEYN (1903–76)[205] as Chief Justice in 1959 was not without controversy. Born at Bothaville, Orange Free State, he was educated in Kroonstad and then at the University of Stellenbosch. Here he attained the degrees of BA (1923), LL B (1926), and LL D (1931), the last for a thesis entitled *Die Staat se Aanspreeklikheid vir Onregmatige Ampsdade* (The Responsibility of the State for Unlawful Official Actions). Steyn was a lecturer in law at Stellenbosch from 1927 to 1928, but following his admission as an advocate in 1928 he became assistant to the Attorney-General of South West Africa. He was himself appointed Attorney-General of South West Africa in 1931.

From 1933 to 1951 Steyn was a Government Law Adviser. He took silk in 1943. In his leisure time he produced a treatise entitled *Uitleg van Wette* (Interpretation of Statutes), published in 1946 and which remained for many years the standard text in this field. Steyn was on four occasions a member of the South African delegation to the United Nations. He represented the country in the International Court of Justice's deliberations over South West Africa. He was elevated to the bench of the Transvaal Provincial Division in 1951. This appointment deviated from the convention that judges should be selected from the ranks of practising senior advocates, and it provoked loud criticism. Attention was drawn to the new appointee's lack of practical experience in litigation. Nevertheless, he was

---

[204] Dion Basson, *South Africa's Interim Constitution: Text and Notes* (1994), 142 sqq.; Kahn, *Essays Corbett* (n. 116), 31 sqq.

[205] Forsyth (n. 138), 10; Kahn (n. 69), 255 sqq.; Ellison Kahn, 'Retirement of the Chief Justice, Mr Justice L. C. Steyn', (1971) 88 *SALJ* 1 sqq. For a highly critical assessment of his career see Edwin Cameron, 'Legal Chauvinism, Executive-mindedness and Justice: L. C. Steyn's Impact on South African Law', (1982) 99 *SALJ* 38 sqq. See also David Dyzenhaus, 'L. C. Steyn in Perspective', (1982) 99 *SALJ* 380 sqq. A volume of essays in L. C. Steyn's honour has appeared under the title *Petere Fontes: LC Steyn-Gedenkbundel* (ed. D. J. Joubert, undated).

made a Judge of Appeal in 1955 and served as Chief Justice from 1959 until 1971. One highly critical review of his chief justiceship argues that:

L. C. Steyn had a towering but parsimonious intellect; that he was a scrupulous but ungenerous judge; that his attempt to rid South African law of its unique and fundamental connection with English law was not only jurisprudentially and historically unjustified, but ultimately quixotic; that he was an unfettered but—of his own volition—executive-minded judge; and that during his term of office a legal temperature, already chill for the survival of human values and the preservation of fundamental freedoms, turned several degrees colder.[206]

Steyn's successor as Chief Justice in 1971, NEWTON OGILVIE THOMPSON (1904–92),[207] was born at Butterworth, Cape and educated at St Andrew's College, Grahamstown. Thereafter he attended the University of Cape Town, obtaining a BA and an LL B (with distinction) in 1924. After a period as registrar to Sir Malcolm Searle, the then Judge President of the Cape Provincial Division, he commenced practice at the Cape bar in 1926. He took silk in 1944; at the time his practice 'was one of the largest at the Cape Bar and he had earned for himself a reputation as one its hardest-working and most conscientious members'.[208] He was elevated to the bench of the Cape Provincial Division in 1949. In 1958 he became a Judge of Appeal, generally regarded as a strong appointment, with a reputation for being both sound and hard-working. His particular expertise was commercial cases, especially those involving income tax, trade marks, and patents. His period as Chief Justice was comparatively short (just less than three years) and not especially notable, though 'he proved a fine administrator'.[209] He was awarded two honorary doctorates, LL D *honoris causa*: by Rhodes University (1972) and the University of Cape Town (1974).

FRANS LOURENS HERMAN RUMPFF (1919–92),[210] successor to Ogilvie Thompson as Chief Justice in 1974 and Judge of Appeal from 1961 to 1974, was born at Standerton and educated at the Hogere Oost-Eind School, Pretoria. He then attended the University of Pretoria, obtaining the degrees of BA (1933) and LL B (1935). On graduating he joined the Department of Justice for a brief period before becoming a clerk to Maritz J.[211] He practised at the Pretoria bar from 1938 to 1953, taking silk in 1951. He was a judge of the Transvaal Provincial Division from 1953 to 1961, and

---

[206] For development of these themes see Cameron, (1982) 99 *SALJ* 38 sqq.

[207] Forsyth (n. 138), 10; The Hon. Mr Justice N. Ogilvie Thompson, (1949) 66 *SALJ* 375 sq.; M. M. Corbett, '*In memoriam*: The Hon. Newton Ogilvie Thompson', (1992) 109 *SALJ* 680 sqq.

[208] Corbett, (1992), 109 *SALJ* 681.   [209] Ibid.

[210] Forsyth (n. 138), 10; Ellison Kahn, 'Retirement of the Chief Justice, Mr Justice F. L. H. Rumpff', (1982) 99 *SALJ* 438 sqq.; M. M. Corbett, '*In memoriam*: The Hon. Frans Lourens Herman Rumpff', (1992) 109 *SALJ* 684 sqq.

[211] On Gerhardus Jacobus Maritz, judge of the Transvaal Provincial Division from 1930, see Roberts (n. 19) 371.

Judge President from 1959 to 1961. In 1961 Rumpff was raised to the Appellate Division. His *alma mater*, the University of Pretoria, honoured him with the award of an LL D *honoris causa* in 1978. Concerning private law legal doctrine, Rumpff CJ did not shy away from far-ranging innovations; thus, in *Administrateur, Natal v. Trust Bank van Afrika Bpk*[212] he opened the door for the recovery of pure economic loss according to Aquilian principles, and in *Minister van Polisie v. Ewels*[213] he equally boldly generalized delictual liability for omissions. At a gathering in his memory, Corbett CJ remarked that:

Hy het 'n groot liefde vir, en 'n helder insig in, ons oorspronklike regsbronne, die Romeinse reg en die Romeins-Hollandse reg, gehad en sonder om dogmaties of fanatiek daaroor te wees, het hy hom beywer vir die handhawing van die egte beginsels van ons gemene reg en, waar nodig, die verwydering van uitheemse neigings in ons regspleging wat nie by ons regstelsel ingepas het nie. Nogtans het hy meermaal getoon dat hy begrip het vir die waarde van 'n vergelykende benadering tot regsprobleme en in dié verband het hy by tye elders gesoek om te sien of die jurisprudensies van, byvoorbeeld, Engeland en Wes-Europa, oplossing bied vir die besondere vraag waarmee hy gemoeid was.[214]

On the retirement of Rumpff CJ in 1982, he was succeeded by PIETER JACOBUS RABIE (1917–),[215] who had been Judge of Appeal since 1970. Rabie CJ was born at Jacobsdal, Orange Free State and educated at Koffiefontein and then the University of Stellenbosch. Here he obtained two MA degrees *cum laude*, in Latin and in Greek. He was awarded a Queen Victoria Scholarship in 1939 and proceeded to the University of Michigan where he gained a Ph.D. in Latin in 1943. On his return to South Africa he was a Lecturer in Latin and Greek at Stellenbosch from 1944 to 1948. During this period he studied part-time for the LL B and was awarded the degree *cum laude* in 1948. He immediately commenced practice at the Pretoria bar and took silk in 1962. In 1965 he appeared before the International Court of Justice at The Hague in the South West Africa case. One year later, in 1966, he became a judge of the Transvaal Provincial Division. During his period of office as a Judge of Appeal he was the Chairman of the South African Law Commission. On reaching the official

---

[212] 1979 (3) SA 824 (A). [213] 1975 (3) SA 590 (A).

[214] (He had a great love of, and a clear insight into, our original sources of law, i.e. Roman and Roman-Dutch law, and, without being dogmatic or fanatical about it, he has endeavoured to apply the true principles of our common law and, wherever necessary, to remove foreign inclinations in our administration of justice that did not fit in with our legal system. Nevertheless, he has demonstrated on several occasions that he appreciated the value of a comparative approach to legal problems, and in this context he has, time and again, made the effort to find out whether the jurisprudence of, for example, England and Western Europe, offers solutions for the specific question at issue): Corbett, (1992) 109 *SALJ* 684 sq.

[215] *Who's Who in South African Law* (1992), 211; Forsyth (n. 138), 10; (1982) 99 *SALJ* 448 sqq.

retirement age in 1987 he served two more years as Acting CJ until the post went to Michael McGregor Corbett.

MICHAEL McGREGOR CORBETT (1923–),[216] the present Chief Justice, was born at Pretoria where his father was the Commissioner for Inland Revenue. He completed his schooling at Rondebosch Boys High School in Cape Town. He then enrolled at the University of Cape Town where he was awarded a BA in 1941 and, on his return from active service, an LL B in 1946. On graduating, Corbett was awarded an Elsie Ballot Scholarship and entered Trinity Hall, Cambridge. Here he obtained a First in Part II of the Law Tripos (BA, 1947) and, one year later, an LL B, also First Class. On his return to the Cape from South Africa, Corbett read in the chambers of Marius Diemont (later to become Judge of Appeal) for about six weeks and then commenced practice. He made rapid progress, taking silk in 1961. In 1960 he was responsible, with J. L. Buchanan, for an important practitioner's treatise: *The Quantum of Damages in Bodily and Fatal Injury Cases*. He was appointed to the bench of the Cape Provincial Division in 1963 and was made a Judge of Appeal in 1974. During this period of his life he made another important contribution to South African legal literature by co-authoring the standard textbook on the law of succession.[217] He assumed the chief justiceship in 1989 and has served in this capacity with great distinction. Five universities have awarded him the degree of LL D *honoris causa*: Cape Town (1982), Orange Free State (1990), Rhodes (1990), Pretoria (1993), and Witwatersrand (1994). On 13 May 1991 he was elected an Honorary Bencher of Lincoln's Inn and on 13 June 1992 Trinity Hall, Cambridge elected him to an Honorary Fellowship. Although reaching the statutory retirement age of seventy in 1993, his term of office has twice been extended and he is now due to retire in June 1996.[218]

---

[216] Forsyth (n. 138), 8; Kahn (n. 116), 1 sqq.; Ellison Kahn, 'Mr Justice M. M. Corbett, Chief Justice', (1989) 106 *SALJ* 147 sqq. In 1995 a *Festschrift* in his honour has been published: Ellison Kahn (ed.), *The Quest for Justice: Essays in Honour of Michael McGregor Corbett*.

[217] *The Law of Succession in South Africa* (1980). The other authors are H. R. Hahlo, Gys Hofmeyr, and Ellison Kahn.

[218] Among the judges who have, over the last thirty years, served on the Appellate Division, two names will be mentioned particularly often in the pages that follow. (Dr C.P.) Joubert JA today appears to be the specialist on old authorities to whom cases requiring a thorough historical investigation seem usually to be assigned. As a young man, he studied first at Pretoria, then at Leyden and published a thesis on '*Stigting in die Romeins-Hollandse Reg en in die Suid-Afrikaanse Reg*' (The Foundation in Roman Law and in South African Law) (1951). The other judge renowned for his meticulous probing of Roman and Roman-Dutch sources was Jansen JA. His judgments, however, display a fundamentally different approach towards the old authorities; this comes out particularly clearly in the conflicting views of Joubert JA and Jansen JA on the role of equity in contract law; cf. the clash of opinion in *Bank of Lisbon and South Africa Ltd v. De Ornelas* 1988 (3) SA 580 (A) 592 sqq., 611 sqq.: Reinhard Zimmermann, 'Roman Law in a Mixed Legal System: The South African Experience', in: Robin Evans-Jones (ed.), *The Civil Law Tradition in Scotland* (1995), 58 sq. Concerning Jansen JA, see the analysis by Carole Lewis, 'Towards an Equitable Theory of Contract: The Contribution of Mr.

V. CONCLUSION

'The courts are the capitals of law's empire, and judges are its princes.'[219] In South Africa the reputation of some of the princes is not without blemish, but the country has nonetheless produced judges of great moral stature.[220] The constraints of this book dictate that the above biographies must be concise, and therefore only the briefest of glimpses could be given of the judges' strengths and weaknesses. The emphasis has been on highlighting the attitudes of the judges towards the twin constituent elements of South African law.

Among those judges who have played a prominent role in the crafting of South Africa's mixed legal system during the last two centuries, both Roman Dutch and English law have had powerful champions; the result is that each of these roots is firmly embedded in the system. Education clearly was an important influence in determining the approach of each individual judge, but often the predictive elements in their biographies failed to produce the expected results. Thus, on one hand, the attitudes of judges like John Wylde and William Menzies or O. D. Schreiner and L.C. Steyn mirrored their legal training closely. On the other hand, the training of Sir Henry Connor or F. L. H. Rumpff contained nothing which could have explained their subsequent appreciation of, respectively, Roman-Dutch and English law. Of course, socio-political factors were of some consequence in the making of the mixed system, with support for either English or Roman-Dutch law (especially in the last fifty years) becoming an extension of the political struggle between the Afrikaans- and English-speaking sections of the erstwhile Settler community. Often, however, the facts also contradict this generalization. Thus, for instance, Henry Fagan was a strong opponent of the Government (having entered opposition politics after his retirement[221]) but a great exponent of Roman-Dutch law; similarly, the current Chief Justice, Michael Corbett, has staunchly defended the rule of law, without inclining to remould South African private law in the English image: for he displays a great knowledge of, and respect for, the Roman-Dutch authorities.

Justice E. L. Jansen to the South African Law of Contract', (1991) 108 *SALJ* 249 sqq.; on *Bank of Lisbon* see the contribution by Reinhard Zimmermann to the present volume. A judge who 'wrote with a raciness of style, a verve and a turn of phrase all of his own [and who was] fond of rich imagery and flights of rhetoric' was Holmes JA, on whom see Kahn (n. 69), 95 sq.; for a collection of famous 'Holmesiana', see J. J. Gauntlett, (1974) 37 *THRHR* 169 sqq.

[219] Ronald Dworkin, *Law's Empire* (1986), 407.

[220] See generally Corder (n. 139); Forsyth (n. 138); Stephen Ellmann, *In a Time of Trouble: Law and Liberty in South Africa's State of Emergency* (1992).

[221] Adrienne E. van Blerk, 'Judicial Appointments: Some Reflections' (1992) 55 *THRHR* 559, 573.

Perhaps the most important fact to emerge from these biographies is that so many of the important judges consciously strove to create a balance between Roman-Dutch and English law. The even-handed approach and intellectual honesty of the early protagonists of the South African legal system, Lord de Villiers and Sir James Rose Innes, set a tone which was to survive all later partisan attempts to narrow the base of South African law. As a result, it is widely accepted today that South African law has acquired its own identity which is neither purely Roman-Dutch nor purely English.[222]

[222] D. P. Visser, 'Daedalus in the Supreme Court: The Common Law Today', (1986) 49 *THRHR* 127 sqq.; Zimmermann, *Civil Law Tradition* (n. 218), 50 sqq.

4: *The Interaction of Substantive Law and Procedure*

H. J. ERASMUS

I. INTRODUCTION

South African law is an uncodified civil law system with Roman-Dutch law, and originally Roman law, as its major formative element. Since the beginning of the nineteenth century a strong thread of English law has been woven into the fabric of that system. In particular, procedural techniques have largely assimilated the English patterns. The purpose of this essay is to examine the effect of the superimposition upon the Roman-Dutch law, during the formative years of modern South African law, of a judicial and procedural framework of common law origin.[1] This is preceded by a brief sketch of the nature of civil procedure in Roman-Dutch law,[2] and of the main features of the procedural system in use at the Cape under Dutch rule.

II. ROMAN-DUTCH LAW

The medieval romano-canonical (learned) procedure spread through the countries of Europe from the twelfth century onwards.[3] It established itself in the French courts, from whence, from about the middle of the fourteenth century, it started to exert its influence in the Low Countries. The *Practijke Civile* of Philips Wielant (written about 1519 and printed in Antwerp in 1558) played a vital role in the penetration of the learned procedure in the Low Countries: '[F]irst in Flanders, then in Brabant and after the middle of the sixteenth century, in Holland, medieval practice was gradually replaced by new forms of process typical of the modern age'.[4] Particularly

---

[1] This Chapter is an elaboration of a preliminary survey of the topic which I undertook in an article entitled 'The Interaction of Substantive and Procedural Law: the Southern African Experience in Historical and Comparative Perspective', (1990) 1 *Stellenbosch LR* 348 sqq.

[2] For a comprehensive discusssion see Gero R. Dolezalek, 'Das Zivilprozessrecht', in: Robert Feenstra, Reinhard Zimmermann (eds.), *Das römisch-holländische Recht: Fortschritte des Zivilrechts im 17. und 18. Jahrhundert* (1992), 59 sqq.

[3] On the spread of the learned procedure in Europe see R. C. van Caenegem, 'History of European Civil Procedure', in: *International Encyclopedia of Comparative Law*, vol. XVI, ch. 2 (1973).

[4] Van Caenegem (n. 3), 34.

influential in the northern Netherlands was Joost van Damhouder's *Praxis rerum civilium*[5] which, in fact, was merely a Latin version of Wielant's work.[6]

Procedure in the Low Countries was affected not only by the practice of the French courts but also by that of the *Reichskammergericht*.[7] A major influence in this regard was the commentary of Andreas Gail on the practice and procedure of that Court.[8] It was regarded by the Dutch jurists as a work of the highest authority and was quoted by them as if it were a work on the practice of their own courts.[9] A Dutch translation appeared in 1656.[10]

In the Republic of the United Netherlands, created by the Union of Utrecht in 1579, no court had jurisdiction, either original or appellate, over the whole of the Republic. Each of the seven constituent provinces had its own judicial hierarchy.[11] In the province of Holland the inferior courts were those of *schout* and *schepenen*. Next in rank were the courts of *baljuw en welgeboren mannen* (*Hooghe Vierschaar*). The *Hof van Holland, Zeeland en West-Vriesland* was the supreme court.

As a result of the establishment of the Republic of the United Netherlands, the jurisdiction which the *Groote Raad van Mechelen* had exercised over the northern Netherlands ceased to exist. In an endeavour to create a supreme court with jurisdiction over the entire Republic, the *Staten van Holland* in 1581 established a *Hooge Raad* with its seat in The Hague. The other provinces, however, with the exception of Zeeland, declined to submit to the jurisdiction of the *Hooge Raad* which thus became known as the *Hooge Raad van Holland en Zeeland*.[12]

[5] (1567), also published in Dutch under the title *Practijke in civile saecke* (1626). See further W. G. P. E. Wedekind, *Bijdrage tot de Kennis van de Ontwikkeling van de Procesgang in civiele Zaken van het Hof van Holland in de eerste Helft van de zestiende Eeuw* (1938).

[6] On the 'plundering' (as he terms it) of Wielant's work by Damhouder, see J. C. de Wet, *Die Ou Skrywers in Perspektief* (1988), 114; cf. A. A. Roberts, *A South African Legal Bibliography* (1942), 101.

[7] See Paul L. Nève, 'Enige Opmerkingen over de Betekenis van het Rijkskamergerecht voor de Receptie van het geleerde Recht in de Nederlanden (1495–1550)', (1980) 48 *Tijdschrift voor rechtsgeschiedenis* 151–79.

[8] *Practicarum observationum tam ad processum iudiciarium praesertim Imperialis Camerae quam causarum decisiones pertinentium libri duo* (1578/80). Colin B. Prest, *Interlocutory Interdicts* (1993), 18, fn. 64, observes that neither Philips Wielant nor Damhouder refer to the *mandament poenaal*, a remedy often mentioned by the Dutch jurists and frequently employed in the Dutch courts. The remedy derives from the *Mandatsprozess* of the *Reichskammergericht* and Gail is quoted as an authority on the *mandament poenaal* e.g. by Pieter Bort, *Nagelate Werken* (1745), 1, 25, 1; Simon van Leeuwen, *Het Rooms-Hollands-Regt* (1664), 5, 11, 10; Fransciscus Lievens Kersteman, *Hollandsch Rechtsgeleerd Woordenboek* (1768), 273; see further Prest, 14 sqq.

[9] See J. W. Wessels, *History of Roman Dutch Law* (1908), 234.

[10] *Observantien van de Kayserlyke Practyke, rakende so wel de judiciele processen [voornamentlijk der Kaiserlijke Kamere] als der selver saken decisien . . . uyt het Latijn overgeset door A. van Nispen* (1656).

[11] See H. R. Hahlo, Ellison Kahn, *The South African Legal System and its Background* (1968), 473–6, 541–3.

[12] A. S. de Blécourt, 'De Geboorte van den Hoogen Raad van Holland en Zeeland', (1920–21) 2 *Tijdschrift voor rechtsgeschiedenis* 428 sqq.

Proceedings in the *Hof van Holland, Zeeland en West-Vriesland* were conducted in accordance with the Instructions issued by Charles V on 20 August 1531.[13] These instructions, which were modelled on the Instructions for the Council of Flanders, in turn provided the inspiration for the instructions of the *Hooge Raad* of 31 May 1582.[14] In the courts of *baljuw en welgeboren mannen* proceedings were conducted in accordance with the Ordinance on Civil Procedure of 1580.[15] In addition, many cities in Holland had their own local ordinances on civil procedure; Merula mentions the examples of Amsterdam, Leiden, Rotterdam, and The Hague.[16]

The various procedural ordinances of the superior and inferior courts in Holland contained rules of practice ultimately derived from the romano-canonical procedure which had originated in the medieval ecclesiastical courts. The law of civil procedure in Holland, like Roman-Dutch law in general, was therefore not peculiarly Dutch but formed part and parcel of the European *ius commune* of the fifteenth to the eighteenth centuries.[17] In their commentaries on the law of civil procedure in Holland, the Dutch jurists sought guidance from the Corpus Juris Civilis, the Corpus Juris Canonici, and the works of scholars from the entire area of the *ius commune*: notably France, Italy, Spain, and Germany.[18] The principal writers on the law of civil procedure were Willem van Alphen,[19] Gerard van Wassenaar,[20] Paulus Merula,[21] Simon van Leeuwen[22] and Johannes van der Linden.[23]

III. THE CAPE OF GOOD HOPE (1652–1827)

This period can be subdivided into (i) the rule of the Dutch East India Company (1652–1795); (ii) the first British occupation (1795–1803); (iii) the Batavian period (1803–1806), and (iv) the second British occupation up to the time of the First Charter of Justice (1806–27).

---

[13] Instructie van den Hove van Hollandt, Zeelandt ende Vrieslandt, *Groot Placaet-Boek*, vol. II, 703 sqq.

[14] Ordonnantie ende Instructie van den Hoogen Raedt van Appel in Hollandt, *Groot Placaet-Boek*, vol. II, 789 sqq.; vol. V, 866 sqq. (A. S. de Blécourt, N. Japikse, *Klein Plakkaatboek van Nederland* (1919), 144 sqq.)

[15] Ordonnantie van de Iustitie binnen den steden en ten platten lande van Hollandt, *Groot Placaet-Boek*, vol. II, 695 sqq.; see also Paulus Merula, *Manier van Procederen in de Provintien van Holland, Zeeland ende West-Vriesland* (1705), 2, 1, 1.

[16] Merula (n. 15), 2, Synopsis Tit. I, fn. 1.   [17] See Dolezalek (n. 2), 61, 66.

[18] Ibid. (n. 2), 66.   [19] *Papegay ofte formulier-Boek* (1642).

[20] *Praktyk judicieel, ofte Instructie op de Forme en Manier van Procedeeren voor Hoven en Rechtbanken* (1660).

[21] See above, n. 15.   [22] *Manier van Procedeeren in civiele en criminele Saaken* (1664).

[23] *Verhandeling over de Judicieele Practijcq of Form van Procedeeren voor de Hoven van Holland gebruikelijk* (1794); see also his *Rechtsgeleerd Practicaal en Koopmans Handboek* (1806).

During this period the general organization of the administration of justice at the Cape remained remarkably consistent. Relatively few changes were made.[24] The *Raad van Justitie*, which came into being in 1656 as a specially composed council in judicial matters, was the highest civil and criminal court. Appeal could be brought against its judgments before the High Court of Justice at Batavia which, however, entailed great expense and delay.[25] During the first British occupation this appeal was abolished and in 1797 the governor was vested with an appellate jurisdiction in certain cases with the possibility of a further appeal to the King-in-Council. During the Batavian period (1803–6) appeals lay to the *Hoog Nationaal Gerechtshof* in The Hague. The procedure established in 1797 was re-introduced during the second British occupation with the creation of a Court of Appeal in Civil Cases headed by the governor, with a final appeal to the Privy Council in London. The period 1806–27 saw further changes in the form of the introduction of a Vice-Admiralty Court, the creation of circuit courts in 1811, the opening of the doors of the courts to the public in 1813, and the replacement in 1825–6 of Dutch by English as the official language of the courts.[26]

At the lower level there were several courts. In 1682 a court was established for the hearing of petty cases, the *Collegie van Commissarissen van de Cleijne Zaken*. In 1711 this was merged with the *Collegie van Commissarissen van Huwelijks Zaken* which had come into being in 1676, charged mainly with the issuing of certificates of non-impediment to marriage, necessary for the publication of banns and the subsequent religious marriage ceremony. Expansion of the settlement at the Cape into the interior led to the establishment of local governments of *landdrosten* and *heemraden*, the first being established at Stellenbosch in 1682. In the outlying areas these colleges of *landdrosten* and *heemraden* served as courts of law in petty civil and criminal cases. Appeal lay to the *Raad van Justitie* in Cape Town.[27]

[24] See G. G. Visagie, *Regspleging en Reg aan die Kaap van 1652 tot 1806* (1969), 40 sqq. (parts of this work have also been published under the title 'Die Regsbedeling aan die Kaap onder die VOC', in 1963 *Acta Juridica* 118 sqq.); Hahlo/Kahn (n. 11) 566 sqq.; H. R. Hahlo and Ellison Kahn, *The Union of South Africa: The Development of its Laws and Constitution* (1960), 200 sqq.; P. J. van der Merwe, *Regsinstellings en Reg aan die Kaap van 1806 tot 1834* (unpublished LL D thesis, University of the Western Cape, 1984); G. G. Visagie, 'The Law applied at the Cape from 1652 to 1828', in: G. G. Visagie *et al.*, *Die Kaapse Regspraak-Projek: Die Raad van Justisie, Hofstukke en Uitsprake wat betrekking het op siviele sake 1806–1827* (1989), also published in 1988 *Miscellanea Forensia Historica* 325 sqq.

[25] See C. H. van Zyl, 'The Batavian and the Cape *plakaten*. An Historical Narrative', (1908) 25 *SALJ* 246, 260.

[26] Hahlo/Kahn (n. 24), 204; Van der Merwe (n. 24), 64 sqq.; G. G. Visagie, *Regsveranderinge aan die Kaap tussen 1823 en 1838* (unpublished MA thesis, University of Cape Town, 1954).

[27] On the inferior courts at the Cape see Visagie, *Regspleging* (n. 24), 52 sqq.; C. Graham Botha, 'The early inferior Courts of Justice at the Cape', (1921) 38 *SALJ* 406; P. J. Venter, 'Landdros en Heemraden', in: *Archives Year Book for South African History*, Third Year, vol. II (1940).

No rules of procedure were promulgated specifically for the Cape, under the rule of the Dutch East India Company.[28] From the documents of the *Raad van Justitie*, preserved in the Cape archives, it is clear that the civil procedure followed by the *Raad* was based on the ordinance on civil procure of 1580.[29] The works on civil procedure of the Roman-Dutch jurists were in regular use. The recorded cases contain references to the relevant books by Andreas Gail, Joost van Damhouder, Paulus Merula, Simon van Leeuwen, and Gerard van Wassenaar.[30] According to an inventory dating from 1793, the library of the *Raad van Justitie* contained works on civil procedure by those authors and by Willem de Groot and Willem van Alphen.[31]

Sir John Truter, the last president of the *Raad van Justitie*, confirmed the position outlined above in his evidence before the commission of inquiry into the administration of justice at the Cape.[32] In its report the commission stated that:

... the Forms of Civil Process have remained in the same state in which they had existed between the first Capture in 1796 and the evacuation of the Colony in 1803. They do not appear to vary in any great degree from the Forms that have been adopted in the Tribunals of those Countries in which the Civil Law has been retained ...[33]

A recent study[34] of the records of the *Raad van Justitie* in the Cape archives has shown that civil procedure at the Cape during the period from 1807 to 1827 showed only minor (local) variations from the procedure described by Johannes van der Linden,[35] the last of the Roman-Dutch writers on civil procedure, who gives an authoritative exposition of Dutch procedure at the end of the eighteenth century.

---

[28] On civil procedure at the Cape under the rule of the Dutch East India Company see Jerold Taitz, 'A further Tribute to the Charter of Justice', (1979) 96 *SALJ* 470 sqq.; C. Graham Botha, *The Public Archives of South Africa* (1928), 15 sqq.; Visagie, *Regspleging* (n. 24), 46.

[29] See above, n. 15.

[30] Visagie, *The Law Applied at the Cape from 1652 to 1828* (n. 24), 15; *idem*, *Regspleging* (n. 24), 46, fn. 49; Van der Merwe (n. 24), 231, 233.

[31] See Visagie, *Regspleging* (n. 24), *Bylae* III, 120–2. In *Bylae* II at 118 sq. Visagie reproduces the list of books sold at the auction of Aletta Corssenaar, the widow of governor A. van Kervel, which also contains all the principal Roman-Dutch writings on civil procedure.

[32] G. M. Theal, *Records of the Cape Colony* (1897–1905), vol. XXXIII, 364.

[33] Ibid. vol. XXVI, 5.

[34] G. G. Visagie et al., *Die Kaapse Regspraak-Projek: Die Siviele Appèlhof en die Raad van Justisie, Hofstukke en Uitsprake wat betrekking het op siviele sake 1806–1827: 'n Evaluëring van Capita Selecta uit bepaalde Gebiede van die Reg aan die Kaap* (1992), J 41; see also Taitz, (1979) 96 *SALJ* 473.

[35] See above, n. 23.

IV. THE CHARTERS OF JUSTICE

The British were not impresssed by the state of the administration of justice at the Cape.[36] In 1821 the Deputy Colonial Secretary, Henry Ellis, submitted a strongly critical report.[37] A commission was appointed in 1823 to look into the matter.[38] In its report, dated 6 September 1826, the commission recommended that the existing judicial machinery and procedural institutions be reshaped along English lines.[39] By letters patent of 24 August 1827, commonly known as the First Charter of Justice, the *Raad van Justitie* was replaced by the Supreme Court of the Colony of the Cape of Good Hope. The First Charter was superseded by the Second Charter constituted by letters patent of 4 May 1834.[40]

Following the First Charter, s. 31 of the Second Charter provided that the Supreme Court of the Colony of the Cape of Good Hope was to excercise its jurisdiction 'according to the laws now in force within Our said Colony, and all such other laws as shall at any time thereafter be made'.

Once the decision was taken to retain the Roman-Dutch law as the law of the Cape there could be no separate administration, as in English law, of law and equity. Hence the statement by Viscount Goderich, the Secretary for the Colonies, in a letter dated 5 August 1827 to Major-General Burke in Cape Town:[41] 'It results from this determination that the Office of Chancellor, as a distinct Judicial Office, will not be established by the Charter of Justice.'

Under the system introduced by the British at the Cape of Good Hope there was, therefore, neither a Court of Chancery nor a Chancery jurisdiction. The Charter of Justice provided for the creation of a unitary Supreme Court of the Colony of the Cape of Good Hope consisting of a chief justice and two puisne judges.[42]

The newly established Supreme Court of the Colony of the Cape of Good Hope was given extensive powers to make rules for the practice and pleading in civil matters.[43] Under s. 46 of the Charter of Justice, all rules and forms of practice, process, and proceeding made by the Supreme Court had

---

[36] C. Graham Botha, 'The early Influence of the English Law upon the Roman-Dutch law in South Africa', (1923) 40 *SALJ* 396–406.

[37] Theal (n. 32), vol. XIV, 183 sqq.

[38] The commissioners were John Thomas Brigge, a former chief justice of Trinidad, and Major W. M. G Colebrooke. See further Van der Merwe (n. 24), 239 sqq.

[39] Theal (n. 32), vol. XVII, 333 sqq.; vol. XXVIII, 1 sqq.

[40] On the Charters of Justice see Taitz (n. 28); Van der Merwe (n. 24), 287 sqq.; G. G. Visagie, *The Charter of Justice: A short commemorative history* (1978).

[41] Theal (n. 32), vol. XXXII, 256.   [42] S. 3, Second Charter of Justice.

[43] The power was conferred by s. 46 of the Charter of Justice. See H. J. Erasmus, 'The History of the Rule-making Power of the Supreme Court of South Africa', (1991) 108 *SALJ* 476–84.

to be framed 'so far as the circumstances of the said Colony may permit, . . . with reference to the corresponding rules and forms in use in Our Courts of record at Westminster'.

The first rules, promulgated in open court on 1, 24, and 31 January 1828 and 27 and 31 March 1828, were drafted by William Westbrooke Burton, second puisne judge of the Cape Supreme Court from 1827 to 1832.[44]

Since there was to be no separate administration of law and of equity, the forms of procedure taken over from England had to be adapted for use at the Cape.[45] The rules made provision for two forms of proceeding before the Supreme Court, namely proceedings by way of motion[46] and those by way of summons.[47] Proceedings by way of motion were reminiscent of the practice in the Court of Chancery in so far as they were mainly on paper and 'little adapted for the determination of controverted issues of fact'.[48] Proceedings by way of summons introduced a system of pre-trial pleading, by which the issues in dispute are defined for determination at a trial at which *viva voce* evidence is heard.

The rules provided for a modified form of common law pleading without any of the substantive elements of the English forms of action being integrated therein. The pleadings for which the rules made provision were the declaration, plea or answer, replication or reply, rejoinder, and pleadings in reconvention.[49] Further pleadings, bearing their English common law names,[50] were possible with leave of the court or of a judge in chambers. Rule 18 required the plaintiff to set out in his declaration 'the nature, extent

---

[44] See C. Graham Botha, 'The Honourable William Menzies 1795–1850', (1910) 33 *SALJ* 385, 394; Stephen Darryl Girvin, *The Influence of British Legal Education and Practice at the Bar on the Judges appointed to the Supreme Courts of Southern Africa 1827–1910* (unpublished Ph. D. thesis, University of Aberdeen, 1990), 222.

[45] See, in general, H. J. Erasmus, 'Historical Foundations of the South African Law of Civil Procedure', (1991) 108 *SALJ* 265–76.

[46] Rules 6 and 41, both promulgated on 1 January 1828.

[47] Rule 11, promulgated on 1 February 1828.

[48] Lord Bowen, 'Progress in the Administration of Justice during the Victorian Period', in: T. II. Ward (ed.), *The Reign of Queen Victoria: A Survey of Fifty Years of Progress*, vol. I (1887), 281, reprinted in: *Select Essays in Anglo-American Legal History* (compiled and edited by a Committee of the Association of American Law Schools) vol. I (1907), 517 sq.

[49] Claims in reconvention were recognized in Roman-Dutch procedure; see Merula (n. 15), 4, 43; Johannes Voet, *Commentarius ad Pandectas*, 5, 1, 78; Van der Linden, *Verhandeling over de Judicieele Practijcq* (n. 23), 2, 4, 12 sq. The term 'reconvention' derives from Roman-Dutch practice: Voet uses the word *reconventio* while Van der Linden uses the verb *reconvenieeren* and the nouns *reconventie* and *wedereisch*. Procedure by way of counterclaim was introduced into English procedure by s. 24(3) of the Judicature Act 1873. In New York provision was made by amendment of the Field Code in 1852 for what was given the new name of 'counterclaims': see Robert W. Millar, 'The Old Régime and the New in Civil Procedure', (1936) 14 *New York University Law Quarterly Review* 1, 17.

[50] In *Deneys & Co v. Elliott & Still, Executors of George* (1841) 2 Menz 120 the plaintiffs filed a surrejoinder to the rejoinder of the defendants. In modern practice these further pleadings are denoted in Afrikaans by terms derived from Roman-Dutch law: rejoinder = *dupliek*; surrejoinder = *tripliek*; rebutter = *tweede dupliek*; surrebutter = *tweede tripliek*.

and grounds of the cause of Action, Complaint, or Demand; and such conclusions as, according to the form of the particular Action, the Plaintiff shall by Law be entitled to deduce therefrom.'

Rule 19 required that the defendant 'in his Plea or Answer, shall either admit, deny, or confess and avoid, all the material Facts alleged in the Declaration or Claim of the Plaintiff and shall clearly and concisely state and set forth the same.'

Thus, a system of fact-pleading was introduced at the Cape a considerable time before this was achieved in New York in the Field Code of 1848[51] or in England under the Judicature Acts of 1873 and 1875.[52]

The demurrer of English law also found a place in the rules, but as Robert W. Millar has pointed out: 'as happened in Louisiana, deference to the pre-existing law of procedure mistakenly caused it to assume the name of "exception".'[53]

The forms of procedure devised under the First and Second Charters of Justice of 1828 and 1834 display the fundamental features characteristic of proceedings at common law:[54] the adversary character of the system, the predominant role of the parties in the conduct of the litigation, and the orality, immediacy, and publicity of its proceedings.[55] It should, however, be remembered that the common law model of civil procedure was introduced at the Cape prior to the fundamental reform of the administration of civil justice in England during the nineteenth century.[56] To a large extent, therefore, the South African law of civil procedure steered an independent course in its development. Although it was, from time to time, influenced by events

[51] The Code required the plaintiff's statement of complaint to contain 'a plain and concise statement of the facts constituting a cause of action without unnecessary repetition.'

[52] Cape rules 18 and 19 were replaced in 1880 by rule 330 (Government Notice 340 of 26 March 1880). The new rule, undoubtedly inspired by the rules made in England under the Judicature Act of 1875, introduced greater specificity in pleading but no change of principle; see J. A. Faris, 'The Formation of the *ficta confessio* as a Principle of Pleading in South African Civil Procedural Law' in: *A Consideration of Certain Aspects of South African Civil Procedural Law and Civil Jurisdiction* (unpublished LL M thesis, University of Cape Town, 1989, 75 sqq., 130–2.

[53] Robert W. Millar, 'The Fortunes of the Demurrer', (1936/37) 31 *Illinois LR* 429–62, 596–630. In fact, a curious development took place in South African law which turned the demurrer of English law into an exception and the *exceptie* of Roman-Dutch law into a special plea; see Erasmus, (1991) 108 *SALJ* 272–5.

[54] See, in general, Wouter le R. de Vos, *Grondslae van die Siviele Prosesreg* (unpublished LL D thesis, Rand Afrikaans University, 1988).

[55] Jack I. H. Jacob, 'Civil Procedure since 1800', in: *The Reform of Civil Procedural Law and other Essays in Civil Procedure* (1982), 205; J. A. Jolowicz, 'Orality and Immediacy in English Civil Procedure', (1975) 8 *Boletin Mexicano de Derecho Comparado* 595–608.

[56] Sir Jack Jacob has pointed out that in England 'the present system of the administration of civil justice bears hardly any resemblance to the system prevailing at the beginning of the 19th C.' (n. 55), 205. The Second Charter of Justice was more or less contemporaneous with the new general rules of pleading, the so-called Hilary Rules, made by the judges in 1834: W. S. Holdsworth, 'The New Rules of Pleading of the Hilary Term 1834', (1923) 1 *Cambridge LJ*, 261–78. They never applied at the Cape.

in England,[57] there have always been some considerable differences in terminology and detail between the civil procedure of South Africa and that of England.

Despite the replacement of the Roman-Dutch mode of civil practice by a common law model, several Roman-Dutch remedies were retained, notably *namptissement* (provisional sentence)[58] and the *mandament van spolie* (spoliation order).[59] Jerold Taitz has rightly stressed that in this regard the difference between a remedy and the procedure necessary to obtain that remedy should not be overlooked.[60] Thus the *mandament van spolie* is usually obtained by way of motion proceedings, while the rules of court, including the earliest Cape rules, prescribe a special summons for obtaining provisional sentence.[61]

V. CHANGES IN JUDICIAL STYLE

The introduction of the English procedural model amounted to much more than the mere adoption of a new set of rules for the conduct of a civil suit. It caused the severance of the Roman-Dutch law from its own procedural tradition and its substitution by a procedural system with a different history, methodology, and intellectual tradition.[62]

The introduction of the English mode of trial, manner of pleading, and law of evidence brought about changes which completely altered the judicial and procedural style at the Cape. The role and status of both the judge and the legal representative underwent fundamental change.[63] The judge

---

[57] Thus, some of the amendments to the rules introduced by Government Notice 340 of 1880 were undoubtedly inspired by the rules made in England under the Judicature Act of 1875.

[58] On the origin of provisional sentence in the early romano-canonical executory procedure of Italian law and its adoption into Roman-Dutch law see F. R. Malan *et al., Provisional Sentence on Bills of Exchange, Cheques and Promissory Notes* (1986), 4 sqq.

[59] Faris (n. 52) mentions also 'the *cautio iuratoria* and although on a tenuous footing, the *interrogatio iure*'. On the latter see further J. A. Faris, 'The *interrogatio iure* and the Principle of Fact-disclosure in South African Civil Procedural Law', in: *A Consideration of Certain Aspects of South African Civil Procedural Law and Civil Jurisdiction* (unpublished LL M thesis, University of Cape Town, 1989), 5 sqq. On the *mandament van spolie* see D. G. Kleyn, *Die Mandament van Spolie in die Suid-Afrikaanse Reg* (unpublished LL D thesis, University of Pretoria, 1986); and see the contribution by the same author to the present volume.

[60] Taitz, (1979) 96 *SALJ* 476.

[61] Cape rule 12, promulgated on 1 Feb. 1828, made provision for 'all Cases, where by Law, any Person may be summoned to hear Claim made for obtaining a provisional Sentence'. The rule also contained the Form of Summons for provisional sentence. Today, provisional sentence is governed by rule 8 of the Uniform Rules, the prescribed form of summons being Form 3 in the First Schedule to the rules; see H. J. Erasmus, *Superior Court Practice* (1994), B–61 sqq.

[62] See Erasmus, (1990) 1 *Stellenbosch LR* 355 sqq.

[63] The contrast between civil law and common law procedural styles is brilliantly encapsulated by A. T. von Mehren, 'The Significance for Procedural Practice and Theory of the Concentrated Trial: Comparative Remarks', in: *Europäisches Rechtsdenken in Geschichte und Gegenwart: Festschrift für Helmut Coing* (1982), vol. II, 361–71.

assumed the passive role characteristic of the common law; in most modern continental systems, by contrast, the judge is an active participant in the proceedings.[64] In contrast to his continental counterpart (who has to avoid any appearance of influencing those who may later be called to give evidence), the common law legal representative actively seeks out possible witnesses, interviews them, decides whether or not a particular witness is to be called, examines them in court and cross-examines the witnesses called by the other party.[65]

One of the most important changes[66] was the adoption of the English style of judgment, personal and individualistic, with the possibility of publishing dissenting opinions, in stark contrast to the stilted formalism of the collegiate judgments of continental courts.[67] Not only was the English *style* of judgment adopted: judgments of the Cape Supreme Court were also accorded the same *status* as the judgments of the English superior courts in the sense that the doctrine of precedent was soon to be invoked[68] by both practitioners[69] and the court itself.[70]

[64] See D. E. van Loggerenberg, *Hofbeheer en Partybeheer in die Burgerlike Litigasieproses: 'n Regshervormingsondersoek* (unpublished LL D thesis, University of Port Elizabeth, 1987).

[65] See e.g. Benjamin Kaplan, 'Civil Pocedure: Reflections on the Comparison of Systems', (1959/60) 9 *Buffalo LR* 409–32; Hein Kötz, 'Zur Funktionsteilung zwischen Richter und Anwalt im deutschen und englischen Zivilprozess', in: *Festschrift für Imre Zajtay* (1982), 277 sqq.; David Luban, 'The Sources of Legal Ethics: a German-American Comparison of Lawyers' Professional Duties', (1984) 48 *RabelsZ* 245 sqq.; Hein Kötz, 'The Role of the Judge in the Courtroom: the Common Law and the Civil Law Compared', 1987 *TSAR* 35 sqq.; Wouter le R. de Vos, 'Die Rol van die Hof en die Partye in die Engelse en Franse Siviele Proses', 1988 *TSAR* 216 sqq.; C. N. Ngwasiri, 'The Role of the Judge in French Civil Proceedings', (1990) 9 *Civil Justice Quarterly* 167 sqq.; Lord Goff of Chievely, 'The Role of the Judge in England', (1994) 58 *RabelsZ* 443–8; Hans-Peter Kirchof, 'Werdegang und Tätigkeit der Richter in Deutschland', (1994) 58 *RabelsZ* 449–55.

[66] Other changes included the adoption of the common law approach in appeals, according to which the proceedings on appeal, though often described as a 'rehearing', fall well short of a complete *novum iudicium*. According to the continental procedural model, the court of second instance may re-examine the witnesses heard below and the record may be supplemented by the addition of new 'proofs'. See J. A. Jolowicz, 'Managing Overload in Appellate Courts: "Western Countries" ', in: W. Wedekind (ed.), *Justice and Efficiency* (Eighth World Conference on Procedural Law, 1987), 76 sq.; Martin Shapiro, *Courts: A Comparative and Political Analysis* (1981), 38–56.

[67] See A. T. von Mehren, J. R. Gordley, *The Civil Law System: An Introduction to the Comparative Study of Law* (2nd edn., 1977), 1140; Bernard Rudden, 'Courts and Codes in England, France and Soviet Russia', (1974) 48 *Tulane LR* 1010–28; B. S. Markesinis, 'Conceptualism, Pragmatism and Courage: a Common Lawyer looks at some Judgments of the German Federal Court', (1986) 34 *American Journal of Comparative Law* 349–67; Hein Kötz, 'Scholarship and the Courts: a Comparative Survey', in: David S. Clark (ed.), *Comparative and Private International Law: Essays in Honor of John Henry Merryman* (1990), 183–95.

[68] See Ellison Kahn, 'The Rules of Precedent applied in the South African Courts', (1967) 84 *SALJ* 43 sqq., 175 sqq., 308 sqq.; *idem*, 'The Role of Doctrine and Judicial Decisions in South African law', in: Joseph Dainow (ed.), *The Role of Judicial Decisions and Doctrine in Civil Law and in Mixed Jurisdictions* (1974), 224–71; Hahlo/Kahn (n. 11), 240 sqq. In Visagie, *Regspleging* (n. 24), 70 it is made clear that the doctrine of precedent did not apply at the Cape under Dutch rule, and in *Trade Fairs & Promotions (Pty) Ltd v. Thomson* 1984 (4) SA 177 (W) 184 it is stressed that '*stare decisis* is part of our English heritage'. That English influence began to assert

VI. THE INTERACTION OF SUBSTANTIVE AND PROCEDURAL LAW

1. Cause of action

As noted above, the rules promulgated under the Charters of Justice provided for an early system of fact-pleading without any integration of the substantive elements of the English forms of action. In a system of fact-pleading the plaintiff's statement of claim must disclose a 'cause of action', a phrase which had already appeared in Cape rule 18, promulgated on 2 March 1829. Diplock LJ has described a cause of action as 'simply a factual situation the existence of which entitles one person to obtain from the court a remedy against another person'.[71]

The factual situation on which the plaintiff relies must, therefore, be capable of being recognized by the law as giving the plaintiff a substantive right to bring the claim against the defendant for the relief or remedy that he is seeking. This means that the South African pleader must (in many cases) look to Roman-Dutch law to determine whether a given factual situation entitles the plaintiff to relief or to a remedy, but that he has to plead the existence of the factual situation by means of an English procedural mechanism which was in origin inextricably interwoven with English substantive law.[72] Thus the *cause célèbre* of contractual theory at the beginning of this century, the question whether the *iusta causa* of Roman-Dutch law was identical with the requirement of consideration of English law,[73] had

---

itself even prior to the First Charter of Justice is apparent from defamation cases decided in the period 1807–27: see 'Laster' by N. J. J. Olivier, in: *Die Kaapse Regspraak-Projek* (n. 34), H 33.

[69] See e.g. *Witham v. Venables* (1828) 1 Menz 291; *Brand v. Mulder* (1829) 1 Menz 25; *Executors of Hoets v. De Vos* (1837) 2 Menz 53; *Koemans v. Van der Walt* (1838) 1 Menz 36; *Watermeyer v. Theron & Meyring* (1833) 2 Menz 14; *Bestandig v. Bestandig* (1847) 1 Menz 280.

[70] See e.g. *In re Taute* (1830) 1 Menz 497; *Meyer v. Louw* (1832) 2 Menz 8; *Executors of Hoets v. De Vos* (1837) 2 Menz 53; *Koemans v. Van der Walt* (1838) 1 Menz 36; *Wood v. Gilmour* (1840) 3 Menz 159; *Southey v. Borcherds* (1844) 1 Menz 22.

[71] *Letang v. Cooper* [1965] 1 QB 232, 242. The definition of the concept by Lord Esher MR in *Read v. Brown* (1888) 22 QBD 128, 131 has been adopted in South Africa by the Appellate Division in *McKenzie v. Farmers' Co-operative Meat Industries Ltd* 1922 AD 16, 23; *Dusheiko v. Milburn* 1964 (4) SA 648 (A) 656 sq.; *Evins v. Shield Insurance Co Ltd* 1980 (2) SA 814 (A) 838. See further the discussion in Jack Jacob, Iain S. Goldrein, *Pleadings: Principles and Practice* (1990), 75–8; H. J. Erasmus, D. E. van Loggerenberg, *Jones and Buckle: The Civil Practice of the Magistrates' Courts in South Africa* (8th edn., 1989), vol. I, 52.

[72] In his study of English pleading O. Hartwig observes that 'die Pleading-Regeln ihrem Inhalt nach in der Übergangszone zwischen Verfahrensrecht und materiellem Recht angesiedelt sind' (the pleading rules are located, as far as their content is concerned, in the transitional area between procedural law and substantive law): *Die Kunst des Sachvortrags im Zivilprozess: Eine rechtsvergleichende Studie zur Arbeitsweise des englischen Pleading-Systems* (1988), 72.

[73] See Reinhard Zimmermann, *The Law of Obligations: Roman Foundations of the Civilian Tradition* (1990, reprint 1993), 556 sqq.; Schalk van der Merwe, L. F. van Huyssteen *et al.*, *Contract: General Principles* (1993), 141 sq.

its origin in an exception to a summons on the ground that the contract referred to was void for want of consideration.[74]

Two further factors should not be overlooked: (i) the common law procedural model was adopted at the Cape at a time when procedure in the English courts was still regulated by the forms of action; and (ii) in spite of the abolition of the forms of action and the introduction of a system of fact-pleading in England by the Common Law Procedure Act of 1852[75] and the Judicature Act of 1875[76] lawyers found it convenient:

to continue to use, to describe the various categories of factual situation which entitled one person to obtain from the court a remedy against another, the names of the various 'forms of action' by which formerly the remedy appropriate to the particular factual situation was obtained.[77]

All of this is clearly manifested in the early reported cases by the authorities cited by both practitioners and the courts. On questions of substantive law there is extensive reference to the writers on Roman-Dutch law; on questions of practice and procedure reference is made to the standard English works. A good early example is *Rogerson v. Meyer & Berning*[78] in which counsel and the court refer to texts from Justinian's Code, numerous passages from Voet, Van Leeuwen's *Censura Forensis*, Van der Linden's *Koopmans Handboek*, and Pothier's *Traité des obligations*. In the same case, on questions of procedure, reference is made to Harrison's *Digest*, Tidd on *Practice*, Chitty on *Pleading*,[79] Archbold on *Pleading*, and Stephen on *Pleading*.[80] All these works deal with the common law rules prior to the abolition of the forms of action.

2. Forms of action

It is, therefore, not surprising that traces of the forms of action are found in nineteenth-century South African cases. For example, in the 1846 case of *Norden v. Oppenheim*[81] it was held that the proper 'form of action' in that case was 'an action for damages, and not for verbal injury'.[82] In argument, the attorney-general, for the plaintiff, distinguished between an 'action for

---

[74] *Alexander v. Perry* 1874 Buch 59. The issue was resolved by the Appellate Division in *Conradie v. Rossouw* 1919 AD 279, also a case decided on an exception to a declaration as being bad in law on the ground that no consideration was alleged to have been given.

[75] 15 & 16 Vict. c. 76.   [76] 38 & 39 Vict. c. 77.

[77] *Letang v. Cooper* [1965] 1 QB 232, 242, *per* Diplock J.   [78] (1837) 2 Menz 38.

[79] See also *Dixon v. Grainger* (1842) 3 Menz 369; *Rose v. Cloete* (1847) 3 Menz 377.

[80] See also *Dixon v. Grainger* (n. 79). The work of Stephen, first published in 1825, was particularly influential in England at the time, its author also being the inspiration behind the Hilary rules of 1834 (W. S. Holdsworth, 1923 *Cambridge LJ* 263, 269 sq.).

[81] (1846) 3 Menz 42.

[82] See the headnote and 46 sq. Cf. the remarks of Connor CJ in *Lumley v. Owen* (1882) 3 NLR 185, 186.

slander' and an 'action on the case to recover damages'.[83] In its judgment, the Court projected this distinction and the peculiarly English concept of an 'action on the case'[84] into the 'law of Holland' by equating the *actio iniuriarum* with an action for slander, and the *actio ad damnum et interesse* with an action on the case for damages.[85]

In the 1882 case of *Holland v. Scott,*[86] the Court held that the Roman-Dutch and English laws of 'nuisance' were 'in every respect similar'; both, after all, recognized the principle *sic utere tuo ut alienum non laedas*. Thus, the Court proceeded to apply the English law. Both Barry JP[87] and Shippard J[88] remarked on the fact that the declaration in this case was drawn on the model of the English case of *Elliotson v. Feetham.*[89] Shortly afterwards, in *Watson v. Geard,*[90] Shippard J said that as to 'what constitutes an actionable nuisance, English decisions are of course authorities of great value and utility'. Though the incidents of the English form of action were not taken over,[91] the substantive components of the English law of nuisance exercised a distinct influence through the agency of a procedural mechanism which was, in origin, inextricably linked to the particular form of action. The overruling of *Holland v. Scott* by the Appellate Division in *Regal v. African Superslate (Pty) Ltd*[92] has given rise to a controversy that has not yet abated.[93]

The action for trespass has been a source of confusion in South African law in more than one respect.[94] First, since trespass is a wrong to possession, an owner who has parted with possession was held to have no remedy for interference with his land unless he could show that his reversionary right to possession was injured by the trespass.[95] This anomaly was removed by the Appellate Division in *Hefer v. Van Greuning,*[96] where the Court recognized that in Roman-Dutch law this kind of owner is not precluded from proceeding under the *actio legis Aquiliae* for appropriate relief. The Court stressed that trespass is a term of art denoting a particular tort which

---

[83] At 50.
[84] See John G. Fleming, *Law of Torts* (8th edn., 1992), 16–18.
[85] At 55, on the basis of an incorrect interpretation, it is submitted, of an opinion of three Dutch lawyers reported in *Utrechtse Consultatien*, vol. II (1684), 414.
[86] (1882) 2 EDC 307.   [87] At 313.
[88] Who adds (at 317) that it was a case 'wherein the only point virtually established was one of pleading'.
[89] (1835) 2 Bing NC 134.   [90] (1884) 3 EDC 417, 427.
[91] See the remarks of Warner AJ in *Assegay Quarries v. Hobbs* 1960 (4) SA 237 (N) 239.
[92] 1963 (1) SA 102 (A).
[93] The various points of view are considered by P. Q. R. Boberg, *The Law of Delict*, vol. I (1984), 247–9. Cf. the contribution by D. van der Merwe to the present volume.
[94] See Erasmus, (1990) 1 *Stellenbosch LR* 364 sq.
[95] *Van Rensburg's Estate v. Fischat* 1938 EDL 65, 69; *Thomas v. Guirgis* 1953 (2) SA 36 (W) 38; *Morkel's Transport (Pty) Ltd v. Melrose Foods (Pty) Ltd* 1972 (2) SA 464 (W) 480.
[96] 1979 (4) SA 952 (A).

occupies a central position in the historical development of English law and procedure,[97] and that its use was not appropriate in South African law.[98]

Problems also arose from the fact that in English law trespass is a tort actionable *per se* and an action for trespass may be brought to vindicate a right, in which case, in the absence of proof of 'special damage' by the plaintiff, the court may award him 'nominal damages'.[99] This course of action was adopted in a number of cases towards the end of the nineteenth century.[100] In Natal, Connor J strongly objected to this practice, stating that '[h]e did not understand nominal damages, and had been sorry to see them introduced into the procedure of this Court, because they meant nothing'.[101] In *Edwards v. Hyde*[102] Innes CJ and Solomon J attempted to justify the practice. Both Price[103] and Boberg[104] have criticized these efforts, the latter arguing that 'the formal requirements of the ancient writ of trespass find no echo in the broad principles of delictual liability under the *actio legis Aquiliae* and the *actio iniuriarum*'.

It is particularly noticable from the judgment of Innes CJ[105] that he was strongly influenced in his thinking by the English form of action. As Price puts it:

his whole mode of expression, his whole cast of thought, is unconsciously on the model of the English law, with the result that, while purporting to distinguish it from the Roman-Dutch law, he invents for the latter a form of action existing only in the former. It is significant that he gives as an example of an action 'brought to vindicate a right', an action for trespass.[106]

Although, in the cases of both nuisance and trespass, the adoption of the term of art from English law caused confusion in South Africa for some time, the substantive incidents of the two actions were ultimately not taken over. In other cases the influence exerted by the common law procedural model was much more pervasive and enduring. Two examples of such influ-

---

[97] At 957G.   [98] At 960F.

[99] See I. A. Ogus, *The Law of Damages* (1973), 22 sq.

[100] See e.g. *Jansen v. Pienaar* (1880) 1 SC 276; *London and South Africa Exploration Co Ltd v. Howe & Co* (1886) 4 HCG 214; *Beukes v. Uys* (1887) 2 SAR 153. On nominal damages in South African law see H. J. Erasmus, J. J. Gauntlett, 'Damages', in: W. A. Joubert (ed.), *The Law of South Africa,* vol. 7 (1979), § 12.

[101] *MacGreal v. Murray & Burril* 1872 NLR 19, 23. Peter Spiller, *A History of the District and Supreme Courts of Natal 1846–1910* (1986), describes Henry Connor (1817–90) as 'indisputably the finest judge who served in colonial Natal. In comparison with those around him, he stood out as a giant of ability, intellect and learning.'

[102] 1903 TS 381.

[103] "Patrimonial Loss and Aquilian Liability', (1950) 13 *THRHR* 87, 100–2.

[104] *Delict* (n. 93), 170.

[105] *Edwards v. Hyde* 1903 TS 381, 385: 'But there were other actions [i.e. other than the action under the *lex Aquilia*] in which it was not necessary to prove specific damages—for instance, those actions in which the element of *contumelia* was present; so also with regard to actions for damages for trespass, brought to vindicate some right.'

[106] (1950) 13 *THRHR* 87, 100–1.

ence are apparent in the law relating to damages and the action for defamation.

3. Damages

The superimposition of a common law judicial and procedural framework upon the Roman-Dutch law has had a profound influence upon the evolution of the South African law of damages.[107] Early decisions on matters of practice and pleading which reflect English influence include (a) that a claim for damages cannot be brought on motion[108] and (b) that where a plaintiff in his pleadings claims specific performance only, he is not entitled under the prayer for other relief to a judgment for damages.[109] English practice and pleading in claims for damages led to the introduction of the terminology of the English law of damages. Even in the earliest reports references are made to vindictive damages,[110] nominal damages,[111] special damages[112] and sentimental damages.[113]

There is a close relationship between the law of evidence and the law of damages. The adoption of the English law of evidence at the Cape[114] brought to South Africa the characteristically English division between the functions of judge and jury. In this division of functions, the assessment of damages is a question of fact which falls within the province of the jury.[115] The jury, of course, need not give reasons for its findings. Thus, in the early years principles of assessment were not stated and the assessment of the quantum was disposed of in a few sentences.[116] The courts, however, were quick to follow new developments in English law and the rules of assessment set out in *Phillips v. London and South Western Rail Co*,[117] the first

---

[107] See H. J Erasmus, 'Aspects of the History of the South African Law of Damages', (1975) 38 *THRHR* 120 sqq., 268 sqq., 362 sqq.

[108] *Orphan Chamber v. Truter* (1830) 1 Menz 452.

[109] *Smith v. Skinner* (1847) 3 Menz 188.

[110] *Keyter v. Le Roux* (1841) 3 Menz 23, 31; *De Villiers v. Van Zyl* (1897) 14 SC 384.

[111] *Breda v. Muller* (1829) 1 Menz 425; *Cawoods v. Simpson* (1845) 3 Menz 542; *Hart & Canstatt v. Norden* (1845) 3 Menz 548. See further Erasmus, (1975) 38 *THRHR* 280 sqq., 366 sqq.

[112] *Cawoods v. Simpson* (1845) 3 Menz 542.

[113] *Matthews v. Young* 1922 AD 492, 503, 505.

[114] By Cape Ordinance 72 of 1830 (Evidence).

[115] See *Biccard v. Biccard* (1892) 9 SC 473, at 477: 'In estimating the amount of damages, which is a jury question . . .'

[116] Thus, in *Durham v. Cape Town and Wellington Railway Co* 1869 Buch 302, in a claim for bodily injuries and loss of business arising from the injuries, a lump sum award of £3,000 (large for the time) was made without any exposition of the principles of assessment and with an extremely brief statement of the factual findings on which the assessment was based. Though Bell J (at 309) states that 'the chief difficulty I have felt in the case had been to fix the amount of damage', he deals with the question of quantum in a few sentences; cf. Denyssen J in his concurring judgment (at 311).

[117] (1879) 4 QBD 406, affirmed (1879) QBD 78 and (1879) 5 CPD 280.

important English authority on personal injury damages, were adopted in South Africa soon after that judgment was handed down.[118]

The early case reports give the impression that, as a result of the lingering influence of the English forms of action, the courts initially had some difficulty in distinguishing clearly between the Roman-Dutch *actio iniuriarum*, where the award was essentially punitive, and those torts of English law in which damages were 'at large' and a punitive award could be made without proof of partrimonial loss. While the statement in *Edwards v. Hyde*[119] that 'where the tort is committed under circumstances which amount to *contumelia*, and in these cases, though no actual damages are proved, the court is entitled to give the plaintiff substantial damages' purports to lay down Roman-Dutch law, it shows that the Court was still haunted by the torts of English law in which damages are 'at large' and the jury can express its disapproval of the defendant's wilful interference with the rights of another by an award of exemplary damages.[120] Once the courts differentiated between the fundamental object of the Aquilian action and that of the *actio iniuriarum*, it was possible to distinguish the two forms of redress available to a plaintiff: compensation or reparation under the *actio iniuriarum* for the wrong done to him (so-called sentimental damages) and compensation under the *lex Aquilia* for any patrimonial loss he has suffered.[121] The influence of the English law lingered in so far as the former is styled general damages and the latter special damages which have to be specially pleaded and proved.[122]

The introduction of the common law procedural model and the adoption of the English law of evidence which gave rise to the use of the English terminology concerning damages and to the application of English rules of assessment have brought about an interesting dichotomy in South African law: whereas the existence of liability is determined in accordance with the substantive law of Roman-Dutch origin, the quantification of liability is largely governed by rules and concepts derived from English law. To meet the demands of modern times the South African courts continue to seek guidance in English decisions, but the use of English authority has become selective; in cases of death and personal injury, for instance, the South African courts do not share the reluctance of the English courts to make use of actuarial evidence. Indeed, Harry Street has remarked on the 'sophis-

---

[118] *Hume v. Divisional Council of Cradock* (1880) 1 EDC 104, 134; affirmed (1881) 1 Buch AC 27.

[119] 1903 TS 381, 387.

[120] See e.g. *Stuurman v. Van Rooyen* (1893) 10 SC 35; *Nicholson v. Myburgh* (1897) 14 SC 384.

[121] *Matthews v. Young* 1922 AD 492, 505.

[122] *Die Spoorbond v. South African Railways* 1946 AD 999, 1011; Erasmus/Gauntlett (n. 100) § 96.

ticated approach of the South African courts' in their use of actuarial evidence.[123]

4. Defamation

Boberg has pointed out[124] that the law of defamation occupies a special place in South African jurisprudence in that it served as the focal point of the purist-pragmatist controversy of the 1950s: the debate, acrimonious at times, about the true sources of South African law.[125] Defamation was indeed a branch of the law where habits of thought engendered by English procedural techniques had strongly asserted themselves.[126]

As noted above, the second British occupation brought no immediate change in the procedural sphere at the Cape. In the considerable number of defamation cases decided during this period[127] the 'pleadings', drawn in accordance with Roman-Dutch procedural principles, contain statements of fact, evidence, and legal argument. The first major defamation case decided after the promulgation of the First Charter of Justice was the sensational cause of *Mackay v. Philip*.[128] The declaration[129] stated that 'the defendant, intending to injure the said plaintiff, in his good name, fame, credit, and reputation ... in or about the month of April, 1828, did compose, write, edit, and publish ... a certain book, entitled *Researches in South Africa* ... and which has been read and circulated in this colony, and which said book, contains the false, malicious, and defamatory libellous matter, of and concerning the said plaintiff, as follows, that is to say ...'

Similarly, in *Botha v. Brink*[130] the plaintiff averred in his declaration that the defendant 'falsely and maliciously spoke and published of and concerning the plaintiff words the following ...'.[131] The declaration in each case

---

[123] *Principles of the Law of Damages* (1962), 137, fn. 8. On the use of actuarial evidence in South African law see Robert J. Koch, *Damages for Lost Income* (1984); *idem*, *The Reduced Utility of a Life Plan as Basis for Assessment of Damages for Personal Injury and Death* (unpublished LLD thesis, University of Stellenbosch, 1993). The multiplier method employed by the English courts has not found favour in South Africa.

[124] P. Q. R. Boberg, 'Defamation South African Style: The Odyssey of *animus iniuriandi*', in: Coenraad Visser (ed.), *Essays in Honour of Ellison Kahn* (1989), 35. On the development of the law of defamation in South Africa cf. Helge Walter, *Actio iniuriarum: Der Schutz der Persönlichkeit im südafrikanischen Recht* (1996) and the contribution by Jonathan Burchell to the present volume.

[125] See Proculus, '*Bellum Juridicum*: Two Approaches to South African Law', (1951) 68 *SALJ* 306–13; G. A. Mulligan, '*Bellum Juridicum* (3): Purists, Pollutionists and Pragmatists', (1952) 69 *SALJ* 25–32. Cf. Reinhard Zimmermann, 'Roman Law in a Mixed Legal System: The South African Experience', in: Robin Evans-Jones (ed.), *The Civil Law Tradition in Scotland* (1995), 50 sqq.

[126] Erasmus, (1990) 1 *Stellenbosch LR* 368.

[127] The defamation cases decided in the period 1807–27 are considered by N. J. J. Olivier, in: *Die Kaapse Regspraak Projek* (n. 34), H 1 sqq.

[128] (1830) 1 Menz 455.   [129] Cited at 455 of the report.

[130] (1878) 8 Buch 118.   [131] Cited at 119 of the report.

was drawn in accordance with English precedent. The following features of the manner in which the plaintiff's claim is set out in both cases, are of particular interest:

(a) In both *Mackay v. Philip*[132] and *Botha v. Brink*[133] the *publication* of defamatory matter *of and concerning* the plaintiff is alleged. The emphasis on these elements of defamation derive from English law.[134]

(b) In English law it is usually alleged in a statement of claim that the words were published 'falsely and maliciously' though falsity of the words is always presumed in the plaintiff's favour, and no issue of malice arises unless the occasion of publication is one of qualified privilege.[135] In South African law, as De Villiers CJ was to hold in *Botha v. Brink*,[136] truth alone is not an adequate defence: some public benefit has to be derived from the publication of the truth. Indeed, in the 1830 case of *Mackay v. Philip*[137] it had already been made clear that publication of the truth may be justified only in certain circumstances.

(c) In *Botha v. Brink*[138] the defamatory words complained of in the declaration were to the effect that the plaintiff 'had been brought up not only for perjury, but for rape also', the following innuendo being added: 'meaning thereby that the plaintiff was a man of bad reputation, and that he had been charged as a criminal with the crimes of perjury and rape respectively'.[139] The distinction between the primary (*per se* or ordinary) meaning of words and an innuendo was not known to Roman-Dutch law: the distinction and all the rules relating to the pleading of an innuendo and a 'quasi-innuendo' are derived from English law.[140]

(d) The declaration in *Mackay v. Philip*[141] alleges that the defendant 'intending to injure' published a book which contained 'malicious' libellous matter. The declaration in *Botha v. Brink*[142] alleges that the defendant 'maliciously' published the defamatory words. Although recognition was given in the early cases to the Roman-Dutch requirement of *animus iniuriandi*, a tendency to equate this requirement with the 'malice' of English law manifested itself in the defamation cases decided at the Cape during the second British occupation prior to the First Charter.[143] Subsequently, in

---

[132] (1830) 1 Menz 455.   [133] (1878) 8 Buch 118.

[134] See C. F. Amerasinghe, *Defamation and other Aspects of the* actio iniuriarum *in Roman Dutch Law* (1968), 55 sqq.; Jonathan M. Burchell, *The Law of Defamation in South Africa* (1985), 67 sqq., 128 sqq.

[135] Jack I. H. Jacob (ed.), *Bullen and Leake and Jacob's Precedents of Pleading* (12th edn., 1975), 625, citing *Bromage v. Prosser* (1825) 4 B & C 247, 255.

[136] (1878) 8 Buch 118, 124.   [137] (1830) 1 Menz 455, 463.

[138] (1878) 8 Buch 118.

[139] The innuendo contained in the declaration is set out at 119 of the case report.

[140] See Burchell (n. 134), 14, fn. 100, 84 sqq. On the rules of pleading see L. T. C. Harms, *Amler's Precedents of Pleadings* (3rd edn., 1989), 98 sqq.

[141] (1830) 1 Menz 455.   [142] (1878) 8 Buch 118, 119.

[143] See Olivier, in: *Die Kaapse Regspraak-Projek* (n. 34).

Botha v. Brink,[144] De Villiers CJ not only expressed a preference for the term 'malice' but he also equated *animus iniuriandi* to malice by assiging to the former the meaning which the latter bears in English law.[145] This 'terminological germ', which found its way into the system via the pleadings, was 'bound to infect the thinking on substantive law'.[146] The stereotyped defences of English law were incorporated as instances of the rebuttal of the presumption of *animus iniuriandi* arising from publication. The next step was to apply the objective criteria of the English law in determining the availability of these defences.[147] The mere absence of any intention to insult was no longer a viable defence: *animus iniuriandi* ceased to be an essential element of defamation and was reduced to a 'hollow fiction'.[148] Only in 1960 was *animus iniuriandi* reinstated as an essential element of defamation.[149]

(e) In *Botha v. Brink*[150] the main defence pleaded was that the words in question were spoken without malice and upon an occasion and under circumstances which justified the speaking. This case is thus also illustrative of the manner in which the English mode of pleading opened the door for the 'defences' (grounds of justification) of English law.[151]

(f) In Roman-Dutch law the remedy for defamation was not an award of damages but the *amende profitable* (monetary penalty) and the *amende honorable* (recantation and apology).[152] In the practice of the *Raad van Justitie* at the Cape the *amende profitable* was applied *ad pias causas*. In *Meres v. Dixon*, decided in 1814, the claim was formulated as follows:[153]

The Respondent is bound and obliged to amend the injury and that he may be condemned to amend the same honorably by appearing before Gentlemen Commissioners of the Worshipful the Court of Justice and there to ask forgiveness of the appellant declaring that the Respondent is heartily sorry for the injurious expressions he has made to the Appellant, and that he acknowledges the Appellant to be an honest man against whose honor, comportment and character he cannot allege anything—And profitably to pay to the Reformed Church of this Town or to such other fund as it may please this Right Honourable Court of Appeals to direct, a sum of One Hundred Silver Duccatoons or so much as the said Court in good justice may deem meet.

---

[144] (1878) 8 Buch 118. [145] At 123. [146] Zimmermann (n. 73), 1079.

[147] See P. Q. R. Boberg, 'Oak Tree or Acorn?: Conflicting Approaches to our Law of Delict', (1966) 83 *SALJ* 150 sqq., 164.

[148] R. G. McKerron, 'Fact and Fiction in the Law of Defamation', (1931) 48 *SALJ* 154, 172.

[149] In *Maisel v. Van Naeren* 1960 (4) SA 836 (C); see further Boberg (n. 124).

[150] (1878) 8 Buch 118. [151] See Boberg, (1996) 83 *SALJ* 150 sqq.

[152] On the history and relationship of these remedies see Melius de Villiers, *The Roman and Roman-Dutch Law of Injuries* (1899), 177–81; Zimmermann (n. 73), 1070–4.

[153] The case and the text of the prayer for relief are cited by Olivier, *Kaapse Regspraak-Projek* (n. 34), H 5.

In defamation cases decided at the Cape during the second British occupation prior to the First Charter, the Appeal Court tended to set aside awards for an *amende honorable* and to confirm only awards for an *amende profitable*, a tendency which may be ascribed to the influence of the English practice of awarding (compensatory) damages in defamation cases.[154] In *Mackay v. Philip*,[155] decided in 1830 soon after the establishment of the Cape Supreme Court, the Court 'gave judgment for the plaintiff, damages £200, with costs . . .'.[156] The Charters of Justice did not, however, bring about the immediate demise of the *amende honorable et profitable*. In *Russouw v. Sturt*,[157] a case from 1829, the plaintiff sued the defendant on the ground of an assault for an *amende honorable* and for an *amende profitable* of £500 'to be paid to the English Church at Simons Town'. *Wolff v. Van Hellings*,[158] decided in 1831, was 'an action for the *amende honorable et profitable* of £15, to the South African College' on the ground of verbal injury. In 1865 in *Hare v. White*[159] Cloete J stated that the *amende honorable et profitable* had come to be discontinued because it was often found that it had to be enforced by civil imprisonment.[160] In Natal the *amende honorable* was in 1882 held to be 'an archaism';[161] in *Ward-Jackson v. Cape Times Ltd*[162] it was said that 'the practice seems to have fallen into desuetude'.[163] As the influence of the English law asserted itself the action changed from a penal to a compensatory action with the punitive element intruding, as in English law, upon proof of express malice.[164]

In recent years the adequacy of an award of damages as a remedy for a plaintiff's loss of reputation has been questioned.[165] Burchell[166] has pleaded for the reintroduction of retraction and apology, not as a *remedy* but rather as a *defence* to an action for damages.

In spite of the efforts to re-establish its Roman-Dutch character, the South African law of defamation is, in the eyes of the comparative lawyer, 'pure Common Law'.[167] The whole 'idiom', and indeed the social function, of the law of defamation in South Africa is that of the common law and not that of modern civil law.[168]

---

[154] *Kaapse Regspraak-Projek* (n. 34), H 33.   [155] (1830) 1 Menz 455.   [156] At 464.
[157] (1829) 1 Menz 378.   [158] (1831) 1 Menz 529.   [159] (1865) 1 Roscoe 246.
[160] At 247; see also the remarks of Watermeyer J at 250.
[161] *Lumley v. Owen* (1882) 3 NLR 185, 186.   [162] 1910 WLD 257, 263.
[163] In *Swarts v. Lion Bottle Store* 1927 TPD 316, at 318 Tindall J found it unnecessary to express an opinion as to whether or not the action for *amende honorable* is obsolete in South African law.
[164] *Diepnaar v. Haumann* (1878) 3 Roscoe 39, 45 sq.
[165] See e.g. the remarks in *Kritzinger v. Perskorporasie van Suid-Afrika (Edms) Bpk* 1981 (2) SA 373 (O) 389G-H.
[166] Burchell (n. 134), 318.
[167] Konrad Zweigert, Hein Kötz, *Introduction to Comparative Law*, vol. I (2nd edn. trans. Tony Weir, 1987), 243.
[168] On the fate of the *actio iniuriarum* in modern German law see Zimmermann (n. 73), 1085 sqq.

VII. CONCLUSION

The adoption of a new procedural model is not merely a matter of form: a complex process of interaction is set in motion. The introduction into South Africa of the common law procedural model has had a decisive influence on South African judicial style: the infrastructure and arrangement of its legal institutions, the pattern of the legal profession, its procedure and evidence are all unmistakably of a common law mould. The introduction of the English mode of pleading, with the concomitant requirement that a statement of claim must disclose a 'cause of action', has firmly placed South African substantive law within a framework of English procedural mechanisms which were in origin inextricably interwoven with English substantive law.

The result is a unique system in which 'the elements of Roman-Dutch law and English law are so intermixed that it cannot without distortion be put in one or other pigeon-hole'.[169]

[169] Zweigert/Kötz (n. 167), 243.

PART II

General Principles of
Contractual Liability

5: *Contract Formation*

DALE HUTCHISON

I. INTRODUCTION

When Jan van Riebeeck landed at the Cape in 1652 the Roman-Dutch law of contract was already based simply on consensus.[1] Notwithstanding Simon van Leeuwen's assertion to the contrary,[2] it is clear from other contemporary writers that the old principle of *nuda pactio obligationem non parit* had finally been rejected, in theory as well as in practice, together with all the formalities and artificial distinctions of the Roman system of contracts.[3] It was no longer necessary to bring an agreement within the scope of one of the established heads of contract, for the old division between enforceable contracts and bare pacts had disappeared and every agreement, no matter how informally made, was now enforceable, provided it had a reasonable cause.[4]

In a sense, therefore, the foundations of the modern law of contract had already been laid, and all that remained for the early South African courts and writers was to complete the work on the superstructure. As regards the formation of contract, however, there were still uncertainties that went to the very basis of contractual liability. What precisely was meant by the requirement that a contract should have a 'reasonable cause', and did this concept bear any relation to the English notion of 'valuable consideration'? What, moreover, was the meaning of consensus, and how was its existence to be determined in practice, particularly when the parties contracted at a distance from each other? Was a subjective meeting of the minds to be required in all cases, or were there circumstances in which a party's reasonable reliance on the objective appearance of consensus might be upheld? Put otherwise, what was the effect on the validity of a contract of a material mistake on the part of one or both parties? These are all questions that have greatly exercised the minds of judges and writers in the course of the

---

[1] See e.g. Robert Feenstra, 'Die Klagbarkeit der *pacta nuda*', in: Robert Feenstra, Reinhard Zimmermann (eds.), *Das römisch-holländische Recht: Fortschritte des Zivilrechts im 17. und 18. Jahrhundert* (1992), 123 sqq.; R. W. Lee, *Introduction to Roman-Dutch Law* (5th edn., 1953), 223; D. J. Joubert, *General Principles of the Law of Contract* (1987), 27.

[2] *Censura forensis theoretico-practica*, 1, 4, 2, 2.

[3] See Reinhard Zimmermann, *The Law of Obligations: Roman Foundations of the Civilian Tradition* (1990, reprint 1993), 539 sqq., and authorities there cited.

[4] See Lee (n. 1), 223, and authorities there cited.

historical development of South African contract law, and accordingly this Chapter focuses on these particular issues.

II. *IUSTA CAUSA* AND THE DOCTRINE OF CONSIDERATION

Whatever its demerits, the Roman principle that bare pacts were unenforceable served at least to protect the inexperienced or careless from binding themselves without adequate reflection. Acceptance of the modern consensual notion of contract carried with it the need for a rule to ensure that only agreements which were seriously intended to create binding obligations would be enforceable.[5] It seems that the medieval lawyers developed the doctrine of *iusta causa* from a few Roman texts with this purpose in mind.[6] However, the requirement of *animus contrahendi* is implicit in the notion of consensus, so that once it is clearly established in its own right the need for *iusta causa* should fall away. Some writers boldly say that by the seventeenth century the doctrine of *causa* had already played out its historically most important role of facilitating the transition 'from a closed shop of (enforceable) *pacta vestita* to the principle of modern law that every agreement begets an action', and was also on the way out in Germany and in the Netherlands.[7] That might explain why the Roman-Dutch writers, while still insisting on the need for *iusta causa* or *redelijke oorzaak*, are less than clear on what they mean by this term.[8]

Be that as it may, the uncertainty surrounding the whole concept led to one of the most celebrated and protracted disputes in the history of South African law when the Chief Justice of the Cape Supreme Court, Sir Henry (later Lord) de Villiers attempted to equate *iusta causa* with the English requirement of valuable consideration.

It is difficult to define exactly the practice at the Cape prior to 1874. In two early cases, decided in 1830 and 1841 respectively, the Cape Supreme Court unhesitatingly enforced gratuitous promises that were seriously made.[9] While it made no mention whatsoever of *iusta causa*, the Court

[5] Zimmermann (n. 3), 549.   [6] Ibid. sqq.   [7] Ibid. 553, 557 sq.

[8] See e.g. Hugo Grotius, *Inleiding tot de Hollandsche Rechtsgeleertheyd*, 3, 1, 52; D. G. van der Keessel, *Praelectiones iuris hodierni ad Hugonis Grotii introductionem ad iurisprudentiam Hollandicam*, Th. 484 ad Gr. 3, 1, 52; Simon van Leeuwen, *Het Rooms-Hollands-Regt* (ed. C. W. Decker, 1780, trans. by J. G. Kotzé, 1881 sqq.), 4, 1, 4, 5, 6.

[9] *Louisa and Protector of Slaves v. Van den Berg* (1830) 1 Menz 471; *Jacobson v. Norton* (1841) 2 Menz 218. See also *Cawood v. Lane* (1867) 5 Searle 264; Louis van Huyssteen, 'Some Notes on Roman-Dutch Law at the Cape Under British Rule: Evaluation of a few general principles of the law of contract as applied by the Court of Justice between 1806 and 1827', (1994) 62 *Tijdschrift voor rechtsgeschiedenis* 357, 359 sq., where the conclusion is reached, on the basis of the limited information available in the Government Archives at Cape Town, that 'in the practice at the Cape until 1827 the courts accepted that consensus with an intention to be bound in law was all that was necessary to create a contract (probably subject to the qualification expressed above [i.e. that the agreement should not be an illegal one]) and that valuable consideration as a constitutive element was not yet a part of the law of contract.'

expressly stated in the second case that, according to Cape law, no consideration in the sense of a *quid pro quo* was necessary to support a promise to pay. Thereafter, however, the idea seemed to take hold that consideration was indeed required,[10] which is not altogether surprising given the strong influence exerted by English law at the time.

The first reported case in which this was expressly so held was *Alexander v. Perry*.[11] The defendant had repudiated his contract of service with the plaintiff who claimed damages for the breach. An exception was taken to the summons on the ground that the contract was void for want of consideration for the defendant's services. The magistrate upheld the exception and, on appeal, counsel for the plaintiff actually conceded that 'by the Roman law an agreement without *causa*, i.e. consideration, gave no right of action'[12] but argued that the consideration actually agreed upon need not appear *ex facie* the contract document. By a majority of two to one the Supreme Court dismissed the appeal. In a judgment remarkable only for its brevity De Villiers CJ expressed the view, after a cursory reference to some of the Roman-Dutch authorities, that it 'was only natural that the law should not enable a person to enforce a contract for which there had been no consideration at all'.[13] Fitzpatrick J concurred, saying that it was well known that the practice and the feeling of the country was in favour of such a requirement: 'The consideration might be very slight, but there should be something to sustain a contract'.[14] Denyssen J dissented, declining to rule on such a 'very important question' when it was not properly raised in the pleadings.[15]

The decision in *Alexander v. Perry* was followed six years later by the same court in *Malan & Van der Merwe v. Secretan, Boon & Co*[16] and thereafter in two further cases by the Eastern Districts' Court.[17] In the former case an agreement amongst creditors to accept a composition of five shillings in the pound was held, in the absence of consideration, sufficient to give rise to a defence but not to an action. The notion that *iusta causa* was to all intents and purposes the same as the consideration of English law was by now so entrenched in the law of the colony, said De Villiers CJ, that it was 'too late, even if it were wise, to eliminate it'.[18] Somewhat inconsistently, however, the learned judge exempted the contract of donation from the requirement.[19]

---

[10] Cf. *Tradesmen's Benefit Society v. Du Preez* (1887) 5 SC 269, 275, where De Villiers CJ said that the early cases of *Louisa* and *Jacobson* (n. 9) 'do not appear to be quite consistent with the numerous subsequent unreported cases, in which this Court has refused to give provisional sentence on promissory notes and acknowledgements of debt, for which the defendants respectively had received no consideration'.

[11] (1874) 4 Buch 59. [12] At 60. [13] At 61.

[14] At 62. [15] At 61. [16] 1880 Foord 94.

[17] *Hansen & Schrader v. Quirk* (1885) 5 EDL 35, *Midgley v. Tarrant* (1885) 5 EDL 57.

[18] 1880 Foord 94, 100.

[19] 1880 Foord 94, 98. See also *Joubert v. Enslin* 1910 AD 6, 18 sq., where Lord De Villiers tried to justify this special treatment of the contract of donation.

This rather blatant attempt to smuggle the doctrine of consideration into South African law under the guise of *iusta causa* was soon challenged. In 1886 John Kotzé, the Chief Justice of the Transvaal, published an annotated translation into English of Van Leeuwen's *Het Rooms-Hollands-Regt*,[20] and in a lengthy note at the end of Book IV, chapter II, he convincingly demonstrated that the overwhelming weight of Roman-Dutch opinion was against the view of De Villiers. *Causa* denoted 'the ground, reason or object of a promise'[21] and hence bore a much wider meaning than consideration as generally understood. The feeling of the country might well be in favour of requiring consideration, as Fitzpatrick J had said, 'but until the legislature steps in and makes the necessary alteration, the judges must administer the existing law, and not alter or mould it'.[22]

If De Villiers was impressed by this display of learning he certainly did not show it. He was, however, forced onto the defensive. In *Tradesmen's Benefit Society v. Du Preez*,[23] the following year he canvassed the opinions of the old Dutch writers in much greater detail than he had hitherto done, and cannily relied on Kotzé's own translation of an ambiguous passage from Van Leeuwen in support of his view.[24] Given the high authority of Van Leeuwen, he charged, Kotzé was not justified in reproaching the Cape judges with altering the existing law:[25]

In view of the conflicting meanings attached to the term 'cause' by Roman-Dutch lawyers, I felt myself justified in adopting a meaning which is not in conflict with modern English and colonial mercantile usage, which, although not recognized in Scotland, has been adopted ... by the Courts of all English Colonies in which the Civil law prevails ...[26]

There the matter rested for a while, unresolved; and the Natal Court, when it was afforded the chance of taking sides in or at least contributing to the debate, equivocated by holding that compounding creditors constitute a valuable consideration among themselves.[27] In 1904 the dispute was brought to a head when, in *Rood v. Wallach*,[28] a Full Bench of the Transvaal Court clashed head-on with its counterpart in the Cape by preferring the view of Kotzé to that of De Villiers. In his leading and quite masterly judgment, Innes CJ gave a convincing explanation of the *causa* requirement in the Roman-Dutch law of contract. The disappearance of the old rule *ex nudo pacto non oritur actio* did not mean that every accepted promise, no matter what its nature, was now enforceable: the agreement must have been entered into with a serious and deliberate mind, and for a

---

[20] J.G. Kotzé, *Simon van Leeuwen's Commentaries on Roman-Dutch Law* (ed. C. W. Decker, 1780) revised and edited, with notes, in 2 vols. (vol. I, 1881; vol. II, 1886).

[21] Ibid. vol. II, 30. [22] Ibid. vol. II, 31. [23] (1887) 5 SC 269.

[24] Van Leeuwen (n. 8), 2, 1, 4 (p. 6 of Kotzé's translation). [25] (1887) 5 SC 269, 273.

[26] At 275. [27] *Walter & Co v. Wolder & Co* (1888) 9 NLR 56.

[28] 1904 TS 187.

lawful purpose. It was therefore necessary to have regard to the origin of the agreement; hence the rule that a contract should have a proper or reasonable cause. The Dutch word *oorzaak* used in this connection could only mean 'the ground or reason of the contract—that which brought it about'.[29] Again and again the Dutch writers used the term in this sense, and never in any sense equivalent to the English 'consideration'. That being so, the Court was precluded from adopting a doctrine peculiar to English law and in conflict with the principles of Roman-Dutch law, which it was obliged to apply. Nor would it be advisable to do so, even if it were permissible:

[T]o pluck the English doctrine from its surroundings and from a system of which it forms a well understood part, and to graft it upon our legal system, to which in my opinion it is wholly foreign; to curtail its scope by excluding from its operation all contracts of donation; and to recognise in conjunction with it the inconsistent doctrine that contracts without consideration are valid for all purposes of defence— to adopt such a course would not, I think, be expedient even if it were possible.[30]

De Villiers still obstinately refused to back down, reiterating his view immediately thereafter in *Mtembu v. Webster*,[31] a case involving a right of pre-emption gratuitously given. In his view, Innes' criticism did less than justice to the role played by the Cape Court in developing the law of contract. Since there was no precise English equivalent for the Dutch expression *redelijke oorzaak*, what was more natural than for the Court to adopt the nearest equivalent: valuable consideration?[32] The intention had never been to transplant the whole of the English doctrine of consideration into South African law; but the only practical test for the existence of a reasonable cause was the giving of a *quid pro quo*. 'This is a test which the simplest mind can understand and appreciate, and which in practice is found to solve every difficulty'.[33] Moreover, even if the Court had been wrong in adopting that test, this was a clear case where the principle *communis error facit ius* should apply.[34]

With the advent of Union in 1910 a resolution of this long-running dispute by the newly created Appellate Division of the Supreme Court of South Africa was keenly awaited. Although Lord De Villiers (as he had now become) was the first Chief Justice of that Court, his brethren on the Bench included Innes and Solomon (who had sat in *Rood v. Wallach*) and others known to oppose his view. Indeed, the whole tide of judicial and academic opinion[35] was now running against De Villiers, and he knew it, but none the less tried by every means to save face and postpone the inevitable. Thus,

---

[29] At 199. [30] At 202. [31] (1904) 21 SC 323.
[32] At 339. [33] At 339. [34] At 345.
[35] Apart from Kotzé, prominent critics of Lord De Villiers' view included A. F. S. Maasdorp, the Chief Justice of the Orange Free State (*Institutes of Cape Law*, vol. 3, *The Law of Contracts* (1903), 34), and J. W. Wessels, subsequently the Chief Justice of South Africa (*History of the Roman-Dutch Law* (1908), ch. 14). See *Conradie v. Rossouw* 1919 AD 279, 296.

in 1914, when the matter might finally have been resolved on a cross-appeal in *Green v. Fitzgerald*,[36] he directed that judgment on the issue of consideration should be postponed for further and fuller argument—as if the whole question had not already been exhaustively debated in the courts of the land! Kotzé complained in a private letter to Professor R. W. Lee[37] that '[t]he case has not been handled as it should have been by the highest tribunal in the Union of South Africa . . . The Chief Justice either cannot or will not see that he has erred in *Mtembu v. Webster* and does not like to palinode.' There was a delay in re-arguing the matter, apparently because one side felt they had nothing further to add,[38] and then suddenly Lord De Villiers died, his pride intact, and the opportunity was lost.

It was another five years before the controversy was finally settled in *Conradie v. Rossouw*.[39] In upholding the validity of a gratuitous option, the Appellate Division unanimously and decisively rejected the view that consideration is required by South African law, and ruled that any promise made seriously and deliberately and with the intention of establishing a lawful obligation could found a good cause of action.[40] Sir John Kotzé could be forgiven a feeling of triumph; Lord De Villiers probably stirred in his grave.

Significantly, however, while all the members of the Court were agreed that *causa* did not mean consideration, only two of them were prepared to say what it did mean—and their opinions clashed. Solomon ACJ followed the dominant view of Kotzé and Innes by repeating what he had said in *Rood v. Wallach*: by *causa* jurists simply meant the reason for a promise and by *iusta causa* that the reason should be 'a good and legitimate one and not one contrary to law or morality or public policy'.[41] (Jacob) de Villiers AJA, on the other hand, insisted that *causa* referred to 'the particular transaction out of which the obligation is said to arise, be it sale, hire, donation or any other contract or *handeling*',[42] a view that found few supporters and which Kotzé convincingly criticized in a subsequent monograph for failing to distinguish between *causa contractus* and *causa obligationis*.[43] This difference of opinion at the highest level allowed the debate to ramble on for a few years, mainly in the pages of the *South African Law Journal*: Judge Jacob de Villiers defended his minority view[44] while Melius de Villiers tried in vain to resurrect the thesis of his brother, the late baron.[45]

---

[36] 1914 AD 88.   [37] Dated 30 Jan. 1914 and published in (1950) 67 *SALJ* 176 sq.
[38] See Kotzé's letter to Lee of 5 June 1914: (1950) 67 *SALJ* 177.   [39] 1919 AD 279.
[40] See the headnote to the case, the wording of which is taken from the short judgment of Wessels AJA (at 324) summing up the view of the Court.
[41] 1919 AD 279, 288.   [42] At 314.
[43] John G. Kotzé, *Causa in the Roman and Roman-Dutch Law of Contract* (1922), 56.
[44] Jacob de Villiers, 'The Elements of the *Causa* Problem in Roman-Dutch Law', (1922) 39 *SALJ* 169 sqq.
[45] Melius de Villiers, 'Is Consideration an Alien Element?', (1921) 38 *SALJ* 271 sqq.; *idem*, 'Consideration Reconsidered', (1922) 39 *SALJ* 422 sqq., (1923) 40 *SALJ* 15 sqq.; *idem*,

Since there was unanimity in the Appellate Division on what was necessary and sufficient to constitute a contract in modern law, this debate on the meaning of *causa* seemed to be primarily of academic or historical significance. Indeed, given that any deliberate agreement neither immoral nor illegal and not invalidated by some special defect might be enforced,[46] the conclusion seemed inescapable that *iusta causa* had finally been swallowed up by other requirements for contractual validity, in particular by the requirements of legality and serious intention to contract. The text writers certainly began to draw this conclusion: Wessels, for example, said that the requirement of reasonable cause 'does not add to or take away much from our idea of a contract',[47] while Lee opined that the retention of the phrase might be justified 'as a compendious form of expression' but that its demise 'would leave the substance of the law unimpaired'.[48] Later writers omitted it from their list of requirements altogether.[49]

The same tendency has to some extent manifested itself in the subsequent case-law, but less clearly, and in a manner which unfortunately suggests that the problem of *iusta causa* has not entirely disappeared from our law. In *Kennedy v. Steenkamp*,[50] for example, the question was whether a promissory note given in respect of a debt arising out of an illegal transaction was enforceable. The Court held that it was not, and based its decision on the absence of a reasonable cause for the promise. The *causa* of an obligation, said Watermeyer AJP, expressly adopting the view of Kotzé in preference to that of Jacob de Villiers, meant the ground or reason for entering into it, and this had to be legitimate. If the underlying purpose for making a promise were illicit then the promise would be unenforceable, even though it appeared lawful.

More recently, the Appellate Division has twice pronounced on the matter in disputes about the validity of cheques. The Bills of Exchange Act 1964, modelled on that of English Law, provides that valuable consideration for a bill may be constituted, *inter alia*, by any cause sufficient to support an action founded on contract or agreement.[51] In *Froman v.*

Consideration in the Roman and Roman-Dutch Law of Contract (monograph published by the Speciality Press, no date). According to Kotzé (letter to R. W. Lee, (1950) 67 *SALJ* 266), 'no one takes what Melius has written seriously'.

[46] This was how *Conradie v. Rossouw* was interpreted by Innes CJ in *McCullogh v. Fernwood Estate Ltd* 1920 AD 204, 206.

[47] J. W. Wessels, *The Law of Contract in South Africa*, vol. I (2nd edn., 1951), 72.

[48] Lee (n. 1), 224. In the first edition of this work, published in 1915, Lee had already expressed doubt as to whether the doctrine of *causa*, which he called 'a juristic figment' (a description he omitted in later editions), had 'really occupied the important place in the Roman-Dutch law which has been assigned to it in modern discussions' (198). See too H. R. Hahlo, Ellison Kahn, *The Union of South Africa: the Development of its Laws and Constitution* (1960), 481 sq.; Zimmermann (n. 3), 557.

[49] See e.g. J. C. de Wet, J. P. Yeats, *Die Suid-Afrikaanse Kontraktereg en Handelsreg* (1st edn., 1949), ch. IV.

[50] 1936 CPD 113.   [51] Act 34 of 1964, s. 25(1).

Robertson,[52] Corbett AJA held that this referred to the common law concept of *iusta causa*,[53] which was a requirement for all contracts.[54] There was no need to choose between the various meanings advanced for this concept because, in his view, the authorities clearly established: (i) that the requirement was sufficiently satisfied if the promise was made seriously and deliberately with the intention that a lawful obligation be created; and (ii) that in determining whether the promise is founded upon a *iusta causa* the ground or reason for the promise should be examined.[55] In the case of a cheque, therefore, the court should have regard to the underlying transaction in order to determine whether the drawer intended to establish a binding obligation.[56] Normally, the cheque would have been drawn and issued in order to discharge a pre-existing debt of the drawer but if, as in this case, the intention was to discharge the debt of another, that would supply the necessary *iusta causa*.[57]

In *Saambou-Nasionale Bouvereniging v. Friedman*[58] Jansen JA questioned this tendency on the part of courts and writers to merge *iusta causa* with other requirements for contractual validity. It would lead to greater clarity if in future *animus contrahendi* and *iusta causa* were kept apart, he said. In the case of an accessory contract, such as suretyship or the agreement reflected by a cheque, he suggested that the *causa* might be found in the underlying principal agreement or obligation, so that if the latter failed so too would the accessory contract. However, this result would only follow, apparently, if it were the common intention of the parties to link the principal and accessory agreements in this manner.

Quite what to make of all this is still unclear. Some commentators[59] have interpreted the *Saambou* decision as meaning that in modern law *iusta causa* is a requirement only in the case of accessory agreements. However, even there it seems that the concept has no independent role to play, because if it is required that the parties should expressly or implicitly have agreed to make the validity of the accessory agreement dependent on the existence of a valid principal agreement or obligation, then the so-called *iusta causa* is no more than a term of the accessory agreement: more particularly a condition or common supposition.[60] Indeed, any reason for contracting which the parties elevate to the status of a fundamental supposition should then qualify as a *iusta causa*. This is borne out by the subsequent case of *Tauber v. Van Abo*,[61] in which the plaintiff sued upon an acknowledgement of debt given in exchange for his releasing the defendant from an option agreement. Since the acknowledgement had been signed by both parties on the false

---

[52] 1971 (1) SA 115 (A).   [53] At 127.   [54] At 120G.   [55] At 121.
[56] At 122.   [57] At 127.   [58] 1979 (3) SA 978 (A) 990–2.
[59] M. F. B. Reinecke, S. W. J. van der Merwe, (1979) 42 *THRHR* 435 sqq.
[60] Ibid.; see too J. C. Stassen, '*Causa* in die Kontraktereg', (1979) 42 *THRHR* 357 sqq., esp. 374.
[61] 1984 (4) SA 482 (E).

assumption that the option was valid and binding it could not found a good cause of action, held the court, basing its decision on two alternative grounds: failure of a common supposition, and lack of *iusta causa*.

The only conclusion that may safely be drawn from these cases is that the last word has yet to be spoken on the meaning and role of *iusta causa* in the modern South African law of contract.[62] This is an unfortunate state of affairs, and it is ardently hoped that, when next it has an opportunity to pronounce on the matter, the Appellate Division will unequivocally declare that the *iusta causa* requirement, having served its historically important purpose, has now become redundant.[63] Such a pronouncement would not only reflect the preponderant weight of academic opinion in the country today,[64] it would also finally conclude a chapter of our legal history that has already dragged on for far too long.

III. REACHING AGREEMENT: THE TIME AND PLACE OF CONTRACTING

Once it is accepted that a contract may be based on mere agreement it obviously becomes vital to determine precisely how and when such agreement comes into existence. Today, of course, the process of reaching agreement is analysed in terms of a fairly sophisticated offer and acceptance theory, but this analysis is of relatively recent origin. The Romans never delved too deeply into the notion of *consensus*, focusing their gaze more on the completed agreement as an undivided unit than on the process by which it came about.[65] It was only in the seventeenth century that the natural lawyers, led by Grotius, began to analyse contract in terms of two coinciding declarations of will, and later still when offer and acceptance were clearly distinguished and discussed, as the consensual theory of contract developed.[66] The analysis was greatly furthered by English judges and writers in the nineteenth century, but since these jurists were strongly influenced by the translated works of continental theorists (especially Pothier, and later Savigny[67]) the modern South African law on offer and acceptance may fairly be regarded as an anglicized version of an essentially civilian doctrine.

Of the many issues in this area that required clarification by the early

---

[62] Reinecke/Van der Merwe, (n. 59), 437 sq.
[63] Cf. Zimmermann (n. 3), 559.
[64] Cf. J. C. de Wet, A. H. van Wyk, *Die Suid-Afrikaanse Kontraktereg en Handelsreg*, vol. I (5th edn., 1992), 90, fn. 43; Joubert (n. 1), 32 sqq.; A. J. Kerr, *The Principles of the Law of Contract* (4th edn., 1989), 139 sqq.; R. H. Christie, *The Law of Contract in South Africa* (2nd edn., 1991), 105 sq.; Schalk van der Merwe, L. F. van Huyssteen, M. F. B. Reinecke, G. F. Lubbe, J. G. Lotz, *Contract: General Principles* (1993), 141 sq.
[65] Zimmermann (n. 3) 563, fn. 118.
[66] Ibid. 565 sqq.   [67] Ibid. 569 sqq.

South African courts, undoubtedly the most interesting and fundamental was the much debated question of the time and place of formation of a contract concluded *inter absentes*. The Roman-Dutch authorities clearly established that a contract only came into being when the offer was accepted;[68] apart from *pollicitatio*,[69] a unilateral promise or unaccepted offer had no binding effect and could thus be revoked.[70] But what exactly did this imply when the parties contracted at a distance rather than face to face? Was the contract concluded as soon as the offeree declared his acceptance (the 'declaration theory'), or only when the offeror was informed of such acceptance (the 'information theory')? In the case of acceptance by post, was the contract concluded as soon as the letter of acceptance was posted (the 'expedition theory') or when it reached the address of the offeror (the 'reception theory')?

On this point there was little clarity in Roman-Dutch law. Grotius, one of the first writers to deal explicitly with the problem, favoured the information theory: unless the parties had agreed otherwise, the contract should be taken to have been concluded only when the offeror learned of the acceptance.[71] Voet seemed to agree, but his comments could also be read to support the reception theory.[72] Huber, on the other hand, expressly declined to follow Grotius, holding that the contract was complete as soon as the acceptance was declared.[73]

Later writers in Holland and in other parts of Europe were equally divided.[74] Only in England was there unanimity. There the courts had decided in the first half of the nineteenth century, on the basis of commercial convenience, that an offer made through the post was converted into a contract as soon as the letter of acceptance was posted.[75] Since this rule hardly fitted the then dominant idea that contract required a genuine meeting of the minds of the parties, the courts later attempted to justify it by

[68] See e.g. Hugo Grotius, *De jure belli ac pacis libri tres*, 2, 11, 14, and *Inleiding* (n. 8), 3, 1, 11, 48; Johannes Voet, *Commentarius ad Pandectas* (ed. used: *The Selective Voet*, translated by Percival Gane, 1956) 50, 12 (with exceptions listed); Van Leeuwen (n. 8) 4, 1, 3; Ulrich Huber, *De jure civitatis libri tres, rudimentum juris publici universalis exhibentes*, 2, 3, 2, 4.

[69] See Zimmermann (n. 3), 572 sqq.; Lee (n. 1), 211; Wessels (n. 47), 16, fn. 21. Sir Percival Gane's suggestion in his note to Voet (n. 68), 50, 12 that more use might be made in South Africa of this chapter on *pollicitatio* has thus far not been taken up by the courts; see Zimmermann (n. 3), 576.

[70] Cf. *Gous v. Van der Hoff* (1903) 20 SC 237; B. Beinart, 'Offers Stipulating a Period for Acceptance', 1964 *Acta Juridica* 200 sqq.

[71] Grotius, *De jure belli ac pacis*, 2, 11, 15.

[72] Voet (n. 68), 5, 1, 73. The ambiguity of this passage has frequently been noted by South African judges in the cases that follow.

[73] Huber (n. 68), 2, 5, 3, 9.

[74] See the detailed examination of these authorities by Kotzé JP in *Cape Explosives Works Ltd v. South African Oil and Fat Industries Ltd, Cape Explosives Works Ltd v. Lever Brothers (South Africa) Ltd* 1921 CPD 244, 258 sqq.

[75] *Adams v. Lindsell* (1818) 1 B & Ald 681, approved by the House of Lords in *Dunlop v. Higgins* (1848) 1 HL Cas 381.

saying that communication of acceptance, while generally required to conclude the contract, might be dispensed with where the offeror expressly or
impliedly authorized a different method of acceptance. On this reasoning,
an offeror who used the postal services impliedly authorized the offeror to
do the same and the Post Office thereby became the common agent of both
parties.[76]

The first South African case in which the question arose was *The Fern
Gold Mining Co v. Tobias.*[77] In a letter dated 6 February 1889, T had
applied for 500 shares in the F company, and on 18 February the directors
of the company allotted the shares to him. The next day, before he had
learned of this acceptance of his offer and even before the letter of acceptance had been posted to him, T sought to withdraw his application by written notice to the local agent of the company. In an action brought by the
company it was held by the Supreme Court of the old South African
Republic (Transvaal) that on the facts no contract had been concluded.
Kotzé CJ referred to the conflicting opinions of the Roman-Dutch and
other European writers, and to the various theories advanced by them. He
noted also that the English courts had opted for the expedition theory, but
expressed his own preference for the 'far more logical and scientific' information theory, saying that it was unclear to him why so much importance
was attached to the posting of the letter of acceptance since this was at most
simply evidence of the juristic fact of acceptance and could not take the
place of that fact itself.[78] On either approach, however, no contract had
been formed in the case before him because the withdrawal of the offer had
preceded the posting of the acceptance. The learned judge accordingly
refrained from making a final election between the theories and carefully
framed the following proposition in the alternative:

That an offer made by letter, although accepted by the person to whom it is made,
does not establish a contract until the acceptance has come to the knowledge of the
offeror, or at any rate until an answer by means of a posted letter has been sent to
the offeror.[79]

The matter was again left open by the Transvaal Supreme Court twelve
years later in *Bal v. Van Staden.*[80] B had an option to purchase V's farm,
exercisable at any time prior to 5 August 1900. On 28 July 1900 B purported
to exercise the option by posting a letter of acceptance to V and on 3 August
he posted two further letters of identical import, but owing to the Boer War

---

[76] See, in particular, the judgment of Bowen LJ in *Carlill v. Carbolic Smoke Ball Company*
(1893) (CA) 1 QB 256, 269 sq., explaining the decisions in *In re Imperial Land Company of
Marseilles (Harris' Case)* (1872) LR 7 Ch App 587 and *Brogden v. Metropolitan Railway Co*
(1877) 2 App Cas 666. See also *Household Fire and Carriage Accident Insurance Co Ltd v. Grant*
(1879) 4 Ex D 216; *Henthorn v. Fraser* [1892] 2 Ch 27; C. C. Turpin, 'Acceptance of Offer:
Instantaneous Communication', (1956) 73 *SALJ* 77.

[77] (1890) 3 SAR 134.   [78] At 138.   [79] *Ibid.*   [80] 1902 TS 128.

the postal service was interrupted and only one of the letters reached V— after the expiry date. In these circumstances, held the Court, no contract had been concluded, because even on the test most favourable to the plaintiff, the English expedition theory, his case had to fail. The reason, according to Innes CJ and Solomon J, was that the English doctrine rested on a tacit authority to use the Post Office as a means of communicating acceptance, and such authority could hardly be held to exist where the chosen channel of communication was not functioning owing to war.[81]

If it is possible to detect in *Bal's* case some leaning towards the English point of view[82] that tendency was very much more marked in the Cape case of *Naude v. Malcolm*,[83] decided in the same year, although no authorities, English or otherwise, were cited by the Court. Again the lessee of a farm with an option to purchase attempted to exercise his option by posting a letter to the lessor, who in this case was resident in England. The letter was sent to the only ascertainable address of the lessor but failed to reach him and was eventually returned from the dead letter office, after the period for acceptance had expired. The Court held that the option had been validly exercised because the lessee had done all that could reasonably be required of him to give the requisite notice of his acceptance.[84]

Like their English counterparts many years before, the South African courts were at this stage clearly torn between the expedition and information theories. The perceived needs of commercial practice dictated the former theory, legal principle the latter. How could the two be reconciled? Quite obviously, by adopting the reasoning of the English cases:[85] as a general rule, consensus is reached only when the offeror is made aware of the acceptance; as the initiator of the contract, however, the offeror may require or authorize a different method of acceptance, and compliance by the offeree with such method, even though not brought to the knowledge of the offeror, will suffice to conclude the contract. The fact that Grotius[86] could be invoked in support of this reasoning made it all the more persuasive.

The first cases in which this new approach was adopted did not involve correspondence through the post. In *Dietrichsen v. Dietrichsen*[87] a family agreement for the sale of a farm was reduced to writing and signed by two of the parties but not at first by the third, who went off with the document and only later appended his signature, without informing the others of this

---

[81] At 136 sq., 144 sq. Smith J decided that on its wording the contract required B to declare his acceptance to V, which he interpreted to mean actual communication of acceptance to the mind of V (at 149).

[82] Cf. the comments of Kotzé JP in the *Cape Explosives* case (n. 74), 264.

[83] (1902) 19 SC 482.

[84] At 487, *per* De Villiers CJ (Buchanan and Maasdorp JJ concurring). See also *Baker v. Marshall and Edwards* 1913 WLD 156 where the case was similarly decided on the basis that the Post Office was the common agent of the parties.

[85] See n. 76.   [86] See n. 71.   [87] 1911 TPD 486.

fact. The Transvaal Court had no hesitation in holding that under the circumstances no contract had been concluded and in the process firmly asserted the primacy of the information theory. As a general rule, said Wessels J, South African law required not only that an offer should be accepted but that acceptance should be communicated to the offeror within a reasonable time; in certain cases, however (he went on to say) this rule might be departed from, such as where acceptance by post was tacitly authorized.[88] Innes CJ said virtually the same thing in *Bloom v. American Swiss Watch Company*,[89] where the Appellate Division applied similar reasoning to an offer of a reward:

Under ordinary circumstances the direct communication of the acceptance to the person making the offer is essential to the constitution of a contractual *vinculum*. But it is always open to the offeror to indicate any special mode in which acceptance may be manifested.

Thus a person who consciously supplied the necessary information or did the required deed thereby accepted the offer of reward.

An opportunity to apply this reasoning to a concrete case of contracting through the post arose in 1921 in the well known case of *Cape Explosives Works Ltd v. South African Oil and Fat Industries Ltd*,[90] in which the Court was obliged to determine the place of contracting because of a challenge to its jurisdiction. Interestingly, the leading judgment was delivered by Kotzé JP, who had earlier, in *Tobias'* case, expressed his preference for the information theory.[91] This time the Court opted firmly for the expedition theory, holding that where in the ordinary course the Post Office is used as the channel of communication, a written offer made through the post becomes a contract at the time when and the place where the letter of acceptance is posted, unless a contrary intention is indicated.[92] However, while Searle J followed the recent trend by treating this principle as an exception to the generally applicable information theory,[93] the approach of Kotzé JP was somewhat different.[94] In his view the cases requiring communication of acceptance to the offeror were ambiguous, since in a case such as this communication could refer either to the posting of the letter of acceptance or to the moment when the offeror learned of the acceptance.[95] A clear choice had to be made between the two theories and, while in *Tobias'* case he had been disposed to favour the information theory because philosophically it had much to commend it, he was now persuaded that, from a practical and

---

[88] At 495. See also *R. v. Dembovsky* 1918 CPD 230, 240 sq. where Juta JP accepted this fundamental rule and supported it by reference to the English cases.

[89] 1915 AD 100, 102 sq.   [90] 1921 CPD 244.   [91] See nn. 77 sq.

[92] See esp. 266.   [93] At 275 sqq.

[94] Cf. the observations of Flemming J in *Hawkins v. Contract Design Centre (Cape Division) (Pty) Ltd* 1983 (4) SA 296 (T) 301.

[95] At 264.

business point of view, the expedition theory had the balance of convenience on its side and should be adopted.[96]

We should bear in mind that law in its development is apt to proceed on practical in preference to philosophical lines. The practice of law, as a living system, is based rather on human necessities and experience of the actual affairs of men, than on notions of a purely philosophical kind.[97]

In 1939, when the Appellate Division placed its seal of approval on the *Cape Explosives* decision, in *Kergeulen Sealing & Whaling Co Ltd v. Commissioner for Inland Revenue*,[98] it seemed that the matter had finally been laid to rest. In fact, however, the scope and ramifications of the new doctrine had still to be worked out, and the many criticisms levelled at it by writers have led the courts not only to keep the doctrine within fairly narrow limits but also, more recently, to question it themselves.

In *Yates v. Dalton*[99] the doctrine was extended, reasonably enough, to contracts concluded by telegram, but the attempt to apply it also to contracts by telephone[100] attracted much criticism and has since been rejected.[101] Telephonic communication being instantaneous, the parties are virtually *inter praesentes*, and the offeror, by choosing to make his offer in this way, can hardly be taken to have authorized an acceptance that might prove to be inaudible. The position with regard to contracts by telex, fax, and e-mail is probably the same, but remains undecided.[102]

The chief criticism of the *Cape Explosives* doctrine has always been that it rests on fallacious reasoning.[103] It is one thing to say that the offeror may dispense with the need for acceptance to be communicated to him, but quite another to assume that he does so whenever he makes his offer through the post. Even if an authorization to reply by post may be inferred in such circumstances, that does not necessarily imply that the mere posting of the letter of acceptance should conclude the contract. The truth of the matter is that an intention is fictitiously imputed to the offeror because, in the old days, it seemed fair and commercially sensible to do so:

When in England the post superseded the private hand as a means of commercial communication the problem of the risk involved in using a third party as agent was

---

[96] At 263 sqq.   [97] At 265.

[98] 1939 AD 487. However, doubts have been expressed about whether this case concerned a contract by post at all, and therefore about its binding effect: see nn. 111 sq., and the text thereto.

[99] 1938 EDL 177.   [100] In *Wolmer v. Rees* 1935 TPD 319.

[101] *Tel Peda Investigation Bureau (Pty) Ltd v. Van Zyl* 1965 (4) SA 475 (E), approved in *S. v. Henckert* 1981 (3) SA 445 (A) 451. Cf. *Millman v. Klein* 1986 (1) SA 465 (C); *Entores Ltd v. Miles Far East Corp* [1955] 2 QB 327, [1955] 2 All ER 493.

[102] See A. J. Kerr, 'Contracts by Telex and by Telephone: When and Where Entered Into', (1982) 99 *SALJ* 642; G. A. M. Radesich, 'The Formation of Telex Contracts', (1987) 9 *Modern Business Law* 40.

[103] See e.g. *Anonymous*, 'Smeiman Revisited', (1955) 72 *SALJ* 308, 309; Turpin, (1956) 73 *SALJ* 80; De Wet and Van Wyk (n. 64), 39 sq.; Joubert (n. 1), 48.

solved by the implied authorization doctrine. The risk of not knowing if or when the contract was concluded was laid upon the offeror, since it was he who assumed it by setting commerce in motion in those new and dangerous conditions. But we are not now in a milieu of highwaymen and Dick King—the post is the everyday vehicle of communication.[104]

If it is artificial to infer an authorization to accept by post from the mere fact that the offer was made in that manner, how much more so when the offer is made *inter praesentes*. However, there is some English and American authority to support such an inference where the parties reside at a distance and where a subsequent personal meeting is not contemplated.[105] Nevertheless, in 1954 the Cape Court quite rightly refused to apply the *Cape Explosives* principle in circumstances such as these, holding in *Smeiman v. Volkersz*[106] that it would be 'contrary to the basic principles of contract, as well as likely to be productive of considerable difficulties in practice to do so'.

A further complaint against the *Cape Explosives* principle is that it would seem, as a matter of logic, to preclude the offeree from neutralizing his posted letter of acceptance before its receipt by the offeror, for example by means of a telephonic instruction to ignore it.[107] This indeed was the view taken by the court *a quo* in the case of *A to Z Bazaars (Pty) Ltd v. Minister of Agriculture*,[108] but on appeal Jansen JA in the Appellate Division said that this result did not necessarily follow, since the principle was 'mainly conceived for the protection of the offeree'.[109] The learned judge avoided the issue by deciding the case on other, technical grounds, but in the course of his judgment he reflected the growing unease with the *Cape Explosives* principle, saying that although it had now been reinforced by long recognition, it was 'difficult to shut one's eyes' to the many criticisms that had been raised against it, and suggested that it was probably appropriate only to commercial contracts.[110]

This judicial undermining of an established doctrine was taken a step further by Flemming J in his minority judgment in *Hawkins v. Contract Design Centre (Cape Division) (Pty) Ltd*.[111] After casting doubt on whether the *Kergeulen* case[112] (which approved the *Cape Explosives* decision) had concerned a postal contract at all, the learned judge indicated that the case was difficult to reconcile with the later case of *Driftwood Properties (Pty) Ltd*

---

[104] *Anonymous*, (1955) 72 *SALJ* 309.

[105] *Henthorn v. Fraser* [1892] 2 Ch 27; *Bruner v. Moore* [1904] 1 Ch 305; Samuel Williston, *A Treatise on the Law of Contracts* (3rd edn., 1957), 83.

[106] 1954 (4) SA 170 (C) 179 (*per* Ogilvie Thompson J).

[107] See e.g. E. M. Meijers, 'Overeenkomsten per Brief en Telegram Gesloten', (1937) 1 *THRHR* 63 sqq.; De Wet and Yeats (n. 49), 21.

[108] 1974 (4) SA 392 (C).   [109] 1975 (3) SA 468 (A) 476.   [110] Ibid.

[111] 1983 (4) SA 296 (T) 300 sqq. See discussion of the case by J. P. Vorster, 'Waar kom 'n kontrak inter absentes gesluit tot stand?', (1984) 2 *TSAR* 196 sqq.

[112] See n. 98.

v. McLean,[113] in which the Appellate Division had reaffirmed the primacy in South African law of the information theory.[114] In the light of the latter decision, he said, 'it must be taken that communication of acceptance is necessary for the conclusion of a contract unless and until a sufficient factual basis for reaching the conclusion that a contrary intention should prevail, is established'.[115]

The *Cape Explosives* case was authority for the view that where the parties in the ordinary course used the post as a channel of communication a contrary conclusion was indicated, but Flemming J was critical of this 'forced reasoning'.[116] He warned that particular care should be taken to avoid giving such weight to certain, specific factors in assessing the intention of the parties, that the basic principle of South African law—the information theory—is no longer truly honoured, but rather reduced to the point of being a theoretical rule only.[117]

Only time will tell whether these attempts to rid the law of the expedition theory will ultimately prove successful. Meanwhile, despite doubts as to the wisdom of the *Cape Explosive* decision, the prevailing view remains that contracts concluded through the post constitute an exception to the general principle that acceptance must be communicated to the offeror.[118]

IV. *DISSENSUS* AND THE DOCTRINE OF MISTAKE

If consensus is the basis of contract and is achieved through a process of communicating declarations of contractual intention, there can obviously be no contract when neither the wills nor the declarations of the contracting parties concur. What is the position, however, if owing to some mistake a party declares one thing but means another, so that there is an outward appearance of consensus but no actual meeting of the minds of the parties? On a subjective approach to contract formation, emphasizing the will to be bound, there can in these circumstances be no question of a binding contract, while on an objective approach the concurrence of declarations suffices and there is no room for a defence of mistake. Neither approach is entirely satisfactory: the former because it creates legal uncertainty and fails to protect the legitimate expectations of the non-mistaken party, the latter because

---

[113] 1971 (3) SA 591 (A).

[114] Ever since *Dietrichsen's* case (n. 87) the courts have consistently adhered to the view that, as a general rule, communication of acceptance is required. See, in addition to the cases already cited above, *R. v. Nel* 1921 AD 339, 344, 352; *McKenzie v. Farmers' Co-operative Meat Industries Ltd* 1922 AD 16, 22; *Hersch v. Nel* 1948 (3) SA 686 (A) 702; *Ficksburg Transport (Edms) Bpk v. Rautenbach* 1988 (1) SA 318 (A) 332; *Amcoal Collieries Ltd v. Truter* 1990 (1) SA 1 (A) 4.

[115] 1983 (4) SA 296 (T) 301.   [116] At 302.   [117] At 302.

[118] See e.g. Kerr (n. 64), 98; Joubert (n. 1), 47 sqq.; De Wet and Van Wyk (n. 64), 38 sqq.; Christie (n. 64), 76 sqq.; Van der Merwe, Van Huyssteen *et al.* (n. 64), 51 sqq.

it provides harsh and inequitable results. Invariably, therefore, developed legal systems strike some balance between the two approaches. If the subjective 'will theory' is chosen as the point of departure, some effort is made to protect the reasonable reliance of the other party, often by limiting the type of mistake that will afford an escape from the contract. Conversely, if the approach adopted proceeds from the objective 'declaration theory', the interests of the mistaken party are usually accommodated to some extent by allowing mistake to operate as a defence in a limited number of situations.[119]

South Africa, with its mixed legal heritage, has since the earliest colonial days vacillated between these two approaches. The Roman-Dutch writers, in line with the general trend in the *ius commune*,[120] adopted an essentially subjective approach to contract formation.[121] To what extent the reasonable reliance of the non-mistaken party was protected is not altogether clear. As in Roman law, a mistake was operative only if it related to one of the essential elements of the contract, but whether it also had to be reasonable in the circumstances is uncertain.[122] Voet appeared to support a requirement of *iustus error*,[123] but Grotius took the view that, since the creation of a contract required a free exercise of will, a person could not be held bound by something done in *error*.[124] (Radically, however, he advocated holding a culpably mistaken party liable in damages to the other party[125]—a bold innovation that later formed the basis of Rudolf von Jhering's doctrine of *culpa in contrahendo*.[126])

[119] Zimmermann (n. 3) 584 sqq.

[120] Ibid. 609 sqq. In Roman law there was 'a gradual development from a strictly objective, declaration-oriented approach towards a more flexible and individualistic one': 604.

[121] See generally Laurens Winkel, 'Die Irrtumslehre', in: Feenstra/Zimmermann (n. 1) 225 sqq.; J. C. de Wet, *Dwaling en Bedrog by die Kontraksluiting*, Annale van die Universiteit van Stellenbosch (1943), 9 sqq.; Joubert (n. 1), 75 sqq.

[122] In Roman law a general distinction was drawn between *error iuris* and *error facti* (D. 22, 6; C. 1, 18) and *iustus error* afforded a ground for *restitutio in integrum* (D. 4, 1, 2); but to what extent these general doctrines found specific application in the formation of a contract is uncertain. The same uncertainty infects Roman-Dutch law. See De Wet and Van Wyk (n. 64), 18 sqq. and authorities there cited; Winkel (n. 121), 276 sqq.; Zimmermann (n. 3), 602 sqq.

[123] In his discussion of the *error iuris/error facti* distinction Voet limits the relevance of a mistake of fact by insisting that it should be reasonable in the circumstances, not *supina et affectata* (*Commentarius ad Pandectas* (n. 68), 22, 6, 6); and in his discussion of just causes for granting *restitutio in integrum* he seems to say clearly that a contract may be set aside for *iustus error*: 'Apart from this case of minority, restitution may be prayed against a contract or other transaction made or performed, as when one through fear, fraud or slip due to mistake has experienced loss in contracting, compromising, paying, standing surety, adiating an inheritance or other similar way' (4, 1, 29, Gane's translation; in 4, 1, 26 Voet makes it clear that by mistake he means *iustus error*). [124] *Inleiding* (n. 8), 3, 1, 19; 3, 14, 4.

[125] *De jure belli ac pacis*, 2, 11, 6, 3: '*quod si promissor negligens fuit in re exploranda, aut in sensu suo exprimendo, et damnum inde alter passus sit, tenebitur id resarcire promissor, non ex vi promissionis, sed ex damno per culpam dato . . .*' (if, however, the promisor was careless in investigating the matter, or in expressing his thought, and another suffered loss therefrom, the promisor will be bound to make this loss good not from the force of the promise, but by reason of the loss suffered through his fault . . .)

[126] The idea was taken still further by the drafters of the German BGB who granted a claim

In nineteenth-century England, on the other hand, the courts, despite their attachment at the time to the notion of *consensus ad idem*,[127] favoured a more objective approach. What really mattered in their eyes was not what the parties intended but how they expressed their intentions, because 'the Devil himself knows not the intent of a man' and the reasonable impression or belief created in the mind of the other party had to be protected.[128] This viewpoint was memorably expressed by Blackburn J in the famous case of *Smith v. Hughes*.[129] After declaring that 'if the parties are not *ad idem*, there is no contract, unless the circumstances are such as to preclude one of the parties from denying that he has agreed to the terms of the other', he said that the rule of law was as follows:

If, whatever a man's real intention may be, he so conducts himself that a reasonable man would believe that he was assenting to the terms proposed by the other party, and that other party upon that belief enters into the contract with him, the man thus conducting himself would be equally bound as if he had intended to agree to the other party's terms.[130]

This meant that in the absence of true mutual assent a contract might none the less be founded upon what was termed 'quasi-mutual assent', a doctrine that clearly had much in common with that of estoppel.[131]

As we shall presently see, the South African courts have at various stages adopted either a *iustus error* or a quasi-mutual assent type of approach to the problem of mistake in contract. Only recently has some sort of reconciliation been effected. Consequently, it has long been a controversial question whether South African law proceeds from an objective or a subjective premise. In the 1924 case of *South African Railways and Harbours v. National Bank of South Africa Ltd*,[132] in a passage often quoted with

for reliance damages even in the absence of fault: § 122 BGB; Zimmermann (n. 3), 614. In modern South African law the non-mistaken party would usually be given the benefit of a concluded contract rather than simply a claim for damages (see the discussion below), but with the development in recent times of a right to recover delictual damages for pure economic loss there seems no reason in principle why such a claim should not be granted.

[127] Cf. Zimmermann (n. 3), 601.

[128] Ibid., repeating the oft-quoted observation of Brian CJ in a case decided in 1478 (Anon. YB 17 Edw IV, Pasch. f. 1, pl. 2) and reported in C. H. S. Fifoot, *History and Sources of the Common Law* (1949) 252 sqq., 253.

[129] (1871) LR 6 QB 597.

[130] At 607. This rule derives from a similar but less elegant statement in *Freeman v. Cooke* (1848) 2 Exch 654, 154 ER 652. See too *Cornish v. Abington* (1859) 28 LJ Exch 262, 157 ER 956.

[131] Cf. Ellison Kahn, 'Estoppel and the Conclusion of a Contract', (1959) 76 *SALJ* 123 sqq.; G. A. Mulligan, 'Consent and Estoppel', (1959) 76 *SALJ* 276 sqq.; C. C. Turpin, 1958 *Annual Survey of South African Law*, 46 sqq.; R. H. Christie, 'The Doctrine of Quasi-Mutual Assent', 1976 *Acta Juridica* 149, 153 sqq. See also *Van Ryn Wine and Spirit Co v. Chandos Bar* 1928 TPD 417, 424; *Peri-Urban Areas Health Board v. Breet* 1958 (3) SA 783 (T) 790 (both cases are discussed below).

[132] 1924 AD 704, 715 sq. (Innes CJ, De Villiers JA and Kotzé JA concurred.) See also e.g. the passage from *I Pieters & Co v. Salomon* 1911 AD 121, 137, quoted below (text to n. 167); and the *dicta* in *National and Overseas Distributors Corporation (Pty) Ltd v. Potato Board* 1958

approval in subsequent cases, Wessels JA came close to espousing the extremely objective declaration theory:

The law does not concern itself with the working of the minds of parties to a contract, but with the external manifestation of their minds. Even therefore if from a philosophical standpoint the minds of the parties do not meet, yet, if by their acts their minds seem to have met, the law will, where fraud is not alleged, look to their acts and assume that their minds did meet and that they contracted in accordance with what the parties purport to accept as a record of their agreement. This is the only practical way in which Courts of law can determine the terms of a contract.

On the other hand, many cases attach primary importance to the subjective intentions of the parties. In *Saambou-Nasionale Bouvereniging v. Friedman*,[133] for example, Jansen JA said it was generally accepted that consensus in a subjective sense is the primary basis of contractual liability in our law, and that in a case involving mistake the will theory should serve as the point of departure. However, whichever theoretical perspective is adopted, in practice the results are usually the same. As Zimmermann observes: 'Abstract theorizing in terms of will and declaration theory does not normally affect the direction of the law in action'.[134]

Before tracing the development of the doctrine of mistake through the cases, it is worth mentioning briefly that in modern South African law mistake vitiates a contract only if it is 'material', i.e. if it excludes consensus[135] and (perhaps) played some role in the decision to contract.[136] In this regard the Roman classification of mistake into *error in negotio, error in corpore*, and so on has been of some assistance to the courts, but they have not felt bound by it: the modern approach to *error in substantia* and *error in persona*, for example, is different to that of Roman and Roman-Dutch law.[137] The vital distinction today, following Savigny,[138] is that between errors

(2) SA 473 (A) 479; *Allen v. Sixteen Stirling Investments (Pty) Ltd* 1974 (4) SA 164 (D) 172; *Springvale Ltd v. Edwards* 1969 (1) SA 464 (RAD) 469.

[133] 1979 (3) SA 978 (A) 993, 995 sq. See similar statements by the same judge in *Mondorp Fiendomsagentskap (Edms) Bpk v. Kemp & De Beer* 1979 (4) SA 74 (A) 78; *Cinema City (Pty) Ltd v. Morgenstern Family Estates (Pty) Ltd* 1980 (1) SA 796 (A) 804; and *Société Commerciale De Moteurs v. Ackermann* 1981 (3) SA 422 (A) 428. For earlier *dicta* supporting a subjective approach see e.g. *Rose-Innes Diamond Mining Co Ltd v. Central Diamond Mining Co Ltd* (1884) 2 HCG 272, 308; *Potgieter v. New York Mutual Life Insurance Society* (1900) 17 SC 67, at 70; *Joubert v. Enslin* 1910 AD 6, 23; more recently, *Steyn v. LSA Motors Ltd* 1994 (1) SA 49 (A) 61. [134] Zimmermann (n. 3), 587.

[135] See e.g. Van der Merwe, Van Huyssteen *et al.* (n. 64), 34; *Diedericks v. Minister of Lands* 1964 (1) SA 49 (N) 54, 56; *Gollach & Gomperts (1967) (Pty) Ltd v. Universal Mills & Produce Co (Pty) Ltd* 1978 (1) SA 914 (A) 927; *Trollip v. Jordaan* 1961 (1) SA 238 (A) 252, 254.

[136] Cf. *Khan v. Naidoo* 1989 (3) SA 724 (N); *Trust Bank of Africa Ltd v. Frysch* 1977 (3) SA 562 (A) 587; De Wet and Van Wyk (n. 64), 9 sqq.; Van der Merwe, Van Huyssteen *et al.* (n. 64), 17.

[137] See Van der Merwe, Van Huyssteen *et al.* (n. 64), 17 sqq.

[138] F. C. von Savigny, *System des heutigen Römischen Rechts* (1840), vol. III, §§ 134 sqq.; Beylage VIII, §§ VII sqq.

which relate only to a person's reasons for contracting (errors in motive, which are not material) and errors which relate to a vital aspect of the contract and hence exclude consensus.[139]

Not surprisingly, the earliest recorded cases of mistake do not reveal a consistent approach by the courts.[140] No clear distinction was drawn between material and immaterial mistakes, and there was very little clarity on the effect of a mistake on the validity of a contract. In line with the Roman-Dutch authorities, which were occasionally cited, the general idea seems to have been that mistake nullifies consensus and hence also the contract; but already there were indications that this result would follow only if the mistake had been a reasonable one to make in the circumstances.

The first reported case, *Fry v. Reynolds*,[141] concerned an immaterial mistake, possibly an *error in substantia*. R was mistaken as to the extent of a farm he had bought from F, but since this mistake, though innocently induced by F, had affected neither the price nor R's decision to purchase, the Cape Supreme Court rightly held that it could not affect the validity of the contract. So too in *Riddelsdell v. Williams*,[142] where the mistake was one in motive only. W had signed an undertaking to vacate premises by a certain date in the mistaken belief that his lease expired a year earlier than it in fact did. In an action for ejectment brought by the new owner of the property his counsel argued that the undertaking was not binding, because '[a]ll contracts derived their validity from the mutual and free consent of the parties, and were not binding when made in error, as in this case';[143] but the Court held that W had been guilty of 'culpable negligence' in not ascertaining the terms of his lease before signing the undertaking, and thus had to suffer the consequences of it.[144] In *Beyers v. McKenzie*[145] the Court accepted without hesitation that an *error in persona* nullifies a contract, and in *Kimberley Share Exchange Co v. Hampson*[146] rejected out of hand an attempt to escape from an agreement on the basis of an *error iuris*.

From about 1887 onwards the courts began to talk in terms of granting *restitutio in integrum* on the ground of *iustus error*. The idea clearly came directly from Voet's discussion of certain texts in the Digest,[147] but these

---

[139] De Wet/Van Wyk (n. 64), 10; above, n. 135.

[140] Archival records relating to cases decided by the Court of Justice (*Raad van Justisie*) in the period 1806–27 reveal similar uncertainty about the consequences of mistake: see Van Huyssteen (n. 9), 360 sqq.

[141] (1848) 2 Menz 153.   [142] 1874 Buch 11.

[143] At 14: Maasdorp, citing Roman-Dutch authority; opposing counsel cited English authority, including *Freeman v. Cooke* (n. 130).

[144] *Per* Denyssen J, 15; no authorities were cited.

[145] 1880 Foord 125. See too *Gous v. De Kock, Combrinck v. De Kock* (1887) 5 SC 405; but cf. *Gounder v. Saunders* 1935 NPD 219, 226, where the scope of operative *error in persona* was restricted in line with the view of Pothier (*Traité des obligations*, § 19).

[146] (1883) 1 HCG 340. The effect of an *error iuris* today is uncertain: cf. De Wet/Van Wyk (n. 64) 28.

[147] See n. 123.

sources were cited only much later. The first case to reflect the new terminology, albeit only in the headnote and in counsel's argument, was *Heatlie
v. The Colonial Government*.[148] The defendant had advertised for sale a piece
of waste land in Worcester, reserving to itself certain rights but not those it
held in a cottage that stood on the land. The reason for this oversight was
that when the land had last been surveyed the cottage was not yet in existence. H bought the land at a very low price and in the *bona fide* belief, so
he said, that the cottage was included in the purchase, attributing his bargain to the absence of other bidders. In an action for ejectment one of the
defences raised was mutual mistake, but the Court appeared to accept the
argument of H's counsel[149] that 'the defendant cannot claim *restitutio in
integrum* on the ground of *error* when he has been guilty of gross negligence'. The plaintiff 'had no reason to suppose that the Surveyor-General
would be ignorant of the existence of the cottage, and there certainly was
nothing fraudulent in [his] silence upon the subject', said De Villiers CJ,[150]
so he ought not now to be deprived of his bargain.

The law was very much more clearly stated by the same judge in *Logan
v. Beit*.[151] B had bought a number of shares from L '*cum* rights', which
phrase he interpreted as entitling him to certain additional bonus shares that
had accrued to L prior to the sale; failing which, he demanded cancellation
and *restitutio in integrum*. In the Court *a quo*,[152] Laurence JP adopted a subjective approach, saying that B was entitled to *restitutio in integrum* since
'there was no *consensus ad idem*; the plaintiff understood one thing and the
defendant another, and consequently there was no completed contract'.[153]
On appeal, however, De Villiers CJ disagreed: 'By our law *error* or mistake
on the part of one of the parties to a contract will, under certain circumstances, entitle him to restitution, but it must be *justus error*, that is to say,
a mistake which is reasonable and justifiable'.[154]

Here the *error* in his view was not *justus*. The phrase '*cum* rights' *prima
facie* referred to rights accruing at or after the date of the sale and not to
bonus shares already accrued and distributed. If B did not know that such
shares had already been distributed prior to the sale, he could by making
proper enquiries have ascertained this fact; at all events L was not responsible for B's ignorance. Moreover, there was no finding that L, as the seller
of the shares, knew or had reason to know that B misapprehended the terms
of the contract, but left him under such apprehension, relying on the literal
meaning of the phrase to protect himself against an action for the bonus
shares.

[148] (1887) 5 SC 353.
[149] Leonard QC and Innes, 355.
[150] At 356. No authorities were cited.
[151] (1890) 7 SC 197.
[152] High Court of Griqualand West; the judgment of the Court is reported in (1890) 7 SC
197 together with that of the Cape Supreme Court.
[153] At 212.
[154] At 216.

From this exposition by De Villiers CJ it seems that an *error* is *iustus* if (i) it is a reasonable one to make in the circumstances, or (ii) if it is induced by the other party, or (iii) if the other party is or ought to be aware of the mistake but remains silent in order to snatch a bargain. Seldom since has the position been so clearly stated.

Ironically, the language of restitution for reasonable error, though taken from the Roman-Dutch law, implies a fundamentally objective approach to contract: despite the absence of consensus, the parties are bound by their declared agreement unless or until it is set aside by the court. It also implies that mistake renders a contract voidable rather than void *ab initio*. How could this be reconciled with the consensual basis of our law of contract? Troubling thoughts such as these surfaced a few years later in the case of *Maritz v. Pratley*.[155] At a public auction P had made the highest bid for lot 1208 which he thought included not only a marble mantelpiece but also a 'pier-glass' standing on top of it. In fact the mirror was lot 1209 and when the auctioneer proceeded to offer it for sale, P objected immediately and refused to take lot 1208. In an action against P to recover the price and the auctioneer's commission, it was argued by Innes QC for the appellant that a purchaser who has been guilty of gross negligence in making a mistake as to the article being sold is estopped from setting up that mistake[156]: a clever way of having your cake and eating it: consensus is required for a valid contract, but a party guilty of an *iniustus error* may not assert the absence of consensus. Juta QC, for the respondent, replied that the question here was not one of restitution on the ground of mistake, but whether there was ever a complete contract in the absence of consensus.[157] The Court held, reasonably enough, that no sale had been concluded, but the reasoning of De Villiers CJ is singularly unconvincing: 'By negativing *consensus*, mistake can prevent the conclusion of a contract; but that is a defence which should not be easily allowed; there must be clear and definite proof of a mistake; where the mistake is coupled with gross negligence, the court would be very loth to find that there was a mistake at all'.[158]

In the present case, said the Court, there was a *bona fide* mistake and no negligence; hence there was no contract. What this amounted to was the following: a *iustus error* renders a contract void *ab initio*, while an *iniustus error* is not a mistake at all! By these means the pretence was maintained that in a case of *iniustus error consensus* remains the basis of the contract.

Despite these difficulties the courts adhered closely to the *iustus error* approach in all the mistake cases that came before them in the course of the following three decades.[159] The tension between the consensual basis of con-

---

[155] (1894) 11 SC 345.   [156] At 346.   [157] At 347.   [158] At 347.
[159] *Van der Byl v. Van der Byl & Co* (1899) 16 SC 338; *Wiggins v. Colonial Government* (1899) 16 SC 425; *Klette v. South African Cycle Factory Ltd* (1899) 16 SC 240; *Merrington v. Davidson* (1905) 22 SC 148; *Umhlebi v. Estate of Umhlebi and Fina Umhlebi* (1905) 19 EDL

tract and the notion of *iustus error* remained unresolved, however, as appears clearly from the case of *Van Rensburg v. Rice*.[160] R had intended to sell his limited rights in a piece of ground to V, but according to the deed of sale what he sold was the ground itself, and this was what V *bona fide* believed he was buying. Despite the self-evident negligence of R the Court held that in the circumstances his error was excusable and granted *restitutio in integrum*. '[W]hat constitutes just error', said McGregor J, citing the Roman and Roman-Dutch authorities referred to earlier,[161] 'must always, to some extent, be a question of fact depending on the circumstances of the particular case; one cannot lay down an absolute rule, or seek to catch every possible colour of circumstance'.[162] The Court's reluctance to uphold the agreement seems to have stemmed from its strongly subjective view of contractual liability. 'After all', said the judge, 'subject to rules of evidence and considerations of public policy, one must endeavour to give effect to what parties intended—to let *consensus* govern'.[163]

Then suddenly, in two cases decided within a space of a few weeks in 1928, the Cape and Transvaal Courts appeared to adopt a new approach to mistake in contract—one which, though taken from English law, was more consistent with the consensual theory of contract. In terms of this new approach, the vital question was not whether the error was *iustus* but rather whether the other party's belief in the existence of consensus was reasonable, for in the absence of mutual assent a contract might none the less be established on the basis of 'quasi-mutual assent'. This was of course the principle expounded by Blackburn J in *Smith v. Hughes*[164] and it was now embraced with enthusiasm by the South African courts. Thus in *Hodgson Bros v. South African Railways*,[165] where the defendants had objectively accepted an offer to buy the plaintiffs' lorry for £500 though they had actually intended to pay only £300, the Court held that 'having induced the erroneous belief in the minds of plaintiffs, they were bound thereby, whatever their actual intention may have been'.[166] The decision was consistent with what Innes JA had stated earlier in *I. Pieters and Company v. Salomon*:[167]

When a man makes an offer in plain and unambiguous language, which is understood in its ordinary sense by the person to whom it is addressed, and accepted by him *bona fide* in that sense, then there is a concluded contract. Any unexpressed reservations hidden in the mind of the promissor are in such circumstances irrelevant. He cannot be heard to say that he meant his promise to be subject to a condition which he omitted to mention, and of which the other party was unaware.

237; *Hoffmann v. SA Conservatorium of Music* (1908) 25 SC 24, 18 CTR 52; *De Villiers v. Parys Town Council* 1910 OPD 55; *Natal Bank v. Kuranda* 1907 TH 155; *Van Rensburg v. Rice* 1914 EDL 217; *Bushby v. Guardian Assurance Co Ltd* 1916 AD 488, 492. Cf. *I Pieters & Co v. Salomon* 1911 AD 121; *McAlpine v. Celliers* 1921 EDL 112.

[160] 1914 EDL 217.
[161] See nn. 122, 123.
[162] At 227.
[163] At 226.
[164] See n. 130.
[165] 1928 CPD 257.
[166] At 261.
[167] 1911 AD 121, 137.

Although this passage was cited to the Court by counsel, no mention was made of it in the judgment; instead, the Court quoted with approval Blackburn's *dictum* in *Smith v. Hughes*. There was no reference to the *iustus error* cases, nor any attempt to explain the theoretical basis of the new principle.

In *Van Ryn Wine and Spirit Co v. Chandos Bar*,[168] on the other hand, where the principle in *Smith v. Hughes* was again referred to with approval (though not applied on the facts) the Court said that the principle was not founded on any doctrine peculiar to English law, and was part of the Roman-Dutch law. The doctrine, said Greenberg J, was one of estoppel, which the courts had already decided was as much a part of South African law as it was of English law;[169] and to back up this assertion he quoted a passage from Glück's Commentary on the Pandects.[170]

Having adopted this new approach to mistake the courts adhered to it consistently for the next thirty years, with nary a mention of the concept of *iustus error*.[171] The idea that the theoretical basis of the new approach was the doctrine of estoppel, though endorsed by the influential Professor J. C. de Wet,[172] never gained full acceptance, however.[173] If taken seriously, it would mean that the person invoking the principle in *Smith v. Hughes* would have to prove all the requirements of estoppel in order to succeed, including prejudice, i.e. detrimental reliance on the representation, and (perhaps) fault in making the representation;[174] but these requirements were usually not referred to at all by the courts when applying the principle.[175] Even in England there were doubts as to whether the principle was based on estoppel.[176] Nevertheless in *Peri-Urban Areas Health Board v. Breet*,[177] Trollip AJ decided that the principle 'is really one of ordinary estoppel' and

---

[168] 1928 TPD 417.

[169] At 424, referring to *Baumann v. Thomas* 1920 AD 428. On the reception of this doctrine see J. C. de Wet, *'Estoppel by Representation' in die Suid-Afrikaanse Reg* (1939); on its scope and operation in modern law see P. J. Rabie, *The Law of Estoppel in South Africa* (1992).

[170] C. F. Glück, *Ausführliche Erläuterung der Pandekten* (Erlangen, 1797 sqq.), vol. IV, 88 sqq.

[171] See e.g. *Irvin and Johnson (SA) Ltd v. Kaplan* 1940 CPD 647; *Diamond v. Kernick* 1947 (3) SA 69 (A); *Collen v. Rietfontein Engineering Works* 1948 (1) SA 413 (A); *Peri-Urban Areas Health Board v. Breet* 1958 (3) SA 783 (T); but cf. *Maduray v. Simpson* 1932 NLR 521.

[172] *Dwaling en Bedrog* (n. 121), 4 sqq., 16 sqq.: application of the reliance theory (*vertrouensteorie*) is an expression of the principle of estoppel by representation, which in turn is founded on the fault principle.

[173] See e.g. the authors cited in n. 131 and the discussion below.

[174] Whether fault is a general requirement for the operation of estoppel remains a controversial point even today: see Rabie (n. 169), 83 sqq.; *Sonday v. Surrey Estate Modern Meat Market (Pty) Ltd* 1983 (2) SA 521 (C). Where an estoppel is raised to defeat an owner's right to vindicate, fault is required: *Johaadien v. Stanley Porter (Paarl) (Pty) Ltd* 1970 (1) SA 394 (A).

[175] See the cases cited in nn. 165, 168, 171; cf. *Petit v. Abrahamson (II)* 1946 NPD 673, 682.

[176] See the authorities referred to by Trollip AJ in *Peri-Urban Areas Health Board v. Breet* 1958 (3) SA 783 (T) 790.

[177] *Loc. cit.*

accordingly that 'some kind of prejudice' is required. The reason why prejudice had not been mentioned as a requirement in earlier cases, he suggested rather unconvincingly, was because it had such a wide connotation in relation to estoppel, and:

the very act of the one contracting party in entering into the contract in reliance on the other's conduct will be regarded in most bilateral contracts as a sufficient alteration of his position to his detriment to meet the requirement of prejudice.[178]

At this stage one might have been forgiven for believing that the *iustus error* doctrine had been well and truly laid to rest; but that would have been a mistake. In two cases decided on the same day in 1958 the Appellate Division carefully resurrected the doctrine and breathed new life into it. In *National and Overseas Distributors Corporation (Pty) Ltd v. Potato Board*[179] Schreiner JA, delivering the judgment of the Court, and after referring to 'the generally objective approach to the creation of contracts which our law follows', said:

Our law allows a party to set up his own mistake in certain circumstances in order to escape liability under a contract into which he has entered. But where the other party has not made any misrepresentation and had not appreciated at the time of acceptance that his offer was being accepted under a misapprehension, the scope for a defence of unilateral mistake is very narrow, if it exists at all. At least the mistake (error) would have to be reasonable (justus) and it would have to be pleaded.

This pronouncement still left unclear what was meant by a *iustus error*, and how that concept related to the doctrine of quasi-mutual assent. Fagan CJ attempted to clarify these issues in *George v. Fairmead (Pty) Ltd*:[180]

When can an error be said to be *justus* for the purpose of entitling a man to repudiate his apparent assent to a contractual term? As I read the decisions, our Courts, in applying the test, have taken into account the fact that there is another party involved and have considered his position. They have, in effect, said: Has the first party—the one who is trying to resile—been to blame in the sense that by his conduct he has led the other party, as a reasonable man, to believe that he was binding himself? . . . If his mistake is due to a misrepresentation, whether innocent or fraudulent, by the other party, then, of course, it is the second party who is to blame and the first party is not bound.

This admirable attempt to reconcile the doctrines of *iustus error* and quasi-mutual assent (or estoppel) unfortunately met with little success at first. In the years that followed, despite a flood of academic writings on the subject,[181] the law relating to mistake in contract became ever more confused

---

[178] *Loc. cit.*   [179] 1958 (2) SA 473 (A) 479.   [180] Ibid. 471.
[181] See e.g. B. R. Bamford, 'Mistake and Contract', (1955) 72 *SALJ* 166, 282; W.A. Ramsden, '*Iustus error* Reconsidered', (1973) 90 *SALJ* 393; Wouter de Vos, 'Mistake in Contract', 1976 *Acta Juridica* 177; R. H. Christie, 'The Doctrine of Quasi-Mutual Assent', 1976 *Acta Juridica* 149 sqq.; Schalk van der Merwe, 'Die Duiwel, die Hof en die Wil van 'n

and uncertain as the courts veered between the two doctrines, sometimes proclaiming an objective approach tempered by the defence of *iustus error*,[182] at other times adopting an essentially subjective approach, with or without the qualification of the principle in *Smith v. Hughes*.[183] And whether the latter principle constituted an independent doctrine or merely an application of the doctrine of estoppel—the requirements of which were in turn unclear—remained a source of debate.[184]

In the *Saambou* case,[185] decided in 1979, Jansen JA attempted to sort out the mess by introducing into his judgment a discussion of the various theories of contract—a highly unusual step for a South African judge. In his view, as noted earlier, it had come to be generally accepted that the will theory served as the point of departure in determining the existence of a contract, with the result that genuine consensus formed the primary basis of contractual liability in South African law. In suitable cases, however, the will theory was tempered by an application of the reliance theory, in the form of the principle enunciated by Blackburn J in *Smith v. Hughes*. The doctrine of estoppel appeared to overlap somewhat with the reliance theory but, he said—with a pointed reference to the *Peri-Urban Areas Health Board* case[186]—it would lead to greater clarity of thought if in this context one refrained from talking of estoppel. In this way a watering down of the requirements of estoppel could be avoided.

Just a few years later, however, the Appellate Division not only reaffirmed but extended the *iustus error* doctrine without any enquiry into the

---

Kontraktant', in: J. J. Gauntlett (ed.), *J. C. Noster: 'n Feesbundel* (1979), 13; Konrad M. Kritzinger, 'Approach to Contract: A Reconciliation', (1983) 100 *SALJ* 47; M. F. B. Reinecke, Schalk van der Merwe, 'Dwaling by Kontraksluiting', 1984 *TSAR* 290; R. D. Sharrock, 'Fault and *Iustus Error*', (1985) 102 *SALJ* 1; A. D. J. van Rensburg, 'Die Grondslag van Kontraktuele Gebondenheid', (1986) 49 *THRHR* 448; Carole Lewis, '*Caveat Subscriptor* and the Doctrine of *Iustus error*', (1987) 104 *SALJ* 371; Dale Hutchison, B. J. van Heerden, 'Mistake in Contract: A Comedy of (*Justus*) Errors', (1987) 104 *SALJ* 523.

[182] See e.g. *Diedericks v. Minister of Lands* 1964 (1) SA 49 (N); *Allen v. Sixteen Stirling Investments (Pty) Ltd* 1974 (4) SA 164 (D); *Springvale Ltd v. Edwards* 1969 (1) SA 464 (RA). In the latter case Macdonald JA regarded the objective approach as now 'firmly established' and seemed reluctant to allow the defence of unilateral mistake any existence at all: 'To admit such a defence would once more introduce a conflicting subjective element and this conflict would be only partially removed by a requirement that such mistake must be *justus*' (470). See also *Trollip v. Jordaan* 1961 (1) SA 238 (A) (majority judgment).

[183] See e.g. *Lindner v. National Bakery (Pty) Ltd* 1961 (1) SA 372 (O); the minority judgment of Steyn CJ in *Trollip v. Jordaan* 1961 (1) SA 238 (A); *Ocean Cargo Line v. F R Waring (Pty) Ltd* 1963 (4) SA 641 (A); cf. *Usher v. AWS Louw Elektriese Kontrakteurs* 1979 (2) SA 1059 (O).

[184] Cf. *Springvale Ltd v. Edwards* 1969 (1) SA 464 (RA) 470; *Usher v. AWS Louw Elektriese Kontrakteurs* 1979 (2) SA 1059 (O) 1063 sqq.

[185] *Saambou-Nasionale Bouvereniging v. Friedman* 1979 (3) SA 978 (A) 993, 995 sq. See n. 133 above for references to similar statements by the same judge in other cases.

[186] See n. 176.

reasonableness of the reliance on the appearance of consensus[187]. The question had to be asked: how could the courts approach the same problem of mistake from such divergent angles without ensuring that, no matter which approach was adopted, the same result would be obtained? Fortunately, in most cases an application of either the *iustus error* or the quasi-mutual assent doctrine would yield the same result; but what would the courts do in a case where the doctrines appeared to clash, for example where there was an unreasonable error on one side and an unreasonable reliance on the other? The answer was not long in coming because, by sheer coincidence, two cases of this very nature arose for decision at this juncture.

In *Horty Investments (Pty) Ltd v. Interior Acoustics (Pty) Ltd*[188] a lessor had intended to let his property for two years but, owing to a careless typing error on his part, the contract document stated that the lease was to endure (at a fixed rental) for twelve years. The problem was that the lessee, an elderly and inexperienced businessman, had signed the contract in the *bona fide* belief that he was getting a twelve-year lease. The Court, adopting the *iustus error* approach, said that the mistaken party could not rely on the lack of true consensus to escape liability if the mistake was due to his own fault, because then the other party could rely on the doctrine of quasi-mutual assent to uphold the contract despite the *dissensus*.[189] Instead of focusing on the undoubted negligence of the lessor in making the error, however, the Court shifted the enquiry to the reasonableness of the lessee's conduct and, having decided that a reasonable person in his position would have detected the typing error, held that there was in the circumstances no room for an application of the quasi-mutual assent doctrine.[190] In effect, therefore, though the Court did not say so, the lessor's error was *iustus* because the lessee's reliance on the appearance of consensus was unreasonable. Indeed, this was clearly stated in the second case, *Nasionale Behuisingskommissie v. Greyling*[191] where the facts were similar: because Greyling should have been aware of the other party's careless error, he bore substantial contributory blame for its perpetuation. This meant that the appellant's error was *iustus*. '*Miskien ietwat anders gestel, die appellant se*

---

[187] See *Du Toit v. Atkinson's Motors Bpk* 1985 (2) SA 893 (A) and *Spindrifter (Pty) Ltd v. Lester Donovan (Pty) Ltd* 1986 (1) SA 303 (A), where the court held that a failure by one party to draw attention to an onerous clause in a standard form contract, in circumstances where there was a legal duty to do so, constituted a misrepresentation by silence which misled the other party and rendered his mistake as to the contents of the contract *iustus*. For similar reasoning in subsequent cases see *Kempston Hire (Pty) Ltd v. Snyman* 1988 (4) SA 465 (T); *Keens Group Co (Pty) Ltd v. Lötter* 1989 (1) SA 585 (C); *Maresky v. Morkel* 1994 (1) SA 249 (C); *Dlovu v. Brian Porter Motors Ltd t/a Port Motors, Newlands* 1994 (2) SA 518 (C); cf. *Diner's Club SA (Pty) Ltd v. Thorburn* 1990 (2) SA 870 (C). See also *Shepherd v. Farrell's Estate Agency* 1921 TPD 62; *Van Wyk v. Otten* 1963 (1) SA 415 (O); *Janowski v. Fourie* 1978 (3) SA 16 (O).
[188] 1984 (3) SA 537 (W).   [189] At 539 sq.   [190] At 541 sq.
[191] 1986 (4) SA 917 (T).

error was justus *omdat dit in die omstandighede geen redelike vertroue van wilsooreenstemming kon verwek het nie'.*[192]

What these cases clearly demonstrated was that, in a clash between the doctrines of *iustus error* and quasi-mutual assent, the latter would prevail: unreasonable reliance trumped an unreasonable error. If *iustus error* was to survive, therefore, it would have to be defined in terms of quasi-mutual assent in order to ensure a complete reconciliation between the two doctrines. An error would thus be *iustus* when one or more of the requirements of quasi-mutual assent (or the reliance theory) was not satisfied.[193] This might seem contrived, even a negation of the original doctrine of *iustus error*, but any other interpretation carried with it the unthinkable possibility that, approached from one side, A could resile for *iustus error*, while approached from the other side, B could uphold the contract on the basis of quasi-mutual assent. Moreover, this interpretation of the concept of *iustus error*, which could be traced back to the *dictum* of Fagan CJ in *George v. Fairmead (Pty) Ltd*,[194] fitted with fundamental contractual theory: consensus remained the primary basis of contract, but in cases of *dissensus* a secondary basis might be found in the one party's reasonable reliance on the appearance of consensus[195].

In a very recent case, *Sonap Petroleum (SA) (Pty) Ltd v. Pappadogianis*[196] the Appellate Division has at last placed its seal of approval on the aforegoing line of reasoning and has thereby effected the long-sought reconciliation of the two approaches to mistake. The facts were similar to those in the *Horty* case. In drafting an addendum to a contract of lease between the parties, S's attorney had by mistake shortened the lease period from twenty to fifteen years. P, who stood to gain by this error, signed the addendum without comment, claiming to have believed that P really intended to amend the period of the lease. Was the *addendum* of any force or effect? Answering this question in the negative, Harms AJA took the opportunity to review the law relating to mistake in contract.[197] Whilst the law, as a general rule, concerned itself only with the external manifestations of the minds of parties to a contract, it did have regard to other considerations in cases

---

[192] (Perhaps put somewhat differently, the appellant's error was *iustus* because, under the circumstances, it could not engender reasonable reliance concerning a meeting of the minds): 927, *per* Schabort J (Daniels J concurred).

[193] See Hutchison/Van Heerden, (1987) 104 *SALJ* 523 sqq.; cf. G. F. Lubbe, C. M. Murray, *Farlam & Hathaway, Contract: Cases, Materials and Commentary* (3rd edn., 1988), 164, fn. 3; Van der Merwe, Van Huyssteen *et al.* (n. 64), 40 sq.

[194] See n. 180.

[195] Cf. Lubbe/Murray (n. 193), 96, 114, fn. 5; Van der Merwe, Van Huyssteen *et al.* (n. 64), 29 sqq.

[196] 1992 (3) SA 234 (A). The case is discussed by Schalk van der Merwe, Louis van Huyssteen, 'Kontraksluiting en Toerekenbare Skyn', 1993 *TSAR* 493 sqq.; see also *Steyn v. LSA Motors Ltd* 1994 (1) SA 49 (A).

[197] At 238 sqq.

of alleged *dissensus*. In such cases, he said, citing the *Saambou* decision, resort had to be had to the reliance theory in order to determine whether or not a contract had come into existence. In the *Fairmead* and *Potato Board* cases the Court had dealt authoritatively with the question of *iustus error* in the context of mistake, but if one had regard to the authorities referred to by the judges in those cases, it seemed that what they had in fact done was to adapt, for the purposes of the facts in their respective cases, the well known *dictum* of Blackburn J in *Smith v. Hughes*:

> In my view, therefore, the decisive question in a case like the present is this: did the party whose actual intention did not conform to the common intention expressed, lead the other party, as a reasonable man, to believe that his declared intention represented his actual intention? ... To answer this question, a three-fold enquiry is usually necessary, namely, firstly, was there a misrepresentation as to the one party's intention; secondly, who made that representation; and thirdly, was the other party misled thereby? ... The last question postulates two possibilities: was he actually misled and would a reasonable man have been misled?[198]

It was unnecessary, said Harms AJA, to enquire whether the mistaken party had been at fault in making the error, and unhelpful to introduce the notion of estoppel: 'it may be that estoppel merely bedevils the enquiry and that reliance thereon is not conducive to clear thinking.'[199] On all the evidence in the present case, he was satisfied that P was alive to the real possibility of a mistake but deliberately kept quiet in order to snatch a bargain. There was therefore no consensus, actual or imputed, on the amendment of the period of the lease and the *addendum* was to that extent void.[200]

This important decision at last makes the resolution of the mistake problem a fairly simple matter. In all cases of alleged mistake one should merely ask: did the parties reach consensus? If not, did one party induce in the mind of the other the reasonable belief that consensus had been reached? If neither of these foundations of liability are present, there is nothing on which the supposed contract can rest and it is accordingly void *ab initio*; or, if one prefers to phrase the matter in this misleading manner, the error is *iustus*.[201]

V. CONCLUSION

The Roman-Dutch law relating to the formation of a contract has undergone considerable development in its new setting in South Africa, and there can be little doubt that the modern law in this area is much clearer and a distinct improvement on that of eighteenth-century Holland. The

---

[198] At 239 sq. [199] At 240. [200] At 242.
[201] Cf. Hutchison/Van Heerden, (1987) 104 *SALJ* 530.

uncertainties surrounding the nebulous concept of *iusta causa* have largely been dispelled; the offer and acceptance analysis has been developed into a sophisticated doctrine with sufficient particularity in its detailed rules to afford clear answers to almost all questions relating to whether, when, or where a contract has been concluded; and after a protracted period of confusion and uncertainty the law relating to mistake in the formation of a contract seems (to this writer at least) at last to have crystallized into a clear and workable set of rules and principles.

In all three of the areas discussed in this paper the influence of English law has been strongly felt, and in some cases has been highly beneficial. The misguided attempt by Lord De Villiers to introduce the doctrine of consideration under the guise of the *iusta causa* concept mercifully failed, thanks to the vigilance of jurists steeped in the Roman-Dutch tradition, such as Kotzé and Innes. Surely nobody even remotely acquainted with that 'complex and multifarious body of rules'[202] in English law today can seriously question the wisdom of its rejection in South African law. On the other hand, our law on offer and acceptance would be very much poorer had it not had the assistance and guidance of the English cases, and the importation of the principle in *Smith v. Hughes* has likewise been enormously beneficial in developing a secondary basis for contractual liability.

Much of the credit for the improvement of the South African law on formation of contract must go to our judges, who have been highly selective in their borrowings from other systems and have relied on their own sense of practicality and fairness to develop the law. Particularly in the area of mistake, they have woven together various strands of legal tradition to create a body of law that, while sharing many features with other systems, is distinctly South African in its final form.

[202] G. H. Treitel, *The Law of Contract* (8th edn., 1991), 63.

6: *Interpretation of Contracts*

CAROLE LEWIS

I. INTRODUCTION

Ascertaining the intention of the parties to a contract is a matter of considerable complexity in modern South African law. That is nothing new. As I hope to show in this Chapter, the difficulties that have beset jurists and courts (in the classical Roman period, in the period of Roman-Dutch law, and still now) are substantially similar. This Chapter does not purport to be a comprehensive study of the development of the law: its theme is that whereas the theory of contractual formation has moved in a subjective direction—certainly in the last couple of decades in South African law—the construction of the content of a contract has moved in an objective direction. In deciding whether a contract has come into existence, our law has moved from *verba* to *voluntas*: from objective formalism to ascertaining real consensus. However, in determining the meaning of a contract we have moved largely from *voluntas* to *verba*.

I examine below the possible explanations for the dichotomy, and hope to show why the underlying theory of contract should also inform our approach to interpretation, and that we need now to seize the opportunity to bring them together. In doing so, I endeavour to show that such a move is not only required by logic and equity, but is in accord with the spirit which prevailed in Roman Law and which determined the development of Roman-Dutch contract law.

II. THE ROMAN AND ROMAN-DUTCH ROOTS

The starting point of any discussion of the interpretation of contract in Roman-Dutch law must be the respective texts of Pothier, *Obligations*[1] and Van der Linden, *Koopmans Handboek*[2] which takes from the twelve 'rules' listed by Pothier nine which he considers paramount. These rules are in turn

---

[1] *Traité des obligations*, §§ 91 sqq. See the translation by W. D. Evans, *A Treaty on the Law of Obligations or Contracts* (1802).

[2] Johannes van der Linden, *Rechtsgeleerd, Practicaal, en Koopmans Handboek* (1806). The commonly used translation in English is H. Juta, *Institutes of Holland* (1884), the last edition of which was published in Cape Town in 1906.

taken largely from Justinian's Digest, and apply not only to the interpretation of contracts but also to legislation.

The first of these is referred to as the primary, or golden rule: 'In the interpretation of the contract we must follow the general will and intention of the parties rather than the literal sense of the words'.[3] This rule has been the object of controversy, since although none would dispute that the search for the parties' intention is paramount, the very meaning of intention, and the method of ascertaining it, have been vexed issues for decades. This Chapter concentrates principally on the search for intention in the development of the law. The secondary rules discussed by Pothier and Van der Linden, and their status and operation, will also be discussed.[4] These are the guides to the meaning of the contract that may be resorted to if, and only if, the words of the contract do not themselves reveal a clear meaning—in other words, if there is ambiguity or lack of clarity in the contract.[5]

First: how has the search for intention, where no apparent ambiguity exists, been undertaken? In the process of looking at the approach of the courts to this undertaking we shall see that English law in this regard had a substantial impact on South African law, particularly in the early years of this century.

III. THE INFLUENCE OF ENGLISH LAW

1. The parol evidence rule

Sir John Wessels, the foremost exponent of the Roman-Dutch law of contract for many decades, a jurist who had a significant influence on the development of the law, wrote in his classic work on contract:[6]

We have seen what rules of evidence must be followed in order to prove to the Court what the actual terms of a contract are, and we have seen that these rules are taken from the law of England. Although we know what the terms of a contract are, we

---

[3] Pothier (n. 1), § 91. Van der Linden (n. 2), 1, 14, 4 states (transl. Juta): 'In agreements we should consider what was the general intention of the contracting parties rather than follow the literal meaning of the words.' This is drawn largely from D. 50, 16, 219: 'In conventionibus contrahentium voluntatem potius quam verba spectari placuit'. The rule was referred to with approval by Innes JA in *Joubert v. Enslin* 1910 AD 6; and in *West Rand Estates Ltd v. New Zealand Insurance Co Ltd* 1925 AD 245, Kotzé JA said that the rule as set forth by Pothier was 'universally recognized'. On the interpretation of contracts in Roman law, and in the later *ius commune* generally see Reinhard Zimmermann, *The Law of Obligations: Roman Foundations of the Civilian Tradition* (1990, reprint 1993), 622 sqq., 635 sqq. with further references.

[4] Below, section VI.

[5] See R. H. Christie, *The Law of Contract in South Africa* (2nd edn., 1991).

[6] J. W. Wessels, *The Law of Contract in South Africa* (2nd edn., ed. A. A. Roberts, 1951), § 1894.

may not know the exact meaning of these terms. To ascertain their true meaning, we must have recourse to certain rules of construction as laid down by the Roman-Dutch Law. It is only with regard to the proof of the contract that we invoke the law of England: in order to ascertain the meaning of the contract when proved—the interpretation of the contract—we must go primarily to the Civil Law for guidance. As, however, the rules of construction which prevail in the English courts are largely based upon the principles of the Civil Law, the difference between the two systems of law with regard to the interpretation of contracts is not great.

Whatever the differences, Wessels and his contemporaries drew very heavily on English law and were particularly affected by the operation of English rules of evidence, especially the parol evidence rule,[7] in ascertaining intention. The rule, also referred to in the context of interpretation as the 'integration rule',[8] has been enunciated thus by the Appellate Division in *Union Government v. Vianini Ferro-Concrete Pipes (Pty) Ltd*:[9]

Now this Court has accepted the rule that when a contract has been reduced to writing, the writing is, in general, regarded as the exclusive memorial of the transaction and in a suit between the parties no evidence to prove its terms may be given save the document or secondary evidence of its contents, nor may the contents of such document be contradicted, altered, added to or varied by parol evidence.

In the *National Board* case[10] Botha JA said: 'When a jural act is embodied in a single memorial, all other utterances of the parties on that topic are legally immaterial for the purpose of determining what are the terms of their act'. The rule clearly has an impact on the construction of terms of a contract: for the evolution of the law has been such that no evidence may be given to alter what appears to be the clear and unambiguous meaning of a contract. The impact is well illustrated by the approach of Watermeyer AJA in *Rand Rietfontein Estates Ltd v. Cohn*:[11]

[T]his Court has accepted the proposition that in the interpretation of contracts what is being sought is the common intention of the parties. . . . The difficulty which arises in practice, however, is not connected with the aim of the enquiry but with the limitations imposed by the rules of evidence upon the conduct of the enquiry. These rules limit the material which can be placed before the Court in order to ascertain the intention of the parties. In the first place there is the well known rule that when a contract has been reduced to writing no oral evidence may be given to contradict, alter, add to or vary the written terms, and in the second place there is

---

[7] L. H. Hoffmann, D. T. Zeffertt, *The South African Law of Evidence* (4th edn., ed. D. Zefffertt, 1981) say of this 'rule' at 293 that it is misleading in all 3 of its constituent parts: it is not a rule; it refers not only to parol (oral) evidence but to all forms of evidence; and it is not a rule of evidence but one of substantive law.

[8] A phrase used by John Henry Wigmore, *Evidence* (3rd edn., 1940), vol. IX, 2425, and accepted by Jansen JA in *Venter v. Birchholtz* 1972 (1) SA 276 (A) and by Botha JA in *National Board (Pretoria) (Pty) Ltd v. Estate Swanepoel* 1975 (3) SA 16 (A).

[9] 1941 AD 43, 47, *per* Watermeyer JA.

[10] See above, n. 8, 26.   [11] 1937 AD 317, 326.

another rule the effect of which is that when the terms of a contract are clear and unambiguous no evidence may be given to alter such plain meaning. This latter rule has been the subject of controversy. Wigmore (secs. 2461 and 2462) regards it as unsound both in theory and in policy. But the rule undoubtedly exists and must be applied.

2. The ambiguity principle

The application of the rule has led to the formulation of the principle that extrinsic evidence of intention may be led only where there is an ambiguity in the words of a contract, objectively construed.[12] In *Rand Rietfontein* Watermeyer AJA, in discussing counsel's contention that a court is always entitled to put itself 'in thought' in the same position as were the parties when they entered into the contract (that is, to be informed of the 'surrounding circumstances'), put the principle as follows:[13]

Now it is quite true that the Court may look at the surrounding circumstances in order to apply the words to the facts but, as I have pointed out, it is not entitled to make use of that evidence in order to vary the meaning of language, the grammatical meaning of which is clear. This is emphasised both by Lord Atkinson and Lord Shaw in the case of *Great Western Railway and Midland Railway v. Bristol Corporation* (87 LJ Ch 414), the latter remarking that the attempt seems to be inevitable to elude the distinction which the rule lays down and confuse evidence of a writer's intention as such with the intention conveyed by the words he employed.

This was not the view taken by De Wet JA in the same case, however. Stating that he could not agree with the conclusion arrived at by Watermeyer AJA, De Wet JA said:[14]

I have always regarded it as a cardinal requisite for interpretation that the Court which has to construe a document ought to know the surrounding circumstances at the time when it was executed so as to place itself, as nearly as possible, in the position of the parties; the intention of the parties is expressed in the words, *used as they were with regard to the particular circumstances and facts*. This is the rule deduced from the welter of English decisions by Halsbury (*Laws of England*, 2nd edn., vol. 10, s. 336). It seems to me that this requisite is necessary to carry out the first rule of interpretation laid down by van der Linden (*Institutes*, bk. 1, cap. 14, sec. 4) and taken by him from Pothier (*Obligations*, s. 91). It is as follows: 'In the interpretation of the agreement we must follow the general will and intention of the parties in preference to the literal sense of the words.' I am prepared to concede that this rule does not apply where the words used are so clear and precise that they are capable of one and only one meaning. *But with the imperfections of human language such cases are rare. In most cases the words used are capable of two or more meanings according to the context and circumstances.*[15]

[12] Whether words are ever capable of objective construction is a moot point, discussed below.

[13] See above, n. 11, 328.   [14] At 329.   [15] Emphasis added.

However, Watermeyer AJA's approach won the day.[16] And certainly there was ample authority prior to *Rand Rietfontein* to buttress the refusal to look at extrinsic evidence. The 'objectification' of the process of interpretation had as a consequence the principle that was expressed earlier by Innes CJ thus:[17]

The rule itself is clear: apart from cases where words or expressions are used in a technical or special sense, extrinsic evidence is only admissible to explain the construction of a document where words occur which are ambiguous either in themselves or as read with their context.

Wessels himself took an objective approach. Referring to the Digest rule that one must have regard to the intention of the parties rather than the words used,[18] he said that if the literal and grammatical sense of words used are sufficient to determine the 'nature and scope of the contract', the rule as to intention should not be invoked. 'It is not the function of the judge to decide whether the words used by the parties do not possess some hidden meaning different from their true [sic] meaning. The surest method of arriving at the true meaning of the parties is to assume that they intended their words to have their ordinary grammatical meaning'.[19]

Accordingly, unless the document itself is unclear or ambiguous, evidence may not be led as to any factor that sheds light upon the real meaning of the words in the document, or what the parties intended them to cover. Although extrinsic evidence may be given of facts which will place the court,

[16] This difference in approach, although ignored for many years because of the subsequent endorsement of the rule enunciated by Watermeyer AJA by Schreiner JA in *Delmas Milling Co Ltd v. Du Plessis* 1955 (3) SA 447 (A) is reflected in the seminal decision of the Appellate Division in *Commissioner of Customs and Excise v. Randles, Brothers and Hudson Ltd* 1941 AD 369, where again Watermeyer (then JA) and De Wet (then CJ) differed as to contractual intention, though in a different context. The De Wet approach—one of substance over form—has been echoed in a number of decisions of Jansen JA more recently. See below.
[17] In *Richter v. Bloemfontein Town Council* 1922 AD 57, 69 sq. See also the *dictum* of Solomon J in *Van Pletsen v. Henning* 1913 AD 82, at 99: 'The intention of the parties must be gathered from their language, not from what either of them may have had in mind.'
[18] D. 50, 16, 219; see n. 3 above.
[19] Wessels (n. 6), § 1900. See also *Hansen, Schrader, & Co v. De Gasperi* 1903 TH 100, 103, and the various cases referred to as authority for the literal approach by Wessels (n. 6), § 1907. R. H. Christie, *The Law of Contract in South Africa* (2nd edn., 1991) also endorses a purely literal approach, though not expressly. See his discussion, 247 sqq., of 'Lord Wensleydale's golden rule' enunciated in *Grey v. Pearson* (1857) 6 HL Cas 61, 106–108, 10 ER 1216, 1234. The rule (that in construing written instruments, including contracts, the grammatical and ordinary sense of the words is to be followed unless inconsistent with the rest of the instrument) is no more, says Christie, than an application of the Roman-Dutch golden rule that we establish the parties' intention by examining the words used. He states, at 248: 'The key to understanding the modern law is the concept of the common intention of the parties, which may be a very different thing from the actual intention locked up in the mind of each party at the time of contracting, and even more different from what, after a dispute has arisen, each party honestly or dishonestly maintains his intention then to have been.' This view negates entirely the notion of intention, relegating what the parties wanted to a fiction. It is entirely out of keeping with the subjective basis of contract: consensus.

as far as possible, in the situation of the parties when they entered into the contract, and of facts which will enable the identification of people or things referred to in the document, no evidence may be led for the purpose of interpreting the language used.[20]

For decades following *Richter* and *Rand Rietfontein* the courts insisted that intention was to be ascertained from a literal interpretation of the document recording the agreement of the parties. One of the bluntest expositions of this principle is to be found in the judgment of Greenberg JA in *Worman v. Hughes*:[21]

It must be borne in mind that in an action on a contract, the *rule of interpretation is to ascertain, not what the parties' intention was, but what the language used in the contract means, i.e. what their intention was as expressed in the contract.*[22]

Any controversy that there might have been as to the exclusion of extrinsic evidence, or the application of the rule, was effectively obliterated by Schreiner JA in his judgment in *Delmas Milling Co Ltd v. Du Plessis*:[23]

There appear to be three broad classes of evidence that are usable in different kinds of cases. Where although there is difficulty, perhaps serious difficulty, in interpretation but it can nevertheless be cleared up by linguistic treatment this must be done. The only permissible additional evidence in such cases is of an identificatory nature; such evidence is really not used for interpretation but only to apply the contract to the facts. Such application may, of course, be itself the cause of the difficulty, giving rise to what is sometimes called a latent ambiguity. If the difficulty cannot be cleared up with sufficient certainty by studying the language, recourse may be had to 'surrounding circumstances', i.e. matters that were probably present to the minds of the parties when they contracted (but not actual negotiations and similar statements). It is commonly said that the Court is entitled to be informed of all such circumstances in all cases ... But this does not mean that if sufficient certainty as to the meaning can be gathered from the language alone it is nevertheless permissible to reach a different result by drawing inferences from the surrounding circumstances. Whether there is sufficient certainty in the language of even very badly drafted contracts to make it unnecessary and therefore wrong to draw inferences from the surrounding circumstances is a matter of individual judicial opinion on each case. Cases of this class, though they are generally spoken of as cases of ambiguity, might conveniently be given some such name as 'cases of uncertainty' to distinguish them from the third class of case where even the use of surrounding circumstances does not provide 'sufficient certainty'. These are cases of ambiguity in the narrow sense, where after the surrounding circumstances have been considered there is still no substantial balance in favour of one meaning rather than another ... In these cases, which will naturally be much rarer than those of uncertainty, recourse may be had to what passed between the parties on the subject of the contract.

---

[20] *Richter v. Bloemfontein Town Council* 1922 AD 57, 69 sq.
[21] 1948 (3) SA 495 (A) 505.   [22] Emphasis added.
[23] 1955 (3) SA 447 (A) 454 sq.

3. 'Facility and certainty of interpretation'

This strict, literal approach to the construction of a contract has been followed by the courts with little deviation, though with some difficulty as to when there is ambiguity, since *Delmas Milling*. Although it has occasionally been argued by counsel that the refusal to allow evidence of surrounding circumstances where there is no apparent uncertainty, or ambiguity, will result in a false reconstruction of the agreement of the parties, this argument has had little success. Attempts to temper the rule have not been far-reaching. Thus, for example, in *List v. Jungers*,[24] in determining the meaning ascribed by the parties to the word 'guarantee', Diemont JA said:

It is, in my view, an unrewarding and misleading exercise to seize on one word in a document, determine its more usual or ordinary meaning, and then, having done so, to seek to interpret the document in the light of the meaning so ascribed to that word . . . It must be borne in mind that this Court has held that it can be informed of the background circumstances under which a contract was concluded so as to enable it to understand the broad context in which the words to be interpreted were used.

The Appellate Division thus made it clear that words cannot be looked at in isolation: they must be read within the context of the contract as a whole. However, a court still cannot examine surrounding circumstances and factors known to the parties at the time of contracting unless there is uncertainty or ambiguity.

What has made South African law, following the early English approach to the exclusion of extrinsic evidence, take this direction? One of the answers is the need for certainty. Once the parties have reduced their contract to writing—and if there is no ambiguity in its provisions—they ought to have a document on which to rely in regulating their relationship: they should not have to undertake extensive, expensive litigation in order to conduct an

---

[24] 1979 (3) SA 106 (A) 118, 120. See also *Van Rensburg v. Taute* 1975 (1) SA 279 (A), *Swart v. Cape Fabrix (Pty) Ltd* 1979 (1) SA 195 (A), *Sassoon Confirming and Acceptance Co (Pty) Ltd v. Barclays National Bank Ltd* 1974 (1) SA 641 (A), *Van Rensburg v. City Credit (Natal) (Pty) Ltd* 1980 (4) SA 500 (N) 506 sq.; *Sonarep (SA) (Pty) Ltd v. Motorcraft (Pty) Ltd* 1981 (1) SA 889 (N) 895–7. In the latter case Kumleben J, after referring to the more liberal approach of the English courts, said: 'This view, which appears to dispense with the requirement of uncertainty or ambiguity before evidence of surrounding circumstances is held to be admissible, may reflect an attractive and more logical approach to language and its meaning. We are, however, bound by the explicit pronouncements of the Appellate Division in this regard.' In *Van Rensburg v. City Credit (Natal) (Pty) Ltd* 1980 (4) SA 500 (N) Kriek J said that the three classes of evidence are 'like the colours of a spectrum with diffused borders between the different colours' (506). This approach would allow a court to look at background factors despite the absence of ambiguity. It has not, however, received any subsequent judicial support.

historical-psychological investigation into their real intentions at the time of entering into the contract.[25]

A protagonist of the view that once a contract has been concluded, its written form takes on a life of its own, is the American jurist, Samuel Williston,[26] whose work has also had an impact on the decisions of South African courts. Williston argued that giving a contract a meaning different from that ascribed to it by the parties was justified by the 'facility and certainty of interpretation' so obtained.[27] This is the rationale used for the literal, objective approach to interpretation. The merits of the approach are strongly argued by Lubbe and Murray. They state:[28]

An alternative approach [that is, to the one that investigates actual intention] is to regard [the process of interpretation] as an objective, normative process, directed towards establishing the legal consequences of a transaction with reference not merely to the intention of the parties, but also in view of relevant considerations of legal policy . . . From such a perspective, the traditional view of the parol evidence rule in the present context becomes intelligible. It seeks to protect judges against intractable disputes of fact regarding subjective states of mind and the concomitant risks of fraud and perjury that will undoubtedly arise should parties be entitled to resort freely to extrinsic evidence during the process of interpretation . . . There are, in fact, indications that the parties, for reasons of convenience and costs, are often more interested in obtaining a decision on linguistic grounds than facing the uncertainty and risks attendant on a recourse to extrinsic evidence.

The authors cite as authority for this view the judgment of Schreiner JA in *Delmas Milling*[29] where reference is made to *Frumer v. Maitland*,[30] a case in which the Court, *per* Schreiner JA (Hoexter and Greenberg JJA concurring, Van den Heever JA dissenting, though not on this issue) adopted the literal approach. No reason for the adoption of the literal approach was, however, advanced in the various judgments of the Court, so clear was it that the objective approach had become embedded in our law.

[25] This is the view of Gerhard Lubbe and Christina Murray, *Farlam and Hathaway, Contract: Cases, Materials and Commentary* (3rd edn., 1988). Lubbe and Murray argue at 463: 'Interpretation need not necessarily, however, bear a wholly historical-psychological stamp. An alternative approach is to regard it as an objective, normative process, directed towards establishing the legal consequences of a transaction with reference not merely to the intention of the parties, but also in view of relevant considerations of legal policy . . . From such a perspective, the traditional view of the parol evidence rule in the present context becomes intelligible. It seeks to protect judges against intractable disputes of fact regarding subjective states of mind and the concomitant risks of fraud and perjury that will undoubtedly arise should parties be entitled to resort freely to extrinsic evidence during the process of interpretation . . . There are, in fact, indications that the parties, for reasons of convenience and costs, are often more interested in obtaining a decision on linguistic grounds than facing the uncertainty and risks attendant on a recourse to extrinsic evidence.'

[26] Samuel Williston, *A Treatise on the Law of Contracts* (3rd edn., ed. Walter H. E. Jaeger, 1957–76), 603. See also John D. Calamari and Joseph M. Perillo, *The Law of Contracts* (1970), 116–23.

[27] § 612, 577.

[28] Lubbe/Murray (n. 25), 463.

[29] See above, n. 16, 455.

[30] 1954 (3) SA 840 (A).

Lubbe and Murray continue:[31]

What is required is that gaps in the contractual intention be filled in a manner consistent with the terms of the agreement and in accordance with business efficacy and fairness. The traditional approach to interpretation, precisely because of its formalistic nature, affords judges the opportunity of fulfilling this function.[32]

4. Do words have a different meaning?

An entirely different approach was, however, taken in a number of the judgments of Jansen JA. In *Sassoon Confirming & Acceptance Co (Pty) Ltd v. Barclays National Bank Ltd*[33] Jansen JA said:

The first step in construing a contract is to determine the ordinary grammatical meaning of the words used by the parties (*Jonnes v. Anglo-African Shipping Co (1936) Ltd* 1972 (2) SA 827 (AD) 834E). Very few words, however, bear a single meaning, and the 'ordinary' meaning of words appearing in a contract will necessarily depend upon the context in which they are used, their interrelation, and the nature of the transaction as it appears from the entire contract. It may, for example, be quite plain from reading the contract as a whole that a certain word or words are not used in their popular everyday meaning, but are employed in a somewhat exceptional, or even technical sense. The meaning of a contract is, therefore, not necessarily determined by merely taking each individual word and applying to it one of its ordinary meanings.

Referring then to a passage from Wessels[34] dealing with the discovery of the parties' intention in relation to the fulfilment of a condition, in which Wessels said that '[t]he Court must gather from the surrounding circumstances what the parties contemplated. It must take into consideration everything which can give a clue to the intention of the parties',[35] Jansen JA pointed out that the rule as stated in Wessels 'lets in the surrounding circumstances as material from which to gather the intention of the parties without reference to any prerequisite of ambiguity or uncertainty in the language of the contract'. This was said *obiter*, however, since the judge found

---

[31] *Ibid.*

[32] The linguistic approach to interpretation was also favoured by George Findlay and F. C. Kirk-Cohen, (1953) 70 *SALJ* 145, who argued (152) that it is a good thing for courts to pretend 'to interpret while they are really modifying', for '[w]e have not yet found and explained the principles of contractual modification—at least not with sufficient clarity to act upon them boldly'. But see P. J. J. Olivier, *Legal Fictions in Practice and Legal Science* (1975), 127. Olivier said of the rules that South African courts have adopted in relation to interpretation: 'It is remarkable that a legal system, which has rejected the normative approach to interpretation and which clearly accepts the intention of the parties as the ultimate criterion, should at the same time limit evidence by which the intention can be proved. This is not only contradictory but self-defeating and leads to practical absurdities, *inter alia* that the court is forced to speculate as to the intention of the parties although evidence is available as to their intention.'

[33] 1974 (1) SA 641 (A) 646. [34] Wessels (n. 6), §§ 1334 sq.

[35] The passage was applied in *Hanomag SA (Pty) Ltd v. Otto* 1940 CPD 437, 443–6.

that in any event there was sufficient uncertainty in the language of the contract to allow evidence of surrounding circumstances.[36]

Jansen JA, in suggesting that courts should not be bound rigidly by the rule that extrinsic evidence should be led only in cases where there is ambiguity or uncertainty in a contract, was influenced to a considerable extent by changes in the English approach—which had affected the golden rule of interpretation in the first place—and by the writings of another American jurist, Arthur Linton Corbin.[37]

The English courts have to some extent, moved away, from the inflexible literal approach. A start was made by Denning LJ in dealing with the doctrine of frustration in a case where the literal words of a contract covered a new situation which had not and could not have been in the contemplation of the parties at the time of entering into the contract.[38] In reaching the conclusion that it would be unjust to allow the literal meaning of the contract to prevail, Denning LJ said:

This does not mean that the courts no longer insist on the binding force of contracts deliberately made. It only means that they will not allow the words, in which they happen to be phrased, to become tyrannical masters . . . The day is done when we can excuse an unforeseen injustice by saying to the sufferer 'It is your own folly. You ought not to have passed that form of words. You ought to have put in a clause to protect yourself'. We no longer credit a party with the foresight of a prophet or his lawyer with the draftsmanship of a Chalmers.

[36] See above, n. 33, 648. This approach was endorsed also by Kumleben J in *Sonarep (SA) (Pty) Ltd v. Motorcraft (Pty) Ltd* 1981 (1) SA 889 (N) 895–7. Stating that the more liberal approach was attractive, Kumleben J none the less held that he was bound by the 'explicit pronouncements of the Appellate Division in this regard'.

[37] *Corbin on Contracts* (1962–3), vol. III, § 536. See also A. J. Kerr, *The Principles of the Law of Contract* (3rd edn., 1980), 240 sqq. (relied on by Jansen JA; the 4th edn. of the book was published in 1989: see 300 sqq.); and for approval of the more liberal approach, and the views of Corbin, see D. T. Zeffertt and A. Paizes, *Parol Evidence with Particular Reference to Contract* (published by the Centre for Banking Law, Rand Afrikaans University, 1986), 79 sqq., Hoffmann/Zeffertt (n. 7), 321 sqq.

[38] *British Movietonews Ltd v. London and District Cinemas Ltd* [1951] 1 KB 190 (CA) 201 sq. The decision was overturned on appeal ([1952] AC 166 (HL)), the House of Lords finding that Denning LJ had misinterpreted earlier decisions on frustration. But there was no criticism of his view that words should not become 'tyrannical masters'. Indeed, Viscount Simon said (185) that if 'a consideration of the terms of the contract, in the light of circumstances existing when it was made, shows that they never agreed to be bound in a fundamentally different situation which has now unexpectedly emerged, the contract ceases to bind at that point—not because the court in its discretion thinks it just and reasonable to qualify the terms of the contract, but because on its true construction it does not apply in that situation.' See also, on the doctrine of frustration, *Davis Contractors v. Fareham UDC* [1956] AC 696, where the Court, in discussing the principle that the court must look to what the parties, as fair and reasonable men, must have intended, said (at 728): 'By this time it might seem that the parties have become so far disembodied spirits that their actual persons should be allowed to rest in peace. In their place there rises the figure of the fair and reasonable man. And the spokesman of the fair and reasonable man, who represents after all no more than the anthropomorphic conception of justice, is, and must be, the court itself.'

More recently, Lord Wilberforce, in two seminal judgments of the House of Lords,[39] made it clear that uncertainty and ambiguity are not the only reasons to look beyond the words of a document to determine intention. In *Prenn v. Simmonds* he said:

> The time has long passed when agreements, even those under seal, were isolated from the matrix of facts in which they were set and interpreted purely on internal linguistic considerations . . . We must . . . enquire beyond the language and see what the circumstances were with reference to which the words were used, and the object, appearing from those circumstances, which the person using them had in view.

It is important to note that Lord Wilberforce was not prepared to allow all evidence to be admitted: thus evidence of negotiations, of what had passed between the parties, is still inadmissible in English law.

These *dicta* were set out by Jansen JA in *Cinema City (Pty) Ltd v. Morgenstern Family Estates (Pty) Ltd.*[40] The judge went on to say[41] that allowing 'evidence of surrounding circumstances in all cases as an aid to interpretation would be consistent with modern thinking on language and its meaning'. However, because the disputed phrase in the contract in question was considered to be ambiguous, and evidence of surrounding circumstances was therefore admissible, he found it unnecessary to 'express any opinion' as to whether South African law had reached the 'stage of development' where the 'open sesame of uncertainty may be dispensed with as a prerequisite to opening the door to evidence of surrounding circumstances'.[42]

This more liberal approach to interpretation is founded on the assumption that words do not have a fixed meaning, a view which has been argued vigorously by Corbin.[43] The essence of his approach is this:[44]

> [I]t can hardly be insisted on too often or too vigorously that language at its best is always a defective and uncertain instrument, that words do not define themselves, that terms and sentences in a contract, a deed, or a will do not apply themselves to external objects and performances, that the meaning of such terms and sentences consists of the ideas that they induce in the mind of some individual person who uses or hears or reads them, and that seldom in a litigated case do the words of a contract convey one identical meaning to the two contracting parties or to third

---

[39] *Prenn v. Simmonds* [1971] 3 All ER 237 (HL) 239 sq.; *Reardon Smith Line Ltd v. Hansen Tangen* [1976] 3 All ER 570 (HL) 574. See also *Rabin v. Gerson Berger Association Ltd* [1983] 1 All ER 374 (CA).

[40] 1980 (1) SA 796 (A) 804 sq.   [41] At 805.

[42] At 805 sq. See also *Sassoon Confirming and Acceptance Co (Pty) Ltd v. Barclays National Bank Ltd* 1974 (1) SA 641 (A) 646, where Jansen JA found that the words 'final judgment against [X]' were uncertain, and that evidence of surrounding circumstances could be admitted to show that the parties had intended to include a judgment against X's trustee. His views on interpretation are also to be found in the text of the L. C Steyn Memorial Lecture delivered by him in August 1980 at the Rand Afrikaans University, printed in 1981 *TSAR* 97.

[43] See above, n. 37.   [44] § 536, 27 sq. See also 535, 17 sq., and 542, 111 sq.

persons. Therefore, it is invariably necessary, before a court can give any meaning to the words of a contract and can select one meaning rather than other possible ones as the basis for the determination of rights and other legal effects, that extrinsic evidence shall be heard to make the court aware of the 'surrounding circumstances', including the persons, objects and events to which the words can be applied and which caused the words to be used.[45]

However, that liberal approach did not gain even a foothold. It has not been dwelt upon in any case subsequent to *Cinema City*, and even Jansen JA, in *Pritchard Properties (Pty) Ltd v. Koulis*,[46] in which the Court did not consider looking for the real intention of the parties beyond the four corners of the document, did not suggest in his dissenting judgment looking to extrinsic evidence to determine the intention of the parties.[47]

Thus one of the ultimate ironies in the development of South African law has been the way in which English rules of evidence have led to the adoption of an objective, literal approach to the ascertainment of the intention of the parties to a contract, whereas English law itself has now adopted a more flexible approach to interpretation. A further anomaly is that the South African courts have moved to a more subjective approach in determining whether a contract has come into existence at all: yet in the interpretation of a contract a rigid, objective approach holds sway.

IV. THE BIFURCATION OF CONTRACTUAL THEORY AND CONTRACTUAL INTERPRETATION

The effect of resorting to an objective, literal approach to interpretation is in a sense a return to the formalism of ancient Roman law where, once the proper form was complied with, the absence of agreement and the intention of the parties were irrelevant. Thus this aspect of the law has not developed in consonance with the jurisprudential basis of contractual liability. Here too the English law has had an effect, though not one which is consistent. The famous expression in England of the theory of quasi-mutual assent, or the reliance theory of contract, which starts (one assumes) from a subjective postulate but allows for liability—in spite of the absence of true consensus—on the basis of reasonable reliance, is that of Blackburn J in *Smith v. Hughes*:[48] '[I]f, whatever a man's real intention may be, he so conducts himself that a reasonable man would believe that he was assenting to the

---

[45] See also Zeffertt/Paizes (n. 7), 82.   [46] 1986 (2) SA 1 (A).

[47] The *Delmas Milling* principles were reaffirmed yet again in *Total South Africa (Pty) Ltd v. Bekker* 1992 (1) SA 617 (A) and in *OK Bazaars (1929) Ltd v. Grosvenor Buildings (Pty) Ltd* 1993 (3) SA 471 (A).

[48] (1871) LR 6 QB 597, 607. Cf. the contribution 'Formation of Contract' by Dale Hutchison to this volume.

terms proposed by the other party, and that other party upon that belief enters into the contract with him, the man thus conducting himself would be equally bound as if he had intended to agree to the other party's terms'. The reliance theory has now finally found acceptance in South African law.[49]

While there have been leanings to an entirely objective theory of contractual liability,[50] the weight of decisions has been in favour of the reliance theory.[51] The essence of this approach is that consensus forms the basis of contractual liability. But if there is in fact no true agreement, and one party has led the other reasonably to believe that there is agreement on certain terms, the former will be bound. Therefore only when the party who relies on a particular meaning has misled the other into believing that he meant something else will he be bound by the appearance that he gave, rather than his subjective state of mind. In the absence of misleading behaviour, culpable or otherwise, a party will not be bound by a contract to which he did not really assent. This is the theory that appeared to find favour in *Spes Bona Bank Ltd v. Portals Water Treatment South Africa (Pty) Ltd*[52] and which was applied in *Sonap Petroleum (SA) (Pty) Ltd v. Pappadogianis.*[53]

The decisive question in cases where there is a dispute as to the terms of a contract is, said Harms AJA in *Sonap*:[54]

[D]id the party whose actual intention did not conform to the common intention expressed, lead the other party, as a reasonable man, to believe that his declared intention represented his actual intention? . . . To answer this question, a three-fold enquiry is usually necessary, namely, firstly, was there a misrepresentation as to one party's intention; secondly, who made that representation; and thirdly, was the other

---

[49] Indeed, as early as 1911, in *I Pieters v. Salomon* 1911 AD 121, Innes J, without reference to *Smith v. Hughes*, said (137): 'When a man makes an offer in plain and unambiguous language, which is understood in its ordinary sense by the person to whom it is addressed, and accepted by him *bona fide* in that sense, then there is a concluded contract. Any unexpressed reservations hidden in the mind of the promisor are in such circumstances irrelevant.'

[50] The clearest statement of an objective approach is that of Wessels JA in *South African Railways and Harbours v. National Bank of South Africa Ltd* 1925 AD 704, 715 sq.: 'The law does not concern itself with the workings of the minds of parties to a contract, but with the external manifestation of their minds. Even therefore if from a philosophical standpoint the minds of the parties do not meet, yet, if by their acts their minds seem to have met, the law will, where fraud is not alleged, look to their acts and assume that their minds did meet and that they contracted in accordance with what the parties purport to accept as a record of their agreement. This is the only practical way in which courts of law can determine the terms of a contract'.

[51] See *contra* Konrad M. Kritzinger, 'Approach to Contract: A Reconciliation', (1983) 100 *SALJ* 47.

[52] 1983 (1) SA 978 (A). And see the comments on the case by Kritzinger (n. 51) and in (1983) 100 *SALJ* 569; R. D. Sharrock, (1984) 101 *SALJ* 1. See also Zeffertt/Paizes (n. 37), 93 sqq. The various theories of contract were discussed by Jansen JA in *Saambou-Nasionale Bouvereeniging v. Friedman* 1979 (3) SA 978 (A); no indication was given, however, as to which of them the Court should adopt.

[53] 1992 (3) SA 234 (A) 239 sq.   [54] At 239 sq.

party misled thereby? . . . The last question postulates two possibilities: Was he actually misled and would a reasonable man have been misled?

The debate about the underlying theory of contractual liability thus seems to be over. However, it is surely unacceptable to follow one approach in determining whether there is a contract at all, and another to determine what the terms of the contract mean.[55] That is the unfortunate result of refusing to ascertain the real intention of the parties. Zeffertt and Paizes have suggested that where there is *dissensus* as to the meaning of a contract the defendant should be penalized for not performing in accordance with the plaintiff's different interpretation if the defendant has at any time, by words or conduct, led the plaintiff reasonably to believe that he interpreted the contract in the same way as the plaintiff did.[56] Thus, in any enquiry as to the existence and meaning of a contract, one should ask first whether the parties have concluded a valid contract (looking first for *consensus*, and only if there is none invoking the reliance theory); then what are the terms of the contract, and finally, what do the terms mean. The reliance theory, say Zeffertt and Paizes,[57] should apply in the answering of the second and third questions as well.

V. SUBSTANCE AND FORM

If we are to ask why South African courts have persisted with a literal approach to the interpretation of contracts, I believe that the answer would, in large measure, lie in the differences in judicial attitudes to the substance of contracts. These differences are exemplified in two decisions in which two judges of appeal, Watermeyer and De Wet, took entirely opposite views. These are *Rand Rietfontein Estates Ltd v. Cohn*[58] and *Commissioner of Customs and Excise v. Randles, Brothers and Hudson Ltd*.[59] In the former case, as we have seen, the Court was concerned with the meaning of the contract before it. Watermeyer AJA adopted the literal approach to interpretation. De Wet JA, dissenting, preferred to allow extrinsic evidence of surrounding circumstances in order to ascertain what the parties had really intended. In concluding that the Court *a quo* had been correct in admitting evidence 'as to the circumstances existing at the time when the agreement was made and as to the facts to which the words of the agreement relate',[60] De Wet JA was bolstered in his approach by reference to Sir John Wessels' *Law of Contract*,[61] which argued that '[t]he Court will lean to that interpretation

---

[55] See in this regard Zeffertt/Paizes (n. 7), 101. This is also the approach of other writers: see e.g. Calamari/Perillo (n. 26), 121.

[56] Zeffertt/Paizes (n. 7), 87.   [57] Ibid. 101 sq.

[58] 1937 AD 317. See above, *sub* II.   [59] 1941 AD 369.   [60] At 330.

[61] 1st edn., vol. I, 1974, referred to at 330 sq. of De Wet JA's judgment.

which will put an equitable construction upon the contract and will not, unless the intention of the parties is manifest, so construe the contract as to give one of the parties an unfair or unreasonable advantage over the other'.

Whilst having regard to substance will not always ensure that equity will prevail, in the case of interpretation it is submitted that establishing the real intention of the parties must be more equitable than construing the contract in a way which none of the parties might ever have intended. In the case of *Commissioner of Customs and Excise* equity was not in issue. In dispute was the intention of the importer of materials to transfer ownership of the materials to various manufacturers, and their respective intentions to acquire ownership. In order to obtain a rebate on customs duty the respondent had purported to sell and transfer ownership of material to various manufacturers, subject to limitations on what the manufacturers could do with it: they had, *inter alia*, to resell the material duly made into garments (at a price equal to the price at which the material was sold to the manufacturer, plus the cost of making up the garments) and made in accordance with the instructions of the respondent, to the respondent, who at all times bore the risk of loss or damage. The majority judgment, delivered by Watermeyer JA (Centlivres JA delivered a separate concurring judgment), found that the parties had so much wanted to transfer and acquire ownership respectively, albeit that the transfer was but a vehicle to achieve some other purpose, that they must have intended ownership to pass. There was no requirement, the Court considered, that the right transferred had to be untrammeled. The minority judges, in particular De Wet CJ,[62] preferred to look to the substance of the contract between the parties, and concluded that they could not possibly have intended ownership to pass when what the buyer actually acquired was an empty shell devoid of any content.[63]

There have thus emerged two clear schools of thought relating to the ascertainment of intention. In the process of contractual interpretation, the approach has been to look at form: to take the literal meaning of the language used in a document and to give it its usual, or ordinary meaning. In other contexts, notably in determining whether there is contractual liability, the courts have veered in the direction of the subjective, but tempered it

---

[62] The other being Tindall JA.

[63] The De Wet approach was followed by Rabie JA (though without any acknowledgment, or perhaps any awareness, that he was doing so) in *Skjelbreds Rederi A/S v. Hartless (Pty) Ltd* 1982 (2) SA 710 (A). In *Vasco Dry Cleaners v. Twycross* 1979 (1) SA 603 (A) the Appellate Division (*per* Hoexter JA) insisted on looking at all the peculiarities of a contract, ostensibly for the transfer of ownership, in determining the real intention of the parties. Thus instead of looking only at the actual words used in a contract for the purpose of ascertaining whether there is a genuine intention to transfer ownership (both in cases dealing with *iusta causa traditionis* and with those considering whether ownership has been passed by *constitutum possessorium*) some judges have looked at all the available evidence. The Watermeyer approach in *Commissioner of Customs and Excise* has, however, prevailed in other cases: see e.g. *Hippo Quarries (Tvl) (Pty) Ltd v. Eardley* 1991 (1) SA 867 (A).

with the theory of quasi-mutual assent (the reliance theory). In ascertaining intention for the purpose of determining whether ownership has been transferred, the courts have adopted different approaches: in some cases looking at form only and in others examining the substance of a transaction: what was truly intended.

VI. THE SECONDARY RULES

As we have seen, the primary rule of interpretation is taken from Pothier and Van der Linden[64] who were, for the most part, relying on texts in the *Digest*. The secondary rules have the same sources. However, their status has never been made absolutely clear and it must be assumed that they were always regarded as guides to the meaning of a contract where intention could not be determined. A resort to any of these rules or guides is thus an implementation of a construction put on a contract by a court, which might bear little, if any, relation to what was actually intended by the parties. There is no hierarchy in the application of the rules, and indeed some have rarely been applied by South African courts, if ever.[65] Lubbe and Murray[66] suggest that the secondary rules 'indicate normative considerations of policy relevant to problems of interpretation'. In support of this proposition they cite the *dictum* of Schreiner JA in *Kliptown Clothing Industries (Pty) Ltd v. Marine and Trade Insurance Co of South Africa Ltd*:[67] the secondary rules, he held, are 'directed to the ascertainment, not of the meaning of the language as understood by the Court, but of the meaning which the law says ought in the circumstances to be given to it'.

1. The context rule[68]

'*Incivile est, nisi tota lege perspecta, una aliqua particula eius proposita, judicare vel respondere*'.[69] Pothier renders the rule thus:[70] 'We must interpret

---

[64] Pothier (n. 1); Van der Linden (n. 3).

[65] I shall discuss only those rules which have been applied by South African courts. Not all of Pothier's or even Van der Linden's principles of interpretation have been invoked, and the division into 'rules' is somewhat arbitrary since some may be subdivided into yet others, and some are merely different aspects of what is essentially the same principle. Paul van Warmelo, 'Die Uitleg van Kontrakte', (1960) 77 *SALJ* 69 sqq., finds well over 40 rules in the *Corpus Juris*.

[66] Lubbe/Murray (n. 25), 466 sqq.   [67] 1961 (1) SA 103 (A) 107.

[68] In discussing the secondary rules I shall follow the order adopted by Wessels (n. 6), §§ 1915 sqq.

[69] D. 1, 3, 24. Wessels, § 1915, follows Monro's translation: 'It is not like a lawyer to take hold of one particular portion of a statute and found a judgment or opinion upon it without examining the whole statute.' Whether one should render '*incivile est*' as 'it is not like a lawyer' is questionable.

[70] Pothier (n. 1), rule 6.

every term of a contract by the other terms of the same contract whether they precede or follow it.' Van der Linden states:[71] 'A stipulation must be construed by the aid of the other stipulations contained in the contract, whether they precede or follow it.'

The same principle is invoked in English law, as in the judgment of Lord Halsbury in *Elderslie Steamship Co v. Borthwick*.[72] It has also frequently been invoked in South African cases.[73] In *Swart v. Cape Fabrix (Pty) Ltd* Rumpff CJ said:

Wat natuurlik aanvaar moet word, is dat, wanneer die betekenis van woorde in 'n kontrak bepaal moet word, die woorde onmoontlik uitgeknip en op 'n skoon stuk papier geplak kan word en dan beoordeel moet word om die betekenis daarvan te bepaal. Dit is vir my vanselfsprekend dat 'n mens na die betrokke woorde moet kyk met inagneming van die aard en opset van die kontrak, en ook na die samehang van die woorde in die kontrak as geheel.[74]

Note that the context may be examined simply in order to ascertain the ordinary meaning of the words used: *Jaga v. Dönges*.[75]

2. The validity rule

'When a contract or clause in a contract is capable of being taken in two senses, it must be construed in that sense which will give effect to the instrument as a legal contract rather than in a sense which will render it inoperative'.[76] Again, there are a number of supporting statements in the *Digest*, the best known of which is in D. 1, 3, 18 and D. 34, 5, 12: '*Interpretatio chartarum benigne facienda est ut res magis valeat quam pereat.*' The chief application of this principle has been to rescue contracts from illegality or from inefficacy.[77]

---

[71] Van der Linden (n. 2). [72] [1905] AC 93.

[73] See the list of authorities cited by Christie (n. 5), 244, fn. 46.

[74] 1979 (1) SA 195 (A) 202. (What must, of course, be accepted is that when the meaning of words in a contract has to be ascertained it is impossible to cut out the words and put them on a clean sheet of paper and look at them in order to determine their meaning. It is self-evident that one has to look at the words concerned, taking account of the type and purpose of the contract, and also at the interrelationship of the words in the contract as a whole.) See also *List v. Jungers* 1979 (3) SA 106 (A), where Diemont JA said (118): 'It is, in my view, an unrewarding and misleading exercise to seize on one word in a document, determine its more usual or ordinary meaning, and then, having done so, to seek to interpret the document in the light of the meaning so ascribed to that word . . . It must be borne in mind that this court has held that it can be informed of the background circumstances under which a contract was concluded so as to enable it to understand the broad context in which the words to be interpreted were used.'

[75] 1950 (4) SA 653 (A) 664. Another approach would be that resort should be had to the context only where the clear meaning of the disputed words is not apparent. But this would not be consonant with the *dicta* in *Swart* and in *List* above.

[76] Pothier (n. 1), rule 2, § 92. The Van der Linden rule reads: 'When a stipulation is capable of two meanings, it should rather be construed in that sense in which it can have some operation than in that in which it cannot have any': 1, 14, 4, rule 2.

[77] See the list of cases in which the maxim has been applied in Christie (n. 19), 253 sq.

3. The conformity to the contract rule

'When the words of a contract may be taken in two ways, they must be construed in that way which is most agreeable to the nature of the contract'.[78]

4. Customary meaning rule

'Custom or usage is of such authority in the interpretation of contracts that a contract is understood to contain the customary clauses although they are not expressed'.[79] A term based on custom or trade usage will be implied into a contract where:

it is shown to be universally and uniformly observed within the particular trade concerned, long-established, notorious, reasonable and certain, and does not conflict with positive law (in the sense of endeavouring to alter a rule of law which the parties could not alter by their agreement) or with the clear provisions of the contract.[80]

In *Alfred McAlpine and Son (Pty) Ltd v. Transvaal Provincial Administration*[81] Corbett AJA suggested that trade usages and customary terms are but instances of implied terms—*naturalia*—of a contract: that is, terms implied by the law, or in this specific instance by custom or usage, rather than by the facts (in which case such terms would be 'tacit' rather than implied). Note, however, that in a number of early cases, reliance was placed on *Halsbury*,[82] which distinguished between custom and usage on the basis that custom is a rule which has existed, actually or presumptively, since time immemorial, and which has applied in a place even if contrary to the general law of a country.[83] Usages, on the other hand, need not have existed since time immemorial, they need not be confined to a particular locality, and they may not be contrary to positive law.[84] Recent cases in South Africa, notably *Alfred McAlpine*, have made it clear that this distinction no

---

[78] Pothier (n. 1), rule 3, § 93. Van der Linden writes: 'Whenever the words of a contract are capable of two meanings, it should rather be construed in that sense which is most agreeable to the nature of the agreement': 1, 14, 4. A number of passages from the Digest express this principle: see e.g. D. 50, 17, 67. The principle underlies the decision in *AA Farm Sales (Pty) Ltd (t/a AA Farms) v. Kirkaldy* 1980 (1) SA 13 (A).

[79] Pothier (n. 1), rule 5, § 95. Van der Linden has 2 rules to this effect: his 4th rule is: 'That which appears ambiguous in a contract should be construed according to usage of the place where the contract was made.' The 5th rule states: 'Usage has such weight in the construction of agreements that the usual stipulations are understood to be included in them, although not expressly mentioned': 1, 14, 4.

[80] *Per* Corbett J in *Golden Cape Fruits (Pty) Ltd v. Fotoplate (Pty) Ltd* 1973 (2) SA 642 (C) 645.

[81] 1974 (3) SA 506 (A).

[82] The principles reflected in *Halsbury* are to be found in the 4th edn., vol. XII, §§ 400–5.

[83] Halsbury (n. 82), §§ 401 sq.

[84] Ibid. § 405. See Christie (n. 19), 189 for references to the cases in which Halsbury's rules have been applied.

longer obtains: neither custom nor trade usage may be contrary to the general provisions of the law.

5. Restriction of general words

Pothier sets out two rules in this regard, one a qualification of the other: 'However general the expressions in a contract may be, they are restricted in interpretation to those matters only which were contemplated by the parties at the time the contract was made, and are not extended to matters of which they never thought'.[85] The qualification is: 'When the object of the agreement is universally to include everything of a given nature, the general description will comprise all particular articles, although they may not have been in the knowledge of the parties'.[86] Often referred to as the *eiusdem generis*—or *noscitur a sociis*—rule, it is difficult to apply. (It has had particular application in contracts of insurance, however.[87])

In *Grobbelaar v. Van der Vyver*[88] Schreiner JA said:

The application of the *ejusdem generis* principle of interpretation often gives rise to difficult problems. It is not possible to lay down any simple rule which will provide clear guidance as to when wide general language is to be given its full independent width and when it is to be narrowed down to conform with the scope of associated words: nor can the reasons which may lead to the association in a contract or a statute of narrow, specific words with wide, general ones be summarised with any approach to completeness and accuracy . . . . [T]he instrument of interpretation denoted by *ejusdem generis* or *noscitur a sociis* must always be borne in mind where the meaning of general words in association with specific words has to be ascertained, but that what is often a useful means of finding out what was meant by a provision in a contract or statute must not be allowed to substitute an artificial intention for what was clearly the real one.[89]

6. General words not restricted by special example

'If a special case is mentioned in a contract on account of a doubt whether the contract would extend to such a case or in order to explain the nature of the obligation, the parties are not thereby understood to restrict the scope of the contract in respect of other cases not expressed'.[90] The maxim

[85] Rule 8, § 98. See D. 2, 15, 9, 3: '*Iniquum est peremi pacto id de quo non cogitatur.*'

[86] Rule 9. Van der Linden's version is: 'However general the expressions may be in which an agreement is framed, they only include the matters in respect of which it appears that the contracting parties intended to contract, and not those which they did not contemplate': 1, 14, 4, rule 8.

[87] See Wessels (n. 6), § 1946.   [88] 1954 (1) SA 248 (A) 254 sq.

[89] Contrast this statement with Schreiner JA's approach to ascertaining the *real* intention of the parties, expressed in *Delmas Milling*, discussed above.

[90] Pothier (n. 1), rule 10, § 100. The rule originates from Papinian D. 50, 17, 81: '*Quae dubitationis causa contractibus inseruntur, ius commune non laedunt.*'

inclusio unius est exclusio alterius is a negation of this principle, and is thus rarely invoked.[91] Essentially, the rule requires one to consider whether special examples have been included *ex abundanti cautela*, or whether their inclusion requires one to exclude all other possibilities covered by the general words.

7. The *contra stipulatorem* or *contra proferentem* rule

'In case of doubt, a clause ought to be interpreted against the person who stipulates for a thing, and in favour of a person who contracts the obligation'.[92] Of course, we no longer recognize stipulation as a method of concluding a contract, and so modern law has adapted the rule to penalize the party responsible for the wording or the drafting of the ambiguous provision. Wessels says of this rule:[93]

If we mean by interpretation or construction of a contract an endeavour to find out the intention of the parties, then this rule is out of place here. It does not help solve the difficulty of knowing what the parties intended; it cuts the Gordian knot and arbitrarily determines against the stipulator. Faber and Lord Bacon point out that it should be the last recourse of the judge. It is only to be invoked if no other rule of construction can be applied.

The observation that the rule does not help us in finding the true intention of the parties is equally applicable to all the other secondary principles of interpretation. Perhaps, however, the *contra proferentem* rule is singled out by Wessels as being unhelpful in the search for intention because it is so arbitrary in its application.

The *contra proferentem* rule is discussed at length, as is its history, in the judgment of Davis AJA in *Cairns (Pty) Ltd v. Playdon & Co Ltd*.[94] Having traced the rule from its Roman antecedents through the writings of the Roman-Dutch authorities, Davis AJA pointed out that the *contra stipulatorem* rule is but an instance of the rule that a provision must be construed against the *proferens*. He indicated also that a third aspect of the rule is that 'in case of doubt, a burden is to be construed as lightly as possible'.[95] While recognizing that the rule does not lead one to discovering the parties' intention, Davis AJA held that in the case before him the contract was so badly

---

[91] See Christie (n. 5), 257 (notes 91 and 92) for cases where the general principle has prevailed, and those where the maxim *inclusio unius est exclusio alterius* has been applied.

[92] Pothier (n. 1), rule 7, § 97. Van der Linden (n. 2), 1, 14, 4, in the 7th rule, states: 'In cases of ambiguity a stipulation must be construed against the party who has stipulated for anything, and in favour of the release of the party who has contracted the obligation.' See also D. 45, 1, 48, 18: '*In stipulationibus cum quaeritur quid actum sit verba contra stipulatorem interpretanda sunt.*' For details see Zimmermann (n. 3), 639 sqq.

[93] Wessels (n. 6), § 1956.   [94] 1948 (3) SA 99 (A).

[95] 122 sq. As authority Davis AJA cites D. 50, 17, 9: ('*Semper in obscuris quod minimum est sequimur*') as well as the *Restatement of the Law, Contracts*, § 236 (d).

drafted that he had to apply the rule and, in Wessels' words, 'cut the Gordian knot'.[96]

VII. EXCLUSION OR EXEMPTION CLAUSES

A full treatment of clauses which exempt a party from liability on certain grounds, or generally, is beyond the scope of this paper. However, it is important to note that South African courts have interpreted such provisions differently from other provisions in contracts in two respects. First, public policy is invoked in the application of exemption clauses. In *Morrison v. Angelo Deep Gold Mines Ltd*[97] Innes CJ said:

Now it is a general principle that a man contracting without duress, without fraud, and understanding what he does, may freely waive any of his rights. There are certain exceptions to that rule, and certainly the law will not recognise any arrangement which is contrary to public policy.

Applying this principle in *Wells v. SA Alumenite Co*,[98] Innes CJ stated:

On grounds of public policy the law will not recognise an undertaking by which one of the contracting parties binds himself to condone and submit to the fraudulent conduct of the other. The Courts will not lend themselves to the enforcement of such a stipulation; for to do so would be to protect and encourage fraud ... Hence contractual conditions by which one of the parties engages to verify all representations for himself, and not to rely upon them as inducing the contract, must be confined to honest mistake or honest misrepresentations.[99] However wide the language, the Court will cut down and confine its operations within those limits.

Secondly, although not expressly done, clauses excluding liability tend to be strictly construed, *contra proferentem*: although this rule is not expressly invoked in the process of construction.[100]

VIII. CONCLUSION

The application of the secondary rules of interpretation, while in some instances facilitating the ascertainment of the parties' genuine intention, has often required courts to ignore the primary rule that requires them always to ascertain what the parties themselves meant by the words they used. Although the secondary rules have been invoked rarely, because the courts

---

[96] At 123.   [97] 1905 TS 775, 779.   [98] 1927 AD 69, 72.
[99] The term 'honest' encompasses 'negligent'. This has been clear since *Central South African Railways v. Adlington & Co* 1906 TS 964.
[100] See Christie (n. 19), 214 sqq. and Lubbe/Murray (n. 25), 466 sqq. See also *Lawrence v. Kondotel Inns (Pty) Ltd* 1989 (1) SA 44 (D) 53 sqq.

have more often than not considered it possible to construe provisions 'linguistically', they do obscure the search for genuine intention. This has not yet caused difficulty because the literal, objective approach to interpretation itself does not anyway require the discovery of true intention.[101] However, the application of the literal approach coupled with the application of the secondary rules must inevitably result in inequity, particularly in view of the prevalence of standard form contracts, the high rate of illiteracy, and the notorious inequality in bargaining power in South African society.

The purpose of this Chapter is to trace the development of the Roman-Dutch law relating to the interpretation of contracts in South Africa. As has been shown, there are different threads, often knotted rather than woven together. The courts have moved towards the objective, on the assumption that a linguistic treatment of the parties' words will reveal what the contract means. They have consistently cited the golden, primary rule of construction—that the parties' intention must be ascertained—as being the base from which they must proceed. However, they have rarely stopped to examine what the texts of the Roman and European writers (principally those of Pothier and Van der Linden) requiring a search for the intention of the parties really mean. With few exceptions[102] they have assumed that an objective, linguistic approach is necessary and indeeed possible.[103]

Whether such an approach is warranted is debatable, as I have indicated; that it should continue in dissonance with the underlying theories of contract is clearly unacceptable. The time has now come for an overhaul of the South African approach to the interpretation of contracts. I believe that a re-examination of the foundations of the law, and an explicit statement of judicial policy on the ascertainment of intention, would be of value. Not only could it lead to the reconciliation of approaches to the interpretation of contract on one hand, and to the theory of contractual liability on the other, but it might also lead to a triumph of equity and substance over form, a result that would be in keeping with a society now in search of greater justice than has existed before.

---

[101] According to Lubbe/Murray (n. 25), 469, a normative, rather than a historical, psychological approach is desirable. And, they say: 'Explicit recognition of [a normative] judicial role will promote the just enforcement of contracts. It will provide a mechanism by which South African contract doctrine can move away from a rigidly individualistic stance to one which takes account of the structural inequalities within society.'

[102] Notably the judgments of De Wet CJ and Jansen JA, discussed above.

[103] See the passage from Corbin (n. 37), and the views of Jansen JA set out above.

7: *Good Faith and Equity*

REINHARD ZIMMERMANN*

I. INTRODUCTION: EQUITY, *BONA FIDES*, *EXCEPTIO DOLI*

Modern South African law is one of a handful of 'mixed' legal systems.[1] It is based firmly on the continental civilian heritage but has also been influenced to a considerable extent by the English common law. The process that transformed South African law into a mixed legal system originated in the British occupation of the Cape of Good Hope in 1806;[2] and one of the main factors facilitating it was the reception of the English law of procedure and evidence within a court system remodelled according to the English pattern.[3] One characteristic aspect of the English court system was, however, never received in South Africa: the distinction between courts of law and courts of equity. If, therefore, it was often said that the Cape Supreme Court (and later the South African Supreme Court) was a court of equity[4] as well as of law, this was taken to mean that the Court had 'the power to exercise an equitable jurisdiction', but only 'insofar as it is not inconsistent with the fixed principles of the Dutch law'.[5] The law that had originally

---

* This paper was first presented at a conference in Jerusalem in May 1993 (on which see 1993 Zeitschrift für Europäisches Privatrecht, 628 sqq.). A volume containing all contributions to this conference will be edited by A. M. Rabello under the title *Aequitas and Equity: Equity in Civil Law and Mixed Jurisdictions*.

[1] For details and further references cf. Reinhard Zimmermann, 'Roman Law in a Mixed Legal System—The South African Experience', in: Robin Evans-Jones (ed.), *The Civil Law Tradition in Scotland* (1995), 41 sqq.

[2] On the reception of English law at the Cape see e.g. H. R. Hahlo, Ellison Kahn, *The Union of South Africa: The Development of its Laws and Constitution* (1960), 17 sqq.; Ben Beinart, 'The English Legal Contribution in South Africa: The Interaction of Civil and Common Law', 1981 *Acta Juridica* 7 sqq.; Reinhard Zimmermann, 'Die Rechtsprechung des Supreme Court of the Cape of Good Hope am Ende der sechziger Jahre des 19. Jahrhunderts', in: *Huldigingsbundel Paul van Warmelo* (1984), 286 sqq. See also the contribution by Eduard Fagan in this volume.

[3] Cf. esp. H. J. Erasmus, 'The interaction of substantive and procedural law: the Southern African experience in historical and comparative perspective', (1990) 1 *Stellenbosch LR* 348 sqq.; *idem*, 'Historical Foundations of the South African Law of Civil Procedure', (1991) 108 *SALJ* 265 sqq. See also the contribution by the same author in this volume.

[4] See specifically, the statement by Graham, JP, in *Ferreira v. Ferreira* 1915 EDL 9 (15 sq.), set out below in n. 48.

[5] *Estate Thomas v. Kerr* (1903) 20 SC 354 (366) (*per* De Villiers CJ). See e.g. *Bothwell v. Union Government*, as reported in 1917 AD 262 (269) (*per* Kotzé JA); *Weinerlein v. Goch Buildings Ltd* 1925 AD 282 (295) (*per* Kotzé JA); *Bank of Lisbon and South Africa Ltd v. De Ornelas* 1988 (3) SA 580 (A) 606 (*per* Joubert JA).

been transplanted to the Cape by Dutch settlers in 1652, the so-called Roman-Dutch law,[6] always remained the common law of the country and had to be administered by its courts; and thus, these courts were essentially courts of law. But Roman-Dutch law was, in itself, inherently equitable;[7] equity was not a body of rules outside of and apart from the 'common' law, but thoroughly pervading and informing it. The 'equitable jurisdiction' was thus taken to be part and parcel of the general mission of the courts to administer the (South African, i.e. essentially Roman-Dutch) 'common law'.[8]

A great variety of rules and legal institutions find their origin in this kind of 'built-in' equity;[9] the whole law of unjustified enrichment, for instance, reflects the principle according to which it is in the nature of things fair *neminem cum alterius detrimento fieri locupletiorem*.[10] For present purposes, however, we have to focus our attention on the law of contract; and here we find one specific device that, more than any other, infused this branch of the law with an equitable spirit: the concept of *bona fides*, or good faith. *Bona fides* was one of the most fertile agents in the development of Roman contract law.[11] In relation to *iudicia stricti iuris* it gained its influence as a result of a specific standard clause, inserted into the procedural formula at the request of the defendant. This clause was known as an *exceptio doli* and it was worded in the alternative: *si in ea re nihil dolo malo A^i A^i factum sit neque fiat*.[12] *Factum est* referred to fraudulent behaviour before the institution of the action (against which the *exceptio* was now raised), particularly in the act of concluding the contract.[13] *Fiat*, on the other hand, comprised all cases where the bringing of the action itself could be taken to constitute *dolus*. It was particulary this second alternative that made the *exceptio doli* such a powerful instrument for bringing about a just solution, for it invited an answer which located *dolus* not so much in personal misconduct, but rather in an inequity or injustice that would flow from the action being

---

[6] Cf. Reinhard Zimmermann, *Das römisch-holländische Recht in Südafrika* (1983), 1 sqq.

[7] See e.g. Kotzé J in *Estate Thomas v. Kerr* (1903) 20 SC 354 (374): 'Indeed its broad equitable spirit is one of the most noteworthy characteristics of Roman-Dutch law'. For a recent reassertion cf. *Bank of Lisbon and South Africa Ltd v. De Ornelas* 1988 (3) SA 580 (A) 606.

[8] On the meaning of the term 'common law' in South Africa see D. P. Visser, 'Daedalus in the Supreme Court: the common law today', (1986) 49 *THRHR* 127 sqq.

[9] H. R. Hahlo, Ellison Kahn, *The South African Legal System and its Background* (1968), 137 sq.

[10] (. . . to render nobody richer at the expense of another): Paul. D. 12, 6, 14; cf. D. 50, 17, 206; on which see Reinhard Zimmermann, *The Law of Obligations: Roman Foundations of the Civilian Tradition* (reprint 1993), 851 sqq., 873, 885 sqq.

[11] Cf. Emilio Betti, 'Der Grundsatz von Treu und Glauben in rechtsgeschichtlicher und -vergleichender Betrachtung', in: *Festgabe für Müller-Erzbach* (1954), 16; Max Kaser, *Das römische Privatrecht, Erster Abschnitt* (2nd edn., 1971), 485; Detlef Liebs, *Römisches Recht* (3rd edn., 1987), 264 sqq.

[12] Gai. IV, 119.

[13] On *dolus in contrahendo* see Peter Stein, *Fault in the Formation of Contract* (1958).

countenanced.[14] Ultimately, therefore, it gave the judge an equitable discretion to decide the case before him in accordance with what appeared to be fair and reasonable.[15]

This, essentially, was the regime applicable to the one cornerstone of the Roman contractual system, the stipulation, for it was governed by the *iudicium stricti iuris par excellence*, the *condictio*.[16] The other—in the long run even more durable—cornerstone was the consensual contract. A specific procedural device in the form of an *exceptio doli* was not necessary here to check the improper exercise of contractual rights.[17] The judge had this discretion anyway, for he was, according the formulae applicable to these kinds of contracts, instructed to condemn the defendant into *quidquid ob eam rem N^m N^m A° A° dare facere oportet ex fide bona*. The substantive content of the *exceptio doli*, in other words, was absorbed into the requirement of good faith according to which the dispute had to be decided.

The essential prerequisite for the growth of the modern generalized theory of contract was the replacement of the Roman *numerus clausus* of contracts concluded *nudo consensu* with the idea that, in principle, all informal agreements are binding.[18] It was nearly universally recognized in seventeenth and eighteenth century Roman-Dutch law[19] and has therefore also become the basis of modern South African contract law. Yet in a streamlined, general system of contract law it makes no sense to perpetuate two (technically, not substantially) different regimes of making the evaluation of contractual rights and duties dependent on the standard of good faith. Which of them was to prevail? Roman-Dutch law was no longer actional law: *ubi ius ibi remedium* had for many centuries been the maxim governing the relationship between substantive law and procedure. The term *exceptio* therefore no longer had a specific technical significance. Furthermore, in the course of the Middle Ages the stipulation had lost its appeal as a viable legal institution and slowly faded into obscurity.[20] The modern theory of contract thus descends in direct line from the consensual contracts of Roman law; it was based, historically, on a generalization of their field

[14] Geoffrey MacCormack, 'Dolus in the Law of the Early Classical Period (Labeo-Celsus)', (1986) 52 *Studia et documenta historiae et iuris*, 263 sq.

[15] On *bona fides* and *dolus* and on the meaning of *dolus* in the present context see *Law of Obligations* (n. 10) 667 sqq.

[16] For details see *Law of Obligations* (n. 10) 68 sqq.

[17] Cf., D. 30, 84, 5: ' . . . *quia hoc iudicium fidei bonae est et continet in se doli mali exceptionem*'; Bernhard Windscheid, Theodor Kipp, *Lehrbuch des Pandektenrechts* (9th edn., 1906), 47, n. 7.

[18] For an account of this development see *Law of Obligations* (n. 10) 508 sqq., 537 sqq. and the contributions to John Barton (ed.), *Towards a General Law of Contract* (1990).

[19] Reinhard Zimmermann, 'Roman-Dutch Jurisprudence and its Contribution to European Private Law', (1992) 66 *Tulane LR* 1689 sqq.; Robert Feenstra, 'Die Klagbarkeit der *pacta nuda*', in: Robert Feenstra, Reinhard Zimmermann (eds.), *Das römisch-holländische Recht: Fortschritte des Zivilrechts im 17. und 18. Jahrhundert* (1992), 123 sqq.

[20] Cf. *Law of Obligations* (n. 10) 546 sqq.

of application rather than on a 'deformalization' of the type of contract that had, even in Roman law, been universally applicable.

The consequence was obvious, and it was particularly clearly spelt out by the late eighteenth century Amsterdam advocate Cornelis Willem Decker in his annotations to Van Leeuwen, *Het Rooms-Hollands-Regt*: '. . . we may also conveniently dispense with the division of contracts into *stricti juris* and *bonae fidei*', he wrote, 'for according to our customs all contracts are considered to be *bonae fidei*, which necessarily follows, if we hold that with us all contracts are constituted by consent'.[21] Whether this was recognized as unequivocally by all the other Roman-Dutch authors; whether the further consequences flowing from this statement were in fact drawn in theory and practice; and whether the Roman-Dutch courts actually used the discretion thus conferred upon them:[22] these are questions that need not detain us here. Suffice it to say that modern South African courts and writers generally consider contracts to have been *bonae fidei* in 'classical' Roman-Dutch law. 'That is to say', as Joubert JA puts it,[23] 'the contracting parties were bound to everything which good faith reasonably and equitably demanded'. Or, in the words of Jansen JA: 'On principle this meant that the courts should have had wide powers to read into a contract any term that justice required'.[24]

Somewhat surprisingly, in view of this, the expression '*exceptio doli*' continued to be used in Roman-Dutch law as well as elsewhere in the European *ius commune*;[25] it has also surfaced in modern South African law. If, therefore, we want to assess the role of equity in modern Roman-Dutch law we will have to proceed in two stages. First, we have to discuss the significance of the *exceptio doli*; secondly, we have to explore the implications of the statement that all contracts are *bonae fidei*.

---

[21] *Simon van Leeuwen's Commentaries on Roman-Dutch Law*, revised and edited with notes, in two volumes, by C. W. Decker, trans. J. G. Kotzé (1886), Bk. IV, Ch. II, ad § 1 (vol. II, 11). Cf. the references in A. D. Botha, *Die exceptio doli generalis in die Suid-Afrikaanse Reg* (unpublished LL D thesis, University of the Orange Free State, 1981), 83 sqq.; *idem*, 'Die *exceptio doli generalis*, rektifikasie en estoppel', (1980) 43 *THRHR* 261 sqq.

[22] Cf. in this context the observations by Jansen JA in *Tuckers Land and Development Corporation (Pty) Ltd v. Hovis* 1980 (1) SA 645 (A) 651 sq. and David Carey Miller, '*Judicia bonae fidei*: A new development in contract?', (1980) 97 *SALJ* 532 sq.

[23] *Bank of Lisbon and South Africa Ltd v. De Ornelas* 1988 (3) SA 580 (A) 601.

[24] *Tuckers Land and Development Corporation (Pty) Ltd v. Hovis*, see n. 22 above, 1980 (1) SA 645 (A) 652.

[25] Cf. the references in Botha (n. 21) 79 sqq., 89 sqq.

II. *EXCEPTIO DOLI*

1. Estoppel

(a) The reception of estoppel

As far as can be ascertained from the printed law reports, the *exceptio doli* made its Southern African début[26] in a case reported *sub nomine Smith and Rance v. Philips* and *B Lazarus v. Levy and the Glencairn GM Co.*[27] It dealt, *inter alia*, with the application of the doctrine of estoppel, and in the course of his judgment Kotzé CJ stated that '[this] doctrine is . . . recognised by our law, as sufficiently appears from the *exceptio doli mali*, the rule *nemo ex suo delicto meliorem condicionem suam facere potest*, and others'.[28] In the case at hand he was, however, unable to find 'that the circumstances of this case entitle the respondents successfully to set up the *exceptio doli mali* against the applicants'.[29]

Kotzé, at that stage Chief Justice of the South African Republic (which was to become, within the Union of 1910, the Province of Transvaal) was one of the great judges of the late nineteenth and early twentieth centuries who laid the foundations of modern South African law.[30] He was as learned in Roman-Dutch as in English law and constantly attempted to elaborate the Roman-Dutch principles whithout necessarily rejecting whatever had, over the previous decades, been received from English law. *Smith and Rance* presents a good example of how he tried to accommodate an English doctrine within the framework of the civilian heritage. For the concept of estoppel had come from English Equity to Southern Africa and had been applied long before 1893. This was acknowledged by Kotzé CJ in the passage quoted above, and it is also obvious, as far as the Cape Colony is concerned, from a statement by De Villiers CJ[31] in *Merriman v. Williams*, a case decided in 1880. Even at that stage, the principles relating to estoppel appear to have been so widely recognized in practice that the Chief Justice felt compelled to raise his doubts as to whether they were applicable, without modification, to the law of the Cape.[32] This, however, did not mean that 'the doctrine of estoppel is entirely unknown in our law', as he clarified in the 1904 case of *Van Blommestein v. Holliday*.[33] At the same time, like

---

[26] I rely in this regard on Botha (n. 21) 181 sq.
[27] 1893 Hertzog 50.
[28] Ibid. 60.
[29] Ibid. 60 sq.
[30] Cf. Zimmermann (n. 6) 22 sq.; Ellison Kahn, *Law, Life and Laughter: Legal Andecdotes and Portraits* (1991), 115 sqq.; Sir John Kotzé, Biographical Memoirs and Reminiscences (no year); *idem*, Memoirs and Reminiscences (vol. II, no year, ed. B. A. Tindall). Unfortunately there is not yet a substantial biography.
[31] On whom see E. A. Walker, *Lord de Villiers and His Times* (1925); cf. Reinhard Zimmermann, 'De Villiers, John Henry', in: Michael Stolleis (ed.), *Juristen: Ein biographisches Lexikon* (1995), 160 sq.
[32] 1880 Foord 135 (172).
[33] (1904) 21 SC 11 (17 sq.).

Kotzé CJ before him, he sought to justify its importation from English law by referring to the legal sources he was supposed to apply; neither under Roman nor under Dutch law, he asserted, 'would a person who, by his words or conduct, has wilfully or negligently induced another to alter his own position in the belief that a certain state of facts exists, have been allowed to assert a right against such other person inconsistent with such state of facts'.[34] He did not mention the *exceptio doli* but it is obvious that this defence would have covered that type of situation in Roman law.

Very soon afterwards, the Transvaal Supreme Court had another opportunity to pronounce on the matter. Somewhat more cautiously than Kotzé CJ the Court now stated that the doctrine of estoppel *in pais*,[35] as expounded 'by the later decisions in England and America', though not known 'to our law' under that name, 'is analogous to what was known in Roman law as the *exceptio doli mali*'.[36] Curlewis J went on to explain the significance of the *exceptio doli* in Roman law; a consideration of the many instances given in D. 44, 4 of the range of application of this defence led him to describe the doctrine of estoppel as being 'merely an extended interpretation' of the principles underlying the *exceptio doli mali*.[37] The term estoppel, which has 'indeed been generally adopted in practice in South Africa', is then described as 'a more convenient expression for that form of defence which was known under the Roman law as the *exceptio doli mali*'; and the principles of the English doctrine of estoppel 'may, I think, be equally applied in our courts in the consideration of a defence such as is raised in the present case'.[38]

These statements can hardly be regarded as models of precision, for the exact relationship between the *exceptio doli* and estoppel disappears behind a smokescreen of nebulous phrases ('analogous', 'extended interpretation', 'more convenient expression'). However, two things become clear. Despite the protestations by De Villiers CJ, it is the English doctrine of estoppel that has been received;[39] no mention is made of any 'modification'. And the Roman-Dutch niche for it is the *exceptio doli*—no matter whether it covers the same,[40] a similar, a more restricted, or a more extended ground. After Union this position was affirmed by the Appellate Division of the Supreme

---

[34] *Van Blommestein v. Holliday* (1904) 21 SC 11 (17 sq.)

[35] On the term estoppel '*in pais*' (an ancient expression in English law which, as far as South African law is concerned, is 'neither enlightening nor useful') cf. P. J. Rabie, *The Law of Estoppel in South Africa* (1992), 17.

[36] *Waterval Estate & Gold Mining Co Ltd v. New Bullion Gold Mining Co Ltd* 1905 TS 717 (722). On which see Tebbutt J in *Sonday v. Surrey Estate Modern Meat Market (Pty) Ltd* 1983 (2) SA 521 (C) 526: 'If not a blood brother, [the English doctrine of estoppel] was a near cousin [of the *exceptio doli*] and therefore to be welcomed as part of the family.'

[37] *Waterval Estate & Gold Mining Co Ltd v. New Bullion Gold Mining Co Ltd* 1905 TS 717 (722).   [38] *Loc. cit.*

[39] This is generally recognized today; cf. esp. J. C. de Wet, *Estoppel by Representation in die Suid-Afrikaanse Reg* (1939), 10 sqq.; Rabie (n. 35) 21.

[40] See e.g. the view expressed by Howard J in the *Oceanair* case as quoted below, n. 44.

Court of South Africa. 'The doctrine of estoppel . . . is as much a part of our law as it is of that of England': this is how Solomon JA described the situation in the 1920 case of *Baumann v. Thomas*;[41] and, since the subject had been much more fully developed by the decisions of the English courts 'than it has been in our own authorities', South African courts 'usually look for guidance to the former rather than to the latter'.[42] Solomon JA also referred to the *exceptio doli* in this context and associated himself with the views expressed by Curlewis in the *Waterval Estate* case. That appeared to settle the matter. *Baumann v. Thomas* became the authoritative point of reference for the proposition that the (English) doctrine of estoppel had become part and parcel of South African law.[43] Further investigations into its relation to the *exceptio doli* were apparently no longer regarded as necessary, and so the Roman institution slowly faded into the background.[44]

(b) The legitimacy of the new doctrine

None of the cases so far mentioned was decided on the basis of the *exceptio doli*; that remedy was never actually applied. Its sole function was to legitimize the introduction of a 'foreign' doctrine. The process was succinctly described by Trollip J when he said: 'The English doctrine of estoppel by representation migrated to this country on the authority of a passport that it approximated the *exceptio doli mali* of Roman Law. However doubtful the validity of that passport might originally have been, the doctrine has now become naturalized and domiciled here as part of our law'.[45] What happened here is typical for the development of South African law. In the nineteenth century judges as well as advocates were continually tempted to refer to English case law or textbooks for guidance; they had been trained in Britain and found it very awkward to apply a law that was, at least initially, not only completely alien to them but also rather inaccessible.[46] Thus,

---

[41] 1920 AD 428 (434).

[42] *Baumann v. Thomas* 1920 AD 428 (435); *Hauptfleisch v. Caledon Divisional Council* 1963 (4) SA 53 (C) 56 (*per* Corbett AJ).

[43] Cf. e.g. *Union Government v. National Bank of South Africa Ltd* 1921 AD 121 (126 sq., 133 sq.): '. . . the doctrine of estoppel is in accordance with the principles of our law and is constantly applied by South African Courts': *per* Innes CJ; 'the doctrine of estoppel is as much part of our law as it is of that of England': *per* Solomon JA; *Union Government v. Vianini Ferro-Concrete Pipes (Pty) Ltd* 1941 AD 43 (49): 'This is a statement of English law, but this Court in several cases . . . has accepted the doctrine of estoppel as part of our law': *per* Watermeyer JA.

[44] But cf. *Oceanair (Natal) (Pty) Ltd v. Sher* 1980 (1) SA 317 (D) 325: '[T]he doctrine of estoppel by conduct as recognized in South African law is derived from the principles underlying the *exceptio doli*. . . . It would therefore be illogical to uphold the defence of estoppel *stante* the finding that in the circumstances of this case the defendant is precluded from relying upon the *exceptio doli* itself as a defence'; for commentary see A. J. Kerr, (1981) 44 *THRHR* 88 sqq. Also, e.g., the reference by Holmes JA in *Oakland Nominees (Pty) Ltd v. Gelria Mining & Investment Co (Pty) Ltd* 1976 (1) SA 441 (A) 452 to 'the broad concept of the *exceptio doli*'.

[45] *Connock's (SA) Motor Co Ltd v. Sentraal Westelike Ko-operatiewe Maatskappy Bpk* 1964 (2) SA 47 (T) 49.

[46] 'It is so much easier to find your law in an English text book or in English reports than

English doctrines managed to creep in on an ever broader front. That process only began to slow down towards the end of the century and under the influence of judges like J. G. Kotzé and Lord de Villiers.[47] Now more serious efforts were made to decide South African cases according to Roman-Dutch law.[48] However, as far as doctrines were concerned, that had already become established, an essentially pragmatic line was taken: as long as they could be reconciled with Roman-Dutch principles they were not to be thrown out again. There came, though, a time when this precarious balance was threatened. For, originating in the Afrikaans-medium law schools of Stellenbosch[49] and Pretoria,[50] a strong tendency began to gain ground not only to preserve the *status quo* but also to remove the English 'pollution' from the South African *usus modernus pandectarum*.[51] By the 1960s, this trend had reached the Appellate Division, for one of its protagonists, L. C. Steyn, had been appointed Chief Justice.[52] Estoppel was one of the doctrines he chose to attack. No court, he said, had the right to substitute the law of another country for 'our common law', and the idea that 'our own authorities' had been replaced by the English doctrine of estoppel was thus to be rejected.[53]

to wade through a sea of Latin or to puzzle your head over old Dutch writers and black letter consultations': Sir John Wessels, 'The Future of Roman-Dutch Law in South Africa', (1929) 37 *SALJ* 276.

[47] Furthermore, tuition in Roman-Dutch law began to be offered in Cape Town in the 1870s (cf. D. V. Cowen, 'The History of the Faculty of Law, University of Cape Town: A Chapter in the Growth of Roman-Dutch Law in South Africa', 1959 *Acta Juridica* 8 sqq.), the first indigenous literature started to appear, and translations of some of the main authorities were undertaken.

[48] For a typical statement concerning equity see Graham JP in *Ferreira v. Ferreira* 1915 EDL 9 (15 sq.): '[He] merely based his argument on the contention that our Courts were courts of equity. No doubt that remark is true in a general sense; but it does not necessarily mean that every rule and principle of the English law of equity is a part of the Roman-Dutch law. . . . one must not too hastily conclude that because our Courts are courts of equity, the equity they administer must needs throughout be the body of rules administered as such by the English Courts.'

[49] On its history see A. H. van Wyk, 'Die Stellenbosse Regsfakulteit 1920—1989', 1989 *Consultus* 42 sqq.; on its most influential member cf. Reinhard Zimmermann, Charl Hugo, 'Fortschritte der südafrikanischen Rechtswissenschaft im 20. Jahrhundert: Der Beitrag von J. C. de Wet (1912—1990)', (1992) 60 *Tijdschrift voor rechtsgeschiedenis* 157 sqq.

[50] See Kobus van Rooyen, 'Die Regsfakulteit, Universiteit van Pretoria: Meer as Tagtig Jaar Regsonderrig', 1991 *Consultus* 49 sqq.

[51] On the '*bellum juridicum*' about the true sources of South African law that ensued cf., e.g., Proculus *Redivivus*, 'South African Law at the Crossroads or What is Our Common Law?', (1965) 82 *SALJ* 17 sqq.; C. F. Forsyth, *In Danger for Their Talents: A Study of the Appellate Division of the Supreme Court of South Africa from 1950—1980* (1985), 182 sqq.; Reinhard Zimmermann, 'Synthesis in South African Private Law: Civil Law, Common Law and *Usus Hodiernus Pandectarum*', (1986) 103 *SALJ* 259 sqq.

[52] For a critical assessment of his role see Edwin Cameron, 'Legal Chauvinism, Executive-mindedness and Justice: L. C. Steyn's Impact on South African Law', (1982) 99 *SALJ* 38 sqq. The law of delict especially was reshaped by him; cf. Forsyth (n. 51) 197 sqq.

[53] *Trust Bank van Afrika Bpk v. Eksteen* 1964 (3) SA 402 (A). Cf. the majority of the Court, led by Steyn CJ in *Johaadien v. Stanley Porter (Paarl) (Pty) Ltd* 1970 (1) SA 394 (A).

This approach might well have heralded the revival of the *exceptio doli*. Ultimately, however, it did not. By and large, it is the more pragmatic view of Rumpff JA that has prevailed; he expressed himself in favour of accepting as a *fait accompli* that the doctrine of estoppel was received into South African law from English law.[54] A very similar attitude had already been adopted by the main exponent of 'purism' among South African academics, Professor J. C. de Wet,[55] when he had written, as far back as 1939: 'Ons howe stel ons voor 'n voldonge feit'.[56] Later, he went so far as to contend that the principles underlying estoppel were not foreign to Roman-Dutch law, and that their reception was therefore not to be condemned.[57]

(c) South African usus modernus

This does not, however, imply that modern South African and English law are necessarily identical on each and every point. For, 'as [so] often happens with foreign principles and doctrines, once they have permanently settled here, they tend to develop along lines that are peculiar to South Africa in conformity with the fundamental concepts of our own law'.[58] The Appellate Division of the Supreme Court continues to apply and develop the doctrine of estoppel,[59] its essence being that a person is precluded from denying the truth of a representation previously made by him to another person if the latter, believing in the truth of the representation, acted thereon to his prejudice.[60] Its field of application is very wide; estoppel can, to mention three of its most significant and distinctive consequences, remedy the lack of *consensus* required for the conclusion of a contract,[61] enable someone who has contracted with an agent to claim from the principal even though there was

[54] *Johaadien v. Stanley Porter*, n. 53 above, 409 sq. He added, however, that the doctrine could not and ought not to be allowed to operate in a way that would be in conflict with, or divorced from, the foundations 'of our own law'. Cf. also Rabie (n. 35) 28 sqq. and Tebbutt J in *Sonday v. Surrey Estate Modern Meat Market (Pty) Ltd* 1983 (2) SA 521 (C) 524.

[55] For a more detailed analysis of his attitude see Zimmermann/Hugo, (1992) 60 *Tijdschrift voor rechtsgeschiedenis* 157 sqq., 168 sq.

[56] (Our courts present us with a fait accompli): De Wet (n. 39) 15. At the same time, however, he set out to prove that the Roman and Roman-Dutch law relied upon by the courts did not justify the importation of the doctrine of estoppel. Cf., as far as the *exceptio doli* is concerned, De Wet (n. 39) 83 sqq.

[57] Cf. J. C. de Wet, A. H. van Wyk, *Die Suid-Afrikaanse Kontraktereg en Handelsreg*, vol. I, ed. G. F. Lubbe, (5th edn., 1992), 22, n. 58.

[58] *Connock's (SA) Motor Co Ltd v. Sentraal Westelike Ko-operatiewe Maatskappy Bpk* 1964 (2) SA 47 (T) 49; *Sonday v. Surrey Estate Modern Meat Market (Pty) Ltd* 1983 (2) SA 521 (C) 527: 'Like any other immigrant that has been here for some time, the original "Englishness" has to a certain extent faded in favour of a more South African appearance. But the immigrant's background remains and our Courts have not overlooked it in adopting it into the South African legal milieu.'

[59] For a comprehensive, modern analysis: Rabie (n. 35).

[60] *Aris Enterprises (Finance) (Pty) Ltd v. Protea Assurance Co Ltd* 1981 (3) SA 274 (A) 291.

[61] *Van Ryn Wine and Spirit Co v. Chandos Bar* 1928 TPD 417; *Peri-Urban Areas Health Board v. Breet* 1958 (3) SA 783 (T); De Wet (n. 39) 72 sqq.; D. J. Joubert, *General Principles of the Law of Contract* (1987), 82 sqq.

no valid authority,[62] and can also defeat an owner's *rei vindicatio*.[63] Arguably, in all these cases, we are even able to dispense with the specific estoppel terminology. For we are dealing, effectively, with the protection of reasonable reliance induced by a contracting party in cases of *dissensus* in the first case;[64] with a specific kind of agency based on what a German lawyer would call *Rechtsschein* in the second;[65] and with a new mode of acquiring *bona fide* ownership in the third.[66]

Estoppel can thus be seen to provide a *nucleus* around which new principles and doctrines can conveniently crystallize; based ultimately on equitable considerations, they gradually acquire their own distinctive form and substance until they become a self-contained and independent part of the doctrinal establishment. This, in fact, appears to be the most important function which estoppel in South African law shares with the *exceptio doli* and its modern equivalents such as § 242 BGB. Apart from that, of course, it remains a residual means of attaining equitable results in individual cases.[67] It may well be asked whether, in view of these developments, it is still possible to carve out certain general requirements applying to estoppel in all its emanations. According to the latest monograph in the field, fault should be considered as one of them.[68] Others, however, tend to confine fault to the sphere of the vindicatory action; this appears to be the prevailing view today.[69] But whichever side one takes in this dispute:[70] the recognition of fault as an element of at least some aspects of estoppel probably constitutes the most important deviation from the English doctrine.[71]

The South African history of the doctrine of estoppel is instructive in that it shows how the 'productive force'[72] of the *exceptio doli* could be deployed in a manner entirely uncontemplated by the creator of that remedy; neither

---

[62] Cf. *Strachan v. Blackbeard and Son* 1910 AD 282; *Monzali v. Smith* 1929 AD 382; De Wet (n. 39) 69 sqq.; Rabie (n. 35) 95 sqq.

[63] De Wet (n. 39) 56 sqq.; C.G. van der Merwe, *Sakereg* (2nd edn., 1989), 368 sqq.

[64] Gerhard Lubbe, Christina Murray, *Farlam and Hathaway, Contract: Cases, Materials and Commentary* (1988), 178 sqq.

[65] Cf. the criticism of the prevailing estoppel doctrine by D. H. Bester, 'The Scope of an Agent's Power of Representation', (1972) 89 *SALJ* 49 sqq.

[66] Cf. H. J. O. van Heerden, 'Estoppel: 'n Wyse van Eiendomsverkryging?', (1970) 33 *THRHR* 19 sqq.; J. W. Louw, 'Estoppel en die Rei Vindicatio', (1975) 38 *THRHR* 218 sqq.

[67] G. F. Lubbe, 'Estoppel, vertrouensbeskerming en die struktuur van die Suid-Afrikaanse privaatreg', 1991 *TSAR* 1 sqq.

[68] Rabie (n. 35) 83 sqq.; De Wet (n. 39) 38 sqq.

[69] *Grosvenor Motors (Potchefstroom) Ltd v. Douglas* 1956 (3) SA 420 (A) 426 sq. and the detailed discussion by Tebbutt J in *Sonday v. Surrey Estate Modern Meat Market (Pty) Ltd* 1983 (2) SA 521 (C). But cf. Rumpff JA in his dissenting opinion in *Johaadien v. Stanley Porter (Paarl) (Pty) Ltd* 1970 (1) SA 394 (A) 411 sq. and Steyn CJ, ibid. 409.

[70] Cf. Lubbe, 1991 *TSAR* 1 sqq. who rejects the differentiation between vindicatory and other estoppel with regard to fault and who argues that the fault requirement depends on the nature of the conduct constituting the representation giving rise to the estoppel.

[71] Tebbutt J in *Sonday's* case (n. 69) on 530, referring to the standard text of Spencer Bower.

[72] Heinrich Dernburg, *Pandekten*, vol. I (6th edn., 1900), 138, 4 *in fine*.

an ancient Roman nor a modern German lawyer would have associated the protection of reliance in the conclusion of a contract or acquisition of ownership with the principle of *bona fides*. Yet estoppel is only one important example of an English equitable doctrine that migrated to South Africa on the authority of a passport marked '*exceptio doli*'. The defence of rectification of a written contract is another case in point.

2. Rectification

(a) The reception of the doctrine of rectification

When a contract has been reduced to writing the document drawn up by the parties is generally regarded as the exclusive memorial of the transaction, and in a suit between the parties it may not be contradicted, added to, or varied by oral evidence.[73] This is the so-called parol evidence (or integration) rule which was taken over as part and parcel of the English law of evidence.[74] Proof of a contract has traditionally been considered as belonging to the law of evidence[75] which, in turn, had been taken over as early as 1830 and by way of legislation.[76] However, it can be grossly inequitable if a party can under no circumstances aver that the document did not accurately reflects the actual agreement reached. For the other party might then even be allowed to enforce a document in full knowledge of the fact that it was based on a mistake. English law therefore recognizes the equitable doctrine of rectification[77] which, while ultimately allowing the real agreement to prevail, still requires that agreement to be reflected in the—rectified—document. In this way the parol evidence rule can still be preserved, at least formally, since the document may now again be attributed sole and indisputable authority to evidence the rights and duties of the parties *vis-à-vis* each other.

In 1925 the Appellate Division of the Supreme Court of South Africa had to decide a case[78] in which the plaintiffs based their claim on a written agreement according to which one piece of land described as No. 859 had been sold to the defendant and an adjacent piece (No. 857) to the plaintiffs. This document, however, did not correctly reflect the parties' intention since they had previously agreed verbally that part of No. 857 should also be

---

[73] *Union Government v. Vianini Ferro-Concrete Pipes (Pty) Ltd* 1941 AD 43 (47); *National Board (Pretoria) (Pty) Ltd v. Estate Swanepoel* 1975 (3) SA 16 (A) 26; *Johnston v. Leal* 1980 (3) SA 927 (A) 938, 943; D. T. Zeffertt, A. Paizes, *Parol Evidence with Particular Reference to Contract* (1986); Lubbe/Murray (n. 64) 215 sqq.

[74] See *Brown v. Selwin* (1734) Cases T. Talbot 240 (242); Konrad Zweigert, Hein Kötz, *Einführung in die Rechtsvergleichung auf dem Gebiete des Privatrechts* (3rd edn., 1996), 402 sq. On its reception in South Africa see e.g. Zeffertt and Paizes (n. 73) 6 sqq.

[75] Cf. *Cassiem v. Standard Bank of South Africa Ltd* 1930 AD 366.

[76] Ord. 72 (Cape of Good Hope); see further C. W. H. Schmidt, *Bewysreg* (3rd edn., 1989), 12 sqq.

[77] Cf. today G.H. Treitel, *The Law of Contract* (8th ed., 1991), 285 sqq.

[78] *Weinerlein v. Goch Buildings Ltd* 1925 AD 282.

transferred to the defendant. The defendant had built on that part of No. 857 and the plaintiffs now claimed the value of the land so appropriated plus damages. The Court dismissed the claim and allowed rectification of the written contract as well as of the deeds registry. Two of the three judges of appeal referred to the *exceptio doli* in this context. According to Wessels JA[79] Roman law had from the earliest times set its face against a person benefiting himself by his own fraud or by a mutual mistake even if the strict interpretation of the law seemed, at first blush, to give him that right. Even though, strictly speaking, the plaintiffs might have to be considered owners of the disputed part of No. 857, the civil law would not have allowed them to claim removal of the buildings or damages, because such a claim could have been met by the *exceptio doli*. In order to succeed in this *exceptio doli* it was not necessary to prove fraud; '[it] lies whenever the court regards it as a fraudulent act to rely on your *summum jus* when you know full well that your claim is founded on mutual error'.[80] Kotzé JA[81] observed that the rectification of a written document, on good cause shown, was a well settled rule in South Africa, and he proceeded to demonstrate that it found a basis in 'equitable considerations, which have been adopted and become part of the civil law'.[82] These equitable considerations, according to Kotzé JA, were first introduced by the *praetor* in the form of an *exceptio doli*.

   Weinerlein v. Goch Buildings Ltd has become the leading case on rectification,[83] and once again the *exceptio doli* has been instrumental in making that equitable remedy palatable to South African lawyers. For rectification of written documents had long been recognized; in the 1899 case of *Van der Byl v. Van der Byl & Co*[84] De Villiers CJ already referred to an 'established practice' at the Cape. It is obvious that the courts had simply been following English practice; De Villiers CJ had justified this reception by stating that the relief thus granted was founded upon 'the same broad principles of equity'[85] (as constitute the foundations of *in integrum restitutio*).

(b)   Rectification and exceptio doli

'It is clear that the defence of rectification of a written contract is based on the *exceptio doli generalis*':[86] this would appear to be the prevailing view today. Yet there is something strange about it. For the raising of the *excep-*

---

[79] *Weinerlein v. Goch Buildings Ltd* 1925 AD 291 sqq.   [80] At 292.
[81] *Weinerlein v. Goch Buildings Ltd* 1925 AD 282 (293 sqq.)[82] At 297.
[83] *Meyer v. Merchants' Trust Ltd* 1942 AD 244; *Mouton v. Hanekom* 1959 (3) SA 35 (A); *Benjamin v. Gurewitz* 1973 (1) SA 418 (A); *Lubbe/Murray* (n. 64) 225 sqq.; A.J. Kerr, *The Principles of the Law of Contract* (4th edn., 1989), 123 sqq.; Schalk van der Merwe, L. F. van Huyssteen, M. F. B. Reinecke, G. F. Lubbe, J. G. Lotz, *Contract: General Principles* (1993), 128 sqq.
[84] (1899) 16 SC 338; cf. Joubert (n. 61) 163.
[85] *Van der Byl v. Van der Byl & Co* (1899) 16 SC 338 (349).
[86] *Neuhoff v. York Timbers Ltd* 1981 (4) SA 666 (T) 673 (*per* Ackerman J); Kerr (n. 83) 491 sqq.; cf. Joubert (n. 61) 163 sq.

tio doli should in itself have been sufficient to defeat the claim. Rectification of the written document, in addition, is neither necessary nor logically inferable. For the *exceptio doli* merely constitutes a defence and does not grant a right to change the text of a document. Nor, incidentally, does an '*exceptio*' help a *plaintiff* who wishes to rely on an agreement which differs from the document. The possibility therefore exists that, as far as the defendant is concerned, rectification and the *exceptio doli* have to be regarded as separate remedies.[87] Yet, even if this were the case, the *Bank of Lisbon* decision[88] would have sounded the death knell for the latter. Thus, on both views rectification remains the only relief to mitigate the harshness of the parol evidence rule.

But if rectification was so firmly established in South African law by 1925, what was the point of the elaborate discussion in *Weinerlein v. Goch Buildings Ltd*? Central to the decision was a problem which had not yet been settled in English law. For whilst it was generally recognized that rectification required a previous agreement between the parties that had not been properly reflected in the document, it was uncertain whether this agreement, in itself, had to constitute a valid contract. This was not the case in *Weinerlein*, since according to s. 30 of the Transfer Duty Proclamation of 1902 any contract for sale of land required an agreement in writing.[89] Thus, by granting rectification, the Court extended the range of application of that equitable relief not inconsiderably, without receiving any guidance from English law.[90] This may have prompted the court to explore in depth the continental foundations of rectification.

3. Innocent misrepresentation

Another particularly interesting development that has to be discussed in the present context has occurred in the field of misrepresentation. A misrepresentation is a false statement of fact made by one party to the other before or at the time of concluding the contract.[91] It is obvious that a claim for damages lies whenever such misrepresentation was fraudulent;[92] and the scope of the Aquilian action, as extended by the Appellate Division in

---

[87] Cf. Botha (n. 21) 207 sqq.; *idem*, (1980) 43 *THRHR* 264; Lubbe/Murray (n. 64) 225.

[88] See below, text after n. 134.

[89] Cf. esp. the opinion of De Villiers JA in *Weinerlein v. Goch Buildings Ltd* 1925 AD 282 (287 sq.).

[90] In England the question was only settled by the decision of the Court of Appeal in *Joscelyne v. Nissen* [1970] 2 QB 86.

[91] Dale Hutchison (ed.), *Wille's Principles of South African Law* (1991), 440.

[92] Certain difficulties have been experienced with regard to the calculation of damages in cases of *dolus incidens*; cf. *Bill Harvey's Investment (Pty) Ltd v. Oranjezicht Citrus Estates* 1958 (1) SA 479 (A); *Scheepers v. Handley* 1960 (3) SA 54 (A); *De Jager v. Grunder* 1964 (1) SA 446 (A); *Ranger v. Wykerd* 1977 (2) SA 976 (A).

Administrateur, Natal v. Trust Bank van Afrika Bpk [93] appears to be broad enough to allow also the recovery of damages in cases of negligent misrepresentations.[94] But what about the *contract* that was induced by the misrepresentation? Is it still enforceable, is it void, or can it be rescinded? In classical Roman law no action could be granted on the basis of *negotia bonae fidei* affected by fraud; in all other cases relief had to be sought by raising the *exceptio doli* or by instituting the *actio de dolo*.[95] With the advent of the modern general law of contract the regime applicable to *iudicia bonae fidei* should ultimately have prevailed. However, for a variety of reasons *ipso iure* invalidity of the contract induced by fraud did not appear to be a suitable solution, and thus it came to be recognized that the effect of fraud was at most to render the contract voidable at the instance of the innocent party.[96] But does this kind of rescission really depend on fraudulent behaviour, *stricto sensu*, on the part of the other party to the contract? In other words, does it require an intentional misstatement of an existing material fact?

This was the problem addressed for the first time in South African law by Solomon J in *Viljoen v. Hillier*, decided in 1904.[97] The judge not only rejected the proposition that, in order successfully to defend himself against the contractual claim, the defendant had to prove a fraudulent misrepresentation on the part of the plaintiff; he did not even regard proof of negligence as necessary. Fault was thus considered to be entirely irrelevant. Under Roman law, Solomon J argued, the defendant could have raised the *exceptio doli* under such circumstances, 'the *dolus* consisting not in fraud at the initiation of the contract, but in the fact that it is against good faith for a man to insist upon enforcing a contract which he has secured by his own misrepresentation'.[98] Once again, however, the *exceptio doli* provided a convenient screen behind which an entirely new doctrine could be introduced into the emerging South African version of Roman-Dutch law. For Solomon J quite clearly took his lead from English law and simply adopted the doctrine of innocent misrepresentation, as he perceived it to have been developed in Equity. This is evident from his conspicuous remark that in

[93] 1979 (3) SA 824 (A), the 'Hedley Byrne' of South African law in which recoverability in delict of pure economic loss was authoritatively (re-)established.

[94] *Kern Trust (Edms) Bpk v. Hurter* 1981 (3) SA 607 (C); Hutchison, (1981) 98 *SALJ* 486 sqq.; *Bayer South Africa (Pty) Ltd v. Frost* 1991 (3) SA 559 (A); Lewis, (1992) 109 *SALJ* 381 sqq.; Hutchison, in: Wille (n. 91) 443 sq.; Van der Merwe/Van Huyssteen *et al.* (n. 83) 112 sq. Dale Hutchison, Reinhard Zimmermann, 'Fahrlässige irreführende Angaben im vorvertraglichen Bereich: Zur Haftung für reine Vermögensschäden nach modernem römisch-holländischem Recht', (1995) 3 *Zeitschrift für Europäisches Privatrecht* 271 sqq.

[95] *Law of Obligations* (n. 10) 663 sq.

[96] *Law of Obligations* (n. 10) 671 sq. As far as the requirements for rescission in modern South African law are concerned, see Joubert (n. 61) 92 sqq.; Lubbe/Murray (n. 64) 335 sqq.; Hutchison, in: Wille (n. 91) 441 sq.

[97] 1904 TS 312.   [98] *Viljoen v. Hillier* 1904 TS 312 (315 sq.).

his opinion 'by our law as well as by the English law the facts above enumerated would constitute a good defence';[99] and also, particularly, from his reference to the decision of the Chancery Division in *Redgrave v. Hurd*, where Jessel MR had stated that it would be 'moral delinquency' if the law were to allow a man to enforce a contract obtained by a statement which he *now* knew to be false.[100]

What thus came to be received by the Transvaal Supreme Court was not, however, a well established principle of English Equity but a comparatively recent doctrinal innovation even in its country of origin.[101] Nevertheless, rescission of contracts induced by innocent misrepresentation managed to establish itself in Southern Africa and was finally recognized by the Appellate Division of the Supreme Court.[102] In 1929[103] Wessels JA re-emphasized that a defendant is entitled to succeed if he can establish that the representation of the plaintiff was material and that he entered into the contract on the faith of such representation. He referred to *Viljoen v. Hillier* as well as to *Redgrave v. Hurd*; he also stressed the identity of these principles in the civil law and in the law of England. Recognition of the doctrine of innocent misrepresentation[104] has effectively meant that unilateral mistakes of motive, induced by the other party, are to be accorded legal effect;[105] for if the mistake induced by the misrepresentation relates to one of the material elements of the contract, lack of *consensus* prevents the formation of a contract in the first place.[106] Obviously, therefore, the *exceptio doli* has once again facilitated major doctrinal developments in the general law of contract.

---

[99] Ibid.   [100] (1881) 20 ChD 1 (12 sq.).

[101] Cf. the fascinating analysis of its development by G. F. Lubbe, 'The Origin and Development of the Doctrine of Innocent Misrepresentation', in: J. J. Gauntlett (ed.), *J. C. Noster, 'n Feesbundel* (1979), 113 sqq. The first unambiguous statement of the new principle was that of Lord Herschell in *Derry v. Peek* (1889) 14 App Cas 337 (359): for purposes of rescission it was 'only necessary to prove that there was misrepresentation: then, however honestly it may have been made, however free from blame the person who made it, the contract having been obtained by misrepresentation cannot stand'. For an interpretation of *Redgrave v. Hurd* (the case usually referred to for this principle by South African courts) cf. Lubbe, 129 sqq. See also the contribution by the same author to this volume.

[102] *Karroo and Eastern Board of Executors & Trust Co v. Farr* 1921 AD 413 (415).

[103] *Sampson v. Union & Rhodesia Wholesale Ltd (in liquidation)* 1929 AD 468 (480).

[104] See, as well as the references given above, *Parke v. Hamman* 1907 TH 47 (52); *Bowditch v. Peel and Magill* 1921 AD 561 (572); *Harper v. Webster* 1956 (2) SA 495 (FC) 501; *Trollip v. Jordaan* 1961 (1) SA 238 (A) 252; Lubbe, *J. C. Noster* (n. 101) 135 sqq.; Joubert (n. 61) 97 sq.; Kerr (n. 83) 214 sqq.; Van der Merwe/Van Huyssteen *et al.* (n. 83) 100 sqq.; on the various attempts of modern commentators to find a theoretical basis for rescission in cases of innocent misrepresentation: Lubbe/Murray (n. 64) 341.

[105] Lubbe, *J. C. Noster* (n. 101) 137.

[106] For an overview see Lubbe/Murray (n. 64) 95 sqq.; *Law of Obligations* (n. 10) 584 sqq.; Hutchison, in: Wille (n. 91) 416 sqq.

4. The subsequent fate of the *exceptio doli*

(a) *Zuurbekom's case*

It will have been noted that in none of the cases discussed so far was the *exceptio doli* ever applied *per se*; it provided a convenient cover for the application of doctrines to be received from English law. Thus, it has been one of the crucial devices, as far as the law of contract is concerned, for bringing about the kind of integration between Roman-Dutch and English law that has become the most conspicuous characteristic of the South African *usus modernus pandectarum*.[107] Otherwise, however, the *exceptio doli* (in its own right!) has not been of great practical significance in South African law.[108] It has repeatedly been discussed by the various Divisions of the Supreme Court but it has hardly ever actually been applied. Usually, the endorsement of this remedy was either *obiter*,[109] or the remedy was held not to be applicable to the facts of the case at hand. One of the great and often quoted *causes célèbres* dealing with the *exceptio doli, Zuurbekom Ltd v. Union Corporation Ltd*, falls into the second category.[110] It dealt with the question of whether an unreasonable delay by a creditor in enforcing a right could result in refusal by a court to enforce it because enforcement would cause prejudice to the debtor. In English law this type of situation was traditionally covered by the equitable doctrine of laches,[111] and for a long time this doctrine appeared about to be received into South African law.[112] The pattern was the one familiar from estoppel, rectification, and innocent misrepresentation: the doctrine of laches was described as 'the *exceptio . . . doli* of the Roman-Dutch law under a new name' and therefore being 'nothing

---

[107] This is a particularly interesting reflection of the 'ongoingness' and of the vitality inherent in the Western legal tradition: cf. Reinhard Zimmermann, 'Das römisch-kanonische *ius commune* als Grundlage europäischer Rechtseinheit', 1992 *Juristenzeitung* 8 sqq.

[108] See also Botha, (1980) 43 *THRHR* 263; C. F. C. van der Walt, 'Die huidige posisie in die Suid-Afrikaanse reg met betrekking tot onbillike kontraksbedinge', (1986) 103 *SALJ* 650 sqq.; Vermooten J in *Edwards v. Tuckers Land and Development Corp. (Pty) Ltd* 1983 (1) SA 617 (W) 627.

[109] See esp. *Edwards v. Tuckers Land and Development Corp. (Pty) Ltd* 1983 (1) SA 617 (W) 625 sqq: 'In view of the conclusion I have reached on the first submission it is not necessary for me to deal with the second, but I do wish to express my view in regard to the third defence raised, namely the *exceptio doli*.'

[110] 1947 (1) SA 514 (A); cf. further *North Vaal Mineral Co Ltd v. Lovasz* 1961 (3) SA 604 (T); *Rashid v. Durban City Council* 1975 (3) SA 920 (D); *Paddock Motors (Pty) Ltd v. Igesund* 1976 (3) SA 16 (A); *Aris Enterprises (Finance) (Pty) Ltd v. Waterberg Koelkamers (Pty) Ltd* 1977 (2) SA 425 (A); *Oceanair (Natal) (Pty) Ltd v. Sher* 1980 (1) SA 317 (D); *Neuhoff v. York Timbers Ltd* 1981 (4) SA 666 (T).

[111] The case most often referred to in South Africa is *Lindsay Petroleum Co v. Hurd* 1874 LR 5 PC 221.

[112] Botha (n. 21) 200 even claims: 'Die Engelsregtelike leerstuk van "laches" het oorspronklik deel uitgemaak van die Suid-Afrikaanse reg' (The English legal doctrine of 'laches' has originally been part of South African law). See esp. *Pathescope (Union) of SA Ltd v. Mallinick* 1927 AD 292 (305) (*per* Stratford JA).

new in our law'.[113] However, Tindall JA conclusively rejected this view in *Zuurbekom's* case[114] and thus ended the South African career of the law relating to laches. South African courts, he held, in order to assist the debtor in cases of this nature, could resort only to the *exceptio doli*. He accepted that 'something falling short of conduct constituting an estoppel'[115] could be embraced by that defence; but it would have to be shown that, in the circumstances of the particular case, the enforcement of that remedy by the creditor would cause some great inequity and would amount to unconscionable conduct on his part. In the present case, the defence could not be taken to have satisfied this test.

(b) A distinct field of application?

Zuurbekom's case offers some insight into two of the main reasons why the *exceptio doli*, in its own right, was only very rarely raised successfully in South African courts. On one hand, it can operate usefully, as Jansen J once put it metaphorically, only 'when a claim has run the gauntlett of all other principles and still survives (otherwise the *exceptio* would be mere surplusage). It cannot rest on error, fraud, or duress in the ordinary legal sence of these words nor is it estoppel. To be distinctive it must transcend the principles associated with these concepts'.[116] Estoppel, in particular, covers (or can be made to cover) much of the ground claimed by the *exceptio doli*, but so do the defences of rectification and misrepresentation. With every new sub-doctrine to which it gives birth, the range of application of the *exceptio doli* is reduced. In a way, it is a case of the children swallowing up their mother. Coetzee J certainly went too far when he claimed that '[i]n a fully developed system of law such an instrument has no meaningful *raison d'être*, and, if anything, is a superfluous anachronism'.[117] But even Jansen J, the great champion of an equitable theory of contract,[118] found it 'extremely difficult to envisage an appropriate field of operation for a distinctive *exceptio doli*'.[119]

---

[113] *Schwarzer v. John Roderick's Motors (Pty) Ltd* 1940 CPD 170 (181) (*per* Van den Heever J). Also *Zuurbekom Ltd v. Union Corporation Ltd* 1947 (1) SA 514 (A) 533: '. . . he contended that Union Corporation's claim to an interdict is barred by its laches (to use the terminology of the English law), or, so it was contended, by the *exceptio doli* (to use the terminology of the Roman law and the commentators thereon).'

[114] *Zuurbekom Ltd v. Union Corporation Ltd* 1947 (1) SA 514 (A) 535.

[115] At 537.

[116] *North Vaal Mineral Co Ltd v. Lovasz* 1961 (3) SA 604 (T) 607; Van der Walt, (1986) 103 *SALJ* 652.

[117] *Aris Enterprises (Finance) (Pty) Ltd v. Waterberg Koelkamers (Pty) Ltd* 1977 (2) SA 436 (T) 438.

[118] Carole Lewis, 'Towards an Equitable Theory of Contract: The Contribution of Mr. Justice E. L. Jansen to the South African Law of Contract', (1991) 108 *SALJ* 249 sqq.

[119] *North Vaal Mineral Co Ltd v. Lovasz* 1961 (3) SA 604 (T) 608. Along very similar lines see the argument by Carole Lewis, 'The Demise of the *Exceptio Doli*: Is There Another Route to Contractual Equity?', (1990) 107 *SALJ* 26 sqq.

On the other hand, *Zuurbekom* has become the *fons et origo* in South African law of a narrow view of the *exceptio doli*.[120] For the test proposed by Tindall JA and widely applied in practice[121] required not only unconscionable conduct on the part of the plaintiff but also 'some great inequity' to the defendant flowing from such conduct.[122] The policy behind these stringent formulations is obvious: the courts are striving to preserve legal certainty and therefore do not wish to arrogate to themselves a jurisdiction to regulate contractual relationships merely on the ground that they regard the terms agreed upon by the parties as harsh or unfair.[123] Yet there are also somewhat more lenient formulations opening up, theoretically at least, a greater sphere of intervention for the courts. Thus, a passage from Sohm's *Institutes*[124] has often been referred to, with apparent approval, according to which the *exceptio* was the instrument employed, both in the theory and practice of Roman law, for effecting such modifications of the material law as equity seemed to require; it was available 'wherever the raising of the action constituted objectively a breach of good faith', the judge being empowered 'to take account of every single circumstance that would render the condemnation of the defendant substantially unjust'. Wessels JA, in *Weinerlein's* case, also spoke of the 'inherent equitable jurisdiction' of the courts to refuse to entertain unconscionable claims 'even though [they] might be supported by a strict reading of the law'.[125]

(c) The Rand Bank *case*

The only case of—potential—consequence[126] in which the *exceptio doli* was held to have been successfully invoked is *Rand Bank Ltd v. Rubenstein*.[127]

---

[120] For a very useful survey of the various attempts by South African courts to define the scope of application of the *exceptio doli* see Peter Aronstam, *Consumer Protection, Freedom of Contract and the Law* (1979), 173 sqq.

[121] *Paddock Motors (Pty) Ltd v. Igesund* 1975 (3) SA 294 (D) 297 sq.; *Novick v. Comair Holdings Ltd* 1979 (2) SA 116 (W) 156 sq.

[122] *Zuurbekom* (n. 114 above) 537. Botha (n. 21) 191 sqq. (cf. (1980) 43 *THRHR* 265) argues that Tindall JA merely projected the requirements of the doctrine of laches onto the *exceptio doli*.

[123] *Rashid v. Durban City Council* 1975 (3) SA 920 (D) 927; *Paddock Motors (Pty) Ltd v. Igesund* 1976 (3) SA 16 (A) 28; *Novick v. Comair Holdings Ltd* 1979 (2) SA 116 (W) 157. This inflexible approach is criticized by Aronstam (n. 120) 168 sqq., 182 sq.; also C. F. C. van der Walt, (1986) 103 *SALJ* 651.

[124] *The Institutes: A Textbook of the History and System of Roman Private Law*, trans. by James Crawford Ledlie (3rd edn., 1907), 280.

[125] *Weinerlein v. Goch Buildings Ltd* 1925 AD 282 (292 sq.). Cf. *MacDuff & Co Ltd (in liquidation) v. Johannesburg Consolidated Investment Co Ltd* 1924 AD 573 (609 sqq.) *per* Kotzé JA; *Sonday v. Surrey Estate Modern Meat Market (Pty) Ltd* 1983 (2) SA 521 (C) 531, *per* Tebbutt J: '. . . it seems clear that [the limits of the field of application of the *exceptio*] have been extended from the comparatively limited area embraced by Tindall JA's "great inequity" or "unconscionable conduct" '; cf. ibid. 532.

[126] Cf. *Edwards v. Tuckers Land and Development Corporation (Pty) Ltd* 1983 (1) SA 617 (W) 625 sqq.; C. F. C. van der Walt, (1986) 103 *SALJ* 651.

[127] 1981 (2) SA 207 (W).

The plaintiff, in the opinion of the Court, attempted to enforce a right acquired for one purpose in order to achieve another, unrelated and uncontemplated, purpose; relying on the wide wording of a deed of suretyship he sought to make the surety responsible for a debt to which the deed was not intended to refer. Botha J regarded this as 'a clear exhibition of bad faith'[128] on the part of the plaintiff; enforcement of the deed of suretyship would, in the circumstances, 'undoubtedly' constitute unconscionable conduct and also cause 'gross injustice or great inequity' towards the defendant. Even on the more stringent test, therefore, the requirements of the *exceptio doli* were met; the judge even went so far as to describe the case as 'tailor-made' for the application of the general defence of the *exceptio doli*.[129] Arguably, however, the decision could also have been explained on the basis of the accessory nature of the surety's liability,[130] and reference to the *exceptio doli* may thus have been, even in this exceptional case, unnecessary.

(d) Requiescat in pace? *(Bank of Lisbon, part I)*

It is a matter for speculation whether the *Rand Bank* case had the potential of instilling a new lease on life into the *exceptio doli*. As it turned out, it merely brought about a final flare-up. The remedy had already been threatened by extinction for some time. The most influential writer in the field of contract law, Professor J. C. de Wet,[131] had argued as far back as 1939[132] that the *exceptio doli* did not embody any particular substantive principle of liability. More recently, judicial scepticism as to whether it had become or remained part of Roman-Dutch law had been expressed.[133]. All doubts in this regard were finally laid to rest by an extraordinary judgment of the Appellate Division.[134] Joubert JA, speaking for the majority of the Court, took the opportunity to embark upon a detailed analysis of Roman and Roman-Dutch law. His opinion bristles with references to Gaius and Papinian, to Van Oven, Sohm, and Moyle, to Donellus and Cujacius, to Van Leeuwen, Grotius, and Tuldenus. A dazzling erudition is displayed in order to substantiate a rather straightforward conclusion. 'The *raison d'être* of the *exceptio doli generalis*', as Joubert JA summed up his views,[135] 'had disappeared in the law of contract at the end of the Middle Ages ... [and therefore a]ll things considered, the time has now arrived, in my judgment, once and for all, to bury the *exceptio doli generalis* as a superfluous, defunct

---

[128] Ibid. 215.   [129] Ibid. 214.

[130] Cf. Lubbe/Murray (n. 64) 389 sq. For different solutions to the problem raised in the *Rand Bank* case see Lewis, (1990) 107 *SALJ* 33 sqq.; Kerr (n. 83) 498 sqq.

[131] Cf. above, n. 55.   [132] De Wet (n. 39) 83 sqq.

[133] See esp. *Aris Enterprises (Finance) (Pty) Ltd v. Waterberg Koelkamers (Pty) Ltd* 1977 (2) SA 436 (T) 437 sqq.; *Novick v. Comair Holdings Ltd* 1979 (2) SA 116 (W) 156 sq.

[134] *Bank of Lisbon and South Africa Ltd v. De Ornelas* 1988 (3) SA 580 (A).

[135] Ibid. 605, 607. Cf. the words used by Coetzee J in *Aris Enterprises (Finance) (Pty) Ltd v. Waterberg Koelkamers (Pty) Ltd* 1977 (2) SA 436 (T) 438.

anachronism'. And he added, for good measure: '*Requiescat in pace.*' This appears[136] to have brought to an end the surprising afterlife of the *exceptio doli* in South African law. Having fulfilled its historic mission of authorizing the entry into South African law of doctrinal immigrants from English equity and of fashioning them to the local mould, it could ultimately be discarded.

But does the demise of the *exceptio doli* entail a substantive shift of approach? Has the crucial device for introducing equitable elements been abandoned and have the South African courts thus lost that flexibility in the evaluation of contractual rights and duties which has enabled them to adapt the law of contract to the demands of changing times by developing new or productively incorporating seemingly foreign strands of legal tradition?[137]

III. *DOLUS*

In the first place it must be remembered that the removal of the *exceptio doli* as a device available to a defendant to plead fraud on the part of the plaintiff has not removed the concept of *dolus* from the legal scene. *Dolus* today is usually equated with fraud, and fraud implies an intention to deceive.[138] Fraudulent misrepresentation , as we have seen, entitles the innocent party to rescind the contract and to claim damages.[139] There have, however, been situations where *dolus* has been given a less restricted meaning and where, as a result, it has fulfilled a similar function to the *exceptio doli*. The two most significant examples relate to the doctrines of notice and undue influence.

1. The doctrine of notice

Under the doctrine of notice a person who acquires an asset may be bound to give effect to a right which his predecessor in title had granted, if he knew about his predecessor's undertaking.[140] For instance, a purchaser of land will be obliged to register a right of servitude granted by the vendor to a

---

[136] But cf. *Van der Merwe v. Meades* 1991 (2) SA 1 (A) confirming the existence of the *replicatio doli*; see A. J. Kerr, 'The *replicatio doli* reaffirmed: The *exceptio doli* available in our law', (1991) 108 *SALJ* 583 sqq.

[137] Cf. Zimmermann, 1992 *Juristenzeitung* 11 sq.

[138] Cf. Sir John Wessels, *The Law of Contract in South Africa*, vol. II (2nd edn., 1951), §§ 1066 sqq.; Hahlo/Kahn (n. 2) 463 sqq. The German equivalent is the '*arglistige Täuschung*' of § 123 BGB.

[139] Cf. above, *sub* II. 1.

[140] Cf. generally Zimmermann (n. 6) 132 sq.; Lubbe/Murray (n. 64) 15 sqq. (both with further references).

third party if he bought the land in the knowledge of this undertaking.[141] The same applies in the case of a double sale: provided the second purchaser knew about the first sale, the first purchaser is not only able to prevent transfer of ownership to the second purchaser but can also, if such transfer has already taken place, demand transfer of ownership from the second purchaser.[142] This is a doctrinal anomaly, since a position which is, conceptually, purely obligatory is turned, under the doctrine of notice, into a real right.[143] It was justified, in one of the first and most influential decisions on the matter, by claiming that the (second) acquirer had acted fraudulently; his behaviour was to be regarded as 'a species of fraud and *dolus malus*'.[144] Clearly, however, the characterization of the doctrine of notice as a species of fraud is merely a fiction to provide it with theoretical support:[145] '. . . 'n aanknopingspunt in die regsisteem ter onderskraging van die kennisleer', to quote the words of Van Heerden AJA in *Associated South African Bakeries (Pty) Ltd v. Oryx & Vereinigte Bäckereien (Pty) Ltd*.[146] The consequence is obvious. *Mala fides* on the part of the acquirer need not be proved; all that is necessary is that he should have had knowledge of the prior right of another party. Fraud is thus construed on the basis of mere knowledge.[147] This is, as Lubbe and Murray have pointed out,[148] in line with the equitable principles of the English law of trusts which appear to have influenced Barry JP in his opinion in *Judd v. Fourie*. Distinct notice to a purchaser, the Judge President said,[149] that the seller has sold the object in question to another obliges the purchaser either to desist from purchasing or to hold himself as trustee for the previous purchaser. Furthermore, Barry JP quoted[150] extensively from Story's *Equity Jurisprudence* where it is stated as a general rule that the parties to a contract shall not only act *bona fide* as between themselves, but also not transact *mala fide* in respect of other persons who stand in such relation to either of them as to be affected by the contract or its

---

[141] *Judd v. Fourie* (1881) 2 EDC 41; *Richards v. Nash* (1881) 1 SC 312; *Jansen v. Fincham* (1892) 9 SC 289; *Ridler v. Gartner* 1920 TPD 249; D. L. Carey Miller, *The Acquisition and Protection of Ownership* (1986) 198 sqq.; Van der Merwe (n. 63) 526 sqq.

[142] *Cohen v. Shires, McHattie & King* (1882) 1 SAR 41; *Tiger-Eye Investments (Pty) Ltd v. Riverview Diamond Fields (Pty) Ltd* 1971 (1) SA 351 (C); *Kazazis v. Georghiades* 1979 (3) SA 886 (T); E. M. Burchell, 'Successive Sales', (1974) 91 *SALJ* 40 sqq.

[143] The rule 'sale does not break hire' (*huur gaat voor koop*) presents a similar exception; cf. *Law of Obligations* (n. 10) 381 sq.

[144] *Judd v. Fourie* (1881) 2 EDC 41 (53, 76) (*per* Buchanan J and Barry JP, both referring to Lord Chancellor Hardwicke). Cf. Kotzé CJ in *Cohen v. Shires, McHattie & King* (1882) 1 SAR 41 (46).

[145] Lubbe/Murray (n. 64) 16.

[146] (A point of reference in the legal system to support the doctrine of notice.) 1982 (3) SA 893 (A) 910; cf. *Kazazis v. Georghiades* 1979 (3) SA 886 893.

[147] 'Bedrog word dus uit blote kennis gekonstrueer': Van Heerden AJA in *Associated South African Bakeries (Pty) Ltd v. Oryx & Vereinigte Bäckereien (Pty) Ltd* 1982 (3) SA 893 (A) 910.

[148] Lubbe/Murray (n. 64) 16.   [149] (1881) 2 EDC 41 (76).

[150] Ibid. (75 sq.)

consequences. Finally, he referred to the English Lord Chancellor Hardwicke in whose view the taking of a legal estate after notice of a prior right makes the person a *mala fide* purchaser. According to Lord Hardwicke, this is a species of fraud, and 'exactly agrees with the definition of the Civil Law of *dolus malus*'.[151]

2. Undue influence

Of central importance for the other example in point is the decision of the Appellate Division of the Supreme Court in *Preller v. Jordaan*.[152] Referring to Labeo's famous definition of *dolus* ('. . . *dolum malum esse omnem calliditatem fallaciam machinationem ad circumveniendum fallendum decipiendum alterum adhibitum*'[153]) Fagan JA expressed the opinion that it was broader than the concept of fraud since it did not carry such a strong connotation of moral censure.[154] He pointed out that *dolus* in terms of the *exceptio doli* was taken to comprise conduct that could merely be described as inequitable (*onbillik*) and quoted a judgment by Kotzé JA,[155] who had in turn relied on Savigny and Heumann for the proposition that *dolus* indicated 'anything which the law does not allow, anything inequitable, done with the consciousness that one is acting contrary to the law and good faith'. Fagan JA then explored the range of application of the term *dolus* among the 'classical' Roman-Dutch authors and finally came to the conclusion that it was broad enough to cover the case 'where one person obtains an influence over another which weakens the latter's resistance and makes his will pliable, and where such a person then brings his influence to bear in an unscrupulous manner in order to prevail upon the other to agree to a prejudicial transaction which he would not normally have entered into of his own free will'.[156] The innocent party, under these circumstances, may rescind the contract and claim *restitutio in integrum*.

Preller v. Jordaan constitutes the most serious, and ultimately successful, attempt to domesticate a doctrine which had already been repeatedly acknowledged and in some cases even applied:[157] the doctrine of undue

[151] (1881) 2 EDC 41 (76); cf. pp. 53 (*per* Buchanan J) and 67 sq. (*per* Shippard J). Also Kotzé CJ in *Cohen v. Shires, McHattie & King* (1882) 1 SAR 41 (46) who refers to Lord Hardwicke and Story on *Equity*, but in addition quotes Loenius, *Decisiones*, cas. 80.

[152] 1956 (1) SA 483 (A).   [153] Ulp. D. 4, 3, 1, 2.

[154] *Preller v. Jordaan* 1956 (1) SA 483 (A) 491.

[155] *MacDuff & Co Ltd (in liquidation) v. Johannesburg Consolidated Investment Co Ltd* 1924 AD 573 (610).

[156] *Preller v. Jordaan*, (above n. 154) 492 (trans. from the Afrikaans original). Cf. also already Wessels (n. 138) § 1209 ('This our courts call undue influence, though the Roman-Dutch lawyers merely regarded it as one of the Protean forms of *dolus*').

[157] Cf. *Executors of Cerfonteyn v. O'Haire* (1873) 3 SC 476; *Armstrong v. Magid* 1937 AD 260 (273, 276); *Katzenellenbogen v. Katzenellenbogen and Joseph* 1947 (2) SA 528 (W) 540; *Mauerberger v. Mauerberger* 1948 (4) SA 902 (C) 910. But cf. Van den Heever JA in *Preller v. Jordaan* 1956 (1) SA 483 (A) 504 sqq.; L. F. van Huyssteen, *Onbehoorlike Beïnvloeding en*

influence, as developed by the English courts of Equity.[158] Again, therefore, *dolus* has proved to be the most suitable[159] port of entry for an equitable doctrine which had become an established part of South African private law.[160] Whatever the attitude of the Roman-Dutch authorities may have been,[161] it is clear that classical Roman law offers some support for Fagan JA's proposition. For there even the confines of the Labeonic definition had not been taken too seriously and the misconduct of a party could well be labelled 'fraudulent' if it fell short of deceit or trickery.[162] Whenever the behaviour of the plaintiff did not conform to the overriding standard of good faith, the *exceptio doli* could be granted; ultimately the same criterion determined whether or not the *actio de dolo* could be brought successfully. '*Palam est autem hanc exceptionem ex eadem causa propositam, ex qua causa proposita est de dolo malo actio*' said Ulpian,[163] making it clear that *actio* and *exceptio* did not refer to different types of situation.

IV. BONA FIDES

1. 'All contracts are *bonae fidei*'

This brings us to the role of *bona fides* in South African contract law. Obviously, this is the most potentially powerful agent for bringing equitable considerations to bear upon the law; and its significance has now been accentuated by the demise of the *exceptio doli*. From a purely technical point of view the historical deductions of the majority in the *Bank of Lisbon* case cannot, of course, be faulted. If, as has been pointed out above, the modern theory of contract descends from the consensual contracts of Roman law, there is no longer any room for a specific procedural device such as the *exceptio doli*. The substantive content of that *exceptio* had been absorbed into the requirement of good faith underlying the operation of all

---

Misbruik van Omstandighede in die Suid-Afrikaanse Verbintenisreg (1980), 108 sqq. See also the contribution by Gerhard Lubbe to this volume.

[158] Cf. Treitel (n. 77) 366 sqq.; Wessels (n. 138) §§ 1208 sqq.

[159] On *metus* as an alternative basis for undue influence cf. *Preller v. Jordaan* 1956 (1) SA 483 (A) 489 sqq.; also earlier cases e.g. *Van Pletsen v. Henning* 1913 AD 82 (94) (*per* Innes JA); *Ferreira v. Ferreira* 1915 EDL 9 (15 sq.).

[160] *Patel v. Grobbelaar* 1974 (1) SA 532 (A); Wessels (n. 138) §§ 1208 sqq.; Hahlo/Kahn (n. 2) 470 sqq.; Joubert (n. 61) 116 sqq.; Lubbe/Murray (n. 64) 374 sqq.; De Wet/Van Wyk (n. 57) 51 sqq.; Hutchison, in: *Wille* (n. 91) 448 sqq.; Van der Merwe/Van Huyssteen *et al.* (n. 83) 91 sqq.

[161] For criticism of Fagan JA's analysis of the sources (*Preller v. Jordaan* 1956 (1) SA 483 (A) 491 sqq.) e.g. De Wet/Van Wyk, *loc. cit.*; Van Huyssteen (n. 157) 115 sqq.; Van den Heever JA in his dissenting opinion in *Preller v. Jordaan* 1956 (1) SA 483 (A) 497 sqq.

[162] Cf. *Law of Obligations* (n. 10) 667 sq.; *Van der Merwe v. Meades* 1991 (2) SA 1 (A) 4.

[163] D. 44, 4, 2 pr.; cf. also Ulp. D. 4, 3, 7, 8 and Andreas Wacke, 'Zum *dolus*-Begriff der *actio de dolo*', (1980) 27 *Revue internationale des droits de l'antiquité* 371 sqq.

consensual contracts. Therefore, from about the seventeenth century onwards,[164] whenever the term *'exceptio doli'* was used,[165] it was a mere *façon de parler*—a convenient way for a defendant to allege that the plaintiff's behaviour constituted an infringement of the principles of *bona fides*. Significantly, for example, Barry JP justified acknowledgement of the doctrine of notice not only with reference to fraud or *dolus* but also by pointing out that 'the doctrine seems to be that good faith is required in all contracts'.[166]

In more recent years it has been asserted again and again that in modern South African law all contracts are *bonae fidei*.[167] The requirement of *bona fides* thus underlies and informs the South African law of contract.[168] However, the implications of these bland statements are far from clear. For South African courts have traditionally been reluctant to interfere openly with the freedom of the parties to make their own bargain. 'In our system of society', in the words of Millner,[169] 'paternalism is not a characteristic of the economic relations of men nor of the common law which mirrors those relations.' Statements like these essentially reflect classical nineteenth-century contract theory as articulated in Sir George Jessel MR's celebrated statement that 'if there is one thing which more than another public policy requires it is that men of full age and competent understanding shall have the utmost liberty of contracting, and that their contracts when entered into freely and voluntarily shall be held sacred and shall not be enforced by courts of justice'.[170] The private autonomy of contracting parties must be accorded paramount importance;[171] and thus it is hardly surprising that

---

[164] I.e. the time of the decisive break-through towards recognition of the principle of *'ex nudo pacto oritur actio'*; cf. above, n. 18.

[165] As for 'classical' Roman-Dutch law see Botha (n. 21) 89 sqq.; on the writers of *usus modernus* and pandectism see 79 sqq. Cf. *Law of Obligations* (n. 10) 674 sqq.

[166] *Judd v. Fourie* (1881) 2 EDC 41 (76).

[167] *Meskin v. Anglo-American Corporation of SA Ltd* 1968 (4) SA 793 (W) 804 (*per* Jansen J); *Paddock Motors (Pty) Ltd v. Igesund* 1976 (3) SA 16 (A) 28; *Tuckers Land and Development Corporation (Pty) Ltd v. Hovis* 1980 (1) SA 645 (A) 651 sq. (*per* Jansen JA); *Mutual and Federal Insurance Co Ltd v. Oudtshoorn Municipality* 1985 (1) SA 419 (A) 433 (*per* Joubert JA); *Bank of Lisbon and South Africa Ltd v. De Ornelas* 1988 (3) SA 580 (A) 599, 601 (*per* Joubert JA); *LTA Construction Bpk v. Administrateur, Transvaal* 1992 (1) SA 473 (A) 480 (*per* Joubert JA).

[168] For a particularly clear statement see Jansen JA in *Tuckers Land and Development Corporation (Pty) Ltd v. Hovis* 1980 (1) SA 645 (A) 652; also Wessels (n. 138) §§ 1976, 1997.

[169] M. A. Millner, 'Fraudulent Non-Disclosure', (1957) 74 *SALJ* 183.

[170] *Printing and Numerical Registering Co v. Sampson* (1875) LR 19 Eq 462 (465); references in *Law of Obligations* (n. 10) 576 sq. It has repeatedly been quoted in South Africa: e.g. Innes CJ in *Wells v. South African Alumenite Co* 1927 AD 69 (73); *Edouard v. Administrator, Natal* 1989 (2) SA 368 (D) 379; M. M. Corbett, 'Aspects of the Role of Policy in the Evolution of Our Common Law', (1987) 104 *SALJ* 64; Ellison Kahn, *Contract and Mercantile Law: A Source Book*, vol. I (2nd edn., 1988), 31 ('almost a matter of legal etiquette'); Cockrell, (1992) 109 *SALJ* 46 ('. . . arguably the most privileged statement of all').

[171] 'In this respect, South African contract law bears more than a superficial resemblance to the so-called classical theory of contract': Lubbe/Murray (n. 64) 20. Further: Alfred Cockrell, 'Substance and Form in the South African Law of Contract', (1992) 109 *SALJ* 40 sqq.

public policy has, until quite recently, generally been taken to require the strict enforcement of contractual obligations.[172] This accounts for the lack of academic attention devoted to the role of *bona fides*; indeed, some of the leading South African textbooks still do not consider it a concept worth discussing in its own right.[173] No comprehensive anlaysis has yet appeared of how the principle of good faith operates and what its various functions are;[174] and the courts also have contributed little to its conceptual clarification. It is obvious that good faith has not become a general principle enabling courts to alter the agreement of the parties merely because they consider it reasonable to do so; nor does it give the court general power to refuse to enforce a contractual obligation which it considers harsh or inequitable. At the same time, however, good faith has recognizably shaped South African contract law in much more subtle ways; for it has worked its way into the system in many different places, largely within the framework of existing legal concepts.[175] Since it is impossible, within the limited space presently available, to survey the whole law of contract, we must content ourselves with a few typical illustrations.

2. Offer and acceptance and performance of contract

One of the earliest examples of an overt exploitation of *bona fides* is provided by the decision in *Neugebauer & Co v. Hermann*.[176] The plaintiff had conspired with a number of likely buyers at an auction in order to buy galvanized iron piping cheaply. Innes CJ refused to hold the seller bound by the plaintiff's bid. This, he said, is 'not so much a question of public policy as of the requirements of good faith. The principle is fundamental that *bona fides* is required from both parties to a contract of sale. . . . [F]or buyers to conspire in order to deprive [the seller] for their own benefit of that upon which they know that the whole transaction is based is not consistent with good faith. It is a fraud upon the seller'.[177] In an unreserved auction[178] the seller is bound to allow the article to go to the highest bidder; but that, according to Innes CJ, must mean to the highest *bona fide* bidder.

---

[172] Cf. *SA Sentrale Ko-op Graanmaatskappy Bpk v. Shifren* 1964 (4) SA 760 (A) 767; *Magna Alloys and Research (SA) (Pty) Ltd v. Ellis* 1984 (4) SA 874 (A) 893 sq.; *Edouard v. Administrator, Natal* 1989 (2) SA 368 (D) 378 sq.

[173] See esp. De Wet/Van Wyk (n. 57); but cf. R. H. Christie, *The Law of Contract in South Africa* (2nd edn., 1991), and Kerr (n. 83); cf. in this context Joubert JA in *Bank of Lisbon and South Africa Ltd v. De Ornelas* 1988 (3) SA 580 (A) 610 who notes (with apparent approval) that '[e]ven in our modern textbooks on the law of contract hardly any mention is made of *bona fides* unless it is based on some substantive rule of law'. But the situation is changing. In Lubbe/Murray the index has a whole list of entries under the headword '*Bona Fides*' (p. 775); cf. also Van der Merwe/Van Huyssteen *et al.* (n. 83) 230 sqq.

[174] Cf. the criticism by Gerhard Lubbe, '*Bona fides*, billikheid en die openbare belang in die Suid-Afrikaanse kontraktereg', (1990) 1 *Stellenbosch LR* 19.

[175] Cf. Cockrell, (1992) 109 *SALJ* 55 sqq.   [176] 1923 AD 564.

[177] Ibid. (573 sq.).   [178] Cf. generally Joubert (n. 61) 50 sqq.; Christie (n. 173) 46 sqq.

Neugebauer & Co v. Hermann thus illustrates the role of good faith in the evaluation of the declarations leading to a contract; but it also shows, once again, how closely the concepts of good faith and fraud are related. Incidentally, if it is not the bidder who infringes the precepts of good faith but the auctioneer who employs sham bids in order to raise the price, he is usually taken to have committed a fraud on the innocent bidders who are therefore able to rescind the contract.[179]

Most obviously, once a contract has been concluded one would expect good faith to be of central importance for evaluating the conduct of the parties in respect of its performance. If this is only rarely stressed,[180] the main reason appears to be that the *exceptio doli* used to be available to the party prejudiced by the other's *mala fide* acts. More particularly, we are dealing here with the domain of the doctrine of estoppel as it has come to be received within the framework of that remedy.[181] In other cases a creditor may be taken to have waived his rights. Occasionally the courts find it difficult to decide into which of these two pigeonholes to fit a case. In *Garlick Ltd v. Phillips* that was held not to matter: 'Whether the legal principle involved in the modification of contractual rights and duties by a long continued course of conduct, consisting of defective performance by one party acquiesced in by the other, be given the name of waiver or acquiescence or of estoppel there is no doubt that modification by conduct of the obligations under an executory contract can occur'.[182] Clearly, the idea informing this statement is the implementation of the standards of good faith in a contractual context.[183] The same can be said about the various ways in which the courts try to grant relief to a party prejudiced by the other's enforcement of a so-called non-variation clause.[184]

3. Interpretation of contracts

Good faith is also a relevant criterion in the interpretation of contracts. For whilst the courts are not entitled to depart from the clearly expressed intention of the parties because they consider the contract to be unfair to one of

---

[179] Joubert (n. 61) 51.

[180] But cf. Wessels (n. 138) § 1997; *Meskin v. Anglo-American Corporation of SA Ltd* 1968 (4) SA 793 (W) 802.

[181] Cf. above, *sub* II. 1.					[182] 1949 (1) SA 121 (A) 130 sq., *per* Watermeyer CJ.

[183] Cockrell, (1992) 109 *SALJ* 59. Cf. *Phillips v. Miller (2)* 1976 (4) SA 88 (W) 93 discussing *Garlick v. Phillips* in terms of the *exceptio doli*.

[184] I.e. a clause by means of which the parties to a written contract have prescribed writing as a formal prerequisite for variation of the contract. Such clauses are, as a rule, enforced in the face of subsequent agreement by the parties to alter their contract. However, a waiver has been held not to be subject to a non-variation clause; a party may be precluded from relying on a non-variation clause by virtue of the doctrine of estoppel; and in *Van As v. Du Preez* 1981 (3) SA 760 (T) 765 it was said that '[a] non-variation clause would of course not protect a party against his own fraud'. For details see Lubbe/Murray (n. 64) 182 sqq., 191 sq.; Van der Merwe/Van Huyssteen *et al.* (n. 83) 117 sqq.; cf. Cockrell, (1992) 109 *SALJ* 58 sq.

them, the matter is different when the wording is ambiguous. If an expression is capable of two constructions, and if there is nothing in the context which points specially to either of them, then 'it would be proper to avoid a manifestly inequitable result'. This is how Innes CJ expressed the position as long ago as 1916.[185] Some twenty years later De Wet JA quoted with approval the following statement from Sir John Wessels' textbook on contract:[186] 'The Court will lean to that interpretation which will put an equitable construction upon the contract and will not, unless the intention of the parties is manifest, so construe the contract as to give one of the parties an unfair or unreasonable advantage over the other'.[187] However, since the courts primarily profess to establish the common intention of the parties[188] and since, moreover, a whole range of guidelines, or 'presumptions', have been developed to assist the courts in ascertaining that intention,[189] the scope of the equitable interpretation rule appears to be limited. Yet in practice the process of interpretation is not merely a psychological inquiry into what the parties to the contract thought at that particular moment when the contract was concluded. Many of the so-called secondary rules of interpretation (also, for instance, the approach adopted by South African courts towards the use of extrinsic evidence) reveal a normative dimension[190] so that 'considerations of fairness and policy contribute to the shaping of contractual content'.[191] Like their colleagues in many other countries, South African judges tend to avail themselves of covert tools in order to achieve reasonable solutions without openly attacking the 'idol' of freedom of contract.[192] The theoretical basis for this kind of judicial activism, however, appears to be the overriding notion of good faith.[193]

---

[185] *Trustee, Estate Cresswell & Durbach v. Coetzee* 1916 AD 14 (19); cf. *Van Rensburg v. Straughan* 1914 AD 317 (326).

[186] Wessels (n. 138) § 1974.

[187] *Rand Rietfontein Estates Ltd v. Cohn* 1937 AD 317 (330).

[188] Cf. generally Wessels (n. 138) §§ 1899 sqq.; E. L. Jansen, 'Uitleg van kontrakte en die bedoeling van die partye', 1981 *TSAR* 97 sqq.; Zeffertt/Paizes (n. 73) 79 sqq.; Joubert (n. 61) 59 sqq.; Kerr (n. 83) 300 sqq.; Lubbe/Murray (n. 64) 451 sqq.; Hutchison, in: *Wille* (n. 91) 460 sqq.; Van der Merwe/Van Huyssteen *et al.* (n. 83) 218 sqq., all with many references.

[189] Cf. Wessels (n. 138) §§ 1915 sqq.; Joubert (n. 61) 62 sqq.; Lubbe/Murray (n. 64) 466 sqq.; Van der Merwe/Van Huyssteen *et al.* (n. 83) 221 sq.; *Law of Obligations* (n. 10) 637 sq.

[190] Cf. Schalk van der Merwe, Gerhard Lubbe, '*Bona Fides* and Public Policy in Contract', (1991) 2 *Stellenbosch LR* 98 sq., discussing *Joosub Investments (Pty) Ltd v. Maritime & General Insurance Co Ltd* 1990 (3) SA 373 (C).

[191] Lubbe/Murray (n. 64) 469. Cf. George Findlay, F. C. Kirk-Cohen, 'On Fictitious Interpretation', (1953) 70 *SALJ* 145 sqq.

[192] '[Judges] still had before them the idol "freedom of contract". They still knelt down and worshipped it, but they concealed under their cloaks a secret weapon. They used it to stab the idol in the back. This weapon was called the "true construction of the contract" ': Lord Denning in *George Mitchell (Chesterhall) Ltd v. Finney Locky Seeds Ltd* [1983] 1 All ER 108 (CA) 113.

[193] Lubbe/Murray (n. 64) 464, 469; Van der Merwe/Van Huyssteen *et al.* (n. 83) 219.

4. Tacit terms and terms implied by law

Closely related is another rather open-ended device for determining the content of a contract: reading into it a 'tacit term'. A tacit term (or a 'term implied in fact') is usually described as an unexpressed provision of the contract which derives from the common intention of the parties, as inferred by the Court from the express terms of the contract and the surrounding circumstances.[194] The courts profess reluctance to import such provisions into a contract.[195] They also stress the need to base it on the actual (albeit unexpressed) intention of the parties. Again, however, this process is usually fictitious in nature: the courts, more often than not, undertake to establish what the parties *must be taken* to have intended.[196] Common intention comprehends not only actual intention but also imputed intention.[197] The focus of the inquiry thus easily shifts onto what an officious bystander[198] would have expected reasonable parties to have agreed upon in the circumstances of the particular case. Obviously, therefore, this is another covert way in which the precepts of good faith may assert themselves.

This brings us to the role of terms implied by law.[199] For if tacit terms

---

[194] *Minister van Landbou-Tegniese Dienste v. Scholtz* 1971 (3) SA 188 (A) 197; *Alfred McAlpine & Son (Pty) Ltd v. Transvaal Provincial Administration* 1974 (3) SA 506 (A) 531 (*per* Corbett, AJA); Joubert (n. 61) 66 sqq.; Lubbe/Murray (n. 64) 416 sqq.; Christie (n. 173) 194 sqq.; Van der Merwe/Van Huyssteen *et al.* (n. 83) 197 sqq.

[195] *Liquidator of Booysen's Race Club Ltd v. Burton* 1910 TPD 597 (601); *Alfred McAlpine & Son (Pty) Ltd v. Transvaal Provincial Administration* 1974 (3) SA 506 (A) 532; *Union National South British Insurance Co Ltd v. Padayachee* 1985 (1) SA 551 (A) 559.

[196] Corbett AJA in *Alfred McAlpine & Son (Pty) Ltd v. Transvaal Provincial Administration* (above, n. 194) 532, quoting Van den Heever JA in *Van der Merwe v. Viljoen* 1953 (1) SA 60 (A) 65: '*wat die partye bedoel het, of geag moet word te bedoel het*' (what the parties have intended, or what they must be taken to have intended).

[197] *Alfred McAlpine & Son (Pty) Ltd v. Transvaal Provincial Administration* 1974 (n. 194) 532. Also e.g. *Van den Berg v. Tenner* 1975 (2) SA 268 (A) 277 (*per* Botha JA); and (for Germany) Werner Flume, *Allgemeiner Teil des Bürgerlichen Rechts*, vol. II, *Das Rechtsgeschäft* (3rd edn., 1976), § 16.

[198] From whose perspective it must be determined whether or not a term should be implied; cf. the references collected by Joubert (n. 61) 68 and Christie (n. 173) 198 sqq. The officious bystander test is an import from England; cf. *Reigate v. Union Manufacturing Co (Ramsbottom)* [1918] 1 KB 592 (605).

[199] Both the terminology and the doctrine of implied conditions were adopted from English law. Cf. *Phillips v. Bulawayo Market and Offices Co* (1899) 16 SC 432 (437); *Douglas v. Baynes* 1908 TS 1207 (1210); also J. P. Vorster, 'The Influence of English Law on the Implication of Terms in the South African Law of Contract', (1987) 104 *SALJ* 588 sqq. Colman J in *Techni-Pak Sales (Pty) Ltd v. Hall* 1968 (3) SA 231 (W) 236 even contended that the South African law relating to the implication of terms is identical to the English law. The implication of terms had become a fashionable device in 19th C. English decisions, designed, in terms of the prevailing will theories of contract, to impute to the intention of the parties what appeared to be a fair and reasonable solution. Of particular significance was the implication of conditions, a device which the English courts had taken over from continental jurisprudence. For details see Reinhard Zimmermann, ' "Heard melodies are sweet, but those unheard are sweeter ...", *Condicio tacita*, implied condition und die Fortbildung des europäischen Vertragsrechts', (1993) 193 *Archiv für die civilistische Praxis* 121 sqq.

may be based on an imputed intention,[200] the line between these two conceptually distinct determinants of contractual content becomes rather difficult to draw.[201] Implied terms are unexpressed provisions of a contract which do not originate in the contractual *consensus*; they are imposed from without, and as a matter of course.[202] The actual intention of the parties is referred to only to the extent that no term may normally be implied which conflicts with the express provisions of the contract. These kinds of terms, normally connected with or 'naturally' flowing from a specific type of contract, are referred to in the civilian tradition as *naturalia negotii*.[203] They help to determine the rights and duties of contracting parties and the effects of their agreements. Examples abound. Thus, a seller need not transfer ownership, but must grant the purchaser undisturbed possession.[204] He must carry the risk of accidental destruction, *emptione perfecta*, even before delivery.[205] He is liable for latent defects under aedilitian principles, but if he has fraudulenty concealed the defect or has specifically warranted the absence of defects, he will be liable to pay damages.[206] A lessor must deliver and maintain the property in the condition it was in at the time when the lease was concluded.[207] A carrier by sea is subject to strict *receptum* liability.[208] All these[209] and many other *naturalia negotii* recognized in modern South African contract law are derived from Roman law, and usually reflect Roman notions of what is right and equitable in a contract of that type.[210] They are, in other words, concrete manifestations of the basic principle of *bona fides*. However, they do not form a *numerus clausus*. New *naturalia* may be developed and existing ones extended or restricted in order to adjust the law to changing circumstances.[211] This is a constant process[212] which, once again, provides much scope for imbuing the law of contract with an equitable spirit.[213]

---

[200] *Naturalia negotii*, in turn, often derive historically from (express or tacit) *accidentalia negotii*, regularly agreed upon by the parties. For an example see *Law of Obligations* (n. 10) 519 sq.

[201] See (1993) 193 *Archiv für die civilistische Praxis* 168.

[202] *Minister van Landbou-Tegniese Dienste v. Scholtz* 1971 (3) SA 188 (A) 197; *Alfred McAlpine & Son (Pty) Ltd v. Transvaal Provincial Administration* (above, n. 194); and see Joubert (n. 61) 65 sq.; Lubbe/Murray (n. 64) 422 sqq.; Christie (n. 173) 184 sqq.; Van der Merwe/Van Huyssteen *et al.* (n. 83) 200 sq.

[203] Cf. *Law of Obligations* (n. 10) 234.   [204] Cf. Hutchison, in: *Wille* (n. 91) 534.

[205] Ibid. 533.   [206] Ibid. 536 sqq.   [207] Ibid. 549.

[208] Ibid. 584 sqq.

[209] Cf. *Law of Obligations* (n. 10) 293 sqq., 281 sqq., 305 sqq., 360, 514 sqq.

[210] See, in this regard, *A Becker & Co (Pty) Ltd v. Becker* 1981 (3) SA 406 (A) 419.

[211] Ibid.

[212] Cf. *Phame (Pty) Ltd v. Paizes* 1973 (3) SA 397 (A); *Tregidga & Co v. Sivewright* (1897) 14 SC 76 (81 sq.); *Hall–Thermotank Africa Ltd v. Prinsloo* 1979 (4) SA 91 (T) as *causes célèbres* in the law of sale and *receptum nautarum* respectively. Cf. *Law of Obligations* (n. 10) 329 sq., 522; *Stocks & Stocks (Pty) Ltd v. T J Daly & Sons (Pty) Ltd* 1979 (3) SA 754 (A); and the examples provided in the works cited above, n. 202.

[213] Cf. Lubbe/Murray (n. 64) 425; Vorster, (1987) 104 *SALJ* 592.

5. Good faith *in contrahendo*

(a) *Contracts* uberrimae fidei

Last but not least, good faith may also operate *in contrahendo*. 'The proposition that by our law all contracts are *bonae fidei* is not confined to matters that arise after *consensus* has been reached; it applies to the very process of reaching *consensus*'.[214] The main problem[215] arising in this context is whether failure by one of the parties to disclose information reasonably relevant to the other party's decision to contract, or failure to remove a wrong impression which to his knowledge exists in the mind of that other party, constitutes a misrepresentation entitling the latter to rescind the contract, or even to claim damages.[216] According to the traditional view, as a rule it does not.[217] Snatching a bargain is not, in principle, frowned upon in an individualistic society where it is expected 'that each must pit his skill, enterprise, *acumen* and energy against those of his neighbour. Each must look to his own interests, inform himself, so far as possible by reasonable enquiry, of the nature and circumstances of the subject-matter of his bargains, and safeguard himself by contractual stipulations'.[218] There are, however, exceptions. Particularly, in a contract of insurance the party wishing to be insured must disclose to the insurer any fact that might reasonably affect the risk to be insured, whether or not he has been asked specifically about such facts.[219] Equally onerous duties have been recognized in contracts of agency[220] and partnership.[221] All these transactions, it has been pointed out, are characterized by a fiduciary relationship or relationship of close trust;

---

[214] *Savage and Lovemore Mining (Pty) Ltd v. International Shipping Co (Pty) Ltd* 1987 (2) SA 149 (W) 198.

[215] Generally on *culpa in contrahendo* in South African law cf. now Van der Merwe/Van Huyssteen *et al.* (n. 83) 69 sq.

[216] Cf. generally Joubert (n. 61) 94 sqq.; Lubbe/Murray (n. 64) 336 sq.; Kerr (n. 83) 220 sqq.; Christie (n. 173) 332 sqq.; Hutchison, in: *Wille* (n. 91) 444 sqq.

[217] Cf. *Speight v. Glass* 1961 (1) SA 778 (D) 781.

[218] Millner, (1957) 74 *SALJ* 183.

[219] *Malcher and Malcomess v. Kingwilliamstown Fire and Marine Insurance and Trust Co* (1883) 3 EDC 271 (279, 287 sq.); *Fine v. General Accident, Fire and Life Assurance Corp Ltd* 1915 AD 213; *Colonial Industries Ltd v. Provincial Insurance Co Ltd* 1922 AD 33; *Pereira v. Marine and Trade Insurance Co Ltd* 1975 (4) SA 745 (A) 755 (*per* Corbett JA); *Mutual and Federal Insurance Co Ltd v. Oudtshoorn Municipality* 1985 (1) SA 419 (A); Schalk van der Merwe, '*Uberrima fides* en die beraming van die risiko voor sluiting van 'n versekeringskontrak', (1977) 40 *THRHR* 1 sqq.; A. N. Oelofse, *Die uberrima fides-leerstuk in die versekeringsreg* (1983), 141 sqq.; M. F. B. Reinecke, S. W. J. van der Merwe, *General Principles of Insurance* (1989), nn. 120, 132 sqq.

[220] *Page v. Ross* (1885) 2 Buch AC 52 (65) (*per* De Villiers CJ); *Transvaal Cold Storage Co Ltd v. Palmer* 1904 TS 4 (20, 33); *Hargreaves v. Anderson* 1915 AD 519; *Robinson v. Randfontein Goldmining Co Ltd* 1921 AD 168 (177 sqq., 229 sqq.).

[221] *Matabele Syndicate v. Lippert* (1897) 4 OR 372 (385); *Purdon v. Muller* 1961 (2) SA 211 (A) 230.

many material facts are accessible to one party only so that the other party is obliged to depend on him.[222]

If this is the substantive basis for the imposition of a duty to disclose, South African courts and legal writers have tended to encapsulate it in a rather strange expression adopted from English law.[223] They attached the label *uberrima fides* to those types of contract for which they were prepared to recognize a duty of disclosure—contracts requiring not only good faith but the utmost good faith. This was not a very happy terminological invention, for it appeared to imply the recognition of varying standards of honesty.[224] However, whilst one may be less than honest, one can hardly be more honest than honest.[225] Obviously, therefore, the expression 'contracts *uberrimae fidei*' could never be taken—and in fact never was taken—literally.[226] Nevertheless, in one of his extraordinary and entirely unrestrained judgments, Joubert JA took the opportunity to cast out the uncouth foreign intruder. 'In my opinion', he said,[227] '*uberrima fides* is an alien, vague, useless expression without any particular meaning in law. . . . [I]t cannot be used in our law for the purpose of explaining the juristic basis of the duty to disclose a material fact before the conclusion of a contract of insurance'. Strangely, however, this finding (supported as it is by a wide-ranging investigation into the 'true' sources of Roman-Dutch insurance law[228]) was without any relevance to the case before the Court. Joubert JA held that insured and insurer are indeed both under a duty to disclose facts which are material to either risk or premium.

But what, after *Oudtshoorn Municipality*, is the legal basis of this duty? According to Joubert JA it is 'the correlative of a right of disclosure which is a legal principle of the law of insurance'.[229] It is neither based upon an implied term of the contract of insurance nor flowing from the requirement of *bona fides*. Moreover, it is not common to all types of contract but is restricted 'to those contracts, such as contracts of insurance, where it is imposed *ex lege*'.[230] The reference to duties of disclosure imposed *ex lege* is,

---

[222] Millner, (1957) 74 *SALJ* 189; Hutchison (n. 91) 445.

[223] Wessels (n. 138) §§ 1035 sqq.; Erwin Spiro, '*Uberrima Fides*', (1961) 24 *THRHR* 196 sqq.; Oelofse (n. 219) 1 sq.

[224] Cf. Millner, (1957) 74 *SALJ* 188.

[225] *Mutual and Federal Insurance Co Ltd v. Oudtshoorn Municipality* 1985 (1) SA 419 (A) 443 (*per* Miller JA).

[226] *Ibid.*, Miller JA; Van der Merwe, (1985) 48 *THRHR* 459; Reinecke/Van der Merwe (n. 219) n. 120.

[227] *Oudtshoorn Municipality* (above, n. 225). For comment see Schalk van der Merwe, 'Insurance and good faith: exit *uberrima fides*—enter what?', (1985) 48 *THRHR* 457 sqq.; Van Zyl J in *Trust Bank van Afrika Bpk v. President Versekeringsmaatskappy Bpk* 1988 (1) SA 546 (W) 552 sq.; see also the contribution by Van Niekerk to this volume.

[228] *Oudtshoorn Municipality* (above, n. 225) 426–433 ('The contract of insurance was unknown to Roman law. . . '). Cf. Reinecke/Van der Merwe (n. 219) nn. 7 sqq.

[229] *Oudtshoorn Municipality* (above, n. 225) 432.   [230] *Ibid.* 433.

however, obscure and their restriction to specific types of contract is both illogical and *obiter*.[231]

(b) Duties of disclosure

In the light of the above, there is much to commend the different view put forward most forcefully by Jansen J in the case of *Meskin v. Anglo-American Corporation of SA Ltd*.[232] '[T]here can be no doubt', he argued,[233] 'that *in contrahendo* our law expressly requires *bona fides*, a concept of variable content in the light of changing *mores* and circumstances.' However, whilst resting ultimately on an ethical basis, good faith does not require the evaluation of business transactions according to abstract ethical ideals but with a view to ordinary business decency.[234] On this approach, good faith does not require a duty of disclosure in all circumstances and in every situation.[235] On the other hand, however, its field of operation is not limited to a specific *numerus clausus* of contracts, and therefore duties of disclosure may well arise in transactions other than those which used to be classified as *uberrimae fidei*.[236] What matters is the element of 'involuntary dependance'[237] obliging one party to repose confidence in the other, not the abstract categorization of the contract. '[T]he determination of the extent of the disclosure does not depend oñ the label we choose to stick on a contract. The principles applicable to contracts of insurance do not differ in essence from those applicable to other kinds of contracts', Roberts AJ opined as far back as 1961,[238] and he proceeded to apply these principles to suretyship.[239] Duties of disclosure have also, in the past, been recognized with regard to contracts of sale.[240] A seller of land was held liable for failing to disclose that it had previously been used as a graveyard;[241] the seller of a hotel for not revealing that the local municipality had withdrawn its consent to the hotel's septic tank remaining on adjacent ground belonging to the municipality.[242] And finally: all sellers are required to disclose latent

---

[231] Cf. Reinecke/Van der Merwe (n. 219) n. 134, n. 6.   [232] 1968 (4) SA 793 (W).
[233] Ibid. 804.
[234] Ibid. 802 sq.; see generally *Law of Obligations* (n. 10) 256 sqq., 669 sq.
[235] Cf. Lubbe/Murray (n. 64) 337; Reinecke/Van der Merwe (n. 219) 120.
[236] This view is predominantly held by modern South African academic writers; cf. Joubert (n. 61) 95 sq.; Lubbe/Murray (n. 64) 336 sqq.; Christie (n. 173) 334 sqq.; Hutchison, in: *Wille* (n. 91) 445; Van der Merwe/Van Huyssteen *et al.* (n. 83) 78 sq. Cf. also earlier Millner, (1957) 74 *SALJ* 189.
[237] Millner, (1957) 74 *SALJ* 189.
[238] *Iscor Pension Fund v. Marine and Trade Insurance Co Ltd* 1961 (1) SA 178 (T).
[239] According to *Caney's The Law of Suretyship* (3rd edn., 1982) by C. F. Forsyth, 32 sqq., however, suretyship is not a contract *uberrimae fidei*. Cf. Oelofse (n. 219) 4 sq.
[240] Cf. the discussion by Kerr (n. 83) 221 sqq. But cf. also decisions like *Speight v. Glass* 1961 (1) SA 778 (D) 781.
[241] *Dibley v. Furter* 1951 (4) SA 73 (C).
[242] *Cloete v. Smithfield Hotel (Pty) Ltd* 1955 (2) SA 622 (O).

defects in their wares.[243] This rule has been preserved from Roman law where, as part of the aedilitian remedies, it was read into the *'oportere ex bona fide'* clause of the general action on sale.[244] Significantly, therefore, it resulted from a refined interpretation of what was owed in good faith under the *actio empti*.

6. Fictional fulfilment of conditions

Bona fides also provides the point of departure for more specific rules of contract law. Some of these derive from Roman law. The doctrine of fictional fulfilment of conditions is an example which features particularly prominently in South African case law.[245] It was recognized at an early stage that a condition must be deemed satisfied if its actual satisfaction has been prevented by the party to whose disadvantage it would have operated (i.e. who would have been bound by the obligation that had been subjected to the condition). This principle it was at first applied in a straightforward manner and without refined reflections on its precise ambit.[246] Occasionally it was justified by a statement to the effect that the behaviour of a person preventing a condition from materializing was contrary to good faith.[247] In 1918 De Villiers AJ cast doubt over its general applicability by suggesting that the rule might have been intended to apply only to cases where fulfilment is prevented fraudulently or in a manner contrary to good faith.[248] This suggestion found an echo in the leading case of *MacDuff & Co Ltd (in liquidation) v. Johannesburg Consolidated Investment Co Ltd*.[249] Here the rule was, on the one hand, specifically based on the precepts of good faith.[250] On the other hand, however, both Innes CJ and Kotzé JA linked its application to the requirement of *dolus* on the part of the (conditional) debtor.[251] Thus, it is now widely accepted that the 'prevention equals satisfaction' rule can only be invoked by a party whose opponent has acted intentionally, i.e. with the

---

[243] Cf. *Glaston House (Pty) Ltd v. Inag (Pty) Ltd* 1977 (2) SA 846 (A) 867 sqq. (*per* Galgut AJA) and the references in Joubert (n. 61) 95, n. 48.

[244] *Law of Obligations* (n. 10) 321 sq.

[245] Cf. generally Wessels (n. 138) §§ 1346 sqq.; Joubert (n. 61) 175 sqq.; Lubbe/Murray (n. 64) 441 sqq.; Kerr (n. 83) 343 sqq.; Christie (n. 173) 171 sqq.; Hutchison, in: *Wille* (n. 91) 457 sq.; Van der Merwe/Van Huyssteen *et al.* (n. 83) 206 sqq.

[246] Cf. *Myburgh & Co v. Protecteur Fire Assurance Co* (1878) 8 Buch 152 (157) (*per* De Villiers CJ).

[247] *Stephen v. Pepler* 1921 EDL 70 (85 sq.).

[248] *Boose v. Zeederberg and Duncan* 1918 CPD 283 (292 sq.)   [249] 1924 AD 573.

[250] Ibid. 589: 'Now a person conditionally under an obligation who takes steps for the very purpose of preventing the condition from happening must speaking generally do so in order to escape the obligation. And to do so is not consistent with good faith'; 610: 'Thus understood, we see at once that the reason for the general rule laid down by the Roman jurists, as particularly expressed by Julian and Ulpian . . . is to be found in the principle of equity which permeates Roman jurisprudence.'

[251] Ibid. 589 sqq., 610 sq.; cf. De Villiers JA 608.

object of frustrating satisfaction of the condition.[252] Significantly, however, South African judges have been at pains to stress that *dolus* must be interpreted 'in its more extended and general sense as indicating anything which the law does not allow, anything inequitable'.[253] Yet the fact remains that *dolus* (in the sense of an infringement of the precepts of good faith[254]) is usually regarded as a specific (additional) requirement for the application of the rule, and no longer as its *fons et origo*. This is in line with developments in other modern legal systems; § 162 BGB is a typical example.[255] The intellectual link is furnished by nineteenth century German literature, particularly Savigny's *System des heutigen römischen Rechts*, referred to by Innes CJ, De Villiers JA, and Kotzé JA in *MacDuff's* case.[256]

Yet, at least in classical Roman law the position was different. Why the (conditional) debtor had prevented the condition from materializing was relevant to the extent that his failure to act had to be 'attributable' to him (*si per eum steterit quo minus impleatur*[257]). This did not imply an intention to defraud the other party, nor plain *dolus*, nor even fault in general.[258] Provided only that the reason for the non-perfection of the transaction fell within his sphere of responsibility, the debtor's refusal to treat the contract as valid was apparently seen as an infringement of the precepts of good faith. A return to the Roman approach does not appear impossible. The South African courts have stressed that the nature of the contract is always an important element in determining whether prevention equals satisfaction.[259] Furthermore, despite frequent statements to the effect that a deliberate action of the debtor is required, it has never been authoritatively ruled out that, in certain circumstances, negligence might be sufficient.[260] But if one accepts the explanation of the rule offered by Holmes JA in *Scott v.*

---

[252] Cf. *Scott v. Poupard* 1971 (2) SA 373 (A) 378 sq., and references in the literature quoted above, n. 245.

[253] *MacDuff* (above, n. 249) 610. Cf. Wessels CJ in *Koenig v. Johnson & Co Ltd* 1935 AD 262 (271): '. . . it will be manifest that the term *"dolus"* is used by Innes CJ in its widest sense, not in the narrow sense of fraud or want of good faith'; Stratford JA in *Koenig v. Johnson* 281: 'That *"dolus"* was not used in the modern sense of fraud is, I think, clear.' See also Joubert (n. 61) 176.

[254] Cf. esp. *Gowan v. Bowern* 1924 AD 550 (553) (*per* Innes CJ).

[255] Cf. *Law of Obligations* (n. 10) 746. For a critical evaluation see Rolf Knütel, 'Zur sogenannten Erfüllungs- und Nichterfüllungsfiktion bei der Bedingung', 1976 *Juristische Blätter* 615 sqq. 162 BGB is referred to in *Bark v. Boesch* 1959 (2) SA 377 (T).

[256] 1924 AD 573 (589, 608, 610).   [257] Cf. Ulp. D. 18, 1, 50.

[258] Cf. *Law of Obligations* (n. 10) 105 sq., 730.

[259] Cf. Innes CJ in *Gowan v. Bowern* (above, n. 254): 'The test to be applied is *dolus*: whether it is consistent with good faith for the promisor to have prevented the fulfilment of the condition. And that must be gathered from the nature and terms of the contract and from all the relevant circumstances'; *Koenig v. Johnson* (above, n. 253) 272.

[260] *Gowan v. Bowern* (above, n. 254) 552: 'It is difficult to see how the principle of fictional fulfilment of a condition can operate on the mere ground of *culpa*'. But cf. *Ferndale Investments (Pty) Ltd v. DICK Trust (Pty) Ltd* 1968 (1) SA 392 (A) 395, as interpreted by P. M. A. Hunt, 'General Principles of Contract', *Annual Survey of South African Law* (1968), 104; Hutchison, in: *Wille* (n. 91) 457 sq.

Poupard that 'a party must not be allowed to take advantage of his own default, to the loss or injury of another',[261] we are dealing with an equitable doctrine, the application of which should depend on neither intention nor negligence.[262] Whether or not prevention can be equated with satisfaction is essentially a matter of interpretation;[263] and such interpretation must be guided by the precepts of good faith.[264]

7. Repudiation

(a) Reception of the doctrine of repudiation

There are, of course, many other rules which have an equitable basis. Protection of a debtor who, as a result of cession of a claim, is suddenly faced with a new creditor for example, has been a matter of concern. Two new rules have emerged over the last few decades in this regard: if the debtor has paid in good faith to the cedent he is immune from liability towards the cessionary;[265] and cession does not deprive the debtor of the procedural advantages of the reconvention procedure if it was entered into *mala fide*, i.e. if cedent and cessionary had effected the transfer of the claim deliberately to deprive the debtor of these advantages.[266] However, since the South African courts have not resorted directly to the principle of good faith but have based their decisions on more specific Roman-Dutch and Roman sources, we will not deal with these decisions. Rather, we will turn our attention to the one case in which the concept of *bona fides* has been exploited in the grand style and in a manner very similar to that in which the *exceptio doli* used to be applied. This is the celebrated decision of the Appeal Court in *Tuckers Land and Development Corporation (Pty) Ltd v. Hovis, per* Jansen JA.[267] This takes us into the field of repudiation.

Where a party to a contract manifests an unequivocal intention not to perform his obligation, the other party should not be expected to wait until

---

[261] 1971 (2) SA 373 (A) 378.　　　　　　　　　　[262] Cf. also Hunt (n. 260) 104.

[263] Generally, Knütel, 1976 *Juristische Blätter* 615 sqq.

[264] In this sense, cf. the remarks by Lubbe/Murray (n. 64) 442; Van der Merwe/Van Huyssteen *et al.* (n. 83) 207.

[265] *Brook v. Jones* 1964 (1) SA 765 (N); *Agricultural & Industrial Mechanisation (Vereeniging) (Edms) Bpk v. Lombard* 1974 (3) SA 485 (O); *Pillay v. Harichand* 1976 (2) SA 681 (D); *Illings (Acceptance) Co (Pty) Ltd v. Ensor* 1982 (1) SA 570 (A); see also P. M. Nienaber, 'The Inactive Cessionary', 1964 *Acta Juridica* 115 sqq.; Susan Scott, *The Law of Cession* (2nd edn., 1991), 111 sq., 120 sqq.; Lubbe/Murray (n. 64) 683 sqq.; Van der Merwe/Van Huyssteen *et al.* (n. 83) 343 sqq. Previously, the relevant criterion was notice to the debtor of the cession.

[266] *LTA Engineering Co Ltd v. Seacat Investments (Pty) Ltd* 1974 (1) SA 747 (A); on which see Paul van Warmelo, '*Mala Fide* Cession, *Stare Decisis* and Abrogation by Disuse', (1974) 91 *SALJ* 298 sqq.; Zimmermann (n. 6) 66 sq.; Lubbe/Murray (n. 64) 677 sqq.; Scott (n. 265) 197 sqq.; Lewis, (1991) 108 *SALJ* 252 sqq.; Van der Merwe/Van Huyssteen *et al.* (n. 83) 341 sq.

[267] 1980 (1) SA 645 (A).

the due date before taking legal action.[268] Therefore modern legal systems tend to grant to that other party a remedy for breach of contract *in antici-pando*.[269] South African courts took over and applied[270] the English doctrine of repudiation as it had been established in the mid-twentieth century.[271] They did not at first realize that 'an entirely new doctrine, unknown to Roman-Dutch law, thereby came to form part and parcel of South African law . . . and if ever a twinge of doubt was experienced this was finally laid to rest in *Dennill v. Atkins & Co*', when Innes CJ declared that it was too late to question this position.[272] English authorities were regularly quoted 'and so it hardly occasions surprise that not only the principle, but the underlying reasons for the principle as expressed in the leading English cases, were adopted'.[273] The introduction of this specific type of breach of contract was generally welcomed as 'both useful and convenient'[274] while being at the same time consonant with the basic principles of Roman-Dutch law.[275] Final confirmation came with the decision of the Appellate Division in *Novick v. Benjamin*.[276]

(b) Doctrinal foundations

However, there were always pecularities arising, by and large[277], from the specific way in which the English courts had attempted to explain the fact that the creditor, confronted with the debtor's declared intention not to perform by the due date, was entitled to terminate the contract. Termination,

---

[268] Cf. the policy considerations advanced by Lord Campbell in *Hochster v. De la Tour* (1853) 2 El & Bl 678.

[269] In German law the rules relating to positive malperformance are usually applied: cf. Volker Emmerich, in: *Münchener Kommentar*, vol. II (3rd edn., 1994), Vor 275, nn. 274 sqq. On historical and comparative aspects of the doctrine of anticipatory breach see Francis Dawson, 'Metaphors and Anticipatory Breach of Contract', (1981) 40 *Cambridge LJ* 83 sqq.; James C. Gulotta Jr., 'Anticipatory Breach: A Comparative Analysis', (1975–6) 50 *Tulane LR* 927 sqq.

[270] For details see P. M. Nienaber, *Anticipatory Repudiation in English and South African Law of Contract* (unpublished Ph. D. thesis, University of Cambridge, not available to me); cf. also Wessels (n. 138) §§ 2935 sqq.

[271] Cf. Nienaber (n. 270); cf. also *idem*, 'The Effect of Anticipatory Repudiation: Principle and policy', 1962 *Cambridge LJ* 213 sqq.; *idem*, 'Enkele Beskouinge oor Kontrakbreuk *in antic-ipando*', (1963) 26 *THRHR* 22 sqq. The leading case is *Hochster v. De la Tour* (1853) 2 El & Bl 678.

[272] 1905 TS 282 (288).

[273] Nienaber (n. 270) 111 sqq., quoted by Holmes JA in *Crest Enterprises (Pty) Ltd v. Rycklof Beleggings (Edms) Bpk* 1972 (2) SA 863 (A) 869. On the position in Roman-Dutch law cf. Nienaber, (1963) 26 *THRHR* 29 sq.; but see also Wouter de Vos, *Verrykingsaanspreeklikheid in die Suid-Afrikaanse Reg* (3rd edn., 1987), 65.

[274] Joubert (n. 61) 211.

[275] De Wet/Van Wyk (n. 57) 169: '*Dit . . . bots nie met die grondbeginsels van ons reg nie*' (This . . . does not conflict with the basic principles of our law).

[276] 1972 (2) SA 842 (A) (*per* Jansen JA and Trollip JA). Cf. *Crest Enterprises (Pty) Ltd v. Rycklof Beleggings (Edms) Bpk* 1972 (2) SA 863 (A) (*per* Holmes JA).

[277] Cf. the analysis by Nienaber, (1963) 26 *THRHR* 27 sqq.; also Hutchison, in: *Wille* (n. 91) 512 sq.

it was argued, required an agreement between the parties to that effect; and so repudiation came to be interpreted as an offer which still had to be accepted by the other party. Thus, the perception gained ground that repudiation, unlike all other forms of breach of contract, required 'acceptance'.[278] Only slowly did the South African courts manage to disentangle themselves from this kind of theoretical framework and to recognize that repudiation is in itself a breach of contract.[279] The innocent party may now decide either to stand by the contract or to terminate it. By ignoring the repudiation he chooses the first alternative. By 'accepting' it, he exercises his election to terminate the contract. Thus, it is not the repudiation that terminates the contract;[280] nor does the contract come to an end as a result of an agreement between the parties.[281] Termination of the contract does not prevent the innocent party from claiming damages (for breach of contract); the ordinary principles governing assessment of his loss apply.[282] In *Tuckers'* case, Jansen JA essentially accepted these principles and proposed, 'in order to obtain clarity of thought', finally 'to jettison the terminology of offer and acceptance'.[283]

But he went much further. For he took the opportunity to redefine the doctrinal foundations of repudiation:

It could be said that it is now, and has been for some time, felt in our domain, no doubt under the influence of English law, that in all fairness there should be a duty upon a promisor not to commit an anticipatory breach of contract, and such a duty has in fact often been enforced by our courts. It would be consonant with the history of our law, and also legal principle, to construe this as an application of the wide jurisdiction to imply terms conferred upon a court by Roman law in respect of the *judicia bonae fidei*. It would not then be inapt to say, elliptically, that the duty

---

[278] *Hochster v. De la Tour* (above, n. 271); and cf., e.g., *White & Carter (Councils) Ltd v. McGregor* [1961] 3 All ER 1178 (1181) (*per* Lord Reid); *Denmark Productions Ltd v. Boscobel Productions Ltd* [1968] 3 All ER 513 (CA) (on which see *Stewart Wrightson (Pty) Ltd v. Thorpe* 1977 (2) SA 943 (A) 952).

[279] Cf. generally *Nash v. Golden Dumps (Pty) Ltd* 1985 (3) SA 1 (A) 22 (*per* Corbett JA); Joubert (n. 61) 210 sqq.; Lubbe/Murray (n. 64) 476 sqq.; De Wet/Van Wyk (n. 57) 168 sqq.; Hutchison, in: *Wille* (n. 91) 510 sqq.; Van der Merwe/Van Huyssteen *et al.* (n. 83) 256 sqq.; and specifically P. M. Nienaber, 'Kontrakbreuk *in anticipando* in retrospek', 1989 *TSAR* 1 sqq.

[280] As had been thought by the Court in *Kameel Tin Co (Pty) Ltd v. Brollomar Tin Exploration Ltd* 1928 TPD 726. An act of repudiation not 'accepted' has been described as 'a thing writ in water': cf. *Culverwell v. Brown* 1990 (1) SA 7 (A) 28 referring to *Howard v. Pickford Co Ltd* [1951] 1 KB 417 (421), but this goes too far. After all, the repudiation in itself constitutes a breach of contract. Cf. *Moodley v. Moodley* 1990 (1) SA 427 (D); Nienaber, 1989 *TSAR* 12 sq.; Van der Merwe/Van Huyssteen *et al.* (n. 83) 261.

[281] As suggested in *Myers v. Abramson* 1952 (3) SA 121 (C); cf. now *Stewart Wrightson (Pty) Ltd v. Thorpe* 1977 (2) SA 943 (A).

[282] In principle, damages must therefore be calculated from the date of performance rather than from the breach: *Novick v. Benjamin* 1972 (2) SA 842 (A).

[283] Nevertheless, the traditional construction of repudiation still occasionally resurfaces; cf. *HMBMP Properties (Pty) Ltd v. King* 1981 (1) SA 906 (N) and the criticism by Nienaber, 1989 *TSAR* 9 sqq.

flows from the requirement of bona fides to which our contracts are subject, and that such duty is implied in law and not in fact.[284]

IIe also referred to modern German law which had developed along broadly similar lines and emphasized again that an anticipatory breach is the violation of an obligation *ex lege*, flowing from the requirement of *bona fides* which underlies the South African law of contract. The critical and essential step, as pointed out by Carey Miller,[285] in Jansen's process of reasoning is the return to classical Roman law and the resuscitation of the power of the Roman *iudex*, within the framework of *iudicia bonae fidei*, to decide in accordance with what appeared to be equitable under the circumstances. In principle, according to Jansen JA,[286] this meant that the Dutch courts should have had the same wide powers to read into a contract any term that justice required; and in spite of the fact that the Dutch courts do not seem to have made any creative use of these powers,[287] they still vest in the modern South African courts.

8. *Bank of Lisbon* (part II)

Tuckers' case appeared to indicate that the South African courts might be prepared, at long last, to abandon their reluctance to interfere with the principle of *pacta sunt servanda* and openly to exercise a large-scale equitable jurisdiction. The South African law of contract thus seemed to have acquired a new dimension in which policy and other external criteria determine the decisions of the courts.[288] More particularly, the substantive fairness of a contract appeared to have become an issue which could no longer be regarded as irrelevant.[289] On the other hand, however, it was pointed out that predictability and consistency would be sacrificed, at least *pro tempore*.[290] Reference was made in this context to the way in which § 242 BGB had been used as a vehicle to relieve parties of onerous contractual conditions and as an instrument of judicial law-making even within a codified legal system.[291] But whatever hopes, or fears, the decision in *Tuckers'* case may have engendered, they were soon to be quashed. For in the *Bank of Lisbon* case the Appellate Division of the Supreme Court not only rejected

---

[284] *Tuckers Land & Development Corporation (Pty) Ltd v. Hovis* 1980 (1) SA 645 (A) 652.

[285] 'Judicia Bonae Fidei: A New Development in Contract?', (1980) 97 *SALJ* 532. For further comment on Jansen's views of repudiation see Nienaber, 1989 *TSAR* 8 sq.; Kahn (n. 170) 32, 718; Lewis, (1991) 108 *SALJ* 249 sqq.

[286] *Tuckers Land & Development Corp. (Pty) Ltd v. Hovis* 1980 (1) SA 645 (A) 652.

[287] Jansen, in *Tuckers'* case at 652, referring to De Blécourt/Fischer, *Kort Begrip van het Oud-Nederlands-Burgerlijk Recht* (7th edn., 1969), 193.

[288] Carey Miller, (1980) 97 *SALJ* 531 sqq. (537); cf. Lewis, (1991) 108 *SALJ* 251.

[289] C. F. C. van der Walt, (1986) 103 *SALJ* 646 sqq.

[290] Carey Miller, (1980) 97 *SALJ* 537.

[291] *Tuckers'* case (above, n. 286); Carey Miller, (1980) 97 *SALJ* 534 sqq.

the *exceptio doli* but also attempted to eradicate the most obvious alternative basis for an equitable jurisdiction. For whilst the Court recognized that in modern law all contracts are *bonae fidei*,[292] it rejected the proposition that *bona fides* had developed to fulfil the function of the *exceptio doli*.[293] Good faith, the Court appears to say, was the fountainhead of a whole variety of rules of substantive law and has rendered Roman-Dutch law an 'inherently ... equitable' system.[294] Even in Roman-Dutch law, however, it was no longer conceived as conferring wide powers on the court either to complement or to restrict the duties of the parties or to imply terms in accordance with the requirements of justice, reasonableness, and fairness. Still less, therefore, could it be used today to subvert established rules of contract law.[295]

V. EQUITY AFTER *BANK OF LISBON*

1. From freedom of contract to social responsibility

Does this mean that as a result of the 'formalistic and clinical'[296] conclusions of the majority in the *Bank of Lisbon* case the Roman-Dutch law in South Africa should, in a particularly crucial area, have lost the very feature which enabled it to survive in the modern world, its flexibility to react to new challenges and to accommodate new problems, its potential for growth and for organic change, and its openness to considerations of policy?[297] 'Should the description of Roman-Dutch law as a strong and vibrant

---

[292] *Bank of Lisbon and South Africa Ltd v. De Ornelas*, 1988 (3) SA 580 (A) 599, 601; cf. above, n. 167.

[293] Cf.esp. *ibid.* 605, 609 sq.; also Jansen JA in his minority opinion (616) who for this very reason asserts that the *exceptio doli* has not yet become redundant as a specific mechanism of equity.

[294] Ibid. 606; on this 'cryptic' assertion cf. Lubbe/Murray (n. 64) 391. For further comment see Michael A. Lambiris, 'The *exceptio doli generalis*: an obituary', (1988) 105 *SALJ* 648 sq.; Kerr (n. 83) 479 sqq.; Lewis, (1990) 107 *SALJ* 26 sqq.

[295] In line with this approach, the Appellate Division of the Supreme Court (*per* Joubert JA) has recently confirmed the prohibition on interest in *duplum* (as taken over from classical Roman law through Roman-Dutch law; cf. Zimmermann, in: Evans-Jones (n. 1) 60) without considering the suggestion by Lubbe, (1990) 53 *THRHR* 190 sqq. that this rule be related to the operation of the norm of *bona fides*: *LTA Construction Bpk v. Administrateur, Transvaal* 1992 (1) SA 473 (A).

[296] S. W. J. van der Merwe, G. F. Lubbe, L. F. van Huyssteen, 'The *exceptio doli generalis: requiescat in pace—vivat aequitas*', (1989) 106 *SALJ* 239.

[297] Cf., as far as modern South African common law is concerned, Corbett, (1987) 104 *SALJ* 52 sqq. For criticism of the *Bank of Lisbon* decision along the lines suggested in the text see H. J. Erasmus, 'Roman Law in South Africa Today', (1989) 106 *SALJ* 676 sq.; Van der Merwe/Lubbe/Van Huyssteen, (1989) 106 *SALJ* 235 sqq.; Kerr (n. 83) 483 sqq., 488 sqq.; Lubbe/Murray (n. 64) 391; Lewis, (1991) 108 *SALJ* 262 sqq.; Reinhard Zimmermann, 'The Law of Obligations: Character and Influence of the Civilian Tradition', (1992) 3 *Stellenbosch LR* 5 sqq.

legal system with a powerful inherent capacity for growth, [have become] pure hypocrisy? Should the Roman-Dutch law perhaps have started to suffer from the modern disease of sclerosis?'[298]

It is unlikely that *Bank of Lisbon* will remain the last word on the matter of good faith and contract law.[299] As Jansen JA pointed out in his minority judgment,[300] the twin concepts of freedom of contract and *pacta sunt servanda* have, in the course of this century, increasingly come under assault as a result of, *inter alia*, rampant inflation, monopolistic practices giving rise to unequal bargaining power, and the large-scale use of standard form contracts. The heyday of extreme individualism was shortlived and thus we are witnessing today, all over the world, a transition from freedom of contract to social responsibility. In a broader context, the development can be described as a return to the ethical foundations of the earlier *ius commune*.[301] Yet, while many of the doctrines designed to accommodate this concern for substantive justice have been abandoned,[302] the will theories of contract replacing them have now turned out to be in many ways deficient.[303] In certain fields the South African legislature has intervened to readjust the balance. Particularly important, in this regard, are the Credit Agreements Act,[304] the Usury Act,[305] and the Alienation of Land Act.[306] Section 3 of the Conventional Penalties Act[307] gives the courts power to reduce a penalty found to be excessive to such 'extent as it may consider equitable in the circumstances'.[308]

However, the perception has been gaining ground that the problem of unfair contract terms will have to be tackled in a more fundamental, less

---

[298] Rumpff JA in *Nortje v. Pool* 1966 (3) SA 96 (A) 113 (translated from the Afrikaans original). This *dictum* referred to the law of unjustified enrichment where the South African courts have also, thus far, endeavoured to keep a principle 'vibrant with life ... locked ... in tight compartments': cf. *Da Costa v. Bank of Ceylon* (1970) 72 *New Law Reports* (Ceylon) 457 (544 sq.); see generally *Law of Obligations* (n. 10) 886 sq. But cf. recently *Blesbok Eiendomsagentskap v. Cantamessa* 1991 (2) SA 712 (T) *per* Van Zyl J; D. H. van Zyl, 'The General Enrichment Action is Alive and Well', in: *Unjustified Enrichment, Essays in Honour of Wouter de Vos* (1992), 115 sqq.; see also the contribution by Visser to this volume.

[299] Cf. n. 136 above; *Law of Obligations* (n. 10) 677.

[300] *Bank of Lisbon* 613.

[301] Cf. on the topic of equality in exchange, James Gordley, (1981) 69 *California LR* 1587 sqq.; *Law of Obligations* (n. 10) 259 sqq., 268 sq. ('renaissance' of the *laesio enormis*).

[302] Thus, for instance, the *clausula rebus sic stantibus* (on which see *Law of Obligations* (n. 10) 579 sqq.) is not applied in South Africa (cf. Lubbe/Murray (n. 64) 773); and *laesio enormis* (*Law of Obligations* (n. 10) 259 sqq.) was formally abolished by s. 25 of the General Law Amendment Act 32 of 1952; see H. R. Hahlo, Ellison Kahn, 'Good-Bye *Laesio Enormis*', (1952) 69 *SALJ* 392 sqq.; Lubbe/Murray (n. 64) 387.

[303] For an analysis of this development see James Gordley, *Philosophical Origins of Modern Contract Doctrine* (1991).

[304] Act 75 of 1980 (replacing the Hire Purchase Act 36 of 1942).

[305] Act 73 of 1968.

[306] Act 68 of 1981 (replacing the Sale of Land on Instalments Act 72 of 1971).

[307] Act 15 of 1962. This provision essentially reinstates the common law; cf. *Law of Obligations* (n. 10) 108 sqq.

[308] On these and other statuory enactments cf. Aronstam (n. 120) 49 sqq.

fragmentary manner.[309] The doctrine of undue influence, according to Van Huyssteen,[310] has paved the way for the recognition of 'abuse of circumstances' as a general ground for the rescission of contracts. Nonetheless, this proposal still essentially accepts the parameters set by the will theories: the courts are merely concerned with the fairness of the bargaining process, the assumption being that the result of fair negotiations is likely also to be substantially fair. Hence the defences of fraud, misrepresentation, duress, and undue influence. Abuse of circumstances would merely extend this list. Alternatively, a more enlightened approach to the construction of contracts has been advocated to avoid the inequity which has arisen in cases like *Bank of Lisbon* and *Rand Bank v. Rubenstein*.[311] But it would be naïve to assume[312] that this is the only remaining problem area for which, after the demise of the *exceptio doli*, another route to contractual equity has to be devised. Others have argued that a change of circumstances may effectively render a contract unenforceable; and they have based their argument on the concept of good faith in contract law.[313] There are, however, no signs of this kind of renaissance of the *clausula rebus sic stantibus* in South African case law. But it has also been submitted that legislative intervention will be necessary to enable South African courts openly to perform their duty of policing unfair contract terms.[314] A rather sweeping proposal along these lines has been submitted to the South African Law Commission.[315] Its framework of reference is not confined to standard form contracts; a statutory provision is recommended according to which the courts may either declare invalid or modify any contract or any clause within a contract which, in the light of all the circumstances, does not conform to the standard of good faith. If adopted, this provision would effectively overrule *Bank of Lisbon*.

---

[309] Cf. C. F. C. van der Walt, 'Die huidige posisie in die Suid-Afrikaanse reg met betrekking tot onbillike kontraksbedinge', (1986) 103 *SALJ* 646 sqq.

[310] Van Huyssteen (n. 157) 127 sqq. [311] Lewis, (1990) 107 *SALJ* 26 sqq.

[312] But see Lewis, (1990) 107 *SALJ* 33.

[313] L. F. van Huyssteen, Schalk van der Merwe, 'Good Faith in Contract: Proper Behaviour Amidst Changing Circumstances', (1990) 1 *Stellenbosch LR* 244 sqq.; cf. Lubbe/Murray (n. 64) 773 sq.

[314] Cf. earlier Aronstam (n. 120) 184: 'It is submitted that, because the South African courts are extremely reluctant to extend the principles of the common law to vest themselves with a jurisdiction based on principles of equity to deal with problems caused by unconscionable contractual conduct, the legislature should introduce or create such a general jurisdiction for them.'

[315] See C. F. C. van der Walt, 'Kontrakte en beheer oor kontrakteervryheid in 'n nuwe Suid-Afrika', (1991) 54 *THRHR* 367 sqq.; *idem*, 'Aangepaste voorstelle vir 'n stelsel van voorkomende beheer oor kontrakteervryheid in die Suid-Afrikaanse reg', (1993) 56 *THRHR* 65 sqq.

2. Public interest

In the meantime, however, there has been a line of cases in which the courts have begun to explore a new point of departure. In the important case of *Magna Alloys and Research (SA) (Pty) Ltd v. Ellis*[316] the Appellate Division of the Supreme Court rejected the English approach to agreements in restraint of trade[317] which had been followed in South Africa for many years.[318] Preferring sanctity of contract to freedom of trade,[319] the Court held that agreements in restraint of trade should no longer be regarded as *prima facie* void. Enforcement may only be refused if the person bound by the restraint is able to show that such enforcement would be prejudicial to the public interest (*openbare belang*). In so determining, the reasonableness of the restraint still appears to be a relevant consideration.[320] Apart from its immediate relevance for agreements in restraint of trade, *Magna Alloys*[321] contains, or at least implies, a number of propositions of a far-reaching and fundamental character. They can be summarized as follows. (1) *Openbare belang*, i.e. public interest or public policy, is an essential factor in determining the (common law) legality or otherwise of contracts. Or, to put the matter differently: agreements contrary to public policy are illegal and cannot therefore be enforced. (2) Public interest generally favours the sanctity of contracts. (3) Public interest, however, also requires that certain limitations must be placed on freedom of contract. (4) The unreasonableness *inter partes* of a contract, whilst not in itself constituting a good reason to refuse its enforcement, is a factor to be taken into account when determining what public policy requires. (5) Public policy is a dynamic concept.[322] It is bound to reflect changing attitudes and social policies and may thus vary from time to time. More particularly, there is no *numerus clausus* of types of agreements that can be regarded as contrary to public policy.

[316] 1984 (4) SA 874 (A) (*per* Rabie CJ).
[317] Cf. *Van de Pol v. Silbermann* 1952 (2) SA 561 (A) 569; Hahlo/Kahn (n. 2) 476; Ellison Kahn, 'The Rules Relating to Contracts in Restraint of Trade: Whence and Whither', (1968) 85 *SALJ* 391 sqq.
[318] Cf. Treitel (n. 77) 401 sqq.
[319] Cf. Didcott J in *Roffey v. Catterall, Edwards & Goudré (Pty) Ltd* 1977 (4) SA 494 (N) 505: 'I am satisfied that South African law prefers the sanctity of contracts. . . . Freedom of trade does not vibrate nearly as strongly through our jurisprudence . . . it is intrinsically the less commanding of the two ideas'; see also the criticism by J. T. Schoombee, 'Agreements in Restraint of Trade: The Appellate Division confirms new principles', (1985) 48 *THRHR* 127 sqq., 139 sq.
[320] *Magna Alloys* (above, n. 316) 897.
[321] For academic comment see Schoombee, (1985) 48 *THRHR* 127 sqq.; Lubbe/Murray (n. 64) 255 sqq.; A. J. Kerr, 'Restraint of Trade After *Magna Alloys*', in: *Essays in Honour of Ellison Kahn* (1989), 186 sqq.; Van der Merwe/Van Huyssteen *et al.* (n. 83) 155 sqq.
[322] *Magna Alloys* (above, n. 316) 891; cf. Corbett, (1987) 104 *SALJ* 64; Gerhard Lubbe, '*Bona fides*, billikheid en die openbare belang in die Suid-Afrikaanse kontraktereg', (1990) 1 *Stellenbosch LR* 11 sqq.

These are the main premises which enabled the Appellate Division some five years after *Magna Alloys* to take another bold step forward. In *Sasfin (Pty) Ltd v. Beukes*,[323] the Court struck down a deed of cession which, while placing the one party economically almost entirely at the other party's mercy, far exceeded the protection of the latter's reasonable interests.[324] An agreement of this kind, it was held, was 'clearly unconscionable and incompatible with the public interest, and therefore contrary to public policy'.[325] This result can hardly be regarded as startling; a German court would probably have regarded the transaction as what has come to be termed *Knebelungsvertrag* and would thus have held it to be *contra bonos mores* in terms of 138 I BGB.[326] Startling, however, are some of the pronouncements made in the course of the judgment to substantiate the result. For, in considering whether the transaction was enforceable, the Court declared it to be 'relevant and not unimportant' that 'public policy should properly take into account the doing of simple justice between man and man'.[327]

The implications of this rather 'cursory and unelaborated'[328] approach, confirmed in *Botha (now Griessel) v. Financredit (Pty) Ltd*,[329] are not entirely clear and still need to be worked out in greater detail. It is obvious, however, that *Sasfin* is an important decision, following which the concept of *bona fides*, thrown out in *Bank of Lisbon*, may yet again assert its influence. Good faith, it could be argued,[330] requires that parties to a contract show a minimum level of respect for each other's interest. The unreasonable and one-sided promotion of one's own interest at the expense of the other

---

[323] 1989 (1) SA 1 (A).

[324] Sasfin, a Finance Company, was effectively put in control of all of Beukes' (a specialist anaesthesist) professional earnings from the date of cession and at all times thereafter; Sasfin was also entitled, on notice of cession to Beukes' debtors, to recover all of Beukes' book debts and to retain all amounts recovered, irrespective of whether Beukes was indebted to Sasfin in a lesser amount or at all. Beukes was, furthermore, rendered powerless to end this situation.

[325] *Sasfin* (above, n. 323) 13 sq.

[326] On the distinction (if there is any!) between the *boni mores*, public policy, and public interest in South African law see *Sasfin* (above, n. 323) 8; Joubert (n. 61) 132 sqq.; Lubbe/Murray (n. 64) 237 sqq.; Hutchison, in: *Wille* (n. 91) 428 sqq.; Van der Merwe/Van Huyssteen *et al.* (n. 83) 139 sqq. ('not at all clear'); Lubbe, (1990) 1 *Stellenbosch LR* 11; cf. *Edouard v. Administrator, Natal* 1989 (2) SA 368 (D) 378 referring to a *dictum* by Benjamin Cardozo according to which a contract must be regarded as illegal if it infringes 'some fundamental principle of justice, some prevalent conception of good morals, some deep-rooted tradition of the common weal'. Hoexter JA in *Botha (now Griessel) v. Financredit (Pty) Ltd* 1989 (3) SA 773 (A) 780 (confirming the Sasfin approach) draws no distinction between contracts *contra bonos mores*, inimical to the interest of the community, unconscionable and contrary to public policy.

[327] *Sasfin* (above, n. 323) 9 referring to the famous decision in *Jajbhay v. Cassim* 1939 AD 537 (544) where the same criterion had been used to determine whether an enrichment claim is barred on account of the *in pari turpitudine* rule; cf. *Law of Obligations* (n. 10) 865 sq.; Leon E. Trakman, 'The Effect of Illegality in South African Law', (1977) 94 *SALJ* 330, 476; Lubbe, (1990) 1 *Stellenbosch LR* 17 sq.

[328] Lubbe, (1990) 1 *Stellenbosch LR* 25.

[329] 1989 (3) SA 773 (A) 783. Cf. Schalk van der Merwe, Gerhard Lubbe, '*Bona Fides* and Public Policy in Contract', (1991) 2 *Stellenbosch LR* 91 sqq.

[330] Lubbe, (1990) 1 *Stellenbosch LR* 17 sqq.

infringes the principle of good faith to such a degree as to outweigh the public interest in the sanctity of contracts. Public policy, under these circumstances, rather requires the courts to refuse to enforce the contract. From the point of view of the appropriate doctrinal pigeonholes, conduct contrary to good faith may thus be classified as illegal.[331] How far this argument will carry is, however, uncertain. At present the courts appear to be busy exploring the consequences of the *Sasfin* approach for (usually standardized) deeds of suretyship.[332] A German lawyer is bound to be reminded of the way in which § 138 was initially used as a screen behind which the courts began to police unfair standard contract terms.[333] In the final analysis, however, these recent tendencies show that the development of the law cannot be artificially stifled by unimaginative and formalistic conclusions like those reached in the *Bank of Lisbon* case. Some kind of residual mechanism must remain available to keep the law in tune with the demands of equity or, in the imagery of Rumpff CJ,[334] to prevent its death by sclerosis.

---

[331] Van der Merwe/Lubbe, (1991) 2 *Stellenbosch LR* 97; Van der Merwe/Van Huyssteen *et al.* (n. 83) 160, 234.

[332] *D Engineering Co (Pty) Ltd v. Morkel* 1992 (3) Commercial Law Digest 228 (T); *Interland Durban (Pty) Ltd v. Walters* 1993 (1) SA 223 (C); *Mark Enterprises Incorporated v. Malberand (Pty) Ltd* 1992 (4) Commercial Law Digest 331 (W); *Pangbourne Properties Ltd v. Nitor Construction* 1992 (4) Commercial Law Digest 314 (W); *Conshu Holdings Ltd v. Lawless* 1992 (4) Commercial Law Digest 301 (W); *Standard Bank Financial Nominees (Pty) Ltd v. Bamberger* 1992 (4) Commercial Law Digest 308 (W). The yardstick often applied in these cases to determine whether a contract is unconscionable is whether it serves the legitimate security requirements of the creditor or whether it unnecessarily exceeds the purpose which a transaction of this kind is normally designed to serve. Cf. Lubbe, (1990) 1 *Stellenbosch LR* 23 sq.

[333] Cf. Ludwig Raiser, *Das Recht der allgemeinen Geschäftsbedingungen* (1961), 277 sqq.; Wilhelm Weber, *Die Allgemeinen Geschäftsbedingungen* (1967), nn. 333 sqq., 344 sqq., 373 sqq.

[334] Cf. above, n. 298.

8: *Voidable Contracts*

GERHARD LUBBE

I. INTRODUCTION

When dealing with the defeasibility of contracts South African courts have traditionally referred to the grounds for *restitutio in integrum* in Roman-Dutch law.[1] In the former South African Republic the treatment of *dolus* and *metus* by certain old authorities was enshrined as the law of the land by a single *lex citandi*.[2] However, modern sources reveal that South African law has moved beyond the classic themes of *dolus* and *metus* as grounds justifying the rescission of a contract. Undue influence has found recognition as an additional ground,[3] and there is today no doubt that a contract induced by misrepresentation may be set aside irrespective of whether the representor had been at fault, whether in the form of *dolus* or *culpa*.[4] According to the prevailing view,[5] these grounds for avoidance—all of them instances of procedural irregularities during the process of bargaining—constitute a *numerus clausus*. This reveals a further remarkable feature of South African law. The doctrine of *laesio enormis* does not form part of modern law. That product of the '*cerebrina aequitas* of Constantinople and Berytus',[6] which permitted *restitutio in integrum* of contracts of sale on account of a substantive imbalance in the performances agreed upon[7] was

---

[1] *White Bros v. Treasurer-General* (1883) 2 SC 322; *Stewart's Assignee v. Wall's Trustee* (1885) 3 SC 246; *Durr v. Bam* (1891) 8 SC 22, 25; *Vlotman v. Landsberg* (1890) 7 SC 301; *Tait v. Wicht* (1890) 7 SC 158.

[2] See *Volksraadsbesluit* of 19 Sept. 1859, art. 52, and the discussion by Maurits Josson, *Schets van het Recht van de Zuid-Afrikaansche Republiek* (Gent, 1897), 10 sqq., 188 sqq.

[3] *Preller v. Jordaan* 1956 (1) SA 483 (A); *Patel v. Grobbelaar* 1974 (1) SA 532 (A).

[4] *Karroo & Eastern Board of Executors and Trust Co v. Farr* 1918 AD 413; *Reyneke v. Botha* 1977 (3) SA 20 (T); *Novick v. Comair Holdings Ltd* 1979 (2) SA 116 (W). The remarks to the contrary by Van den Heever JA in *Tjollo Ateljees (Eins) Bpk v. Small* 1949 (1) SA 856 (A) 871, 872 are incorrect.

[5] *Hare's Brickfields Ltd v. Cape Town City Council* 1985 (1) SA 769 (C) 774. Cf. David Joubert, *General Principles of the Law of Contract* (1988), 89 sqq., 104 sqq., 111 sqq.; R. H. Christie, *The Law of Contract* (2nd edn., 1991), 325 sqq., 367 sqq. But see Schalk van der Merwe, Louis van Huyssteen, Michiel Reinecke, Gerhard Lubbe, Jan Lotz, *Contract: General Principles* (1993), 73, who propose with reference to *Plaaslike Boerediensте (Edms) Bpk v. Chemfos Bpk* 1986 (1) SA 819 (A) that the various grounds for rescission be subsumed under one single ground, namely improperly obtained consensus.

[6] *Tjollo Ateljees (Eins) Bpk v. Small* (above, n. 4), 862.

[7] Reinhard Zimmermann, *The Law of Obligations: Roman Foundations of the Civilian Tradition* (1990, reprint 1993), 259 sqq.

finally and formally abolished in 1952,[8] apparently in response to criticism in the judgments handed down in *Tjollo Ateljees (Eins) Bpk v. Small*.[9]

This Chapter attempts to explain the development of the grounds for rescission in South African law, a process generally attributed to the adoption of the doctrines of innocent misrepresentation and undue influence from English Equity jurisprudence by the South African courts.

The discussion is restricted to a consideration of the circumstances in which rescission is permitted. It seems to have been accepted at an early stage that *metus* and *dolus* render a contract voidable rather than void,[10] and neither this aspect nor the legal nature of *restitutio in integrum*, as received in South African law, will be considered here. Although it seems that there is nothing to prevent a party from seeking a formal decree rescinding a contract,[11] this is not strictly a requirement. A contract may be terminated, extra-judicially by means of a unilateral act, and courts need only be approached to enforce the consequences of such a course of action.[12] Furthermore, it seems that *restitutio in integrum* in modern law merely refers to the enforcement of a claim for the restitution of benefits

---

[8] Section 25 of the General Law Amendment Act 32 of 1952, concerning Natal and the Transvaal. On the abolition of *laesio enormis* in the Cape and the Orange Free State see s. 8 of Act 8 of 1879 (Cape); s. 6 of Ordinance 5 of 1902 (OFS); and presently s. 4 of the Pre-Union Statute Law Revision Act 43 of 1977. See generally Johannes Christiaan de Wet, Andreas van Wyk, *Kontraktereg en Handelsreg*, vol. I (5th edn., 1992), 53; Louis van Huyssteen, *Onbehoorlike Beïnvloeding en Misbruik van Omstandighede in die Suid-Afrikaanse Reg* (1980), 121 sqq.; Peter Aronstam, *Consumer Protection, Freedom of Contract and the Law* (1979), 44 sqq.

[9] Above, n. 4.

[10] On misrepresentation see *Gous v. De Kock* (1887) 5 SC 405, 408; *Adamanta Diamond Mining Co Ltd v. Wege* (1883) 2 HCG 172, 179; *Vigne v. Leo* (1902) 9 HCG 196; *Woodstock, Claremont, Mowbray and Rondebosch Councils v. Smith* (1909) 26 SC 681; *Van Geems v. Fitt* (1910) 20 CTR 537; *Frost v. Leslie* 1923 AD 276, 279. See also *Broodryk v. Smuts* 1942 TPD 47 (*metus*); *Preller v. Jordaan* (n. 3), 494 (undue influence); and see generally: Robert Warden Lee, *An Introduction to Roman Dutch Law* (1915), 227; Sir John Wessels, *The Law of Contract in South Africa* (1937), § 1126. *Contra*: Andries Maasdorp, *The Institutes of Cape Law*, vol. III (1907), 64 sqq.

[11] *Sonia (Pty) Ltd v. Wheeler* 1958 (1) SA 555 (A) 561.

[12] While it was undoubtedly established practice for a considerable time to seek a formal court order setting aside the contract (e.g. *Vlotman v. Landsberg* (above, n. 1); *Forbes v. Behr* (1896) 13 SC 304; *Schoenemann v. Cape Lime Co* (1897) 7 CTR 350) this is no indication that South African courts ever enjoyed a prerogative power to grant relief against valid contracts (*Tjollo Ateljees (Eins) Bpk v. Small* 1949 (above, n. 4) 871; D. P. Visser, 'Rethinking Unjustified Enrichment', 1992 *Acta Juridica* 203, 220–2). References in the law reports to the legitimate 'repudiation' of a contract on account of e.g. misrepresentation suggest that contracts were eventually regarded as being rescinded by extra-judicial action by the representee. See e.g. *Stellenbosch Municipality v. Lindenburg* (1860) 3 Searle 345; *Wilson v. Hjul* (1882) 1 HCG 67; *Atlas Diamond Mining Co v. Poole* (1882) 1 HCG 20, 30; *Macrae & Nicholay v. Matthysen* (1889) 3 SAR 72; *Lothian Gold Mining Co Ltd v. Lister* (1890) 11 NLR 78; *Begley v. Denton & Thomas* (1897) 14 SC 344; *Bodasingh v. Massey-Harris* 1932 AD 39). This approach can be traced to English decisions such as *Reese River Silver Mining Co v. Smith* (1869) LR 4 HL 64, 73 and *United Shoe Machinery Co of Canada v. Brunnet* [1909] AC 330 (PC), explicitly endorsed in *Lebedina v. Schechter and Haskell* 1931 WLD 247, 252.

derived from a contract which has been rescinded after performance has occurred.[13]

The inquiry reveals that decisive reception of the English doctrines is a relatively recent occurrence. Such information as is available suggests that before 1828[14] there was no discernible English influence in the decisions of the Court of Justice at the Cape, and that Roman-Dutch principles were applied in respect of contracts induced by fraud.[15] Although some English influence is apparent from about the middle of the nineteenth century,[16] the case-law indicates that even in the penultimate decade of that century, Roman Dutch law still constituted the judicial point of departure.[17] The truly important developments, at least as regards misrepresentation, only came about after 1890 in consequence of the House of Lords decision in *Derry v. Peek*.[18] The treatment of misrepresentation in the present paper is accordingly divided into two sections, dealing with the periods before and after 1890. An excursus into developments in English law offers a perspective on South African judgments on misrepresentation. An evaluation of the treatment of misrepresentation will also provide a touchstone for a discussion of the introduction of the doctrine of undue influence into South African law and of its relationship to the established doctrine of *metus*. This study focuses on rescission, but occasional remarks are necessary on the related issue of the recovery of delictual damages on account of improper behaviour *in contrahendo*. Although the principles applicable to rescission and damages were initially regarded as identical, the growing influence of English law has led to a divergence.[19]

---

[13] *Lebedina v. Schechter* (above, n. 12); *Tjollo Ateljees (Eins) Bpk v. Small* (above, n. 4) 872; *Vryburg Garage v. Steinmann* 1939 GWLD 34; *Van Schalkwyk v. Griesel* 1948 (4) SA 460 (A); *Yorkshire Insurance Co v. Ishmail* 1957 (1) SA 353 (T); *Davidson v. Bonafede* 1981 (2) SA 501 (C) 505; *Johnson v. Jainodien* 1982 (4) SA 599 (C) 605; *Visser*, 1993 *Acta Juridica* 203, 211; Joubert (n. 5) 242; Wouter de Vos, *Verrykingsaanspreeklikheid in die Suid-Afrikaanse Reg* (3rd edn., 1987), 158 sqq. *Contra*, but on unconvincing grounds: Michael Lambiris, *Orders for Specific Performance and* Restitutio in Integrum *in South African law* (1989), 198 sqq.

[14] This date marks the inception of reported decisions of the Cape Supreme Court, instituted by the First and Second Charters of Justice of 1827 and 1832. See Reinhard Zimmermann, *Das römisch-holländische Recht in Südafrika* (1983), 11.

[15] Louis van Huyssteen, 'Some notes on Roman-Dutch Law at the Cape under British rule', (1994) 62 *Tijdschrift voor rechtsgeschiedenis* 357 sqq., suggests that during this period contracts induced by fraud were regarded as void rather than voidable. See also *Tjollo Ateljees (Eins) Bpk v. Small* (above, n. 4), 870; Zimmermann (n. 7), 670; De Wet/Van Wyk (n. 8), 42 sqq. and Joubert (n. 5), 91 on the uncertainty of Roman-Dutch texts on this point.

[16] See below, II. 1.   [17] Above, n. 1.

[18] (1889) 14 App Cas 337. See below, II. 3.

[19] See *Nathan, Michaelis & Jacobs v. Blake's Executors* 1904 TS 626, 631: requirements for *restitutio in integrum* and damages said to be 'entirely different'.

II. FROM FRAUD TO MISREPRESENTATION

1. Developments prior to 1890

The South African law regarding rescission for misrepresentation was authoritatively stated by the Appellate Division in *Karroo & Eastern Board of Executors & Trust Co v. Farr*.[20] Whoever avers misrepresentation,[21] must prove that the representee entered into the contract on the faith of false representations of fact of a material nature, made to him by the other contractant or his authorized agent, in order to induce him to enter into the contract.[22] Solomon JA's expressed relief at not having to investigate a charge of fraud[23] vividly emphasizes that *dolus*, in the sense of a fraudulent intent, does not form part of the cause of action. The absence of any dispute between the parties with regard to the law governing the case[24] confirms that in permitting rescission without proof of fault the Appellate Division was not breaking new ground but merely adopting a position entrenched in previous case-law.

The so-called doctrine of innocent misrepresentation[25] is a late development in South African law. In *Tait v. Wicht*,[26] for instance, De Villiers CJ had no difficulty in describing the affirmation in the 'very recent case' of *Derry v. Peek*[27] that 'actual fraud'[28] was an element in an action for damages for deceit in English law as 'quite consistent with the views of Roman Dutch authors in reference to *restitutio in integrum* for fraud'.[29] In fact between the establishment of the Cape Supreme Court in 1828[30] and 1890 the redress of misrepresentation in a contractual context (both in respect of a delictual claim for damages and the setting aside of a contract thereby induced) depended on proof of fraudulent intent on the part of the representor.[31] The case-law after 1828 did not therefore depart radically from the

---

[20] (Above, n. 4), 415.

[21] Irrespective of whether this occurs by way of a defence to a claim on a contract or at the initiative of the representee in order to set aside a contract.

[22] (Above, n. 4), 415. [23] Ibid. [24] Ibid.

[25] The term is a misnomer in that there is no need to establish that the behaviour of the representor is free from *dolus* or *culpa*. This aspect is simply irrelevant. The connotation is the same in English law after *Derry v. Peek* (above, n. 18). See Harold Hanbury, Ronald Maudsley, Jill Martin, *Modern Equity* (13th edn., 1989), 786. Before 1889 the term referred an honest but negligent misrepresentation. See below, II. 2.

[26] (1890) 7 SC 158. [27] Above, n. 18.

[28] Entailing proof of a false representation which has been made knowingly, without belief in its truth, or recklessly, without caring whether it be true or false. See *Derry v. Peek* (above, n. 18), 360 sq.

[29] *Tait v. Wicht* (n. 1), 166. [30] Zimmermann (n. 14), 11.

[31] On damages see: *Lawton v. Rens* (1842) 3 Menz 483; *Commissioners of the Municipality of Cape Town v. Truter* (1866) 1 Roscoe 412; *Lippert & Co v. Smit* (1878) 8 Buch 95; *Tait v. Wicht* (above, n. 29). In regard to rescission see: *Farmer v. Findlay & Chisholm* (1837) 2 Menz 97; *Smith, Hooper & Co v. Steyn* 1867 NLR 102; *Blamire's Executor v. Milner & Wirsing* 1869

Roman-Dutch principles as they seem to have been adhered to in pre-1828 Cape law.[32]

Tait v. Wicht[33] also echoes earlier cases[34] in its emphasis on Labeo's classic definition of *dolus malus* as comprising[35] '*omnis calliditas, fallacia, machinatio ad circumveniendum, fallendum decipiendum alterum adhibita*'. The proscription of all conduct characterized by an 'intention on the part of the wrongdoer to bring about a result of circumventing, cheating or deceiving someone',[36] covers an enormously wide field, irrespective of the means adopted by the wrongdoer. In fact, whether because of inadequate reporting or not, the term 'fraud' is used in the earliest cases in precisely such a wide and undifferentiated way. Behaviour is treated as fraudulent without any particular concern for the substantive categories in which the relevant situations would be placed today. Cases relating to *fraus creditorum*,[37] machinations to defeat prior rights,[38] and instances of disagreement[39] are thus all dealt with as fraud, together with misrepresentation inducing a contract, the 'mechanics of deceit' apparently being of little relevance.[40] Similarly, the elements of fraudulent behaviour initially received only scant analytical attention.[41] Apart from any other consideration,[42] this lack of analytical elaboration may be attributable as much to the paucity of cases dealing with misrepresentation in a contractual context[43] as to the crude nature of frauds produced by the relatively unsophisticated communities of

---

NLR 39; *Riddelsdell v. Williams* (1874) 4 Buch 11; *Levisohn v. Williams* (1875) 5 Buch 108; *Alexander v. Owen* (1882) 1 Buch AC 159; *Adamanta Diamond Mining Co Ltd v. Smythe* (1883) 1 HCG 406; *Macrae & Nicolay v. Matthysen* (1889) 3 SAR 72; *Tait v. Wicht* (n. 29); *Vlotman v. Landsberg* (above, n. 1); *Lothian Gold Mining Co Ltd v. Lister* (above, n. 12); *Young v. Kruger* (1890) 11 NLR 239; *Durr v. Bam* (above, n. 1).

[32] Above, n. 15. [33] Above, n. 29.

[34] E.g. *Harris v. Prince & Co and Norden* (1854) 2 Searle 83. For later cases see: *Frenkel & Co v. Freisman & Shapiro* (1897) 4 OR 227; *Crowley v. Bergtheil* (1899) 20 NLR 67 (PC); *Ross v. Van Vueren* (1896) 17 NLR 25.

[35] D. 4, 3, 2, 1. [36] *Tait v. Wicht* (above, n. 29), 165.

[37] *Harris v. Prince & Co and Norden* (above, n. 34).

[38] On fraud in relation to the so-called doctrine of notice see *Cohen v. Shires, McHattie & King* (1882) 1 SAR 41; *Coaton v. Alexander* 1879 Buch 17; *Richards v. Nash* (1881) 1 SC 312; *Grant v. Stonestreet* 1968 (4) SA 1 (A); *Reynders v. Rand Bank Bpk* 1978 (2) SA 630 (T).

[39] *Preuss & Seligmann v. Prins* (1864) 1 Roscoe 198.

[40] Cf. Zimmermann (n. 7), 666 on *dolus* in Roman law. The open-ended approach of Roman-Dutch authors is apparent from *Josson* (n. 2), 190.

[41] *Farmer v. Findlay & Chisholm* (n. 31); *Lawton v. Rens* (1842) 3 Menz 483; *Commissioners of the Municipality of Cape Town v. Truter* (1866) 1 Roscoe 412; *Smith, Hooper & Co v. Steyn* 1867 NLR 102; *Riddelsdell v. Williams* (n. 31).

[42] For aspects of the legal profession and the structure of the courts in the early colonial period which might have a bearing on this issue see Zimmermann (n. 14), 13 sqq.

[43] Apart from the low level of business activity, the extensive use of promissory notes as a payment mechanism in early Cape law, as is evident from the great number of cases dealing with provisional sentence proceedings in Menzies' reports, seems to have hampered the development of substantive law.

the early colonial period.[44] As might be expected, noticeable developments came only with the stimulus of economic activity following the discovery of diamonds at Kimberley in 1870 and of gold on the Rand in 1886.[45]

From early in the nineteenth century the courts tended to resort to English sources to flesh out Labeo's injunction against fraud. References in *Steytler v. Brink*[46] to the notions of 'moral' as against 'legal' fraud, while not particularly significant for the decision of the case, reflect an acquaintance with contemporary doctrinal themes of English equity jurisprudence.[47] The citation of English precedents and treatises, both in judgments and the arguments of counsel, reinforces this conclusion.[48] Perhaps in response to these influences, a differentiated approach, strongly reminiscent of the English equitable doctrine concerning misrepresentation,[49] is evident in *Stellenbosch Municipality v. Lindenburg*.[50] In a judgment of some sophistication, misrepresentation[51] and inducement[52] emerge as distinct elements which must be established, in addition to knowledge of the falsity of the representation,[53] in order to avoid a contract. The influence of English

---

[44] See *Preuss & Seligmann v. Prins* (above, n. 39): contents of document in pencil effaced by means of an 'india-rubber', and completed in fraud of signor; *Kitshoff v. Daly's Trustees* (1866) 5 Searle 213: mortgagee's name substituted on bond; *Gous v. De Kock* (1887) 5 SC 405: impersonation of contracting party. Cases relating to the propensities of milk cows and the quality of forage fed to them abound in the reports. See *Stibbs v. Le Roux* (1884) 3 HCG 356; *Durr v. Bam* (above, n. 1), 25; *Vlotman v. Landsberg* (above, n. 1); *Young v. Kruger* (above, n. 31); *Commissioners of the Municipality of Cape Town v. Truter* (1866) 1 Roscoe 412; *Bouwer v. Ferguson* (1884) 4 EDC 90.

[45] See e.g. *Atlas Diamond Mining Co Ltd v. Poole* (above, n. 12); *Geddes v. Kaiser Wilhelm Gold Mining Co* (1888) 5 HCG 178, 182; *Macrae & Nicolay v. Matthysen* (above, n. 12); *Lothian Gold Mining Co Ltd v. Lister* (above, n. 12); *Laughton v. Griffiths* (1893) 14 NLR 84, referring to a 'great impulse to deal in shares', amounting to a 'mad frenzy'.

[46] (1851) 1 Searle 123, 130.

[47] See Zimmermann (n. 14), 13–5 on circumstances conducive to the reception of English influence.

[48] *Lawton v. Rens* (above, n. 31); *Harris v. Prince & Co and Norden* (above, n. 34), 85; *Stellenbosch Municipality v. Lindenburg* (above, n. 12), 348; *Preuss & Seligmann v. Prins* (above, n. 39); *Riddelsdell v. Williams* (1874) 4 Buch 11; *Lippert & Co v. Smit* (1878) 8 Buch 95 sq.; *Atlas Diamond Mining Co Ltd v. Poole* (above, n. 12), 28; *Adamanta Diamond Mining Co Ltd v. Wege* (above, n. 10), 177, 181; *Alexander v. Owen* (1882) 1 Buch AC 159, 161; *Geddes v. Kaiser Wilhelm Gold Mining Co* (1888) 5 HCG 178, 181; *Tait v. Wicht* (above, n. 1), 165, 166–9; *Young v. Kruger* (above, n. 31).

[49] See below, II. 2.   [50] (1860) 3 Searle 345.   [51] See the arguments of counsel at 348.

[52] 350. See also: *Vlotman v. Landsberg* (n. 1); *Durr v. Bam* (n. 1).

[53] Although the pleadings in *Stellenbosch Municipality v. Lindenburg* (n. 12) make no mention of fraud, the judgment affords no basis for the conclusion that *mala fides* was regarded as irrelevant. See Gerhard Lubbe, 'The Origin and Development of the Doctrine of Innocent Misrepresentation', in: Jeremy Gauntlett (ed.), *J. C. Noster: 'n Feesbundel aangebied deur oud-studente van professor J. C. de Wet* (1979), 116, 135, fn. 176. See generally on a fraudulent state of mind as an element for relief during this period: *Lawton v. Rens* (n. 31); *Lippert & Co v. Smith* 1878 8 Buch 95; *Alexander v. Owen* (1882) 1 Buch AC 159; *Tait v. Wicht* (n. 1), 166; *Lothian Gold Mining Co Ltd v. Lister* (n. 12); *Young v. Kruger* (n. 31). The suggestion in *Bouwer v. Ferguson* (1884) 4 EDC 90 that, despite the abolition of *laesio enormis* in the Cape in 1879, a gross disproportion between the value of performances agreed upon might constitute evidence of fraud did not find acceptance.

sources is apparent in the treatment of each of these elements in later decisions. Fundamentally, relief came to be restricted to instances of misrepresentation, that is to say, untrue statements of fact as opposed to mere statements of opinion,[54] whether made expressly or by conduct,[55] provided that such statements emanated from the other contractant or his authorized representative.[56] English authorities also provided the impulse for a further refinement, namely a distinction between misrepresentations of fact and statements expressing an intention to act in a certain way in the future: the frustration of expectations engendered by a statement of future intention may in appropriate circumstances give rise to remedies in contract[57] but does not generally afford relief on account of misrepresentation.[58] Whether a misrepresentation had induced a contract was, and still is today, dealt with as a factual issue subject to proof.[59] The early South African cases dealing with this question clearly held that an awareness of uncertainty regarding the outcome of inherently speculative business ventures entails an assumption of responsibility which excludes inducement.[60] The treatment of inducement in the early cases does not reflect the classic civilian distinction between *dolus dans locum contractui* and *dolus incidens* in regard to the voidability of the transaction.[61]

Apart from the relevance which the bearing of the representee subsequent

---

[54] *Adamanta Diamond Mining Co Ltd v. Wege* (n. 10), 177, 180; *Atlas Diamond Mining Co Ltd v. Poole* (n. 12), 32–4; *Alexander v. Owen* (n. 53); *Adamanta Diamond Mining Co Ltd v. Smythe* (n. 31); *Durr v. Bam* (n. 1). On the position in Equity see: *Jennings v. Broughton* (1853) 5 De G M & G 126, 134; *Leyland v. Illingworth* (1860) 2 De G F & J 243; *Mathias v. Yetts* (1882) 46 LT 497; *In re Metropolitan Coal Consumers Association: Kalberg's case* (1892) 3 Ch 1; Lubbe (n. 53), 126.

[55] Whether by way of *suggestio falsi* or, in appropriate circumstances, *supressio veri*. See *Commissioners of the Municipality of Cape Town v. Truter* (n. 41); *Lothian Gold Mining Co Ltd v. Lister* (n. 12).

[56] *Tait v. Wicht* (n. 1); *Riddelsdell v. Williams* (n. 31); *Adamanta Diamond Mining Co Ltd v. Wege* (n. 10), 179.

[57] *Geddes v. Kaiser Wilhelm Gold Mining Co* (n. 48), 182. On the Equity doctrine in this regard, see *Vernon v. Keys* (1810) 2 East 632; *Hemingway v. Hamilton* (1838) 4 M & W 115; *Beattie v. Lord Edbury* (1872) 7 Ch App 777, 804; *Jorden v. Money* (1854) 5 HL Cas 185; *Bold v. Hutchinson* (1855) 5 De G M & G 558; *Chadwick v. Manning* [1896] AC 231.

[58] A person who willfully misrepresents his future course of action is guilty of misrepresentation, the state of a man's mind being 'as much a fact as the state of his digestion' (*Edgington v. Fitzmaurice* (1885) 29 ChD 459 (CA) 483; *Van Heerden v. Smith* 1956 (3) SA 273 (O); *Feinstein v. Niggli* 1981 (2) SA 684 (A) 695. See also Lubbe (n. 53), 126.

[59] *Gous v. De Kock* (1887) 5 SC 405, 407 sq.; *Atlas Diamond Mining Co Ltd v. Poole* (n. 12), 31; and see on the position in Equity: *Rawlins v. Wickham* (1858) 3 De G & J 304; *Coneybeare v. The New Brunswick and Canada Railway Co* (1869) 1 De G F & J 578, 594 sq.; *Torrance v. Bolton* (1872) 8 Ch App 118; Lubbe (n. 53) 128.

[60] *Adamanta Diamond Mining Co Ltd v. Wege* (n. 10), 178 sq., 181; *Atlas Diamond Mining Co Ltd v. Poole* (n. 12), 31, 34 sq.

[61] The distinction is referred to, without elaboration, in *Macrae & Nicolay v. Matthysen* (n. 31); and see *Geddes v. Kaiser Wilhelm Gold Mining Co* (n. 48), 182 for an inconclusive reference.

to the transaction might have[62] on the question of relief for misrepresentation, such relief depends to a considerable extent on social perceptions of
proper behaviour *in contrahendo*. Thus in Roman law a departure from the
'basic ethical precept of fidelity'—which seems ultimately to have been the
test for *dolus malus*[63]—was determined 'in accordance with prevailing and
average business decency'.[64] No relief was therefore granted for *dolus bonus*,
nor more importantly, in cases of *sollertia*, where the conduct complained
of, although not wholly proper, nevertheless accorded with pragmatic standards of trade and practice.[65] *Bouwer v. Ferguson*,[66] decided in an agricultural context in the Eastern Cape after the abolition of *laesio enormis* in
1879, deals with this issue in largely civilian terms.[67] In contrast, judgments
in cases engendered by the heady atmosphere of the Kimberley diamond
fields reveal the more ruggedly individualistic approach to relations *in contrahendo* of the English notion of materiality.[68] A representee who genuinely
invested in, and did not merely speculate with, the shares of a diamond mining company was accordingly expected to make independent enquiries using
ordinary caution, and to disregard exaggerated statements regarding the
prospects of the venture and statements of opinion on matters inherently
uncertain.[69] This emphasis on the plaintiff's own responsibility in the face
of representations *in contrahendo* did, of course, echo the principle underlying the notion of *sollertia*. As a result of English influence, however, this
premise found expression in rules of thumb based on the nature, form, and
subject matter of the conduct complained of.[70]

The developments referred to did not constitute a radical break with the

---

[62] See Lubbe (n. 53), 128 on the effect of an inability to make restitution, a delay in the
exercise of the election, or an affirmation of the contract. Cf. Visser, 1992 *Acta Juridica* 203,
213 sq.

[63] Zimmermann (n. 7), 669 sq.   [64] Ibid.   [65] Ibid.

[66] (1884) 4 EDC 90.

[67] At 95 Johannes Voet, *Commentarius ad Pandectas*, 19, 1, 15, is cited to the effect that a
vendor would not incur liability for statements merely made by way of commendation, and
that although parties are entitled, within limits, to overreach each other about the price, good
faith is required on both sides of the transaction.

[68] This entailed the denial of relief for statements of opinion (*New Brunswick Railway &
Land Co v. Coneybeare* (1862) 9 HL Cas 711; *Melbourne Bank Corp v. Brougham* (1882) 7 App
Cas 307 (PC)) and mere predictions as to the future course of events (*Ex parte Burrel* (1876)
1 ChD 537, 552, *Beaumont v. Dukes* (1882) Jac 422) and for statements of fact which, because
of their form or subject matter were of such a nature as to have put a reasonable person in the
position of the representee upon enquiry: *Haycraft v. Creasy* (1801) 2 East 92; *Attwood v. Small*
(1838) 6 Cl & Fin 232; *Higgins v. Samuels* (1862) 2 J & H 460; *Greenwood v. Greenwood* (1863)
2 De G J & S 28; *Traill v. Baring* (1864) 2 De G J & S 318; *Kisch v. Central Venezuela Railway
Co* (1865) 3 De G J & S 122; *Dimmock v. Hallet* (1866) 2 ChD 27–29; *Torrance v. Bolton* (1872)
8 Ch App 118.

[69] *Adamanta Diamond Mining Co Ltd v. Wege* (n. 12), 178 sq., 180; *Atlas Diamond Mining
Co Ltd v. Poole* (n. 12); *Lothian Gold Mining Co Ltd v. Lister* (n. 12), 81.

[70] Although Van den Heever J was accurate in ascribing an English origin to the treatment
of materiality in our courts (*Van Niekerk & Van der Westhuizen v. Weps & Morris* 1937 SWA
99) his criticism of its adoption has gone unheeded.

Roman-Dutch tradition. The guidelines regarding materiality can relatively easily be seen as more or less implicit in the Labeonic understanding of *dolus*. By the 1880s, however, more fundamental challenges to the established doctrine were emerging from the hurly-burly of the Kimberley diamond fields. In *Atlas Diamond Mining Co (Bultfontein Mine) Ltd v. Poole*,[71] for instance, rescission was sought of a contract to take shares in a company, on the ground that the transaction had been induced by untrue statements in the company's prospectus. This document was alleged to have been published by promotors of the company:[72]

as facts within their own knowledge, with the object of inducing the defendant and others, on faith of and in reliance on the said statements, to apply for shares . . . without any belief in their truth, or without any reasonable grounds for such belief, or in wilful and reckless ignorance as to their truth or otherwise, and without adopting ordinary business-like precautions in order to test their accuracy.

In response to the argument that the plea made no allegations of fraud or wilful concealment[73] counsel for Poole relied on English authorities for the proposition that in a claim for rescission the representor could not escape responsibility for false statements put forth recklessly merely because they were thought to be true.[74] Buchanan JP's difficulty in understanding whether 'fraud is or is not directly imputed' in the plea[75] attests to the novelty of this contention in the South African context. The judge eventually concluded (correctly, it is submitted) that the defendant had 'not relied directly on fraud, but on misrepresentation'.[76] The question of whether what would today be termed 'negligent' misrepresentation[77] provided a basis for rescission was, however, sidestepped by the Court's factual findings[78] and the judgments handed down do not contain even an *obiter dictum* on the issue. The question of laches regarding the 'repudiation' of a contract by a representee proved decisive in *Adamanta Diamond Mining Co Ltd v. Wege*[79] but Laurence J nevertheless set out the elements of the defence of misrepresentation. Fraud was not mentioned.[80] No authority was referred to. In line with this approach is *Geddes v. Kaiser Wilhelm Gold Mining Co*[81] which concerned a claim for the rescission of a contract as hav-

---

[71] Above, n. 12.   [72] See the plea at 22.   [73] 28.

[74] 29. Reference was made to *Reese River Silver Mining Co v. Smith* (n. 12), 73; *Peeke v. Gurney* (1873) LR 6 HL 377; *Smith v. Chadwick* (1882) 20 ChD 27. Interestingly, counsel for the defendant was driven to concede (at 30) that 'even negligent misrepresentation' might afford a ground for relief, his argument being that Poole had not been misled by the prospectus.

[75] 30.   [76] 31.

[77] This is implicit in the assertion, at 22, that the promotors were guilty of failing to adopt 'ordinary business-like precautions' in respect of the accuracy of the statements, and was explicitly acknowledged in the admission by counsel for the defendant, referred to in note 74.

[78] There was no evidence of either misrepresentation or inducement, and Poole had in any event not instituted proceedings within a reasonable time. See 32, 33–5.

[79] Above, n. 10.   [80] 179.   [81] (Note 48), 182.

ing been induced by a material misrepresentation without any allegation of
fraud, and where it was stated that 'if [the plaintiff] can establish this he is
no doubt entitled to relief'.[82] Once again, however, this statement is *obiter*,
the decision going against the plaintiff in the absence of a misrepresentation
of fact[83]. These judgments seem to have been edging, albeit in a tentative
way, towards recognizing that rescissory relief might, in the absence of
fraud, be based on negligence and, more specifically, on the failure of the
representor to take 'ordinary business-like precautions'.[84]

These significant developments were, as far as can be ascertained,
restricted to the High Court of Griqualand West. Contemporary judgments
of the Cape Supreme Court certainly do not reveal a similar tendency.
Although De Villiers CJ at one stage favoured the view that negligent misrepresentation might be sufficient to found an action for delictual damages,[85] *Tait v. Wicht*[86] indicates that as late as 1890 the Cape Supreme
Court still emphatically required proof of fraud for rescission. Interestingly
enough, this proposition was justified with reference to English authority.[87]
The *Griqualand West* cases, on the other hand, make it abundantly clear
that the movement towards the recognition of negligent misrepresentation
in that jurisdiction was inspired by leading cases from the Court of
Chancery's jurisdiction in respect of misrepresentation.[88]

In order to establish whether the South African courts were confused
about the English authorities they were purporting to rely on, or whether
those authorities were in themselves contradictory, it is necessary to consider aspects of the equitable doctrine of misrepresentation in its country of
origin.

2. Misrepresentation in English Equity

Dissonances in South African case law of the late nineteenth century relating to misrepresentation reflect a central feature of English law, namely the
duality of common law and Equity. More particularly, the differences of
opinion between the Cape Supreme Court and the High Court of
Griqualand West echoed the culmination of an epic struggle between the
Chancery and common law Courts regarding the redress of misrepresenta-

---

[82] 182.   [83] 182 sq.
[84] *Atlas Diamond Mining Co Ltd v. Poole* (above, n. 12), 22.
[85] *Cape of Good Hope Bank v. Fischer* (1886) 4 SC 368, 376.   [86] Above, n. 1, 166.
[87] See the reference in *Tait v. Wicht* (above, n. 1), 166 to the 'very recent' English decision
of *Derry v. Peek* (n. 18) and De Villiers' statement in *Cape of Good Hope Bank v. Fischer* (1886)
4 SC 368, 378 that he was unaware 'of any English case expressly deciding that a false representation without fraud and irrespective of contract is actionable'.
[88] See *Atlas Diamond Mining Co Ltd v. Poole* (n. 12), 29 for references to: *Reese River Silver
Mining Co v. Smith* (n. 12); *Peeke v. Gurney* (1873) LR 6 HL 377; *Smith v. Chadwick* (1882)
20 ChD 27.

tion[89] which left English law in a confusing state of flux during the decisive stages of the reception in South Africa.

Matters which would be characterized today as involving misrepresentation occupied the attention of the Chancellor at an early stage[90] but it has been asserted that the beginnings of the modern doctrines of fraud and misrepresentation in Equity may be traced to developments during the last quarter of the seventeenth century.[91] During this period fraud was a 'hold-all' concept with a wider meaning than today.[92] Equitable fraud encompassed not merely instances of wilfully false misrepresentations inducing a contract but also a diverse range of situations that had in common only a failure to meet the standard of conscientious behaviour required by the Court of Chancery.[93] While it is often difficult to distinguish fraudulent misrepresentation from other aspects of the Chancellor's jurisdiction in respect of fraud in the early cases,[94] the development of the law brought about some differentiation. Cases of so-called actual fraud, relating to misrepresentation *in contrahendo*, came to be distinguished from those concerning constructive fraud.[95] Apart from certain instances of illegal agreements[96] the jurisdiction in respect of constructive fraud related mainly to relief against unconscionable bargains concluded by weak and disadvantaged persons, the sanctioning of breaches of fiduciary duties, and the rescission of contracts brought about by undue influence.[97]

[89] According to Harold Hanbury, *Modern Equity* (2nd edn., 1937), 607, practitioners of both systems 'quarrelled over possession of the word "fraud" like two dogs over a bone, off which neither side was sufficiently strong to tear all the meat'.

[90] William Baildon, *Select Cases in Chancery (1364–1471), Publications of the Selden Society*, vol. X (1896), esp. case 2, p. 2; W. T. Barbour, 'Contract in Early English Equity', in: Paul Vinogradof (ed.), *Oxford Studies in Social and Legal History*, vol. IV (1914), 84, 122; William Holdsworth, *A History of English Law*, vol. V (2nd edn., 1937), 212, 292, 326, 328; L. A. Sheridan, *Fraud in Equity* (1957), 4 sq.; Harold Potter, *An Historical Introduction to English Law* (1932), 500 sqq.

[91] See Lubbe (n. 53), 115, fn. 15 and David Allen, *Misrepresentation* (1968), 1–3 on the tangled relationship of the concepts 'deceit' and 'warranty' under the common law.

[92] Cf. the annotation following the cases grouped under the heading 'Fraud' in 2 Bro CC 201; Sheridan (n. 90), 7; Hanbury (n. 89), 609 (fraud in Equity a 'generic term'); *Torrance v. Bolton* (1872) 8 Ch App. 118 (fraud a *'nomen generalissimum'*).

[93] *Nocton v. Lord Ashburton* [1914] AC 932, 934; Hanbury (n. 89), 607.

[94] The facts of the early reports often suggest wilful misrepresentation, but the victims are generally of a type that attracted special attention from the Chancellor. See *Evans v. Llewellyn* (1787) 2 Bro CC 150; *Pusey v. Desbouverie* (1734) 3 P Wms 316; cf. Arthur Leff, 'Unconscionability and the Code: the Emperor's new Clause', (1967) 115 *University of Pennsylvania LR* 485, 532.

[95] *Nocton v. Lord Ashburton* [1914] AC 932; *Torrance v. Bolton* (1872) 8 Ch App 118, 124 sq.; see also *Earl of Chesterfield v. Janssen* (1751) 2 Ves Sen 125, 155–7 and the treatment by Joseph Story, *Commentaries on Equity Jurisprudence* (2nd English edn., 1892), chs. VI and VII.

[96] Story (n. 95), 167; Sheridan (n. 90), 7, 173–6.

[97] See generally Story (n. 95), 166 sqq.; Thomas Snow, *Leading Cases in Equity*, vol. I (7th edn., 1897), 266 sqq.; Hanbury/Maudsley (n. 25), 546 sqq. These sources indicate that the divisions mentioned in the text were not watertight, and also by no means exhaustive of the notion of constructive fraud. See generally Sheridan (n. 90), 1–9.

Three areas are relevant to the jurisdiction in respect of misrepresentation. Misrepresentation might firstly constitute a defence against a claim for specific performance.[98] In addition, a representor might in certain circumstances be compelled 'to make good his representation', or to make monetary compensation to the representee should that not be possible.[99] Lastly, it was regarded as a 'constant rule' that either *suppressio veri* or *suggestio falsi* during negotiations would serve to avoid a legal transaction.[100] With regard to rescission, it was initially necessary to establish that the representor should have been aware of the falsity of the representation which had induced the contract.[101] This pattern persisted into the nineteenth century[102] but after certain intimations that the requirement of fraud might be relaxed[103] it was held in *Pulsford v. Richards*[104] that misrepresentation would affect the contract not merely if, to the knowledge of the representor, the statement was false but also if it emanated from 'persons who believed them to be true, if in the discharge of their duty, they ought to have known, or if they had formerly known and ought to have remembered the fact which negatives the representation made'.[105]

This approach was confirmed in *Jennings v. Broughton*[106] but with additional emphasis on whether the representor had reasonable grounds for his belief in the truth of his assertions. *Rawlins v. Wickham*[107] finally settled the

---

[98] *Phillips v. Bucks (Duke of)* (1863) 1 Vern 227.

[99] According to Lord Eldon this was a 'very old head of Equity' (*Evans v. Bicknell* (1801) 6 Ves 182). Later cases make it clear that this was not a claim for damages but one 'to make restitution, or to compensate the plaintiff by putting him in as good a position pecuniarily as that in which he was before the injury'. See *Nocton v. Ashburton* (n. 95), 952; *Ex Parte Adamson* (1878) 8 ChD 807, 819; Ian Davidson, 'The Equitable Remedy of Compensation', (1982) 13 *Melbourne University LR* 349, 351–3 for differences between restitution and damages. In earlier cases the distinction is not so clear and there is some evidence of confusion. See *Hill v. Lane* (1870–71) LR 11 Eq 215; *Taylor v. Ashton* (1843) 11 M & W 401. See also: Sheridan, 'Equitable Estoppel Today', (1952) 15 *Modern LR* 325 sqq.; Simon Stoljar, *Mistake and Misrepresentation* (1968), 87; Allen (n. 91), 3 sq.; Frederick Pollock, *The Law of Fraud, Misrepresentation and Mistake in British India* (Tagore Law Lectures, 1894), 31.

[100] *Jarvis et Uxor v. Duke* (1681) 2 Vern 20; *Broderick v. Broderick* (1713) 1 P Wms 239; cf. *Tuck v. Pattison* (1613) Tothill 170; *Otby v. Daniel* (1629–30) Tothill 26.

[101] *Wangen v. Kett* (1701) 12 Mod 558, 2 Eq Cas Abr 478 n. 7 (dealer, heavily indebted to another, procured a settlement by representing that he was financially embarrassed by 'absconding, skulking and shutting down shop'); *Barney v. Beak* (1682) 2 Chan Cas 138; *Wood v. Fenwick* (1702) Prec Ch 204, 2 P Wms 204; *Ramsden v. Hylton* (1751) 2 Ves Sen 304; *Butler v. Butler* (1780) 1 Bro PC 383; *Sowerby v. Ward* (1791) 2 Cox 267.

[102] *Edwards v. M'Leay* (1818) 2 Swan 289; *Attwood v. Small* (1838) 6 Cl & Fin 232; cf. Sheridan (n. 90), 27; Lubbe (n. 53), 119 sq. on developments during the 18th C.

[103] *Gibson v. D'Este* (1843) 2 Y & C Ch Cas 542; *Clarke v. Manning* (1844) 7 Beav 162.

[104] (1853) 17 Beav 87.

[105] 94. The impulse for this development came from decisions relating to Equity's jurisdiction to the making good of misrepresentations. See the confusion of gross negligence evident in *Burrowes v. Locke* (1805) 10 Ves 470, as well as *Evans v. Bicknell* (1801) 6 Ves 174; cf. Lubbe (n. 53), 122–4.

[106] (1853) 17 Beav 234, confirmed on appeal (1858) 5 De G M & G 126.

[107] (1858) 3 De G & J 304.

principle that even in the absence of what was now called moral (or actual) fraud[108] rescission could be granted where the representor had, without excuse, acted in breach of a duty of care owed to the representee.[109] Midway through the nineteenth century, therefore, an honest but negligently made misrepresentation provided a sufficient ground for the rescission of a contract[110] provided that the misrepresentation was material[111] and had induced the contract.[112]

The doctrine of legal fraud, occasionally dubbed 'innocent misrepresentation',[113] was based on the premise that those who took it upon themselves to make representations during the negotiations leading to a contract were duty-bound to speak truthfully.[114] This duty was derived from Equity's 'rigid adherence to truth'[115] and a negligent breach of that duty was considered to found liability.[116]

The rise of legal fraud was attended by controversy and opposition. Whatever its true nature,[117] the remedy of compensation, or indemnity, was perceived to be a claim for damages; and when it was recognized that it lay in Equity for non-fraudulent (though negligent) misrepresentation, legal fraud was bound to come into conflict with the common law action for damages for deceit and its requirement of fraudulent intent.[118] The resultant struggle between the Chancery and common law courts was conducted

---

[108] Cf. 301 and 316.

[109] 312 sq. Because of the formal nature of land law fraud was still required for the rescission of executed conveyances of interests in real property.

[110] See, on the details of this development, Lubbe (n. 53), 124 sq.; H. A. Hammelmann, 'Seddon v. North Eastern Salt Co', (1939) 55 *LQR* 90 sqq. That the doctrine of legal fraud entailed a form of negligence liability is apparent from the exasperated comments of Bramwell CJ in *Weir v. Bell* (1878) Ex D 243: 'I do not understand legal fraud. To my mind it has no more meaning than legal heat or legal cold, legal light or legal shade. There can never be a well-founded complaint of legal fraud, or of anything else, except where some duty is shown and correlative right, and some violation of that duty and right. And when these exist it is much better that they should be stated and acted on, than that recourse should be had to a phrase illogical and unmeaning with the consequent uncertainty.'

[111] See n. 68; cf. Lubbe (n. 53), 126–8.

[112] *Lowndes v. Lane* (1789) 2 Cox 363; *Grant v. Munt* (1815) Coop G 173; *Attwood v. Small* (1838) 6 Cl & Fin 232; *Pulsford v. Richards* (1853) 17 Beav 87; *Jennings v. Broughton* (1853) 5 De G M & G 126; *Rolt v. White* (1862) 3 De G J & S 360.

[113] See the passing remarks in *Newbigging v. Adam* (1886) 34 ChD 582, 591 and *Arkwright v. Newbold* (1881) 17 ChD 301, at 320.

[114] *Pulsford v. Richards* (n. 112); *Jennings v. Broughton* (n. 112); *Rawlins v. Wickham* (1858) 3 De G & J 304; *Ayre's Case: In re The Deposity and General Life Insurance Co* (1858) 25 Beav 512; *Hart v. Swaine* (1877) 7 ChD 42; *Mathias v. Yetts* (1882) 46 LT 497, 503; *Peek v. Derry* (1887) 37 ChD 541; Hammelmann, (1939) 55 *LQR* 94; John Pomeroy, *Treatise on Equity Jurisprudence* (1882), 372; Pollock (n. 99), 93 sqq. On the socio-economic context of the development of legal fraud see Lubbe (n. 53), 124; Hammelmann, (1939) 55 *LQR* 95; Peter Stein, *Fault in the Formation of Contract* (1958), 187 sq.

[115] *Pulsford v. Richards* (n. 112); *Dimmock v. Hallet* (1866) 2 ChD 27, 28.

[116] See Lubbe (n. 53), 125 on the extent of this duty.   [117] See n. 99.

[118] See e.g. *Taylor v. Ashton* (1843) 11 M & W 401, decided in the Court of Exchequer in 1843; *Hill v. Lane* (1870–71) LR 11 Eq 215; Sheridan, (1952) 15 *Modern LR* 330; P. S. Atiyah, Misrepresentation, Warranty and Estoppel, (1971) 9 *Alberta LR* 347, 372.

with great acrimony[119] and created considerable difficulties after the fusion of the dual court system by the Judicature Acts.[120] Matters came to a head in *Derry v. Peek*[121] where the House of Lords, by reaffirming the *scienter* requirement of the common law action of deceit,[122] rejected the ruling of the Court of Appeal according to which an action of deceit lay in Equity where the representor had acted honestly but negligently and without reasonable grounds for his belief.[123] The opinions of both Lord Herschell and Lord Bramwell were generally perceived to imply a rejection of the proposition that a person who made a material statement to another and intended that it should be acted upon by him was under a duty to take care that he had reasonable grounds for his belief in the assertions.[124] This left without any theoretical basis the line of cases that had established Equity's jurisdiction to ensure that negligent misrepresentations were made good. These cases, accordingly, ceased to be of any practical importance[125] except in so far as the doctrine of estoppel by representation was concerned.[126] Applied consistently, the reasoning in *Derry v. Peek* would also have left the courts without a leg to stand on in matters concerning rescission. Lord Herschell, however, seized the opportunity to restate the doctrine of rescission for misrepresentation in a way which suggested that it did not depend on the representor's fault:[127]

Where rescission is claimed it is only necessary to prove that there was misrepresentation; then, however honestly it may have been made, however free from blame the person who made it, the contract, having been obtained by misrepresentation, cannot stand.

No authority was cited for this proposition for which, in fact, there was none in the Equity jurisprudence.

[119] See the acerbic comments of Bramwell J, cited in n. 110.
[120] Supreme Court of Judicature Act (36 & 38 Vict. c. 66) and Supreme Court of Judicature Act (38 & 39 Vict. c. 77). For a discussion see George Keeton and L. A. Sheridan, *Equity* (2nd edn., 1976), 53 sqq.
[121] (1889) 14 App Cas 337.
[122] 359 sqq., holding that a statement was fraudulent not only where it was false to the knowledge of the person making it, but also where it was made recklessly, without caring whether it be true or false. Cf. *Evans v. Edmonds* (1853) 13 CB 777.
[123] 361. This conclusion was reached with 'some reluctance', Lord Herschell expressing the view that people seeking to raise money for commercial ventures 'ought to be careful'; at the same time, however, it was the responsibility of the legislature to make 'the want of reasonable care to see that statements made under such circumstances are true' into an actionable wrong (376). The Directors' Liability Act of 1890 (53 & 54 Vict. c. 64) was passed in response to these remarks.
[124] Pollock (n. 99), 93. Cf. Atiyah, (n. 118), 372, who describes the decision as constituting an 'unexpected check to a general current of authority'.
[125] Pollock (n. 99), 31; cf. *Le Lievre and Dennes v. Gould* [1893] 1 QB 491.
[126] Estoppel survived by being portrayed as a rule of evidence rather than a substantive cause of action: Atiyah (n. 118), 372.
[127] 359; cf. the remarks of Lord Bramwell at 347.

Considerable confusion existed after *Derry v. Peek* as to when, and on what basis, a contract could be rescinded for honest misrepresentation.[128] Some commentators attempted to rationalize the rule laid down by Lord Herschell by assimilating it to the common law principle that a contract could be avoided on account of a failure of consideration.[129] This was based on the adoption of the civilian learning concerning *error in substantia* in *Kennedy v. Panama Mail Co*[130] as the criterion to determine failure of consideration. By arguing that an honest misrepresentation would lead to an *error in substantialibus*, provided it was material and was related to the subject matter of the transaction, it could be taken to constitute a ground for relief,[131] albeit on a narrower basis than under the doctrine of misrepresentation.[132] Other commentators sought to provide a conceptual basis for the extension of the remedy of rescission by resorting to the formulation of legal fraud, some years previously, in *Redgrave v. Hurd*.[133] This case decided that honest belief in the truth of the representation would not preclude rescission because, in the words of Jessel MR, the representor 'ought to have found that out before he made [the statement]'[134] or because an insistence on a contract obtained by a statement, now known to be false, in itself constituted moral delinquency.[135] These propositions were clearly meant to be read together as alternative formulations of the same principle. What the Master of Rolls intended to convey was that an attempt to enforce a contract obtained by misrepresentation would constitute a moral delinquency if the representation had been made in breach of a duty to take care.[136] With the disappearance of the duty to take care as a result of *Derry v. Peek*, this statement acquired a new significance. Insistence on a contract obtained by misrepresentation in itself amounted to improper behaviour, quite irrespective of fraud or negligence: this notion was seized upon by commentators as a theoretical basis for a doctrine of innocent misrepresentation under

---

[128] Lubbe (n. 53), 132 sq.; cf. William Kerr, *A Treatise on the Law of Fraud and Mistake* (3rd edn., 1902), 17 who described *Derry v. Peek* as having 'given rise to an extraordinary amount of doubt, difficulty, discussion and vigorous dissent'.

[129] See Sydney Hastings, *A Short Treatise on the Law relating to Fraud and Misrepresentation* (1893), 76 sq.; Kerr (n. 128), 96 sqq.; Edward Fry, *A Treatise on the Specific Performance of Contracts* (4th edn., 1903), 326.

[130] (1867) LR 2 QB 580, 587, with reference to D. 18, 4, 9 and 10, 11.

[131] See esp. Kerr (n. 128), 96 sq., 100 sq.

[132] See the discussion, examples, and the actual decision in *Kennedy v. Panama Mail Co* (1867) LR 2 QB 580.

[133] (1881) 20 ChD 1.　　　　　　　　　　[134] I.e. the statement was unfounded.

[135] 12 sq.

[136] See the judgment of Jessel MR in *Mathias v. Yetts* (1882) 46 LT 497, where rescission was made to depend on the representor being aware of the falsity of the statement, or on the misrepresentation relating to 'some matter upon which [the representor] had means of enquiring and ought to have enquired'. *Redgrave v. Hurd* was treated as being fully in line with this approach. Cf. Lubbe (n. 53), 130 sq.

which the culpability of the representor at the time of making the representation became wholly irrelevant.[137]

Derry v. Peek should not be seen as the culmination of a development of a general theory of rescission for misrepresentation. In fact it was the beginning of a process which resulted in the replacement of a well developed system of fault liability[138] by one which permitted rescission irrespective of whether the representation was culpable.[139] This development occurred in a haphazard fashion, largely, it seems, because of the difficulties experienced in the wake of the fusion of the dual court system. Neither the concept of *ex post facto* fraud nor the attempt to construe innocent misrepresentation as a failure of consideration ever played a significant role in later judicial pronouncements, and the doctrine of rescission for mere misrepresentation was soon unquestioningly accepted as part of English law.[140]

3. South African law in the aftermath of *Derry v. Peek*

Developments in misrepresentation after 1890 took place in a socio-economic context of greater diversity than had existed before. The law reports of the time convey a sense of burgeoning urban development,[141] a more varied range of economic and commercial activities,[142] mining frauds,[143] and even fraud in the field of early show business.[144] While the courts continued to refer to Roman Dutch sources, English law gained an ever-increasing influence. While, in a general sense, the impact of English law served to simplify the substance of the Roman-Dutch law (which was

---

[137] Melville Bigelow, *A Treatise on the Law of Fraud on its civil side* (1890), 11, 410 sq.; Hastings (n. 129), 4, 6, 88; Frances Moncreiff, *A Treatise on the Law relating to Fraud and Misrepresentation* (1891), 218.

[138] Lubbe (n. 53), 135; cf. Atiyah, (n. 118), 372 who refers to 'generations of lawyers . . . to whom *Derry v. Peek* was the starting point in the law of misrepresentation rather than an unexpected check to a general current of authority'.

[139] Allen (n. 91), 6, fn. 35.

[140] See Hammelmann, (1939) 55 *LQR* 94; Lubbe (n. 53), 133 on *Seddon v. North Eastern Salt Co* (1905) 1 ChD 326 where rescission was restricted to executory contracts.

[141] See e.g. *Crews v. Zweigenhaft* (1898) 8 CTR 193; *Provident Land Trust v. Thomas* (1909) 19 CTR 1043; *Roorda v. Cohn* 1903 TS 279; *Croeser v. African Realty Trust* (1908) 25 SC 304; *Jenkins v. Durban Bay Land Co Ltd* (1905) 26 NLR 455; *Woodstock, Claremont, Mowbray and Rondebosch Councils v. Smith* (1909) 26 SC 681.

[142] See e.g. *Klette v. SA Cycle Factory Ltd* (1899) 16 SC 240; *Begley v. Denton & Thomas* (1897) 14 SC 344; *Schoenemann v. Cape Lime Co* (1897) 7 CTR 350; *Robinson v. Ryves* (1898) 8 CTR 414; *Viljoen v. Hillier* 1904 TS 312; *Hain & Son v. Elandslaagte Colliery Co Ltd & Young* (1903) 24 NLR 363; *American Medicine Co v. Stantial & Allerston* (1905) 26 NLR 22.

[143] *Orange River Asbestos Co v. Hirsche, King & Weingarten* (1893) 10 SC 71; *Josephi v. Parkes* 1906 EDC 138.

[144] *St Marc v. Harvey* (1893) 10 SC 267, concerning a tour of the Cape by 'Princess Topaze', billed as the smallest woman in the world; the promoter of the tour wanted to cancel the contract concluded with her manager because she was only 10 years old and not 16 as represented.

perceived to contain 'ancient',[145] overly artificial, and technical limitations[146]) the landmark decision of the House of Lords in *Derry v. Peek*[147] affected South African law particularly profoundly.

In the first place, it was held in a number of decisions that there was no substantial difference between South African law and the doctrine of *Derry v. Peek* as regards the action for deceit.[148] This settled the contours of the *scienter* element of fraud as a cause of action. Lord Herschell's statement, that fraud existed not merely where a representor was positively aware of the falsity of his assertion but also where a statement was made recklessly, without caring whether it be true or false,[149] was adopted as the test for *dolus malus* in respect of both rescission[150] and a claim for damages.[151]

As for the claim for damages *ex delicto*, South African judgments recognized that the House of Lords had 'practically abolished the doctrine of constructive, as distinguished from actual, fraud';[152] this greatly contributed to the obliteration of the suggestion in *Cape of Good Hope Bank v. Fischer*[153] that negligent misrepresentation might be sufficient to found liability. Not even the example of the recognition by American courts of liability for negligent misrepresentation under an extended definition of fraud[154] could persuade South African judges to follow a course independent of *Derry v. Peek*.[155] In the

---

[145] See e.g. the strictures of the Privy Council on the notion that the action for damages is an *actio famosa*, involving infamy to the person against whom fraud was proved, in *Douglas v. Sanders* (1902) 23 NLR 201.

[146] See e.g. *Hain & Son v. Elandslaagte Colliery Co Ltd & Young* (n. 142).

[147] (1889) 14 App Cas 337.

[148] *Tait v. Wicht* (n. 1); *Benjamin v. Minter* (1896) 8 HCG 37, 53; *African Banking Corp v. Goldbard* (1897) 4 OR 402. In *Tait's* case, at 166, De Villiers CJ held, contrary to Lord Herschell's finding in *Derry v. Peek*, that Labeo's definition enshrined a fraudulent motive as an essential element of fraud as a cause of action (cf. *Roorda v. Cohn* 1903 TH 279). De Villiers CJ's spirited defence of this aspect of Roman-Dutch law, as he conceived it, has had no influence: see *Robinson v. Ryves* (n. 142), 416; *Fraser v. Solomon* (1898) 8 CTR 22, 24; *Eaton Trust v. Schoevers* (1909) 19 CTR 532; *Berkenmeyer v. Woolf* 1929 CPD 235; *Frenkel & Co v. Freisman & Shapiro* (1897) 4 OR 227; *Schickerling v. Schickerling* 1936 CPD 269; *Macduff & Co Ltd (in liquidation) v. Johannesburg Consolidated Investment Co Ltd* 1924 AD 573; *Koenig v. Johnson & Co Ltd* 1935 AD 262.

[149] (1889) 14 App Cas 337; cf. *Evans v. Edmonds* (1853) 13 CB 777; *Reese River Silver Mining Co v. Smith* (n. 12).

[150] *Vlotman v. Landsberg* (n. 1), 302; *Durr v. Bam* (n. 1), 24–5; *Young v. Kruger* (n. 31); Maasdorp (n. 10), 63; Lee (n. 10), 202; Manfred Nathan, *The Common Law of South Africa*, vol. II (1904), 525.

[151] *Dickson & Co v. Levy* (1894) 11 SC 33; *African Banking Corp v. Lewis Goldbard* (1897) 4 OR 402; *Shauban v. Goveia* (1901) 11 CTR 289; *Vivian v. Woodburn* 1910 TPD 1285; *De Kock v. Gafney* 1914 CPD 377, 382.

[152] *Trustees of the Orange River Land & Asbestos Co v. King* (1892) 6 HCG 260, 291.

[153] (1886) 4 SC 368.

[154] Discussed with approval by Frederick Pollock, *The Law of Torts* (4th edn., 1895), 265.

[155] *African Banking Corp v. Goldbard* (n. 151); *Dickson & Co v. Levy* (n. 151); *Frenkel & Co v. Freisman & Shapiro* (n. 148); *Skippon v. De Witt* (1904) CTR 747; *Saacks v. Thomas* (1906) 16 CTR 825; *Eaton Trust v. Schoevers* (1909) 19 CTR 532; *Vivian v. Woodburn* 1910 TPD 1285; *De Kock v. Gafney* (n. 151).

result, a duty to provide correct information *in contrahendo* arose only where it was imposed by contract[156] or statute.[157]

In contrast to its restrictive impact on the recovery of damages caused by misrepresentation, *Derry v. Peek*[158] had the opposite effect in regard to the availability of rescissionary relief. The initial focus of developments regarding rescission in this period was the Cape Supreme Court. At the outset, the emphasis was on the retention of fraud as a requirement for rescission,[159] developments in English law being approached with considerable diffidence. In *Forbes v. Behr*,[160] for instance, Innes QC relied on the equitable doctrine of legal fraud for the argument that an honest but negligent misrepresentation would permit rescission, although proof of negligence had been made redundant by *Derry v. Peek*.[161] Because no material misrepresentation appeared from the evidence, the issue of relief for non-fraudulent misrepresentation was not addressed by the Court.[162] After some vacillation on the part of De Villiers CJ[163] the matter came up for consideration once again in *Van der Byl v. Van der Byl*.[164] The arguments addressed to the Court clearly demarcated the issue that had to be decided. Innes QC, on behalf of the representors, contended strongly that the 'equitable doctrine ... in England that innocent misrepresentation, if material, is sufficient defence to liability on contract induced thereby' was contrary to Roman-Dutch law which permitted *restitutio in integrum* on the basis of fraud and *iustus error*, but not innocent misrepresentation.[165] On the other hand, counsel for the representee relied on Moyle's treatise on the Roman law of sale[166] for the proposition that leading English cases were compatible with the principles of Roman law.[167] The resultant judgment, alas, is not a model of clarity.

---

[156] *Dickson & Co v. Levy* (n. 155); *Skippon v. De Witt* (1904) CTR 747; *Saacks v. Thomas* (n. 155); *Eaton Trust v. Schoevers* (n. 155).

[157] *See Benjamin v. Minter* (1896) 8 HCG 37 on ss. 91–5 of the Griqualand West Companies Act of 1892, which took over the provisions of the Directors's Liability Act of 1890 (53 & 54 Vict. c. 64).

[158] (1889) 14 AC 337.

[159] *Forbes v. Behr* (1896) 13 SC 304, 311; *Begley v. Denton & Thomas* (1897) 14 SC 344; *Schoenemann v. Cape Lime Co* (1897) 7 CTR 350; *Robinson v. Ryves* (1898) 8 CTR 414.

[160] (1896) 13 SC 304.

[161] 309. Also of interest is the explicit attempt in the argument to avoid English law altogether, and to base rescission of a contract of sale for non-fraudulent misrepresentation on the aedilitian remedies for an unfounded *dictum et promissum* (307).

[162] 309.

[163] *Fraser v. Solomon* (1898) 8 CTR 22 distinguished between fraud and misrepresentation as defences to a claim on a contract, but judgment was given without counsel for the plaintiff being heard and without any citation of authority. *Klette v. SA Cycle Factory Ltd* (n. 142), 242 thereafter reaffirmed fraudulent intent as a requirement.

[164] (1899) 16 SC 338, also reported in (1899) 9 CTR 343. This was an action to rescind a lease granted by the plaintiff to a firm of attorneys on the honest but unfounded assurance that its terms reflected that of a previous lease between the firm and the plaintiff's late father.

[165] At 346. [166] John Moyle, *The Contract of Sale in the Civil Law* (1892), 190.

[167] See 349 of the report in the *Cape Times Law Reports*, (1899) 9 CTR 343. The passages relied on (190) do not support the contention sought to be drawn from it. Moyle seems to

De Villiers CJ accepted (a) absence of fraud on the part of the defendants[168] and (b) that the plaintiff would not have signed the document had he been aware of the true facts.[169] He had no doubt, under these circumstances, that the plaintiff was entitled to relief. However, he was extremely vague as to the principle involved. In the final analysis the *ratio decidendi* seems to have been that the plaintiff was entitled to rectification of the document since it incorrectly reflected the common intention of the parties.[170] The decision does not provide authority for rescission on the basis of misrepresentation irrespective of fraud on the part of the representor, and the traditional position was endorsed in a later Cape case.[171]

Cases decided in other jurisdictions after the hiatus of the Anglo–Boer war also reveal judicial preoccupation with the conceptual domestication of rescission for non-fraudulent misrepresentation. After citing *Derry v. Peek* with approval, the High Court of Griqualand in *Vigne v. Leo*[172] went on to say that in order to justify rescission, an honest misrepresentation[173] 'must be in the nature of a warranty, or must at all events have induced the other party to enter into the contract; or, in other words, it must have been a term or condition of the contract.' This qualification denies the existence of innocent misrepresentation as a distinctive ground for relief and thus goes against the reasoning in *Derry v. Peek*.

A further attempt to find a conceptual basis for the notion of innocent misrepresentation is evident from the Natal case of *Jenkins v. Durban Bay Land Co Ltd*.[174] By way of an *obiter dictum*—no misrepresentation being established on the facts—the Court referred to *Kennedy v. Panama Mail Co*[175] for the view that apart from fraud, innocent misrepresentation could only constitute a ground for rescission where it resulted in 'a complete difference in substance between the thing bargained for and that obtained, so as to constitute a failure of consideration'. This reasoning should not be seen as proposing the establishment of the doctrine of consideration: what the Natal Supreme Court found attractive was the attempt in *Kennedy's* case to adopt the civilian learning regarding *error in substantia* as the criterion for the existence of a failure of consideration. However, the suggestion that the doctrine of innocent misrepresentation should be absorbed into South African law by assimilating it to the Roman doctrine of mistake,[176] did not meet with success.[177]

suggest that English law in *Newbigging v. Adam* (1886) 34 ChD 582 and *Redgrave v. Hurd* (1881) 20 ChD 1 had developed beyond Roman law in permitting rescission for non-fraudulent misrepresentation.

[168] (1899) 16 SC 338, 347. [169] Ibid. [170] Ibid. 348 sq.
[171] *Elliott v. McKillop* (1902) 19 SC 350. [172] (1902) 9 HCG 196.
[173] 203. [174] (1905) 26 NLR 455.
[175] (1867) LR 2 QB 580; cf. Hastings (n. 129), 77.
[176] Every legally relevant misrepresentation, of course, results in a mistake on the part of the representee: *Trollip v. Jordaan* 1961 (1) SA 238 (A) 252.
[177] It is generally accepted that *error in substantia* does not form part of modern South

The decisive initiative to abandon fraud as an element for rescission came from the Transvaal. There the courts had initially subscribed to the traditional approach.[178] In *Viljoen v. Hillier*,[179] however, Solomon J stated that a material misrepresentation made by a contracting party or his agent constituted a defence to a claim on the contract provided that the representee had been induced by the misrepresentation to conclude the contract. Proof that the plaintiff had been aware of the falsity of the representation when making it was held to be irrelevant.[180] Although strictly an *obiter dictum*,[181] this judgment set South African courts on the path of *Derry v. Peek* by holding that it was against good faith to insist on enforcing a contract which had resulted from a statement now known to be false.[182] The judgment explicitly coupled the *exceptio doli generalis* of Roman law with the notion of *ex post facto* fraud enunciated in *Redgrave v. Hurd*.[183] No other authorities were cited, and no reference was made to an earlier attempt to link *Redgrave v. Hurd* to the principles of Roman law.[184]

The passport under which the doctrine of innocent misrepresentation entered South African law was therefore the elastic but also somewhat artificial notion of *dolus praesens*,[185] rather than the doctrine of *error in substantia* or any theory of implied condition. In *Parke v. Hamman*[186] it was suggested in an *obiter dictum* that rescission could be had upon proof of mere misrepresentation,[187] and in *Hartogh v. National Bank Ltd*,[188] Bristowe J cemented the reasoning in *Viljoen v. Hillier* by the confident assertion that 'an innocent misrepresentation may be *dolus malus*'. *Wiley v. African Realty Trust Ltd*[189] provides the first example of a contract actually rescinded irrespective of fraud, that is to say merely on proof of its having been induced by a false, material misrepresentation made for the purpose of inducing the contract.[190] *Viljoen v. Hillier*, and its resort to the *exceptio*

African law. See *Papadopoulos v. Trans-State Properties & Investments Ltd* 1979 (1) SA 682 (W); *Trollip v. Jordaan* 1961 (1) SA 238 (A); Gerhard Lubbe, Christina Murray, *Contract: Cases, Materials and Commentary*, (1988), 125, n. 4.

[178] *Roorda v. Cohn* 1903 TH 279. [179] 1904 TS 312.

[180] 315. No opinion was expressed regarding the requirements for an action for damages.

[181] No misrepresentation was proved: see 316. It has been contended that the case really involved a disagreement between the parties: see Johannes Christiaan de Wet, *Estoppel by Representation in die Suid-Afrikaanse Reg* (1939), 87.

[182] 315 sq. [183] Note the extensive quotation from the judgment of Jessel MR at 316.

[184] See text to nn. 166 sq.

[185] As pointed out by De Wet (n. 181), 85, the bringing of an action in cases where the *exceptio doli generalis* is applied is regarded as improper because of circumstances attendant on the conclusion of the contract, or subsequent events. When such circumstances are recognized explicitly as legally relevant the need for the *exceptio doli* falls away. See also Lubbe (n. 53). 136 sq.

[186] 1907 TH 47.

[187] 52. Relief was denied because the representee was unable to restore what he had received from the representor.

[188] 1907 TH 207, 210. [189] 1908 TH 104.

[190] 110, relying on *Viljoen v. Hillier* 1904 TS 312.

doli, received the approval of the Cape Supreme Court in *Woodstock, Claremont, Mowbray and Rondebosch Councils v. Smith.*[191] It was against good faith to enforce an executory contract in the knowledge that it had been secured by misrepresentation; the same applied, according to De Villiers CJ, to attempts to 'insist upon retaining the benefit of an executed contract for the purpose of securing which he had made a false statement'.[192] Thus, the South African version of the rule in *Derry v. Peek* was liberated from the arbitrary limitation of the English doctrine which excluded rescission in respect of executed contracts.[193]

In a host of subsequent cases[194] the doctrine of innocent misrepresentation was so widely recognized that in *Welgemoed v. Cohen*[195] it was held that the term 'false representation' *prima facie* meant simply an incorrect or untrue representation, rather than a misrepresentation which the representor knew to be false. Accordingly, it was not *per se* defamatory to state that a person had made a false representation. The Appellate Division was not required to deal with innocent misrepresentation in its South African guise in *Geldenhuys & Neethling v. Beuthin,*[196] nor in *Lamb v. Walters,*[197] although in the latter case fraud was clearly regarded as irrelevant to rescission. In *Sampson v. Union & Rhodesia Wholesale Ltd (in Liquidation),*[198] however, the notion that rescission could be had on account of an honest misrepresentation which had induced a contract was finally approved by the Appellate Division with reference to *Viljoen v. Hillier* and its resort to the *exceptio doli generalis.* With this decision, the reception in South African law of the principle established in *Derry v. Peek* was finally complete.[199]

In respect of the technical requirements for rescission on account of misrepresentation, the pattern adopted from English law even before 1890[200] was retained and developed.[201] Thus, apart from stressing the fundamental requirement of misrepresentation,[202] judgments after 1890 accepted that

[191] (1909) 26 SC 681, 700 sq. [192] 701. [193] See note 140.
[194] *Caithness v. Fowlds* 1910 EDL 261; *Symons & Moses v. Davies* (1911) 32 NLR 69; *Van der Riet v. Steytler's Executors* 1912 CPD 2; *Corbett v. Harris* 1914 CPD 535, 545; *Brink v. Robinson & Wife* 1916 OPD 88; *Krupal v. Brooklands Dairies Ltd* 1921 TPD 541, 543; *McAlpine v. Celliers* 1921 EDL 112; *Koch v. Du Plessis* 1923 OPD 113, 114; *Glass v. Hyde* 1932 WLD 19; *Sim v. Fox* 1934 EDL 91.
[195] 1937 TPD 134, 137. [196] 1918 AD 426. [197] 1926 AD 358.
[198] 1929 AD 468, 480.
[199] For a recent statement see *Reyneke v. Botha* 1977 (3) SA 20 (T) 25; *Novick v. Comair Holdings Ltd* 1979 (2) SA 116 (W).
[200] See above, II. 1.
[201] For a full treatment of the present doctrine see Christie (n. 5), 325 sqq.
[202] See *Hain & Son v. Elandslaagte Colliery Co Ltd & Young* (1903) 24 NLR 363; *Josephi v. Parkes* (n. 143); *Erasmus v. Russel's Executor* 1905 TS 365 (distinction between *suggestio falsi* and *supressio veri*); *Begley v. Denton & Thomas* (n. 142); *Klette v. SA Cycle Factory Ltd* (n. 142); *Jenkins v. Durban Bay Land Co Ltd* (n. 141); *Woodstock, Claremont, Mowbray and Rondebosch Councils v. Smith* (n. 141; false statement of fact intended to be acted upon is required); *Vlotman v. Landsberg* (n. 1); *Durr v. Bam* (n. 1); *Capstick v. Keen* 1933 NPD 556; *Reyneke v. Botha* (n. 199), 26: exemption clauses exclude cause of action except in cases of fraud.

relief could only be based on a material misrepresentation.[203] Despite criticism[204] the approach in regard to materiality was that of English law. Whether a misrepresentation is 'of such a nature as would be likely to induce a person to enter into the contract'[205] is therefore determined with respect to whether it is one of fact or not,[206] how it is phrased,[207] and the relative position of the parties.[208] These factors do not purport to embody rigid rules but merely serve as guidelines regarding the application of the underlying principle, namely that a misrepresentation is improper or wrongful where it entails an unreasonably high risk of harm to the representee. On the other hand, where a person is misled by a misrepresentation which would not have deceived a reasonably careful person no liability ensues.[209] In any event it is clear that in respect of a statement intentionally made during negotiations in order to induce the representee to conclude the transaction, the degree of circumspection expected of the latter is not too exacting. Thus, a twenty-three-year-old constable in the South African police was held to have acted reasonably in concluding a contract for a series of body-building exercises with a 'physical culture expert' on the strength of the fol-

---

[203] *Robinson v. Ryves* (n. 142); *Klette v. SA Cycle Factory Ltd* (n. 142); *Corbett v. Harris* 1914 CPD 535; *Wilmot v. Sutherland* 1914 CPD 873; *Geldenhuys & Neethling v. Beuthin* 1918 AD 426; *Karroo & Eastern Board of Executors & Trust Co v. Farr* 1921 AD 413.

[204] See *Van Niekerk & Van der Westhuizen v. Weps & Morris* 1937 SWA 99, 105: materiality 'not quite co-extensive' with the requirements of Roman-Dutch law; cf. Lubbe/Murray (n. 177), 338, n. 5 for a discussion of the literature.

[205] *Karroo & Eastern Board of Executors & Trust Co v. Farr* (n. 203), 420 citing *Smith v. Chadwick* (1884) 9 AC 187. The test imports the notion of objective reasonableness: see *Pathescope (Union) of South Africa Ltd v. Mallinick* 1927 AD 292, at 307.

[206] Provided they are honestly entertained, no liability attaches to statements of intention and prophecies as to the future which do not come to fruition. *Jenkins v. Durban Bay Land Co Ltd* (n. 141); *American Medicine Co v. Stantial & Allerston* (1905) 26 NLR 22; *Feinstein v. Niggli* 1981 (2) SA 684 (A) 695. See, on the exclusion of relief in cases of mere opinions and statements which express value judgments or personal preferences on issues upon which different perceptions may legitimately be entertained, *Begley v. Denton & Thomas* (n. 142); *Corbett v. Harris* (n. 203); *Naude v. Harrison* 1925 CPD 84; *Lamb v. Walters* 1926 AD 358; *Sampson v. Union & Rhodesia Wholesale Ltd (in liquidation)* 1929 AD 468; *Feinstein v. Niggli* (n. 206).

[207] Statements which are so vague, ambiguous or exaggerated as to betray their uncertainty and unreliability provide no ground for relief. See *Roorda v. Cohn* (n. 148); *Provident Land Trust v. Thomas* (1909) 19 CTR 1043; *Wilmot v. Sutherland* 1914 CPD 873; *Adam v. The Curlewis Citrus Farms Ltd* 1930 TPD 68; *Geldenhuys & Neethling v. Beuthin* (n. 203); *Pathescope (Union) of South Africa Ltd v. Mallinick* (n. 205); *Bodasingh v. Massey-Harris* 1932 AD 39; *Van Niekerk & Van der Westhuizen v. Weps & Morris* (n. 204).

[208] Statements containing definite assertions of fact upon a matter within the sphere of knowledge of the representor and relevant to the contractual purpose of the representee are generally regarded as material: see *Bodasingh v. Massey-Harris* (n. 207).

[209] It should therefore come as no surprise that there are instances where the issue of materiality was decided directly with reference to the fundamental principle and without resort to the guidelines. See *Fraser v. Solomon* (n. 163); *Pietersen v. Joyce & McGregor* (1909) 19 CTR 121, where the representees were denied relief on the basis of a failure to exercise reasonable precautions.

lowing advertisment: 'Weakness is a Crime—Be strong! Strength doubled in twelve lessons (guaranteed)'.[210]

Gane AJ upheld the finding of the magistrate that the contract had been concluded on the faith of the representation[211] and also found for the defendant concerning the issue of materiality. According to the Court, there was 'no evidence that the respondent's belief was necessarily unreasonable', and that on the facts there was 'nothing to show that he should have regarded a doubling of such power as beyond the possibilities of an expert trainer'.[212]

The question of whether rescission is available even where the representation affected only the terms of a contract which would have been concluded in any event, or whether it is restricted to cases where the representee would not have contracted at all in the absence of a representation,[213] was not decisively addressed in *Woodstock, Claremont, Mowbray and Rondebosch Councils v. Smith*.[214] Similarly, in *Douglass v. Dersley*[215] the refusal of rescission seems to have been based on the absence of any causal significance of the representation rather than on the conclusion—as suggested by the headnote[216]—that the representation had only an incidental effect.[217] Decisive authority against the recognition of the distinction between *dolus dans* and *dolus incidens* is, however, to be found in *Karroo & Eastern Board of Executors & Trust Co v. Farr*.[218] Here the representee was held entitled to rescission in spite of an explicit finding that he would, in the absence of the misrepresentation, in all probability still have concluded a contract, albeit on different terms.[219]

4. Evaluation

It is not surprising that the *exceptio doli generalis* rather than an analysis in terms of *error in substantia* should have been preferred as a basis for the

---

[210] *McAlpine v. Celliers* 1921 EDL 112. The representation in the advertisment was subsequently repeated verbally and in writing by the plaintiff who billed himself as the 'strongest man in Africa, the modern Irish Samson' (at 113). The representee rescinded the contract upon being told, at the first session, that it was impossible to double his capacity to lift 150lbs. Instead, it was claimed that his overall prowess in 4 different feats of strenght would be doubled.

[211] 113.

[212] 115 sq. The enigmatic statement from the bench that 'I happen to know that a lift of 300 lbs is not beyond human capacity' seems to have played a part in this conclusion, but the judgment expressly disavows being based on 'private knowledge' only.

[213] See Zimmermann (n. 7), 670 sqq. on the civilian distinction between *dolus incidens* and *dolus causam dans*.

[214] Above, n. 191. Although seemingly favouring the view that rescission is permissible also in cases of *dolus incidens* (699 sq.) the judgment deals in the main with a question of evidential significance, namely the methods by which what would have happened in the absence of the misrepresentation might be established (700–2).

[215] 1917 EDL 221.   [216] 222.   [217] 230 sq.   [218] 1921 AD 413.

[219] 422 sq. See also Wouter de Vos, 'Skadevergoeding en Terugtrede weens Bedrog by Kontrakbreuk', 1964 *Acta Juridica* 26 sqq.

introduction of English principles. In a number of other situations the *exceptio doli* in fact served a similar function during this period.[220] What is peculiar about the development in respect of misrepresentation is that resort was had to the *exceptio doli* merely on the strength of the alternative explanation of the doctrine of legal fraud in *Redgrave v. Hurd*,[221] without any attempt[222] to establish whether Roman-Dutch sources permitted its application in cases of innocent misrepresentation.[223] That Solomon J misunderstood the tenor of *Redgrave v. Hurd* in his decision in *Viljoen v. Hillier* is of no import.[224] Of greater interest is whether the concurrence in reasoning was coincidental, or whether it is indicative of a deeper interrelationship between the notion of fraud in Equity and the principles of the civil law.[225]

The impact on South African law of importing the doctrine of innocent misrepresentation has been profound. By permitting, in effect, redress for mistakes in motive induced by a contracting party on a broad and flexible basis, this doctrine obviates the need for an exception to the general rule that such mistakes are legally irrelevant. The doctrine of *error in substantia* has accordingly been supplanted by the possibility of rescission on account of mere misrepresentation, and this venerable, if problematic, institution therefore no longer forms part of modern South African law.[226] The theoretical and practical difficulties inherent in the civilian approach to the problem of disappointed expectations has as a result been replaced by a solution which bases relief on objective considerations, and which, by adopting the construction of voidability rather than imposing nullity as an invariable consequence, respects the autonomous decision of the disadvantaged party regarding the fate of the transaction. Interestingly, the development in the uncodified South African legal system parallels that in the Netherlands under the former civil code, in terms of which the operation of 'Dwaling in de zelfstandigheid der zaak'[227] was ultimately limited to situations where it was imputable to the misleading conduct of the party seeking to enforce the contract.[228]

---

[220] See on the role of the *exceptio doli generalis* in the reception of estoppel *United SA Association v. Cohn* 1905 TH 169; *Waterfall Estate and GM Co v. New Bullion GM Co Ltd* 1905 TS 717; *Connock's (SA) Motor Co Ltd v. Sentraal Westelike Ko-operatiewe Maatskappy Bpk* 1964 (2) SA 47 (T); De Wet (n. 181), 10–13. On rectification see *Weinerlein v. Goch Buildings Ltd* 1925 AD 282, 292. For a general discussion see the contribution by Reinhard Zimmermann to this volume.   [221] See above, II. 2.

[222] That is, apart from the attempt of counsel in *Forbes v. Behr* (1896) 13 SC 304, 307 to link relief for mere misrepresentation to the aedilitian edict.

[223] See Zimmermann (n. 7), 673, fn. 166.

[224] In terms of the doctrine of legal fraud, 'moral delinquency' (or *dolus praesens*) would have been present only where the representor had acted negligently, in breach of a duty to take care. At least some of the English commentators trying to make sense of *Derry v. Peek* shared this misapprehension. See above, II. 3.

[225] See below, IV.   [226] N. 177.   [227] S. 1358 BW.

[228] See J. M. van Dunné, 'De Misrepresentation Act 1966: In Engeland is het goed dwalen', 1967 *Nederlands Juristenblad* 974; C. A. Uniken Venema, *Van Common Law en Civil Law*

This apparently simple solution, generally accepted today by South African commentators,[229] did not come without a price. The extension of the remedy of rescission brought with it the restriction of the delictual action for damages occasioned by misrepresentation, as established by *Derry v. Peek*.[230] Rescission is a drastic remedy which often operates harshly[231] and which lacks the suppleness of an action for damages. A corrective tendency to extend contractual liability, coinciding with the reception of innocent misrepresentation,[232] was cut short by the emergence of a firm distinction between terms and mere representations.[233] A further corrective development, entailing the extension of the aedilitian remedies to cases of innocent misrepresentation, was discernible at an early stage[234] and came to fruition in *Phame (Pty) Ltd v. Paizes*.[235] In spite of negative comments[236] it served, to some extent, to remedy the denial of delictual liability for economic loss caused by negligent misrepresentation, a deficiency remedied only after considerable delay and after a period of great uncertainty.[237]

From a theoretical perspective, rescission on account of a mere misrepresentation is currently understood as based upon a delict committed by the representor against the representee.[238] However, the emphasis on improper or wrongful behaviour obscures a doctrinally satisfactory explanation for the relief granted to the representee. While wrongful behaviour explains why the perpetrator ought not to be permitted to retain ill-gotten gains, the

(1971), 142; Gerhard Lubbe, 'Onskuldige Wanvoorstelling', (1978) 41 *THRHR* 374, 389–92. See Art. 6:228 NBW; cf. Jac Hijma, Art. 6:228–30 NBW, in: C. J. Brunner and E. H. Hondius, *Verbintenissenrecht* (1994).

[229] Joubert (n. 5), 98, Christie (n. 5), 325 sq.   [230] See text to nn. 152–7.

[231] George Mulligan, 'No Orchids for Misrepresentation?', (1951) 68 *SALJ* 157; Peter Hunt, 'Contract', 1963 *Annual Survey of South African Law* 124; Wouter de Vos, 'Skadevergoeding en Terugtrede weens bedrog by kontraksluiting', 1964 *Acta Juridica* 26.

[232] See *Wheeler v. Woodhouse* (1900) 21 NLR 162; *Vivian v. Woodburn* 1910 TPD 1285; *Peabody & Co v. Deane* (1913) 34 NLR 37; *Eales & Harris v. Hartigan & Forsyth* 1915 EDL 436. See also *Vorster v. Louw* 1910 TPD 1099; *Vivian v. Woodburn* 1910 TPD 1285 and *Koch v. Du Plessis* (n. 194) on the rejection of the doctrine, initiated in *Irvine & Co v. Berg* (1879) 9 Buch 183, that after delivery a purchaser is restricted to the aedilitian remedies.

[233] E.g. *Naude v. Harrison* (n. 206).

[234] *Douglass v. Dersley* 1917 EDL 221, 229; *Naude v. Harrison* (n. 206), 89; *Brink v. Robinson & Wife* (n. 194); *Hall v. Milner* 1959 (2) SA 304(0); *Jack van Niekerk v. Thompson Motors* 1966 (2) PH A70.   [235] 1973 (3) SA 397 (A).

[236] E.g. in *Steyn v. Davis & Darlow* 1927 TPD 651; *Glass v. Hyde* 1932 WLD 19; *Ramon Jackson* 1955 (1) PH A 6, 19.

[237] See Zimmermann (n. 7), 674, fn. 169 for an overview. Cf. *Bayer SA (Pty) Ltd v. Frost* 1991 (4) SA 559 (A), on which see Dale Hutchison, Reinhard Zimmermann, 'Fahrlässige irreführende Angaben im vorvertraglichen Bereich: Zur Haftung für reine Vermögensschäden nach modernem römisch-holländischem Recht' (1995) 3 *Zeitschrift für Europäisches Privatrecht* 271 sqq.

[238] De Wet/Van Wyk (n. 8), 47; Van der Merwe, Van Huyssteen *et al.* (n. 5), 76; R. H. Christie, 'Contract', in: W. A. Joubert (ed.), *The Law of South Africa*, vol. 5 (first reissue, 1994), § 147.

significance of the mistake induced in the other party militates against the imposition of liability and ought not to be overlooked. Apart from the need to develop a theoretical framework which takes account of all relevant factual circumstances, an analysis which focuses on only one dimension of the situation might also lead to unacceptable practical results. There may, for instance, be circumstances in which a reliance on a mistake in motive, although not induced by the other party, appears to be justifiable.[239] The absence of a developed notion of defective volition (or 'defect of the will')[240] also seems to contribute to the obscurity surrounding the nature of the duties to make restitution which arise upon rescission of the contract.[241] All in all, however, there can be no doubt that the Labeonic definition of fraud, consistently applied by the courts in the period under consideration, amounts to the recognition of a general norm of proper behaviour *in contrahendo* as a fundamental principle of South African law. Therefore, to the extent that rescission for a material misrepresentation rests on the recognition of such a norm, its reception cannot be regarded as conflicting with the fundamental premises of the Roman-Dutch foundations of South African law.

III. CONTRACTS 'GOTTEN BY THREATS AND PRACTICE'

Another aspect of the Equity jurisdiction regarding constructive fraud relates to undue influence[242] or, as it was initially put, contracts 'gotten by threats and practice'.[243] It served to mitigate the rigidity of the common law principle of duress. Relief for duress was initially restricted to cases where the contract was induced by the exercise of actual violence or threats against the life or bodily integrity of the victim.[244] Undue influence, on the other

---

[239] Instances of common mistake provide just such a case. The notion is poorly developed in South African law, being dealt with, uncomfortably, by means of the theory of implied terms. See Lubbe/Murray (n. 177), 135, n. 3.

[240] As opposed to cases of disagreement.

[241] The current analysis which ascribes a contractual nature to the duties to make restitution (*Johnson v. Jainodien* 1982 (4) SA 599 (C); *Davidson v. Bonafede* 1981 (2) SA 501 (C); De Vos (n. 13), 158 sq.) is not wholly satisfactory. A developed notion of defective (or frustrated) volition, might very well open the way for an analysis which characterizes performances rendered under a contract induced by misrepresentation as having been made *sine causa*. See Pierre Olivier, 'Die Aediliese Aksie weens verborge gebreke', (1963) 26 *THRHR* 173, and *idem*, 'Aanspreeklikheid weens onskuldige wanvoorstelling by kontraksluiting', (1964) 27 *THRHR* 20; Visser, 1993 *Acta Juridica* 203; cf. also Reinhard Zimmermann, 'A Road through the Enrichment Forest? Experiences with a General Enrichment Action', (1985) 18 *CILSA* 1.

[242] See above, II. 2.

[243] Harold Potter, *An Introduction to the History of Equity and its Courts* (1931), 58.

[244] See *Barton v. Armstrong* [1976] AC 1041 (PC); Robert Goff, Gareth Jones, *The Law of Restitution* (3rd edn., 1986), 204; G. H. Treitel, *The Law of Contract* (8th edn., 1991), 363; Hugh Beale, 'Duress and Undue Influence', in: Anthony Guest (ed.), *Chitty on Contracts* (27th edn., 1994), 399 sqq. See *Skeate v. Beale* (1841) 11 Ad & El 983 on the exclusion of so-called

hand, permitted rescission where power enjoyed by one person over another was abused so as to bring about a contract that was not based on the exercise of independent judgment by the victim.[245] Where contracting parties stood in a confidential relationship to one another the existence of undue influence over the weaker party was presumed, and it was for the party enforcing the contract to establish that the contract resulted from an informed and independent decision of the other party.[246] In the absence of such a special relationship, the latter had to establish that the contract had been brought about by 'some unfair and improper conduct' on the part of the former.[247]

Despite the assertion in *Katzenellenbogen v. Katzenellenbogen & Joseph*[248] that the English doctrine of undue influence was received in South Africa 'as fully consistent with the principles of the Roman-Dutch law', it is clear that no general reception took place before 1937.[249] The earliest references to the doctrine are tentative and unclear[250] and while some decisions in the Cape and Transvaal assumed the English doctrine to be part of Southern African law, such remarks were clearly *obiter* and hence inconclusive.[251] In *Armitage Trustees v. Allison*,[252] however, the Natal Supreme Court applied English law in setting aside a transaction between a legal advisor and his client because the latter had not had the benefit of independent advice.[253] Roman-Dutch authority on undue influence being 'somewhat scanty', and in the absence of authority favouring a presumption of undue influence, the Appellate Division declined to adopt English law in *Van Pletsen v. Henning*,[254] deciding to leave the matter open for future decision. After

duress of goods. And see Goff/Jones, 204 sqq. on the extension of duress in the 20th C. and under the influence of the equitable doctrine of undue influence, so as to permit rescission on account of any pressure which the law regards as illegitimate.

[245] See *Allcard v. Skinner* (1887) 36 ChD 145, 186 and, generally, Goff/Jones (n. 244), 248 who trace the formulation of the doctrine of undue influence to the judgment of Lord Hardwicke in *Morris v. Burroughs* (1737) 1 Atk 398, but see *Blundell & Hester v. Baker* (1720) 1 P Wms 634.

[246] *Allcard v. Skinner* (n. 245), 171; Goff/Jones (n. 244), 249–53.

[247] *Allcard v. Skinner* (n. 245), 181. See e.g. *Nottidge v. Prince* (1860) 2 Giff 246 (person of weak intellect manipulated by claim of supernatural powers); *Norton v. Relly* (1764) 2 Eden 286 (exploitation of religious delusions); *Lyon v. Home* (1868) LR 6 Eq 655 (belief in spiritualism); *William v. Bayley* (1866) LR 1 HL 200 (threat to prosecute son for a crime carrying penalty of life transportation).

[248] 1947 (2) SA 528 (W) 540.

[249] *Preller v. Jordaan* 1956 (n. 3), 506 (Van den Heever JA).

[250] *Nourse v. Steyn, Wife of Griffiths* (1847) 1 Menz 23; *Mostert v. SA Assoc* 1868 Buch 286; *Morkel v. Bain* (1872) 2 Roscoe 81.

[251] *Executors of Cerfonteyn v. O'Haire* (1873) 3 Buch 47; *Hough v. Van Eyk* (1898) 8 CTR 463; *Yates v. Yates* (1903) 20 SC 35; *Ex Parte Morum* (1904) 14 CTR 381; *Stride v. Wepener* 1903 TH 386, 386 sq.

[252] (1911) 32 NLR 88, 103.

[253] At 106, with reference to *Yates v. Yates* (n. 251), described as the 'only South African case which we have been able to find dealing with these principles'.

[254] 1913 AD 82, 94.

further conflicting provincial decisions[255] the Appellate Division again side-stepped the issue in *Penny v. Walker*.[256] The spirited argument before the Court[257] seems to have had some effect, however, for in *Armstrong v. Magid*[258] three judges of appeal were prepared to assume that a contract could be rescinded on the ground of undue influence.[259] Subsequently, the acceptance of undue influence in a number of provincial decisions[260] culminated in its final approval as part of South African law in *Preller v. Jordaan*.[261] In its South African guise, the doctrine permits rescission:

> where one person acquires an influence over another which weakens the latter's resistance and makes his will pliable and where such a person then uses his influence in an unscrupulous manner in order to prevail upon the other to agree to a prejudicial transaction into which, with normal freedom of will, he would not have entered.[262]

The formulation of the doctrine adopted by the Appellate Division leaves no room for the operation of a presumption of undue influence in the case of confidential relationships[263] and to this extent South African courts have adopted a line independent of English law. In contrast to the position in regard to misrepresentation, rescission for undue influence does not merely depend upon the unconscionable conduct of the party asserting the contract but presupposes defective (as opposed to absence of) volition on the part of the victim.[264] Interestingly enough, the absence of 'true consent' is also stressed in judicial restatements of the doctrine of *metus*.[265]

In spite of an initial criticism directed against its adoption[266] the concept

[255] Natal decisions such as *Foxon v. Foxon* (1914) 35 NLR 9 and *Moborak Ally v. Pathon* (1915) 36 NLR 363 favoured the doctrine, whereas *Ferreira v. Ferreira* 1915 EDL 9, 15 sq. shares the doubts expressed in *Van Pletsen v. Henning* (n. 254).

[256] 1936 AD 241. [257] 244. [258] 1937 AD 260.

[259] Stratford ACJ (270) and De Villiers JA (272) assumed this without any citation of authority, whereas De Wet JA (276) relied on *Yates v. Yates* (n. 251) and *Armitage Trustees v. Allison* (1911) 32 NLR 88 for the proposition that '[t]here seems to be no reason for holding that these principles are not in accordance with the principles of our law'.

[260] *Katzenellenbogen v. Katzenellenbogen & Joseph* 1947 (2) SA 528 (W); *Mauerberger v. Mauerberger* 1948 (4) SA 902 (C); *Ratanee v. Maharaj* 1950 (2) SA 538 (D); *Silver Garbus & Co (Pty) Ltd v. Teichert* 1954 (2) SA 198 (N).

[261] See n. 3.

[262] *Per* Corbett J, in *Miller v. Muller* 1965 (4) SA 458 (C), following the formulation in *Preller v. Jordaan* (n. 3).

[263] *Preller v. Jordaan* (n. 3), *Patel v. Grobbelaar* 1974 (1) SA 532 (A) 533 sq.; *Miller v. Muller* (n. 262), 463. For indications to the contrary, see *Armstrong v. Magid* (n. 258), 275 sq.; *Katzenellenbogen v. Katzenellenbogen & Joseph* (n. 260), 540 sq.; *Mauerberger v. Mauerberger* (n. 260).

[264] See above, II. 4.

[265] *Steiger v. Union Gov* (1919) 40 NLR 75; *Broodryk v. Smuts* 1942 TPD 47; *Arend v. Astra Furnishers (Pty) Ltd* 1974 (1) SA 298 (C). See Pierre Olivier, 'Onregmatige Vreesaanjaging', (1965) 28 *THRHR* 187, 199 on the implications for the notion of *voluntas coacta tamen est voluntas* (D. 4, 2, 21, 5).

[266] See e.g. J. C. de Wet and J. Yeats, *Kontraktereg en Handelsreg* (2nd edn., 1953), 36 sqq.; H. R. Hahlo, Ellison Kahn, *The Union of South Africa: The Development of its Laws and Constitution* (1960), 471.

of undue influence, viewed from a functional perspective, seems to have played a vital, corrective role in a number of distinctive areas. It has often been resorted to in cases involving persons of limited intellectual capacity who, physically and psychologically isolated from the outside world, fall prey to shady and unscrupulous characters. The former often face evidential difficulties when seeking relief from oppressive transactions on grounds such as mental incompetence, misrepresentation, duress, or other traditional defences. As far as both the memory of past events and the ability to communicate these to the court is concerned, the traditional defences often demand too much of the disadvantaged party. The doctrine of undue influence was resorted to in a number of cases in order to counter such evidential difficulties.[267] More fundamentally, however, it has remedied deficiencies in the substantive law by permitting redress in situations where certain principles available today to disadvantaged parties were still imperfectly developed or not recognized at all.[268] Furthermore, there were those cases in which the requirements of established doctrines were found to be too restrictive to satisfy the postulates of fairness and where resort to an equitable expedient was therefore considered necessary. Of especial importance is recourse to the doctrine of undue influence where contracts were concluded in response to threats and pressure below the level of *metus* as traditionally understood by the courts.

It has been remarked that D 4, 2 still exercises a dominant influence on the perception of *metus* in the South African courts.[269] Although a leading case such as *Broodryk v. Smuts*[270] requires the behaviour inducing the contract to be *contra bonos mores*, or unlawful, the implications of this general criterion have only recently been taken seriously.[271] Especially in the years before the introduction of the doctrine of undue influence, the emphasis has instead been on threats of evil directed against the victim or his family.[272]

---

[267] See *Preller v. Jordaan* (n. 3); *Patel v. Grobbelaar* (n. 263); *Armstrong v. Magid* (n. 263); *Mauerberger v. Mauerberger* (n. 260) on problems of this nature in respect of mental incompetence and misrepresentation. In *Penny v. Walker* (n. 256) the trial court explicitly adverted to difficulties of proof where the victim was a person of limited intellectual abilities. Here the difficulties were of such an order that relief was granted on the basis of the interpretation of the contract rather than undue influence. See also *Preller v. Jordaan*, 503 (*per* Van den Heever JA) on the possibility of a defence based on breach of contract.

[268] See *Armitage Trustees v. Allison* (n. 259): recovery of economic loss as a result of negligent misrepresentation; *Mostert v. SA Assoc* (n. 250); *Morkel v. Bain* (n. 250), *Hough v. Van Eyk* (n. 251: reliance on disagreement); cf. the facts of *Van Pletsen v. Henning* (n. 254).

[269] Zimmermann (n. 7), 658.   [270] Note 265.

[271] See, in regard to threats of criminal prosecution, *Arend v. Astra Furnishers (Pty) Ltd* (n. 265), *Ilanga Wholesalers v. Ebrahim* 1974 (2) SA 292 (D); *Machanick Steel & Fencing (Pty) Ltd v. Wesrhodan (Pty) Ltd* 1979 (1) SA 265 (W). The courts have not yet accepted the possibility that a threat of civil action may be illegal where the ends sought to be achieved are improper. See *Sievers v. Bonthuys* 1911 EDL 525; *Salter v. Haskins* 1914 TPD 264; *Houtappel v. Kersten* 1940 EDL 221; Olivier (n. 265) 201.

[272] *Broodryk v. Smuts* (n. 265).

Duress of goods, for instance, remains an obscure matter,[273] and the problems of economic duress are still inadequately dealt with.[274] While the criterion of ordinary firmness has been adopted in respect of the degree of pressure required,[275] and in spite of some indications of an individualized approach taking into account the circumstances of the victim,[276] the requirement of *iustus metus*, importing a considerable evil of an imminent and inevitable nature, still stands.[277]

This is the background for the resort to undue influence in some of the more important decisions. It is questionable, for instance, whether the facts in *Executors of Cerfonteyn v. O'Haire*[278] could have been brought home under the rubric *metus* as understood at the time of the decision. Here relentless pressure from a priest resulted in an elderly and debilitated woman naming him the guardian of her children in a codicil to her will, executed hours before her death.[279] Although the codicil was set aside on the ground that the *testatrix* lacked the requisite mental capacity,[280] the majority of the Court indicated that relief could also have been granted on the basis of undue influence. Both judges phrased this issue in language appropriate to *metus*, requiring that the conduct complained of should amount to 'force and coercion destroying free agency'.[281] *Metus* was not brought into play, however, perhaps because of uncertainty about the evaluation of the conduct of both the perpetrator and the victim in the unique circumstances of the case.[282] This conclusion also holds true of *Mauerberger v. Mauerberger*,[283] albeit in a more materialistic context. Here the plaintiff was

[273] *White Bros v. Treasurer-General* (1883) 2 SC 322; *Cupido v. Brendon* 1912 CPD 64; *Union Gov (Minister of Finance) v. Gowar* 1915 AD 426; *Hendricks v. Barnett* 1975 (1) SA 765 (N).
[274] *Insolvent Estate Evans v. SA Breweries Ltd* (1901) 22 NLR 115; *Lombard v. Pongola Sugar Milling Co Ltd* 1963 (4) SA 860 (A); *Caterers Ltd v. Bell & Anders* 1915 AD 698; *Lilienfeld & Co v. Bourke* 1921 TPD 365.
[275] *Freedman v. Kruger* 1906 TS 817; *Block v. Dogon, Dreier & Co* 1910 WLD 330; *Salter v. Haskins* 1914 TPD 264; *Union Gov (Minister of Finance) v. Gowar* (n. 273); *Steiger v. Union Gov* (n. 265); *Broodryk v. Smuts* (n. 265).
[276] Cf. *Freedman v. Kruger* (n. 275); *Block v. Dogon, Dreier & Co* 1910 WLD 330; *Salter v. Haskins* (n. 275); *Steiger v. Union Gov* (n. 265).
[277] *Freeman v. Corporation of Maritzburg* (1882) 3 NLR 117; *Salter v. Haskins* (n. 275); *Kilroe v. Bayer* 1915 CPD 717; *Steiger v. Union Gov* (n. 265), 73; *Lilienfeld & Co v. Bourke* (n. 274); *Broodryk v. Smuts* (n. 265); *Paragon Business Forms (Pty) Ltd v. Du Preez* 1994 (1) SA 434 (E).
[278] (1873) 3 Buch 47.
[279] This would have resulted in the children being brought up in their mother's church rather than in that of their late father (73, 74).
[280] 69.   [281] 76, per Denyssen J; cf. also Bell J, 74.
[282] The *testatrix* complied with the demand after confession and absolution was withheld from her and after she had been told that failure to execute the codicil was a sin for which her legal advisor would be unable to intercede for her (73 sq., 77).
[283] 1948 (4) SA 902 (C). It is important to note that this case was decided on exception, and that the only question in issue was whether, as an abstract legal issue, undue influence was recognized under South African law. No finding was made on the allegations relied upon by the plaintiff, nor was there any finding as to whether the allegations, if held to be well founded on a subsequent trial, would constitute undue influence.

held entitled to attempt to make a case of undue influence in order to avoid an extraordinary agreement entered into with his father,[284] although what was alleged were, on one hand, 'coercive and threatening acts . . . in the nature of duress'[285] and, on the other hand, 'misrepresentation and fraud'.[286] Any reliance on—innocent or fraudulent—misrepresentation or *metus* would, however, have faced insurmountable problems[287] in the former case, from the issue of materiality.[288] The recognition of undue influence as a distinct cause of action therefore afforded the plaintiff an opportunity of obtaining relief from a suspiciously one-sided transaction by adducing evidence of improper conduct on the part of the party enforcing the contract, irrespective of the limitations of *metus* or misrepresentation as conceived at that time.[289]

The corrective function of the doctrine of undue influence is also evident from the grounds adduced for its justification. The blithe assumption in *Katzenellenbogen v. Katzenellenbogen & Joseph*[290] that English law had been adopted in South Africa, elicited renewed attempts to domesticate the foreign import. *Mauerberger v. Mauerberger*[291] referred to Roman-Dutch authorities to the effect that *restitutio in integrum* could be obtained on any

---

[284] In the agreement, entered into after the plaintiff had divorced his wife, he renounced his position as shareholder in a number of companies and all benefits under a family trust. This allegedly constituted a loss to the plaintiff of at least £100,000 (906). In return the father undertook to pay the son £10,000 and an annuity of £1,200. In addition, the defendant entrusted the custody of the child—vested in him under the divorce settlement, 'but with the right to pass [it] to the plaintiff' (906)—to the plaintiff.

[285] 910. The father was alleged to have threatened to 'reduce the plaintiff to the gutter'.

[286] See 910 for the allegation that the father had indicated that the proposed steps had already been put into effect.

[287] There was hardly any question of an imminent or inevitable evil, and in the absence of information as to the personal circumstances of the plaintiff his reaction seems to have been vain and foolish, and not that of a person of ordinary firmness. Nothing was made of the pressure exercised by means of the extraordinary provision concerning the custody of the issue of the marriage.

[288] See text to nn. 62–70; *Karroo & Eastern Board of Executors and Trust Co v. Farr* (n. 4); *Reyneke v. Botha* (n. 4); *Novick v. Comair Holdings Ltd* (n. 4). The possibility that the requirement of materiality might require qualification in cases of fraudulent misrepresentation is of a relatively late origin. Cf. *Lourens v. Genis* 1962 (1) SA 431 (T) and *Otto v. Heymans* 1971 (4) SA 148 (T).

[289] For further examples of threats being dealt with as undue influence see *Ferreira v. Ferreira* (n. 254); *Patel v. Grobbelaar* 1974 (1) SA 532 (A). In *Katzenellenbogen v. Katzenellenbogen & Joseph* (n. 260), too, the plaintiff exacted a prejudicial divorce settlement from his wife by threatening to expose in court her adulterous relationship with her legal advisor. The threats were made by the plaintiff's legal advisors through the medium of the adulterous attorney. The husband conceded that his conduct 'was a pistol held at the heads of the plaintiff and Joseph' (537) and both his legal advisors and the judge agreed with Joseph's assessment that he and his lover had been subjected to 'legal blackmail' (535, the judge, however, feeling the epithet 'legal' to be 'hardly appropriate'). Here the resort to undue influence rather than *metus* resulted in a finding that the contract was not voidable. The plaintiff, it was found, had consulted her father and had accordingly acted on independent advice. See 539–40, 542.

[290] 1947 (2) SA 528 (W).   [291] 1948 (4) SA 902 (C).

just or reasonable cause[292] in order to demonstrate that this remedy encompassed instances of undue influence. Biting criticism of this view[293] resulted in an about-face in *Preller v. Jordaan*.[294] Although some reference was made to texts relating to *metus reverentialis*[295] the treatment of *dolus* in the old sources was regarded as being of greater importance.[296] With reference to the adoption of the Labeonic definition of fraud by Voet[297] and Van Leeuwen[298] the majority of the Court concluded that *dolus* in Roman-Dutch law had a more extended connotation than fraud in modern law. Whereas, according to Fagan JA, fraud is often taken today to refer exclusively to fraudulent misrepresentation,[299] *dolus* in Roman Dutch law insinuated *calliditas* or *malitas*, which was to be understood in the sense of 'cunning, craft, slyness, artfulness'.[300] While accepting that *restitutio in integrum* did not depend merely on the discretion of the judge,[301] *dolus* was understood to constitute an elastic criterion, dependent ultimately on an open-ended distinction between proper and improper conduct.[302] Crucially, the definition of *dolus* in *Macduff & Co Ltd (in liq.) v. Johannesburg Consolidated Investment Co Ltd*[303] ('anything which the law does not allow, anything inequitable, done with the consciousness that one is acting contrary to the law and good faith'), was cited in support of what amounted to the recognition of a general norm enjoining proper and reasonable behaviour *in contrahendo*.[304]

This approach, it is important to note, did not originate in *Preller's* case. In *Ferreira v. Ferreira*[305] McGregor J, although sharing the doubts of Innes JA in *Van Pletsen v. Henning*[306] as to the Roman-Dutch pedigree of undue influence, nevertheless suggested that 'the idea of undue influence could in principle be found to some extent embodied in the more general conception of *dolus* (whether as a cause of action or a defence)' of Roman-Dutch law.[307] In the judgment of De Wet JA in *Armstrong v. Magid*[308] *restitutio in integrum* was said (with reference to D 4, 3, 1) to aim at rendering 'assis-

---

[292] Simon van Leeuwen, *Rooms-Hollands-Regt*, 4, 42, 1 (as translated by John Kotzé, 1886), vol. II, 342, 345; Ulrich Huber, *Hedendaagse Rechtsgeleertheyt*, 4, 41, 7 (trans. Percival Gane, 1939), vol. II, 172.

[293] De Wet/Yeats (n. 266), 36 sqq.   [294] 1956 (1) SA 483 (A).

[295] Johannes Voet (n. 67), 4, 2, 11; 2, 14, 9, 18, 19; cf. the minority judgment of Van den Heever JA in *Preller v. Jordaan* (n. 3), 500; Hahlo/Kahn (n. 266), 471; J. E. Scholtens, 'Undue Influence', 1960 *Acta Juridica* 276.

[296] 491 sq.   [297] *Commentarius ad Pandectas* (n. 67), 4, 3, 1.

[298] Simon van Leeuwen, *Censura Forensis*, 1, 4, 40, 10; 1, 4, 42, 1.

[299] See, in this sense, *Preller v. Jordaan* (n. 3), 501 (Van den Heever JA).

[300] 491.

[301] At 492, with reference to Huber (n. 292), 4, 41, 7–9 and Voet (n. 67), 4, 6, 8–11, thereby rejecting the reasoning in *Mauerberger v. Mauerberger* (n. 260).

[302] 493. Cf. *Ratanee v. Maharaj* 1954 (2) SA 98 (N) 549 sq.

[303] 1924 AD 573, 610.   [304] *Preller v. Jordaan* (n. 3), 491.

[305] 1915 EDL 9 16.   [306] 1913 AD 82.

[307] 16.   [308] 1937 AD 260, 277 sq.

tance against shifty and deceitful persons who use some kind of craft to the prejudice of other persons, the object being to secure that the former shall not profit by their cunning and the latter shall not lose by their simplicity'. Finally, in *Mauerberger v. Mauerberger*[309] undue influence was linked to the concept of *dolus* in the general sense, quite independently of the argument based on the existence of a general equitable ground for *restitutio in integrum*. It was emphasized that the wide meaning of *dolus* as it is evident from D 4, 3, 1, 2 reverberated throughout South African case-law.[310] Reference was made to a number of decisions, all of which recognize not only the Labeonic definition of fraud but also the importance of the *exceptio doli generalis* as a device to provide redress in cases of improper conduct contrary to good faith (i.e. fraud in the extended sense).[311]

As in the case of misrepresentation, the English law of undue influence constituted the impulse for a development which, rather than leading to the reception of a foreign doctrine, entailed the rediscovery of the principle underlying the broad civilian definition of *dolus*, namely a general norm requiring proper behaviour, particularly *in contrahendo*. In this sense the development of the doctrine of undue influence in South Africa parallels that of innocent misrepresentation. Ultimately, both doctrines are based on an essentially similar reasoning.[312] Perhaps because *Derry v. Peek* stood in the way of the explicit recognition of such a norm, the introduction of innocent misrepresentation proceeded by way of the *exceptio doli generalis*, with the concept of *dolus praesens* serving to mask the inarticulate premise. By 1956, however, the recognition of the notion of wrongfulness had advanced to such a degree[313] that there were no obstacles to the explicit recognition of a general norm prescribing proper behaviour *in contrahendo*.

Criticism that the casuistry of Roman-Dutch law does not contain any indication that instances of undue influence were in fact redressed under the rubric of *dolus*[314] appears to be misplaced. The Labeonic definition of fraud imports an open-ended standard of behaviour. It depends on societal conceptions of proper and improper conduct, which are variable over time.[315] There can therefore be no objection to a reinterpretation of the imperatives of such a general norm in any given era. That the recognition of undue influence amounted in essence to the adoption of such a general norm is evident from the collapse of conceptual barriers between undue influence and

---

[309] 1948 (4) SA 902 (C).   [310] 911.

[311] See 911, where reference is made to *Estate Schickerling v. Schickerling* 1936 CPD 269, 276; *Tait v. Wicht* (n. 1), 165; *Sampson v. Union & Rhodesia Wholesale Ltd (in liq.)* 1929 AD 468; *Macduff & Co Ltd (in liq.) v. Johannesburg Consolidated Investment Co Ltd* 1924 AD 573, 610; *Zuurbekom Ltd v. Union Corporation Ltd* 1947 (1) SA 514 (A) 533.

[312] See above, II. 3.   [313] Esp. in view of *Herschel v. Mrupe* 1954 (3) SA 464 (A).

[314] An objection raised by Van den Heever JA in *Preller v. Jordaan* (n. 3), 502; Hahlo/Kahn (n. 266), 471. See, however, Scholtens (n. 295), 280, 288 on historical antecedents for the view adopted in *Preller v. Jordaan*.

[315] See Zimmermann (n. 7), 668–70.

metus in subsequent decisions.[316] Henceforth, it seems, these categories will serve as *Fallgruppen* constituting applications of the general principle, rather than distinct substantive categories.[317]

IV. '. . . THERE IS NO SUBSTANTIAL DIFFERENCE BETWEEN OUR LAW AND THE LAW OF ENGLAND ON THE SUBJECT'[318]

The equitable doctrines presently under consideration do not constitute exceptions to the growing appreciation of the interrelationship between English law and the legal systems derived from Roman law.[319] In addition to all the other circumstances which facilitated civilian influences on the English legal culture[320] the personnel,[321] procedure,[322] and institutional character[323] of the Court of Chancery rendered the jurisprudence of Equity particularly receptive to 'foreign' influence. The eventual secularization of the Chancellory shifted the focus of such influence from the canon law[324] to civilian sources in a broader sense.[325]

Even a cursory overview of decisions and treatises on Equity during the nineteenth century reveals a multitude of points of contact between Equity and the civilian sources. In regard to misleading conduct *in contrahendo*, the

[316] See *Savvides v. Savvides* 1986 (2) SA 325 (T); *Malilang v. MV Houda Pearl* 1986 (2) SA 714 (A).

[317] Van der Merwe, Van Huyssteen *et al.* (n. 5) 73.

[318] *Benjamin v. Minter* (1896) 8 HCG 37, 53.

[319] For a full discussion of the need to revise the concept of the 'noble isolation' of English law and an overview of the relevant literature see Reinhard Zimmermann, 'Der Europäische Charakter des englischen Rechts', (1993) 1 *Zeitschrift für Europäisches Privatrecht* 4, 9–46. Civilian influence initially penetrated the English legal culture in the late 12th and early 13th centuries, and then again in the early 16th C. A third era of influence stretches from 1600 to 1900. See Peter Stein, 'Continental Influences on English Legal Thought, 1600–1900', in: *idem, The Character and Influence of the Roman Civil Law* (1988), 209.

[320] These range from the Norman Conquest of England, the role of the Catholic Church and the economic integration of the British Isles in mediaeval Europe, to shared intellectual traditions. See Zimmermann, (1993) 1 *Zeitschrift für Europäisches Privatrecht* 9–46.

[321] See, on the clerical background of the Chancellors manning the Court of Chancery, Zimmermann, ibid. 27 sq.; cf. Thomas Edward Scrutton, *The Influence of the Roman Law on the Law of England* (1885), 152, 155; Carleton K. Allen, *Law in the Making* (6th edn., 1958), 389–92, 407.

[322] Zimmermann (n. 320), 28.

[323] On the Court of Chancery as a court of conscience, initially concerned with the redress of sin and the salvation of the sinner, see Zimmermann (n. 320), 28; Holdsworth (n. 90) vol. VIII (2nd edn., 1937), 50; Barbour (n. 90), 50; Scrutton (n. 321), 161; S. F. C. Milsom, *Historical Foundations of the Common Law* (2nd edn., 1981), 82 sq.; A. W. B. Simpson, *History of the Common Law of Contract* (1975), 379.

[324] According to Barbour (n. 90), 68, 'reason and conscience should be taken as a term of art, a broad, flexible principle derived from canon law, with a content sufficiently certain to guide the conscience of the chancellor'. See Zimmermann (n. 320), 28 sq. on the influence of canon law on the law of contract.

[325] On the tendency to identify 'conscience' with fairness and the demands of good faith, see Scrutton (n. 321), 161; Allen (n. 321), 389–92, 407; Zimmermann (n. 320), 28.

fundamental concept of misrepresentation is treated as consisting in *suggestio falsi*, whether expressly or by conduct, or even *suppressio veri* in appropriate circumstances.[326] Particularly influential was the treatment in civilian sources of Cicero's discussion of the question of non-disclosure.[327] Another essential element of relief for misrepresentation, implicit in late eighteenth- and early nineteenth-century case-law,[328] namely that of inducement, is brought into analytic focus in later decisions by means of the notion of *dolus dans causam contractui.*[329] In respect of materiality[330] Joseph Story relates the *simplex commendatio* of Roman law to the criteria of English law for distinguishing between misrepresentation and mere puffing.[331] While the origins of the dual test for *sciens* in regard to fraudulent misrepresentation[332] are obscure, Moyle, for one, endeavoured to provide an explanation with reference to 'the broad principle that . . . gross negligence is to be treated as equivalent to fraud'.[333] Although the Roman sources putting *culpa lata* on an equal footing with *dolus* are not quoted in

---

[326] *Jarvis and Wife v. Duke* (1681) 2 Vern 20; *Broderick v. Broderick* (1713) 1 P Wms 239; *Osmond v. Fitzroy* (1720) 3 P Wms 131; *Pusey v. Desbouverie* (1734) 3 P Wms 316; *Evans v. Bicknell* (1801) 6 Ves 174; *Central Railway Co of Venezuela v. Kisch* (1867) 15 WR 821 825; Edward Fry, *Treatise on the Specific Performance of Contracts* (1858), 206. The precise origin of the terminology employed is obscure but reference is often made to D 18, 1, 43, 2. See Story (n. 95), 118 who also refers to D 2, 14, 7, 9; Moyle (n. 166), 191.

[327] See *Carter v. Boehm* (1766) 3 Burr 1905 (*per* Lord Mansfield); *Gibson v. D'Este* (1843) 2 Y & C Ch Cas 542, 571; *Nelthorpe v. Holgate* (1844) 1 Coll 203; *Turner v. Green* (1895) 2 ChD 205 209; Fry (n. 326), 206 sqq. who refers to Cicero, *De officiis,* III, 12; Hugo Grotius, *De jure belli ac pacis,* 2, 12, 9; Robert Joseph Pothier, *Traité du contrat de vente,* 2, 2 without an indication of the editions concerned, or whether the original or the English translations were being referred to (see in regard to the latter Zimmermann, (n. 230), 47. On civilian influence in regard to *suppressio veri* generally see George Spencer Bower, *The Law Relating to Actionable Non-Disclosure and Other Breaches of Duty in Relations of Confidence and Influence* (London, 1915), 601 sqq.; Story (n. 95), 118, 131–6.

[328] *Lowndes v. Lane* (1789) 2 Cox 363; *Grant v. Munt* (1815) G Coop 173; *Smith v. Clark* (1806) 12 Ves 484.

[329] *Attwood v. Small* (1838) 6 Cl & Fin 232; *Pulsford v. Richards* (1853) 17 Beav 87; *Jennings v. Broughton* (1853) 5 De G M & G 126; *Rolt v. White* (1862) 3 De G J & S 360. Cf. Story (n. 95), 128, referring to Pothier (n. 327), § 210.

[330] See nn. 68, 111 and text to nn. 201–19.

[331] Story (n. 95), 121 refers to Jean Domat, *Loix civiles dans leur ordre naturel* (trans. William Strahan as *The Civil Law in the Natural Order: Together with the Publick Law,* London, 1722) I, 2, 11, 12 for the proposition that there is no misrepresentation where a misstatement is inconsequential, and to Pothier, *Traité des obligations* (trans. William Evans, Philadelphia, 1806), §§ 17–20 and fn. (a) in support of the view that an unfounded opinion leads to liability if, under the circumstances, it is reasonable to rely on it. Later (128) Story equates the equitable guidelines regarding puffing to the maxim *simplex commendatio non obligat,* referring to D 18, 1, 43 for the proposition that 'if the means of knowledge are not equally open, the same law [Roman law] pronounced a different doctrine', a rule which, it is stated, is also borne out by English decisions. Cf. Lubbe (n. 53), 127.

[332] Above, II. 2, n. 122.

[333] See Moyle (n. 166), 59 sq. for an attempt to link *Evans v. Edmonds* (1853) 13 CB 777; *Weir v. Bell* (1898) 3 Ex D 238 CA; and *Reese River Silver Mining Co v. Smith* (n. 12), 79 (which held that untrue statements about the subject matter of the contract, in reckless ignorance as to their truth or falsehood, amounted to fraud) to D 19, 1, 13, 3.

the relevant cases, the shift in Equity towards the recognition of liability for honest but negligent misrepresentations[334] seems to have come about as a result of an equation of gross negligence with fraud.[335] Similar tendencies are evident with regard to that part of equitable fraud that is normally classified under the rubric constructive fraud.

Apart from decisions on unconscionable bargains concluded with expectant heirs, in which references to the *Senatusconsultum Macedonianum* occur,[336] civilian sources also play a role in cases dealing with the quintessentially English doctrine of undue influence. Nineteenth-century treatise writers, for example, frequently cite Pothier, generally in order to relate the individualized test of *metus* to the doctrine of undue influence.[337] Keeton and Sheridan[338] go even further and attribute the development of a general doctrine of undue influence to Pothier. The Court of Chancery, they write, struggling during the nineteenth century with 'the problem of the undue influence exercised upon wives to compel them to surrender their property', 'lent a ready ear' to Pothier's suggestion that gifts between persons in relationships of dependency ought as a general rule to be regarded with disfavour.[339] *Huguenin v. Basely*,[340] often referred to as providing the foundation of undue influence,[341] is the only case cited by Keeton and Sheridan in support of their contention. Lord Eldon's judgment, however, contains no reference to Pothier. Keeton and Sheridan's claim seems to be based on the heads of argument presented to the Court by Samuel Romilly. At issue in this case was whether relief for undue influence was restricted to contracts resulting from relationships such as that between guardian and ward and administrator and beneficiary, or whether it also extended to transactions brought about by the 'spiritual ascendency' of a religious advisor over his disciple.[342] On the assumption that there was no direct authority in the case-law for such an extension[343] recourse was had to Pothier

---

[334] See text to nn. 103–9, section II. 2.

[335] See the treatment of *Evans v. Bicknell* (1801) 6 Ves 174 in *Burrowes v. Locke* (1805) 10 Ves 470; cf. Lubbe (n. 53), 122–4; Davidson (1982) 13 *Melbourne University LR* 349, 356–61.

[336] *Earl of Chesterfield v. Janssen* (1751) 2 Vessen 125, 157 sq.; *Gwynne v. Heaton* (1778) 1 Bro CC 1.

[337] See Story (n. 95), 149, n. 5. He states that 'the doctrine of the common law, upon the subject of avoiding contracts upon the ground of mental weakness, or force, or undue influence, does not seem, in any essential manner, to differ from that adopted in Roman law, or in the law of modern continental Europe'. After a discussion of *metus* in the civil law (based on D 4, 2, 1–6) he cites Domat (n. 331), 1, 18, 2, arts. 1–10 and Pothier (n. 331), 1, 1, 3, 2, 25; cf. Kerr (n. 128) 167, fn. (p).

[338] Keeton/Sheridan (n. 120), 230.

[339] The authors refer to Robert Joseph Pothier, *Traité des donations entre-vifs* and *Traité des personnes et des choses*.

[340] (1807) 14 Ves 273.   [341] Goff/Jones (n. 244), 248.

[342] (1807) 14 Ves 273, 284, 279 sq.

[343] Both counsel and the Court overlooked *Norton v. Relly* (1764) 2 Eden 286, where Lord Northington declared that 'the constitution itself would be in danger' if a court were unable to relieve a spinster from a detrimental transaction concluded with an 'independent' preacher

concerning the position under French law. A spirited counter-argument was made, *inter alia*, to the effect that Pothier was dealing with an ancient French ordinance, and that the civil law at large did not support the proposition contended for. This elicited from Romilly a 'celebrated reply',[344] full of rhetorical flourish, in which he argued, referring to Cicero,[345] that relief 'stands on a general principle applying to all varieties of relationships in which *dominium* may be exercised by one person over another'.[346] The extension of relief was presented as an *a fortiori* case, with religious influence being portrayed as infinitely more powerful than a position based on the relationship between ward and guardian.[347] The significance of this excursion lies in the fact that Romilly's reply was accorded 'quasi-judicial authority' by being 'textually adopted' in subsequent judgments[348] to such an extent that *Huguenin v. Basely* has been described as 'perhaps the only modern case in which a reported argument has acquired by later judicial approval an authority equal to that of the judgment itself'.[349]

Any conclusion about the validity of the contention that the development of undue influence during the nineteenth century was fundamentally inspired by Pothier, and any final judgment as to the role of civilian institutions in determining the technicalities of misrepresentation, requires detailed analysis of numerous judgments and treatises and is beyond the scope of this Chapter. It is clear, however, that considerable subtlety is necessary in order to establish not only the extent but also the nature of the civilian influence. Although it has been described as considerable, it has been said to have been 'more subtle and elusive' during the period from 1600 to 1900 than in previous eras, affecting 'not so much the substance of the law as the way lawyers looked at it, and the way they presented and expounded it'.[350]

References to civilian sources in treatises, for example, must be approached with caution. Thus, Story's influential treatise on Equity, in

whom he described as 'a subtle sectary who preys upon his deluded hearers, and robs them under the mask of religion; an itinerant who propagates his fanaticism even in the cold northern countries, where one should scarcely suppose that it could enter'.

[344] For the extraordinary deference accorded to Romilly's argument in *Huguenin v. Basely*, esp. his 'reply', in subsequent cases, see e.g., *Hunter v. Atkins* (1834) 3 My & K 113, 139 sq. where Lord Brougham speaks of 'the famous case of *Huguenin v. Basely*, remarkable amongst other things, for the display of these transcendant talents, and that pure taste, by which amongst many other accomplishments, Sir Samuel Romilly elevated and adorned the bar'. In *Dent v. Bennet* (1839) 4 My & Cr 269, 277, Cottenham LC speaks of 'the celebrated reply in *Huguenin v. Basely*, from which I received so much pleasure that the recollection of it has not been diminished by the lapse of more than 30 years'. Cf. *Nottidge v. Prince* (1860) 2 Giff 246, 263; *Cavendish v. Strutt* (1903) 19 TLR 483. See, however, Spencer Bower (n. 327), 370 fn. (c) for a more jaundiced view of the 'uncritical raptures' with which Romilly's argument was treated in later cases.

[345] *De Officiis*, I, 13.   [346] 285 sq.   [347] 288, 286.
[348] Spencer Bower (n. 327), 369, 370, fn. (c).
[349] Frederick Pollock, *Preface, Revised Reports* (London, 1893), vol. IX, vi.
[350] Stein (n. 319), 209.

conformity with the author's intention,[351] reads to some extent as a comparative study of Equity and civil law. The manner of treatment in itself, however, does not indicate whether the parallels so documented are the result of independent evolution, or reflect, if only partially, inspiration derived from civilian sources. At the same time, the traditional reticence of English judges concerning the citation of textbooks, added to the often anecdotal style and haphazard citation of authorities evident from many of the Chancery judgments, stand in the way of any attempt to establish the substantive effect of such references in legal literature on the case-law.

The question of the possible role of the *exceptio doli generalis* in the doctrine of legal fraud gives some indication of the difficulty of assaying the nature of civilian influence on equitable doctrines. The assertion in *Redgrave v. Hurd* by Jessel MR that insistence on a contract obtained by a statement now known to be false constitutes a moral delinquency,[352] reveals such an obvious affinity to the reasoning underlying the *exceptio doli* that it served as the basis for the introduction of innocent misrepresentation into South African law.[353] English commentaries, however, which in the aftermath of *Derry v. Peek* seized on the notion of *ex post facto* fraud to preserve the equitable doctrine of rescission for misrepresentation, provide no basis for assuming a link with the *exceptio doli*[354] and this also holds true of such works as could be consulted from the era before *Derry v. Peek*.[355] The judgment in *Redgrave v. Hurd* itself sheds very little additional light on whether Jessel MR was thinking in terms of the *exceptio doli* or not.[356] A non-civilian origin for the notion of *ex post facto* fraud cannot therefore be excluded. It may conceivably have been derived from certain cases in which it was held that a failure to disclose the subsequent falsehood of an assertion amounted in itself to misrepresentation,[357] and there is a tendency in

---

[351] Story (n. 95), ix sq. (preface to the original edn., 1835).

[352] See above, II. 2, text to n. 135.

[353] See above, II. 3, and for a similar conclusion by a Scottish jurist, T. B. Smith, *British Justice: The Scottish Contribution* (Hamlyn Lectures, 1961), 178.

[354] Moyle (n. 166), 65 did not link the *exceptio doli* and the doctrine of *Redgrave v. Hurd* even though he suggested that according to Roman law the *exceptio* was available where a person who was sued under a contract was unable to rely on *metus* because the threats made against him were not of a sufficiently 'serious character'. Indeed, Moyle portrays the English law regarding misrepresentation as going beyond the confines of the civil law (190). Bigelow (n. 137), who hailed fraud 'by conduct subsequent' as being of considerable significance, treated it as a conceptual innovation 'whose existence . . . has not before been pointed out' (lxiii).

[355] William Anson, *Principles of the English Law of Contract* (2nd edn., 1882), 144 does refer to *ex post facto* fraud but regards it as 'calculated to create additional confusion in a subject already difficult' (146 sq.).

[356] In *Reese River Silver Mining Co v. Smith* (n. 12), the only other decision referred to by Jessel MR, the Court merely stated the doctrine of legal fraud in the traditional way as involving a breach of duty on the part of the representor.

[357] *Reynell v. Sprye* (1851) 1 De G M & G 660, 709; *Arkwright v. Newbold* (1881) 17 ChD 301, at 315.

the literature to link these situations.[358] Other indications seem to point in a different direction. The cases decided in Equity do occasionally betray an awareness of the *exceptio doli*[359] and there are formulations which seem to express the idea articulated in *Redgrave v. Hurd*. There is also the statement of Lord Justice Turner in *Rawlins v. Wickham*[360] that the notion of legal fraud is based on the consideration that a representor 'surely cannot be heard to say that he knew nothing of the truth or falsehood of that which he represented, and still more surely, he cannot be allowed to retain any benefit which he has derived if the representation he has made turns out to be untrue'; one may add to it the pronouncement in *Torrance v. Bolton*[361] that rescission is permissible even in the absence of actual fraud in cases in which 'the court is of the opinion that it is unconscientious for a person to avail himself of the legal advantage which he has obtained'.

The idea that insistence on a contract is improper on account of prior conduct falling short of actual fraud reflects the reasoning in those cases where specific performance was denied by the Court of Chancery for contracts induced by misrepresentation.[362] Here we have the first instance of the legal recognition in Equity of non-fraudulent misrepresentation[363] and it seems to have originated in the doctrine of clean hands, by which relief was denied in circumstances where the conduct of the plaintiff was unreasonable.[364] While not inherently implausible, the existence of a link between the principle of clean hands and the civilian idea of *dolus praesens* is obscured by the briefness of the judgments applying a principle regarded as so self-evident as not to require any elaboration.[365]

A further dimension emerges if circumstances beyond the textual manifestations of thoughts long gone are taken into account. George Jessel's knowledge of the civil law, and indeed the law of continental Europe, is well documented[366] and the resort, in Redgrave's case, to a formulation typically Roman might conceivably be nothing more than an expression of his personal orientation and style, rather than an indication of an established

---

[358] Fry (n. 326), 275; Bigelow (n. 137), 11, 410–12; Moncreiff (n. 137), 314; Frederick Pollock, *The Principles of Contract* (9th edn., 1921), 603.

[359] *Kennel v. Abbot* (1797) 4 Ves 803. The case does not concern misrepresentation, and the reference to the *exceptio* seems misplaced.

[360] 316.   [361] (1872) 8 Ch 118, 124.

[362] It is well to remember that in *Redgrave v. Hurd* (1881) 20 ChD 1 rescission was raised as a defence to a claim for specific performance.

[363] Above, II. 2.

[364] See *Cadman v. Horner* (1810) 18 Ves 11; *Clermont v. Tasburgh* (1819) 1 Jac & W 112; H. Maddock, *Treatise on the Principles and Practice of the High Court of Chancery* (1815), 321.

[365] *Wall v. Stubbs* (1815) 1 Madd 80.

[366] Holdsworth (n. 90), vol. XVI (1966), 121 describes Jessel as 'something of a jurist', who had 'studied Roman law and the foreign codes based on it'. Cf. Gerry R. Rubin, 'Jessel, Sir George', in: A. W. B. Simpson (ed.), *Biographical Dictionary of the Common Law* (1984), 280 sqq. ('A deeply learned man, he had mastered Roman law and the foreign codes founded on it').

convention in the conceptual armoury of Equity jurisprudence. Reference to the civilian sources may thus, in this as in many other instances, ultimately amount to nothing more than a rhetorical flourish, a *topos* to enhance an argument or to embellish a conclusion already reached upon other grounds. A clear example is presented by *Attwood v. Small*.[367] In a general statement of the requirements for rescission on account of fraudulent misrepresentation the Court stressed that the representation should have induced the contract. What was required was not merely a misrepresentation but, 'in the language of the civil law', *dolus dans causam contractui*. Only then, it was said,[368] 'comes in the equitable principle of the civil law, which forms a part of all other systems of jurisprudence, whether founded upon it or not, being grounded on the highest consideration of natural equity, *ex dolo non oritur contractus*'. By this time causation was already well established as an element of relief;[369] in the absence of any indication of the adoption of the distinction between *dolus dans* and *dolus incidens*[370] the recourse to Roman law in this and other instances[371] seems to have served a confirmatory function only. This view is endorsed by Spencer Bower who calls attention to the 'not infrequent or unimportant' references in the case-law to civilian sources in respect of the problem of non-disclosure and good faith, but adds that in most cases '. . . the principles of Roman jurisprudence are appealed to in support of established rules of English law'; only in exceptional instances did judges resort to the civil law to advance 'personal predilections' regarding the substance of the law.[372]

The possibility that some references to civilian sources are merely of peripheral or superficial significance does not, of course, exclude the existence of a fundamental substantive interrelationship in other instances. This becomes apparent if the focus is shifted from the level of technicalities to that of general principles. Although there are of course examples of unsuccessful attempts to remould English institutions in the image of the civil law on account of 'personal predilections',[373] such projects did not necessarily end in failure.

In both *Mauerberger v. Mauerberger*[374] and *Preller v. Jordaan*[375] reference is made to *Allcard v. Skinner*, decided in the Chancery Division in 1887.[376] The judgment in this case is, once again, marked by a concern to state the law relating to undue influence in terms of a coherent principle, namely the protection of unsuspecting members of the community 'from

---

[367] (1838) 6 Cl & Fin 232.   [368] 444 sq.   [369] See nn. 112, 328.
[370] After a discussion of the civilian distinction Kerr (n. 128), 39 n. (s) comments, that it 'does not obtain in the common law, and is not admitted in Equity'.
[371] See n. 329.   [372] Spencer Bower (n. 327), 614.
[373] See e.g. the comments of Lord Eldon LC in *Conolly v. Parsons* (1797) 3 Ves 625 on the reform attempts of Lord Mansfield CJ; cf. Holdsworth (n. 90), vol. XII (1938), 477, 517 sq.; *Lee v. Jones* (1864) 17 CB NS 482 Exch Ch.
[374] 1948 (4) SA 902 (C).   [375] 1956 (1) SA 483 (A).
[376] (1887) 36 ChD 145.

being forced, tricked or misled, *in any way*,[377] by others into parting with their property'.[378] It was also stressed that undue influence was one of the heads of constructive fraud which, in conjunction with actual fraud,[379] constituted fraud in Equity. According to Lindley LJ[380] the doctrine of undue influence grew out of 'the necessity of grappling with insidious forms of spiritual tyranny and with the infinite varieties of fraud'. To this end it required a general formulation, rather than a definition, of fraud which, indeed, the courts of Equity had never attempted to provide.[381] At the end of the nineteenth century this orientation still echoes the views of one of the principal founders of the doctrine of equitable fraud, the celebrated Chancellor Lord Hardwicke[382] who had famously stated:[383]

Fraud is infinite, and were a court of Equity to lay down rules, how far they would go, and no farther, in extending their relief against it or to define strictly the species of evidence of it, the jurisdiction would be cramped, and perpetually eluded by new schemes which the fertility of man's invention would contrive.

Hardwicke's open-ended categorization of the heads of fraud in *Earl of Chesterfield v. Janssen*[384] similarly attempts to reduce the importance of the manner in which the overreaching takes place. In this fundamental respect[385] equitable fraud not only parallels the Labeonic concept of fraud[386] but seems in fact to have been derived from it. Hardwicke was an 'accomplished Roman lawyer';[387] and prior to *Janssen*'s case he had adopted D 4, 3, 1, 2 in another famous decision, *Le Neve v. Le Neve*.[388] This approach to the notion of equitable fraud remained engrained in the equitable treatment of fraud in subsequent cases[389] and commentaries.[390]

---

[377] My emphasis.

[378] See 183, 171, 189 sq.; Leonard Sealy, 'Fiduciary Relationships', 1961–62 *Cambridge LJ* 69, 78.

[379] *Earl of Chesterfield v. Jannsen* (1751) 2 Ves Sen 125, 155 sq.   [380] 183.

[381] Ibid. Cf. Story (n. 95), 115 ('extensive signification' of fraud in equity); *Torrance v. Bolton* (1872) 8 Ch App 118 (fraud is *nomen generalissimum*').

[382] See Holdsworth (n. 373), 237–96 for an assessment of Hardwicke's enormous contribution to the modern system of Equity.

[383] 1759, in a letter to Lord Kames, reproduced by Parkes, *History of the Court of Chancery* (1828), 506–9. See Keeton/Sheridan (n. 120), 42; Holdsworth (n. 373), 262.

[384] (1751) 2 Ves Sen 125, 155–7.

[385] Also included under the rubric 'equitable fraud' were instances of agreements regarded as illegal on account of public policy or of 'some fixed artificial policy of the law': see Story (n. 95), 167 sqq. for a discussion; cf. *Earl of Chesterfield v. Janssen* (n. 379), 155–7.

[386] Zimmermann (n. 7), 666.

[387] Holdsworth (n. 373), 280. Cf. Gareth H. Jones *'Yorke, Philip (Earl of Hardwicke)'*, in: Simpson (n. 366), 555 sqq. ('Hardwicke . . . combined mastery of technical rules with a power of generalisation which owed much to his study of Roman law and the civilian codes').

[388] (1748) 3 Atk 647, 654, where he also stated it to be a maxim of English law that: *fraus et dolus nemini patrocinari debent.*

[389] *Stikeman v. Dawson* (1847) 1 De G & Sm 90; *Thompson v. Hopper* (1858) E B & E 1038; *Lee v. Jones* (1864) 17 CB NS 482 Exch. Ch.; *Crowley v. Bergtheil* [1899] AC 374 PC.

[390] See e.g. Spencer Bower (n. 327), 602: 'Roman jurisprudence shrank from restricting the

This perspective is essential for an understanding of the notion of equitable fraud. As indicated above,[391] fraud in Equity encompassed, not only wilfully false misrepresentations inducing a contract but also any conduct 'in breach of the sort of obligation which is enforced by a court that regarded itself from the beginning as a court of conscience'.[392] The emphasis is not on form but on the redress of conduct flouting 'the dictates of conscience as defined by the court'.[393] The term 'conscience', initially bearing a religious connotation and thus reflecting the ecclesiastical origins of the Court of Chancery, later became a secularized term of art and was employed to express the standard of behaviour required by Equity for human intercourse. Not unnaturally, it has been identified with the praetorian notion of good faith.[394] Indeed, in *Earl of Chesterfield v. Janssen*[395] Lord Hardwicke explicitly stated that 'persons in contract shall not only transact *bona fide* between themselves, but should not transact *mala fide* in respect of other persons'.[396]

'[T]he history of Roman law in England has yet to be written . . . ';[397] this assertion made one hundred years ago is probably still true today. At the same time, however, there is some basis for saying that the doctrine of equitable fraud seems not only to have proceeded originally from a premise similar to that of the civil law but actually to have been inspired by it. In view of this the occasional scornful reaction[398] to the vital role of English precedents in shaping the South African approach to voidable contracts can hardly be regarded as well founded. For in a fundamental sense the reception process has not diverted South African law from its 'pure' Roman-Dutch origins. Rather, it has resulted in the rediscovery of a basic premise of its civilian heritage, namely that a reasonable concern for the interests of others is required of those engaging in commercial activities. Ultimately, the equitable doctrines of misrepresentation and undue influence are not alien to Roman-Dutch principles: this assertion by South African judges is thus substantially correct.

meaning or range of *dolus* . . . just as the term "fraud" has been extended by our equity judges to embrace a similarly miscellaneous assortment of transgressions against *aequum et bonum*'. Cf. Fry (n. 326), 206; Kerr (n. 128), 1–3; Scrutton (n. 321), 161; H. Gibson Rivington, A. Clifford Fountaine, *Snell's Principles of Equity* (19th edn., 1925), 441; Sheridan (n. 90), 167; Davidson (1982) 13 *Melbourne University LR* 349, 358.

[391] Above, II. 2, text to nn. 90–7.

[392] *Per* Viscount Haldane LC, in *Nocton v. Lord Ashburton* (n. 95) 951–4.

[393] *Nocton v. Lord Ashburton* (n. 95), 952. Cf. Hans W. Goldschmidt, *English Law from the Foreign Standpoint* (1937), 107.

[394] See n. 325.   [395] (1751) 2 Ves Sen 125, 155–7.

[396] The latter aspect refers to that dimension of constructive fraud which concerns matters of public policy rather than issues of interpersonal good faith.

[397] Scrutton (n. 321), 195.   [398] *Preller v. Jordaan* (n. 3), 504.

9: *Breach of Contract*

ALFRED COCKRELL

I. INTRODUCTION

This Chapter explores some aspects of the development of the South African law relating to breach of contract from its Roman-Dutch roots to the present day. In order to reduce the topic to manageable proportions I have chosen to restrict myself to a discussion of the following three processes: (1) the process by means of which the concept of breach of contract has fractured into a number of 'specific types of breach'; (2) the process by means of which a 'generalized' right of cancellation for breach of contract has evolved in the case law; and (3) the process by means of which specific performance has come to be regarded as the 'routine' remedy for breach of contract. While a number of related issues will be touched on under these broad headings, this Chapter makes no claim to deal comprehensively with the topic of breach as a whole. Most obviously, nothing is said about the development of the legal rules relating to the quantification of contractual damages, a matter which has been comprehensively dealt with elsewhere.[1] This Chapter concludes with an attempt to distil some general principles out of the historical discussion which forms its major focus.

II. FISSURING THE CONCEPT OF 'BREACH OF CONTRACT'

In its modern guise, South African law is characterized by what I propose to call a 'fissured concept of breach'. By this I mean that in our modern law the generic concept of 'breach of contract' has become fractured into a number of distinct types of breach, and these 'specific breaches' act as doctrinal pigeon-holes into which the promisor's conduct must be slotted before it can attract the consequences of breach of contract.[2] There is, of course, considerable controversy regarding the number of pigeon-holes which exist

---

[1] See esp. H. J. Erasmus, 'Aspects of the History of the South African Law of Damages', (1975) 38 *THRHR* 104, 268, 382; P. J. Visser, J. M. Potgieter, *Law of Damages* (1993), 8–15; Reinhard Zimmermann, *The Law of Obligations: Roman Foundations of the Civilian Tradition* (1990, reprint 1993), 824–33.

[2] Gerhard Lubbe, Christina Murray, *Farlam & Hathaway, Contract: Cases, Materials and Commentary* (3rd edn., 1988), 471.

and the labels which should be attached to them,[3] but it does seem to be generally accepted that our modern notion of breach of contract is fractured along some or other lines.

The evolution of such a fissured concept of breach is noteworthy for at least three reasons. First, the fissures in modern South African law seem to cut deeper than in the English law; the latter system appears to operate a more 'unitary' concept of breach.[4] Secondly, a perusal of the Roman-Dutch writers reveals no attempt to carve up the terrain of breach of contract in a sharply delineated way. This statement must immediately be qualified. No doubt there are, submerged within the institutional writings, a number of indications and hints regarding the diverse ways in which a contract might be breached; my point is simply that the doctrinal pigeon-holes had not yet acquired the 'hard edges' which they have in the modern law.

The third reason can be stated cryptically as follows: while the history of South African contract law is essentially the story of a movement from a 'theory of specific contracts' to a generalized 'theory of contract', the concept of breach has been moving—in an opposite direction, as it were—towards an increasingly fissured notion of 'specific breaches'. It is well known that the rise of *pacta sunt servanda* subsumed an earlier *numerus clausus* of nominate contracts under a generalized theory for the ascription of contractual responsibility based on an abstract principle of consensuality.[5] This was in essence a movement from the *specific* to the *general* in the context of the ascription of contractual responsibility. However, the devel-

---

[3] For a laconic overview of the different classifications adopted by the textbooks see Zimmermann (n. 1), 815, fn. 228.

[4] Zimmermann (n. 1), 814; G. H. Treitel, *Remedies for Breach of Contract: A Comparative Account* (1988), 130 sq.; cf. J. W. Carter, *Breach of Contract* (2nd edn., 1991), 21. Certainly it can be said that the treatment of breach of contract in a standard English textbook such as Treitel, *The Law of Contract* (8th edn., 1991), ch. 19 strikes one as being superficially more 'unitary' than the approach adopted by any of the modern South African textbooks. (Peter Cane points out that little more than 10 out of 800 or so pages of the 7th edn. of Treitel's *Contract* textbook are devoted to explicit discussion of what amounts to breach of contract: see Peter Cane, 'The Basis of Tortious Liability', in: Peter Cane and Jane Stapleton (eds.), *Essays for Patrick Atiyah* (1991), 351 sqq., 372, fn. 49.) Yet perhaps not too much should be made of this point, since it may be that many English law rules peculiar to 'specific forms of breach' are simply factored in at different places in the equation. See e.g. Treitel's discussion of 'stipulations as to time' at 724–30 of his *Contract* textbook, in the chapter entitled 'Performance'. Furthermore, it will become apparent from the discussion below that a number of the rules peculiar to 'specific types of breach' in modern South African law were in fact imported from English law.

[5] This story has been told on numerous occasions: see e.g. Coenraad Visser, 'The Principle *Pacta Servanda Sunt* in Roman and Roman-Dutch Law, With Specific Reference to Contracts in Restraint of Trade', (1984) 101 *SALJ* 641; Zimmermann (n. 1), 508 sqq., 537 sqq. For an illuminating recent account of this development in an international context see James Gordley, *The Philosophical Origins of Modern Contract Doctrine* (1991). Concerning 17th and 18th C. Dutch law see Robert Feenstra, 'Die Klagbarkeit der *pacta nuda*', in: Robert Feenstra, Reinhard Zimmermann (eds.), *Das römisch-holländische Recht: Fortschritte des Zivilrechts im 17. und 18. Jahrhundert* (1992), 123 sqq.

opment of the law relating to breach of contract over the period under discussion seems to pull in the opposite direction, demonstrating an increasing willingness to fracture itself into nominate 'specific types of breach'. This tension need not necessarily indicate incoherence or contradiction: it could be cogently argued that the policy issues which govern *the ascription of contractual responsibility* differ from those which govern the *award of remedies for enforcement*.[6] Nevertheless, on a superficial level these two contexts do seem to be characterized by disparate 'strains of commitment' within the common law,[7] and this justifies some examination of the historical process by means of which 'specific breaches' have become entrenched in the modern South African law.

It is this process which is examined below. Crucial to the fissured concept of breach in the modern law is the distinction—largely suppressed in English law[8]—between *time* and *content* of performance. The failure to perform timeously is said to amount to a specific form of breach known as *negative malperformance* (which comprises *mora debitoris* and *mora creditoris*); performance in a manner that fails to correspond with the content of the contractual duty is known as *positive malperformance*.[9] Writing in 1929, Van Zijl Steyn admitted that this distinction had been largely elided by judges and writers:

> *Die verhouding tussen wanprestasie en mora debitoris het nog nie die aandag van ons skrywers en Howe geniet nie. Daar word in die algemeen alleen gepraat van 'breach of contract', en daaronder word dan wanprestasie sowel as mora debitoris ingesluit.*[10]

Largely as a result of Van Zijl Steyn's own efforts, this fundamental fissure has become entrenched in our law during the course of this century,[11]

---

[6] Hugh Collins, *The Law of Contract* (1986), 179. See further the discussion in text to nn. 168–70 below.

[7] It might be argued that this 'divergence' is more apparent than real. The generalized theory for the ascription of contractual responsibility does not deny that 'specific contracts' continue to exist in modern law, albeit under the umbrella of an abstract consensual theory. Continuing in that vein, 'specific types of breach' in modern law might be said to be nominate forms which huddle together under the umbrella of a higher-level, 'unitary' concept of breach. That higher-level principles of law *do* exist in the context of breach of contract is evidenced by the ease with which we speak (for example) of a 'generalized right of cancellation for breach': see discussion in section III below, esp. n. 106. Perhaps it was this sort of linkage which informed the complaint of Watermeyer CJ in *Aucamp v. Morton* 1949 (3) SA 611 (A) 619, when he despaired of formulating a single test to govern the right of cancellation 'because *contracts* and *breaches of contract* take so many forms' (my emphasis).

[8] Sir J. W. Wessels, *The Law of Contract in South Africa*, vol. II (2nd edn., 1951), § 776.

[9] The *locus classicus* on the importance and origin of this distinction is I. van Zijl Steyn, *Mora Debitoris volgens die Hedendaagse Romeins-Hollandse Reg* (1929), 3–10.

[10] (The relationship between malperformance and *mora debitoris* has not yet attracted the attention of our writers and courts. Reference is merely made, as a rule, to 'breach of contract', and under this term malperformance as well as *mora debitoris* are included.) Van Zijl Steyn (n. 9), 4.

[11] See esp. *Sweet v. Ragerguhara* 1978 (1) SA 131 (D) 138. However, it has not been all one-way traffic. Some of the South African textbooks dating from the middle of the century

and it will be discussed further below. The other crucial development in the evolution of a fissured concept of breach was the reception into our law of a doctrine of 'anticipatory breach' from English law. This type of breach, which is itself said to take two different forms ('repudiation' and 'prevention of performance'), is also discussed below.

1. Negative malperformance

(a) Mora debitoris

In modern South African law *mora debitoris* is defined as culpable delay on the part of the debtor in performing an obligation that is due and enforceable, and that remains capable of performance in spite of such delay. Most of the reported judgments from the nineteenth century dealing with conduct that would today be subsumed under the heading of *mora debitoris* failed to mention such a label, and approached the issue of the debtor's delay in performance in a remarkably intuitive way.[12] However from the turn of the century, and especially after the publication of Van Zijl Steyn's thesis,[13] we begin to find in the case-law attempts to articulate the rules relating to *mora debitoris* as a form of breach in a more explicit and rigorous fashion.

The argument developed here is that judicial development of the principles of *mora debitoris* at that stage occurred under the influence of two rival gravitational forces: while the principles relating to the requirements for *mora debitoris* were articulated with reference to the Roman-Dutch writers, the rules allowing for cancellation on account of *mora debitoris* were developed largely on the basis of English law authorities. In the result, twin tracks of authority evolved to govern these two different spheres, and it is hardly surprising that the sticking points in the modern law of *mora debitoris* are situated at precisely those points where the two tracks have run into one another. In order to bolster this argument I discuss first the development of the law relating to the requirements for *mora debitoris*, and secondly the evolution of a right to cancel for *mora debitoris*.

The requirements for *mora debitoris*[14] were, at a fairly early stage,

---

presented a unitary notion of breach which seemed to fudge the distinction between positive and negative malperformance. For example, the first edn. of R. W. Lee, A. M. Honoré, *The South African Law of Obligations* (1950), 46 stated the principle of breach in very general terms: 'When a party to a contract, from whom performance is due, without lawful excuse fails to perform his promise, the contract is broken.' See also R. W. Lee, *An Introduction to Roman-Dutch Law* (4th edn., 1946), 264 sq. (although cf. App. H at 445–8). This distinction continues to be played down in the latest edition of a leading South African textbook: A. J. Kerr, *The Principles of the Law of Contract* (4th edn., 1989), ch. 20. Some judges have also claimed that the distinction is unhelpful: see *Broderick Properties Ltd v. Rood* 1962 (4) SA 447 (T) 450C.

[12] See e.g. *Richards Slater & Co v. Fuller & Co* (1880) 1 EDC 1; *Philip v. Metropolitan and Suburban Railway Co* (1893) 10 SC 52; *Searle & Son v. Arkell and Douglas* (1899) 16 SC 522.
[13] *Mora Debitoris Volgens die Hedendaagse Romeins-Hollandse Reg* (1929).
[14] On which see generally Zimmermann (n. 1), 791–9; Steyn (n. 9), 52 sqq.

anchored in the writings of the Roman-Dutch jurists. Thus, for example, two early judgments cited Voet, Van der Linden, and Van Leeuwen in support of the rule that *dies interpellat pro homine* in those situations where the contract expressly stipulated a date for performance.[15] The most fundamental distinction of all, that between *mora ex re* and *mora ex persona*,[16] was entrenched in South African law by the Appellate Division shortly after that Court's formation.[17] The need for an *interpellatio* to trigger *mora ex persona* was traced back to Roman-Dutch law,[18] as was the need for fault on the part of the debtor as a condition precedent for *mora debitoris*.[19] These fundamental requirements for *mora debitoris* have come down to us in the modern law in an almost unaltered form[20] (although the current practice seems not to require fault to be either specifically pleaded or proved by the creditor[21]).

The evolution of the innocent party's right to cancel the contract on account of *mora debitoris* followed a very different path. According to Roman-Dutch law, the innocent party was not allowed to cancel the contract on account of *mora debitoris* unless that power had been expressly conferred by a *lex commissoria*.[22] From the middle of the nineteenth century, however, we find judicial statements in South Africa which expressed a much broader principle in the language of a canonical formula allowing for cancellation 'where time was of the essence of the contract'.[23] This formula was expressly borrowed from English law, as was the test of Equity which

---

[15] *Thibart v. Thibart* (1840) 3 Menz 472; *Kessel v. Davis* 1905 TS 731, 733; cf. *Lee* (n. 11), 446–7.

[16] See Johannes Voet, *Commentarius ad Pandectas* (in: The Selective Voet, trans. Percival Gane, Durban, 1956), 20, 1, 25 sqq.; Simon van Leeuwen, *Censura Forensis* (trans. S. H. Barber and W. A. MacFadyen, Cape Town, 1896), 1, 4, 4, 21 sqq.; Willem Schorer, *Aantekeningen over de Inleidinge tot de Hollandsche Rechtsgeleerdheid van Hugo de Groot* (in: The Introduction to Dutch Jurisprudence of Hugo Grotius with an Appendix containing selections from the notes of Willem Schorer, trans. A. F. S. Maasdorp, 2nd edn., 1888), 2, 46, 6.

[17] *Victoria Falls and Transvaal Power Co Ltd v. Consolidated Langlaagte Mines Ltd* 1915 AD 1, 31.

[18] *Breytenbach v. Van Wijk* 1923 AD 541, 549; Steyn (n. 9), 52–64.

[19] *Victoria Falls and Transvaal Power Co Ltd v. Consolidated Langlaagte Mines Ltd* (n. 17), 32; *West Rand Estates Ltd v. New Zealand Insurance Co Ltd* 1926 AD 173; Steyn (n. 9), 43–51.

[20] See esp. *Hammer v. Klein* 1951 (2) SA 101 (A); *Nel v. Cloete* 1972 (2) SA 150 (A); *C & T Products (Pty) Ltd v. MH Goldschmidt (Pty) Ltd* 1981 (3) SA 619 (C); *Ver Elst v. Sabena Belgian World Airlines* 1983 (3) SA 637 (A); *Du Toit v. Standard General Insurance Co Ltd* 1994 (1) SA 682 (W). But cf. the discussion in the text below of the 'maverick' cases cited in n. 35.

[21] *Legogote Development Co (Pty) Ltd v. Delta Trust and Finance Co* 1970 (1) SA 584 (T) 587F; D. J. Joubert, *General Principles of the Law of Contract* (1987), 205.

[22] See the exhaustive discussion of the old authorities in Van Zijl Steyn (n. 9), 94 sqq., and the judgment of Maasdorp J in *Hiddingh v. Von Schade* (1899) 16 SC 128, 133. But cf. Wouter de Vos, *Verrykingsaanspreeklikheid in die Suid-Afrikaanse Reg* (3rd edn., 1987), 65, fn. 22.

[23] *Mitchell v. Howard Farrar & Co* (1886) 5 EDC 131; the judgment of Lord De Villiers CJ in *Hiddingh v. Von Schade* (n. 22); *Bergl & Co v. Trott Bros* (1903) 24 NLR 503; *Murphy v. Labuschagne & Central Coronation Syndicate Ltd* 1903 TS 393; *Hayward v. Berlin* 1914 EDL 57; *Bernard v. Sanderson* 1916 TPD 673; *Radue v. Kirsch* 1920 OPD 181; *Cowley v. Estate Loumeau* 1925 AD 392; *Lewis & Co v. Malkin* 1926 TPD 665.

had triumphed in England in 1873[24] for determining whether or not time should be taken to be of the essence in any particular contract. Indeed there can be little doubt that the English law rules regarding cancellation were simply taken over holus-bolus at the time, with no more than throw-away comments to the effect that these rules could be taken to be consistent with the principles of Roman-Dutch law.[25]

With hindsight we can now see that a remarkably dexterous fusion of sources was occurring in the law relating to *mora debitoris*: while the Roman-Dutch authorities were employed to determine the requirements for *mora debitoris* (and also one of the 'consequences' of *mora*, namely the payment of damages[26]), it fell to English law authorities to determine whether the innocent party should have a right to cancel for *mora debitoris* on the basis that 'time was of the essence of the contract'. Such a two-track approach to the sources can clearly be seen in the leading case of *Nel v. Cloete*.[27] In this case a majority of the Appellate Division held that it should be accepted as part of South African law that a creditor might 'make time of the essence' by unilaterally serving a so-called 'notice of rescission' on the debtor, reserving the right to cancel the contract if performance were not made by a stipulated date. While the Court accepted that such a right of cancellation was foreign to Roman-Dutch law,[28] the majority judgment also went out of its way to modify the English law principles relating to 'notices of rescission' so as to make those principles more harmonious with the Roman-Dutch institution of *mora debitoris*:

Vir sover die kennisweging op *in mora*-stelling gerig is, het dit werking volgens die reeds erkende beginsels van die Romeins-Hollandse reg. Vir sover die kennisgewing op moontlike terugtrede gerig is, slaan dit slegs op die bykomstige uitbreiding van 'n skuldeiser se regte waar mora intree. Dit is ook oorbodig om die verlening van hierdie reg tot terugtrede enigsins te koppel aan beginsels van die Engelse reg wat daarop betrekking het.[29]

---

[24] Section 25(7) Judicature Act 1873, replaced by s. 41 of the Law of Property Act 1925.

[25] In *Mitchell v. Howard Farrar & Co* (1886) 5 EDC 131, at 140, Barry JP stated that 'the rule of equity is now the general rule of English law (and as I think it has always been of Roman Dutch jurisprudence)'. In *Radue v. Kirsch* (n. 23), 187, McGregor J claimed that the expression regarding time being of the essence 'in substance doubtless accords sufficiently with the principles of Roman and Roman-Dutch law regarding the effect to be given to stipulations respecting time'. But cf. the divergent approaches adopted in the judgments delivered by De Villiers CJ and Maasdorp J in *Hiddingh v. Von Schade* (n. 22).

[26] *Silverton Estates Co v. Bellevue Syndicate* 1904 TS 462.   [27] 1972 (2) SA 150 (A).

[28] '*Ek het hierbo daarna gewys dat daar wel 'n leemte in ons reg was, wat daartoe gelei het dat die regspraak verplig was om 'n reg van terugtrede op grond van mora te erken in omstandighede waar sodanige verligting nie deur Romeinse- of Romeins-Hollandsereg geoorloof was nie*' (I have pointed out above that there was indeed a gap in our law with the result that the courts were obliged to recognize a right or rescission on the basis of *mora* in circumstances where such relief was not allowed in Roman or Roman-Dutch law) (*per* Wessels JA, 162 *in fine*).

[29] (As far as the giving of notice aims at placing [the other party] *in mora*, it operates according to the principles of Roman-Dutch law that have already been recognized. As far as the giving of notice aims at a possible rescission, it merely entails the incidental extension of a

This is pragmatism of the highest order. The Roman-Dutch *institution* of *mora* remained unaltered, but an additional *remedy* of cancellation (derived from English law) was superimposed thereon. This might be termed a strategy of 'divide and rule': having demarcated a division between the *institution* of *mora debitoris* and its *consequences*, the historic influence of English law sources could be restricted to the latter sphere while Roman-Dutch sources retained their overall hegemony. This was, no doubt, a neat and remarkably agile fusion of sources. However, such doctrinal subtlety comes at a price, for the strategy of divide and rule is apt to mislead those judges and commentators who find themselves unable to cope with the tortuous mental dexterity which the strategy demands. In the two instances next described the strategy of 'divide'—and, by extension, the strategy of 'rule'— has threatened to break down.

The first instance is this: although the majority judgment in *Nel v. Cloete* rejected a wholesale assimilation of the English law rules regarding cancellation for *mora debitoris*, it seemed to endorse the continued use of the expression 'time being of the essence'. A reasonable interpretation of that judgment might have claimed that cancellation would henceforth be allowed in three situations: first, where time was expressly of the essence (by virtue of an express *lex commissoria*); secondly, where time was 'impliedly of the essence'; and thirdly, where the creditor makes time of the essence by serving a notice of rescission. My concern here is with the second situation, where time is 'impliedly' of the essence of the contract. As we have already seen,[30] the early judgments had interpreted this phrase in an English law sense and so were prepared to follow English law presumptions (for example, to the effect that time was always of the essence in mercantile transactions[31]). However, a more recent judgment of the Appellate Division has suggested that this second category requires proof of a tacit *lex commissoria*.[32] This approach divorces the expression 'time being of the essence' from its English law roots, and reinstates to a position of prominence the Roman-Dutch centerpiece of a *lex commissoria* which now has to be *implied* into the contract.[33] If, though, it is intended that the tacit *lex commissoria* must now be capable of implication according to the full-blown test for tacit terms, then this amounts to an implicit rejection of the earlier case-law which had followed the English law test for determining whether 'time was

plaintiff's rights in case of *mora*. It is also unnecessary to link the granting of this right of rescission in any way to the principles of English law relating to it.) *Per* Wessels JA 163 *in fine-* 164A.

[30] See cases cited in n. 23 above.   [31] *Lewis & Co v. Malkin* 1926 TPD 665.

[32] *Greenfield Manufacturers (Temba) (Pty) Ltd v. Royton Electrical Engineering (Pty) Ltd* 1976 (2) SA 565 (A) 569B-F, 571F-H.

[33] This was the approach advocated by Van Zijl Steyn (n. 9), 104–5, who urged that the expression 'time being of the essence' should be rejected outright in favour of 'ons eie terminologie: *lex commissoria*' (112).

of the essence' without going through the motions of applying the officious-bystander test for tacit terms.[34] In other words, to retain the English law expression 'time being of the essence' as an empty conceptual vessel which is henceforth to be filled with the Roman-Dutch notion of a tacit *lex commissoria* amounts to judicial sleight of hand.

A second instance of the breakdown of the strategy of divide and rule is encapsulated within a run of cases initiated by *Federal Tobacco Works v. Baron and Co.*[35] This line of authority provides that in contracts where 'time is of the essence' the debtor will automatically fall into *mora* after the elapse of a reasonable time, even though no date for performance was stipulated in the contract itself. For those who have mastered the doctrinal strategy of divide and rule the error is immediately obvious: the reference to 'time being of the essence' is quite simply a *non sequitur* at that point in the equation, since this expression refers 'to the *consequences* of the breach and not to the *breach itself*'.[36] That is, this English law expression is to be restricted to a limited sphere of operation in the context of the consequences of *mora*; it has nothing to tell us about the requirements for (or the institution of) *mora debitoris*. The almost unanimous view of commentators that this line of cases is wrongly decided thus originates from those who believe that at the level of sources the distinction between the *requirements for* and the *consequences of mora debitoris* should be preserved.[37]

(b) Mora creditoris

While *mora debitoris* has now become firmly entrenched as a 'specific breach' in modern South African law, its counterpart of *mora creditoris* occupies a much more shadowy position and is still shrouded in enigma. Considered analytically, it makes sense to treat *mora creditoris* as a separate form of breach only if it is possible to explain why the 'duty' on party A to co-operate with party B in the discharge of B's contractual obligation is significantly different from the sort of duty that would fall under the heading of *mora debitoris*. That is, it must be explained how the duty on A *qua creditor* is in some essential respect different from a duty that rests on A *qua*

---

[34] Cf. Schalk van der Merwe, L. F. van Huyssteen, M. F. B. Reinecke, G. F. Lubbe, J. G. Lotz, *Contract: General Principles* (1993), 249. Thus Joubert (n. 21), 238 suggests that 'since the real intention of the parties rests on a supposition and cannot be contradicted, it may be easier to infer a term implied by the law'.

[35] 1904 TS 483. The cases which followed this judgment include: *Benoni Produce and Coal Co Ltd v. Gundelfinger* 1918 TPD 453; *Graf & Co v. Bassa* (1925) 25 NPD 1; *Crook v. Pedersen Ltd* 1927 WLD 62; *Meyerowiz v. Annetts* 1937 NPD 140; *Broderick Properties Ltd v. Rood* 1962 (4) SA 447 (T).

[36] *Per* Trengove J in *Alfred McAlpine & Son (Pty) Ltd v. Transvaal Provincial Administration* 1977 (4) SA 310 (T) 347G-H (emphasis added).

[37] See *Nel v. Cloete* 1972 (2) SA 150 (A) 177B-D; Wouter de Vos, '*Mora Debitoris* and Rescission', (1970) 87 *SALJ* 304, 313–6; J. C. de Wet, A. H. van Wyk, *Die Suid-Afrikaanse Kontraktereg en Handelsreg,* vol. I (5th edn., 1992), 161 sqq. But cf. Kerr (n. 11), 453–6.

debtor. Roman law and Roman-Dutch law (unlike English law) were prepared to offer such an explanation, and so treated *mora creditoris* as a separate form of breach.[38] Building on the Roman-Dutch texts, it has fallen in particular to A. B. de Villiers[39] and J. C. de Wet[40] to develop *mora creditoris* as a distinct type of breach in South African law, and these rules have largely tracked the analogous rules in the context of *mora debitoris*.[41]

The courts, in contrast, have been somewhat tardy in accepting the challenge. As recently as 1984, Coetzee J complained that counsel in a case before him had resisted a suggestion from the bench that he should apply the principles of *mora creditoris*:

I mentioned to Mr. Schutz in argument that it seemed to be a case of mora creditoris and that its principles should be applied. Counsel however eschewed this legal concept and still persisted therein at the stage of the application for leave to appeal. He dealt with it as if it were an invention of De Wet and Yeats.[42]

While it may be conceded that *mora creditoris* is not 'an invention of De Wet and Yeats', nonetheless there are to my knowledge only ten South African judgments in which its existence as an independent form of breach has been referred to. Many of the early judgments cited by De Wet in this context failed to refer expressly to *mora creditoris* as a type of breach, and so cannot be said to advance the argument in any significant way.[43] Of those judgments which did refer expressly to *mora creditoris*, five involved no more than a passing reference that was probably *obiter* in each case,[44] and two judgments involved the quoting of passages from the textbook of De Wet and Yeats.[45]

That leaves merely three judgments of which it could be said that the existence of *mora creditoris* as an independent type of breach was integral to

---

[38] Zimmermann (n. 1), 817–23; generally on *mora creditoris* in modern comparative law cf. *idem*, 'Konturen eines Europäischen Vertragsrechts', 1995 *Juristenzeitung* 489 sq.

[39] *Mora creditoris as Vorm van Kontrakbreuk* (unpublished LL D thesis, Stellenbosch, 1953). This thesis is cited by De Wet/Van Wyk (n. 37), 180, fn. 142, but is not available to me.

[40] De Wet/Van Wyk (n. 37), 180–93.

[41] For a detailed discussion of the modern law see Joubert (n. 21), 214 sqq.

[42] *Ranch International Pipelines (Transvaal) (Pty) Ltd v. LMG Construction (City) (Pty) Ltd* 1984 (3) SA 861 (W) 877B.

[43] In this category I would include cases such as: *Jacobs v. Maree* (1902) 19 SC 152; *National Bank of South Africa Ltd v. Leon Levson Studios Ltd* 1913 AD 213; *Jacobson v. Haddad & Co* 1920 OPD 116; *Gibson Bros v. Abrahamson and Son* 1921 CPD 622; *Leviseur v. A Rosin & Co* 1921 OPD 62; *Leviseur v. Frankfort Boere Ko-operatiewe Vereeniging* 1921 OPD 80; *M Leviseur & Co v. Highveld Supply Stores* 1922 OPD 233; *Van Loggenberg v. Sachs* 1940 WLD 253.

[44] *Wingerin v. Ross* 1951 (2) SA 82 (C) 86D-E; *Forfif v. MacBain* 1984 (3) SA 611 (W); *Boland Bank v. Pienaar* 1988 (3) SA 618 (A) 622J; *Chrysafis v. Katsapas* 1988 (4) SA 818 (A) 827H-J; *CIR v. First National Industrial Bank* 1990 (3) SA 641 (A) 651H.

[45] *Aubrey Feinberg Investments (Pty) Ltd v. Runge* 1981 (2) SA 598 (T) 606; *Le Roux v. Yskor Landgoed (Edms) Bpk* 1984 (4) SA 252 (T) 258D.

the *ratio*.[46] The ambivalent attitude of our courts to the subject is well captured by the fact that the seminal judgment of the Appellate Division in the
McAlpine case[47] has been cited in support of both *mora debitoris*[48] and *mora
creditoris*.[49] Perhaps the most that can be said is that *mora creditoris* is an
'inchoate' type of breach, firmly rooted in Roman-Dutch principle but still
waiting to be fully developed in modern case-law.

2. Positive malperformance

While a lawyer trained in the common law tradition would be likely to think
of 'positive malperformance' as the primary category of breach, this form
of breach enjoys a curiously marginalized status in the Roman-Dutch
authorities and in modern South African textbooks. It seems to occupy
something of a residual position: a convenient grab-bag in which are stuffed
all those breaches which cannot be accommodated elsewhere. Academic
interest regarding the requirements for positive malperformance has focused
on the need for fault on the side of the breaching party. While the Roman-
Dutch writers provide little assistance in this regard, there is some modern
academic writing which takes the view that fault is a requirement for positive malperformance in South African law.[50] This proposition would if
adopted set our law apart from English law in a most significant way,[51] but
it must be approached with some caution: to my knowledge there are no
cases which stipulate that fault is a requirement for positive malperformance, and there is at least one Appellate Division *dictum* to the contrary.[52]

By far the most interesting development in the context of this form of
breach is the evolution of a generalized right to cancel the contract for positive malperformance. Roman-Dutch law allowed for cancellation if the

---

[46] *Ranch International Pipelines (Transvaal) (Pty) Ltd v. LMG Construction (City) (Pty)
Ltd* (n. 42) in which Coetzee J at 877C described *mora creditoris* as 'an important and valuable doctrine in our law'; *Erasmus v. Pienaar* 1984 (4) SA 9 (T) 20–21; *LTA Construction Ltd
v. Minister of Public Works and Land Affairs* 1992 (1) SA 837 (C) 848–849.

[47] *Alfred McAlpine & Son (Pty) Ltd v. TPA* 1974 (3) SA 506 (A).

[48] *Alfred McAlpine & Son (Pty) Ltd v. TPA* (n. 36), 338 sqq.

[49] *Ranch International Pipelines (Transvaal) (Pty) Ltd v. LMG Construction (City) (Pty)
Ltd* (n. 42), 878. Coetzee J argued that the *mora creditoris* interpretation was 'the purer
approach, juridically speaking, one which is more firmly rooted, to my mind, in the principles
and system of Roman-Dutch law' (882D-E).

[50] A. D. J. van Rensburg, J. G. Lotz, T. A. R. van Rhijn, 'Contract' in: W. A. Joubert (ed.),
The Law of South Africa, vol. 5 (1978), § 221; P. M. Nienaber, 'Kontrakbreuk *in Anticipando*
in Retrospek', (1989) *TSAR* 6; N. J van der Merwe, P. J. J. Olivier, *Die Onregmatige Daad in
die Suid-Afrikaanse Reg* (6th edn., 1989), 479 sqq.; Van der Merwe, Van Huyssteen *et al.* (n.
34), 237–8.

[51] Cf. Zimmermann (n. 1), 815; Treitel, *Remedies* (n. 4), 8–9; Carter (n. 4), 38.

[52] *Per* Van Heerden JA in *Administrator Natal v. Edouard* 1990 (3) SA 581 (A) 597E-F:
'fault is not a requirement for a claim for damages based upon a breach of contract.' Due to
constraints of space it is not possible for me to consider the role of 'supervening impossibility
of performance (without fault)' in this context.

contract expressly reserved such a right by means of a so-called *lex commissoria*, and otherwise in very restricted circumstances.[53] Since the middle of the nineteenth century, however, South African courts have been moving in the direction of creating a generalized right to cancel the contract when the positive malperformance is 'sufficiently material'. The test for 'materiality' justifying cancellation has been expressed in various ways at different times. The early cases required the defective performance to 'concern a vital part of the contract'[54] or to 'amount to a failure to substantially perform'[55], or to amount to a breach of 'condition' in the English law sense of that term.[56] In recent cases the right to cancel has become completely generalized, and the currently preferred terminology requires that the defect must 'go to the root of the contract'.[57] There is no doubt that this highly significant development occurred under the direct influence of English law. Most of the tests which have been employed for 'materiality' in this context can be traced back to English law,[58] and indeed the courts have been unusually candid in acknowledging the location of their sources in the common law tradition.[59]

Constraints of space prohibit any detailed discussion here of the *exceptio non adimpleti contractus*. The *exceptio non adimpleti contractus* is primarily relevant to the order in which contractual performances must occur, but can also provide a defence when a defendant is sued *ex contractu* by a plaintiff who had earlier rendered defective performance of an *obligatio faciendi*.[60] In a famous trilogy of cases decided at the turn of the century the Appellate Division held that in certain circumstances a plaintiff in this scenario might have an enrichment-based remedy against a defendant who was utilizing the defective performance.[61] Sixty-five years later the relevant principles were comprehensively redrafted by Jansen JA in the leading case of *BK Tooling*[62]

---

[53] See the Roman-Dutch authorities cited in De Wet/Van Wyk (n. 37), 179, fn. 129. See further nn. 104, 105 below.

[54] *Strachan v. Prinsloo* 1925 TPD 709, at 718.

[55] *Cedarmont Store v. Webster & Co* 1922 TPD 106. Cf. *Holz v. Thurston & Co* 1908 TS 158; *Trinder v. Taylor* 1921 TPD 517.

[56] *MacDonald v. Hume* 1875 Buch 8.

[57] *Oatarian Properties (Pty) Ltd v. Maroun* 1973 (3) SA 779 (A) 784G; *Elgin Brown & Hamer (Pty) Ltd v. Industrial Machinery Suppliers (Pty) Ltd* 1993 (3) SA 424 (A) 430I-J. For earlier use of this formulation see *Transvaal Cold Storage Co v. SA Meat Export Co Ltd* 1917 TPD 413.

[58] The complexity of this aspect of English law is notorious. For a modern statement of the applicable principles see Treitel, *Contract* (n. 4), 659 sqq.

[59] See esp. *Strachan v. Prinsloo* (n. 54); *Aucamp v. Morton* 1949 (3) SA 611 (A). But cf. *Radiotronics (Pty) Ltd v. Scot Lindberg & Co Ltd* 1951 (1) SA 312 (C) 329C, where Van Zyl J stated that '[t]he right to rescind upon a breach of a material term is merely a *lex commissoria* implied by the operation of law'. On the influence of Pothier in this development see text to nn. 115–17 below.

[60] On the background see Zimmermann (n. 1), 801, fn. 133.

[61] *Hauman v. Nortje* 1914 AD 293; *Breslin v. Hichens* 1914 AD 312; *Van Rensburg v. Straughan* 1914 AD 317.

[62] *BK Tooling (Edms) Bpk v. Scope Precision Engineering (Edms) Bpk* 1979 (1) SA 391 (A).

so as to create a discretionary power in the court to relax the principle of reciprocity in circumstances where equity required that the plaintiff should have a contractual remedy for a reduced price. This remarkable judgment was an outstanding blend of legal scholarship and pragmatic common sense, an erudite fusion of civilian and common law sources. In the development of an indigenous South African law of breach of contract, the case of *BK Tooling* stands alone as a towering high point.[63]

3. Anticipatory breach

(a) Anticipatory repudiation

The Roman-Dutch writers did not recognize the type of breach now known in South African law as anticipatory repudiation[64] and it is unanimously accepted that the doctrine was received into our law from English law. The early cases adopted a flamboyantly cavalier stance in this regard, citing English judgments on anticipatory repudiation with full-scale approval and implying in throw-away judicial asides that our law could simply be taken to correspond with English principles.[65] Notwithstanding the lack of Roman-Dutch authority, it has been accepted by the Appellate Division[66] and even by J. C. de Wet[67] that anticipatory repudiation is now firmly established as part of modern South African law.

More recently, however, some attempts have been made to integrate the

---

[63] It is worth noting that the academic subtleties of the judgment in *BK Tooling* have not always been appreciated by hard-pressed practitioners. For recent examples of parties who have noticeably failed to plead and prove in accordance with the *ratio* of *BK Tooling* see *Fritsch v. Eckrats (Pty) Ltd t/a Wally Pools* 1990 (3) SA 242 (N); *N. Goodwin Design (Pty) Ltd v. Moscak* 1992 (1) SA 154 (C); *Retail Management Services (Edms) Bpk v. Schwartz* 1992 (2) SA 22 (W). A book widely used in practice, L. T. C. Harms, *Amler's Precedents of Pleadings* (4th edn., 1993), 140–2, gives in my view a slightly misleading account of the implications of *BK Tooling* for this area of law.

[64] On the lack of Roman-Dutch authority see P. M. Nienaber, 'Enkele Beskouinge oor Kontrakbreuk *in Anticipando*', (1963) 26 *THRHR* 19, 29–30; *Crest Enterprises (Pty) Ltd v. Rycklof Beleggings (Edms) Bpk* 1972 (2) SA 863 (A) 869D, which quotes with approval from an unpublished thesis by P. M. Nienaber, *Anticipatory Repudiation in English and South African Law of Contract*; Joubert (n. 21), 210. But cf. De Vos (n. 22), 65, fn. 22.

[65] See e.g. *Executors of Evans v. Stranack* (1890) 11 NLR 12 (quoting with approval at 22 from the English case of *Johnstone v. Milling* (1886) 16 QBD 460); *Bergl & Co v. Trott Bros.* (1903) 24 NLR 503, 515–16; *Delany v. Medefindt* 1908 EDC 200 (citing the leading English case of *Hochster v. De la Tour* (1853) 2 El & Bl 678); *De Wet v. Kuhn* 1910 CPD 263 (citing *Johnstone v. Milling (supra)*); *Bernard v. Sanderson* 1916 TPD 673 (where De Villiers JP asserted, at 676, that '[o]ur law is the same as the English law on that point'); *Machanick v. Bernstein* 1920 CPD 380 (quoting with approval from *Frost v. Knight* 26 LT 77 (= (1872) LR 7 Exch 111)); *Strachan v. Lloyd Levy* 1923 AD 670 (in which De Villiers JA quoted from *Johnstone v. Milling (supra)* and concluded, at 671: '[t]hat is our law as well as the English law').

[66] *Novick v. Benjamin* 1972 (2) SA 842 (A); *Crest Enterprises (Pty) Ltd v. Rycklof Beleggings (Edms) Bpk* (n. 64); *Tuckers Land and Development Corp (Pty) Ltd v. Hovis* 1980 (1) SA 645 (A); *Culverwell v. Brown* 1990 (1) SA 7 (A).

[67] De Wet/Van Wyk (n. 37), 169.

English doctrine of anticipatory repudiation with the underlying principles of Roman-Dutch law. The most celebrated attempt at integration occurred in *Tuckers Land and Development Corporation (Pty) Ltd v. Hovis*,[68] where Jansen JA grafted anticipatory breach onto South African law by depicting it as 'the violation of an obligation *ex lege*, flowing from the requirement of *bona fides* which underlies our law of contract'.[69] While this attempt to make the concept of *bona fides* carry such a heavy load has been criticized,[70] in my view the judgment stands out as a remarkably innovative instance of doctrinal fusion in that it resurrected a Roman-Dutch doctrine often marginalized within mainstream contract law in order to effect the graft.

Another example of an attempt to superimpose Roman-Dutch principles onto the common law doctrine of anticipatory repudiation challenges the orthodox 'offer and acceptance' model for repudiation. The case-law from the turn of the century consistently adopted the following construction regarding the consequences of repudiation: the innocent party could either 'accept the repudiation' (thereby cancelling the contract) or 'reject the repudiation' (in which case the act of repudiation would effectively fall away).[71] This offer-and-acceptance construction was clearly borrowed from English law:

Die leerstuk van kontrakbreuk in anticipando *is van betreklike resente oorsprong, 'n maaksel van die Engelse regters oor die laaste 50 jaar of wat van die vorige eeu. Daar mag spore van so-iets in die Romeins-Hollandse reg wees maar as 'n leerstuk op sy eie is dit nooit beskryf nie. Dit het ons via die Engelse reg bereik. Die eienaardighede van die leerstuk, soos die gedagte dat aanvaarding deur die onskuldige die skuldige se kontrakbreuk voltooi, kom holus bolus daarvandaan.*[72]

In an influential article published in 1963 P. M. Nienaber argued that the offer-and-acceptance model was internally incoherent, had no Roman-Dutch basis, and should be rejected in favour of a construction which would regard repudiation as an immediate breach which puts the innocent party to an election but does not require 'acceptance' in order to become complete.[73] The foundational premise for Nienaber's argument was that the

---

[68] N. 66.   [69] At 652G.

[70] P. M. Nienaber, 'Kontrakbreuk *in Anticipando* in Retrospek', 1989 *TSAR* 1, 8–9. Cf. *Dawnford Investments CC v. Schuurman* 1994 (2) SA 412 (N) 418H–419D.

[71] In addition to the cases cited in n. 65 above see *Bacon v. Hartshorne* (1899) 16 SC 230; *Geldenhuys and Neethling v. Beuthin* 1918 AD 426 at 444; *Kameel Tin Co (Pty) Ltd v. Brollomar Tin Exploration Ltd* 1928 TPD 726; *Central Produce Co v. Hirschowitz* 1938 TPD 350.

[72] (The doctrine of anticipatory breach of contract is of rather recent origin, a product of the English courts over the last 50 years or so of the last century. There may be traces of something like it in Roman-Dutch law but it has never been described as a doctrine in its own right. It has reached us via English law. The characteristic features of the doctrine, such as the idea that an acceptance on the part of the innocent party completes the other party's breach, derive holus bolus from thence.) Nienaber, 1989 *TSAR* 15.

[73] Nienaber, (1963) 26 *THRHR* 32 sqq.

English tradition which gave us the doctrine of anticipatory repudiation was rich in detail but poor in systematic principle; his recasting of the rules was expressly an attempt to reconcile the institution of repudiation with Roman-Dutch principles of contract law.[74] This very persuasive argument has enjoyed a mixed reception in the case-law, where it has been partially endorsed[75] but also emphatically denounced.[76] The most recent judgments of the Appellate Division, seemingly oblivious to the existence of the debate, continue to use the language of 'offer and acceptance' in the context of anticipatory repudiation[77]—indeed on one occasion this was said to be 'trite' law.[78] The modern law on this topic is most unsatisfactory, and the confusion is a direct result of the hodge-podge of historical sources which have gone into the brew.

A more successful illustration of the way in which Roman-Dutch principle might be fused with an English law institution is provided by consideration of the manner in which damages are assessed for anticipatory repudiation. Jansen JA signposted the proposed fusion clearly in 1972:

The concept of an unlawful repudiation before the appointed time of performance as constituting a breach, enabling the innocent party to sue for damages immediately if he so elects, is derived from English law, and represents a departure from the Roman-Dutch law. It does not follow, however, that such departure should affect the fundamentals of that law in respect of the assessment of damages. On the contrary, principle would dictate a retention of those fundamentals even in relation to a novel form of breach.[79]

Jansen JA went on to hold that in the case of an 'accepted' anticipatory breach damages are to be assessed in relation to the date of performance (subject to the mitigation rule). It so happened that this rule did correspond (fortuitously) with the English rule[80] but in the South African context the justification was said to be that the rule was 'squarely based on the fundamental principle of our law that the innocent party should be placed in the position he would have occupied had the contract been performed'.[81]

---

[74] See esp. Nienaber, 1989 *TSAR* 15.

[75] *NKP Kunsmisverspreiders (Edms) Bpk v. Sentrale Kunsmiskorporasie (Edms) Bpk* 1973 (2) SA 680 (T); *Tuckers Land and Development Corporation (Pty) Ltd v. Hovis* (n. 66), 652G; *Erasmus v. Pienaar* 1984 (4) SA 9 (T); *Moodley v. Moodley* 1990 (1) SA 427 (D); *Dawnford Investments C.C. v. Schuurman* (n. 70), 419–20.

[76] *HMBMP Properties (Pty) Ltd v. King* 1981 (1) SA 906 (N) 912. Cf. *Veneta Mineraria Spa v. Carolina Collieries (Pty) Ltd* 1985 (3) SA 633 (D) 644 where the dispute was referred to but not resolved.

[77] *Nash v. Golden Dumps (Pty) Ltd* 1985 (3) SA 1 (A) 22E; *Atteridgeville Town Council v. Livanos t/a Livanos Bros Electrical* 1992 (1) SA 296 (A) 304B-C; *OK Bazaars (1929) Ltd v. Grosvenor Buildings (Pty) Ltd* 1993 (3) SA 471 (A) 481D.

[78] *Culverwell v. Brown* (n. 66), 28G.

[79] *Novick v. Benjamin* (n. 66), 853H-854A.   [80] Ibid. 857E.

[81] At 857G. See also *Culverwell v. Brown* (n. 66), 25 sqq.

(b) Prevention of performance

According to Roman-Dutch law, the doctrine of supervening impossibility of performance operated to discharge the obligations of the contracting parties without breach as long as there was no fault on the part of the contractors.[82] What would be the position if the contracting party disabled himself from performing the contract by virtue of his own default before the arrival of the date for performance? Although some Roman-Dutch texts suggest that such conduct would amount to breach,[83] these authorities noticeably fail to provide us with any detailed exposition of the legal rules.[84] In *McCabe v. Burisch*[85] Tindall J said that he could find little guidance on this issue in the Roman-Dutch authorities, but stated that he would expect any 'rational system of law' to take the view that such conduct amounted to breach of contract.[86] Today it is generally accepted that culpable conduct which renders performance absolutely or relatively impossible amounts to a form of breach known as 'prevention of performance',[87] although there have been very few cases on the point.

In a sense, the answer to the stated question is inevitable if the antecedent acceptance of 'anticipatory repudiation' is accepted as a form of breach in South African law. If a party who indicates in advance of the date set for performance that he has no intention of performing is held to commit a breach at that stage, why should the law treat more favourably a party who disables himself from performing on the set date? Interestingly, this seems to have been the chronological direction of development in South African case-law: from the initial reception of *repudiation* to the subsequent acceptance of *prevention of performance* as a form of breach. In a 1930 judgment Tindall J expressed the point as follows:

The principle of 'anticipatory breach' by a total refusal, even before the time of performance has arrived, to perform the contract, has often been applied by our courts. If that doctrine is part of our law, I know of no reason for saying that the doctrine applied in *Ford v. Tiley* [see n. 89] and *Lovelock v. Franklyn* [see n. 89] is not in accordance with the principles of our law. After all, the doctrine is only common sense.[88]

This amounts to a complete reversal of the direction of development followed in English law. The English courts had accepted at an early stage that

[82] Consideration of this doctrine falls outside of the scope of the present article. See generally W. A. Ramsden, *Supervening Impossibility of Performance in the South African Law of Contract* (1985).
[83] See e.g. Hugo Grotius, *Inleiding tot de Hollandsche Rechtsgeleertheyd*, 3, 46, 3; Voet (n. 16), 45, 1, 24; Van Leeuwen (n. 16), 1, 4, 39, 1.
[84] Van Rensburg/Lotz/Van Rhijn (n. 50), § 231, fn. 1.
[85] 1930 TPD 261.
[86] At 268. See also *Marquard & Co v. Biccard* 1921 AD 366, 378; *Loubser v. Vorster and Vorster* 1944 CPD 380.
[87] See, for example, De Wet/Van Wyk (n. 37), 172 sqq.
[88] *McCabe v. Burisch* (n. 85), 268–9.

a party who disabled himself from performing by his own default was liable for breach of contract even though the date for performance had not yet arrived.[89] Though we tend to forget the point today, the landmark 1853 judgment in *Hochster v. De la Tour*[90] built on those earlier decisions in extending the doctrine of anticipatory breach to include the intimation of a refusal to perform on the set date.[91]

Perhaps this curious reversal of direction in South African law explains why the outlines of prevention of performance as a form of breach have not yet been clearly drawn in modern law, and why its relationship with repudiation continues to be obscure.[92] De Wet, for example, takes the view that prevention of performance as a form of breach exists whether the performance has been rendered absolutely or relatively impossible.[93] Nienaber, in contrast, is of the opinion that relative prevention of performance is indistinguishable from repudiation and should be treated as such.[94] The latter view seemed to enjoy the support of Jansen JA in the *Hovis* case,[95] where he intimated that the *genus* of 'anticipatory breach' should not be subdivided in a random and *ad hoc* way. The matter, however, has still to be resolved with judicial rigour.

4. Conclusion: the development of 'specific breaches'

The preceding discussion has sought to marshal evidence in support of the following proposition: within the past hundred years the concept of breach of contract in South African law has been fracturing into a number of 'specific breaches', separated from one another by increasingly deep-set doctrinal chasms. In some instances (most notably in the case of *mora debitoris*) the historical roots can be traced back to Roman-Dutch law. In other instances (of which repudiation provides the best example) the roots penetrate deep into English law. Academic writings have been exceptionally influential in the process of fissure, and it is noteworthy that the modern rules regarding three forms of breach have to a large extent been articulated in three separate doctoral dissertations.[96]

One risk attends such a process of fissure: specific breaches which have

---

[89] *Bowdell v. Parsons* (1808) 10 East 359, 103 ER 811; *Lovelock v. Franklyn* (1846) 8 QB 371, 115 ER 916; *Ford v. Tiley* (1827) 6 B & C 325, 108 ER 472.

[90] (1853) 2 El & Bl 678.

[91] A point emphasized by Nienaber, (1963) 26 *THRHR* 23–6.

[92] The confusion is illustrated by *Stern v. Vesta Industries (Pty) Ltd* 1976 (1) SA 81 (W) 85, where Colman J seemed to interprete *McCabe v. Burisch* (n. 85) as a case about *repudiation*.

[93] De Wet/Van Wyk (n. 37), 176–7. See also Van Rensburg/Lotz/Van Rhijn (n. 50) 228.

[94] Nienaber, (1963) 26 *THRHR* 36; *idem*, 1989 *TSAR* 1–2.

[95] *Tuckers Land and Development Corporation (Pty) Ltd v. Hovis* (n. 66), 652H–653A.

[96] Van Zijl Steyn on *mora debitoris* (n. 9), De Villiers on *mora creditoris* (n. 39), and Nienaber on repudiation (n. 64).

developed independently will almost inevitably come into conflict where they are forced to 'cross' one another. A survey of the history of breach of contract reveals numerous instances of such dissonance, where the principles articulated in the context of one type of breach do not gel with the rules of another 'independent' form of breach. A ready example is provided by comparing *mora debitoris* with positive malperformance. It has recently been said that 'these two forms of breach of contract are different in character and that different rules relating to the right to cancel apply to each'.[97] That is no doubt correct as a matter of law, and yet the application of those different rules can lead to dissonance in the case of a contract that does not contain a *lex commissoria*. It is anomalous that a debtor in this situation who fails to perform a vital term is better placed than one whose timeous performance is materially defective; yet in the former case the debtor must receive a 'notice of rescission' before a right to cancel accrues, while in the latter case the creditor can cancel immediately.[98]

Given that different legal consequences attach to different types of breach, much is made to turn on which 'pigeon-hole' the conduct of the party in breach is slotted into. A historical survey of South African contract law reveals numerous penumbral cases where the choice of the correct pigeon-hole was a matter of some difficulty. In terms of 'strict theory' it can be said that there are judgments in which *mora creditoris* has mistakenly been labelled as *mora debitoris*,[99] repudiation has been confused with *mora debitoris*,[100] *mora debitoris* has incorrectly been conflated with positive malperformance,[101] and prevention of performance has been wrongly interpreted as repudiation.[102] While modern contract theorists often find it necessary to lament these supposedly fundamental errors,[103] the truth is that such problems of characterization are an inevitable by-product of the movement in our law towards an increasingly fissured notion of breach of contract.

---

[97] *Sweet v. Ragerguhara* 1978 (1) SA 131 (D) 138E (*per* Kumleben J).

[98] Ibid. 138F-H. One method of reconciling the outcome in each case would be to imply a tacit *lex commissoria* into the former contract on the basis that 'time was of the essence': see n. 32 above. On the different consequences that will attach to conduct in breach depending on whether the conduct is pigeonholed as 'repudiation' or '*mora creditoris*' see *Erasmus v. Pienaar* (n. 75), 18 sqq.

[99] See the differing interpretations placed upon *Alfred McAlpine & Son (Pty) Ltd v. TPA* 1974 (3) SA 506 (A) in the 2 cases cited in nn. 48 and 49 above.

[100] *Crook v. Pedersen Ltd* 1927 WLD 62; *Strachan & Co Ltd v. Natal Milling Co (Pty) Ltd* 1936 NPD 327.

[101] *Young v. Land Values Ltd* 1924 WLD 216; *Broderick Properties Ltd v. Rood* 1962 (4) SA 447 (T).

[102] *Stern v. Vesta Industries (Pty) Ltd* (n. 92), 85, and cf. the discussion in text to n. 94 above.

[103] See esp. De Vos, (1970) 87 *SALJ* 304, 318-23.

III. CANCELLATION AS A REMEDY FOR BREACH OF CONTRACT

1. Availability of the remedy of cancellation

The discussion of the different types of breach of contract in Section II above canvassed the circumstances in which cancellation for each type of breach will be permitted. Indeed a significant function of the fissured concept of breach in South African law is to characterize the different types of conduct which will allow an innocent party to 'exit' from the contract. I shall not repeat those specific observations here, but make instead some more general remarks about the development of the right to cancel for breach of contract.

The most significant point is this: although Roman-Dutch law casuistically recognized certain specific instances of cancellation for breach (such as the *actio redhibitoria* for latent defects in contracts of sale[104]) it had no general rule allowing for cancellation on account of breach.[105] In modern law, however, our courts have come to recognize a right to cancel for breach of contract which is generalized in such a way as to operate outside of the catalogue of Roman-Dutch instances of cancellation.[106] Although this development is often traced to the turn of the century[107] the precise date is difficult to pinpoint. It is possible to locate reported judgments from the end of the nineteenth century and the early years of the twentieth century which allowed for cancellation on the basis of what appears to be a generalized

---

[104] For a full discussion of the circumstances in which Roman-Dutch law allowed for cancellation in contracts of sale and lease see J. R. Harker, *The Nature and Scope of Rescission as a Remedy for Breach of Contract* (unpublished Ph.D. thesis, University of Natal, 1981), 181 sqq.

[105] *Stewart Wrightson (Pty) Ltd v. Thorpe* 1977 (2) SA 943 (A) 953A-B; *Goldberg v. Buytendag Boerdery Beleggings (Edms) Bpk* 1980 (4) SA 775 (A) 791A-B; *Spies v. Lombard* 1950 (3) SA 469 (A) 487B-C; Van Zijl Steyn (n. 9) 95 sqq.; Zimmermann (n. 1), 800 sqq.; Harker (n. 104), 180, 211; *idem*, 'The Nature and Scope of Rescission as a Remedy for Breach of Contract in American and South African Law', 1980 *Acta Juridica* 61, 69 sq.; *idem*, 'Damages for Breach of Contract: Negative or Positive interesse', (1994) 111 *SALJ* 5, 8. The formulation in the text should perhaps be qualifed by the following 2 riders. First, it seems likely that a more general right to cancel for breach began to evolve in the later period of Roman-Dutch law: see Harker (n. 104), 190 sqq. Secondly, the Roman-Dutch law of *locatio conductio* allowed for cancellation in a less circumscribed list of circumstances than did the law of sale: see Harker (n. 104), 204 sqq.

[106] Harker (n. 104), 211 has pointed out that '[i]nasmuch as it did not have a generelized [sic] theory of contract, Roman-Dutch law also did not develop a general notion which entitled a party aggrieved by breach to claim to be relieved of his obligations arising out of a contract'. This is true, but it should be borne in mind that on a different level the concept of breach of contract is itself a 'fissured' one in the modern law: it is the *type* of breach which functions to determine the specific circumstances in which the 'generalized' right of cancellation can be exercised by an aggrieved party.

[107] This is the time-frame adopted by most of the authorities cited in n. 105.

right.[108] In 1883, however, Connor CJ stated: '[i]t seems to be settled in our law, that an express contract cannot, in general, be withdrawn from, at the will of one of the parties only'.[109] In 1905 Innes CJ stated that he preferred to leave open the question whether breach of an essential term justified cancellation:

No authority in point has been quoted to us from the Roman-Dutch law. We have been referred to English law, and to the French Civil Code; but this court administers Roman-Dutch law .... I wish to guard myself against deciding the point, because it is not necessary to do so.[110]

As late as 1951, Wessels asserted that South African law differed from English law in that 'our law does not allow one party to rescind or cancel a contract without the consent of the other'.[111]

Whatever the difficulties attendant on the charting of the time-frame of this development, there is no doubt that in modern South African law the right of cancellation for breach of contract has become more generalized than it was in Roman-Dutch law. The recognition of such a generalized power of cancellation was, in my view, the single most important development in the history of our law relating to breach of contract. This development can be traced back to the influence of two sources: English law and Pothier's writings on French law.[112]

The influence of English law was by far the more important of the two.[113] I have described above the manner in which English legal authorities pertaining to cancellation were adopted by our courts in the context of specific types of breach. The impact of English law was critically acknowledged by Joubert JA (in the context of *mora debitoris*) in the following terms:

Ons uitsprakereg het egter onder die invloed van die Engelse reg in die rigting ontwikkel waarvolgens 'n onskuldige party deur middel van 'n kennisgewing van ontbinding 'n terugtredingsreg teenoor 'n skuldige party weens sy kontrakbreuk kan verwerf. (Ek mag hier daarop wys dat indien die Romeins-Hollandse reg, soos die Franse reg voor die Franse Revolusie, die Romeinse reg suiwer toegepas het dan sou dit wel in die algemeen 'n terugtredingsreg weens kontrakbreuk by wederkerige kontrakte

---

[108] See e.g. *Van der Hoeven v. Trustee of De Wit* 1879 Buch 127 (although it has been suggested that Roman-Dutch law would have allowed for cancellation in this case: see Harker (n. 104), 272–3); *Emslie v. African Merchants Ltd* 1908 EDC 82, 88.

[109] *McRoberts v. Povall* (1883) 4 NLR 1, 2.

[110] *Weinberg v. Aristo Egyptian Cigarette Co* 1905 TS 760, 764.

[111] Wessels (n. 8), § 836. Note, however, that a brief footnote (not reprinted here) does serve to qualify the statement quoted in the text.

[112] Harker, 1980 *Acta Juridica* 70.

[113] For a recent (critical) account of the English law on this topic see Roger Brownsword, 'Retrieving Reasons, Retrieving Rationality? A New Look at the Right to Withdraw for Breach of Contract', (1992) 5 *Journal of Contract Law* 83.

erken het en sou daar geen noodsaak gewees het om toevlug tot die Engelse reg oor hierdie aangeleentheid te neem nie).[114]

While the influence of English law has been striking, the writings of Pothier have played a rather more marginalized role. During the sixteenth and seventeenth centuries French law had been moving in the direction of recognizing a right on the side of the aggrieved party to cancel a contract in the event of a material breach in the case of all reciprocal contracts (notwithstanding the absence of an express *lex commissoria*).[115] Pothier is sometimes regarded as having fathered this generalized notion of a right to cancel a contract in the event of material breach,[116] and some early judgments referred to Pothier as authority for the development of a parallel right in South African law.[117]

2. Consequences of cancellation

While the generalized right of cancellation for breach entered our law via the English law, I have been at pains to stress the various ways in which our courts have attempted to flesh out the implications of that remedy by adherence to Roman-Dutch principles. Thus, for example, it has been judicially stated that the juristic nature of the act of cancellation must be located 'in the basic principles of our own law'[118] rather than in English law. Similarly, South African courts have noticeably refrained from adopting the English rules in connection with the legal consequences of cancellation, but have instead developed those principles with reference to analogous Roman-Dutch rules.[119] The development of those rules relating to the consequences of cancellation are considered in this Section.

The extension of the remedy of cancellation beyond instances recognized in Roman-Dutch law has been accompanied by the development of a rule

[114] (Our case-law has, however, under the influence of English law developed in the direction that an innocent party may gain a right of rescission against the party in breach by means of a notice of rescission. (I may take the opportunity to point out that if Roman-Dutch law, like French law before the French Revolution, had followed the pure Roman law, it would indeed have recognized in general a right of rescission on account of breach of contract with regard to reciprocal contracts and it would thus not have been necessary to have recourse to the English law concerning this matter.)) *Goldberg v. Buytendag Boerdery Beleggings (Edms) Bpk* (n. 105), 793A-B. *In Stewart Wrightson (Pty) Ltd v. Thorpe* (n. 105), 953C, Jansen JA affirmed that '[i]t is difficult to resist the inference that this [recognition of a generalized right to cancel for breach] was under the influence of English law'.

[115] *Goldberg v. Buytendag Boerdery Beleggings (Edms) Bpk* (n. 105), 790A-B; Harker (n. 104), 142 sqq.; *idem*, 1980 *Acta Juridica* 69.

[116] Harker (n. 104), 146.

[117] *Young v. Land Values Ltd* (n. 101); *Du Toit v. Lange* 1930 CPD 315.

[118] *Stewart Wrightson (Pty) Ltd v. Thorpe* (n. 105), 953E (*per* Jansen JA).

[119] Harker, 1980 *Acta Juridica* 70. *Idem* (n. 104), 269 sqq. stresses that South African law did not 'take over the English remedy of rescission for breach of contract'. In this context he lays particular emphasis on a distinction (foreign to English law and which he traces back to Roman-Dutch law) between 'successive' and 'instantaneous' contracts: see esp. 211 sqq.

that both contracting parties are required to make restitution of any benefits transferred under the contract.[120] This rule has been developed with reference to the Roman-Dutch learning on the consequences which attached to cancellation in three analogous contexts: on the basis of an express *lex commissoria*;[121] on the basis of the *actio redhibitoria*;[122] and *restitutio in integrum* consequent upon rescission of a 'voidable' contract.[123] In this way the rules regarding restitution of benefits have come to be developed by an incremental process of judicial reasoning committed to the virtues of 'coherence':[124] the ambit of the existing Roman-Dutch rules was extended so as to accommodate a generalized right of cancellation, itself imported from English law.

More mysterious has been the development of the rules regarding the effect of cancellation on accrued rights of performance. A number of cases from the first part of this century took the view that a plaintiff who had cancelled a contract for breach could not thereafter sue the defendant for performance which was already due at the date of cancellation.[125] A contrary view was taken by Greenberg J in 1930, when he held (without citing any authority) that cancellation only affected the executory portion of the contract: 'where a certain right has accrued to the one party before the election [to cancel], such right is not affected after the election.'[126] The view of Greenberg J has now clearly triumphed in decisions of the Appellate Division of the last two decades.[127] It is interesting to note that the victory of this view has been attributed to the fact that the rule is not only fair but also in accordance with English law. In the leading case, Holmes JA reasoned that the rule in *Walker's Fruit Farms* is worth preserving, *inter alia*,

---

[120] See generally D. P. Visser, 'Rethinking Unjustified Enrichment: A Perspective on the Competition between Contractual and Enrichment Remedies', 1992 *Acta Juridica* 203, 225 sqq.; Harker (n. 104), 472 sqq.; *idem*, 1980 *Acta Juridica* 100 sqq.

[121] For Roman-Dutch authority on this topic see esp. Voet (n. 16), 18, 3, 2 sqq. See further the discussion of the Roman-Dutch law in *Barenblatt & Son v. Dixon* 1917 CPD 319, 322–3; *Mangold Bros v. Greyling's Trustee* 1910 EDC 471, 475–6; *Bonne Fortune Beleggings Bpk v. Kalahari Salt Works (Pty) Ltd* 1974 (1) SA 414 (NC) 424C-F.

[122] For a statement of the Roman-Dutch principle see Voet (n. 16), 21, 1, 4. See further the early cases of *Irvine & Co v. Berg* 1879 Buch 183; *Pringle v. Ellis & Son* (1897) 12 EDC 119.

[123] See e.g. *Radiotronics (Pty) Ltd v. Scott Lindberg & Co Ltd* 1951 (1) SA 312 (C) 329–30; *Bonne Fortune Beleggings Bpk v. Kalahari Salt Works (Pty) Ltd* (n. 121), 425–6; *Hall-Thermotank Natal (Pty) Ltd v. Hardman* 1968 (4) SA 818 (D) 826 sqq. Cf. *Baker v. Probert* 1985 (3) SA 429 (A) 439B-C.

[124] I use this term in the rich sense which has been colonized by Neil MacCormick, *Legal Reasoning and Legal Theory* (1978), 152 sqq.

[125] *Webster v. Varley* 1915 WLD 79; *Bloch v. Michal* 1924 TPD 54; *Hall v. Cox* 1926 CPD 228; *De Lange v. Herselman* 1941 WLD 13.

[126] *Walker's Fruit Farms Ltd v. Sumner* 1930 TPD 394, 401.

[127] *Crest Enterprises (Pty) Ltd v. Rycklof Beleggings (Edms) Bpk* (n. 64); *BK Tooling* (n. 62), 424G-H; *Nash v. Golden Dumps (Pty) Ltd* 1985 (n. 77). See generally Harker, 1980 *Acta Juridica* 95 sqq.

because '[i]t accords with English principles, which are relevant since the doctrine of anticipatory repudiation came to us from England'.[128]

Even more mysterious is the derivation of those statements in modern law which claim that cancellation has the effect of terminating the 'primary' obligations to perform, while simultaneously activating certain 'secondary' obligations (such as an obligation to pay damages and to make restitution). This terminology of primary/secondary obligations has been endorsed by the Appellate Division in two very recent cases.[129] To my knowledge there is no Roman-Dutch authority for this gloss on the consequences of cancellation[130] and the question might well be asked: what is the source of this doctrine? Although traces of the distinction apparently exist within the German law of obligations,[131] I suspect that any lawyer trained in the common law tradition would give the intuitive answer that this distinctive terminology derives from a well known series of judgments delivered by Lord Diplock in the English courts. In a long line of cases, of which the most famous is *Photo Production Ltd v. Securicor Transport Ltd*,[132] Lord Diplock formulated an elegant model of contractual undertakings premised on the

---

[128] *Crest Enterprises (Pty) Ltd v. Rycklof Beleggings (Edms) Bpk* (n. 64), 870F (and see *Nash v. Golden Dumps (Pty) Ltd* (n. 77), 22H-I). Note that it has subsequently been held that this rule is *not* restricted to cancellation following repudiation, but applies to cancellation for *all* forms of breach: see *Thomas Construction (Pty) Ltd v. Grafton Furniture Manufacturers (Pty) Ltd* 1988 (2) SA 546 (A) 564C.

[129] In *Atteridgeville Town Council v. Livanos* (n. 77), 304D-E Smalberger JA stated that cancellation 'puts an end (in the case of a contract that is executory) to the primary obligations of the parties to perform in terms of their contract. Certain secondary obligations, for example, the duty to compensate for damages arising from wrongful repudiation, however, remain.' In *CIR v. Collins* 1992 (3) SA 698 (A) 711E-F Botha JA said that 'in the case of a unilateral cancellation on breach it is to be noted that secondary rights and obligations flowing from the contract and its breach, for example in regard to damages, may be said to remain'. See also *LTA Construction Ltd v. Minister of Public Works and Land Affairs* 1992 (1) SA 837 (C) 850A-C.

[130] Voet, for example, stated that if a seller cancelled a contract of sale on the basis of a *lex commissoria*, then the contract is *ipso jure* dissolved ('*ipso jure contractus resolvitur*'): Voet (n. 16), 18, 3, 2. This passage (quoted with approval in *Provident Land Trust Ltd v. Union Gov* 1911 CPD 510, 516 and *Schuurman v. Davey* 1908 TS 664, 670) fails to make any distinction between termination *of the contract* and termination *of the principal obligation of performance*: see Harker (n. 104), 449, fn. 52. Cf. Van Zijl Steyn (n. 9), 3; J. G. Lotz, 'Obligations', in: W. A. Joubert, *The Law of South Africa*, vol. 19 (1983), § 247. See also the heads of argument of counsel in *Crest Enterprises (Pty) Ltd v. Rycklof Beleggings (Edms) Bpk* (n. 64), 866F-H.

[131] See Brice Dickson, 'The Contribution of Lord Diplock to the General Law of Contract', (1989) 9 *Oxford JLS* 441, 449.

[132] [1980] AC 827 (HL) 846 sqq. The other judgments delivered by Lord Diplock in this line include *C. Czarnikow Ltd v. Koufos* [1966] 2 QB 695 (CA) 730–1; *Rodophone Facilities Ltd v. Blank* [1966] 1 WLR 1428 (CA) 1446; *R V Ward Ltd v. Bignall* [1967] 1 QB 534 (CA) 548; *Moschi v. Lep Air Services Ltd* [1973] AC 331 (HL) 350; *Bremer Vulkan Schiffbau und Maschinenfabrik v. South India Shipping Corp Ltd* [1981] AC 909 (HL) 982; *Sudbrook Trading Estate Ltd v. Eggleton* [1983] 1 AC 444 (HL) 478; *Paal Wilson & Co v. Partenreederei Hannah Blumenthal* [1983] 1 AC 854 (HL) 916; *Afovos Shipping Co SA v. Pagnan* [1983] 1 WLR 195 (HL) 203. For a full discussion see Dickson, (1989) 9 *Oxford JLS* 448 sqq.

juxtaposition between the primary obligation to perform and the secondary obligation to pay damages after cancellation. The curious thing is that, as far as I am aware, Lord Diplock has never been acknowledged as the source of the terminology regarding primary/secondary obligations in our law.[133] In the result, the derivation of this doctrine in modern South African law remains very obscure indeed.

IV. THE AVAILABILITY OF SPECIFIC PERFORMANCE AS A REMEDY FOR BREACH

Modern South African law regarding the availability of specific performance as a remedy for breach represents the outcome of an extremely nuanced process of historical development. At stake is one fundamental issue of principle: should the law regard damages or specific performance as being the routine remedy for breach of contract? While the majority of Roman-Dutch writers took the view that specific performance was the usual remedy for breach, the competing rules of English Equity have proceeded on the assumption that specific performance is an exceptional remedy only to be ordered if an award of damages would be inadequate. These conflicting viewpoints have been bouncing against one another throughout the South African case-law of the last century. The net result is that our modern law adheres to a hybrid position—which is, unfortunately, not always distinguished by its internal coherence. This historical development is described below.

On one side, then, we have the Roman-Dutch law. The circumstances in which specific performance was available under the law of Holland was the subject of a vigorous controversy amongst Dutch jurists. The details of that dispute have been comprehensively rehearsed elsewhere and are therefore not dealt with here.[134] Suffice it to say that some Roman-Dutch jurists seemed to suggest that a promisor could not be forced into rendering specific performance, but could release himself from a contractual undertaking by paying damages to the other party.[135] Other writers claimed that it was not open to a promisor to release himself by the payment of damages, and that the promisor could always be compelled by civil imprisonment to the

[133] A passing reference to Lord Diplock's speech in the *Photo Production* case is contained in *Mitchell Cotts Engineering (Pty) Ltd v. Epic Oil Mills (Pty) Ltd* 1982 (2) SA 467 (W) 469E.
[134] The leading discussion is that of J. W. Wessels, *History of the Roman-Dutch Law* (1908), 612 sqq. See also J. W. Wessels, *The Law of Contract in South Africa*, vol. II (2nd edn., 1951), 825 sqq.; Philip Gross, 'Specific Performance of Contracts in South Africa', (1934) 51 *SALJ* 347, 348–51; R. W. Lee, *An Introduction to Roman-Dutch Law* (4th edn., 1946), 268 sqq.; M. A. Lambiris, *Orders of Specific Performance and Restitutio in Integrum in South African Law* (1989), 35 sqq.; Zimmermann (n. 1), 775 sqq.; *idem*, 'Roman-Dutch Jurisprudence and its Contribution to European Private Law', (1992) 66 *Tulane LR* 1698 sqq.
[135] See esp. Voet (n. 16), 19, 1, 14; Grotius (n. 83), 3, 3, 41 (but cf. 3, 15, 6 and 3, 31, 9).

strict fulfilment of his contractual undertaking.[136] The majority of modern commentators have taken the view that the prevailing position in Roman-Dutch law was that the creditor was entitled as of right to claim specific performance of all obligations, whether *ad dundum* or *ad faciendum*.[137]

On the other side of the divide we have the English position. After a bitter conflict between the jurisdictions of the courts of common law and those of Equity, specific performance eventually came to be regarded as an 'exceptional' remedy, available at the discretion of the court where damages were inadequate as a remedy.[138] A number of sub-rules evolved to designate the circumstances in which an award of specific performance would not be considered appropriate. Underlying the foundational rule was the principle that damages were to be regarded as the normal remedy for breach of contract. It is this principle which explains the force behind Holmes's unsettling *dictum* that '[t]he duty to keep a contract at common law means a prediction that you must pay damages if you do not keep it—and nothing else'.[139]

The chasm which separated the majority view of the Roman-Dutch writers from the English law was so deep that there was always likely to be discord within the South African judgments. A number of reported judgments from the mid-nineteenth century recited that specific performance was ordered by various courts, but these judgments provide little instruction today since they are often silent as to the legal principles which justified the award in each case.[140] However, once the judgments began to articulate more explicitly the legal principles applied they quickly fell into two distinct

---

[136] See esp. Simon van Groenewegen van der Made, *Ad Inleidinge* (edn.: The Introduction to Dutch Jurisprudence of Hugo Grotius with notes by Simon à Groenewegen van der Made, trans. A. F. S. Maasdorp, Cape Town, 1878), 3, 3, 41; Simon van Groenewegen van der Made, *Tractatus de Legibus Abrogatis et Inusitatis in Hollandia Vicinisque Regionibus* (edn.: A Treatise on the Laws Abrogated and no longer in use in Holland and Neighbouring Regions, trans. B. Beinart, Johannesburg, 1975), ad D. 42, 1, 13, 1; ad C. 4, 49, 4; Van Leeuwen (n. 16), 1, 4, 19, 10; Simon van Leeuwen, *Het Rooms-Hollands-Regt* (edn.: Commentaries on Roman-Dutch Law, trans. J. G. Kotzé, London, 1886), 4, 14, 3; 4, 18, 1.

[137] See the commentators cited in n. 134 above, as well as De Wet/Van Wyk (n. 37), 209. After an extensive survey of the controversy in *Cohen v. Shires McHattie and King* (1882) 1 SAR 41, Kotzé CJ concluded, at 45, that '[t]he Roman-Dutch law, therefore, clearly recognises the right to a specific performance of a contract.' In *Wheeldon v. Moldenhauer* 1910 EDL 97 Kotzé JP concluded, at 98, that the remedy of specific performance is 'well established in our Roman-Dutch law'. In *Moffat v. Touyz & Co* 1918 EDL 316 Kotzé AJP surveyed the institutional authorities and concluded that the power to decree specific performance of obligations *to do* as well as obligations *to give* was clearly established by Roman-Dutch law.

[138] See Zimmermann (n. 1), 776 sqq.; H. G. Hanbury & R. H. Maudsley, *Modern Equity* (12th edn., 1985), 659 sqq.; Treitel, *Contract* (n. 4), 902 sqq.

[139] Mr. Justice Holmes, 'The Path of the Law', (1897) 10 *Harvard LR* 457, 462. Somewhat less pithily, Voet stated that 'in all obligations to do a thing the rule is that he who does not fulfil the act can discharge his duty by the monetary making good of damages': Voet (n. 16), 19, 1, 14.

[140] See e.g. *Twentyman v. Hewitt* (1833) 1 Menz 156; *Wolhuter v. De Villiers* (1837) 2 Menz 37; *Knox v. Blackhurst* (1880) 1 NLR 73; *Trollip v. Tromp & Van Zweel* (1880) 1 NLR 166; *Kettles v. Bennett* (1893) 8 EDC 82.

camps: one endorsed the English rules of Equity and the other relied on Roman-Dutch law. I will refer to each of these camps in turn.

Early judgments in the 'English Equity camp' asserted that the court had an overriding discretion to order specific performance.[141] These judgments tended to track the rules of English Equity by endorsing sub-rules which operated to determine the circumstances in which specific performance should be refused in the exercise of the court's discretion. Thus, for example, judgments from the early part of this century expressly referred to English authorities in support of the contentions that specific performance should be refused where it would be unjust,[142] where the court could not enforce such an order,[143] where damages would be an adequate remedy,[144] or where the contract was one of employment.[145]

Cases in the rival camp rejected the relevance of English authorities and defined the correct approach to specific performance by reference to Roman-Dutch writers. In the leading case from the nineteenth century, Kotzé CJ held that '[b]y the well established practice of South Africa, agreeing with the Roman-Dutch law, suits for specific performance are matters of daily occurrence'.[146] These judgments, holding that the plaintiff was entitled to claim specific performance as of right, seemed to reject the view that South African courts possessed the wide discretion of English courts:

The English courts undoubtedly exercise a discretion in such cases to refuse specific performance, but I am not quite sure that our courts possess the same power because where specific performance is claimable under our law, it is a legal right of which the person entitled to it may demand the enforcement.[147]

[141] In *Shakinovsky v. Lawson and Smulowitz* 1904 TS 326, at 330, Innes CJ formulated the legal position as follows: 'Now a plaintiff has always the right to claim specific performance of a contract which the defendant has refused to carry out, but it is in the discretion of the court either to grant such an order or not.' See also *Stansfeld v. Kuhn* 1940 NPD 238.

[142] A vivid illustration is provided by *Atkinson v. Vause's Executors* (1892) 13 NLR 85, where Wragg J allowed parol evidence to be led in order to show whether it would be 'unconscientious in the plaintiff to insist upon, and unjust in the court to decree, the specific performance' (92). Cf. the invocation of the English doctrine of part performance in *Pauline Colliery and Developing Syndicate v. Natal Land and Colonisation Co Ltd* (1902) 23 NLR 166.

[143] In *Ingle Colonial Broom Co Ltd v. Hocking* 1914 CPD 495, at 499, Searle J stated that '[a]s a general rule the court will not make an order which the court cannot see carried out'. See also *Barker v. Beckett & Co Ltd* 1911 TPD 151; *Keyter v. Terblanche* 1935 EDL 186.

[144] See *Visser v. Neethling* 1921 CPD 176, where Benjamin J refused specific performance of a contract of purchase on the basis that the *res vendita* 'had no special and peculiar value' to the purchaser.

[145] The leading case from this early period was *Schierhout v. Minister of Justice* 1926 AD 99, in which Innes CJ stated (108) that 'it may be taken that South African practice in regard to the remedy of an ordinary servant for wrongful dismissal is the same as the practice of the courts in England'.

[146] *Cohen v. Shires McHattie and King* (n. 137), 45.

[147] *Amoils v. Amoils* 1924 WLD 88, 98 (*per* Mason JP). For the expression of similar conclusions in cases from this period see *Bergl & Co v. Trott Bros* (1903) 24 NLR 503; *Newton v. Lotter* (1909) EDC 159; *Wheeldon v. Moldenhauer* (n. 137); *Du Pisani v. Watson* 1914 EDL 242; *Moffat v. Touyz & Co* 1918 EDL 316.

The early judgments of these two camps offered radically divergent interpretations of the institution of specific performance. While judges in both
camps would have agreed that courts were competent to order specific performance, they disagreed about whether the order of specific performance
was available to a plaintiff *as of right*. In doctrinal terms, these divergent
understandings were often most clearly revealed in judicial discussion of the
nature of the court's discretion in the making of an award of specific performance. These were undoubtedly fundamental points of disagreement,
and so it is suprising to note that in many cases dating from this period
there was no proper appreciation of the significance of the issues in dispute.
For example, in *Manasewitz v. Oosthuizen*[148] Kotzé J held that '[i]t is a well
recognized rule of the Roman-Dutch law that in a case of purchase and sale
the court would recognize a claim for specific performance'.[149] Hardly paus-
ing for breath, he added that 'the question is always in the discretion of the
court whether, under the circumstances before the court, it would be doing
right to grant a claim for specific performance'.[150] The same tension can be
identified in *Thompson v. Pullinger*,[151] where Kotzé CJ affirmed the Roman-
Dutch view that '[t]he right of a plaintiff to the specific performance of a
contract . . . is beyond all doubt'[152] but saw no incongruity in tacking on a
rider to the effect that specific performance should (as a 'general rule') not
be decreed in the case of 'shares in companies which can daily be obtained
on the market without difficulty'.[153]

The tensions within many of the judgments from this period emanated
from the slippage between the so-called 'right to specific performance' on
one hand and the overriding discretion of the court to refuse specific performance on the other. The underlying difficulty was that the 'discretion' of
the court to refuse specific performance was fundamentally at odds with the
supposed 'right' of the promisee to claim specific performance. This explains
why those judgments which lurched between talk of 'the right to specific
performance' and talk of 'the court's overriding discretion' seemed to be
engaged in a conjuring trick which involved giving with one hand and taking away with the other.

This fundamental tension was clearly operating beneath the surface of the
Appellate Division judgments on the subject. In 1912 the highest court of
the land affirmed that a plaintiff has a '*prima facie* right' to specific performance, but immediately added the rider that the award was subject to the
discretion of the court.[154] This approach was endorsed nine years later:

The plaintiff is broadly speaking entitled to claim the performance of a contract
where it is possible for the other party to perform it. But the court has a discretion

---

[148] 1914 CPD 328.　　　　　[149] 331.　　　　　　　[150] 331.　　　　　[151] (1894) 1 OR 298.
[152] 301.　　　　[153] 301.　　　　　[154] *Farmers' Co-operative Soc v. Berry* 1912 AD 343.

to say whether in any particular case specific performance is the proper and appropriate remedy.[155]

Five years later the Appellate Division suggested that the South African practice followed the well established English rule in refusing to order specific performance of a contract of employment.[156] In 1937 the Appellate Division stated that the adequacy of damages as a remedy did not negate the right of a plaintiff to claim specific performance.[157] In 1951 Schreiner JA seemingly endorsed the language of English equity when he stated that 'specific performance will be refused where it would be "inequitable in all the circumstances"'.[158] In the same year the Appellate Division stated authoritatively that while the plaintiff had a right in South African law to claim specific performance, the court had a discretion to refuse to order it in appropriate circumstances:

As examples of the grounds on which the courts have exercised their discretion in refusing to order specific performance, although performance was not impossible, may be mentioned: (a) where damages would adequately compensate the plaintiff; (b) where it would be difficult for the court to enforce its decree; (c)_where the thing claimed can readily be bought elsewhere; (d) where specific performance entails the rendering of services of a personal nature . . .; [and] (e) where it would operate unreasonably hardly on the defendant, or where the agreement giving rise to the claim is unreasonable, or where the decree would produce injustice, or would be inequitable under all the circumstances.[159]

The judgment in *Haynes v. Kingwilliamstown Municipality*, for many years regarded as the leading statement on specific performance in South African law, clearly equivocates on the fundamental issue of principle. The Roman-Dutch right to specific performance, affirmed as part of modern South African law, was effectively negated by the court's subsequent endorsement of crystallized instances—borrowed from English law—in which specific performance should be refused. For this reason the judgment was subjected to strenuous criticism thirty-five years later in what is now regarded as the leading case: *Benson v. SA Mutual Life Assurance Society*.[160] In *Benson* the Appellate Division affirmed three principles. First: the 'right to specific performance' is 'the cornerstone of our law relating to specific performance'.[161] Secondly: although the right is subject to a judicial discretion to refuse specific performance, that discretion cannot be regulated by any 'rules' which

---

[155] *Woods v. Walters* 1921 AD 303, 309 (*per* Innes CJ).

[156] *Schierhout v. Minister of Justice* 1926 AD 99 at 108.

[157] *Shill v. Milner* 1937 AD 101.

[158] *R v. Milne and Erleigh* 1951 (1) SA 791 (A) 873H. The quotation by Schreiner JA derives from Wessels (n. 8), § 3119, who took the view that the rules of English equity were 'in harmony with the principles of the Roman-Dutch Law'.

[159] *Haynes v. Kingwilliamstown Municipality* 1951 (2) SA 371 (A) 378H–379A (*per* De Villiers AJA).

[160] 1986 (1) SA 776 (A).   [161] 782I-J.

would curtail the court's discretion and erode the posited right to specific performance.[162] Thirdly: the English legal guidelines regarding the circumstances in which specific performance is an inappropriate remedy cannot fetter the discretion of a South African court (although they may continue to be relevant as factors to be considered in a pool of relevant considerations).[163]

Benson's case purported to vindicate the Roman-Dutch position by reinstating the right to specific performance at the centre of South African law.[164] Yet I would argue that the fundamental tension in this area of law was not properly addressed by the judgment, and that the cumulative effect of the three propositions extracted above perpetuates internal incoherence. Bear in mind that those modern continental jurisdictions which endorse a right to specific performance as a cornerstone admit 'exceptions' to specific enforceability, but do not usually retain the sort of freewheeling *discretion* to refuse performance which is affirmed in *Benson*.[165] How is one to take seriously the claim that a plaintiff has a right to specific performance, if that right can be trumped by competing considerations of social policy within the overriding discretion of the court?[166] The underlying difficulty is that the discretion (essentially the English law artefact) still seems to cut the ground from beneath the right (which is the Roman-Dutch artefact). The precariousness of the modern position is apparent from the following passage of the *Benson* judgment, in which Hefer JA equivocates uncomfortably on the nature of the discretion involved:

[T]heoretically, I suppose, there may be a rule which regulates the exercise of the discretion without actually curtailing it but, apart from the rule that the discretion is to be exercised judicially upon a consideration of all relevant facts, it is difficult to conceive of one. Practically speaking it follows that, apart from the rule just referred to, no rules can be prescribed to regulate the exercise of the court's discretion. This does not mean that the discretion is in all respects completely unfettered. It remains, after all, a judicial discretion . . .[167]

Notwithstanding these criticisms, the judgment in *Benson* still stands as the definitive statement of the modern South African law on specific performance, and succeeds in setting it apart from common law jurisdictions in a most striking manner. It is worth making one final observation. There is no 'logic' internal to contract doctrine itself which dictates that specific performance must be the routine remedy for breach. From the antecedent fact

---

[162] 782I–783C.   [163] 785F–G.

[164] Hefer JA stated (785F) that there is 'neither need nor reason' to continue to follow the English rules of Equity as regards when specific performance should be refused.

[165] Zimmermann (n. 1), 782; Treitel, *Remedies* (n. 4), 51 sqq.

[166] In a very different context cf. the arguments of Ronald Dworkin, *Taking Rights Seriously* (1977), 14 sqq.

[167] 783B–C.

that a contract is 'binding' we cannot read any conclusion about the nature of the remedy which the state should grant for a failure to perform the contractual undertaking. There would be no contradiction involved in affirming the principle of *pacta sunt servanda* at the level of the ascription of contractual responsibility, and still maintaining that for policy reasons the law should restrict the availability of specific performance as a remedy in favour of an award of damages.[168] For example, it might be argued that for reasons of 'justice' specific performance should be refused where such an award would be unduly intrusive and oppressive.[169] Alternatively, economic goals of efficiency and wealth-maximization might be said to militate against making specific performance the routine remedy for breach of contract.[170] I do not claim that these are knock-down arguments against the general availability of specific performance; my point is that these are the sorts of policy issues which need to be addressed in order to offer a rational defence of the South African rules. The judgment in *Benson*, by failing to consider these policy issues, generates more heat than light and fails to provide a firm foundation for South African law on the availability of specific performance.

In concluding this Section, it is noteworthy that modern statutory provisions have exerted a profound impact on the existing methods for enforcement of specific performance orders. In Roman-Dutch law an order of specific performance was enforceable by depriving the debtor of his or her liberty in the practice of *gijzeling* (civil imprisonment).[171] Civil imprisonment of a debtor for failure to satisfy a monetary judgment has now been abolished in South Africa by statute.[172] In modern Supreme Court practice, an order *ad pecuniam solvendam* will be enforced by attachment of the judgment debtor's property and subsequent sale in execution.[173] While a judgment debtor who refuses to comply with an order *ad factum praestandum* may be committed for contempt of court,[174] the modern position is that contempt proceedings are not available in the Supreme Court in respect

---

[168] Cf. Collins (n. 6), 179 sqq.; Cane (n. 4), 353.

[169] Anthony Ogus, 'Remedies', in: Donald Harris, Dennis Tallon (eds.), *Contract Law Today: Anglo-French Comparisons* (1989), 243, 256 sqq.

[170] This issue forms the subject matter of a well known debate within Anglo-American law: see Anthony Kronman, 'Specific Performance', (1978) 45 *University of Chicago LR* 351; Alan Schwartz, 'The Case for Specific Performance', (1979) 89 *Yale LJ* 271. Cf. Donald Harris, Anthony Ogus, Jennifer Phillips, 'Contract Remedies and the Consumer Surplus', (1979) 95 *LQR* 581. For discussion regarding the efficiency of the South African rules see B. J. van Heerden, 'An Exploratory Introduction to the Economic Analysis of Law', (1981) 4 *Responsa Meridiana* 152 sqq.

[171] Johannes van der Linden, *Regtsgeleerd, Practicaal, en Koopmans Handboek*, 3, 9, 9. See further *Woods v. Walters* 1921 AD 303, 309–10; Lambiris (n. 134), 40–1.

[172] The Abolition of Civil Imprisonment Act 2 of 1977. See also the earlier Civil Imprisonment Restriction Act 21 of 1942.

[173] Uniform Rules of Court, rr. 45–6.

[174] L. T. C. Harms, *Civil Procedure in the Supreme Court* (1990), 577.

of an order *ad pecuniam solvendam*.[175] For magistrates' courts the legislature has created a battery of procedures to enforce judgments.[176]
Anomalously, these lower courts *are* empowered to commit a judgment
debtor for contempt of court even for failure to comply with an order *ad
pecuniam solvendam*.[177] The jurisdiction of the magistrates' courts to order
specific performance without an alternative of payment of damages is, however, severely limited by statute.[178]

V. CONCLUSION

I wish to distil three conclusions from the preceding discussion of the historical development of the South African law relating to breach of contract.
My first conclusion involves the obvious fact that it has been left almost
entirely to the courts to develop the law relating to breach of contract. The
legislature has contributed little to the subject; the only noteworthy statutory intervention is the regulation of methods for the enforcement of orders
of specific performance.[179]

My second conclusion relates to the manner in which the courts have
deployed 'authority reasons'[180] in developing the law relating to breach. I
have sought several times in the Chapter to emphasize the extent to which
the courts have relied on both Roman-Dutch and English authorities in the
development of new legal doctrines. In some situations the skilful fusion of
authorities has produced a seamless legal artefact: the South African law
relating to cancellation for breach of contract provides the best example.
Elsewhere, however, the mixture of authorities has proved rather less successful: the modern South African law regarding specific performance is a

---

[175] *Metropolitan Industrial Corporation (Pty) Ltd v. Hughes* 1969 (1) SA 224 (T) 227F.

[176] See chapter IX Magistrates' Courts Act 32 of 1944, and rr. 36–48, Magistrates' Courts
Rules of Court.

[177] Magistrates' Courts Act 32 of 1944, s. 65F read with s. 65A(1). It should be borne in
mind that Supreme Court judgments for payment of sums of money may also be enforced in
the magistrates' courts under s. 65M Magistrates' Courts Act 32 of 1944. See further H. J.
Erasmus, D. E. van Loggerenberg, *Jones and Buckle: The Civil Practice of the Magistrates'
Courts in South Africa* (8th edn., 1988), 237, 262 sqq.; Lambiris (n. 134), 51. It has been argued
by a public interest attorney that imprisonment for contempt in the lower courts is in practice
usually controlled by the creditor so as to amount to 'nothing more than old fashioned imprisonment for non-payment of debt, dressed up in the flimsy clothing of the contempt offence':
see Matthew Walton, 'The rich get richer . . . and the poor go to prison', *Weekly Mail &
Guardian Review/Law*, Vol. 2 No. 1, Mar. 1994, 12. See also 'Civil imprisonment: LRC rec-
ommends abolition' (anon.) in: (1994) No. 1 *Legal Resources Centre Review* 4.

[178] Magistrates' Courts Act 32 of 1944, s. 46(2)(c).

[179] See text to nn. 172–8 above. Although I have not discussed contractual damages in this
article (see n. 1 above) for the sake of completeness it should be added that the Conventional
Penalties Act 15 of 1962 represents the legislature's most significant intervention into the arena
of breach of contract.

[180] For this terminology see Robert Summers, 'Two Types of Substantive Reasons: The
Core of a Theory of Common-Law Justification', (1978) 63 *Cornell LR* 707, 724 sqq.

good example of the doctrinal dissonance which can result from superimposing English law onto incompatible Roman-Dutch principles. It is, in my view, beyond dispute that elements from diverse legal traditions have been smelted in the crucible of judicial reasoning to produce the unique alloy which is the modern South African law relating to breach of contract.

My third conclusion relates to the courts' use of 'substantive reasons'[181] (i.e. policy-driven justifications employed when the 'authority reasons' prove insufficiently determinate to generate an outcome in a hard case). It will be apparent from the above that the South African courts have generally been reluctant to deploy substantive reasons explicitly in the development of the principles relating to breach, and have on the whole preferred to take refuge within the safe harbor of authority reasons.[182] This is well illustrated by the development of the law relating to the availability of specific performance, where the courts have conspicuously shied away from unpacking the legal principles and engaging in the enterprise of substantive reasoning.

It is increasingly accepted today that the most important function of modern contract law is to regulate the functioning of market relations.[183] American commentators are fond of pointing out that the legal rules relating to breach of contract are also in many ways *the most* important part of the law of contract, since people tend to have recourse to the law only after the contractual relationship has broken down. If those points are accepted then it follows that the modern South African law relating to breach of contract needs to be assessed instrumentally in terms of its commercial appropriateness, and not merely in terms of the internal elegance of its doctrines. Unfortunately, there is insufficient evidence to allow us to appraise the law of breach in such instrumental terms. Certainly we have no empirical studies (such as those of Anglo-American jurisdictions[184]) to help us assess the extent to which commercial contractors actually rely on the law of contract when it comes to sorting out their exchange relationships. For this reason the final conclusion to this article must be somewhat rueful. We know that the extraordinarily elaborate juggling of the diverse sources of the modern South African law of breach has produced legal doctrines of great finesse.

---

[181] Summers, (1978) 63 *Cornell LR* 716 sqq.; cf. Alfred Cockrell, 'Adjudication styles in South African private law', (1993) 56 *THRHR* 590.

[182] This reluctance to engage in 'substantive reasoning' may well change in the light of South Africa's new 'Interim Bill of Rights', which came into operation on 27 Apr. 1994. Section 35(3) of the Constitution of the Republic of South Africa 1993 instructs that in 'the application and development of the common law . . . a court shall have due regard to the spirit, purport and objects of [Chapter 3 of the constitution, the so-called 'interim bill of rights']'. I would argue that this subsection has the effect of mandating judges to be more openly 'pragmatist' in their deployment of 'substantive reasons' in the development of the common law relating to breach.

[183] See e.g. Collins (n. 6), 1 sqq.; Harker (n. 104), 14 sqq.

[184] See e.g. Hugh Beale, Tony Dugdale, 'Contracts between Businessmen: Planning and the Use of Contractual Remedies', (1975) 2 *British Journal of Law and Society* 45.

But can we also be certain that this end-product has been utilized by the people out there in the 'legal market-place'? In other words, do our legal principles satisfy the needs of a group of people notorious for their lack of brand-loyalty, namely the consumers of legal doctrine? On that rather different question the jury is unfortunately still out.

10: *Agency and* Stipulatio Alteri

DAVID J. JOUBERT

I. INTRODUCTION

Agency was not completely unknown in Roman law, for although the Romans did not have a general concept of agency they did recognize indirect representation and allowed a variety of exceptions to the rule against agency. In the course of the development of the *ius commune* this rule was progressively eroded, paving the way for the modern concept of direct agency. It is true that the Roman law of mandate and various other actions (such as the *actio institoria*, the *actio exercitoria*, and the *actio ad exemplum institoriae actionis*) probably provided some basis for this development, but it would clearly be wrong to state, as did Wessels,[1] that the rules of Roman law relating to agency were taken over almost in their entirety. (He probably had in mind that the contract of mandate regulated the relationship between 'principal' and 'agent' in situations of indirect agency and that the institutional writers, with some exceptions, by and large adopted the Roman approach to privity of contract.)

By the seventeenth century the Roman-Dutch variant of the *ius commune* had accepted the fundamental tenet of the modern law of agency, namely that an agent can in certain circumstances directly bind the principal. The institution of agency proved to be of great commercial importance. Wealthy landowners, like the feudal lords of earlier times, employed stewards to buy and sell as well as to collect rents or feudal dues on their behalf. Manufacturers and merchants often did not trade personally, but employed a *koopman* to sell goods in a shop or on board a ship, or to barter their products for others to resell in Holland. Likewise, producers of agricultural products often consigned their produce to factors to sell either wholesale or retail.

II. AGENCY IN SOUTH AFRICA: AN OVERVIEW

The Roman-Dutch law with regard to agency is generally regarded as being 'little developed'.[2] First, there was not much of a theoretical foundation,

---

[1] Sir John Wessels, *History of the Roman-Dutch Law* (1908), § 586.
[2] Jonathan Silke, *De Villiers & Macintosh: The Law of Agency in South Africa* (3rd edn., 1981), 4. Cf. R. W. Lee, *An Introduction to Roman-Dutch Law* (5th edn., 1953), 310 and the authorities cited below.

and secondly, many of the details of this crucially important institution were not fully worked out. Consequently, courts and practitioners were required to solve problems for which the old sources provided no ready answers. Thus a new paradigm made its appearance, allowing new uses for agency, but also bringing new problems to the fore.

This does not mean, however, that South African law has developed a complete modern theory, nor that answers would be possible on a level comparable with, say, modern European legal theory. Contemporary continental theory, for example, distinguishes between direct and indirect agency;[3] but owing to the absence of a comprehensive theory of agency in the Roman-Dutch legal sources[4] and the use of the doctrine of the undisclosed principal, this theoretical distinction is seldom used in modern South African legal theory, and when it is, it is often blurred.

The law of agency developed gradually and kept pace with economic and commercial development in South Africa. When the Dutch East India Company founded its settlement at the Cape trade was principally in the hands of the Company. The Company bought produce from local farmers or producers and traded with passing ships and merchants. It employed agents (*koopmanne*). However, for ordinary *burgers* and farmers agency must have been a concept of little relevance. With the passing of time, however, commercial activity was freed from the control of the Company and, as a result, the need for agency surfaced. The farmer sometimes sold or consigned his produce to a factor. The passing merchant fleet carried agents who purchased fresh produce and sold trade goods for their principals. At first all transactions were probably conducted on a cash or barter basis, so that rules of agency were not needed; but during the course of the eighteenth century, as commerce gained an increasing level of sophistication, the need for a law of agency became acute. Since the community was agrarian, agency developed a distinctly agrarian aspect. The common law auctioneer was well known in the settled Cape community[5] and was probably invaluable in determining what the market could afford. Selling to the highest bidder at an auction sale was a popular method of disposing of all sorts of assets; and such sales enjoyed a good reputation. The factor to whom goods were consigned for sale out of hand or over the counter also continued to play a role. The market agent who sold agricultural produce at market was perhaps one of the best known examples.

Of course, the discovery of gold and diamonds gave a strong impetus to economic development, with a consequent increase in the use of agents who

[3] J. C. van der Horst, *Die Leerstuk van die* 'Undisclosed Principal' (1971), 1 sqq.; Reinhard Zimmermann, *The Law of Obligations: Roman Foundations of the Civilian Tradition* (1990, reprint 1993), 49 sq.

[4] Silke (n. 2), 5.

[5] C. G. Hall, *Maasdorp's Institutes of South African Law*, vol. 3: *The Law of Contracts* (1970), 247.

bought and sold land, mining claims, diamonds, gold, shares and debentures, as well as food; who arranged finance and loans; and who floated commercial enterprises. New needs also arose: in the nineteenth century a stock exchange emerged, selling stocks and shares in companies and other enterprises.[6] At the same time the estate agent, who brokered the sale of immovable property by finding a potential buyer and intervening so as to help seller and buyer reach consensus, made his appearance. Later still, travel agents became commonplace, as did agents in various other spheres.

The types of problems encountered in agency varied with the passage of time. Naturally, the relationship between principal and agent has always been central to every instance of agency. Initially, the key question was whether the principal could sue or be sued on the contract entered into by his agent. In the late nineteenth century, with the advent of the mining industry, greed and graft made their appearance on a grand scale and the duty of good faith became a focal point for litigation. During the twentieth century a serious attempt was made to elucidate the legal issues involved in agency and, gradually, greater clarity was achieved.

The relationship between agency and cession is one of the areas in which significant progress towards lucidity was made. As is well known, the Romans used an irrevocable mandate *in rem suam* to achieve the same result as the transfer of a personal right. Today parties still use the guise of agency to approximate the effect of the transfer of a personal right when they purport to appoint an agent *in rem suam*. Although, as explained below, the courts seem still to experience difficulty in dealing with the notions of agency and cession, and in divining the intention of the parties,[7] the difference between them is clear, at least at a conceptual level: if the parties intend to transfer the right, the transferee acts in his own name and there is a cession; if they intend agency, the agent must act in the name of his principal.[8]

Another noteworthy modern notion is that of the nominee. When one party sells to another, the latter may act for himself 'and/or for a nominee'. A sale is completed, but the intention is to create the possibility for the buyer to transfer both rights and duties arising from the contract to a third party, who would then essentially assume the position of the buyer. Nevertheless, the transaction between the person nominating and the nominee is not a sale.[9] The jurisprudential challenge has been to find a proper explanation for this practice, and the courts have adopted the common law principle of delegation in this regard. The third party, tacitly or impliedly,

---

[6] Hall (n. 5), 246.

[7] *Skjelbreds Rederi A/S v. Hartless (Pty) Ltd* 1982 (2) SA 710 (A); *Hippo Quarries (Tvl) (Pty) Ltd v. Eardley* 1992 (1) SA 867 (A).

[8] *Bird v. Lawclaims (Pty) Ltd* 1976 (4) SA 726 (D); *Portion 1 of 46 Wadeville (Pty) Ltd v. Unity Cutlery (Pty) Ltd* 1984 (1) SA 61 (A); *Spendiff v. JAJ Distributors (Pty) Ltd* 1989 (4) SA 126 (C); *Hippo Quarries (Tvl) (Pty) Ltd v. Eardley* (n. 7).

[9] *Jassat v. Jassat* 1980 (4) SA 231 (W).

consents in advance to a delegation of the buyer's duties (flowing from the contract) to a nominee still to be chosen. The rights are then ceded.[10]

A person who merely holds property for another is a separate type of nominee and may be described as an agent with limited authority.[11] The role of the 'stakeholder' is important here.[12] A contract of sale may provide that the buyer of (usually immovable) property is to deposit the price with a third party (usually the estate agent). If the contract fails and the money has to be refunded to the buyer, the question arises whether the third party was an agent for the seller (in which case the seller, as principal, must refund the money) or a true stakeholder (in which case he, the recipient, and not the seller, must refund the money). The answer depends upon the facts and upon the intention of the parties.

In modern law the contract between a builder (contractor) and a building owner may provide for an architect to issue certificates stipulating that the work has reached a certain stage, whereupon the builder becomes entitled to payment of specified sums of money. The question arises: is the architect an agent of building owner?[13] The answer depends upon the intention of the parties, but usually the architect would not be classified as an agent. It is important to bear in mind that the word 'agent' is sometimes used in a loose sense, to denote someone who does something for or in the interest of another, without necessarily affecting the latter's legal relations with others.[14] In law an agent is someone who has been given authority to perform a juristic act, affecting the legal relations of the person who gave him such authority.

Furthermore, agency doctrines have been introduced into novel fields. Such doctrines have always been applied in respect of property,[15] where ownership could be acquired or alienated by an agent or property could be held in possession by an agent. Likewise, the agent was a familiar figure in contractual relations as well as in respect of making and receiving payment. Now, however, agency is also employed in connection with the receipt of information or notices[16] and waiver.[17] In some of these cases the courts have been able to resort to Roman-Dutch common law authority. In others they found it convenient to refer to English law, as described in more detail below.

Over the years there have also been a number of statutes dealing with

---

[10] *Botha v. Van Niekerk* 1983 (3) SA 513 (W) 525, 527.
[11] *Ocean Commodities Inc v. Standard Bank of SA Ltd* 1978 (2) SA 367 (W).
[12] Cf. *Probert v. Baker* 1983 (3) SA 229 (D); *Baker v. Probert* 1985 (3) SA 429 (A).
[13] *Randcon (Natal) (Pty) Ltd v. Florida Twin Estates (Pty) Ltd* 1973 (4) SA 181 (D).
[14] *Fish v. Adam t/a Charter Bazaar* 1978 (2) SA 313 (R).
[15] *Mbuku v. Mdinwa* 1982 (1) SA 219 (Tk) 221.
[16] *Swart v. Vosloo* 1965 (1) SA 100 (A) 116.   [17] *Wright v. Wright* 1978 (3) SA 47 (EC).

agency matters.[18] Clearly, new situations sometimes require legislation to ensure clarity or to introduce a special ruling. Nevertheless unsettled questions remain: can an agent, on behalf of a principal, contract with himself?[19] Can he, on behalf of one principal, contract with himself on behalf of another?[20]

III. THE INFLUENCE OF ENGLISH LAW

The British occupation of the Cape gave rise to a situation in which English law exercised an important influence on the formulation and development of the law by the courts. One of the areas strongly affected was the law of agency.[21] The following facets of the law of agency deserve mention as having been thus influenced:

(1) the relationship between the third party, and principal and agent, in cases of undisclosed agency;[22]
(2) the doctrine of estoppel;[23]
(3) the doctrine of the implied warranty of authority;[24]
(4) the use of the term 'contract of agency'; and
(5) the notion of irrevocable authority.[25]

Instances where English precedent or the contributions of academic lawyers have assisted in the development of this field of law are plentiful and include the relationship between banker and client.[26] The general

---

[18] One might mention e.g. the former s. 311 Merchant Shipping Act 57 of 1951, which dealt with the position of maritime agents, making them liable to third parties on the contracts of their principals for reasons of convenience (repealed by s. 5 of the Carriage of Goods by Sea Act 1 of 1986). Section 23(2) Close Corporations Act 67 of 1984 renders signatories for a close corporation personally liable if they state the name of the close corporation incorrectly. The form of signature of a company is regulated by s. 70 Companies Act 61 of 1973. If the name of the company is not properly disclosed the director signing is personally liable: H. S. Cilliers, M. L. Benade, D. H. Botha, M. J. Oosthuizen, E. M. de la Rey, *Korporatiewe Reg* (1987), 47. Cf. Marketing Act 59 of 1969, as amended; Agricultural Produce Agents Act 12 of 1992 (replacing older statutory regulations); Estate Agents Act 112 of 1976; Travel Agents and Travel Agencies Act 58 of 1983.

[19] J. C. de Wet, 'Agency and Representation', in: W. A. Joubert (ed.), *The Law of South Africa*, vol. 1 (1976) (hereinafter *LawSA*) § 107; 'Agency and Representation' (revised by A. G. du Plessis), in: W. A. Joubert (founding editor), L. T. C. Harms, G. J. Pienaar, P. J. Rabie (eds.), *The Law of South Africa*, vol. 1 (first re-issue, 1993), (hereinafter *LawSA*, first re-issue), § 106.

[20] J. C. De Wet, 'Agency and Representation', in: *LawSA* (n. 19), § 102; 'Agency and Representation' (revised by A. G. du Plessis) in: *LawSA*, first re-issue (n. 19), § 107.

[21] H. R. Hahlo, Ellison Kahn, *The South African Legal System and its Background* (1968), 578 regard the influence as 'fairly strong'.

[22] Van der Horst (n. 3), 21; De Wet, *LawSA* (n. 19), § 148; David Joubert, *Die Suid-Afrikaanse Verteenwoordigingsreg* (1979), 17.

[23] Joubert (n. 22), 17. [24] Ibid.

[25] De Wet, *LawSA* (n. 19), § 125.

[26] *Rousseau v. Standard Bank of SA Ltd* 1976 (4) SA 104 (C).

approach of the courts towards English law may be gleaned from the following remark by Smith J in *Faure v. Louw*:[27]

As there is an absence of any clear authority upon the point raised in the present case [i.e. ostensible authority], either in Roman or Roman-Dutch law, and as there is only one reported case in this Court bearing upon it, and as the authorities in English law are conflicting, it is necessary to consider the principles upon which a commercial agency is constituted and the rules by which it is governed.[28]

The Court went on to establish these principles with reference to English, Scottish, and Continental sources. In *Blower v. Van Noorden*[29] it was confirmed, in an oft quoted statement, that the South African courts would not follow Roman-Dutch law slavishly:

There come times in the growth of every living system of law when old practice and ancient formulae must be modified in order to keep in touch with the expansion of legal ideas, and to keep pace with the requirements of changing conditions. And it is for the courts to decide when the modifications, which time has proved to be desirable, are of a nature to be affected by judicial decision, and when they are so important or so radical that they should be left to the legislature.[30]

The nature of commerce at a particular stage in history obviously has a bearing on the approach to and the nature of agency.[31] De Wet and Yeats[32] report that the rules of agency in Roman-Dutch law were difficult to find because the writers occupied themselves with mandate whilst largely ignoring agency.[33] In so far as the institutional writers actually dealt with agency, they often did so in a cursory manner, without much attention to detail.[34] Kerr[35] points out in the preface to his work on agency that he had greatly relied on the French writer, Pothier, because of, *inter alia*, 'the fullness of his exposition'. This highlights the lack in the Roman-Dutch common law sources of sufficient detail to answer the questions posed by modern legal practice. The similarity between English law and Roman-Dutch law facili-

---

[27] (1880) 1 SC 3 (17).   [28] 24.   [29] 1909 TS 890 (905).

[30] Cf. *Goodriche & Son v. Auto Protection Insurance Co Ltd (in liq.)* 1967 (2) SA 501 (W) 503–4; Hall (n. 5), 242; Dale Hutchison, Belinda van Heerden, D. P. Visser, C. G. van der Merwe, *Wille's Principles of South African Law* (8th edn., 1991), 592; Joubert (n. 22), 8; Lee (n. 2), 310; Deon van Zyl, *Geskiedenis van die Romeins-Hollandse Reg* (1979), 478–94; Hahlo/Kahn (n. 21), 582; Silke (n. 2), 11–12; S. R. van Jaarsveld, *Die Leerstuk van Ratifikasie in die Suid-Afrikaanse Reg* (1974), 185; S. R. van Jaarsveld *et al.*, *Suid-Afrikaanse Handelsreg* (3rd edn., 1988), 208.

[31] Hall (n. 5), 242.

[32] J. C. de Wet, J. P. Yeats, *Die Suid-Afrikaanse Kontraktereg en Handelsreg* (2nd edn., 1953), 75.

[33] Cf. J. C. de Wet, A. H. van Wyk, *Die Suid-Afrikaanse Kontraktereg en Handelsreg*, vol. 1 (5th edn., 1992), 75.

[34] J. C. de Wet, A. H. van Wyk, *De Wet and Yeats: Die Suid-Afrikaanse Kontraktereg en Handelsreg* (4th edn., 1978), 85; Joubert (n. 22), 17; Van Jaarsveld *et al.* (n. 33), 208.

[35] A. J. Kerr, *The Law of Agency* (3rd edn., 1991), v.

tated the adoption of English rules.[36] Frequent references to English writers and cases do indeed occur in our cases and textbooks.[37]

The fact that the great majority of judgments of the courts were delivered in English opened the door to English terminology, which became predominant; this has given modern expositions of the law of agency a distinctly English flavour.[38] Even the expressions *per procurationem* and *qualitate qua*, or their abbreviations,[39] have acquired a foreign content.[40] American law, too, has exerted some influence.[41] The work of Joseph Story[42] has featured particularly prominently, while the American *Restatement, Law of Agency* has also provided a source of reference.[43] The result of this, according to Gibson,[44] is that South African law combines the Roman-Dutch law of mandate and the modern Anglo-American principles of commercial agency.[45] However, it does not merely duplicate Anglo-American law. There is still much that is Roman and Roman-Dutch; for instance, the English doctrine of agency of necessity has not been adopted.

In matters related to contract,[46] in particular, the courts have applied Roman-Dutch law. Here the main problem distinguish between agency and mandate.[47] The distinction between authority and instructions was facilitated to a large degree by the recognition that the relationship between principal and agent (i.e. a person with authority) can be regulated by a contract other than mandate.[48] Furthermore, there are many references to continental doctrine and theory in the modern textbooks. Thus the agent is distinguished from the messenger or *nuntius*[49] and the rule is stated that the agent must be able to formulate an intention, but does not have to have full contractual capacity.[50]

---

[36] Van Jaarsveld *et al.* (n. 30), 208. Cf. Kerr (n. 35), 293.

[37] E.g. Kerr (n. 35), 5 refers to F. M. B. Reynolds, *Bowstead on Agency* (15th edn., 1985), a well known English textbook, and at 45 he quotes from a judgment of Lord Denning in *Stevenson Jordan & Harrison Ltd v. MacDonald & Evans* [1952] 1 TLR 101.

[38] Joubert (n. 22) 17.   [39] *Kruger v. Rheeder* 1972 (2) SA 391 (O) 393.

[40] Cf. *Hersch v. Nel* 1948 (3) SA 686 (A) 703: the Court refers to the English case of *Smith v. M'Guire* 27 LJ Exch 485 to explain the meaning of the term *per procurationem*.

[41] Hutchison *et al.* (n. 30), 592.

[42] Joseph Story, *Commentaries on the Law of Agency* (5th ed, 1857).

[43] Joubert (n. 22), 17; *Kerr* (n. 38), v, acknowledges the granting of permission to print extracts from the *American Restatement*.

[44] J. T. R. Gibson, *Wille's Principles of South African Law* (6th edn., 1970), 449.

[45] Joubert (n. 22), 18.

[46] Silke (n. 2), 12.

[47] J. C. de Wet, J. P. Yeats, *Die Suid-Afrikaanse Kontraktereg en Handelsreg* (3rd edn., 1964) 81. Cf. De Wet/Van Wyk (n. 34), 100, 340.   [48] De Wet/Yeats, 3rd edn. (n. 47), 81.

[49] De Wet/Yeats, 2nd edn. (n. 32), 76.   [50] De Wet/Yeats, 2nd edn. (n. 32), 76.

IV. THE RELATIONSHIP BETWEEN THE PRINCIPAL AND THE THIRD
PARTY

1. The undisclosed principal

The essential basis of agency is authority: the power to affect the legal relations of another.[51] The Roman idea of a *mandatum*, mandate, or *lastgeving*
is still found in modern parlance. The English word 'authority' has, however, become the customary term.

The other usual element in bringing about a change in the principal's
legal position is the manner in which the authority is exercised. The terms
'direct agency' and 'indirect agency', often used in continental legal systems
in this connection, were not adopted in South Africa.[52] The Roman-Dutch
writers drew a clear distinction between those instances where an agent
acted in the name of the principal and with his authority and those instances
where he did not. If he did, the third party and the principal could sue each
other directly with no cession of action.[53] This supports the conclusion of
these writers that the contract was entered into between the principal and
the third party.[54] Modern South African law has made no theoretical
advance on this proposition: it has merely taken note of the European discussion.[55]

A special feature of the South African law of agency is the partial adoption of the English doctrine of the undisclosed principal.[56] When an agent
receives authority from a principal but acts in his own name, the question
arises whether the principal and agent have any rights of action against the
third party and/or the third party against principal or agent with no cession
of rights or delegation of duties. The English law admits such an action on
the basis that the contract was in truth made by the principal. It has been
argued that is not so in Roman-Dutch law.[57] In *Lippert & Co v. Desbats*[58]
and *O'Leary v. Harbord*[59] South African courts adopted the English law
and held that the third party and the principal could sue each other directly
without cession of rights or delegation of duties. Van der Horst[60] contends
that the facts of these cases did not necessitate this decision, but the state-

---

[51] Called 'the principal'.   [52] But cf. De Wet/Yeats, 2nd edn. (n. 32), 75.
[53] Johannes Voet, *Commentarius ad Pandectas*, 17, 1, 9; 19, 1, 16; 45, 1, 3; Ulrich Huber,
Disputationes Juridicae pro Eunomia Romana (Franeker, 1692), 60, 9.
[54] Hugo Grotius, *De Jure Belli ac Pacis*, 2, 2, 12.
[55] Van der Horst (n. 3), 7.   [56] Ibid. 76–7.
[57] Van der Horst, however, ignores the actions against the *institor* (or *faktoor*) and the
exercitor (or ship's captain) found in Roman and Roman-Dutch law, and the extension of
these actions to other situations. He also ignores the Roman rules allowing the principal to sue
the third party. Cf. Joubert (n. 22), 13–16.
[58] 1869 Buch 189.   [59] (1888) 5 HCG 1.
[60] Van der Horst (n. 3) 116.

ment of the law, whether *obiter dictum* or not, became authoritative by virtue of its long-standing acceptance by courts and legal practitioners. The South African courts, however, did not take over the English doctrine *in toto*.[61] In *Natal Trading & Milling Co Ltd v. Inglis*[62] the Transvaal Provincial Division of the Supreme Court held that the principal and the agent were liable in the alternative. The reasoning in certain American decisions was adopted because it was 'satisfactory'[63] and 'more convincing'.[64] It is important to note that the requirement of actual authority was maintained[65] and that set-off or *compensatio* was permitted in respect of claims owed by the third party to the agent.[66] This was the result of the courts having referred to the Roman-Dutch common law relating to cession, as set out by Voet[67] and Van der Keessel.[68] These decisions have demonstrated the independence of South African law from English law regarding the details of the doctrine of the undisclosed principal. When it became necessary to decide whether the third party could plead payment to the agent, the courts again decided differently from the English courts and held that he could.[69]

The case of the undisclosed principal, whose existence is kept secret, is sometimes distinguished from that of the unnamed principal, whose existence is known but whose identity is not revealed.[70] When the agent, acting with authority, concludes a contract with the intention of carrying out the principal's instructions, he intends to contract for the benefit of the principal rather than for himself. However, this depends upon both his (and the other party's) intentions and the interpretation of the contract concluded by the agent with the other party.

As for written contracts, it has been difficult to justify the rule that a principal may always sue on a contract concluded by his agent, for the English doctrine of parol evidence should logically exclude evidence of the authority. However, the courts have held that such evidence did not violate the rule and was therefore admissible.[71] This approach could not solve all cases, but it did reaffirm that English law was not the sole basis of South African law in this respect.

The doctrine of the undisclosed principal has attracted trenchant criticism[72] and was eventually challenged directly. In *Noordkaaplandse*

---

[61] Ibid. 134–6 lists the differences.   [62] 1925 TPD 724.   [63] 733.   [64] 741.

[65] *Judelson & Cohen v. Bootha* 1913 TPD 747; Van der Horst (n. 3), 76.

[66] *Heydenrych v. Woolven* (1897) 14 SC 376; *Symon v. Brecker* 1904 TS 745; Van der Horst (n. 3), 76.

[67] Voet (n. 53), 16, 2, 10.

[68] Dionysius Godefriedus van der Keessel, *Theses selectae juris Hollandici et Zeelandici: ad supplendam Hugonis Grotii introductionem ad jurisprudentiam Hollandicam,* trans. A. Lorenz as *Select Theses of the Law of Holland and Zeeland* (1868), Th. 826.

[69] *Avis v. Highveld Supply Stores* 1925 AD 410.

[70] Hutchison *et al.* (n. 30), 605.   [71] *Cook v. Aldred* 1909 TS 150.

[72] De Wet/Yeats, (n. 47) 88–9; De Wet, *LawSA* (n. 19), § 149, and *LawSA*, first re-issue (n. 19), § 148.

Aartappel-kernmoerkwekers Ko-operasie Bpk v. Cullinan[73] De Vos Hugo J called it a *Fremdkörper*, inelegant and indefensible. It was also maintained that the doctrine had been adopted without adequate investigation of the Roman-Dutch common law. However, in *Cullinan v. Noordkaaplandse Aartappelkernmoerkwekers Koöperasie Bpk*[74] the Appellate Division held that the doctrine of the undisclosed principal had been accepted as part of South African law for such a long time that it could no longer be excised judicially.[75] Such an excision would have retrospective effect, which was undesirable.[76] Although the doctrine was admittedly contrary to the basic principles of South African law (according to which the contract would be entered into by the agent and cession of rights as well as delegation of duties would be necessary to bring the principal into a direct relationship with the third party[77]) it was nevertheless neither unfair nor ineffective.[78] However, the Court held that the doctrine should not be extended. Where a number of undisclosed principals existed, none could claim a proportionate share of the performance owed by the third party as they could have done if they were mere co-creditors.[79] An obligation, it was argued, may not be carved up, because cession of a part of an obligation is not recognized.[80] It has been noted[81] that this decision is evidence of a more moderate or tolerant attitude to the influence of English law.

2. Authority

Agency is dependent upon the authority of the agent. Roman-Dutch common law sources relating to authority often refer to it as though all authority (*mandatum* or *last*) were explicit or express.[82] This does not, of course, accord with reality. Thus, the Romans stated that a person who knowingly allows another to act in his name is deemed to have given authority (a mandate) for this purpose.[83] In *Faure v. Louw*[84] a father had for years allowed his son to act in his name and when the son performed an act which had not been specifically authorized the Court applied this Roman rule and held that he had been given authority to act.[85] Silence only gives rise to this inference if there is a duty to speak.[86]

Reference has sometimes been made to 'implied authority'.[87] This is a real, albeit tacit, authority.[88] Roman and Roman-Dutch law, however, also

---

[73] 1971 (3) SA 417 (NC) 423.   [74] 1972 (1) SA 761 (A).   [75] 767.
[76] 769.   [77] 767.   [78] 768.   [79] 770.
[80] 771.   [81] Van Zyl (n. 30), 487.   [82] Cf. Ulp. D. 46, 3, 3.
[83] Ulp. D. 17, 1, 18; Scaev. D. 17, 1, 60.   [84] (1880) 1 SC 3.
[85] 7–8. Cf. *Coetzer v. Mosenthals Ltd* 1963 (4) SA 22 (A) 23.
[86] *Parsons v. Langemann* 1948 (4) SA 258 (C) 263.
[87] *Broderick Motors Distributors (Pty) Ltd v. Beyers* 1968 (2) SA 1 (O); *Tuckers Land & Development Corporation (Pty) Ltd v. Perpellief* 1978 (2) SA 11 (T) 14.
[88] Cf. *Forder Ritch & Eriksson v. Engar's Heirs* 1973 (1) SA 719 (N) 724.

recognized liability in the absence of express or tacit (real) authority. For instance, the Roman-Dutch sources record a case where a person was held liable on the basis of his former partner's acts because he had not given notice to customers of the dissolution of the partnership.[89] This approach has been expanded, under the guidance of English law, to create a doctrine of 'ostensible authority' or 'apparent authority'.[90] In *Faure v. Louw*[91] the Cape Supreme Court held a 'principal' to be bound by his conduct where he had led another to believe that he had given the 'agent' authority to act in his (the 'principal's') name.[92] This applied particularly where he had appointed a person to a position in which the latter would normally have authority to perform certain acts, but had not in fact been granted that authority in the particular case.[93] It also applied where a person consigned to another goods for sale together with the instruments of title, which enabled the consignee to appear as the owner or at least as someone authorized to dispose of the goods.[94]

Was this rule based on estoppel? If so this would merely be a situation where someone has created the impression that he had given another person authority to act on his behalf and would therefore be precluded from denying that such authority existed[95]. Estoppel is of course an English doctrine, accepted into South African law under the guise of the *exceptio doli*. The following requirements for the application of the doctrine in the sphere of agency have been accepted over the years:

(1) an act or omission by the principal creating the belief that authority was granted or existed.[96] This belief, or impression, may be created indirectly by giving the agent the means with which to create such a false impression;[97]

(2) belief in the mind of the third party that the agent had authority, engendered by the act or omission of the principal;

---

[89] Cf. *Hollandsche Consultatien* (ed. Rotterdam, 1645), Lib. 5, Casus 92. Compare also the position of a husband married in community of property under the old common law, who does not notify third parties that he has revoked consent given his wife to act as public trader, where she continues to act as such in spite of the withdrawal of consent.

[90] *Stephen v. Pepler* 1921 EDL 70 (80).   [91] Above, n. 84.   [92] 10, 12.

[93] *Senior Service (Pvt.) Ltd v. Nyoni* 1987 (2) SA 762 (ZS) 766: secret instructions did not bind a third party who was unaware of them.

[94] *Akojee v. Sibanyoni* 1976 (3) SA 440 (W) 442; *Pretorius v. Loudon* 1985 (3) SA 845 (A) 859.

[95] *Weedon v. Bawa* 1959 (4) SA 735 (D) 741; *Inter-Continental Finance & Leasing Corp (Pty) Ltd v. Stands 56 & 57 Industria Ltd* 1979 (3) SA 740 (W) 743; *Big Dutchman (SA) (Pty) Ltd v. Barclays National Bank Ltd* 1979 (3) SA 267 (W) 282; *Thompson v. Voges* 1988 (1) SA 691 (A) 708.

[96] *Weedon v. Bawa* 1959 (4) SA 735 (D) 741; *Van Rooyen v. Minister van Openbare Werke en Gemeenskapsbou* 1978 (2) SA 835 (A) 849.

[97] *Saambou-Nasionale Bouvereniging v. Friedman* 1979 (3) SA 978 (A) 1002.

(3) an act performed on the strength of, i.e. caused by, the false belief[98] to the detriment of the third party acting in reliance on such belief;[99]
(4) fault.[100]

This English doctrine fitted well with the law of agency and has never been challenged.[101] The position that has emerged is therefore that where the agent alone creates the false belief the principal is not liable. The same is true where the third party draws his own incorrect conclusions without any act by either the agent or the principal. The principal may not evade liability by a private arrangement with the agent.[102] A fairly recent development in the law of agency is that the principal has come to be held liable for misrepresentations made by his agent.[103] Thus the conduct of the agent may make the contract voidable and also give rise to actions for damages based on delict.[104]

Another novel aspect which had to be considered was whether a contract for sale of a vehicle would be valid where the principal, in ignorance of the fact that it was stolen, authorized an agent to sell it. In *Germie Motors (Pty) Ltd v. Erikssen*[105] it was held that a mandate had been given for an illegitimate purpose and was therefore invalid. The contract with the third party was thus also invalid.

In Roman-Dutch common law the termination of authority was governed by the rules laid down for the termination of a mandate.[106] In modern South African law, however, certain novel problems had to be dealt with. It was held by the Witwatersrand Local Division of the Supreme Court that authority to act for a principal during his absence terminates upon his return.[107] On appeal the Appellate Division[108] distinguished between the contract of mandate (which creates the authority) and the authority itself, and held that there was no rule that the agent's authority came to an end

---

[98] *Barclays Western Bank Ltd v. Fourie* 1979 (4) SA 157 (C).

[99] *Peri-Urban Areas Health Board v. Breet* 1958 (3) SA 783 (T); *Albatross Fishing Corp (Pty) Ltd v. Ramsay* 1968 (2) SA 217 (C).

[100] *Kajee v. H. M. Gough (Edms) Bpk* 1971 (3) SA 99 (N); *Southern Life Assoc Ltd v. Beyleveld* 1989 (1) SA 496 (A) 501; but *contra*: *Sonday v. Surrey Estate Modern Meat Market (Pty) Ltd* 1983 (2) SA 521 (C) 534 sq.

[101] Cf. *Lee* (n. 2), 430; De Wet, *LawSA* (n. 19), §§ 135 sq.

[102] *Haddad v. Livestock Products Central Co-op Ltd* 1961 (2) SA 363 (W) 367. This is the case of private instructions referred to in n. 95, above.

[103] *Davidson v. Bonafede* 1981 (2) SA 501 (C) 504.

[104] *Standard Bank of South Africa Ltd v. Coetzee* 1981 (1) SA 1131 (A) 1138; cf. *Randbank Bpk v. Santam Versekeringsmaatskappy Bpk* 1965 (2) SA 456 (W) and 1965 (4) SA 363 (A) 372.

[105] 1985 (2) SA 389 (C).

[106] E.g. where the principal has become insane: *Molyneux v. Natal Land & Colonization Co Ltd* [1905] AC 569 (PC); Ulp. D. 46, 3, 3; Robert Joseph Pothier, *Traité des obligations*, § 81; where the agent has become insolvent: *McEwen v. Hansa* 1968 (1) SA 465 (A); *Voet* (n. 53), 17, 1, 17; Pothier, *loc. cit.*, § 120.

[107] *National Board (Pretoria) (Pty) Ltd v. Swanepoel* 1975 (1) SA 904 (W) 910.

[108] *National Board (Pretoria) (Pty) Ltd v. Estate Swanepoel* 1975 (3) SA 16 (A).

when the principal returned. This was based, *inter alia*, on Pothier[109] and Story.[110] In *A N & G Coal Mining Co (Pty) Ltd v. Stuart*[111] the same Local Division held that a material supervening change in circumstances, which had not been within the contemplation of the parties, terminates the agent's authority.

The courts accepted the Roman-Dutch common law principle that the principal could revoke the agent's authority at will[112] even if this constituted a breach of contract.[113] Certain exceptions were, however, recognized where the principal could not revoke the agent's authority, the most important being where such authority was coupled with an interest.[114] Upon a strict interpretation of the old authorities one may easily conclude that the courts have, in this regard, misconstrued the Roman-Dutch common law. They were apparently influenced by the mandate *in rem suam*, which was used in Roman and Roman-Dutch law to transfer a personal right.[115] Today cession fulfils that function. This development does not prevent a creditor from giving an 'agent' a mandate to claim on his behalf or to collect a claim due to him, but such a mandate is not a cession and is not irrevocable, even if the parties call it a cession *in rem suam*.[116] However, once the courts had recognized the existence of an irrevocable authority in one case, they opened the door to its recognition in other cases: where it is part of a contract,[117] and where revocation would expose the agent to loss.[118] It could not, however, be used to circumvent the rule against *parate executie*[119] of immovable property.[120]

3. Delegation of authority

The development of South African law necessitated the solution of problems relating to delegation of authority. The Romans permitted the mandatary to delegate his position unless he was forbidden to do so. Thus he could employ another to carry out the task which he had undertaken. In

---

[109] Pothier (n. 106), § 119. [110] Story (n. 42), § 480.

[111] 1981 (3) SA 521 (W) 529.

[112] *Consolidated Frame Cotton Corp Ltd v. Sithole* 1985 (2) SA 18 (N) 22; *Standard Bank of SA Ltd v. Ocean Commodities Inc.* 1983 (1) SA 276 (A) 290.

[113] *Joel Melamed & Hurwitz v. Cleveland Estates (Pty) Ltd, Joel Melamed & Hurwitz v. Vorner Investments (Pty) Ltd* 1984 (3) SA 155 (A) 171.

[114] *Natal Bank Ltd v. Natorp & Registrar of Deeds* 1908 TS 1016; *Kotsopoulos v. Bilardi* 1970 (2) SA 391 (C).

[115] Hall (n. 5), 276; De Wet/Van Wyk (n. 34), 108; *LawSA* (n. 19), § 124.

[116] Cf. *Waikiwi Shipping Co Ltd v. Thomas Barlow & Sons (Natal) Ltd* 1978 (1) SA 671 (A) 675.

[117] *Consolidated Frame Cotton Corp Ltd v. Sithole* (n. 112), 25.

[118] *Magua v. Kahn* 1981 (1) SA 1239 (W).

[119] The agreement that gave a secured creditor the right to sell the security if he was not paid.

[120] *Mardin Agency (Pty) Ltd v. Rand Townships Registrar* 1978 (3) SA 947 (W) 954.

South African law, due in part to two contradictory opinions by Van Leeuwen,[121] the opposite rule has been adopted: the agent may not delegate his authority unless permitted to do so—an approach which refers back to the rule that a procurator was not allowed to effect a delegation.[122] The failure to distinguish clearly between delegation of a mandate and delegation of authority resulted in a lack of clarity. The simple fact is that an agent may, for example, employ another to keep or to deliver goods bought or sold.[123] The agent may also delegate other tasks, as a result of which the delegatee is also empowered to exercise the authority to perform the task in the principal's name.

4. Ratification

The Roman doctrine of *ratihabitio* or ratification is a field which has remained relatively untouched by modern influences. The basic Roman-Dutch law rule was that authority to act could be given *ex post facto*. There were, however, lacunae in the Roman-Dutch law, with the result that South African courts had recourse to English law for guidance.[124] Since the English law of ratification was a highly functional system with a Roman basis, corresponding to civil law systems, it could easily be assimilated.[125]

The Roman-Dutch doctrine was that ratification had retrospective effect, thus rendering the act valid as though authority to act had been granted at the time when it was performed. Since this was a factual impossibility if the principal did not exist at that time, it was accepted in South Africa that ratification is excluded in such circumstances.[126] In other words, the basic requirement of ratification came to be that the principal must have existed at the time when the act to be ratified was performed.[127] This presented a problem for contracts entered into on behalf of companies still to be incorporated[128] and the matter was therefore regulated by statute.[129]

A second basic requirement that has become accepted in South African law is that the agent must have purported to act in the name of the alleged principal who now wishes to ratify.[130]

Thirdly, ratification may be express or implied. Since silence is also a form of conduct it may amount to ratification, provided the circumstances support the inference of positive acceptance. This is the case where the law

---

[121] Joubert (n. 22), 201.   [122] Ulp. D. 14, 1, 1, 5; Macer D. 49, 1, 4, 5.
[123] Cf. *Donaldson Investments (Pty) Ltd v. Anglo Transvaal Collieries Ltd* 1979 (1) SA 959 (W) 970.
[124] Van Jaarsveld (n. 30), 186.   [125] Ibid. 256.
[126] De Wet, *LawSA* (n. 19), § 111.   [127] Van Jaarsveld (n. 30), 213–57.
[128] *Sentrale Kunsmis Korporasie (Edms.) Bpk v. NKP Kunsmis Verspreiders (Edms) Bpk* 1970 (3) SA 367 (A) 390; *Swart v. Mbutzi Development (Edms.) Bpk* 1975 (1) SA 544 (T) 550.
[129] Section 35, Companies Act 61 of 1973.   [130] *Erasmus v. Strick* (1969) 1 PH A2 (T).

places a duty on the alleged principal to speak if he acquires knowledge of the conduct of the professed agent.[131]

The question arose in the South African courts whether non-compliance with formalities was fatal: *Nampak Products Ltd t/a Nampak Flexible Packaging v. Sweetcor (Pty) Ltd*[132] held that it was. The courts were also called upon to decide whether the ratification, which bound the principal to the third party, amounted to ratification of the conduct of the agent as against the principal, if the agent had acted contrary to his actual mandate. In *Mine Workers' Union v. Brodrick*[133] the Appellate Division held that it did not.

Certain theoretical problems have, however, remained. It is unclear whether the third party may renounce the contract before ratification. Grotius[134] said that the third party could withdraw. This was confirmed by Van der Keessel.[135] In *Ottawa Rhodesia (Pvt) Ltd v. Burger*[136] this approach was accepted.[137]

5. Lack of authority

The normal result of an act performed without authority is undoubtedly that it does not affect the legal position of the principal. However, South African courts have been faced with a number of difficult situations. For example, in *Ficksburg Transport (Edms) Bpk v. Rautenbach*[138] the addressee handed his acceptance of an offer to a person ostensibly in charge of the property of the offeror. This person had not been authorized to receive the acceptance. Also, no apparent authority existed. The unauthorized act did not bind the principal and the knowledge possessed by the recipient did not constitute knowledge on the part of his employer, so that it could not be held that the principal had been informed of the acceptance.

An agent who uses his authority to perform an act for his own advantage is unauthorized, even if otherwise within the scope of the authority actually given.[139]

---

[131] *Wilmot Motors (Pty) Ltd v. Tucker's Fresh Meat Supply Ltd* 1969 (4) SA 474 (T) 477; *Alli v. De Lira* 1973 (4) SA 635 (T) 639.

[132] 1981 (4) SA 919 (T) 922.　　　　　　　　[133] 1948 (4) SA 959 (A) 979.

[134] Grotius (n. 54), 2, 11, 18.

[135] Dionysius Godefridus van der Keessel, *Praelectiones juris hodierni ad Hugonis Grotii introductionem ad jurisprudentiam Hollandicam* (ed. by van Warmelo, L. I. Coertze, H. L. Gonin, D. Pont, Amsterdam and Cape Town, 1961–71), ad Gr. 3, 3, 38.

[136] 1975 (1) SA 462 (R).

[137] Van Jaarsveld *et al.* (n. 30), 220; Van Jaarsveld (n. 30), 227.

[138] 1988 (1) SA 318 (A).　　　　　　　　[139] *S v. Heller* 1971 (2) SA 29 (A) 53.

6. Formalities

Since the early stages of South African law statutes have required formalities for valid authorization in certain cases.[140] A question which often arises is whether the statute is applicable to mandataries only or to all representatives (i.e. persons who have authority) such as partners and company officers and employees. The answer depends on the interpretation of the statute in question. The courts have adopted the traditional view that not all persons with authority to act are covered by the term 'agent', but it is, of course, always a question of fact whether the authority was given in terms of the relevant statute. For example, it was held in one case that a particular statute using this term did apply to the exercise of an option in an agreement subsequently embodied in a court order.[141]

7. Married women

The development of the law of agency did not merely involve additions to the undeveloped Roman-Dutch law: in certain prevailing circumstances social and economic conditions led to certain rules falling away. Under Roman-Dutch common law a husband was vested with so-called 'marital power' and managed the joint estate if the parties were married in community of property. He could give his wife consent to contract and so make her competent to contract in her own name. If the spouses were married out of community of property, but with retention of marital power (as was the case in most common law marriages between black persons prior to the Marriage and Matrimonial Property Law Amendment Act[142]) he could give his wife authority to act for him. Could he also give her authority to act in his name if they were married in community of property? The Court in *Cross v. Pienaar*[143] answered this question in the affirmative. Marital power has now been abolished[144] in respect of all marriages.

V. THE RELATIONSHIP BETWEEN AGENT AND THIRD PARTY

The agent acting with authority 'in the name of the principal' not only brings his principal into the legal relationship but also excludes his own personal involvement (liability and/or right to claim performance) as far as the third party is concerned. He is, in short, not a party to the act. It is cru-

---

[140] See currently e.g. s. 2(1), Alienation of Land Act 68 of 1981, which requires that an authority to buy or sell immovable property be in writing.

[141] *De Ujfalussy v. De Ujfalussy* 1989 (3) SA 18 (A).

[142] Act 3 of 1988.   [143] 1978 (4) SA 943 (T) 949.

[144] Section 11, Matrimonial Property Act 88 of 1984, as amended by the Fourth General Law Amendment Act 132 of 1993.

cially important, in this regard, to determine what indications are sufficient to show that the act was performed in the name of the principal. The courts interpret the contract in order to determine the intention of the parties.[145] The legislature has also occasionally intervened to regulate these matters, as illustrated by the legislation dealing with negotiable instruments.[146]

The result is that unless the agent excludes his own involvement as a party when concluding a contract he is personally liable as debtor and entitled as creditor, subject to the operation of the doctrine of the undisclosed principal.

The agent may also contract in such a way as to render the principal a party to the contract and at the same time to create rights and/or duties for himself. The courts have accepted that he may bind himself as surety or co-debtor.[147] He may also acquire a right against the third party, as in the case of an agent who has a mandate to sell and who adds a clause to the contract between the principal and the third party that third party will pay his commission, either absolutely or in certain circumstances. This gives him a right as a third party.[148]

One of the most important legal developments was the introduction of the warranty of authority, where an agent has acted without authority. Under Roman-Dutch common law the agent was personally liable under the contract, but South African courts regarded this as an old-fashioned solution. English law provided differently. In English law an agent was held liable, not on the contract as the principal, but on a supplementary contract in which he warranted that he had authority to enter into the contract. This appealed to the Transvaal Supreme Court in *Blower v. Van Noorden*,[149] and the warranty was held to be an actual warranty, and not a warranty implied merely by virtue of a legal rule. This meant that the parties could adduce proof of the circumstances under which the contract had been entered into to show that the parties had excluded such a warranty and that the third party had taken the risk that the ostensible authority existed.[150] It has been argued that a preferable doctrine would be that an agent who falsely pretends to have authority makes a misrepresentation and is liable in delict on the basis of this false statement.[151] This suggestion has not, however, been accepted.

---

[145] Cf. *Ericsen v. Germie Motors (Edms.) Bpk* 1986 (4) SA 67 (A).

[146] Section 24(1), Bills of Exchange Act 34 of 1964.

[147] Cf. *Slabbert, Verster & Malherbe (Noord Vrystaat) (Edms) Bpk v. Gellie Slaghuise (Edms) Bpk* 1984 (1) SA 491 (O).

[148] *Cowley v. Hahn* 1987 (1) SA 440 (E). Cf. *Goodclaims (Pty) Ltd v. Globus-Reederei GmbH* 1981 (3) SA 485 (D) 492, where a maritime agent entered into a contract with the customs officer in favour of prospective claimants. Contracts in favour of third parties are considered further below.   [149] 1909 TS 890.

[150] Cf. *Nordis Construction Co (Pty) Ltd v. Theron, Burke & Isaac* 1972 (2) SA 535 (D); *Terblanche v. Nothnagel* 1975 (4) SA 405 (C).

[151] Cf. *Claude Neon Lights (SA) Ltd v. Daniel* 1976 (4) SA 403 (A).

In the case of a non-existent principal the third party has no claim under this warranty because he would not have been able to claim anything from the person named as principal.[152] In such a case, following English law, the agent is liable under the contract, unless both parties believed that the principal was in existence.[153]

An agent is not automatically liable for false statements made by him to the third party during the contractual process.[154] He is only liable if there was fault on his part. He may also avoid liability for any negligent mis-statements,[155] unless he has acted in bad faith.

VI. THE RELATIONSHIP BETWEEN THE PRINCIPAL AND THE AGENT

Roman-Dutch law recognized *mandatum* and *locatio conductio* as contracts regulating the provision of service and services. Agency has always been associated with mandate for unstated but obvious reasons.[156] The problem was that the Roman contract of mandate required performance of the mandate without reward, although receipt of an *honorarium* was not regarded as infringing the essential nature of the contract. In modern law a new approach was required. One possibility was to refer simply to 'a contract of agency' and to ignore the Roman-Dutch heritage, except in defining the duties of the parties. Another approach was to accept that in modern law mandate is no longer limited to gratuitous services.[157] According to a third suggestion there could be a contract of mandate if there was no remuneration, or a contract of either *locatio conductio operis*[158] or *locatio conductio operarum*[159] when remuneration was promised. This latter approach necessitated the use of the term 'authority' instead of 'mandate' in relation to the task undertaken by the agent.[160]

Once remuneration was introduced a variety of problems arose requiring solutions in law. It had to be determined whether remuneration was promised (expressly or impliedly);[161] the amount of such remuneration or

---

[152] *Indrieri v. Du Preez* 1989 (2) SA 721 (C).

[153] *Nordis Construction Co (Pty) Ltd v. Theron Burke & Isaac* (n. 150); disputed by De Wet, *LawSA* (n. 19), § 111.

[154] *Administrator, Natal v. Bijo* 1978 (2) SA 256 (N).

[155] *Faure v. Joubert* 1979 (4) SA 939 (A) 945.

[156] Cf. *Benson v. Walters* 1984 (1) SA 73 (A) 83, where it was accepted that an attorney was employed under a contract of mandate.

[157] Hall (n. 5), 242; De Wet/Yeats (n. 32), 277.

[158] *Ese Financial Services (Pty) Ltd v. Cramer* 1973 (2) SA 805 (C) 811; Silke (n. 2), 9.

[159] *Smit v. Workmen's Compensation Commissioner* 1979 (1) SA 51 (A) 68; Gibson (n. 44), 450.

[160] Silke (n. 2), 11.

[161] *Verenigde Adverteerders (Edms) Bpk v. Tanner* 1947 (2) SA 1128 (T); Gibson (n. 44), 458.

the formula to be used in calculating it;[162] and lastly at what stage it was earned and/or became payable. The existence of remuneration also had an influence on the right of the agent, as mandatary, to renounce the authority or contract of mandate. De Wet and Van Wyk[163] argue that such renunciation may constitute a breach of contract.

The idea of *quantum meruit* is often encountered: it is used to indicate that an agent is entitled to a reasonable remuneration, when an agreement exists to reward him without specifying the amount of such reward or the formula for determining it. This notion has its roots in Roman law.

Special problems have arisen with regard to estate agents: they are not true agents, having no authority, but they are nevertheless called 'agents'. Their remuneration, referred to as commission, must be earned and accrue (i.e. become payable) before it can be claimed. It is earned when the contract is concluded between the third party and the principal, and it accrues when the price is paid by the third party. Nevertheless, difficulties may arise, for instance the collapse of the contract of sale, or the conclusion of a contract of sale at a price different from that in the mandate of the estate agent on the basis of which the remuneration was determined,[164] or the use of a second agent. All these cases have called for new answers.

The Roman idea that mandate was an unremunerated contract raised the question whether the agent was bound to perform or whether he could simply renounce the mandate (authority). In *Blooms Woollens (Pty) Ltd v. Taylor*[165] it was held that he was bound to perform.

Significant developments took place with regard to the concept of good faith. The Roman lawyers subscribed to the basic principle that the mandatary should render an account in respect of whatever he had received *ex mandato, contra mandatum*, and *occasione mandati*.[166] This principle has been applied not only to bribes received from someone who wishes the agent to use his powers contrary to the best interests of his principal[167] but also to 'secret profits', where the agent buys from the principal and sells at a profit, or buying in his own name that which he is authorized to buy for the principal and then selling it to the principal for a profit, or using information garnered in the service of the mandator to make a profit.[168]

The first rule relevant in the present context is that any act which conflicts with the principle of good faith is unauthorized.[169] Secondly, the onus is on the agent to show that he acted in good faith once a conflict of

---

[162] *Quality Machine Builder v. MI Thermocouples (Pty) Ltd* 1982 (4) SA 591 (W): a fair and reasonable remuneration; Gibson (n. 44), 459.

[163] De Wet/Van Wyk (n. 34), 389.

[164] Cf. *Van Zyl en Seuns (Edms) Bpk v. Nel* 1975 (3) SA 983 (N).

[165] 1962 (2) SA 532 (A).   [166] See Paul. D. 17, 1, 20 and Gai. D. 3, 3, 46.

[167] *South African Fabrics Ltd v. Millman* 1972 (4) SA 592 (A) 596.

[168] *Premier Medical & Industrial Equipment (Pty) Ltd v. Winkler* 1971 (3) SA 866 (W) 868.

[169] *Leites v. Contemporary Refrigeration (Pty) Ltd* 1968 (1) SA 58 (A).

interest was proved.[170] The Roman sanction of accounting for the profits of his breach was retained, without the necessity of proving a breach of contract.[171] It was, however, founded on the fiduciary duty of the agent not to use confidential information to his own advantage,[172] as in English Equity. The agent was considered to be under a duty of trust.[173] As regards the rendering of an account, we find references to the English practice of claiming an account.[174] The normal remedy is to demand an account and upon receipt of it to claim what is due, according to either the account or the evidence adduced by the principal. The principal has no right to call the agent as a witness and cross-examine him. Of course, various modern procedures exist to establish the amount payable, such as the pre-trial conference, or the appointment of a referee.[175]

The problem of bribery also experienced a marked English influence.[176] In English law it is presumed that an agent who accepts an unauthorized gift is thereby influenced to act to the detriment of his principal.[177] The principal then has the right to cancel his contract with the third party.[178] The means by which the consent of the agent was obtained are regarded as being contrary to law and a sufficient ground for this step, even though no fraud in the conventional sense was committed.[179] Public policy prevents the third party from enforcing his bargain.[180] The principal may also claim damages from the third party.[181] Furthermore, he may claim the secret profit from the agent or sue him for damages.[182] In addition, the agent forfeits any right to his commission.[183]

The Roman rules preventing the mandatary from exceeding the bounds of his mandate must also be judged in a new setting. The principal may lose ownership of his goods or be bound by the act of the agent. Modern law gives him an action for damages in such cases.[184]

Where the agent is permitted to use the services of another, he remains responsible for the actions of his own assistant or 'agent'.[185] Where he is permitted to delegate, there are two possibilities: he may appoint a second

---

[170] *Mallinson v. Tanner* 1947 (4) SA 681 (T).

[171] *Uni-Erections v. Continental Engineering Co Ltd* 1981 (1) SA 240 (W) 252.

[172] *Stellenbosch Wine Trust Ltd v. Oude Meester Group Ltd* 1972 (3) SA 152 (C) 160.

[173] *Tobacco Sales Floor Ltd v. Chimwala* 1988 (3) SA 427 (ZS) 432.

[174] Cf. *Doyle v. Fleet Motors PE (Pty) Ltd* 1971 (3) SA 760 (A).   [175] Ibid.

[176] Cf. *Mangold Bros Ltd v. Minnaar & Minnaar* 1936 TPD 48 55 sqq.

[177] *Plaaslike Boeredienste (Edms) Bpk v. Chemfos Bpk* 1986 (1) SA 819 (A) 840–6.

[178] 846.   [179] 848.   [180] 849.

[181] *Nathan, Michaelis, & Jacobs v. Blake's Executors* 1904 TS 626.

[182] *Balmoral Diamond Syndicate Ltd (in liq.) v. Liddle, Smith, Leeb, Harger & Schuller* 1907 WLD 89.

[183] *Hay v. Executors of the late James Roberts* 1907 ORC 64; *Levin v. Levy* 1917 TPD 702; *Le Grange v. Faure* 1921 CPD 764.

[184] *Umtali Farmers' Co-op Ltd v. Sunnyside Coffee Estates (Pvt) Ltd* 1972 1 SA 449 (R).

[185] *Turkstra v. Kaplan* 1953 (2) SA 300 (T).

agent for the principal in substitution for himself or he may appoint a sub-agent who is responsible to the agent.[186]

VII. SPECIAL CASES

The well known example of the auctioneer has already been mentioned; nothing particularly important has been added to his position in modern law. Whereas modern law requires a sale of immovable property to be in writing, it has made an exception for the sale of such property at an auction.[187]

The broker, too, has been mentioned above. He is not normally a factor to whom goods are assigned, but an agent who arranges a sale by acting as a middleman. The best known commercial agent referred to as a broker today is the sharebroker. However, it cannot be said that a sharebroker concludes a contract for his principal with a third party. He does not act as a middleman who brings the principal into contractual relations with a third party. He buys 'for the principal' but in his own name, and then allocates shares to his principal; he sells the principal's shares in a transaction in his own name and delivers the shares to carry out his part of the bargain. This relationship is regulated by statute.[188]

VIII. STIPULATIONS IN FAVOUR OF THIRD PARTIES

Although the rule *alteri stipulari nemo potest* was generally followed in the Roman law[189] there were both exceptions and avoidance techniques, which led to the *stipulatio alteri* becoming a well known and useful instrument.[190] The Roman-Dutch writers held such stipulations to be binding if accepted by the party intended to be benefited.[191] The *stipulatio alteri* is still available and has proved its versatility in contemporary situations.

The modern insurance policy, for instance, often contains a provision nominating a beneficiary, and such a clause can be interpreted as a stipulation in favour of a third party. Furthermore, in the case of a trust *inter vivos* the courts have found the construction of a *stipulatio alteri* useful in order to explain its operation.[192] In cases where A has agreed to give property to

---

[186] *Karaolias v. Sulam t/a Jack's Garage* 1975 (3) SA 873 (R) 875.
[187] Section 3(1), Alienation of Land Act 68 of 1981.
[188] Cf. ss. 22, 25 Stock Exchange Act 1 of 1985.
[189] Silke (n. 2), 6; Zimmermann (n. 3), 34 sqq.
[190] Cf. Wessels (n. 1), 583; Zimmermann (n. 3), 38 sqq.
[191] Cf. Wessels (n. 1), 584–5; Zimmermann (n. 3), 43 sq. J. C. de Wet, *Die ontwikkeling van die ooreenkoms ten behoewe van 'n derde* (doctoral thesis, University of Leiden, 1940) discussed this aspect in detail and came to a different conclusion.
[192] *Crookes v. Watson* 1956 (1) SA 277 (A).

B to hold for some other beneficiary, on the basis that a discretionary distribution of capital and/or income is to take place, the courts have construed the agreement as a stipulation in favour of a third party, with all the
consequences entailed by this construction. According to the accepted construction of the stipulation in favour of a third party, this would mean that
the third party acquires a right of action only after he has accepted the
benefit provided for in the contract. This explanation so impressed
Swanepoel[193] that he conceived a theory which used the *stipulatio alteri* to
explain not only the trust but also the *modus* and other legal institutions
(such as the *fideicommissum inter vivos*) on this basis.

A stipulation in favour of a third party must be distinguished from
agency or representation.[194] It differs from agency in that the *stipulans*, by
contrast with the agent, acts in his own name and for himself.[195] In order
to illustrate this we must note the significant characteristics of the contract
in favour of a third party. The parties A (*stipulans*) and B (*promissor*) contract, each in his own name but with the intention of creating an opportunity for C (the third party) to acquire rights and duties, if he should so wish,
against B. This results in a contract between A and B; C is not a party.[196]
De Wet and Van Wyk[197] ascribe this rule to Grotius.[198] The consequences
of this construction of the stipulation have not been spelt out in detail. We
can, however, conclude that the named third party has an opportunity to
elect whether to ignore (refuse) or to accept the benefit in his favour. This
construction is criticized by De Wet and Van Wyk[199] who maintain that
such a stipulation is not a true contract in favour of a third party. They
argue that the third party immediately acquires a conditional right, from
which the *stipulans* is able to release the *promissor* until the moment of
acceptance, when the right of A (*stipulans*) to release B (the *promissor*) is
extinguished.

A special rule applicable to stipulations in favour of third parties is that
the third party need not exist when the contract is concluded between A and
B. This makes the contract in favour of a third party suitable to benefit
unborn members of the family, or to secure benefits for companies in the
process of registration or formation. The fact that the law has created a
statutory alternative in order to achieve the same purpose has not caused
this option to fall into disuse. However, some uncertainty still prevails in
the case of a stipulation in favour of a third party who is not yet in exis-

---

[193] H. L. Swanepoel, *Oor Stigting, Trust, Fideicommissum, Modus en Beding ten behoewe van
'n Derde* (1961).
[194] *Malelane Suikerkorporasie (Edms) Bpk v. Streak* 1970 (4) SA 478 (T).
[195] De Wet/Yeats, (n. 32), 76; De Wet/Van Wyk (n. 32), 105–9; De Wet, *LawSA* (n. 19),
§ 103.
[196] *Contra*: De Wet/Yeats (n. 32), 82.
[197] De Wet/Van Wyk (n. 34), 93; *idem.* (n. 32), 104.   [198] Grotius (n. 54), 2, 11, 18.
[199] De Wet/Van Wyk (n. 34), 94–6; *idem.* (n. 32), 104–9.

tence, because the third party may not come into existence and, even if he does, may not accept the benefit. In such cases the second contract, intended to exist between the *promissor* and the third party, neither comes into existence nor becomes executory between the two original parties, unless they have agreed specifically that this will be the case. This possibility opens the door for A (*stipulans*) to provide for alternative plans to meet this eventuality. He may, for example, contract with a view to the benefit being obtained by a company in which he will have an interest or, if this proves impossible, seek to obtain the benefit and corresponding duties in his own name.

IX. CONCLUSION

We have seen that the South African law of agency has undergone considerable development, and differs in many respects from the Dutch law of the sixteenth, seventeenth, and eighteenth centuries. A solid Roman legal basis underlies the contract between principal and agent, with additions and alterations to take account of modern problems. The use of comparative law was, for historical and linguistic reasons, limited to Anglo-American sources. The Roman-Dutch concept of agency has been expanded under English influence to include the doctrines of the undisclosed principal, and estoppel, or ostensible authority. This reception of these doctrines has been criticized, but they are now so firmly entrenched that only legislation could dislodge them. Difference of opinion also exists as to whether this would be desirable. The law may be weak in theory but it is strong in providing practical solutions for most modern situations.

PART III

Obligations in a Commercial Context

11: *Purchase and Sale*

JAN LOTZ

I. INTRODUCTION

The South African law of purchase and sale has come down in uncodified form from Roman law via Roman-Dutch law. It has undergone remarkably little change since the seventeenth century, which is not really surprising in view of the following: first, the development of rules relating to contracts of sale was 'one of the most remarkable achievements of Roman jurisprudence';[1] secondly, during the eleven centuries between Justinian's codification and Jan van Riebeeck's landing at the Cape this construct was progressively refined in day-to-day practice and studied, analysed and commented upon by generations of jurists of great erudition; while thirdly, the economic function which contracts of sale were required to fulfil remained basically unchanged even though economic life became increasingly sophisticated. For more than three hundred years, therefore, the South African judicial system has been called upon, as far as the contract of sale is concerned, merely to cross a few t's and dot a few i's. For the rest, answers to questions which arose could be (and indeed were) found mainly in the treatises of the Roman-Dutch authors of the seventeenth and eighteenth centuries. Those legislative provisions which have been introduced over the past fifty years or so to meet the perceived need for consumer protection, as far as they relate to contracts of sale, have for the most part taken the form of restrictions on a seller's power to impose unreasonable *incidentalia* on his buyer and have left the *essentialia* and *naturalia* of the contract largely unchanged.[2]

The static nature of the law of sale presents a problem for any writer attempting to describe the fortunes of such contracts since 1806. Should only the relatively few developments that have taken place be included? Or should a holistic approach be adopted? I argue that the durability of the basic features of the contract of sale is in itself of historical interest and therefore I do not limit the description to those aspects which have undergone change, but present (as fully as possible within the confines of this

---

[1] Reinhard Zimmermann, *The Law of Obligations: Roman Foundations of the Civilian Tradition* (1990, reprint 1993), at 230.
[2] See e.g. s. 6(1), Credit Agreements Act 75 of 1980; s. 5(1), Property Time-Sharing Control Act 75 of 1983; s. 15(1), Alienation of Land Act 68 of 1981.

article) an overview of the current law of purchase and sale in South Africa. At the outset it should be mentioned that according to South African law all contracts are consensual. Contracts of sale therefore, in principle, derive their binding force from the mere agreement between a buyer and a seller, as was the case in Roman and Roman-Dutch law. For the validity of a sale of immovable property a further requirement has, however, been introduced by legislation:[3] the contract must be in writing and signed by the parties or their agents acting on their written authority.

II. DEFINITION AND CHARACTERISTICS OF A CONTRACT OF SALE

De Wet and Van Wyk define a contract of sale in modern South African law as a reciprocal agreement by which one person, the seller, undertakes to deliver an object (*res*) to the other, the buyer, and the latter undertakes to pay the former a sum of money in exchange for that object.[4] According to this definition there are only two *essentialia* for a contract of sale, namely the undertaking by one party to deliver an object and the undertaking by the other to pay a sum of money in exchange. This view has its roots in the works of the institutional writers. Thus Van der Linden[5] describes the contract of sale as the agreement to transfer a certain object, for a fixed price, to someone else ('*de overeenkomst, om een zeker goed, voor eenen bepaalden prijs, aan een ander over te doen*'). These two *essentialia* are sufficient to distinguish a contract of sale from other contracts. *Consensus*, sometimes mentioned as a third *essentiale*,[6] is required in South African law for the validity of any contract. It is not a specific characteristic of contracts of sale. The position mirrors Roman-Dutch law.[7]

In South African (as in Roman-Dutch) law, a seller's undertaking to deliver an object to the buyer does not involve an undertaking by him to

---

[3] At present the relevant provision is s. 2(1), Alienation of Land Act 68 of 1981. Before this section was enacted sales of land were governed by the Formalities in respect of Contracts of Sale of Land Act 71 of 1969 which, in turn, was preceded by s. 1, General Law Amendment Act 68 of 1957. Before 1957 there were legislative provisions in the Transvaal (in s. 30, Procl. 8 of 1902) and Orange Free State (in s. 49, Ordinance 12 of 1906) which required writing for the validity of contracts of sale of land in those two provinces. In Natal ss. 1 and 2 of the Natal Act 12 of 1894 contained evidentiary directives relating to sales of land in that province but did not require writing for the validity of the relevant contracts. In the Cape Province there was no legislation on the subject.

[4] J. C. de Wet and A. H. van Wyk, *Die Suid-Afrikaanse Kontraktereg en Handelsreg*, vol. I (5th edn., 1992), 313.

[5] Johannes van der Linden, *Koopmans Handboek*, 1, 15, 8. Cf. Ulrich Huber, *Praelectiones juris civilis*, 3, 24, 2.

[6] See e.g. Simon van Leeuwen, *Censura Forensis*, 4, 19, 1; Johannes Voet, *Commentarius ad Pandectas*, 18, 1, 1.

[7] Reinhard Zimmermann, 'Der Kaufvertrag', in: Robert Feenstra/Reinhard Zimmermann (eds.), *Das römisch-holländische Recht: Fortschritte des Zivilrechts im 17. und 18. Jahrhundert* (1992), 147 (text to fn. 9).

make the buyer owner of that object.[8] It does, however, impose on him the duty to transfer all his rights to the object, including the right of ownership if it vests in him, unreservedly to the buyer. Consequently, neither a contract which *as part of its performance* requires the transferee to return the *res* to the transferor at some stage[9] nor a contract which permanently reserves the ownership of the *res* to the purported seller[10] can be a contract of sale.

In South African law a contract of sale is a purely obligatory agreement. As in Roman and Roman-Dutch law, performance of the obligations takes place by separate legal acts. These acts involve, in the case of corporeal property, the physical delivery of the object accompanied by an 'abstract' agreement relating purely to the transfer of property *(dinglicher Vertrag)*,[11] and in the case of an incorporeal object such agreement alone.

III. THE THING SOLD (*RES VENDITA, MERX*)

The object of a contract of sale may be, in the words of Van der Linden,[12] *'alle dingen, die van den handel niet zijn uitgesloten'* (all objects which are not excluded from trade) or, in the earlier words of Paul,[13] all objects *'quas quis habere vel possidere vel persequi potest'* (which someone can have, possess, or claim). In other words the *res vendita* may be corporeal or incorporeal, movable or immovable, it may be an object which already exists or which is to come into existence in the future. Purported sales may sometimes be void for reasons connected with the object of the sale. Those reasons have, in South African law, always been sought in the general principles of the

---

[8] See *Kleynhans Bros v. Wessels' Trustee* 1927 AD 271, 282.

[9] A contract of sale may, of course, provide for the return of the *res vendita* on the fulfilment of a resolutive condition or the non-fulfilment of a suspensive condition or the exercise of a *lex commissoria*. In such cases, however, the return of the *res* does not take place *in performance of the contract*; it takes place after the contractual obligations *have been terminated*.

[10] D. 18, 1, 80, 3 and Voet (n. 6), 18, 1, 26. Incidentally, a mistaken interpretation of these texts led the South African courts to assume that in cases of a *temporary* reservation of ownership until the purchase price has been paid there is no contract of sale, as long as the price has not been paid. In *Tuckers Land and Development Corp (Pty) Ltd v. Strydom* 1984 (1) SA 1 (A) 17 this view was rejected. But the erroneous view concerning the effect of a temporary reservation of ownership led to another mistake: the courts expressed the opinion that a suspensive condition in an intended contract of sale prevents the contract from coming into existence until the condition has been fulfilled, although 'a very real and definite contractual relationship' exists between the parties pending fulfilment: see *Corondimas v. Badat* 1946 AD 548; *Palm Fifteen (Pty) Ltd v. Cotton Tail Homes (Pty) Ltd* 1978 (2) SA 872 (A). In *Tuckers Land and Development Corp* (above) the Court acknowledged that the *Corondimas* approach was wrong but refused to overrule it: see *Tucker's* case, 18.

[11] See e.g. *Commissioner of Customs and Excise v. Randles, Brothers and Hudson Ltd* 1941 AD 369, 398.

[12] Van der Linden (n. 5), 1, 15, 8. See also Voet (n. 6), 18, 1, 13; Hugo Grotius, *Inleiding tot de Hollandsche Rechtsgeleertheyd*, 3, 14, 9.

[13] D. 18, 1, 34, 1.

law of contract—mistake, impossibility of performance, illegality—rather than in specific rules relating to contracts of sale. The relevant cases discussed by the institutional writers in their treatises on the law of sale are, in fact, merely examples of the application of general contractual principles. However, over the years the South African legislature has introduced a large number of prohibitions and restrictions on the sale of specific objects.[14]

The best known examples of the sale of *res futurae* in South African law, are (i) a thing to be manufactured by the seller from his own material,[15] (ii) the *emptio rei speratae*, and (iii) the *emptio spei*.

In Roman law the sale of an object which the parties expected to come into existence in the (near) future—the *emptio rei speratae*—was regarded as a sale subject to a condition.[16] Zimmermann explains the position thus: 'Only if it eventually transpired that there was an object did the contract of sale become effective (*ex tunc*, i.e. with retroactive effect). If the crop failed, the contract of sale failed too.'[17]

This seems also to have been the position in Roman-Dutch law. In his discussion of what might be the object of a sale, Voet stated that 'if after an unqualified sale of the fruits of the following year no fruits have grown, then no sale has ensued'.[18] This statement clearly implies that the nature of the contract is for a sale subject to a condition.

The *emptio rei speratae* is still regarded as a conditional sale by some South African authors.[19] This approach ignores the problems which arise when the seller prevents fulfilment of the 'condition' and the doctrine of the fictional fulfilment of the condition consequently finds application. The simpler and, it is suggested, preferable construction is that an *emptio rei speratae* is an unconditional sale of a *res futura*.[20] To a modern South African lawyer a seller's undertaking to deliver an object does not imply that the object is already in existence, and its non-existence does not preclude an unconditional undertaking to deliver it. On this construction it is a *naturale* of every *emptio rei speratae* that the seller will do everything in his power to bring the object into existence so that he can deliver it to the buyer. If as a result of *vis maior* or *casus fortuitus* it does not come into existence then the rules relating to supervening impossibility of performance come into operation: the seller's duty to deliver is extinguished, and with it the buyer's

---

[14] For examples see ss. 18, 35, Arms and Ammunition Act 75 of 1969; ss. 6(2), 12(1), Radio Act 3 of 1952; ss. 14, 18, 19, 22A, Medicines and Related Substances Control Act 101 of 1965; ss. 2(1) and 3(1), Foodstuffs, Cosmetics and Disinfectants Act 54 of 1972.

[15] If the material is supplied by the alleged buyer the contract is one of *locatio conductio operis* and not of sale—see e.g. *SA Wood Turning Mills (Pty) Ltd v. Price Bros (Pty) Ltd* 1962 (4) SA 263 (T); *S v. Progress Dental Laboratory (Pty) Ltd* 1965 (3) SA 192 (T).

[16] See Zimmermann (n. 1), 246 and the authorities quoted by him. [17] *Loc. cit.*

[18] Voet (n. 6), 18, 1, 13 (trans. Percival Gane, *The Selective Voet* (1955 sqq.))

[19] See A. J. Kerr, *The Law of Sale and Lease* (1984), 19 sq.; G. R. J. Hackwill, *MacKeurtan's Sale of Goods in South Africa* (5th edn., 1984), § 2, 2, 2.

[20] Cf. D. F. Mostert, D. J. Joubert and G. Viljoen, *Die Koopkontrak* (1972), 22 sq.

duty to pay the purchase price. The buyer cannot insist on immediate delivery because he must give the seller a reasonable time to perform, and the seller, in effect, bears the risk of the *res* not coming into existence because that is what the parties have agreed, whether expressly or tacitly. On this view a seller who deliberately prevents the *res* from coming into existence will be liable for a breach of contract.

In the case of speculative sales where the purchaser is to bear the risk of the object of sale not coming into existence—the *emptiones spei*—the contract in Roman law was not conditional but came into existence immediately.[21] The position was the same in Roman-Dutch law. Voet explains that in this instance 'a mere expectation *(spes)* has been purchased ... [and] ... the expectation takes the place of the thing'.[22] However, there are objections to regarding an *emptio spei* as the sale of a *spes*, or chance.[23] To regard a *spes* as a *res* is to strain that term beyond reasonable limits. It is suggested that in the case of an *emptio spei*, too, there is an immediate and unconditional sale of a *res futura*, again implying that the seller will do everything in his power to ensure that the object comes into existence. If, however, owing to *vis maior* or *casus fortuitus*, the object of the sale does not come into existence the rules relating to impossibility of performance do not come into operation in this situation. While the seller's duty to deliver the object is extinguished by the impossibility the buyer's duty to pay the purchase price is not.[24] Once again, this result is based on the intention (actual or presumed) of the parties.

For a South African lawyer, as for his Roman-Dutch predecessor, there is nothing strange in the notion of a purely generic sale and there are consequently no restrictions on such sales in South African law. If the sale is from an unlimited *genus* the rule *genus non perit* applies.[25]

Inasmuch as a South African seller (like his precursors in ancient Rome and seventeenth-century Holland) does not undertake to transfer ownership of the *merx* to the buyer, it is possible, as in Roman and Roman-Dutch law, for a seller to sell a *res aliena*[26]— as long as it does not belong to the buyer.[27]

---

[21] Zimmermann (n. 1), 248. [22] Voet (n. 6), 18, 1, 13 (trans. Gane).
[23] Among modern South African authors, see Kerr (n. 19), 20–2; Hackwill (n. 19), § 2, 2, 2; Mostert/Joubert/Viljoen (n. 20), 24 sq.
[24] Cf. Mostert/Joubert/Viljoen (n. 20), 24 sq.
[25] Cf. *Hersman v. Shapiro and Co* 1926 TPD 367.
[26] See e.g. *Kleynhans Bros v. Wessels' Trustee* 1927 AD 271; *Frye's (Pty) Ltd v. Ries* 1957 (3) SA 575 (A); *Shaw v. Arami* 1913 WLD 105; *Ensor v. Kader* 1960 (3) SA 458 (D).
[27] It is impossible to 'deliver' a thing to a buyer who is already the unrestricted owner thereof; the purported sale is therefore void: cf. *Cawcutt v. Teperson and Saacks* 1916 CPD 406. But an owner may validly buy the limited interest which another may have in his property: cf. *Hilton Quarries Employees' Social and Athletic Club v. Commissioner for Inland Revenue* 1956 (3) SA 108 (N); *Venter v. Rosmead Railway Recreation Club* 1960 (4) SA 183 (E). See also the note by J. E. Scholtens in (1960) 77 *SALJ* 288 sqq. and the one by P. Q. R. Boberg in *Annual Survey of South African Law* (1960), 107 sqq., 106–8.

IV. THE PURCHASE PRICE (*PRETIUM*)

As in both Roman law (after acceptance of the Proculian view) and Roman-Dutch law,[28] the purchase price in South African law must be in money or, more accurately, at least partly in money. Therefore if the parties agree to exchange objects the contract is not one of sale.[29] However, if one of them promises payment of a sum of money *plus* delivery of an object, this may be classified as a contract of sale. The nature of such contracts is discussed, generally, in connection with trade-in agreements which are common in the motor trade. The crucial issue in these cases is usually whether the aedilitian actions may be brought on the grounds of either a defect in the object traded in, or a *dictum et promissum* relating to it.

Voet states:

If partly money and partly something else is given for a thing, we must look to see what was in the mind of the contracting parties, whether purchase or barter. If that matter is not clear, the transaction must be classified according to the leading factor. Thus if there is more in money, and less in the value of other things given, the contract ought to be one of sale; but the contrary if there is more in the thing given than in the money.[30]

A subtle variation of Voet's approach was accepted in *Mountbatten Investments (Pty.) Ltd v. Mahomed.*[31] Bristowe J summarized the approach to be followed in determining whether an agreement, in which the price is not wholly in money, is a contract of sale as follows:[32]

(a) If no part of the consideration for the delivery of a merx is in cash the contract cannot be classified as a sale and must be regarded as a barter.

(b) If part of the consideration is in cash and part is in kind the intention of the parties must be looked to in order to determine whether the contract is truly a sale or whether it is a barter.

(c) If the parties disagree as to their intention or if there is reason not to accept their description of what contract they intended to enter into, the relative values of the cash and kind should be looked to as one of the factors relevant to a determination of the issue. There may of course be other factors.

(d) Only if all else fails or is equivocal should the presumption described by Voet and Huber be resorted to.[33]

However, it cannot be said that this question has been settled in South African law. The courts have vacillated about the true nature of the trade-

---

[28] See Zimmermann (n. 1), 250 sqq. (Roman law); *idem* (n. 7), 159 sqq. (Roman-Dutch law).
[29] *Rand Water Board v. Receiver of Revenue* 1907 TH 215; *Pretoria Townships Ltd v. Pretoria Municipality* 1913 TPD 362.
[30] Voet (n. 6), 18, 1, 22 (trans. Gane).   [31] 1989 (1) SA 172 (D).   [32] 178A-C.
[33] The presumption that, in case of doubt, the contract must be regarded as a contract of sale: see Voet (n. 6), 18, 1, 22; Ulrich Huber, *Heedendaegse Rechtsgeleertheyt*, 3, 4, 3.

in transaction. At various times it has been suggested that such a transaction embodies two contracts of sale;[34] that the transaction is one of exchange (barter)—at least where the major consideration on each side is property and not money[35]—and, finally and most often, that it is a (single) contract of sale.[36] Even if a trade-in transaction is regarded as a contract of sale, however, it remains unclear whether the aedilitian actions will lie in respect of the object which is traded in and how the trade-in part of the agreement is to be construed. In *Wastie v. Security Motors (Pty) Ltd*[37] an *actio quanti minoris* was allowed on the ground of a defect in the motor car which was traded in, but this decision was criticized by Bristowe J in *Mountbatten Investments (Pty) Ltd v. Mahomed*[38] in which an *actio quanti minoris* was refused on the ground of a *dictum et promissum*. In neither case was the nature of a trade-in satisfactorily explained. Academic writers have also remained divided. De Wet and Van Wyk[39] and Luanda Hawthorne[40] submit that the trading in of a vehicle (or other object) constitutes a *datio in solutum* of part of the purchase price. M. F. B. Reinecke, however, argues[41] that the so-called trade-in transaction is best explained by the concept of an *obligatio facultativa*: the parties agree that the buyer is bound to pay a purchase price sounding wholly in money but has the option of substituting another (specified) performance for a part of the price. Perhaps the true position is that the parties sometimes intend an *obligatio facultativa* for the buyer and at other times a *datio in solutum*.

The Roman requirement that the purchase price must be certain—in the sense of being at least ascertainable by reference to some objective standard[42]—has never been questioned in South African law. This is clear from a long line of cases since 1905.[43] However, as in Roman-Dutch law, cases

---

[34] This view was advanced, but rejected, in *Massyn's Motors v. Van Rooyen* 1965 (3) SA 717 (O).

[35] A view which found some support in *R v. Van Heerden* 1935 EDL 292 and *Vizirgianakis v. Karp* 1965 (2) SA 145 (W).

[36] A view accepted in *Antonie v. The Price Controller* 1946 TPD 190; *Bouwer v. Adelford Motors (Pty) Ltd* 1970 (4) SA 286 (E), *Wastie v. Security Motors (Pty) Ltd* 1972 (2) SA 129 (C); *Mountbatten Investments (Pty) Ltd v. Mahomed* (n. 31) and *Bloemfontein Market Garage (Edms) Bpk v. Pieterse* 1991 (2) SA 208 (O). M. F. B. Reinecke, in a case note in 1989 *TSAR* 442 sqq., made the valid point that while the parties' classification of their contract may be useful, too much weight cannot be attached to it. How a contract should be classified is a question of law and the parties are, as a rule, not legal experts. Reinecke suggests that the answer to the question of classification is to be sought in the *essentialia* to which the parties have agreed.

[37] Above, n. 36.

[38] Above, n. 31. See also *Bloemfontein Market Garage (Edms) Bpk v. Pieterse* (n. 36).

[39] De Wet/Van Wyk (n. 4), 314, fn. 5.

[40] In 2 case notes, in 1990 (53) *THRHR* 116 sqq., and in 1992 (55) *THRHR* 143 sqq.

[41] In the case note cited in n. 36.

[42] Zimmermann (n. 1), 253 sqq. (Roman law); *idem* (n. 7), 160 sq. (Roman-Dutch law).

[43] See e.g. *Colonial Gov v. De Beers Consolidated Mines Ltd* (1905) 25 SC 452; *Douglas v. Baynes* 1907 TS 508, 1908 TS 1207; *R v. Caplin* 1931 OPD 172; *Cassimjee v. Cassimjee* 1947 (3) SA 701 (N); *Erasmus v. Arcade Electric* 1962 (3) SA 418 (T).

have come before the courts where the particular standard in question produces unsatisfactory results. Thus, a problem arises when a third person whom the parties have appointed for that purpose fixes a price that is palpably out of proportion to the object sold.[44] Voet[45] suggests that in such cases the 'award is to be corrected in goodness and in fairness by a *bonae fidei* judicial proceeding, that is to say, by the judge doing his duty in accord with the nature of *bonae fidei* transactions'. His solution is echoed, albeit in a somewhat modified form, in *Total South Africa (Pty) Ltd v. Bonaiti Developments (Pty) Ltd; Valdave Investments (Pty) Ltd; Dave White Holdings (Pty) Ltd;* and *Dave White Investments (Pty) Ltd.*[46] Friedman J summarized the position as follows:

Where parties to a contract make provision for the valuation of the subject-matter of the contract by a third party, neither party can be held to that valuation if it is one that is so grossly excessive (or in suitable cases so grossly less than the true value) that it bears no reasonable relationship at all to the true value of the property. The party in whose favour the valuation would appear to be cannot compel the other party to the contract to perform it at that valuation or, to put it conversely, the party aggrieved by the valuation can refuse to pay a price or rental based on that valuation. In the event, however, that the aggrieved party resists performance based upon the excessive valuation, the non-aggrieved party has the right to elect whether to resile from the contract or to carry it out upon the basis of the valuation found by the Court to be a true or fair valuation of the res vendita or the leased property.[47]

While the current price of an article is an acceptable objective norm for determining the purchase price in a specific case, a 'reasonable price' for an article apparently is not,[48] as was also the case in Roman-Dutch law.[49] However, in *Genac Properties Jhb (Pty) Ltd v. NBC Administrators CC (previously NBC Administrators (Pty) Ltd)*[50] Nicholas AJA observed that 'it is difficult to see on what principle a sale for a reasonable price, or a lease for a reasonable rent, should be regarded as invalid'.[51] The remark was *obiter*, but indicates that the last word on the possibility of selling at a reasonable price may not yet have been spoken.[52] In *Erasmus v. Arcade Electric*[53] Voet's statement that an agreement to sell for a just price did not

---

[44] See *Gillig v. Sonnenberg* 1953 (4) SA 675 (T); *Dublin v. Diner* 1964 (1) SA 799 (D); *Bekker v. RSA Factors* 1983 (4) SA 568 (T).

[45] Voet (n. 6), 18, 1, 23 (trans. Gane). Cf. Zimmermann (n. 7), 160 sq.

[46] 1981 (2) SA 263 (D).

[47] At 266 sq. of the report. See also *Hurwitz v. Table Bay Engineering (Pty) Ltd* 1994 (3) SA 449 (C).

[48] See *Erasmus v. Arcade Electric* (n. 43); *Adcorp Spares PE (Pty) Ltd v. Hydromulch (Pty) Ltd* 1972 (3) SA 663 (T).

[49] Zimmermann (n. 7), 161; Arnoldus Vinnius, *Institutiones*, 3, 24, 1, 2; Voet (n. 6), 28, 1, 2.

[50] 1992 (1) SA 566 (A). [51] 577G.

[52] See also H. J. Erasmus, P. van Warmelo and D. Zeffertt, 'Pretium Certum and the *Hooge Raad*', (1975) 92 *SALJ* 267 sqq. in this regard.

[53] Above, n. 43.

constitute a valid contract was expressly followed and this remains the law.

Sales of an unweighed, unmeasured, or uncounted quantity of goods at an agreed price per unit, on the other hand, are valid; once weighing, measuring, or counting has taken place the total price may be determined by a simple calculation. Problems have arisen from time to time when, in a sale of land, the total price was calculated at an agreed price per unit and the number of units was stated in the contract but it later emerged that the actual extent of the land was greater or smaller than had been stated. This kind of sale may be by measure (*ad mensuram, ad quantitatem*) or by the piece (*ad corpus*), but in either case the question is whether the price has to be adjusted to compensate for the discrepancy. An answer was provided, *obiter*, by Jansen JA in *Welgemoed v. Sauer*.[54] As far as both sales *ad quantitatem* and sales *ad corpus* are concerned, he held, the purchase price must be adjusted in proportion to the excess or shortfall, unless there is an agreement to the contrary. In a sale *ad quantitatem* such adjustment takes place in the normal course of events; in a sale *ad corpus* only if the discrepancy is sufficiently large. This accords with Roman-Dutch law.[55]

The doctrine of *laesio enormis*, which formed part of the Roman-Dutch common law,[56] has been abolished by statute in all parts of South Africa.[57] There is consequently no requirement in modern South African law for the purchase price to bear any relation to the intrinsic or market value of the object concerned, nor that it must be a just price (*iustum pretium*).

V. THE DUTIES OF THE PARTIES IN TERMS OF THE *ESSENTIALIA* OF A CONTRACT OF SALE

The *essentialia* of a contract of sale give rise to two obligations. One requires the buyer to pay the purchase price to the seller, the other imposes a duty on the seller to deliver the *res vendita* to the buyer. As stated above, these duties are performed by the parties through legal acts which are distinct from the agreement creating the obligations.

With regard to the currency in which the price has to be paid, we find

[54] 1974 (4) SA 1 (A) 16B-C.

[55] Prior to *Welgemoed v. Sauer* there were cases in which it was held that in a sale *ad corpus* no adjustment is made for an excess or shortfall in the *res vendita*, unless the seller has misstated its extent with fraudulent intent: see e.g. *Elliott v. McKillop* (1902) 19 SC 350; *Dingley v. Cornforth* (1917) 38 NLR 386. But a question mark must now be placed against those cases. See further the notes on the *Welgemoed* case by P. van Warmelo in (1975) 92 *SALJ* 12 sqq. and D. J. Joubert in (1975) 38 *THRHR* 177 sqq.

[56] Zimmermann (n. 1), 259 sqq. (Roman law); Christoph Becker, 'Das Problem der Austauschgerechtigkeit', in: Feenstra/Zimmermann (eds.), (n. 7), 201 sqq. (Roman-Dutch law).

[57] In the Cape by s. 8, Act 8 of 1879 (Cape); in the Free State by s. 6, Ordinance 5 of 1902 (OFS); and in Transvaal and Natal by s. 25, Act 32 of 1952.

among the institutional writers a reasonable, if somewhat *laissez-faire*,
approach to what is deemed acceptable. Ulrich Huber informs us that: 'He
who owes a sum of money can pay it in all kinds of current coin, but if he
owes certain denominations of money, then the creditor can be given no
money from which he might suffer any loss, but, it appears, may be given
another class which cannot be attended by any loss'.[58]

Nowadays, payment must be effected in South African legal tender unless
the parties have agreed otherwise.[59] This means, *inter alia*, that a seller may
refuse payment by cheque, bill of exchange, postal order, money order, etc.
It has, however, been held that

> ... in an ordinary commercial contract, in the absence of anything signifying the
> contrary, only some slight indication in the contract or evidence would generally suf-
> fice for inferring or implying that payment of the creditor can be effected by cheque,
> because that is now a widely used and recognised *medium* of payment in such trans-
> actions.[60]

At Roman-Dutch common law, faithful to the position in Roman law
where *emptio venditio* did not imply a warranty of title,[61] a seller discharged
his duty to deliver a movable object of sale by providing the buyer with
vacua possessio (undisturbed possession) of the object. This meant that the
buyer had to obtain physical occupation of the object free from lawful or
unlawful interference by anyone else.[62] However, although the duty of the
seller was in principle 'to deliver' and not to pass ownership, he had in fact
a qualified duty to pass ownership. For a seller was under a duty to transfer all his rights in the *res vendita* to the buyer, including the right of ownership if he was owner. Grotius[63] sets out the position as follows: 'On the

---

[58] Huber (n. 33), 3, 38, 10.

[59] What constitutes legal tender in the Republic of South Africa is set out in s. 17, South
African Reserve Bank Act 90 of 1989. When parties express a money debt (e.g. the price) to
be payable, in the Republic, in a foreign currency, payment may be made in the South African
currency equivalent of the foreign currency. In the absence of a contrary agreement, the rate
of exchange at which the conversion to the South African currency is to take place is that
which prevails at the time of payment. See e.g. *Barry Colne and Co (Tvl.) Ltd v. Jackson's Ltd*
1922 CPD 372; *Bassa Ltd v. East Asiatic (SA) Co Ltd* 1932 NLR 386; *Murata Machinery Ltd
v. Capelon Yarns (Pty) Ltd* 1986 (4) SA 671 (C); *Elgin Brown and Hamer (Pty) Ltd v.
Dampskibsselskabet Torm Ltd* 1988 (4) SA 671 (N); *Barclays Bank of Swaziland Ltd v.
Mnyeketi* 1992 (3) SA 425 (W). A contract may, of course, stipulate that payment must be
made in the foreign currency but such a payment may be prohibited by exchange control regulations in which case the contract will be unenforceable. Matters were different in the
Netherlands of the 17th and 18th centuries where foreign coins were apparently in common
use; see Voet (n. 6), 46, 3, 9; Huber (n. 33), 3, 38, 10.

[60] In *Esterhuyse v. Selection Cartage (Pty) Ltd* 1965 (1) SA 360 (W) *per* Trollip J. Payment
by cheque is, however, regarded as a conditional or provisional payment until the cheque has
been honoured: see *Eriksen Motors (Welkom) Ltd v. Protea Motors, Warrenton* 1973 (3) SA
685 (A); D. H. van Zyl, 'Payment by cheque: cash or credit?', (1974) 91 *SALJ* 337.

[61] Zimmermann (n. 1), 278 sqq. (Roman law); *idem* (n. 7), 163 sqq. (Roman-Dutch law).

[62] Mostert/Joubert/Viljoen (n. 20), 155 sqq.

[63] Grotius (n. 12), 3, 15, 4 (trans. R. W. Lee, *The Jurisprudence of Holland*, vol. I (1926)).

seller's side the execution of the contract consists in the seller's duty, if he is owner of the thing sold, to make the buyer owner of it. . . . If the seller is not owner, he must deliver to the buyer vacant possession (*vrij bezit*).' This approach still holds true today.[64]

In South African law transfer of ownership of a movable requires not only physical delivery but also an agreement between the parties that ownership be transferred from the owner/seller to the purchaser.[65] Although it is generally accepted that the rule of Inst. II, 1, 41 (ownership does not pass under a contract of sale unless the price has been paid or credit been given) still forms part of South African law,[66] payment of the price or the giving of credit is, at most, evidence of the intention of the parties and not an independant legal requirement for the passing of ownership. In *Eriksen Motors (Welkom) Ltd v. Protea Motors, Warrenton*,[67] for instance, the Appellate Division held that although a motor car had been sold for cash and the purchase price had not been paid, the ownership of the car had nevertheless passed to the buyer because the parties had intended such transfer of ownership. Conversely, in most instalment sales of movables ownership is reserved to the seller until the last instalment of the price has been paid, notwithstanding that credit has been given to the buyer. The *Eriksen Motors* case has been strongly criticized by some authors[68] and equally strongly supported by others.[69]

For sales of immovable property the common law appears to have been amended by s. 72 of the Insolvency Act, 1916, Amendment Act of 1926,[70] which provided that a purchaser of immovable property who had undertaken to pay the purchase price in instalments and had paid at least 50 per cent of the price was entitled to demand transfer of the property from the seller against registration of a first mortgage bond over the property to secure the balance of the price and interest. This section appeared to place a *duty* on the seller of immovable property by instalments to *transfer ownership* to the buyer.[71] Section 72 of the Insolvency Act, 1916, Amendment

---

[64] Mostert/Joubert/Viljoen (n. 20), 135, 143 sqq., and the authorities there cited.

[65] See *Commissioner of Customs and Excise v. Randles, Brothers and Hudson Ltd* (n. 11) 398 sq., 411.

[66] See e.g. Robert Feenstra, 'Eigendomsovergang bij koop en terugvorderingsrecht van de onbetaalde verkoper: Romeins recht en Middeleeuws handelsrecht', (1987) 50 *THRHR* 127 sqq.

[67] Above, n. 60. Cf. *Lendalease Finance (Pty) Ltd v. Corporacion de Mercadeo Agricola* 1976 (4) SA 464 (A).

[68] E.g. D. H. van Zyl (1974) 91 *SALJ* 339 sqq.; D. J. Pavlich, *Annual Survey of South African Law* (1973), 204; J. R. Harker, 'Cash and Credit Sales', (1974) 91 *SALJ* 350 sqq.; De Wet/Van Wyk (n. 4), 352, fn. 241.

[69] E.g. David Zeffertt in his note to the *Eriksen Motors* case in: Ellison Kahn, *Contract and Mercantile Law through the Cases*, vol. II (2nd edn., 1985), 237.

[70] Act 29 of 1926.

[71] See Mostert/Joubert/Viljoen (n. 20), 145. A case where ownership does not pass with registration of the transfer will always be exceptional, e.g. where the transferor is still the registered owner of the property but someone else has acquired ownership by prescription.

Act was repealed by the Alienation of Land Act[72] but was, at the same time, re-enacted as s. 27 of the latter Act. Failure by the seller to comply with the buyer's demand for transfer within three months entitles the buyer to cancel the contract[73] but apparently does not entitle him to an order for specific performance. In *York & Co (Pvt) Ltd v. Jones (1)*[74] Murray CJ declared that:

[a] seller of immovable property is under at least three duties to the purchaser in regard to the delivery of the property. He is firstly bound to effect transfer in the Deeds Office into the purchaser's name. Secondly, he is obliged to give physical possession of the property to the purchaser on or before the stipulated date. Thirdly, he is under duty, even after transfer and giving of possession, to guarantee the purchaser against eviction ...

In spite of its generality, this *dictum* may not be the unequivocal acknowledgement of a duty on the seller of immovable property to transfer ownership to the buyer which it might seem, for Murray CJ may have intended to restrict his remarks to the situation where a seller has specifically contracted to transfer ownership. This is what had happened in *York & Co (Pvt) Ltd v. Jones (1)*.

The remedies of a seller for the buyer's breach of duty to pay the purchase price and those of a buyer on the ground of the seller's breach of duty to deliver the *res vendita* must, in South African law, be sought in the general principles of the law of contract. A buyer, like any other contracting party, is in principle entitled to an order for specific performance, but the courts have a discretion to refuse such an order.[75]

VI. THE DUTIES AND LIABILITIES OF THE PARTIES IN TERMS OF THE *NATURALIA* OF THE CONTRACT OF SALE

1. The duties and liability of the buyer

The duties and liability of a buyer in terms of the *naturalia* of a contract of sale are unchanged from Roman and Roman-Dutch law. The buyer must reimburse the seller for necessary expenses incurred by the latter on the *res vendita* between sale and delivery.[76] If delivery takes place before the purchase price is paid the buyer is liable to pay interest on the price.[77] Mostert, Joubert, and Viljoen[78] are of the opinion that the buyer's liability for

---

[72] Act 68 of 1981. [73] Section 27(3), Act 68 of 1981. [74] 1962 (1) SA 65 (SR) 66G.
[75] See *Farmers' Co-operative Soc v. Berry* 1912 AD 343; *Haynes v. Kingwilliamstown Municipality* 1951 (2) SA 371 (A).
[76] See e.g. D. 19, 1, 13, 22; Grotius (n. 12), 3, 15, 1; De Wet/Van Wyk (n. 4), 347.
[77] See e.g. D. 19, 1, 13, 20; Grotius (n. 12), 3, 15, 1; De Wet/Van Wyk (n. 4), 159.
[78] Above, n. 20, 264.

expenses incurred by the seller in looking after the object of sale depends on the incidence of the risk[79] and that it only arises where the buyer bears the risk of damage to, or destruction of, the object sold. As far as the buyer's liability for interest is concerned, I. van Zijl Steyn in his doctoral thesis on *mora debitoris*[80] concluded that it does not depend on *mora debitoris* but is based entirely on equitable considerations. This view was vindicated in *Milner v. Friedman's Trustee*.[81] The equitable rule was also referred to in *George Loader & Co v. Vosloo*;[82] however, in *Hanekom v. Bosman*[83] it was said that it ought not to be applied too rigidly as a buyer must often keep the purchase price ready for payment at short notice, so that he derives no benefit from the money in the meantime. However, other cases lend support to the view that a buyer can only be held liable for interest when he is *in mora*.[84]

2. The duties and liability of the seller

(a) The seller's duty of custody

In the period between the conclusion of a contract of sale and the delivery of the *res vendita* to the buyer a seller is under a duty 'to look after [the property sold] as would a *bonus paterfamilias* and if he fails in that duty the purchaser will be entitled to claim damages or, if, but only if, the result of the vendor's neglect is that the thing sold is materially different from the thing tendered, to repudiate the contract and refuse to take delivery'.[85] When the buyer is *in mora creditoris* the seller's liability is restricted to gross negligence and fraud, but when the seller is *in mora debitoris* he escapes liability only if he can show that the object would have been damaged or lost even if it had been delivered on time.[86] Where the damage or loss is imputable to the fault of a third person, the seller incurs no liability but must cede to the buyer any claim which he may have against the third party, provided, of course, that the risk is on the buyer.[87] All these rules stem from Roman-Dutch law.[88]

---

[79] On the risk in contracts of sale see below, Section VIII.

[80] Published as *Mora debitoris volgens die hedendaagse Romeins-Hollandse reg* (1929), 73.

[81] 1925 OPD 296, *per* McGregor J.   [82] 1939 OPD 151, 155.

[83] 1943 CPD 327, 331.

[84] *Milner v. Friedman's Trustee* (n. 81), *per* Blaine J; *Applebee v. Berkovitch* 1951 (3) SA 236 (C) (described by De Wet/Van Wyk (n. 4), 159 as unconvincing); *Schoeman v. Botha* 1968 (1) SA 637 (T).

[85] *Per* Schreiner JA in *Frumer v. Maitland* 1954 (3) SA 840 (A) 845. Cf. also *Frenkel v. Ohlssons Cape Breweries Ltd* 1909 TS 957 and *Weiner v. Calderbank* 1929 TPD 654.

[86] See Voet (n. 6), 18, 6, 2; Grotius (n. 12), 3, 14, 34; De Wet/Van Wyk (n. 4), 329; Hackwill (n. 19), § 6, 5, 5.

[87] See *Grobbelaar v. Van Heerden* 1906 EDC 229; *Schackell v. Lippert* 7 SC 75; *Van Wyk v. Herbst* 1954 (2) SA 571 (T); De Wet/Van Wyk (n. 4), 329; Hackwill (n. 19), § 6, 5, 6.

[88] Cf. Voet (n. 6), 18, 6, 2; Grotius (n. 12), 3, 14, 34.

(b) The seller's liability for eviction

As stated above[89] the validity of a contract of sale does not require that the seller owns the object sold. Nor need he undertake to make the buyer owner. On the other hand, it is almost always the intention of the parties to a contract of sale that the buyer should acquire the ownership of the object bought and exercise the powers of an owner over it. These conflicting positions were reconciled: it became a *naturale* of contracts of sale that the seller warrants that no one with a better title to the object will deprive the buyer wholly or partly of his use and enjoyment of the *res vendita*; that is, of the use and enjoyment which he would have had, had he become owner. This is the essence of the liability for eviction,[90] as was also recognized in Roman and Roman-Dutch law.[91] However, in South Africa 'the warranty against eviction has in certain respects been modified in the direction of providing more effective help to the buyer'.[92] That modification took place in two directions, with respect to what constitutes eviction, and with respect to the remedies of a buyer who has been evicted.

As far as the first of these issues is concerned, the original meaning of eviction, namely the dispossession of a buyer by judicial decree, has been extended to include cases where the court order in question has not in fact *deprived* the buyer of his possession of the *res vendita*, and also cases where the buyer has voluntarily surrendered, or undertaken to surrender, the *res vendita* to a claimant. A buyer compelled by a court order to pay a sum of money in order to retain the object of the sale is considered to have been evicted[93] and so is an intermediate buyer in a chain of sales who has to make reparation to *his* buyer when the latter is evicted.[94] A buyer who voluntarily surrenders, or undertakes to surrender, the object of sale to a claimant alleging a superior title can be considered to have been evicted only if he is able to prove that the claimant's title was incontestable and eviction thus inevitable.[95]

Turning to the remedies of an evicted buyer, there has been some amplification of two special requirements for a seller's liability on the ground of

---

[89] Sections II and III.

[90] See generally Mostert/Joubert/Viljoen (n. 20), 161 sqq.; De Wet/Van Wyk (n. 4), 329 sqq.; Hackwill (n. 19), ch. 12.

[91] See e.g. Voet (n. 6), 21, 2, 1; Zimmermann (n. 1), 293 sqq.; *idem* (n. 7), 171 sqq.

[92] *Per* Schreiner JA in *Lammers and Lammers v. Giovannoni* 1955 (3) SA 385 (A) 390.

[93] Hackwill (n. 19), § 12, 2.

[94] See *Olivier v. Van der Bergh* 1956 (1) SA 802 (C) 804; *Westeel Engineering (Pty) Ltd v. Sidney Clow & Co Ltd* 1968 (3) SA 458 (T); *Garden City Motors (Pty) Ltd v. Bank of the Orange Free State Ltd* 1983 (2) SA 104 (N) 107; *Louis Botha Motors v. James & Slabbert Motors (Pty) Ltd* 1983 (3) SA 793 (A).

[95] See *Nunan v. Meyer* (1905) 22 SC 203; *Lammers and Lammers v. Giovannoni* (n. 92), 391; *Olivier v. Van der Bergh* (n. 94); *Westeel Engineering (Pty) Ltd v. Sidney Clow & Co Ltd* (n. 94).

eviction: that a buyer must notify his seller of an imminent eviction[96] and that a buyer must offer a *virilis defensio* if the seller, in spite of having been notified of the imminent eviction, does not come forward to assist the buyer in defending the action.[97] In Roman-Dutch law there was some doubt whether an exception to the notification rule existed in cases where the claimant's title was incontestable.[98] In South African law such an exception does exist, so that a buyer who has failed to inform his seller of the impending eviction can still succeed in an action against the latter if he can prove that the claimant's title was incontestable.[99] Concerning the *virilis defensio*, uncertainty existed about what would be required for it. In *York & Co (Pvt) Ltd v. Jones (2)*[100] Beadle CJ expressed the opinion 'on reading these authorities, that nothing more is expected of a purchaser than that he should conduct his case as a reasonable litigant'.[101] This seems to be the correct approach. It means that what will constitute a *virilis defensio* will depend on the circumstances of each case. Factors which led Beadle CJ to conclude in *York & Co* that there had indeed been a *virilis defensio* were that (a) the plaintiff company employed an attorney and an advocate to act on its behalf; (b) the proceedings were brought in the proper form; (c) the pertinent facts were laid before the court; (d) no manifest error in law was made in the presentation of the case to the court; and (e) no erroneous concessions of fact or law were made. However, the question remains whether a South African buyer still needs to conduct a *virilis defensio* as a prerequisite for holding the seller liable. In *Lammers and Lammers v. Giovannoni*[102] it was said that:

whatever may have been the position under the Roman law it is clear from what has been said above that today the buyer is not obliged to put up any, let alone a vigorous, defence against the true owner on pain of being unable to recover from the seller[103] . . . [and] . . . [t]he existence of such risks and uncertainties is not, of course, a ground for making a seller liable for loss caused by the unreasonable conduct of the buyer, but it is a reason for holding that where the seller has called upon the seller timeously to come to his aid the latter, being in breach, should pay the penalty if he refuses to help and in the result the buyer's dealings with the true owner leave him a loser.[104]

These *dicta* make it clear (a) that a buyer who is able to prove that a claimant's title is incontestable is not required to put up a *virilis defensio* as a prerequisite for a successful action against the seller and (b) that a buyer

---

[96] See e.g. Grotius (n. 12), 3, 15, 4; Voet (n. 6), 21, 2, 20; *Lammers and Lammers v. Giovannoni* (n. 92), 391.

[97] See e.g. Voet (n. 6), 21, 2, 20; *York & Co (Pvt) Ltd v. Jones (1)* (n. 74).

[98] Zimmermann (n. 7), 177.

[99] *Nunan v. Meyer* (n. 95); *Weber and Pretorius v. Gavronsky Bros* 1920 AD 48; *Lammers and Lammers v. Giovannoni* (n. 92); *Olivier v. Van der Bergh* (n. 94), 804.

[100] 1962 (1) SA 72 (SR).   [101] 83.   [102] Above, n. 92.

[103] Schreiner JA, 391H.   [104] *Idem*, 393B.

who has failed to put up a *virilis defensio* and is also unable to prove that the claimant's title was incontestable may nevertheless be granted recourse against the seller unless he acted unreasonably.

Futhermore, uncertainty exists on a second aspect of an evicted buyer's remedies, namely as to what exactly he can recover from the seller. It is submitted that the correct approach is that expressed by De Wet and Van Wyk,[105] namely that the buyer's remedies are the normal remedies of a buyer on breach of contract by the seller. Those remedies are rescission of the contract (with return of the purchase price) if the breach is sufficiently serious, and/or a claim for damages. On this approach total eviction of a buyer will always be a breach sufficiently serious to justify rescission. However, in *Hendler Bros Garage (Pty) Ltd v. Lambons Ltd*[106] it was held that an evicted buyer is not entitled to the return of the purchase price but only to the value of the *res vendita* at the time of eviction. This case was overruled in *Alpha Trust (Edms) Bpk v. Van der Watt*.[107] Yet, contrary to what one would have expected, the Appellate Division did not hold that a buyer who was entitled to rescind the contract could claim the return of the purchase price and compensation for any loss that he may have suffered; it held that the *actio empti*, in the case of eviction, was aimed at obtaining compensation for the damage suffered but with the purchase price as the minimum amount recoverable.[108] The purchase price, in other words, is recovered *qua* damages even though the contract is upheld and not, as is normally the case, by way of restitution after rescission of the contract. (Botha JA raised the possibility that where a buyer had for a considerable time had the use of an object which is either consumable or rapidly wearing, the court could possibly refuse to award the full purchase price, but he expressly refrained from venturing an opinion on the matter.[109])

Apart from the purchase price, a buyer may also claim compensation for other losses sustained as a result of the eviction, but to determine the amount of damages to be awarded in respect of such losses the ordinary contractual principles must be applied. This entails that only such damages are recoverable as were, at the time of contracting, either foreseeable or within the contemplation of the parties. For instance, if the value of the *res vendita* at the time of eviction exceeds the purchase price, the evicted purchaser is entitled to both the purchase price and as much of the difference between the price and the value as was contemplated or foreseeable by the parties when they entered into the contract.[110] A person who knowingly buys a *res aliena* but without agreeing (either expressly or tacitly) to accept

---

[105] De Wet/Van Wyk (n. 4), 330 sq.   [106] 1967 (4) SA 115 (O).
[107] 1975 (3) SA 734 (A).   [108] *Per* Botha JA, 747.
[109] 749. See also S. R. van Jaarsveld, 'Die Verhaalsreg van die Koper in geval van Uitwinning', (1976) 39 *THRHR* 336 sqq.
[110] See *Watt v. Standard Bank Industrial Credit Corp* 1982 (2) SA 47 (D).

the risk of being evicted is entitled, upon eviction to the return of the purchase price but not to his *id quod interest*.[111]

When a seller misleads the buyer about his lack of title, whether by positive statement or by non-disclosure, the latter has the normal remedies for misrepresentation. He can sue for misrepresentation without having to wait until he is evicted.[112]

(c) The seller's liability for latent defects

According to De Wet and Van Wyk[113] the South African courts have developed a set of rules concerning a seller's liability for latent defects which are logical, refined, and practical, even if they no longer reflect pure Roman-Dutch law.[114] Furthermore, they do not conflict with the basic principles of South African law relating to the recovery of damages for breach of contract.

In *Holmdene Brickworks (Pty) Ltd v. Roberts Construction Co Ltd*[115] Corbett JA stated that 'a defect may be described as an abnormal quality or attribute which destroys or substantially impairs the utility or effectiveness of the *res vendita*, for the purpose for which it has been sold or for which it is commonly used'.[116] Whilst in line with what Ulpian set out in D. 21, 1, 1, 8, fitness for use is, as Zimmermann has pointed out,[117] not a particularly convenient criterion when it comes to the sale of fake paintings or imitation pearls. Furthermore, it must be taken into account that where a buyer buys an object for a special purpose known to the seller, the latter may normally be assumed to have guaranteed (or, depending on the circumstances, to have represented) that the object was fit for that specific purpose.[118] If not, a misrepresentation or a breach of contract is committed the remedy for which is usually referred to as the *actio empti* in order to distinguish it from the (more limited) aedilitian remedies. South African courts have, on occasion, regarded an undisclosed servitude as a latent defect.[119] This approach has been

---

[111] *Van der Westhuizen v. Yskor Werknemers se Onderlinge Bystandsvereniging* 1960 (4) SA 803 (T).

[112] See Schalk van der Merwe, L. F. van Huyssteen, M. F. B. Reinecke, G. F. Lubbe, J. G. Lotz, *Contract: General Principles* (1993), 73–85, 99–115 on liability for misrepresentation.

[113] De Wet/Van Wyk (n. 4), 338.

[114] On the position in Roman-Dutch law see Zimmermann (n. 7), 181 sqq.

[115] 1977 (3) SA 670 (A).

[116] 683. For similar definitions see, e.g. *Dibley v. Furter* 1951 (4) SA 73 (C) 80–2; *Knight v. Trollip* 1948 (3) SA 1009 (D) 1012 sq.; *Curtaincrafts (Pty) Ltd v. Wilson* 1969 (4) SA 221 (E) 222; and almost any textbook on the South African law of sale.

[117] Zimmermann (n. 1), 327.

[118] See e.g. *Kroomer v. Hess & Co* 1919 AD 204; *Bower v. Sparks, Young and Farmers' Meat Industries Ltd* 1936 NPD 1; and esp. *Minister van Landbou-Tegniese Dienste v. Scholtz* 1971 (3) SA 188 (A).

[119] See e.g. *Southern Life Assoc v. Segall* 1925 OPD 11; *Overdale Estates (Pty) Ltd v. Harvey Greenacre & Co Ltd* 1962 (3) SA 767 (D).

criticized by De Wet and Van Wyk[120] who support the view of Grotius[121] that a claim to a servitude constitutes a partial eviction.

In South African law both the *actio empti* and the aedilitian remedies are more clearly defined than in Roman-Dutch law.

In accordance with the general principles of the South African law of contract, an *actio empti* will lie for a breach of contract or a misrepresentation. In the context of a *res vendita* with a latent defect it will therefore be available (a) when the seller has expressly or tacitly guaranteed the absence of defects or the presence of certain qualities[122] and (b) when the seller has made a representation to this effect.[123] The buyer can bring a claim for damages based on breach of contract and if the breach is sufficiently serious he may also cancel the contract.[124] On an intentional or negligent misrepresentation the buyer is entitled to rescind the contract and/or to claim damages;[125] in the event of an innocent misrepresentation he is entitled to rescind.[126] The right of rescission based on innocent misrepresentation appears to derive from English rather than Roman-Dutch law.[127] In two situations a buyer is allowed to bring the *actio empti*, enabling him to claim damages for consequential loss, even though there has been neither guarantee nor misrepresentation regarding the *res vendita*: where the seller is the manufacturer of the object sold and where he is a merchant-seller dealing in those types of goods. This was based, respectively, on Voet[128] and Pothier.[129] However, while Pothier does say that a merchant is liable by

[120] De Wet/Van Wyk (n. 4) 330, fn. 97.   [121] Grotius (n. 12), 3, 15, 5.

[122] See e.g. *Kroomer v. Hess & Co* (n. 118); *Marais v. Commercial General Agency Ltd* 1922 TPD 440; *Evans and Plows v. Willis & Co* 1923 CPD 496; *Kock v. Du Plessis* 1923 OPD 113; *Naude v. Harrison* 1925 CPD 84; *Bower v. Sparks, Young and Farmers' Meat Industries Ltd* (n. 118), *Minister van Landbou-Tegniese Dienste v. Scholtz* (n. 118).

[123] See e.g. *S Hain and Son v. Elandslaagte Colliery Co Ltd and Young* (1903) 24 NLR 363; *Vivian v. Woodburn* 1910 TPD 1285; *Kock v. Du Plessis* (n. 122); *Cullen v. Zuidema* 1951 (3) SA 817 (C); *Cloete v. Smithfield Hotel (Pty) Ltd* 1955 (2) SA 622 (O); *Knight v. Hemming* 1959 (1) SA 288 (FC); *De Jager v. Grunder* 1964 (1) SA 446 (A); *Glaston House (Pty) Ltd v. Inag (Pty) Ltd* 1977 (2) SA 846 (A); *Ranger v. Wykerd* 1977 (2) SA 976 (A).

[124] See Van der Merwe/Van Huyssteen *et al.* (n. 112), 301 sqq. on the amount of damages recoverable for breach of contract; 286 sqq. on the right to cancel.

[125] See *De Jager v. Grunder* (n. 123) and *Ranger v. Wykerd* 1977 (2) SA 976 (A) on intentional misrepresentation, and *Kern Trust (Edms) Bpk v. Hurter* 1981 (3) SA 607 (C) and *Bayer South Africa (Pty) Ltd v. Frost* 1991 (4) SA 559 (A) on negligent misrepresentation. See also Van der Merwe/Van Huyssteen *et al.* (n. 112), 99 sqq.; Dale Hutchison, Reinhard Zimmermann, 'Fahrlässige irreführende Angaben im vorvertraglichen Bereich', (1995) 3 *Zeitschrift für Europäisches Privatrecht* 271 sqq.

[126] See e.g. *Viljoen v. Hillier* 1904 TS 312; *Parke v. Hamman* 1907 TH 47; *Wiley v. African Realty Trust Ltd* 1908 TH 104; *Fitt v. Louw* 1970 (3) SA 73 (T); *Reyneke v. Botha* 1977 (3) SA 20 (T).

[127] See De Wet/Van Wyk (n. 4), 46 sq., and esp. the contribution by Gerhard Lubbe to this volume. In issue here is not an *actio redhibitoria* granted on the ground of a *dictum et promissum* but a general right of rescission from *any* contract on the ground of innocent misrepresentation.

[128] Voet (n. 6), 21, 1, 10.

[129] Robert Joseph Pothier, *Traité du contrat de vente*, § 214.

virtue of selling 'articles of his own make, or articles of commerce which it is his business to supply',[130] the version of the 'Pothier rule' approved by the South African Appellate Division[131] is that 'liability for consequential damage caused by latent defect attaches to a merchant seller, who was unaware of the defect, where he publicly professes to have attributes of skill and expert knowledge in relation to the kind of goods sold'. It is not clear when it can be said that a merchant publicly professes to have attributes of skill and expert knowledge in relation to the kind of goods that he sells. It is also unclear whether the liability of the manufacturer-seller or the merchant-seller must be regarded as being founded on breach of contract or misrepresentation; the matter was expressly left open by Corbett JA in *Holmdene Brickworks (Pty) Ltd v. Roberts Construction Co Ltd.*[132]

Like his Dutch and Roman predecessors, a South African seller incurs liability for latent defects even in the absence of warranty or misrepresentation and even though he might not have known of the defect. However, his liability is then restricted to redhibition under the *actio redhibitoria* or to a reduction in price under the *actio quanti minoris*; always provided, of course, that he is not the manufacturer of the article or a merchant who professes to have expert knowledge regarding such articles. Liability under these aedilitian remedies presupposes (a) that the defect is not insignificant,[133] (b) that it is latent,[134] (c) that the buyer is unaware of it,[135] and

---

[130] See *Young's Provision Stores (Pty) Ltd v. Van Ryneveld* 1936 CPD 87, 92.

[131] In *Kroonstad Westelike Boere-Ko-operatiewe Vereniging Bpk v. Botha* 1964 (3) SA 561 (A) 571.

[132] Above, n. 115; and see Zimmermann (n. 1), 334 sq.

[133] *Townsend v. Campbell* (1905) 26 NLR 356. This is but a manifestation of the rule *de minimis non curat lex*.

[134] *G Blaine v. E Moller & Co* (1889) 10 NLR 96; *Muller v. Hobbs* (1904) 21 SC 669; *Deutschman v. Graham* 1912 EDL 214. In *Zieve v. Verster & Co* 1918 CPD 296 a defect was said to be latent if it could as easily be missed as noticed, and in *Holmdene Brickworks (Pty) Ltd v. Roberts Construction Co Ltd* (n. 115), 684 Corbett JA declared that a defect is latent 'when it is . . . not visible or discoverable upon an inspection of the *res vendita*'. The test is an objective one, i.e. the question is whether a reasonable person would have noticed the defect had he inspected the object. How thorough an inspection a reasonable man would have conducted depends on the circumstances of the case: cf. *Lakier v. Hager* 1958 (4) SA 180 (T).

[135] *Cullen v. Zuidema* 1951 (3) SA 817 (C). The approach suggested by Voet (n. 6), 21, 1, 9 (knowledge of a defect to be ascribed to an expert buyer even if in fact he did not know of it) was rejected in *Schwarzer v. John Roderick's Motors (Pty) Ltd* 1940 OPD 170. In *Knight v. Hemming* 1959 (1) SA 288 (FC) Clayden FJ declared (292 sq.) that 'the balance of authority seems to be against any rule that a purchaser who has employed an expert is taken to have known of a defect which should have been discoverable by that expert. But the fact that there has been expert examination may in some cases go to show that there was in fact knowledge of the defect.' Zeffertt in his note to *Knight v. Hemming* (in: Kahn (n. 69), 151) submits that 'the correct rule is that if the seller knows and fails to disclose to the buyer a non-obvious defect, the buyer will not have the remedy of rescission and damages if he has actual, personal knowledge of the defect; but if the seller is unaware of the defect, a buyer who is an expert or who has employed one will be taken to have known of a defect easily discoverable by himself or that expert'.

(d) that the defect existed at the time the contract was entered into.[136] These requirements are not new, but some aspects of the seller's liability have been more precisely defined in South African law than in Roman and Roman-Dutch law. Thus, the *actio redhibitoria* lies if the buyer is able to prove that a reasonable person would not have bought the article had he been aware of the defect. In less serious cases—that is, where a reasonable person would still have bought the article—only the *actio quanti minoris* is available.[137] With the *actio redhibitoria* the buyer may claim the return of the purchase price, plus interest and compensation for the reasonable expenses incurred in connection with the delivery, preservation, and maintenance of the *res vendita*. He, in turn, has to restore the *res vendita* and its fruits to the seller.[138] The *actio quanti minoris* allows the buyer to claim a reduction of the purchase price while retaining the *res vendita*. The amount of the reduction is the difference between the purchase price and the value of the defective article.[139] Since a buyer who avails himself of the *actio redhibitoria* has to restore the *res vendita* to the seller, he may not resort to that remedy if he is unable to effect such restoration (he may, of course, still be able to bring the *actio quanti minoris*).[140] However, this is not an inflexible rule. It may be departed from in order to allow redhibition in spite of the buyer's inability to render restitution 'when justice and equity demand such a departure'.[141] This is the case, especially, where the damage to, or destruction of, the *res vendita* preventing restitution resulted, directly or indirectly, from the

---

[136] *Pitcairn v. Heywood & Son* (1924) 45 NLR 79; *J. & H. du Plessis v. African Supply and Agency Co* 1910 EDL 496; *Van Zyl v. Crause* 1945 OPD 168. The onus of proof that the defect existed when the contract was entered into is on the buyer: see *Seboko v. Soll* 1949 (3) SA 337 (T) in which it was held that there is no *presumption* that the defect existed at the time of contracting even if an animal dies shortly after the conclusion of the sale.

[137] See e.g. *Wiid v. Murison* (1896) 13 SC 444; *Corbett v. Harris* 1914 CPD 535; *Reed Bros v. Bosch* 1914 TPD 578; *J Jones v. W Cotts & Co* (1902) 23 NLR 269; *De Vries v. Wholesale Cars* 1986 (2) SA 22 (O). As for Roman and Roman-Dutch law, see Zimmermann (n. 1), 325 sq.; *idem* (n. 7), 187 sq. There can, of course, be no objection to a buyer bringing the *actio quanti minoris* in place of the *actio redhibitoria*, just as there can be no objection to a buyer who is entitled to bring the *actio empti* electing to bring one of the aedilitian actions (provided, of course, that the requirements for aedilitian relief are met): cf. *S Hain & Son v. Elandslaagte Colliery Co Ltd and Young* (n. 123); *Wilson v. Simon and Lazarus* 1921 OPD 32 and the judgment of Schreiner JA in *Hackett v. G & G Radio and Refrigerator Corp* 1949 (3) SA 664 (A).

[138] See e.g. *Nourse v. Malan* 1909 TS 202; *Seggie v. Philip Bros* 1915 CPD 292; *Inhambane Oil and Mineral Development Syndicate Ltd v. Mears and Ford* (1906) 23 SC 250.

[139] See *South African Oil and Fat Industries Ltd v. Park Rynie Whaling Co Ltd* 1916 AD 400; *Cugno v. Nel* 1932 TPD 289; *Labuschagne Broers v. Spring Farm (Pty) Ltd* 1976 (2) SA 824 (T); *Gannet Manufacturing Co (Pty) Ltd v. Postaflex (Pty) Ltd* 1981 (3) SA 216 (C). The difference between the purchase price and the value of the defective article is an unsatisfactory measure of *quanti minoris* relief where the purchase price is higher than the value of an article without defects would have been: see G. A. Mulligan, 'Quanti Minoris Than What?', (1953) 70 *SALJ* 132 sqq.

[140] *South African Oil and Fat Industries Ltd v. Park Rynie Whaling Co Ltd* (n. 139).

[141] Zeffertt in his note to *South African Oil and Fat Industries Ltd v. Park Rynie Whaling Co Ltd* (in: Kahn (n. 69), 167).

latent defect.[142] Where the damage to the *res vendita*, although caused by the fault of the buyer, is slight, redhibition is also possible, provided that the buyer is prepared to compensate the seller for that damage.[143]

In *Phame (Pty) Ltd v. Paizes*[144] it was held by the Appellate Division that the *actiones redhibitoria* and *quanti minoris* are available to a buyer not only on the ground of a latent defect but also 'if the seller made a *dictum et promissum* to the buyer on the faith of which the buyer entered into the contract or agreed to the price in question; and it turned out to be unfounded'.[145] A *dictum et promissum* was defined as 'a material statement made by the seller to the buyer during the negotiations, bearing on the quality of the *res vendita* and going beyond mere praise and commendation'.[146] This confirmed a direction which had already been taken by some of the Provincial Divisions of the Supreme Court.[147] *Phame (Pty) Ltd v. Paizes* was subjected to sharp criticism[148] as being in conflict with Roman and Roman-Dutch law, but Zimmermann[149] argues that the conclusions arrived at by the Court do not clash with the Roman law in point and, furthermore, that they fit into a general trend in South African law towards imposing liability for non-fraudulent misrepresentation.

As one would expect, the aedilitian liability of the seller provides the buyer not only with a cause of action but also with a defence.[150]

From the old authorities we learn that, inasmuch as a seller's liability for latent defects is a (mere) *naturale* of a contract of sale, it may be excluded by agreement between the parties. This remains the position in South Africa. A sale in which the seller's liability is thus excluded is known as a *voetstoots* sale: even if the term *voetstoots* is not expressly used in the clause which excludes liability.[151] Is a seller still protected by a *voetstoots* clause if

---

[142] *Dodd v. Spitaleri* (1910) 27 SC 196; *Marks Ltd v. Laughton* 1920 AD 12; *African Organic Fertilizers & Associated Industries Ltd v. Sieling* 1949 (2) SA 131 (W); *Schwarzer v. John Roderick's Motors (Pty) Ltd* 1940 OPD 170.

[143] *Schwarzer v. John Roderick's Motors (Pty) Ltd* (n. 142); *Seggie v. Philip Bros* (n. 138); *Harper v. Webster* 1956 (2) SA 495 (FC).

[144] 1973 (3) SA 397 (A).   [145] 417 sq.   [146] 418.

[147] See *Hall v. Milner* 1959 (2) SA 304 (O); *Van Schalkwyk v. Prinsloo* 1961 (1) SA 665 (T); *Overdale Estates (Pty) Ltd v. Harvey Greenacre & Co Ltd* (n. 119); *Elsie Motors (Edms) Bpk v. Breedt* 1963 (2) SA 36 (O).

[148] See e.g. De Wet and Van Wyk (n. 4) 346 sq. and the case note by S. W. J. van der Merwe and, M. F. B. Reinecke, 1974 (37) *THRHR* 175 sqq.

[149] *Law of Obligations* (n. 1), 329 sq.

[150] See *Wilson v. Simon and Lazarus* (n. 137); *McDaid v. De Villiers* 1942 CPD 220; *Skead v. Swanepoel* 1949 (4) SA 763 (T); cf. *Davenport Corner Tea Room (Pty) Ltd v. Joubert* 1962 (2) SA 709 (D).

[151] Grotius (n. 12), 3, 14, 12 states that one may sell a thing as it is '*'t welck men noemt met de voet stooten*' (this is called 'kicking with the foot'); cf. Zimmermann (n. 7), 187, fn. 262. On *voetstoots* sales see e.g. *Fichardts Motors (Prop.) Ltd v. Nienaber* 1936 OPD 221; *Bosman Bros v. Van Niekerk* 1928 CPD 67; *Uhlmann v. Grindley-Ferris* 1947 (2) SA 459 (C); *Knight v. Trollip* (n. 116); *Greyling v. Fick* 1969 (3) SA 579 (T); *Boere Handelhuis (Edms) Bpk v. Pelser* 1969 (3) SA 171 (O).

he had induced the buyer by a misrepresentation to agree to it? According to the general principles of South African contract law, a buyer should be able, under these circumstances, to have the exemption clause set aside; and unless the seller's liability for a negligent, or innocent misrepresentation has also been excluded, it should make no difference whether the misrepresentation was fraudulent, negligent or innocent and whether it was made *per commissionem* or *per omissionem* (that is, by non-disclosure of a defect of which the seller was aware).[152] However, that is not how the courts have seen the matter as far as misrepresentations *per omissionem* were concerned. The Natal Provincial Division held that a seller loses the protection of a *voetstoots* clause (and may thus be held responsible by the buyer in spite of the clause) only if he had 'designedly concealed' the defects from the buyer or had 'craftily refrained' from informing the buyer of their presence: in other words, if there was fraudulent non-disclosure.[153] In the Transvaal, on the other hand, it was held that mere non-disclosure by a seller with knowledge of the defect enables the buyer to escape the effect of the *voetstoots* clause.[154] The Appellate Division recently approved the Natal approach,[155] in spite of the fact that it appears to conflict with general principles. In any event, however, non-disclosure of a defect will avoid a *voetstoots* clause only if the seller had actual, personal knowledge of the defect; knowledge imputed to the seller on the ground that he is an expert is not sufficient.[156] On the effect of non-fraudulent misrepresentations *per commissionem* there is also no unanimity: contrast *Le Marchand v. Creeke*,[157] which held that a *voetstoots* buyer cannot rely on an innocent misrepresentation to avoid the exemption clause, with *Wright v. Pandell*[158] and *Cockroft v. Baxter*,[159] which held that he can. In South African law liability for a fraudulent misrepresentation cannot be excluded by agreement.[160] Liability for non-fraudulent misrepresentation may be excluded[161] but a *voetstoots* clause is not taken to embody an agreement to exclude liability for misrepresentation.[162]

Until 30 November 1970 the *actiones redhibitoria* and *quanti minoris* were subject to a shorter prescription period (one year) than the *actio*

[152] See above, Section VI. 2. (c).

[153] See *Knight v. Trollip* (n. 116); *Crawley v. Frank Pepper (Pty) Ltd* 1970 (1) SA 29 (N); cf. *Glaston House (Pty) Ltd v. Inag (Pty) Ltd* (n. 123).

[154] See *Hadley v. Savory* 1916 TPD 385; *Van der Merwe v. Culhane* 1952 (3) SA 42 (T); cf. *Dibley v. Furter* (n. 116); *Cloete v. Smithfield Hotel (Pty) Ltd* 1955 (2) SA 622 (O).

[155] In *Van der Merwe v. Meades* 1991 (2) SA 1 (A).

[156] *Die Trust Bank van Afrika Bpk v. Bekker* 1961 (3) SA 236 (T).

[157] 1953 (1) SA 186 (N).   [158] 1949 (2) SA 279 (C).

[159] 1955 (4) SA 93 (C). See also *Schmidt v. Dwyer* 1959 (3) SA 896 (C).

[160] *Wells v. South African Alumenite Co* 1927 AD 69.

[161] *Trollip v. Jordaan* 1961 (1) SA 238 (A) 252H; *Wells v. South African Alumenite Co* (n. 160), 72 sq.

[162] *Wright v. Pandell* (n. 158); *Cockroft v. Baxter* (n. 159). But cf. *Le Marchand v. Creeke* (n. 157).

empti.[163] Since 1 December 1970, however, all three actions are subject to the general prescription period of three years.[164]

VII. THE DUTIES AND LIABILITIES OF THE PARTIES IN TERMS OF THE *INCIDENTALIA NEGOTII*

Like the parties to any other contract, a buyer and a seller may add any number of (lawful) terms to their contract to supplement or modify the *naturalia* or to supplement the *essentialia negotii*. The duties and liabilities of the parties in terms of such *incidentalia* are governed by the general principles of the law of contract and nothing further need therefore be said about them in the present context.

VIII. THE PASSING OF THE RISK

According to the South African law of sale, the general risk rule is still *emptione perfecta periculum est emptoris.*[165] Inasmuch as a seller is liable for *culpa levis* in his custody of the *res vendita*[166] (rather than for *custodia*, as in classical Roman law) the risk that passes to the buyer upon perfection of the contract is that of *any* accidental destruction or deterioration of the *res vendita* and not only of destruction or deterioration due to *vis maior*. (The terms 'destruction' and 'deterioration' are here used in a wide sense. They refer not only to physical harm which may befall the object of the sale but also, for instance, to an act of expropriation by the state[167] or to the imposition of a tax on the object concerned.[168]) As in Roman and Roman-Dutch law, a contract of sale is *perfecta* if the parties have agreed on the object of their sale, if the price has been determined (or is determinable by a simple calculation), and if the sale is unconditional.

South African courts have been concerned mainly with determining when exactly a particular contract becomes *perfecta* and which type of risk passes

---

[163] In terms of s. 3(2)(b)(ii) and (iii), Prescription Act 18 of 1943.

[164] In terms of s. 11(d), Prescription Act 68 of 1969.

[165] (With the perfection of the contract of sale, the risk is on the buyer). See Zimmermann (n. 1), 281 sqq. (Roman law); *idem* (n. 7), 168 sqq. (Roman-Dutch law). As for South African law see e.g. *Poppe, Schunhoff and Guttery v. Mosenthal & Co* 1879 Buch 91 and *Taylor & Co v. Mackie, Dunn & Co* 1879 Buch 166. The risk in issue in these two cases (an increase in excise duty on brandy after conclusion of the sale of the brandy) has, incidentally, since been placed on the buyer by legislation: see s. 59, Customs and Excise Act 91 of 1964. The benefit of a decrease in duty also accrues to the buyer in terms of the legislation.

[166] See above, Section VI. 2. (a).

[167] *Rood's Trustees v. Scott and De Villiers* 1910 TPD 47.

[168] *Poppe, Schunhoff and Guttery v. Mosenthal & Co* (n. 165); *Taylor & Co v. Mackie, Dunn & Co* (n. 165).

to the buyer. The answers have not always been logically consistent, particularly in the case of conditional contracts. David Zeffertt has suggested that it is perhaps best 'not to regard the rules of the risk as the logical consequences of a principle, and to regard them as arbitrary'.[169] For instance, no satisfactory explanation has as yet been found why the South African courts have drawn a distinction, pending fulfilment of a suspensive condition, between the risks of destruction of, and damage to, the *res vendita*.[170]

As in Roman and Roman-Dutch law, whoever bears the risk of the destruction of, or of damage to, the *merx* is entitled to any benefit which may accrue: '*commodum eius esse debet, cuius periculum est*'.[171] This not only includes the civil and natural fruits produced by the *merx* but also benefits which take the place of the *merx* (the 'substitutionary *commodum*') as, for example, compensation for a *merx* which is expropriated.[172] It has, however, been held that the seller of a house which burnt down after it had been sold was not obliged to pay to the buyer compensation received from the insurer because such compensation was not taken to constitute a *commodum*.[173]

IX. AGREEMENTS WHICH MAY LEAD TO CONTRACTS OF SALE

In the South African law of sale two of the *pacta de contrahendo* are of importance: the option contract and the contract of preference (*voorkeurkontrak*). The latter, in the context of purchase and sale, confers a right of pre-emption.[174] An option is generally taken to comprise a substantive offer (to buy or to sell) made by the option grantor to the option holder (grantee) and an agreement between the parties in which the grantor undertakes not to revoke the offer for a specific period.[175] The validity of the substantive offer and of the agreement entrenching that offer, as well as consequences of a breach of the option contract, are governed by the general principles of the law of contract and need no elaboration here. An attempted revoca-

---

[169] Note to *Schultz v. Morton & Co* 1918 TPD 343 (in: *Kahn* (n. 69), 185).

[170] Cf., however, M. A. K. Lambiris, 'The Incidence of Risk in Conditional Sales', (1984) 101 *SALJ* 656 sqq. For a discussion of cases with complicating factors other than suspensive conditions see Mostert/Joubert/Viljoen (n. 20), 90–108; Hackwill (n. 19), §§ 13, 3, 1–13, 7, 4.

[171] (The benefit has to accrue to him, who bears the risk.) See e.g. *De Kock v. Fincham* (1902) 19 SC 136; *Walker v. Wales* 1922 CPD 49; *Meintjes v. Manley & Co* 1922 CPD 151; *Kidney v. Garner* 1929 CPD 163.

[172] See *Mnyandu v. Mnyandu* 1964 (1) SA 418 (N) and the note on this case by W. J. Hosten, (1964) 27 *THRHR* 151 sqq.

[173] *Van Deventer v. Erasmus* 1960 (4) SA 100 (T).

[174] For a discussion of *pacta de contrahendo* in South African law see Van der Merwe, Van Huyssteen *et al.* (n. 112), 56–70.

[175] *Venter v. Birchholtz* 1972 (1) SA 276 (A) 283; P. M. Nienaber, 'Formaliteite by koop en sessie ten opsigte van grond: Die jongste beslissings', (1964) 27 *THRHR* 44, 44.

tion of the substantive offer does, at any rate, not preclude the exercise of the option.[176]

While neither the statutory nor the contractual *naastingsrecht* of Roman-Dutch law[177] was received into South African law, the contractual right of pre-emption was adopted; even a statutory right of pre-emption is not unknown.[178] The South-African right of pre-emption, however, no longer reflects pure Roman-Dutch law; it has been influenced by both English law and the German concept of *Gestaltungsrecht*.[179]

In a right of pre-emption the grantor may not sell a particular object before the grantee has been given the opportunity to buy it at a price and on terms which are determined, or objectively determinable, or which are, in principle, within the discretion of the grantor.[180] As far as the due exercise of this right is concerned there are three main possibilities:[181]

(a) If, in the contract of pre-emption, the parties determine exactly how the offer (to sell) has to be made to the grantee, effect must be given to those provisions and the grantee can apparently insist that an offer *in forma specifica* be made to him.[182]

(b) If the grantor of the right of pre-emption sells the object to a third person in breach of the grantee's right of pre-emption, the latter can, by a unilateral declaration addressed to the grantor, bring a contract of sale into existence between himself and the grantor on the same terms as had been agreed between the grantor and the third person.[183] It has been pointed out[184] that the grantee can probably act in this way only if all the *incidentalia* of the contract of sale between the grantor and the third person are able to be implemented between the grantor and the grantee. Also, it is

---

[176] *Thompson v. Van der Vyver* 1954 (2) SA 192 (C).

[177] For details see Zimmermann (n. 7), 190 sqq.

[178] See e.g. C. G. van der Merwe, D. W. Butler, *Sectional Titles, Share Blocks and Time-Sharing* (1985), 136–8. On the right of pre-emption generally see T. B. Floyd, 'Die Voorkoopreg', (1986) 49 *THRHR* 253 sqq.; M. F. B. Reinecke, J. M. Otto, 'Voorkope en ander voorkeur-kontrakte', 1986 *TSAR* 18 sqq.

[179] This appears from *Associated South African Bakeries (Pty) Ltd v. Oryx & Vereinigte Bäckereien (Pty) Ltd* 1982 (3) SA 893 (A) 907.

[180] A. D. J. van Rensburg, 'Formaliteitsvoorskrifte, Voorkoopregte en Opsies', (1986) 49 *THRHR* 208, 209, referring to *Hattingh v. Van Rensburg* 1964 (1) SA 578 (T) 582 and *Bellairs v. Hodnett* 1978 (1) SA 1109 (A) 1138 sq.

[181] Cf. Van Rensburg, (1986) 49 *THRHR* 209–11.

[182] Support for an order for specific performance is found in e.g. *Owsianick v. African Consolidated Theatres (Pty) Ltd* 1967 (3) SA 310 (A) 318–20, 327B-E; *Soteriou v. Retco Poyntons (Pty) Ltd* 1985 (2) SA 922 (A) 932G-I. But see the *obiter dictum* in *Bellairs v. Hodnett* 1978 (1) SA 1109 (A) 1139F-H.

[183] *Associated South African Bakeries (Pty) Ltd v. Oryx & Vereinigte Bäckereien (Pty) Ltd* (n. 179). The terminology used in this case is somewhat misleading. The Court speaks of the grantee 'stepping into the shoes' of the third party, but it is quite clear from the decision that the grantee, through his declaration, creates a new contract between himself and the grantor, leaving the contract between the grantor and the third person unaffected.

[184] (1986) 49 *THRHR* 208, 210.

likely that the grantee may bring into existence a contract between himself and the grantor merely on the basis of an offer made by the grantor to a third person.[185]

(c) If the contract of pre-emption is silent as to how the right of pre-emption is to be exercised, and the grantee is not able to exercise it by way of a unilateral declaration, he may request the grantor to make a *bona fide* offer to him in order to enable him to exercise his right. Such an offer may not be more onerous than that which the grantor is prepared to make to, or accept from, a third person.[186]

Do option contracts and contracts of pre-emption have to comply with the formalities prescribed for the contract of sale to which the option or right of pre-emption will lead? This question has been discussed mainly in connection with the formalities prescribed for the sale of land (writing and signature by the parties). It has been argued, it is submitted correctly, that an option contract need not, whereas a contract of pre-emption must, comply with those formalities.[187] After all, in the case of an option the substantive offer has already been made. If that offer is in writing a written acceptance of it will bring a written contract into existence even though the agreement to keep the offer open may have been oral. In the case of a contract of pre-emption, however, the grantor undertakes to make an offer at a later stage. If that undertaking is not in writing and is later to be specifically enforced then

the anomalous situation would arise that on the strength of a verbal contract the grantee of the right of pre-emption could, on the happening of the relevant contingencies, become the purchaser of land. This would be contrary to the intention and objects of the Formalities Act.[188]

Double sales present a common complication in the case of options and rights of pre-emption. Where a double sale has occurred and delivery of the object sold has not yet taken place, the personal right of the holder of the option or of the right of pre-emption enjoys preference over the personal right of the third party (provided, of course, that the option or right of pre-emption was granted before the sale to the third person took place).[189] However, where the object has been delivered to the third party, the real right of the latter trumps the personal right of the holder of the option or right of pre-emption, unless the third party had knowledge of the prior personal right. If the third person did indeed have such knowledge, the grantee

---

[185] Cf. *Hirschowitz v. Moolman* 1985 (3) SA 739 (A) 763F-G.

[186] Cf. *Soteriou v. Retco Poyntons (Pty) Ltd* (n. 182).

[187] Van Rensburg, (1986) 49 *THRHR* 208, 215.

[188] *Hirschowitz v. Moolman* (n. 185) 767G-H (*per* Corbett JA).

[189] Cf. *Le Roux v. Odendaal* 1954 (4) SA 432 (N); *Botes v. Botes* 1964 (1) SA 623 (O); *Campbell v. First Consolidated Holdings (Pty) Ltd* 1977 (3) SA 924 (W); *Barnard v. Thelander* 1977 (3) SA 932 (C); *Krauze v. Van Wyk* 1986 (1) SA 158 (A).

of the option or of the right of pre-emption may claim the thing from him.[190] It is uncertain at what stage the third party must have had the relevant knowledge: at the time the contract was concluded or at the moment of delivery of the object sold to him.[191]

X. CONCLUSION

The development of the law of purchase and sale in South Africa has amounted to little more than a reaffirmation of the rules and principles of Roman and Roman-Dutch law based, as they were, on a philosophy of economic liberalism. In certain respects the basic stance of Roman-Dutch law was given an even sharper edge due to the fact that essentially socially oriented (if not always sophisticated) institutions such as *naastingsrecht* (*ius retractus, retractus conventionalis*) and *laesio enormis* were either never received or received and subsequently abolished in South African law.[192] Consumer-orientated legislation of more recent date has not affected the essential structure of the contract.[193] It remains to be seen whether the climate created by the new constitutional dispensation in South Africa will allow the present balance between private autonomy and social justice to remain as it is.

---

[190] Cf. *De Jager v. Sisana* 1930 AD 71; *Le Roux v. Odendaal* (n. 189).

[191] See *Associated South African* Bakeries *(Pty) Ltd v. Oryx & Vereinigte Bäckereien (Pty) Ltd* (n. 179) 908G-H; *Botes v. Botes* (n. 189), 628 E, 629G-H.

[192] Cf. Zimmermann (n. 1), 264–70; *idem* (n. 7), 190 sqq.

[193] See above, text to n. 2.

12: *Employment Relations*

BARNEY JORDAAN

Gentlemen, you have heard what has been said in this case by the lawyers, the rascals! . . . They talk of law. Why, gentlemen, It is not law that we want, But justice! They would govern us by the Common law of England. Common sense is a much safer guide. . . . A clear head and an honest heart are worth more than all the law of all the lawyers. . . . It is our duty to do justice between the parties, not by any quirks of the law out of Coke and Blackstone—books that I never read and never will.[1]

I. INTRODUCTION

In South African law the orthodox view of the relationship between employer and employee has always been that the common law, in the guise of *locatio conductio operarum*, serves as the foundation of the relationship, with individual agreement, statute, and collective bargaining—the principal sources of the parties' rights, duties, and remedies—operating as complementary institutions. The contemporary model of *locatio conductio operarum* in South African law, although Roman-Dutch in origin, was deeply influenced during the nineteenth century by principles of English law although the law relating to the contract of employment was still very much in its formative stages in contemporary England.

This Chapter is primarily concerned with the development of the contract of employment by the courts during the nineteenth and early twentieth centuries and, more particularly, with those aspects of it which were most strongly influenced by English law. These were: vicarious liability; specific performance; forfeiture of wages in the event of desertion; and the employee's obligation to exercise care and skill as well as good faith in the execution of his duties. For the sake of perspective, reference is also made to instances where the courts have steered well clear of English law, for example the termination of contracts for an indefinite period and the employee's entitlement to wages during periods of illness.

The influence of English law was not restricted to the contract of employ-

---

[1] Dean Griswold, *Law and Lawyers in the United States* (1964), 12 sq., quoted in: P. Q. R. Boberg, 'Oak Tree or Acorn? Conflicting Approaches to Our Law of Delict', (1966) 74 *SALJ* 172.

ment, however. Legislation concerning the relationship between master and servant introduced in Southern Africa during the nineteenth century was to a large extent modelled on English statutes. While modern employment legislation increasingly tends to codify the rules pertaining to the employment relationship—and as a result may well have stifled the further development of common law principles[2]—early legislation[3] left much scope for the courts to fashion and develop the content of the rules governing employment matters.

II. ROMAN LAW

In Roman law[4] the letting and hiring of the labour or services of free men could take two forms: the letting and hiring of personal services (*locatio conductio operarum*, as it was termed by the pandectists) or the letting and hiring of a particular piece of work or job to be done as a whole (*locatio conductio operis*). Since a slave was a mere thing (*res*) he was incapable of letting his own labour or services, but if his owner rented out his services the contract between the owner and the lessee was construed as an instance of *locatio conductio rei*.

Locatio conductio operarum was a consensual contract which an employee (*locator operarum*) undertook to place his personal services for a certain period of time at the disposal of an employer (*conductor operarum*) who in turn undertook to pay the employee the remuneration agreed upon in consideration of his services. The subject-matter of *locatio conductio operarum* was the labour as such,[5] as long, of course, as such labour was not rendered by slaves. At the upper end of the social scale, too, there was a range of services which were largely excluded from this type of contract: the *artes liberales*, i.e. those activities which could be regarded as worthy of a free man. Among the higher echelons of Roman society it was regarded as unseemly

---

[2] See generally Adrian Merritt, 'The Historical Role of Law in the Regulation of Employment: Abstentionist or Interventionist?', (1982) 1 *Australian Journal of Law and Society* 56 sqq.

[3] Which only applied to a limited category of 'masters' and 'servants' and only regulated some aspects of the relationship even between these persons. The categories of 'master' and 'servant' were later extended to include persons who under Roman-Dutch law were not employed under a contract of *locatio conductio operarum* but under a contract of mandate or who were regarded as independent contractors. See *Smit v. Workmen's Compensation Commissioner* 1979 (1) SA 51 (A) 59B.

[4] Max Kaser, *Das römische Privatrecht*, vol. I (2nd edn., 1971), 568 sqq.; Reinhard Zimmermann, *The Law of Obligations: Roman Foundations of the Civilian Tradition* (1990, reprint 1993), 384 sqq.

[5] *Locatio conductio operis*, on the other hand, involved an agreement in terms of which the workman (*conductor operis*) undertook to execute a particular piece of work as a whole for the employer (*locator operis*) in return for a fixed sum of money; for details see Zimmermann (n. 4), 393 sqq.

to work for a wage and if professional services were rendered it was normally under a (nominally gratuitous) contract of mandate.

As a result of these and other factors[6] *locatio conductio operarum* received relatively little attention by Roman jurists.

III. ROMAN-DUTCH LAW

Roman-Dutch jurists also treated the contract of employment as a species of lease under the heading of *locatio conductio operarum*, although it differed in some important respects from its Roman ancestor. First, its range of application had grown quite considerably, although services rendered by members of the (free) professions were still excluded and fell within the compass of the contract of mandate. Secondly, the content of the most prevalent form of employment relationship, namely that involving domestic servants and agricultural labourers, was to a very large extent regulated by statute.[7] Finally, of course, the *locatio servi* had been abandoned. This brought about a radical change in the underlying economic relationship between the parties concerned. What had once been a simple economic transaction, by which someone temporarily assigned a thing (the slave) to someone else in return for a sum of money, was now conceived to be a free exchange between employer and employee who, as equal individuals, asserted their own free will over the letting and hiring of the employee's services.

Nevertheless, none of the writers on Roman-Dutch law dealt with the employment relationship as an autonomous institution.[8] They were all content to discuss it in the context of the lease of things, or with reference to statutory provisions or local customs applicable to particular situations.[9] Even so, their opinions on important issues peculiar to the employment relationship, such as the employer's vicarious liability for the unlawful acts of his employees, sometimes differed.[10] As described below, such differences of opinion contributed to the assimilation of principles derived from English law into the South African law of employment.

---

[6] See Zimmermann (n. 4), 387 sqq.

[7] E.g. the *placaat* of 2 Sept. 1597 which dealt only with apprentices; the *placaat* of 1 May 1608 which also dealt with journeymen but was confined in its operation mainly to the Hague; and the *placaat* of 29 Nov. 1679 which dealt with domestic servants (*dienstboden*). See James Fourie, *Die Dienskontrak in die Suid-Afrikaanse Arbeidsreg* (unpublished LL D thesis, University of South Africa, 1976), 24 sqq. for further examples. This legislation never acquired the force of law in South Africa: see *Smit v. Workmen's Compensation Commissioner* (n. 3) 59H; *Spencer v. Gostelow* 1920 AD 617, 628.

[8] The exception was domestic service, which received prominent attention. For a more comprehensive treatment of the position of domestic workers in Roman-Dutch law see Paul Benjamin, 'The contract of employment and domestic workers', (1980) 1 *Industrial LJ* 187 sqq.

[9] See Fourie (n. 7), 28 sq.; *Spencer v. Gostelow* (n. 7), 628 sq., 638.

[10] See *Mkize v. Martens* 1914 AD 382.

IV. ENGLISH LAW

Three types of employment relationship existed in England[11] at the turn of the eighteenth century. First, there was the traditional, quasi-servile relationship which prevailed on the farm or in the household between the employer and his menial employees and which was partly shaped by the criminal law, operating through a line of statutes of ancient origin, and partly by the law of persons. Secondly, there was the relationship between principal and independent contractor, as in the case of manufacturer and artisan, which fell outside the ambit of the master and servant statutes. Thirdly, there was the emerging relationship between employer and urban wage-labourer which took some of its characteristics from the domestic and agricultural service relationship[12] but which was, for the rest, governed largely by the legislation concerning master and servant. A developed contract model for the employment relationship did not yet exist.

Statutory regulation of the employment relationship in England dates back to the middle of the fourteenth century when the Statutes of Labourers were passed in order to combat the shortage of labour following upon the Black Death.[13] These statutes were replaced by the Statute of Artificers and Apprentices of 1562, which empowered Justices of the Peace to direct all those having no 'visible effects' to compulsory work and which also allowed them to fix wages. Criminal sanctions were harnessed to ensure obedience and proper work performance. The Poor Law Act of 1601 extended the compulsion to work to children whose parents were regarded as unable to maintain them. Such children could be apprenticed until they came of age. While the coverage of the early legislation was limited to specific classes of 'servants' in specific sectors, such as those employed in husbandry, agricultural labourers, domestic servants, and artisans, legislation passed during the eighteenth and nineteenth centuries, when the emerging process of industrialization began to change patterns of work, steadily increased the range of persons falling within the scope of the statutory provisions.[14] While these early statutes regarded the relationship between 'master' and 'servant', or apprentice, as contractual in origin, they effectively created a type of sta-

---

[11] The following sources were consulted: Otto Kahn-Freund, 'Blackstone's Neglected Child: The Contract of Employment', (1977) 93 *LQR* 508 sqq.; John Cairns, 'Blackstone, Kahn-Freund and the Contract of Employment', (1989) 105 *LQR* 300 sqq.; Bruno Veneziani, 'The Evolution of the Contract of Employment', in: Bob Hepple (ed.), *The Making of Labour Law in Europe* (1980), 33 sqq.; William Holdsworth, *A History of English Law*, vol. II (4th edn., 1936), 459 sqq.; vol. IV (2nd edn., 1937), 379 sqq.; vol. XV (1965), 17 sqq.

[12] Merritt, (1982) 1 *Australian Journal of Law and Society* 57.

[13] Holdsworth, vol. II (n. 11), 461 sq.

[14] Masters and servants legislation was revised in 1747 and again in 1823. See Holdsworth, vol. XV (n. 11), 20 for details.

tus relationship because the rights and duties of the parties were not determined by agreement but fixed by law.[15]

The industrial revolution which began during the latter half of the eighteenth century brought in its wake new industries, a revolution in transport, massive development of trade, and the emergence of a new class of urban wage-labourer.[16] It also spawned a fervent belief in contract doctrine as the cure for all social ills.[17] However, it was some time before contract doctrine was also allowed free reign over the employment relationship. Even as late as 1865, legislation as to master and servant still relied on criminal sanctions to deal with breaches of contract. Only after 1867 were the first steps taken to untie the contract of employment from the field of criminal law. Thus, the imprisonment of 'servants' for breach of contract was restricted to aggravated instances of misconduct. Compensation orders then became the primary remedy for breaches of a less serious nature. The Conspiracy and Protection of Property Act of 1875 crowned this development by completely removing criminal sanctions for breach of contract; employees were thus placed, in this regard, on the same footing as their employers.[18]

The early development of the contract of employment in English law displays a number of peculiar characteristics. First, while *locatio conductio operarum* had already been firmly established in continental systems,[19] the contract model was recognized in England only at a relatively late stage. This reflects the different ways in which the labour market was organized in the English and continental systems. While the latter left the allocation of resources to the individual parties, statutory regulation was the outstanding characteristic of the English labour market until the mid-nineteenth century.[20] Even after that date the labour market in England continued to be regulated by statute. Yet the philosophy[21] and coverage[22] of legislation after 1875 differed considerably from that of the earlier statutes.

---

[15] See Holdsworth, vol. II (n. 11), 462 who compares the employment relationship under the statutes to marriage.

[16] See Holdsworth, vol. IV (n. 11), 386.

[17] Veneziani (n. 11), 33; Brian Napier, 'The Contract of Employment', in: Paul Lewis (ed.), *Labour Law in Britain* (1986), 328. Otto Kahn-Freund, 'Servants and Independent Contractors', (1951) 14 Modern LR 508 reflects on the fact that, although developments in English law and in the civil law systems of the continent progressed along different routes, the end result, i.e. contractual regulation of the employment relationship, was nevertheless the same. He ascribes this to 'the irresistible power of economic necessities'.

[18] Holdsworth, vol. XV (n. 11), 20. See also Veneziani (n. 11), 33; Napier (n. 11), 328.

[19] Veneziani (n. 11), 32 sq.; Kahn-Freund, (1951) 14 Modern LR 504, 514 sq.

[20] Kahn-Freund (n. 19), 514–6. See also Napier (n. 11), 328; Holdsworth, vol. IV (n. 11), 385 sqq.

[21] While the earlier statutes were punitive in nature, the more modern forms of employment legislation are concerned with the protection of individual employees and provide for minimum terms of employment.

[22] Both skilled and unskilled services where brought within the statutory ambit. See Merritt, (1982) 1 *Australian Journal of Law and Society* 56, 58–60.

Secondly, the lack of a contract model for the employment relationship, defined by legislation, meant that the contract, freed of the constraints of criminal law, had to be constructed on the basis of implied terms, an approach adopted by South African courts in connection with the employee's implied duties of fidelity and competent service.[23] Thirdly, the fact that the employment relationship has, since the mid-nineteenth century, been regulated by both contract and statute resulted in a schism which English law has never been able completely to bridge. Instead of viewing contract and legislation as complementary institutions, the former providing the general framework within which mandatory norms function, statute came to be regarded as operating largely outside the framework of the contract.[24] Finally, a gradual synthesis took place between the legal positions of those who were traditionally regarded as menial servants and those whose services were of a skilled nature and who would previously have been classified as independent contractors. Because of the expansion of large-scale industry, employment legislation from the mid-nineteenth century onwards steadily extended the ambit of its coverage: from 'servants' to 'workmen', and, eventually to all persons employed in trade or industry. In this way, the skilled services of persons who, as 'independent contractors' fell outside the range of application of the Statutes of Labourers and the Poor Laws, were brought within the legislative framework.[25] Merritt explains the consequences of this development as follows:[26]

The culmination of this gradual shift in concepts, then, is the present law where there are two basic categories of worker—the employee and the independent contractor. The first category includes those who would previously have been defined as servants, and persons performing types of work initially done under arrangements allowing the worker a considerable degree of independence . . . This independence has now evaporated for these people, just as many of the skills out of which that independent position was forged, have been swept away by mechanisation and by a continual 'segmentation' of the work-processes involved. The second category is made up of those workers whose independent position survived—plumbers, carpenters, lawyers, doctors, artists, etc.

As a result, a clear distinction between independent contractors and employees emerged only late in the nineteenth century.[27]

---

[23] Veneziani (n. 11), 66.

[24] Veneziani (n. 11), 61; Kahn-Freund, (1977) 93 *LQR* 508, 527.

[25] Veneziani (n. 11), 65. What united them was the fact that they were subject to the control of their employers and therefore subordinate to them. See Veneziani (n. 11) 64 sq.; Kahn-Freund, (1977) 93 *LQR* 508, 511–13.

[26] Merritt, (1982) 1 *Australian Journal of Law and Society* 56, 59.

[27] The *locus classicus* of the definition of an employee is *Yewens v. Noakes* (1880) 6 QBD 530, 532 sq.

V. DIFFERENCES BETWEEN THE ENGLISH AND ROMAN-DUTCH LAW OF EMPLOYMENT

While the concept of a contract of employment—based, in principle, on the notions of freedom of contract and equality between the contracting parties—was firmly established in Roman-Dutch law, a similarly general concept evolved in England only in the course of the eighteenth century. Until then employment relationships were dealt with either as part of the law of persons or by statutes which applied to particular industries and particular classes of persons, such as those employed in agriculture or animal husbandry, artificers or colliers. The scope of employment law was therefore not determined by the type of contract under which a person was employed, but by the nature of his work.

The initiative for the development of a general concept of a contract of employment eventually came from the courts who, in the wake of the industrial revolution, had to accommodate new industrial employments falling outside the range of the Statutes of Labourers and Poor Laws.[28] This development was aided by statutory reform as the coverage of employment statutes was gradually extended. It culminated in 1875 with the passage of the Master and Servant Act which welded together true servants, i.e. those employed in agriculture or domestic service, and persons who were previously marked out as independent contractors, such as artisans and other skilled workers.[29] Legislative initiative also rounded off the development with the repeal in 1875 of the penal provisions of master and servant statutes. From then on, disputes between employer and employee resulting from breach of contract were governed by the law of contract rather than by criminal law.

VI. EMPLOYMENT RELATIONS IN THE CAPE OF GOOD HOPE

1. The labour market[30]

At the time of the second British occupation, the population at the Cape of Good Hope consisted of approximately 22,000 settlers, 25,000 (mainly imported) slaves, and an indeterminate number of indigenous Khoisan. The economy was based mainly on subsistence and demand for labour was

---

[28] However, the courts' view of the content of the contract, and esp. of the notion of subordination, was largely modelled on statutory examples. See Veneziani (n. 11), 63 sqq.

[29] Merritt, (1982) 1 *Australian Journal of Law and Society* 56, 64.

[30] The following sources were consulted: J. D. Omer-Cooper, *History of Southern Africa* (1987); P. Wickins, *An Economic History of Southern Africa* (1981); E. Wilson, L. Thompson, *Oxford History of Southern Africa* (1969).

therefore low. Such demand as there was, particularly in domestic service and in agriculture, was, at least until 1834, largely satisfied by the availability of slave labour.[31] With the abolition of slavery in England in 1807, slave imports to the Cape ended, which resulted in a serious shortage of labour, especially on farms. A proclamation was issued in the same year which compelled every Khoisan to have a fixed and registered place of residence and to be in possession of a certificate in order to travel between districts. In this way many of the indigenous inhabitants were compelled to live, and thus work, on farms. A proclamation issued in 1812 also allowed farmers to apprentice children over the age of eight for a period of ten years. However, the Cape authorities, partly as a result of pressure from the Missionary Society, passed an ordinance in 1828[32] which guaranteed to all 'hottentots and other free persons of colour' the same freedom and protection as was enjoyed by the settlers. As a result Khoi labour became scarce and more expensive. After their emancipation in 1834 slaves also attained the legal status won by the Khoi in 1828, but they were frequently still tied to their owners as apprentices for periods of between four and six years. Many remained on the farms, either because of the difficulties they faced in making a living on the open market or because they were detained after having been advanced goods or money for which they had to give value by labour. Many of the slaves were artisans and their emancipation thus led to the growth of a new class of urban artisan who practiced traditional crafts such as shoe-making, tailoring, and wagon-building.

2. Masters and servants legislation

Numerous laws dealing with relations between employer and employee were passed at the Cape between 1657 and 1800.[33] They regulated matters such as vicarious liability of employers for the wrongful acts of their employees, the carrying of passes by indigenous people, and the services rendered by free persons from outside the Colony. The first general enactment on the subject was an Ordinance of 1 March 1841 which served as a model for similar enactments in Natal (1850), Transvaal (1880), and the Orange Free State (1904).[34] It repealed legislation dating from 1787 and various other ordinances and proclamations passed in between.[35] The Ordinance itself was repealed in 1856 and replaced by the Master and Servant Act 15 of 1856. Like its predecessor, the Act only applied to a limited class of employ-

---

[31] Report of the Commission of Inquiry into Industrial Legislation (Botha Commission) UG 62 of 1951, 199.

[32] Act 50 of 1828.   [33] See *Spencer v. Gostelow* (n. 7), 628 sq.

[34] While the legislation in the Cape Colony and the Transvaal was colour-blind, the Natal and Orange Free State statutes applied only to 'coloured' servants.

[35] See Sections I and II of Ch. 1 above.

ees.[36] It regulated such matters as the duration of employment contracts, notice periods, sick leave, provision of food and lodging, termination of the contract in the event of the employer's insolvency or the death of one of the parties, and the payment of wages. The Act also contained a disciplinary code of sorts and prescribed criminal sanctions, including imprisonment with or without hard labour, spare diet, and solitary confinement for misconduct, disobedience, negligence, and desertion. The Act was extensively amended by Act 18 of 1873 and finally repealed by the General Law Amendment Act 94 of 1974.

Although the 1856 Act, like its predecessor, introduced rights and obligations for 'masters' and 'servants' which were foreign to the common law,[37] it was nevertheless based squarely on a contractual foundation. Section 1, Chapter 1 of the Act provided that the courts, in all matters:

arising out of or respecting the formation or dissolution of contracts of service or apprenticeship, or touching or concerning any rights, duties, obligations, powers, liabilities, or other matters or things arising out of or proceeding from any contracts of service or apprenticeship, or any of the mutual relations subsisting between masters and servants or apprentices, shall respectively try, judge and determine the said causes according to the law of this Colony, respecting and applicable to bi-lateral contracts in general, except when other provisions touching and concerning such matter and thing as aforesaid shall have been made in this Act.[38]

VI. THE INFLUENCE OF ENGLISH LAW

1. Vicarious liability

Roman law had no general rule according to which one person may be held liable for the delicts of another.[39] In the absence of personal fault[40] a *paterfamilias* was not normally liable for the unlawful conduct of those under his *potestas*. However, certain exceptions to the general rule were recognized,

---

[36] A 'servant' was defined as 'any person employed for remuneration to perfom any handicraft or other bodily labour in agriculture or manufacture or in domestic service or as a boatman, porter or other occupation of a like nature'.

[37] E.g. the duration of contracts was limited to specified periods (1 year in the event of verbal contracts); paid sick-leave was provided for; and masters were obliged to provide food and lodging unless it was agreed otherwise. Probably the most important deviation from the common law was the fact that exclusive penal sanctions were prescribed for breach of contract by master and servant, although only servants were liable to be imprisoned.

[38] Section III, Chapter 1 of the 1841 Ordinance contained a similar provision.

[39] For a fuller account of the position in Roman law see T. B. Barlow, *The South African Law of Vicarious Liability* (1939), 12 sqq. See also W. W. Buckland, *A Text-Book of Roman Law* (3rd edn., 1963), 599 sqq.; Zimmermann (n. 4), 399 sqq., 1118 sqq.; and *Hirsch Appliance Specialists v. Shield Security Natal (Pty) Ltd* 1992 (3) SA 643 (D) 647.

[40] E.g. where the *paterfamilias* ordered his servant to perform a wrongful act, in which event he was liable as if he had committed the act himself.

such as noxal liability,[41] *custodia* liability,[42] and liability under the *receptum nautarum cauponum stabulariorum*.[43] Liability in these instances did not, however, depend on the existence of a contract of employment.[44]

The position in Roman-Dutch law is uncertain.[45] Some jurists, such as Grotius,[46] Groenewegen,[47] and Van der Keessel,[48] held the view that an employer was only liable for the unlawful acts of his employees in exceptional instances.[49] Other writers amongst whom Johannes Voet[50] was the most prominent,[51] recognized a general liability *in solidum* for unlawful acts committed in the course of employment (*in officio aut ministerio*). However, they all acknowledged that an employer could also be held liable for acts committed outside the scope of employment, but only to the extent of wages due when the unlawful act was committed.[52]

While there is some uncertainty about the precise origins of the doctrine in English law[53] its history has been one of a gradual evolution from lim-

---

[41] Originally, noxal liability entailed an obligation on the *paterfamilias* to surrender the wrongdoer, whether slave, *filius-*, or *filiafamilias*, to the injured person in order to allow the latter to wreak his vengance on the wrongdoer. During the classical period the custom arose of buying off the vengeance of the latter, although this required the consent of the injured party who could still demand the surrender of the wrongdoer. In the post-classical period the payment of a sum of money to the injured party became compulsory where the wrongdoer was *sui iuris*. Where the wrongdoer was *alieni iuris* the payment of a sum of money as an alternative to the surrender of the wrongdoer remained completely voluntary. Noxal liability in respect of sons and daughters under paternal power was eventually abolished. See Barlow (n. 39), 12–15; Zimmermann (n. 4), 1099 sqq., 1118 sq.

[42] Where goods were entrusted to another for safekeeping, repair, or workmanship the custodian was responsible also for the conduct of his servants in connection with the thing left in his custody. See Barlow (n. 39), 17 sq.; Zimmermann (n. 4), 399 sq.

[43] This included liability of inn-keepers, sea carriers, and stable-keepers for theft, damage, and other unlawful acts committed by their servants. For details see Zimmermann (n. 4), 514 sqq.

[44] W. E. Scott, *Middelikke Aanspreeklikheid in die Suid-Afrikaanse Reg* (1983), 3.

[45] See *Lewis v. The Salisbury Gold Mining Co* (1894) 1 OR 1; *Mkize v. Martens* (n. 10); and, generally, Barlow (n. 39), 61 sqq.

[46] Hugo Grotius, *Inleiding tot de Hollandsche Rechtsgeleertheyd*, 3, 1, 34; 3, 38, 3.

[47] Simon van Groenewegen van der Made, *Tractatus de legibus abrogatis vel inusitatis in Hollandia vicinisque regionibus*, ad Dig. 15, 1.

[48] Dionysius Godefridus van der Keessel, *Theses selectae juris Hollandici et Zelandici*, 477.

[49] Grotius (n. 46), 3, 38, 9 mentions liability imposed by statute as an exception to the general rule.

[50] Johannes Voet, *Commentarius ad Pandectas*, 9, 4, 10. He states that the basis of liability is the employer's fault in selecting an incompetent or negligent servant (*culpa in eligendo*). There is a difference of opinion on whether Voet acknowledged a general liability only in relation to the unlawful acts of domestic servants or to employees at large. See Scott (n. 44), 9 sq. In *Estate van der Byl v. Swanepoel* 1927 AD 141, 153 sq. Kotzé JA appears to accept that the liability was of broader application.

[51] See also Simon van Leeuwen, *Het Rooms-Hollands-Regt*, 4, 39, 2 and *Censura Forensis*, 2, 12, 3.

[52] See e.g. Grotius (n. 46), 3, 38, 3; Voet (n. 50), 9, 4, 10; 14, 1, 11.

[53] Barlow (n. 39), 37. See also Scott (n. 44), 11; Reinhard Zimmermann, '*Effusum vel deiectum*', in: *Festschrift für Hermann Lange* (1992), 301, 319 sqq.

ited liability in exceptional instances[54] to a general liability, even for the intentional acts of employees. By the time the doctrine was first adopted in South African law it was already reaching maturity in England.[55]

There is no evidence of a gradual evolution of the doctrine in South African law.[56] South African courts have never regarded the doctrine as controversial and have paid little attention to the considerable differences of opinion among the Roman-Dutch jurists on the subject.[57] On the mistaken assumption that it reflected the general position in Roman-Dutch law[58] they adopted the opinion of those who, like Voet, favoured a general principle of liablity *in solidum*. Decisions handed down during the second half of the nineteenth century—with only one exception[59]—failed to engage in a thorough investigation of the opinions of those of the old writers who did not support the general principle. In the earliest reported case in point[60] Voet was the only authority referred to,[61] while in other cases the principle was adopted without reference to any of the old writers.[62] When the question of vicarious liability was considered for the first time by the Appellate Division[63] the Court regarded the doctrine as well established. Only the most superficial examination of the old authorities was undertaken by the members of the Court.[64] *Feldman (Pty) Ltd v. Mall*[65] perhaps best illustrates the extent of the Court's unwillingness to engage in an analysis of the position in Roman-Dutch law. After stating that the doctrine of vicarious liability had become established by precedent,[66] it was held that, South African law on the subject being 'the same as the English law', it was

---

[54] See Barlow (n. 39), 36 sqq. He demonstrates that there are similarities between the position in England during the formative years of the doctrine and the position in postclassical Roman law and he suggests that this may be attributable to the subconscious influence of the late Roman jurists on English judges.

[55] Barlow (n. 39), 43 sqq. See also *Estate Van der Byl v. Swanepoel* (n. 50), 148.

[56] It was already regarded as established in *Hilpert v. Castle Mail Packets Co* (1897) 12 EDC 38. See also *Gifford v. Table Bay Dock & Breakwater Management Commission* (18/4) 4 Buch 96; *Weir v. Union Steamship Co* 1874 NLR 61.

[57] The exception was the judgment of Kotzé CJ in *Lewis v. Salisbury Gold Mining Co* (n. 45); cf. Zimmermann (n. 4), 1124.

[58] See e.g. *Mkize v. Martens* (n. 10), 389, 393. While Kotzé JA in *Estate van der Byl v. Swanepoel* (n. 50) felt that the rule concerning liability for unpaid wages for unlawful acts committed outside the scope of employment was also part of South African law, it has never been applied by South African courts and must therefore be regarded as having been abrogated by disuse. See *April v. Pretorius* 1906 TS 824, 826; Barlow (n. 39), 85.

[59] See n. 57.   [60] *Dreyer v. Van Reenen* (1845) 3 Menz 375.

[61] However, the reference by counsel in the matter was to Voet, *Commentarius ad Pandectas*, 27, 10, 3 which has no bearing on the issue of vicarious liability.

[62] See e.g. *Reid v. Bouverie* (1914) 35 NLR 203.

[63] *Mkize v. Martens* (n. 20).

[64] De Villiers CJ candidly referred (at 386) to the Roman-Dutch authorities as being 'in hopeless conflict with each other'; the other members of the Court, however, felt that the law applicable to the matter was 'fairly clear' (389; 393).

[65] 1945 AD 733.   [66] 736.

unnecessary to examine whether the doctrine ever applied in Roman-Dutch law.[67]

It has been suggested[68] that the views of those Roman-Dutch authorities who favoured the doctrine of vicarious liability were not accidentally adopted. The courts referred to them because these opinions accorded with the position in English law and therefore served as a convenient port of entry for the almost wholesale importation of the (by then well developed) principles of English law in regard to vicarious liability.[69] While the courts have at times denied a reception from English law[70] there can be little doubt that the fabric of the doctrine as it exists in South African law today is decidedly English in orientation and derivation.[71] Its subsequent history also confirms the overriding influence of English law,[72] particularly with regard to two of its cardinal features: the definition of an employee[73] and

[67] Much later, in *Hirsch Appliance Special lists v. Shield Security Natal (Pty) Ltd* (n. 39), Booysen J referred to the differences of opinion among the old writers as being 'not important' in view of the fact that the doctrine has long been accepted as established. Cf. Boberg, (1966) 74 *SALJ* 150, 170; Barlow (n. 39), 84 sqq.

[68] Boberg (n. 67). See also Scott (n. 44), 10 sq.

[69] The ease with which the courts drew on English precedents is apparent even in some of the first reported decisions on the question of vicarious liability, such as *Gifford v. Table Bay Docks and Breakwater Management Commission* (n. 56), 114 and *Hilpert v. Castle Mail Packets Co* (n. 56), 38. In *Mkize v. Martens* (n. 10), 390 Innes JA boldly stated that the views of those jurists who favoured vicarious liability were 'identical with the English rule that a master is answerable for the torts of a servant committed in the course of his employment'.

[70] See Kotzé JA in *Estate Van der Byl v. Swanepoel* (n. 50), 153: 'I am aware that more recently the view has been advanced that the doctrine of a master's liability for the negligence of his servants, acting within the scope of their duty, is foreign to the principles of Roman-Dutch law, and is entirely based on the law of England. Such a view is a mistaken one, and rests on a misconception of the true development of the Roman-Dutch law and of the English law; for the source of the master's liability for the negligence of those whom he keeps and employs in his service is . . . derived from the *Corpus Juris*'. See also *Feldman (Pty) Ltd v. Mall* 1945 AD 733, at 738. For criticism of the courts' incorrect historical perspective in other cases, see Barlow (n. 39), 86 sq.

[71] Boberg, (n. 67), 170; Scott (n. 44), 10 sq. Barlow (n. 39), 82, while acknowledging the important influence of English law, nevertheless argues that the doctrine is firmly rooted in Roman-Dutch law, since writers who supported a general principle of vicarious liability, even though their opinions may have been based on an incorrect interpretation of Roman law, 'by their very numerical strength' established the principle of liability *in solidum* as the rule of Roman-Dutch law.

[72] So much so that the doctrine of vicarious liability has been described as 'perhaps the most comprehensive and far-reaching innovation we have taken from English law': Boberg, (n. 67), 169. See also *Feldman (Pty) Ltd v. Mall* (n. 70), 736; *HK Manufacturing Co (Pty) Ltd v. Sadowitz* 1965 (3) SA 328 (C) 337D-E.

[73] South African courts have consistently adopted the same, or similar, standards to distinguish between contracts of employment and contracts for services. As in English law, the right of control was initially regarded as the distinguishing feature of the contract of employment. See e.g. *Colonial Life Assurance Soc Ltd v. Macdonald* 1931 AD 412, 426, 432 and, before that, *Kotze v. Ohlssons Breweries* (1892) 9 SC 319; *Newman v. East London Town Council* (1895) 12 SC 61. (It is noteworthy that in Roman-Dutch law the distinction between *locatio conductio operarum* and *locatio conductio operis* lay in their economic purpose, not in the employer's right of control. See Barlow (n. 39), 96, fn. 12. In England, on the other hand, the 'control test' had its origin in the statutes of labourers and Poor Laws. See Kahn-Freund, (n. 24), 511–12. But

the scope of his employment.[74] It would, however, be incorrect to conclude that the courts were entirely uncritical in their acceptance of English law. Thus, they refused to adopt the English doctrine of common employment, which excludes the employer's liability for delicts committed by one employee against another on the basis of *volenti non fit iniuria*.[75] It must also be said that, in spite of their adherence to principles of English law, the courts have from the outset sought to find a basis for the doctrine in Roman-Dutch law. This remains the case today.[76]

2. Forfeiture of wages

In *Spencer v. Gostelow*[77] the Appellate Division held that an employee dismissed for serious misconduct did not forfeit his wages for services rendered prior to his dismissal. Thus the Court brought an abrupt end to the ascendancy of a contrary rule, established for more than thirty years. However, the Court left open the question whether deserters forfeited their wages for services rendered up to the date of their desertion.

There was no general rule of forfeiture of wages in the event of desertion or dismissal for serious misconduct in Roman-Dutch law.[78] However, an exception was recognized in respect of domestic and other servants who stood in a close relationship to their employers:[79] they were taken to have

see now *Smit v. Workmen's Compensation Commissioner* (n. 3), 62C where the Court stated that it had been unnecessary for courts in earlier decisions to have regard to English law since the control test was firmly rooted in Roman-Dutch law). The 'organization test' was first formulated by Lord Denning in *Stevenson, Jordan & Harrison Ltd v. MacDonald & Evans* [1952] 1 TLR 101 (CA). It made its South African appearance in *R v. AMCA Services Ltd* 1959 (4) SA 207 (A). A third test, the 'dominant impression test', was first formulated in *Ongevallekommissaris v. Onderlinge Versekeringsgenootskap AVBOB* 1976 (4) SA 446 (A) and was endorsed in *Smit v. Workmen's Compensation Commissioner* (n. 3). It is virtually identical with the modern test applied in English law. For a fuller account see Etienne Mureinik, 'The Contract of Employment: An Easy Test for Hard Cases', (1980) 97 *SALJ* 246 sqq.

[74] See, for example, *Feldman (Pty) Ltd v. Mall* (n 70); *HK Manufacturing Co (Pty) Ltd v. Sadowitz* (n. 72).

[75] See *Lewis v. Salisbury Gold Mining Co* (n. 45); *Waring & Gillow Ltd v. Sherborne* 1904 TS 340.

[76] See *Smit v. Workmen's Compensation Commissioner* (n. 3), 62C; *HK Manufacturing Co (Pty) Ltd v. Sadowitz* 1965 (3) SA 328 (C) 337E and *Feldman (Pty) Ltd v. Mall* (n. 70), 744.

[77] Above, n. 7.

[78] See the thorough discussion of the position in Roman-Dutch law in the judgment of Wessels J in the Court *a quo* in *Spencer v. Gostelow* (n. 7). See also J. Labuschagne, 'Die Droster se verdiende loon?', 1970 *Speculum Juris* 48 sqq.

[79] Both Voet (n. 50), 19, 2, 27 and Simon van Leeuwen, *Censura Forensis*, 1, 4, 22, 11 restrict the exception to *famuli* and *servi*. See the judgment of Wessels J in the Court *a quo* in *Spencer v. Gostelow* (n. 7) where the conclusion is reached, after an investigation into the grammatical and common law meaning of the terms, that they referred to domestic servants and servants *eiusdem generis*, e.g. stablehands, coachmen, etc. The correctness of this interpretation is fortified by the fact that the statutes on which the exception was based applied only to domestic servants. See Labuschagne, 1970 *Speculum Juris* 48, at 53 sq. and the judgment of Mason AJA in *Spencer v. Gostelow* (n. 7), 639.

forfeited whatever wages were due to them when they deserted or were dismissed.[80] This exception was based on local ordinances as well as statutes of more general application.[81] Employees not included within the statutory exceptions remained, however, entitled to payment for their services rendered. Johannes Voet states the general rule as follows:[82] 'Then again if it is the fault of one who has let his services that he has not rendered them, the wages must be diminished according to the time during which the services were not rendered.'

The passage then mentions the two instances in which an employer may insist on completion of the period of service, namely where apprentices abandon their apprenticeship and where domestic servants depart before the expiry of the period of service.

In English law since the early part of the nineteenth century[83] the position has been that an employee who deserted or who was justifiably dismissed for breach of contract forfeited his wages for the period during which he had in fact rendered his services.[84] No distinction is made between domestic servants and other employees. Thus, whereas Roman-Dutch law regarded forfeiture of wages as an exception to the rule that an employee had to be paid for services rendered, even in the event of justified dismissal or desertion, English law considered forfeiture of wages to be the general rule.

It was the English rather than the Roman-Dutch approach which became established in South African law. However, the reception occurred in a far less overt fashion than was the case with the doctrine of vicarious liability. In fact, references in older cases to English law are few and far between.[85] Yet the general rule of forfeiture which was eventually abandoned in *Spencer v. Gostelow* was undoubtedly of English origin.

The first traces of a general rule of forfeiture appeared in *Bassaramadoo v. Morris*,[86] which concerned the claim for wages by a hotel waiter who had

---

[80] See Voet (n. 50), 19, 2, 27 where it is stated that, in exceptional circumstances, an employer may compel an unwilling servant to complete the full term agreed upon (before becoming liable for payment of any wages).

[81] See *Spencer v. Gostelow* (n. 7), 626–8, 638 sq.; Labuschagne, 1970 *Speculum Juris* 48, 53, fn. 31 for details of the various instruments.

[82] *Commentarius ad Pandectas*, 19, 2, 72 (trans. Percival Gane, *The Selective Voet* (1955 sqq.)).

[83] See Mark Freedland, *The Contract of Employment* (1976), 227 sqq. for the history of the rule. The leading case on the subject is *Turner v. Robinson* (1853) 5 B & Ald 789.

[84] The reasons are not clear. See Freedland (n. 83), 227.

[85] But see the judgment of Wessels J in the Court *a quo* in *Spencer v. Gostelow* (n. 7), 620. In *Bassaramadoo v. Morris* (n. 86) Smith J did refer to the general rule of English law but added that, as there was some controversy over whether it applied in South Africa, he did not wish to express an opinion upon it.

[86] (1888) 6 SC 28. In *Mawele v. Zietsman* (1886) 7 NLR 3 it was still held that a deserter was entitled to be paid for the period for which he had worked. The employer's remedy, according to Connor CJ, lay in a counterclaim for damages.

deserted his employer's service. De Villiers CJ found that, under the common law, an employee who deserted or deliberately misconducted himself 'with the object of inducing his master to dismiss him' was not entitled to wages for the period of service preceding desertion or dismissal. He relied for this statement on Voet[87] and Van Leeuwen.[88] Smith J, who clearly regarded the employee in this case as a domestic servant,[89] went much further. In an *obiter dictum* he added that wages were also forfeited in the case of an employee dismissed for misconduct in the middle of the month for 'some such act as wilful disobedience to orders, theft, or gross moral misconduct'. While the Chief Justice justified the forfeiture of wages on the basis that it would be 'most unreasonable' to allow an employee who wilfully deserted to benefit from his actions, Smith J (adopting the terminology of English law) argued that the contract of emloyment was an 'entire one' which required the period of service to be completed before any claim for wages could be entertained.

Several aspects of the decision call for comment. First, the Chief Justice's view that any deserting employee should forfeit wages for the period preceding his desertion does not accord with the general rule as stated by Voet. Voet, as we have seen, asserted that wages are only forfeited for the period during which *no work* was done, save in the two exceptional circumstances mentioned above. The Chief Justice effectively promoted these exceptions to a general rule for, without distinguishing between domestic servants and other employees,[90] he took the two exceptions as a basis for the proposition that 'if the master does not consent to the diminution of the term of service, he ought not to be compelled to pay for any part of such service'.[91] Secondly, the Chief Justice attempted to substantiate his view that the deserting employee forfeited wages even for the period during which he had in fact worked with an analogy to the case of a lessee whom the lessor had ejected deliberately and without justification from the premises.[92] However, the ejected lessee would clearly still be liable for rent for the period during which he was in occupation.[93] Had he carried the analogy through to its logical conclusion, De Villiers CJ would have had to conclude that the employer still had to pay the deserting employee his wages for services rendered up to the date of his desertion.

---

[87] Voet (n. 50), 19, 2, 27, incorrectly cited in his judgment as Voet, 16, 2, 27.

[88] *Censura Forensis*, 1, 4, 22, 11. [89] 31.

[90] He used the term 'servants' without any qualification. But as the judgment of Wessels J in *Spencer v. Gostelow* (n. 7), 618 sq., illustrates, the exceptional position which Voet sketched related to domestic servants only. See also the judgment of Mason AJA (639 sq.) and *Muller v. Grobbelaar* 1946 OPD 272 (*per* Van den Heever J).

[91] 30. Of course, it does not follow that, because an employer may under certain circumstances compel a servant to complete his period of service, he is entitled to withhold wages for the period during which the employee worked.

[92] 30. [93] Voet (n. 50), 19, 2, 23.

Thirdly, his statements in the *Bassaramadoo* case contradict the view which the Chief Justice had earlier expressed in *Nixon v. Blaine*,[94] according to which an employer who dismissed his employee for misconduct could not avail himself of such misconduct to evade payment of wages for the period during which he had had the use of the employee's services. In *Bassaramadoo*[95] De Villiers CJ argued that his remarks in *Nixon v. Blaine* were not intended to apply to those employees who deserted their employers or whose conduct demonstrated that they were unlikely to serve their employers faithfully for the full term agreed upon,[96] but only to those still willing and able to complete their term of service. The general rule as stated by Voet, he said, would be fully applicable in the latter instance but not in the former. Voet, however, does not draw such a distinction—it appears to be solely based on the Chief Justice's notions of what was just and fair.[97]

Smith J, as indicated, went considerably further, although his statements were *obiter*. He argued that employees who committed acts of misconduct *equivalent to desertion*, such as 'wilful disobedience to lawful orders, theft or gross moral misconduct', also forfeited wages for the period during which services had in fact been rendered.[98] Although the Judge deliberately avoided reference to English cases,[99] his remarks mirrored the position in contemporary English law. They were also subsequently relied upon in other decisions as a correct statement of the South African common law on the subject.

In spite of its somewhat shaky doctrinal foundation, *Bassaramadoo v. Morris* remained for more than thirty years the leading case on forfeiture of wages and the principles established in this decision were gradually extended. This is illustrated by a decision from the Transvaal, *Smith v. Federal Cold Storage Ltd*,[100] which dealt with a total refusal to work. The employee's services had been taken over by the defendant company after the latter had acquired the business. Refusing to obey an instruction to transfer to another location, the employee was dismissed. His claim for arrears of wages and damages for wrongful dismissal was turned down. Innes CJ held that his refusal to obey the order amounted to a refusal to do any of the work which he had been employed to do and therefore constituted misconduct 'equivalent to desertion'. Accordingly, he was not entitled to wages for the period preceding his dismissal. As his dismissal had been justified, he was also not entitled to any damages.[101]

[94] (1879) 9 Buch 217.   [95] 29.

[96] The Chief Justice mentions the situation of employees who misconduct themselves 'with the object of inducing their masters to dismiss them'.

[97] Cf. Labuschagne, 1970 *Speculum Juris* 48, 51.   [98] Above, n. 86, 32.

[99] The reason mentioned was the uncertainty over whether 'our law is in agreement with English law': 32.

[100] 1905 TS 734.

[101] See also *Robertson & Co v. Heathorn* (1904) 21 SC 427 where it was held that concealment of money was 'equivalent to leaving service'.

Hutchinson v. Ramdas[102] was concerned with a partial refusal to work. The employee refused to obey an instruction to clean a door, in spite of having spent some time in gaol for refusing to obey a similar instruction. He was dismissed and thereafter sued his employer, *inter alia*, for wages to the date of his dismissal. The trial magistrate, after indicating that in English law the claim would have been disallowed, was nevertheless prepared to grant it on the basis that this would better conform to the spirit of South African law. However, the decision was overturned on appeal on the strength of *Bassaramadoo*. Finnemore ACJ recognized that the analogy drawn in *Bassaramadoo* between the deserting employee and the position of the lessee ejected without good cause should have led to the conclusion that the latter be entitled to payment for his services rendered.[103] Yet he relied on the provisions of a *placaat* of 29 November 1679[104] as authority for denying the employee's claim. Bird J, in turn, followed the lead of Smith J in *Bassaramadoo* and distinguished between various species of misconduct, only some of which would result in forfeiture of wages. Unlike Smith J, however, he did not limit forfeiture of wages to instances of dismissal for misconduct 'equivalent to desertion'[105] but extended it to any misconduct 'so serious as to make it practically impossible for the employer to work with the servant' and as a result of which it is 'really necessary for the employer to dismiss the servant'.[106]

This line of decisions reached its apex in *Rene v. Alexander*.[107] The appellant, who had been a chef in the service of the respondent, was dismissed for various instances of misconduct, including intoxication, absence without leave, and disobedience. Kotzé J correctly stated that cases such as *Robertson & Co v. Heathorn*[108] and *Smith v. Federal Cold Storage* were not concerned with desertion, or acts of misconduct amounting to desertion, but he then concluded that the true principle established in these and other cases was that wages were forfeited in the event of dismissal for *any* form of serious misconduct.[109] In support of his opinion he cited those Dutch *placaaten* and ordinances which imposed a penalty of forfeiture of wages on domestic servants who deserted their employers' service, and argued that some of these enactments, because they were of general application, formed part of South African law.

In *Spencer v. Gostelow* the Appellate Division of the Supreme Court eventually rejected the rule laid down in *Bassaramadoo* and subsequent decisions. The Court held that any employee dismissed for serious misconduct

---

[102] (1904) 25 NLR 165, the first reported decision in Natal on this point.

[103] See Voet (n. 50), 14, 2, 26.

[104] Which made provision for forfeiture of wages in the case of domestic servants who deserted their employers.

[105] Cf. *Field v. Grace* 1911 TPD 949 which held that wages were forfeited where the misconduct was of a gross or flagrant nature.

[106] 169 sq.   [107] 1916 CPD 608.   [108] Above, n. 101.   [109] 612 sq.

was entitled to wages for the period prior to dismissal during which he had rendered his services. Innes CJ motivated his reasoning as follows:[110]

Speaking generally, the letting of services is regulated in Roman-Dutch law by the same principles as the letting of property. The servant is the locator in the one case; the landlord in the other. Now where the lessee of land has not had the enjoyment of the leased property for the full contractual term, by reason either of premature ejectment or of justifiable abandonment, he is not liable for the full rent. But he is, speaking generally, liable for a part of it, proportionate to the time during which he had occupation—saving in certain cases his claim for damages for breach of contract (Voet, 19. 2, secs. 23 and 26). The fact that, through no fault of his own, he has not had the benefit of the property for part of the term does not absolve him from liability in respect of the period of his usual enjoyment. Applying the same principle to the case of a *locatio operarum*, it would follow that an employer who justifiably terminates the contract by dismissing the servant, though he is not liable for future wages is still bound to pay for services rendered prior to the date of dismissal. Voet (19. 2, sec. 27), discussing the case where a servant has failed to serve for the full period, states that the wages must be rateably diminished; but there is nothing in his remarks to countenance the idea that by common law a master who has properly dismissed his servant is absolved from liability for wages in respect of past services.

The employer's liability, according to Innes CJ, rested 'on the equitable doctrine that no man is allowed to enrich himself at the expense of another'.[111]

   Both Innes CJ and Mason AJA held that the rule mentioned by some Roman-Dutch jurists,[112] namely that domestic servants forfeited wages upon desertion, was not founded on any general principle of law but on the provisions of *placaaten* and ordinances which did not form part of South African law.[113]

   As indicated above, the Court left open the question whether deserters forfeited wages for the period for which they had worked prior to their desertion, although Mason AJA's broad statement of the general principle arguably includes deserters.[114] However, subsequent decisions have held that deserters constitute an exception to the general rule and therefore for-

---

[110] 626 sq.

[111] 627. For criticism of the Chief Justice's reliance on an enrichment action in these circumstances see J. C. De Wet, A. H. van Wyk, *Kontraktereg en Handelsreg*, vol. I (5th edn., 1992), 208; but cf. Wouter de Vos, *Verrykingsaanspreeklikheid in die Suid-Afrikaanse Reg* (3rd edn., 1987), 296.

[112] Apart from Voet (n. 50), 14, 2, 27 see also Van Leeuwen (n. 79), 4, 22, 11; Van der Keessel (n. 48), 679.

[113] 628; 640–3. Wessels J in the Court *a quo*, however, appears to have accepted that the rule does indeed form part of South African law but that it should be restricted in its application to domestic servants or servants *eiusdem generis*. See 1920 AD 617, 621.

[114] He stated (643) that 'the master is not entitled to refuse the payment of arrear wages to a servant whom he has dismissed *for whatever cause* so far as he has benefited by the work of the dismissed servant' (emphasis added).

feit whatever wages may be due to them for services rendered up to the date of their desertion.[115] This is still the position today.[116]

3. Specific performance

The history of specific performance of contracts of employment is characterized by an uncritical acceptance of the principles of English law by South African courts, in spite of the fact that English law differed considerably from Roman-Dutch law in this respect. As a general rule, an employee is not entitled to demand that his employer should employ him or keep him occupied.[117] Therefore, an employee who is unlawfully dismissed by his employer would not, save in exceptional circumstances,[118] be able to claim an order *ad factum praestandum*.[119] However, until the decision in *Stewart Wrightson (Pty) Ltd v. Thorpe*[120] it was a truism that an employee who was wrongfully dismissed was also not entitled to an order *ad pecuniam solvendam*. His sole remedy was a claim for damages on account of his unlawful dismissal.[121] The rule against the granting of specific performance also prevented the unlawfully dismissed employee from enforcing such ancillary benefits as the right to remain in occupation of the employer's premises, and the right to a hearing before dismissal.[122] The courts were, however, prepared to issue orders *ad pecuniam solvendam*[123] or even *ad factum praestandum*[124] where the unlawfully dismissed employee was a public servant,[125] or was dismissed contrary to the provisions of a statute.

The rule against specific performance of contracts of employment in English law developed during the nineteenth century;[126] before then such

[115] *Malan v. Van der Merwe* 1937 TPD 244; *Muller v. Grobbelaar* (n. 90). But see the judgment of Van den Heever AJA where he states, at 277, that 'I cannot see how [our law] can countenance a form of forfeiture which has no contractual foundation and an extremely shaky foundation in law'.

[116] See Gerhard Lubbe, Christina Murray, *Farlam & Hathaway on Contract: Cases, Materials and Commentary* (1989), 572; but cf. De Wet/Van Wyk (n. 111), 188. *Valasek v, Consolidated Frame Cotton Corp Ltd* 1983 (1) SA 694 (N) offers authority for the proposition that the deserting employee ought to be treated in the same way as one lawfully dismissed before the expiry of the term of the contract.

[117] See generally, M. S. M. Brassey, 'Specific Performance: A New Stage for Labour's Lost Love', (1981) 2 *Industrial LJ* 57.

[118] See *Stewart Wrightson (Pty) Ltd v. Thorpe* 1974 (4) SA 67 (D) 77 sq. and the cases there cited.

[119] In what follows, specific performance refers to orders *ad pecuniam solvendam*.

[120] *Above* n. 118.

[121] See e.g. *Farrington v. Arkin* 1921 CPD 286, 289.

[122] See e.g. *International Correspondence Schools Ltd v. Robertson* 1910 CTR 355; *Venter v. Livni* 1950 (1) SA 524 (T).

[123] E.g. *Schierhout v. Minister of Justice* 1926 AD 99 at 107.

[124] E.g. *Somers v. Director of Indian Education* 1979 (4) SA 713 (D); *Rogers v. Durban Corp* 1950 (1) SA 65 (D).

[125] But see now *Bramdaw v. Union Gov* 1931 NLR 57, 78 sq., where it is stated that there is no difference in principle between the position of a public servant and an ordinary employee.

[126] See Freedland (n. 83), 273, fn. 4, and the cases there cited.

orders were not uncommon.[127] Several reasons have been put forward by English courts for their refusal to entertain claims for specific performance, most of them based on considerations of social policy.[128]

South African courts, ignoring the fact that specific performance was an equitable remedy in English law, justified their refusal to grant specific performance with regard to contracts of employment on the same grounds as their English counterparts. While most of these were grounded in social policy,[129] one was based in legal theory: it was said that any dismissal, even a wrongful one, had the effect of terminating the contract of employment immediately, leaving the wrongfully dismissed employee with nothing but a claim for damages.[130] While some earlier decisions[131] had queried the validity of this doctrine of 'automatic termination', *Thorpe's* case unequivocally put an end to it by holding that an unlawful dismissal amounted to a repudiation of the contract of employment which vested the dismissed employee with the option of either enforcing the contract by claiming wages or terminating it.[132] In *National Union of Textile Workers v. Stag Packings (Pty) Ltd*[133] (a case which dealt with the dismissal of employees contrary to the provisions of a statute) the Transvaal Provincial Division of the Supreme Court stated the general rule as follows:[134] 'As a general rule a party to a contract which has been wrongfully rescinded by the other party can hold the other party to the contract if he so elects. There is, in my view, no reason why this general rule should not also be applicable to contracts of employment.'

The policy considerations[135] adduced in support of the refusal to grant specific performance were: the inadvisability of compelling someone to continue employing a person whom he does not trust in a position involving a close relationship;[136] the absence of 'mutuality';[137] and the fact that it would be difficult for the courts to ensure compliance with an order of specific per-

---

[127] See ibid. 272; *Schierhout v. Minister of Justice* (n. 123), 107.

[128] See generally Freedland (n. 83), 273 sqq.

[129] See Brassey, (1981) 2 *Industrial LJ* 57, 58.

[130] See e.g. *Gracie v. Hull, Blythe & Co (SA) Ltd* 1931 CPD 539, 541; *Beeton v. Peninsula Transport Co (Pty) Ltd* 1934 CPD 53.

[131] It was already rejected in *Strachan v. Lloyd Levy* 1923 AD 670, 671, a decision which was not referred to in *Thorpe's* case. See also *Myers v. Abramson* 1952 (3) SA 121 (C); *Venter v. Livni* 1950 (1) SA 524 (T). However, De Villiers JA in *Strachan v. Lloyd Levy* held that repudiation by the employer constitutes an offer of termination which may be accepted by the employee, with the result that the contract is terminated by consent. However, this so-called *consensus* doctrine was rejected in *Thorpe's* case.

[132] 952A.　　　　　　　　　　　　　　　　[133] 1982 (4) SA 151 (T).

[134] 156H. There is, however, no reference to *Thorpe's* case in the judgment.

[135] See *Schierhout v. Minister of Justice* (n. 123), 107.

[136] In *Pougnet v. Ramlakan* 1961 (2) SA 163 (D) 166 sq. it was held, with reference to English authority, that specific performance will not be granted even in situations where employer and employee are unlikely to come into frequent personal contact.

[137] 'Mutuality' concerns the availability to the parties of equal or comparable remedies. The English courts of equity were not prepared to grant a remedy to one party unless it was also possible to grant a comparable remedy to the other party if appropriate. Thus, 'just as a court

formance.[138] However, in *National Union of Textile Workers v. Stag Packings (Pty) Ltd* it was held that these were practical considerations rather than legal principles[139] and therefore could not fetter the Court's discretion of whether to grant an order of specific performance or not. Subsequent decisions have consistently followed this approach.[140]

The precise origins of the rule against specific performance of contracts of employment in South African law are obscure, but decisions such as *Venables v. Jarvis*,[141] *Haupt v. Diebel Brothers*,[142] and *Thompson v. Pullinger*[143] show that such orders were not uncommon during the nineteenth century.[144] The remedy was, undoubtedly, recognized in Roman-Dutch law, also in the context of *locatio conductio*.[145] Nevertheless, in *Schierhout v. Minister of Justice*[146] Innes CJ regarded it as unnecessary to consider the Roman-Dutch law on the subject because 'it may be taken that South African practice in regard to the remedy of an ordinary servant for wrongful dismissal is the same as the practice of the courts of England'.[147] The only cases cited in this context were *Hunt v. Eastern Province Boating Co*[148] and *Wolhuter v. Lieberman & Buirski*;[149] yet neither of them offers support for the established practice referred to by the Chief Justice.

Hunt v. Eastern Province Boating Co has also been relied upon in other cases refusing an order of specific performance.[150] It was, however, not at

is unlikely to grant an employer specific performance by requiring an employee to work (this would amount to forced labour) neither should the employee succeed in a claim for specific performance': Lubbe/Murray (n. 116), 544.

[138] See *Colonial Broom Co Ltd v. Hocking* 1914 CPD 495; *Grundlingh v. Beyers* 1967 (2) SA 131 (W) 146A. [139] 157C.

[140] See e.g. *Myburgh v. Daniëlskuil Munisipaliteit* 1985 (3) SA 335 (NC); *Consolidated Frame Cotton Corp Ltd v. President of the Industrial Court* 1985 (3) SA 150 (N); *Tshabalala v. Minister of Health* 1987 (1) SA 513 (W).

[141] (1828) 1 Menz 314. Salary was awarded for the remainder of the month in the course of which the employee had been unlawfully dismissed. He had originally claimed salary for the remainder of the year but did not succeed in proving that he had been hired for the year.

[142] (1888) 4 HCG 185, where it was held that an employer who had unlawfully dismissed an employee should have allowed the employee to serve for the remainder of his term, or paid him wages in lieu thereof.

[143] (1894) 1 OR 298. Specific performance of an ancillary employment benefit (an option to buy shares) was awarded to a mine manager who had been unlawfully dismissed. See also *Farmer's Co-operative Soc v. Berry* 1912 AD 343.

[144] See also *Suffield v. Natal Drug Co Ltd* (1891) 12 NLR 156.

[145] It is stated in Voet (n. 51), 19, 2, 2 that the lessor may demand rent for the whole period where the lessee quit the property before the end of the term. See on specific performance in Roman-Dutch law generally J. J. du Plessis, 'Spesifieke nakoming: 'n regshistoriese herwaardering', (1988) 51 *THRHR* 349 sqq.; *Cohen v. Shires, McHattie & King* (1882) 1 SAR 41; see Zimmermann (n. 4), 781 sq.

[146] Above, n. 123. [147] 108. [148] 1883 EDC 12. [149] 1892 CTR 116.

[150] See e.g. *Farrington v. Arkin* (n. 121), 289 where it was held by Searle J that 'whatever the form in which these cases were discussed by some of the Roman-Dutch text writers, at all events the practice of our courts has always been that when a contract of service has been wrongfully terminated . . . the action which arises therefrom has been a claim for damages for wrongful dismissal and not for a balance of salary for the period during which the plaintiff was prevented from performing his service'.

all concerned with such an order. The plaintiff had sued his former company *for damages* arising from his unlawful dismissal. Barry JP, in awarding him damages equivalent to the wages for the unexpired portion of his term of employment, considered whether the rule of English law applied in South Africa according to which an unlawfully dismissed employee is compelled to look for alternative employment in an effort to minimize the extent of his losses:[151]

> In the present case there is no evidence that plaintiff, thrown out of service, has or could have obtained beneficial or lucrative employment elsewhere. If there had been, then, according to the decisions ... in England the plaintiff would not have been entitled to recover salary for the whole unexpired term; but I am not at present, without hearing argument, prepared to say that that is our law, for there is some authority for the contention that where a man has been wrongfully prevented from performing his services, he may recover as damages the whole amount of his salary.

In *Wolhuter's* case, on the other hand, the Court was concerned with an exception to the plaintiff's claim for wages. The trial magistrate had upheld the exception that the claim for wages had been premature in that it was brought in the form of an action not for damages, but for salary. De Villiers CJ, without any reference to authority,[152] confirmed the decision of the magistrate and granted leave for the plaintiff's summons to be amended.

Maasdorp's *Institutes of Cape Law*[153] also suggest that the practice at the Cape at the turn of the century was probably not in accordance with English law. Maasdorp stated,[154] with reference to Voet and Van Leeuwen, that the employee's services must be paid for even if not actually rendered if the employer was responsible for the failure to render those services. He mentioned the example of an employee who has been unlawfully dismissed. He also stated that 'a servant may even be compelled by an action for specific performance to carry out his contract'.[155]

The rule laid down in *Schierhout's* case survived for more than fifty years. Only after the decision in *National Union of Textile Workers v. Stag Packings* did orders for specific performance of contracts of employment become more common. However, as a result of the establishment in 1980[156] of a specialized tribunal dealing with employment disputes involving alleged unfair labour practices, further development of the common law remedy has effectively been halted. This tribunal enjoys a very wide statutory jurisdiction, which includes the power to order the reinstatement of employees found to have been unfairly dismissed.

---

[151] 23 sq.
[152] *Hunt's* case was, however, referred to in argument by counsel for the defendant.
[153] Vol. 3 (1913).   [154] 250.   [155] 255.
[156] Under Labour Relations Act 28 of 1956, as amended.

4. The effect of illness on the contract of employment

The smooth acceptance of the principles of English law concerning specific performance of contracts of employment by South African courts is contrasted by their emphatic rejection of English principles concerning an employee's entitlement to payment of wages during periods of illness.[157] The doctrine of 'frustration', by which a contract is discharged by reason of events or circumstances which were not in the contemplation of the parties at the time of the conclusion of the contract, was also judicially applied to contracts of employment in the eighteenth century. However, a distinction was made between contracts for an indefinite period (terminable on notice), contracts entered into for a fixed period, and short-term contracts entered into for a specific purpose. Only contracts of employment for indefinite periods are here discussed in any detail.[158]

In contracts of employment for an indefinite period, the absence of the employee due to illness did not automatically bring the contract to an end; the contract had to be terminated by the employer on due notice. In the absence of a stipulation to the contrary, the employee was also entitled to wages to the date at which the period of notice expired.[159] In the case of contracts for a fixed period, the risk of the employee's temporary incapacity fell on the employer who remained liable for wages during the period of illness. The employer could only escape liability for wages when the employee became permanently incapacitated.[160] Later, however, it was held that the employer could also allege that the contract had been frustrated when the employee's illness, although not of a permanent nature, defeated the commercial purpose of the contract.[161] Finally, where the contract had been entered into for a short term and for a specific purpose, it could be terminated under the doctrine of frustration if the employee, as a result of his illness, had been prevented from fulfilling his obligations. The employee was thus relieved of his obligation to perform services or pay damages, while the employer was able to find a substitute to replace the incapacitated employee.[162]

In South Africa the common law right of a person employed for an indefinite period to wages for the period of his illness is governed by the decision of the Appellate Division in *Boyd v. Stuttaford & Co.*[163] The employee in that case had fallen ill and thereafter claimed wages for the period of his

[157] See Freedland (n. 83), 302 sqq.
[158] First, because contracts for an indefinite period are by far the most common in South African law and, secondly, because it is only in the context of this type of contract that consideration has been given to English law.
[159] Freedland (n. 83), 307.
[160] *Cuckson v. Stones* (1858) 1 E & E 248, referred to in Freedland (n. 83), 305.
[161] Freedland (n. 83), 305–7.   [162] Ibid. 303 sq.
[163] 1910 AD 101.

absence. His contract of employment did not deal with the matter and he was also not covered by the provisions of the Masters and Servants Act of 1856, which provided for payment of one month's wages in the event of illness. In the Court *a quo* Hopley J, relying on Voet,[164] rejected the approach adopted in English law and held that under South African law the employee was not entitled to payment during the period of his illness in the absence of a contractual or statutory provision to that effect.[165] Dealing with the exception in respect of domestic servants mentioned by Voet,[166] Hopley J found that it could not be extended to other employees.[167]

On appeal, Hopley J's judgment was adopted in its entirety by De Villiers CJ, Innes J, and Solomon J. References to English law by counsel for the employee were brushed aside on the basis that 'the law of South Africa seems to be reasonably clear'. The judgments of Hopley J in the Court *a quo* and Innes J in the Appellate Division reveal that the adoption of the general rule stated by Voet was not motivated solely by the clarity with which Voet expressed the law, but also by their own views on the commercial soundness of that rule. Hopley J considered that the English rule, in terms of which the employer in the present case would have been obliged to pay the employee's wages unless he had terminated the contract by giving notice, operated 'with unhuman harshness' against both employer and employee. The employer, he argued, may be put into the 'embarrassing position' of having to dismiss his employee in order to escape liability, or else pay him for services which had not been rendered. He regarded the latter alternative as 'unbusiness-like'. The rule as stated by Voet, however, allowed the employer 'to keep open his servant's situation, if he be considerate to do so, in order that the servant may on his recovery at once have the means of earning a livelihood', without incurring liability for services not rendered.[168] This rule, according to Hopley J, was 'much more in accordance with common sense, equity, and human kindness'. Innes J was of the same opinion; he stated that the absence of a right to payment effectively served to protect the employee against dismissal. The employer who knew that he was not in law liable to pay wages 'is more likely to keep [the employee's] position open . . . than would otherwise be the case'.[169]

Solomon J, on the other hand, was clearly less convinced about the fairness of the general rule; he would have liked to have been able to hold 'that the exception mentioned by Voet [in regard to domestic servants] . . . could

---

[164] Voet (n. 50) 19, 2, 27.   [165] Above, n. 163, 104.

[166] Voet (n. 50), 19, 2, 27 states that if domestic servants have only failed for a short time to render their services as a result of incapacity arising from illness their wages ought not to be reduced for the period of absence.

[167] 105. He ascribed the reason for the exception to the fact that domestic servants could ill afford to be subjected to the general rule laid down by Voet as they were 'peculiarly at the mercy of their employers'.

[168] 108 sq.   [169] 120.

be extended to apply to all servants or employees'. After stating that he found it difficult to understand why this exception should have been introduced in favour of domestic servants only, he considered that 'it would be a fair and equitable principle to apply not only to that case, but also to all contracts of service'.[170] He was, however, not prepared to extend the exception, for the duty of the Court 'is not to say what the law should be, but what it is'.[171]

In view of the fact that all employees outside the public sector have since 1993 had a limited statutory right to payment of wages during periods of illness, the law as stated in *Boyd v. Stuttaford & Co* today applies only to claims for wages for periods of illness which exceed the statutory limits.

5. Implied terms of the contract

Except for the extensive treatment generally given to the incidents of the relationship between employer and domestic servants (largely drawn from the provisions of specific statutes) Roman-Dutch lawyers treated the employment relationship as a commercial transaction governed by the principles of lease.[172] It is probably for this reason that incidents peculiar to the employment relationship, such as the employee's duty to serve the employer in good faith and to exercise reasonable competence in the performance of his duties, did not receive specific mention.

The courts bridged the gap, first, by borrowing extensively from English law, and secondly, by extending principles applicable to other branches of the law to the employment relationship. As for the influence of English law, it has already been pointed out that, in view of the fact that English law lacked a developed contract model for the employment relationship, eighteenth-century English courts availed themselves of the device of the implied term to provide a framework for the contract of employment. Many of these terms originated in the courts' own views as to what the appropriate content of the relationship ought to be.[173]

(a) The employee's duty to serve the employer in good faith

The leading South African case concerning the employee's duty to serve his employer in good faith is *Premier Medical & Industrial Equipment (Pty) Ltd v. Winkler*.[174] The Court referred with approval to the rule expressed in *Robb v. Green*[175] (a leading English authority) that it was a necessary implication of any contract of employment that an employee must 'honestly and

---

[170] 121.   [171] *Ibid.*

[172] Cf. Eltjo Schrage, 'Locatio conductio', in: Robert Feenstra, Reinhard Zimmermann (eds.), *Das römisch-holländische Recht: Fortschritte des Zivilrechts im 17. und 18. Jahrhundert* (1992), 262 sqq.

[173] See P. Davies, M. Freedland, *Labour Law: Text and Materials* (1st edn., 1979), 240 sqq.

[174] 1971 (3) SA 866 (W).   [175] (1895) 2 QBD 1.

faithfully serve his master; ... not abuse his confidence in matters apper-
taining to his service, and ... by all reasonable means in his power, protect
his master's interests in respect to matters confided to him in the course of
his service'.[176]

In the earliest reported case on the subject,[177] De Villiers CJ held that[178]

> included in the services which a servant lets is the personal element of fidelity to his
> master's interests in the particular trade or occupation to which such services are to
> be applied ... The servant is bound to give faithful personal service to his master
> and, as a consequence, to refrain from any course of conduct the natural tendency
> of which must be to injure his master's trade or business.

In spite of the absence of any reference to authority, it is safe to assume that
the Chief Justice followed the English law since that was all that counsel
had referred to in his argument.

In *Jones v. East Rand Extension Gold Mining Co Ltd*[179] extensive reference was made by counsel for both parties to *Robb v. Green* and other
English cases on the subject of the employee's duty to serve the employer
in good faith. However, the Court (*per* Bristowe J), also with reference to
English authority, founded the employee's duty of fidelity on a dubious
analogy between the position of an employee and that of a partner. Thus it
was held that 'the principles which apply in the case of partners also apply
to the case of master and servant'.[180]

(b) The employee's duty to serve the employer competently

According to English law, an employee is taken to have promised that he
possesses the skills necessary for the proper performance of his work and
that he is going to exercise the required degree of care. The origin of this
implied obligation lies in the case of *Harmer v. Cornelius*,[181] where the
Court extended the employer's right to dismiss an employee for misconduct
to cases of incompetence. The employee had applied for a position as 'scene
painter' which the employer had advertised. He was dismissed within two
days because the employer considered him to be incapable of doing the
work for which he had been employed. The Court upheld the dismissal on
the basis that the employee had misconducted himself by failing 'to afford
the requisite skill which had been expressly or impliedly promised'. It
stated:[182] 'When a skilled labourer, artisan or artist is employed, there is on
his part an implied warranty that he is of skill reasonably competent to the
task he undertakes.'

The decision in *Harmer v. Cornelius* has been followed by South African

---

[176] *Premier Medical & Industrial Equipment (Pty) Ltd v. Winkler* (n. 174), 867 sq.
[177] *R v. Eayrs* (1894) 11 SC 330.
[178] See also the judgment of Buchanan J, 334.   [179] 1903 TH 325.
[180] 335.   [181] (1858) 5 CBNS 236.   [182] 246.

courts.[183] In spite of the fact that *Harmer's* case had dealt with a skilled employee, the Court in *Ndamase v. Fyfe-King*[184] applied the same principle to a person employed on probation as a storeman and lorry driver. The reasoning mirrors the approach adopted in *Harmer*: an employee who turns out to be incompetent is guilty of misconduct for failing to comply with an implied warranty to be qualified for the post that accepted.[185]

VII. CONCLUSION

At first sight there is no particular pattern or logic to the frequency with which South African courts have borrowed from English law in order to shape the common law contract of employment. However, closer analysis suggests that such reception occurred where the position in Roman-Dutch law was either uncertain (as in the problem of vicarious liability) or where it did not deal with the matter in issue (as, for instance, with the employee's implied duties of fidelity and competent service). Yet even in these instances the courts generally sought to justify the adoption of rules of English law by trying to fit them into the principles of the Roman-Dutch law, primarily those relating to the lease of things. The one exception was the courts' refusal to enforce contracts of employment *in specie*.

Where certain rules of English law were rejected (such as those concerning forfeiture of wages and payment of wages during periods of illness), this was because the relevant principles of Roman-Dutch law were found to be both clear and fair.

All in all, therefore, the following statement by Holmes J in *ex parte De Winnaar*[186] appears to apply to the nature of the common law contract of employment in contemporary South African law:

Our country has reached a stage in its national development when its existing law can better be described as South African than Roman Dutch ... No doubt its roots are Roman Dutch, and splendid roots they are. But continuous development has come through adaptation to modern conditions, through case law, through statutes, and through the adaptation of certain principles and features of English law ... The original sources of the Roman-Dutch law are important, but exclusive preoccupation with them is like trying to return an oak tree to its acorn. It is looking ever backwards. Lot's wife looked back. Our national jurisprudence moves forward where necessary, laying aside its swaddling clothes.

---

[183] Although it has not always been referred to in the judgments of the courts it has often been cited in argument. See e.g. *Edgcombe v. Pitman* (1881) 2 NLR 73; *Pindar v. Malcomess & Co Ltd* 1905 EDC 266; *Ndamase v. Fyfe-King* 1939 EDL 259.

[184] Above, n. 183; here the Court regarded the misconduct as an instance of negligence.

[185] The risk of the inability to perform is thus placed entirely on the employee. However, his inability to perform may also be due to factors such as a lack of training or poor recruitment and selection by the employer. See also Freedland (n. 83), 202.

[186] 1959 (1) SA 837 (N) 839, also quoted by Boberg, (1966) 74 *SALJ* 150, 173.

13: *Suretyship*

C. F. FORSYTH

I. INTRODUCTION

A lawyer practising in the Cape in the early nineteenth century, would if he could be transported by the magic of time travel to the present day be amazed by the changes in the operation of the law of suretyship.[1] Many of the earliest suretyship cases decided in the Cape concern sureties for various obligations arising out of the purchase and sale of slaves.[2] And almost invariably, sureties undertook their promises in respect of the obligations of natural persons. In those days too, contracts of suretyship were not required to be in writing. Those contracts that were written were individually drafted and drawn up to suit the particular circumstances of the parties. Today slavery is long gone and surety agreements most often concern the obligations of private companies of which the sureties are directors and controlling shareholders. Although suretyship is still a means whereby persons of means help friends and relatives to borrow money, an important modern purpose of suretyship is to place the assets of a company's major shareholders at the disposal of its creditors in the event of the debtor company defaulting. The commercial ends to which suretyship is directed have thus changed dramatically.[3] Moreover, all deeds of suretyship are now required to be in writing and, more importantly, this almost invariably takes the form of a printed standard-form contract drawn up by the creditor.

But if our Cape lawyer were of a thoughtful disposition he would note that, beneath the changes wrought by the vast social, political, and commercial upheavals, the law of suretyship itself remained much as Justinian had left it. Changes in the formal law there have indeed been, but it is far more remark-

---

[1] And much else, of course.

[2] See e.g. *Rosseau v. Bierman* (1828) 1 Menz 338 (a surety for a debt, which was to be further secured by the mortgage of slaves, was released when it transpired that that mortgage was invalid); *Surrurier v. Langeveld* (1828) 1 Menz 316 (a surety who had renounced the benefit of excussion could not raise as a defence the plaintiff's failure to excuss first the special mortgage of 2 slaves which also secured the debt: *Karnspeck v. Rutgers* (10 Jan. 1822, unreported, overruled)).

[3] This fundamental change in the uses to which suretyship is put should not surprise us. After all, suretyship derives from the technicalities of litigation in Rome prior to the Twelve Tables; and then it was transmuted into a form of securing ordinary commercial obligations. Such changes in use are commonplace. See C. F. Forsyth, J. T. Pretorius, *Caney's The Law of Suretyship* (4th edn., 1992), ch. 1.

able how much has remained the same. Intriguingly, as will be seen from this Chapter, many of the most recent changes in the formal law result from judges in the modern age returning to the ancient civilian sources.

This Chapter traces the formal changes (first the legislative and then the judicial) in the law of suretyship. It also identifies some of the major changes in the operation of the law.

II. LEGISLATIVE CHANGES IN THE LAW OF SURETYSHIP

1. The formalities necessary for a valid contract of suretyship[4]

While the classical Roman-Dutch law did not require any formalities for a contract of suretyship,[5] the Natal legislature enacted in 1884[6] (under the influence of the English Statute of Frauds 1677[7]) required that contracts of suretyship must be evidenced by writing. More recently, s. 6 of the General Law Amendment Act 50 of 1956, which applies to all parts of South Africa, requires that the terms of every 'contract of suretyship' should be 'embodied in a written document signed by or on behalf of the surety'.[8]

The reasons why the Parliament of the then Union of South Africa enacted this measure are impossible to fathom with any degree of certainty, since its introduction was not preceded by any official report explaining its necessity. Nor was s. 6 mentioned in the parliamentary debates on the Act.[9] No comment in the learned journals at the time gives any insight.

In *Fourlamel (Pty) Ltd v. Maddison,*[10] however, Miller JA put forward two objects which 'the Legislature may have had in mind': first, the advancement of legal certainty (minimizing the possibilities of perjury, fraud, and unnecessary litigation), and secondly, making sure that the surety realized the onerous nature of the obligation he was undertaking. Grové's comparative review of the formalities required in other legal systems reveals that most require, in one way or another, that contracts of suretyship should be in writing.[11] Moreover, it appears for doctrinal rea-

---

[4] See generally N. J. Grové, *Die Formaliteitsvereiste by Borgstelling* (unpublished LL M dissertation, University of Pretoria, 1984).

[5] *Stride v. Wepener* 1903 TH 383, 386, 387; *Silver Garbus & Co (Pty) Ltd v. Teichert* 1954 (2) SA 98 (N) 105; Grové (n.4), 2 sqq.; J. T. Pretorius, 'Die Formaliteitsvereiste by Borgstelling', (1988) 10 *Modern Business Law* 122.

[6] Law 12 of 1884.

[7] The debates on the law before the Legislative Council in Natal, although seldom touching upon suretyship *eo nomine*, leave no doubt that the legislative draughtsman was guided by English law, esp. the Statute of Frauds of 1677. See *Debates of the Legislative Council* (1884), 24, 45–8, 61, 86–7, 171–2, 213.

[8] Excluding 'the liability of the signer of an aval'.

[9] *Hansard*, 22 May 1956, col. 6203.   [10] 1977 (1) SA 333 (A) 342 sq.

[11] Grové (n. 4), ch. II.

sons, as well as the words of the statute, that the requirement of writing is a substantive one, i.e. it is a precondition for the validity of the contract, not simply a requisite for the proof of the contract in a court of law.[12]

Whatever the legislature's object in enacting s. 6, the introduction of the formal requirement of writing has occasioned a change in focus and emphasis in several areas of the law. The 'terms' of the contract must be embodied in the writing, so the 'terms' of the contract have become the object of judicial attention and have been defined with more clarity than was previously the case.[13] Also, as we shall see, since other forms of intercession are not required to be in writing, the requirement of writing has made it necessary to sharpen the distinction between suretyship and these other forms, such as guarantee. Moreover, the insistence on writing doubtless strengthened the movement towards standard form contracts: since the contract had to be in writing, one of the parties, almost invariably the creditor, would bring a printed standard-form contract to the meeting at which agreement was reached.

2. The fall of women's suretyship benefits

From the days of the Roman Empire until 1971 women enjoyed a remarkable degree of protection from the normal consequences of undertaking the obligations of a surety. *Propter sexus imbecillitatem* women were prohibited from interceding in respect of another person by the *Senatusconsultum Velleianum* of AD 46 and Justinian in AD 556 enacted the *Authentica si qua mulier* which prohibited women from standing surety for their husbands.[14] Although there was little criticism of this state of affairs during the nineteenth century, the matter became controversial during the twentieth. The balance of the debate was clearly in favour of reform.

In a world were sexual equality was being increasingly taken for granted this was bound to be the case. Van den Heever J put the point ironically in oft cited words in *Van Rensburg v. Minnie*:[15]

---

[12] Ibid. 63.

[13] In *Sapirstein v. Anglo African Shipping Co (SA) Ltd* 1978 (4) SA 1 (A) the Appellate Division held that the 'terms' of a suretyship were: the identity of the creditor; the identity of the debtor; and the nature and amount of the principal debt. But a meticulous description of the 'terms' is not required: *Credit Guarantee Insurance Corp of South Africa Ltd v. Schreiber* 1987 (3) SA 523 (W) 525. Furthermore, there is sufficient compliance when the suretyship omits an essential term but refers to another document containing that term since *certum est quod certum reddi potest*.

[14] For the details of the benefits see L. R. Caney, *The Law of Suretyship* (2nd edn., 1970); William Burge, *Commentaries on the Law of Suretyship* (1849). Briefer accounts are found in C. F. Forsyth, *Caney's The Law of Suretyship* (3rd edn., 1982); Reinhard Zimmermann, *The Law of Obligations: Roman Foundations of the Civilian Tradition* (1990, reprint 1993), 145–52.

[15] 1942 OPD 257, 259. For further criticism see Sir John Wessels, *The Law of Contract in South Africa* (1937), § 3872, who states that the benefits 'hinder trade, interfere with credit and are often the source of trickery' and that the special defence 'belongs to the dead past ...'

One of the incongruities of this inconsequent age is the fact that women, while enjoying full rights of citizenship, including that of making or marring the policies of State as effectively as any male, are able in their private affairs to invoke a defence based on their innate fecklessness and incapacity and so avoid obligations which they have deliberately assumed.

What was surprising was how long it took for reform to take place in South Africa. The benefits were abolished in France as early as 1606 and the BGB in 1900 repealed them in those parts of Germany which had not already done so. In Ceylon they were abolished in 1924 and in Zimbabwe in 1959.[16] Yet in 1965 the South African Law Revision Committee reported that the benefits should be retained, although preferably strengthened.[17] However, wiser councils prevailed and the Suretyship Amendment Act 57 of 1971 was in due course enacted—although not without opposition[18]—and the long history of the *Senantusconsultum Velleianum* and the *Authentica si qua mulier* came to an end in Roman-Dutch law[19].

The opposition to reform was not based on any question of legal principle. At its best it was based simply on a sincere, if patronizing, belief that women were inferior to men in their financial acumen and appreciation of the consequences of binding themselves for the debts of another.[20] The more cynical might be forgiven for pointing out, however, that the almost invariable renunciation of the benefits was often done formally by notarial act; and notaries were usually local attorneys, who were well paid for this service. Thus the motives of some in the legal profession who spoke against reform may be open to question. The precise reasons why the movement for reform did not succeed earlier may long remain a matter of dispute, but it was not simply a matter of crass male prejudice.

---

[16] Forsyth/Pretorius (n. 3), 23.

[17] Ellison Kahn, 'Farewell *Senatusconsultum Velleianum* and *Authentica Si Qua Mulier*', (1971) 88 *SALJ* 364.

[18] Kahn (n. 17), 366 gives the details.

[19] Prior to the Suretyship Amendment Act 1971 the legislature provided on several occasions that in certain circumstances or for particular transactions women were deemed to have renounced the benefits (e.g. accepting or endorsing a bill of exchange, borrowing money, or standing surety for a loan from a building society or the land bank). For the statutory authority for these exemptions see Forsyth (n. 14), 178, fn. 10.

[20] See e.g. the Hon. L. C. Caney, the author of the standard work on suretyship, who opposed reform before the Select Committee on the grounds that 'a woman tended to be too kind-hearted and sentimental, [and] too optimistic about the likelihood of her being called upon in practice to make good her promise . . .' (Kahn, (1971) 88 *SALJ* 367).

III. JUDICIAL CHANGES IN THE LAW OF SURETYSHIP

1. The definition of suretyship

The old authorities did not distinguish themselves in defining the contract of suretyship.[21] Generally they do not take the matter much further than to establish that suretyship is a form of intercession, where one person undertakes liability for the debt of another,[22] and that the surety's obligation is accessory to that of the principal debtor.[23] The clearest judicial pronouncement in the nineteenth century is that of Connor J in *Murray and Burrill v. Buck and Buck*[24] where a surety was said 'to engage his own liability in respect of another's debt' but this is plainly far too wide.

However, a distinctly more thoughtful and analytical approach becomes evident on the strong Transvaal bench during the early part of this century. This is most clearly seen in Innes CJ's judgment in *Corrans v. Transvaal Gov and Coull's Trustee*,[25] where the Chief Justice said that the definitions of the old authorities came down to this, 'that the undertaking of the surety is accessory to the main contract, the liability under which he does not disturb, but it is an undertaking that the obligation of the principal debtor will be discharged and, if not, that the creditor will be indemnified'. Here are all the essentials, and in reliance upon this and similar *dicta* successive editions of the standard textbook on the law of suretyship, *Caney's The Law of Suretyship*, put forward a definition that has attracted growing academic and judicial support. It has been referred to with approval by the Appellate Division on three occasions in recent years[26] and must now be considered the orthodox view. That definition reads as follows:

[21] See Forsyth/Pretorius (n. 3), 24 referring esp. to Johannes Voet, *Commentarius ad Pandectas*, 46, 1, 1; Johannes van der Linden, *Koopmans Handboek*, 1, 14, 10; Hugo Grotius, *Inleiding tot de Hollandsche Rechtsgeleertheyd*, 3, 3, 12, and Simon van Leeuwen, *Censura Forensis*, 4, 4, 2. See also Robert Joseph Pothier, *Traité des obligations*, § 365. From time to time there has been judicial approval of one of these definitions. See e.g. *Malmesbury Board of Executors and Trust Co v. Duckitt and Bam* 1924 CPD 101, 108 (approving Voet); *Langeberg Kooperasie Bpk. v. Inverdoorn Farming and Trading Co Ltd* 1965 (2) SA 597 (A) 560 (approving Pothier).

[22] There are, of course, other forms of intercession, e.g. where by novation the new debtor is substituted for the old.

[23] I.e. that the surety's obligation is conditional upon the existence of a valid principal obligation. See Forsyth/Pretorius (n. 3), 27.

[24] 1870 NLR 155, 156.

[25] 1909 TS 605, 612 sq. See also *Union Gov v. Van der Merwe* 1921 TPD 318, 321.

[26] These occasions are: (1) Corbett JA (Jansen JA concurring) in *Trust Bank of Africa Ltd v. Frysch* 1977 (3) SA 562 (A) 548F; (2) Trengove AJA (Wessels ACJ, Jansen, Muller, and Joubert JJA concurring) in *Sapirstein v. Anglo African Shipping Co (SA) Ltd* (n. 13); and (3) Corbett CJ (Hefer, Nestadt, Grosskopf JJA, and Nicholas AJA concurring) in *Nedbank Ltd v. Van Zyl* 1990 (2) SA 469 (A) 473I. J. Lotz, 'Suretyship', in: W. A. Joubert (ed.), *The Law of South Africa*, vol. 26 (1986), § 152 criticizes the fact that in terms of this definition the surety

Suretyship is an accessory contract by which a person (the surety) undertakes to the creditor of another (the principal debtor) primarily that the principal debtor, who remains bound, will perform his obligation to the creditor and, secondarily, that if and so far as the principal debtor fails to do so, the surety will perform it, or failing that, indemnify the creditor.[27]

What is interesting about the emergence of this definition is that it has not been prompted or used for any of the more obvious purposes. It has not been a direct response to the need to define the contract so that the reach of the formalities legislation can be determined.[28] Further, although there has been much debate in the literature over the differences between guarantee and suretyship, suretyship and insurance, suretyship and indemnity,[29] and considerable progress has been made (especially in regard to the distinction between guarantee and suretyship) this has tended to be at a theoretical level. When that issue arises in the courts it is usually in the context of the interpretation of the words used, particularly whether words 'to guarantee' means to enter a contract of suretyship.[30] In recent years, when the courts have made reference to the definition of suretyship, it has been on issues such as whether a suretyship could be undertaken in respect of a principal debt not yet in existence[31] and whether a person can stand surety for himself.[32]

2. The right to contribution between co-sureties arises *ex jure*

Roman Law did not accord to a surety who had paid the creditor any right to a contribution from co-sureties, in the absence of a cession of actions from the creditor either at or before payment by the surety.[33] Where there

undertakes *primarily* that the debtor will perform, suggesting that such an undertaking is 'somewhat pointless'. However, as pointed out in Forsyth/Pretorius (n. 3), 26–7, this definition captures a nuance at the heart of suretyship: that the surety expects that the debtor will perform and promises that on pain of having to perform himself.

[27] Forsyth/Pretorius (n. 3), 26–7.

[28] The reach of the formalities legislation has turned on the 'terms' of the contract and what precisely is required to comply with the legislation. See above, n. 13.

[29] See Forsyth/Pretorius (n. 3), 29–34 for an introduction to the discussion.

[30] See e.g. *Mouton v. Mynwerkersunie* 1977 (1) SA 119 (A); *List v. Jungers* 1979 (3) SA 106 (A).

[31] See *Trust Bank of Africa Ltd v. Frysch* (n. 26).

[32] As in *Nedbank Ltd v. Van Zyl* (n. 26).

[33] The Roman law governing cession of actions by the creditor to the surety was unsatisfactory. The problem was that payment by a surety extinguished the principal obligation at the moment of payment and consequently released the debtor as well as any sureties: D. 46, 1, 39; Voet (n. 20), 46, 1, 30; Forsyth/Pretorius (n. 3), 127–8; Zimmermann (n. 14), 132–7. As a general rule the surety would still have a right of recourse against the debtor, based either on a contract of mandate (where he had undertaken the suretyship at the debtor's request) or on the *actio negotiorum gestorum contraria* (where the debtor did not know of the suretyship). But equity also called for the surety who had paid the debt to be able to turn to co-sureties for a contribution; this was achieved by the development of the benefit of cession of actions.

was no cession of actions, or where the cession took place after payment, the paying surety had no rights against the other co-sureties. Some Roman-Dutch writers, understandably taking the view that this was inequitable, held that cession could take place even after payment.[34] In the leading case of *Kroon v. Enschede*[35] Wessels J held that the commentators who took this view 'made a great innovation on the Roman Law'. However, the balance of opinion among Roman-Dutch jurists was that, in the absence of any cession of actions, a surety could not proceed against his co-sureties. There were some opinions to the contrary, however, and the weighty support of Pothier. Moreover, no cession of actions was required in 'any of the states of Europe that adopt the civil law' nor the law of Scotland or England.

All this emboldened Wessels J to make the further 'great innovation' of holding that 'the principle of the modern Roman-Dutch law is [that] no cession of action is required where sureties guarantee a debt in one instrument, and that the right to contribution is a right which the surety possesses *de jure*'. Moreover, it has since been held in *Hart v. Corder*[36] that even where the sureties undertake liability in separate instruments and are unaware of each other, a right to contribution arises without cession of actions.

Most noteworthy in this development is the judgment of Wessels J. It has been described as 'an essay in historical and comparative law'.[37] Naturally, the learned judge canvasses the development of the Roman-Dutch law in some depth; but he also looks far beyond the Roman-Dutch law to the codified civilian systems, as well as to English law. Imbued with the equitable spirit of the Roman-Dutch law, he seeks to develop the law in ways that will achieve justice and mesh easily with the other leading legal systems of the world. The judgment sets a standard that has seldom been matched.

---

[34] Simon van Groenewegen van der Made, *De legibus abrogatis*, ad Cod. 8, 41, 11; Voet (n. 21), 46, 1, 30 *in fine*; Van Leeuwen (n. 21), 1, 1, 4, 10; *contra*: Grotius (n. 21), 3, 3, 31; Ulrich Huber, *Heedendaegse Rechtsgeleertheyt*, 3, 26, 27. This is also the position in the modern Roman-Dutch law: *Pearce v. De Jager* 1924 CPD 455.

[35] 1909 TS 374.

[36] 1973 (3) SA 11 (N), approved in *Fircone Investments (Pty) Ltd v. Bank of Lisbon and South Africa Ltd* 1981 (3) SA 141 (W) 142; *Fircone Investments (Pty) Ltd v. Bank of Lisbon and South Africa Ltd* 1982 (3) SA 700 (T) 703; but in *Nelson v. Hodgetts Timbers (East London) (Pty) Ltd* 1973 (3) SA 37 (A) 45 the issue was left open. See further J. T. Pretorius, 'A Running Contribution between Co-Sureties', (1983) 100 *SALJ* 387, 390. The difficulty with the extension in *Hart's* case is identifying the juristic basis of the obligation between the sureties. In *Kroon v. Enschede* (n. 35), Wessels J said 'where several sureties agree to become such in one instrument, they must be presumed to have intended that each one could be sued for his share by any one of them' (383). But such an intent can surely not be presumed where the sureties are unaware of each others' existence. Both Pothier (n. 21), § 445 and Burge (n. 14), 381 sqq., however, support the equitable solution, as does *Lever v. Buhrmann* 1925 TPD 254.

[37] H. R. Hahlo, Ellison Kahn, *The Union of South Africa: The Development of its Laws and Constitution* (1960), 710, fn. 68.

3. The extent of the co-surety's right to contribution from his fellows

Under modern circumstances (discussed more fully below) the benefit of division is almost invariably renounced by sureties; thus when the creditor turns to the surety the surety will generally be called upon to pay the full amount due. If there are co-sureties, the surety who has paid (the 'paying surety') will, of course, turn to them for a contribution to ease his burden. In the absence of some contrary agreement, the co-sureties will, in principle, have to bear the burden equally. Does that mean that the paying surety can recover from each co-surety only that surety's share of the burden, or can the paying surety recover the full amount of the debt (less the paying surety's share) from any one of the co-sureties, leaving that surety to seek an appropriate contribution from the others remaining?

Where a surety who has paid the full sum sues a co-surety in reliance on his right to contribution (as developed in *Kroon v. Enschede*) it seems clear that the co-surety is only bound to pay his *aliquot* share; the other sureties must be sued for the balance.[38] However, where the surety has taken cession of actions, can he recover everything that the cedent could have recovered, i.e. the entire amount (less, of course, the surety's share of the debt)? Or can he recover from the co-surety only that co-surety's share of the debt?

This was the crucial doctrinal issue, much debated amongst the old authorities, raised in *Gerber v. Wolson*.[39] The decision is unsatisfactory for, although the doctrinal issue was discussed, the parties were in fact more akin to co-debtors rather than co-sureties, and moreover the case was decided on the narrow ground that the extent of the right to a contribution was governed by a contract between the co-debtors. None the less, the judgment of Van den Heever JA especially, as well as Steyn J's judgment in the Court below, contain much discussion of the Roman-Dutch law. The issue may be presented most simply as a clash between the Roman-Dutch writers (who considered that the greater amount could be recovered)[40] and Pothier (who restricts recovery to the *aliquot* share).[41]

The most persuasive judgment, albeit a dissenting one, is that of Van den Heever JA who, although paying due respect to Pothier, rejects his views cogently.[42] The majority judgments have found little favour with the com-

---

[38] Forsyth/Pretorius (n. 3), 154 sqq. On the question of whether a surety can recover from the co-sureties when he has not yet paid the full amount see Forsyth/Pretorius (n. 3), 158–62, discussing *ASA Investments (Pty) Ltd v. Smit* 1980 (1) SA 897 (C).

[39] 1955 (1) SA 158 (A).

[40] Primarily Voet (n. 21), 46, 1, 29; Joannis à Sande, *De actionum cessione*, 6, 33; *contra*: Van Leeuwen (n. 21), 1, 4, 17, 24.

[41] Pothier (n. 21), § 281.

[42] Pothier argues that there is a circuity of actions (i.e. the same issue would need to be relitigated between the same parties) if a sum greater than the co-surety's *aliquot* share could be recovered by the paying surety. If there were 4 sureties, A, B, C, and D, and A paid the full sum (R 4,000), unless recovery was restricted A would sue B for R 3,000, whereupon B could

mentators[43] and it is submitted that Van den Heever JA's judgment stands the test of time and reveals the true position of the Roman-Dutch law. Even so, it must be remarked that, the debate concerning Pothier aside, the judgment is not distinguished by its comparative analysis.

4. The demise of the *exceptio doli generalis*

For much of the review period it was accepted that the *exceptio doli generalis* was available to a surety, as to all contractual parties, as a defence of last resort.[44] This defence existed to protect a surety when a creditor sought to use the suretyship for a purpose never envisaged by the parties at the time they made their original contract. The clearest example of a proper use of this defence was when the creditor seeks to hold the surety liable for some subsequent and extraneous debt which, although arguably within the terms of a widely phrased suretyship, it was never part of the parties' purpose in contracting to secure.[45] However, in a recent suretyship decision, *Bank of Lisbon and South Africa Ltd v. De Ornelas*,[46] the Appellate Division has ejected this defence from South African law.

In this case the bank had extended overdraft facilities to a fishing company and that overdraft was secured by deeds of suretyship executed by the joint managing directors (the respondents) of the company as well as mortgage bonds in favour of the bank passed over the respondents' dwellings. In due course the company discharged its entire indebtedness to the bank under the overdraft and the sureties sought the discharge of the deeds of suretyship and the mortgage bonds. The bank resisted this on the ground that it had an unsettled claim against the company arising out of a forward

---

sue A for R 2,000, whereupon A could sue B for R 1,000 etc. But, as Van den Heever JA points out, this reasoning contains an 'obvious fallacy', namely, that cession of actions gives A all the creditor's actions including that against A himself. But this is not so: only the creditor's rights of action against B, C, and D are ceded to A when A pays the full sum. And, of course, when B pays A the full amount (less A's share), A cedes to B only the actions against C and D, etc. In this way equity is achieved between the sureties and there is no circuity of actions. Fagan JA's statement (183) that he sees 'no way out of this [circuity of actions] impasse except the one indicated by Pothier' is, it is submitted, fully answered by Van den Heever JA.

[43] J. E. Scholtens, 'Recourse of a Surety against his Co-Sureties', (1955) 72 *SALJ* 355; Paul van Warmelo, 'Gerber v. Wolson 1955 (1) SA 188 (AD)' 1955 *Butterworth's South African LR* 147; Forsyth/Pretorius (n. 3), 131–5. Cf., however, Zimmermann (n. 14), 143 arguing that Pothier scored an 'indirect victory' in this case.

[44] The Appellate Division decisions which recognized that the *exceptio doli generalis* formed part of Roman-Dutch law are: *Weinerlein v. Goch Buildings Ltd* 1925 AD 282; *Zuurbekom Ltd v. Union Corp Ltd* 1947 (1) SA 514 (A); *Paddock Motors (Pty) Ltd v. Igesund* 1976 (3) SA 16 (A) 27G-H.

[45] In *Rand Bank Ltd v. Rubenstein* 1981 (2) SA 207 (W) such a case was described as 'tailor-made for the general defence of the *exceptio doli*' (214H). For other ways, apart from public policy discussed below, in which it is occasionally possible to discover an implied term restricting the operation of a widely phrased suretyship see Forsyth/Pretorius (n. 3), 77–9.

[46] 1988 (3) SA 580 (A).

purchase of foreign exchange on its behalf. The deeds of suretyship provided that the sureties undertook liability for 'the payment of every sum
. . . of money . . . owing by [the company to the bank] from whatsoever
cause . . . arising'. The foreign exchange dispute was thus apparently within
the words of the suretyship although this dispute had nothing to do with
the original overdraft; and unless the *exceptio doli* were available the sureties
would remain liable. Without any investigation into whether the bank's
conduct amounted to *dolus*, the Appellate Division held that the *exceptio
doli generalis* never formed part of Roman-Dutch law, thus it was not part
of modern South African law. It followed that the sureties could not raise
the *exceptio doli* as a defence.

Although the issue arose in the context of suretyship, the decision was
based upon general grounds and is discussed in more detail elsewhere in this
volume.[47] However, two points are relevant here: first, both the majority
judgment (of Joubert JA with Rabie ACJ, Hefer, and Grosskopf JJA concurring) and the minority judgment of Jansen JA are almost entirely
enmeshed in the historical and technical developments of Roman and
Roman-Dutch law; there is little comparative analysis nor are there express
considerations of justice and equity. The judgment is thus antiquarian in
tone and effect and contrary to the best traditions of the Roman-Dutch law.
One reads these judgments in vain in search of an *usus hodiernus pandectarum*.

Secondly, in contemporary circumstances, when practically every contract of suretyship is printed on a standard form drafted by creditors in
terms that are invariably contrary to the interests of the surety, there is a
need for a defence of last resort based upon equitable principles. The demise
of the *exceptio doli* has simply cast public policy into a new role as a defence
of last resort (as Jansen JA in his dissenting judgment in the *Bank of Lisbon*
case pointed out);[48] and litigants have not been slow to raise public policy
as a defence. In the context of suretyship the Appellate Division has thus
far spoken only once in *Botha (now Griessel) v. Finanscredit (Pty) Ltd*,[49]
where Hoexter JA laid down that faced with such a defence the court should
consider whether the clauses in question were 'clearly inimical to the interests of the community, whether they are contrary to law or morality, or run

---

[47] For my more detailed views see Forsyth/Pretorius (n. 3), 191, fn. 163; C. F. Forsyth,
J. T. Pretorius, 'Recent Developments in the Law of Suretyship', (1993) 5 *SA Mercantile Law
Journal* 181. The decision has occasioned much comment, most of it critical: see Carole Lewis,
'Demise of the *Exceptio Doli*: Is there Another Route to Contractual Equity?', (1990) 107
SALJ 26; S. W. J. van der Merwe, G. F. Lubbe, L. F. van Huyssteen, 'The *Exceptio Doli
Generalis*: Requiescat in Pace—*Vivat Aequitas*', (1989) 106 *SALJ* 235; M. A. Lambiris, 'The
Exceptio Doli Generalis: An Obituary', (1988) 105 *SALJ* 644. And see the contribution by
Reinhard Zimmermann to the present volume.
[48] 617G.
[49] 1989 (3) SA 773 (A). *Sasfin (Pty) Ltd v. Beukes* 1989 (1) SA 1 (A) was the first post-*De
Ornelas* decision in which public policy was successfully raised in this way.

counter to social or economic expedience' but should bear in mind the following: '(a) that, while public policy generally favours the utmost freedom of contract, it nevertheless properly takes into account the necessity for doing simple justice between man and man; and (b) that a court's power to declare contracts contrary to public policy should be exercised sparingly and only in cases in which the impropriety of the transaction and the element of public harm are manifest'.[50]

This lapidary *dictum*, perhaps inevitably, lacks precision and when the lower courts have been asked to apply it confusion has often resulted. In *Botha (now Griessel) v. Finanscredit (Pty) Ltd* the Appellate Division held that a clause providing that the suretyship 'shall not be cancelled without the written consent of the creditor' was not contrary to public policy, since it was not morally unacceptable and did not leave the surety 'helpless in the clutches of the plaintiff'. He could always discharge the principal debt and the suretyship would fall away.

For the rest, however, confusion reigns. Most of the controversy has raged over whether a clause which provides that 'a certificate of balance' drawn up by the creditor can be 'conclusive proof of the amount owing by the debtor' is invalid as being contrary to public policy.[51] Although in common use, the Appellate Division cast doubt on such clauses in *Sasfin (Pty) Ltd v. Beukes*.[52] This case dealt with cession rather than suretyship and was decided within the matrix of many other draconian clauses which imposed exceptionally onerous burdens on the debtor. The Appellate Division indeed held that the debtor 'was virtually . . . relegated to the position of a slave'.[53] So *Sasfin* was not conclusive as far as a straightforward suretyship case was concerned. Several cases have, however, held that such clauses are invalid,[54] while others have held that, in the absence of additional draconian *Sasfin* type clauses, they are valid.[55] After all, where, as is very often the case, the creditor is a bank and the surety is the managing director of the principal debtor (a private company with an overdraft at the bank), the surety will have regular access to bank statements setting out the extent of indebtedness and errors can be easily corrected long before the matter comes to court. If the bank refuses to correct clear errors drawn to its attention it is simply laying the foundation for the surety's defence of fraud. Even so, the Appellate Division has just held in *ex parte the Minister of Justice:*

---

[50] 728I–783C.

[51] Such a clause prevents the contract being a valid liquid document for the purposes of provisional sentence: F. R. Malan, A. N. Oelofse, W. de Vos, J. T. Pretorius, C. Nangel, *Provisional Sentence on Bills of Exchange, Cheques and Promissory Notes* (1986), 20–21.

[52] Above, n. 49.   [53] 13H.

[54] *Nedbank Ltd v. Abstein Distributors (Pty) Ltd* 1989 (3) SA 750 (T). But the clause was severable from the rest of the contract, so that the whole suretyship did not fall with the 'conclusive proof' clause.

[55] *Donnelly v. Barclays National Bank Ltd* 1990 (1) SA 375 (W).

in re Nedbank Ltd v. Abstein Distributors (Pty) Ltd[56] that such clauses are *contra bonos mores* and invalid.

5. The demise of correality

Here we must tread warily for we are warned that 'theorizing in terms of "solidarity" and "correality" should be avoided' for it is an 'ahistorical enterprise' and 'unsound lecture-room jurisprudence'.[57] Yet the issue is worth considering in the context of the history of suretyship. For in *Rand Bank Ltd v. De Jager*,[58] one of the most interesting of the modern decisions, the surety's obligation to the creditor and the principal debt were held not to be correal, with the consequence that the surety's obligation could prescribe independently of the principal obligation.[59]

This conclusion in a learned judgment from Baker J rejected a line of

---

[56] 1995(3) SA 1(A).

[57] Zimmermann (n. 14), 129. The final epithet in fact comes from Jhering, *Geist des römischen Rechts*, cited by Zimmermann.

[58] 1982 (3) SA 418 (C).

[59] A note may be devoted here to an explanation of the distinction between the solidary and correal forms of liability *singuli in solidum*. In the classical law once *litis contestatio* was reached the original obligation was extinguished. If a creditor proceeded against only one of his co-debtors to the point of *litis contestatio*, were the other co-debtors released? This would be very inconvenient should the sued co-debtor turn out to be a man of straw. Indeed in the context of suretyship *litis contestatio* in an action against the principal debtor would release the sureties. The jurists devoted considerable ingenuity in various attempts to avoid this inconvenient result (see Forsyth/Pretorius (n. 3), 11–12). However, Justinian deployed the all-powerful wand of legislation by providing in C. 8, 40 (41), 28 that 'through the selection [for suing] of one of the sureties, or of the principal debtor, the others shall not be released . . . [T]he rights of [the creditor] shall remain unimpaired until the entire sum of money to which he is entitled has been paid, or his claim is satisfied in some other way' (trans. Scott). This was the movement from *Konsumptionskonkurrenz* to *Solutionskonkurrenz* (Zimmermann (n. 14), 126–8), release by payment rather than by legal process.

Justinian, indeed, attempted to excise this result of *litis contestatio* throughout the *Corpus Juris*. But, inadvertently, he left several leading texts unchanged (e.g. Paul. D. 11, 1, 8), so that this effect of *litis contestatio* apparently remained in some cases (said by the commentators to be 'correal'), but where the co-debtors were only released by *solutio* the liability was said to be 'solidary'.

Although Zimmermann (n. 14), 128 considers that 'the most dramatic confusion was bound to arise as soon as legal writers set themselves the task of constructing a logically consistent doctrinal building on the basis of the Roman sources—on the basis, that is, of a veritable heap of ruins' the distinction has intrigued Romanists for centuries. The distinction was explained by arguing that with correal liability only *one* obligation was created (although there might be several debtors), thus when that obligation was extinguished (whether by prescription or *litis contestatio*) there was nothing left for the others to owe. While with solidary liability there were several obligations (although their content might be identical) linking the co-debtors with the creditor and one of those obligations might be extinguished (by prescription or *litis contestatio*) without affecting the others.

On correality and solidarity see C. F. Forsyth, 'Suretyship and Prescription: A New Direction', (1984) 101 *SALJ* 237, 243–4; Zimmermann (n. 14), 125–9; J. Kerr Wylie, *Solidarity and Correality* (1923); W. W. Buckland, *Textbook of Roman Law* (3rd edn., 1963, corrected reprint 1975, by Peter Stein).

authority that stretched back to a constitution of the Emperor Justinian enacted in Constantinople on the calends of September AD 531. The authorities rejected include two stalwarts of the law of suretyship, Voet and Pothier. The Appellate Division has not yet approved Baker J's conclusions[60] but the decision none the less provides a useful prism through which to view developments in the law of suretyship.

As adumbrated the issue arises in the context of prescription of the surety's obligation. Colonial and thereafter Union legislation provided that interruption of prescription against the principal debtor also interrupted prescription against the surety.[61] However, Prescription Act No. 68 of 1969 contained no similar provisions, leaving the matter to be governed by the common law (interpreting that phrase sufficiently widely to include Justinian's legislation). In a wide-ranging judgment that canvassed French, German, Austrian, Dutch, Italian, American, and English law as well as, of course, the Roman and Roman-Dutch authorities, Baker J reached some interesting conclusions. In C. 8, 39 (40), 4 (5), the crucial but rather discursive text, Justinian provides that 'it seems to us to be consistent with the dictates of humanity that where prescription has been interrupted, or acknowledgement of debt has been made with reference to one and the same contract, all the parties should be compelled to pay the debt at the same time'. This was the text that Voet had relied upon more than 1,000 years later to conclude that if 'a demand has indeed been made upon the principal debtor, but on the surety never, not even in a whole thirty years, the surety would nevertheless not be able to defend himself with prescription'.[62]

The reason given by Voet is that 'it is more in accord with nature' that the accessory obligation should prescribe with the principal obligation. However, this reasoning is more rhetorical than logical. For anything approaching cogent justification for the rule we must turn to Pothier. He argues in fn. 664 of his *Traité des obligations* that principal and surety were bound by the *same* obligation and thus the fate of the surety should follow that of the principal debtor. This reasoning contains a strong echo of the proposition that surety and principal debtor 'were comprised in the term *correi*; since they are *rei ejuisdem obligationis . . .*';[63] in other words the relationship between surety, principal debtor and creditor was correal. Was this in fact the case?

Baker J concluded that Voet in his commentary ad D. 46, 1, 36 had not stated the common law correctly. There were several reasons for this, the crucial one being that Voet had failed to appreciate the distinction between

---

[60] In *Kilroe-Daley v. Barclays National Bank Ltd* 1984 (4) SA 609 (A) 628D a unanimous Appellate Division said: 'nothing in this judgment must be read to mean that this Court agrees or disagrees with what is said in *Rand Bank Ltd v. De Jager . . .*'

[61] See e.g. Prescription Act 18 of 1943, s. 6(2).

[62] Voet (n. 21), 46, 1, 36.

[63] Pothier (n. 21), n. 664.

the correality of co-debtors and the accessoriality of sureties.[64] As Professor Kerr Wylie remarks: 'Accessoriality, like correality, is based on a conception of the unity of obligation, but, unlike correality, it does not place the different debtors or creditors on a co-ordinate footing'.[65]

This rejection of correality may be presented narrowly as simply a restrictive interpretation of C. 8, 39 (40), 4 (5) correcting an error made by many others (including Voet and Pothier). Indeed, Baker J's judgment contemplates that the old rule continues to apply to co-debtors liable *in solidum* since they clearly fall within the terms of the text.[66] Reliance is placed in this context on the writing of Professor J. C. de Wet particularly in regard to prescription. Professor de Wet *ex natura* takes the view that C. 8, 39 (40), 4 (5) is contrary to principle and should be rejected altogether. Thus, at the more profound level *Rand Bank Ltd v. De Jager* adumbrates the sweeping away of the entire heap of ruins so castigated by Zimmermann across the entire law, not just in the law of suretyship.

IV. CHANGES IN THE OPERATION OF THE LAW

Outlined above are the most important of the formal changes in the law of suretyship over the past two centuries or so. However, more profound, in my view, have been the changes in the actual operation of the law.

During the review period technological changes have meant that printed or photocopied standard-form contracts are both cheap and readily available. Moreover, the financial institutions which are now the primary creditors have grown in size and complexity; this has created considerable pressures toward uniform contracts within those institutions. As we have seen, contracts of suretyship now have to be in writing. Thus contracts of suretyship are almost invariably entered into on printed standard-form contracts.

These contracts, as a rule, also contain similar terms. For instance, one of the commonest provisions to be found in a deed of suretyship is that the surety undertakes liability as 'surety and co-principal debtor'. It was held in *Neon and Cold Cathode Illuminations (Pty) Ltd v. Ephron*[67] that 'generally the only consequence . . . that flows from the surety also undertaking liability as a co-principal is that *vis-à-vis* the creditor he thereby tacitly renounces the ordinary benefits available to the surety, such as those of excussion and division and he becomes liable jointly and severally with the principal debtor'.[68] This consequence of binding oneself as 'surety and co-

---

[64] 444C-D.
[65] Kerr Wylie (n. 59), 23 sq.
[66] 454G-H.
[67] 1978 (1) SA 463 (A) 472A.
[68] This does not mean that the surety and co-principal debtor undertakes a separate and independent liability; he remains a surety (*Maasdorp v. Graaff-Reinet Board of Executors* (1909) 3 Buch AC 482, 490; Forsyth/Pretorius (n. 3), 51) although without the benefits of excussion or division.

principal debtor' has an ancient (though post-Justinianic) origin.[69] The effect of the standard-form contract has been that these benefits, unchanged for centuries (and in formal law still unchanged), have effectively been abolished.

This state of affairs harks back to the pre-Roman Germanic law of sureties; and the emergence of such a phenomenon, albeit without any change in the formal law, has led some to conclude that 'the history of suretyship could indeed be written as a struggle of indigenous custom against the received rules of Roman law'.[70] More straightforwardly modern English law does not allow the surety a benefit similar or analogous to the benefit of excussion;[71] this development simply brings the Roman-Dutch law of sureties into line. In my view, however, this is not the result of an antiquarian struggle for 'indigenous custom' but simply a reflection of the fact that it is creditors who dictate the terms of standard-form contracts and they do not wish to have to excuss the debtor first or not to be able to recover the full sum owing from a surety. Those who advise financial institutions to include such provisions in their standard form contracts probably do not have Germanic custom in mind.

The example of a surety undertaking liability as a co-principal debtor is simply a particular example of a wider phenomenon. Although the creditor must always have held the whip hand as far as the terms of a contract of suretyship were concerned, under the commercial conditions of today this tendency has strengthened considerably. Typically, a financial institution will insist upon sureties, on stringent terms, before advancing funds to the debtor. Thus, although there has been little change in the formal law, the surety's position has generally been weakened through the years. This, as seen above, has cast the potential defences to unconscionable contracts into sharp relief. The demise of the *exceptio doli* and the rise to greater prominence of the public policy exception portends a profound change in the law of suretyship. Texts on the law of suretyship will need to concentrate in the future on marking the boundary between acceptable and unacceptable clauses. That is an uncertain boundary, but more importantly it is not defined by any questions of principle that a traditional lawyer would

[69] See Antonius Heringius, *Tractatus de fideiussoribus* (1575), fn. 62 (quoting Hippolytus), followed by Andreas Gaill, *Practicae Observationes* (1653), Book II, Obs. 28. See further Voet (n. 21), 46, 1, 16 and 24; Pothier (n. 21), §§ 408, 416. Cf. D. 46, 1, 27, 4.

[70] Zimmermann (n. 14), 145, relying on Feenstra, 'Die Bürgschaft im römischen Recht und ihr Einfluss auf die mittelalterliche und spätere Rechtslehre,' (1974) 28 *Recueils de la société Jean Bodin pour l'histoire comparative des institutions* 295, 322 sqq. For the German customary law see J. W. Wessels, *History of the Roman-Dutch Law* (1908), 587–91 and J. W. Wessels, A. A. Roberts, *The Law of Contract* (2nd edn., 1951), § 3777. As in Roman law the surety was born as a hostage (Forsyth/Pretorius (n. 3), 4).

[71] A. K. R. Kiralfy, 'History of the Law of Personal Guarantee (Suretyship) in England since 1500', (1971) 29 *Recueils de la société Jean Bodin pour l'histoire comparative des institutions* 399, 413–14 relying on *Wright v. Simpson* (1802) 6 Ves 714, 734. But medieval English law was influenced by Roman Law and the creditor had first to execute against the debtor: Statute of Merchants 1285 (13 Edward 1).

recognize, nor are there any but the most general way-markers to be found in the ancient texts, whose principles have thus far proved so enduring. The imposition by creditors of ever harsher clauses in standard form contracts has called forth a reaction in the form of a greater role for public policy. That reaction, while undoubtedly necessary, may have the effect of sweeping away centuries of legal learning. The effective demise of the benefits of excussion and division are but the harbingers of this change.

V. CONCLUSIONS

In assessing the way in which the formal institutions of the law have been developed by judges in Southern Africa since 1806, I wish to make use of a distinction I have developed elsewhere: between *purism* and *antiquarianism* in the judicial process.[72] Antiquarians used to assert that the common law of South Africa is that which was applicable in seventeenth-century Holland, and that the task of the judge is simply to identify and to apply that law (altered where necessary by subsequent legislation). The comparative analysis of legal problems was of little value to the judge; if the law so identified was unsuited to modern needs that was a matter for the legislature, not for the judiciary.

On the other hand, purists take the classical Roman-Dutch law as their starting point but not their end point. Both the ancient rules and the modern precedents were to be subjected to intensive and extensive historical and comparative analysis; and only if that analysis revealed the established rule to be logically and systematically correct should it be followed. The purists did not, like the antiquarians, seek a legal system in which the pedigree of each rule was historically legitimate, but a system in which each rule fitted into a logically coherent framework of legal principle. Purism has often been antagonistic to English law, which it has seen, sometimes with justice, as backward and unsystematic. However, when shorn of this antagonism it comes close, at its best, to the ideal *usus hodiernus pandectarum* for which Reinhard Zimmermann has argued so powerfully.[73]

---

[72] In C. F. Forsyth, *In Danger for Their Talents: A Study of the Appellate Division of the Supreme Court of South Africa 1950–80* (1985), ch. IV, 182–6. See also C. F. Forsyth, 'The Juristic Basis of the Testamentary Trust, the Principle of Non-delegation of Will-making Power and the Purism Movement', (1986) 103 *SALJ* 513, 520 (on the perils of antiquarianism). Mention should also be made of the pollutionists—who sought to supplant the Roman-Dutch law with English law—and the pragmatists who considered that the English influence had on the whole been benign but in the future solutions to legal problems should address the needs of society and be based on sound policy. These two attitudes, however, have been of little importance to the development of the law of suretyship.

[73] Reinhard Zimmermann, 'Synthesis in South African Private Law: Civil Law, Common Law and *Usus Hodiernus Pandectarum*', (1986) 103 *SALJ* 259.

Against this background the following points may be made. First, there are many commendable decisions in which the judge has undertaken both an historical and a comparative review of the law before making his decision. Decisions such as *Kroon v. Enschede, African Guarantee and Indemnity Co Ltd v. Thorpe*,[74] and *Rand Bank v. De Jager* are marked by the depth of their investigation of the Roman-Dutch law as well as the width of their comparative analysis. English law is given its proper place; it has no especial role but is one of the leading European legal systems to which thoughtful regard is had in developing the Roman-Dutch law. If anywhere, it is here that the *usus hodiernus pandectarum* is found.

Secondly, however, this comparative and historical review casts a far from uncritical eye upon other legal systems. One could indeed see many of the developments—over the right of recourse, over correality and prescription, and over the benefit of cession of actions—as a dialogue between the true Roman-Dutch jurists and the French civilians Pothier and Troplong. While, on the whole, the Roman-Dutch jurists and the French civilians have marched together, the modern Roman-Dutch judges have not been slow to depart from Pothier and follow the Roman-Dutch writers (as Van den Heever JA did in his brilliant dissenting judgment in *Gerber v. Wolson*) or where necessary to depart from both, as Baker J did in his profoundly convincing judgment in *Rand Bank v. De Jager*.[75]

This view of the best of the judgments in suretyship cases striving towards the approved ideal is, however, marred by a distinctly antiquarian strain, exemplified by *De Ornelas*. Here was ejected from the modern Roman-Dutch law, not an inappropriate English import, not a rule unsuited to modern conditions, but an institution of the law that prevented the modern suretyship contract which often contains harsh terms dictated by the creditor from being transmuted into an engine of injustice. The decision has cast the law into a considerable degree of uncertainty and, with respect, has deflected attention from the true problems at hand. These are the perennial flaws with antiquarianism.

This is the point at which to turn from analysis of the formal developments in the law to the most spectacular but also the most worrying changes: those in the actual operation of the law. As we have seen the move towards standard-form contracts has rendered large parts of the law redundant, even if not formally repealed. Moreover, there are signs that the

---

[74] 1933 AD 330, leading judgment by Wessels CJ.

[75] See Reinhard Zimmermann, 'Der Einfluss Pothiers auf das römisch-hollandische Recht in Südafrika', (1985) 102 *Zeitschrift der Savigny-Stiftung für Rechtsgeschichte (Germanistische Abteilung)* 168; Zimmermann (n. 73), 271–4 who, with respect, underplays those opinions of Pothier's that have not been accepted by modern judges. Surely Baker J and Van den Heever JA were right to reject Pothier's opinions in the two examples cited. Even Homer must nod from time to time.

kernel of the law may no longer be the ancient law of Justinian, but a new law whose heart will be present-day public policy. It would be sadly ironic if the antiquarianism of decisions such *De Ornelas* cast the classical Roman-Dutch law of suretyship onto the scrap-heap of history.

14: *Insurance Law*

J. P. VAN NIEKERK

I. GENERAL INTRODUCTION

Insurance law no doubt formed part of the law transplanted to the Cape of Good Hope by the Dutch in 1652. From the beginning of the golden age of the seventeenth century, and for the larger part of the eighteenth century, the insurance law of the Netherlands in general, and of the province of Holland in particular, constituted a cardinal and highly developed part of Roman-Dutch law.[1] Its importance as such was fully recognized[2] and it had a significant influence elsewhere in Europe.[3]

The fate of the Roman-Dutch law of insurance in South Africa may be described as a gradual but inevitable decline which commenced in the nineteenth century; a relatively recent revival in theory; and an uncertain future in practice.[4] Although in many respects no more than an example of the fate of Roman-Dutch law and of the interaction between that system and English law in general, in other respects the history of Roman-Dutch insurance law in South Africa sheds fresh light on the evolution of the particular hybridity by which South African law is characterized.

[1] Its importance is reflected in Van der Keessel's remark at the end of the 18th C. that insurance contracts had become the most common transaction in the Netherlands after contracts of sale and loan: see Dionysius Godefridus van der Keessel, *Praelectiones iuris hodierni ad Hugonis Grotii introductionem ad iurisprudentiam Hollandicam*, 3, 24, 3.

[2] One example of such recognition is the prominent position conferred upon Dutch insurance law (esp. Dutch insurance legislation) by the London-based German merchant and underwriter, Nicolas Magens, in his treatise on insurance law, *Versuch über Assecuranzen, Haveryen und Bodmeryen* (1753), which subsequently appeared in a translated and expanded version in 2 vols. as *An Essay on Insurances, Explaining the Nature of the Various Kinds of Insurance Practiced by the Different Commercial States of Europe*, and *Shewing Their Consistency or Inconsistency with Equity and the Public Good* (1755).

[3] E.g. Colbert's *Ordonnance de la Marine* of 1861 was influenced by the then existing Dutch (esp. Rotterdam) maritime and insurance law (see e.g. R. Warlomont, 'Les sources néerlandaises de l'ordonnance maritime de Colbert (1681)', (1955) 33 *Revue belge de philologie et d'histoire* 333; for the consultative role played in this regard by the well known Roman-Dutch maritime lawyer, Adriaen Verwer, see B. H. D. Hermesdorf, 'Adriaen Verwer (1655–1717) en de *Ordonnance de la Marine* (1681): Een Amsterdammer geworden zoon van Rotterdam als mens en schrijver', (1967) 5 *Rotterdamsch Jaarboekje* 227. The Dutch example also influenced the development of insurance law in Germany, including the important Hamburg insurance legislation of 1731 (see e.g. Thomas Dreyer, *Die 'Assecuranz- und Haverey-Ordnung' der Freien und Hansestadt Hamburg von 1731* (1990), *passim*).

[4] See J. P. van Niekerk, *The Decline, Revival and Future of the Roman-Dutch Law of Insurance in South Africa* (1986); this Chapter is based on that earlier work.

The decision of the Appellate Division some ten years ago in *Mutual & Federal Insurance Co Ltd v. Oudtshoorn Municipality*[5] was arguably the most important decision yet on South African insurance law. It raised anew the vital question of the relative value to be attached to the various sources of South African insurance law, in particular Roman-Dutch law and English law. Even more than that, it necessitated a reappraisal of existing views on the relevance of these two sources in determining the content of South African insurance law and in further developing and, where necessary, reforming it.

II. THE EARLY INFLUENCE OF ENGLISH LAW

There is a dearth of information on the state and practice of insurance law at the Cape in the seventeenth and eighteenth centuries. Importantly, the Dutch East India Company did not as a rule insure its own ships and cargoes but chose instead to bear its own risks. It may be surmised that at least some of the other ships sailing past and entering Table Bay, as well as the cargoes they carried, were insured. Insurance practice in Amsterdam, Rotterdam, and other Dutch towns at the time was more than familiar with insuring a ship not only, for example, for the outward voyage to the East Indies but also for the return voyage. Similarly, goods exported from and imported into the Netherlands were insured on the Dutch markets. In the light of these factors, and given the nature and the economic development of the settlement there, it is unlikely that many, if any, insurances (marine or otherwise) were concluded in Cape Town itself.

By the same token there is nothing to suggest that when the Cape came under permanent British rule in 1806 the Roman-Dutch insurance law, being part of the transplanted Roman-Dutch law, was not the law commonly applied by the Cape courts.[6]

Soon after 1806 the first complaints were registered about the inconvenience and disadvantage to British merchants of the use of Roman-Dutch procedures and the Dutch language in, and the incompetence of the mem-

---

[5] 1985 (1) SA 419 (A).

[6] A Commercial Court, *Kamer van Commercie*, was established at the Cape in May 1804. Its aim was to provide merchants with an informal and inexpensive option for settling their commercial disputes. The Court had jurisdiction over '[a]*lle veschillen over zaaken den handel betreffende*' (all differences on matters concerning the trade) which arose between local merchants, between a local and a foreign merchant, and even between foreign merchants (see further *Kaapse Plakkaatboek* (1803–6), vol. VI (1951), 143–5; G. G. Visagie, *Regspleging en Reg aan die Kaap van 1652 tot 1806* (1969), 111). Whether this court and the other courts at the Cape ever considered insurance contracts, and if so what sources were relied upon, remains to be determined by future archival research.

bers of, the local courts.[7] No doubt as a result of such grievances, the British government considered[8] but eventually rejected the formal replacement of Roman-Dutch law by English law,[9] preferring instead to permit and await a gradual infiltration of English law into the local legal system.

From early on the informal influence of English law in practice was noticeable and was predominant particularly in the field of mercantile law where it was more readily regarded as natural and necessary.[10] Prevailing conditions at the Cape during the nineteenth century provided numerous reasons for the growing influence of English mercantile law.[11] Local commerce and trade, awakening from a rural slumber, were in the hands of English businessmen and entrepreneurs who followed English mercantile practices and usages. The legal environment in which the mercantile law in general and insurance law in particular were to operate and to be applied became progressively more anglicized: a court structure along English lines was instituted, the English law of evidence and procedure was followed, and

[7] In a letter written by Henry Ellis, Deputy Secretary to the Government of the Cape of Good Hope, in 1821 it was pointed out that whilst the imports and exports of the colony were almost entirely in the hands of British merchants, 'yet the various cases incident to English Shipping and English commerce generally, are tried in a foreign language before a Court, the members of which, if not wholly unacquainted with the English language, are certainly quite incompetent to decide on the interpretation of contracts, *policies of insurances*, licences and other similar matters submitted to their decision' (see George McCall Theal (ed.), *Records of the Cape Colony*, vol. XIV (1905), 183 sqq., 185; italics added).

[8] In 1823 it appointed a Commission to inquire into the judicial system and the administration of justice at the Cape. One of the commissioners, John Thomas Bigge, reported in Sept. 1826, and although not advocating the immediate abolition of the Roman-Dutch law in favour of English law he recommended the gradual importation and infiltration of English law. Regarding Dutch mercantile law, Bigge specifically remarked that '[u]pon commercial questions the Dutch law is singularly deficient, but the Judges are enjoined to follow the principles and practice of those States which are most distinguished by their commercial enterprise and experience' (see Theal (n. 7), vol. XXVIII, 1–111, for Bigge's Report; the quotation is on 14). Generally on the early approach in commercial matters see e.g. C. Graham Botha, 'The Early Influences of the English Law Upon the Roman Dutch Law in South Africa', (1923) 40 *SALJ* 396; J. C. de Wet, 'Die Romeins-Hollandse Reg in Suid-Afrika na 1806', (1958) 21 *THRHR* 239; D. H. van Zyl, *Geskiedenis van die Romeins-Hollandse Reg* (1979), 453–8; and Ellison Kahn, 'The Reception and Development of Roman-Dutch Law in South Africa', (1985) 1 *Lesotho LJ* 69, 69–72.

[9] The First Charter of Justice of 6 Aug. 1827 and the Second Charter of Justice of 11 May 1832 confirmed this by providing for the courts to exercise their jurisdiction according to the local laws in force in the Colony.

[10] See e.g. X, 'What Is the Law?', (1884) 1 *Cape LJ* 272, 273; S. B. K., 'English Influences on the Common Law of South Africa', (1913) 30 *SALJ* 304, 308; R. W. Lee, 'What Has Become of Roman-Dutch Law?: A Vanished Friend', (1930) 47 *SALJ* 274, 277; H. R. Hahlo, E. Kahn, *The Union of South Africa: The Development of Its Laws and Constitution* (1960), 17 sq., 42, 668–70.

[11] See further H. R. Hahlo, E. Kahn, *The South African Legal System and its Background* (1968), 324, 575–8; H. D. J. Bodenstein, 'English Influence on the Common Law of South Africa', (1915) 32 *SALJ* 337, 352 sq.; Imre Zajtay, W. J. Hosten, 'The Permanence of Roman Law Concepts in the Continental Legal Systems and in South African Law', (1969) 2 *CILSA* 181, 193–6; Reinhard Zimmermann, *Das römisch-holländische Recht in Südafrika* (1983), 8 sqq.; and see the contribution by Eduard Fagan to the present volume.

the doctrine of *stare decisis* was applied. The lawyers of the time, being trained in English law, generally lacked any fundamental acquaintance with the Roman-Dutch legal system or any practical knowledge of its languages, Dutch and Latin; and the Roman-Dutch sources which were in any event never freely available were therefore largely inaccessible to legal practitioners. They were, therefore, generally ignorant of the advanced state of development of the Roman-Dutch mercantile law and of its inherent adaptability to modern requirements. This flexibility of the Roman-Dutch law, characterized by the abstract and general nature of its legal principles, itself promoted the advancement of English mercantile law and made possible what was often perceived as its 'modernization' or 'adaptation' with reference to English law with which, because of their common origin in the medieval law merchant, it was readily presumed to correspond.

English law made its presence and influence felt in two ways. Initially there was merely an informal judicial 'modification' of the prevailing Roman-Dutch law. The local courts tacitly permitted, and in some cases even actively encouraged, the adoption of specific rules of English mercantile law which resulted in the inevitable decline of the relevant general principles of Roman-Dutch mercantile law. At a later stage formal legislative modification of Roman-Dutch law became the vogue and played a significant role. English statutes were in certain instances wholly repromulgated at the Cape, while in other cases English law was taken over by being referred to in local legislation.[12]

Roman-Dutch insurance law did not escape a liberal dose of English influence[13] during the nineteenth century. Firstly, as with mercantile law in general, the principles and details of Roman-Dutch insurance law, based largely upon general European legal principles and usages as they had developed up to the end of the eighteenth century, were often regarded as being applicable only to peculiar conditions prevailing in Holland in the seventeenth and eighteenth centuries and therefore unsuited to local conditions. In comparison with the more recently developed and continuously developing English insurance law it was considered outdated. Secondly, the possibility of any further evolution of the general principles of Roman-Dutch insurance law and of their adaptation to modern circumstances was either not recognized or not seriously considered as a viable option in developing a local system of insurance law.[14] Further evolution was also hampered by

---

[12] Thus e.g. the Local Merchant Seaman's Act 13 of 1855 (Cape) was taken over from the British Merchant Shipping Act of 1854 (17 & 18 Vict. c. 104). It may be surmised that had a codification of English marine insurance law in the form of the Marine Insurance Act of 1906 (6 Edw. VII, c. 41) existed earlier in the 19th C. it may well have been repromulgated at the Cape.

[13] See Hahlo/Kahn (n. 10), 716.

[14] But see V. Sampson, 'Sources of Cape Law', (1887) 4 *Cape LJ* 109, 116 who seems to have recognized this possibility.

the fact that the many Roman-Dutch authors who dealt with insurance law were principally concerned with the most prevalent form of insurance of their time, namely marine insurance. This in itself was probably regarded as an insurmountable obstacle to the application of the general principles worked out in Roman-Dutch law to any of the more recently developed forms of insurance (mainly fire and life insurance) then in use at the Cape. Ignorance of developments in insurance law in Europe during the nineteenth century, the fact that local insurance practices and policies closely resembled those followed and used in England, and the influence of English insurance companies and their agents and subsidiaries conducting insurance business at the Cape[15] no doubt further contributed to the gradual but irresistible informal growth of the English influence on local insurance law. As the further development and adaptation of Roman-Dutch law at the Cape during the nineteenth century would have required some legal and judicial innovation which the local lawyers were generally ill equipped to perform, it is not surprising that reference to the more readily available English sources in preference to the voluminous but largely inaccessible body of Roman-Dutch insurance law was increasingly regarded as an eminently practical, natural, and comparatively effortless alternative.

For some illustration of the judicial approach and legal practice in insurance matters during the early period, reference may be had to reported cases.[16] Unfortunately a very small number of insurance or insurance-

[15] The first signs of an emerging local insurance practice date from not long after the British take-over. Initially the importance of the insurance market was no doubt insignificant. The official tariff of stamp duties in the Colony in 1812 (and at least until 1824), while listing various documents, including bottomry bonds, charterparties, bills of lading, sea protests, and numerous Admiralty forms, did not mention insurance policies (see Theal (n. 7), vol. VIII, 412–20, vol. XXV, 194–203, 215–24). But the market soon grew sufficiently to attract British insurers to the Cape. At first they conducted their business through local agents but by 1826 one of them had established a local branch office. This example was soon followed by other British insurance companies. The first local insurance company was established not much later, in 1831. But foreign, mainly British, companies dominated the local insurance industry throughout the 19th C. and thereafter. For the history of the South African insurance industry see e.g. H. Spyrou, 'The Development of Insurance Business in the Union of South Africa', (1955) 23 *South African Journal of Economics* 325–40; J. J. du Plessis, *Die Ontstaan en Ontwikkeling van Versekeringswese met Spesiale Verwysing na die Na-oorlogse Omvang en Ekonomiese Betekenis van Brand-, See- en Algemene Versekering in die Unie van Suid-Afrika* (unpublished M Comm thesis, University of Potchefstroom, 1958), 51–6; M. H. Hirsch, 'Early Days of Insurance in South Africa 1826–1860', (1962) 38 (7) *African Insurance Record (AIR)* 25–7, (1962) 38 (8) *AIR* 39–43, (1963) 38 (11) *AIR* 19–22, (1963) 38 (12) *AIR* 19–23; and Gideon Jacobus de Klerk, *Versekeringswese: 'n Historiese Oorsig en Enkele Bedryfs-Ekonomiese Aspekte met Spesiale Verwysing na Groepsversekering* (unpublished D Comm. thesis, University of Potchefstroom, 1978), 95–108. With the British companies, of course, came British insurance policy forms and practices.

[16] It appears that not many insurance cases were heard before law reporting commenced in 1828. The records of only 3 insurance cases are found in the archives of the Cape Court of Justice and Court of Appeal (see G. G. Visagie, L. F. van Huyssteen, C. R. de Beer, N. J. J. Olivier, P. J. van der Merwe, W. du Plessis, *Die Kaapse Regspraak-Projek. Die Raad van Justisie, Hofstukke en Uitsprake wat Betrekking het op Siviele Sake, 1806–27* (1989), Appendix

related cases were reported during the first fifty years of law reporting at the Cape.[17] Furthermore, quite a few of these were decided with no reference to authority in the reported judgment itself. Nevertheless, a general idea of the respective roles played by Roman-Dutch and English law may be gleaned from a selection of these cases.

Hollet v. Nisbet & Dickson,[18] the first insurance case to be reported, concerned an action for the delivery of a marine insurance policy after the occurrence of a loss. It raised the question: when a binding insurance contract, negotiated through agents, was concluded, and whether, in the absence of a stipulation in the policy to the contrary, the prior payment of the premium was necessary to render the insurer liable. The Court referred to Van der Keessel, Van der Linden and Pothier for an exposition of the 'law of Holland, or of this colony',[19] and to Marshall's work on insurance for the position in English law. It was pointed out that as regards an insurer's right to claim the premium in the case where the insurance contract had been effected by a broker or agent the legal position in England and in Holland was the same.[20] In *Chiappini & Co v. Jones*[21] the burden of proof in respect of the seaworthiness of an insured ship and the right of the plaintiff company, which had advanced money for the repair of the vessel, to abandon her were the issues. In argument, counsel referred to the English writers Marshall and Park for authority on the first issue, and to Van der Linden for authority on the latter issue. In *Calf v. Jarvis*,[22] a case dealing with the effect of a breach of a condition precedent or warranty in a fire insurance policy, counsel on both sides referred to English authorities (to Smith's work on mercantile law, to the work on fire insurance by Ellis, and to the insurance texts of Marshall and Hughes) and also to decided cases. E. B. Watermeyer, who was to become a judge in the Cape Supreme Court,

6). The cases are *Kirstens v. School Commission* (1812) GH 48/2/6, *Murray v. Van der Tuiik* (1812) GH 48/2/55, and *Huntley v. Horne & Co* (1824) GH 48/2/66. It appears that in the last of these decisions English sources were referred to (see G. G. Visagie, 'The Law Applied at the Cape from 1652 to 1826', in: Visagie *et al.* (above), App. 4, 19, fn. 76).

[17] For the period 1828–78 only about 20 cases dealing with insurance could be traced.

[18] (1829) 1 Menz 391. The defendants were the local agents of the Alliance British and Foreign Fire and Life Insurance Co, the first foreign company to establish a branch office at the Cape: see above, n. 15.

[19] 395.   [20] 396.

[21] (1837) 3 Menz 181. C. H. van Zyl, 'Codification', (1895) 12 *Cape LJ* 16, referring to the unsatisfactory state of the law as a result of the uncertainty as to its sources, mentions by way of example (28 sq.) that 'in the case of *Chiappini* in 1856 . . . and in several others, forgotten *Placaaten*, not heard of before, were suddenly brought to light by the Supreme Court'. This, however, is not borne out by the report of the *Chiappini* case and, if regard is had to the date of 1856, it may be that the author had the case of *De Pass v. Commercial Marine Assurance Co* (below, n. 27) in mind and not that of *Chiappini*. Chiappini was one of the directors of the first local insurance company, established in 1831, the South Africa Life and Fire Assurance Co Other directors included well known Cape names such as Cloete, Silberbauer, and Zeederberg (see authorities referred to in n. 15 above).

[22] (1850) 1 Searle 1.

for the defendant 'quoted *Dutch Mercantile Code* ... and French Commercial Code ... to show that the principles in other commercial countries were the same as those in England'.[23] *Levy v. Calf*[24] concerned the proof of seaworthiness of a ship, the liability of part-owners of the ship to the shippers of goods damaged as a result of the vessel's unseaworthiness, and whether an agent failing to effect insurance on the goods, as instructed, could charge the premium against his principal on undertaking to be liable himself as an insurer of those goods in the event of their loss or damage. In argument before the Court reference was made to a number of Roman-Dutch authorities (Grotius; Coren; Van der Linden) and 'in confirmation'[25] to English (Smith; Abbott; Park; Arnould) and American (Kent) authorities. In its judgment the Court referred to Park and Arnould on the question of seaworthiness and, concerning the liability of part-owners of an unseaworthy vessel, to Coren and Van Bynkershoek for 'a doctrine long established in the Dutch Law ... and now adopted into the English Law by [the Merchant Shipping Act, 1854], part IX,—which part IX is applicable to the whole of Her Majesty's dominions ...'.[26]

In 1857 the important case of *De Pass v. Commercial Marine Assurance Co*[27] was decided. In issue was the scope of a master's authority to abandon a damaged ship and to sell her for the account of her insurers. In the course of his judgment, Bell J made the following instructive comment:

When the matter was argued at the bar, a great many authorities were referred to, but not one of those authorities was from the Roman-Dutch law, which is the law of this Court. It is necessary for me, therefore, to take a view of that law, but I shall do so shortly, leaving it to my brothers, who are more conversant with Roman-Dutch law than I am, to go into the subject at greater length, if they shall be so disposed ...[28]

Having then referred to Roman-Dutch authorities (Grotius; Voet; Van der Keessel) and to numerous English decisions and authors (Abbott; Arnould) as well as to the American writer Kent (who 'lays down a law not much different from that I have read from English authorities'),[29] Bell J took pains to emphasize that, on the point to be decided, the Dutch and English law 'in effect, is not much different. It comes to the same result, but only by a different road'.[30] Cloete J, with his Roman-Dutch background,[31] remarked in his concurring judgment:

---

[23] 4. As to Egidius Benedictus Watermeyer, who obtained an LL D *cum laude* at Leiden in 1843 at the age of 19, see A. A. Roberts, *A South African Legal Bibliography* (1942), 382.

[24] (1857) Watermeyer 1.

[25] 3.   [26] 5.   [27] (1857) 3 Searle 46.   [28] 49.   [29] 55.

[30] 55; similar sentiments are expressed at 49, 51 and 52 of the report.

[31] Hendrik Cloete had obtained the LL D degree in Leiden in 1811 as a pupil of Van der Keessel and had also been admitted to the English bar: see further Roberts (n. 23), 353.

We had a very able discussion and argument from counsel on both sides, but which appeared to me to be altogether based upon authorities taken from English and American authors and judges, and it could not but strike one that no reference was made on either side to any of the important Roman-Dutch authorities which bear upon the case, and which ought to be referred to in deciding it.[32]

Referring to the principle laid down by the Roman-Dutch authorities, Cloete J warned that it 'must, . . . at the present day, be understood *cum grano salis*. These old *Placaats* of the fifteenth and sixteenth centuries were based upon, or had reference to the state of navigation of the day . . .'[33] His Lordship continued by noting a case decided by the mercantile tribunal at Amsterdam and reported by Van Bynkershoek, and which he regarded as bearing most fully upon the point to be decided in the case before him. Watermeyer J's concurring judgment[34] is impressive for the wealth of Roman-Dutch authority referred to. In addition to Voet, Van Bynkershoek and Van der Keessel, and the Dutch insurance *placaaten* of 1563 and 1570, he also quoted from the various sections of the municipal ordinances, or *keuren*, on insurance of Amsterdam, Rotterdam, and Middelburg (mentioning that 'the Dutch doctrine of insurance is regulated by the *Placaat* of 1570, and by the Maritime Ordinances of Amsterdam, Rotterdam and Middelburg'[35]) and from the 'Hamburg Ordinance attached to the Dutch edition of Roccus, and which is there stated to give succinctly the general maritime law'.[36]

In *Cock v. Cape of Good Hope Marine Assurance Co*[37] the Court had to

[32] 57.   [33] 58.

[34] Interestingly enough Watermeyer J, in concurring in the decision of the Court, was only prepared to state (60) that '[t]he law on this subject, according to the Dutch authorities, comes very nearly to the same result'.

[35] 60.

[36] 61. In the same year *Willey v. Russel* 1857 Watermeyer 25, a case dealing with general average and a claim for a general average contribution, was decided. Although not strictly concerned with insurance law, the decision is noteworthy for the number of Roman-Dutch authorities referred to by the Court in addition to the mainly English (Arnould; Abbott; Stevens) and American sources relied upon by counsel. Reference was made to the Digest, the *Consolato del Mare*, the Dutch maritime *placaat* of 1563, the Dutch *Consultatien*, the French author Emerigon, and to Voet and Van Bynkershoek. It was pointed out at 34 that '[b]oth of these great authorities [i.e. Voet and Van Bynkershoek], to whom a Court, administering the laws of Holland must necessarily pay the utmost respect, concur in the opinion that . . . It will be observed, also, that both these learned jurists refer to the *Placaat* . . . of 1563, which embodies the Maritime Law . . .' It is furthermore instructive that in this case Roman-Dutch authority provided an answer, supported by American authority, on a point which at the time had not finally been settled in English law. In this regard it was noted in the course of the judgment (34 sq.) that '[i]t seems clear, then, that whatever the doubts which may have arisen in the English and American Courts, the Dutch authorities have held uniform language respecting the legitimacy of a claim for contribution [in circumstances such as those in this case]. The decision . . . [in this case is] in accordance with the Dutch authorities, fortified by the deliberate judgment of Mr Justice Story, which has settled the American Law, and which will undoubtedly influence the decision of this question in the English Courts, if it should directly arise there . . .'

[37] (1858) 3 Searle 114.

decide whether the loss of an insured vessel had occurred within the duration of a marine insurance policy. After mentioning that in argument reference had been made to English authorities on the method by which a period of time was to be computed, Watermeyer J stated that '[v]ery slight allusion was made to the mode in which time is computed according to the law of this Colony, although a plain and an intelligible principle is established, which obviates most of the difficulties with which questions of this nature would otherwise be attended'.[38] His Lordship then proceeded to decide the issue with reference to Roman-Dutch authority.

In 1859 the noteworthy marine insurance case of *Namaqua Mining Co v. Commercial Marine & Fire Insurance Co*,[39] which concerned the implied warranty of seaworthiness, arose for decision. In their judgments Hodges CJ and Bell J referred to numerous English decisions and to the works of the Americans Phillips and Kent. Cloete J, in addition to a reference to the work of Smith, mentioned a Roman law text, Van Bynkershoek and Van der Keessel. The decision of the Cape Supreme Court went on appeal to the Privy Council[40] where, in partially reversing the judgment *a quo*,[41] no specific mention was made of the fact that Roman-Dutch law governed the case. Only English decisions were referred to.[42]

Cape of Good Hope Marine Insurance Co v. Berg[43] dealt with an insurer's right to the proceeds of a sale (by the agent of the owner of the carrying ship) of insured goods which had been abandoned by the consignees to the insurer. In the course of the judgment reference was made to an English decision, the view of the Italian Roccus, and to a decision reported by Coren. Watermeyer J pointed out that:

[n]o case exactly similar to this appears to have occurred in England, Holland, France, or America, so far as we can ascertain from the books. But it seems to me not difficult to arrive at the right conclusion by the application of the same principles of maritime law which have produced the decisions that have taken place. If there be any difference between the law of England and the law of Holland on the subject, the latter must prevail. It is, indeed, desirable never to lose from view that, to use Lord Mansfield's words and adopt his quotation, in *Luke vs. Lyde* [(1759) 2 Burr 882 at 887, 97 ER 614 at 617], 'the maritime law is not the law of a particular country, but the general law of nations . . .'. And it is to be regretted that the

---

[38] 117. [39] (1859) 3 Searle 231.

[40] (1861) 3 Searle 242, also reported as *Biccard v. Shepherd* (1861) 14 Moo PCC 471, 15 ER 383.

[41] Further local proceedings followed in order to determine the construction of the Privy Council judgment: see *Namaqua Mining Co v. Commercial Marine Insurance Co* (1862) 1 Roscoe 47.

[42] In *Butcher & Co v. Hawes & Hedley* (1859) 3 Searle 270 (cf. *De Pass & Co v. Trustees Frontier Fire & Marine Insurance Co* 1868 Buch 28) the Court referred only to a work by the English author Manley Hopkins. The case concerned, amongst other issues, the interpretation of a 'free of particular average' clause in a marine policy.

[43] (1865) 1 Roscoe 289.

tendency of the later English decisions has been rather to depart from this whole-some rule . . .[44]

His Lordship then referred to decisions of the various Dutch courts in a case on the subject which is mentioned by Barels in his opinions on commercial and maritime law, and pointed out that Van Bynkershoek, Van der Keessel, the relevant sections of the Wisby Maritime Code ('the foundation of the Maritime Jurisprudence of Northern Europe') and of the Dutch *placaaten* of 1563 and 1570, and 'in fact, the universal Maritime Law, all tend to this conclusion'.[45]

A fire insurance policy,[46] the question of double insurance, and the inter-pretation of a clause requiring notice of any other insurance effected on the same property fell to be considered in *O'Flynn v. Equitable Fire Insurance & Trust Co.*[47] With reference to the clause in question, it was pointed out that it 'is not a clause peculiar to the offices of this Colony, for the sub-stance of it is . . . to be found in the regulations of every insurance office in the United Kingdom'.[48] In his judgment Cloete J referred to a work on fire insurance by one Dowdeswell, pointing out that similar clauses usually inserted in the policies of English insurers were less harsh than the clause in the policy before him. The reason, he thought, was that '[i]n this Colony there were until recently very few insurance companies; but many English, Indian and other companies advertised for business, and . . . the principal reason why that very stringent clause was introduced into the colonial poli-cies was the great importance that the colonial companies should know who were their co-obligors'.[49] In *Lange & Co v. South African Fire & Life Assurance Co,*[50] which also concerned a fire policy as well as the issue of double insurance and contribution, Bell J referred to the analogous position in the case of marine insurance, mentioned the British Marine Insurance Act of 1745[51] and, almost as an afterthought, added that '[i]n consonance with this are Articles 20 and 23 of the Ordinance of Amsterdam'.[52]

Roman-Dutch insurance law, no doubt to the consternation of many legal practitioners and the local business fraternity in general, was being kept alive, at least in marine insurance cases, by a few judges conversant with that legal system. The ascendancy of English law, however, had cre-ated a dichotomy between the strict legal position and the practical reali-

---

[44] 297 sq.   [45] 300.
[46] Cf. *Cornelissen v. Equitable Fire Insurance Co* (1861) 4 Searle 35, where, in a fire insur-ance case, reference was made to English and American decisions.
[47] (1866) 1 Roscoe 372.   [48] 375.
[49] 378 sq. The Indian companies referred to were probably British insurance companies which conducted insurance business at the Cape through their branch offices in Calcutta. See e.g. the advertisement of Nisbet & Dickson (n. 18, above) as agents for a number of Calcutta insurance companies which appeared in *The South African Almanack and Directory* for 1827, 85.
[50] (1867) 5 Searle 358.   [51] 19 Geo. II, c. 37.   [52] 369.

ties. It was merely a question of time before it was accorded legislative recognition as the law applicable to insurance disputes in the Cape Colony. In this process John Henry de Villiers, Chief Justice at the Cape from 1873 until 1910, was to play a leading role.[53]

III. THE FORMAL INTRODUCTION OF ENGLISH INSURANCE LAW IN 1879

In a letter to the High Commissioner, Sir Henry Barkley, in 1877, De Villiers wrote: '[t]he Common Law of South Africa is the Roman-Dutch Law ... But the old Commercial Law of Holland ... has been gradually superseded by the English Merchant Law throughout South Africa'.[54] Still, as long as any direct conflict between the Roman-Dutch law (formally the law of the country) and English law (informally applied) could be avoided there seemed little need for any formal intervention. De Villiers's approach towards reconciling theory and practice in mercantile disputes, his attitude towards the relevance of Roman-Dutch mercantile law, and his failure to appreciate the inherent adaptability of Roman-Dutch principles to modern requirements[55] are illustrated by his judgment in *London & South African Bank v. Donald Currie & Co*,[56] a case dealing with a bill of lading. After referring to English authority on the nature of a bill of lading, De Villiers CJ continued as follows:

No Roman-Dutch law authorities have been quoted in this case, nor indeed are they likely to be of much assistance to the Court in a question affecting the merchant law of the present day. The enormous development of commerce in recent times requires a corresponding development of the mercantile law, so that it becomes impossible *rigidly to apply* the rules which obtained in Holland in the beginning of the present century to questions which arise out of customs of a later growth. It is satisfactory, however, to find that the views which I have already expressed are not in any way inconsistent with any general principle of the Roman-Dutch Law. That law clearly recognises the validity of a constructive delivery to pass the property in goods as opposed to an actual delivery ... In the famous case of *Lickbarrow v. Mason* [(1794) 5 Term Rep 683, 101 ER 380] I find a reference made to the practice of merchants in

---

[53] See esp. Anon., 'Sir J. H. de Villiers', (1910) 27 *SALJ* 1; E. A. Walker, *Lord de Villiers and His Times: South Africa 1842–1914* (1925), *passim*; G. E. Devenish, 'Our Legal Heritage: Lord de Villiers and the Cape Colony 1828–1910', 1978 *De Rebus* 48; Reinhard Zimmermann, 'De Villiers, John Henry', in: Michael Stolleis (ed.), *Juristen: Ein biographisches Lexikon* (1995), 160 sq.

[54] Quoted in Walker (n. 53), 77.

[55] The Chief Justice was no doubt even then well aware of the existence of the large body of Roman-Dutch insurance law. Some years later, in *Viviers v. Juta & Co* (1902) 19 SC 222, 223, for example, he pointed out that '[t]he Roman law knew nothing about insurance, but in Holland insurances were well established at the time the latest text books were written ...'

[56] (1875) 5 Buch 29.

Holland as to bills of lading in the latter end of the last century which strongly confirms this view . . . [F]or my present purpose the case is useful to show that the Court
of Amsterdam considered the bill of lading as the symbol of the property . . .[57]

However, in 1878 a case came before the Cape Supreme Court which illustrated that Roman-Dutch law and English law could not in all instances be
reconciled and that the time had arrived for the abolition of the Roman-
Dutch common law and for its replacement by English law in certain areas
of mercantile law. *Smith v. Davis*[58] involved a collision between two ships
in Cape territorial waters. Although the Vice-Admiralty Court at the Cape[59]
had jurisdiction over the matter and would have had to apply English maritime law,[60] the resulting action for damages was brought in the Supreme
Court which had to apply the municipal Roman-Dutch law.[61] On the ques-

[57] 34 sq. (italics added). In *Myburgh & Co v. Protecteur Insurance Co* (1878) 3 Roscoe 19,
(1878) 8 Buch 152, a fire insurance case, De Villiers CJ nevertheless referred to Pothier as
authority for a general principle of contract law applicable to the case before him.

[58] (1878) 8 Buch 66.

[59] The Vice-Admiralty Court at the Cape was created in 1797 during the first British occupation, and revived after the second occupation in 1806 (see Theal (n. 7), vol. II, 27, vol. VI,
31 for the 2 Commissions respectively). The Court was a court of prize and of first instance.
Its jurisdiction extended from Cape Negro on the coast of West Africa to Cape Corrento on
the coast of East Africa, it had a largely criminal jurisdiction to try all 'piracies, felonies and
robberies and all accessories thereto', and it had to apply 'the civil law and the methods and
rules of the Admiralty' (see generally Visagie (n. 6), 94; Petrus Johannes van der Merwe,
Regsinstellings en die Reg aan die Kaap van 1806 tot 1834 (unpublished LL D thesis, University
of the Western Cape, 1984), 44–6, 83 sq., 187–9; E. S. Roscoe, *Studies in the History of the
Admiralty and Prize Courts* (1932), whose information on the Cape Admiralty Court (19), however, is not quite correct). Appeals against the decisions of the Cape Vice-Admiralty Court lay
to the High Court of Admiralty in London. It does not appear from any of the reported decisions of the local Court, nor from any of the reported appeals, that the Vice-Admiralty Court
ever determined an insurance case. In *The Elizabeth* (1824) 1 Hagg 226, 166 ER 81 the appeal
from the Cape Vice-Admiralty Court concerned an undertaking by local merchants at the Cape
in terms of a charterparty to 'insure' the shipowner 'against all such risks as underwriters run'.
This was probably not an insurance proper but rather an undertaking on the part of the char-
terers to indemnify the shipowner against loss.

[60] For further details see Clare Dillon, J. P. van Niekerk, *South African Maritime Law and
Marine Insurance: Selected Topics* (1983), 14 sq.

[61] The overlapping jurisdictions of the Vice-Admiralty Court and the ordinary civil courts
at the Cape had given rise to numerous squabbles in the past, e.g. in 1809 when the Admiralty
Court exercised jurisdiction over breaches of the Navigation Laws and matters of slavery (see
Theal (n. 7), vol. VI, 330–3, 497 sq.) The most serious confrontation erupted in 1820, with the
Governor issuing a prohibition against the Admiralty Court to prevent any further impinge-
ment upon the jurisdiction of the then High Court of Justice (see Theal (n. 7), vol. XIII, 371,
377–84, 421–3, 451–3, 486 sq. for some of the correspondence surrounding the jurisdictional
dispute). At the time it was said that 'the Town is quite divided into parties on the subject' (see
Theal (n. 7), vol. XXX, 252). This concurrent jurisdiction, exacerbated at the time by the fact
that the 2 courts involved applied different legal systems to the same issues, continued to exist
even after the replacement of the Vice-Admiralty Court by a Colonial Court of Admiralty in
1891 (see further Dillon/Van Niekerk (n. 60), 20; Christopher Forsyth, 'The Conflict Between
Modern Roman-Dutch Law and the Law of Admiralty as Administered by South African
Courts', (1982) 99 *SALJ* 255). The matter was finally resolved by the Admiralty Jurisdiction
Regulation Act 105 of 1983, which conferred exclusive jurisdiction on the Admiralty Court
over maritime matters (see further below, text to n. 204).

tion of the apportionment of damages Roman-Dutch law produced a result substantially different to that which would have followed from an application of English law. In the course of argument De Villiers CJ probed various reasons why Roman-Dutch law could possibly be held not to apply: the relevant Roman-Dutch rules were based upon purely local custom, probably already abolished even in Holland; foreign law was not to apply to British ships in British waters, and in any event English maritime law extended to the colonies; there was no reason why, if English law was to be applied by the Cape Supreme Court exercising its admiralty jurisdiction, it should not also be applicable if the Court exercised its municipal jurisdiction—after all, as Chief Justice he presided over both courts.[62] However, the defendant in the case at hand accepted that Roman-Dutch law was the law to be applied and the Chief Justice had no choice but to proceed with its application. In his judgment he referred to Voet, Van Bynkershoek, Van der Keessel and to a collection of decisions generally ascribed to Neostadius, although he made it clear that he did not intend to say 'that merely local rules relating to Dutch navigation have any force in this Colony'.[63] Fitzpatrick J, justifying the need for his concurrent but separate judgment, demonstrated a completely different approach to the role of the relevant Roman-Dutch principles:

[D]uring the hearing of the case there seemed to be a fear [no doubt inspired by De Villiers CJ's questions *in arguendo*] that the Court would not recognise the Roman-Dutch law. I think that judgment is in no way inconsistent with the principles of that law. *These abstract principles are of themselves necessarily open to a liberal construction under a new set of circumstances.*[64]

As chairman of a Commission on Law Reform in 1879, De Villiers recommended the introduction of English law in certain areas of the local maritime and mercantile law as 'a highly necessary and important change in the laws of the Colony. The great bulk of these laws is derived from the laws of Holland as it existed at the beginning of the past century ... Considerable portions are, and have always been, unsuited to the requirements of the Colony'.[65] The bill drafted by De Villiers to put his recommendations into effect became the General Law Amendment Act, 8 of 1879, virtually without amendment.[66]

---

[62] 69 sq.   [63] 71.

[64] 73 (italics added). James Coleman Fitzpatrick was Irish educated and the father of Sir Percy Fitzpatrick (see Roberts (n. 23), 360 sq.; Ellison Kahn, *Law, Life and Laughter* (1991), 61 sqq.).

[65] Quoted by Walker (n. 53), 80. See in general Walker 79–90; Ben Beinart, 'The English Legal Contribution in South Africa: The Interaction of Civil and Common Law', 1981 *Acta Juridica* 7, 14.

[66] It may be surmised that, in drafting this measure, De Villiers may have had the Ceylonese example in mind. English law had been adopted by statute in Ceylon in respect of all contracts or questions relating to shipping (including marine insurance) 'and generally to all maritime

The Preamble to this Act stated the reason for its introduction as follows:

[T]he existing general law of the Colony is in several instances unsuited to the advancing trade and the altered circumstances of the country   [A]lso, many portions of such law are uncertain, and partly, if not entirely obselete [sic] . . . [I]t is desirable to alter and amend such laws as are in conflict or inconsistent with modern principles of legislation . . .

The far-reaching changes and the 'brutal injection of English law'[67] effected by the General Law Amendment Act were for obvious reasons widely welcomed as highly practical and necessary. Not only did the view that Dutch commercial law was singularly deficient have 'considerable justification'[68] but 'the provisions . . . of the Act were not intended to effect a revolution, but merely to give legislative sanction to an existing practice'.[69] However, it has also been remarked that the English influence in the field of mercantile law 'did not imply that Roman-Dutch law was inherently incapable of developing a viable mercantile law',[70] but merely that 'it lacked the academic and practical jurists to accomplish this task'.[71] The opinion has even been expressed that '[w]ith the high development of Roman-Dutch shipping law, the Act would appear to have been unnecessary'.[72]

Apart from a few procedural and contractual matters[73] the General Law Amendment Act mainly concerned maritime and mercantile law. Section 1 provided for the application of English law '[i]n all questions relating to maritime and shipping law in respect of which the Supreme Court has concurrent jurisdiction with the Vice Admiralty Court', thereby eliminating, in part, the conflict which arose in *Smith v. Davis*.[74] Section 2 provided as follows:

matters' (by s. 1, Civil Ordinance, 5 of 1852), in respect of bills of exchange (by s. 2 of the same Ordinance), and in respect of all questions arising in connection with fire and life insurance (by s. 1, Ordinance 22 of 1866): see further, e.g. T. Nadaraja, *The Legal System of Ceylon in its Historical Setting* (1972), 238 sq.; H. W. Tambiah, *Principles of Ceylon Law* (1972), 528–30; L. J. M. Cooray, 'The Reception of Roman-Dutch Law in Sri Lanka', (1974) 7 *CILSA* 255; C. G. Weeramantry, 'The Reception and Development of the Roman-Dutch Law in Sri Lanka', (1985) 1 *Lesotho LJ* 135, 155–7.

    [67] Hahlo/Kahn (n. 10), 670.
    [68] Kahn, (1985) 1 *Lesotho LJ* 71. See also e.g. Anon., (1901) 18 *SALJ* 1, 5; Hahlo/Kahn (n. 10), 18.
    [69] See Lee, (1930) 47 *SALJ* 278.   [70] See Devenish, 1978 *De Rebus* 485.
    [71] See Zajtay/Hosten, (1969) 2 *CILSA* 193; Reinhard Zimmermann, 'Roman-Dutch Law in South Africa: Aspects of the Reception Process', (1985) 1 *Lesotho LJ* 97, 104 sq.
    [72] See B. R. Bamford, *The Law of Shipping and Carriage in South Africa* (1983), 4, fn. 27.
    [73] See ss. 6 (civil imprisonment), 7 (leases of land), 8 (*laesio enormis*).
    [74] See n. 58, above. In *Anderson & Murison v. Colonial Govt* (1891) 8 SC 293, 296, De Villiers CJ explained that '[t]he object of this section was to put an end to the absurd state of law which often required the Vice-Admiralty Court in cases such as that of collision, to apply different rules for ascertaining damages from those which, if the cases had been brought in the Supreme Court, would have been applied by that Court. But the section was certainly not intended to have the far-reaching effect of applying to this Colony every provision of the Merchant Shipping Act which, on the face of it, was confined in its operation to the United Kingdom.' In *De Howarth v. SS India* 1921 CPD 451, 458, Gardiner J, in interpreting s. 1, pointed out

In every suit, action, and cause having reference to questions of fire, life, and marine assurance, stoppage in transit, and bills of lading, which shall henceforth be brought in the Supreme Court, or in any other competent court of this Colony, the law administered by the High Court of Justice in England for the time being, so far as the same shall not be repugnant to, or in conflict with, any Ordinance, Act of Parliament, or other statute having the force of law in the Colony, shall be the law to be administered by the said Supreme Court or other competent court.

Section 3 made clear that the application of English law provided for in ss. 1 and 2 was not to 'have the effect of giving force in this Colony to any statutory enactment made and passed by the Imperial Parliament after the taking effect of this Act, unless the same shall be re-enacted here'.[75]

Before turning to the application and interpretation of the General Law Amendment Act by the courts, the formal extension of its influence to another part of the future South Africa may be noted briefly. After the annexation of the Orange Free State by the British in May 1902 it was provided that the Roman-Dutch law was to continue in force as the common law of that colony.[76] However, the Free State legislature, which generally followed the Cape more closely in its legislation than the Transvaal,[77] was quick to pass the General Law Amendment Ordinance, 5 of 1902, which virtually[78] re-enacted the Cape Act of 1879. Section 1 of the Ordinance provided that in every action having reference to questions of fire, life, and marine assurance brought in a Free State court after the taking effect of the Ordinance,[79] the law administered by the Cape Supreme Court for the time being was to be the law to be administered by such court. English law was therefore indirectly introduced into the Orange Free State via the Cape General Law Amendment Act of 1879.

IV. THE APPLICATION AND INTERPRETATION OF THE GENERAL LAW AMENDMENT ACT

1. General

Although the General Law Amendment Act was drafted in fairly simple and general terms, this very simplicity and generality on quite a few occasions that 'the legislature did not give a very wide meaning to the words "maritime and shipping law" [as] is shown by s. 2, for it was thought necessary to make provision by that section for the introduction of the law of maritime insurance and bills of lading'. Section 1 did not, of course, eliminate the concurrent jurisdictions of the ordinary and the Admiralty courts.

[75] Section 4 provided that the introduction of English law was to have no effect on existing rules and forms of pleading, procedure, and evidence, the notarial practice, or the nature and extent of the jurisdiction of the courts in the colony.
[76] See s. 1, Laws Settlement and Interpretation Ordinance, 3 of 1902.
[77] See Hahlo/Kahn (n. 10), 23.
[78] Only ss. 1 and 5 of the Cape Act, dealing with maritime and shipping law, were omitted.
[79] On 30 July 1902.

resulted in the need for a judicial interpretation of the Act in general,[80] and of ss. 2 and 3 in insurance disputes[81] in particular. From the various insurance cases concerning the construction of the Act it appears that considerable uncertainty existed as to the exact meaning and scope of its provisions.[82] Thus in *Mutual Life Insurance Co of New York v. Hotz*,[83] Innes J, in considering the Act, was driven to remark in the presence of De Villiers CJ that '[t]he language of the second section is not very precise, and I do not propose to attempt any complete definition of its scope'.[84] Upon consideration of the relevant provisions of the Act, particularly in view of subsequently altered insurance practices, law, and theory, it is clear that it was a rather unfortunate piece of legislation which considerably hampered the development by the courts of a South African insurance law during a period when such development was taking place in many other areas of the law.

As a *lex correctiva*, abolishing the common law to the extent to which it applied,[85] one would in many cases have expected the Act to have been restrictively interpreted: an expectation based on the presumption that in cases of uncertainty the legislature intended to alter the existing law no more than necessary. Although the courts have indeed generally limited the scope and application of the Act, this has not invariably and consistently been the case. The courts do not always seem to have appreciated that a broad or narrow interpretation of the Act often effectively determined the respective scope of application of English and Roman-Dutch law. They treated the issue rather as one of determining whether English law was to be regarded as binding or merely, and in preference to Roman-Dutch law, as persuasive authority. Problems relating to the interpretation of the Act, therefore, were often not sufficiently closely and seriously examined, or they simply never arose for consideration. In consequence, it is submitted, the importance of a restrictive interpretation of the provisions of the General Law Amend-

---

[80] Walker (n. 53), 80, notes that '[De Villiers] knew what he meant to convey in the meaning of the act . . . Others do not find that meaning in the words.'

[81] For a case involving s. 2 and stoppage *in transitu* see e.g. *Scheinfield's Trustee v. Murray & Co* 1920 CPD 87, at 93; for a case dealing with the interpretation of a bill of lading see *Thomson Watson & Co v. Poverty Bay Farmer's Meat Co Ltd* 1924 CPD 380 where, by reason of s. 2, the Court (386) looked 'first to the law administered by the High Court in England for guidance as to the interpretation of the exception' contained in the bill of lading, and then referred also (389) to American and Roman-Dutch authority.

[82] See generally B. R. Bamford, 'Marine Insurance Law in South Africa: An Historical Anomaly', 1975 *Lloyd's Maritime & Commercial LQ* 171.

[83] 1911 AD 556.   [84] 564.

[85] See e.g. *United Mines of Bultfontein v. De Beers Consolidated Mines* (1900) 17 SC 419, 423: 'the intention [with Act 8 of 1879] was to assimilate our law to that of England'—*per* De Villiers CJ *in arguendo*, and 427: 'the intention of the General Law Amendment Act was to place our law upon the same footing as the law of England and to alter it from the position in which it was before'—*per* Buchanan J; and *Strauss v. Van Zyl* 1958 (3) SA 563 (o) 565. But in *Salisbury Building & Investment Soc v. British South Africa Co* (1904) 21 SC 238, at 241, De Villiers CJ remarked to counsel: 'You assume that the object of Act 8 of 1879 was to assimilate our law to the English law. The Act does not say so.'

ment Act was not always recognized. This resulted in the Act enjoying an unjustifiably wide application and influence which considerably aided the impact of English law on insurance law in South Africa.

2. 'Fire, life, and marine assurance'

Concerning the type of insurance policy to which, under the Act, English law was made applicable, one would have thought that English law was accorded binding authority only in disputes involving those classes of insurance specifically enumerated in the Act. In all other instances the principles of Roman-Dutch law ought to have been applied and English law could, at the most, have been regarded as persuasive authority. However, it has been argued that under the Act English law was to be applied to all forms of insurance since the legislature had intended to cover them all. Fire, life, and marine insurance were mentioned specifically because those were the only forms known at the Cape in 1879.[86]

No South African case ever directly decided this issue, but English law, whether as binding or merely as persuasive authority, was generally followed in cases concerning forms of insurance other than those mentioned in the Act. For example, in *London & Scottish Assurance Corp Ltd v. Venter*[87] where a question of misrepresentation of the ownership of an insured motor vehicle arose for decision, the Court merely stated that '[i]t may be well to notice at the outset that our law as to fire insurance is that obtaining in the Cape Province, and that the law there administered is "the law administered by the High Court of Justice in England for the time being" '.[88] A problem in this regard, admittedly arising only after the introduction of the Act in 1879, was of course that it is not always a simple

---

[86] See D. M. Davis, *Gordon and Getz on The South African Law of Insurance* (4th edn., 1993), 3.

[87] 1923 OPD 209.

[88] 213. In *Scottish Union & National Insurance Co Ltd v. Native Recruiting Corp Ltd* 1934 AD 458, a case dealing with a policy covering loss by theft or fraud, it was merely said (469) that '*[i]n die Kaapprovinsie en die Oranje Vrystaat word die Engelse reg op versekering toegepas*' (in the Cape Province and the Orange Free State the English law is applied to insurance). In *Horne v. Newport-Gwilt* 1961 (3) SA 342 (SR), where the Court had to interpret a motor vehicle policy which also provided cover against fire damage, the question arose whether a particular decision of the House of Lords was binding upon the Court. Because the policy in question was not regarded as a fire policy the Court assumed that the decision was not binding but nevertheless accorded it very high persuasive authority. Maisels J explained as follows (353): 'I may mention that when ... Act 8 of 1879 (Cape) [was] enacted, it is unlikely that there were any motor-car policies. In any event I shall assume ... that the decision of the House of Lords is not binding on me. It is also undoubtedly true ... that the Roman-Dutch Law and not the English Law applies to this Colony [Southern Rhodesia] ... But ... the Roman-Dutch Law is acquainted with marine and fire insurance, but life, accident and other insurance are of a later date ... [P]artly by legislative enactment and partly by decisions of our Courts, we have introduced into South Africa the law of insurance as it prevails in England ... Nevertheless, it seems to me I would have to construe this policy under the Roman-Dutch Law'.

matter to determine whether or not a particular policy is a fire (or life or marine) policy. The advent of comprehensive or multi-peril policies made any such classification difficult if not impossible. Even determination of the nature of a claim on a particular policy may not always be decisive; an insured person may, for instance, suffer and claim for a fire as well as a non-fire loss under his comprehensive policy.

An instructive decision, running counter to the approach generally followed in South Africa, is that of a Ceylonese Court in *Haniffa v. Ocean Accident & Guarantee Corp Ltd.*[89] For jurisdictional purposes it was necessary to decide whether Roman-Dutch or English law was applicable in order to determine where the cause of action on the insurance policy before the Court had arisen. English law had been introduced in Ceylon in respect of all questions relating to fire and life insurance.[90] The policy in question was described as 'a form of insurance generally referred to as accident insurance. The obligation which was undertaken by the defendant company was to indemnify the insured in respect of the motor vehicle in question . . . in respect of claims resulting from death or bodily injury to third parties and accidental damage to property and various other risks among them damage by fire.'[91] The Court disagreed with the view that, inasmuch as some of the risks covered by this policy related to death and fire damage, it was sufficiently close to a life and fire policy for English law to be applicable. Garvin ACJ argued as follows:

An examination of the policy and all its terms and conditions clearly takes it outside both the category of life insurance and that of fire insurance . . . The main purpose of [the policy] is to indemnify the insured against damage from accident . . . The matter, therefore, must be determined with reference to the rules of the Roman-Dutch law. Contracts of indemnity are not unknown to that system . . .[92]

3. 'Having reference to questions of . . . assurance'

Section 2 of the General Law Amendment Act provided for the introduction of English law in every action 'having reference to questions of . . . assurance'. The question soon arose whether English law was to be applied to all the issues arising in the course of an insurance dispute, or whether its application was to be limited to issues specifically relating to insurance.[93] In other words, was English law in general or only English insurance law to be followed in insurance disputes?

Some six years after the introduction of the Act De Villiers CJ had the opportunity to provide some guidance in the case of *Davies v. South British Insurance Co.*[94] In the course of his judgment he noted:

[89] (1933) 35 New LR 216 (DC Kandy).   [90] See above. n. 66.   [91] 218.
[92] 218 sq.   [93] See, in general, Gordon/Getz (n. 86), 3; Hahlo/Kahn (n. 10), 716.
[94] (1885) 3 SC 416.

It seems to have been taken for granted by counsel on both sides that by Act 8 of 1879, the question at issue between the parties ought to be decided under the law of England and not under the law of this Colony. In this view I entirely agree, if the question were one relating to . . . *any of those legal incidents which are common to all fire insurances.* But I cannot concur in the view that the Act was intended to apply to every legal question that may incidentally arise in the course of an action upon a policy of insurance.[95]

Although the test laid down by De Villers CJ was referred to in subsequent cases[96] it was not in all respects satisfactory. Many legal incidents common to all insurances (or matters belonging to the essence of insurance) can arguably also arise in non-insurance disputes. In *Mutual Life Insurance Co of New York v. Hotz*[97] Innes J, confronted with the question whether or not English law was to be applied in terms of the Act, formulated the relevant criterion as follows:

[Section 2] certainly does not purport to introduce the English law in every case springing from a policy of insurance. It applies that law only to suits 'having reference to questions of fire, life and marine insurance, etc'. Now the present litigation is not concerned with *any principle peculiar to life assurance.* It relates to the rights of third parties in respect of contracts made in their favour by others. It so happens that the sum at issue represents the proceeds of a policy. But a position identical in all essentials and governed by the same legal principles might have arisen from a transaction of quite another kind. So that the questions to which this suit has reference are questions, not of life assurance, but of the general law regulating contracts; and the matter therefore does not come within the provisions of the Act of 1879.[98]

In terms of this test, therefore, English law was binding authority as regards matters or principles 'peculiar to insurance' (or insurance contracts?), that is, matters which could only arise in insurance disputes; it was not binding as regards matters concerning contracts (including insurance contracts?) in general or as regards principles forming part of the general law of contract. Put differently, the General Law Amendment Act introduced as binding authority in insurance disputes only English insurance law, and not English contract law or English law in general.[99]

[95] 422 (italics added). De Villiers CJ also referred (422) to 'matters which . . . belong to the essence of the law of fire insurance'.
[96] See e.g. *Irving v. Sun Insurance Office* 1906 ORC 24, 36.
[97] 1911 AD 556.   [98] 565 (italics added).
[99] In Ceylon English law was made applicable in respect of all questions arising in connection with life and fire insurance (see above, n. 66). Notwithstanding the general way in which it was introduced, the intention was to incorporate English law 'so far only as relates to the distinctive features of the different subjects enumerated' and not 'into all other matters wherever such matters happen to be connected with a contract or question relating to' life or fire insurance: see Nadaraja (n. 66), 268, fn. 142; but cf. *Sirimane v. New India Assurance Co Ltd* (1934) 35 New LR 413 (DC Kandy), where it was stated that '[i]t may not be possible in the present state of the law to argue that English law is not applicable in all matters relating to contracts of fire insurance'.

Some matters are clearly not peculiar to insurance and the courts have accordingly held that the relevant principles of Roman-Dutch law, as developed and applied in South Africa, rather than English law, were to govern them. Thus, in *Trautman v. Imperial Fire Insurance Co*[100] rights under a fire policy had been ceded by the insured as security for a debt, and De Villiers CJ pointed out that '[w]e adopted the English law of insurance, but we have not adopted the English law relating to cession'.[101] In *Mutual Life Insurance Co of New York v. Hotz*,[102] a decision on appeal from the Transvaal, the question arose of the right of a beneficiary under a life policy which expressly made the law of the Orange Free State applicable. The Court applied South African law relating to stipulations in favour of a third party.[103] As to the argument that, if English law were to be followed in so far as it affects the law of insurance, the effect of the appointment of a beneficiary in a life policy would be to create a trust in favour of such beneficiary, De Villiers CJ replied *in arguendo* that '[t]he law as to trustees is general law and not insurance law'.[104] Furthermore, for example, questions pertaining to the legality of an insurance contract[105] and the effect of the renewal of an insurance policy[106] have been regarded as not being peculiar to insurance.

However, in numerous other cases English law has been followed and applied in terms of the General Law Amendment Act in respect of matters which, upon consideration, cannot clearly be regarded as peculiar to insurance because they could also arise in other disputes.[107] Thus, as regards the question of pre-contractual misrepresentation and the related English doctrine of *uberrima fides*, Barry JP in *Malcher & Malcomess v.*

---

[100] (1895) 12 SC 38.

[101] 42. The matter was apparently not regarded as beyond doubt in *South British Insurance Co v. Union Govt (Minister of Finance)* 1914 CPD 822, 826. But in *Northern Assurance Co Ltd v. Methuen* 1937 SR 103, which involved the difference between the assignment of an insurance contract and the cession of a right of action in terms of an insurance contract, the approach in *Trautman* was endorsed and South African law was applied in preference to English law.

[102] 1911 AD 556.

[103] See Innes J 565 (quoted above, n. 98); cf. the remarks by Ward J in the Court *a quo* in *Hotz v. Mutual Life Insurance Co of New York* 1910 WLD 334, 336.

[104] 560.

[105] See *Irving v. Sun Insurance Office* 1906 ORC 24, 36, where the Court nevertheless followed English law because 'in questions as to what contracts are illegal on the grounds of their being opposed to public policy, our law is substantially the same as the law of England'.

[106] See *Licences & General Insurance Co v. Bassano* 1936 CPD 179, where Davis J, after referring to common law authority dealing with the renewal of a contract of lease, stated (186) that 'just as the renewal of a lease is a new contract, so is the renewal of an insurance policy such as the present one'. Reference was then nevertheless made to English authority which supported the result of the analogy drawn between contracts of lease and insurance.

[107] But see Gordon/Getz (n. 86), 3 who mention the following examples of matters peculiar to insurance: 'warranties, insurable interest, the principle of subrogation, "good faith" '. At 380 they refer to 'a number of principles which are peculiar to the law of marine insurance'.

Kingwilliamstown Fire & Marine Insurance & Trust Co[108] simply referred to
the General Law Amendment Act as introducing the English law of insurance[109] and declared that '[t]he law, as to misrepresentation, is clearly laid
down by Lord Mansfield in *Carter v. Boehm* [(1766) 3 Burr 1905, 97 ER
1162] ... and the other authorities cited in *Bunyan* [sic] *on insurance*'.[110]
Similarly, in *Drysdale v. Union Fire Insurance Co Ltd*,[111] where the effect of
a misstatement in an insurance proposal form completed by an agent of the
insurer had to be considered, De Villiers CJ averred that

[t]his being an action 'which has reference to questions of fire insurance' the law of
England is applicable under Act No 8 of 1879. I may therefore aptly preface our
judgment with some pregnant remarks made by *Lord Mansfield* in the case of Carter
vs. Boehm ... remarks which are the more valuable to us as being founded upon
well established principles of the Roman law.[112]

Furthermore, concerning the effect of certain essential terms found in insurance contracts and known in English law as 'warranties', the courts have
also ignored the general principles of the law of contract and have introduced English law under the guise of the General Law Amendment Act. In
Colonial Mutual Life Assurance Society Ltd v. De Bruyn,[113] for example, the
question of the legal effect of a breach of contract (i.e. breach of an 'insurance warranty') was, with reference to s. 2, regarded as one to be 'decided
in accordance with English law'.[114] In *Jordan v. New Zealand Insurance Co
Ltd*[115] the Court referred to the exposition of the law relating to insurance
warranties in an English work on insurance and declared that '[t]hat of
course is our law'.[116] Even more blatant was the course adopted in
Ackerman v. Loubser[117] with regard to the doctrine of subrogation.
Acknowledging that '[t]his principle of subrogation is not peculiar to
the English law nor is it confined to the matter of insurance',[118] Ward J

---

[108] (1883) 3 EDC 271   [109] 279.
[110] 282. Buchanan J apparently regarded the existence of a conflicting local statute as the
only limitation placed upon the introduction of English law by the Act (283 sq.), and in connection with the question of non-disclosure or concealment of facts by an insured party he
referred (288) to 'the masterly exposition of some of the leading principles of insurance law
contained in the judgment of Lord Chief Justice Mansfield [in *Carter v. Boehm*]'.
[111] (1890) 8 SC 63.
[112] 65. Subsequently, in *Colonial Industries Ltd v. Provincial Insurance Co Ltd* 1922 AD 33,
a case on appeal from the CPD and dealing with the duty of a proposer for insurance to disclose material facts beyond the scope of specific questions in the proposal form, the Court
referred to an *obiter dictum* in an English decision for an exposition of the doctrine of *uberrima fides* and declared (40): 'there is no doubt that this is a correct exposition of the English
law with which our law agrees.'
[113] 1911 CPD 103.
[114] 126. See further e.g. *Morris v. Northern Assurance Co Ltd* 1911 CPD 293, 304; *Broli v.
London Assurance Co* 1931 EDL 186, 192.
[115] 1968 (2) SA 238 (E).   [116] 243.   [117] 1918 OPD 31.
[118] 34. See further below, n. 237.

nevertheless referred to 'a long and unanimous series of English decisions'[119] and continued as follows:

[Counsel] has taken his stand not on the law of insurance but on the law of torts, and . . . I would like to refer to a passage from a standard work on that subject, namely Addison on Torts. The quotation is a rather long one but it contains a comprehensive statement of the law which, as provided by Ordinance 5 of 1902 combined with Act 8 of 1879 of the Cape, is the law of this Province.[120]

The question of insurable interest, and in particular the role it plays in distinguishing insurance contracts from wagers and in the application of the principle of indemnity, has from early on been regarded as a matter governed by English law, no doubt partly as a result of English legislation touching upon the issue.[121] In considering the nature of an indemnity insurance contract and the function of the requirement of an insurable interest in this regard, Buchanan J referred extensively to English authorities in *Malcher & Malcomess v. Kingwilliamstown Fire & Marine Insurance & Trust Co.*[122] Ironically, in view of the fact that Roman-Dutch insurance law had just been abolished, his reference to Arnould included a quotation by the latter from Straccha's *De Assecurationibus*. In *Van der Westhuizen v. Santam Versekeringsmaatskappy Bpk*[123] the following was remarked in regard to the insurable interest of a seller of insured property:

Daar blyk geen direkte gesag in ons reg te wees nie oor hierdie vraagstuk, behalwe die volgende passasie (waarvoor die geleerde skrywer op Engelse skrywers staat maak) uit Gordon . . . . Dit is nogtans onnodig om te beklemtoon dat . . . die beginsels van die Engelse reg van versekering in die huidige saak van toepassing is, in die afwesigheid van gesaghebbende Suid-Afrikaanse gesag.[124]

Other matters which have—incorrectly, it is submitted—been regarded as peculiar to insurance, and which have thus been taken to be governed by English law, include the question of whether the purchaser of insured property can claim on the seller's policy,[125] the effect of an insurance policy issued in consequence of a c.i.f. contract,[126] the proof of the fraudulence of

---

[119] 35. [120] 36. [121] See further n. 145 below.

[122] (1883) 3 EDC 271, 284–7. In *Old Mutual Fire & General Insurance Co of Rhodesia Ltd v. Springer* 1963 R & N 90 (HC SR), Lewis J rejected the proposition, for which no authority was quoted, that the lack of an insurable interest in Roman-Dutch law is not fatal to the validity of an insurance contract. He pointed out that South African cases seem to assume that an insurable interest is necessary in an insurance contract and declared (96): 'I have no doubt, therefore, that under our common law the position is the same as in English law.'

[123] 1975 (1) SA 236 (E).

[124] (There appears to be no direct authority in our law on this issue, except the following passage (for which the learned writer relies on English writers) from Gordon . . . It is, however, unnecessary to emphasize that . . . the principles of the English law of insurance are applicable in the present case, in the absence of relevant South-African authority): 238.

[125] See *Mendelsohn v. Estate Morom* 1912 CPD 690, 693, where it was pointed out with reference to s. 2 that '[t]he English authorities are . . . not only instructive but authoritative'.

[126] See *Birbeck & Rose-Innes v. Hill* 1915 CPD 687, 698.

an insurance claim,[127] and the effect and possibility of a waiver of the provisions of an arbitration clause contained in an insurance policy.[128] In some decisions the interpretation of an insurance contract was regarded as a matter peculiar to insurance and therefore as being governed by English law in terms of the General Law Amendment Act. Even where English law was not regarded as binding it was often taken to provide at least persuasive authority and was thus applied in preference to the general principles of Roman-Dutch law on the interpretation of contracts.[129]

From the decisions, in which the application of English law in terms of the General Law Amendment Act was directly or indirectly considered, it appears that the courts had some difficulty with a restrictive interpretation of the phrase 'having reference to questions of . . . assurance' in s. 2 as well as with the application of the criterion laid down in the *Hotz* case. In a number of decisions English law was applied to matters arguably not peculiar to insurance, thereby unjustifiably extending the influence of English law on South African insurance law. It should also be mentioned that in many more decisions the courts applied English law without considering whether the matters at issue were covered by the Act. Often, however, they merely followed earlier decisions in which, on a strict interpretation of section 2, the incorporation of English law was unjustified. The distinction between matters peculiar to insurance and matters pertaining to the general law of contract was not satisfactory. Insurance law and contract law, for instance, are often so entwined that it is difficult if not impossible to determine whether or not a particular matter is peculiar to insurance. The distinction may not even be valid, for it may be asked whether there are in fact any principles peculiar to insurance. Arguably, there are merely general principles of the law of contract which have attained a particular importance and are applied in a peculiar manner in the insurance context. The following argument, considered but rejected in *Jordaan v. Scottish Assurance Corp*,[130] should have merited closer attention.

It is . . . contended . . . that the point in question depends not on any law peculiar to . . . insurance but on the general principles of law, and that, accordingly, the [Act] has no application. This contention is in my opinion wrongly taken. It may well be that the point is governed by the general principles underlying the whole body of English law . . . for I take it that the whole of the English common law of . . .

---

[127] See *Papas v. General Accident, Fire & Life Assurance Corp Ltd* 1916 CPD 619, 636.

[128] See *Jordaan v. Scottish Assurance Corp* 1922 OPD 129, where De Villiers JP stated (134): '[i]t may well be that the point is governed by general principles underlying the whole body of English law, but that does not prevent it from being a "question of fire insurance" within the meaning of Statute 5 of 1902' and thereby ignored the interpretation of s. 2 and the test laid down by the Appellate Division in the *Hotz* case: see above, n. 98.

[129] For a discussion of these cases on the interpretation of insurance contracts see Van Niekerk (n. 4), 35–8.

[130] 1922 OPD 129.

insurance is governed by the same identical principles which govern the remainder of English common law. The contention would therefore destroy the law of . . . insurance altogether and leave nothing for the [Act] to operate on.[131]

4. 'The law administered by the High Court of Justice in England for the time being'

Section 2 of the General Law Amendment Act introduced English insurance law as binding authority, but only in so far as it did not conflict with any local legislative enactment[132] or any other statute having the force of law in the Cape Province. The law to be administered by the relevant local courts was stated to be 'the law administered by the High Court of Justice in England for the time being'. The precise meaning of these words was never considered in any insurance decision. The Act did not specifically receive English law as it existed at the date of its coming into operation. It seems to have been generally accepted, however, that the law to be applied was English law as at 1879, and that subsequent decisions and developments in England had merely persuasive authority.[133]

It has been explained[134] that the law administered by the High Court of Justice:[135]

will, in accordance with the strict English doctrine of precedent, be at the very least the law laid down by the Appellate Committee of the House of Lords, the judgments of which are absolutely binding on all other courts . . . It is very arguable that the phrase also embraces a judgment of the Court of Appeal, for its judgments bind the High Court . . . The same could be contended for a decision of the Divisional Court of the High Court . . . As the Privy Council does not pronounce on the law administered by the High Court, its decisions would not be binding. On appeal from South Africa[136] when that was possible, the Privy Council should have applied the law

---

[131] 134, *per* De Villiers JP.

[132] E.g. Insurance Act 37 of 1923, or its successor, Insurance Act 27 of 1943.

[133] See e.g. Bamford, 1975 *Lloyd's Maritime & Commercial LQ* 171; cf. Gordon/Getz (n. 86), 380, who nevertheless (381) regard English authorities prior to 1906 as being of particular importance (1906 is the year when the British Marine Insurance Act—which never applied in South Africa—came into force). See, too, *Table Bay Harbour Board v. City Line Ltd* (1905) 22 SC 511, 520: in connection with s. 1 of the Act the Court referred to 'the English law in force when our Act of 1879 was passed'.

[134] See Ellison Kahn, 'Have Certain English Precedents Binding Force in South Africa?', (1965) 82 *SALJ* 526, 527. See also generally *idem*, 'The Rules of Precedent Applied in South African Courts', (1967) 84 *SALJ* 308, 326–30.

[135] Since the Supreme Court of Judicature Act of 1873 (36 & 37 Vict. c. 66) the various divisions of the High Court—i.e. the Queen's Bench Division (prior to 1881: the separate courts of Queen's Bench, Exchequer, and Common Pleas), the Chancery Division, and the Probate, Divorce and Admiralty Division (since 1970: the Family Division)—together with the Court of Appeal have formed the Supreme Court of Judicature.

[136] More specifically: only on an appeal from South Africa in a case originating in the Cape or Orange Free State, for only there was the law administered by the High Court of Justice applicable.

administered by the High Court.[137] In the event of a decision on such an appeal conflicting with a decision of one of these English courts, it would appear that the latter prevailed.

5. English statutes

Section 3 of the General Law Amendment Act expressly excluded English
statutes made and passed after the introduction of the Act in 1879, unless
such statutes were locally re-enacted. English statutes passed after 1879,
such as the Merchant Shipping Act of 1894,[138] the Marine Insurance Act of
1906,[139] and the Marine Insurance (Gambling Policies) Act of 1909[140] therefore did not apply in any part of South Africa as they were never re-enacted
by any local legislature.[141] Section 3 was considered in *R v. McGarth*,[142] a
case dealing with the application of the British Merchant Shipping Act of
1894 and, more particularly, with provisions specifically extended to the
colonies. In view of the Colonial Laws Validity Act of 1865[143] which provided that no colonial legislature could pass an Act which was repugnant
to the provisions of an Imperial Act which had either expressly or by necessary implication been extended to the colonies, the Court pointed out that
'[s]ection 3 of Act 8 of [1879] can therefore only be operative in so far as
concerns an Imperial Act not expressly or by necessary implication extended
to the Cape Province. In so far as it went further and required re-enactment
of an Imperial Act expressed to apply to this Province it would have been
ultra vires'.[144]

However, the General Law Amendment Act was silent on English
statutes passed prior to 1879. It has been suggested that in view of the
expressio unius est exclusio alterius rule such Acts, in so far as they related
to 'substantive insurance law', were by implication incorporated by the Act
of 1879.[145] This view receives some support from *Malcher & Malcomess v.*

---

[137] I.e. from 1879 when the General Law Amendment Act was introduced until 1950 when
appeals to the Privy Council were abolished by the Privy Council Appeals Act 16 of 1950.
Thus, the Privy Council decision in the *Namaqua Mining* case in 1861 (above, n. 40) was not
binding authority in terms of the Act of 1879.
[138] 57 & 58 Vict. c. 60.   [139] 6 Edw. VII, c. 41.   [140] 9 Edw. VII, c. 12.
[141] In Ceylon the Marine Insurance Act of 1906 was expressly made applicable: see e.g.
Chatoor v. General Assurance Soc Ltd (1958) 60 New LR 169 (DC Colombo).
[142] 1949 (4) SA 207 (C).   [143] 28 & 29 Vict. c. 63.
[144] 210. The effect of this decision was not, as has been suggested by Theodorus E.
Scheepers, *Die Romeins-Hollandse Seeversekeringsreg tot en met 1809* (unpublished LL B dissertation, University of the Orange Free State, 1976), 7, that the Marine Insurance Act of 1906
applied in parts of South Africa.
[145] See e.g. Gordon/Getz (n. 86), 2. *Wetzlar v. General Insurance Co* (1884) 3 SC 86, a case
in which the application of the English law (including English statutes) relating to statutory
declarations in the case of claims on fire insurance policies was considered and in which
De Villiers CJ stated (88): 'it is true that Act 8 of 1879 incorporates the English law of insurance into the law of this Colony, but it certainly does not incorporate the law to statutory

Kingwilliamstown Fire & Marine Insurance & Trust Co[146] where Buchanan
J, in connection with speculative policies of insurance, referred to the existence of 'express legislation on the subject, the Act 14, Geo. III, c. 48, commonly called the Gambling Act, having been passed to prevent wagering
policies'.[147] Although never arising in any reported insurance decision, a
number of pre-1879 English statutes still in force in 1879 may therefore have
been applicable in parts of South Africa, in many cases long after their subsequent repeal in England itself.[148] To what extent these Acts related to
'substantive insurance law' or to matters peculiar to insurance, however, is
now a matter for conjecture and merely of academic interest.[149]

V. FURTHER DEVELOPMENT OF THE ANGLO-SOUTH AFRICAN INSURANCE LAW

In Natal the Roman-Dutch law as accepted and administered by the Cape
courts had been received.[150] Oddly enough, however, the Cape example of
incorporating English insurance law was never emulated, in spite of agitation
by the local business community for the abolition of Roman-Dutch law and
the introduction of English law in mercantile matters.[151] In the Transvaal,
too, Roman-Dutch law was preserved after the British occupation.[152] Unlike
in the Orange Free State, the Cape Act of 1879 was never taken over.[153]

declarations' provides no authority to the contrary as the case concerned procedural matters
(in respect of which s. 4 of the Act expressly preserved the local law; see above, n. 75) and not
matters of insurance.

[146] (1883) 3 EDC 271.   [147] 285.

[148] E.g. Marine Insurance Act of 1745 (19 Geo. III, c. 48); Life Assurance Act (or Gambling
Act as it is commonly referred to) of 1774 (14 Geo. III, c. 48); ss. 83, 86, Fire Prevention
(Metropolis) Act of 1774 (14 Geo. III, c. 78); Marine Insurance Act of 1788 (28 Geo. III, c.
56); s. 55, Merchant Shipping Act Amendment Act of 1862 (25 & 26 Vict., c. 63) (see
Gordon/Getz (n. 86), 383, fn. 23); ss. 4, 7, 8 Customs and Inland Revenue Act of 1867 (30 &
31 Vict., c. 23) (see Gordon/Getz (n. 86), 383, fn. 24, and 386, fn. 63); Policies of Assurance
Act of 1867 (30 & 31 Vict., c. 144); Policies of Marine Assurance Act of 1868 (31 & 32 Vict.,
c. 86); and Sea Insurance (Stamps Policies) Amendment Act of 1876 (39 Vict., c. 6).

[149] Gordon/Getz (n. 86), 92 sq. regard the Life Assurance (or Gambling) Act of 1774 as having been incorporated by the General Law Amendment Act of 1879, but not the Gaming Act
of 1845 (8 & 9 Vict., c. 109) (because the latter was not peculiar to insurance law). But see the
contrary views on the Life Assurance Act of 1774 (and the Marine Insurance Act of 1745)
of M. F. B. Reinecke, 'Versekering Sonder Versekerbare Belang?', (1971) 4 *CILSA* 193,
197–202; and *idem*, 'Die Rol van die *Life Assurance Act* van 1774 in die Suid-Afrikaanse
Versekeringsreg', 1977 *TSAR* 159.

[150] Under Ordinance for Establishing the Roman-Dutch Law in and for the District of
Natal, 12 of 1845 (Cape).

[151] See F. G. Richings, 'Some Aspects of the Influence of English Law in Natal During the
19th Century', 1973 *Natal University LR* 51, 53, who notes that '[a]s the merchant community
at the seaport of Durban expanded, so the rules of Roman-Dutch law in commercial matters
were found increasingly irksome and objections against its continued use began to be heard'.

[152] See s. 17, Administration of Justice Proclamation, 14 of 1902 (Transvaal).

[153] Thus, the Roman-Dutch law of insurance as set out e.g. in M. Josson, *Schets van het
Recht van de Zuid-Afrikaansche Republiek* (1897), 339–52, mainly with reference to Van der
Linden's *Rechtsgeleerd Practicaal en Koopmans Handboek*, continued to apply.

Although insurance law in Natal and in the Transvaal escaped the formal introduction of English law, it nevertheless enjoyed considerable informal influence.[154] For reasons largely similar to those which had encouraged the advancement of English insurance law at the Cape, but also because of the existence of a growing body of precedents from the Cape courts in insurance matters, the Natal and Transvaal courts never seriously considered the application and development of the relevant Roman-Dutch principles in insurance cases. From early on English precedents were generally accorded high persuasive authority. The judicial approach in insurance disputes in these two provinces may be illustrated by reference to a few of the insurance cases reported in the early years.

The decision in *Spencer v. London & Lancashire Insurance Co*[155] is exceptional in that the judgment of Connor CJ[156] provides an excellent example of the approach which the Natal and Transvaal courts could have, but did not in fact choose to follow in insurance cases.[157] In a claim on a fire insurance policy questions of interpretation and the issue of misrepresentation had to be considered. Concerning the interpretation of the insurance contract, his Lordship referred to a number of civilian sources (including Peckius, Grotius, Van Bynkershoek, Van der Linden, Averanius, and Pothier) and remarked *obiter* that '[t]he words in these conditions are those of the Insurance Company . . . and it is a settled rule of construction, in our, as in other systems of law, that in written contracts, as to what is doubtful, words are to be construed strictly against the party using them, because he ought to have expressed himself more clearly'.[158] Proceeding to the issue of misrepresentation, the Chief Justice declared that he preferred to base his judgment 'upon what appears to me to be *our law of insurance*',[159] and made reference to Grotius, Van Bynkershoek, Van der Keessel, Pothier, and Santerna. Then, in order to justify his subsequent reference to English authority[160] including 'the leading English case of *Carter v. Boehm*' he noted that '[t]he law of insurance is part of the general mercantile law, and therefore, presumably, the principles of it in civilized countries correspond'.[161]

---

[154] See, in general, Gordon/Getz (n. 86), 4 sq., 380 sq.; Hahlo/Kahn (n. 10), 717.
[155] (1884) 5 NLR 37.
[156] On Sir Henry Connor, a noted expert on Roman-Dutch law, see Roberts (n. 23), 354.
[157] Other early Natal decisions of note include: *Defiance Co v. Foster* 1871 NLR 94 and *In re the ship 'Defiance'* 1871 NLR 60 and 199, where, in addition to English authorities, reference was also made to Grotius, Vinnius, Van der Linden, the French *Code civil*, the maritime law of Amsterdam, and the *placaat* of Philip II; and *Storm v. Gilmore* (1895) 16 NLR 39, where, in deciding a claim for the reimbursement of an amount deposited in general average, Cape decisions were held not to be authoritative in Natal on account of the Act of 1879.
[158] 40.   [159] 42 (italics added).
[160] See e.g. M. Nathan, *The Common Law of South Africa*, vol. III (1906), 1324; *contra* Gordon/Getz (n. 86), 4, who state that the Court 'then applied English law'.
[161] 43.

Finally, '[t]o come nearer to our own law',[162] Connor CJ also referred to the *Code Napoleon*.

In *Kantor Bros v. Transatlantic Fire Assurance Co*[163] De Korte J, after distinguishing the Cape case of *Davies v. South British Insurance Co*,[164] nevertheless remarked: 'I quite agree with the decision in that case . . . and with what was said by the very learned Chief Justice, who delivered the judgment of the Court, with regard to the principles of the Roman-Dutch Law and the English Law on the subject of the binding force of an arbitration clause in a policy of insurance'.[165] His Lordship then quoted at length from an English decision, stating: 'I entirely accept this statement of law'.[166] In *Ehrig & Weyer v. Transatlantic Fire Insurance Co*[167] Innes CJ had to determine the correctness of an answer on a proposal form for fire insurance. He referred to and applied a decision of the Privy Council in an appeal from Australia, declaring that 'a decision by the Privy Council upon a matter not of English as distinct from Roman-Dutch law, but of legal construction . . . is binding upon this Court . . . In this instance it leads to an equitable result; but we would be bound by it even if it did not'.[168] In *Littlejohn v. Norwich Union Fire Insurance Society*, a case concerning insurable interest,[169] Wessels J ('who often urged that the purity of the Roman-Dutch inheritance should be preserved'[170]) remarked: '[o]ur Roman-Dutch law books, as far as I can see, throw but little light upon the subject, and therefore we must have recourse to English and American decisions'.[171] Coming from such an authority on and champion of the (Roman-Dutch) common law, this passage subsequently gained wide acceptance as virtually indisputable proof of the fact that Roman-Dutch law no longer had any relevance for the development of insurance law in South Africa.[172]

Subsequent Natal and Transvaal insurance decisions demonstrate an almost consistent application of English authority in the absence of any

---

[162] 44 (italics added).

[163] (1892) 4 SAR 185.

[164] (1885) 3 SC 416; see above, n. 94.

[165] 188 sq.

[166] 190.

[167] 1905 TS 557.

[168] 560 sq.; see also Curlewis J, 562. In the Court *a quo* (1905 TH 117, 122) Wessels J decided the issue on another ground. He referred to, but distinguished, English decisions '[w]ithout expressing any opinion as to whether those decisions are sound as regards our system of jurisprudence'.

[169] 1905 TH 374.

[170] See Hahlo/Kahn (n. 11), 586. On Sir Johannes Wilhelmus Wessels and his interest in and support of Roman-Dutch law see Roberts (n. 23), 382 sq.; cf. Kahn (n. 64), 337 sqq.

[171] 378. That the Roman-Dutch sources proved of little assistance is not surprising, for one would not expect them to provide much guidance, if any, on a legal doctrine which crystallized only in the course of the 19th C. and which acquired a particularly English flavour.

[172] Wessels subsequently argued the need for the codification of Roman-Dutch law (see J. W. Wessels, 'The Future of Roman-Dutch Law in South Africa', (1920) 37 *SALJ* 265) and suggested (283) that '[w]here we have abandoned the old Dutch law and sought refuge in statutes founded on English law, as in our . . . insurance laws . . . we will revise these Acts and state them in the form of a code and in the simple language which modern codes adopt'.

local precedents. In one respect the approach of the Transvaal courts to insurance disputes differed during the early years from that of the Cape and Free State courts. Due to the absence of any formal importation of English insurance law as binding authority in insurance matters, the Transvaal courts chose to follow a more 'liberal comparative approach',[173] referring particularly frequently to American authority. Thus, in *Littlejohn v. Norwich Union Fire Insurance Society*[174] the Court relied on American cases in addition to English authorities on the question of insurable interest. Concerning the issue of interpretation of the insurance contract, too, the Court was referred to an American case which occasioned the following remark by Wessels J:

This Court is not bound by the decision, for the decision is one of the Supreme Court of Pennsylvania .... I admit that I had grave doubts whether this view was correct, ... but as this very clause in a policy has received judicial interpretation in an American court of high authority I should feel great diffidence in taking another view. The American courts have had a great experience in insurance cases, and even English text-book writers on insurance of wide reputation ... are constantly citing American cases with approval .... No other case has been quoted to me expressing a different view either from the South African courts, the English courts or indeed from any other court. I feel therefore constrained sitting here as a single judge to adopt the view of the Supreme Court of Pennsylvania.[175]

The Appellate Division generally favoured the application of English law in insurance matters.[176] There is little to suggest that it treated insurance disputes arising in Natal and in the Transvaal any differently from those originating in the Cape or Orange Free State. Thus, in *Fine v. General Accident, Fire & Life Assurance Corp Ltd*[177] the Court regarded a clause in an

---

[173] See Gordon/Getz (n. 86), 5, fn. 55. See, in general, Peter Spiller, 'The Role of American Authorities in the Early Development of South African Law', (1985) 18 *CILSA* 106. The approach in the Cape and Free State is illustrated by the remarks of McGregor J in *London & Scottish Assurance Corp Ltd v. Venter* 1923 OPD 209, 213: '[T]wo Scottish decisions (and perhaps, by reference, one or two American decisions) were referred to as authoritative; but while these would be heard with respect they would not under the circumstances govern in so far as they ran counter to English law. In so far as this might not be the case, they must needs be of high instructive value and might prove materially helpful.'

[174] 1905 TH 374.

[175] 385 sq. See too e.g. *Sacks v. Western Assurance Co* 1907 TH 257, 260, where Wessels J noted: 'I have not been referred to any English cases, and have myself had no time to investigate the English reports. I can find none in the ordinary English text-books. In America, however, a country very fruitful in insurance decisions, there are a large number'. In *Nafte v. Atlas Assurance Co* 1924 WLD 239 the Court referred to a number of Canadian and Scottish decisions and an Irish decision in addition to English cases on the question of indemnity and ascertaining the real or actual value of insured goods.

[176] On general issues, however, Roman-Dutch law was still applied: see e.g. *National Bank of South Africa Ltd v. Cohen's Trustee* 1911 AD 235, 247, where De Villiers CJ, in dealing with the effect of the cession of a life policy *in securitatem debiti*, explained: 'I have not referred to the English law bearing upon the subject, because the principles guiding the English Courts in cases like the present are somewhat different from those of our law.'

[177] 1915 AD 213, on appeal from the WLD.

insurance policy, according to which the insurer's liability in the event of any omission to disclose material facts was excluded, as being for all practical purposes 'merely a statement of the common law on this subject' and referred to English cases explaining the 'well-settled law that insurance policies are contracts *uberrimae fidei*'.[178] *Scottish Union & National Insurance Co Ltd v. Native Recruiting Corp Ltd*[179] finally brought the Transvaal, and with it Natal, into line with the rest of South Africa. The Court *a quo* had accepted American rather than English authority in a case concerning the interpretation of insurance contracts. In a brief concurring judgment Beyers JA sealed the fate of the 'liberal comparative approach'[180] in the Transvaal with the following words:

In die Kaapprovinsie en die Oranje Vrystaat word die Engelse reg op versekering toegepas, en, ek meen, ook in Natal. Waar ons dus twee rigtinge het in die beslissinge van die Amerikaanse howe en die Engelse howe, lê dit voor die hand dat eenvormigheidshalwe ons vir die Transvaal Provinsie die Engelse rigting behoort te volg.[181]

Thus, for all practical purposes English law had permeated the insurance law throughout South Africa. Apart from a few isolated instances[182] no serious attempts were made to refer to or to apply the relevant principles of Roman-Dutch law in insurance disputes.[183] In spite of the formal difference in the various provinces as to the sources of insurance law, a uniform system of insurance law had emerged and was in the process of further development in South Africa. It may be characterized as a hybrid Anglo-South African insurance law.

---

[178] 218 sq.   [179] 1934 AD 458, on appeal from the WLD.

[180] It is submitted, however, that the decision did not abolish the Roman-Dutch insurance law as the common law of the Transvaal and Natal, as is suggested by L. Roeleveld, *Suid-Afrikaanse Lewensversekeringsreg* (1982), 21, fn. 5.

[181] (In the Cape Province and the Orange Free State the English law of insurance is applied and also, I think, in Natal. Where we therefore have two directions in the decisions of the American courts and the English courts, it is obvious that for the sake of uniformity we have to follow the English direction for the Province of Transvaal). 469. See, too, De Villiers JA, 472. Cf. J. P. van Niekerk, 'The Reform of South African Insurance Law: A Preliminary Inquiry', (1983) 5 *Modern Business Law* 88, 93 sq.

[182] See e.g. *Iscor Pension Fund v. Marine & Trade Insurance Co Ltd* 1961 (1) SA 178 (T) 183 sq.; cf. *Trans-Africa Credit & Saving Bank Ltd v. Union Guarantee & Insurance Co Ltd* 1963 (2) SA 92 (C) 98), where extensive reference was made to Troplong on the difference between guarantee, or suretyship, and insurance; *Lake v. Reinsurance Corp* 1967 (3) SA 124 (W) 127 sq., where reference was made to Roman-Dutch authority on the question of the formation of an insurance contract; *Sydmore Engineering Works Ltd v. Fidelity Guards Ltd* 1972 (1) SA 478 (W) 480, where Grotius's definition of insurance was referred to.

[183] Counsel usually did little to assist the courts in this regard: see e.g. the argument advanced in *Bodemer v. American Insurance Co* 1961 (2) SA 662 (A) 664.

VI. THE REPEAL OF THE GENERAL LAW AMENDMENT ACT IN 1977

In the law of contract in general, and with regard to certain specific contracts such as sale, loan, lease, and suretyship, the English influence on South African law has been relatively weak. In contrast, the effect of English law on mercantile law in general and on contracts customarily treated as mercantile contracts, such as those relating to insurance, carriage, shipping, and negotiable instruments, was far more substantial.[184] The distinction between so-called mercantile contracts and other specific contracts is, like the distinction between mercantile law and private law in general, not clear-cut.[185] For instance, the development of the modern insurance contract is historically closely linked to the contracts of loan and sale. Nevertheless, the English influence on mercantile law in general, and on the law of insurance in particular, has for a long time been regarded as natural, beneficial, and irreversible, even by those strongly supportive of the Roman-Dutch heritage.[186] The relevant principles of Roman-Dutch law have been thought to be insufficient, underdeveloped, and not adaptable to new situations, while attention has also been drawn to the fact that English mercantile law, deriving from the continental *ius mercatorum*, cannot merely be regarded as a branch of the English common law.[187]

More recently, however, the reception of English insurance law, and in particular the method of its introduction into South African law, has evoked some adverse comment. Ellison Kahn, in an article on the binding authority conferred upon English decisions by the General Law Amendment Act, noted that:

[t]he prospect of even our Appellate Division being bound by decisions of English courts is not a happy one. Fortunately, there seems a simple remedy. Neither the Transvaal nor the Natal courts have found the absence of the Cape and Free State legislation irksome. Where necessary they have used English case-law as persuasive authority. It is suggested, therefore, that the legislation be repealed. The common

---

[184] See in general e.g. Hahlo/Kahn (n. 10), 42 sq.; Hahlo/Kahn (n. 11), 578; Zajtay/Hosten, (1969) 2 *CILSA* 194 sq.; Beinart, 1981 *Acta Juridica* 46.

[185] See e.g. Hahlo/Kahn (n. 11), 123, 126. Kahn, (1985) 1 *Lesotho LJ* 81, noting the minimal English influence in certain areas of South African law, mentions the specific contracts, 'in particular sale and lease; but particularly not insurance, where Roman-Dutch law was very undeveloped, and recourse has always been had to Anglo-American law'.

[186] See e.g. Bodenstein, (1915) 32 *SALJ* 352 sq.; A. A. Roberts, 'Handhaaf die Gemenereg', (1938) 2 *THRHR* 202, 210; D. F. Mostert, *Die Romeins-Hollandse Reg in Oënskou* (1969), 10 sq.

[187] See e.g. T. B. Smith, 'The Common Law Cuckoo: Problems of "Mixed" Legal Systems with Special Reference to Restrictive Interpretations in the Scots Law of Obligations', (1956) 3 *Butterworth's South African LR* 147, 152; Hahlo/Kahn (n. 11), 576; Kahn, (1985) 1 *Lesotho LJ* 76.

law—such as it is—will then be the same in the Cape and Free State as in the Transvaal and Natal.[188]

Brian Bamford regarded the introduction of English law as having been unnecessary because of the high development of Roman-Dutch shipping law in general[189] and suggested that a strong case could be made out for the repeal of the General Law Amendment Act.[190] Elsewhere, referring to the anomalies and problems created by this Act, he noted the absence of any agitation for its repeal and of any consideration by the authorities as to how to remedy the unhealthy state of affairs.[191]

In 1977, presumably as a result of representations to the South African Law Commission, the General Law Amendment Act, 8 of 1879 (Cape), and the General Law Amendment Ordinance, 5 of 1902 (Orange Free State), 'were (at last) repealed'[192] by the Pre-Union Statute Law Revision Act, 43 of 1977.[193]

This repeal was generally regarded as of little practical significance. Although it was stated that the Act of 1977 achieved uniformity of insurance law throughout South Africa[194] it is submitted that for all practical purposes such uniformity had already been attained as a result of judicial activity. The Act merely effected the formal removal of the existing difference concerning the sources of insurance law in the various provinces. Even though it was recognized that theoretically[195] and in principle[196] Roman-Dutch law was again the common-law source of insurance in South Africa, it was not thought that the Act would have any tangible effect in practice upon South African insurance law or its future development.[197] English law, though no longer binding authority in the Cape and Free State after 1977,

---

[188] See Kahn (1965) 82 *SALJ* 527. See, too, Wessels' calls for revision of these Acts, referred to in n. 172, above.

[189] See above n. 72; cf. e.g. Scheepers (n. 107), 2.

[190] See B. R. Bamford, *The Law of Shipping and Carriage in South Africa* (2nd edn., 1973), 2.

[191] See Bamford, 1975 *Lloyd's Maritime & Commercial LQ* 172.

[192] Bamford (n. 72), 4, fn. 27, who also argued that s. 1, Act of 1879 may by implication have been repealed by the Admiralty Jurisdiction Regulation Act 5 of 1972 (which, however, never came into force).

[193] Section 1 of this Act provides that '[t]he laws specified in the Schedule are hereby repealed to the extent set out in the third column of the Schedule'. The Schedule to the Act contains references to the Cape Act and Free State Ordinance, the unrepealed sections of which are indicated to be repealed by the Act.

[194] See e.g. Lionel H. Hodes, 1977 *Annual Survey of South African Law* 338, 339; Gordon/Getz (n. 86), 5, 381.

[195] See Dillon/Van Niekerk (n. 60), 107.   [196] See Gordon/Getz (n. 86), 5.

[197] Various reasons were advanced in this regard: the extensive influence English law had already had on our law; the inadequacy of the Roman-Dutch insurance law; the common origin of English and Roman-Dutch insurance law; the fact that existing differences between the 2 systems may be of form rather than of substance; and the influence of English insurance practices and usages in South Africa. See e.g. Dillon/Van Niekerk (n. 60), 112; Gordon/Getz (n. 86), 5.

would continue to enjoy considerable persuasive authority[198] and would also, from a comparative point of view, provide the most important insurance system.[199] These conclusions were generally supported by the cases on insurance law reported after the introduction of the Act of 1977.[200] In view of the fact that the Act did not operate retrospectively it was assumed that the principles already taken over from English law by the Cape and Free State courts before 1977 would still bind[201] and that existing local precedents would in future constitute an increasingly important source of South African insurance law. A conscious return to the sources of Roman-Dutch insurance law was regarded as either unlikely, or at least not immediately viable in view of the lack of comprehensive research into these sources.[202] One commentator, however, suggested that the local precedents based on English law could no longer be regarded as binding authority.[203]

VII. THE ADMIRALTY JURISDICTION REGULATION ACT OF 1983

An investigation by the South African Law Commission into the possible reform of admiralty law in South Africa resulted in the Admiralty Jurisdiction Regulation Act, 105 of 1983, being passed.[204] The basis of the reforms suggested by the Law Commission and introduced by the Act was the existing admiralty law, based upon English maritime law. However, various claims not previously included within the admiralty jurisdiction of South African courts, such as claims relating to marine insurance, general average, and charterparties, were included in the courts' extended admiralty jurisdiction. Now 'with regard to the extensions of the jurisdiction the basis

---

[198] See e.g. Gordon/Getz (n. 86), 381; Reinecke, 1977 *TSAR* 164.

[199] See Dillon/Van Niekerk (n. 60), 114.

[200] Thus, in *Zahn Investments v. General Accident Insurance Co* 1981 (4) SA 143 (SEC) 148, English law was recognized as being of 'great persuasive authority'; in *Blackshaws Ltd v. Constantia Insurance Ltd* 1983 (1) SA 120 (A) 126, the Court, being referred to English cases in the absence of South African authority, pointed out: '[a]lthough these decisions are not of binding force on this Court, they are certainly entitled to respect and are of persuasive authority, for there does not appear to be any fundamental difference in the principles of construction of a policy of insurance between our law and the English law . . . The degree of authority any such case possesses would naturally depend upon the quality of the Judge's reasoning and the status of the Court in question.'

[201] Dillon/Van Niekerk (n. 60), 107.

[202] Ibid. 109.

[203] See Roeleveld (n. 180), 22, who was criticized on this point (wrongly, as appeared from subsequent developments) by the present author in (1985) 48 *THRHR* 373, 374.

[204] For further background see generally, e.g. Dillon/Van Niekerk (n. 60), 3–34; H. Booysen, 'South Africa's New Admiralty Act: A Maritime Disaster?', (1984) 6 *Modern Business Law* 75; Alan Rycroft, 'Changes in South African Admiralty Jurisdiction', 1984 *Lloyd's Maritime & Commercial LQ* 417; Hilton Staniland, 'The Implementation of the Admiralty Jurisdiction Regulation Act in South Africa', 1985 *Lloyd's Maritime & Commercial LQ* 462; D. J. Shaw, *Admiralty Jurisdiction and Practice in South Africa* (1987).

[was] again the existing system of law, that is the Roman-Dutch law'.[205] Section 6(1) of the Act provides as follows:

Notwithstanding anything to the contrary in any law or the common law a court in the exercise of its admiralty jurisdiction shall-
(a) with regard to any matter in respect of which a court of admiralty of the Republic referred to in the Colonial Courts of Admiralty Act, 1890, of the United Kingdom, had jurisdiction immediately before the commencement of this Act, apply the law which the High Court of Justice of the United Kingdom in the exercise of its admiralty jurisdiction would have applied with respect to such matter at such commencement, in so far as that law can be applied;
(b) with regard to any other matter, apply the Roman-Dutch law applicable in the Republic.

Whether English law or Roman-Dutch law is to be applied to claims on marine insurance contracts in terms of section 6(1) depends upon whether marine insurance claims were previously within the admiralty jurisdiction of South African courts. That, in turn, depends upon whether the matter was within the jurisdiction of the English Admiralty Court in 1890. It has generally been accepted that marine insurance claims are not a matter previously within that admiralty jurisdiction.[206] Accordingly, in terms of section 6(1)(b), 'the Roman-Dutch law applicable in the Republic' applies to such claims.

Although statutory recognition was now for the first time given to the application of Roman-Dutch law in the context of (marine) insurance, the precise meaning of section 6(1) was (and still is) uncertain in numerous respects.[207] In terms of subsection (b) Roman-Dutch law is to be applied '[n]otwithstanding anything to the contrary in any law or the common law', and this appears to suggest[208] that Roman-Dutch law must be applied in preference, for example, to those rules of English law already taken over by South African courts as a result of the legislative measures discussed above. The phrase 'Roman-Dutch law as applicable', as opposed to 'Roman-Dutch law as applied', seems to indicate that in marine insurance cases South African courts are required to turn to the old sources and to apply and, where necessary, adapt the principles of Roman-Dutch insurance law.[209]

---

[205] Bamford (n. 72), 195, fn. 1 refers to this arrangement as 'an ingenious compromise between the pro-Admiralty and pro-Roman-Dutch lobbies'.

[206] See J. P. van Niekerk, 'Marine Insurance Claims in the Admiralty Court: An Historical Conspectus', (1994) 6 *South African Mercantile LJ* 26 where this aspect is canvassed in further detail. For a contrary view see Hilton Staniland, 'What Is the Law to be Applied to a Contract of Marine Insurance in Terms of Section 6(1) of the Admiralty Jurisdiction Regulation Act 105 of 1983?', (1994) 6 *South African Mercantile LJ* 16.

[207] See the questions raised by Van Niekerk (n. 206), 29, fn. 18.

[208] Although not clearly so, for the signed Afrikaans version of the Act reads '[o]ndanks *andersluidende bepalings van die een of ander wet of die gemene reg*'.

[209] But again this view is not confirmed by the signed Afrikaans version of the Act which merely refers to '*die Romeins-Hollandse reg . . . soos dit in die Republiek geld*' (the Roman-Dutch law . . . as it applies in the Republic).

Further problems may yet be encountered with section 6(5) which states that the provisions of subsection (1) are not to 'supersede any agreement relating to the system of law to be applied in the event of any dispute'. Although a choice of foreign (English) law clause in a local marine insurance policy will therefore be valid, it may, in the light of the insured party's unilateral right to exclude a choice of law as provided for in section 63(1) of the Insurance Act, 27 of 1943, not invariably result in English law being applied by a South African court.[210]

Thus, by compelling the courts to apply Roman-Dutch law, the Admiralty Jurisdiction Regulation Act created an important distinction as far as the sources of the law of marine insurance compared with those for insurance law generally were concerned.[211]

In 1984 the first decision in a marine insurance action under the Admiralty Jurisdiction Regulation Act was reported. *Shooter t/a Shooter's Fisheries v. Incorporated General Insurances Ltd*[212] dealt with the confiscation of an insured fishing vessel, the *Morning Star*, by the Mozambican authorities and the consequent claim by her owners on hull and war-risk policies which were identical in form to those in general use in England. The Court noted that the claim was a maritime claim in the terms of the Act and that, since the Court did not have admiralty jurisdiction in respect of such a claim prior to 1983, the action was by section 6(1)(b) to be decided 'by means of the application of the principles of Roman-Dutch law'.[213]

One of the issues arising for decision was whether the loss in this case was covered by the words 'arrests restraints and detainment of all kings princes and people of what nation condition or quality soever'. This involved the interpretation of the policies in question. They were in the form of the well known Lloyd's 'SG policy' which has often been interpreted (but is now abolished). The Court was referred to one of the rules of construction contained in the First Schedule to the British Marine Insurance Act, 1906. Friedman J commented:

The English Marine Insurance Act, of course, purports to codify the English law relating to marine insurance and most, if not all, of the rules of construction contained in the First Schedule to the Act are derived from earlier judicial decisions, interpreting the usual Lloyd's form of policy. An English Court is obliged by s 30(2) of the Act to give to the words and expressions in the First Schedule the meanings and expressions therein assigned to them unless the context otherwise indicates . . . I am, of course, under no such obligation although, quite obviously, any statements

---

[210] As to the effect of s. 63(1) see e.g. Dillon/Van Niekerk (n. 60), 109–11; J. P. van Niekerk, 'The Proper Law of a Marine Insurance Contract: The *Al Wahab* Case', (1984) *Modern Business Law* 87, 93.

[211] Legislation compelling the application in certain provinces of English law had simply been repealed. Thus, there no longer existed any statutory compulsion to apply any particular system of law in insurance matters coming before any South African courts.

[212] 1984 (4) SA 269 (D).   [213] 272I–273A; see too 285C.

in English judicial decisions relevant to the matter will be of great persuasive authority, more particularly as the words to be interpreted are of long and ancient English pedigree.[214]

After referring to an English case in which the specific rule of construction under consideration had its origin, the Court discussed and followed a subsequent English decision in which the words in question had been interpreted. Furthermore, the Court, with reference to *Blackshaws Ltd v. Constantia Insurance Ltd*,[215] reiterated the general principle that:

the rules governing different types of insurance policies are no different to the rules governing the interpretation of contracts in general, which in turn are no different to the rules governing the interpretation of written documents generally; in the absence of any particular trade or customary usage, words which are unambiguous must be given their ordinary grammatical meaning, and are to be understood in their plain and popular sense.[216]

Another question which arose in the *Shooter* case was whether any notice of abandonment of the insured vessel to the insurer was required at common law. The Court decided that, in view of the insurer's unequivocal repudiation of liability on the grounds of an alleged breach of contract,[217] such notice, even if required at common law, had become unnecessary; any such requirement had been waived by the insurer.[218] The views expressed on the common law requirement of a notice of abandonment may therefore be regarded as *obiter dicta*. Nevertheless, the approach of the Court in applying Roman-Dutch law is of sufficient interest and import to warrant some closer examination.

In attempting to apply 'the Roman-Dutch law applicable in the Republic', the Court unfortunately received little assistance from counsel who, in support of his allegation that a notice of abandonment by the insured was required under Roman-Dutch law, 'simply and solely' referred to the brief and superficial discussion in Gordon and Getz.[219] The latter

---

[214] 274I–275A.   [215] 1983 (1) SA 120 (A) 127 (see above, n. 200).

[216] 278G-H. It has been suggested that the question of interpretation in this case was not decided according to the accepted Roman-Dutch rule of construction, by which words must be given their grammatical meaning, but rather according to English law (see Alan Rycroft, 'The *Morning Star*: An Omen for the Law of Marine Insurance?', (1984) *South African Insurance LJ* 73, 74). It may be argued, though, that the words to be interpreted had by 'particular trade or customary usage' acquired a technical meaning which, in terms of the well recognized exception to the Roman-Dutch rule (see e.g. Gordon/Getz (n. 86), 244), would have excluded their ordinary grammatical meaning. The suggestion, furthermore, that by reason of the use of an English policy form a Court should regard English law as binding authority (see Rycroft, above, 75; Gordon/Getz (n. 86), 384) does not seem to be supported by the approach adopted by the Court. That English law was, at most, regarded as 'of great persuasive authority' is borne out also by the fact that Friedman J exercised a choice in following the English case in point when he stated that '[t]he reasoning . . . in the . . . case appeals to me as being correct' (276G).

[217] It was held that the term in question had in fact not been breached (279–82).

[218] 287.   [219] 285B and 286B of the report.

state[220] that under Roman-Dutch law an insured party, in order to claim for a total loss, had to abandon the subject-matter to the insurer by giving proper notice of abandonment.[221] For this proposition the authors rely on Van der Keessel and Van der Linden. Apart from these two writers, the Court referred to Grotius for the necessity to provide a notice of loss and a notice of abandonment, of which the latter had to be in writing and served upon the insurer by a messenger of the local chamber of maritime affairs; but the Court noted that the three authors in question relied on various Dutch municipal ordinances or *keuren*. Thus, the question arose 'whether or not the provisions of these ordinances can be said to be part of the "Roman-Dutch law applicable in the Republic" '. Friedman J answered this question as follows:

I do not propose to enter upon a detailed discussion of precisely what is embraced by the notion of Roman-Dutch law applicable in the Republic where one is concerned, not with the Roman common law received in the Netherlands, but with Dutch statutory law. There have been a number of learned treatises on the subject and not all of the conclusions reached are harmonious. What does, however, seem to be reasonably clear is that statutory requirements in the various provinces of Holland [sic] of a fiscal or purely local nature, whether passed before or after the year 1652, are not part of the law of the Republic . . . In my view, the requirements of the various ordinances . . . referred to above are, by their very nature, of local application only. I conclude therefore that these requirements are not part of the Roman-Dutch law applicable in the Republic.[222]

The extent to which Roman-Dutch statutory law forms part of modern South African law is moot.[223] It appears, in the first place, that post-1652 Dutch statutory provisions, or rather the principles introduced or modified by such measures, form part of our law in so far as they have been incorporated into South African common law by the institutional writers.[224]

---

[220] Gordon/Getz (n, 86), 406.

[221] The distinction in English law between a constructive total loss and an actual total loss was not recognized in Roman-Dutch law (see 285A of the report and further Gordon/Getz (n. 86), 406); the formal distinction between an act of abandonment—in the case of a constructive and an actual total loss—and notice of abandonment—only in the case of a constructive total loss—seems therefore to be of no significance in Roman-Dutch law. For a more detailed discussion of the Roman-Dutch law of abandonment, including the differences from English law, see J. P. van Niekerk, 'Marine Insurance', in: W. A. Joubert (ed.), *The Law of South Africa*, vol. 12 (1988), § 307; Christiaan Georg Marnewick, *A Critical Analysis of the Law to be Applied in Respect of a Maritime Claim for Marine Insurance, with Reference to Non disclosure and Abandonment, and the Need for Codification* (unpublished LL M dissertation, University of Natal, 1991), 152–212; Engela Catherina Schlemmer, *Verkryging van Eiendomsreg deur 'n Versekeraar in Geval van Diefstal van 'n Versekerde Saak* (unpublsihed LL M dissertation, Rand Afrikaans University, 1991), 43–55.

[222] 286C-E. It is, however, not clear whether the Court thought that the ordinances in question were, in their entirety, not part of South African law.

[223] See generally Hahlo/Kahn (n. 11), 572 sq.; Van Zyl (n. 8), 438–40.

[224] See e.g. *Estate Heinamann v. Heinamann* 1919 AD 99, 114; *R v. Harrison & Dryburgh* 1922 AD 320, 336. In *Spies v. Lombard* 1950 (3) SA 469 (A) 483, it was said that 'because

Secondly, a Dutch statute dating after 1652 which has not been so incorporated is part of South African law only if it has been promulgated in South Africa. However, statutes which are *ex facie* of universal application are presumed to have been promulgated in South Africa. Statutes *ex facie* of merely local application, or of a fiscal nature are presumed not to have been promulgated in South Africa.[225] Furthermore, the fact that part of a Dutch statute is of a local (or fiscal) nature is not sufficient to exclude its operation as regards other non-local (or non-fiscal) matters dealt with in that statute.[226] Finally, a statute 'has to be given the meaning it bore at the time of its promulgation' in the Netherlands.[227]

In view of these guidelines it is submitted that the principles contained in the various municipal insurance ordinances, or *keuren*, do form part of South African law in so far as they have been incorporated into Roman-Dutch law by the institutional writers. Since these ordinances, containing largely identical provisions, were usually merely local re-enactments of the provisions contained in the earlier insurance *placaaten* of Philip II of 1563 and 1570, if not even a statutory embodiment of the European *ius commune* on insurance matters,[228] it cannot be said that the general principles embodied in these statutes were of a merely local nature.[229] It is also submitted that, in the light of the guidelines just mentioned, a notice of abandonment is clearly required in terms of the Roman-Dutch law applicable in South Africa. It is equally obvious, as Friedman J recognized,[230] that not all of the particulars concerning such notice, as set out in the various ordinances (such as that the notice had to be given to the insurer through the local chamber of assurance or maritime board) can still be applied today. In this

Holland was more advanced than the other provinces and had more institutional law books, statutory rules which did not operate *proprio vigore* found ready reception in the body of our law *via* the writings of the jurists of Holland'.

[225] See e.g. *R v. Harrison & Dryburgh* (n. 224), 331, 333; *R v. Sacks* 1943 AD 413, 422 sq.

[226] See e.g. *Green v. Griffiths* (1886) 4 SC 346, 349; *Seaville v. Colley* (1891) 9 SC 39; *R v. Harrison & Dryburgh* (n. 224), 329; *Spies v. Lombard* (n. 224), 483 sq.

[227] See *Spies v. Lombard* (n. 224), 477.

[228] J. W. Wessels, *History of the Roman-Dutch Law* (1908), 229, referring to the statutory provisions made in the various seaport towns on marine insurance matters, notes that '[t]hese laws were constantly amended and amplified during the seventeenth and eighteenth centuries, and if we examine them we find that they contain all the fundamental principles of maritime insurance that are in vogue today in all the great commercial countries of Europe'. For further details on the Roman-Dutch statutory insurance law see J. P. van Niekerk, *An Introduction to and Some Perspectives on the Sources of Roman-Dutch Insurance Law With Appendices Containing the More Important Roman-Dutch Insurance Legislation* (1988), 31–63.

[229] They were in fact referred to and quoted in *De Pass v. Commercial Marine Assurance Co* (1857) 3 Searle 46 (n. 27), a case which ironically also concerned the issue of abandonment but which was overlooked by both counsel and the Court in the *Shooter* decision. There Watermeyer J had pointed out (60) that '[t]he Dutch doctrine of insurance is regulated by the *Placaat* of 1570, and by the Maritime Ordinances of Amsterdam, Rotterdam, and Middelburg'.

[230] 287A.

respect, the relevant provisions of the ordinances were merely of local application in that they were geared specifically to the conditions prevailing and the bodies existing in the various Dutch cities at that time, and are thus not part of South African law. The remaining requirement of a notice of abandonment to the insurer in writing[231] is by no means out of tune with modern practices and should accordingly still be taken to constitute modern South African law.[232]

The *Shooter* decision went on appeal.[233] Although counsel paid much more attention to the relevant principles of Roman-Dutch law than before, the Appellate Division chose to base its decision on an interpretation of the policies in question. In this regard Galgut AJA, for the majority, noted that Roman-Dutch law was applicable in terms of section 6(1)(b) of the Admiralty Jurisdiction Regulation Act, and that the interpretation of clauses in an insurance policy was, generally, a question of law: 'It follows that in interpreting the policies the law to be applied is the Roman-Dutch law but that English decisions as to the meaning of expressions used in the policy are of assistance and are persuasive authority.'[234]

In a minority judgment, Viljoen JA took a different point of view. He argued that by making use of a marine insurance policy in the form of the Lloyd's SG policy the parties by implication chose English law as the proper law of their contract. English law was therefore the binding, as opposed to the merely persuasive, authority with reference to which the policies in question had to be interpreted. Moreover Viljoen JA proceeded from the assumption that the marine contract involved concepts peculiar to itself and not governed by the general law of contract. The concepts mentioned in this regard included subrogation, suing and labouring clauses, and abandonment. This occasioned the following:

Subrogation is a well-known concept in South African law but the others . . . are completely foreign to our law and peculiar to English marine insurance law . . . If the other issues [that is, other than the interpretation of the policies] had to be resolved I fail to see how it could have been done without applying English marine insurance law as it has evolved around the type of Lloyd's policy concerned.[235]

These views call for a few brief comments. Suing and labouring, and abandonment, are not in fact foreign to South African law: both concepts were well developed in Roman-Dutch law and were discussed in great detail in the sources; furthermore, they are not confined in their application to

---

[231] An insurer can of course agree to accept oral notice of abandonment or, in appropriate cases, be held to have waived the requirement of written notice of abandonment.

[232] This is also the view of Gordon/Getz (n. 86), 411, fn. 322.

[233] See *Incorporated General Insurances Ltd v. Shooter t/a Shooter's Fisheries* 1987 (1) SA 842 (A). It may be noted that the appeal was heard after the Appellate Division had delivered judgment in the *Oudtshoorn Municipality* case (n. 241 below).

[234] 857E.

[235] 864H, 865I.

marine insurance but constitute particular applications of principles encountered also outside the field of insurance.[236] Ironically, however, subrogation (though peculiar neither to marine insurance nor even to insurance in general) is foreign to Roman-Dutch law, having been taken over from English law.[237] In principle, therefore, English marine insurance law is not the only system which may conceivably govern the law relating to these concepts. Furthermore, it is debatable whether the use of a form of policy similar to the Lloyd's SG policy can be said to amount to an implied choice of English law. Although of longstanding English use and interpretation,[238] it has become an international form of policy which merely happens to be drafted in the English language; there are probably as many non-English decisions interpreting phrases found in that policy as there are English decisions. In any event, the Lloyd's SG policy form has now been abolished and the link between the new policy forms and clauses and English (marine insurance) law has become even more tenuous.

The reintroduction of Roman-Dutch law in marine insurance matters, and the rather unsatisfactory beginnings of this process in the *Shooter* decision by the court *a quo*, was bound to evoke hostile comment. Rycroft[239] deplored the fact that marine insurance issues now had to be decided 'by an underdeveloped and uncertain system of law' and expressed the opinion that South African courts would largely avoid any systematic effort to rediscover Roman-Dutch law. He called for legislative intervention in order to extend the application of English law in terms of the Admiralty Jurisdiction Regulation Act to the new areas of admiralty jurisdiction, such as marine insurance; alternatively, he argued that the South African law of marine insurance law should be codified. Davis[240] wondered:

whether *Shooter's* case . . . is going to herald a mechanistic return to an idiosyncratic view of Roman-Dutch law in the area of marine insurance rather than giving s 6(1)(b) of the Admiralty Jurisdiction Regulation Act a broad interpretation so that the courts . . . can have recourse to a body of law which is more in tune with the demands of commercial practice than that of the scattered literature on the subject which is to be found in the old authorities.

[236] As to the former, see J. P. van Niekerk, 'Suing, Labouring and the Insured's Duty to Avert or Minimise Loss', (1987) 9 *Modern Business Law* 144; as to the latter see the sources referred to in n. 221 above.

[237] See further Johan Petrus van Niekerk, *Subrogasie in die Versekeringsreg* (unpublished LL M dissertation, University of South Africa, 1979), *passim*.

[238] But not of English origin: see Eiichi Kimura, 'Der Ursprung der Lloyd's Seeversicherungspolice', (1965) 3 *Hitotsubashi Journal of Commerce and Management* 27; *idem*, 'Die Entstehung der Lloyd's Seeversicherungspolice', (1972) 7 *Hitotsubashi Journal of Commerce and Management* 1.

[239] Rycroft, (1984) 8 *South African Insurance LJ* 78.

[240] D. M. Davis, '*Shooter* Revisited', (1984) 8 *South African Insurance LJ* 92, 95.

The answer to this query was soon provided by a majority of the Appellate Division in the case of *Mutual & Federal Insurance Co Ltd v. Oudtshoorn Municipality*.[241]

VIII. THE *OUDTSHOORN MUNICIPALITY* DECISION IN 1985

For present purposes the importance of the majority judgment delivered by Joubert JA[242] in *Oudtshoorn Municipality* lies in the fact that judicial consideration was for the first time given to the effect of the repeal of the General Law Amendmend Act in 1977 on the sources of South African insurance law.[243] The judgment provided some clarity, but also raised further questions as to the future role of Roman-Dutch and English insurance law in the development of South African law. In essence, the Appellate Division restored the Roman-Dutch insurance law to its full extent as the primary source of South African law. Not surprisingly, the judgment elicited a veritable flood of conflicting comment from which it appeared that the ageing purist–pragmatist debate was far from dead. Indeed, the potential effect of the *Oudtshoorn Municipality* decision upon insurance law in South Africa is enormous.

In the first place, it appeared from the general tenor of the majority judgment that any future development of South African insurance law would involve a conscious return to the Roman-Dutch sources of South African law. Referring to the repeal of the Cape General Law Amendment Act and its Free State counterpart, Joubert JA noted that English law was no longer binding authority in these two provinces and proceeded to declare that 'the South African law of insurance is governed mainly by Roman-Dutch law as our common law'.[244] Thus, in addition to the statutory basis for the application of Roman-Dutch law in marine insurance cases, the judgment provided judicial authority for its application in this field of insurance law in general. Some commentators, attributing antiquarian intentions to Joubert JA, have expressed their indignation at the idea that the judgment may herald a return to an outdated system of insurance law comprised of 'a motley assortment of seventeenth and eighteenth century texts'.[245] The response to these misgivings is that Roman-Dutch insurance law does not constitute the South African law of insurance; it merely provides its historical point of reference. Nobody would seriously suggest today that Roman-Dutch law provides ready-made answers to all insurance issues which may

---

[241] 1985 (1) SA 419 (A).

[242] Cillié JA, Viljoen JA, and Galgut JA concurring, although the latter is reported to have concurred also in the minority judgment delivered by Miller JA.

[243] No less important, although not relevant to this discussion, is the Court's actual decision on the issue of non-disclosure in the context of insurance contracts.

[244] 430G.   [245] See the editorial in (1984) 8 *South African Insurance LJ* 83.

arise in modern society. However, Roman-Dutch law constitutes the basis from which, by historical and comparative methods,[246] a viable system of South African insurance law may be developed. In some instances reference to the Roman-Dutch sources may provide acceptable solutions; in other cases the relevant Roman-Dutch principles may have to be adapted to suit present-day requirements.[247]

Secondly, if Roman-Dutch law is the primary source of South African insurance law, it follows that the principles of Roman-Dutch law in general, as applied in South Africa today, should also be brought to bear on insurance cases. By an 'examination of analogous material within the fabric of our own law',[248] insurance law can be developed as an integral part of private law in general, in the same way as the Dutch courts and jurists 'collectively succeeded in moulding the principles of marine insurance as an integral part of Roman-Dutch law'.[249] In particular it seems that the general principles of the South African law of contract and delict can fruitfully be employed so as to replace those rules of English law which have, under the guise of 'matters peculiar to insurance', been incorporated into local insurance law as if the latter constituted an isolated compartment without any connection to such general principles.

In the third place, it is significant that Joubert JA took pains to point out that both Roman-Dutch and English marine insurance law have their origin in the medieval *lex mercatorum*.[250] This argument has often been used in the past to justify the application of English law in preference to any proper investigation of Roman-Dutch law. By the same token, there can hardly be any objection to an application in insurance disputes of the Roman-Dutch principles of insurance law in preference to English sources.

Fourthly, in stating that '[t]he principles of the Roman-Dutch law of marine insurance are indeed capable of application, with adaptation if necessary, to other forms of insurance to meet the requirements of our modern society',[251] Joubert JA rejected the view, often expressed in the past in order to justify the application of English law in preference to Roman-Dutch law, that the Dutch jurists and legislators concerned themselves almost exclusively with marine insurance and that therefore the Roman-Dutch law of

---

[246] By these very methods the indigenous Dutch law had developed with reference to Roman law, even in the case of the insurance contract: see J. E. Scholtens, 'Early Roman-Dutch Law', 1979 *Acta Juridica* 74, 82.

[247] It should be borne in mind that Roman-Dutch law 'is a virile, living system of law, ever seeking, as every such system must, to adapt itself consistently with its inherent basic principles to deal effectively with the increasing complexities of modern organised society' (*per* Lord Tomlin in *Pearl Assurance Co v. Union Govt* 1934 AD 560 (PC) 563, [1934] AC 570 (PC) 579, also referred to by Joubert JA at 430D of the report). See further e.g. Zajtay/Hosten, (1969) 2 *CILSA* 200 sq.; Van Zyl (n. 8), 479 sq.

[248] *Per* Holmes JA in *Govt of RSA v. Ngubane* 1972 (2) SA 601 (A) 605 sq.

[249] Joubert JA, 430A.   [250] 427G, 428F, 430G, and 431D of the report.

[251] 430C.

insurance could not be of any assistance in non-marine insurance issues. It is obvious that the general principles of Roman-Dutch marine insurance are indeed capable of being applied in connection with other derivative forms of indemnity insurance. The Dutch themselves applied those principles to fire and land transit insurances in the eighteenth century. The trump card of those advocating recourse to English law was no doubt the question of life insurance (and other forms of 'non-indemnity' insurance), the more so because, in addition to statutory prohibitions on life insurance at the time,[252] there was uncertainty among the Roman-Dutch authors as to whether contracts of life insurance were legally valid according to Roman-Dutch common law. However, recent research has shown that traditional views on the position of life insurance in Roman-Dutch law may well have been mistaken, especially if seen against the broader background of European insurance practices of that time. In any event, neither the specific prohibitions nor the general uncertainty prevented the Dutch from developing a viable mutual life insurance industry.[253]

Fifthly, the majority decision in *Oudtshoorn Municipality* provided some useful guidance as to the sources of Roman-Dutch insurance law. It is clear from a passage of Johannes Voet's *Commentarius ad Pandectas*, quoted by Joubert JA,[254] that Dutch insurance statutes (such as the *placaaten* of 1563 and 1570 and the numerous subsequent municipal ordinances on insurance[255]) form part of the sources of Roman-Dutch law. Furthermore, the term 'Roman-Dutch law' was used in its liberal sense,[256] as being part and parcel of the European *ius commune*.[257]

In the sixth place it appeared that, in the light of the retrospective effect attributed to the repeal of the General Law Amendment Act, local

---

[252] 428I.

[253] See further Roeleveld (n. 180), 26–31; Peter Henry Havenga, *The Origins and Nature of the Life Insurance Contract in South African Law With Specific Reference to the Requirement of an Insurable Interest* (unpublished LL D thesis, University of South Africa, 1993), 31–61.

[254] 426I–427E. The passage was from Johannes Voet, *Commentarius ad Pandectas*, 22, 2, 3.

[255] 428H-I.

[256] See e.g. Van Zyl (n. 8), 7 sq., 265–89, 329 sq., 490–2, 498 sq. Although supported by the majority of commentators, this wide view has not yet gained a consistent acceptance by the courts: see further D. P. Visser, 'Daedalus in the Supreme Court: The Common Law Today', (1986) 49 *THRHR* 127, 135 sq. as to the uncertainty in this regard.

[257] Joubert JA remarked at 427F and I that '*Voet's* reference to the sources of the law of insurance in the Netherlands is by no means exhaustive. It is of great significance that he referred not only to the legislation of the Netherlands and France on marine insurance but also to the treatises of *Petrus de Santerna* and *Benevenutus Straccha* on the law of insurance . . . *Voet* . . . referred to these two treatises as sources of the Roman-Dutch law of insurance.' See generally Reinhard Zimmermann, 'Synthesis in South African Private Law: Civil Law, Common Law and *Usus Hodiernus Pandectarum*', (1986) 103 *SALJ* 259, 270 sq. where Joubert JA's approach in the *Oudtshoorn Municipality* case is characterized as 'very broadly based and *ius commune*-orientated'; cf. *idem*, '*Usus Hodiernus Pandectarum*', in: Reiner Schulze (ed.), *Europäische Rechts- und Verfassungsgeschichte* (1991), 61 sqq.

precedents will for the time being be of a somewhat diminished authority.[258] The restrictive influence of the doctrine of *stare decisis* on the development of a South African insurance law based upon general Roman-Dutch principles has virtually been eliminated by the *Oudtshoorn Municipality* judgment.[259]

In the seventh place, the *Oudtshoorn Municipality* decision highlighted the increasingly important role that a comparative approach will play in the development of a South African insurance law. Where Roman-Dutch law does not provide acceptable solutions to particular questions arising in insurance disputes, South African courts and insurance lawyers, like their Dutch predecessors, will of necessity have to employ comparative methods.[260] It is in this context that English law may well come into consideration again: no longer as a binding source but as comparative material which may or may not be found to provide persuasive solutions to individual problems.

Finally, the *Oudtshoorn Municipality* decision necessitated a reappraisal of the reform, possibly even codification of South African insurance law. Reform is urgently needed,[261] and the application of Roman-Dutch principles will certainly not obviate that need. However, before any reform can effectively be undertaken there must be clarity as to what it is which needs reform. It is submitted that the subject of reform should be the Roman-Dutch rather than the existing Anglo-South African insurance law.[262] In some instances the application of Roman-Dutch principles will eliminate or reduce, in others it may generate, the need to reform the Anglo-South African insurance law thusfar developed. A codification of the South African law of marine insurance, which has been proposed,[263] appears to

---

[258] At 435D Joubert JA pointed out that the judgment in *Colonial Industries Ltd v. Provincial Insurance Co Ltd* 1922 AD 33, insofar as it was based on English law, was no longer binding by virtue of the 1977 repeal. It could also be argued, of course, that because the issue involved in that case was not 'a matter peculiar to insurance', the reliance on English law in that case was in any event erroneous (see n. 75 above).

[259] D. M. Davis, 'The Roman Dutch Mist Over the Duty of Disclosure', (1985) 9 *South African Insurance LJ* 12, 15 sq. regarded this aspect of the judgment as the most disturbing because, in his view, 'much of our law is built upon an indigenous basis'. Even if 'indigenous basis' is taken to refer to local decisions *specifically*, and not to Roman-Dutch law in general, this statement is patently incorrect.

[260] See generally D. H. van Zyl, *Beginsels van Regsvergelyking* (1981), 14–16; Zimmermann, (1986) 103 *SALJ* 259 sqq. On the application of what is termed an open method in those cases where comparative materials have to be consulted because of the deficiency of Roman-Dutch insurance law, see Theo de Jager, *The Roots and Future of the South African Law of Marine Insurance*, Publications of the Institute of Marine Law, Number 18 (1993), 150–3.

[261] See Van Niekerk, (1983) 5 *Modern Business Law* 181.

[262] Attempts at reforming South African insurance law have so far been disappointing. See generally Coenraad Visser, 'Two Insurance Bills and Insurance Contract-Law: A Furtive Reconnaissance', (1991) 3 *South African Mercantile LJ* 19.

[263] See Marnewick (n. 221), 213–43. In both Roman-Dutch and English law marine insurance was and is exceptional for being largely contained in and regulated by statute. Codification is not therefore offensive to the Roman-Dutch approach to marine insurance.

raise similar issues. For, again, such codification would in the first instance have to draw on the Roman-Dutch sources of South African law rather than on the English law of marine insurance.[264]

IX. THE FUTURE OF ROMAN-DUTCH INSURANCE LAW IN SOUTH AFRICA

The revival of Roman-Dutch insurance law has occurred in three stages: the repeal of the General Law Amendment Act in 1977, the passing of the Admiralty Jurisdiction Regulation Act in 1983, and the decision of the Appellate Division in the *Oudtshoorn Municipality* case in 1985.

Thus far, however, this revival has remained on an academic level. Legal practice has not been greatly influenced by it. Counsel continue to take their arguments from, and the courts continue to base their decisions on English legal sources. In the case of *Trust Bank van Afrika Bpk v. President Versekeringsmaatskappy Bpk*[265] the need for a reappraisal appeared to have been recognized.[266] However, in *Videtsky v. Liberty Life Insurance Association of Africa Ltd*[267] Flemming J expressed a starkly contrasting view:

I believe that the law of insurance is a field in which there has been [a] large extent of reception of the English law. The belief does not rest upon my lack of enthusiasm for South Africa in splendid isolation wending its own way via a return to the rare and bare comments in the Netherlands, frequently found only in inaccessible sources, to the Netherlands of centuries ago, and doing so despite what practitioners have been doing here from day to day—where the living law is found—and despite this country's involvement with the outside world in areas of maritime insurance, export insurance, re-insurance etc. I will accordingly, as a starting point, take

---

[264] See also De Jager (n. 260), 159 who, while not of the opinion that codification is necessary, nevertheless agrees that if it is to occur then the open method (see n. 260) would have to be employed. The suggestion by Bamford, 1975 *Lloyd's Maritime & Commercial LQ* 1/2, of 'a local codification (which would obviously draw heavily on the [British] 1906 Act)' is therefore not acceptable. Nor is the Draft Proposal for a Marine Insurance Act in South Africa, submitted to the Maritime Law Association in 1988 (the proposal is reproduced in Marnewick (n. 221), App H): the Act proposed is for all intents and purposes the British Marine Insurance Act. The only significant change is the substitution of the words 'Roman-Dutch law as applied in the Republic' for the words 'common law including the law merchant' in s. 91(2). This section provides that, save insofar as they are inconsistent with the express provisions of the Act, the rules of the 'common law including the law merchant' are to continue to apply to contracts of marine insurance.

[265] 1988 (1) SA 546 (W).

[266] At 552 Van Zyl J, referring to the *Oudtshoorn Municipality* decision, spoke of the need for a new approach to long-established principles of insurance law and noted that this could occur, as in that decision, by a renewed investigation and evaluation of Roman-Dutch sources. Significantly, his Lordship also indicated that he did not understand the *Oudtshoorn Municipality* decision to reject English insurance law as one of the sources of South African law.

[267] 1990 (1) SA 386 (W).

at face value the proposition that English law on the subject is a good indication of what South African law is.[268]

His Lordship did not, of course, suggest that any South African court is bound by English insurance law. However, since it is 'a good indication of what South African law is', he appears to attribute very considerable persuasive authority to English law. Three comments are called for. In the first place, it is emphasized again that the Roman-Dutch law 'of centuries ago' does not constitute modern South African law. It is merely its primary source, or one of its primary sources. Secondly, the assumption may be questioned that a modern South African insurance law drawing primarily upon Roman-Dutch—as opposed to English—sources would find itself out of step with other insurance systems in the world. In spite of its Roman-Dutch foundation, neither South African contract law in general nor the law pertaining to specific contracts (such as sale, lease, and loan) are recognizably backward when compared to other legal systems. It is not apparent why this should be different in the case of insurance contracts, which after all are (or should be) governed by the same general principles of contract law. Thirdly, the mere fact that South African practitioners do not refer to the sources of Roman-Dutch law would appear to be of no consequence for insurance law, unless it is suggested that Roman-Dutch law has fallen into desuetude.

The place of Roman-Dutch insurance law would possibly have been secure today had its revival occurred some decades earlier. As things now stand its relevance in a contemporary South African law is precarious, its future uncertain.

[268] 390I—391B.

15: *Negotiable Instruments*

CHARL HUGO*

I. INTRODUCTION

There is no branch of South African law in which the influence of English law has been more marked than that dealing with negotiable instruments.[1]

This strong statement by Cowen and Gering may be an overstatement. However, it cannot be doubted that the development of the South African law of negotiable instruments from 1806 to the present day is largely dominated by the interaction of English and Roman-Dutch law, as well as the reaction to the problems caused by the coexistence of these two systems. The very term 'negotiable instrument' is, for instance, firmly rooted in English law[2] and it appears to be generally agreed that the term defies precise definition.[3] Although the concept was known earlier,[4] the term itself dates back only to the nineteenth century.[5] The following comprehensive and workable definition is also offered by Cowen and Gering:

* The financial assistance of the University of Stellenbosch and the research assistance of Elizabeth van Wyk are gratefully acknowledged.

[1] Denis Cowen, Leonard Gering, *The Law of Negotiable Instruments in South Africa*, vol. I (5th edn., 1985), 146.

[2] F. R. Malan, C. R. de Beer, *Bills of Exchange, Cheques and Promissory Notes in South African Law* (1983), § 8. The clearest statement in this regard that I could find in South African case-law is that of Connor J in *Escombe v. Henderson and Scott* 1872 NLR 124, 130: 'The term *negotiable instrument* does not . . . appear to me to be applicable to our law here'.

[3] Cowen/Gering (n. 1), 49–52; Leonard Gering, *Handbook on the Law of Negotiable Instruments* (1993), 6; Malan/De Beer (n. 2), §§ 8–10. See also *Impala Plastics (Pty) Ltd v. Coetzer* 1984 (2) SA 392 (W) 394: 'Attempts to define a "negotiable instrument" have generally all been unacceptable to the next critic'.

[4] See esp. Francois Retief Malan, *Die Reëlmatige Houer in die Wisselreg* (1975), 150–6. The role of Lord Mansfield, Chief Justice of England from 1756–88, is often emphasized in this regard. See Cowen/Gering (n. 1), 59, fn. 224. J. Milnes Holden, *The History of the Law of Negotiable Instruments in English Law* (1955), 113 describes his role as follows: '[T]he doctrine of negotiability . . . had been recognised by C. J. Holt in 1696. But it fell to Mansfield to explain the doctrine in language so well chosen that it normally forms the starting point in any exposition of the history of the subject at the present day.'

[5] See Cowen/Gering (n. 1), 59, fn. 224, who trace the term back to the decision in *Wookey v. Pole* (1820) 4 B & Ald 1. An early definition is that adopted by Blackburn J in the case *Crouch v. Credit Foncier of England Ltd* (1873) LR 8 QB 374, 381: 'It may therefore be laid down as a safe rule that where an instrument is by the custom of trade transferable, like cash, by delivery, and is also capable of being sued upon by the person holding it *pro tempore*, then it is entitled to the name of a *negotiable instrument*, and the property in it passes to a *bona fide* transferee for value, though the transfer may not have taken place in market overt.'

A negotiable instrument is a document of title embodying rights to the payment of money or the security for money, which, by custom or legislation, is (a) transferable by delivery (or by indorsement and delivery) in such a way that the holder *pro tempore* may sue on it in his own name and in his own right, and (b) a *bona fide* transferee *ex causa onerosa* may acquire a good and complete title to the document and the rights embodied therein, notwithstanding that his predecessor had a defective title or no title at all.[6]

This Chapter, however, focuses on a more restricted category of documents, namely bills of exchange (which include cheques) and promissory notes. This is indeed also the focus of all the major treatises[7] on the South African law of negotiable instruments,[8] for a number of good reasons. In the first place, bills of exchange and promissory notes are the most important and prevalent[9] negotiable instruments.[10] Secondly, these instruments, and only these instruments, are governed in South Africa by legislation based on the English Bills of Exchange Act of 1882.[11] As such they have a history of their own, closely associated with the adoption, interpretation, and development of this legislation in South Africa. The legislation concerned has undoubtedly been the main vehicle for the importation of English law. Negotiable instruments other than bills of exchange and promissory notes, not being governed by this legislation, have remained largely unaffected by English law.[12]

---

[6] Cowen/Gering (n. 1), 52.

[7] Malan/De Beer (n. 2); J. C. de Wet, A. H. van Wyk, *Die Suid-Afrikaanse Kontraktereg en Handelsreg* (4th edn., 1978), 744 sqq.; Denis Cowen, Leonard Gering, *The Law of Negotiable Instruments in South Africa* (4th edn., 1966); Gering (n. 3); Louise Tager, 'Negotiable Instruments', in: W. A. Joubert (ed.), *The Law of South Africa*, vol. 19 (1983).

[8] There is indeed a difference of opinion amongst South African commentators as to whether the English negotiable instrument concept is the proper theoretical framework in which the law of bills of exchange and promissory notes should be examined. This debate is, in a sense, a reflection of the dual heritage of South African law. Malan/De Beer (n. 2), §§ 6–8 and De Wet/Van Wyk (n. 7), 744 prefer regarding bills of exchange and promissory notes as species of the continental (predominantly German) *Wertpapier* and *Legitimationspapier* concepts and they de-emphasize the role of the English negotiable instrument. Cowen/Gering (n. 1), 71–111 and Gering (n. 3), 19–21, on the other hand, regard the German theory as being of little assistance and view bills of exchange and promissory notes as species of the English negotiable instrument.

[9] It is estimated that in South Africa more than 500 million cheques are issued annually (Robert Sharrock, Michael Kidd, *Understanding Cheque Law* (1992), 1).

[10] Other important negotiable instruments which do not fall under the Bills of Exchange Act 34 of 1964 are traveller's cheques and treasury bills. Traveller's cheques do not generally comply with the definition of a bill of exchange due to the fact that the order is not unconditional: see s. 2(1), Bills of Exchange Act and *S v. Katsikaris* 1980 (3) SA 580 (A). A treasury bill (the South African equivalent to the English exchequer bill) is clearly not a bill of exchange and is generally regarded as falling outside the provisions of the Bills of Exchange Act. See Cowen/Gering (n. 1), 258 sq. Treasury bills do, however, in many respects resemble promissory notes. In *Secfin Bank Ltd v. Mercantile Bank Ltd* 1993 (2) SA 34 (W) 37 this possibility was raised but not decided.

[11] 45 and 46 Vict c. 61.

[12] See *Kahn v. Volschenk* 1986 (3) SA 84 (A); *Secfin Bank Ltd v. Mercantile Bank Ltd* (n. 10).

Generally speaking, it is possible to discern three periods in the development of the South African law of bills of exchange and promissory notes. The first is that prior to the British occupation of the Cape Colony in 1806. During this period the Roman-Dutch *wisselrecht*, unaffected by English law, presumably applied. However, no reported decisions from this era exist and very little is known about it.

The second period starts with the British occupation in 1806 and ends with the introduction of bills of exchange legislation based on the English model, first in Natal in 1887,[13] then in the Cape in 1893,[14] and finally in the Transvaal[15] and Orange Free State[16] in 1902. During this period the Roman-Dutch law remained, in theory, the law of the land, but references to English case-law and textbooks were common.[17] English law was cited alongside Roman-Dutch law in a context in which it was assumed that there were no fundamental differences between the two systems. There is, of course, much truth in this point of view: the roots of both the Roman-Dutch and the English law of bills of exchange lie in the medieval *lex mercatoria*.[18]

The third period follows the introduction of the provincial legislation modelled on the English Bills of Exchange Act of 1882. The role of English law during this period was immense. Although the *wisselrecht* was not totally abolished by the legislation it has very little relevance today. The situation was expressed as follows by Curlewis JA in *Estate Liebenberg v. Standard Bank of South Africa Ltd*:

I cannot agree that we must regard the law merchant as to Bills of Exchange as having ceased to exist. Any provision of the law merchant which is inconsistent with the

---

[13] Bills of Exchange Law, Natal Law 8 of 1887.

[14] Bills of Exchange Act 19 of 1893 (Cape).

[15] Bills of Exchange Proclamation 11 of 1902 (Transvaal).

[16] Bills of Exchange Ordinance 28 of 1902 (Orange Free State).

[17] In this respect the evidence given by Sir John Truter before a commission of enquiry into the administration of justice in the Cape Colony in 1827 is instructive. The question was: 'Do you permit the practitioners to appeal to English authorities in their pleadings?' To this he answered as follows: 'They do appeal to those authorities, but we do not consider them as law except in some commercial cases. The Dutch Laws upon these subjects are rather antiquated, but it is considered by the commentators that reference may be made to the laws of other nations in deciding commercial questions. We are also influenced by the circumstance of the greatest part of the commercial questions that come before the court having arisen between English Merchants or out of transactions that have taken place in England.' See George McCall Theal, *Records of the Cape Colony*, vol. 33 (1905), 267. See further C. R. de Beer, 'Wisselreg aan die Kaap van 1807 tot 1826', (1993) 26 *De Jure* 308, 311–18 who discusses several unreported cases on bills of exchange before the *Raad van Justitie* during the period 1807–29. These include references to Chitty, Blackstone, and Comyns. See further for examples of English law being consulted in bills of exchange cases: *Caro v. Enslin and Zinn* (1860) 3 Searle 351; *Preuss and Seligmann v. Prins* (1864) 1 Roscoe 198; and *Mills and Sons v. Trustees of Benjamin Bros* (1876) 6 Buch 115.

[18] See the discussion below. The Roman-Dutch *wisselrecht* is sometimes referred to as the *law merchant*. See e.g. *Estate Liebenberg v. Standard Bank of SA Ltd* 1927 AD 502, 527.

provisions of the Statute must of course give way to the latter. The Statute embodies many of the provisions of the law merchant, but where the Statute is silent on a particular point and the law merchant can assist us, I do not think that we are debarred from resorting to the latter.[19]

However, the English Bills of Exchange Act of 1882, drafted by Sir MacKenzie Dalzell Chalmers, was 'an Act to codify the law relating to Bills of Exchange, Cheques, and Promissory Notes'.[20] As such it attempted to make reference to the common law superfluous, a task in which it largely succeeded.[21] As a consequence it stands to reason that in South Africa reference to the *wisselrecht* is seldom necessary.[22]

The influence of English law during this period was enhanced by the fact that not only was the English legislation itself imported but, to a large degree, also the interpretation applied to that legislation in the English courts. Thus we find the following remark in *Estate Wege v. Strauss*:

It may be stated as a general proposition that our courts would, as a general rule, follow the authoritative interpretation of a section in an English statute as laid down by the higher English courts if that section occurs in a Union statute which in all its essentials is the same as the English statute in which the section occurs.[23]

Two important legislative events occurred during this period. The Bills of Exchange Amendment Act 25 of 1943 brought about certain substantial changes to the legislation,[24] and then the provincial legislation was consolidated in the Bills of Exchange Act 34 of 1964.[25]

Finally, work was started in 1983, under the auspices of the South African Law Commission, to bring about a complete revision of the Bills of Exchange Act. This project was led by Professor Frans Malan of the Rand Afrikaans University. A scholarly report, inviting comment, was eventually published in 1988.[26] As yet, however, none of the suggested reforms have been implemented. Instead, an attempt has been made to politicize the issue. In the preface to his book published in 1993 Gering states:

---

[19] 1927 AD 502, 527.

[20] Title of the Bills of Exchange Act, 1882 (45 and 46 Vict. c. 61.)

[21] This Act has been described as 'the best drafted Act of Parliament which was ever passed' (*Bank Polski v. K J Mulder and Co* [1942] 1 All ER 396 (CA) 398). M. D. Chalmers, in his introduction to the 3rd edn. of *A Digest of the Law of Bills of Exchange, Promissory Notes, Cheques, and Negotiable Securities*, remarks: 'The Act has now been in operation for more than eight years, so that some estimate can be formed as to its results . . . As regards particular cases which arise, it is seldom necessary to go beyond the Act itself.' (5th edn., 1896), xlvii (reproduction of the preface to the 3rd edn.)

[22] De Beer, (1993) 26 *De Jure* 309 and Cowen/Gering (n. 1), 134 regard the *wisselrecht* as of importance only in regard to the aval and the concept of value (both in the sense of *iusta causa* and acquisition *ex causa onerosa*).

[23] 1932 AD 76, 80 sq.   [24] See the discussion below.

[25] According to the title of the Act it is intended '[t]o consolidate and amend the laws relating to bills of exchange, cheques and promissory notes'.

[26] F. R. Malan, A. N. Oelofse, J. T. Pretorius, *Proposals for the Reform of the Bills of Exchange Act 1964*, Working Paper 22 of the South African Law Commission (1988).

I am of course aware that proposals have been made on behalf of the SA Law Commission to replace the Bills of Exchange Act of 1964. I venture to suggest that when for the first time—and hopefully in the near future—there will be a government in South Africa based on the will of all the people of this land . . . its priorities will be to address the vast social and economic problems affecting the lives of millions of citizens, and not to replace a statute based on the English Bills of Exchange Act, which has been referred to as the 'best drafted Act of Parliament which was ever passed'. In any event, the SA Law Commission itself will no doubt require transformation.[27]

Thus, the future of the Bills of Exchange Act remains uncertain.

The history of bills of exchange in this country is a broad topic; this necessitates, for the purposes of this Chapter, the selection of those *capita* which have a particularly significant or interesting history. These are: (1) the protection of the *bona fide* transferee *ex causa onerosa*; (2) the position of the aval; (3) the interpretation of 'value' in the Bills of Exchange Act; and (4) the liability of the collecting bank. Before dealing with these topics, however, some comments on the Roman-Dutch *wisselrecht* are called for.

II. THE ROMAN-DUTCH *WISSELRECHT* IN PERSPECTIVE

1. The *wisselrecht* as part of the *lex mercatoria*

The law of bills of exchange, as part of mercantile law,[28] is considerably more uniform in common and civil law jurisdictions than most other areas of law. This is of course an essential feature of this 'most cosmopolitan of all contracts'.[29] The reason is that, in mercantile law more than in the traditional fields of private law, the common and civil law jurisdictions share the same root: the medieval European *lex mercatoria*.[30] The nature of the *lex mercatoria* was succinctly stated as follows by Bärmann:

---

[27] Gering (n. 3), v. But see Cowen/Gering (n. 1), 141: 'That there is a need for a careful and comprehensive revision of the South African Act has long been obvious.'

[28] The very existence of 'mercantile' or 'commercial law' as distinct from civil law is questioned by several modern commentators. See esp. Filip de Ly, *International Business Law and Lex Mercatoria* (1992), 41 sq., who writes of the 'fading relevance of the distinction'. It is not my intention to enter into this debate. I use the term here in its historical sense as that portion of private law which, due to a history distinct from that of other parts of private law, acquired the name of 'mercantile law'. See H. F. W. D. Fischer, 'Het oudvaderlandse handelsrecht en Hugo de Groot', (1952) *rechtsgeleerd magazijn Themis* 598, 599 sq.

[29] Chalmers (n. 21) xlviii (from the 'Introduction to Third Edition' as reproduced in the 5th edn.)

[30] Also termed *ius mercatorum* or *stilus mercatorum*. See Ernst von Caemmerer, 'The Influence of the Law of International Trade on the Development and Character of the Commercial Law in the Civil law Countries', in: H. G. Leser (ed.), *Ernst von Caemmerer: Gesammelte Schriften*, vol. I (1968), 11. Gerard Malynes, *Consuetudo vel lex mercatoria or the Ancient Law Merchant* (1622), in his introduction, opts for *lex mercatoria* instead of *ius mercatorum* 'because it is a Customary Law approued by the authoritie of all Kingdomes and

[D]as Handelsrecht des Mittelalters [ist] keineswegs ein nationales Recht eines Staates und auch nicht das uniforme Recht mehrerer Staaten . . . , sondern [wird] allein gebildet . . . durch die Gewohnheiten und Praktiken einer sozialen Klasse, nämlich der Kaufleute, wie sie in allen Ländern und Städten existiert mit der gleichen Mentalität, den gleichen Gewohnheiten und den gleichen Notwendigkeiten. Insofern allerdings kann man von einem gemeinen Recht aller Kaufleute verschiedener Nationalität und verschiedener juristischer Systeme sprechen, das in jedem Land neben dem nationalen Zivilrecht besteht.[31]

Generally speaking,[32] therefore, the *lex mercatoria* amounted to a universal customary law. Whatever its earliest origins may have been[33] it is clear that from the eleventh century onwards it developed mainly in the Italian cities and then spread to Spain, France, Germany, and England.[34] Several factors (apart from the customs of the social class of international merchants[35])

Commonweales, and not a Law established by the Soveraigntie of any Prince'. On this name see further J. Bärmann, 'Ist internationales Recht kodifizierbar', in: W. Flume (ed.), *Internationales Recht und Wirtschaftsordnung, Festschrift für F. A. Mann* (1977), 548; and, more recently, Uwe Blaurock, 'Übernationales Recht des Internationalen Handels', (1993) 1 *Zeitschrift für Europäisches Privatrecht* 247 sqq.; Rudolf Meyer, *Bona fides und lex mercatoria in der europäischen Rechtstradition* (1994), 13 sqq.

[31] (The mercantile law of the Middle Ages is by no means the national law of one state, and also not the uniform law of a number of states . . . but is derived from the customs and practices of a social class, i.e. the merchants, as they existed in all countries and cities sharing the same mentality, customs, and circumstances. In this sense only is it possible to speak of a common law of all merchants from different nationalities and legal systems, existing in each country side by side with the national private law): Bärmann (n. 30), 559.

[32] Differences, esp. in the earlier stages of the development of the *lex mercatoria* in the European cities and fairs, did exist. See W. Mitchell, *An essay on the early history of the law merchant* (1904), 7, who nevertheless concludes that 'in spite of minor differences, the international character of the Law Merchant . . . cannot be denied'.

[33] With reference to early sources W. A. Bewes, *Romance of the Law Merchant* (1923), 1 sq., argues as follows: 'It has been too confidently assumed by most writers that the law merchants (*sic*) arose in Italy in the central part of the Middle Ages . . . International trade is in some measure a constant thing. Although a great revival took place after the new contact with the East which was made by the Crusades, commerce at that time simply changed hands, leaving the Arabs . . . and being undertaken by the Italians . . . . But before the Arabs came the Romans, and before the Romans the Greeks, and before the Greeks the Phoenicians.' He also points out that in Europe at the time of the trade revival canon law was the prevailing authority and must have extended its influence over the law merchant, especially as the Church was a considerable trader during the Middle Ages. Egyptian, Babylonian, Assyrian, Phoenician, Greek, Roman, and Arabian sources are also discussed in the major treatise of L. Goldschmidt, *Universalgeschichte des Handelsrechts* (1891), 48–100. On the history of the *lex mercatoria* prior to the 11th C. see further Mitchell (n. 32), 22–6; L. E. Trakman, *The Law Merchant: The Evolution of Commercial Law* (1983), 8.

[34] Mitchell (n. 32), 29–38; von Caemmerer (n. 30), 11; Goldschmidt (n. 33), 142–200; H. Kellenbenz, 'Handelsrecht', in: Adalbert Erler, Ekkehard Kaufmann (eds.), *Handwörterbuch zur deutschen Rechtsgeschichte*, vol. I (1971), col. 1943.

[35] On the customary nature of the *lex mercatoria* see Mitchell (n. 32), 9–12 who regards it as 'by far the most decisive factor in its development'. See also Trakman (n. 33), 1 sq., 9–11; Bärmann (n. 30), 555–60; Clive M. Schmitthoff, 'Das neue Recht des Welthandels', (1964) 28 *RabelsZ* 48 sq.; the works by Blaurock and Meyer cited in n. 30.

contributed to the universal nature of the *lex mercatoria*[36]. For instance, the uniform manner in which the great international fairs were regulated[37] might be mentioned, as might the general correspondence of the rules of sea traffic;[38] very important, furthermore, was the creation of special mercantile courts throughout most of Europe, in which cases were decided according to the customs of merchants.[39]

It is of note, however, that the position was somewhat different in the Northern European states and especially in the Netherlands. Here a *lex mercatoria* in the guise of a separate body of law, applicable to the specific social class of merchants and existing side by side with the national law, was unknown.[40] Instead, a vast body of regional and municipal legislation arose, much of which dealt with mercantile matters. This legislation applied not only to merchants but to all citizens. Nevertheless, this does not mean that the substantive mercantile law in the Netherlands differed much from that applied elsewhere. The sources of the legislation were undoubtedly the customs of the merchants, which transcended national boundaries.

The question may be posed why the *lex mercatoria* presented itself in a different guise in the Netherlands than elsewhere in Europe. Asser suggests that the answer lies in the structure of society itself:

In Holland and Zeeland feudalism and the dominant position of the nobility had dwindled and the cities with their free population of craftsmen and merchants played by far the most influential role in the provincial government . . . [L]ocal government was for a great deal in the hands of a relatively small group of 'regents', who were, in many cases, members of important business houses themselves. From this it becomes clear that there was little need for a separate judicature where matters of commerce were concerned. There was, so to speak, no mercantile class, well

---

[36] On the universal nature of the *lex mercatoria* in general see Mitchell (n. 32), 20 sq.; Bärmann (n. 30), 555–60; Schmitthoff, (1964) 28 *RabelsZ* 49.

[37] Mitchell (n. 32), 5–8; Schmitthoff, (1964) 28 *RabelsZ* 49. Amongst the well known international fairs were those of Champagne, Lyon, Frankfurt-am-Main, Leipzig, and Bruges. See von Caemmerer (n. 30), 11; Bärmann (n. 30), 556.

[38] Schmitthoff, (1964) 28 *RabelsZ* 49.

[39] Ibid. Mitchell (n. 32), 39–78 contains a detailed discussion of the role of the special mercantile courts. A feature of these courts often encountered was the so-called 'half-tongue jury', i.e. a jury of which half the members were local merchants and the other half foreign merchants.

[40] This is the prevailing view. See esp. W. L. P. A. Molengraaff, *Leidraad bij de Beoefening van het Nederlandsche Handelsrecht* (6th edn., 1930), 6: '*In . . . Nederland . . . geen bijzondere gerechten voor de leden van de gilden der handelaars . . . Daar ook geen handelsrecht, afgescheiden van en naast het burgerlijk recht, maar voor een ieder geldendende landswetten, gewestelijke of stedelijke keuren en ordonanties*' (In . . . the Netherlands . . . [there were] no specific courts for the members of the merchant guilds . . . There also no seperate mercantile law co-existing with civil law, but for all the statutory law in force, the regional and municipal *keuren* and *ordonanties*.) See also Fischer, (1952) *rechtsgeleerd magazijn Themis* 598; A. van Oven, Monica van Bruining-Volmer, *Handelsrecht* (1981), 4. For a different view see W. F. Lichtenauer, 'Burgerlijk en Handelsrecht', in: *Rechtskundige Opstellen op 2 November 1935 door oud-leerlinge aangeboden aan Prof. Mr. E. M. Meijers* (1935), 337–65.

distinguished from the nobility . . . A judicature established by and reserved for the members of that class was therefore out of the question.[41]

Similar nationalization of mercantile law occurred somewhat later in the other European states. From the eighteenth century onwards the *lex mercatoria* was received into the different national legal systems.[42] On the continent this nationalization of the *lex mercatoria* took the form of the adoption of national codifications.[43] In England the special mercantile courts initially had to give way to the common law courts. Subsequently, under Lord Mansfield in particular, the rules of the *lex mercatoria* were incorporated into the common law[44] and eventually, in the latter half of the nineteenth century, the most important parts of commercial law were codified in England.[45] However, in spite of this nationalization of commercial law throughout Europe the common foundation is still clear today.

2. The main sources of the *wisselrecht*

In one of the earliest works on the common law of South Africa, Manfred Nathan remarked that the law of bills of exchange and promissory notes was a subject which was 'scarcely if at all known to the Roman jurists; and it was not much more extensively treated in the Roman-Dutch law'.[46] However, this statement, in so far as it pertains to the Roman-Dutch authorities, is not a fair reflection of the actual state of affairs. Although it is true that the leading Roman-Dutch writers of the seventeenth century,

---

[41] W. D. J. Asser, 'Bills of Exchange and Agency in the 18th Century Law of Holland and Zeeland', in: Vito Piergiovanni (ed.), *The Courts and the Development of Commercial Law* (1987), 108. See also Lichtenauer (n. 40), 351 sq. who accepts that the merchants did not constitute a separate social class and that mercantile law therefore could not be regarded as '*beroepsrecht*'; thus, in contrast to other writers, he does not dispute its existence.

[42] Von Caemmerer (n. 30), 12–17; Schmitthoff, (1964) 28 *RabelsZ* 49–55.

[43] The Napoleonic *Code de Commerce* of 1807 was the first major commercial code. In Germany commercial law was first codified in 1861 in the *Allgemeines Deutsches Handelsgesetzbuch*. The law of bills of exchange had by then already been codified in the *Allgemeine Deutsche Wechsel-Ordnung* of 1848; for details see Ulrich Huber, 'Das Reichsgesetz über die Einführung einer allgemeinen Wechselordnung für Deutschland vom 26. November 1848', 1978 *Juristenzeitung* 785 sqq. See in general on the codification of commercial law in continental Europe Schmitthoff, (1964) 28 *RabelsZ* 50–4; von Caemmerer (n. 30), 13 sq.

[44] At first the common law courts treated the rules of the *lex mercatoria* simply as commercial usage, which had to be proved. However, in Lord Mansfield's time the *lex mercatoria* acquired the status of law, and was incorporated into the common law. See von Caemmerer (n. 30), 12; Schmitthoff, (1964) 28 *RabelsZ* 52 sq.; Reinhard Zimmermann, 'Der europäische Charakter des englischen Rechts: Historische Verbindungen zwischen civil law und common law', (1993) 1 *Zeitschrift für Europäisches Privatrecht* 29 sqq., 34 sqq. On Lord Mansfield's role in this respect see esp. C. H. S. Fifoot, *Lord Mansfield* (1977), 82–157.

[45] The law of sale of goods, bills of exchange, carriers, marine insurance, merchant shipping, bills of lading, partnership and companies was codified. See von Caemmerer (n. 30), 12 sq.; Schmitthoff, (1964) 28 *RabelsZ* 50–3.

[46] Manfred Nathan, *Common Law of South Africa*, vol. III (1904), 1382.

such as Grotius[47] and Voet,[48] paid scant attention to the law of bills of exchange, the same cannot be said of the eighteenth-century writers. Both Van der Keessel[49] and Van der Linden[50] devoted considerable attention to the topic. Much can also be learned from the compilations of the decisions of the *Hooge Raad* by Van Bynkershoek and Pauw.[51]

Apart from the writers mentioned above, who are all authorities on the general body of Roman-Dutch law, two important specialized works were written in the eighteenth century: Phoonsen's *Wissel-Styl tot Amsterdam*[52] and Heineccius' *Grondbeginselen van het Wisselrecht* (translated into Dutch by K. K. Reitz).[53] To these may be added Van der Linden's translation of Pothier's *Traité du Contrat de Change*, prompted by the fact that Van der Linden held Pothier's treatise[54] in high regard, but did not think much of the work of either Phoonsen or Heineccius.[55] In fairness, however, it must

---

[47] Hugo Grotius, *Inleiding tot de Hollandsche Rechtsgeleertheyd*, 3, 13, 45. (Each title comprises one page only.)

[48] Johannes Voet, *Commentarius ad Pandectas*, 22, 2, 5–10. This portion of Voet was not deemed worthy of translation by Sir Percival Gane due to the fact that he could find only one reference to it in the case-law. See Johannes Voet, *The Selective Voet being the Commentary on the Pandects by Johannes Voet* (trans. Percival Gane), vol. III (1956), 723 (translator's note).

[49] D. G. van der Keessel, *Praelectiones iuris hodierni ad Hugonis Grotii Introductionem ad Jurisprudentiam Hollandicam*, Th. 574–628; Th. 838–73.

[50] Johannes van der Linden, *Regtsgeleerd, Practicaal, en Koopmans Handboek*, 4, 7.

[51] Cornelis van Bynkershoek, *Observationes Tumultuariae* (eds. E. M. Meijers *et al.*, Haarlem 1926–62); Willem Pauw, *Observationes Tumultuariae Novae* (eds. R. Feenstra, W. L. de Koning-Bey, L. E. van Holk, H. W. van Soest, Haarlem 1967).

[52] J. Phoonsen, *Wissel-Styl tot Amsterdam* (*en daarna vervolgt en tot op dezen tyd verbetert door I. le Long*) (ed. Rotterdam, 1755).

[53] J. G. Heineccius, *Grondbeginselen van het Wisselrecht (naar de zevende uitgaaf vertaald, en met de noodige aanmerkingen verrykt en opgehelderd door Karel Koenraad Reitz)* (Middelburg, 1774).

[54] He terms it a '*keurlijk zamenstel van 't Wissel-recht ... waar in men, behalven den doorzichtigsten Rechtsgeleerden, ook te gelijk den Man opmerkt, die de gebruiken van den Koophandel, en de wel doorgedachte begrippen van ervaarene Kooplieden, eerbiedigde*'. (An elegant compilation of the law of bills of exchange ... in which one perceives not only the thorough jurist but also a person who honours mercantile custom and the considered concepts of experienced merchants.) See Robert Joseph Pothier, *Verhandeling van het Wisselrecht (Naar het Fransch: door Johannes van der Linden)* (ed. Leyden, 1801), *Voorbericht van den Vertaaler*, x.

[55] With reference to Heineccius he remarks: '*Zonder te kort te doen aan de verdiensten van Heineccius, mogen wij met reden zeggen, dat, welk een groot en onvergelijkelijk Man hij ook in Letterkunde, in Oudheden, en in't Romeinsche Recht geweest moge zijn, het schrijven van een Werk, dat in den Koophandel een waar nut moet aanbrengen, de paalen van zijn vak scheen te buiten te gaan*'. (Without detracting from the merit of Heineccius we have reason to say that, however good and incomparable a man he may have been in literature, history and Roman law, by the writing of a work endeavouring to be of use in trade, he appears to have ventured out of the area of his competence.) Phoonsen is dismissed in the following terms: '*behalven den duisteren en verveelenden stijl, die de leezing van dit Werk alleronaangenaamst maakt, ziet men 'er, ja wel, den Koopman in, maar men derft den Rechtsgeleerden.*' (apart from the incomprehensible and boring style which renders the reading of this work exceptionally unpleasant, one recognizes therein the merchant, but the jurist is absent). See Pothier (n. 54), *Voorbericht van den Vertaaler*, vii–viii.

be remarked that Phoonsen was held in high esteem by others,[56] a fact borne out by his work having been translated into German and French.[57]

Furthermore, as noted above, much of the *lex mercatoria* in Roman-Dutch law is to be found in the different local and regional ordinances. Phoonsen's *Wissel-Styl*, for instance, contains *inter aliu* the text of the *Willekeuren der Stadt Amsterdam*, the *Keure ende Ordonnantie der Stadt Rotterdam*, and the *Ordonnantie van Keyser Karel tot Antwerpen gepubliceert*, as well as extracts from the influential *Costuymen van Antwerpen*.[58]

3. The *wisselrecht* and the modern bill of exchange

The bill of exchange known to the Roman-Dutch authors differed in several important respects from that known and in use today.

First, the legal nature of the bill itself (the *wisselbrief*) in Roman-Dutch times differed materially from its modern counterpart. Roman-Dutch law differentiates between the contract of exchange (*cambium*) and the bill of exchange (*wisselbrief*). In this respect Pothier's treatment is especially clear. He defines the contract of exchange as:

een Contract, waar bij ik u geef, of my verbinde om u te geven, eene zekere somme, op een zekere plaats, om en tot verwisseling van eene somme gelds, welke gij u verbindt om mij op eene andere plaats te doen toetellen.[59]

The bill of exchange (*wisselbrief*) itself was merely an instrument of proof of the exchange contract and the means by which the exchange contract was executed. The drawing or delivery of the bill of exchange did not in itself give rise to any obligations. Pothier explains as follows:

Men moet den Wisselbrief met het Wissel-Contract niet verwarren. De Wisselbrief behoort tot de uitvoering van het Wissel-Contract; hij is het middel, waar door dit Contract ter uitvoer gebragt word, hij veronderstelt het zelve, en brengt het niet in werking; maar hij is het Contract zelve niet.[60]

On the other hand, the drawing, that is the signing and delivery, of the modern bill of exchange gives rise to a contract founded on the bill itself[61].

[56] Asser (n. 41), 107 terms him '[a]n outstanding authority on the exchange law of Amsterdam'.

[57] Asser, ibid.

[58] On this codification in general as well as its introduction into Holland and Zeeland see Asser (n. 41), 105–7.

[59] (a contract in terms of which I give to you, or bind myself to give to you, a certain sum at a certain place to accomplish the exchange of a sum of money which you bind yourself to provide me with at a different place): Pothier (n. 54), § 2.

[60] (One should not confuse the bill of exchange with the contract of exchange. The bill of exchange has to do with the execution of the contract of exchange; it is the means by which the contract is executed, it implies the same and does not bring it into operation; but it is not the contract itself): Pothier (n. 54), § 2.

[61] See ss. 19(1), 53(1), Bills of Exchange Act 34 of 1964.

Secondly, the functions of the bill of exchange have been substantially extended. The function of the Roman-Dutch bill of exchange was to transport funds without the risks associated with the physical transport of money. The drawer, in terms of his exchange contract with the remitter, undertook to repay money (or value of some other kind) received from the remitter in a different place (the requirement of *distantia loci*)[62] and often also in a different coin (the requirement of *diversitas monetarum*).[63] The drawer executed this contract, as noted above, by instructing his mandatory in a *wisselbrief* to pay the representative or mandatory of the remitter, or the remitter himself, or in accordance with an indorsement of the remitter.[64]

The modern bill of exchange, although still employed to transport money, has developed several more prominent functions not evident in Roman-Dutch times. In the guise of the cheque it has become a simple instrument of payment; in the guise of the trade bill, a credit instrument; in the guise of the banker's acceptance, a financing instrument; and in the guise of the capital project bill, an investment instrument.[65]

Finally it must be noted that the bill of exchange developed into its modern form very much earlier in England than on the European continent. In the introduction to the third edition of his seminal *A Digest of the Law of Bills of Exchange*, Chalmers makes the following instructive comments in this regard:

A reference to Marius' treatise on Bills of Exchange, written about 1670, or Beawes' *Lex Mercatoria*, written about 1720, will show that the law, or perhaps rather the practice, as to bills of exchange, was even then pretty well defined. Comparing the usage of that time with the law as it now stands, it will be seen that it has been modified in some important respects. Comparing English law with French, it will be seen that, for the most part, where they differ, French law is in strict accordance with the rules laid down by Beawes. The fact is, that when Beawes wrote, the law or practice of both nations on this subject was uniform. The French law, however, was embodied in a Code by the *Ordonance de 1673*, which is amplified but substantially adopted by the *Code de Commerce* of 1818. Its development was thus arrested, and it remains in substance what it was 200 years ago. English law has been developed piecemeal by judicial decision founded on custom. The result has been to work out a theory of bills widely different from the original.[66]

What was said of French law applied largely as to the Netherlands, since French law was very influential in this field.[67] By the end of the eighteenth century, the law of bills of exchange on the European continent had not reached a stage of development comparable to that in England. The

---

[62] Pothier (n. 54), 4, 6; Van der Keessel (n. 49), Th. 597; Van der Linden (n. 50), 4, 7, 2.
[63] F. R. Malan, 'Evolusie van die Wisselreg', 1976 *TSAR* 1, 2.
[64] Malan/De Beer (n. 2), § 21; Malan, 1976 *TSAR* 1 sq.; Chalmers (n. 21), lvii.
[65] Cowen/Gering (n. 1), 180–4, 185–213; Chalmers (n. 21), lvii; Malan, 1976 *TSAR* 2 sq.
[66] Chalmers (n. 21), lvi–lvii.

development of a modern theory of bills of exchange on the continent was left to the nineteenth and twentieth centuries.[68]

What, then, are the consequences of the comparative lack of sophistication of the *wisselrecht* for South African law? There appears to be a general consensus that since the adoption of the English legislation the Roman Dutch *wisselrecht* has become largely irrelevant.[69] The most important exceptions relate to the positions of the *bona fide* transferee *ex causa onerosa*, and the aval. Both are dealt with below as *capita selecta*.

However, a final matter must be stressed: although in the South African law of bills of exchange the *wisselrecht* has become largely redundant, the same cannot be said of the Roman-Dutch law in its entirety. The general principles of the Roman-Dutch law of obligations have played and continue to play an important role in the South African law of bills of exchange.[70] Two fascinating developments have been the interpretation of the concept of 'value' in the Bills of Exchange Act, and the development of a delictual action against a bank negligently collecting a cheque. These two topics are the final matters to be considered in this contribution.

III. THE PROTECTION OF THE *BONA FIDE* TRANSFEREE *EX CAUSA ONEROSA*

The Roman-Dutch authors did not devote much attention to the protection of the *bona fide* transferee *ex causa onerosa* of a bill of exchange. Dealing with the fraudulent transfer of bills, Van der Keessel suggests certain general principles to assist in determining who must bear the loss. These include: '*quod quis iuris ipse non habet, illud in alterum transferre non potest*' and '*qui cum aliquo contrahit, videre debet cui fidat et eius condicionis non debet esse ignarus*'.[71] These remarks, echoed by Van der Keessel,[72] hold little comfort for the *bona fide* transferee of a bill of exchange. He can acquire no better title than that of the transferor, and he must seek his compensation from him whom he trusted.

There are, however, indications in the Roman-Dutch law that situations existed in which the *bona fide* transferee *ex causa onerosa* was protected. Van der Keessel himself, for instance, states that the *exceptio non numeratae pecuniae* is not available to a drawer sued by the indorsee of a bill of

---

[67] Malan (n. 4), 56. See also Van der Linden's praise of Pothier mentioned in n. 54 above.

[68] Malan, 1976 *TSAR* 1–24; *idem* (n. 4), 88–123.

[69] Cowen/Gering (n. 1), 134; De Beer, (1993) 26 *De Jure* 309.

[70] See Malan/De Beer (n. 2), § 20.

[71] (A right which a person himself does not have cannot be transferred to another; He who contracts with another must ensure that he is not ignorant either of the person whom he trusts or of that person's legal position): Van der Keessel (n. 49), Th. 871.

[72] Van der Keessel (n. 49), Th. 623, Th. 873.

exchange.[73] Malan and De Beer,[74] as well as Cowen and Gering[75] cite the *Discursus legales de Commercio* of Casaregis[76] in support of the proposition that an acceptor is not entitled to raise against a *bona fide* indorsee *ex causa onerosa* defences he may have had against the indorser.

Another possible exception to Van der Keessel's general rule is that the vindication of negotiable instruments payable to bearer from a *bona fide* transferee *ex causa onerosa* may well have been restricted in Holland by the end of the eighteenth century. This matter gained prominence in the recent decision of the Appellate Division in *Kahn v. Volschenk*.[77] In an erudite judgment Joubert JA, referring to several cases heard in the *Hooge Raad* between 1652 and 1777, traces a development in that Court from a position where it allowed the vindication of negotiable instruments payable to bearer from someone who acquired them *bona fide ex causa onerosa* to a situation where such actions were no longer successful. Joubert concludes as follows:

> *Uit die voorgaande blyk dit dat die Romeins-Hollandse reg aan die einde van die 18de eeu as gevolg van die beslissing van die Hooge Raad op 15 April 1777 hom op die standpunt gestel het dat die vindikasie van openbare toonderdokumente beperk is en nie ontvanklik teen 'n* bona fide *houer vir waarde is nie.*[78]

However, the matter is not completely free from doubt. Van der Keessel,[79] writing after 1777 and without referring to the abovementioned development in the *Hooge Raad*, still supports the view that the *rei vindicatio* should succeed in the circumstances.[80] Thus, one may conclude generally that,

---

[73] Ibid. Th. 600.

[74] Malan/De Beer (n. 2), § 176, fn. 21.

[75] Denis Cowen, Leonard Gering, *The Law of Negotiable Instruments in South Africa* (4th edn., 1966), 284 sq., fn. 315.

[76] (1733), 48, 19. I rely here on the interpretation of the authors mentioned above.

[77] 1986 (3) SA 84 (A). See also *Secfin Bank Ltd v. Mercantile Bank Ltd* (n. 10).

[78] (From the aforegoing it is clear that by the end of the 18th C. Roman-Dutch law, as a consequence of the decision of the *Hooge Raad* on 15 Apr. 1777, had taken the stance that the vindication of public bearer documents was limited and not available against a bona fide holder for value). The first authority mentioned is Van der Keessel (n. 49), Th. 183 who refers to a decision of the *Hooge Raad* in 1652 in which the *rei vindicatio* of public bearer bonds was allowed against a *bona fide* holder *ex causa onerosa*. The *Hooge Raad* gave similar decisions in 1716 and 1720 (Van Bynkershoek (n. 51), Obs. 1222 and 1694). Of major importance, however, was the fact that in both these decisions Van Bynkershoek himself gave dissenting minority judgments: '*jure defendi non posse vindicari; nam recte cedit cautione, qui creditor est, creditor autem est den thoonder, neque alius*' (I took the view that [a public bearer bond] could not be vindicated; for he who is the creditor with right cedes [it] in security, and the creditor is the bearer and no-one else) (1222) and '*[p]raeter eas rationes, quas attuli d. n. 1222, etiam nunc ajebam, dat immers een houder van een wisselbrief, in blanko geëndorseert, daarvan eigenaar was*' (Apart from those reasons which I mentioned in 1222 I have always said that after all the holder of a bill of exchange, indorsed in blank, was owner thereof) (1694). The minority view of Van Bynkershoek eventually triumphed in 1777 when the *Hooge Raad* refused the *rei vindicatio* of a public bearer bond from a *bona fide* pledgee (Pauw (n. 51), Obs. 1383).

[79] Van der Keessel (n. 49), Th. 183.

[80] The difference of opinion between Van der Keessel and the *Hooge Raad* raises the interesting question as to the status of the *Hooge Raad* decisions. It is clear that they are not

although the Roman-Dutch law awarded some protection to the *bona fide* transferee *ex causa onerosa*, his position was by no means certain, nor secure.

The position in England was very different. By the end of the seventeenth century it was clear that the '*bona fide* holder for value' (the English equivalent for the *bona fide* transferee *ex causa onerosa*) enjoyed a preferential status.[81] His position was entrenched in a trilogy of cases between 1696 and 1699.[82]

The first case was *Hussey v. Jacob*.[83] The payee of a bill, given to him by the drawer to settle a gaming debt, sued the acceptor of the bill. This being an illegal consideration, the claim was denied. Significant, however, was an *obiter dictum* of Lord Holt that if a bill is 'given to the winner or order, and the winner indorsed it to a stranger for a just debt, and the person upon whom the bill was drawn, accepts it in the hands of the stranger, the acceptor would be liable'.[84] Shortly thereafter, in a decision in the Court of Chancery, Lord Somers decided that the holder of a bill which he had acquired 'for an honest debt' could enforce payment against the drawer, in spite of the fact that the bill had in the first instance been given without any consideration 'because it would tend to destroy trade which is carried on every where by bills of exchange'.[85] Finally, in a 1699 decision, Lord Holt found that although a person who had lost a bill payable to bearer could maintain an action of trover against the person who found the bill, such action could not succeed against a person who had acquired such bill for a good consideration from the finder thereof 'by reason of the course of trade, which creates a property in the assignee or bearer'.[86] As Holden eloquently notes:

A chariot had been driven through the hitherto impregnable lines of the common law maxim *nemo dat quod non habet*. That chariot was driven by Holt CJ and by Somers LC and the motive power was simply 'the course of trade'; in other words, the custom of merchants.[87]

The privileged status of the *bona fide* holder for value, of course, found its way into the English Bills of Exchange Act, and from there into the South African legislation. In the respective statutes this kind of holder acquired the less cumbersome title of a 'holder in due course'.[88] The English notion

---

precedents: see H. R. Hahlo, Ellison Kahn, *The South African Legal System and its Background* (1968), 543–6. It is suggested that, in view of the brevity of the case summaries, it is dangerous to award them too high a status especially when in conflict with the views of an established Roman-Dutch writer.

[81] This was not the case in earlier times. See J. Milnes Holden, *The History of Negotiable Instruments in English Law* (1955), 51.

[82] Ibid. 63–5; Malan (n. 3), 150–3.   [83] (1892) 1 Comyns 4.   [84] (1892) 1 Comyns 4 (6).

[85] (1892) 1 Comyns 4 (43).   [86] *Anon.* 1 Salkeld 126.   [87] Holden (n. 81), 64 sq.

[88] See s. 29, English Bills of Exchange Act and s. 27 of its South African counterpart.

of the holder in due course thus, by statute, forms an important and integral part of the South African law of bills of exchange.

However, the South African courts did not wait on legislation to adopt the principles of English law in this regard. This became apparent as early as 1841 in the case *Cape of Good Hope Bank v. Elliot Brothers and Sutherland*.[89] Elliot Brothers had given several promissory notes to Sutherland. Certain of these notes were handed to the plaintiff, who discounted them in good faith. The question before the Court was whether Elliot Brothers could successfully raise against the plaintiff bank the defences of prior payment and usurious interest (defences which Elliot Brothers[90] had raised successfully in two earlier cases against the payee of one of the notes as well as against the indorsee without value of two further notes). The Court held that the *bona fide* indorsees were 'entitled to Provisional Sentence, notwithstanding that the Defendant had a good Defence against the Payee'.[91] No authority, English or Roman-Dutch, is quoted in the reports of any one of these cases. From the state of the law in the respective legal systems as well as from the terminology employed in the cases,[92] there is little doubt, however, that the Court followed the principles of English law.

Some twenty-five years later, a *dictum* of Bell J in *Blackburn's Trustees v. Landsberg and Son*[93] must have dispelled any doubts in this regard. Having been referred exclusively to English authorities, he stated the law as follows:

[I]t is altogether a mistake to say that J. D. Cilliers' last blank endorsement could convey to Blackburn no further right than was in Cilliers himself; for the doctrine is quite trite, in the law of bills of exchange, that the holder for value, without notice, takes full right, without respect to the equities which may exist between prior endorsers.

Thus by the time the English legislation was adopted in South Africa the holder in due course, or as he was known at that stage 'the *bona fide* holder for value without notice',[94] and the privileged position of such holder, clearly formed part of South African law.

IV. THE AVAL

1. Roman-Dutch law and its interpretation in South Africa

In order to enhance the value of bills of exchange and promissory notes, the guarantee of a surety is often sought that the instrument will be paid. The

---

[89] (1841) 1 Menz 102.
[90] *Sutherland v. Elliot Bros* (1841) 1 Menz 99; *Taylor v. Elliot Bros* (1841) 1 Menz 101.
[91] 102 (headnote).   [92] E.g. '*bona fide* indorsee' and 'indorsee without value'.
[93] (1866) 5 Searle 180, 181 sq.
[94] David A. L. Smout, *Chalmers on Bills of Exchange* (13th edn., 1964), 94; Malan/De Beer (n. 2), § 172.

Roman-Dutch *wisselrecht* admitted of two different ways in which this could be accomplished: (i) the surety could enter into a separate contract of suretyship *dehors* the instrument; or (ii) the surety could simply evidence his undertaking by signing the instrument, in which case the surety was termed an 'aval'.[95] Pothier defines the aval as follows:

> Aval i*s de Borgtocht van hem, die zig bij een Wisselbrief, voor den Trekker, of voor één der* Endossanten, *of voor den* Acceptant, *tot Borg stelt: de form daar van is, dat de Borg Zijne handteekening stelt onder die van den geen, voor wien hij Borg blijft.*[96]

The difference between the aval and the surety binding himself on a separate instrument is that the aval is deprived of the *beneficia excussionis et divisionis* customary to suretyship.[97] The aval is accordingly a surety who has tacitly renounced the *beneficia*.[98]

However, this was not always appreciated in early South African caselaw. In *Norton v. Satchwell*,[99] the first reported decision in point,[100] the Cape Supreme Court refused provisional sentence against an aval due to the absence of liquid liability. The basis of the decision appears to be that an aval leads to the same position as suretyship, and that the benefit of excussion precludes liquid liability.[101] This, in any event, is how the decision was later interpreted.[102] Thereafter the Cape Court in a series of decisions con-

---

[95] Heineccius (n. 53), 3, 26; Van der Keessel (n. 49), Th. 594.

[96] (Aval is a form of suretyship in terms of which a person binds himself on a bill of exchange as surety for the drawer, or indorsers or acceptor: it takes the form of the surety affixing his signature below that of the person for whom he binds himself as surety): Pothier (n. 54), 3, 20.

[97] Pothier (n. 54), 4, 74: '*Het is iets bijzonders in deeze zoort van Borgtochten, die bij wijze van* Aval *gesteld worden . . . dat zij de voorrechten van uitwinning en schuldsplitsing, die aan gewoone Borgen zijn toegestaan, (*exceptiones excussionis and divisionis,*) geen gebruik kunnen maaken*' (There is something exceptional in this type of suretyship arising from *Aval . . .* that it disallows the benefits of excussion and division of action awarded normal sureties). See also Reitz's note 57 to Heineccius (n. 53), 3, 28; Van der Keessel (n. 49), Th. 594.

[98] Heineccius (n. 53), 6, 10; *Moti and Co v. Cassim's Trustee* 1924 AD 720, 726.

[99] (1840) 1 Menz 77.

[100] For a discussion of three earlier unreported judgments, one of which did in fact exhibit an appreciation of the difference between a surety and an aval, see De Beer, (1993) 26 *De Jure* 319–24.

[101] Significantly, the only authority referred to in the judgment is Van der Linden (n. 50), 4, 7, 5 who, without any discussion, simply lists as one of the possible parties to a bill of exchange '*[b]orgen van den betrokkenen*' (sureties of the drawee), and explains: '*Deze borgtocht word genoemd aval*' (this suretyship is termed *aval*). Van der Linden's references to Heineccius and Pothier were clearly not followed up.

[102] *Ullman Bros and Davidson v. Railton* 1903 TS 596, 600: 'If we look into the reason why provisional sentence has been refused in the cases I have referred to, the reason seems perfectly clear. The courts have held that an indorsement on a note as surety does not necessarily imply a renunciation of the benefit of excussion; because if it did, then the signatory would become a co-principal debtor, and provisional sentence would be given. His obligation would be a liquid one.'

sidered itself bound by the *Norton* case[103] in spite of having realized later that it was not in accordance with Roman-Dutch law.[104] The Transvaal Supreme Court followed suit.[105] In 1924 the Appellate Division was eventually called upon to adjudicate this matter in *Moti and Co v. Cassim's Trustee*.[106] Having reviewed both the Roman-Dutch authorities and previous case-law, Innes CJ remarked that the principle of *Norton v. Satchwell* had been 'adopted and acted upon by South African Courts for more than half a century', and that 'a doctrine thus authoritatively laid down and acted upon in regard to so important a subject matter should not be interfered with by the Courts'.[107] In his judgment Kotzé JA concurs despite confessing that '[i]t would certainly be more in the interests of commercial dealings to hold that a party, whose name figures on a bill or note, is primarily liable thereon'.[108]

2. English law and the bills of exchange legislation

The English common law has no institution comparable to the Roman-Dutch aval. A stranger who signs a bill, that is a person who is neither drawer, acceptor nor indorser, would not in English law be liable to the holder.[109] To bridge this difficulty s. 56 of the English Bills of Exchange Act provides as follows: 'Where a person signs a bill otherwise than as drawer or acceptor, he thereby incurs the liabilities of an indorser to a holder in due course.' This provision was faithfully reproduced in the bills of exchange legislation first introduced into South Africa and, as s. 54, remains part of the current South African Bills of Exchange Act.

The interpretation of section 54 against the different common law background of the aval has proved vexing. Soon after the introduction of the English legislation, De Villiers CJ expressed the opinion that the Act did not 'alter the rule that a person who indorses a non-negotiable note *prima facie*

---

[103] *De Kock v. Russouw and Van der Poel* (1841) 1 Menz 78; *Coetzee v. Tiran* 1880 Foord 12; *Bevern v. Jacobse* (1889) 7 SC 65; *Klopper v. Van Straaten* (1894) 11 SC 94; *Stephan Bros v. Engelbrecht* (1894) 11 SC 248; *Verster, Van Wijk & Co v. Pienaar* (1904) 21 SC 386; *Du Plessis v. Greef and Walter* (1905) 22 SC 580; *Maasdorp v. Graaff Reinet Board of Executors* (1909) 3 Buch AC 482. Sureties binding themselves as 'sureties and co-principal debtors' or simply as 'co-debtors' were, however, held to have renounced the *beneficia*. See *Van der Vyver v. De Wayer* (1861) 4 Searle 27; *Gildenhuys v. Swart* (1865) 5 Searle 165.

[104] In *Coetzee v. Tiran* (n. 103), 43 De Villiers CJ remarked as follows: 'According to Heineccius . . . such an endorsement creates an obligation of suretyship, and was known in the Dutch law . . . as *aval*. The holder had his summary remedy against the guarantor *jure cambiali*, but the practice of giving provisional sentence against such endorsers has never been followed in this Court'.

[105] *Ullman Bros and Davidson v. Railton* (n. 102); *Arnoldi v. Klazenga, Alberts and Dreyer* 1905 TS 533.

[106] 1924 AD 720. [107] 727. [108] 740.

[109] To hold him liable would violate the doctrine of privity of contract as well as the English Statute of Frauds. See A. G. Guest, *Chalmers and Guest on Bills of Exchange, Cheques and Promissory Notes* (14th edn., 1991), 456; Cowen/Gering (n. 75), 220.

incurs the liability of an "aval", or surety'.[110] However, this was *obiter dictum*, as the instrument in question was made prior to the passing of the legislation. A few years later Innes CJ in *Ullman Bros and Davidson v. Railton*[111] also rejected the contention that s. 54 had altered the legal position of a stranger signing a bill. The decision is, however, of little use as it is based on the fact that the plaintiff did not qualify as holder in due course and therefore s. 54 was not applicable.[112] However, in *National Bank of SA Ltd v. Seligson* Mason J remarked that s. 54 was 'clearly intended to embrace every other person who indorsed a bill whether as holder competent to convey title, or whether as an aval or surety'.[113]

The most authoritative pronouncement on the problem of reconciling the provisions of s. 54 with the position of the aval was that of the Appellate Division in *Moti and Co v. Cassim's Trustee*.[114] The Court had to decide whether the appellant who had signed a promissory note prior to it being indorsed by the payee thereof was liable as indorser or as surety (aval) for the maker. A decision holding the appellant liable as indorser would have implied that, in so far as the holder in due course is concerned, 'the contract of aval . . . has been abolished'[115] by s. 54. The Court rejected this view. In what has become a classical *dictum* Innes CJ found that 'a person who has placed his signature on the back of a promissory note before delivery to or endorsement by the payee is upon these facts liable as surety under an aval and is not in the position of an ordinary endorser'.[116] In his concurring judgment Wessels JA also aligned himself 'with the view that . . . s. 54 should not be so interpreted as to alter the obligations of an aval as they existed before that Proclamation'.[117] This problem came before the Appellate Division again in *Peimer v. Finbro Furnishers (Pty) Ltd*.[118] Following the *Moti* case De Villiers JA found that 'it was neither the object of the Act as a whole, nor of s. 54 in particular, to alter the obligations of the signer of an aval'.[119] Finally, even though these *dicta* carry considerable weight, it must be remarked that they are *obiter*[120] since in both the *Moti* and the *Peimer* cases the plaintiffs were found not to be holders in due course.

Although the effect of s. 54 on the aval is by no means clear[121] the current position may be rendered as follows:

---

[110] *Klopper v. Van Straaten* (1894) (n. 103), 97 sq.   [111] 1903 TS 596.

[112] 599: 'It is clear that if a third person indorses a note to which he is no party, he is considered to have undertaken the obligations of a surety or aval . . . But the magistrate held (and that was the ground of his decision) that that law had been altered by s. 54 . . . The magistrate decided that the plaintiff in this case was a holder in due course, and therefore the persons who indorsed this note before it became negotiable were liable as indorsers. In my opinion his decision was quite wrong, *because the plaintiff was not a holder in due course*' (italics added).

[113] 1921 WLD 108, 116.   [114] Above, n. 106.   [115] 727.

[116] 733.   [117] 744.   [118] 1936 AD 177.   [119] 183.

[120] De Wet/Van Wyk (n. 7), 769, fn. 214.

[121] See N. J. van der Merwe, 'Enkele Probleme wat uit ons Wisselwetgewing Voortspruit', (1959) 22 *THRHR* 275, 278–81; C. J. Rowland, 'Some Aspects of the Contract of Aval', (1965)

(1) It is clear that s. 54 only applies against a holder in due course. It does not therefore affect the liability of an aval *vis-à-vis* any other holder.

(2) In the event of the signatory expressly indicating that he signs as aval or surety, he should be held liable as such, also as against a holder in due course. There is authority for this point of view in the case-law. In *National Acceptance Co (Pty) Ltd v. Robertson*[122] Howes J took the view that it would not make sense to apply s. 54 to an 'express contract of suretyship merely because it happens to be inscribed on the face of the note'[123] while the same section is clearly not applicable to a suretyship embodied in a different document. There is, however, another possible approach. Section 14 of the Act provides as follows:

The drawer and any indorser of a bill may insert therein an express stipulation—
(a) negativing or limiting his own liability to the holder;
(b) waiving as regards himself some or all of the holder's duties.

It has been argued that even if the signatory is regarded as an indorser by virtue of the provisions of s. 54, s. 14 may be invoked to limit his liability to that of an aval.[124]

(3) In the event of the signatory not indicating expressly that he signs as an aval, his liability as against a holder in due course is unclear. *Obiter dicta* in the *Moti* case[125] suggest that if the signature is placed on the bill before its negotiation (that is before the payee's indorsement) the signatory is liable as an aval due to 'a usage admitted and sanctioned by the South African courts . . . that if a stranger puts his name on a bill before negotiation, his placing his name there is equivalent to writing on the bill that he is liable as a surety and no more'.[126] However, the precise content of this usage has recently been questioned.[127] If the signature does not precede that of the payee s. 54 may well be applicable and render the signatory liable as an indorser.

From this it is clear that s. 54 has made no positive contribution to South African law and should indeed be scrapped. However, the proposals of the South African Law Commission dealing with the reform of the Bills of

---

28 *THRHR* 30–45; Cowen/Gering (n. 75), 225–37; De Wet/Van Wyk (n. 7), 769 sq.; Malan/De Beer (n. 2), §§ 239–43; Malan/Oelofse/Pretorius (n. 26), 309–21.

[122] 1938 CPD 175. See also the *obiter dicta* of Wessels JA in *Moti and Co v. Cassim's Trustee* (n. 106), 744.

[123] At 181.

[124] Rowland, (1965) 28 *THRHR* 30, 40; Malan/Oelofse/Pretorius (n. 26) 311.

[125] At 733 and 744.

[126] *Moti and Co v. Cassim's Trustee* (n. 106), 744. See also *Lion Mill Manufacturing Co (Pty) Ltd v. New York Shipping Co (Pty) Ltd* 1974 (4) SA 984 (T) 990: 'Where a person signs on the reverse side of a note and indicates expressly *or otherwise* that he is merely signing as surety, the provisions of s. 54 are in my view excluded. Where *ex facie a note it is obvious that the signatory is an aval*, his liability is that of a surety and no more' (italics added).

[127] Malan/Oelofse/Pretorius (n. 26), 312.

Exchange Act go one step further: legislation is suggested which would in effect restore the *aval* of Roman-Dutch law, that is a surety who has renounced the *beneficia*. This proposal is based upon a belief that the interests of commerce require that provisional sentence be possible against an *aval* without the necessity of first excussing the principal debtor.[128] As noted above[129] the future of the proposals published by the Law Commission is uncertain. However, developments in England may well give added impetus to this specific amendment, irrespective of the fate of the other proposals. Guest concludes his commentary on s. 56 of the English Bills of Exchange Act with the following paragraph:

The Government has declared its intention to give legal recognition to the *aval*, as mentioned in the report of the Review Committee on Banking Services Law and Practice. It proposes to introduce legislation to amend the Act so as to recognise a guarantee given by way of *aval*.[130]

In the event of this happening it would be most peculiar if the South African legislature were to retain s. 54.

V. 'VALUE' IN THE BILLS OF EXCHANGE ACT

1. Introduction

The word 'value' has long been associated with bills of exchange. The bill of exchange of the Roman-Dutch *wisselrecht* invariably contained a value clause,[131] the most typical of which was that value was received in money (*'de waarde per cassa ontfangen'*[132]), or in goods (*'waarde in koopmanschappen ontfangen'*[133]). The value clause was accordingly an indication that the drawer had received value for the bill from the remitter. In this sense the value was the *quid pro quo* or the *causa* for the bill of exchange.[134] If there was no value clause the instrument was not a bill of exchange.[135]

Although retained longer on the continent, the value clause was dispensed with at an early stage in England, where value was presumed.[136] It would appear also that from an early stage the value clause was not required in South Africa.[137] The word 'value' was, however, incorporated into several provisions

---

[128] Malan/Oelofse/Pretorius (n. 26), 319 sq.   [129] Section I, above.
[130] Chalmers/Guest (n. 109), 461.
[131] For a detailed discussion of the different value clauses and their significance see Malan (n. 4), 64–7.
[132] Van der Keessel (n. 49), Th. 598; Pothier (n. 54) 1, 4; Van der Linden (n. 50), 4, 7, 4.
[133] Pothier (n. 54), 1, 4; Van der Keessel (n. 49), Th. 598.   [134] Malan (n. 4), 64.
[135] Van der Keessel (n. 49), Th. 598; Van der Linden (n. 50), 4, 7, 6, 5.
[136] Chalmers (n. 21), lvii; Malan (n. 4), 67.
[137] *Watermeyer v. Neethling qq.* [sic] *Denyssen* (1831) 1 Menz 26; *Low v. Oberholtzer* (1835) 1 Menz 43; *Rens v. Smith* (1850) 1 Menz 13.

of the English Bills of Exchange Act, and from there found its way into the South African legislation. The interpretation of these provisions has proved to be a major problem in the South African law of bills of exchange.[138] This is a direct consequence of the difficulty of interpreting legislation in South Africa which was drafted against the background of the English common law.

2. English law

The English Bills of Exchange Act defines 'value' as 'valuable consideration',[139] a concept with which English lawyers are well acquainted. In English law any simple contract must be supported by a valuable consideration[140] in order to be enforceable. The rule is *ex nudo pacto non oritur actio*; the *pactum* must be clothed by valuable consideration. The classical definition is that valuable consideration may be 'some right, interest, profit, or benefit accruing to the one party, or some forbearance, detriment, loss, or responsibility given, suffered, or undertaken by the other'.[141] A mere moral obligation does not constitute valuable consideration;[142] neither does a consideration founded in mere affection or gratitude.[143] Past consideration, such as an antecedent debt, also does not constitute valuable consideration.[144] Valuable consideration accordingly amounts to a *quid pro quo* or, to use a term employed by Chalmers, 'onerosity'.[145] Finally, English law requires that consideration move from the promisee, although not necessarily to the promissor.[146]

Against this background the English Bills of Exchange Act, having equated 'value' and 'valuable consideration',[147] provides that valuable consideration for a bill may be constituted by 'any consideration sufficient to support a simple contract'.[148] By this provision the Act simply places bills and notes upon the same footing as other simple contracts.[149]

---

[138] Much has been written in this regard. See Cowen/Gering (n. 75), 82–102; Malan/De Beer (n. 2), §§ 73–86; June D. Peterson, 'The Chameleon-Like Quality of "Value" in the Bills of Exchange Act', (1971) 88 *SALJ* 155; F. R. Malan, 'Oor Waarde, Banke en die Reëlmatige Houer', (1977) 40 *THRHR* 126; G. Viljoen, ' "Waarde" in die Suid-Afrikaanse Wisselreg', in: D. J. Joubert (ed.), *E. M. Hamman Gedenkbundel* (1984), 1.

[139] S. 2. Doubt has been expressed as to whether 'valuable consideration' and 'value' are in fact exactly convertible terms. See Cowen/Gering (n. 75), 87 sq.

[140] *Rann v. Hughes* (1788) 7 Term Rep 350. A simple contract is an unsealed contract, i.e. a contract not made in the form of a deed. See Cowen/Gering (n. 75), 84; Malan (n. 4), § 73.

[141] *Currie v. Misa* (1875) LR 10 Exch 153, 162; Chalmers (n. 21), 81; Joseph Story, *Commentaries on the Law of Bills of Exchange, Foreign and Inland, as Administered in England and America* (2nd edn., 1847), 212.

[142] Chalmers (n. 21), 80; Holden (n. 81), 138.   [143] Story (n. 141), 210.

[144] Cowen/Gering (n. 75), 84; Malan/De Beer (n. 2), § 73.   [145] Chalmers (n. 21), 81.

[146] Cowen/Gering (n. 75), 86; Malan/De Beer (n. 2), § 73.   [147] S. 2.

[148] S. 27(1)(a).

[149] Although the applicability of the doctrine of consideration to bills of exchange was questioned during the 17th and 18th centuries, most clearly by Lord Mansfield in *Pillans and Rose v. Van Mierop and Hopkins* (1765) 3 Burr 1663, it was eventually placed on a firm footing by the House of Lords in *Rann v. Hughes* (n. 140).

In furtherance of the interests of commercial dealing the Act, however, contains a number of provisions which, in the case of bills of exchange and promissory notes, broaden the common law concept of valuable consideration. In the first place, s. 27(1)(b) provides that valuable consideration may be constituted by an 'antecedent debt or liability . . . whether the bill is payable on demand or at a future time'.[150] The rule that past consideration is no consideration does not therefore apply to bills and notes. As Evershed MR stated in *Oliver v. Davis and Woodcock*:[151]

[T]he proper construction of the words antecedent debt or liability in paragraph (b) is that they refer to an antecedent debt or liability of the promissor or drawer of the bill and are intended to get over what would otherwise have been *prima facie* the result that at common law the giving of a cheque for an amount for which you are already indebted imports no consideration since the obligation is past and has already been incurred.

Secondly, s. 27(2) provides that where 'value has at any time been given for a bill or note the holder is deemed to be a holder for value as regards the acceptor or maker and all parties to the instrument who became such prior to such time'. This provision accordingly does away with the rule that consideration must move from the promisee.[152]

In the third place, s. 28 provides that 'a person who has signed a bill as drawer, acceptor or indorser, without receiving value therefor, and for the purpose of lending his name to some other person . . . is liable on the bill to a holder for value' thereby rendering the so-called accommodation party liable in spite of the absence of consideration on his part.[153]

Finally, it is noteworthy that bills of exchange, unlike any other simple contract, enjoy the privilege of being presumed to be founded upon valid and valuable consideration.[154]

From the aforegoing one may conclude in general that in English law the holder for value is (i) a holder who has given a *quid pro quo* for the instrument; and (ii) a holder whose entitlement is established by the principles of the law relating to simple contracts. However, contractual liability being

---

[150] Prior to the enactment of s. 27(1)(b) it was argued that an antecedent debt could constitute consideration for a bill payable in future in the sense that the suspension of the creditor's remedies during the currency of the instrument constituted valuable consideration, but that this argument could not be extended to bills payable on demand. The case-law was inconclusive. See *Currie v. Misa* (n. 141), (1876) 1 App Cas 554; *Holden* (n. 81), 139, fn. 4; Chalmers (n. 21), 81 sq. The wording of s. 27(1)(b) suggests an intention of clearing up this uncertainty.

[151] [1949] 2 KB 727, 735.

[152] Its effect is illustrated by Cowen/Gering (n. 75), 87: 'If A gratuitously makes a note in favour of B, who gratuitously indorses it to C, the maker will incur no liability to either B or C thereon. But if C indorses it for consideration to D, the latter may enforce it against A, B or C; and if D gratuitously indorses it to E, the latter may similarly enforce it against A, B or C, but not against D.'

[153] See Cowen/Gering (n. 75), 95; Malan/De Beer (n. 2) § 82.

[154] S. 30(1), Bills of Exchange Act 34 of 1964. See also Story (n. 143), 203.

dependent upon valuable consideration, these two characteristics in fact amount to very much the same thing.

3. South African law

The doctrine of valuable consideration is a peculiarity of English law and unknown in Roman-Dutch law. Its essential role in English law was to distinguish between promissory transactions which are binding, and those which are not: a role which in Roman-Dutch law was fulfilled by the doctrine of *iusta causa* or *redelicke oorzaecke*.[155] The classical formulation is that of Grotius: '*toezegginghen die uit eenighe redelicke oorzaecken geschieden . . . recht gaven om te eisschen.*'[156] In Roman-Dutch law any promise based on a *iusta causa* is accordingly enforceable.

However, this does not mean that *iusta causa* must be regarded as a separate element of the definition of a contract;[157] in the theory of contract the *iusta causa* concept has become largely redundant. In a watershed decision the Appellate Division in *Conradie v. Rossouw* defined the *causa* requirement as follows: 'A good cause of action can be founded on a promise made seriously and deliberately and with the intention that a lawful obligation should be established'.[158] Thus, in requiring of a contract that it be founded on a *iusta causa*, one is saying no more than that it must have been entered into seriously and deliberately, and must not be unlawful.[159]

Although this interpretation of *iusta causa* is widely accepted in South Africa today this was not always the case. Dealing with the history of the doctrines of *iusta causa* and valuable consideration in South Africa, Zimmermann remarks that both are 'refined legal doctrines' which are 'highly problematic'. He continues as follows: 'These problems are, of course, exacerbated if a legal system starts confounding the two doctrines. Such a legal system may well, as a result, land in "a nightmare of confusion" '.[160] This is precisely what happened in South Africa. Despite earlier judicial recognition of the fact that the doctrine of valuable consideration did not form part of Roman-Dutch law,[161] Lord De Villiers, in a series of decisions between 1874 and 1904,[162] equated the doctrines of *iusta causa*

---

[155] See Reinhard Zimmermann, *The Law of Obligations: Roman Foundations of the Civilian Tradition* (1990, reprint 1993), 556.

[156] (Promises arising from a *redelicke oorzaecke* give rise to a claim): (n. 47), 3, 1, 52.

[157] As argued by Sir John Kotzé, *Causa in the Roman and Roman-Dutch Law of Contract* (1922), 45 sq. This idea lives on in French law. See Zimmermann (n. 155), 553.

[158] 1919 AD 279 (headnote).

[159] This, too, is the conclusion of Zimmermann (n. 155), 559.

[160] Zimmermann (n. 155), 556. And see Dale Hutchison ('Formation of Contract') above.

[161] *Louisa and Protector of Slaves v. Van den Berg* (1830) 1 Menz 471; *Jacobson v. Norton* (1841) 2 Menz 218.

[162] *Alexander v. Perry* (1874) 4 Buch 59; *Malan and Van der Merwe v. Secretan, Boon & Co* 1880 Foord 94; *Tradesmen's Benefit Soc v. Du Preez* (1887) 5 SC 269; *Mtembu v. Webster* (1904) 21 SC 323.

and valuable consideration.[163] Only in the 1919 case of *Conradie v. Rossouw*[164] did the Appellate Division reject this view.

Bills of exchange legislation modelled on the English Act was first introduced into South Africa between 1887 and 1902, in the very midst of the 'nightmare of confusion'[165] resulting from the confounding of the doctrines of *causa* and consideration. Natal was the first province to legislate.[166] As in England, the legislation equates the concepts 'value' and 'valuable consideration', the latter being defined in the exact terms of the English Act, as 'any consideration sufficient to support a simple contract'.[167] Significantly, however, the provisions of the English legislation are supplemented by s. 26(2): 'Valuable consideration for a bill is not necessary to entitle the holder to sue therefor.'

The legislation introduced somewhat later in the Cape, Transvaal, and Orange Free State[168] (henceforth the Cape legislation) differs from the aforementioned in two respects: (i) there is no provision akin to the Natal s. 26(2); and (ii) 'valuable consideration' is defined as 'any *cause* sufficient to support an action founded on contract or agreement'.[169] When the different provincial statutes were eventually consolidated in 1964 into a single national Bills of Exchange Act, the provisions of the Cape legislation prevailed.[170]

The provisions of the different provincial legislations warrant two observations. In the first place, the incorporation of s. 26(2) into the Natal legislation is a clear indication that the Natal legislature appreciated that the doctrine of valuable consideration was not part of our common law. Kotzé draws the same conclusion in respect of the substitution of the term 'cause' for 'consideration' in the Cape legislation.[171] But is this conclusion warranted? Another, and it is submitted better, interpretation is that the Cape legislature, by substituting 'cause' for 'consideration', simply codified the viewpoints of its own Chief Justice, Lord de Villiers. They were as follows: (i) *iusta causa* and valuable consideration are the same thing; (ii) the common law of the Cape Province is the Roman-Dutch law; and (iii) therefore, why not opt for the Roman-Dutch rather than the English term?[172]

Secondly, the confusion resulting from the confounding of *causa* and consideration is already evident in the very wording of the legislation. '*Valuable consideration* for a bill', so s. 25(1) of the Cape legislation provided 'may be

---

[163] An opposing point of view was adopted by Innes CJ in the Transvaal. See *Rood v. Wallach* 1904 TS 187.
[164] 1919 AD 279.   [165] Ibid. 323.   [166] See n. 13, above.
[167] S. 26(1), Bills of Exchange Law, Natal Law 8 of 1887.   [168] See nn. 14–16 above.
[169] S. 25(1), Bills of Exchange Act 19 of 1893 (Cape) (italics added).
[170] See s. 25(1), Bills of Exchange Act 34 of 1964.   [171] 101 sq.
[172] Viljoen (n. 138), 6 sq.: '*Dit is ondenkbaar dat die Kaapse wetgewer sou waag om 'n wet te giet in terme wat onbestaanbaar is met die reg soos deur die howe gespreek.*' (It is unthinkable that the Cape legislature would have utilized terminology which is not reconcilable with existing case-law.)

constituted by ... [a]ny *cause* sufficient to support an action on contract'. A gratuitous promise could be enforced in Roman-Dutch law; therefore, to use the terminology employed in the Cape legislation, a gratuitous promise amounted to valuable consideration! This unfortunate wording has nevertheless survived.[173]

'Value' as defined in section 25(1) was, however, eventually interpreted authoritatively by the Appellate Division. The rejection of the consideration doctrine in *Conradie v. Rossouw* paved the way, and in 1971 Corbett AJA had the opportunity in *Froman v. Robertson* to deal with *iusta causa* specifically in the context of cheques:

In applying the requirements of *justa causa* to the engagements of the drawer, regard must always be had to the special characteristics of a cheque. In modern usage a valid cheque represents money and is a generally accepted medium for the payment of a monetary obligation ... Such an obligation generally arises from some transaction, contractual or otherwise, extraneous to the drawing and issue of the cheque itself but nevertheless constituting the ground or reason therefor. Accordingly, any investigation as to the existence or validity of the causa for the engagements of the drawer must necessarily embrace this underlying transaction.[174]

Thus, a holder for value, at least for the purposes of s. 25(1) of the Bills of Exchange Act, is a holder who holds the bill as a consequence of a valid underlying transaction, such as a contract of sale or a donation; but this is in effect to say no more than that the bill of exchange contract is valid. The value of the concept of *iusta causa*, also in the case of bills of exchange, is therefore questionable.[175]

However, the South African legislation not only adopted the English definition of value (albeit in a modified form) but also faithfully reproduced the other provisions in the English Act regarding value. Thus, for instance, s. 25(1)(b) observes that valuable consideration may also be constituted by an 'antecedent debt or liability', which provision is not so much problematical as totally redundant. More problematic, though, is the interpretation of s. 27(1) which provides that a holder in due course must have acquired the bill 'for value'. The question arises whether the meaning ascribed to 'value' in s. 25(1)(a) is equally applicable in this instance.

---

[173] The very different policy followed in the erstwhile Ceylon (Sri Lanka) is especially noteworthy. By providing that value may be constituted by 'any consideration *which by the law of England* is sufficient to support a simple contract' (s. 27(1)(a), Ceylon Ordinance), the confusion rampant in the South African legislation has been avoided. This provision is strengthened by s. 97(2) of the Ceylon Ordinance: 'The rules of the common law of England, including the law merchant, save in so far as they are inconsistent with the express provisions of this Ordinance ... shall apply to bills of exchange, promissory notes and cheques'. See Cowen/Gering (n. 75), 90, fn. 46.

[174] 1971 (1) SA 115 (A) 121 sq. See also *Saambou-Nasionale Bouvereniging v. Friedman* 1979 (3) SA 978 (A) in which the concept that the underlying contract constituted the *causa* for the bill was further entrenched.

[175] Viljoen (n. 138), 9 sq.

The holder in due course enjoys a very privileged status. In terms of s. 36(b) 'he holds the bill free from any defects in the title of prior parties, as well as mere personal defences available to prior parties among themselves, and may enforce payment against all parties liable on the bill'.[176] Should the extraordinary protection awarded to the holder in due course be available to a gratuitous holder? The question has never been investigated in any depth in South African case-law. Most commentators, however, are in agreement that the answer should be negative.[177] This would also appear to be more in line with the position in South African common law which, as noted above,[178] offered limited protection to *onerous* transferees in good faith.

Another point raised by Malan is that the definition of value contained in s. 25(1)(a) applies only in terms of the Act, 'unless the context otherwise indicates'.[179] Malan indicates that s. 27 attempts to define the '*bona fide* holder for value without notice'[180] of the English common law, and must accordingly be interpreted with reference to the English common law; and the English common law, of course, required not only acquisition through contract but also for a *quid pro quo*. Hence a similar interpretation is allowed by the Act.[181] Viljoen, on the other hand, rejects this view on the basis that the context of s. 27 itself does not indicate the necessity for an interpretation of value different from that contained in s. 25.[182]

It would seem, though, that South African case-law, despite the absence of any comprehensive judicial interpretation, has accepted that 'value' in the definition of the holder in due course means a *quid pro quo*.[183] There is also support for this view in the case-law prior to the Bills of Exchange legislation.[184] It is accordingly suggested that, in spite of Viljoen's reasoning, it is highly unlikely (and, it is submitted, not in accordance with commercial expectations) that a court would at this stage award the privileges of a holder in due course to a gratuitous holder. 'Value' in this context accordingly means *quid pro quo*.[185]

---

[176] S. 36(c)(i) provides that if a person with a defective title 'negotiates the bill to a holder in due course, that holder obtains a good and complete title to the bill'. In the same vein, s. 19(3) provides: 'If a bill is in the hands of a holder in due course a valid delivery of such bill by all parties prior to him, so as to make them liable to him, is conclusively presumed.'

[177] Cowen/Gering (n. 75), 283 sq.; Malan/De Beer (n. 2), §§ 174–7. But see Viljoen (n. 138), 15–17.

[178] Above, Section III.   [179] Section 1.   [180] Malan (n. 94), 94.

[181] Malan/De Beer (n. 2), § 174.   [182] Viljoen (n. 138), 15–17.

[183] *Netherlands Bank of SA Ltd v. Smith* 1971 (3) SA 647 (W) 652; *Haynes Industries (Pty) Ltd v. North Coast Industries (Pty) Ltd* 1978 (1) SA 1087 (D) 1090.

[184] In *Kennel v. Harries* (1830) 1 Menz 85 the privileged holder who was later to become known as a 'holder in due course' is referred to simply as an 'onerous indorsee'. See also *Hovil and Mathew v. Wood* (1840) 1 Menz 97.

[185] That is so not only in s. 27(1), which lists the requirements for holding in due course, but also in s. 28(2), which provides that every holder is deemed to be a holder in due course until the acceptance, issue, or negotiation of the bill is proved or admitted to be tainted, after

Once this is accepted the 'chameleon-like quality'[186] of 'value' in South African law becomes apparent. In some instances it means *iusta causa* in the sense of a valid underlying agreement; in others a *quid pro quo*. Thus, wherever the term is employed in the Bills of Exchange Act, its interpretation is fraught with difficulty. One example suffices: the provisions of the Act relating to accommodation.

A typical example of accommodation is the banker's acceptance.[187] A bill is drawn by the client of a bank and accepted by the bank in furtherance of a prior undertaking to its client to do so. Once accepted by the bank (a creditworthy institution) the bill can readily be discounted in the money market. The client thereby acquires financing on the strength of the bank's creditworthiness. The understanding between the bank and its client is, however, that the client will provide the bank with the necessary funds to meet the bill on maturity. The bank (accommodation party) clearly does not intend to become liable to its client (accommodated party) on the bill of exchange. It merely lends its creditworthiness to the bill so as to enable the accommodated party to discount it to a subsequent holder. On the other hand, it is to this holder, who finances the accommodated party, that the bank deliberately and seriously intends to make itself liable. The South African law of contract is perfectly capable of giving effect to such an arrangement.

In the wake of the English Act, however, s. 26(1) of the South African Bills of Exchange Act defines the accommodation party as a person who has signed a bill with the purpose of lending his name to another 'without receiving value therefor', and who in terms of s. 26(2) is rendered liable on the bill to 'a holder for value'. In England, as noted above,[188] these provisions were necessary due to the consideration doctrine; but how must they be interpreted in South Africa? Does 'value' in s. 26(1) mean a *quid pro quo*? No, says Malan: the words simply signify that the accommodation party has not concluded a bill of exchange contract with the accommodated party; in other words 'value' must be interpreted here as *iusta causa*.[189] On the other hand, Gering takes the view that the words do indeed mean a *quid pro quo*, for 'one would not ordinarily speak of "receiving" any "cause sufficient to support an action founded on contract" '.[190] What about 'value' in

---

which the holder, to avail himself of the presumption, must prove that he gave 'value' in good faith subsequent to the tainting of the bill. See *Netherlands Bank of SA Ltd v. Smith* (n. 183); *Haynes Industries (Pty) Ltd v. North Coast Industries (Pty) Ltd* (n. 183).

[186] Peterson, (1971) 88 *SALJ* 155.   [187] Cowen/Gering (n. 1), 186.
[188] Above, Section V. 2.
[189] F. R. Malan, 'Die Aanspreeklikheid van die Akkommodasieparty', 1976 *TSAR* 241, 242 sq. See further Malan/De Beer (n. 2), § 83; C. J. Nagel, 'Enkele Gedagtes oor die Akkommodasiefiguur' (1985) 18 *De Jure* 23, 26–9.
[190] Gering (n. 3), 168.

s. 26(2)? Case-law suggests that it means a *quid pro quo*;[191] but this too can be explained simply with reference to the law of contract, for, as Cowen and Gering state, 'the deliberate intention of the accommodation party is to incur liability only to a holder who finances the party accommodated'. Thus, as the learned authors continue: 'The reproduction in the South African legislation of the English section on accommodation parties was ... not only redundant; it is also perplexing and another potential source of what was avoidable litigation'.[192]

To conclude this topic, it is of note that the proposals for the reform of the Bills of Exchange Act published by the South African Law Commission would do away with all provisions relating to value (including the accommodation party) with the single exception that the holder in due course must have acquired the bill 'for value'.[193] In this respect the proposed legislation defines 'value' as follows: 'For the purposes of this Act, a person takes an instrument for value if he acquires it under onerous title'.[194]

VI. THE NEGLIGENT COLLECTING BANK

1. Introduction

Is a bank that negligently collects a cheque on behalf of a client who is not the true owner of the cheque liable to the true owner? This question, in the history of the law of bills of exchange in South Africa, has attracted most attention in academic writing.[195] Since the recent cases *Indac Electronics (Pty) Ltd v. Volkskas Bank Ltd*,[196] and *Fedgen Insurance Ltd v. Bankorp*

---

[191] *Dimart Discounting (Pty) Ltd v. Deals Furnishers (Pty) Ltd* 1973 (1) SA 458 (T) 461: 'It is clear that if the plaintiff took the cheque gratuitously he cannot claim from the accommodation party.'

[192] Cowen/Gering (n. 75), 95 sq.   [193] Malan/Oelofse/Pretorius (n. 26), 181–7.

[194] Ibid. 40 (s. 1(4)).

[195] Apart from the standard textbooks, see e.g. C. R. De Beer, 'Die Aanspreeklikheid van die Invorderingsbankier teenoor die Ware Eienaar van 'n Tjek', (1977) 40 *THRHR* 360; F. R. Malan, 'Professional Responsibility and the Payment and Collection of Cheques', 1978 *De Jure* 326 and 1979 *De Jure* 31; *idem*, 'Once More on Professional Liability', 1979 *De Jure* 363; Louise Tager, 'The Collecting Bank's Liability to the True Owner of a Lost or Stolen Cheque', (1979) 96 *SALJ* 372; Denis Cowen, 'The Liability of a Bank in the Computer Age in Respect of a Stolen Cheque', 1981 *TSAR* 193; J. T. Pretorius, 'Professionele Aanspreeklikheid, die Invorderingsbank en Regshervorming', 1987 *Moderne Besigheidsreg* 56; Malan/Oelofse/Pretorius (n. 26), 581–637; F. R. Malan, J. T. Pretorius, 'The Collecting Bank Revisited', (1991) 54 *THRHR* 705; Charl Hugo, 'The Negligent Collecting Bank: Recent Decisions Introduce a New Era', (1992) 3 *Stellenbosch LR* 115; C. J. Nagel, Melanie Greef, 'Die Deliktuele Aanspreeklikheid van die Invorderingsbank', (1992) 55 *THRHR* 314; Michael Kidd, 'Can a Collecting Banker be Held Liable under the *Lex Aquilia*? Recent Developments and Some Thoughts on the Future', (1993) 110 *SALJ* 1; F. R. Malan, J. T. Pretorius, 'Questions of Negligence and the Collecting Bank: A Brief History of the *Bonitas* Trilogy', (1994) 6 *South African Mercantile Law Journal* 116.

[196] 1992 (1) SA 783 (A).

Ltd[197] there can be little doubt that the question must be answered in the affirmative; but the recognition of this action has had a long and fascinating history, fraught with difficulties.

The question, when first posed in *Yorkshire Insurance Co Ltd v. Standard Bank of SA Ltd*,[198] was argued on two bases: (i) on the legislation governing bills of exchange, and (ii) on the general principles of the Roman-Dutch law of delict. This distinction is useful as the statutory and delictual liability of the collecting bank, although not totally unrelated, have undergone separate historical development.

2. The statutory liability of the collecting bank

The plaintiff in the *Yorkshire* case proceeded partly on the basis that a bank which collects a cheque negligently is liable to the true owner by virtue of s. 80 of the Transvaal Bills of Exchange Proclamation, which provides as follows:

Where a banker in good faith and without negligence receives payment for a customer of a cheque crossed generally or specially to himself, and the customer has no title or a defective title thereto, the banker shall not incur any liability to the true owner of the cheque by reason only of having received such payment.

This was taken verbatim from s. 82 of the English Bills of Exchange Act. However, s. 82 was designed to protect the bank collecting a crossed cheque from an action based on the tort of conversion. This action, peculiar to English law, allowed the true owner of stolen property to recover damages from any person who possessed or 'converted' the property subsequent to the theft, irrespective of whether such possessor was in good or bad faith. In order to be protected by s. 82 the bank had to fulfil three requirements: it must have collected 'for a customer',[199] 'in good faith',[200] and 'without negligence'.[201]

This statutory provision, as Tindall J points out, suggests an intention to protect the bank against an existing liability and not to impose a liability

---

[197] 1994 (2) SA 399 (W).   [198] 1928 WLD 251.

[199] In *Capital and Counties Bank v. Gordon, London City and Midlands Bank v. Gordon* [1903] AC 240, 249 the House of Lords ruled that once the collecting bank had credited its client with the amount of a cheque deposited with him for collection, the bank no longer collected 'for a customer' in terms of s. 82 and could be held liable. This caused the English legislature to intervene. The Bills of Exchange (Crossed Cheques) Act 1906 (6 Edw. 7 c. 17) provides where the bank 'credits the customer's account with the amount of the cheque before receiving payment thereof' it still collects 'for a customer' for the purposes of s. 82. Should the banker, however, allow his client to draw against an uncleared cheque, or where there is an agreement to that effect between the banker and his client, the banker no longer collects 'for a customer' but as a 'holder for value'. See Frank R. Ryder, Antonio Bueno, *Byles on Bills of Exchange* (26th edn., 1988), 316–19; De Beer, (1977) 40 *THRHR* 362.

[200] See Ryder/Bueno (n. 199), 313–23.   [201] Ibid.

where none existed before.[202] In English law there is such an existing liability; in South African law there is not. Therefore this section could not be relied on to found an action, and was meaningless in South Africa.

This finding led to intervention of the legislature in 1943. The Bills of Exchange Amendment Act of that year repealed the meaningless s. 80 of the Transvaal Proclamation and enacted a new s. 80, which in 1964 became s. 81 of the South African Bills of Exchange Act. Section 81(1) provides as follows:

If a cheque was stolen or lost while it was crossed as authorized by this Act, and while it bore on it the words 'not negotiable', and it was paid by the banker upon whom it was drawn, under circumstances which do not render such banker liable in terms of this Act to the true owner of the cheque for any loss he may sustain owing to the cheque having been paid, the true owner shall, if he suffered any loss as a result of the theft or loss of the cheque, be entitled to recover from any person who was a possessor thereof after the theft or loss, and either gave a consideration therefor or took it as a donee, an amount equal to the true owner's said loss or the amount of the cheque, whichever is the lesser.

This section adopts the English action of conversion but limits its application to crossed cheques marked 'not negotiable'.[203] By virtue of this provision the true owner of such a cheque in certain circumstances now has an action also against a person who possessed the cheque in good faith after the theft or loss.

Someone through whose hands such a cheque must necessarily pass is the collecting bank. The dictates of commerce require that a collecting bank must be protected against this statutory conversion action. By virtue of s. 81(1) any possessor of the cheque 'who gave a consideration therefor or took it as a donee' is liable to the true owner. In terms of s. 81(5), however, the collecting bank is not regarded as having given a consideration for the cheque 'merely because he has in his own books credited his customer's account with the amount of the cheque before receiving payment thereof, or because any such payment is applied towards the reduction or settlement of any debt owed by the customer to the banker'. This provision relates to the requirement in s. 82 of the English Bills of Exchange Act, which in 1957 was superseded by s. 4 of the English Cheques Act,[204] that for the collecting bank to escape conversion liability it must have collected 'for a customer'.

However, a bank which allows its client to draw against a cheque deposited by him for collection before having received the proceeds of the

---

[202] 1928 WLD 251 (280). This was also the interpretation of De Villiers CJ in the earlier decision *Liquidators of Cape of Good Hope Building Soc v. Bank of Africa* (1900) 17 SC 480, 493. See also M. O. Evans, *Law of Bills of Exchange, Promissory Notes, Cheques and Banks in South Africa* (2nd edn., 1926), 235 sq.

[203] See Cowen/Gering (n. 75), 434.   [204] 5 and 6 Eliz. 2 c. 36 (1957).

cheque from the drawee has, for the purposes of s. 81, given a consideration for the cheque, and is not protected by s. 81(5).[205] The same probably
holds true when the bank, as a consideration for the specific cheque, agrees
to allow its client to draw against that cheque. A general agreement by
which the client is allowed to draw against deposited cheques is more problematical. Under s. 81 consideration must be given 'therefor', that is for the
specific cheque in question.[206] The wording of all the relevant subsections
suggests reciprocity, a true *quid pro quo*. Such a general agreement, it is submitted, will not suffice.[207]

Finally, the ambit of the English legislation protecting the collecting bank
from conversion liability is expressly limited to a bank collecting in good
faith and without negligence. The South African legislation has no comparable provision. This led to the *obiter* contention in *National Housing
Commission v. Cape of Good Hope Savings Bank Soc*[208] that the words 'in
good faith and without negligence' were left out of s. 81(5) *per incuriam*.
This point of view has not found favour elsewhere.[209] Consequently, the liability of the collecting bank for bad faith and negligence after the 1943
amendments must still be determined with reference to South African common law.

---

[205] See *Fonds Adviseurs Bpk v. Trust Bank van Afrika Bpk* 1974 (4) SA 883 (A) in which it
was found that 'consideration' for the purposes of s. 81 is a *quid pro quo*. Thus the 'consideration' of s. 81 differs from the 'valuable consideration' or 'value' of s. 1 read with s. 25(1). The
fact that the collecting bank has for the purposes of s. 81 given consideration therefore does
not imply that the bank, by virtue of the provisions of s. 84 or otherwise, qualifies as a holder
for value of the cheque. As stated by Malan/De Beer (n. 2), § 143 it is not 'the mere giving of
value or the mere payment of a cheque drawn against uncleared effects' which constitutes the
bank a holder for value, but an 'express or implied agreement to this effect'. See also *Haynes
Industries (Pty) Ltd v. North Coast Industries (Pty) Ltd* (n. 183), 1090–2; *Bloems Timber Kilns
(Pty) Ltd v. Volkskas Bpk* 1976 (4) SA 677 (A) 687E. For the purposes of the South African
conversion liability of the collecting banker (the s. 81 liability), the distinction of English law
between the banker acting as collecting agent or as holder for value (see Ryder/Bueno (n. 199),
316) cannot be adopted. The relevant distinction is between a banker acting as collection agent
and the banker who has given consideration for the cheque. As apparent from the *Haynes* and
Bloems Timber cases, the totally different question of whether the collecting banker qualifies
as holder for value is of importance in a different situation, i.e. where the banker wishes to
enforce payment of the cheque.

[206] See s. 81(1)–(5).

[207] A general agreement in terms of which the collecting banker allows his client to draw
against deposited uncleared cheques does, however, constitute 'value'. See *Haynes Industries
(Pty) Ltd v. North Coast Industries (Pty) Ltd* (n. 183), 1090–2; *Bloems Timber Kilns (Pty) Ltd
v. Volkskas Bpk* (n. 205).

[208] 1963 (1) SA 230 (C) 237.

[209] This contention has not found favour elsewhere. See Cowen/Gering (n. 75), 439;
Malan/De Beer (n. 2), § 339, fn. 82.

3. The common law liability of the collecting bank

(a) The actio ad exhibendum

In the *Yorkshire* case Tindall J equates the position of a bank collecting a cheque on behalf of someone who is not the true owner to that of a person who has purchased stolen property.[210] In an earlier decision, *Leal and Co v. Williams*, Innes CJ described the position of the true owner of stolen property under Roman-Dutch common law as follows:

> He may follow his property and vindicate it anywhere provided it is *in esse*. And he may bring an action *ad exhibendum* to recover the property or its value (should it have been consumed) against the thief or his heirs, or against any person who has received it with knowledge of the tainted title. The fact that these are the only remedies allowed by our law is inconsistent with the doctrine of conversion . . .[211]

In the same vein Tindall J states in the *Yorkshire* case:

> The Roman-Dutch authorities[212] deal particularly with the specific case of the person who innocently received stolen property and has parted with it innocently[213] . . . such a person is not liable to the true owner for the value of the property . . . It is true that in the passages in question the authors are dealing with the vindicatory *actio ad exhibendum* . . . but they state definitely that the purchaser who buys the stolen article in good faith and disposes of it in good faith is not liable on any ground, neither *ex delicto* nor upon contract or quasi-contract nor in natural equity.[214]

His finding is clear: the matter is exhaustively dealt with under the *actio ad exhibendum*, and consequently there is no room for liability under the *lex Aquilia*.[215] In a subsequent case, *Atkinson Oates Motors Ltd v. Trust Bank of Africa Ltd*, the *ratio decidendi* of the *Yorkshire case* was stated thus: 'A collecting banker owes no duty of care, at common law, to the true owner of a cheque . . . and is not liable to him for negligence *as opposed to knowledge, direct or constructive*'.[216]

But what amounts to constructive knowledge? The answer, it is submitted, can be gleaned from the *Yorkshire* case itself: 'If the officials of the bank

---

[210] 281 sq.

[211] 1906 TS 554, 558 sq. See also *John Bell and Co Ltd v. Esselen* 1954 (1) SA 147 (A) 153.

[212] Tindall J relies especially on Johannes Voet (n. 48), 6, 1, 10. On this passage in this context see De Beer (1977) 40 *THRHR* 368 sq.; Tager (1979) 96 *SALJ* 381 sq.

[213] It would seem from the context that Tindall J by 'innocently' does not mean 'without negligence' but 'in good faith'.

[214] 281 sq.

[215] Tager, (1979) 96 *SALJ* 387 sq., is correct in submitting that the Court 'did not approach the question of the collecting banker's liability squarely on the basis of Aquilian liability. It simply denied the existence of an action in negligence on the ground that a *bona fide* purchaser who has negligently parted with the property of another could not be liable.' See also her arguments on 385 sq.

[216] 1977 (3) SA 188 (W) 191.

deliberately shut their eyes to what was going on, it could not then be said that the defendants "did not have knowledge" '.[217]

From the aforegoing two conclusions may be drawn as to 'constructive knowledge'. In the first place, the test for constructive knowledge, unlike the test for negligence,[218] is subjective. Secondly, the term may also relate to the imputation of the knowledge of officials or employees of a juristic person to that person. In this respect the following *dictum* of Nicholas AJA in *Anderson Shipping (Pty) Ltd v. Guardian National Insurance Co Ltd* is apposite:

[I]t was argued that Anderson [the plaintiff company] had constructive knowledge because Roos's knowledge was to be imputed to the company. The applicable rule was summarized by Trollip J . . . There may be imputed to a company 'the knowledge of any of its agents or servants possessed and acquired by him in the course of his employment under such circumstances and being of such a nature that it was his duty to communicate it to the proper authority in the company . . . unless that agent or servant is perpetrating a fraud on the company in relation to the matters of which he so possesses or acquires knowledge.[219]

In practical terms: if a thief deposits a stolen cheque for collection, in circumstances where the bank official accepting the deposit suspects that all is not well with the cheque but nevertheless simply closes his eyes to this fact, the *actio ad exhibendum* will be available to the true owner against the bank.

(b) The actio legis Aquiliae

The infliction of damage is actionable only if both unlawful and negligent. Consequently, the true owner of a lost or stolen cheque, in order to hold the collecting bank liable, must show that the bank had a legal duty[220] not to cause him economic loss. The existence of such a duty was denied in the *Yorkshire* case in 1928. Almost fifty years transpired before a South African court, in *Atkinson Oates Motors Ltd v. Trust Bank of Africa Ltd*[221] had the opportunity to consider this question again. The Court regarded itself as bound by the *Yorkshire* case.

In the meanwhile, however, the same question had come up for decision

---

[217] 283.

[218] See also the judgment of Lord de Villiers in *Cape of Good Hope Building Soc v. Bank of Africa* (1900) 17 SC 480, 487–9, who cites as examples of knowledge the situation where a party has the means to obtain knowledge and willingly shuts his eyes, or has a suspicion which he wilfully disregards. A different test for constructive knowledge may apply in the law of insurance in the context of the duty on the proposer to disclose facts within his knowledge which may affect the risk. See *Anderson Shipping (Pty) Ltd v. Guardian National Insurance Co Ltd* 1987 (3) SA 506 (A), 516 sq.

[219] (n. 218), 518.

[220] The term 'legal duty' is better than the often encountered term 'duty of care' which involves both the issue of unlawfulness and fault. See J. Neethling, J. M. Potgieter, P. J. Visser, *Deliktereg* (2nd edn., 1992), 140 sq.

[221] 1977 (3) SA 188 (W).

in what was then Rhodesia, a country also governed by Roman-Dutch law.[222] In *Rhostar (Pvt) Ltd v. Netherlands Bank of Rhodesia Ltd*[223] the High Court of Rhodesia, arguing that banking practice had changed since the *Yorkshire* case, accepted the existence of such a legal duty. This finding was soon followed thereafter in another Rhodesian case *Philsam Investments (Pvt) Ltd v. Beverley Building Society.*[224]

The *Atkinson Oates, Rhostar*, and *Philsam* cases sparked off much academic discussion. It was generally accepted that policy considerations were crucial in determining the liability of the collecting banker.[225] Amongst the arguments raised in favour of the *Yorkshire status quo* was the fact that the potential liability of the collecting bank would detrimentally affect the speed and cost of the collection process.[226] It was further argued that it was undesirable for the courts to interfere with the law as laid down over a long period of time, especially where legislation, based on the premise that the *Yorkshire* case had been correctly decided, had been enacted.[227]

In support of the existence of a legal duty on the part of the collecting bank towards the true owner of a cheque, reliance was placed on the function of the collecting bank. As stated by Goldin J: '[t]he collecting banker is the only one who is in a position to know whether or not the cheque is being collected on behalf of the person who is entitled to receive payment.'[228] This consideration, as well as an appreciation of the fact that the practice of crossing cheques originated from a desire to make cheque payments safer,[229] favour the acceptance of a legal duty on the part of the collecting bank towards the true owner.

During 1978 and 1979 the argument for recognition of such a duty gained impetus from two important events. The first was the publication of a series of articles on the question by Professor Malan in which a new, and possibly the strongest argument favouring such a duty was first raised.[230] With reference to developments in England, he said:

The momentous decision in *Hedley Byrne and Co Ltd v. Heller and Partners*[231] is a judgement of policy. The House of Lords held that economic loss caused by a negligent misrepresentation was actionable because the law implies a duty of care when someone seeks information from one possessing certain skills and relies on him to exercise due care in furnishing that information . . . This was a case of the recovery of economic loss. It was also an instance of professional liability . . . It is in the fas-

---

[222] See Reinhard Zimmermann, 'Das römisch-holländische Recht in Zimbabwe', (1991) 55 *RabelsZ* 505 sqq.
[223] 1972 (2) SA 703 (R).   [224] 1977 (2) SA 546 (R).
[225] See Malan, (1979) 12 *De Jure* 32, 37; Tager, (n. 215), 392; Cowen, 1981 *TSAR* 195, 204.
[226] Cowen, (n. 225), 220.   [227] Ibid. 220 sq.
[228] *Rhostar* (n. 223), 715. See also Malan (1979) 12 *De Jure* 37.
[229] See Holden (n. 81), 229–43; Malan, (1978) 11 *De Jure* 335.
[230] Malan, (n. 229), 326; *idem* (n. 228), 31, 363.
[231] [1964] AC 465, [1963] 2 All ER 575 (HL).

cinating field of professional liability that the basis for the responsibility of the paying and collecting bank to the owner of a lost or stolen cheque has to be found. The law imposes upon those engaged in a calling which requires skill and competence the duty to exercise their profession with reasonable care and skill.[232]

The second important event was the decision of the Appellate Division in *Administrateur, Natal v. Trust Bank van Afrika Bpk*[233] in which the principle of delictual liability for pure economic loss was unequivocally accepted.[234] This case necessitated a re-evaluation of the *Yorkshire* and *Atkinson Oates* decisions in the light of the material growth of the law of delict.[235] As pointed out a few years later by Gubbay JA in *Zimbabwe Banking Corporation Ltd v. Pyramid Motor Corporation (Pvt) Ltd*[236]—in which the Zimbabwean Supreme Court once again evaluated and approved the stance it had taken in the *Rhostar* and *Philsam* cases—the *Yorkshire* decision 'came during an era when the concept of liability for pure economic loss unintentionally caused had never been contemplated, let alone considered by the courts'.[237]

Finally, in 1988, in the form of a Working Paper of the South African Law Commission, Malan, Oelofse, and Pretorius's *Proposals for the Reform of the Bills of Exchange Act, 1964* was published. The authors recognized the existence in principle of a duty (in the policy sense) on the part of a collecting banker to avoid causing loss to the owner of a lost or stolen cheque by dealing with it negligently.[238] Thus the stage was set for a South African court to re-evaluate the previous South African decisions.

The first opportunity arose in *Worcester Advice Office v. First National Bank of SA Ltd.*[239] This was only the third case in which a South African court was called upon to decide whether a collecting banker can be held liable by the true owner of a stolen cheque for its negligent collection. It was a decision by the Cape Provincial Provision of the Supreme Court, which was not bound by the *Yorkshire* and *Atkinson Oates* cases. The facts were typical. The plaintiff was the true owner of a cheque which was stolen. The thief had opened an account in a name similar to that of the payee at the defendant bank. The cheque was deposited into this account and collected by the defendant bank. The plaintiff instituted action on the basis that the

---

[232] 1979 *De Jure* 32–4.

[233] 1979 (3) SA 824 (A). For a detailed discussion see Dale Hutchison, 'Aquilian Liability II' Ch. 18, below.

[234] 832H–833A. The extension of Aquilian liability to pure economic loss was also favourably commented upon by Hoexter J in *Greenfield Engineering Works (Pty) Ltd v. NKR Construction (Pty) Ltd* 1978 (4) SA 901 (N) 913–7. See also the much earlier *obiter dictum* of Innes CJ in *Leal and Co v. Williams* 1906 TS 554, 559.

[235] See Tager, (1979) 96 *SALJ* 387; Pretorius, 1987 *Moderne Besigheidsreg* 61 sq.; Malan/Oelofse/ Pretorius (n. 26), 596.

[236] 1985 (4) SA 553 (ZS); on which see Zimmermann (1991) 55 *RabelsZ* 525 sq.

[237] 563.   [238] Malan/Oelofse/Pretorius (n. 26), 582.

[239] 1990 (4) SA 811 (C).

defendant bank was liable in delict for its negligence in not properly verifying the identity of its client when opening the account. The defendant excepted to the particulars of the claim on the basis that it owed no duty towards the plaintiff.

In their judgment Van Niekerk J and Comrie AJ gave a clear exposition of all the arguments raised in the Zimbabwean decisions and academic writing in support of the existence of such a duty of care. They continued as follows: 'This is undoubtedly an impressive set of reasons. However, we are unpersuaded that we should change the settled law of South Africa, which has stood for sixty years, or adopt the law of the Zimbabwean Courts'.[240] Two reasons for the decision were advanced: (i) although the vigilance and expertise required of the collecting banker may not seem too much to ask in an individual case, cumulatively, with reference to the aggregate of cheques collected through the clearing system, it would be 'too great burden' to be placed upon collecting bankers and spread among its customers. Part of the 'too great a burden' would be the necessity to make proper enquiry as to the identity and commercial standing of someone wanting to open an account.[241] (ii) Issues of causation and contributory negligence would be likely to prove intractable, with the result that bankers would be tempted to pay rather than tie up their officials in court and face adverse publicity. Thus the suggested duty may operate unfairly towards the banks.[242]

These reasons are not convincing. The first does not take account of the fact, as pointed out by Malan and Pretorius, that '[a] duty of care arises only if the apprehended damage could be prevented by reasonable, practicable and affordable measures'.[243]

To this may be added the fact that in countries such as Zimbabwe, England,[244] and Germany[245] where an action against the negligent collecting bank is admitted, this has not proven to be 'too great a burden'.

Malan and Pretorius also dismiss as 'simply not correct' the second reason advanced by the Court.[246] They refer to South African decisions in which the issues of contributory negligence as well as causation in the context of the drawing of cheques were satisfactorily dealt with by the courts in question.[247]

[240] 819F. [241] 819 sq. [242] 820I.
[243] (1991) 54 *THRHR* 713. See also Malan/Pretorius (1994) 6 *South African Mercantile Law Journal* 116, 120: '[T]here is no absolute duty—only one to take reasonable care.'
[244] The liability arises as a consequence of the collecting bank negligently forfeiting its statutory protection against the conversion action. See s. 4(1), Cheques Act 1957 (5 and 6 Eliz. 2, c. 12).
[245] For a brief but well documented discussion see Malan (1978) 11 *De Jure* 326, 338–42.
[246] (1991) 54 *THRHR* 714.
[247] See e.g. *Greenfield Engineering Works (Pty) Ltd v. NKR Construction (Pty) Ltd* (n. 234), 912G-H in which the Court concluded that the drawer of the cheque had acted negligently by drawing the cheque 'in an improper and unbusinesslike manner' and that the 'issue of causality [did not] provide any substantial problems'. See also *Barclays Bank DCO v. Straw* 1965 (2) SA 93 (O).

In the meantime, in the case *Bonitas Medical Aid Fund v. Volkskas Bank Ltd*,[248] the Witwatersrand Local Division had the opportunity to reconsider its stance.[249] The defendant bank had collected a non-transferable cheque on the account of a person other than the payee (the defendant bank itself was the payee). Esselen J dismissed the defendant bank's exception to the claim. With reference to the legal duty owed by defendant bank he remarked as follows:

[I]n principle, and in the absence of any authority to the contrary, there appears to be no valid objection to accepting that the effect of crossing the said cheque *in casu* imposed on the collecting bank (who was the payee) the duty to the drawer of dealing with the cheque in the particular manner indicated on the face thereof, namely to avoid transfer or payment thereof to any party other than itself.[250]

However, the *Yorkshire* and *Atkinson Oates* cases were not overruled but merely distinguished:

[I]t is vitally important to bear in mind that the Court in those cases was concerned with the duty of care on the part of the collecting bank to the payee or true owner of the cheque and not with the duty of care to the drawer of the cheque (who, after proper delivery to first defendant, was not the true owner of the cheque) with which the court is presently concerned. It follows that they are not of assistance *in casu*.[251]

The extensive academic writing in support of the acceptance of a duty on the part of a collecting bank was dismissed on the same basis. Having distinguished the case-law and academic writing, it would appear that Esselen J accepted in principle the possibility of the collecting bank owing a duty to the drawer (the first true owner)[252] but not to subsequent true owners. This approach, however, is not sound. Policy considerations must determine whether the collecting bank has such a duty. The policy considerations favouring the existence of such a duty to the first true owner apply equally to subsequent true owners.[253] Esselen's decision, with its rather forced distinction, nevertheless heralded a marked change in attitude.

---

[248] 1991 (2) SA 231 (W). See C. R. De Beer, N. J. J. Olivier, 'Aanspreeklikheid weens Verhandeling van 'n nie-oordraagbare Tjek', (1991) 16 *Tydskrif vir Regswetenskap* 152 for a discussion of the case.

[249] The *Bonitas* case, although reported later, was heard earlier than the *Worcester* case (22 Mar. 1990 and 10 Sep. 1990 respectively).   [250] 235I.   [251] 236E.

[252] Cf. the following *dictum* on 235: 'In principle, and in the absence of any authority to the contrary, there appears to be no valid objection to accepting that the effect of crossing the said cheque *in casu* imposed on the collecting bank (who was the payee) the duty to the drawer of dealing with the cheque in the particular manner indicated on the face thereof, namely to avoid transfer or payment thereof to any party other than itself.'

[253] See also Malan/Pretorius (1991) 54 *THRHR* 714 who, with reference to the question whether there can be a difference in principle between the position of the collecting bank *vis-à-vis* the drawer or true owner, state as follows: 'There can be no cogent reason for a distinction in this regard, since the drawer may well be the true owner of a lost or stolen cheque. Ordinary principles of the law of property are used to determine who the true owner of a cheque is. It is trite law that it is the *owner* of a cheque who usually suffers loss in the event of theft or forgery.'

The *Bonitas* case subsequently came before Plewman J to be decided on its merits. He stated expressly his opinion that the Zimbabwean approach would lead to a more practical result but considered himself bound by *Yorkshire* and *Atkinson Oates*.[254] He nevertheless managed to find the defendant bank liable on the basis of *mala fides*:

[T]he teller who received the cheque directed no attention to the crossing, or even to the fact that Volkskas itself was named as payee. That would seem to me to be 'shutting one's eyes' . . . The Volkskas officials must be considered to have had, at least, constructive knowledge that the proceeds of the cheque were being applied to the credit of a person not entitled thereto in terms of the instrument itself.[255]

One may well ask whether in this instance the Court applied the proper subjective test for *mala fides*. The *dictum* has an aura of the objective test for negligence about it. At the very least, it is submitted, one may state that Plewman J leant over backwards to find *mala fides*. As such the decision certainly contributed to the breaking down of the *Yorkshire* stronghold.

The *coup de grace* followed shortly thereafter. In *Indac Electronics (Pty) Ltd v. Volkskas Bank Ltd*[256] defendant bank was sued for collecting on behalf of one Le Roux a cheque *ex facie* payable to Indac Electronics. Defendant bank's exception was upheld in the Transvaal Provincial Division. The plaintiff appealed. Viviers JA introduced his judgment with a thorough analysis of the *Yorkshire*, *Rhostar*, *Atkinson Oates*, and *Pyramid* cases.[257] He proceeded as follows:

The correctness of the decisions in *Yorkshire Insurance* and *Atkinson Oates* must today be considered in the light of the subsequent development of our law . . . Aquilian liability for pure economic loss was . . . recognised by this court in 1979 in the case of *Administrateur, Natal* . . . In view of the decision of the *Administrateur, Natal* case . . . the *Yorkshire Insurance* case . . . can, in my view, no longer be regarded as authority for the proposition that no delictual liability lies against a collecting banker who has negligently caused loss to the true owner of the cheque. There can now be no reason in principle why a collecting banker should not be held liable under the extended *lex Aquilia* for negligence to a true owner of a cheque, provided all the elements or requirements of Aquilian liability have been met.[258]

The *Indac* decision has introduced a new era for the law relating to the Aquilian liability of the collecting bank. The focus has now shifted from the question of whether such an action is possible in principle to the question of what constitutes negligence. The collecting banker is a professional; the standard against which his conduct should be measured is accordingly that of the *bonus argentarius*.[259] The standard of care required will be determined

---

[254] 48F.   [255] 49C.   [256] 1992 (1) SA 783 (A).   [257] 789–795.   [258] 796C.
[259] Malan (1979) 12 *De Jure* 39. See also Ryder/Bueno (n. 199), 320 who formulate the test as follows: 'The presence or absence of negligence is to be determined by reference to the practice of reasonable men carrying on the business of bankers.'

by many factors including 'the likelihood of injury and the cost and practicability of taking measures guarding against it'.[260] On the negligence issue, valuable guidance may be obtained from English case-law.[261]

If the decision of Van Zyl J in *Fedgen Insurance Ltd v. Bankorp Ltd*[262] is to be taken as the norm, a reasonably conservative approach is to be expected. Referring to the standard of the *bonus argentarius*, Van Zyl J remarks:

> It is clear that this does not mean that the banker must examine every cheque minutely to determine whether the customer has title thereto. But if, in the course of the transaction, something unusual, untoward or anomalous should attract his attention or arouse his suspicion, it may reasonably be expected of him to institute an inquiry and to take such steps as may be required to prevent loss or damage.

In casu the cheque was made payable to 'R. H. Johnson Crane Hire (Pty) Ltd', but indorsed by means of a rubber stamp by 'R. H. Johnson Crane Hire PO Box 22 Edenvale 1610'. The failure of the teller to notice anything unusual was not deemed negligent.

What then will constitute negligence? In most instances where a cheque is stolen the thief acquires the proceeds in one of two ways: he opens an account in the name of the payee or a similar name,[263] or he simply deposits the cheque into his account with or without a forged endorsement.[264] With reference to the first possibility, it is submitted that a collecting bank is clearly negligent if it opens an account for a prospective client without at the very least properly verifying his identity.[265] With reference to the second possibility, the bank should be regarded as negligent where it collects a cheque for one customer whilst the cheque is *ex facie* clearly payable to someone else.[266] Furthermore, it is submitted that the bank would also be negligent if it collected a non-transferable cheque on behalf of a customer who purports to be holding under an indorsement.[267] In all these instances the loss may be prevented by the adoption of simple measures which are neither impracticable nor expensive. In many other situations the negligence question will undoubtedly be more problematic and will require careful consideration of all the surrounding circumstances.

---

[260] *Indac* (n. 256), 798H; Malan (n. 259).

[261] For a list of what has been held to be negligent conduct in English case-law see Malan (1978) 11 *De Jure* 336 sq. See also Ryder/Bueno (n. 199), 320–3.

[262] 1994 (2) SA 399 (W). [263] As was done in the *Worcester* case.

[264] As was done in the *Indac* case.

[265] See Ryder/Bueno (n. 199), 321 sq. who mention that even failure to make inquiries as to the respectability of a proposed customer may be sufficient to constitute negligence.

[266] Ryder/Bueno (n. 199), 321 formulate the following rule: 'Generally speaking, where there is something on the face (and perhaps the back) of the cheque, taken in relation to the customer for whom it is collected, which should put the banker on inquiry, he ignores it at his peril.'

[267] As in the *Bonitas* case.

4. *Gore v. Saficon Industrial (Pty) Ltd*

After the *Indac* and *Fedgen* cases banking lawyers may have been forgiven for succumbing to a feeling of complacency as to the delictual liability question. The law, so one was inclined to think, had reached its logical conclusion. This complacency, it is suggested, may be shattered by the *Gore* case[268] which dealt with the *actio ad exhibendum*. Zulman J, having stated that knowledge is a requirement for such liability, went on to say: '[K]nowledge may be actual knowledge or may be constructive knowledge which is to be derived from the circumstances of a particular case. *Mala fides* in the limited sense of the word is, to my mind, unnecessary'.[269] He continued: 'It is sufficient, I reiterate, for the purpose of an action for wrongful disposal, that the defendant could reasonably have acquired knowledge . . .'[270]

Thus, it would appear that constructive knowledge is knowledge which the person concerned would have had but for his negligence. If Zulman J's view of constructive knowledge is correct, which with respect I think is not the case,[271] the consequences are far-reaching. This is illustrated by the following example: X steals a cheque from A, forges A's indorsement, and utilizes the cheque to pay for goods he purchases from B. If the cheque is paid under circumstances entitling the drawee bank to debit the drawer's account, the true owner (A) suffers a loss. B is not a bank and owes A no duty of care. B is accordingly not liable under the *lex Aquilia*. However, Zulman's judgment seems to suggest that B will be liable under the *actio ad exhibendum* if he 'could reasonably have acquired knowledge' that the cheque was stolen. It is suggested that Zulman J's judgment, if correct and if applied in this context, may have a detrimental effect on commerce and on the free negotiability of commercial paper.

VII. CONCLUSION

What general conclusions can be offered on the history of negotiable instruments in South Africa? In the first place it is clear that the main problems experienced in the South African legal theory of bills of exchange are generally a consequence of the wholesale incorporation of English legislation. The past century's jurisprudence has, however, crystallized these problems to a large degree. It is therefore submitted that the time is ripe for new legislation. One can but hope that the South African Law Commission's initiatives in this regard will not be shelved indefinitely. Secondly, one can glean from this history the impressive ability of the Roman-Dutch law to grow with the times. As a consequence, there is little doubt that Roman-Dutch law will continue developing in, and contribute to the development of the new South Africa.

[268] 1994 (4) SA 536 (W). [269] 549 sq. [270] 550.
[271] See the text to nn. 216–19 above.

PART IV

Obligations arising neither from Contract nor from Delict

16: *Unjustified Enrichment*

DANIEL VISSER

I. INTRODUCTION

In the South African law of unjustified enrichment Pomponius' celebrated principle that no one should be enriched to the detriment of another[1] has, like one of Michaelangelo's captive giants, struggled mightily to emerge fully from the matter which gave it substance: but has succeeded only in revealing an unfinished vision of its form and power. Ironically, this principle had managed to emerge much more fully in the Dutch law of the seventeenth and eighteenth centuries[2] which was destined to form the basis of South African law. However, in the arid conditions of the colonial settlement at the Cape its features were eroded, and the task of carving out the principle had to begin anew.

The process of shaping the present South African law of unjustified enrichment began in earnest in the second half of the nineteenth century. The preceding period (i.e. from the arrival of the first Dutch colonists in the mid-seventeenth century), it is true, witnessed, as part of a wider process, the reception of Roman-Dutch enrichment law.[3] However, there was no law

---

[1] D. 12, 6, 14: '*Nam hoc natura aequum est neminem cum alterius detrimento fieri locupletiorem*' (For it is naturally just that nobody be rendered richer to the detriment of another). See also D. 50, 17, 206; and generally Max Kaser, *Das römische Privatrecht*, vol. I (2nd edn., 1971), 592 sqq.; Reinhard Zimmermann, *The Law of Obligations: Roman Foundations of the Civilian Tradition* (1990, reprint 1993), 834 sqq.; Wouter de Vos, *Verrykingsaanspreeklikheid in die Suid-Afrikaanse Reg* (3rd edn., 1987), 5.

[2] See Robert Feenstra, 'De Betekenis van De Groot en Huber voor de Ontwikkeling van een Algemene Actie uit Ongerechtvaardigde Verrijking', in: *Uit het Recht: Opstellen aangeboden aan Mr P. J. Verdam* (1971), 137 sqq.; *idem*, 'L'influence de la scolastique espagnole sur Grotius en droit privé: quelques experiences dans des questions de fond et de forme, concernant notamment les doctrines de l'erreur et de l'enrichissement sans cause', in: *Fata Iuris Romani: Etudes d'histoire du droit* (1974), 338 sqq.; *idem*, 'Grotius' Doctrine of Unjust Enrichment as a Source of Obligation: its Origin and its Influence in Roman-Dutch Law', in: Eltjo J. H. Schrage (ed.), *Unjust Enrichment* (1995), 197 sqq.; *idem*, 'Die ungerechtfertigte Bereicherung in dogmengeschichtlicher Sicht', (1972) 29 *Ankara Üniversitesi Hukuk Fakültesi Dergisi* 289 sqq.; J. E. Scholtens, 'The General Enrichment Action That Was', (1966) 83 *SALJ* 394 *sqq.;* D. H. van Zyl, 'The General Action is Alive and Well', 1992 *Acta Juridica* 115, 120 sqq.; Daniel Visser, 'Das Recht der ungerechtfertigten Bereicherung', in: Robert Feenstra, Reinhard Zimmermann (eds.), *Das römisch-holländische Recht: Fortschritte des Zivilrechts im 17. und 18. Jahrhundert* (1992), 370 sqq.

[3] See generally H. R. Hahlo, Ellison Kahn, *The South African Legal System and its Background* (1973), 566 sqq.; J. C. de Wet, *Die Ou Skrywers in Perspektief* (1988), 18 sqq.; Reinhard Zimmermann, *Das römisch-holländische Recht in Südafrika* (1983), 4 sqq.

reporting, so if any development did indeed take place during this period it could not be drawn upon in later decisions.[4] The result was a hiatus in the continuity of the development of South African law. When law reporting was initiated in the course of the nineteenth century[5] (in the wake of the gradual acceptance of the principle of *stare decisis* under the influence of English law) the South African law generally, and the law of unjustified enrichment in particular, began to develop its own distinctive form.

The courts found their initial inspiration for the development of the law in continental legal literature and English case-law. The European sources that influenced the courts were not limited to the Roman-Dutch authorities and the other civilian literature of the seventeenth and eighteenth centuries, but included also the contemporary writings of the German pandectists, with the result that the received Roman-Dutch law of enrichment was reshaped with distinctive nineteenth-century features. Furthermore, although it has not been acknowledged in the South African literature on unjustified enrichment, the English law of the nineteenth and early twentieth centuries also had a considerable influence on this area of the law. Of course 'unjustified enrichment' or 'restitution' did not form a separate, accepted category in English law at that time,[6] but the problems typically dealt with in this field of law did. The English training of many of the judges led to the common law solutions to such problems finding their way, although often in disguised form, into South African law. Thus enrichment law, traditionally regarded (like the law of property) as purely civilian, has come to display an androgynous face.

Although the law of enrichment developed in a variety of ways during the twentieth century, in many respects it never lost its nineteenth century aspect. Several reasons for its *fin de siècle* veneer may be advanced. After the codification of Dutch law in 1838 German law, the last comparative source of the *ius commune* as a living system, provided important inspiration for adapting the Roman-Dutch law to modern conditions. When German law was codified in 1900 the South African courts did not transfer

---

[4] Since the first chair in law was only founded in 1859 at the then South African College (later to become the University of Cape Town) there was also no academic writing to make up for the lack of judicial development of the law. (On the founding of the law faculty in Cape Town see D. V. Cowen, 'The History of the Faculty of Law, University of Cape Town: a Chapter in the Growth of Roman-Dutch Law in South Africa', 1959 *Acta Juridica* 8 sqq.; D. P. Visser 'As Durable as the Mountain: The Story of the Cape Town Law School since 1859', 1992 *Consultus* 32 sqq.; on the emergence of an indigenous legal literature see Wouter de Vos, *Regsgeskiedenis* (1992), 264.

[5] On the history of law reporting in South Africa see Hahlo/Kahn (n. 3), 282 sqq.

[6] Only with the publication of the first edition of Goff & Jones in 1966 (see now Lord Goff of Chieveley, Gareth Jones, *The Law of Restitution* (4th edn., 1993)) did the concept of restitution based on unjust(ified) enrichment begin to gain currency, and not until the last decade of this century did it gain judicial acceptance: *Lipkin Gorman (A Firm) v. Karpnale Ltd* [1991] 2 AC 548, [1992] 4 All ER 512; *Woolwich Equitable Building Soc v. Inland Revenue Commissioners* [1993] AC 70.

their attention to the new code. They continued to refer to the pandectists, partly, one imagines, because they were unfamiliar with the sources of the new law, and partly because they simply did not (and could not have been expected to) realize that the German codification, together with the other European codifications, was just another phase within the history of the *ius commune*.[7] Furthermore, the South African textbook on enrichment law which dominated its development during the second half of the twentieth century accorded the pandectists special weight. This contributed in an important way to confirming its nineteenth-century character.[8] Modern English law too, having until the very last decade of this century hidden its solutions to restitution problems behind the opaque screen of quasi-contract, was able to influence solutions to particular problems but was incapable of providing an overall model for South African law.

However, the law of this country did not respond only to influences from the laws of the European colonial powers; it also developed its own solutions in many instances. Sometimes this happened by design, sometimes by accident; sometimes with happy results, sometimes with rather startling consequences. In certain respects the law merely stagnated, due at least partly to the relatively low volume of cases in this area and the dearth of academic writing on the subject. The result is that the law of enrichment in many ways reflects the character which South African law generally has developed over the past three centuries. In certain respects it has unmitigated antiquarian features. In others it displays a refreshing modernity. On important occasions it has shrunk from taking the bold step required; in others it has rushed ahead without proper caution. Often, however, it has found just the right balance. Thus, it embraces many of the solid, classical solutions of the *ius commune* while at the same time having rough, unhewn aspects which cry out to be fashioned properly.

In this Chapter my purpose is to describe how these features of the South African law of unjustified enrichment came about, and to ask what is to be learnt from this historical process for the future development of this field of the law.

---

[7] See Reinhard Zimmermann, 'Das römisch-kanonische *ius commune* als Grundlage europäischer Rechtseinheit', 1992 *Juristenzeitung* 8, 20; *idem*, 'Civil Code and Civil Law: The "Europeanization" of Private Law within the European Community and the Re-emergence of a European Legal Science', (1994/95) 1 *Columbia Journal of European Law* 86 sqq.

[8] Wouter de Vos, *Verrykingsaaspreeklikheid in die Suid-Afrikaanse Reg*, first published 1958, and now in its third edition (1987).

II. THE PANDECTIST VENEER: THE GERMAN INFLUENCE

1. The approach to loss of enrichment as a defence

If Bernard Windscheid were to chance upon a copy of the standard South African textbook[9] on enrichment in the *Juristenhimmel* he would probably find its general structure and much of the substance very familiar. For the work deals, first, with all the *condictiones* in much the same way that he and his contemporaries did. Then are discussed the other actions that have been regarded as enrichment actions since Roman times, namely the *actio negotiorum gestorum contraria*, the action of a person who has contracted with an unassisted minor, and the action for improvements to the property of another.[10] It is true that Windscheid would be unfamiliar with some of the extensions or refinements which these actions have evolved. There are also a few instances of enrichment liability which would be completely new to him. However, on the whole he would have before him the traditional contours of the enrichment law of his day.[11]

Clearly Roman-Dutch and nineteenth-century German enrichment law had much in common, since both systems were after all merely specific variations of the European *ius commune*. Therefore, more often than not, the substantive rules that governed a particular situation corresponded, broadly speaking, with each other; and when it is said that South African law has in the course of its development acquired certain pandectist features, reference is made to the general approach or style, rather than to the actual rules (although even the Roman-Dutch rules themselves have, in some instances, changed under German influence).

The law relating to the defence of 'loss of enrichment' before *litis contestatio* (or 'change of position' as it is known in English law) provides a good example of the German mould in which South African enrichment law is cast. Roman law dealt rather strictly with recipients of unjustified enrichment. The aim of the *condictiones* was to recover that which had been given,

---

⁹ Above, n. 8.　　　　　　　　　　　　　¹⁰ See generally De Vos (n. 1), 153 sqq.
¹¹ Cf. De Vos (n. 1), 244 sqq. The German influence on South African law during this period is not entirely surprising: during the 19th C. German legal scholarship had an impact throughout the Western world; see e.g. M. Reimann, 'Holmes's Common Law and German Legal Science', in: R. W. Gordon (ed.) *The Legacy of Oliver Wendell Holmes Jr* (1992), 72 sqq.; the Rt. Hon. Lord Rodger of Earlsferry, 'Scottish Advocates in the Nineteenth Century: The German Connection', (1994) 110 *LQR* 563 sqq.; G. Edward White, 'The Impact of Legal Science on Tort Law, 1880–1910', (1978) 78 *Columbia LR* 213 sqq.; M. H. Hoeflich, 'Roman Law in American Legal Culture', (1992) 66 *Tulane LR* 1723 sqq. In South Africa this influence was of course not limited to the law of unjustified enrichment. See generally D. P. Visser, 'The "Absoluteness" of Ownership: The South African Common Law in Perspective', 1985 *Acta Juridica* 39 sqq.; A. J. van der Walt, 'Gedagtes oor die Herkoms en Ontwikkeling van die Suid-Afrikaanse Eiendomsreg', 1988 *De Jure* 16 sqq.

rather than to restore the balance of enrichment remaining with the recipient; the *condictiones* were focused, *in concreto*, on the return of the *res* or its substitute. Thus, in the case of a lost fungible the recipient could not escape liability on account of that loss because a fungible can always be substituted. (The matter was different with regard to non-fungible objects, which of course cannot be substituted.) The basic stance of the law was therefore that unjustified enrichment *received* (rather than unjustified enrichment *remaining*) should be returned.[12] This position was carried through to the *ius commune* (including Roman-Dutch law[13]) and was thus received into South African law with the rest of the law of unjustified enrichment.

In the course of the nineteenth century, however, the basic approach to this matter began to change in Germany. The fact that the principle against unjustified enrichment gained ground in contemporary German law necessitated, as Reinhard Zimmermann[14] explains, that the recognition of new instances of enrichment liability be balanced by the greater protection of the reasonable reliance of those who have used up or disposed of what they had received. As a result it became one of the central tenets of German law that the enrichment debtor could never be expected to return more than the remaining enrichment (unless, of course, the enrichment debtor was to blame for the loss).[15] Dawson[16] points out that, in adopting a clearly over-protective approach towards the enrichment debtor, 'the Pandectist authors and their followers gave a basic misdirection by segregating as a privileged class, entitled to special leniency, all "innocent receivers" of unjustified gain'.

Significantly, when in the middle of this century the matter was seriously considered in South Africa for the first time[17] the Court referred to a number of authors of the *ius commune*, including Glück and Windscheid. The earlier authors were, however, freely interpreted and the position adopted was essentially that of the pandectist school. De Vos, in his work which appeared shortly afterwards, also embraced the position of the German school.[18] When the highest Court in the country eventually came to consider the matter its heavy reliance on De Vos ensured that Glück's interpretation of the *Corpus Iuris* became orthodoxy in South Africa.[19] Since

---

[12] See Werner Flume, 'Der Wegfall der Bereicherung in der Entwicklung vom römischen zum geltenden Recht', in: *Festschrift für Hans Niedermeyer* (1953), 124; Zimmermann (n. 1), 896 sqq.; D. P. Visser, 'Responsibility to Return Lost Enrichment', 1992 *Acta Juridica* 175 sqq.

[13] Visser, (1992) *Acta Juridica* 183 sq.   [14] Zimmermann (n. 1), 900.

[15] See Flume (n. 12), 145 sqq.; Zimmermann (n. 1), 900; J. P. Dawson, 'Erasable Enrichment in German Law', (1981) 61 *Boston University LR* 306; Visser, 1992 *Acta Juridica* 185 sq.

[16] (1981) 61 *Boston University LR* 306, with reference to RGZ 118, 185, 187 (1927) and BGHZ 1, 75, 81 (1951). See also Zimmermann (n. 1), 900.

[17] *King v. Cohen Benjamin and Co* 1953 (4) SA 641 (W).

[18] De Vos (n. 1), 200 sqq.

[19] *African Diamond Exporters (Pty) Ltd v. Barclays Bank International Ltd* 1978 (3) SA 699 (A).

then the South African courts have shown themselves totally unmoved by
the strict approach of English law towards loss of enrichment[20] and have
consistently accepted that the enrichment debtor is to be protected against
all 'innocent loss' of enrichment, without enquiring into, to quote Dawson
once more, 'the really relevant issues, such as how the gain was originally
acquired and why it has been dissipated'.[21]

2. The development of the rule *error iuris nocet*

In 1888 a South African court (the Supreme Court of the *Zuid-Afrikaansche
Republiek*) had the first opportunity to consider in depth a question that has
intrigued scholars and courts throughout the development of both the civil
law and the common law, namely whether an error of law should be a bar
to the recovery of money or property paid or transferred in circumstances
where it was not owed. The case was *Rooth v. The State*.[22] The features
which it gave the law of enrichment in South Africa endured for more than
a century. In fact, in certain respects they still do. Before *Rooth's* case there
had been strong English influence in this area. In *Port Elizabeth Divisional
Council v. Uitenhage Divisional Council*, for instance, counsel for the respondent stated (with reference to the dispute between the authorities of the *ius
commune* regarding mistake of law in the context of the *condictio indebiti*)
that it was an accepted principle that 'where there is such conflict among
the civilians, and one of the conflicting doctrines is the doctrine of the courts
of law in England, this Court favours the doctrine which so co-incides with
the English law, rather than that which contradicts'.[23] However, the
approach in *Rooth's* case was ultimately to gain acceptance. The case presents a very useful demonstration of the reception of German thought into
this area of South African law. In order to understand the significance of
this decision for the development of the law of unjustified enrichment it is,
however, necessary first to explain the attitude of the pandectists (or the

[20] The defence was only accepted as part of English law in 1991 in *Lipkin Gorman (A Firm)
v. Karpnale Ltd* (n. 6), and then only with great caution. See generally Goff/Jones (n. 6), 739
sqq.; Andrew Burrows, *The Law of Restitution* (1993), 421 sqq.
[21] Dawson, (1981) 61 *Boston University LR* 306.   [22] (1888) 2 SAR 259.
[23] 1868 Buch 221, discussed by Reinhard Zimmermann, 'Die Rechtsprechung des Supreme
Court of the Cape of Good Hope am Ende der sechziger Jahre des 19. Jahrhunderts', in:
Huldigingsbundel Paul van Warmelo (1984), 285 sqq., 303 sqq. Referring to this case and to the
way in which it had been used in the later decision of *Britannia Gold Mining Co v. Yockmonitz*
(1889) 7 SC 218, Zimmermann (304) notes: '*Man sieht, wie der kleinste Anhaltspunkt dankbar
aufgenommen wird, das "koloniale" Recht mit dem der Rechtsordnung des Mutterlandes,
England, in Einklang zu bringen*' (One notices how the smallest foothold was gratefully utilized
to bring the 'colonial law' into harmony with that of the legal order of the mother country,
England). On the role of the English law on the South African law of unjustified enrichment
generally see Ben Beinart, 'The English Legal Contribution in South Africa: The Interaction
of Civil and Common Law', 1981 *Acta Juridica* 7, 50 sqq.

'modernists' as they were then sometimes called) towards the question of error in relation to the *condictio indebiti*.

(a) Pandectist thought on the role of error in regard to the recovery of a payment not owed

The majority opinion among the exponents of the Historical School and its pandectist branch may be summarized in the words of Vangerow:[24] 'only excusable error, but then every excusable error, without distinction as to whether it is an error of law or an error of fact' is sufficient to found the *condictio indebiti*.[25] In these words are encapsulated a sophisticated argument regarding the centuries-old dispute about whether an error of law bars the recovery of a payment that was not owed. Until the nineteenth century the debate surrounding this question was focused almost exclusively on the distinction between error of law and error of fact, and the question asked was simply: did the *Corpus Iuris* allow the *condictio indebiti* in case of an error of law, or did it not? In this controversy excusability featured as a separate requirement, linked to error of fact.[26] The pandectists, however, broke through this mould and, in a bold re-interpretation of the sources, elevated the excusability of the error—rather than the distinction between error of law and fact—to the central concern regarding the return of *indebitum solutum*.

Vangerow opined that one would have had to assume that excusability constituted a necessary requirement, even if not a single text had declared it be relevant to the *condictio indebiti*.[27] However, he was careful to point out that such texts did in fact exist. As proof for his contention that a

[24] Karl Adolph von Vangerow, *Lehrbuch der Pandekten*, vol. III (7th edn., 1876), 397. On the pandectists see generally Robert Feenstra, 'Romeins Recht en Europese Rechtswetenschap', in: J. E. Spruit (ed.), *Coniectanea Neerlandici Iuris Romani: Inleidende Opstellen over Romeins Recht* (1974), 123 sqq.

[25] Those who share this point of view are Bernhard Windscheid, *Lehrbuch des Pandektenrechts*, vol. II (9th edn., 1906), 896 sqq.; Ludwig Arndts von Arnesberg, *Lehrbuch der Pandekten* (11th edn., 1883), 636; H. Witte, *Die Bereicherungsklagen des Gemeinen Rechts* (1859), 99; A. Erxleben, *Die condictiones sine causa: condictio indebiti* (1853), 62 sqq.; and E. Haniel, *Beitrag zur Lehre vom Wesen und Beweis des Irrthums bei der condictio indebiti unter Berücksichtigung der neuern Gesetzgebung* (Dr. iur. thesis, University of Göttingen, 1893), 18. Savigny's view accords with Vangerow's approach, although he places the emphasis somewhat differently. He begins by saying that the *condictio indebiti* is not normally available in cases of an error of law, but immediately adds that there are exceptions (Friedrich Karl von Savigny, *System des heutigen römischen Rechts*, vol. III (1840), 447, 448–51), and elsewhere (*op. cit.*, 114) he states explicitly that in certain circumstances an error of law could be 'excusable and thus operative' (see also Savigny, 447, fn. (a)). C. F. F. Sintenis, *Das Practische Gemeine Civilrecht*, vol. II (1844–51), 525 and H. Dernburg, *Pandekten* (8th edn., 1910–12), 840, place the emphasis in the same way as Savigny.

[26] See Visser (n. 2), 388 sqq.; *idem*, *Die Rol van Dwaling by die condictio indebiti: 'n Regshistoriese Perspektief met 'n Regsvergelykende Ekskursus* (Dr. iur. thesis, University of Leiden, 1985), 66 sqq.

[27] Vangerow (n. 24), 397. A. F. J. Thibaut, *Civilistische Abhandelungen* (1814), 189, shares this view. See further Windscheid (n. 25), 410–13; Dernburg (n. 25), 840; Erxleben (n. 25), 90.

particular quality of error was required he mentioned, for instance, the direct statement in D. 22, 3, 25 referring to a *iusta causa ignorantiae* as a precondition for the successful institution of the *condictio indebiti*, and the fact that *normally* recovery is excluded in case of an error of law.[28] This, he argued, was evidence that the distinction between *error iuris* and *error facti* in the *Corpus Iuris* was merely an expression of the more fundamental distinction between excusable and inexcusable error.

Bähr,[29] like Vangerow and Savigny, classified the *condictio indebiti* as a remedy which, by way of exception, allows error to function as the basis for undermining the validity of a completed juridical act. Consequently he too insisted on excusability. Remedies of this kind, he argued, always require *iustus* or *probabilis* error, *supina ignorantia* being insufficient for these purposes.[30] Furthermore, Bähr held that the excusability requirement was indispensable from a procedural point of view. It was, he maintained, a necessary step in proving the even more basic fact that the payment that was made was indeed an *indebitum*:

Die Nichtschuld wird erst völlig glaubhaft durch den Irrthum; der Irrthum durch seine Entschuldbarkeit[31] ... [and] *Die innere Annäherung zwischen Entschuldbarkeit und Beweisbarkeit des Irrthums findet einen Ausdruck in der Bezeichnung des rechtswirksamen Irrthums als* error probabilis *welches Wort doppelsinnig auf beide Momente hinweist.*[32]

An error of *law* was usually inexcusable, although it could be held to be excusable by way of exception,[33] while the converse was true of an error of *fact*.[34]

The writers defended the equity of requiring an error to be excusable in order for it to found a successful claim in terms of the *condictio indebiti* in different ways. The most important justifications appear from the works of Witte[35] and Bähr[36] (with whom Windscheid[37] agreed). The essence of their arguments was that the main purpose of the requirement was to protect the recipient. Thus, Witte[38] defended excusability on the basis of the protection of a recipient who had changed his position. If one were to allow unconditional recovery, he maintained, the transferor would be unduly advantaged.

---

[28] Vangerow (n. 24), 397.

[29] O. Bähr, *Die Anerkennung als Verpflichtungsgrund* (2nd edn., 1867), 76. See also Savigny (n. 25), 114, 448.

[30] Bähr (n. 29), 76.

[31] (The fact that no debt exists becomes fully credible by virtue of the error; and the error by virtue of its excusability): Bähr (n. 29), 75.

[32] (The inner approximation between excusability and provability of the error finds expression in the description of the legally effective error as *error probabilis*—a word referring, with its double-meaning, to both aspects): Bähr (n. 29), 75.

[33] Vangerow (n. 24), 121; Haniel (n. 25), 18–19.

[34] Vangerow, *loc. cit.*, and Haniel, *loc. cit.*; see also Savigny (n. 25), 114, 332–8.

[35] Above, n. 25, 98 sqq.

[36] Above, n. 29, 74 sqq.

[37] Above, n. 25, 898, fn. 14.

[38] Above, n. 25, 99.

Allowing recovery only in the case of an excusable error provided a better balance between the interests of transferor and recipient.[39] This notion, added Witte, was already inherent in the *Digest*; he referred to the well known text about proof in respect of the *condictio indebiti*, namely D. 22, 3, 25. (The requirement of excusability should be disregarded, he felt, if it appeared in a particular case that the recipient had not in fact detrimentally altered his position.[40])

In taking this approach, the nineteenth-century jurists vindicated the lone stance of an eighteenth-century author, Augustin Leyser,[41] who had argued that there was very little value in making a distinction between *error iuris* and *error facti* and that a distinction should rather be made *inter ignorantiam vincibilem et invincibilem*.[42]

(b) Rooth v. The State *and its interpretation of the civilian authorities*

In *Rooth v. The State*[43] the High Court of the South African Republic (Transvaal) initially emphasized that in order to answer the question whether an error of law may found the *condictio indebiti*, 'recourse [must be had] to the Civil Law', and it proceeded to list those in favour of and those against the recoverability of a payment made in error of law amongst 'the commentators and expounders of the Roman law'.[44] In analyzing the

---

[39] *Ibid.*

[40] Witte (n. 25), 100. Bähr's defence of the requirement of excusability ties in with that of Witte. He too emphasizes that, although the recipient might be expected to investigate whether or not the debt exists, the material basis of this requirement is not '*[daß] die Nachlässigkeit des leichtsinnig Zahlenden gestraft werden soll, sondern ... der Schutz, den dadurch der Empfänger genießt*' (that the negligence of a person who pays carelessly should be punished, but the protection that the recipient thereby enjoys). For Vangerow and Dernburg the equity of regarding an error of law, as opposed to an error of fact, as generally inexcusable is to be found in the fact that every citizen is obliged to acquaint himself with the law: at least insofar as it pertains to his own affairs. Since the law is finite and static (!), they argued, this is not a particularly difficult task. On the other hand, the facts that might be relevant to a particular situation are myriad, and therefore even a careful person could easily err in respect of them. Nevertheless, even an error of fact must be excusable '*im Interesse des Verkehrs und der guten Ordnung, wäre doch sonst der Unaufmerksame und Nachlässige dem Aufmerksamen und Sorgfältigen gegenüber im Vorteil*' (in the interest of commerce and good order, otherwise an inattentive and negligent person would have an advantage over an attentive and careful person). Although a minority opinion also existed during this period that every error, whether *iuris* or *facti*, excusable or inexcusable, should be sufficient to found a claim based on the *condictio indebiti*, the view that the distinction between error of law and error of fact could in essence be traced to the requirement of excusability (*error iuris* and *error facti* being the archetypes of inexcusable and excusable error) was firmly established.

[41] August Leyser, *Meditationes ad Pandectas*, vol. VI (edn. Lipsiae et Guelpherbyti, 1741–62), Spec. 289, 1–2.

[42] (... between ignorance that is excusable and that which is not): ibid.

[43] Above, n. 22.

[44] The Court made the following remark in regard to the sources by which it considered itself bound: 'Mr Wessels in very learned argument, maintained with great force that this question [whether the applicants are entitled to the *condictio indebiti* by reason of their mistake of law] should be answered in the affirmative, inasmuch as Van der Linden, Van Leeuwen, and Grotius give it as their opinion that money paid under a mistake of law can be reclaimed, and

judgment it is important to remember that Roman-Dutch law, although ambivalent as to whether recovery should be allowed in case of an error of law, *did not require excusability in any circumstances.*[45] The Court, however, did not confine itself to Roman-Dutch authority. It also canvassed the view of the exponents of the German *usus modernus pandectarum*, the French humanists, and the pandectists. Van Leeuwen, Huber, Coccecius, Peckius, Carpzovius, Vinnius, D'Aguesseau, the *Hollandsche Consultatien*, Leyser, and Mühlenbruch were listed by the Court as being in favour of the availability of the *condictio indebiti* in case of an error of law. As representatives of the opposite point of view Cujacius, Donellus, Merenda, Brunnemann, Domat, Voet, Glück, Savigny, Mackeldey, Goudsmit, and Windscheid were cited.

Concerning the arguments of those who would allow the *condicti indebiti* in all instances of mistake of law, the Court stated that they:

appear . . . sufficiently refuted by Voet, Glück and Savigny, who observe that where the leges are clear and specially lay down as a well recognized rule (or, as Windsheid puts it, axiom) of law, that in the case of *error juris* the *condictio indebiti* does not lie (*vid.* Cod. 1, 18, 10; Dig. 22, 6. 9, pr.), there can be no question of natural equity.[46]

Later in the judgment the Court added:

It appears . . . that the jurists of our own time [i.e. the pandectist authors] . . . are more or less inclined to adopt the middle view, and (as Glück expresses it) discard the distinction between mistake of law and mistake of fact, and simply consider if the error, whether *juris* or *facti* be excusable (*verzeilich, entschuldbar*) or not.[47]

The Court then stated that, since in the case before it there existed no element of excusability, it was not necessary to decide 'whether, according to the strict interpretation of the Roman law, we are justified in adopting this view of the modern school as correct'.[48]

Even though the Court did not accept the doctrine as part of the *ratio decidendi*, its sympathetic treatment of the pandectist approach was to exercise a powerful and lasting influence on the law in regard to this matter.

(c) Development after Rooth v. The State

The basic approach of *Rooth v. The State*, namely that a mistake of law is in principle not sufficient to found the *condictio indebiti*, was consistently

according to App. 1 to the *Grondwet* [i.e. the Constitution of the South African Republic] . . . the court is bound to follow the text-books of these writers. But in answer to that I must observe that the Appendix in question likewise provides that in the interpretation and use of these text-books the Court shall always proceed in the manner prescribed by paragraph 31 of the thirty-three Articles, where it is laid down: "In all instances wherein these [i.e. the local] laws fail, the Dutch (i.e. the Roman-Dutch) law shall serve as a basis, yet upon a reasonable system and in accordance with the usage of South Africa, and for the benefit and welfare of the community" '. See generally in regard to the sources of law in the Transvaal Republic D. H. van Zyl, *Die Geskiedenis van die Romeins-Hollandse Reg* (1979), 460 sqq.

[45] See Visser (n. 2), 405 sqq.   [46] 263.   [47] 265.   [48] Ibid.

followed, albeit often with a marked reluctance and accompanied by a number of exceptions, until 1992.[49] During this period the basic sympathy for the pandectist approach manifested in *Rooth v. The State* also found expression in a variety of subsequent judgments. In *Miller v. Bellville Municipality*[50] the Court opined that if the Appellate Division were in future to adopt (as it was put) the 'equitable discretion' to assist the claimant in instances of error of law, this discretion should be confined to situations in which the error was excusable. This view was prophetic, for the early signal in *Rahim v. The Minister of Justice*[51] (a case dealing with error of fact in which the requirement of excusability was reaffirmed with reference to the nineteenth-century German authors) was carried through when the Appellate Division decided, in *Willis Faber Enthoven (Pty) Ltd v. Receiver of Revenue*,[52] that error of law was no longer an obstacle to the successful institution of the *condictio indebiti*, provided such error was excusable.

Thus, the pandectist approach has triumphed in South African law. Is this a good thing? It is not possible in the present context to discuss this question in any detail; suffice it to say that the arguments of the nineteenth-century German authors in favour of excusability have many weak spots. For example, the emphasis on the protection of the recipient ignores the fact that usually the recipient would be labouring under exactly the same 'inexcusable' mistake as the transferor and would therefore hardly merit the protection. In any event, the defence of 'change of position' adequately protects the recipient when the enrichment is lost. Furthermore, the protective approach towards the recipient has a hollow ring to it when the recipient is, for instance, the taxman. It may safely be assumed that the history of this particular aspect of the law of enrichment is not yet over.

III. A DIFFERENT GRAIN UNDER THE SURFACE: THE BALANCING INFLUENCE OF ENGLISH LAW

1. Reciprocity and claims after breach of contract

The influence of English law on the shaping of unjustified enrichment is less obvious than that of German law, but if one looks closely the evidence is

---

[49] The Appellate Division changed the rule in *Willis Faber Enthoven (Pty) Ltd v. Receiver of Revenue* 1992 (4) SA 202 (A): see the discussion directly below.

[50] 1973 (1) SA 914 (C). In this case the Court referred to *Rooth v. The State* (n. 22). See also *Barker v. Bentley* 1978 (4) SA 204 (N) 206E-F; *Rulten v. Herald Industries (Pty) Ltd* 1982 (3) SA 600 (D) 607E-G.   [51] 1964 (4) SA 630 (A).

[52] 1992 (4) SA 202 (A). On this case see D. P. Visser, 'Error of Law and Mistaken Payments: A Milestone', (1992) 109 *SALJ* 177 sqq.; Coenraad Visser, 'The Recovery of Payments under Mistake of Law', (1992) 4 *South African Mercantile LJ* 382 sqq.; C.-J. Pretorius, 'The *Condictio Indebiti*, Error of Law and Excusability: *Willis Faber Enthoven (Pty) Ltd v. Receiver of Revenue*', (1993) 56 *THRHR* 315 sqq.

clear. Sometimes English law was nothing more than a sounding-board which provided the South African courts with the counter-principles and arguments; in other cases it clandestinely influenced this area of the law; and occasionally it had an open and direct bearing on the way in which a particular aspect of unjustified enrichment law developed. The penumbral overlap between enrichment and contract offers one of the most rewarding source of clues.

An example of English law helping to refine South African law by acting as a sounding-board is found in the rules relating to the right of the party in the wrong to claim compensation for work done or services rendered after a breach of contract. Traditionally English law has taken a strict approach to the principle of reciprocity. Cases such as *Munro v. Butt*,[53] *Sumpter v. Hedges*,[54] and *Appleby v. Myers*,[55] all decided in the second half of the nineteenth century, clearly illustrate the fact that English law long insisted that a party to an 'indivisible or entire contract'[56] can 'recover nothing unless the work be done, or it can be shown that it was the defendant's fault that the work was incomplete, or that there is something to justify the conclusion that the parties had entered into a fresh contract'.[57] This requirement of full reciprocity has been mitigated to some degree: (a) by what Goff and Jones have called the 'artificial exception of substantial performance',[58] whereby a party in breach may recover *in contract* if he or she has substantially performed the contract;[59] and (b) by the doctrine of 'free acceptance' of the plaintiff's work,[60] that is, where the defendant may be held to have waived the right to demand full performance.

South African courts were from very early on aware of the English attitude to this issue. In *Hauman v. Nortje*[61] (which was to form, until 1979, the cornerstone of the law on compensation payable to a contractor who had not rendered perfect performance) both Lord de Villiers and Innes JA contrasted the strict English rule that 'no compensation is claimable unless a new contract to do so can be implied' with the more lenient Roman-Dutch approach that compensation was payable unless it was clear from the original contract that such compensation was to be excluded. (Although

---

[53] (1858) 8 E & B 738.   [54] [1898] 1 QB 673.
[55] (1867) LR 3 CP 651, 36 LJ CP 331, 16 LT 669.
[56] See Goff/Jones (n. 6), 409 sqq. The authors explain that an entire contract 'is one which provides expressly or implicitly that a party must perform his part in full before he can recover any part of the price or other consideration due to him under the contract; in particular, in the absence of anything to the contrary, a contract is held implicitly so to provide where the consideration is a lump sum or is otherwise unapportioned, or where the payment of the consideration is postponed until completion of the work' (409).
[57] Goff/Jones (n. 6), 409 sq.   [58] Ibid. 444, fn. 82.
[59] *Boone v. Eyre* (1789) 1 Hy Bl 273, cited by Goff/Jones (n. 6), 441, fn. 54.
[60] Goff/Jones (n. 6), 441 and the cases cited there.
[61] 1914 AD 293. See also *Van Rensburg v. Straughan* 1914 AD 317; Beinart, 1981 *Acta Juridica* 53 sqq.

Roman-Dutch law also adhered to the principle of reciprocity, it allowed the relaxation of the principle under certain circumstances.) Having had the benefit of a comparative analysis, the Court firmly decided to treat incomplete performance by a contractor in the manner set out by the Roman-Dutch authorities. It based the right to compensation of the party in breach of contract on the general principle against unjustified enrichment (which it held to be part of South African law) as well as on the direct authority of Voet, who specifically allowed an enrichment claim to a contractor who had made an incomplete performance. This approach, which did not distinguish between instances where the contract had been cancelled and others where it had not, was followed consistently for almost seven decades.[62] Over the years a number of writers argued strenuously—but incorrectly, it is submitted—that Voet did not really mean to base the right of the contractor on unjustified enrichment where the contract had not been cancelled.[63] They argued that in such cases a *contractual* action for a reduced contract price is the appropriate remedy. Only if the contract had been cancelled and the innocent party had returned what he was able to return would there be room for liability in enrichment for the value of what could not be returned. In 1979 the Appellate Division cautiously approved of this view in *BK Tooling (Edms) Bpk v. Scope Precision Engineering (Edms) Bpk*,[64] but left the door open to the argument that enrichment liability could conceivably exist *stante contractu*.

In one respect, however, the English law may after all have had some influence on this instance of enrichment liability. In the *Hauman v. Nortje*[65] Innes JA, relying on *Scott and Boyd v. Venner* (an unreported Cape case of 1885) confirmed the right of the innocent party to reject an imperfect performance in terms of the principle of reciprocity, and to insist on full performance. The right to compensation which Voet allowed to a contractor who has made an incomplete performance must, he argued, be read not as questioning the principle of reciprocity but as applying 'to cases where an owner took steps to enrich himself at the expense of the contractor by utilizing the fruits of the contract without paying for them'.[66] This approach is subtly reminiscent of the English 'free acceptance' rule and, although the Court was at pains to point out that the South African position was based on the fact of enrichment rather than a waiver or a new contract, it is possible that this refinement of Voet's statement of the law was inspired by

[62] De Vos (n. 1), 280. See too *Breslin v. Hichens* 1914 AD 312, 315.

[63] See J. C. de Wet and A. H. van Wyk, *Die Suid-Afrikaanse Kontraktereg en Handelsreg*, vol. I (5th edn., 1992), 201 sqq.; Schalk van der Merwe, L. F. van Huyssteen, M. F. B. Reinecke, G. F. Lubbe and J. G. Lotz, *Contract: General Principles* (1993), 284.

[64] 1979 (1) SA 391 (A). See further on this case Beinart, 1981 *Acta Juridica* 53; S. J. Hutton, *Restitution after Breach of Contract: A Comparative Study of English and South African Law* (unpublished LL M, University of Oxford, 1994), 73 sqq.

[65] Above, n. 61.   [66] 303 sq. of the report.

cases such as *Forman & Co Proprietary Ltd v. S S Liddesdale*,[67] of which the Court would undoubtedly have been aware. Moreover, South African courts have over many years used the English legal term *quantum meruit* in this regard; this also suggests (even if one concedes that it has not contributed to clarity in South African law) that the courts have consistently borne English law in mind when formulating the law of unjustified enrichment.

2. *Restitutio in integrum*

An instructive example of the clandestine reception of English law is that of the remedy of *restitutio in integrum*. Courts and the academic commentators in South Africa have steadfastly maintained that *restitutio in integrum* is a contractual and not an enrichment remedy. For instance, in *Davidson v. Bonafede*[68] the Court, following De Vos,[69] held that *restitutio in integrum* and enrichment remedies are inherently distinguishable from each other in that (i) innocent loss of the received benefit is a defence against enrichment remedies but not against a claim for *restitutio in integrum*, and (ii) interest is paid *ex nunc* where a *condictio* is concerned, but *ex tunc* in the case of *restitutio in integrum*.[70] I have argued elsewhere[71] that while these differences do in fact exist, they should not be perpetuated; and that eventually the South African legal system is bound to recognize that *restitutio in integrum* is essentially an enrichment action. There can be no doubt that *restitutio in integrum* is based on unjustified enrichment in English law, certainly since the acceptance of unjustified enrichment as a cause of action *eo nomine* in *Lipkin Gorman (a firm) v. Karpnale Ltd*[72] (and in *Woolwich Equitable Building Soc v. CIR*[73]). The mere fact, however, that English and South

[67] [1900] AC 190. See Goff/Jones (n. 6), 441, fn. 57.

[68] 1981 (2) SA 501 (C); but cf. C. F. C. van der Walt 'Die Grondslag van die Teruggaweplig ten opsigte van wat reeds Presteer is waar na Kontrakbreuk Teruggetree word', (1985) 48 *THRHR* 22.

[69] De Vos (n. 1), 158–9.

[70] M. A. Lambiris, *Orders of Specific Performance and restitutio in integrum in South African Law* (1989), 181, 198–200, 319, fn. 7, opines that *restitutio in integrum* is not an enrichment action because it does more than merely restore the parties to their former position. It is, according to him, also the instrument by which a contract is avoided, because a court order is needed to rescind a contract. This is, it is submitted, not correct. Cf. e.g. D. J. Joubert, *General Principles of Contract* (1987), 242: a party with the right to rescind a contract can do so by his own act and need not ask the court to assist in the rescission; he needs the court's assistance only in regard to the enforcement of remedies flowing from the rescission. See *Lebiedina v. Schechter and Haskell* 1931 WLD 247; *Radiotronics (Pty) Ltd v. Scott, Lindberg & Co Ltd* 1951 (1) SA 312 (C); *Swart v. Vosloo* 1965 (1) SA 100 (A). See further Dale Hutchison, Belinda van Heerden, D. P. Visser and C. G. van der Merwe, *Wille's Principles of South African Law* (8th edn., 1991), 521; cf. *Sonia (Pty) Ltd v. Wheeler* 1958 (1) SA 555 (A).

[71] D. P. Visser, 'Rethinking Unjustified Enrichment: A Perspective of the Competition between Contractual and Enrichment Remedies', 1992 *Acta Juridica* 203, 211 sqq.

[72] [1991] 2 AC 548, [1992] 4 All ER 512.

[73] [1993] AC 70 (HL). See generally, on the relevant English law, Goff/Jones (n. 6), 230 sqq.

African law differ on its classification has not prevented the former from influencing the latter in regard to this remedy. This influence manifests itself most clearly in the recognition of innocent misrepresentation[74] and undue influence[75] as grounds for seeking *restitutio in integrum*; but it is also apparent in the gradual relaxation of the rule that the party claiming restitution must himself be willing and able to restore any benefit received under the contract. Strictly speaking rescission was available in Roman-Dutch law (as in the older English law) only when perfect restitution was possible, but this principle has been considerably watered down in English law.[76] Although some cases have affirmed the strict rule of Roman-Dutch law that restitution *in kind* must be possible,[77] other decisions have taken a different line. Thus the Appellate Division has stated that 'since the rule is founded on equity it has been departed from in a number of varying circumstances where considerations of equity and justice have necessitated such departure'.[78] In *Hall-Thermotank Natal (Pty) Ltd v. Hardman*[79] the same approach was adopted.

In developing the remedy of *restitutio in integrum* the South African courts did not as a rule refer to English decisions. However, the position which they have reached is so similar to that of English law (and at the same time so different from that of Roman-Dutch law) that one may safely assume that English law played an important role in the process.

3. Countermanded cheques and the right of banks to recovery

The question of the right of banks to recover money which they have erroneously paid out is one in which the influence exerted by English law was overt (though transitory). The Roman-Dutch sources do not specifically deal with the situation of a bank that pays on the basis of a countermanded cheque, and whether the bank (as opposed to the customer) may reclaim a payment made in such circumstances was therefore bound to occasion difficulty. Clearly the question as to who is impoverished in this situation would depend on the contract between banker and client, and on whether the recipient was enriched. Whether the recipient was enriched, in turn,

---

[74] See *Novick v. Comair Holdings Ltd* 1979 (2) SA 116 (W); for further discussion see Ch. 8 by Gerhard Lubbe above.

[75] See G. F. Lubbe, C. M. Murray, *Farlam and Hathaway, Contract: Cases, Materials and Commentary* (3rd edn., 1988), 374; Goff/Jones (n. 6), 276 sqq. On undue influence in general see L. F. van Huyssteen, *Onbehoorlike Beïnvloeding en Misbruik van Omstandighede in die Suid-Afrikaanse Verbintenisreg* (1980), ch. 16; and Ch. 8 by Gerhard Lubbe, above.

[76] Hugo Grotius, *Inleiding tot de Hollandsche Rechtsgeleertheyd*, 3, 48, 5; Johannes Voet, *Commentarius ad Pandectas*, 4, 1, 22; *Uni-Erections v. Continental Engineering Co Ltd* 1981 (1) SA 240 (W); Lubbe/Murray (n. 75), 344. On the position in English law see Goff/Jones (n. 6), 198 sqq.

[77] See e.g. *Uni-Erections v. Continental Engineering Co Ltd* 1981 (1) SA 240 (W).

[78] *Van Schalkwyk v. Griesel* 1948 (1) SA 460 (A).   [79] 1968 (4) SA 818 (D) 831 sq.

depends on whether or not the law considers a debt to the recipient to be extinguished by the payment in question. Most importantly, a policy decision has to be taken whether it is at all advisable to allow a bank to claim in such circumstances. A South African court was first confronted with this policy decision in 1903. In the case of *Natal Bank v. Roorda*[80] the Transvaal Supreme Court held that the bank in question could reclaim from the recipient the amount of a countermanded cheque that it had erroneously paid. In coming to this conclusion the Court did not investigate the doctrinal intricacies presented by this situation in any sophisticated way, but allowed the claim with reference to a *dictum* in the English case of *Kelly v. Solari*[81] which, however, did not deal with a payment by a bank but was merely to the effect that where money is paid to another under the influence of mistake it can normally be reclaimed. The Court also noted (with reference to an equally general passage in Van Leeuwen's *Rooms-Hollands-Regt*[82]) that Roman-Dutch law was to the same effect. The decision was given shortly after the Anglo-Boer war by Mr Justice Smith (formerly a judge in British Guyana). He was equally at home in both English and Roman-Dutch law (which obtained in that Colony), but it cannot really be said that English law (or Roman-Dutch law for that matter) influenced the decision, for the authority quoted did not really take account of the essential difficulties of the problem before the Court. This influence was to come much later.

Considering the frequency with which banks erroneously pay out stopped cheques, it is remarkable that the problem did not arise again before a South African court until 1984, when the Cape Supreme Court was asked to determine this question in *Govender v. Standard Bank of South Africa Ltd.*[83] Here the Court did not allow the claim. It found on the facts that the debt had been owing to the recipient and that the payment by the bank had extinguished that debt. Therefore the recipient was not (unjustly) enriched and a *condictio* to reclaim the payment was not available. (In any event, the Court also held that the customer had signed an indemnity in favour of the bank in terms of which the latter was empowered to debit its customer's account, which meant that it was not impoverished.)

Some ten years later the question of a mistaken payment on a countermanded cheque arose again in *First National Bank of SA Ltd v. B & H Engineering.*[84] In this case the Transvaal Provincial Division of the Supreme Court held that a bank could recover the amount in question. A prerequisite for an effective payment of a debt, the Court argued, is a valid debt-extinguishing agreement, which presupposes a continuing intention to pay on the part of the payer and a continuing intention to receive payment on the part of the recipient. Since the countermand removed the intention to

---

[80] 1903 TS 298.   [81] (1841) 9 M & W 54.
[82] See Simon van Leeuwen, *Het Rooms-Hollands-Regt*, Bk. 4, Pt. 14.
[83] 1984 (4) SA 392 (C).   [84] 1993 (2) SA 41 (T).

pay this prerequisite was not complied with when the cheque in question was paid, and the debt was therefore not extinguished. The result was that the recipient still had a valid claim against the drawer in spite of having received the payment and was thus enriched. In reaching its decision the Court referred at length to the judgment of Goff J in *Barclays Bank Ltd v. W J Simms Son & Cooke (Southern) Ltd*[85] and the result was on all fours with that case. The following statement by Preiss J sums up the the Court's approach:

I have been careful not to pay undue regard to this decision of the English court in a situation where the *condictio sine causa* [which the Court regarded as the appropriate action in the circumstances], foreign to English law, has to be considered. Nevertheless, the judgment contains a valuable indication in my view as to the precise legal nature of an inadvertent payment by a bank despite the stop instruction.[86]

On a technical level the decision of the English Court differed from that of its South African counterpart. Goff J had reached his conclusion that the erroneous payment of a stopped cheque did not extinguish the underlying debt by holding that a bank paid its client's cheque as an agent, with the result that the withdrawal of authority meant that payment by the bank could not extinguish the client's debt to the recipient. The South African court, on the other hand, did not consider the bank to have paid as the agent of its client, but concluded that the underlying debt had not been extinguished (as explained above) on the basis of the nature of the debt-extinguishing agreement between the drawer and the payee. In spite of this difference, the decisions in the two countries were in agreement on the principle that payment of a countermanded cheque by a bank does not extinguish the underlying debt of the drawer to the payee.

On appeal, however, the decision of the Transvaal Provincial Division was overturned.[87] Although the Appellate Division confirmed a debt-extinguishing agreement to be a condition for a valid payment of the debt, it differed from the court of first instance on a crucial point: a debt-extinguishing agreement, it said, is normally to the effect that even an unauthorized payment by the bank would discharge the debt and therefore it does not assume a continuing intention to pay on the part of the payer; thus any attempt by the payer to stop the payment is irrelevant as far as the extinction of the debt is concerned. The policy behind this thinking may be summarized in this way: (i) since a cheque itself is discharged when a bank pays that cheque—even if the payment is unauthorized—the approach of the court *a quo* would mean that the payee not only would have to return the amount of the cheque, but at the same time would also no longer have the advantage of a liquid document, with its procedural and other advantages;

---

[85] [1980] QB 677, [1979] 3 All ER 522 (QB).   [86] 45J–46A.
[87] *B&H Engineering v. First National Bank of SA Ltd* 1995 (2) SA 279 (A).

and the fact of obtaining a liquid document, after all, ameliorates the risk of non-payment that a creditor runs when accepting payment by cheque. Good commercial practice therefore demands that a continuing authorization should not be held to be part of an ordinary debt-extinguishing agreement. (ii) Commercial convenience further demands that the payee not be drawn into the question as to whether the cheque had been properly countermanded.

Referring to the *Simms* case and its finding that an erroneous payment by a bank of a countermanded cheque does not discharge the drawer's obligation in regard to that cheque, the Court observed:

No reasoning or authority is advanced in support of this proposition. In fact there is authority in English law, not referred to by Goff J, which apparently lays down that the unauthorised payment by a bank of a cheque can serve to extinguish a debt owing by the drawer to the payee . . .[88] I do not think that *Simm's* case accords with our law on this point. Indeed, even in England it has been criticised . . .[89] I consider, therefore, that the learned judge *a quo* in the present matter was mistaken to place reliance on *Simms* case . . .[90]

The Appellate Division probably overstated both the commercial convenience of its decision and the relative weakness of the authority of the *Simms* case. Thus, the last word has probably not yet been spoken on the matter. For present purposes, however, it is not appropriate to delve too deeply into the relative merits of the opposing positions. What is important in the present context is that this issue is evidence of the continuing influence of English law on the South African law of unjustified enrichment. Furthermore, it illustrates rather well that the South African courts are able to ignore doctrinal details and to consider the essence of the relevant English cases when determining whether or not to adopt a specific solution existing in that country.[91]

---

[88] The Court here refers to *B Liggett (Liverpool) Ltd v. Barclays Bank* [1928] 1 KB 48, 58–64 and *Jackson v. White and Midland Bank Ltd* [1967] 2 *Lloyd's Reports* 68 (QB) 80 sq. However, the authority of these cases must be doubted: see e.g. Goff/Jones (n. 6), 624, fn. 63.

[89] Mr Justice Grosskopf refers to R. M. Goode, 'The Bank's Right to Recover Money Paid on a Stopped Cheque' (1981) 97 *LQR* 254; but see Goff/Jones (n. 6), 139, fn. 25.

[90] 294D-F.

[91] On the interaction between civil law and common law in South Africa see generally Beinart, 1981 *Acta Juridica* 7 sqq.; Reinhard Zimmermann, 'Synthesis in South African Private Law: Civil Law, Common Law and *Usus Hodiernus Pandectarum*', (1986) 103 *SALJ* 259 sqq.; D. P. Visser, 'Daedalus in the Supreme Court: The Common Law Today', (1986) 49 *THRHR* 127 sqq.; O. D. Schreiner, *The Contribution of English Law to South African Law; and the Rule of Law in South Africa* (1967), 5 sqq.; Christopher Forsyth, *In Danger for their Talents: A Study of the Appellate Division of the Supreme Court of South Africa 1950–1980* (1985), 182 sqq.; H. J. Erasmus, 'Roman Law in South Africa Today', (1989) 106 *SALJ* 666, 669 sq.; cf. H. B. Fine, *The Administration of Criminal Justice at the Cape of Good Hope 1795–1828* (unpublished Ph.D. thesis, University of Cape Town, 1991), 1–106; Stephen D. Girvin, *The Influence of a British Legal Education and Practice at the Bar on the Judges appointed to the Supreme Court of Southern Africa 1827–1910* (unpublished Ph.D. thesis, University of Aberdeen, 1990).

4. Contracts for the sale of land which are void for lack of writing

From an early stage in the development of South African law certain formalities for the sale of land—most notably that a valid contract must be in writing—have been prescribed by legislation.[92] A typical situation occurring as a result of this kind of legislation was the following: A enters into an oral agreement with B for the sale of a particular piece of land. He pays all or part of the purchase price, but B refuses to transfer the land to A. There are three possibilities. A may have laboured under an (excusable) error of fact that the formalities were complied with. His action may also have been prompted by an error of law, if he thought that such formalities need not be complied with in order for the contract to be valid. The third possibility is that A knew that writing was an essential requirement for the validity of the contract, but nevertheless performed in the assumption that B would transfer the land in spite of the invalidity of the contract. Until recently there would have been no remedy in the second situation, but in the first a *condictio indebiti* would have been available and in the third the *condictio causa data causa non secuta* presented itself as a possible remedy.

When the last situation fell to be considered by the Transvaal Supreme Court in *Carlis v. McCusker*[93] early in this century, the Court, as De Vos[94] points out, approached the matter in the following way: it did not consider at all whether the *condictio indebiti* or the *condictio causa data causa non secuta* was the appropriate remedy in the circumstances, but merely stated that in view of the principle against unjustified enrichment the Court 'would not permit a man, who had verbally agreed to sell landed property, and had on faith of that agreement received the whole or portion of the purchase price, to retain both the money and the land'.[95]

To this general principle the Court added a rider, namely that if the seller 'were willing and able to carry out his part of the inchoate understanding, on faith of which the money was paid ... there would be no equity entitling the buyer to the assistance of the court'.[96] This approach accorded with the position in English law (to which the Court made extensive reference). Here the buyer could, in principle, recover his payment only if there was a total failure of consideration,[97] unless the exception of

---

[92] See e.g. Proclamation 8 of 1902 (Transvaal).   [93] 1904 TS 917.

[94] De Vos (n. 1), 188.   [95] 923.   [96] Ibid.

[97] It should be noted that 'consideration' in the context of a restitutionary action does not mean the same thing as when used as a requirement for the formation of a valid contract in English law. Cf. *Fibrosa Spolka Akcyjna v. Fairbairn Lawson Combe Barbour Ltd* [1943] AC 32, 48, where the distinction was explained in the following way: 'In English law, an enforceable contract may be formed by an exchange of a promise for a promise, or by the exchange of a promise for an act ... and thus, in the law relating to the formation of a contract, the promise to do a thing may often be the consideration, but when one is considering the law of failure of consideration and of the quasi-contractual right to recover money on that ground, it is, generally speaking, not the promise which is referred to as the consideration, but the

Thomas v. Brown[98] applied. In that case it was held that if the seller 'were ready and willing to complete', no action for the recovery of the money was available.

It was this rule that the Transvaal Supreme Court in *Carlis v. McCusker*[99] grafted onto South African law. In *Wilken v. Kohler*[100] the natural corollary of this rule was added, namely that if the defendant had performed in full an action for recovery would likewise be excluded. The rule in *Carlis v. McCusker* was followed consistently in the Transvaal, but it was criticized by De Vos[101] and eventually (in 1979) by the Cape Provincial Division of the Supreme Court.[102] The essence of the criticism was that, depending on the circumstances, the principles of either the *condictio indebiti* or the *condictio causa data causa non secuta* should be applied and that neither of these actions contemplated that a claim for recovery would be excluded merely because the other party to a void contract had performed in full, or was willing to perform. The uncertainty arising as a result of that criticism was resolved when the Alienation of Land Act was promulgated in 1981.[103] In s. 28 it introduced a statutory enrichment action for the recovery of performances made in pursuance of a contract void for failure to comply with the prescribed formalities. This section had the effect of abolishing the rule in *Carlis v. McCusker*. The other party's willingness and ability to perform has thus become irrelevant. However, it effectively retained the extension of the rule in *Wilken v. Kohler*, by providing[104] that a contract which did not conform to the prescribed formalities 'shall in all respects be valid *ab initio* if the alienee had performed in full, in terms of the deed of alienation or contract, and the land in question has been transferred to the alienee.'

IV. INDEPENDENT DEVELOPMENT

1. Illegal contracts and the *par delictum* rule

Roman-Dutch law strictly enforced the principle that a performance made in terms of an illegal contract cannot be reclaimed unless the plaintiff comes with clean hands: *in pari delicto potior est conditio defendentis,* or *nemo auditur suam turpitudinem allegans*, as this principle was proclaimed in the authoritative Roman-Dutch sources of the seventeenth and eighteenth cen-

---

performance of the promise. The money was paid to secure performance and, if performance fails, the inducement which brought about the payment is not fulfilled.' See P. B. H. Birks, *An Introduction to the Law of Restitution* (1985), 219; Hutton (n. 64), 3.

[98] (1876) 1 QBD 714.   [99] Above, n. 93.
[100] 1913 AD 135.   [101] De Vos (n. 1), 187 sqq.
[102] *CD Developments Co (East Rand) (Pty) Ltd v. Novick* 1979 (2) SA 546 (C) 550C–564F. See also Sieg Eiselen and Gerrit Pienaar, *Unjustified Enrichment: A Casebook* (1993), 222.
[103] Act 68 of 1981.   [104] In s. 28(2).

turies.[105] By the end of the eighteenth century the same was true of English law.[106] 'No court will lend its aid to a man who founds his cause on an immoral or illegal act' said Lord Mansfield, and continued: 'if the plaintiff and defendant were to change sides, and the defendant was to bring an action against the plaintiff, the latter would not then have the advantage of it; for where both were equally at fault, *potior est conditio defendentis'*.[107]

South Africa thus inherited, from both its basic sources, an unqualified unwillingness to aid those involved in illegal dealings. For South African courts to have continued in the groove cut for it would, therefore, have been unremarkable. However, in a dramatic departure from precedent the South African Appellate Division decided in the early part of this century not to enforce this rule rigidly. In *Jajbhay v. Cassim*[108] it was held that the *par delictum* rule may be relaxed in the interests of public policy or in order to 'do simple justice between man and man'.

Not everyone has been happy about the flexibility (and consequent uncertainty) created in this way; and there have certainly been some erratic decisions. Generally, however, the rule has stood the test of time: so much so, in fact, that Goff and Jones argue for a similar relaxation in English law with reference to, amongst other authority, *Jajbhay v. Cassim*.[109]

2. Serendipitous advances: the right of *bona fide* occupiers to claim compensation

In Roman law a *bona fide* possessor was limited to a *ius retentionis* in order to enforce a right to compensation for necessary and useful expenses in respect of the property of the *dominus*.[110] By the seventeenth century it had come to be recognized (at least in Holland) that the *bona fide* possessor could claim these expenses by means of an action.[111] The *bona fide*

---

[105] Grotius (n. 76), 3, 1, 13; Simon van Leeuwen, *Censura Forensis*, 1, 4, 14, 8 sqq.; Voet (n. 76), 12, 5, 2; Dionysius Godefridus van der Keessel, *Praelectiones iuris hodierni ad Hugonis Grotii Introductionem ad Iurisprudentiam Hollandicam* (ed. Amsterdam/Cape Town, 1961–71), ad Gr. 3, 1, 43. See generally Robert Feenstra, 'Nemo auditur suam turpitudinem allegans', in: *Brocardica in honorem G. C. J. J. van den Bergh* (1988), 31 sqq.; Visser (n. 2), 412 sq.; Zimmermann (n. 1), 844 sqq., 862 sqq.

[106] Goff/Jones (n. 6), 498.

[107] *Holman v. Johnson* (1775) 1 Cowp 341, 343 (also quoted by Goff/Jones (n. 6), 499).

[108] 1939 AD 537.   [109] See Goff/Jones (n. 6), 522.   [110] D. 12, 6, 51; De Vos (n. 1), 54.

[111] See e.g. Van der Keessel (n. 105), ad Gr. 2, 10, 8. See further De Vos (n. 1), 85, 98. Interestingly, the position regarding the right of a possessor of *movable* property to claim for necessary and useful expenses was uncertain in Roman-Dutch law and remains so in South Africa until this day. The weight of opinion in modern South African law is that the *bona fide* possessor of a movable is able to enforce his claim by way of an action. *Obiter* statements to this effect were made in *Rondalia Bank Bpk v. Pieter Nel Motors (Edms) Bpk* 1979 (4) SA 467 (T) and *Van der Burgh v. Van Dyk* 1993 (3) SA 312 (O). See also De Vos (n. 1), 233. In all probability, then, the view expressed in the old case of *Reed Bros v. Ford* 1923 TPD 150, namely that the *bona fide* possessor did not have an action in these circumstances, will not be followed if the matter were to arise for decision before the Appellate Division.

occupier, on the other hand, had no such action, and the Roman-Dutch law received into South Africa reflected this position.[112] However, by what must be regarded as a rather fortunate accident, South African law was set on a course which was to result in the recognition of an enrichment action for *bona fide* occupiers who had improved the property of others.

In 1874 Lord de Villiers was faced with the following set of facts in *Bellingham v. Bloommetje*.[113] A lessee of agricultural land had erected certain structures on what he assumed to be the rented property. In reality he had encroached upon the neighbouring farm and was thus a *bona fide* occupier of the contiguous property. When the owner of the neighbouring property sought to evict him he insisted on a *ius retentionis* until he was compensated for the improvements. Lord de Villiers allowed the defendant a right of retention. However, it would seem that the learned judge had nodded for a moment and that in all probability he thought that he was dealing with a *bona fide* possessor. Thus De Vos[114] points out that Lord de Villiers had relied on texts of the institutional writers dealing with possessors and had used the terms '*bona fide* possessor' and '*bona fide* occupier' indiscriminately.

Bellingham v. Bloommetje[115] was clearly the weakest possible authority that a *bona fide* occupier was entitled to compensation for improvements made to the property of another and for nearly forty years the question did not arise again. Then in 1911 *Rubin v. Botha*[116] fell to be decided by the newly established Appellate Division of the Supreme Court. Lord de Villiers, now serving as the first Chief Justice of the Union of South Africa, once again presided over the Court that was to decide the matter. In this case the putative 'lessee' of land had been evicted after it was held that the contract of lease was invalid, and he subsequently claimed, as *bona fide* occupier, compensation for buildings that he had erected in terms of the invalid contract.[117] Lord de Villiers took the opportunity to rehabilitate his judgment in *Bellingham v. Bloommetje*. In that case, he stated, he had consciously dealt with the defendant as a *bona fide* occupier and it was therefore authority for that class of plaintiffs to claim compensation. (In the present case, however, judgment was given against the plaintiff because he had already received more compensation from the defendant than he was entitled to.[118])

Sir James Rose Innes, who delivered a separate but concurring judgment, was more sceptical with regard to the *Bloommetje* case. In his view that case had been decided on the basis that the defendant was a *bona fide* possessor,

---

[112] See De Vos (n. 1), 85, 247–9; D. G. John, *'n Oorsig van Ongeregverdigde Verryking as 'n Gedingoorsaak in die Suid-Afrikaanse Reg* (1951), 18–57. Cf. Voet (n. 76), 5, 3, 23; Van der Keessel (n. 105), ad Gr. 2, 10, 8.

[113] (1874) 4 Buch 36.   [114] De Vos (n. 1), 249.   [115] Above, n. 113.
[116] 1911 AD 568.   [117] De Vos (n. 1), 250.   [118] See also ibid. 252.

which meant that it did not provide authority for allowing such a claim in an instance of *bona fide occupatio* as opposed to *bona fide possessio*. Nevertheless, he was prepared, without reference to any authority, to support the Chief Justice in saying that a *bona fide* occupier is entitled to compensation. This attitude of Innes JA prompted De Vos to argue that a general enrichment action had by this time evolved in South African law.[119] Whether that was so or not (we will return to this aspect below) the episode demonstrates that the Appellate Division of the South African Supreme Court was certainly prepared to develop the law of unjustified enrichment in a creative manner. (The right of the *bona fide* occupier to claim compensation was consistently reaffirmed in subsequent cases.[120])

3. The dark side of *Bellingham v. Bloommetje*: the position of *mala fide* possessors and occupiers

The reasonableness of treating the *bona fide* occupier in the same way as the *bona fide* possessor for the purposes of claiming necessary and useful expenses is, I believe, obvious. It is therefore not difficult to appreciate why South African courts consistently favoured the granting of a remedy in this situation. However, when having to decide whether the *mala fide* possessor and the *mala fide* occupier should be granted a similar remedy, the courts have, again understandably, vacillated, since the issues and policy considerations are not nearly as clear as they are in the case of *bona fide* possessors and occupiers.

As far as the position in Roman-Dutch law is concerned, Hugo Grotius,[121] it seems, evaluated the matter with remarkable perspicacity: someone who has built in bad faith on the land of another has no recourse, except for necessary expenses. The policy underlying this approach was probably, that if a *mala fide* possessor is allowed a claim for necessary expenses that would encourage the possessor to preserve the property. On the other hand, there is neither advantage to the owner nor any equitable consideration in favour of the *mala fide* possessor which requires useful expenses to be compensated. However, most of the institutional writers did not follow Grotius in this matter. Van der Keessel did,[122] but Vinnius,[123]

---

[119] Ibid. 251.

[120] See e.g. *Fletcher and Fletcher v. Bulawayo Waterworks Co Ltd* 1915 AD 636, 650; *Nortjé v. Pool* 1966 (3) SA 96 (A); *Weilbach v. Grobler* 1982 (2) SA 15 (O); *Earljay Holdings (Pty) Ltd v. Moldenhauer* 1984 (3) SA 354 (E). (The position of the *bona fide* occupier is slightly different to that of the *bona fide* possessor, in that the owner of the land may set off the value of the occupation of the land against the occupier's claim, whereas the owner has no such right concerning a claim by a possessor. See generally Eiselen/Pienaar (n. 102) 417; J. E. Scholtens, 'Unjustified Enrichment', 1956 *Annual Survey of South African Law* 183.)

[121] Grotius (n. 76), 2, 10, 8.

[122] Van der Keessel (n. 105), ad Gr. 2, 10, 8; De Vos (n. 1), 102, fn. 28.

[123] Arnoldus Vinnius, *In Quatuor Libros Institutionum Imperialum Commentarius*, ad Inst. 2, 1, 30. See also De Vos (n. 1), 102, fn. 28.

Voet,[124] and Groenewegen[125] did not. According to the second group of authors the *mala fide* possessor should be treated in exactly the same way as the *bona fide* possessor, although he may in some circumstances be compelled to remove the improvements. In South African law this curiously generous approach to *mala fide* possessors[126] continued to exert an influence whose roots may be traced, once again, to the decision in *Bellingham v. Bloommetje*. In that case Lord de Villiers stated *obiter* that it was impossible to reconcile the conflicting common law authorities, 'but considering the high respect which this Court has always paid to the opinion of *Groenewegen, Voet and Van Leeuwen* it is not too much to say that the weight of authority is in favour of the right of even the *mala fide* possessor to compensation for *useful expenses*'.[127] (The basis for the *lex citationis* thus invented by Lord de Villiers is not at all clear; Grotius and Van der Keessel cannot be said to be of lesser authority than Voet and Groenewegen.) The Chief Justice went on to hold that a *mala fide* possessor was entitled to claim for necessary *as well as* useful expenses. However, some twenty years later, in *De Beers Consolidated Mines v. London and South African Exploration Co*,[128] Lord de Villiers, again *obiter*, followed the approach of Grotius and restricted the claim of the *mala fide* possessor to necessary expenses.

Both views still survive in South African law. The *Bellingham v. Bloommetje* approach was followed in the Transvaal Republic for the first time in 1890 in *Campbell v. Golden Crescent Gold Mining Co*[129] and in the second half of the twentieth century there have been a number of cases in which the bare assertion was made that South African law allowed *mala fide* possessors to claim for useful expenses.[130] The latest of them was *JOT Motors (Edms) Bpk h/a Vaal Datsun v. Standard Kredietkorporasie Bpk*,[131] where Mr Justice Coetzee had to decide whether a garage had a lien for necessary and useful expenses against the owner (usually the finance company) of a car brought in for repairs by the hire-purchase buyer. The learned Judge regarded the matter as one in which he had to decide the position of the *mala fide* possessor and, in a forceful judgment, held that such a possessor did indeed have a right to both necessary and useful expenses. Unfortunately, however, the garage was not a *mala fide* possessor but a lawful occupier. This mistake (echoing that made in *Bellingham v. Bloommetje*) nullified or at least weakened the force that this judgment would otherwise

---

[124] Voet (n. 76), 5, 3, 21; 5, 2, 23.
[125] Simon van Groenewegen van der Made, *Tractatus de legibus abrogatis et inusitatis in Hollandia vicinisque regionibus*, ad Inst. 2, 1, 30.
[126] See generally Eiselen/Pienaar (n. 102), 395; De Vos (n. 1), 258.
[127] (1874) 4 Buch 36, 39. See also De Vos (n. 1), 235 sqq.
[128] (1893) 10 SC 359. [129] (1890) 3 SAR 248.
[130] See *Spencer v. Gostelow* 1920 AD 617; *Lechoana v. Cloete* 1925 AD 536; *Kommissaris van Binnelandse Inkomste v. Anglo-American (OFS) Housing Co Ltd* 1960 (3) SA 642 (A).
[131] 1984 (2) SA 510 (T).

have had. (On appeal, the Appellate Division of the Supreme Court remarked on the classification of the garage as a *mala fide* possessor, but did not find it necessary to decide the issue.[132]) The matter must therefore still be considered uncertain, although there is powerful backing amongst academic writers in favour of treating the *mala fide* possessor in the same way as the *bona fide* possessor.[133] The sympathy in South African law for the *mala fide* possessor includes the *mala fide* occupier. De Vos,[134] Lotz,[135] Kleyn and Boraine,[136] and Van der Merwe[137] are all prepared to allow compensation for both the necessary and the useful expenses of *mala fide* occupiers. Over the years there has also been judicial support for this view.[138]

The bland assumption which mechanistically equates the *mala fide* possessor (and occupier) with a *bona fide* possessor (and occupier) unfortunately appears too deeply entrenched to be easily unsettled. It is true that the law of unjustified enrichment could not function effectively if it were based solely on vague notions of equity, but to classify enrichment as unjustified without any reference to the equities of the situation has been an unfortunate trend in the development of this branch of South African law.

The unfinished quality of this area of the law of unjustified enrichment is further illustrated by the uncertainty surrounding the actual remedies available to *mala fide* possessors and occupiers. It has not been decided whether a *mala fide* possessor or occupier—if indeed he has a claim—can avail himself of both an action *and* a *ius rententionis*, or only one or the other.[139] Furthermore, it remains uncertain[140] whether the *mala fide* possessor has a *ius rententionis* in regard to useful expenses (as opposed to necessary expenses), while the final and authoritative word on whether the *bona fide* possessor of *movables* may enforce his right by way of an action or only by claiming a *ius rententionis* has also not been spoken.[141]

4. Hubris: the case of the unauthorized administrator who has administered the affairs of another against his wishes.

While the civilian tradition in regard to the unauthorized administration of the affairs of another is based on what one might call a caring, humanitarian

---

[132] *Standard Kredietkorporasie Bpk v. JOT Motors (Edms) Bpk h/a Vaal Motors* 1986 (1) SA 223 (A).

[133] See De Vos (n. 1), 237 sq.   [134] Ibid. 258.

[135] J. G. Lotz, 'Enrichment', in: W. A. Joubert (ed.), *The Law of South Africa*, vol. 9 (1979), § 91.   [136] *Silberberg and Schoeman's The Law of Property* (3rd edn., 1992), 153.

[137] C. G. van der Merwe, *Sakereg* (1989), 162 sq.

[138] See e.g. *Acton v. Motau* 1909 TS 841, a case involving a *mala fide* occupier (although there, once again, the *mala fide* occupier was described as a *mala fide* possessor); and see *Peens v. Botha-Odendaal* 1980 (2) SA 381 (O); *Quarrying Enterprises (Pvt) Ltd v. John Viol (Pvt) Ltd* 1985 (3) SA 575 (ZH); *Boikhutsong Business Undertakings (Pty) Ltd v. Grobler* 1988 (2) SA 676 (BA); Van der Merwe (n. 137), 162 sq.; Kleyn/Boraine (n. 136), 156.

[139] See *Weilbach v. Grobler* 1982 (2) SA 15 (O) at 29 sq.; Eiselen/Pienaar (n. 102), 424.

[140] See generally Eiselen/Pienaar (n. 102), 395.   [141] De Vos (n. 1), 233.

approach, English law, in this respect, emphasizes individualism. Where the civilian tradition encourages the Good Samaritan, English law tends to view the administration of the affairs of another as unwarranted interference.

Reinhard Zimmermann[142] encapsulates the difference between the two approaches in the following way:

English law . . . does not possess a doctrine of *negotiorum gestio* . . . a highly characteristic trait, for it reflects the traditional individualism and the reserved mentality of the English people. Management of another's affairs is regarded, first and foremost, as an undue curtailment of that other person's autonomy, and the unsolicited gestor is often somewhat contemptuously referred to as an officious meddler.

Roman law, on the other hand, reflected the fact that individualism, though not foreign to Roman society, was tempered by the social obligation to assist one's friends. This view of life was clearly influential in the emergence of the institution of *negotiorum gestio*:

It is the prime example of the sober sense of realism with which the Roman lawyers were able to attune law and social ethics to each other and, more specifically, to balance the individualistic interest in not having one's affairs interfered with and the interests of society in encouraging ethically desirable activities on behalf of others.[143]

It must be added, though, (as Zimmermann[144] also points out) that the Good Samaritan is not as unprotected under the common law as it appears at first blush. For instance, those who rescue persons or property from the perils of the sea receive compensation at common law (under the influence of the Italian law merchant and according to the doctrine of 'agency of necessity') and Good Samaritans are helped in a number of further instances which a South African lawyer would classify as unauthorized administration.[145]

The direction taken by the Cape Supreme Court in regard to an unauthorized administrator who acts against the wishes of the *dominus* vividly illustrates that South African courts have not always taken sufficient advantage of the balancing perspective offered by English law. In C. 2, 18, 24 it is clearly stated that the gestor who acts against the express wishes of the *dominus* is not entitled to claim the expenses thus incurred. This view has remained predominant throughout the development of the *ius commune* (including its Roman-Dutch version),[146] although a minority view (with its origin in the twelfth century with the glossator Martinus Gosia[147]) main-

---

[142] Zimmermann (n. 1) 435 sq. [143] Ibid. 436. [144] Ibid. 448.
[145] See Burrows (n. 20), 231 sqq.; Goff/Jones (n. 6), 363 sqq.
[146] See D. H. van Zyl, 'Die Regshistoriese Metode', (1972) 35 *THRHR* 19, 25 sqq.; Albericus de Rosate, *In primam codicis partem commentarii* (ed. Venetiis, 1586), ad C. 2, 18, 24; Leyser (n. 41), Spec. 55, 5 sqq.; Voet (n. 76), 3, 5, 11; Groenewegen (n. 125), ad C. 3, 32, 5.
[147] *Dissensiones dominorum sive controversiae veterum iuris Romani interpretum qui Glossatores vocantur* (ed. Lipsiae, 1834), 275.

tained that such a *gestor* should be granted an action. In South African law the position of the *gestor* acting *domine prohibente* has been uncertain for a long time, with the Orange Free State Provincial Division of the Supreme Court in the 1927 case of *Pretorius v. Van Zyl*[148] expressing support for a claim being recognized in these circumstances, while the Transvaal Provincial Division in the late 1960s[149] leaned in the opposite direction. A decade later the Cape Provincial Division, in *Standard Bank Financial Services Ltd v. Taylam (Pty) Ltd*,[150] allowed an action where a bank had administered the affairs of a client in a way expressly prohibited by the client. The Court relied on the authority of Voet and Groenewegen[151] (which, will be remembered, was also invoked (*obiter*) in *Bellingham v. Bloommetje* in favour of granting the *mala fide* possessor a claim). This is not the place to develop the history of this radical remedy in any detail; it should be pointed out, however, that a sensitivity to the alternative English approach to unauthorized administration of another person's affairs may very well have taken the Cape Supreme Court in a different direction. For the reticence of English law in helping the ordinary *gestor* may have persuaded the Court, not that English law should replace Roman-Dutch law, but that accommodating a *gestor* who acts against the wishes of the *dominus* goes just too far.

V. THE SPIRIT OF THE LAW: THE GENERAL PRINCIPLE AGAINST UNJUSTIFIED ENRICHMENT AND THE NOTION OF A GENERAL ACTION

In the course of the seventeenth and eighteenth centuries the law of Holland distinguished itself within the family of legal systems that formed the *ius commune* by developing a general enrichment action.[152] However, the version of Roman-Dutch law received in South Africa allowed this important fact to become obscured. This development is quite understandable, for some of the sources from which it appears that such an action existed in Holland were published only in the course of the twentieth century. (This applies to both the *Observationes Tumultuariae* of Cornelis van Bynkershoek,[153] the President of the *Hooge Raad*[154] and the *Observationes*

---

[148] 1927 OPD 226. [149] Odendaal v. Van Oudtshoorn 1968 (3) SA 433 (T).
[150] 1979 (2) SA 383 (C). [151] See n. 146 above.
[152] See the literature quoted in n. 2 above.
[153] Ed. E. M. Meijers, A. S. de Blécourt and H. D. J. Bodenstein (1926–47) [vols. 1–3] and E. M. Meijers, H. F. W. D. Fischer and M. S. van Oosten (1962) [vol. 4]. On Cornelius van Bynkershoek see Reinhard Zimmermann, 'Römisch-holländisches Recht: ein Überblick', in: Robert Feenstra/Reinhard Zimmermann (eds.), *Das römisch-holländische Recht: Fortschritte des Zivilrechts im 17. und 18. Jahrhundert* (1992), 32 sqq.; Govaert C. J. J. van den Bergh, 'Der Präsident: Cornelius van Bynkershoek, seine Bedeutung und sein Nachruhm', (1995) 3 *Zeitschrift für Europäisches Privatrecht* 423 sqq.
[154] The highest court in Holland, Zeeland, and West-Friesland, established 1587. See generally Zimmermann (n. 154), 21 sq. with further references.

Tumultuariae Novae of Willem Pauw,[155] who, like his father-in-law Van Bynkershoek, also served as President of the *Hooge Raad*.) Other sources were available but needed a sophisticated interpretation to reveal that they provided evidence of the existence of a general enrichment action. (In this regard Grotius' *Inleiding tot de Hollandsche Rechtsgeleertheyd* is of specific importance.[156]) The result of the opacity of the sources was that in nineteenth and early twentieth centuries South Africa—where scholarship was, to put it mildly, uneven—views varied as to the existence of a general enrichment action.

Shortly after Union in 1910, for instance, we find a strong judge like Sir James Rose Innes supporting the existence of such action. Thus, in *Hauman v. Nortjé*,[157] after a comparative survey of the relief afforded to a contractor who had not completed the work as specified by the contract, he stated:

Turning now to our own law, we find the doctrine well established that no man may enrich himself at the expense or to the detriment of another. Its general operation lies outside the realm of contract, and its most frequent application relates to cases where improvements have been made by a possessor of land. But it was used in *Rubin v. Botha* (1911 AD 568) to prevent enrichment which had its origin not in possession but in an agreement which the parties believed to be binding, but which turned out to be invalid. And there is no reason in principle why it should not be similarly employed where the enrichment would follow in consequence of a contract but would not be covered or contemplated by it.[158]

The judge went on to say that there happened to be direct authority which covered the situation before the Court, but he would clearly have come to the same conclusion even without such a precedent. Indeed, as we have seen, this is exactly what he had previously done in *Rubin v. Botha*.[159]

Statements such as these, even though they emanated from a judge of the Appellate Division, were not enough to convince all or even the majority of judges in provincial and local divisions that a general enrichment action had in fact been developed or acknowledged in South Africa. Consequently many a *dictum* during the first half of this century denied the existence of a general action, a particularly unambiguous formulation being that of Van den Heever J in *Pucjlowski v. Johnston's Executors*:[160]

Save as a rather nebulous generalisation, there was not in Roman law and there is now in Roman-Dutch law no rule which lays down categorically that no person shall be enriched at the expense of another without legal cause. The alleged rule is a generalisation not borne out by legal phenomena; it is mere *causae conjectio* (in the words of *Sabinus*) and in practical application frequently *perdit officium suum*.[161]

During the 1950s two academic lawyers published the findings of their respective investigations into the conflicting signals sent out by the South

---

[155] Ed. R. Feenstra, W. L. de Koning-Bey, L. E. van Holk, H. W. van Soest (1964–72).
[156] See the literature qouted in n. 2 above.   [157] 1914 AD 293.   [158] 301 sq.
[159] 1911 AD 568.   [160] 1946 WLD 1.   [161] 3 sq.

African courts on this issue. D. G. John in 1951[162] did not, on the evidence available, feel free to conclude that a general enrichment action had been established in South Africa. Wouter de Vos in 1958, however, argued that the development in respect of occupiers and contractors, as well as a variety of other incidental acknowledgements of enrichment liability, meant that South African law had indeed come to recognize a subsidiary general action, alongside the 'classic' specific enrichment remedies.[163] From these opposing assessments and subsequent legal uncertainty it was clear that a directive from the Appellate Division was the only way in which the matter could be resolved.

The opportunity for the Appellate Division to provide such directive and to determine the overall structure of enrichment liability in South Africa came in 1966, in the dispute in *Nortjé v. Pool*.[164] It concerned an agreement in terms of which the appellants received the right to prospect for kaolin (and to exploit any kaolin deposits if such were to be found) against the payment of certain sums to the owner of the land. The appellants carried out the prospecting work and uncovered substantial kaolin reserves on the land in question. Unfortunately, however, unbeknown to the parties the contract was invalid because it had not been attested to by a notary under the provisions of Act 50 of 1956. When the owner died the executor of his estate refused *ex post facto* attestation. The appellants instituted an enrichment action against the estate of the owner on the basis that the detection of the kaolin deposits had increased the value of the land; its owner had thus been enriched.[165] On the face of it, an ordinary *bona fide* occupier had improved the property of another (a class of occupier whose right to claim, as we have seen, has been firmly established since *Rubin v. Botha*[166]). However, the sources seem to support only claims relating to tangible improvements and the Court now had to decide whether improvement of the market value of property (for instance by revealing hitherto unknown qualities) could found an enrichment claim.

The claim was excepted to in the court of first instance on the ground, amongst others, that it did not fall within the ambit of one of the recognized enrichment actions; the exception was upheld. On appeal the majority also upheld the exception, on the grounds that (i) the right to compensation for improvements had always been restricted to useful improvements that physically improved the property; (ii) none of the recognized actions covered this instance; and (iii) South African law did not have a general enrichment action.

---

[162] John (n. 112), 141 (but see 137); cf. De Vos (n. 1), 305, fn. 10.
[163] De Vos (n. 1), 304.   [164] 1966 (3) SA 96 (A).
[165] In accordance with South African law, the plaintiffs claimed the owner's enrichment only up to the amount of their own impoverishment.
[166] 1911 AD 568.

Mr Justice Botha, who delivered the judgment of the Court, was persuaded that there were clear policy reasons why the claim should not be allowed.[167] Thus, allowing claims for intangible improvements would create a very large number of new instances where enrichment liability would have to be considered, making it difficult to contain this kind of liability within acceptable bounds. Presumably these policy considerations would also have prevented a successful claim under the general enrichment action had the existence of such an action been acknowledged. This means that the Court could have achieved the same result in this case even if it had found positively in regard to the question of the existence of a general enrichment action. We must therefore conclude that the decision not to recognize a general action was motivated not by expediency, to achieve the result which the Court thought correct in the case at hand, but by a conviction that the existence of such an action was not desirable. The reasons advanced by Mr Justice Botha were two-fold: the lack of authority in Roman-Dutch and South African law for such an action; and considerations of legal certainty.

A survey of the institutional writers brought the Court to the conclusion that a general enrichment action had not existed in Roman-Dutch law: a view which, it is now widely accepted, was based on an erroneous interpretation of the sources. As far as South African authority was concerned, the Court sided with John rather than De Vos and held that the developments, such as there were, did not amount to the recognition of the existence of a general action.[168]

The Court attempted to bolster the conclusion that it drew from the sources with a more fundamental consideration, namely that recognition of a general action 'before the parameters of such a general enrichment action have been clearly established and its requirements clearly defined would make it a mere discretionary remedy which would lead only to uncertainty in the law'.[169]

At the time of the decision in *Nortjé v. Pool* Professor de Vos had already outlined in the first edition of his textbook the requirements he envisaged of a general enrichment action. The Appellate Division seemed to be of the opinion that these were not detailed enough to keep such an action within manageable bounds. The Court preferred an incremental accretion of principles over time, which might eventually lead to the recognition of a general action.[170] The tenor of the judgment was that such future development would have to happen as an analogous extension of the existing actions when specific circumstances were present which pointed to the desirability of the particular extension.[171]

The minority judgment delivered by Mr Justice Ogilvie Thompson had

---

[167] 132 sq. of the report.
[168] 138A-C.
[169] 140A. My translation from the Afrikaans original.
[170] 140A.
[171] See 133D, 139H.

no difficulty in holding that the claim of a *bona fide* occupier included instances where 'the market value of landed property is enhanced by means other than the annexation of a tangible improvement and in circumstances which constitute an unjustified enrichment of the owner of the land'.[172]

Mr Justice Rumpff (who also delivered a minority judgment) held the *condictio indebiti* to be applicable since, in his view, it could be instituted to recover the value of a *factum*. Although it was thus not necessary for him to comment on the question of whether a general action existed in South African law, he nevertheless revealed himself to be favourably disposed towards its recognition. He was of the opinion that the matter had not been fully argued, but indicated that it could very well be that a general action did in fact exist.[173] It would have been surprising, he argued, if the steady progress towards the recognition of a general claim on the European continent since the seventeenth century should not have found an echo in South Africa. The judges who had brought about the changes in South African law probably assumed that enrichment at the expense of another generally founded a claim, provided the enrichment could be branded as unjustified.[174] Concerning the question whether such an action *should* exit, the learned judge displayed a very clear appreciation of the issues involved. In a *cri de coeur* he stated:

If the 'enrichment action' is part of the law, should the use thereof be limited to the instances mentioned in the Roman law and the Roman-Dutch law of the seventeenth and eighteenth centuries? Could it be that the description of the Roman-Dutch law as a strong and vibrant legal system, with a powerful growth potential, is in fact pure hypocrisy? Could it be that Roman-Dutch law has begun to suffer from the 'modern' disease of arteriosclerosis?.[175]

The application of such a general rule against unjustified enrichment, he added later on in the judgment:

does not depend on the capriciousness of individual judges and the rule is not amporhous and without substance—as some seem to think—but must be given form with reference to the law itself, which is, of course, capable of development, especially since the rule [in question] is one which *par excellence* is rooted in equity— and the problem as to what is to be regarded as equitable is, in the same way as any other ethical problem, not static but dynamic.[176]

The judgments of Botha JA and Rumpff JA reflect in a dramatic way the deeply divided approach to the judicial function that existed in South Africa's highest court at that time. Forsyth has described the judgment of Mr Justice Botha as 'plainly antiquarian', since the judge, 'steeped in learning from the old authorities . . . [was] reluctant to step beyond the bounds

---

[172] 105A. [173] 117A. [174] 118E.
[175] 113G-H of the report; my translation from the Afrikaans originial.
[176] 118 of the report; my translation from the Afrikaans original.

which he thought was set by the ancient writers'.[177] This reluctance was no doubt the result of a great many complex influences, but on reading the judgment it is clear that it was at least partly rooted in an unwillingness to deal with open-ended principles and with broadly-formulated standards. In sharp contrast, Rumpff JA in his judgment displayed a confident approach towards the use of general principles. He appreciated that a legal system has a great many restraining devices on which a judge is able to draw in order to keep any broadly defined principle within workable limits.

The fact that the approach of Mr Justice Rumpff did not carry the day in *Nortjé v. Pool* was to prove disastrous for the South African law of unjustified enrichment. The majority of judgments following it brought not incremental development but stagnation. There were, as we have seen, certain significant developments within the confines of the recognized actions, but the essential shape of the body of enrichment law was frozen in a state of suspended animation. It was to be twenty-eight years before the opportunity again arose for the Appellate Division to free the captive form of enrichment law. In *Kommissaris van Binnelandse Inkomste v. Willers*[178] the liquidator of a company had made payments to certain shareholders of that company in, it was averred, the erroneous but *bona fide* belief that these payments were due. In fact the payments were (in part) not due because they included an amount owed by the company to the Commissioner of Inland Revenue as income tax. The shareholders were then sued by the Commissioner on the basis, amongst others, that they were unjustifiably enriched at the expense of the Commissioner in the amount of the *(pro rata)* excess each had received as a result of the liquidator not having taken the Commissioner's claim into account. The desirability of the recognition of a general action was fully argued before the Court by counsel for the appellants, with counsel for the respondents, after initial opposition, conceding that such an action should now be recognized in South African law. Once again, however, the Appellate Division responded in a disappointing way. It ruled, on a technicality, that the question of a general claim was not before the Court. Nevertheless an important step forward was taken, for the Court sought to reinterpret *Nortjé v. Pool* in a way which would allow for greater development of the law of unjustified enrichment. If *Nortjé v. Pool* had held that a general enrichment action did not exist and had to be created by the legislature, said (another) Mr Justice Botha, this did not mean:

that the Court should be prevented from accepting enrichment liability in a particular instance, merely because it had not found acknowledgement before in the same,

[177] Above, n. 91, 214.
[178] 1994 (3) SA 283 (A). For comment on this case see D. P. Visser, 'Not the General Enrichment Action', 1994 *TSAR* 196 sqq.; C.-J. Pretorius, 'Uitbreiding van die Toepassingsgebied van die *condictio indebiti* en die Ontwikkeling van 'n Algemene Verrykingsaksie', (1995) 58 *THRHR* 331 sqq.

or even similar, circumstances. In such an instance attention would naturally have to be devoted to the question whether the extension or new development is necessary or desirable, and, in addition, the existing precedents, old as well as new, would have to be considered, as would, too, the contributions of academic authors who have developed general criteria to found as well as limit liability.[179]

In other words, the judicial and academic interpretation during the last three decades amounted, in the opinion of the Court, to a misunderstanding of *Nortjé v. Pool*, and if that case had only been correctly understood the long years after this judgment need not have been as barren as they had turned out to be.

However, if a generalized claim for the recovery of enrichment unjustifiably retained does not exist then what, one is forced to ask, is the basis of these new instances of enrichment liability? That any development beyond the confines of the traditional actions necessarily implied the existence of a general claim was alluded to by Mr Justice Rumpff when he said in *Nortjé v. Pool* that the development in South African law took place 'precisely because those who implemented the law accepted that enrichment at the expense of another may be a ground for an action, provided that such enrichment is unjustified'.[180] This point was reiterated by Mr Justice van Zyl in a decision by the Transvaal Provincial Division of 1991,[181] where it was pointed out that the past extensions to the existing enrichment actions provided evidence of the existence of a general enrichment claim based on the general principle against unjustified enrichment.[182] The Appellate Division in this case was not moved by this line of reasoning. This leaves South African law with the possibility of further *ad hoc* expansion, but without a clear framework within which to accomplish it. Three and a half centuries after Grotius we have still to regain the ordering power of a general enrichment claim. Only if this is achieved can the mould of the past be broken to reveal the full power of unjustified enrichment as a balancing force within the law of obligations.

---

[179] 333. My translation from the Afrikaans original. [180] 118F-G.

[181] *Blesbok Eiendomsagentskap v. Cantamessa* 1991 (2) SA 712 (T). For comment on this case see G. T. S. Eiselen, 'Herlewing van die algemene Verrykingsaksie', (1992) 55 *THRHR* 124 sqq.; D. P. Visser, 'Unjustified Enrichment', 1991 *Annual Survey of South African Law* 113 sqq.

[182] 719. On the notion of a general enrichment action in South African law see generally Van Zyl, 1992 *Acta Juridica* 115 sqq.; Eiselen/Pienaar (n. 102), 22 sq.; Scholtens, (1966) 83 *SALJ* 394 sqq.; Eiselen, (1992) 55 *THRHR* 124 sqq.; Reinhard Zimmermann, 'A Road through the Enrichment Forest? Experiences with a General Enrichment Action', 1985 *CILSA* 1 sqq.

PART V

The Law of Delict

17: *Aquilian Liability I (Nineteenth Century)*

ANNÉL VAN ASWEGEN

I. INTRODUCTION

It is a truism that the modern South African law of delict is based substantially on the Roman *actiones legis Aquiliae* and *iniuriarum*, as well as on the action for pain and suffering developed in classical Roman-Dutch law, and derived at least partly from Germanic roots.[1] Our concern in this contribution is only with the *actio legis Aquiliae*,[2] the action used today to recover damages for patrimonial loss culpably and wrongfully caused.[3]

It is equally truistic to say that the *actio legis Aquiliae* underwent a process of adaptation by which it was extended far beyond the limited scope of the first and third chapters of the original *lex*. The first chapter provided that the wrongful killing of somebody else's slave or four-footed grazing beast rendered the wrongdoer liable to pay damages to the owner equal to the highest value of that object during the previous year. The third chapter

---

[1] Johannes Voet, *Commentarius ad Pandectas*, 9, 2, 11; Arnoldus Vinnius, *In Quatuor Libros Institutionum Imperialium Commentarius*, 4, 3, 13; Hugo Grotius, *Inleiding tot de Hollandsche Rechtsgeleertheyd*, 3, 34, 2; Johannes van der Linden, *Rechtsgeleerd, Practicaal, en Koopmans Handboek*, 1, 16, 3; cf. in general N. J. J. Olivier, *Die Aksie weens die Nalatige Veroorsaking van Pyn en Lyding* (unpublished Dr. iur. thesis, University of Leiden, 1978), 83 sqq.; P. J. J. Visser, *Kompensasie en Genoegdoening volgens die Aksie weens Pyn en Leed* (unpublished LL D thesis, University of South Africa, 1980), 207–17.

[2] The action for pain and suffering was originally regarded as a form or extension of the *actio legis Aquiliae*: Voet (n. 1), 9, 2, 11; Simon van Groenewegen van der Made, *Tractatus de Legibus Abrogatis et Inusitatis in Hollandia Vicinisque Regionibus*, 9, 3; *Union Govt v. Warneke* 1911 AD 657, 665 sq. In modern South African law this action is generally classified as *sui generis*: see e.g. *Hoffa v. SA Mutual Fire and General Insurance Co Ltd* 1965 (2) SA 944 (C) 950 sq.; *Administrator, Natal v. Edouard* 1990 (3) SA 581 (A) 595; J. Neethling, J. M. Potgieter, P. J. Visser, *Law of Delict* (2nd edn., 1994), 18 sqq.; J. C. van der Walt, *Delict: Principles and Cases* (1979), 19 sq.; Olivier (n. 1), 242 sqq. Some writers still prefer to classify it with the *actio legis Aquiliae*: P. Q. R. Boberg, *The Law of Delict*, vol. I, *Aquilian Liability* (1984, reprint 1989), 517 sqq., 521 sq.; Visser (n. 1), 376 sqq.; cf. H. J. Erasmus, J. J. Gauntlett, 'Damages', in: W. A. Joubert (ed.), *The Law of South Africa*, vol. 7 (1978), §§ 44 sqq., who regard the distinction as 'an academic nicety'. For the purposes of this Chapter it is accepted that the action is *sui generis* and falls outside the ambit of the *actio legis Aquiliae*.

[3] *Matthews v. Young* 1922 AD 492, 504; Neethling/Potgieter/Visser (n. 2), 5 sqq.; Boberg (n. 2), 18 sqq.; Van der Walt (n. 2), 2 sqq.; N. J. J. van der Merwe, P. J. J. Olivier, *Die Onregmatige Daad in die Suid-Afrikaanse Reg* (6th edn., 1989), 226 sqq.; F. P. van den Heever, *Aquilian Damages in South African Law*, vol. I (1945), 35 sqq.

imposed liability for wrongful damage to property, inflicted by burning, breaking, or tearing; here the wrongdoer had to pay the highest value of the object in question within the preceding thirty days.[4] (The second chapter had become obsolete by the time of classical Roman law.) The process of extension commenced with the interpretation of the *lex Aquilia* by Roman lawyers throughout the classical period and down to the days of Justinian. Through extensive interpretation of the words of the *lex*, and by the granting of *actiones in factum* and *actiones utiles* in situations not covered by the provisions of the enactment itself, the Romans brought about a situation where a remedy was available in all cases of wrongful damage to corporeal property, as well as for injuries to slaves and freemen, by means of which the wrongdoer was held liable for *id quod interest*, i.e. including consequential damages, to the owner of the object damaged or to the person injured. In a limited number of cases immaterial damage was covered and occasionally the action was also granted to non-owners.[5]

After the resurgence of Roman law in medieval Europe from the twelfth century onwards, the work of the Glossators, the School of Orléans, the Commentators, the canon lawyers, the humanists, and the natural lawyers contributed to the refinement and adaptation of Roman law in general and of the Roman *actio legis Aquiliae* in particular. The reception of Roman law in Europe, and the gradual formation of an European *iũs commune*, resulted in further development and expansion of the action, which occurred mainly in legal practice and came to be reflected in the works of the writers of the *usus modernus pandectarum*, the 'Historical School' of jurisprudence and the pandectists as well as in the European codifications at the turn of the nineteenth and twentieth centuries.[6]

In the course of the seventeenth century the *actio legis Aquiliae* was transplanted to the Cape of Good Hope as part of the Roman-Dutch law brought by the settlers of the Dutch East India Company.[7] By that time the action had

---

[4] For a full discussion of the text, date, meaning, and effect of the original *lex* see Reinhard Zimmermann, *The Law of Obligations: Roman Foundations of the Civilian Tradition* (1990, reprint 1993), 953–69; Van den Heever (n. 3), 4–20; Aquilius, 'Aantekenings by die Digestetitel op die Aquiliese Wet', (1939) 3 *THRHR* 219 sqq.; Pieter Pauw, 'Once Again on the Origin of the *Lex Aquilia*', (1978) 95 *SALJ* 186 sqq.; Ben Beinart, 'De Lege Aquilia', (1946) 10 *THRHR* 192 sqq.

[5] There is a wealth of literature on the expansion of the *lex Aquilia* in Roman law. For a modern summary see Zimmermann (n. 4), 969–1017; cf. Van den Heever (n. 3), 21–9; F. H. Lawson, *Negligence in the Civil Law* (1950, reprint 1968), 1–79; F. H. Lawson, B. S. Markesinis, *Tortious Liability for Unintentional Harm in the Common Law and the Civil Law*, vol. I (1982), 1–36; Aquilius, 'Aantekenings by die Digestetitel op die Aquiliese Wet', (1940) 4 *THRHR* 53 sqq.; Pieter Pauw, '*Actio in Factum* and the *Lex Aquilia*', (1980) 97 *SALJ* 285 sqq.; Beinart, (1946) 10 *THRHR* 192 sqq.

[6] For details see Helmut Coing, *Europäisches Privatrecht*, vol. I (1985), 508–13; Zimmermann (n. 4), 1017–49; Van den Heever (n. 3), 30–5; Reinhard Zimmermann, '*Usus Modernus Legis Aquiliae* and Delictual Liability Today', (1990) 1 *Stellenbosch LR* 67 sqq.

[7] For details see Ch. 1 by Eduard Fagan, above.

developed to embrace general principles of liability for patrimonial loss to person or property wrongfully and culpably caused. It had lost its (partly) penal nature and become purely compensatory, which was reflected in the rules governing its transmissibility. Liability of joint wrongdoers was no longer cumulative. Furthermore, the action lay for patrimonial loss caused by injury to personality rights, or suffered by dependants as a result of the death of a breadwinner, or by parents or employers as a result of injury to a child or employee, and it was extended to several classes of holders of personal rights to things. Some contend that it even covered every form of patrimonial loss caused wrongfully and culpably in any manner whatsoever.[8]

II. THE *ACTIO LEGIS AQUILIAE* IN SOUTH AFRICA

The historical development of the *actio legis Aquiliae* in South Africa has been the subject of less penetrating analysis than its European history. Much has been written on the general development of Roman-Dutch law in South Africa, and here attention has mainly focused on two aspects, namely the correct meaning of the term Roman-Dutch law and the nature, extent, and desirability of English influence on the development of South African law. No comprehensive study of the history of the *actio legis Aquiliae* in South Africa, however, has been undertaken. Such studies as there are are limited either to fairly general historical overviews usually contained in textbooks, concentrating mainly on the development of Roman and Roman-Dutch law,[9] or to the detailed examination of specific aspects of Aquilian liability, often within the framework of a doctoral thesis.[10]

[8] On the state of development of the *actio legis Aquiliae* in Roman-Dutch law see the authorities quoted in n. 6; cf. Neethling/Potgieter/Visser (n. 2), 10–13; Van der Merwe/Olivier (n. 3), 12 sqq.; Van der Walt (n. 2), 17 sqq., 19 sq.

[9] Cf. e.g. Van den Heever (n. 3), 33–46; J. W. Wessels, *History of the Roman-Dutch Law* (1908), 695–710; H. R. Hahlo, Ellison Kahn, *South Africa: The Development of its Laws and Constitution* (1960), 502–22, 527–57; Neethling/Potgieter/Visser (n. 2), 8–18; Van der Merwe/Olivier (n. 3), 226 sqq.; Van der Walt (n. 2), 11–20; P. R. Spiller, 'The Making of the Law of Delict: A Mélange of Sources', in: D. P. Visser (ed.), *Essays on the History of Law* (1989), 335 sqq.; cf. D. P. Visser, 'The Legal Historian as Subversive or: Killing the Capitoline Geese', in: D. P. Visser (ed.), *Essays on the History of Law* (1989), 1 sqq.

[10] Cf. e.g. T. J. Scott, *Die Geskiedenis van die Oorerflikheid van Aksies op grond van Onregmatige Daad* (unpublished Dr. iur. thesis, University of Leiden, 1976), 175–220; Derek van der Merwe, *Oorlas in die Suid-Afrikaanse Reg* (unpublished LL D thesis, University of Pretoria, 1982), 333 sqq.; C. J. Davel, *Die Dood van 'n Broodwinner as Skadevergoedingsoorsaak* (unpublished LL D thesis, University of Pretoria, 1984), 399–628; J. C. C. van Loggerenberg, *Lex Aquilia en Nalate* (unpublished Dr. iur. thesis, University of Leiden, 1947), 17–128; Ben Beinart, 'The Relationship of *Iniuria* and *Culpa* in the *Lex Aquilia*', in: *Studi in Onore di Vincenzo Arangio-Ruiz*, vol. I (1953), 279–303; idem, '*Culpa in Omittendo*', (1949) 2 *THRHR* 141–69; T. W. Price, 'Aquilian Liability and the "Duty of Care": A Return to the Charge', 1959 *Acta Juridica* 120–83; R. G. McKerron, 'Liability for Mere Pecuniary Loss in an Action under the *Lex Aquilia*', (1973) 90 *SALJ* 1–4; Pieter Pauw, 'Aanspreeklikheid vir "Suiwer Vermoënskade" in die Suid-Afrikaanse Reg', (1975) 8 *De Jure* 23–31; D. B.

The purpose of the present Chapter is to make some attempt to rectify this deficiency. The scope of the subject obviously precludes any attempt at comprehensiveness. This paper could therefore either provide a general overview or a detailed study of one or several specific aspect(s). However, either course would merely conform to the present patterns of analysis. For that reason a somewhat unusual alternative has been chosen. In view of the fact that information on the very beginnings of the process of development is as yet to be found only in case-law, and to some extent in the earliest text-books (now outdated and also out of print), a thorough analysis of the reported South African cases on Aquilian liability up to 1900 is here under-taken. My purpose is to identify trends in, and where possible reasons for, the peculiarly South African slant to the early development of liability under the *actio legis Aquiliae* in this country.

Before embarking on this venture, some attention has to be given to the two main issues referred to above underlying any historical study of South African law. For some time the prevailing view among South African courts and academics has been that the term Roman-Dutch law referred only to the law applicable in the province of Holland, and that consequently only the writers dealing with the law of Holland could be regarded as authoritative sources of the South African common law.[11] The main reason for this narrow understanding of the term was the political history of the coloniza-tion of the Cape of Good Hope.[12] On the other hand, it is undoubtedly true that Roman-Dutch law formed part and parcel of the European *ius commune*, and that the practitioners and writers of the *ius commune* did not limit themselves to their own geographical areas when adjudicating on or dis-cussing non-statutory aspects of the law. Accordingly, it has increasingly been recognized in recent years that the term Roman-Dutch law as South African common law should be understood in a more liberal sense. Writers on the *ius commune* not directly associated with the province of Holland can and should be consulted in order to determine the position in South African law.[13] Such a broad and flexible approach which rests on sound historical arguments promotes the adaptability of the law and is to be welcomed.

Hutchison, 'Negligent Statements: Why the Reluctance to Impose Liability?', (1978) 95 *SALJ* 515–33; J. C. van der Walt, 'Nalatige Wanvoorstelling en Suiwer Vermoënskade: Die Appèlhof Spreek 'n Duidelike Woord', (1979) *TSAR* 145–56.

[11] See *Tjollo Ateljees (Edms) Bpk v. Small* 1949 (1) SA 856 (A) 865 sq.; D. H. van Zyl, *Geskiedenis van die Romeins-Hollandse Reg* (1969), 489–91; Wessels (n. 9), 357; H. R. Hahlo, Ellison Kahn, *The South African Legal System and its Background* (1973), 572; J. C. de Wet, 'Die Resepsie van die Romeins-Hollandse Reg in Suid-Afrika', (1958) 21 *THRHR* 84 sqq.

[12] See Ch. 1 by E. Fagan, above.

[13] On this movement and its rationale see Van Zyl (n.11), 491–4; Reinhard Zimmermann, 'Synthesis in South African Private Law: Civil Law, Common Law and *Usus Hodiernus Pandectarum*', (1986) 103 *SALJ* 259 sqq., 271–4; Pauw, 1980 *TSAR* 32 sqq.; D. P. Visser, 'Daedalus in the Supreme Court: The Common Law Today', (1986) 49 *THRHR* 211 sqq., 135

South African courts, however, who originally did not disdain relying on writers not directly associated with the province of Holland[14] seem to incline towards the narrow view,[15] and it is to be hoped that this trend will be reversed.

The influence of English law on the development of Roman-Dutch law in South Africa is probably one of the most contentious issues in South African legal history. Once again, it arose as a result of political factors, in this case the surrender of the Cape of Good Hope by the Dutch to Great Britain in 1806. Thereafter the Cape Colony, and eventually the whole of Southern Africa that came to be colonized by white settlers, remained or was brought under British rule and administration. Although the law prevailing in the Cape at the time of the British occupation, namely the Roman-Dutch law, remained in force the British system of administration of justice was introduced.[16]

Thus, inevitably, English influence made itself felt over the years, directly and indirectly, on South African substantive law. In the first place important elements of English law were directly incorporated into South African law in statutory form. Secondly, the English law of procedure and evidence was taken over and the English doctrine of *stare decisis* was adopted in a slightly modified form. Thirdly, the fact that for a long time most South African legal practitioners and judges were almost exclusively trained in Britain resulted in English legal principles creeping into the judgments of the South African courts.[17]

In the course of the twentieth century we have witnessed a movement to purify South African private law from English influence; this has led to an

sq.; S. W. J. van der Merwe, G. F. Lubbe, L. F. van Huyssteen, 'The *Exceptio Doli Generalis: Requiescat in Pace—Vivat Aequitas*', (1989) 106 *SALJ* 235 sqq., 238 sq.; Johan Scott, 'The Future of our Roman-Dutch Law: Reflections and a Suggestion', (1993) 26 *De Jure* 394 sqq.; W. du Plessis, N. J. J. Olivier (1988) 21 *De Jure* 371 sqq., 372 sq., 381 sq.; cf. D. P. Visser, D. B. Hutchison, 'Legislation from the Elysian Fields: The Roman-Dutch Authorities Settle an Old Dispute', (1988) 105 SALJ 619 sqq., 630–2.

[14] See Van Zyl (n. 11), 489 sq. and the cases quoted by him in fn. 58. Cf. the following cases, referred to below: *Rooth v. The State* (1888) 2 SAR 259; *Steel v. Pearman* 1877 NLR 22; *Visser v. London en Jagersfontein Diamant Delverij Maatschappij* 1884 Gregorowski 8; *Hall v. Hodgson* (1892) 13 NLR 212; *Freeman v. Colonial Govt* (1888) 9 NLR 181; *Hume v. Divisional Council of Cradock* (1880) 1 EDC 104.

[15] *Du Plessis v. Strauss* 1988 (2) SA 105 (A) 133; *Bank of Lisbon and South Africa Ltd v. De Ornelas* 1988 (3) SA 580 (A) 604.

[16] See Van Zyl (n. 11), 443–76; Hahlo/Kahn (n. 11), 575–8; Wessels (n. 9), 362–71; Hahlo/Kahn (n. 9), 17, 21 sq., 24 sq.

[17] On the nature of, and reasons for, the influence of English law see generally Wessels (n. 9), 386–401; Hahlo/Kahn (n. 11), 576–8; Hahlo/Kahn (n. 9), 17–21; Van Zyl (n. 11), 453–8; O. D. Schreiner, *The Contribution of English Law to South African Law; and the Rule of Law in South Africa* (1967), 10–70; Ben Beinart, 'The English Legal Contribution in South Africa: The Interaction of Civil and Common Law', 1981 *Acta Juridica* 7–13; Reinhard Zimmermann, 'Die Rechtsprechung des *Supreme Court of the Cape of Good Hope* am Ende der sechziger Jahre des 19. Jahrhunderts', in: *Huldigingsbundel Paul van Warmelo* (1984), 286 sqq.

acrimonious battle about the true sources of South African law.[18] Today, however, a pragmatic attitude prevails. Insofar as aspects of the English law have been received, they have become a legitimate part of South African law, which in turn can thus be said to be based on not only Roman-Dutch but also English sources.[19]

III. AQUILIAN LIABILITY IN THE CASES UP TO 1900

It was only in the course of the nineteenth century that regular reporting of the decisions of the courts in Southern Africa began. One is therefore limited to archival material in attempting to form an impression of the early application and development of the law in the Cape Colony. A certain amount of archival research has been undertaken. While some general conclusions can be drawn (*inter alia*, that the courts made use from the outset of mainly Dutch writers in order to determine the law in cases not covered by Dutch or South African statutes, but that they also referred to other writers of the *ius commune* and to Roman law and biblical sources[20]), very little can be gleaned from this material about the fortunes of the *actio legis Aquiliae*. Our study therefore commences with the earliest reported cases. They can be classified conveniently as dealing with: first, general principles of Aquilian liability, secondly, specific instances of liability; and thirdly, specific torts.

1. The area of application of the *actio legis Aquiliae*

Some of the early cases contain general statements to the effect that the *actio legis Aquiliae* governs civil liability for damages for loss wrongfully and culpably caused. In *Port Elizabeth Municipality v. Nightingale*, decided in 1855, it was accepted that the liability of municipal bodies for damage sustained was regulated by the *lex Aquilia* just like that of any private person.[21] This general proposition was confirmed in several later cases. In *Van Reenen v. Cloete*, dealing with liability for damage caused to the property

---

[18] On the purist–pragmatist debate see, in general, Adrienne van Blerk, 'The Genesis of the "Modernist–Purist" Debate: A Historical Bird's-Eye View', (1984) 47 *THRHR* 255 sqq.; *idem*, 'The Irony of Labels', (1982) 99 *SALJ* 365 sqq.; Zimmermann, (1986) 103 *SALJ* 259 sq., 274–6; *Proculus*, '*Bellum Juridicum*: Two Approaches to South African Law', (1951) 68 *SALJ* 306 sqq.; *Proculus Redivivus*, 'South African Law at the Crossroads or What is our Common Law?', (1965) 82 *SALJ* 17 sqq.; P. Q. R. Boberg, 'Oak Tree or Acorn?: Conflicting Approaches to our Law of Delict', (1966) 83 *SALJ* 150 sqq.

[19] See Visser, (1986) 49 *THRHR* 128–34; Zimmermann, (1986) 103 *SALJ* 274–89.

[20] See Van Zyl (n. 11), 440–2; G. G. Visagie, *Regspleging en Reg aan die Kaap* (1969), 69–76, 95–7; J. C. de Wet, ' "Nederlandse" Reg in Suid-Afrika tot 1806', (1958) 21 *THRHR* 162 sqq.

[21] (1855) 2 Searle 214. Authority for this proposition was found in D. 9, 2, 29, described as 'the first principles of Roman-Dutch law'.

of another by a fire, the Court stated unequivocally, with a general reference to Johannes Voet, Commentarius ad Pandectas, that civil liability for
damage in the Cape Colony was regulated by the Aquilian law.[22] In *Hume
v. Divisional Council of Cradock*,[23] Shippard J dealt exhaustively with the
principles of Aquilian liability for negligence in Roman-Dutch law, and
hence also in the Colony. The judgment was basically concerned with the
requirement of negligence, but reiterated the general proposition. In *Hill
and Paddon v. Commissioner of Crown Lands*[24] De Villiers CJ confirmed the
general Roman-Dutch requirements of liability for *damnum iniuria datum*,
namely *iniuria, damnum*, and a direct relationship between damage and
iniuria, without any reference to authority; in *Jordaan v. Worcester
Municipality*[25] he held that Aquilian principles were applicable to damages
caused by commission or omission,[26] with reference only to previous colonial case-law; and in *Eastern and South African Telegraph Company v. Cape
Town Tramways Company*[27] he relied on an example given by Voet[28] as
authority for the proposition that the *actio legis Aquiliae* regulated claims
for damages occasioned by wilfulness or negligence.

The general proposition was also confirmed in respect of the other South
African jurisdictions. The Natal Supreme Court held in *Weir v. Union
Steamship Company*[29] that damage to ships was governed by the *actio legis
Aquiliae* when not covered by the special rules of Admiralty law; and in
Steel v. Pearman,[30] dealing with sports injuries, it was held that compensa-
tion for injury to limb was regulated by the *actio legis Aquiliae*. The former
case contains no references to authority, but in the latter the works of
Huber, Voet, Mühlenbruch, and Westenberg were cited, as well as Roman
texts from both the Digest and the Institutes.[31] In the Orange Free State,
the Court in *Visser v. London en Jagersfontein Diamant Delverij
Maatschappij*[32] referred to previous decisions of the *Hooge Gerechtshof*,
Voet, and Pothier as authority for the proposition that the requirements for
recovering damages under the *lex Aquilia* were *iniuria*, or infringement of a
right, and calculable *damnum*. The Transvaal Supreme Court held, with reference to the Digest, Voet, and Huber, that negligence or *culpa* was a
requirement for Aquilian liability for injury or damage.[33]

In *Hall v. Hodgson*[34] the Natal Supreme Court, citing a passage from
Heineccius, made the surprising statement that the 'modern action in respect

[22] (1869) 2 Buch 219, 226. The reference is simply to Voet 9, 2.
[23] (1880) 1 EDC 104, confirmed on appeal: *Divisional Council of Cradock v. Hume* (1880) 1
Buch AC 27.
[24] (1883) 2 SC 395. [25] (1893) 10 SC 159.
[26] He was dealing with the liability of municipalities, or public bodies, for so-called misfeasance and non-feasance. On which see below, Section 11 (a).
[27] (1900) 17 SC 95. [28] Voet (n. 1), 9, 2, 26.
[29] 1874 NLR 61. [30] 1877 NLR 22.
[31] D. 9, 2, 9, 4; 9, 2, 52, 4; 9, 2, 7, 4; Inst. IV, 3, 5. [32] 1884 Gregorowski 8.
[33] *Walker v. Beeby and Stewart* (1895) 2 OR 148. [34] (1892) 13 NLR 212.

of damage to property or person does not depend on the *lex Aquilia*, but on local law and natural equity'. It is probable that Heineccius, who wrote in the early eighteenth century, was commenting on how far civil liability for damages in the *usus modernus pandectarum* had progressed beyond the original Roman *lex Aquilia*,[35] and that the Court relied too heavily on the literal meaning of the passage, especially in the light of the overwhelming Roman-Dutch and earlier South African case-law authority to the contrary. At any rate, this view found no support in subsequent South African case-law.

The above cases clearly show that the Aquilian action was accepted at an early stage as the basis of delictual liability for patrimonial loss. During this time there was, generally speaking, strict adherence to the Roman-Dutch conception of Aquilian liability; there were no signs yet of a peculiarly South African *usus modernus*. In two instances the courts pronounced upon the extension of the area of application of the *lex Aquilia* in Roman-Dutch law. In a famous statement in *The Cape of Good Hope Bank v. Fischer*[36] De Villiers CJ, referring to a case quoted by Johannes van de Sande and to comments by Matthaeus and Voet, held that the Aquilian law:

had received an extension by analogy to an extent never permitted under the Roman law. The action *in factum* was no longer confined to cases of damage done to corporeal property, but was extended to every kind of loss sustained by a person in consequence of the wrongful acts of another . . .

The same judge expressed similar sentiments in *Liquidator of The Cape Central Railways v. Nöthling* with reference to liability for breach of a statutory duty:[37] 'The provisions of the Aquilian law have, by judicial interpretation, been extended to cases not falling strictly within the terms of that law . . .'

Although the latter statement expressed a general truth about the development of the *actio legis Aquiliae* in South African law, the sentiments articulated in the first case did not accurately reflect the development of South African law at that stage. While it is true that the area of application of the *actio legis Aquiliae* has been extended significantly through the years, especially in regard to liability for omissions, negligent misrepresentation, and pure economic loss, this development came at a much later stage. The statement in *Fischer* can thus be regarded at best as a somewhat optimistic prediction of the future development of the action in South African law. Even today, however, certain limitations exist which qualify the general tenor of the statement, notably with regard to negligent interference with contractual relations and situations of concurrent contractual and delictual liability for damages.[38]

---

[35] For a discussion of this statement and for references see Van den Heever (n. 3), 30.

[36] (1886) 4 SC 368, 376.

[37] (1890) 8 SC 25. In regard to breach of a statutory duty see below, Section 13.

[38] See *Union Govt v. Ocean Accident & Guarantee Corp Ltd* 1956 (1) SA 577 (A); *Lillicrap, Wassenaar and Partners v. Pilkington Bros (SA) (Pty) Ltd* 1985 (1) SA 475 (A).

2. The relationship and distinction between civil and criminal liability

As early as 1829 the Cape Supreme Court relied on passages from Voet in order to hold that the institution of criminal proceedings in a case did not bar a subsequent civil claim for damages on the same facts.[39] This was confirmed in a number of later cases, where either no authority was quoted, or Roman-Dutch law was relied upon.[40] The same proposition was accepted for the Transvaal in respect of a criminal conviction in *Williams v. Young*.[41] The Natal Supreme Court held in *Engelbrecht v. Estate Van der Merwe*[42] that the bringing of a civil action under the *lex Aquilia* did not prevent subsequent criminal proceedings, and relied in its judgment on texts from the Digest and the Institutes, Voet, Van der Linden, and Huber.[43] In *Schoeman v. Goosen*[44] it was decided, the other way round, that 'in our law' there was no bar on civil proceedings before the institution of a criminal trial. Here the Court did not refer to Roman-Dutch authority, but investigated English cases in order to determine whether the doubts existing in that system about this proposition were well founded; even there, it was decided, a criminal trial was no condition precedent. In a number of further cases the possibility of claiming civil damages in a criminal trial was denied without reference to authority, but with an exhortation that the two classes of liability, aimed at compensation and punishment respectively, should be kept distinct.[45]

These cases tend to show that, at least according to the South African judges of the time, the Roman-Dutch sources distinguished with sufficient clarity between criminal and civil liability to keep these forms of liability apart from each other. They thus refute the opinion of some early writers that the English law played an important part in drawing this distinction in South African law, since Roman-Dutch sources (some of which still followed the Roman classification) referred indiscriminately to crimes and delicts.[46] In fact these writers were probably misled by that very classification. Early Roman law recognized no distinction between criminal and civil liability. Over the centuries, however, it came to distinguish between *delicta*

---

[39] *Russouw v. Sturt* (1829) 1 Menz 378. The relevant passages were Voet (n. 1), 44, 2, 3; 47, 10, 17, 18 and 24.

[40] See *Hare v. Kotzé* (1840) 3 Menz 472 (no authority); *Eaton v. Moller* (1872) 2 Roscoe 85 (no authority, but with the query whether this rule also applied to private, as opposed to public, prosecutions); *Mostert v. Fuller* (1875) 5 Buch 23 (no authority); *Colonial Secretary v. Breda's Curator, v. Southey, v. Davidson* (1877) 7 Buch 1 (relying on Roman-Dutch and civil law in general and referring specifically to Matthaeus *De Criminibus*).

[41] 1878 Kotzé 134.   [42] (1889) 10 NLR 117.

[43] D. 9, 2, 5 pr.; 9, 2, 23, 9; Inst. IV, 3, 11; Voet (n. 1), 9, 2, 30.

[44] (1883) 3 EDC 7.

[45] *Queen v. Jim* (1880) 1 EDC 93; *Queen v. Robinson* (1882) 2 EDC 230; *Queen v. Jonas* (1884) 4 EDC 268; *Queen v. Klaas* (1884) 4 EDC 276; *Queen v. Charlie* (1884) 4 EDC 365.

[46] Cf. e.g. Wessels (n. 9), 705 sq.; see also the discussion by Van den Heever (n. 3), 1 sq.

publica and *delicta privata*, but the latter, under which the *actio legis Aquiliae* was classified, were still regarded as (at least partly) penal.[47] In Roman-Dutch law the *actio legis Aquiliae* completely lost its penal character, and several Roman-Dutch writers commented very clearly on the relation and distinction between civil and criminal liability.[48]

3. Wrongfulness

Several early cases unequivocally stated that *iniuria*, or wrongfulness, was an essential requirement for Aquilian liability. They often emphasized that there could be no liability for *damnum absque* (or: *sine*) *iniuria*.[49] In *Freeman v. Colonial Government*[50] it was expressly decided with reference to Roman texts,[51] Pothier, and earlier Natal cases, that *iniuria* in this context meant acting in a manner not permitted by law, or doing what one has no right to do, with the further proviso that the exercise of a right must not be injurious. Two other cases defined *iniuria* as infringement of (another's) legal right.[52]

The issue of wrongfulness also arose in a case where it had to be decided under which circumstances an otherwise lawful act (namely exercising the right of ownership) causing injury to another would be unlawful.[53] With reference to texts from the Digest and Voet, as well as to general maxims of Roman law (like *nemo cum injuria aliorum jure suo uti permittitur*),[54] it was decided that the motive to injure another would render the actor liable. However it was (apparently) also decided that negligence (whether the injury could reasonably have been foreseen and prevented) or imprudence would have the same effect. Two later cases confirm the proposition that

---

[47] Cf. Zimmermann (n. 4), 914–20.

[48] Grotius (n. 1), 3, 32, 7; Vinnius (n. 1), 4, 3, 9; Groenewegen (n. 2), 4, 3, 15; Voet (n. 1), 9, 2, 12. See also Van den Heever (n. 3), 1–3; Annél van Aswegen, *Die Sameloop van Eise om Skadevergoeding uit Kontrakbreuk en Delik* (unpublished LL D thesis, University of South Africa, 1991), 57–9; T. J. Scott, 'Oor die Aard van ons Fundamentele Deliksaksies', (1976) 9 *De Jure* 179 sqq.

[49] See e.g. *Hill and Paddon v. Commissioner of Crown Lands* (1883) 2 SC 395; *Reed v. De Beers Consolidated Mines Ltd* (1892) 6 HCG 179; *Mostert v. De Beers Consolidated Mines Ltd* (1893) 7 HCG 26; *Eastern and South African Telegraph Co v. Cape Town Tramways Co* (1900) 17 SC 95 for the Cape Colony; *Pretorius v. Coetzee* 1879 Kotzé 158 for the Transvaal; *Visser v. London en Jagersfontein Diamant Delverij Maatschappij* 1884 Gregorowski 8 for the Free State; and *Freeman v. Colonial Govt* (1888) 9 NLR 181 for Natal.

[50] (1888) 9 NLR 181.   [51] D. 50, 17, 55; 47, 10, 13, 1.

[52] *Visser v. London en Jagersfontein Diamant Delverij Maatschappij* (n. 14) (with general references to Voet (n. 1), 9, 2, 7 and Pothier); *Hill and Paddon v. Commissioner of Crown Lands* (n. 49) (no reference to authority).

[53] *De Pass & Co v. Rawson* (1863) 1 Roscoe 108 (the court *a quo*) *De Pass & Co v. Rawson* (1863) 5 Searle 1.

[54] The court *a quo* referred to Voet 9, 2, 14 and D. 30, 3, 12; 50, 17, 151; while in the appeal case the references were to Roman maxims and to the Digest in general.

negligently exercising a right would render the actor liable, one with reference to English case-law and the other without authority.[55]

These cases illustrate what has been so well explained by Ben Beinart,[56] namely the interrelationship between *iniuria* and *culpa* in the interpretation of the Roman *lex Aquilia*. It is well known that the Romans extended the original concept of *iniuria* to include blameworthiness or *culpa*, which concept was in turn extended to cover the modern notion of negligence. The earliest and most basic meaning of *iniuria* (i.e. 'contrary to law') was gradually merged with the later meaning (*culpa*) but, according to Beinart, never entirely displaced.[57] It is widely accepted that Roman-Dutch law also implicitly accepted the notion of wrongfulness under cover of a broadly conceived notion of *iniuria*.[58] As in Roman law, however, there was no systematic distinction between wrongfulness and *culpa*.

The original meaning of *iniuria* as wrongfulness was accepted in the first group of cases mentioned above; no mention was then made of *culpa*. Those decisions could thus be interpreted as early indications that South African law was moving towards a systematic distinction between these two issues. The alternative definition ('infringement of a legal right') found in two of these cases further reinforces that interpretation, and may have provided an early point of reference for the acceptance of the doctrine of subjective rights and the concomitant definition of wrongfulness as an infringement of a subjective right.

The second group of cases inclines towards the broader meaning of the concept of *iniuria*, which incorporates *culpa* in precisely the kind of situation that Beinart used as an example to illustrate the position in Roman law: the negligent exercise of a private right can constitute *iniuria*. The blurring of wrongfulness and negligence in these cases provides evidence of the application of Roman-Dutch law in early South African case-law, without any discernible South African development with regard to the concept of *iniuria*.

A variety of further cases determine the question of *iniuria* with reference to the breach of a (legal) duty.[59] The proposition that *iniuria* consists of the breach of a duty may only be another way of expressing either the original Roman meaning of *iniuria* (in which case it will imply a duty to act in accordance with the law) or it may relate to the notion of *culpa* (in which case it will imply a duty not to act negligently). There is only one case where that

---

[55] *February v. Kirby* (1896) 6 CTR 443; *Wright v. Paterson, Bristow v. Paterson* (1864) 5 Searle 29, also reported in (1887) 5 EDC 390.

[56] Beinart (n. 10), 281–95. See also Zimmermann (n. 4), 1004–9.

[57] Beinart (n. 10), 300–2; cf. Zimmermann (n. 4), 998 sqq., 1004, 1006 sq.; Lawson (n. 5), 14 sq., 36 sq.; Lawson/Markesinis (n. 5), 19 sq.; Van der Walt (n. 2), 12.

[58] Voet (n. 1), 47, 1, 1; Grotius (n. 1), 3, 32, 3–6; Zimmermann (n. 4), 1028; Van der Walt (n. 2), 17, 20 sq.

[59] *Schluter v. Thomson, Watson & Co* (1888) 6 SC 97; *Reed v. De Beers Consolidated Mines Ltd* (n. 49); *Eastern and South African Telegraph Co v. Cape Town Tramways Co* (n. 49).

proposition was extensively discussed. It dealt with damage to a mining claim caused by water overflowing from a neighbouring claim.[60] Liability was held to depend on whether the damage was a result of *iniuria*. This question, in turn, depended on whether a duty to work a mining claim 'at least to the extent of keeping [it] free from such a body of water as would damage their neighbours' existed in South African law. Lawrence JP dealt mainly with the question of liability for non-feasance, and although he referred to the Roman maxim of *sic utere tuo ut alienum non laedas*, he held that it was not authorative because it was too vague. He launched an exhaustive inquiry into English case-law in order to extract the principle that a man may use his own property in a natural way. This principle was relied on to decide, contrary to previous colonial cases, that no duty to work a mining claim existed. Thus, it was held that there had been no *iniuria* on the part of the defendant. Since Lawrence JP then proceeded to deal with the question of whether failure to act constituted negligence, it can safely be concluded that the first part of this case dealt with the original meaning of wrongfulness. This indicates that the duty concept with regard to wrongfulness was, at least initially, imported under the influence of English law.

The final issue relevant to the concept of wrongfulness that was raised in some of the early cases is the question of justification. Although it was not expressly considered as a defence excluding *iniuria* in any of them, the possibility of justifying an act for which liability in damages would usually have existed was clearly recognized. In *Schluter v. Thomson, Watson and Company*[61] liability for the detention of a ship was made to depend on the general question of whether there was a breach of duty that was not justified, and in *Hay v. Divisional Council of King William's Town*[62] the breach of a duty imposed by statute was held to be justified by impossibility since the party bound could not provide against an act of God, or *vis maior*. The former case made no reference to any authority, but in the latter English cases were relied on. In *Snodgrass v. Pretorius*[63] the shooting of a dog chasing the defendant's sheep was held to be justified in view of the fact that the chase was still going on. A Roman law textbook was relied on in order to determine under which circumstances force may be used in this type of situation. In *Parker v. Scott*[64] a passage from Voet[65] was referred to in a case concerning provocation: an assault could not be taken to be justified by an insult where a similar insult had previously been forgiven: forgiveness, the Court held, wipes out an injury in the same way as payment or an apology does. In *Spires v. Scheepers*[66] a plaintiff was denied a remedy (available under Roman-Dutch law) against the defendant in his capacity as owner of

---

[60] *Reed v. De Beers Consolidated Mines Ltd* (n. 49).   [61] (1888) 6 SC 97.
[62] (1879) 1 EDC 97.   [63] (1895) 9 EDC 125.
[64] (1894) 15 NLR 218; cf. *Saget v. Bataillou* (1868) 1 Buch 32.
[65] Voet (n. 1), 47, 10, 23.   [66] (1883) 3 EDC 173.

an animal by whom the plaintiff had been injured. The reason was that the plaintiff, a servant of the defendant, knew about the danger emanating from the animal and had expressly undertaken to accept the risk in his contract of employment. Only English authority was relied on in this case. In *Davids v. Mendelsohn*[67] the plaintiff knew of and disregarded an imminent danger and was consequently denied a remedy on the basis of the English maxim of *volenti non fit iniuria.* Here the Roman rule excluding a claim for loss sustained by the injured party's fault[68] was referred to in order to explain that the principle underlying the *volenti* rule in English law was fully recognized in Roman-Dutch law.

Some of these cases can be brought home under the justification grounds known in Roman law, like necessity, defence, and consent[69]. There are, however, no direct references to the relevant Roman texts and English law is extensively quoted. Nevertheless, the rules applied accord substantially with Roman and Roman-Dutch law and there can, accordingly, be no objection in principle to the law as expounded in these cases, albeit under English influence.

4. Negligence (*culpa*)

The general proposition that *culpa*, or negligence, is a requirement for Aquilian liablity was expressly accepted in several early cases.[70] In addition, there are numerous cases in which the requirement of negligence was analysed more closely and in which a number of different tests for negligence were applied. These cases can be divided into different groups.

In the first group, negligence was defined in terms of failure to observe a particular standard of conduct. The defendant was seen to be under an

---

[67] (1898) 15 SC 367.   [68] On which see below, Section 5.

[69] See Zimmermann (n. 4), 999–1004; Lawson (n. 5), 14–16, Lawson/Markesinis (n. 5), 19–22; Van der Walt (n. 2), 12.

[70] See e.g. *Freeman v. Colonial Govt* (1888) 9 NLR 181, where Inst. IV, 3, 2 and 14 were relied on for the proposition that *culpa* was needed for an action under the *lex Aquilia*; *Walker v. Beeby and Stewart* (1895) 2 OR 148 (referring to D. 9, 2, 44 pr., Voet (n. 1), 9, 2, 29, and Ulrich Huber). *Hume v. Divisional Council of Cradock* (n. 23), confirmed on appeal, without reference to authority, in *Divisional Council of Cradock v. Hume* (n. 23). In this case Shippard J appeared to accept that liability of a public body for breach of a statutory duty fell under the *lex Aquilia* and thus required *culpa*; he then proceeded to determine what degree of fault was required to render the public body liable. In the course of his judgment Shippard J dealt exhaustively with Roman and Roman-Dutch sources concerning the various degrees of *culpa* and their distinction from *dolus*. Consulting Roman texts, numerous Dutch authors, notably Voet, Vinnius, Noodt, Van Leeuwen, Antonius Matthaeus, and Van Bynkershoek, and other civilian authorities like Heineccius, Brunnemann, Hasse, Mühlenbruch, and Goudsmit, he concluded that there are only two classes of *culpa*: *culpa lata* and *culpa levis* (or ordinary *culpa*) and that the latter is sufficient to render the council liable. Buchanan J in his judgment expressly stated, with reference to D. 9, 2, 29, 7 and Voet (n. 1), 9, 2, 3, that liability of *magistratus municipales* to make good loss or damage caused by them arose under the *lex Aquilia*.

obligation to act with reasonable diligence,[71] to exercise the degree of prudence, care, and foresight that the public can reasonably expect,[72] not to disregard the care which we are bound by law to exercise towards other people,[73] to exercise due caution,[74] or to apply due or ordinary care, skill, diligence, or skilfulness.[75] No authority was relied on in these cases. In *Clair v. Port Elizabeth Harbour Board, Kennedy v. Port Elizabeth Harbour Board*,[76] however, both Barry JP and Buchanan J referred to a passage by Voet[77] in order to define negligence as a want of ordinary care, or failure to use reasonable care to prevent damages. In similar vein, the failure to observe a certain standard of conduct was expressed in some cases as a breach of a duty to observe that standard of conduct. That duty was formulated either with reference to a particular act, directly connected with the circumstances of the case,[78] or more generally to take due precautions.[79]

In other cases belonging to the same group negligence was described as the failure to avoid or prevent loss or damage by not meeting the required standard of conduct. Thus, the issue of whether the loss could have been prevented was added to the standard of care required. These cases generally held that negligence was present where the injury or loss, or actual occurrence causing such injury or loss, could have been prevented or avoided by the exercise of due, proper, or ordinary care, skill, or diligence.[80] Authority in the form of English law and a previous colonial decision was referred to in only one of these cases.[81]

A second group of cases did not emphasize the failure to meet a particular

---

[71] *Murtha v. Von Beek* (1882) 1 Buch AC 121.

[72] *Bérrange v. Metropolitan and Suburban Railway Co* (1898) 15 SC 73. Cf. *Keet v. Henwood, Solomon and Bradley* (1898) 5 OR 98.

[73] In *Meister v. Town Council of Johannesburg* (1898) 5 OR 307.

[74] *Nederlandse Zuid-Afrikaanse Spoorweg Maatschappij v. Van Rooyen* (1896) 2 OR 103.

[75] See *Eastern and South African Telegraph Co v. Cape Town Tramways Co* (n. 49) (due skill and care in execution); *Meister v. Town Council of Johannesburg* (n. 73) (ordinary care to prevent damages); *Gibson Bros v. Otto* (1898) 8 HCG 193 (ordinary care, diligence, and skilfulness).

[76] (1886) 5 EDC 311.   [77] Voet (n. 1), 9, 3, 5.

[78] *Johannesburg City and Suburban Tramway Co v. Doyle* (1894) 1 OR 205 (duty of tram-driver to look ahead); *Botes v. Nederlands Zuid-Afrikaanse Spoorweg Maatschappij* (1895) 2 OR 136 (duty to keep proper lookout for trains); *Nel v. Nederlands Zuid-Afrikaanse Spoorweg Maatschappij* (1895) 2 OR 162 (duty of train-driver to blow whistle).

[79] *O'Shea v. Port Elizabeth Town Council* (1895) 12 SC 146 (duty to take due precautions); *Lamb v. Colonial Govt* (1894) 14 EDC 103 (duty to take every precaution to guard against damage); *Clair v. Port Elizabeth Harbour Board, Kennedy v. Port Elizabeth Harbour Board* (1886) 5 EDC 311 (Board's duty not to expose the public to danger).

[80] See *Tychsen v. Evans (Emanuel v. Fairy Queen)* (1880) 1 EDC 28 (defendant might by ordinary skill have avoided accident); *Clair v. Port Elizabeth Harbour Board, Kennedy v. Port Elizabeth Harbour Board* (n. 79) (explosion could have been avoided by ordinary care); *McLaren v. Consolidated DM Co Bultfontein* (1888) 5 HCG 202; *Lord v. Union Steamship Co* (1891) 6 EDC 141; *Walker v. Beeby and Stewart* (1895) 2 OR 148; *Appolis v. Jarom* (1898) 12 EDC 187; *Jendraschewitz v. Nederlandse Zuid-Afrikaanse Spoorweg Maatschappij* (1899) 6 OR 60.

[81] *McLaren v. Consolidated DM Co, Bultfontein* (n. 80).

standard of care as such, but formulated a test for negligence by inquiring whether loss or damage was reasonably foreseeable and could have been prevented. Some cases referred only to the issue of foreseeability and held that negligence was present where damage, or the injury causing it could reasonably have been foreseen.[82] References to authority are not generally found in these cases, with the exception of the very earliest finding that negligence was absent in the case of an unforeseen occurrence: here a passage by Voet was relied on.[83] In other cases reasonable foreseeability of harm, alternatively knowledge of danger, and whether the loss could have been prevented were used as a test for negligence.[84] In some of these instances the issue of whether the loss could have been prevented was determined by asking whether adequate precautions were taken. Some further cases applied the question whether loss could have been prevented by taking adequate precuations, as the the sole test for negligence. *Van Reenen v. Cloete*[85] required all precautions to be taken, and it was held, with reference to Van Leeuwen, that negligence was absent where damages could not have been averted by human means. In several later cases negligence was determined by asking whether all reasonable, possible, due, or necessary precautions had been taken to avoid or prevent harm, injury, or loss, once again without any reference to authority.[86] In a number of cases dealing with the liability of public bodies for negligence in exercising statutory duties or powers, negligence was confined to the duty to take reasonable precautions.[87] Again, in only one case was reference made to English case-law in support of this proposition; in the others it was simply accepted.

In two cases forming a third group the maxim *imperitia culpae adnumeratur* was applied and Roman and Roman-Dutch authority referred to.[88]

---

[82] *Brink v. Cloete* (1869) 2 Buch 215; *O'Shea v. Port Elizabeth Town Council* (1895) 12 SC 146; *Newman v. East London Town Council* (1895) 12 SC 61; *Stephenson v. Molyneux* (1895) 16 NLR 140; *Cape Divisional Council v. Langford* (1897) 14 SC 148; *Eastern and South African Telegraph Co v. Cape Town Tramways Co* (n. 49).

[83] Voet (n. 1), 9, 2, 19.

[84] *De Pass & Co v. Rawson* (1863) 5 Searle 1 (*culpa* present if defendant could reasonably have been expected to know of the consequences of his conduct and could have prevented them); *Metropolitan and Suburban Railway Co v. De Villiers* (1893) 10 SC 211 ; *Newman v. East London Town Council* (1895) 12 SC 61; *Walters v. Lucas* (1889) 7SC 153; *Boukamp v. Govt* (1898) 5 OR 140; *Kohne v. Harris* (1899) 16 SC 144.

[85] 1869 Buch 219.

[86] *Solomon v. Du Toit's Pan DM Co Ltd* (1882) 1 HCG 1; *Wiblin v. Webber* (1895) 10 EDC 71; *Walker v. Beeby and Stewart* (1895) 2 OR 148; *Westhuysen v. Lotter* (1898) 19 NLR 162 (with references to English cases).

[87] See *Lamb v. Colonial Govt* (1894) 14 EDC 103; *Fell v. Colonial Govt* (1889) 10 NLR 185; *Jordens v. Cape Divisional Council* (1894) 11 SC 158; *Mills v. Colonial Govt*, (1894) 4 CTR 28; *Searight & Co v. Cape Town Town Council Railway Co* (1900) 17 SC 78; *Jendraschewitz v. Nederlands Zuid-Afrikaanse Spoorweg Maatschappij* (1899) 6 OR 60 (with reference to English cases).

[88] *Gifford v. Table Bay Dock and Breakwater Management Commission* (1874) Buch 96, with reference to D. 50, 17, 132; 19, 2, 9, 5, and Grotius (n. 1), 3, 9, 11; and Watermeyer J in *Elmer v. Warren* (1887) 5 EDC 385, with reference to Voet (n. 1), 9, 2, 13.

The fourth group consists of a single case. In *Newman v. East London Town Council*,[89] the Cape Supreme Court had to decide on the issue of negligence in a situation of sudden peril. Referring to American and previous colonial authority, the Court applied the 'doctrine of sudden emergency'. However, Roman-Dutch law had been drawn upon earlier in the judgment in order to establish reasonable foreseeability of the likelihood of harm as the test for liability for negligent conduct. With regard to the doctrine of sudden emergency, the Court took pains to point out that it only encapsulates what a reasonable man could reasonably be expected to do.

The development of the requirement of *culpa* in Roman law did not involve the formulation of a standardized test for negligence. *Culpa* was seen to be present when a person had behaved as he should not have behaved, which in turn was determined in a casuistic fashion. The *diligens paterfamilias* was used as a role model, but no abstract definition was provided as to what exactly one could expect of him. A general definition of *culpa* as the failure to avert reasonably foreseeable loss was established only at a later stage.[90]

All the cases discussed above reflect the Roman and Roman-Dutch approach to *culpa*, with the emphasis on the general standard of care required (first group), on foreseeability and the possibility of the prevention of loss as concrete expressions of that standard (second group), and on the application of these standards to typical sets of situations (third and fourth groups). Where authority is provided it is usually Roman-Dutch, although English law also features occasionally. Nowhere are concepts entirely alien to either Roman or Roman-Dutch law used to determine negligence, with the exception of the reference to the doctrine of sudden emergency. This is undoubtedly an English import, but its application can be reconciled with Roman-Dutch principles, as the Court attempted to show. It is also possible that the cases mentioned in n. 87 (liability of public bodies for negligence in exercising statutory duties or powers) may have been influenced by the English law concerning liability for breach of a statutory duty. It had, however, been decided earlier[91] that Aquilian principles are applicable to such situations, and the inquiry into whether the harm could have been prevented that was undertaken in these cases was certainly not alien to Roman or Roman-Dutch law. On the whole, therefore, there appear to have been no significant developments beyond Roman-Dutch law concerning the issue of negligence.

---

[89] (1895) 12 SC 61.

[90] Zimmermann (n. 4), 1004–9, 1027–30, 1033–5; Van den Heever (n. 3), 45 sq.; Lawson (n. 5), 36–43; Lawson/Markesinis (n. 5), 14–30; Van der Walt (n. 2), 12 sq.

[91] In *Hume v. Divisional Council of Cradock* (n. 23), confirmed on appeal, without reference to authority, in *Divisional Council of Cradock v. Hume* (n. 23); cf. *Jordaan v. Worcester Municipality* (1893) 10 SC 159. In the former case the proposition referred to was based exclusively on Roman and Roman-Dutch sources (cf. n. 70 above); the latter case relied on the former.

5. Contributory negligence

The issue of contributory negligence arose in several early cases. It was eventually to lead to so much confusion that the legislature had to save the day. In *Hume v. Divisional Council of Cradock* [92] Shippard J, relying entirely on English cases, held that the plaintiff's contributory negligence was a bar to his success in an action for damages based on negligence if his negligence contributed to the accident, provided that it was the proximate or joint proximate cause and not a remote cause. Thus, if the defendant could have avoided the accident in spite of the plaintiff's negligence he would be liable. This exposition was followed in several later colonial cases, all with reference to previous decisions and/or English law. [93] In one of these cases the Court referred in general terms to Roman-Dutch law, but held that it provided a solution identical to that in English law. [94] The causal connection between the plaintiff's negligence and the harm was stressed in other cases, where it was held, without authority, that the defendant was not released from liability unless the accident would not have occurred but for the plaintiff's negligence. [95]

Often, however, judges dealing with contributory negligence stated the principles applicable to cases of this kind more vaguely. In two instances it was simply held, without any further proviso, that a plaintiff's contributory negligence excluded a claim for damages. [96] The Transvaal Court in one instance relied on an English precedent and stated boldly that South African law should be the same. [97] The question of contributory negligence on the part of children was considered in two other Transvaal cases, in both of which it was held that the defendant was liable unless the child's negligence was the only cause of the harm. [98] One of these cases exclusively relied on English authority for this proposition, [99] while the other quoted no source at all.

[92] Above, n. 23.

[93] *Tychsen v. Evans (Emanuel v. Fairy Queen)* (n. 80) (contributory negligence does not absolve defendant who might have avoided accident by ordinary skill); *Ward v. Griqualand West DM Co Ltd* (1888) 5 HCG 70 (plaintiff's negligence alone would have caused same consequence); *Weddovitch v. Donald Currie & Co* (1891) 6 EDC 177 (could defendant have avoided accident?); *Cowell v. Friedman & Co* (1888) 5 HCG 22; *McLaren v. Consolidated DM Co, Bultfontein* (1888) 5 HCG 202 (confirming previous case); *Appolis v. Jarom* (1898) 12 EDC 187 (defendant not absolved by plaintiff's negligence where the former could have avoided the injury).

[94] *Tychsen v. Evans (Emanuel v. Fairy Queen)* (n. 80).

[95] *Hutton v. Black Reef Gold Mining Co* (1889) 7 SC 77; *Jacobson v. City Tramway Co* (1898) 8 CTR 376; *Nederlands Zuid-Afrikaanse Spoorweg Maatschappij v. Van Rooyen* (1896) 2 OR 103; *Gibson Bros v. Otto* (1898) 8 HCG 193.

[96] *Hambly v. Soeker Bros* (1893) 10 SC 229; *Botes v. Nederlands Zuid-Afrikaanse Spoorweg Maatschappij* (1895) 2 OR 136.

[97] *Botes v. NZASM* (1895) 2 OR 136.

[98] *Johannesburg City and Suburban Tramway Co v. Doyle* (1894) 1 OR 205; *Eagleson v. Argus Printing & Publishing Co* (1894) 1 OR 259.

[99] *Eagleson v. Argus Printing & Publishing Co* (n. 98).

These cases might suggest that the English approach to contributory negligence was applied in South Africa without further ado. In fact, however,
there were some attempts to accommodate the Roman-Dutch law on the
subject. In *Kettle v. Storm*[100] the question of negligence on the part of a
plaintiff was determined with reference to the civilian rule of *compensatio
culpae*: where a person suffers damage through his own fault no claim is
granted to him to recover damages.[101] In this regard, it was held, South
African law follows the civil law. In *Priestly v. Dumeyer*[102] the same exposition of the Roman law was given with reference to the same text in the
Digest. However, Grueber's explanation of the reason for that rule (that the
plaintiff's fault interrupted the causal connection between the defendant's
conduct and the harm) was then used to argue that the Roman rule was
consistent with the English case-law. Consequently it was held that the
plaintiff's own negligence did not deprive him of his claim since, *in casu*, the
immediate cause of the harm was the defendant's conduct. Lastly, in *De
Kock v. Town Council of Cape Town*[103] Roman-Dutch law was referred to
in order to determine the *onus* of proof in cases of contributory negligence.

Roman law indeed adopted an all-or-nothing approach to the problem of
contributory negligence which was based on the principle of *compensatio
culpae*: damage caused through the plaintiff's own fault was not recoverable. Whether this was based on considerations of causation is uncertain.
The rule was certainly never conceptualized in these terms by the Roman
lawyers. The principle that the plaintiff's negligence excluded liability
remained in force in Roman-Dutch law.[104] However, it was definitely not
applied in early South African case-law. From the earliest reported decisions it is clear that the position was regulated mainly by English law, and
attempts to relate the English cases to Roman-Dutch principles were not
sufficient to lend a Roman-Dutch character to South African law. In this
instance, then, we are faced with an indigenious development stimulated by
the importation of English law.

6. Causation

The question of whether particular conduct on the part of the defendant
had caused the damage for which compensation was claimed was in some
of the early cases decided simply by asking whether the damage would have
resulted but for the conduct.[105] A number of cases, however, laid down

---

[100] (1893) 14 NLR 275.
[101] Reference was made to Pomp. D. 50, 17, 203, and Domat's *Civil Law*.
[102] (1898) 15 SC 393. The reference is to Grueber's commentary on the Aquilian law.
[103] (1886) 4 SC 458.
[104] Voet (n. 1), 9, 2, 17; Zimmermann (n. 4), 1010–13, 1047–9; Lawson (n. 5), 53–9;
Lawson/Markesinis (n. 5), 33 sq.; Van der Walt (n. 2), 86 sq.
[105] *De Pass & Co v. Rawson* (1863) 5 Searle 1; *Cathcart Divisional Council v. Hart* (1892) 2
CTR 28; cf. *Cape of Good Hope Bank v. Fischer* (1886) 4 SC 368.

more specific tests for causation. In the first place, a proviso was added in *McLaren v. Consolidated DM Company, Bultfontein*[106] to the effect that the but-for test determined causation unless the damage was too remote. In other cases it was decided, without reference to any specific authority, that the cause had to be proximate or immediate, not remote, in order to establish liability.[107] Yet other judgments, again without specific authority, simply required that the damage be the proximate cause of the harm.[108]

However, the majority of cases did not apply the proximate-cause formula to decide when damages could be recovered, but rather worked, on Roman-Dutch authority, either with the concept of the 'direct cause',[109] or, more generally, with a combination of the following terms: ordinary, natural, reasonable, probable, and direct cause of the harm.[110] In only one of these cases English case-law was quoted.[111]

Causation was not regarded as a distinct requirement for Aquilian liability in Roman law; rather it was taken to be implicit in the operative words used by the original *lex*. No theory of causation was thus developed; nor was a specific test devised.[112] In Roman-Dutch law there appears to have been no significant development in this regard beyond attributing liability only to direct or foreseeable consequences.[113] The South African cases referring directly to Roman-Dutch law simply apply these principles; at the same time, however, the influence of English law is apparent in the use of the concepts 'proximate' and 'remote' cause, and in the references to a 'natural', 'probable' and 'reasonable' cause. In some of the cases referred to above, these terms are used in conjunction with the term 'direct' cause. Thus, there

---

[106] (1888) 5 HCG 202.

[107] *Hume v. Divisional Council of Cradock* (n. 23); *De Villiers v. De Villiers* (1887) 5 SC 369; *Hall v. Hodgson* (1892) 13 NLR 212; *Naumann v. Johnson* (1895) 2 OR 188; cf. *Ngai and Assegai v. Ngobozana* (1900) 14 EDC 155, where it was simply decided that the damage was too remote.

[108] *Solomon v. Du Toit's Pan DM Co Ltd* (1882) 1 HCG 1; *Margoschis v. Dutoitspan Mining Board* (1889) 5 HCG 469; *Mostert v. De Beers Consolidated Mines Ltd* (1893) 7 HCG 26. It is interesting to note that in *Newman v. East London Town Council* (1895) 12 SC 61 it was held, with reference to cumulative causation, that the term 'proximate cause' implies only one cause and was not found in Roman-Dutch law; two parties could therefore both be liable for causing the same damage.

[109] *Walkden v. Natal Govt Railways* (1881) 2 NLR 222 (damage directly connected with the object itself: D. 19, 1, 23, 3, Pothier, and Noodt); *Cape of Good Hope Bank v. Fischer* (1886) 4 SC 368 (direct cause, loss directly (*in continenti*) inflicted: Voet (n. 1), 9, 2, 16); *Eastern and South African Telegraph Co v. Cape Town Tramways Co* (1900) 17 SC 95 (direct consequence: Voet (n. 1), 9, 2, 16).

[110] *De Bloemfonteinsche Stadsraad v. Clement* 1883 OFS 23; *Hill and Paddon v. Commissioner of Crown Lands* (1883) 2 SC 395; *McLaren v. Consolidated DM Co Bultfontein* (1888) 5 HCG 202; *Tait v. Wicht* (1890) 7 SC 158; *Hall v. Hodgson* (1892) 13 NLR 212; *Naumann v. Johnson* (1895) 2 OR 188.

[111] *McLaren v. Consolidated DM Co Bultfontein* (n. 110).

[112] Zimmermann (n. 4), 988–93; Lawson (n. 5), 50–3; Lawson/Markesinis (n. 5), 30–3.

[113] Voet (n. 1), 9, 2, 16 and 19; D. G. van der Keessel, *Theses Selectae Iuris Hollandici et Zelandici*, 814; Van der Walt (n. 2), 94; cf. J. C. Macintosh, *Negligence in Delict* (1926), 39.

is as yet no evidence of the later controversy in English law concerning the two tests for remoteness, namely direct consequences *versus* reasonable foreseeability.[114] Nevertheless, the indirect influence of English legal notions on South African law is already apparent in regard to causation in these early cases.

7. Damages

(a) Nominal and exemplary damages

That *damnum*, damage, or loss was a general requirement for Aquilian liability was expressly confirmed in some early cases.[115] At the same time, however, we find several instances of Aquilian liability where damages were awarded in spite of the fact that no actual damage or loss had been proved.

In the first place, the Cape Supreme Court held in *Jansen v. Pienaar*,[116] without specific reference to any authority, that where a plaintiff proves a wrong he is entitled to damages even if not a farthing of actual damage was proved. The Supreme Court of the Orange Free State, however, relying on Roman-Dutch authority, refused to follow this rule in *Visser v. London en Jagersfontein Diamant Delverij Co*.[117] In *Wolfaardt v. Colonial Government*[118] and *London and South Africa Exploration Co v. Haybittel*[119] the Cape Supreme Court and the High Court of Griqualand disallowed claims for negligence in the execution of a writ and for the wrongful sinking of a well on the plaintiff's property, because no damage was proved. The courts did not refer to the *Jansen* case. The Cape Supreme Court did not adduce any authority, while the High Court of Griqualand based its finding on English law. The rule in *Jansen* was also queried by the High Court of Griqualand in *London and South Africa Exploration Co Ltd v. Howe and Co*.[120] Jones J pointed out that the rule had been doubted in the Free State and Transvaal courts and that he himself was unsure whether a plaintiff under Roman-Dutch law could be granted a delictual action if the wrong had not led to any damage. He reluctantly followed the *Jansen* case because his court was bound by that decision of the Cape Supreme Court.

In spite of this divergence of opinions, South African courts continued to grant so-called nominal damages in cases where a wrong was established but no damages could be proved. Reference was usually made to English law,

---

[114] Cf. Macintosh (n. 113), 33–9; Van der Walt (n. 2), 95–104; Lawson/Markesinis (n. 5), 106–40.

[115] *Hill and Paddon v. Commissioner of Crown Lands* (n. 110); *Visser v. London en Jagersfontein Diamant Delverij Maatschappij* 1884 Gregorowski 8; cf. *Cape of Good Hope Bank v. Fischer* (n. 105).

[116] (1881) 1 SC 276. The case deals with enticing away a servant, which was classified by the Court as the tort of seduction.

[117] 1884 Gregorowski 8. The authorities referred to were Voet (n. 1), 9, 2, 7 and Pothier.

[118] (1898) 8 CTR 429.   [119] (1888) 5 HCG 170.   [120] (1886) 5 HCG 214.

if indeed any authority was referred to at all for this proposition. However, all these cases concerned trespass[121] (considered more fully below[122]) and there is some authority to the effect that nominal damages could be awarded only in cases of trespass and not where the basis of the claim was negligence.[123] Yet there is *Canny v. Boorman*[124] where a child had been injured but no damage had been proven. The case could have been brought under trespass to the person. It was, however, not classified as such but was based on negligence. Nevertheless, an award of nominal damages was made.

Secondly, it was accepted in some cases that a sum of money could be awarded without proof of actual loss as vindictive or exemplary damages, i.e. to punish the wrongdoer for reprehensible conduct.[125] (The term nominal damages was in one instance incorrectly used to describe such an award.[126]) Finally, the motive underlying exemplary damages, namely censure of conduct, was in one judgment used against the successful plaintiff to reduce the amount of damages awarded.[127]

(b) General principles

The general principles underlying the assessment of damages were explored in two cases. In *Hume v. Divisional Council of Cradock*[128] it was confirmed (without reference to any authority) that *damnum emergens* as well as *lucrum cessans* could be recovered. Possible loss of profit was excluded as that was not a consequence flowing immediately from the injury (natural and proximate result). The patrimonial nature of the damage was stressed by referring to 'out of pocket' loss. In *Walkden v. Natal Government*

---

[121] *Van Breda v. Muller* (1829) 1 Menz 425; *Pullinger v. Harsant* (1883) 2 HCG 111 (with reference to English cases); *Standard DM Co v. Compagnie Française* (1886) 4 HCG 29 (with reference to English law; *London and South Africa Exploration Co Ltd v. Howe & Co* (1886) 4 HCG 214 (with reference to *Jansen v. Pienaar*); *Beukes v. Uys* (1887) 2 SAR 153; *Nabob Gold Mining Co v. Phoenix Gold Mining Co* (1890) 3 SAR 142; *Trustees of the Mahomedan Mosque and Madrassa at Durban v. Corporation of Durban* (1893) 14 NLR 144.

[122] See below, Section 14 (a).

[123] *Standard DM Co v. Compagnie Française* (n. 121); where English law is relied on. Cf. *Wolfaardt v. Colonial Govt* (1898) 8 CTR 429; *London and South Africa Exploration Co v. Haybittel* (1888) 5 HCG 170.

[124] (1883) 2 SC 282.

[125] In the following cases such damages were expressly awarded: *De Villiers v. Van Zyl* 1880 Foord 77; *Murtha v. Von Beek* (1882) 1 Buch AC 121; *Russouw v. Wilsenach* (1887) 2 SAR 155; *Morkel v. Nederlands Zuid-Afrikaanse Spoorweg Maatschappij* (1896) 3 OR 71; *Nicholson v. Myburgh* (1897) 14 SC 384. In some cases an award was made in order to indicate censure of the defendant's conduct without, however, specifically referring to the notion of exemplary or vindictive damages: *Henwood v. Trafford* (1890) 11 NLR 93; *Hart v. Yates* (1896) 3 OR 201. In *Hume v. Divisional Council of Cradock* (1880) 1 EDC 104 and *Adonis v. Du Toit* (1896) 6 CTR 187 the concept of exemplary damages was recognized in principle, but no award was made *in casu*.

[126] *MacGreal v. Murray and Burrill* 1872 NLR 19, *per* Connor J (disapproving of the concept of nominal damages).

[127] *Van der Byl v. De Smidt* (1869) 2 Buch 183.   [128] Above, n. 23.

Railways[129] the Court relied on Roman and Roman-Dutch authority[130] for the following propositions: the damages must be directly connected to the object damaged at the time of the injury and it must be substantially certain. Consequential, or subsequent, loss can be recovered subject to these principles. It is interesting to note that in both these cases the assessment of damages is made to depend on an inquiry into causation.

(c) Specific instances

As for the measure of damages in specific instances, only damage to person or property was considered. The difficulty of assessing damages was stressed in one case,[131] and in another it was held that the determination of damages was not a question of strict mathematical calculation, but that fair and reasonable compensation should be granted.[132] The measure of damages for the wrongful detention of shares was in the former decision found to be the difference in the price of the shares from the day they were wrongfully detained to the day they were returned. The market value was also relied upon in other cases concerning corporeal objects.[133] In one case the loss of use of a carriage was measured in terms of the costs for a replacement of that carriage[134] and in another, where the plaintiff had been injured and was unable to work, the reasonable costs of a substitute were referred to.[135]

The cases discussed under (a), (b), and (c) show signs of the curiously hybrid nature of the modern South African law of damages. The influence of English law is apparent even at this early stage, particularly in the adoption and application of the notion of damages without proof of loss, such as nominal and exemplary damages. Although the relevant cases rarely refer to English authority, these notions are alien to civilian principles and can therefore only have been borrowed from English law. The same holds for the cases concerning a specific measure of damages in instances of damage to corporeal objects. There is no evidence for this kind of assessment being accepted in Roman or Roman-Dutch law.

The position under the Aquilian action in Roman law had progressed from the somewhat awkwardly drafted and very specific assessment instructions in the original *lex* to an appraisal of what the object concerned had been worth to the individual plaintiff. However, no general conceptual framework for the law of damages was ever developed and little attention

---

[129] Above, n. 109.
[130] D. 19, 1, 23, 3; 19, 1, 21, 3; 9, 2, 29, 3; 9, 2, 37, 1; Voet (n. 1), 19, 1, 20; Pothier, Noodt, Van Bynkershoek, and Van Leeuwen were referred to.
[131] *Van Reenen v. Republic Gold Mining Syndicate Ltd* (1888) 2 SAR 236.
[132] *Clair v. Port Elizabeth Harbour Board, Kennedy v. Port Elizabeth Harbour Board (n. 79)*.
[133] *Barnett & Co v. Van der Merwe* (1889) 3 SAR 106; *Elias Syndicate v. Leyds and the Responsible Clerk of Doornkop* (1897) 4 OR 248.
[134] *Stevens v. Naidoo* (1894) 15 NLR 284.
[135] *McLaren v. Consolidated DM Co, Bultfontein* (n. 110).

was paid to the definition, determination, or calculation of damages. Roman-Dutch law was more advanced only insofar as the influence of the medieval concept of *interesse* had led to some attempts at stating principles for the assessment of damages.[136]

Some of these principles featured prominently in what little early case-law there is on the subject, and in this regard there is as yet no solid evidence of English influence, even though English terminology is used to some extent. Also, there was little evidence of the tremendous development that the South African law of damages was to undergo in later years.

8. Joint wrongdoers

Early case-law unanimously holds each wrongdoer liable for the full amount of damages where the conduct of several wrongdoers contributed to causing the harm. Thus it was held in several cases, of which only one referred to authority in the form of English law, that joint wrongdoers are liable jointly and severally *in solidum* and that any one of them can be sued.[137] There is less certainty about whether payment by one wrongdoer absolves the other(s) and whether, having paid, a wrongdoer has a right of contribution against the others. The cases seem to accept by implication that payment by the one absolves the others. *Nel v. Halse*[138] seems to recognize the existence of a right of contribution, while in *Combrinck v. Wolfaardt*[139] some doubt is evident from the fact that the Court refers to 'a right of contribution, if any'.

Joint and several liability is in accordance with Roman-Dutch law, as is the rule that payment by the one wrongdoer absolves the others.[140] On the other hand, a right of contribution was not, apparently recognized in Roman-Dutch law.[141] The rules applied in these cases, with the exception of those relating to contribution, therefore accord with Roman-Dutch law.

---

[136] Voet (n. 1), 45, 1, 9 and 12; 39, 2, 1; Zimmermann (n, 4), 969–73, 1014 sq.; Lawson/Markesinis (n. 5), 35 sq.; Lawson (n. 5), 59–61; Erasmus/Gauntlett (n. 2), §§ 3–5; P. J. Visser, J. M. Potgieter, *Skadevergoedingsreg* (1993), 9–14; H. J. Erasmus, 'Aspects of the History of the South African Law of Damages', (1975) 38 *THRHR* 104 sqq., 268 sqq., 362 sqq.

[137] *Paterson v. McLoughlin and Solomon & Co* (1876) 6 Buch 62; *Graan v. During* (1883) 2 SC 308; *Nel v. Halse* (1888) 6 SC 275; *Bartlett v. Willimore* (1896) 10 EDC 89 (with reference to the previous 2 cases); *Bessenger v. Dyan, Umhale and Nosequ* (1891) 6 EDC 42; *Pieta v. Mhlom* (1897) 12 EDC 97; *Combrinck v. Wolfaardt* (1901) 9 HCG 139.

[138] Above, n. 137.   [139] Above, n. 137.

[140] Voet (n. 1), 17, 2, 7; 9, 2, 8 and 12; Grotius (n. 1), 3, 34, 6; 3, 32, 15; Van der Walt (n. 2), 109; Macintosh (n. 113), 128 sq. The latter part of the proposition was probably influenced by the fact that the *actio legis Aquiliae* had lost its penal character in Roman-Dutch law. The rule also corresponds with the English law of the time: G. T. Morice, *English and Roman-Dutch Law* (1905), 231.

[141] Voet (n. 1), 9, 2, 20; Macintosh (n. 113), 129; *contra*: Morice (n. 140), 231 sq. Again, the position was the same in English law; see Morice (n. 140), 231; M. Nathan, *South African Law of Torts* (1921), 42 sq.

9. Title to sue

The question of who, apart from the owner of a corporeal asset, has the right to sue for damages under the *actio legis Aquiliae* arose in a number of early cases. Some of them dealt with the title to sue for trespass, which will be considered later.[142]

In *De Pass and Company v. Rawson*[143] and *Umpofana v. Martens*[144] damages for injury to a construction and to crops were awarded to the lessee and occupier of the land on which the construction was built and the crops were growing. In both cases this was done not on the basis of the lease or right of occupation but because the construction and the crops were held to be the property of the lessee, or occupier of the land. In the former case Roman-Dutch authority was relied on,[145] while in the latter the Court avoided reference to authority and classified the claim as being one for trespass. Since the occupier of land could sue for trespass in English law[146] it would have been unnecessary to rely on the notion of ownership in order to establish a claim had English law been applied. These cases therefore do no more than recognize the Roman and Roman-Dutch rule that the owner of the object damaged has title to sue for damages.

The right of a bailee (who was contractually liable to the bailor) to claim damages for injury to the object received in bailment was recognized, apparently on the strength of the availability of such a claim to the borrower in Roman-Dutch law.[147] Furthermore, the possibility of a lessee instituting an action on account of damage to the object leased was considered, but the claim was refused because *in casu* it was considered to be excluded by the terms of the contract.[148] Lastly, the right of a possessor or occupier of land to sue for loss caused by a fire was recognized, but again the claim was refused *in casu*, this time because negligence (of the wrongdoer) could not be proved.[149]

Since the *actio legis Aquiliae* was available to the borrower and possessor in Roman-Dutch law[150] these cases do not indicate any startling new development or expansion. Had the lessee's claim succeeded, it would have constituted an extension of the Roman-Dutch position where the availability of the action was restricted to the lessor of services. One case offers evidence

---

[142] See below, Section 14 (a).   [143] (1863) 5 Searle 1.
[144] 1867 NLR 100.   [145] Voet (n. 1), 1, 8, 4 and 9.
[146] See below, Section 14 (a).
[147] *Bower v. Divisional Council of Albany* (1893) 7 EDC 211. Voet (n. 1), 9, 2, 10 was quoted in argument.
[148] *Cooke v. Allerstone* 1868 NLR 210.
[149] *Brink v. Cloete* (1869) 2 Buch 215. Reference was made to Voet (n. 1), 9, 2, 19 in the part of the decision dealing with negligence.
[150] Voet (n. 1), 9, 2, 10; Van der Walt (n. 2), 17.

of English influence; however, it concerned trespass which is considered below.[151]

10. Immunity

The English rule according to which the Crown is immune from actions for damages for tortious acts of its servants was applied to liability under the *lex Aquilia* in early cases in the Cape Colony, Natal, and Transvaal. The importation of the rule from England was confirmed by the Cape Court in *Binda v. Colonial Government*[152] without any attempt to determine the Roman-Dutch position in this regard. Colonial officials, it was argued, were servants of the Crown and their liability would therefore have to be determined by English law, otherwise the Crown would have been exposed to liability that did not exist in England. The decision was confirmed in Natal, where the Court held that the immunity of the Government was too well established to be upset except by legislation.[153] The principle applied in the *Binda* case was also affirmed in the Transvaal in spite of that country's then independence from England, once again without examining the Roman-Dutch position. It was thought to be based on good grounds.[154] This may have been true of the Cape Colony and Natal, which were under English rule, but was certainly not true (at least not necessarily) in regard to an independent Republic.

11. Omissions

Apart from the general principles of Aquilian liability discussed above, several specific instances of liability received special attention in the early case-law. The first of these, liability for omissions, can be subdivided into two groups: the liability of public bodies and mining cases.

(a) Liability of public bodies

The principles applicable to the liability of public bodies for omissions were first set out in *Port Elizabeth Municipality v. Nightingale*.[155] Having established, with reference to a Roman text, that such liability was regulated by the *lex Aquilia*, Cloete J relied on Voet for the proposition that while omissions did not normally lead to Aquilian liability this did not hold true when there was a duty to act, for then the act of omission was coupled with an

---

[151] See below, Section 14 (a).

[152] (1887) 5 SC 284. The Court approved of an earlier unreported decision of the Natal Supreme Court to the same effect.

[153] *Vos v. Colonial Govt* (1891) 12 NLR 337. Previous Natal cases, a Privy Council decision, and *Binda* were referred to.

[154] *Cullinan, Langebrink and MacEwan v. Reitz* (1899) 6 OR 147.

[155] (1855) 2 Searle 214.

act of commission.[156] He therefore held a municipality which was directed by an Ordinance to keep roads in good repair liable for its omission to do so. This statement was confirmed by the judgments of Shippard and Buchanan JJ in *Hume v. Divisional Council of Cradock*.[157] Shippard J also paid meticulous attention to the form of *culpa*, or negligence, required for liability. Meanwhile it had been decided in *Manuel v. Cape Town Town Council*[158] (without reference to authority) that where a municipality undertakes to carry out work and then performs it improperly or negligently it is liable for damages on the basis of negligence, no matter whether it was bound to carry out the work or not. Finally, in *Kimberley Town Council v. Von Beek*[159] it was held that a municipality was not liable for failing to do what it was only authorized to do, but was liable for misfeasance if it negligently carried out any work it had undertaken.

The position was summarized in *Jordaan v. Worcester Municipality*.[160] Here it was expressly held that Aquilian principles were applicable to both misfeasance and nonfeasance. A public body was liable for misfeasance where work was undertaken, no matter whether a duty to undertake it was imposed by statute or mere permissive powers had been granted. Liability for nonfeasance only arose in cases of a duty imposed, but not of a permissive power granted. In both instances liability was based on negligence. These principles were subsequently applied in several cases,[161] not all of them concerning public bodies.[162] In a solitary Free State case it was decided that a municipality was not liable for damages arising from failure to repair a river which it had no duty to repair, even if it had repaired the river on a previous occasion. Under Roman-Dutch law such liability rested on the State or on the riparian landowners. Thus, the Court did not apply the above-mentioned principles relating to misfeasance, in terms of which

---

[156] The references are to D. 9, 2, 29, and Voet.   [157] Above, n. 23.
[158] (1877) 7 Buch 107.
[159] (1882) 1 Buch AC 101; confirmed in substance in *Kimberley Town Council v. Mathieson* (1882) 1 Buch AC 112; *Murtha v. Kimberley Town Council* (1883) 1 HCG 323 (where it was held that a municipality had assumed control over a drain and was thus liable for failure to maintain it) and, on appeal, *Kimberley Town Council v. Murtha* (1883) 1 Buch AC 282.
[160] (1893) 10 SC 159.
[161] *Rivenhall v. Divisional Council of Tarka* (1887) 5 EDC 355; *Jordens v. Cape Divisional Council* (1894) 11 SC 158; *East London Municipality v. Murray* (1894) 9 EDC 55; *O'Shea v. Port Elizabeth Town Council* (1895) 12 SC 146; *Meister v. Town Council of Johannesburg* (1898) 5 OR 307; *Smith v. Mayor and Councillors of Borough of Pietermaritzburg* (1897) 18 NLR (this was a case of misfeasance; the opinion was, however, expressed that had it been a case of nonfeasance, the position might have had to be reconsidered in the light of later English cases and of Roman-Dutch law.)
[162] *Solomon v. Du Toit's Pan DM Co Ltd* (1882) 1 HCG 1; *Haarhoff's Trustee v. Frieslich* (1894) 11 SC 158; *Sanitary Board of Johannesburg v. Purchase* (1895) 2 OR 44; *Reed v. De Beers Consolidated Mines Ltd* (1892) 6 HCG 179; *Eagleson v. Argus Printing & Publishing Co* (1894) 1 OR 259.

the first act of repair would have been regarded as an assumption of control and thus as an undertaking to carry out the work.[163]

In these cases the first germ of the confusion was laid that was to grow around the prior conduct doctrine and its attendant problems. Although the courts professed to base their views on Roman-Dutch law, English terminology confused the issue and imported essentially English modes of thought into South African law. In addition, Roman-Dutch law was probably interpreted somewhat imperfectly. There, liability for mere omissions had been recognized, in principle, in all circumstances where the law required positive action.[164] In South African law, on the other hand, liability was for a long time limited to the breach of duties imposed by statute or to cases of prior conduct, or assumption of control over a dangerous object. The indirect influence of English law, coupled with an incomplete perusal of the relevant Roman-Dutch sources, contributed to an undesirable and disorderly development of the law which ran counter to the generalized nature of the *usus modernus legis Aquiliae*.

(b) Mining cases

An interesting exception to the generally accepted principle that mere omissions did not give rise to Aquilian liability emerged with regard to mining cases. In *Murtha v. Von Beek*[165] an obligation was held to exist to work a claim with due diligence. Failure to work a claim constituted negligence and led to liability for the damage caused to neighbouring claims. No authority was referred to for these propositions which were confirmed in several later cases.[166] In 1886 Buchanan J imposed liability for damage, independent of negligence, in an action of trespass concerning a mining case.[167] This

---

[163] *Munisipaliteit van Kroonstad v. Coetzer* (1886) 2 Gregorowski 75. The sources relied upon were Van Leeuwen and Grotius (*De jure belli ac pacis*).

[164] As to Roman-Dutch law, see Grotius (n 1), 3, 32, 3, 4, 12 and 14; Zimmermann (n. 4), 1043–5; Van der Walt (n. 2), 17, 29–33; Van den Heever (n. 3), 32 sq., 37–42; cf. Beinart, (1949) 12 *THRHR* 141–69; Van Loggerenberg (n. 10), 62–122 for the Roman sources.

[165] (1882) 1 Buch AC 121. In another case it was decided that the working of a claim in an ordinary manner did not amount to negligence and thus did not give rise to liability: *Goode and Smith v. Hall* (1883) 1 HCG 526, followed in *Hall v. Compagnie Française des Mines de Diamants du Cap* (1883) 1 HCG 464; cf. *Leo, Kennedy and Murray v. Ramsbottom* (1880) 1 Buch AC 40 in regard to the negligent working of a claim. These cases did not, however, concern omissions.

[166] *Hall v. Compagnie Française des Mines de Diamants du Cap* (n. 165) (cf. the judgment of Jones J who referred, with approval, to the rule in *Murtha*); *European DM Co Ltd v. Mylchreest* (1884) 2 HCG 465 (a claimholder was held liable for damage caused by earth dropping from his claim onto an adjacent claim); *Burnett and Taylor v. De Beers Consolidated Mines Ltd* (1895) 8 HCG 5 (cf. the judgment of Hopley J who considered the rule in *Murtha* to be correct and himself to be bound by it); *Standard Bank v. Bisset* (1887) 4 HCG 256 (cf. the judgment of Jones J who referred to the rule but decided the case on other grounds); *Reed v. De Beers Consolidated Mines Ltd* (1892) 6 HCG 179.

[167] *Standard DM Co v. Compagnie Française* (1886) 4 HCG 29.

opened up the possibility of arguing that the rule in *Murtha* might not be
based on negligence; but this was vehemently denied in later cases.[168]

Eventually the rule in *Murtha* became suspect. In *Reed v. De Beers
Consolidatcd Mines Ltd*,[169] Laurence JP refused to extend it to cases of failure to prevent water from escaping from one claim to another. In *Burnett
and Taylor v. De Beers Consolidated Mines Ltd*,[170] Solomon J did not accept
an argument based on an unreported decision by Lord De Villiers that
Murtha was decided incorrectly. *In casu* he did not, however, apply the
Murtha rule, since it was designed to accommodate open mining. In the
meantime underground mining had become the rule, and by-laws had been
issued to provide the necessary protection to neighbouring claim-holders.

The rise and fall of the rule in *Murtha* is an interesting example of an
indigenous South African development concerning Aquilian liability. It
occurred in response to changing industrial and economic circumstances,
namely the prevalence and importance of mining operations, and appears
to have been independent of English influence.

12. Misrepresentation

In one of the earliest reported cases concerning liability for misrepresentation, *Cape of Good Hope Bank v. Fischer*, it was held that negligent
misrepresentation afforded a cause of action in Roman-Dutch law.[171]
Subsequent cases, however, dealt exclusively with fraudulent misrepresentation, and in 1894 it was in fact held that false representations causing damage in a non-contractual context were actionable only in case of fraud.[172]
No authority was provided but it is likely that the English decision in *Derry
v. Peek*[173] influenced the Court.[174] However, the existence of the Roman-
Dutch *actio doli* may also have played a role in this respect.

Be that as it may, the main issue arising in the reported cases on fraudulent misrepresentation was the exact nature of the requirement of fraud.
Incidentally, the focus on fraud entailed that these cases dealt with aspects
of the *actio doli* rather than with the *lex Aquilia*. Later the emphasis shifted;
after all, the principles of Aquilian liability were wide enough to include

---

[168] *Ward v. Griqualand West DM Co Ltd* (1888) 5 HCG 70, where it was held that the statement in the *Standard* case concerning negligence was *obiter*; *Standard Bank v. Bisset* (1887) 4
HCG 256, where negligence was required for liability for earth falling onto another person's
claim.

[169] (1892) 6 HCG 179.   [170] (1895) 8 HCG 5.

[171] (1886) 4 SC 368. The authorities relied upon were Johann van de Sande, Antonius
Matthaeus, and Voet (n. 1), 20, 1, 11.

[172] *Dickson & Co v. Levy* (1894) 11 SC 33; cf. *Lippert & Co v. Smit* (1878) 8 Buch 95.

[173] (1889) 14 AC 337. According to *Derry v. Peek*, negligent misprepresentation did not constitute a cause of action according to English common law.

[174] Cf. e.g. Neethling/Potgieter/Visser (n. 2), 287; Susan Scott, 'Nalatige Wanvoorstelling as
Aksiegrond in die Suid-Afrikaanse Reg', (1977) 40 *THRHR* 58.

actions based on *dolus*. As a result, all cases of misrepresentation today are dealt with as instances of Aquilian liability. The earliest pertinent case simply required an intention to induce the other party to act on the false representations.[175] Another case contained an *obiter* remark to the effect that a bad motive need not be proved in cases of misrepresentation, as long as (a) the representor had known the statement to be false, (b) that statement had been calculated to induce the other party to act, and (c) damage had been incurred.[176] In *Tait v. Wicht*[177] it was decided that in Roman-Dutch law the intention to injure, or cheat, formed the root of fraud. Thus, a representation which the representor knew to be false, or which he made recklessly, was sufficient for liability to arise. While the motive was immaterial, fraud could not exist where intention to injure was absent. The pronouncement in *Tait v. Wicht* and the earlier remark were confirmed in a later case where the defendant was found to have acted *bona fide* since he had believed in the truth of his statement and was thus absolved from liability.[178]

In *African Banking Corporation v. Goldbard*[179] Kotzé CJ expressed a slightly narrower point of view than that adopted in *Tait's* case, holding that a statement which the representor knew to be false, or which he had made recklessly, would lead to liability. *Bona fide* belief in the truth of the statement would, however, exclude fraud. His lordship came to this decision without referring to the intention to deceive. He relied on Roman-Dutch authority[180] and English law, but in fact accepted the requirements as set out in *Derry v. Peek*.[181]

The cases dealing with fraudulent misrepresentation demonstrate how a basic similarity between English and Roman-Dutch law concerning the requirement of fraud was apt to lead to a process of gradual assimilation. However, it also appears to have contributed to the adoption of the English rule that liability for damages is confined to cases of fraudulent misrepresentation. This restriction was in conflict with the general tenor of the development of the *actio legis Aquiliae* in Roman-Dutch law; the English influence retarded the expansion of Aquilian liability in South African law for a considerable period.

13. Breach of a statutory duty

In *Hume v. Divisional Council of Cradock*[182] liability for breach of a statutory duty was held to fall under the *lex Aquilia* and to depend on negligence. Yet determination of the exact form of negligence required for the different types of statutory duties was undertaken with reference to the relevant

---

[175] *Lippert & Co v. Smit* (1878) 8 Buch 95.
[176] *De Villiers v. De Villiers* (1887) 5 SC 369.
[177] (1890) 7 SC 158, with reference to D. 4, 3, 1, and Voet (n. 1), 4, 3, 1 and 2.
[178] *Hosking v. Standard Bank of SA (Ltd)* (1892) 13 NLR 174.
[179] (1897) 4 OR 402.   [180] Voet (n. 1), 4, 3, 1 sqq.
[181] Cf. *Frenkel & Co v. Freisman and Shapiro* (1897) 4 OR 227.   [182] (1880) 1 EDC 104.

English case-law. *Liquidator of the Cape Central Railways v. Nöthling*[183]
gave De Villiers CJ an opportunity to confirm that Aquilian liability had
been extended by judicial interpretation to cases of breach of a statutory
duty. He then referred to specific rules developed in English law in order to
determine under which circumstances such a breach gives rise to a civil remedy for damages. Of central importance were the object and the language
of the statute, not the mere fact that damage had arisen. In *Naumann v.
Johnson*[184] it was decided, again with reference to English cases, that breach
of a statutory duty may give rise to a right of action for damages.

In these cases, a specific form of liability for damages recognized in
English law, but unknown to Roman-Dutch law, was imported into South
African law and subsumed under the general principles of the *lex Aquilia*.
This form of liability, and the special rules relating to it, did not conflict
with the civilian tradition. It thus provides a good example of the enriching
effect of the harmonious fusion of Roman-Dutch and English law.

14. Specific torts

The development of Aquilian liability in South African law was inevitably
influenced by the fact that particular English torts, falling within the normal area of application of the *lex Aquilia*, were recognized and applied in
early South African case-law. References to trespass abound, and the tort
of negligence is also referred to in a variety of cases.

(a) Trespass

Trespass was recognised in some instances[185] in spite of an early Transvaal
case to the effect that trespass disclosed no cause of action.[186] Actions for
trespass were recognized in respect of the unauthorized use of another person's land and served in practice as a mechanism to resolve boundary disputes.[187] The unauthorized erection of an aquaduct, a building or a fence,
and the dumping of rubbish on another person's property were classified as
trespass,[188] as was the cutting of trees on, and the traversing of, somebody
else's land.[189] The action was granted where damage was caused to the

---

[183] (1890) 8 SC 25.   [184] (1895) 2 OR 188.

[185] *Rhodes v. Coetzee* (1865) 1 Roscoe 288; *Preller v. Zeederberg* (1885) 2 SAR 20 (relying
only on English cases and referring to trespass as a common law action).

[186] *Ferguson v. Pretorius* 1879 Kotzé 158 (damage to crops by cattle). Actions for trespass
were nevertheless granted in later Transvaal cases: *Beukes v. Uys* (1887) 2 SAR 153; *Nabob
Gold Mining Co v. Phoenix Gold Mining Co* (1890) 3 SAR 142.

[187] *Gill v. Hirsch* (1891) 1 CTR 53; *Jansen v. Conradie* (1891) 1 CTR 226; *Barrington v.
Barnard* (1891) 1 CTR 292.

[188] *Van den Heever v. Du Toit* (1897) 7 CTR 97; *Christie v. Haarhoff* (1887) 4 HCG 349;
Gavin v. Municipality of Oudtshoorn (1897) 7 CTR 397; *London and South Africa Exploration
Co Ltd v. Howe & Co* (n. 121).

[189] *Liversage v. Kremer* 1867 NLR 57; *Breda v. Hofmeyer* (1837) 3 Menz 459; *Beukes v. Uys*
(n. 186); *Henwood v. Trafford* (1890) 11 NLR 93.

crops of another,[190] whether damage was done by humans or by grazing animals.[191] However, trespass was also recognized as a cause of action in cases of unlawful arrest: trepass to person, as opposed to land.[192]

Several cases dealt with the requirements for an action for trespass. The action was held to be available only to the owner, or lawful occupier or possessor, of the relevant property.[193] Damages were awarded even in the absence of proof of actual loss (nominal damages).[194] In *Standard DM Company v. Compagnie Française*[195] damages were awarded even though there was no negligence. This seems to have been followed in one other case;[196] in another decision the question of negligence as a requirement for a claim based on trespass was raised but not decided.[197]

The importation of the tort of trespass into South African law was neither a necessary nor a welcome development. The relevant cases would in any event have been covered by the principles of the *lex Aquilia* which provided then, as they do today, adequate protection of ownership. Moreover, the requirements for liability for trespass conflict with those of the *lex Aquilia* and this has led to confusion and uncertainty. Finally, certain doctrines incompatible with Roman-Dutch principles of liability have been incorporated into South African law at least partly under the auspices of the tort of trespass, such as the notion of nominal damages.

(b) Negligence

It has been pointed out above that the *lex Aquilia* covered liability for damages caused negligently.[198] The early cases concerning negligence deal mostly with the determination of negligence or with negligence as a requirement for delictual liability. These issues are obviously relevant for the application of the *lex Aquilia*, but they can equally well be associated with the English tort of negligence. In the absence of express indications in the cases concerned it is therefore very difficult to determine whether the courts were in fact applying Aquilian principles or whether they were influenced by the

[190] *Malcolm v. Shaw* (1898) 8 CTR 34.

[191] *Greeff v. Van der Westhuyzen* (1894) 4 CTR 28; *Adonis v. Du Toit* (1896) 6 CTR 187; *Preller v. Zeederberg* (1885) 2 SAR 20; *Umpofana v. Martens* 1867 NLR 100.

[192] *Riggs v. Roper and Jackson* (1885) 4 SC 114; *Pullinger v. Harsant* (1883) 2 HCG 111; *Trustees of the Mahomedan Mosque and Madrassa at Durban v. Corporation of Durban* (1893) 14 NLR 144.

[193] *Breda v. Hofmeyer* (n. 189) (lawful possession or occupation); *Theron v. Nieuwenhuizen* (1898) 15 SC 27 (lawful occupation); *Vos v. Colonial Govt* (1891) 12 NLR 337 (possession); *Du Bois v. Baumann* 1859 Phipson 37 (occupier); *Smith v. Bewick* (1890) 11 NLR 269 (owner or occupier); *Wessels v. Wilson and Hall* (1891) 6 HCG 88 (owner or person with reversionary interest).

[194] *Beukes v. Uys* (n. 186); *Nabob Gold Mining Co v. Phoenix Gold Mining Co* (n. 186); *Pullinger v. Harsant* (n. 192); *London and SA Exploration Co Ltd v. Howe & Co* (1886) 4 HCG 214; *Henwood v. Trafford* (n. 189).

[195] (1886) 4 HCG 29.   [196] *Westhuysen v. Lotter* (1898) 19 NLR 162.

[197] *Nabob Gold Mining Co v. Phoenix Gold Mining Co* (n. 194).   [198] See above, *sub* 1.

requirements of the English tort of negligence. The terminology and turn of phrase in some early cases on negligence seem to indicate that the courts had in mind the tort of negligence,[199] but even if that was so it did not affect the decision. For nothing turns on the question of whether English or Roman-Dutch law was applied in cases dealing with substantially identical requirements of liability. There is, however, one early South African case concerning an issue on which Aquilian principles and the English tort of negligence are at odds. In *Freeman v. Colonial Government*[200] it was held that no negligence arises in respect of any person or object to whom, or to which, the defendant owes no duty. The existence of a duty, which was to develop into a duty of care, had always been a requirement for liability under the tort of negligence in English law. In Roman-Dutch law, on the other hand, there had been occasional references to a concept of duty in discussions surrounding the requirement of *iniuria*. However, no such a duty was ever taken to be owed to a specific person, unlike the English duty of care referred to in the *Freeman* case. Thus, this case imported into South African law the concept of a directional duty of care, which was to cause such confusion and controversy[201] before it eventually matured into a flexible, policy-based test for wrongfulness in cases of liability for omissions, negligent misrepresentation, and purely patrimonial loss.[202]

IV. CONCLUSION

1. Judicial attitudes to the sources of South African law

Before attempting to draw general conclusions about the historical development of the *actio legis Aquiliae* during this period, it is expedient to examine the attitude of South African courts, as it appears from the cases discussed above, toward the sources of law to be consulted when they were faced with new problems.

There are numerous cases during this early period which affirm in general terms that the law applicable in South Africa, or in a specific jurisdiction within that area, is Roman-Dutch law;[203] or even that it is Roman-

---

[199] Cf. e.g. *Van der Byl v. De Smidt* (1869) 2 Buch 183; *Leo, Kennedy and Murray v. Ramsbottom* (1880) 1 Buch AC 40; *Murtha v. Von Beek* (1882) 1 Buch AC 121; *Westhuysen v. Lotter* (1898) 19 NLR 162.

[200] (1888) 9 NLR 181.

[201] Van den Heever (n. 3), 42–4; Price, 1959 *Acta Juridica* 120 sqq.

[202] *Minister van Polisie v. Ewels* 1975 (3) SA 590 (A); *Administrateur, Natal v. Trust Bank van Afrika Bpk* 1979 (3) SA 824 (A); *Indac Electronics (Pty) Ltd v. Volkskas Bank Ltd* 1992 (1) SA 738 (A); Van der Walt (n. 2), 23–9; Neethling/Potgieter/Visser (n. 2), 48–50.

[203] *Viljoen v. Graham* (1878) 3 Roscoe 49; *Schoeman v. Goosen* (1883) 3 EDC 7; *Hilpert v. Castle Mail Packets Co* (1897) 12 EDC 38; *Austen Bros v. Standard DM Co Ltd* (1883) 1 HCG 363; *Rooth v. State* (1888) 2 SAR 259; *Lewis v. Salisbury GM Co* (1894) 1 OR 1; *Hume v. Divisional Council of Cradock* (n. 23).

Dutch as opposed to English law.[204] These statements were not mere lip-service: in many cases the courts did indeed confirm and apply Roman-Dutch law where it was found to differ from English law on a particular point.[205] Yet the general political situation of the Cape, coupled with the anglicization of the administration of justice, also led the courts in some early cases to attribute to English law the status of a secondary source of law. Thus, the position according to English common law was frequently examined and compared with that in Roman-Dutch law, and where the latter was found to be uncertain, or to reveal conflicting opinions, or where it did not appear to deal with a specific issue, English law was applied.[206]

Generally, the courts considered themselves bound to apply Roman-Dutch law. At the same time, however, English legal principles managed to infiltrate South African law in various ways. Thus, the direct importation of a common law rule (such as the immunity of government from being sued for damages) could be justified by reference to British political sovereignty.[207] Much more frequently the courts examined the English position in detail, referred to a similar rule, or (most often) adduced a supporting principle in Roman-Dutch law, and proceeded to apply English law.[208] Where no similar rule or principle was found to exist in Roman-Dutch law, the application of English law could be justified by stating that it was not in conflict with the former.[209] In other cases the courts applied English law, sometimes reluctantly, even where it was found to differ from Roman-Dutch law, because they considered themselves bound by previous decisions of a South African court or of the Privy Council.[210] Thus, the adoption of the English doctrine of *stare decisis* made itself felt on the development of substantive law. Finally, in rare instances South African courts simply applied English law without any attempt to determine the legal position in Roman-Dutch law and without any effort to justify this way of proceeding.[211]

---

[204] E.g. *Schoeman v. Goosen* (1883) 3 EDC 7.

[205] *Lotter v. Rhodes* (1902) 19 SC; *Kettle v. Storm* (1893) 14 NLR 275; *De Kock v. Town Council of Cape Town* (1886) 4 SC 458; *Tychsen v. Evans (Emanuel v. Fairy Queen)* (n. 80) (the point was specifically made; nevertheless, English law was applied *in casu* because it was held to be the same as Roman-Dutch law).

[206] *Du Toit v. De Bot, Du Toit v. Zuidmeer* (1883) 2 SC 213; *Rooth v. State* (n. 203); *Lewis v. Salisbury Gold Mining Co* (n. 203); cf. *Le Roux v. Fick* (1879) 9 Buch 29.

[207] *Binda v. Colonial Govt* (1887) 5 SC 284.

[208] *Tychsen v. Evans (Emanuel v. Fairy Queen)* (n. 80); *Holland v. Scott* (1882) 2 EDC 307; *Snodgrass v. Pretorius* (1895) 9 EDC 125; *Walker v. Beeby and Stewart* (1895) 2 OR 148; *African Banking Corp v. Goldbard* (1897) 4 OR 402; *Priestly v. Dumeyer* (1898) 15 SC 393; *Davids v. Mendelsohn* (1898) 15 SC 367.

[209] *Hilpert v. Castle Mail Packets Co* (1897) 12 EDC 38.

[210] *London & SA Exploration Co Ltd v. Howe & Co* (1886) 4 HCG 214; *Burnett and Taylor v. De Beers Consolidated Mines Ltd* (1895) 8 HCG 5.

[211] Cf. e.g. *Botes v. Nederlands Zuid-Afrikaanse Spoorweg Maatschappij* (1895) 2 OR 136.

2. Aquilian liability in the nineteenth-century case-law

During the period under discussion the *actio legis Aquiliae* remained essentially Roman-Dutch in nature and application. Thus, the basic rules and principles concerning the requirements of liability like, especially: the notions of *iniuria* and *culpa*; the position concerning the liability of joint wrongdoers; and concerning title to sue (in cases not involving trespass) remained substantially unchanged.

However, there were also numerous indications of further development and refinement of Aquilian principles in nineteenth-century South African case-law. They were entirely in accordance with the civilian character of the remedy and were not based on any bias towards English law. Examples are the conceptual distinction between wrongfulness and fault, the recognition of the possibility of a right of contribution between joint wrongdoers, and also the beginnings of the expansion of Aquilian liability to forms of patrimonial loss other than those recognized in Roman-Dutch law. Another development, the rationale of which had nothing to do with English influence even though its form owed more to English than to Roman-Dutch principles, was the development of special rules in mining cases. They constitute a response to economic changes in South African society.

The most significant developments, however, took place under the direct or indirect influence of English law. In some instances rules or principles entirely alien to Roman-Dutch law were incorporated into South African law by direct importation. The immunity of government from liability is a prominent example. The rules relating to contributory negligence also derive essentially from English law.

There are numerous examples of more subtle judicial reception of English rules and principles. The contents of the notion of wrongfulness; the concept of a duty of care; the law of damages; the requirement of causation; liability for omissions, especially of statutory bodies; liability for misrepresentation and for breach of a statutory duty; and the law of trespass: all carry a characteristically English imprint.

One could have thought, in view of the sheer number of common law accretions, that English law was on its way to replacing Roman-Dutch law in South Africa. That this did not happen is largely due to two factors. In the first place, of course, the general structure of delictual liability remained essentially civilian. Secondly, in many of the instances referred to the pertinent English rules or principles were not inconsistent with their Roman-Dutch counterparts and could fairly easily be assimilated. The eventual result was a South African hybrid. Sometimes, of course, the reception of English law led to confusion and uncertainty. It was apt to restrict the area of application of the generalized Aquilian principles and had a retarding effect on the development of South African law. Examples include liability for omissions, especially of statutory bodies, and for negligent misrepresentation, the duty-of-care requirement, and trespass. Fortunately, however, subsequent developments have by and large led to a uniform and internally consistent body of rules governing delictual liability.

The history of the application and development of the *actio legis Aquiliae* in early South African case-law is thus a story of continuity and change, of strife and reconciliation. At least in retrospect, it is a story of enrichment and of growth.

18: *Aquilian Liability II (Twentieth Century)*

DALE HUTCHISON

I. INTRODUCTION

At the dawn of the twentieth century the South African courts seemed poised finally to round off the long process of historical development of the Aquilian action by accepting the simple, general proposition that all damage caused intentionally or negligently is actionable, unless it can be justified. To some extent, such a development had been presaged by the statement of De Villiers CJ in *Cape of Good Hope Bank v. Fischer*[1] that, in the time of Voet and Matthaeus:

> the Aquilian law had received an extension by analogy to a degree never permitted under the Roman law. The action *in factum* was no longer confined to cases of damage done to corporeal property, but was extended to every kind of loss sustained by a person in consequence of the wrongful acts of another . . .

Whether historically correct or not,[2] this statement reflected an admirable willingness on the part of the early South African courts to continue the process of generalization of Aquilian liability. In fact, however, as Van Aswegen has shown,[3] the hard reality was that in the practice of the courts in the late nineteenth century Aquilian liability was still by and large confined to culpable *acts* causing *physical* injury to person or property. The story of the development of the Aquilian action in the twentieth century is largely one of the struggle to free the action from these outdated confines, by extending it to conduct and harm of all kinds. More particularly, it is the story of the development of liability for omissions, for negligent misstatements, and for pure economic loss. As we shall see, these developments have been made possible, or at any rate facilitated, by the resurrection and redefinition of the element of wrongfulness, which has come to serve a very prominent role as a discretionary tool for judicial control in expanding the frontiers of Aquilian liability.

The main focus of this paper is therefore these major developments, with

---

[1] (1886) 4 SC 368, 376.

[2] For doubts about the validity of this sweeping statement see R. G. McKerron, *The Law of Delict* (7th edn., 1971), 8. Cf. the writers cited in n. 96 below.

[3] See Ch. 17, above, Section III. 11, 12.

liability for misstatements being treated as an aspect of the wider problem of liability for negligently inflicted pure economic loss. There have, of course, been other important developments in the field, of arguably equal or greater importance. I have in mind particularly the adoption of the principle of vicarious liability of employers for the delicts of their employees;[4] the creation by statute of rights of contribution between joint wrongdoers, and to apportionment of damages in the case of contributory negligence;[5] the limitation of liability by the concept of legal causation, or 'remoteness';[6] the development of liability for psychiatric injury in the form of 'nervous shock';[7] and, last but not least, the introduction, as in other industrialized countries, of statutory compensation schemes for the victims of industrial[8] and road traffic accidents.[9] Space constraints unfortunately preclude discussion of these topics in this paper.

The main reason for the delay in rounding off the process of development of the Aquilian action—and many would argue that the process is still far from complete—is the extraordinarily strong influence exerted by English law in this field at the turn of the century. This is an historical irony of the first order, given the ancient pedigree of the Aquilian action and the fact that the English tort of negligence was then hardly into its infancy. Be that as it may, the then prevalent tendency to rely on English rather than Roman-Dutch authorities for guidance in developing the law was strongly reinforced in the area of delict by the influence of Robin McKerron, Vinerian scholar and first full-time professor of law at the University of the Witwatersrand, whose *Law of Delicts in South Africa*[10] soon became the leading textbook in the field. McKerron's approach was openly spelled out

[4] See *Mkize v. Martens* 1914 AD 382. For a recent exposition of the law in this regard see J. Neethling, J. M. Potgieter, P. J. Visser, *Law of Delict* (2nd edn., 1993), 352 sqq.

[5] Apportionment of Damages Act 34 of 1956.

[6] Historically, three main tests for determining legal causation have vied for recognition by the courts: the 'direct consequences' test, the 'reasonable foreseeability' test, and the 'adequate cause' test. The Appellate Division has recently refused to accept any one test as determinative of the issue on its own, preferring a more flexible approach which takes into consideration all the traditional tests as well as policy factors. See *Smit v. Abrahams* 1994 (4) SA 1 (A); *International Shipping Co(Pty) Ltd v. Bentley* 1990 (1) SA 680 (A); and in the context of criminal law *S. v. Mokgethi* 1990 (1) SA 32 (A). On the distinction between factual and legal causation see *Minister of Police v. Skosana* 1977 (1) SA 31 (A), 34; Jonathan Burchell, *Principles of Delict* (1993), 114 sqq.

[7] See esp. *Bester v. Commercial Union Versekeringsmaatskappy van Suid-Afrika Bpk* 1973 (1) SA 769 (A). For general expositions see Neethling/Potgieter/Visser (n. 4), 277 sqq.; Burchell (n. 6), 59 sqq.; and for the earlier cases McKerron (n. 2), 154 sqq.

[8] Workmen's Compensation Act 30 of 1941, now repealed and replaced by the Compensation for Occupational Injuries and Diseases Act 130 of 1993.

[9] Motor Vehicle Insurance Act 29 of 1942, subsequently repealed and replaced by the Compulsory Motor Vehicle Insurance Act 56 of 1972; in turn repealed and replaced by the Motor Vehicle Accidents Act 84 of 1986, now largely superseded by the Multilateral Motor Vehicle Accidents Fund Act 93 of 1989. See Burchell (n. 6), 15 sqq.

[10] R. G. McKerron, *The Law of Delicts in South Africa* (1st edn., 1933). The 7th and final edition of this work appeared in 1971.

by himself in the preface to his book: in attempting to expound the principles of liability for civil wrongdoing in South Africa, he sought assistance
from English and American court decisions and textbooks, rather than from
the Roman and Roman-Dutch writers, since 'so much of the law of delicts
has been worked out only in comparatively recent times that in this branch
of the law the old authorities afford little or no guidance'.[11]

Given the tensions in South African law and society in the first half of this
century, McKerron's approach was bound to elicit a strong reaction from
those lawyers who fiercely resisted the steady encroachment of English law;
and it certainly did so, mainly in a series of publications by McKerron's chief
tormentor and antagonist, Professor Tom Price of the University of Cape
Town,[12] ably assisted on the Bench and off it[13] by the brilliant and sternly
individualistic Mr Justice 'Toon' van den Heever, and later by the authors
of a rival textbook in Afrikaans, Professors N. J. van der Merwe and P. J. J.
Olivier.[14] In consequence, the law of delict became one of the prime sites of
the *bellum juridicum* that raged between the 'purists', who adhered strictly to
Roman-Dutch principles, and the more English-oriented 'pragmatists'.[15] The
tone of this debate can be gathered from Van der Merwe's scathing review
of the sixth edition of McKerron's book.[16] Fortunately, however, the war of
words, unpleasant as it was, generated not only heat but also a great deal of
light, as I hope this paper will make clear.

II. SETTING THE SCENE: WRONGFULNESS AND FAULT AT THE TURN OF THE CENTURY

As suggested earlier, the most fundamental question facing the South
African courts at the turn of the century was whether the Aquilian law had

[11] See P. Q. R. Boberg, 'Oak Tree or Acorn?: Conflicting Approaches to our Law of Delict', (1966) 83 *SALJ* 150.

[12] T. W. Price, '*Animus Iniuriandi* in Defamation', (1949) 66 *SALJ* 4 sqq.; *idem*, 'The Conception of "Duty of Care" in the *Actio Legis Aquiliae*', (1949) 66 *SALJ* 171 sqq., 269 sqq.; *idem*, 'Nuisance: the *Canarvon Municipality* Case', (1949) 66 *SALJ* 377 sqq.; *idem*, 'Liability in Delict for "Acts of Omission" ', (1950) 13 *THRHR* 1 sqq., 261 sqq.; *idem*, 'Patrimonial Loss and Aquilian Liability', (1950) 13 *THRHR* 87 sqq.; *idem*, 'Aquilian Liability for Negligent Misstatements', (1950) 67 *SALJ* 138 sqq., 411 sqq., (1951) 68 *SALJ* 78 sqq.; *idem*, 'Volenti Non Fit Iniuria', (1952) 15 *THRHR* 60 sqq.; *idem*, 'The Role of *Casus Fortuitus, Vis Major* and Mistake in Actions for Delict', (1953) 16 *THRHR* 1 sqq.; *idem* 'Is the Rule in *Rylands v. Fletcher* part of Roman-Dutch Law?', (1953) 70 *SALJ* 381 sqq.; *idem*, 'Defence, Necessity and Acts of Authority', 1954 *Butterworth's South African LR* 1 sqq.; *idem*, 'Aquilian Liability and the "Duty of Care": A Return to the Charge', 1959 *Acta Juridica* 120 sqq.; *idem*, 'Aquilian Liability for "Acts of Omission" ', 1962 *Acta Juridica* 76 sqq.

[13] F. P. van den Heever, *Aquilian Damages in South African Law*, vol. I (1945).

[14] N. J. van der Merwe, P. J. J. Olivier, *Die Onregmatige Daad in die Suid-Afrikaanse Reg*. The 1st edn. of this work appeared in 1966, the 6th (and latest) in 1989.

[15] See Boberg, (1966) 83 *SALJ* 150 sqq.

[16] N. J. van der Merwe, (1965) 28 *THRHR* 160 sqq.

developed to the point where all harm culpably caused was *prima facie* wrongful. In other words: was it sufficient for the plaintiff merely to prove the elements of damage, causation, and fault, thereby casting upon the defendant the burden of justifying his conduct? Or did he have to establish at the outset that the conduct complained of was not only culpable but also wrongful, an *iniuria* in the eyes of the law?

These questions raise the difficult issue of the interrelationship between the concepts of wrongfulness and fault, a problem that was by no means resolved at the beginning of this century and one which therefore runs through all the developments outlined in this paper.

As Van Aswegen has pointed out,[17] neither in Roman law, nor in Roman-Dutch law, nor in early South African law was any clear and systematic distinction drawn between wrongfulness and fault. The element of *iniuria* had originally meant simply 'contrary to law' (*non iure*), but had in the classical period of Roman law already come to be submerged under the concept of *culpa*, so that for all practical purposes the delict of *damnum iniuria datum* had become *damnum culpa datum*.[18] At this stage *culpa* was understood in a wide sense: had the defendant behaved as he was allowed by law to behave in the circumstances?[19] Given this meaning, *culpa* could easily cover the same ground as the earlier *iniuria* concept. By the time of Justinian, however, *culpa* had acquired the narrower, more technical meaning it still bears today: had the defendant conducted himself as a *bonus paterfamilias* would have done in the circumstances? This development paved the way for the modern distinction between wrongfulness and fault as distinct elements of liability, since the new criterion of *culpa* hardly provided a suitable test for determining issues of wrongfulness.[20] It is not surprising, therefore, that both under Justinian and later in the *usus modernus* of Roman law the original concept of *iniuria* still lurked in the background, with the result that wrongfulness remained an essential ingredient of Aquilian liability, even though as a matter of terminology it was not clearly distinguished from fault.[21]

The foundations of the modern, generalized law of delict were laid in the seventeenth century by Grotius and Pufendorf, foremost amongst the natural lawyers, who adopted as their fundamental proposition the idea that all harm caused culpably ought to be made good.[22] To what extent this

[17] See Ch. 17 above by Van Aswegen, Section III 3.; see also generally B. Beinart, 'The Relationship of *Iniuria* and *Culpa* in the *Lex Aquilia*', in: *Studi in Onore di Vicenzo Arangio-Ruiz*, vol. I (1953), 279 sqq.; *idem*, 'Culpa in Omittendo', (1949) 12 *THRHR* 141 sqq.

[18] See Reinhard Zimmermann, *The Law of Obligations: Roman Foundations of the Civilian Tradition* (1990, reprint 1993), 1004 sqq.; Beinart, (1949) 12 *THRHR* 148 sqq.; Van den Heever (n. 13), 38.

[19] Zimmermann (n. 18), 1006 sq.; Beinart, (1949) 12 *THRHR* 161.

[20] Zimmermann (n. 18), 1007.   [21] Ibid. 1027 sqq.

[22] Ibid. 1032.

principle was accepted in the law of Holland is disputed,[23] but it received full recognition in the famous general clause (article 1382) of the French *code civil*, which made *culpa* or *faute* the all-embracing criterion of liability.[24] Significantly, although the general clause fails to distinguish between wrongfulness and fault, French legal science treats both concepts as being implicit in the notion of *faute*.[25] In Germany wrongfulness came strongly to the fore in § 823 I BGB (which lists the interests legally protected against culpable invasion), a clear reflection of the desire of the nineteenth-century pandectists to return to the more limited scope of Aquilian liability in Roman law.[26]

So much for the civil law. In late nineteenth-century England, by contrast, the law relating to the compensation of negligently inflicted harm was in a relatively undeveloped state. Negligence had by then come to be defined in terms of the conduct of the hypothetical 'reasonable man',[27] but remained essentially an element of liability in the tort of trespass on the case, rather than an independent tort in its own right.[28] There was no general principle of liability at this stage, merely a list of situations derived from precedent, where the law recognized the existence of a duty to take care: the 'categories of negligence'. In *Heaven v. Pender* Brett MR made a famous attempt to generalize the duty of care by formulating a general principle of liability for negligence based on reasonable foreseeability of the harm;[29] but this doctrine, while hailed by Street as 'the most powerful judicial effort which has ever been put forth to generalise the theory of negligence',[30] was

---

[23] See n. 2 above.

[24] Similar provisions were enacted in the Italian, Spanish, and Austrian codes, and in the Swiss Code of Obligations: see F. H. Lawson, 'The Duty of Care in Negligence: A Comparative Study', (1947) 22 *Tulane LR* 111, 118; F. P. Walton, 'Delictual Responsibility in the Modern Civil Law (More Particularly in the French Law) as compared with the English Law of Torts', (1933) 49 *LQR* 70, 78.

[25] Zimmermann (n. 18), 998, fn. 6, 1036, fn. 248; Lawson, (1947) 22 *Tulane LR* 118; Beinart, (1949) 12 *THRHR* 157.

[26] Zimmermann (n. 18), 1036.

[27] 'Negligence is the omission to do something which a reasonable man, guided upon those considerations which ordinarily regulate the conduct of human affairs, would do, or doing something which a prudent and reasonable man would not do' (*per* Alderson B, in *Blyth v. Company of Proprietors of the Birmingham Waterworks* (1856) 11 Exch 781, 784, 156 ER 1047, 1049).

[28] Cf. Percy H. Winfield, 'The History of Negligence in the Law of Torts', (1926) 42 *LQR* 184, 195 sqq.; Zimmermann (n. 18), 908 sqq.

[29] (1883) 11 QBD 503 (CA) 509: 'whenever one person is by circumstances placed in such a position with regard to another that every one of ordinary sense who did think would at once recognise that if he did not use ordinary care and skill in his own conduct with regard to those circumstances he would cause danger of injury to the person or property of the other, a duty arises to use ordinary care and skill to avoid such danger'.

[30] Thomas Atkins Street, *The Foundations of Legal Liability: a presentation of the Theory and Development of the Common Law*, vol. I (1906), 93, cited by Innes CJ in *Cape Town Municipality v. Paine* 1923 AD 207, 216.

not favourably received by other judges,[31] and ten years later was explained by its author himself in a sense that restricted its operation to cases involving the element of physical proximity.[32] Lord Atkin's 'neighbour principle', formulated nearly fifty years later in the well known case of *Donoghue v. Stevenson*,[33] met with a somewhat better reception, but even today English law favours an 'incremental' approach based on precedent over one based on a sweeping general principle.[34]

III. WEATHERING THE ENGLISH ONSLAUGHT: *CULPA* REMAINS THE KEY TO COMPENSATION

In a series of important cases decided in the early part of this century the South African courts were called upon to determine the liability of an owner of property to a person who ventured onto the premises and suffered injury as a result. Rereading those cases one is struck anew by the force of the pressure then being exerted on the courts to abandon the *lex Aquilia* in favour of the very much more detailed—and rigid—rules of the English common law. Fortunately, as we shall see, the courts managed by and large to resist these pressures—thanks in no small part to the wisdom, learning and vigilance of Sir James Rose Innes—and insisted on retaining the flexibility of the Aquilian principles of liability. In so doing they ensured that *culpa* would remain the key to compensation, at least in cases involving negligent acts that caused injury to person or property.

---

[31] In *Heaven v. Pender* (n. 29) 516 Cotton and Bowen LJJ expressed their unwillingness to concur with the Master of the Rolls in laying down the general principle favoured by him.

[32] *Le Lievre and Dennes v. Gould* [1893] 1 QB 491 (CA) 497. See too the remarks of A. L. Smith LJ, 504.

[33] *M'Alister (or Donoghue) v. Stevenson* [1932] AC 562, 580: 'You must take reasonable care to avoid acts or omissions which you can reasonably foresee would be likely to injure your neighbour. Who, then, in law is my neighbour? The answer seems to be—persons who are so closely and directly affected by my act that I ought reasonably to have them in contemplation as being so affected when I am directing my mind to the acts or omissions which are called in question.' On which see, most recently, Franco Ferrari and Reinhard Zimmermann, (1993) 1 *Zeitschrift für Europäisches Privatrecht* 354 sqq., 435 sqq.

[34] Cf. the rejection of Lord Wilberforce's 'two-stage' test for the existence of a duty of care (formulated in *Anns v. Merton London Borough Council* [1978] AC 728 (HL) 751 sq.) by Brennan J in the Australian case of *Council of the Shire of Sutherland v. Heyman* (1985) 157 CLR 424, 481:'It is preferable . . . that the law should develop novel categories of negligence incrementally and by analogy with established categories, rather than by a massive extension of a *prima facie* duty of care restrained only by indefinable "considerations which ought to negative, or to reduce or limit the scope of the duty or the class of person to whom it is owed" '. The House of Lords has in a number of recent cases expressly favoured this incremental approach of Brennan J: see e.g. *Caparo Industries Plc v. Dickman* [1990] 2 AC 605 (HL) 618, 633 sq.; *Murphy v. Brentwood District Council* [1991] 1 AC 398 (HL) 461. See further Dale Hutchison, 'Murphy's Law: The Recovery of Pure Economic Loss in the Tort of Negligence', (1995) 6 *Stellenbosch LR* 3 sqq.

1. Of invitees, licencees, and mere trespassers

At common law in England, prior to the enactment of the Occupier's Liability Act of 1957, the extent of the duty imposed upon an owner or occupier of premises depended upon an elaborate classification of visitors.[35] At the top end of the scale was a visitor who entered upon the premises in pursuance of a contract with the occupier; to such a person the occupier was deemed to warrant that the premises were as safe as reasonable care and skill could make them. Next came the 'invitee', one who entered on business of interest both to himself and the occupier; in his case the occupier's duty was to prevent damage from any unusual danger of which he was or should have been aware. Below that came the 'licencee', one who entered with the occupier's permission but sharing no common interest with him; to him the duty was merely to warn of any concealed danger or trap of which the occupier had actual knowledge. Finally, there was the trespasser, to whom no duty of care was owed, the occupier being obliged merely to refrain from causing him deliberate or reckless harm.

In *Fleming v. Rietfontein Deep Gold Mining Co Ltd*[36] the plaintiff had in the dark inadvertently strayed from a public road on which he was walking and had fallen down an unfenced shaft which the defendant mining company had sunk at a distance of eighty-two feet from the road. Before the Transvaal Supreme Court it was contended by Advocate Solomon that, as a trespasser on the land, the plaintiff was not entitled to recover damages for negligence.[37] According to the English cases, he argued, an owner of land adjoining a highway, who made an excavation on his land, was not responsible for injury to road-users unless the excavation was so close to the road as to constitute a public nuisance.[38] Innes CJ rejected this argument. After discussing at some length the English and American cases the learned judge held that according to Roman-Dutch law as prevailing in Southern Africa the true test of liability was not whether the excavation constituted a public nuisance but rather whether there was *culpa* on the part of the person who made the excavation. That in turn, he said, relying on Roman and Roman-Dutch texts, depended upon whether or not a reasonably careful man could have foreseen that an accident was likely to happen.[39]

The same approach was adopted in *Skinner v. Johannesburg Turf Club*,[40] where a horse belonging to Skinner was killed when it fell into a hole on the club's ground. In the Court *a quo* Smith J had held that since Skinner

---

[35] See W. V. H. Rogers, *Winfield and Jolowicz on Tort* (14th edn., 1994), 224 sqq.
[36] 1905 TS 111. [37] 112, 114.
[38] The cases cited were *Hardcastle v. South Yorkshire Railway & River Dun Co* (1859) 28 LJ, Exch 139, 157 ER 761; *Binks v. South Yorkshire Railway & River Dun Co* (1862) 32 LJ QB 26, 122 ER 92.
[39] 1905 TS 111, 116 sq.: Mason and Curlewis JJ concurred. [40] 1907 TS 852.

had used the ground for his own benefit and with the club's permission he was a mere licensee and thus not entitled to damages for negligence.[41] Again Innes CJ rejected this slavish adherence to English law. Liability depended upon *culpa*, he said, which was the failure to observe the standard of care of a *diligens paterfamilias* ('the Roman equivalent of the English "reasonable man" ').[42] *Culpa* corresponded almost exactly with the English concept of negligence, but he used the Latin word 'because it is a term appropriate to the civil law; and the definition of *culpa* and its qualities have been carefully examined by Roman lawyers'.[43] It was unnecessary in the present case to decide whether Southern African law recognized all the fine distinctions drawn in the English cases, but those distinctions seemed to rest on the same underlying principle that applied in the civil law, because the relationship between the parties was clearly relevant to the question of how the *diligens paterfamilias* would have conducted himself in the circumstances.[44]

The principle in *Fleming*'s case was applied by the Transvaal Provincial Division in *Hammerstrand v. Pretoria Municipality*[45] and received the seal of approval of the Appellate Division in *Transvaal and Rhodesian Estates Ltd v. Golding*;[46] in both these cases also the plaintiff had fallen at night into an unfenced hole or ditch adjacent to a public road.

One might have expected this finally to put paid to the attempt to introduce the English distinctions into our law, but such was the pressure exerted at the time to follow English law that the matter had once again to be taken all the way to the Appellate Division in *Farmer v. Robinson Gold Mining Company Ltd*.[47] This time the plaintiff was a wilful trespasser—a six-and-a-half year-old boy who had ventured from a public park onto mining land, climbed through a barbed-wire fence and been seriously injured while playing on a large mechanical wheel connected to mining apparatus: in the Court *a quo* Ward J thought this fact made all the difference. In a judgment devoted almost entirely to a discussion of English authorities, he said that while *Fleming*'s case might show that South African law was wider than the English law with regard to the placing of traps near a public way, 'our law does not go to the extent of saying that a piece of machinery fenced off by a substantial barbed-wire fence adjoining a highway is a trap or a nuisance'.[48]

The approach of the Appellate Division was very different. Delivering the leading judgment of the Court,[49] Innes CJ refused to be drawn into a dis-

---

[41] *Skinner v. Johannesburg Turf Club* 1907 TH 186.   [42] 1907 TS 852, 858.
[43] 857.   [44] 859: Solomon and Curlewis JJ concurred.
[45] 1913 TPD 374 (De Villiers JP, Bristowe and Gregorowski JJ concurring).
[46] 1917 AD 18 (Innes CJ, Solomon and C. G. Maasdorp JJA concurring).
[47] 1917 AD 501.
[48] 513 (the judgment of Ward J in the Witwatersrand Local Division is reported in 1917 AD 502 sqq.).
[49] Solomon and C. G. Maasdorp JJA delivered separate, concurring judgments.

cussion of the English cases because, valuable as they were, the principles of South African law were adequate for the solution of the present enquiry, 'and we must be guided by them'.[50] Once again he spelled out those principles, with reference to examples from the *Digest*, and said that the reason why as a general rule an owner is not obliged to be careful in the case of a trespasser is that he cannot be reasonably expected to anticipate his presence. If in any instance a reasonable man would anticipate such presence, however, then the owner should observe towards the trespasser due and reasonable care. The measure of care would depend on all the circumstances, including the fact that a trespasser could be expected to exercise greater circumspection than a person using his accustomed rights. In consequence, South African law probably did not differ much in its final results from English law: but, the learned judge added, as instructive as the English decisions were, '. . . we will do well . . . to adhere to the general principles of the Aquilian law, to leave the enquiry as elastic as possible, and to determine on the facts of each case whether or not there has been *culpa*'.[51]

It should be noted that this was not a chauvinistic rejection of the English law: Innes CJ recognized the value of referring to English sources for comparative purposes, but rightly felt bound to apply the Roman-Dutch law, and stressed the advantages in terms of legal flexibility in doing so. It is also worth noting that, even as he was resisting the encroachment of English law, the learned judge himself was almost unconsciously allowing the English terminology of a 'duty to take care' to creep into his formulation of Aquilian principles. 'It is the right of every man', he said, 'that others shall not by their negligence injure him in his person or property; and that involves the duty on each to exercise due and reasonable care'.[52] As Price pointed out, however, this use of the word duty was still relatively innocuous, since it was synonymous with the basic definition of culpability: 'the duty is a general duty not to behave culpably'.[53] Nevertheless, as we shall see, the seed had been sown of a doctrine that was to give rise to much contention in South African law

2. No law against letting a tumble-down house?

The final formulation of the *culpa* principle, and one which gave considerably more prominence to the notion of a duty to take care, was given, appropriately, by Innes CJ in what became the leading case of *Cape Town Municipality v. Paine*.[54] Once again an attempt was made to introduce a restrictive rule from English law, and once again the attempt was resisted. The defendant municipality was the owner of athletic grounds which it leased to an organization for sporting purposes; the plaintiff, a spectator at

---

[50] 519.   [51] 523.   [52] 521. Maasdorp JA spoke in similar terms at 545.
[53] Price, 1959 *Acta Juridica* 164.   [54] 1923 AD 207.

an athletics meeting held on the grounds, suffered serious injury when a plank on the grandstand gave way as he stood upon it, causing him to fall through the opening. In the ensuing action for damages, counsel for the municipality relied heavily upon English decisions (particularly *Cavalier v. Pope*[55]) to the effect that a landlord who lets property in a dangerous state is not liable to the tenant's customers or guests for accidents happening during the term since 'there is no law against letting a tumble-down house'.[56] The only English case causing difficulty was *Heaven v. Pender*,[57] but the *dicta* of Brett MR in that case had subsequently been considerably narrowed down.[58]

Innes CJ would have none of this. South African law applied a wider test of liability than was recognized by the English courts, and the much criticized doctrine of Brett MR in *Heaven v. Pender* was in accordance with the principles of Roman-Dutch law:[59]

It has repeatedly been laid down in this Court that accountability for unintentioned (*sic*) injury depends upon *culpa*, the failure to observe that degree of care which a reasonable man would have observed. I use the term reasonable man to denote the *diligens paterfamilias* of Roman law, the average prudent person. Every man has a right not to be injured in his person or property by the negligence of another, and that involves a duty on each to exercise due and reasonable care. The question whether, in any given situation a reasonable man would have foreseen the likelihood of harm and governed his conduct accordingly, is one to be decided in each case upon a consideration of all the circumstances. Once it is clear that the danger would have been foreseen and guarded against by the *diligens paterfamilias*, the duty to take care is established, and it only remains to ascertain whether it has been discharged.[60]

These remarks, however, were subject to the important proviso that 'mere omission did not under the *lex Aquilia* constitute *culpa*; it only did so when connected with prior conduct'.[61] It is to that significant qualification that our attention must now turn.

IV. OMISSIONS: THE ELEMENT OF *INIURIA* RAISES ITS HEAD

If *culpa* was to be the all-embracing criterion of liability, one might logically have expected it to apply equally to all forms of conduct, whether acts of

---

[55] 1906 AC 428 (HL).

[56] 430, *per* Lord Macnaghten, quoting with approval the following statement of Erle CJ in *Robbins v. Jones* (1863) 15 CBNS 221: 'A landlord who lets a house in a dangerous state is not liable to the tenant's customers or guests for accidents happening during the term: for, fraud apart, there is no law against letting a tumble-down house; and the tenant's remedy is upon his contract, if any.'

[57] (1883) 11 QBD 503 (CA). See n. 29 above.   [58] See n. 32 and text thereto.

[59] 1923 AD 207, 216.   [60] 216 sq.   [61] 217.

commission or of omission.[62] After all, if the *diligens paterfamilias* would have foreseen and guarded against the harm flowing from the omission, how could it be denied that the person who failed to take equally efficacious measures was guilty of *culpa*?

Indeed, this was the view taken by the natural lawyers such as Grotius,[63] and in Roman-Dutch law it attracted the support of Matthaeus.[64] Voet, on the other hand, adhered to the more individualistic view of the Romans that it would be unjust to impose liability for the slightest *culpa in omittendo*. To take steps to preserve the property of one's neighbour might be the action of a *bonus vir*, he argued, but the law could not impose liability for a failure to do so. Only if the omission was connected with a prior act of commission, or if there had been an express assumption of a duty and a subsequent failure to fulfil it, could there be liability under the *lex Aquilia*.[65]

Which of these divergent opinions would the South African courts adopt? The colonial courts of the nineteenth century had appeared to embrace Voet's view by drawing a clear distinction between misfeasance and nonfeasance: a public authority that was statutorily empowered but not obliged to construct or repair a road might be held liable for damage caused by doing the job badly, but not for damage flowing from a mere failure to do the job at all.[66] This principle owed more to the influence of English law than to any careful study of the Roman-Dutch sources, however.

1. The doctrine of 'prior conduct'

In *Halliwell v. Johannesburg Municipal Council*,[67] the first in a long series of 'municipality' cases decided this century,[68] the Appellate Division was given an opportunity to pronounce on the matter. The plaintiff was injured when his horse slipped on certain cobbles laid by the defendant municipality along the edge of tramlines in a public street. The cobbles were properly laid but had become dangerously slippery because, though originally rough, they had over the years worn smooth. In upholding the claim for damages the Appellate Division established a doctrine on liability for omissions that was to prove very troublesome in the years to follow.

The weight of civilian authority, said Innes ACJ in his leading judgment,[69] was in favour of the view that Aquilian liability was always

---

[62] Cf. Beinart, (1949) 12 *THRHR* 156 sq.

[63] Hugo Grotius, *De Jure Belli ac Pacis,* 2, 17, 1. See also *idem, Inleiding tot de Hollandsche Rechtsgeleertheyd,* 3, 32, 12.

[64] Antonius Matthaeus II, *De Criminibus,* 48, 5, 6.

[65] Johannes Voet, *Commentarius ad Pandectas,* 9, 2, 3.

[66] See Van Aswegen, Ch. 17 above, III 11, *(a)*.   [67] 1912 AD 659.

[68] These cases are listed and discussed by P. Q. R. Boberg, *The Law of Delict,* vol. I, *Aquilian Liability* (1984), 221 sq.

[69] 1912 AD 659, 670 sqq. Maasdorp JP concurred; Laurence and Wessels JJ delivered separate concurring judgments; Solomon J dissented on the facts.

attributable to some act of a positive nature, and that a mere omission, unconnected with any positive act, was insufficient. As Grueber[70] had shown, the apparent instances in the *Digest* of liability for an omission were all explicable on the basis of a prior act of commission which created a duty of taking positive action to prevent injury to others; and the failure to discharge that duty was the *culpa* upon which liability rested.

The same principle was recognized in the law of Holland, said Innes, for the difference of opinion between Voet and Matthaeus was more apparent than real: both accepted that liability for an omission could exist only where there was a legal duty to take positive action.[71] The earlier South African cases had drawn a clear distinction between misfeasance and nonfeasance. Although they had established a principle of municipal immunity for failure to repair a road, in none of these cases had the injury complained of been caused by previous acts of construction, as in this case; the principle accordingly needed to be qualified. Such qualification was to the effect that if a public authority, by constructing or repairing a road, introduced a new source of danger that would not otherwise have existed, then it was obliged to take due steps to guard against that danger. An omission to do so would entail liability since the omission would be connected with a prior positive act that created the danger; and the fault would be one not of mere omission, but of omission and commission combined.[72]

2. 'Let those sweat who cannot abide an antinomy'

This doctrine of 'prior conduct' established by *Halliwell's* case might have seemed reasonable at the time but it gave rise to a great deal of discontent. The main complaint was that it led to an artificial search in many cases for some prior act of commission on which to establish liability when the real reason for the decision clearly lay elsewhere. A good illustration of this tendency is to be found in the case of *South African Railways and Harbours v. Estate Saunders.*[73] The defendant railways had left a trailer at the store of a company to be unloaded and fetched later, in accordance with the usual practice followed by the parties. The servants of the company had unloaded the trailer, pushed it onto an adjacent road, and informed the defendant by telephone that the trailer was ready for collection. On this occasion the railways failed to collect the trailer with the result that it remained on the road after dark without lights. A bus owned by the plaintiff having collided with the trailer, the railways were held liable in damages for negligently failing to remove it, or at least give warning of its presence, when they were informed of its position. According to Stratford JA, this liability was based

---

[70] E. Grueber, *The Roman Law of Damage to Property, being a Commentary on the Title of the Digest Ad Legem Aquiliam* (IX.2) (1886), 208 sqq.
[71] 1912 AD 659, 671 sq.   [72] 673.   [73] 1931 AD 276.

on the prior conduct of the defendant in allowing the trailer to pass out of its custody on the terms and understandings set out above![74]

Another serious difficulty was encountered in determining when the prior conduct created a new source of danger. In *Municipality of Bulawayo v. Stewart*,[75] for example, the laying of a rainwater pipe under the surface of a public footpath was held to satisfy this test, while in *Cape Town Municipality v. Clohessy*[76] the paving of a footpath with tar was held not to satisfy it. In both cases natural erosion of the surface over time had caused the plaintiff to trip and injure herself while walking along the path at night.

Not surprisingly, academic commentators were unimpressed by the results of all this judicial effort. Van den Heever, himself a leading judge, was particularly scathing:[77]

This doctrine of 'previous conduct' is not a harmless shibboleth; it has caused confusion and led our courts to give irreconcilable decisions unless we find the reconciliation in pure casuistry. With all diligence the Municipality builds a road; a portion is paved with cobblestones, the rest with tar macadam. Under the surface of the road they lay a water pipe. Proper materials are used and there is no negligence in construction. In the course of time the cobblestones wear smooth and two potholes develop in the macadam, one directly over the pipe, the other away from it. I slip on the cobblestones and break my leg: the Municipality is liable. I stumble in the pothole away from the pipe and break a leg: the Municipality is not liable. I step into the pothole in which there is a pipe; it trips me and I break a leg: the Municipality is liable. Liability flows from *culpa*, yet is made to hang on the peg of lawful conduct previous to the omission. One can only say with Leibnitz: 'Let those sweat who cannot abide an antinomy'.

According to Van den Heever,[78] whose views were largely shared by Price,[79] the distinction between acts of commission and those of omission was more apparent than real, and both were governed by the same Aquilian principles. In the absence of a statutory or contractual duty to act, an omission would be culpable only if a reasonable man would have taken positive action in the circumstances. In applying that test, however, one had to bear in mind the 'healthy individualism' accepted by our legal system, which was reflected in the view of the average, reasonable citizen that 'a person can never be blameworthy for minding his own business'.[80]

To some extent this criticism was misconceived. It proceeded from a fundamental assumption that in modern law *culpa* had become the all-embracing

---

[74] For criticism of this reasoning and various suggestions as to the true basis of the decision see e.g. McKerron (n. 2), 15; *idem*, (1932) 49 *SALJ* 186; Price, 1962 *Acta Juridica* 77 sq.; Boberg (n. 68), 224 sq.

[75] 1916 AD 357.

[76] 1922 AD 4. Cf. *De Villiers v. Johannesburg Municipality* 1926 AD 401.

[77] Van den Heever (n. 13), 41 sq.   [78] 37 sqq.

[79] Price, (1950) 13 *THRHR* 1 sqq.; *idem, 1962 Acta Juridica* 76 sqq.

[80] Van den Heever (n. 13) 37.

criterion of liability,[81] and that the insistence on prior conduct was designed to satisfy the conduct element of Aquilian liability.[82] In fact, however, the courts were perpetuating an exception to the *culpa* principle by recognizing that there were still situations where, irrespective of the presence of fault, it might not be desirable or appropriate to impose liability.[83] In cases involving omission the failure to act was almost invariably deliberate, but that hardly settled the issue because the vital question was whether there was a legal duty to act in the circumstances.[84] In that inquiry the likely conduct of the hypothetical reasonable man was not altogether relevant. As Stratford JA put it in *Estate Saunders*:[85] 'We cannot invoke the view of the *diligens paterfamilias* as to what conceivably would be his sense of duty in a case of "mere omission"; in such a case it is decided that there is no duty and there can be, therefore, no neglect of a duty.'

In effect, the courts were tacitly recognizing the continued existence and need for wrongfulness as a distinct element of Aquilian liability, independent of and logically anterior to that of fault, or *culpa*. The long-dormant concept of *iniuria* was once again rearing its head. McKerron[86] seems to have been aware of this phenomenon, but the first writer clearly to articulate it in the field of omissions was Beinart.[87] Both recognized, however, that it was a mistake to make the wrongfulness of an omission depend entirely on the existence of a prior act of commission.[88] Other factors might also play an important role in determining whether or not there was a duty to act in the circumstances: for example, the fact that the alleged wrongdoer was in control of a dangerous thing,[89] occupied a public office,[90] or had a special relationship with another person.[91] Policy considerations were relevant too, as the municipality cases showed: it was widely believed,[92] and vir-

---

[81] 38; Price, (1950) 13 *THRHR* 28.

[82] Cf. Van der Walt, 1976 *TSAR* 101, 106; Boberg (n. 68), 215, 221.

[83] Van der Walt (n. 82).   [84] Cf. Beinart, (1949) 12 *THRHR* 158 sqq.

[85] *South African Railways and Harbours v. Estate Saunders* (n. 73), 284. But cf. Beinart (n. 84).

[86] In the earlier editions of his work on delict (nn. 2 and 10), McKerron clearly recognized wrongfulness as a separate element of Aquilian liability, independent of fault (see e.g. the 2nd edn. (1939), 30 sqq.). Surprisingly, however, he appears not to have regarded the problem of liability for omissions as turning on the question of wrongfulness: cf. his discussion of that topic, *ibid.* 22 sqq.

[87] Beinart (n. 84), 141 sqq. (a review article, discussing the thesis of J. C. C. van Loggerenberg, *Lex Aquilia en Nalate* (1947)).

[88] McKerron (2nd edn.) 26 sq.; Beinart (n. 84), 159.

[89] On this basis McKerron (n. 2), 20 sqq. explained cases such as *Cambridge Municipality v. Millard* 1916 CPD 724 and *Administrator, Cape v. Preston* 1961 (3) SA 562 (A), as well as the judgment of Steyn JA in *Silva's Fishing Corp (Pty) Ltd v. Maweza* 1957 (2) SA 256 (A), discussed below.

[90] Cf. *Cape of Good Hope Bank v. Fischer* (1886) 4 SC 368.

[91] Cf. *Mtati v. Minister of Justice* 1958 (1) SA 221 (A), as explained by McKerron (n. 2), 23 sq.

[92] See e.g. Beinart (n. 84), 166 sq.; McKerron (n. 2), 23.

tually conceded by the Appellate Division in *Moulang v. Port Elizabeth Municipality*,[93] that the general immunity of municipalities in relation to their failure to maintain or repair streets was originally based on the consideration that they could ill afford the expense of doing so. If that were no longer so, or if the practical results of the present law were seen on balance to be seriously unsatisfactory, said Schreiner JA, then the remedy lay in legislation.[94] At least in this particular branch of the law on omissions, it seemed, the courts were not prepared to reconsider their doctrine of prior conduct.

V. PURE ECONOMIC LOSS: THE SAME PATTERN EMERGES

The same reluctance to give a free reign to the *culpa* principle manifested itself, though usually in a less obvious manner, in cases involving claims for 'pure' economic loss, i.e. patrimonial loss unaccompanied by any physical injury to the person or property of the plaintiff.

1. A modern distinction?

The distinction between physical and purely financial harm does not feature prominently in the historical sources of our law. In the later period of Roman law an extended Aquilian action had been allowed in at least some situations where there was no physical injury as such, but the better view is that in all these cases there was still a physical dimension to the loss, in that the plaintiff had been deprived of some corporeal asset in his estate.[95] In the law and practice of seventeenth-century Holland, on the other hand, it certainly seems that claims for pure economic loss were sometimes allowed, but whether they were as freely entertained as those in respect of physical injury remains a matter for conjecture. At the very least, however, one can assert that no firm distinction was drawn in principle between the two forms of harm.[96]

This apparently liberal attitude to the recovery of economic loss reflected the view of the natural lawyers and was taken up in the French and Austrian codes,[97] but stood in marked contrast to the restrictive approach

---

[93] 1958 (2) SA 518 (A) 522.   [94] 523.

[95] See e.g. Zimmermann (n. 18), 1022 sqq.; F. H. Lawson, *Negligence in the Civil Law* (1950) 26 sq.; P. Pauw, 'Aanspreeklikheid vir "Suiwer Vermoënskade" in die Suid-Afrikaanse Reg', (1975) 8 *De Jure* 23, 25; *Administrateur, Natal v. Trust Bank van Afrika Bpk* 1979 (3) SA 824 (A) 830. Cf. G. Rotondi, *Scritti Guiridici*, vol. II (1922), 472, 474 sqq.; Price, (1949) 66 *SALJ* 173.

[96] See e.g. Pauw (n. 95); Susan Scott, 'Nalatige Wanvoorstelling as Aksiegrond in die Suid-Afrikaanse Reg', (1976) 39 *THRHR* 347, (1977) 40 *THRHR* 58 sqq., 165 sqq., 172 sqq.; Van den Heever (n. 13), 32; Price, (1950) 13 *THRHR* 89. Cf. McKerron (n. 2), 8.

[97] Zimmermann (n. 18), 1036, with reference to art. 1382 *code civil* and § 1295 ABGB.

adopted in nineteenth-century German[98] and English[99] law, where claims for economic loss were denied. The English attitude, in particular, was to have a marked influence on the development of this aspect of Aquilian liability in South Africa. That influence had already manifested itself strongly at the Cape in the late nineteenth century. In *Cape of Good Hope Bank v. Fischer*,[100] decided in 1886, the Cape Supreme Court had recognized in principle that Aquilian damages might be recovered in respect of a negligent misstatement causing pure economic loss; but eight years later, without so much as a backward glance at its earlier decision, the same Court held that, independently of contract, a false representation causing damage was not actionable unless made fraudulently.[101] It was surely no coincidence that in the intervening period the English courts had finally, after much debate, come to precisely the same conclusion.[102]

Against this background one might have expected the question of liability for negligently inflicted economic loss to have loomed large in the consciousness of the South African judges and writers at the beginning of this century; somewhat surprisingly, it did not. As we shall see, the question was seldom directly addressed and seems, when it was, to have been regarded to a large extent as merely one aspect of the more immediate problem of liability for negligent misstatements.

2. Avoiding the issue

One of the earliest cases in which the Appellate Division was given an opportunity to pronounce on the matter was *Union Government v. National Bank of South Africa Ltd*;[103] it is interesting to observe, first, how the issue was sidestepped, and secondly, how the element of wrongfulness reared its head again. The facts were rather complicated. A number of blank postal order forms had been stolen from the Roodepoort post office in 1914. No money could be paid out on such orders unless they had been signed and stamped with an official date-stamp by a postmaster. Some of the stolen forms found their way into the hands of S who happened to know I, the postmaster at Rietfontein. S persuaded I to allow him the use of his office

[98] Zimmermann (n. 18), 1036 sqq.; § 823 I BGB.

[99] Zimmermann (n. 18), 1038 sq.; P. S. Atiyah, 'Negligence and Economic Loss', (1967) 83 *LQR* 248 sqq.; Jane Stapleton, 'Duty of Care and Economic Loss: A Wider Agenda', (1991) 107 *LQR* 249 sqq. The foundation cases establishing this rule of non-recovery are *Cattle v. Stockton Waterworks Co* (1875) LR 10 QB 453; *Simpson & Co v. Thomson* (1877) 3 App Cas 279 (HL).

[100] (1886) 4 SC 368 (De Villiers CJ, Dwyer, and Smith JJ concurring).

[101] *Dickson and Co v. Levy* (1894) 11 SC 33 (De Villiers CJ, Buchanan, and Upington JJ concurring).

[102] See *Derry v. Peek* (1889) 14 App Cas 337 (HL), as interpreted by the Court of Appeal in *Le Lievre and Dennes v. Gould* [1893] 1 QB 491 (CA).

[103] 1921 AD 121.

on Sundays for study purposes; within the office I had left his official stamp on the counter, instead of under lock and key as post office regulations demanded. By these means S was enabled to stamp the orders in his possession, sign them with initials purporting to be those of an issuing postmaster, and dispose of them to third parties. Some of these falsified postal orders were in due course acquired by the defendant bank from its customers and presented for payment to the postal authorities. Later, when the falsity of the orders was discovered, the government demanded the return of the money wrongly paid out to the bank, suing with the *condictio indebiti*. The bank raised the defence of estoppel and also claimed damages in reconvention, calculated at the face value of the orders in question. Both the defence and the counterclaim were based on the alleged negligence of the plaintiff's employee I in allowing S access to the official stamp. For present purposes it is important to note that the counterclaim concerned loss of a purely economic nature.

The Appellate Division allowed the *condictio indebiti* and rejected the bank's defence and counterclaim for lack of proof of negligence and/or a sufficiently close causal connection between I's conduct and the bank's loss.[104] Innes CJ drew a distinction between 'abstract negligence', or negligence 'in the popular sense', and 'legal negligence'.[105] The latter presupposed a duty to take care in the circumstances, and by our law the test as to the existence of the duty centred on the foresight of a reasonable man. Significantly, however, Innes had some doubt whether that test applied in a case such as the present one:

There are innumerable cases in which South African courts have dealt with these questions by an application of the extended principles of the Aquilian Law. But, speaking generally, there will be found in them this element: that the injury to person or property relied upon was the direct result of the act done or the force set in motion. The obstruction placed in the road, the vehicle unskilfully driven, the fire carelessly kindled, in these and numerous other cases the injury was due to the direct operation of the act or agency complained of. Here the alleged injury did not result from the direct operation of the conduct complained of. It followed from the fact that the postmaster's conduct rendered possible a forgery which resulted in the acquisition by the bank for value of a false instead of a genuine order.[106]

He nonetheless assumed, without deciding, that the usual test applied, and on that basis held that there was no duty because the harm was not reasonably foreseeable. No doubt the postmaster I had been careless and in a

---

[104] Innes CJ based his decision on the absence of a duty of care, and hence of *culpa;* Solomon JA based his on the absence of an adequate causal connection; and Juta JA held that there was neither a duty, nor *culpa*, nor adequate causation of the loss. C. G. Maasdorp JA and J. E. R. de Villiers AJA concurred generally.

[105] 126 sqq.   [106] 129.

general sense negligent towards his employer, but there was no negligence in a legal sense because I owed no duty to the bank.[107]

Solomon JA's approach was similar. Negligence, in his view, was the neglect of a duty, 'and where there is no duty towards the party affected there can be no negligence'.[108] For Juta JA the question of whether a duty was owed to the bank was distinct from, and anterior to, the question of 'whether there was *culpa* under the ordinary principles of our law'.[109]

Despite the attempts to portray the problem in this case as essentially of legal causation, or remoteness, it is hard to avoid the conclusion that what really distinguished it from the other cases mentioned by Innes, and what troubled the judges, was that it involved a claim for pure economic loss.[110] It certainly cannot be denied that the English duty of care concept was suddenly given a new prominence in our law, and that it was made to serve the function performed in modern law by the requirement of wrongfulness.

3. A glimpse of the modern approach

Wrongfulness came to the fore again, and more openly, in *Matthews v. Young*,[111] decided the following year. The plaintiff had lost his job after being expelled from his trade union. Since the procedure followed in expelling him was irregular he managed to get a court order reinstating him as a member of the union; but he could not persuade his erstwhile employer to give him back his job. He therefore sued the members of the union council for the economic loss suffered as a result of the unlawful expulsion, and was successful in the Witwatersrand Local Division, but not on appeal.

Delivering the judgment of the Appellate Division,[112] De Villiers JA decided that the claim was 'an Aquilian action for patrimonial loss based upon *dolus*, an intentional violation of plaintiff's legal rights'.[113] The fact that the loss was purely economic in nature was not considered an insuperable stumbling block, since the Court accepted the *dictum* in *Cape of Good Hope Bank v. Fischer*[114] to the effect that in Roman-Dutch law the Aquilian action was extended to every kind of loss sustained in consequence of the wrongful acts of another. The real issue in this case was whether the defendants had acted wrongfully.

In the Court *a quo* Ward J had relied upon the statement by Bowen LJ in the English case of *Mogul Steamship Co Ltd v. McGregor, Gow and*

---

[107] 130.   [108] 134.   [109] 150.

[110] Cf. the remarks of Barry J in *Alliance Building Soc v. Deretitch* 1941 TPD 203, 209.

[111] 1922 AD 492.   [112] Innes CJ and Kotzé JA concurred.   [113] 505.

[114] See n. 1. Cf. Boberg (n. 68), 24, who regards this statement as being 'too wide for comfort' since it takes no account of the caution with which our courts approach claims for economic loss. See too R.G. McKerron, 'Liability for Mere Pecuniary Loss in an Action under the *Lex Aquilia*', (1973) 90 *SALJ* 1, 2; but cf. Price, (1950) 13 *THRHR* 89 sq.; Pauw (1975) 8 *De Jure* 27 sq.

Co[115] that intentionally to cause damage to another in his property or trade is actionable if without just cause or excuse. De Villiers JA would not accept this statement without qualification:

... I must point out, with great respect to so eminent a judge, that there is no onus upon a defendant until the plaintiff has proved that a legal right of his has been infringed. Under the *lex Aquilia* there is only an action for *damnum iniuria datum*— for pecuniary loss inflicted through a legal injury, and the defendant is not called upon to answer the plaintiff's case before the plaintiff has proved both the pecuniary loss and that it directly results from what is, in the eye of the law, an *iniuria*.[116]

The question, therefore, was whether any right of the plaintiff's had been infringed. Answering that question in the negative, De Villiers JA said:

In the absence of special legal restrictions a person is without doubt entitled to the free exercise of his trade, profession or calling, unless he has bound himself to the contrary. But he cannot claim an absolute right to do so without interference from another. Competition often brings about interference in one way or another about which rivals cannot legitimately complain. But the competition and indeed all activity must itself remain within lawful bounds. All a person can, therefore, claim is the right to exercise his calling without unlawful interference from others. Such an interference would constitute an *iniuria* for which an action under the *lex Aquilia* lies if it has directly resulted in loss.[117]

In casu, the defendants had purported to act as a properly constituted tribunal under the rules of the union and, since they had acted in a quasi-judicial capacity, they were not liable for any damage provided they acted *bona fide* and in the honest discharge of their duties, which indeed they had done.[118]

    Matthews v. Young is a particularly interesting case because in it we can see very clearly the foundations being laid for the modern approach to claims involving economic loss: whilst the nature of the harm does not in itself rule out the recovery of damages, it brings into play the element of wrongfulness, the presence of which, unlike in most cases involving physical injury, cannot be taken for granted, not even when the loss has been inflicted deliberately.[119]

4. Resort to the *actio iniuriarum*

Another notable feature of the case is its very clear and succinct summary of the scope and requirements of the *actio iniuriarum* and the *actio legis*

---

[115] (1889) 23 QBD 598 (CA) 613.   [116] 1922 AD 492, 507.   [117] Ibid.   [118] 509 sq.
[119] Cf. L. B. Behrmann, '*Perlman v. Zoutendyk*', (1941) 58 *SALJ* 25, 30, commenting on the decision in *Matthews'* case: 'We see, therefore, that where the injury in question is injury to property, other than direct physical injury, or injury to trade, it is not enough that the injury be foreseeable to be actionable, it must also involve the breach of a duty owed to the plaintiff.'

Aquiliae respectively.[120] How strange then, one might think cynically, that in *G. A. Fichardt Ltd v. The Friend Newspapers Ltd*,[121] decided just a few years earlier, the Appellate Division had managed to confuse the two actions in a way that ensured, quite coincidentally of course, that South African law on damages for negligent misstatements remained in line with that of English law.[122] During World War I, when anti-German feeling was running so high in parts of South Africa that German businesses were being attacked by unruly mobs, the defendant newspaper company published a report which implied that the plaintiff company was owned by Germans. Alleging that it had been 'seriously injured in its reputation in the way of its business and otherwise and had been and became exposed to the most serious risks affecting its property',[123] the plaintiff instituted an action for defamation, claiming general damages of £20,000.

Not surprisingly, the Appellate Division refused the claim on the grounds that it was not defamatory to call a person a German. At the same time, however, the Court suggested that had the action been differently framed, as one for patrimonial loss caused by a false but non-defamatory statement, it might well have succeeded, on proof of intention to injure the plaintiff in its business; for then the remedy would have taken the form, not of 'an ordinary action for defamation', but of the *actio iniuriarum*, for which proof of *animus iniuriandi* was an essential requirement.[124]

Why not the Aquilian action, one might well ask? Why this transparently erroneous[125] attempt to label a claim for patrimonial damages as the *actio iniuriarum*? The answer can only be that the Court was reluctant to recognize Aquilian liability for a negligent misstatement causing economic loss.[126] By labelling the action as the *actio iniuriarum* the Court was ensuring that only a deliberately false statement would be actionable; and it noted with satisfaction that in the result South African law on the point was in

---

[120] Cf. Boberg (n. 68), 24.   [121] 1916 AD 1.

[122] On the English law of the time on 'injurious falsehood' see *Ratcliffe v. Evans* [1892] 2 QB 524 (CA), referred to by the Court (7, 10).

[123] At 3 of the report.

[124] *Per* Innes CJ, 7. See too the judgment of Solomon JA, 11; and of De Villiers AJA, 13 (where it is said that, on proof of damage and *animus iniuriandi*, the plaintiff 'would have an *actio iniuriarum*, or the *actio doli*'). In modern South African law the action for defamation, though bearing the clear imprint of English influence, is still regarded as a specialized form of the *actio injuriarum*: see e.g. J. Neethling, *Persoonlikheidsreg* (3rd edn., 1991), 125 sqq.; Jonathan Burchell, *The Law of Defamation in South Africa* (1985), 13 sqq.; *Die Spoorbond v. South African Railways* 1946 AD 999, 1010 sq. (Schreiner JA). And see Ch. 19 by Jonathan Burchell, below.

[125] Cf. *Bredell v. Pienaar* 1924 CPD 203, 213; *Van Zyl v. African Theatres Ltd* 1931 CPD 61, 64 sq.; *Die Spoorbond v. South African Railways* 1946 AD 999, 1011; R. G. McKerron, 'Liability for Non-defamatory Statements', (1930) 47 *SALJ* 359, 361 sqq.; Price, (1950) 67 *SALJ* 412. In *Caxton Ltd v. Reeva Forman (Pty) Ltd* 1990 (3) SA 547 (A), 561A, the Appellate Division left open the question whether a claim for damages in such circumstances 'falls under the *actio iniuriarum* or is rather to be classed as Aquilian'.

[126] See n. 102 above, and the text thereto.

substantial agreement with the English law relating to injurious false-hoods.[127]

In *Bredell v. Pienaar*,[128] and again in *Van Zyl v. African Theatres Ltd*[129] Watermeyer J (who subsequently became Chief Justice of South Africa) noted with regret the confusion in the *Fichardt* case but felt himself bound as a court of first instance to accept the law there stated. In *Van Zyl's* case, however, he expressed the view that there was 'a good deal to be said in favour of liability for *negligent* misstatements which cause damage and for being able to recover damages on a wider basis than the accepted one'.[130]

5. Throwing caution to the winds

Three years later, in the now famous case of *Perlman v. Zoutendyk*,[131] Watermeyer overcame his reluctance to disregard the strong *obiter dicta* of the Appellate Division and gave effect to his personal view of the matter. The defendant Z, a sworn appraiser, had issued to X a certificate of valuation in terms of which he grossly over-valued land belonging to X. Acting in reliance on this certificate, the plaintiff P had advanced a considerable sum of money to X on security of the land. Almost all of this money had been lost when X became insolvent and the security proved worthless. P instituted an action for damages against Z, basing his claim squarely upon negligence. Z excepted to the declaration as disclosing no cause of action, relying in particular upon the English cases of *Derry v. Peek*[132] and *Le Lievre v. Gould*.[133]

In dismissing the exception, Watermeyer J said that those cases were very much in point but were neither binding upon him nor in accordance with the principles of Roman-Dutch law.[134] It had to be remembered that the English law of torts, while freely quoted and often followed in the South African courts, was not always a safe guide for solving a problem of Roman-Dutch law. This was due to a fundamental difference in outlook and general approach to new problems. Unlike other European systems, which took a general principle of liability as their starting point, English law asked whether the act causing the damage fell within one of the established torts, or categories of liability, and many writers denied the existence of any broad principle of liability. 'Roman-Dutch law', said Watermeyer,[135] 'approaches a new problem in the continental rather than the English way, because in general all damage caused unjustifiably (*iniuria*) is actionable, whether caused intentionally (*dolo*) or by negligence (*culpa*).' In any event, continued the judge,[136] the former narrow view of liability for negligence in

---

[127] 7. See n. 122 above.   [128] 1924 CPD 203, 213.   [129] 1931 CPD 61, 64 sq.
[130] 66.   [131] 1934 CPD 151 (Sutton J concurring).
[132] Note 102 above.   [133] Ibid.   [134] 1934 CPD 151, 154 sqq.
[135] 155.   [136] 159.

English law seemed to be falling into disfavour, as was evident from the (then) recent decision of the House of Lords in *Donoghue v. Stevenson*.[137] Indeed, Lord Atkin's proposed test for the existence of a duty to take care—the 'neighbour principle'—was expressed in terms remarkably similar to that used years before by Innes CJ in *Cape Town Municipality v. Paine*.[138]

Applying the broad principle in *Paine's* case to the facts stated in the plaintiff's declaration, Watermeyer J held that the defendant had owed the plaintiff a duty to take care because a reasonable appraiser in his position would have foreseen the possibility of the harm occurring.[139]

The decision in *Perlman's* case was highly controversial.[140] To some commentators[141] it was a long overdue affirmation of Roman-Dutch principle and a milestone in the development of Aquilian liability; to others like McKerron[142] it was 'the leading heresy in the law of delict' because it took the general test for a duty of care enunciated in *Cape Town Municipality v. Paine*[143] out of its context of physical injury to person or property and applied it without qualification to a claim for pure economic loss. Reasonable foreseeability of the harm was not the sole criterion in cases involving mere financial loss, argued McKerron: before considering the question of foreseeability the court had first to determine whether the defendant's conduct constituted a wrong to the plaintiff. In the case of conduct involving the risk of physical injury there was always a duty to take care, whereas in the case of conduct not involving such risk no rule could be laid down: '[I]n the absence of precedent, the court must decide the question by balancing the interest of the plaintiff against the social consequences of imposing liability, bearing in mind that the net of liability must not be spread so widely as to discourage human enterprise.'[144]

Despite this controversy the decision in *Perlman* wrought a significant change in the law: in subsequent provincial cases the courts, instead of denying liability for negligent statements, now sought merely to control its ambit,[145] being all too aware of the American judge Cardozo's warning about 'liability in an indeterminate amount for an indeterminate time to an

---

[137] See n. 33 above.   [138] See text to n. 60 above.

[139] 161 sq. It is worth noting, however, that when the matter subsequently came to trial Watermeyer J dismissed the claim on two grounds: lack of proof that the misstatement was the decisive cause of the loss, and contributory negligence on the part of the plaintiff—at that time still a complete defence (1934 CPD 328).

[140] Boberg (n. 68), 66.

[141] See e.g. A. M. Conradie, 'Verhaalbaarheid van Skade aan 'n Werkgewer toegebring deur die Onregmatige Besering van sy Werknemer', (1943) 7 *THRHR* 133, 146 sqq.; Price (1950) 67 *SALJ* 411, 414; Pauw, (1975) 8 *De Jure* 28; J. C. van der Walt, 1977 *TSAR* 269, 270.

[142] McKerron, (1973) 90 *SALJ* 1; *idem*, 'The Duty of Care in South African Law', (1952) 69 *SALJ* 189, 194 sq.; *idem*, (1954) 71 *SALJ* 316 sq. See also Behrmann, (1941) 58 *SALJ* 25, 27.

[143] See text to n. 60, above.   [144] McKerron, (1952) 69 *SALJ* 195.

[145] See *Fichardts Motors (Prop) Ltd v. Nienaber* 1936 OPD 221; *Alliance Building Soc v. Deretitch* 1941 TPD 203; *Western Alarm System (Pty) Ltd v. Coini & Co* 1944 CPD 271.

indeterminate class'.[146] However, the lack of uniformity in the approaches adopted made clarification by the Appellate Division an urgent necessity.

6. *Quot judices, tot sententiae*

An opportunity to dispel the uncertainty presented itself in *Herschel v. Mrupe*,[147] but was unfortunately squandered: each of the five judges of appeal expressed a different view on the matter, making it all but impossible to extract a *ratio decidendi* from the case.[148] The plaintiff claimed damages in respect of the wasted legal expenses incurred as a result of relying on incorrect information supplied by the defendant. By a majority of four to one[149] her claim was denied in the Appellate Division. The principle enunciated in *Perlman's* case was not rejected outright, however; on the contrary, all the judges accepted that in a suitable case liability might be imposed for economic loss caused by a negligent misstatement. The general sentiment was rather that the development of such liability had to be carefully controlled.[150] Even Centlivres CJ, in the minority, was prepared to assume that some limitation might have to be placed upon the application of the sweeping principle propounded by Watermeyer J in *Perlman v. Zoutendyk*.[151]

What is particularly striking about the case, in retrospect, is that only one of the judges expressly stated that the mechanism of limitation was to be found in the requirement of wrongfulness. According to Van den Heever JA, negligence was never the 'sole hook' upon which liability under the *lex Aquilia* depended; the requirement of *iniuria* 'remained throughout'.[152] When Innes CJ stated in *Cape Town Municipality v. Paine*[153] that every man has a right not to be injured in his person or property, he clearly used the word 'injure' in a pregnant sense to bear the same meaning as *iniuria* in the expression *damnum iniuria datum*.[154] So too, said Van den Heever, an essential element had obviously been left out of Lord Atkin's formulation of the neighbour principle in *Donoghue v. Stevenson*:[155] 'the act or omission

---

[146] *Ultramares Corp v. Touche* (1931) 255 NY 170, 174 NE 441, 444; 74 ALR 1139, 1145.

[147] 1954 (3) SA 464 (A).

[148] Cf. G. A. Mulligan, 'Quot judices, tot sententiae', (1954) 7 *SALJ* 321 sqq.; T. W. Price, 'Negligent Misrepresentation Again', 1955 *Butterworth's South African LR* 154, 156 ('As a precedent of any value, this case must be said to fail').

[149] Schreiner, Van den Heever, Hoexter, and Fagan JJA constituted the majority; Centlivres CJ dissented.

[150] In his book on *Aquilian Damages*, Van den Heever (n. 13), 33 sq. appeared to support the decision in *Perlman's* case, saying that 'Roman-Dutch law is rich in principle and is not fond of rules of thumb'. In *Herschel v. Mrupe* (supra, 488), however, he was more cautious: 'If the element of the appraiser's public capacity and function cannot be regarded as having been tacitly assumed in *Perlman's* case, I cannot agree with the reasoning of Watermeyer, J.'

[151] 1954 (3) SA 464 (A) 472.   [152] 487D-E. Cf. *Aquilian Damages* (n. 13), 35 sqq.

[153] See text to n. 60, above.   [154] 1954 (3) SA 464 (A) 484G.

[155] See n. 33 above.

complained of must be an *unlawful* incursion into another's economic sphere'.[156] The element of *iniuria* or wrongfulness was established by proving that the defendant had invaded rights recognized by the law as pertaining to the plaintiff.[157]

At first sight the approach of Schreiner JA in the other leading judgment delivered in this case seems very different. In his view[158] there was no justification for assuming the existence in South African law of an all-embracing general principle applicable whenever negligence was in issue. The principle enunciated in *Paine's* case was an authoritative guide to the decision of cases in the fields in which it was intended to apply, but ought not to be used to provide a universal major premise from which results might be deduced which were not in the contemplation of the judges who stated the principle. In view of the many different problems peculiar to negligence in word, as opposed to deed, it was doubtful whether any advantage was to be gained by treating words simply as another form of conduct to which the *lex Aquilia* applied, and then deciding what exceptions were to be admitted to the application of the *lex* in this field. A better approach, he thought, would be to enquire directly whether and in what circumstances it was convenient and right to allow recovery of loss caused by reliance on a negligent misstatement. On the assumption, which seemed to him reasonable, that there were cases where such an action would lie, even if the loss was purely economic, he knew of no more reasonable summary of the requirements for such an action than that given by Andrews J in the American case *International Products Company v. Erie Railway Company*:[159]

Liability in such cases arises only where there is a duty, if one speaks at all, to give the correct information. And that involves many considerations. There must be knowledge, or its equivalent, that the information is desired for a serious purpose; that he to whom it is given intends to rely and act upon it; that if false or erroneous, he will because of it be injured in person or property. Finally, the relationship of the parties, arising out of contract or otherwise, must be such that in morals and good conscience the one has the right to rely upon the other for information, and the other giving the information owes a duty to give it with care . . .

As commentators[160] have pointed out, though worded very differently the approach of Schreiner is fundamentally similar to that of Van der Heever. Considerations of policy pervade his reasoning, and the requirement of a special relationship between the parties (as formulated in the *Erie Railway*

---

[156] 1954 (3) SA 464 (A) 485A.   [157] 490A.
[158] 477 sqq.   [159] (1927) 244 NY 331; 56 ALR 1377, 1381.
[160] See e.g. Boberg (n. 68), 81 sq.; McKerron, (1954) 71 *SALJ* 321; K. Schwietering, (1957) 20 *THRHR* 56, 57; D. B. Hutchison, 'Negligent Statements: Why the Reluctance to Impose Liability?', (1978) 95 *SALJ* 515, 529 sq. The approach of Fagan JA was very different: he suggested that liability for negligent statements could be adequately controlled by exploiting to the full the elasticity inherent in the test of reasonableness for fault (1954 (3) SA 464 (A) 494).

Company case) is without doubt a test for wrongfulness.[161] McKerron recognized this very clearly:

Whichever approach is adopted it is clear that the real question which confronts the court in determining in a novel case such as the present whether or not liability should be imposed is one of judicial policy. Whether one says that liability depends upon the existence or non-existence of a duty or upon the invasion or non-invasion of a right, in neither case can the answer to the problem be solved solely by logic. The answer can only be reached 'by balancing the social interests involved in order to ascertain how far the defendant's duty and the plaintiff's right may justly and expediently be extended'. There is little doubt that both Schreiner JA and Van den Heever JA impliedly, if not expressly, recognized and accepted this position.[162]

7. Keeping the foot on the brake

In *Herschel v. Mrupe* more emphasis was placed on the nature of the conduct in question than on the nature of the loss. Two years later, however, in *Union Government v. Ocean Accident and Guarantee Corporation Ltd*,[163] the Appellate Division displayed an even more cautious attitude to a claim involving relational economic loss, or negligent interference with contractual relations. The appellant sought to recover the salary that it was contractually obliged to pay to a magistrate who had been absent from duty for a period of ten weeks as a result of a motor accident involving a vehicle insured by the defendant. The claim was unanimously denied, on grounds of policy. Stressing that the law took a conservative attitude on the subject of expansion of the Aquilian remedy,[164] Schreiner JA said that justice might sometimes better be served by denying a remedy than by granting one.[165] If liability in negligence were allowed to extend beyond the person physically injured in an accident to all those who, owing to a contractual or other relationship with the injured person, suffered indirect but material harm through his incapacitation, the situation would become unmanageable.[166]

The same sentiment was expressed nearly twenty years later by Addleson J in a provincial case: 'It is not everyone who is worse off as the result of injury to another, who has an action against the person whose unlawful act caused the injury'.[167] So, too, in *Combrinck Chiropraktiese Kliniek (Edms) Bpk v. Datsun Motor Vehicle Distributors (Pty) Ltd*[168] the Court expressly

---

[161] Boberg (n. 68), 82; *idem*, 1961 *Annual Survey of South African Law* 207; Schwietering, (1957) 20 *THRHR* 57; Hutchison, (1978) 95 *SALJ* 530.
[162] McKerron (n. 160).
[163] 1956 (1) SA 577 (A). The leading judgment of Schreiner JA was concurred in by Fagan, De Beer, and Hall JJA; Reynolds JA delivered a separate concurring judgment.
[164] 587.   [165] 584.   [166] 585.
[167] *De Harde v. Protea Assurance Co Ltd* 1974 (2) SA 109 (E) 114.
[168] 1972 (4) SA 185 (T) (Myburgh J; Human J concurring).

rejected the idea that Aquilian liability extended to all instances of financial loss caused negligently. The claim in this case was brought against a manufacturer for economic loss caused by a defect in the manufactured product. Foreshadowing the later developments in English law,[169] Myburgh J said that to allow a delictual action in such circumstances would constitute an unjustifiable invasion of the field of contract and would do more harm than good.[170] The door to the recovery of pure economic loss seemed well and firmly shut.

VI. THE DUTY TO TAKE CARE: A FIFTH WHEEL ON THE COACH?

By now it had become abundantly clear that the South African courts were not prepared to accept without qualification the idea that all harm caused culpably is *prima facie* actionable. Why then was it that, with a few notable exceptions, so little express recognition was given to wrongfulness as a distinct element of Aquilian liability? The answer is to be found, as usual, in the influence of English law, and more particularly in the concept of a duty to take care.

To English lawyers negligence meant more than just the absence of due care; the term denoted carelessness *where there was a duty to take care*: conduct which was wrongful as well as careless.[171] In the memorable words of Greer LJ in *Haynes v. Harwood*:[172] 'Negligence in the air will not do; negligence, in order to give a cause of action, must be the neglect of some duty owed to the person who makes the claim.'

This notion of an antecedent duty of care limited liability for negligence in two ways: first, by ensuring that there would be no liability to an unforeseeable plaintiff—the duty was owed only to those persons within the reasonable contemplation of the defendant;[173] and secondly, by affording a device of judicial control over the area of actionable negligence on the grounds of policy: where appropriate, the courts could hold that the conduct, though careless, was not an actionable wrong.[174] The first limitation was considered necessary because of the then accepted rule that a person

---

[169] Cf. *Murphy v. Brentwood District Council* [1991] 1 AC 398 (HL).

[170] 1972 (4) SA 185 (T), 192. The decision was hailed by McKerron, (1973) 90 *SALJ* 1 sqq., but criticized by other writers: see esp. Boberg (n. 68), 116; *idem*, 1972 *Annual Survey of South African Law* 131 sqq. Cf. *Tobacco Finance (Pvt) Ltd v. Zimnat Insurance Co Ltd* 1982 (3) SA 55 (ZH) 65, and *Atkinson Oates Motors Ltd v. Trust Bank of Africa Ltd* 1977 (3) SA 188 (W) 198, for doubts about the correctness of the reasoning in *Combrinck's* case.

[171] McKerron (n. 2), 13.   [172] [1935] 1 KB 146 (CA) 152.

[173] Cf. *Hay (or Bourhill) v. Young* [1943] AC 92 (HL); *Palsgraf v. Long Island Railroad Co* (1928) 284 NY 339.

[174] Cf. M. A. Millner, *Negligence in Modern Law* (1967), 26 sq.; McKerron (n. 2), 34 sq.; *idem*, (1952) 69 *SALJ* 190.

was liable for all the direct consequences of his negligence;[175] the second because there were still a number of situations where it was generally felt there ought to be no liability for negligence.[176] Unfortunately, however, judicial formulations of the test for ascertaining the existence of a duty of care created the misleading impression that the sole criterion was whether a reasonable person would have foreseen and guarded against the danger,[177] probably because the judges were reluctant to acknowledge the role played by policy factors in the development of the law.

The *lex Aquilia*, of course, made no reference to this notion of a duty to take care, and when the concept of *culpa* was substituted for that of *iniuria*, it was defined in abstract rather than relative terms:

Culpa, unlike negligence, was not defined with reference to a particular person or class. Failure to take that care which a reasonable man, the *bonus paterfamilias* or *paterfamilias diligens*, would take, was *culpa*, and if damage to property resulted, there was liability (subject only to a causal nexus). This was unlawful damage, *damnum iniuria datum*, and the 'unforeseeable plaintiff' rode home with the rest.[178]

Nevertheless, as already observed, there was a strong tendency in the Appellate Division from its earliest days to allow the notion of 'duty of care' to creep into its formulations of Aquilian liability, ironically in the very cases in which the Court was strenuously resisting the encroachment of English principles of negligence.[179] Initially this practice amounted to little more than a rephrasing of the *culpa* principle, but in *Union Government v. National Bank of South Africa Ltd*[180] a substantive change was effected. As we have seen, in that case Innes CJ for the first time drew a distinction between negligence in the popular sense and 'legal negligence', while Solomon JA said that 'where there is no duty towards the party affected there can be no negligence'.[181] In *Cape Town Municipality v. Paine* De Villiers JA went even further by suggesting, unwisely, that *culpa* implied the existence of a *vinculum juris* between the parties.[182]

The practical effect of this adoption of the duty concept was witnessed in *Workmen's Compensation Commissioner v. De Villiers*.[183] The defendant had with his lorry lightly bumped the door to the Cape Town Municipal Market, thereby dislodging and injuring a carpenter whose ladder had been placed against the inside of the door. The Court held that, while the

---

[175] Cf. *Re Polemis and Furness, Withy & Co Ltd* [1921] 3 KB 560 (CA), [1921] All ER 40. See also McKerron (n. 2), 129 sqq. where the earlier South African cases—which tended to support the direct consequences test for remoteness—are discussed.

[176] See e.g. the writers cited in n. 174, above.

[177] See n. 33 and text to n. 60 above.

[178] Millner (n. 174), 27.

[179] See text to nn. 52 and 60, above.

[180] 1921 AD 121.

[181] See text to nn. 105 and 108, above.

[182] 1923 AD 207, 223. For criticism see Van den Heever (n. 13), 42; Price, 1959 *Acta Juridica* 168.

[183] 1949 (1) SA 474 (C).

defendant had owed a duty of care to the City Council not to damage the door, it owed no duty to the carpenter since his presence behind the door was not reasonably foreseeable.

Predictably, not all commentators welcomed this importation from English law. Van den Heever conceded that *culpa* was unthinkable without a previously existing duty to take care, but he was adamant that this duty was owed to society at large, not to specific individuals whose identity could only be ascertained after the event. 'To regard the duty to take care as something which functions directionally, like a beam, leads to obvious absurdities', he said, and was 'juridically preposterous'.[184] In his view, once an injury *to someone* was foreseeable, any person injured as a direct result might sue *ex delicto*.[185] However, this is not a view that would appeal to many today since, as Millner has observed, it amounts to a theory of strict liability hiding behind the screen of *culpa*.[186]

The most vociferous critic of the duty concept was Price, who conducted a long and acrimonious campaign to rid our law of this 'alien and disturbing element'.[187] Echoing the view of Buckland, who considered the concept 'an unnecessary fifth wheel on the coach, incapable of sound analysis and possibly productive of injustice',[188] Price argued that it was not only confusing and ambiguous but also tautologous, in that it merely repeated the foreseeability test for fault.[189]

This prompted McKerron, the staunchest defender of the duty element, to accuse Price of missing the point by overlooking or ignoring the concept's policy function.[190] The requirement of a duty to take care served to determine not only whether the plaintiff was within the risk of harm created by the defendant's conduct but also, in a difficult or novel case, whether the plaintiff ought to be accorded a remedy for negligence at all. This dual function was lucidly explained by Millner:[191]

The duty concept in negligence operates at two levels. At one level it is fact-based, at another it is policy-based. The fact-based duty of care forms part of the inquiry whether the defendant's behaviour was negligent in the circumstances. The whole inquiry is governed by the foreseeability test, and 'duty of care' in this sense is a convenient but dispensable concept.

On the other hand, the policy-based or notional duty of care is an organic part of the tort; it is basic to the development and growth of negligence and determines its scope, that is to say, the range of relationships and interests protected by it. Here

---

[184] Van den Heever (n. 13), 43. See also his comments in *Herschel v. Mrupe* 1954 (3) SA 464 (A) 489.

[185] Ibid.   [186] Millner (n. 174) 28.

[187] Price (n. 182), 120; *idem*, (1949) 66 *SALJ* 171 sqq., 269 sqq.

[188] W. W. Buckland, 'The Duty to Take Care' (1935) 51 *LQR* 637, 648 sq.

[189] Price (n. 182), 120, 127.   [190] McKerron (n. 2), 34 sq.; *idem*, (1952) 69 *SALJ* 190.

[191] Millner (n. 174), 230, quoted with approval by McKerron (n. 2), 35, and by Rumpff CJ in *Administrateur, Natal v. Trust Bank van Afrika Bpk* 1979 (3) SA 824 (A) 833.

is a concept entirely divorced from foreseeability and governed by the policy of the law.

In the light of the developments outlined above in this Chapter there can be little doubt about the correctness of this analysis. It is indeed, to the modern reader, a striking feature of Price's writing that he never acknowledged the existence of wrongfulness as an element of Aquilian liability. In his view the law had long since outgrown the need for the 'primitive' notion of *iniuria*, and *culpa* was now the sole key to compensation.[192] As we have seen, however, this view was hardly compatible with some of the leading decisions of the Appellate Division; which no doubt explains Price's scornful rejection of them as aberrations brought about by blindly adopting the concept of a duty to take care.[193]

Whatever the merits of the various criticisms levelled at the duty concept (its telescoping of the fault and wrongfulness requirements was obviously not conducive to clear thinking)[194] the Appellate Division in a number of cases indicated that it was in no hurry to jettison the concept. In *Union Government v. Ocean Accident and Guarantee Corporation Ltd*[195] Schreiner JA said:

The expression 'duty of care' has sometimes been criticised as introducing an unnecessary complication into the law of negligence, but, apart from the fact that it is endorsed by considerable authority in this Court, it is so convenient a way of saying that it is the plaintiff himself and no other, whose right must have been invaded by the careless defendant, that the complication seems rather to be introduced by the effort to avoid its use. The duty of care is in our case-law rested upon foreseeability and this gives rise to a measure of artificiality. But this is really unavoidable for, if there is to be control over the range of persons who may sue, the test must be that of the reasonable man; what he would have foreseen and what action he would have taken may not be calculable according to the actual weighing of probabilities, but the device of reasoning on these lines helps to avoid the impression of delivering an unreasoned moral judgment *ex cathedra* as to how the injurer should have behaved. The duty of care fits conveniently into the reasoning process and even if it is no more than a manner of speaking it is a very useful one.

---

[192] See e.g. T. W. Price, 'Some Further Observations on Liability in Delict for "Acts of Omission" ', (1950) 13 *THRHR* 261, who felt constrained to repeat that 'the more primitive conception must in time give way to the more developed one, however slowly and painfully, and that with a fully developed theory of *culpa* in delict there is no longer any room whatsoever for the more primitive notion of *injuria*; it becomes an anachronism, and in so far as it may continue to find a place it does so as an illogical survival'.

[193] See the articles cited in n. 187, above. [194] Cf. Boberg (n. 68), 31.

[195] 1956 (1) SA 577 (A) 585. See also *South African Railways and Harbours v. Marais* 1950 (4) SA 610 (A) 621, where the academic debate on the duty of care was dismissed as irrelevant in view of the many cases accepting the concept as part of South African law.

VII. *BONI MORES* TO THE RESCUE: THE BREAKTHROUGH IN THE FIELD OF OMISSIONS

With the benefit of hindsight it is obvious that the key to solving the seemingly intractable problems of liability for omissions, misstatements, economic loss, and the like lay in the requirement of wrongfulness. For too long obscured by the tendency to make *culpa* the general criterion of Aquilian liability, and by the confusing pretence that foreseeability alone determined the existence of a duty to take care, wrongfulness needed to be acknowledged as an element in its own right, distinct from fault, so that greater attention could be given to its function as a policy instrument facilitating a controlled expansion of liability for negligent conduct. That breakthrough finally occurred in the field of omissions, where discontent with the 'prior conduct' doctrine had long been brewing.

1. A challenge to the established doctrine

The first signs of a change of heart in the Appellate Division appeared in *Silva's Fishing Corporation (Pty) Ltd v. Maweza*.[196] The respondent's husband, a member of the crew of a fishing boat owned by the appellant, drowned at sea when the boat was wrecked after drifting helplessly for nine days with a motor that would not start. The claim for damages was based on the fact that, although the appellant had known of the crew's plight and could have rescued them, it had made no effort to do so.

The court was unanimous in its view that in these circumstances there was a legal duty on the appellant to take available steps to rescue the crew. Though Schreiner JA in his majority judgment did say that a duty to rescue was not subject to special rules and might arise out of the circumstances of the case,[197] he based his decision ultimately on the appellant's 'potentially noxious' prior act in providing the boat for fishing purposes.[198] From an historical point of view the real significance of the case lies in the minority judgment of Steyn JA. In a bold attempt to break free from the shackles of the prior conduct doctrine, he held that a legal duty to act might arise from a wide variety of circumstances, some of them unconnected with prior conduct. What these circumstances were would depend upon 'the conceptions prevailing in a given community at a given time'.[199]

Six years later, as Chief Justice, Steyn gained the support of Ogilvie Thompson and Rumpff JJA for his view, in *Regal v. African Superslate*

---

[196] 1957 (2) SA 256 (A).   [197] 263.   [198] 264.

[199] 265. As Boberg (n. 68), 231 points out, this formulation strongly foreshadowed the criterion subsequently adopted by Rumpff CJ in *Minister van Polisie v. Ewels* 1975 (3) SA 590 (A), discussed below. For comment on the case see, *inter alia*, Price, 1962 *Acta Juridica* 76, 80 sqq.; R. G. McKerron, 'Liability for Omissions', (1957) 74 *SALJ* 257 sqq.

(Pty) Ltd.[200] Although the case involved an application for an interdict rather than a claim for Aquilian damages, it turned essentially on the question of whether a landowner's failure to take steps to prevent slate waste from washing downstream and causing harm to a neighbour constituted a wrongful *omissio*. The slate waste had been deposited in the bed of a river traversing both properties by a predecessor in title of the respondent.

In holding that there was no legal duty to act in the circumstances, a majority of the Court rejected the view that prior conduct was an indispensable requirement for the wrongfulness of an omission[201] and applied instead the far more flexible criterion of what could reasonably be expected of the person in the circumstances. More particularly, the test in a case such as the present was whether there were any 'reasonably practicable' measures that could be taken to prevent the harm.[202] Steyn CJ pointed out that this objective notion of reasonableness should not be confused with the test for *culpa*. For example, he said, if an owner failed to take steps to prevent a nuisance because he had been expertly advised that there were no reasonably practicable means of doing so, his omission could hardly be labelled as negligent but it would nonetheless be wrongful and would afford a right to an interdict if the advice could be shown to be wrong.[203]

Objective reasonableness as a criterion of wrongfulness was espoused with vigour by the authors of a new textbook on delict that appeared at this juncture.[204] According to Van der Merwe and Olivier[205] the wrongfulness of an act or omission consists in the infringement of another's subjective right, and is determined by an *ex post facto* evaluation of the reasonableness of the defendant's conduct, viewed in relation to its consequences. This standard of reasonableness is shaped by the *boni mores* or the general legal convictions of the community, and differs from the test for fault in that it takes account of all the circumstances of the case as subsequently found by a court, not merely those known or foreseeable to a reasonable person in the position of the defendant prior to the accident.

Though scorned at first by other writers,[206] this broader approach to the problem of wrongfulness in delict soon found favour with the courts[207] and, as we shall see, has proved enormously influential in developing liability for omissions and for economic loss.

---

[200] 1963 (1) SA 102 (A), noted by N. J. van der Merwe, (1963) 26 *THRHR* 131 sqq.
[201] 109E-G (Steyn CJ); 116 sq. (Ogilvie Thompson JA); 121 sq. (Rumpff JA).
[202] 111H.   [203] 112A-C.
[204] Van der Merwe/Olivier (n. 14; 1st edn., 1966), 43 sqq.
[205] Van der Merwe/Olivier (6th edn., 1989), 49 sqq.
[206] See reviews by D. R. Stuart, (1967) 84 *SALJ* 362, 363 sq. and J. C. de Wet, (1970) 33 *THRHR* 68, 71. Both suggested that the objective test of reasonableness merely restated the test for fault.
[207] Cf. *Meskin v. Anglo-American Corp of SA Ltd* 1968 (4) SA 793 (W) 800, 807.

2. Liberation from the incubus

The penultimate step to the liberation of South African law from what Boberg[208] calls the 'incubus' of the prior conduct doctrine was taken by the Appellate Division in *Minister of Forestry v. Quathlamba (Pty) Ltd.*[209] In an action for damage caused by a *veld* fire, the Court unanimously approved[210] the minority opinion of Steyn JA in *Maweza's* case[211] and for the first time based liability for an omission squarely on control of property. Once an owner or occupier becomes aware of a fire on rural land under his control, it was held, he is required by law to take reasonable steps to control or extinguish the fire, even though he was not responsible for starting it.[212]

The breakthrough finally came in 1975, in *Minister van Polisie v. Ewels.*[213] Ewels had been assaulted in a café by Barnard, an off-duty police sergeant, and went to the local police station to lay a charge. Barnard followed him there and, in the presence of the policemen on duty at the time, once again beat him up. Ewels sued the Minister in delict, seeking to hold him vicariously liable for the failure by the policemen in charge of the station to come to his assistance and protect him from Barnard. The Appellate Division held that in the circumstances there was a legal duty to intervene and protect Ewels.

Delivering the unanimous opinion of the Court, Rumpff CJ said[214] that the law on omissions had developed through the cases to the stage where a measure of clarity at last prevailed. The point of departure remained that, as a matter of law rather than morality, no general duty existed to take positive action to prevent harm to another, even when such action could easily be taken. In certain circumstances, however, the law did regard an omission as wrongful and thus as capable of giving rise to delictual liability. Such circumstances were not limited to cases involving prior conduct or the control of property, though these were relevant factors in determining the issue of wrongfulness.

It appears that the stage of development has been reached wherein an omission is regarded as unlawful conduct also when the circumstances of the case are of such a nature that the omission not only excites moral indignation but also that the legal convictions of the community demand that the omission should be considered wrongful and that the loss suffered should be made good by the person who neglected to take positive action.[215]

---

[208] Boberg (n. 68), 247.

[209] 1973 (3) SA 69 (A), noted by J. Neethling, A. D. J. van Rensburg, (1973) 36 *THRHR* 427 sqq.; J. J. Reyneke, 'Verantwoordelikheid op Grond van 'n Late', (1974) 91 *SALJ* 310 sqq.

[210] 82.   [211] See text to n. 199 above.   [212] 82.   [213] 1975 (3) SA 590 (A).

[214] 596 sqq.   [215] 597A-B (my translation from the original Afrikaans).

As to when the legal convictions of the community so demanded, no general rule could be laid down: whether there was a legal duty to act depended on all the relevant facts. In the present case the important factors were: the fact that the assault took place in the police station over which the policemen had control; the general duty of the police to protect members of the public from crime; the ease with which the assault could have been prevented or stopped; and the fact that one of the bystanders held a rank equal to that of Barnard.[216]

3. The wider significance of *Ewels*

The significance of *Ewels'* case for the development of the South African law, not merely of omissions but of delict in general, cannot be overemphasized. Indeed, it may without too much exaggeration be likened to the significance of *Donoghue v. Stevenson*[217] for the development of the tort of negligence in English law. In the same way that Lord Atkin's neighbour principle united the various categories of liability for negligence and opened the door to the recognition of new ones, so too Rumpff CJ's broad formula not only explained the existing instances of liability for an omission but also provided an invaluable mechanism for judicial development of the law. The present Chief Justice spelled this out clearly in a public lecture delivered in 1986:

Even in 1975 there were probably still two choices open to the court in the *Ewels* case. The one was to confine liability for an omission to certain stereotypes, possibly adding to them from time to time; the other was to adopt a wider, more open-ended general principle, which, while comprehending existing grounds of liability, would lay the foundation for a more flexible and all-embracing approach to the question whether a person's omission to act should be held unlawful or not. The court made the latter choice; and, of course, in doing so cast the courts for a general policy-making role in this area of the law.[218]

Moreover, just as the significance of *Donoghue v. Stevenson* cannot be limited to the field of products liability, so too that of *Ewels* transcends the bounds of liability for omissions. Not only has it revolutionized the law in that narrow field, sweeping away for example the long established immunity of municipalities,[219] it has also made its influence felt throughout the law of delict, in such disparate but inherently contentious areas as the right

---

[216] 597 sq.

[217] See n. 33, above.

[218] The Hon. Mr Justice M. M. Corbett, 'Aspects of The Role of Policy in the Evolution of our Common Law', (1987) 104 *SALJ* 52 sqq., 56.

[219] See *Van der Merwe Burger v. Munisipaliteit van Warrenton* 1987 (1) SA 899 (NC). Cf. *Blackwell v. Port Elizabeth Municipality* 1978 (2) SA 168 (C); *Cape Town Municipality v. April* 1982 (1) SA 259 (C); *Fourie v. Munisipaliteit van Malmesbury* 1983 (2) SA 748 (C).

to privacy,[220] wrongful competition,[221] and, as we shall see shortly, liability for pure economic loss.

The decision has had this profound influence because it clearly established wrongfulness as a distinct element of liability in which the courts can openly take account of policy considerations in developing the law.[222] For this very reason an eminent judge[223] complained that the decision in *Ewels* created legal uncertainty by substituting judicial discretion for principle;[224] but his was a lone voice amidst the general chorus of approval.[225] It was widely appreciated that if Aquilian liability was to be extended into these new, controversial fields without giving rise to indeterminate liability or undesirable social and economic consequences than a much greater degree of flexibility (or judicial discretion, if you like) would have to be introduced into the tests for liability.

Van Dijkhorst J expressed this sentiment well in a case involving wrongful competition: 'What is needed is a legal standard firm enough to afford guidance to the Court, yet flexible enough to permit the influence of an inherent sense of fair play'.[226] Following in the footsteps of Rumpff CJ, he found such a flexible standard in 'the general sense of justice of the community, the *boni mores*, manifested in public opinion'.[227]

It is not without interest that at much the same time certain English judges, notably Lord Denning and Lord Wilberforce, began to express the need for a consideration of policy factors in determining the existence of a duty of care in the tort of negligence.[228] Even if that approach has since been somewhat discredited,[229] one notes with interest the new prominence given in the common law to 'proximity' and considerations of fairness and reasonableness as additional criteria, beyond foreseeability, in recognizing

---

[220] See e.g. *Universiteit van Pretoria v. Tommie Meyer Films (Edms) Bpk* 1977 (4) SA 376 (T); *Financial Mail (Pty) Ltd v. Sage Holdings Ltd* 1993 (2) SA 451 (A) 462 sq.

[221] See e.g. *Atlas Organic Fertilizers (Pty) Ltd v. Pikkewyn Ghwano (Pty) Ltd* 1981 (2) SA 173 (T) 188 sq.; *Schultz v. Butt* 1986 (3) SA 667 (A) 679.

[222] Cf. the remarks of Conradie J in *Kadir v. Minister of Law and Order* 1992 (3) SA 737 (C) 742.

[223] The Hon. George Colman, former judge of the Transvaal Provincial Division: see Corbett, (1987) 104 *SALJ* 56.

[224] *Amicus Curiae*, 'The Actionable Omission: Another View of *Ewels*' Case', (1976) 93 *SALJ* 85, 87.

[225] See the writers listed by Boberg (n. 68), 266.

[226] *Atlas Organic Fertilizers (Pty) Ltd v. Pikkewyn Ghwano (Pty) Ltd* (n. 221).

[227] Ibid.

[228] See e.g. *Spartan Steel & Alloys Ltd v. Martin & Co (Contractors) Ltd* [1973] 1 QB 27 (CA) 36 sqq. (Lord Denning MR); *Anns v. Merton London Borough Council* [1978] AC 728 (HL) 751 (Lord Wilberforce).

[229] Cf. *Yuen Kun Yeu v. A-G of Hong Kong* [1988] 1 AC 175 (PC) 194; *McLoughlin v. O'Brian* [1983] 1 AC 410 (HL) 430.

the existence of new duties of care.[230] Some of the formulations of these requirements bear a striking resemblance to our requirement of wrongfulness in its new guise.[231] The need for soft concepts as flexible tools for judicial lawmaking in extending the scope of liability for negligent conduct is clearly not limited to South African law.[232]

VIII. NEGLIGENT MISSTATEMENTS AND ECONOMIC LOSS: THE NEXT DOMINO FALLS

The five separate judgments delivered in *Herschel v. Mrupe*[233] caused such legal uncertainty that for the next two decades few litigants were brave enough to base a claim for damages on negligent misstatement. Nor was this hesitation unjustified, as the strong *obiter dicta* of the Appellate Division in *Hamman v. Moolman*[234] made clear. There was no practical necessity for a remedy in delict where a negligent misrepresentation induced a contract between the parties, said Wessels JA,[235] because the existing law already granted adequate protection to the representee in the pre-contractual sphere.

Although pure logic and never-ending development and expansion of legal ideas do not appear to be opposed in principle to a conclusion that in appropriate circumstances an action might be maintained to recover pecuniary loss caused by honest but carelessly made verbal (or written) misrepresentations, there is as yet in our law no authoritative determination or generally accepted definition of the principles to be applied in deciding in what circumstances such an action will lie in the field of contract.[236]

Though not binding, and strongly criticized by academic commentators,[237] these remarks were treated by lower courts as a clear affirmation of judicial policy and were followed, albeit with evident reluctance in some cases.[238] Then suddenly in 1977, two years after the decision in *Ewels*,[239] a swing in

[230] See e.g. *Caparo Industries Plc v. Dickman* [1990] 2 AC 605 (HL) 617 sq., 632 sq.; *Murphy v. Brentwood District Council* [1991] 1 AC 398 (HL) 461, 475, 481, 486; *White v. Jones* [1993] 3 All ER 481 (CA) 488. See generally Hutchison, (1995) *Stellenbosch LR* 3, 4 sqq.

[231] See esp. *Council of the Shire of Sutherland v. Heyman* (1985) 157 CLR 424, 497 sq. (per Deane J).

[232] Cf. Kit Barker, 'Unreliable Assumptions in the Modern Law of Negligence', (1993) 109 *LQR* 461 sqq. Concerning German law, see the remarks and references in Hutchison/Zimmermann, (1995) 3 *Zeitschrift für Europäisches Privatrecht* 283, fn. 39.

[233] 1954 (3) SA 464 (A). See text to n. 147, above. [234] 1968 (4) SA 340 (A).

[235] 348. [236] Ibid.

[237] See e.g. P. M. A. Hunt 'No Damages for Negligent Misrepresentation Inducing Contract?', (1968) 85 *SALJ* 379 sqq.; Dale Hutchison, 'Non-Fraudulent Misrepresentation Inducing Contract', (1975) 3 *Responsa Meridiana* 129 sqq.; but cf. McKerron (n. 2), 221.

[238] *Murray v. McLean* 1970 (1) SA 133 (R); *Latham v. Sher* 1974 (4) SA 687 (W); *Du Plessis v. Semmelink* 1976 (2) SA 500 (T).

[239] *Minister van Polisie v. Ewels* 1975 (3) SA 590 (A). See text to n. 213, above.

judicial opinion began to manifest itself. In *Suid-Afrikaanse Bantoetrust v. Ross en Jacobz*[240] Coetzee J held that it was no longer even arguable that our law failed to recognize liability in delict for a negligent misrepresentation causing economic loss. The problem, he said, was not whether such liability existed, but how to limit it.

These sentiments were quickly endorsed by judges in other provincial divisions[241] so that it became merely a matter of time before the Appellate Division would be asked to reconsider the question. That occurred in 1979, in the now famous case of *Administrateur, Natal v. Trust Bank van Afrika Bpk*,[242] the '*Hedley Byrne* of South African law'.[243]

1. The birth of a problem child

Wishing to expropriate a certain piece of property, the Administrator had sent a notice of expropriation to Bijo, who he thought was the registered owner of the property. In fact Bijo was not the owner, but this did not deter him from showing the notice, which described him as owner, to the Trust Bank with a request to negotiate on his behalf for the payment of compensation. The bank agreed to do so and in its letter to the Administrator repeated the assertion that Bijo was the registered owner of the property in question. In due course the sum of R6,800 was paid as compensation. When the error was discovered the Administrator sued both Bijo and the bank for repayment, basing his claim against the latter on negligent misrepresentation. The Court *a quo* entered default judgment against Bijo but dismissed the claim against the bank on the ground that on the facts there was no legal duty on the bank to check the veracity of the information supplied by Bijo.[244]

This decision was confirmed on appeal. Fortunately, however, the Appellate Division did not leave the matter there but seized the opportunity to establish once and for all that negligently inflicted economic loss is recoverable in appropriate circumstances. The Court, mindful of the American judge Learned Hand's warning against 'anticipating a doctrine which may be in the womb of time, but whose birth is distant',[245] justified its stance by extending the metaphor:

In the present case the birth pangs have already endured for so long that the time has arrived to bring the child into the world, perhaps even by Caesarian section. I

---

[240] 1977 (3) SA 184 (T) 187.
[241] See *Greenfield Engineering Works (Pty) Ltd v. NKR Construction (Pty) Ltd* 1978 (4) SA 901 (N) 915; *EG Electric Co (Pty) Ltd v. Franklin* 1979 (2) SA 702 (E) 705; *Administrateur, Natal v. Bijo* 1978 (2) SA 256 (N).
[242] 1979 (3) SA 824 (A).   [243] Boberg (n. 68), 103.
[244] *Administrator, Natal v. Bijo* (n. 241).
[245] *Spectator Motor Service Inc v. Walsh* 139 F 2d 809 (1944) 823, quoted in (1974) 91 *SALJ* 408 and by Rumpff CJ at 831 of his judgment.

think that one should immediately add that it is predictable that this child will become a problem child. With the necessary love, and especially discipline, however, it can play a useful role in legal life.[246]

The new cause of action, said Rumpff CJ,[247] fell within the extended field of the *lex Aquilia*. From this it followed that both wrongfulness and fault had to be established. The fear of indeterminate liability could only be allayed by requiring the court, in the circumstances of each case, to decide whether the defendant had owed the plaintiff a legal duty to speak with care, and whether the defendant had exercised reasonable care to ensure, for example, that the statement was correct. Liability would further be kept within reasonable bounds by giving proper attention to the nature and interpretation of the statement, and to the problem of causation.

The Court placed particular emphasis on wrongfulness as a means of controlling liability. Although the English concept of a 'duty to take care' was a monstrosity (*onding*) in South African common law, said Rumpff CJ, it corresponded to some extent with the concept of wrongfulness in that, properly understood, it too embraced considerations of policy. In support of this contention he quoted the following passage from Fleming's *Law of Torts*:[248]

In short, recognition of a duty of care is the outcome of a value judgment, that the plaintiff's invaded interest is deemed worthy of legal protection against negligent interference by conduct of the kind alleged against the defendant. In the decision whether or not there is a duty, many factors interplay: the hand of history, our ideas of morals and justice, the convenience of administering the rule and our social ideas as to where the loss should fall. Hence, the incidence and extent of duties are liable to adjustment in the light of the constant shifts and changes in community attitudes.

2. No sparing of the rod

The decision in *Trust Bank* was unanimously hailed by academic commentators,[249] and is undoubtedly one of the milestones in the development of our law of delict. It is important to appreciate, however, that the decision did not do away with the distinction between physical and economic loss, but merely down-graded its significance. Henceforth, the fact that loss was purely economic in character would not necessarily rule out the possibility of recovery, but it would mean that the element of wrongfulness could not be taken for granted, as in most cases of physical harm. Sometimes that initial hurdle has proved difficult to overcome, much to the chagrin of the

---

[246] 1979 (3) SA 824 (A) 831 (my translation from the original Afrikaans).
[247] 832 sq.
[248] John G Fleming, *The Law of Torts* (4th edn., 1971), 136, quoted at 833 sq. of the judgment.
[249] See esp. J. M. Burchell, 'The Birth of a Legal Principle: Negligent Misstatement Causing Pure Economic Loss', (1980) 97 *SALJ* 1 sqq.; J. Neethling, J. M. Potgieter, (1980) 43 *THRHR* 82 sqq.; J. C. van der Walt, 1979 *TSAR* 145 sqq.

commentators.[250] For in the gradual process of development of this new form of liability the courts have deliberately adopted a cautious approach: commendably so in my opinion, though not everyone agrees with this view.[251] By feeling its way slowly forward the Appellate Division has managed to avoid the need for embarrassing u-turns such as that recently executed by the House of Lords in *Murphy v. Brentwood District Council.*[252]

The caution of the highest South African court was most visibly displayed in the case of *Lillicrap, Wassenaar and Partners v. Pilkington Brothers (SA) (Pty) Ltd.*[253] The facts were complicated. For present purposes it suffices to state that the plaintiff had suffered economic loss because its new glass factory was not suitable for the purpose for which it had been built. This loss was allegedly due to negligence by the defendant firm of engineers in performing their contractual duties before and during the process of construction. Having assigned its contractual rights against the defendant to the main building contractor, the plaintiff attempted to short-circuit the contractual chain by suing the defendant in delict: the very sort of claim that had recently been permitted by the House of Lords in *Junior Books Ltd v. Veitchi & Co Ltd.*[254]

By a majority of four to one[255] the Appellate Division upheld the exception taken to the claim, thereby refusing to follow the lead given by the House of Lords. South African law, said Grosskopf AJA, adopted a more cautious approach in extending the scope of Aquilian liability to new situations, doing so only when there were positive policy considerations which favoured such an extension.[256] Negligent breach of a contractual duty would constitute a delict where all the elements of delictual liability were satisfied. In a case such as the present, however, where the loss was purely economic and where the parties to the building contract had regulated their relations *inter se* by contract, the element of wrongfulness was not satisfied, since policy considerations dictated that the negligent breach should not be regarded as a wrongful act for Aquilian purposes. For the reasons spelled out by Lord Brandon in his dissenting judgment in *Junior Books*, 'the Aquilian action does not fit comfortably in a contractual setting like the present'.[257] Was the standard of care, for example, to be determined with

---

[250] See n. 253, below.

[251] See esp. Mervyn Dendy, 'Reflections on Reading Bernstein's Economic Loss', (1994) 111 *SALJ* 592 sqq.

[252] [1991] 1 AC 398 (HL).

[253] 1985 (1) SA 475 (A), noted by P. Q. R. Boberg, 'Back to *Winterbottom v. Wright*? Not Quite!' (1985) 102 *SALJ* 213 sqq.; Andrew Beck, 'Delictual Liability for Breach of Contract', (1985) 102 *SALJ* 222 sqq.; Paul van Warmelo, 'Liability in Contract and in Delict', (1985) 102 *SALJ* 227 sqq.; Dale Hutchison, D. P. Visser, '*Lillicrap* Revisited: Further Thoughts on Pure Economic Loss and Concurrence of Actions', (1985) 102 *SALJ* 587 sqq.

[254] [1983] 1 AC 520 (HL).

[255] The majority judgment of Grosskopf AJA was concurred in by Kotzé, Cillie, and Van Heerden JJA; Smuts AJA dissented.

[256] 504.   [257] 500 G.

reference to the terms of the contract or by the usual test of the *bonus pater-familias*? Arguably, the reasonable man always complied with the standards laid down by a contract to which he was party, but why should the law of delict reinforce the law of contract in this manner? There were no policy considerations to justify such a conclusion.[258]

In many other cases, however, the Appellate Division has displayed a willingness to break new ground. In *Bayer South Africa (Pty) Ltd v. Frost*,[259] for example, the Court rejected as overtaken by events its earlier *dicta* in *Hamman v. Moolman*[260] and allowed a claim for economic loss caused by a negligent misstatement inducing a contract between the parties. And in *Indac Electronics (Pty) Ltd v. Volkskas Bank Ltd*[261] it recognized the principle that a collecting banker may be held liable under the extended *lex Aquilia* to the true owner of a cheque for economic loss caused by its negligence in dealing with a cheque.

The lower courts have in numerous cases gone further, recognizing liability in a wide variety of situations, most of which involve an element of professional negligence.[262] In a recent case[263] which is difficult to reconcile with the decision in *Lillicrap*[264] the Cape Provincial Division declined the invitation to follow *Murphy v. Brentwood District Council*[265] and imposed liability on an engineer. In Natal the courts have recognized the principle of liability for economic loss caused by a negligent disruption of the electricity supply.[266]

As yet, however, there has been no case reported that involves a claim by a 'disappointed beneficiary':[267] we still await a South African *White v. Jones*.[268] Finally, the courts have thus far shown no willingness to allow a

---

[258] 500 sq.

[259] 1991 (4) SA 559 (A), noted by Carole Lewis, 'Damages for Negligent Misrepresentation: The Appellate Division Leaps Forward', (1992) 109 *SALJ* 381 sqq., N. P. Mngqibisa, 'Liability for Negligent Misstatement Inducing a Contract', (1992) 55 *THRHR* 504 sqq.; Dale Hutchison, Reinhard Zimmermann, 'Fahrlässige irreführende Angaben im vorvertraglichen Bereich: Zur Haftung für reine Vermögensschäden nach modernem römisch-holländischem Recht', (1995) 3 *Zeitschrift für Europäisches Privatrecht* 271 sqq. For further misstatement cases (outside of the contractual context) see *Siman & Co (Pty) Ltd v. Barclays National Bank Ltd* 1984 (2) SA 888 (A); *International Shipping Co (Pty) Ltd v. Bentley* 1990 (1) SA 680 (A); *Standard Chartered Bank of Canada v. Nedperm Bank Ltd* 1994 (4) SA 747 (A).

[260] 1968 (4) SA 340 (A).   [261] 1992 (1) SA 783 (A).

[262] See e.g. *Arthur E Abrahams and Gross v. Cohen* 1991 (2) SA 301 (C); *McLelland v. Hulett* 1992 (1) SA 456 (D) (directors of a company); *Tsimatakopolous v. Hemingway, Isaacs and Coetzee CC* 1993 (4) SA 428 (C) (engineer); *Cathkin Park Hotel v. J D Makesch Architects* 1993 (2) SA 98 (W) (architects, engineers, and builders—physical and economic loss).

[263] *Tsimatakopoulos v. Hemingway, Isaacs and Coetzee CC* (n. 262).

[264] See n. 253, above.   [265] [1991] 1 AC 398 (HL).

[266] *Coronation Brick (Pty) Ltd v. Strachan Construction Co (Pty) Ltd* 1982 (4) SA 371 (D).

[267] Cf., however, *Bedford v. Suid-Kaapse Voogdy Bpk* 1968 (1) SA 226 (C); *Arthur E. Abrahams & Gross v. Cohen* (n. 262). See generally Owen Rogers, 'The Action of the Disappointed Beneficiary', (1986) 103 *SALJ* 583 sqq.

[268] [1995] 2 WLR 187, [1995] 1 All ER 691 (HL); on which see Werner Lorenz, 'Anwaltshaftung wegen Untätigkeit bei der Errichtung letztwilliger Verfügungen: ein Rechtsvergleich', 1995 *Juristenzeitung* 317 sqq.

claim for so-called relational economic loss, or negligent interference with contractual relations:[269] for the time being, at any rate, the decision in *Union Government v. Ocean Accident and Guarantee Corporation Ltd*[270] remains good law.

IX. CONCLUSION

As the twentieth century draws to a close, how much nearer is South Africa to accepting of the general principle that all harm culpably caused is actionable unless justified? Has Aquilian liability finally reached the logical endpoint of its long process of historical development? And to what extent, if at all, has it shed its civilian character and taken on that of the English tort of negligence?

The short answer to the first question is: very much nearer. As we have seen, there have been some dramatic developments this century, particularly over the past two decades, opening the door in principle to liability for negligent omissions, negligent misstatements, and for negligently inflicted loss of a purely economic nature. The key to these developments has been the resurrection of the old requirement of *iniuria*, in its new guise of wrongfulness. This requirement, distinct from and logically anterior to that of fault, provides a niche for the open consideration of policy factors in the development of liability for negligent conduct, and hence has come to serve a vital role as a mechanism of control over the gradual expansion of Aquilian liability. Some have objected that it substitutes discretion for principle, but its positive impact on our law is undeniable. Armed with this discretionary tool, the courts have boldly ventured into territory previously thought too hazardous, secure in the knowledge that they can always retreat if the danger becomes too great.

Significant as these developments undoubtedly are, the stage has not yet been reached where it can be said that all financial harm culpably caused is *prima facie* wrongful and therefore actionable. That is certainly true in the field of omissions, where the *boni mores* do not require one to take positive action whenever a failure to do so would foreseeably cause harm to another;[271] and it seems also still to be true in the case of purely economic loss, whether caused by a misstatement or otherwise.[272]

---

[269] See *Shell and BP South African Petroleum Refineries (Pty) Ltd v. Osborne Panama SA* 1980 (3) SA 653 (D); *Franschhoekse Wynkelder (Ko-operatief) Bpk v. South African Railways and Harbours* 1981 (3) SA 36 (C).

[270] 1956 (1) SA 577 (A). See text to n. 163 above.

[271] See e.g. Boberg (n. 68), 211; Burchell (n. 6), 39.

[272] See Hutchison/Visser, (1985) 102 *SALJ* 588 sq. and authorities there cited; *Zimbabwe Banking Corp Ltd v. Pyramid Motor Corp (Pvt.) Ltd* 1985 (4) SA 553 (ZS) 562 sq. Cf. Dendy, (1994) 111 *SALJ* 592 sqq.

The insistence on wrongfulness as a separate element represents a defeat for those such as Price who maintained that there was no need for it in a fully developed system of Aquilian liability based on fault. Ironically, therefore, McKerron's opposing view has triumphed, though his victory is tarnished to some extent by his subsequent[273] adoption of the English practice of telescoping the wrongfulness and fault requirements into one issue, namely whether there was a duty to take care in the circumstances: a practice now frowned upon as being conducive to muddled thinking. The irony lies in the fact that Price was ahead of his time in advocating liability for omissions, misstatements, and for purely economic loss, while McKerron's resistance to these developments grew over the years. Furthermore, as confusing as the concept of a duty to take care might be, its chief function was and remains identical to that served by the requirement of wrongfulness; and in that respect it does operate 'directionally, like a beam', contrary to the view of Van den Heever:[274] there is now general agreement that the wrongfulness of an act is a quality relative to the consequence it produces for a particular plaintiff.[275]

If Aquilian liability is to be reduced to one general principle today, that principle would have to be that all patrimonial loss caused wrongfully and culpably is actionable: which is essentially what Watermeyer J said in *Perlman v. Zoutendyk*.[276] Expressing South African law in this sweeping way certainly emphasizes its inherently civilian nature and makes it look very different to that of England; but outward appearances can sometimes be misleading. It is a notable fact that South African courts still refer far more frequently to English than to continental decisions in developing the law relating to liability for negligence; and if one probes beneath superficial differences it is questionable whether the law 'approaches a new problem in the continental rather than the English way'.[277] That statement tends to overlook not only the extent to which the tort of negligence has been generalized this century, but also the ingrained reluctance of South African courts to commit themselves to sweeping extensions of *prima facie* liability under the *lex Aquilia*.

In order to appreciate the fundamental similarity in approach between the two systems, consider the following. Since at least 1932 the English courts have been trying to formulate a general principle of liability for negligence that would serve to unite the various categories of liability established by precedent and would assist in the recognition of new duties of care. Each significant development along the way has brought English law closer to our own. Thus Lord Atkin's neighbour principle in *Donoghue v. Stevenson*,[278] based essentially on the reasonable foreseeability of the harm,

---

[273] See n. 86, above.
[275] See e.g. Boberg (n. 68), 31.
[277] Ibid.

[274] See n. 184, above and text thereto.
[276] 1934 CPD 151, 155. See text to n. 135, above.
[278] See n. 33, above.

echoed the *culpa* principle enunciated by Innes CJ in *Cape Town Municipality v. Paine*.[279] When negligence began to expand into the realm of misstatements causing economic loss, the need was felt to supplement the foreseeability test with a further element that allowed greater scope for the exercise of judicial discretion and for the open consideration of policy factors. That led to Lord Wilberforce's formulation of a 'two-stage' test for the existence of a duty of care in *Anns v. Merton London Borough Council*.[280] The two elements of that test correspond to some extent with the twin requirements of fault and wrongfulness which had just then begun to be clearly distinguished in South African law, for much the same reason.

This steady movement from precedent to principle as a means of determining the existence of a duty of care caused some tension and recently there has been a backlash.[281] The preferred view today is that the law should develop new categories of negligence incrementally and by analogy with established categories rather than by a massive extension of a *prima facie* duty of care restrained only by indefinable policy considerations[282]. The Wilberforcian 'two-stage' test has been rejected in favour of an updated neighbour test in terms of which 'necessary ingredients' in any situation giving rise to a duty of care include not only that the harm should be reasonably foreseeable but also (i) that there should be a relationship of proximity between the parties and (ii) that it should be 'fair, just and reasonable' to impose a duty in the circumstances.[283] This new test is intended to serve not as a formula by means of which the existence of a duty can be determined directly but rather as an umbrella principle to unite the categories of negligence and to facilitate an incremental expansion in their number and scope.[284] Judges have said that the requirements of proximity and fairness shade into one another and involve value judgments as to whether in a given situation there ought to be liability for negligence;[285] being incapable of precise definition, they are not so much practical tests as convenient labels attached to the features of different situations which the law pragmatically recognizes as giving rise to a duty of care.[286]

I end with these provocative thoughts. The new approach of the English courts seems very different to that of our own, but is it really so different? The issue of wrongfulness clearly involves a value judgment as to whether in a given situation there should be liability for negligence, but is it a test for liability or merely a label attached *ex post facto* to a particular set of facts? It turns on the *boni mores* or legal convictions of the community, but

---

[279] See text to n. 60, above.   [280] See n. 34, above.

[281] For a fuller discussion see Hutchison, (1995) 6 *Stellenbosch LR* 4 sqq.

[282] See n. 34, above.   [283] See n. 230, above.

[284] See esp. the comments of Lords Bridge and Oliver in *Caparo Industries Plc v. Dickman* [1990] 2 AC 605 (HL) 617, 633.

[285] *White v. Jones* [1993] 3 All ER 481 (CA), 488 (Sir Donald Nicholls V-C).

[286] *Caparo Industries Plc v. Dickman* (n. 284), 618 (Lord Bridge), 633 (Lord Oliver).

are these concepts any more capable of precise definition than those of proximity and fairness? Is the broad generalization that harm wrongfully and culpably caused is actionable of any practical utility, or is it merely an umbrella principle covering the various situations where the courts have already decided the issue of wrongfulness? Finally, in view of the often approved assertion by Schreiner JA in the *Ocean Accident* case[287] that 'the law takes a conservative view on the subject of expansion of the Aquilian remedy beyond what the authorities have recognized in the past', can it be denied that South African courts too favour an incremental approach in expanding the boundaries of liability for negligence?

---

[287] *Union Govt v. Ocean Accident and Guarantee Corp Ltd* 1956 (1) SA 577 (A) 587.

19: *The Protection of Personality Rights*

JONATHAN M. BURCHELL*

I. INTRODUCTION

The story of the evolution of the delictual remedy under the Roman *actio iniuriarum* unfolds like a mystery novel, replete with contradictory versions and clues that apparently lead nowhere, but that eventually prove to be authoritative. It is perhaps fitting that the Anglo-American equivalent of the concept of a 'delict' is referred to as a 'tort': a word derived from the Latin *tortus* meaning 'twisted'. The path to the unravelling, or partial unravelling, of the mystery surrounding the *actio iniuriarum* and its governing principles is appropriately tortuous in South Africa.

However, there is some consolation to be gained from an historical analysis of the *staccato* progress of the South African version of the *actio iniuriarum* during the nineteenth and twentieth centuries. The process of demystification of this branch of the law at the hands of commentators[1] and the legal profession has reached an advanced stage and the unveiling of the revised version of the *actio iniuriarum* undoubtedly adds lustre and authority to its orthodox Roman origins. The modern South African law of defamation ranks with the most sophisticated in the Anglo-American legal systems and the cultivation in South African soil of a unique civil law protection of human dignity and privacy, using cuttings from Roman jurisprudence, holds considerable potential for the flourishing symbiosis of common

* Ms. Fiona Humphries, LL M, very kindly collected and collated the nineteenth-century cases on the *actio iniuriarum* for me in the preparation of this Chapter. I am indebted to her for helping me with this demanding task.

[1] In the early formative years the leading academic treatises were Melius de Villiers, *The Roman and Roman-Dutch Law of Injuries* (1899) and W. A. Joubert, *Grondslae van die Persoonlikheidsreg* (1953). More recent specialist works on the *actio iniuriarum*, which have contributed to the development of this action in South Africa, are: Chittharanjan Felix Amerasinghe, *Aspects of the Actio Injuriarum in Roman-Dutch Law* (1966); *idem, Defamation and other Aspects of the Actio Injuriarum in Roman-Dutch Law* (1968); Bhadra Ranchod, *The Foundations of the South African Law of Defamation* (1972); Pieter Pauw, *Persoonlikheidskrenking en skuld in die Suid-Afrikaanse privaatreg: 'n regshistoriese en regsvergelykende ondersoek* (1976); G. J. Davidtsz, *Animus Injuriandi as Vereiste vir Aanspreeklikheid op Grond van Privaatregtelike Laster* (unpublished LL D thesis, University of Potchefstroom, 1976); J. Neethling, *Die Reg op Privaatheid* (unpublished LL D thesis, University of South Africa, 1976); David McQuoid-Mason, *The Law of Privacy in South Africa* (1978); J. Neethling, *Persoonlikheidsreg* (3rd edn., 1991); Jonathan Burchell, *The Law of Defamation in South Africa* (1985).

law and constitutional protection of individual rights. The crucial task, however, still awaits those who play a role in interpreting and applying the law in this field. The principles of the modern *actio iniuriarum* must not only be compatible with but also enhance the protection of fundamental rights in a Bill of Rights.

The *actio iniuriarum* became the general remedy for aggressions upon person, dignity, and reputation long before the time of Justinian[2] and this survey of the development of the action on South African soil[3] will use this hallowed distinction between impairments of reputation (the law of defamation), impairments of dignity (including invasions of privacy, unlawful arrest, and malicious prosecution), and impairments of person. Since, however, in physical injury cases the plaintiff is usually protected by the principles of Aquilian liability (as far as patrimonial loss is concerned) as well as by an action for pain and suffering,[4] we will confine our discussion to the first two types of injuries.

II. THE EVOLUTION IN THE LAW OF DEFAMATION

1. Persistent Roman-Dutch influences

(a) The fluctuating fortunes of animus iniuriandi

When the Dutch settlers arrived at the Cape in 1652 they brought with them the legal system that prevailed in Holland during the seventeenth century. Even when the British arrived in 1795 there was no immediate deviation from Roman-Dutch principles. However, in 1806 when control at the Cape passed into British hands the infiltration of English law began to be felt. This English influence, seen by one prominent writer on delict as a 'contagion',[5] has, for better or for worse, played a significant role in the evolution of the principles of the law of defamation, but the competition between English and Roman-Dutch principles has at times been fierce.

In some instances the Roman-Dutch principles held sway for a considerable time before the English intruder made its presence felt. For instance, in the earliest reported case on defamation in South Africa, *Mackay v. Philip*[6] in 1830, the Cape Supreme Court took it for granted that *animus ini-*

---

[2] For the development of the *actio iniuriarum* in Roman law and under the *ius commune* see Reinhard Zimmermann, *The Law of Obligations: Roman Foundations of the Civilian Tradition* (1990, reprint 1993), 1050 sqq. On the South African *usus modernus* see 1078 sqq.

[3] For a comprehensive historical and comparative discussion see, most recently, Helge Walter, *Actio iniuriarum: Der Schutz der Persönlichkeit im südafrikanischen Privatrecht* (1996).

[4] See e.g. Zimmermann (n. 2), 1084 sq.

[5] T. W. Price, '*Animus Injuriandi* in Defamation', (1949) 66 *SALJ* 4, commenting on his perception of the retarding effect of the English influence in the acceptance of *animus iniuriandi* as a requirement for liability in the law of defamation.

[6] (1830) 1 Menz 455.

uriandi (intention), which was recognized under the Roman and Roman-Dutch law,[7] was an essential for liability for defamation in South Africa. This Roman-Dutch emphasis on *animus iniuriandi* was evident from 1830 to 1915; only in 1916 did the English principle of strict liability exert an influence, albeit briefly.

Although the judgments of the South African courts at this time were pithy, it is possible in some of them to detect a very firm reliance on a broad approach to *animus iniuriandi*, compatible with Roman influences.

For instance, in *Van Reenen v. Mollett*,[8] the plaintiff (a gaoler) in a defamation case alleged that a letter written on the instruction of the defendant imputed that he had substituted diseased rations for healthy food for distribution to the prisoners. Kotzé CJ and Burgers and Brand JJ held that, assuming the letter contained defamatory matter and had been published, if the defendant *bona fide* believed that lungsick meat had been substituted as rations then he was justified in causing the letter to be written. Aside from the potential confusion between a defence excluding *animus iniuriandi* and a ground of justification (or defence excluding unlawfulness) which was only dispelled in the 1970s and 1980s, this judgment is a striking precursor of the reaffirmation of broad Roman-Dutch principles of *animus iniuriandi* in *Maisel v. Van Naeren*.[9]

However, *Van Reenen v. Mollett* is not an isolated instance of a broad Roman-Dutch approach to *animus iniuriandi* taken by the South African courts in the late nineteenth century. In *Fradd v. Jacquelin*[10] the Natal Supreme Court, relying on Roman and Roman-Dutch authority, defined *animus iniuriandi* as intention to offer insult or affront and cited Roman-Dutch authority for regarding anger or provocation as excluding this element of liability.[11] Specifically identifying the difference between English and Roman-Dutch law in this regard, the Court gave a wide meaning to *animus iniuriandi* by indicating that the defendant could rebut the presumption of *animus iniuriandi* in any way he liked.[12]

The courts sometimes defined 'privilege' or 'privileged occasion' as a statement made *bona fide*, with honest belief in the truth and made without

---

[7] See generally Burchell (n. 1), 3 sqq.; Zimmermann (n. 2), 1078 sqq.; Walter (n. 3).

[8] (1881–90) 2 SAR 5.

[9] 1960 (4) SA 836 (C), on which see below, text to n. 28, and Burchell (n. 1), 152 sqq.

[10] (1882) 3 NLR 144.

[11] See also *Harper v. Posnot* (1881) 2 NLR 78 and *Wilhelm v. Beamish* (1894) 11 SC 13 (where it was accepted that insanity or anger could exclude *animus iniuriandi*). Similarly, the Cape Supreme Court in *Botha v. Brink* (1878) 8 Buch 118 recognized the difference between English and Roman-Dutch law on this matter and concluded that the defendant is always in a position to prove that he was not actuated by 'malice'.

[12] Sometimes, however, a court lapsed back into the approach that a *bona fide* mistake (e.g. referring to the wrong person) was not a defence (*Proctor v. Christ* (1894) 11 SC 254) or that the mistake had to be reasonable in order to excuse (*Bulpin v. Jackson* (1896) 13 SC 254).

malice.[13] This is a perplexing definition which may have something to do with the 'anomalous rolled-up plea' of truth for the public benefit and fair comment[14] which has fortunately been rejected in the modern South African law of defamation. However, the definition of 'privilege' also undoubtedly carried the seed of an extremely wide view of *animus iniuriandi*, which can even embrace mistake or ignorance as regards the truth of a statement.

During the period 1830 to 1915 certain common features appeared in cases dealing with *animus iniuriandi*. *Animus iniuriandi* (sometimes incorrectly rendered by judges trained in the English law as 'malice'[15] or even 'malice aforethought'[16]) was undoubtedly a requirement of liability for defamation and the defendant bore a burden of disproving this element.[17] In certain instances a presumption of *animus iniuriandi* arose. The origin of this presumption seems to have lain in the ancient rule that a person is presumed to intend the natural consequences of his act.[18] These early cases also took the view (prompted by an English influence which was later eradicated) that defences such a privilege or truth for the public benefit served to rebut the presumption of *animus iniuriandi*.[19]

A brief interlude, with judicial emphasis on English strict liability principles, intervened from 1916 to 1960 which retarded the full flowering of the Roman-Dutch concept of *animus iniuriandi*. In 1916 the Transvaal Court handed down judgment in *Jooste v. Claassens*[20] and in the course of his judgment the following statement was made by Mason J:

---

[13] See *James v. Oldfield* (1891) 12 NLR 256; *Hofmeyr v. Stigant* (1879) 9 Buch 95; *Bosman v. Bisset* (1880–2) 1 SC 319; *Johnston v. Doig* (1902) 23 NLR 144; *Course v. Household* (1909) 30 NLR 188.

[14] See Burchell (n. 1), 208 sq.

[15] See below, text before n. 48, on the confusion brought about by this infiltration of English terminology.

[16] *De Jager v. Bryant* (1875) 5 Buch 145.

[17] See e.g. *White v. Pilkington* (1851) 1 Searle 107; *Hare v. White* (1865) 1 Roscoe 246; *Henry Jardine v. James Marshall* 1869 NPD 168; *Dippenaar v. Hauman* (1878) 8 Buch 135, 143; *Botha v. Brink* (1878) 8 Buch 118; *Harper v. Posnot* (1881) 2 NLR 78; *Fradd v. Jacquelin* (1882) 3 NLR 144; *Tait v. Schulz* (1886) 7 NLR 40; *Bok v. Erasmus and Toerien* (1887) 2 SAR 164; *Burne v. Proprietor of the 'Weekly News'* (1888) 9 NLR 57 (even in the case of a newspaper defendant!); *Martin v. Pickering* (1890) 11 NLR 86 (where malice was defined as acting 'recklessly, without any serious endeavour to discover the real facts'); *Loveday v. Lombaard* (1896) 3 SAR 38; *Miller v. State* (1899) 6 SAR 76. It is not clear whether the reference to 'burden of proof' in these cases unquestionably places on the defendant a burden of proof on a balance of probabilities or merely an evidential burden to adduce evidence of lack of *animus iniuriandi*. Recent case authority seems to require only an evidential burden and this approach is undoubtedly in keeping with overall dictates of freedom of expression, entrenched in s. 15, Bill of Rights in the Constitution of the Republic of South Africa Act 200 of 1993.

[18] See *Dippenaar v. Hauman* (1878) 8 Buch 135 and, later, *Young v. Kemsley* 1940 AD 258, 277.

[19] *Botha v. Brink* (1878) 8 Buch 118; *Dippenaar v. Hauman* (1878) 8 Buch 135; *Loveday v. Lombaard* (1896) 3 SAR 38; Price, (1949) 66 *SALJ* 8 sqq.

[20] 1916 TPD 723, 732.

It seems to me therefore that a person who like the defendant on an unprivileged occasion repeats slanders to a third party in the course of ordinary conversation cannot escape liability by asserting or even proving that he was a friend of the slandered plaintiff and had no intention of injuring him.

There followed decisions in the Transvaal where the view was taken that the defendant, in rebutting the presumption of 'malice' (the English term was used), is confined to the set defences: he could not simply plead an absence of *animus iniuriandi* or intention to injure.[21]

McKerron, writing in 1931,[22] accordingly had some support for his contention that *animus iniuriandi* was a 'fiction'. However, shortly before the publication of his views Wessels JA had defined *animus iniuriandi* in *Nasionale Pers Bpk. v. Long*[23] in terms of recklessness. Although there was a measure of confusion as to whether he was alluding to an objective element akin to negligence or to intention,[24] these prophetic words have been interpreted as being reconcilable with the recklessness element of *animus iniuriandi*.[25] However, it was still to take time before the ultimate definition of *animus iniuriandi* as subjective intention to defame with knowledge of unlawfulness was finally accepted by the Appellate Division in *O'Malley's* case in 1977.[26]

Apart from the influential judgment of De Villiers AJ in the Cape Court in *Maisel v. Van Naeren*,[27] reaffirming Roman-Dutch principles of *animus iniuriandi* (in their most dramatic form by allowing a *bona fide*, but erroneous, belief in the existence of a privileged occasion to excuse), the milestones in this development were provided by the Appellate Division. Schreiner JA in *Basner v. Trigger*[28] emphasized that *animus iniuriandi* was the gist of the action. From then on the development of *animus iniuriandi* (albeit at times faltering) lay in the hands of a single judge of appeal: Rumpff CJ.

Although three of his judgments on *animus iniuriandi*[29] arguably contributed little to dispel the mist of confusion around the concept, the fourth (*Suid-Afrikaans Uitsaaikorporasie v. O'Malley*[30]) finally established the pre-eminence of *animus iniuriandi* as subjective intention to defame with knowledge of unlawfulness. The Roman-Dutch law had, after considerable opposition from the English strict liability principle, eventually triumphed.

---

[21] Notably *Laloe Janoe v. Bronkhorst* 1918 TPD 165; *Tothill v. Foster* 1925 TPD 857, 862 sq.; see also *Kleinhans v. Usmar* 1929 AD 121, 126; *Edwards v. Stewart* 1917 TPD 159, 163.

[22] 'Fact and Fiction in the Law of Defamation', (1931) 48 *SALJ* 154.

[23] 1930 AD 87, 90–100.

[24] See *Hassen v. Post Newspapers (Pty) Ltd* 1965 (3) SA 562 (W).

[25] *Suid-Afrikaanse Uitsaaikorporasie v. O'Malley* 1977 (3) SA 394 (A) (*per* Rumpff CJ).

[26] Above, n. 25.　　　　　[27] 1960 (4) SA 836 (C).　　　　　[28] 1946 AD 83, 94–5.

[29] *Jordaan v. Van Biljon* 1962 (1) SA 286 (A); *Craig v. Voortrekkerspers Bpk.* 1963 (1) SA 149 (A); *Nydoo v. Vengtas* 1965 (1) SA 1 (A).

[30] 1977 (3) SA 394 (A).

Paradoxically, the very judge of appeal who had nurtured *animus iniuriandi* to its full flowering sowed the seeds of the destruction of *animus iniuriandi* (or any fault element, including negligence, for that matter) as a requirement for the liability of the mass media for defamation. This blow to freedom of expression can hardly go unnoticed by a court which is serious about upholding freedom of the press and other media under a Bill of Rights.[31]

(b) Unlawfulness and fault distinguished

The differentiation between the respective domains of unlawfulness and fault (*animus iniuriandi*) is unquestionably one of the most distinct and beneficial contributions of Roman and Roman-Dutch jurisprudence to the South African law of delict. The recognition of a general criterion of unlawfulness, based upon the legal convictions of the community and distinct from intention or *animus iniuriandi*, stretches back to the Roman *convicium*[32] which emerged from the Praetorian edict of about 200 BC. It was this policy-based concept of unlawfulness which was echoed by *Antonius Matthaeus*[33] when he described an *iniuria* as '*contumelia* contra bonos mores alicui illata'. This emphasis on the element of *contra bonos mores* foreshadows the development of the modern concept of unlawfulness or wrongfulness.

(c) Truth for the public benefit

In stark contrast to the protracted and only partial eradication of the stubborn English principle of strict liability is the relatively painless and complete rejection of the English rule that publication of the truth is a defence to an action for libel and slander.[34] From the nineteenth-century South African cases on defamation it is clear that the publication of the truth on its own is no defence in a defamation action: the publication of the truth must be for the public benefit.[35] This approach was embraced by the Cape Supreme Court and persists in modern case-law.[36]

---

[31] See below, text to n. 44.   [32] See Burchell (n. 1), 4 sqq.; Zimmermann (n. 2), 1053 sq.
[33] Antonius Matthaeus II, *De Criminibus*, 47, 4, 1, 1.

[34] The affirmation of the principle that the publication of the truth was not in itself a defence but required that the publication of the truth be for the public benefit in order to constitute a justification was not entirely straightforward. De Villiers JP in *Liebenguth v. Van Straaten* 1910 TPD 1203, 1206–7 mentioned that the Roman-Dutch law on the point was in dispute and, in fact, at one time the Orange Free State Court took the rather uncharacteristically English approach that truth alone was sufficient while the Cape Court required truth for the public benefit.

[35] *Botha v. Brink* (1878) 8 Buch 118; *Graham v. Ker* (1892) 9 SC 185. See also *Walter v. Powrie* (1877) 7 Buch 35; *Michaelis v. Braun* (1886) 4 SC 205; *Bloem v. Zietsman* (1897) 14 SC 361; and the Natal case of *Weil v. Hardy* (1906) 27 NLR 192.

[36] There was some dispute as to whether the public benefit addition was clearly required under the Roman and Roman-Dutch law; see Burchell (n. 1), 206 sq. andMelius De Villiers (n. 1), 104.

Why did *animus iniuriandi* take so long to find favour and why did the 'truth for the public benefit' rule receive such prompt acceptance? The confusion between 'malice' and *animus iniuriandi* may have played its part in the slow progress of *animus iniuriandi*, but perhaps the answer lies in the inherent pragmatism of judges in the field of defamation. In the development of the true hybrid which is the modern South African law of defamation, this is only one of the examples of judges choosing from the Roman, Roman-Dutch, and English options the principle which they think is best suited to local soil.

2. Indelible English influences

Much has been written about the influence of English law on Roman-Dutch principles.[37] In the law of defamation the English influence has been felt particularly in the test of defamatory matter[38] and the defence of fair comment,[39] both of which are essentially of English, not Roman-Dutch origin. The English law relating to the elements of 'publication' ('identification')[40] and the basis for the liability of distributors of published material[41] has also exerted an influence on the South African law. The Appellate Division in *Pakendorf v. De Flamingh*,[42] in reaching the momentous and debatable[43] conclusion that the press, radio, and television are subject to strict liability for defamation, has stated that this strand of our law of defamation comes from English law.

When the Constitutional Court, or any other court charged with implementing the provisions of the Bill of Rights in South Africa, is confronted with an appropriate case it could significantly advance the freedom of the mass media by requiring fault, at least in the form of negligence, as a requirement for their liability for defamation and invasion of privacy.[44]

---

[37] See e.g. O. D. Schreiner, *The Contribution of English Law to South African Law and the Rule of Law in South Africa* (1967), esp. 61 sq.; *Price*, (1949) 66 SALJ 4; *P. Q. R. Boberg*, 'Oak Tree or Acorn?: Conflicting Approaches to our Law of Delict', (1966) 83 *SALJ* 150.

[38] The hallowed formulation of the test for determining defamatory matter by Lord Atkin in *Sim v. Stretch* [1936] 2 All ER 1237 (HL) has been adopted in South Africa: 'Would the words tend to lower the plaintiff in the estimation of right-thinking people generally?'

[39] Burchell (n. 1), 219 sqq.   [40] Ibid. 71 sqq.

[41] E.g. libraries and newsvendors: see Burchell (n. 1), 175 sqq.

[42] 1982 (3) SA 146 (A) 156.

[43] It is submitted that not only is the South African case authority used by the Appellate Division to support its conclusion shaky, but the practical effect of such a principle on press freedom and the right of the public to be informed is also suspect, particularly as 'freedom of the press and other media' is entrenched in Ch. 3 of the South African Bill of Rights; see further Burchell (n. 1), 181 sqq.

[44] Cf. the analogous approach of the United States Supreme Court, discussed in Burchell (n. 1), 190 sqq.

3. Perplexing influences

(a) Old habits die hard

Judges, very often trained in English law and familiar with English terminology, naturally spoke of 'libel and slander' and 'malice'. Throughout the nineteenth century, South African courts referred to libel and slander, although the odd case revealed the more contemporary terminology of 'defamation' without any reference to the peculiarly English distinction between libel and slander.[45] It was only in 1904 that Bale CJ in the Natal Supreme Court stated: 'I do not think that the English law in this regard is the same as our own. The English law draws a distinction between words spoken and words written, which our own law does not draw.'[46]

Mercifully, the formal distinction between libel (defamation in a permanent form) and slander (spoken words and gestures) has exerted little if any influence on the development of the principles of the law of defamation in South Africa, but occasionally South African judges and the press inadvertently reveal their English roots by using the terminology of libel and slander.

While any damage caused to the fabric of the South African law of defamation by the use of the words of libel and slander was confined to terminology rather than principle, the same cannot be said of the exportation to South African soil of the term 'malice' and the confusion which existed, and still exists, in the English legal system between unlawfulness and fault and the defences excluding these respective elements.

The English law distinguished between 'express' or 'special' malice (which indicated spite, ill-will, or improper motive on the part of the defendant) and 'legal malice' or 'malice in law' (which meant publication without lawful excuse, and bore no relevance to the state of mind of the defendant). The South African courts took some time to emerge from the smog which engulfed the law of defamation as a result of a confusion between malice and *animus iniuriandi*. It was only after *animus iniuriandi* was resurrected, defined and a clear distinction drawn between unlawfulness and fault that the Appellate Division could confine 'malice' to the improper motive, spite, or ill-will which leads to the forfeiture of certain defences such as fair comment and qualified privileged occasion.[47]

---

[45] See e.g. *Fradd v. Jacquelin* (1882) 3 NLR 144.

[46] *Nicolson v. Roberts* (1904) 25 NLR 278, 282.

[47] Corbett JA in *Borgin v. De Villiers* 1980 (3) SA 556 (A), in dealing with the plea of lawful publication of defamatory matter (579F-G), left open the question whether the term 'express malice' is still appropriate. However, it is submitted that a clear distinction is drawn in South African law between express malice and *animus iniuriandi*; thus there can now be no confusion in terminology. Furthermore, Joubert JA's unqualified acceptance in *May v. Udwin* 1981 (1) SA 1 (A) of the term 'malice' (covering improper motive, spite, and ill-will) places the matter of terminology beyond doubt. See also Jansen JA in *Marais v. Richard* 1981 (1) SA 1157 (A) 1170C-D.

Some Roman-Dutch influences were also discarded in the process of developing a truly South African version of the *actio iniuriarum*. The Roman-Dutch principle of honourable amends, which provided for a retraction of defamatory words by the defendant, an acknowledgement of their falsity, and an apology, was referred to in an early Natal case as 'an archaism'.[48] Melius de Villiers[49] pointed out that although the *amende honorable* was regarded as 'obsolete' it had nevertheless appeared more than once in letters of demand and forms of summons. However, in the 1910 case of *Ward-Jackson v. Cape Times Ltd*[50] it was held that in Roman-Dutch law a plaintiff might sue for an apology or *amende honorable*, but that this practice seemed to have fallen into desuetude.

The Roman-Dutch *amende honorable* was an action or more correctly: a remedy, and hence the method of its enforcement was seen as a stumbling-block in certain early South African cases.[51] However, there are, it is submitted, merits in the concept of a general defence of retraction (including acknowledgement of the falsity of words) and an apology.[52]

(b) New habits may be short-lived

English precedent demanded that, while the plaintiff obviously has the burden of proving the elements of an action, the defendant bears the burden of proving the existence of a defence. The South African courts in the late nineteenth and early twentieth centuries, although not drawing a firm distinction between a burden of proof and an evidential burden, simply referred to the defendant 'proving' a defence, e.g. truth for the public benefit.[53]

In the face of this arguably ambivalent precedent, the South African Appellate Division in the late 1970s[54] and early 1980s[55] demonstrated a distinct predilection for placing only an evidential burden (*weerleggingslas*[56])

---

[48] *Per* Cloete J in *Hare v. White* (1865) 1 Roscoe 246, 247.

[49] *The Roman and Roman-Dutch Law of Injuries* (1899), 178. Generally on the *amende honorable* see Zimmermann (n. 2), 1072 sqq

[50] 1910 WLD 257, 263.   [51] Burchell (n. 1), 315 sqq.

[52] These advantages are canvassed in Burchell, (n. 1).

[53] See *Meurant v. Raubenheimer* (1886) 1 Buch AC 87; *Payne v. Sheffield* (1881–2) 2 EDC 166; *Sturrock v. Birt* (1889–91) 8 SC 120; *Bloem v. Zietsman* (1897) 14 SC 361; *Rubel v. Katzenellenbogen* 1915 CPD 627; *Masch v. Leask* 1916 TPD 114 (defendant must prove lack of intention to injure because the words were uttered in jest and would have been understood as such by a reasonable person); and the cases referred to by Burchell (n. 1), 218, fn. 104, 231, fn. 93. That the courts did not draw any analytical distinction between proof on a balance of probabilities and an evidential burden is borne out by the statement of Shippard J in *Q v. Shaw and Fennell* (1884) 3 EDC 323 concerning the accused in a criminal case 'proving' truth. Shippard J must surely have been referring to an evidential burden, not a true burden of proof.

[54] *Suid-Afrikaanse Uitsaaikorporasie v. O'Malley* 1977 (3) SA 394 (A).

[55] *Borgin v. De Villiers* 1980 (3) SA 556 (A) 571E-G; *May v. Udwin* 1981 (1) SA 1 (A); *Marais v. Richard* 1981 (1) SA 1157 (A) 1166H.

[56] The exact origin of the emphasis on such a *weerleggingslas* is unclear, but C. H. W. Schmidt, *Bewysreg* (2nd edn., 1982), 30 and 25 sqq. refers to a *weerleggingslas* as the

on the defendant to adduce evidence of a defence rebutting either the presumption of unlawfulness or of *animus iniuriandi* which arose on the publication of defamatory matter referring to the plaintiff.

As far as the presumption of unlawfulness is concerned, the tide has now turned dramatically, starting with the *obiter* statement of Kotzé JA in *Joubert v. Venter*[57] that the 'question of *weerleggingslas versus* full onus in relation to the plea of qualified privilege should be regarded as being still an open question in our law'. The Appellate Division has now firmly opted for a full onus of proof resting on the defendant to prove the defence of truth for the public benefit and privileged occasion, deriving strength from the English approach.[58]

The days of the *weerleggingslas* in connection with defences excluding unlawfulness may be numbered, but the presumption of *animus iniuriandi* may still be rebutted by the defendant adducing evidence rather than proving a defence excluding *animus iniuriandi*.[59]

Placing a burden of proof on the defendant to prove, for instance, the truth of a statement made may carry adverse implications for freedom of expression and consequent constitutional challenges, particularly in the context of the mass media which are already subject to strict, or no-fault, liability for defamation. The question of allocating an onus of proof is undoubtedly one of public policy[60] but, in determining the relevant policy considerations, sight must not be lost of the demands of free speech and the right of the public to be informed.

Hoexter JA in *Neethling's case*[61] regarded it as inequitable to require of the defendant only that it be 'just as likely as not'[62] that the defamatory allegations are true. This means that truth and falsity would be held in equilibrium. Even the casting of an evidential burden on the defendant to adduce evidence of truth requires more than this equilibrium. Very much as after a claim of *res ipsa loquitur*, where an inference of negligence is drawn, the defendant is called upon to give the other side of the story in order to swing the balance in his favour. This can be done by adducing evidence that he was not negligent. Similarly, in the face of a presumption of unlawfulness arising from the publication of defamatory matter referring to the

equivalent of what Phipson calls an 'evidential burden' (*Phipson on Evidence* (14th edn., 1990), fns. 4 sqq.). Schmidt may have played a significant role in popularizing the notion of a *weerleggingslas*.

[57] 1985 (1) SA 654 (A) 697G-H.
[58] *Neethling v. Du Preez, Neethling v. Weekly Mail* 1994 (1) SA 708 (A) 770I-J.
[59] See the statement of Hoexter JA in *Neethling's* case (n. 58) 767G-I where the judge of appeal appeared to accept the view of Rumpff CJ in *O'Malley* (n. 25) that the burden on the defendant of rebutting the presumption of *animus iniuriandi* is evidential; see also Hoexter JA, 768 sq., who distinguishes between the effect of the presumption of *animus iniuriandi* and that of unlawfulness.
[60] Hoexter JA in *Neethling's* case (n. 58), 770.
[61] *Neethling's* case (n. 58), 770G-H.
[62] Hoexter JA, ibid. 770G-H.

plaintiff, the defendant should be able to rebut this presumption by adducing evidence of a defence excluding unlawfulness. To require him to prove his defence to a defamation action on a balance of probabilities could well result in the unjustifiable curtailment of freedom of speech and, for instance in the case of the mass media, may lead to pressure to disclose confidential sources.[63]

4. Missed opportunities

Before the judges in the Appellate Division finally imposed strict liability on the mass media for defamation[64] they were given numerous opportunities to choose paths which, it is submitted, are not only more enlightened but also in keeping with current notions of press freedom and the right of the public to be informed.

Aside from the compelling judgment of Colman J in *Hassen v. Post Newspapers (Pty) Ltd*[65] in 1965, support for a negligence-based form of liability for defamation for the press can be found in the early Transvaal decision in *Sauer v. Mendelssohn and Scott* in 1887.[66] In this case, although the press were held liable for publishing defamatory matter, it was stated that although the press have no exceptional privileges in commenting on people, editors ought to make every effort to ascertain the truth.

Even if negligence-based liability for defamation (for both the individual and the mass media) does not suit the judicial palate, an acceptable concession to freedom of expression might be to give greater latitude to criticism of the public conduct of public figures. A distinction between the public and private conduct of public figures was in fact drawn in the early Cape case of *De Jager v. Bryant*.[67]

The South African courts have often emphasized that the mass media have no greater rights or privileges than the ordinary citizen in criticizing the acts of others, including public officials.[68] Shippard J in *Payne v. Sheffield*[69] astutely observed:

I take it to be clear that propietors, editors, and publishers of newspapers, important and influential as their functions undoubtedly are, have in the eyes of the law no greater rights, privileges, or exemptions in respect of the publication of libels than all private individuals. The law knows no distinction of persons, and cannot be varied and moulded to suit particular classes. The same rules apply equally to all.

---

[63] The presumption of unlawfulness (and that of *animus iniuriandi*) which arises on the publication of defamatory matter referring to the plaintiff, and the policy factors pertaining to freedom of expression, serve to distinguish the position under the *actio iniuriarum* from that under the Aquilian action where the defendant has to prove a defence excluding unlawfulness.

[64] See *Pakendorf v. De Flamingh* 1982 (3) SA 146 (A).

[65] 1965 (3) SA 562 (W).   [66] (1885–8) 2 SAR 210.

[67] (1875) 3 Buch 145. See also *Watkins v. Ewing* (1883) 3 EDC 155.

[68] See e.g. *Payne v. Sheffield* (1882) 2 EDC 166.   [69] (1882) 2 EDC 166, at 174.

Although this statement was made in the context of setting limits for comment by the press, it can as forcefully be used to emphasize that the position of the mass media should also not be inferior to that of the individual, as has occurred in the wake of the Appellate Division judgment in *Pakendorf v. De Flamingh*.[70]

Another missed opportunity, but which could still be remedied by a change in the final version of the South African Constitution if necessary, is the failure to incorporate into the Bill of Rights an individual right of reply.[71] The African National Congress in its draft Bill of Rights included reference to 'a free press which shall respect the right to reply'. It is unfortunate that this enlightened recommendation, which would have served to continue public debate and to provide speedy recompense for a tarnished reputation or dignity, was neglected in the political bargaining process.

III. IMPAIRMENT OF DIGNITY AND INVASION OF PRIVACY

Legal systems rooted in the English, rather than the Roman, tradition have developed sophisticated protection for reputation in the laws of libel and slander, and they protect physical integrity through civil actions for tresspass to the person, assault, and battery. However, the protection of that precious and inherent attribute of human personality—dignity—does not exist in the common law of these systems. Whatever common law protection of dignity there is depends on the expansive, judicial interpretation of existing torts or, in the case of the United States, constitutional interpretation.[72]

The protection of human dignity under the *actio iniuriarum* is undoubtedly one of the most impressive and enduring legacies of Roman law, and a feature which places the South African law of delict in the forefront of the protection of what is arguably the most fundamental of all human rights. At present the remedy is used to protect an individual from insulting words or conduct, interference with parental authority, breach of promise to marry, adultery, unlawful arrest and detention, malicious prosecution, and invasion of privacy. The further potential which lies within the *actio iniuriarum* to protect dignity in a Bill of Rights era is enormous.

Aside from the controversial issue of whether the Bill of Rights in South Africa operates only vertically (i.e. between individual and State) or also horizontally (between individuals), it is clear that under the limitations

---

[70] 1982 (3) SA 146 (A).

[71] On the French *droit de reponse*, other comparative examples of rights of reply, and the reservations expressed by the Supreme Court in the United States about infringements on the editorial discretion of the media see Burchell (n. 1), 311 sqq.

[72] E.g. the protection of privacy in the United States.

clause (s. 33) a rule of common law can only in specified circumstances limit the protection of fundamental rights entrenched in the Constitution. Rules of the common law of delict, as well as any other rules of the common law, may have to pass this litmus test.

Section 33 of the Bill of Rights of the Interim Constitution of the Republic of South Africa Constitution Act[73] and the injunction in section 35 (that '[i]n the interpretation of any law and the application and development of the common law and customary law, a court shall have due regard to the spirit, purport and object of [the Bill of Rights]') could well provide the spark needed to keep the flame of the *actio iniuriarum* burning, fuelled by its identification with the cause of protecting fundamental human rights.

However, even in Roman law there were texts which supported a broad interpretation of the concept of dignity, analogous to the sense in which the concept is used in the major human rights instruments, both internationally and nationally.[74] Thus, Justinian's Digest provides: if anyone hinders me from fishing in the sea, bathing in a public bathing area, or sitting in a public stall at the theatre I can institute an action for injury against him. In these examples the individual's freedom of movement is unjustifiably curtailed,[75] for which redress under the *actio iniuriarum* would lie.

This broad interpretation of dignity could, for instance, provide a remedy in damages for unlawful discrimination, unlawful dismissal from employment, deprivation of due process safeguards, or denial of prisoners' rights.[76] A culture of respect for human rights can only develop where fundamental rights are protected under the common law and the Bill of Rights.

Some initial confusion in the development of the protection afforded by the *actio iniuriarum* arose from the term *contumelia* used in classical Roman law. Joubert[77] has analysed the various meanings of *contumelia* (namely insulting behaviour and the expression of arrogance) and has concluded that the concept of *contumelia* only played a formative function in the development of the idea of *animus iniuriandi*.

---

[73] 200 of 1993.

[74] See s. 10, Chapter 3 of the Interim Constitution of the Republic of South Africa Constitution Act 200 of 1993.

[75] See further Jonathan Burchell, 'Beyond the Glass Bead Game: Human Dignity in the Law of Delict', (1988) 4 *SAJHR*, 1, 2 sqq. Compare, however, the approach of Neethling (n. 1), 54 and Joubert (n. 1), 95, who take the view that although the Roman texts are not clear on this point they appear to demand some physical interference with rights. This restriction would prevent 'dignity' from being interpreted broadly so as to include the infringement of liberty (without physical interference) and it would preclude the courts from e.g. utilizing the remedy for impairment of dignity to provide redress for unfair discrimination, deprivation of the protection of due process, etc. A broad interpretation of the concept of 'dignity' would allow the South African courts to achieve a similar protection of the right to personal autonomy as that developed by the American courts under the artificially expanded concept of 'privacy'.

[76] See generally Burchell, (1988) 4 *SAJHR* 1 sqq.; *Minister of Justice v. Hofmeyr* 1993 (3) SA 131 (A).

[77] Joubert (n. 1), 92 sq.

It would be far too restrictive to require for an *actio iniuriarum* the presence of *contumelia*, in the form of insult. The Appellate Division has recently seized the opportunity to reject such a limiting requirement and preferred to extend a remedy for invasion of privacy to an artificial or juristic person, who obviously cannot experience insult in the strict sense of the word.[78]

There was no sophisticated concept of privacy in the Roman law, but the Roman jurists recognized a number of specific instances where a remedy (usually under the *actio iniuriarum*) was provided for a wrong which can be interpreted as constituting an impairment of privacy: for instance, invasions of the sanctity of the home.[79] As Blecher concludes: 'The civil law did, to a certain extent, and albeit indirectly, protect what would today be termed privacy, and to the extent that it did not, one can say that the civil law may have lacked the need to protect privacy, not the means.'[80]

During the nineteenth and early twentieth centuries in South Africa there was no recorded case-law which gave any substance to this concept of privacy, but from the 1950s onward a right to be free from unreasonable intrusions of one's private sphere began to develop. While South African jurisprudence cannot claim to have fashioned a clearly defined concept of privacy, the case-law nevertheless provides examples of unreasonable intrusions into the private sphere,[81] public disclosure of private facts,[82] appropriation of name or likeness,[83] and false light cases.[84] The remedy for invasion of privacy has even been extended to a corporate body.[85]

Section 13 of the South African Bill of Rights entrenches the right of every person to 'personal privacy, which shall include the right not to be subject to searches of his or her person, home or property, the seizure of private possessions or the violation of private communications'. This right, however, is subject to the right to free expression protected in s. 15 and any general limitation referred to in s. 33 of the Constitution. In the future the focus will be on the limits, particularly in terms of free speech, which can legitimately be placed on the protection of an individual's privacy,[86] reputation, or dignity.

[78] See Corbett CJ in *Financial Mail (Pty) Ltd v. Sage Holdings Ltd* 1993 (2) SA 451 (A) 460–3, esp. 462A–E.

[79] See M. D. Blecher, 'Privacy in the Civil Law', (1975) 43 *Tijdschrift voor rechtsgeschiedenis* 279–96.

[80] *Loc. cit.*, 296.

[81] See e.g. *S v. A* 1971 (2) SA 293 (T) and the 'Peeping Tom' cases in criminal law, e.g. *R v. Holliday* 1927 CPD 395.

[82] *O'Keeffe v. Argus Printing & Publishing Co Ltd* 1954 (3) SA 244 (C); *Mhlongo v. Bailey* 1958 (1) SA 370 (C); *Rhodesian Printing & Publishing Co Ltd v. Duggan* 1975 (1) SA 590 (R); *La Grange v. Schoeman* 1980 (1) SA 885 (E); *Janssen van Vuuren v. Kruger* 1993 (4) SA 842 (A).

[83] Usually occurring under the defamation remedy.

[84] Also occurring under the defamation remedy.

[85] *Financial Mail (Pty) Ltd v. Sage Holdings Ltd* 1993 (2) SA 451 (A) 460.

[86] E.g. should a corporate body, more particularly a political party, be entitled to sue for

In passing, it is hoped that the courts, including the Constitutional Court, will interpret the concept of dignity widely, including under this concept especially attributes such as self-esteem and individual autonomy. This would be preferable to the American approach which overloads the concept of privacy.

IV. CONCLUSION

It was once said that to attempt to return the South African law to its pure Roman origins and to purge it of its English influence, would be like trying to reduce an oak tree to an acorn.[87] Besides being botanically and legally impossible, this attempt would deprive South Africans of the extensive protection of personality rights provided by the spreading branches of this impressive oak. Symbiotic growth of both the personality rights protected by the *actio iniuriarum* and equivalent rights under the Constitution is inevitable and highly desirable.

defamation or invasion of privacy? (See *Argus Printing & Publishing Co Ltd v. Inkatha Freedom Party* 1992 (3) SA 579 (A), holding that, in principle, it can.) S. 7(3) of the Constitution states that juristic persons are entitled to the rights set out in Ch. 3 'where, and to the extent that, the nature of the right permits', while s. 15 lays down the right to freedom of expression. Does the *Inkatha Freedom Party* case strike the correct balance between these competing rights? Should any limits be placed on 'hate speech'? When does the public interest require exposure of certain information? These and other questions undoubtedly require answers.

[87] See the *dictum* of Holmes J in *Ex parte De Winnaar* 1959 (1) SA 837 (N) 839, adopted by Boberg, (1966) 83 *SALJ* 150, 173.

PART VI

Property Law

20: *Ownership*

J. R. L. MILTON

I. INTRODUCTION

The earliest recorded reference to ownership in South African law occurs just five years or so after the servants of the Dutch East India Company waded ashore in Table Bay on 9 April 1652 to found a European settlement at the Cape of Good Hope. In the journal kept by the commander of the settlement it is noted on 21 February 1657 that grants of land are to be made to certain men '*in vollen eygendom*'.[1] Thereafter, title deeds were issued.[2] The day of issue, 14 April 1657, has been called 'the birthday of [South Africa's] ... present day system of private ownership of land'.[3]

In tracing the later history of *eygendom* in South African law it is helpful to bear in mind the social and economic background of the three and a half centuries which followed the birthday of 14 April 1657.

1. The background[4]

(a) Political

The Dutch, in the form of the Dutch East India Company and its successors, governed the settlement at the Cape until the end of the eighteenth century. At the beginning of the nineteenth century the country was acquired by Britain and thereafter governed as a colony of the British Crown until 1910.

In the 1830s the event known as the Great Trek saw Dutch members of the colonial community—known to history as Boers (meaning 'farmers')—emigrate beyond the boundaries of the colony into an interior inhabited by indigenous African tribespeople. The Boers, by force of arms, annexed the land and established republican states. In this newly acquired territory the Boers distributed the land among themselves, allowing the indigenous

---

[1] B. Bosman, H. B. Thom (eds.), *Daghregister gehouden by den oppercoopman Jan Anthoniz van Riebeeck, 1652–62* (1955), vol. II, 100. '*In vollen eiygendom*' was translated into English as 'in full ownership': see H. B. Thom (ed.), *Journal of Jan van Riebeeck 1651–62* (1954), vol. II, 91.

[2] See below, n. 15.

[3] J. W. S. Heyl, *Grondregistrasie in Suid-Afrika* (1977), 9 (translation).

[4] For a good brief history of South Africa see T. R. H. Davenport, *South Africa: A Modern History* (3rd edn., 1987). Cf. Ch. 1 above, by Eduard Fagan, and the references provided there.

peoples to occupy only scattered remnants, known as 'locations', on a form of precarious communal tenure.[5] The Anglo-Boer War of 1899–1902 saw the Boer Republics colonized by Britain, which in 1910 consolidated the colonies of Southern Africa into the Union of South Africa.

Early practices of social segregation of the white and other races in South Africa, in the mid-twentieth century, became the system of legally enforced apartheid.[6] In 1993 this system was swept away with the enactment of a new constitution which brought into existence a democratic and non-racist constitutional dispensation.

(b) Socio-economic

For almost two hundred years following the arrival of the Dutch the economy of South Africa was essentially rural and agrarian. In such a milieu issues relating to the concept of ownership tended to be focused upon matters such as the recovery of the lost possession of movable property, forms of land tenure, and water rights. The discovery in the latter part of the nineteenth century of gold and diamonds introduced an industrial economy concentrated around the mining industry. In this context issues concerning ownership in minerals emerged as an important factor in shaping the concept of ownership.

(c) Legal

During the Dutch era Roman-Dutch law, as modified by local statute and custom, was the prevailing legal system. When the British acquired the Cape colony Roman-Dutch law was retained as the law of the land. However, there was inevitably an infiltration of English law which to some extent challenged the dominance of Roman-Dutch law. In the mid-twentieth century there was a tendency to 'purify' South African law by rejecting English law and returning to the Roman-Dutch sources.

(d) Historical

When Jan van Riebeeck arrived at the Cape the great Dutch jurist Hugo Grotius had been dead for only seven years. Grotius' famous and influential account of the law of Holland, *Inleiding tot de Hollandsche Rechtsgeleertheyd*, had been published only twenty-one years previously.[7] It contained an innovative and important reformulation of the concept of

---

[5] See Derek van der Merwe, 'Land Tenure in South Africa', 1989 *TSAR* 663, 671 sqq. Since the object of this work is the history of the Roman-Dutch law in South Africa, I have not sought to examine the state or history of land tenures of the indigenous peoples.

[6] Cf. M. Robertson, 'Segregation Land Law', in: H. Corder (ed.), *Law and Social Practice in South Africa* (1988), 285 sqq.

[7] For details see R. Zimmermann, 'Römisch-holländisches Recht', in: R. Feenstra, R. Zimmermann (eds.), *Das römisch-holländische Recht: Fortschritte des Zivilrechts im 17. und 18. Jahrhundert* (1992), 26 sqq.

ownership.[8] Grotius described ownership as being either 'full ownership' (which he called *dominium plenum*) where the title to the property and actual use of it are combined in one hand, or 'incomplete ownership' (*gebreckelicke eigendom,* or *dominium minus plenum*) where title and use are separated, as where the owner grants a usufruct over his property.[9]

Implicit in this formulation is the principle of *dominium plenum* (full ownership) as the pre-eminent right over property.[10] It was this concept of the nature of ownership which travelled with Van Riebeeck on his journey to the tip of Africa in 1652.

II. LAND OWNERSHIP: TENURES (1652–1910)

The available records of the early history of the Roman-Dutch concept of ownership at the settlement at the Cape are almost exclusively concerned with the matter of land ownership, so it is in this field[11] that our exploration must begin.

1. The Dutch era

(a) *Grants* in eigendom

Jan van Riebeeck came to the Cape not to establish a colony of Holland but rather a refreshment station for the trading fleets of his masters, the Dutch East India Company. In 1657, however, the directors of the Company decided that the settlement should become economically self-sufficient. Among other things, it was decided to make grants of land to

---

[8] For Grotius' formulation of ownership see A. J. van der Walt, 'Der Eigentumsbegriff', in: Feenstra/Zimmermann (n. 7), 485 sqq. and the sources and literature there cited, particularly the contributions by R. Feenstra (fn. 3).

[9] Grotius (n. 7), 2, 33, 1.   [10] Van der Walt (n. 8), 453.

[11] I have examined sources relating to slavery in the expectation that they might reveal something about the concept of ownership at this time. Slaves were imported to the Cape (the Company's 'Statutes of India' forbade the enslavement of indigenous persons) in 1658; there were 16,839 slaves in the settlement by 1795. However, these sources reveal that the ownership of slaves was not dealt with under the ordinary Roman-Dutch common law, but in terms of a separate code of slave law, taken over mainly from the Roman law of slavery (see the memorandum of the Fiscal of the Cape (in: G. M. Theal, *Records of the Cape Colony* (1897), vol. IX, 146 sqq.) which indicates that the law relating to slaves at the Cape derived from local *placaaten* (notably the codification of regulations issued in 1754 (S. D. Naudé, *Kaapse Plakkaatboek* (1949), vol. III, 1 sqq.)), the Statutes of India (J. A. van der Chijs (ed.), *Nederlandsche-Indisch Plakkaatboek* (1885–97), vol. I, 537 sqq.), and the Roman law of slavery. This investigation thus revealed nothing about the Roman-Dutch concept of ownership. On slavery at the Cape see A. J. Boeseken, *Slaves and Free Blacks at the Cape, 1658–1700* (1977); R. Ross, *Cape of Torments: Slavery and Resistance in South Africa* (1983); N. Worden, *Slavery in Dutch South Africa* (1985); R. L. Watson, *The Slave Question: Liberty and Property in South Africa* (1990). Cf. D. P, Visser, 'The role of Roman law in the punishment of slaves at the Cape of Good Hope under Dutch rule', in: *Mélanges Felix Wubbe* (1993), 525 sqq.

certain 'freemen', employees of the Company who were released from their contracts.[12]

The decision made by the Commander in Council[13] at the Cape to grant[14] land to freemen[15] referred specifically to the grantee receiving not merely ownership but 'full ownership' (*vollen eigendom*).[16]

It is not entirely clear what the Council meant when it spoke of 'ownership'. It may be that the officials intended to dispense *dominium plenum* as conceived by Grotius. However, given that the Council consisted of laymen, it is more likely that what was intended by the term *eigendom* was some sort of quasi-feudal tenure.[17] This is suggested by the fact that the officials had no scruples about attaching to the grant of *eigendom* 'what must have been, even in those days of patient submission to rigid paternal rule, irritating and difficult conditions [under which *eigendom* was to be enjoyed]'.[18] In the case of the first grants, it is stated[19] that the land 'will . . . remain *their property forever to do with as they like*, that is they may sell, lease or otherwise alienate it, subject to notice being given to the Commander or his authorised representative—this to serve instead of a deed given by way of a mortgage, etc'.

In the *erfbriewen* issued on 14 April 1657, the grant of land was described as being subject to the condition that the 'owners' could 'not sell, let or

---

[12] See generally L. Guelke, 'Freehold Farmers and Frontier Settlers, 1657–1780', in: R. Elphick, H. Giliomee (eds.), *The Shaping of South African Society 1652–1840* (2nd edn., 1989), 66.

[13] More usually known as the *Raad van Politie* (Council of Policy).

[14] It seems that the Company believed itself to have acquired (by *occupatio?*; this is suggested by D. van der Merwe, 1989 *TSAR* 663, 666) the power to dispose of the right of ownership in land at the Cape. It has been doubted whether, in law, the Company enjoyed this power (C. H. van Zyl, 'The Batavian and Cape *Plakaaten*', (1907) 24 *SALJ* 132. Whether true or not, the Company clearly proceeded on the basis that it enjoyed this power. Cf. H. R. Hahlo, Ellison Kahn, *The Union of South Africa: The Development of its Laws and Constitution* (1960), 15, fn. 22.

[15] The grants were made under a decision of the Council of Policy of 21 Feb. 1657 to 2 groups of free *burghers*. They had formed two 'colonies', Harman's *Colonie* and Steven's *Colonie*. Harman's *Colonie* was allocated a piece of land beyond the Liesbeeck River, to be known as *Groeneveldt*; Steven's *Colonie* received land 'this side' of the river '*bij 't ronde doorn bosjen*' (at the round thorn bushes—today the suburb of Rondebosch) to be known as *Hollantsen Tuin*. For these and other details see G. M. Theal, *History of South Africa* (1907), vol. II, 61 sqq. The sites of these first grants are recorded on the map in A. J. Boeseken, *Geskiedenis-Atlas van Suid-Afrika* (2nd edn., 1948), 5. The title deeds (*erfbrieven*) to these properties were issued on 14 Apr. 1657. For the text see Heyl (n. 3), 324–37.

[16] The resolution of the Council of Policy was that the grants would be made in 'full ownership' (see sources cited in n. 1). However, the deed of grant (*erfbrief*) issued in April states that the grants are made 'in ownership' (see Heyl (n. 3), 325 sq.).

[17] H. M. Robertson, 'Some Doubts Concerning Early Land Tenure at the Cape', 1935 *South African Journal of Economics* 162, 169, suggests that this might have been the case, a suggestion thought by the historian Davenport to 'make good sense'. See T. H. R. Davenport, 'Some Reflections on the History of Land Tenure in South Africa, Seen in the Light of Attempts by the State to Impose Political and Social Control', 1985 *Acta Juridica* 53, 55 sq.

[18] See *Cape of Good Hope, Report of the Surveyor General on Tenure of the Land, Land Laws, and Their Results*, G. 30-'76 (1876), 6.

[19] Thom (n. 1), 91.

alienate the same' for a period of twelve years, and then only 'with the knowledge and consent of the authorities'.[20] A title deed, dated 10 October 1657 contained a similarly worded restriction.[21]

Indeed, it seems that in every case[22] in which *eigendom* was granted conditions were imposed which would enable the Company to derive some revenue, whether in cash or kind, from the grant.[23] Usually the conditions required the holder to cultivate the land to its fullest capacity, to pay the government a tenth of the harvest, and to allow the construction of roads on the land without compensation.[24] The land was liable to forfeiture if the conditions were not complied with.

After 1685 the authorities insisted that each such grant be surveyed and registered.[25]

The Council was parsimonious in its grants of land *in eigendom*.[26] Grants were confined to comparatively few parcels of land for residential and agricultural purposes[27] in and around Cape Town[28] itself, and later the village of Stellenbosch.[29] It seems likely that this was because, as the settlement grew more permanent, the company's officials became concerned to retain control over the land for fiscal and policy reasons.[30]

In 1717 the Company instructed that no further grants *in eigendom* should be made.[31]

(b) Loan tenure (leeningsplaatsen)

Since the settlement at the Cape was intended to serve primarily as a supply and refreshment station for the Company's fleets *en route* to the East

---

[20] See the deed reproduced and translated in Heyl (n. 3), 324–37.

[21] The grant is reproduced in *Cape of Good Hope* (n. 18), 30–1. An English translation is provided 11.

[22] Between 1657 and 1662 27 grants *in eigendom* were made (Heyl (n. 3), 7). By 1672 there were some 64 deeds of grants *in eigendom* in the register kept at the Cape (ibid. 9).

[23] R. C. Fisher, *Official Land Tenure Policies in the Cape Colony and Natal 1652–1910* (unpublished M.Phil. thesis, University of Cambridge, 1980), 16 sq.).

[24] *Cape of Good Hope* (n. 18), 5 sq., 11–13.

[25] L. C. Duly, *British Land Policy at the Cape, 1795–1844* (1968), 14. It was the 'inveterate custom' of the Netherlands in the time of Grotius that every sale of land was recorded in a register *coram judice loci rei sitae* (*Houtpoort Mining & Estate Syndicate v. Jacobs* 1904 TS 105, 108). From this beginning sprang the elaborate system of registration of deeds of transfer of ownership (and other real rights) in land which prevails in the Republic of South Africa. See generally Heyl (n. 3).

[26] By 1717 only 400 or so farms were held in ownership, occupying a mere 194 square km. (Guelke (n. 12), 74 and fig. 2). At the end of the Dutch era (*c.* 1800) only 1,364 grants in ownership (comprising some 25,500 hectares) had been made. See Duly (n. 25), 14.

[27] The early grants specified the uses or purposes for which the land was to be used. Thus land was granted as an *erf* or building lot, a *tuin* or garden, or a *plaas* or farm. These descriptions came to be distinct tenures, determining the nature and extent of the use or enjoyment of the land. See G. Denoon, 'Conditions in Deeds', (1948) 65 *SALJ* 362, 363 sq.

[28] Duly (n. 25), 14. [29] Guelke (n. 12), 73.

[30] See G. G. Visagie, *Regspleging en Reg aan die Kaap van 1652 tot 1806* (1969), 80; Duly (n. 25), 14.

[31] Guelke (n. 12), 78, fn. 44.

Indies, the policy of the Company was to encourage agriculture and pastoralism at the Cape to ensure adequate supplies of meat and vegetables for the fleets. To this end, the officials at the Cape decided to lend the Company's land to its servants or freemen,[32] usually without requiring any payment for the privilege.[33]

In the course of the later decades of the seventeenth century pastoralists began to drift away from the nuclear settlement, venturing out beyond the tiny hamlet of Cape Town into the interior of the colony with herds of cattle and sheep.

Removed from the control of the officials at Cape Town, and seeking to avoid the legal obligation to pay rents, these itinerant farmers simply occupied such lands in the interior as they chose without seeking permission.[34] Faced with the reality of this type of colonization of the interior, the Company approved 'loan farms' (*leeninggsplaatsen*)[35] for the graziers on the colony's frontiers. The loan, when granted, was made administratively, not as a legal title but simply as a licence to occupy the land.[36] Originally *leeninggsplaatsen* were obtained without the payment of any fee for the privilege, but after 1714 the occupier of a loan place was required to pay a rent (*recognitie*) to the Company.[37] This form of tenure became the commonest of the Dutch era, some 80 per cent of available land in the colony being held in this way.[38]

Leeninggsplaats tenure was characterized by its informality.[39] A farmer requested[40] permission from a local official to occupy a parcel of land[41] and agreed to pay the annual rent. No survey was made nor any deed drawn up. Although the request was supposed to be forwarded to Cape Town for approval, custom held that once the official had approved the request the applicant was regarded as having some right to the land.

[32] Resolutions of the Council of Policy, 1 Oct. 1655, cited in: C. G. Botha, 'Early Cape Land Tenure', (1919) 36 *SALJ* 149, 151; *Cape of Good Hope* (n. 18), 4.

[33] An arrangement in the nature of the contract of *commodatum* or *bruikleen* of Roman-Dutch law. See Fisher (n. 23), 22.

[34] H. A. Reyburn, 'Studies in Cape Frontier History', 1934 *The Critic* 40, 41; Guelke (n. 12), 78.

[35] The usual name for this type of tenure. Theal (n. 11), vol. VIII, 95; Visagie (n. 30), 83.

[36] Duly (n. 25), 16.

[37] M. K. Jeffreys, S. D. Naudé (eds.), *Kaapse Plakkaatboek, 1652–1806*, 1948, vol. II, 31 (a translation can be found in T. R. H. Davenport, K. S. Hunt, *The Right to the Land* (1974), 2). It was suggested that the levying of a rent converted the tenure into a form of lease. See the letter of 28 June 1811 from the Fiscal, J. A. Truter, to the Colonial Secretary, reproduced in Theal (n. 35), 97. See also Robertson, 1935 *South African Journal of Economics* 162 sqq.; Duly (n. 25), 15 sqq.; Visagie (n. 30), 82; Botha, (1919) 36 *SALJ* 151.

[38] Duly (n. 25), 15.

[39] The procedure for obtaining a loan place is cited by Visagie (n. 30), 82.

[40] Many did not even bother to do this: one study suggests that in the frontier districts only a minority of the farmers even bothered formally to request permission to occupy a *plaats*. See Reyburn (n. 34), 41 sq.

[41] Typically the *leeningsplaats* was some 3,000 *morgen* (16,000 acres; or 9 sq. miles).

For all the legal informality of the grant, *leeningsplaats* tenure was an attractive option to the pastoralists. For one thing, it provided them with cheap land which was easily obtained. For another thing the land was obtained without legal complexities (and attendant costs[42]). In the absence of proper registration and survey, it was often possible to occupy more land than had been granted.[43] Although the tenure was annually renewable, in practice the renewal was 'automatic and unquestioned'.[44] Technically, the holder was not able to subdivide the property; in practice this was permitted on an informal basis.[45] Also, although he had no title to the land, custom allowed the occupier to sell his tenure at a price calculated according to the value of the land.[46]

The result of this state of affairs was that the *leeningsplaats* tenure, though in law of the most precarious nature, in fact provided most, if not all, of the benefits and advantages of *eigendom*.

(c) Loan ownership (leenings eigendom)

In 1743 an attempt was made to regularize loan tenure by a provision which vested some legal right in a portion of a loan place in the occupier. An occupier could apply to have sixty *morgen* of the farm conferred upon him in *leenings eigendom* (in English: 'loan freehold').[47] What was required was a survey of the land, a formal deed of grant, and payment of an annual rental. The holder acquired the legal right to subdivide and to dispose of the land. This form of tenure was conceived as conferring more security than loan place tenure, without conferring ownership upon the tenant.[48] It proved to be of only small attraction to the farmers.[49]

(d) Emphyteusis (erfpacht)

In 1732 the Company introduced *erfpacht* tenure, a form of tenure which enabled persons holding land under *eigendom* to lease adjoining land for fifteen years,[50] the Company retaining ownership of the land. In practice only a very few of these grants were made and this form of tenure fell into desuetude.[51]

---

[42] Particularly those involved in the survey of land grants, a practice introduced in 1685, and in principle a necessary requirement for any grant of land. The costs of survey were borne by the grantee and were often exorbitant. Cf. Duly (n. 25), 42.

[43] Reyburn (n. 34), 40.   [44] Ibid.; Duly (n. 25), 17.

[45] Duly (n. 25), 17.   [46] Ibid.

[47] This came about by the instruction of the Baron Van Imhoff, a director of the Company. See Reports of De Chavonnes and Van Imhoff, cited in Davenport/Hunt (n. 37), 3. See also Visagie (n. 30), 83; Cape of Good Hope (n. 18), 6; Botha, (1919) 36 *SALJ* 152 sq.

[48] Fisher (n. 23), 22.   [49] Duly (n. 25), 18.

[50] See the government notice of 18 Feb. 1732, reproduced in Jeffreys/Naude (n. 37), 151 sq. (translation in Davenport/Hunt (n. 37), 3). On this form of tenure see Fisher (n. 23), 27 sqq.

[51] Duly (n. 25), 15.

(e) Conclusion

The outcome of these practices during the Dutch era was that the owner-ship of land, in the sense of the traditional form of Roman-Dutch *dominium plenum*, was by no means a universal feature of the legal landscape. Indeed, the traditional form of *dominium* occupied an insignificant place in the scheme of things, being confined to a relatively few parcels of urban land, and entirely overshadowed by the more common and preferred 'loan' tenure. The latter was a unique indigenous type of tenure of obscure legal provenance[52] developed from the peculiar customs and practices of the colony.[53] Under it, the formal *dominium* in the land resided in the Company while the land-holder enjoyed customarily determined rights which con-ferred virtually all of the benefits and advantages of *dominium* in the land.[54]

2. The British era

At the beginning of the nineteenth century Britain was engaged in its long struggle with Napoleon. In 1795 and again in 1806 the British captured the strategically important Cape of Good Hope from the Dutch. In 1814, as part of the peace settlement ending the Napoleonic Wars, the Dutch Government permanently ceded the Cape to Britain. The Cape thus became a colony under the British Crown, which succeeded to the prerogatives, powers, and privileges of the previous regime. Following the practice of the time, the Roman-Dutch law was not replaced by English law.[55] Accordingly the system of land tenure which applied in the Cape remained[56] as it was under the Dutch administration.[57]

[52] Indeed, as Robertson (1935 *South African Journal of Economics* 172) has pointed out, in matters of land tenure 'the origins of the landholding methods in use in the Netherlands had been lost sight of, and their true construction was often a matter for speculation. The Cape officials, then, had had to adapt something they did not understand to conditions which they had first to learn by experience'.

[53] It should be borne in mind that the public administration during the Dutch era was largely carried out by men without formal legal training. Furthermore there were few admin-istrators, especially in the vast hinterland. As Duly (n. 25), 3 noted, 'one basic truth' in South African history during the Dutch period 'was that government authority seldom existed at local level: government was always an imperfect and exceedingly primitive force which followed the expansion and development of society'.

[54] Cf. D. van der Merwe, 1989 *TSAR* 667: 'The Company's inability to exercise effective control over its outlying districts paved the way for custom to transform the loan place tenure into a form of private ownership.'

[55] Hahlo/Kahn (n. 14), 17.   [56] See Duly (n. 25), ch. 2.

[57] What did change was terminology. The Dutch nomenclature was translated into English, not literally but rather by reference to the equivalent concept in the English law. Thus the Dutch *eigendom* was rendered in English not as 'ownership' but rather as 'freehold'. In English law the term 'freehold' derived from a form of tenure of land of a feudal overlord held by a freeman and thus free of servile incidents. It was characterized by being a tenure of land inde-terminate in point of time and capable of being inherited. The Dutch *erfpacht*, a tenure in the nature of the Roman emphyteusis was translated as 'quitrent', a term of English law (see

(a) The Cradock Proclamation

British officialdom, however, did not approve of the *leeningsplaats* tenure, which besides its careless informality was depriving the government of substantial revenues.[58] In 1811 the Governor, Sir John Cradock, denounced loan tenures as 'unworthy', 'unfitted to the growing prosperity of the Colony, and only suited to the earliest and rudest institutions of the settlement'.[59] This tenure, he announced, was to be replaced with something more formal and regular.[60] Following lengthy consultation with 'the most eminent Colonial lawyers and heads of departments'[61] the Governor in 1813 introduced a new form of land tenure for the colony.[62] It was to be known as 'perpetual quitrent'.

To this end the Governor issued a Proclamation, 'more like the Edict of a Roman Emperor than a modern Act of Parliament'.[63] In the Preamble it announced that the encouragement of agriculture, essential for the prosperity of the colony, would be encouraged 'by the certainty of tenures and the confidence connected therewith'. It was desirable that 'all improvements to the soil' should 'indisputably belong to the holder as his own' and be 'exclusively secured to him [and] his heirs'. The existing system of loan tenures was 'injurious to that certainty' and accordingly the Governor had 'determined' in the interests of 'giving security to title' to grant 'to the holders of all lands on loan ... their places on *perpetual quitrent*' with 'rights and privileges' and 'on terms and conditions' set out in the Proclamation.

The term 'quitrent', derived from English law, denotes a form of tenure under which a person holding land in freehold is obliged to pay an annual rent to the lord of the manor in order to be 'quit and free of all other services'.[64]

The characterization of the new tenure as quitrent suggests that the intention was to confer *dominium plenum*[65] upon the grantor in return for an

---

below, text to n. 64). The English term 'estate' came to be used to denote a parcel of land. This English legal terminology prevailed in South Africa until well into the 20th C. (even today agents for the sale of land are called 'estate agents' in English; but *eiendomsagente* in Afrikaans). The use of English terminology in this area has had a confusing effect on the understanding of South African land law.

[58] Elphick/Giliomee (n. 12), 502.

[59] Proclamation of 6 Aug. 1813, reproduced in J. Foster, H. Tennant, E. M. Jackson (eds.), *Statutes of the Cape of Good Hope 1652–1886*, vol. II, 485.

[60] See Duly (n. 25), ch. 3.

[61] *Cape of Good Hope* (n. 18), 8. The events preceding the issue of the Proclamation are examined in detail in Duly (n. 25), ch. 3.

[62] Proclamation of 6 Aug. 1813 (n. 59), 481.

[63] De Villiers CJ in *De Villiers v. Cape Divisional Council* (1874) 5 Buch 50, 64.

[64] *Encyclopedia of the Laws of England* (2nd edn., vol. XII, 1908), s.v. 'Quitrent'.

[65] Since *eigendom* (freehold) was known at the Cape, why did Cradock not simply convert loan tenures into freehold tenure? The answer is that he was instructed by his superiors in London that it was not legally possible to do so. At the time the Cape was a territory held under military conquest, and therefore not officially a colony of Britain. International law,

annual rent. The Proclamation did not, however, say this explicitly. Rather it haphazardly set out in its various clauses features that were to characterize the new tenure.

There was a clear intention to create a form of tenure freed from the usual controls of government as *dominus eminens*. The Crown, the document stated, 'has resolved to sacrifice its rights and prerogatives in order to place property upon that solid and secure foundation, without which fair adventure and speculation cannot arise'.[66] The Government was thus 'graciously offering to their acceptance a perfect title to lands, that enables them to provide for their children and descendants, and dispose of them as they please, [and] grants to them, in fact, possession of an estate, and the high character and station of "a real landholder" '.[67]

The essential contents of this 'perfect title' were as follows. The holder obtained the 'right to hold the land hereditarily, and to do with the same as he may think proper, in like manner as with other immovable property'.[68] He was entitled to 'sell or otherwise alienate it, with the usual previous knowledge of Government . . . as free and allodial property'.[69]

The Proclamation stated[70] that the Government 'reserves no other rights but those on mines of precious stones, gold or silver;[71] as also the right of making and repairing public roads, and raising materials for the purpose on the premises . . .'.

The tenure was 'not liable to any other burthens but those to which all freehold lands are already subject, or which may hereafter be further prescribed'[72].

The Proclamation further specified that in regard to judicial decisions relating to the new quitrent tenure 'the same rights, laws and usages shall be observed, which have hitherto been acted upon . . . with respect to freehold lands'.[73] For this 'irrevocable title'[74] the holder was only required 'to pay to the public revenue' a yearly rent.[75]

Cradock's Proclamation, for all its gushing benevolence, was a document of remarkable obscurity.[76] It contained seventeen numbered clauses, some of which related only to the conversion of loan places,[77] and others[78] were

---

Cradock was told, prohibited the implementation of any policies which might curtail the income or preogatives of the future government (whether British or Dutch) of the colony. Thus he could not implement any land policy which might deprive the government of its title in the land. Quitrent, with its continuing obligation to pay rent to the *fiscus*, did not violate this restriction. Duly (n. 25), 44; D. van der Merwe, 1989 *TSAR* 668, fn. 35.

[66] Clause 17.   [67] Ibid.   [68] Clause 3.   [69] Clause 3.   [70] Clause 4.
[71] The Proclamation specified that 'other mines of iron, lead, copper, tin, coals, slate or limestone, are to belong to the proprietor': ibid.
[72] Clause 11.   [73] Clause 6.   [74] Clause 7.   [75] Ibid.
[76] In *De Villiers v. Cape Divisional Council* (1874) 5 Buch 50, 62 the Chief Justice of the Cape Supreme Court said: 'it is impossible to conceive a statute more loosely drawn or more inartistically worded.'
[77] Clauses 1, 7.   [78] Clauses 4, 10, 11.

of a more general application while not necessarily applying to all land granted in quitrent, while yet others[79] applied to all land granted in quitrent. It was not at all clear whether the Proclamation applied only to the conversion of *leeningsplaats* tenure or whether it had a more general application. Nor was the exact juridical nature of the tenure clear.[80]

(b) Quitrent Tenure

For nearly sixty years officials at the Cape implemented the Cradock Proclamation without any clarity as to what exactly were the legal rights and duties of holders of land under this tenure.

The earliest and most important misconception arose with regard to the tenure of the land which formed the subject of the grants issued under the provisions of the Proclamation. Until 1886 the general belief was that the tenure was emphyteutic or *erfpacht*. Thus, the understanding was that the Government had not transferred the *dominium* of the land to the grantee. Another misconception was that the Proclamation was intended to operate merely for the benefit of occupiers of loan land by offering to regrant their land on perpetual quitrent tenure.[81]

Then in 1874 the Cape Supreme Court, in the case of *De Villiers v. Cape Divisional Council*,[82] considered the nature of the tenure created by the Cradock Proclamation. It was, De Villiers CJ stated, 'in all respects identical with the *emphyteusis* of the Roman-Dutch law'.[83] However, he went on to say, the terms of the Cradock Proclamation enhanced the rights of holders under this form of tenure beyond those afforded by the common law emphyteusis. Accordingly, the Chief Justice held, the Proclamation did not merely reformulate the emphyteutic sort of tenure which had existed under the Dutch regime, but was rather a new sort of tenure, whose content was laid down in the clauses of the Proclamation.[84]

---

[79] Clauses 6, 9.

[80] For an analysis of the South African quitrent tenure see C. G. van der Merwe, *Sakereg* (1979), 420 sqq.

[81] This was the construction of the Proclamation adopted by the majority of the Court in *De Villiers v. Cape Divisional Council* (n. 76).

[82] Ibid.   [83] 58.

[84] This construction of the judgment derives from the gloss upon it by De Villiers CJ in the later case of *Colonial Govt v. Fryer and Huysamen* (1886) 4 SC 313, 316, where he observed of his judgment in the *De Villiers* case: 'I held that . . . the statutory conditions introduced by Sir John Cradock's Proclamation . . . excluded the operation of the common law [relating to emphyteusis] altogether. If this view was correct—and the Privy Council held it to be so—the grantee [of perpetual quitrent] really became the owner of the land, subject only to such reservations in favour of the Crown as had been provided for by the Proclamation; in other words, the Crown ceased to have any proprietary rights, but retained only those general rights which belonged to it, not as *dominus* of the land, but as *princeps*, and those special rights which were secured to it by the Proclamation.' This construction of the effect of the Cradock Proclamation, the Judge said, was made clear beyond doubt by the words in the Proclamation cited above in the text to n. 66. However, a reading of the judgment does not reveal the bold and explicit statements about the nature of quitrent tenure which De Villiers claims for it in

When the views of the Chief Justice were upheld on appeal[85] it came to be accepted that the perpetual quitrent tenure of the Cape was not merely the Romanistic emphyteusis, but rather a type of tenure *sui generis*. 'It might perhaps be said', a South African judge has observed, 'that the "Cradock tenure" had been substituted for the "emphyteutic tenure" '.[86] In the result, 'Cradock tenure' was of general application in the Cape colony and created a form of tenure that would be ownership in its Grotian common law sense in all but name.[87]

Curiously enough, this construction of the Proclamation did not receive general application:

a quitrent grant came to be called an *'erfpachtbrief'* or in English a 'quitrent lease' and instead of being filed with the old freehold grants a new set of volumes was established in which the quitrent grants were bound separately, thus creating an unnecessary confusion . . .[88]

In practice, the officials charged with the registration of grants in Cradock tenure 'either did not know the provisions of the Proclamation or disregarded them'.[89] In the result, the judicial identification of Cradock's perpetual quitrent tenure as a form of *dominium plenum* was not realized.

(c) The aftermath

The immediate response to Cradock's tenure was not favourable.[90] This was partly because of the conservatism of the colonists and partly because of inept administration by officialdom. However, in the course of time the tenure became, besides the long-established *eigendom* ('freehold') tenure, the prevailing form of land tenure in the Cape.[91]

In the 1830s the Government, anxious to raise revenue for the colony, instructed that Crown lands should in future be disposed of as freehold by sale at public auction.[92] In 1844 it was made known[93] that no further grants in perpetual quitrent tenure would be made, and all Crown lands were to

the passage quoted above. De Villiers CJ's judgment in the *De Villiers* case seems to have redounded to his fame as a 'Roman-Dutch lawyer': E. A. Walker, *Lord De Villiers and His Times* (1925), 71.

[85] *Divisional Council of the Cape Division v. De Villiers* [1877] 2 AC 567.

[86] Feetham JP in *Odendaal v. Registrar of Deeds* 1939 NPD 327, 338.

[87] See C. G. van der Merwe (n. 80), 425.

[88] Denoon, (1948) 65 *SALJ* 546. As to how this confusion came about, see ibid.

[89] Denoon (n. 88), 549.   [90] See Duly (n. 3), ch. 4.

[91] Because of delays in processing applications for quitrent tenures, a new type of informal tenure, known as 'request tenure' grew up. A person applying for a quitrent tenure would submit an application (request) for a grant to a local official for transmission to the authorities in Cape Town. Thereupon he would be allowed to occupy, and dispose of, the land notwitstanding the fact that his application had not yet been approved and no title deed had been issued. See Fisher (n. 23), 38.

[92] Duly (n. 25), 155 sqq.; Fisher (n. 23), 40; Denoon (n. 88), 554.

[93] Government Notice of 15 May 1844.

be disposed of in freehold.[94] As an added incentive, and in order to raise further revenue, the Government advised that it would allow landholders under Cradock's tenure to extinguish the perpetual obligation to pay rent by a single payment[95] and thereby convert their tenure to 'freehold'.[96]

These efforts at reconstructing the system of land tenure at the Cape as 'freehold' (meaning *eigendom*), in order to bring the colony in line with others in the British Empire,[97] were not welcomed at the Cape and not successful. The simple reason was that for the most part the agricultural community preferred the older loan tenures, and the bureaucrats administering the Lands Department were dismayed at the need to set in motion the cumbersome process of converting all quitrent tenures into freehold.[98] In the result there was little or no progress in the middle decades of the century towards the realization of the policy of establishing *eigendom* as the principal form of land tenure in the Cape colony. Indeed, when the colony obtained self-rule in 1854 the new Government decided to return to Cradock's perpetual quitrent tenure[99] and the conversion of quitrent into freehold was no longer permitted.[100] In 1860 the Crown Lands Act[101] gave legislative effect to the revived system of quitrent tenure.[102]

Quitrent tenure remained a recognized form of tenure in the Cape[103] until the 1930s when, because collection of the quitrent was considered not worth the effort,[104] the obligation to pay quitrent was abolished by the Abolition of Quitrent Act 1934.[105]

However, Sir John Cradock's Proclamation, 'an ancient monument with which it would be sacrilegious to meddle'[106] remained unrepealed. Only in 1968, some 150 years after its promulgation, was it finally removed from the statute book.[107]

[94] *Cape of Good Hope* (n. 18), 10; Duly (n. 25), 174.

[95] Duly (n. 25), 155; Fisher (n. 23), 43; Denoon (n. 88), 550.

[96] Where this was done the officials, demonstrating their intransigent confusion, registered these titles not as freehold but as 'redeemed quitrent land': Denoon (n. 88), 552.

[97] Duly (n. 25), 155.

[98] See Duly (n. 25), 155 sqq.; *Cape of Good Hope* (n. 18), 10.

[99] Government Notice 357 of 31 Oct. 1856. See *Cape of Good Hope* (n. 18), 10; Denoon (n. 88), 559.

[100] Fisher (n. 23), 44.   [101] Act 2 of 1860.   [102] Denoon (n. 88), 560.

[103] For an account of the various forms of legislative meddling with the concept during these years see ibid. 559 sqq.

[104] Ibid. 367.

[105] Act 54 of 1934. The Abolition of Quitrent (Towns and Villages) Act 33 of 1937 abolished quitrent in urban areas.   [106] Denoon (n. 88), 555.

[107] By the Pre-Union Statute Law Revision Act 44 of 1968. This Act, however, retained cl. 4, something which especially angered landowners in the Cape province who were obliged to continue to experience the taking of portions of their land for purposes of constructing roads *without compensation* (see text to n. 70), while their neighbours holding under ordinary freehold received compensation in the ordinary way for such expropriation (see *House of Assembly*, Debates, (1986, vol. 22, col. 2102, 13 Mar. 1968). Only in 1977, by the Pre-Union Statute Law Revision Act 43 of 1977, was this last remnant of the Cradock Proclamation expunged from the statute book.

3. Land ownership in the other colonies in South Africa

In 1836 Dutch-speaking inhabitants of the Cape colony, dissatisfied with British rule, began to emigrate beyond the boundaries of the colony to establish new states where they could rule themselves. The South African Republic (in the territory known as Transvaal) and the Orange Free State were set up in the *hinterland*. In addition Britian acquired territory on the eastern seaboard, to be known as the colony of Natal.

The forms of land tenures in these territories were approximations of the forms of tenure at the Cape, though often modified in some way to suit the peculiar policies or interests of the inhabitants. As a general rule they did not replicate the conditions attached to Cradock's tenure, and by and large they provided for a form of *dominium plenum*, albeit under some other description.[108]

III. LAND OWNERSHIP: CONTENT (*CIRCA* 1860–1900)

1. Introduction

The new system of land tenure introduced in 1813 gradually produced a change in the general attitude of public opinion towards ownership of the soil.[109] The older idea that landholders enjoyed only such rights as were granted by the Company came to be replaced by the view that landholders, as a matter of course, were entitled to certain incidents of enjoyment of the land as 'natural' rights of ownership of property. The concept of a natural right of land ownership was derived not from the Roman-Dutch but from the English law.[110] That English law came to influence the concept of land ownership at this time can be attributed to the fact that from 1828 onwards the Cape judges were, almost to a man, trained in English law. Coincidentally, the English law of land ownership was, as a result of the Industrial Revolution then occurring in Britain, undergoing a transformation. The Industrial Revolution in Britain converted an essentially rural and

---

[108] In *Webb v. Giddy* (1878) 3 App Cas 908, 930 it was held that the Orange Free State had a form of perpetual quitrent not derived from Cradock's Proclamation which had the effect of conferring 'full proprietary rights on the grantees'. In *Odendaal v. Registrar of Deeds* 1939 NPD 327, 354, it was held that the forms of quitrent tenure introduced in Natal 'were never intended to be grants in *empheyteusis*, but were intended to confer rights in the nature of freehold, including mineral rights'. See generally G. Denoon (n. 88), 69 sqq. See also Fisher (n. 23), 59 sqq.; Davenport, 1985 *Acta Juridica* 55 sq.; Davenport/Hunt (n. 37), 1 sqq.

[109] C. G Hall, *The Origin and Development of Water Rights in South Africa* (1939), 29.

[110] Hall (n. 109), suggests that the process whereby this change in the perception of the nature of land ownership came about was that '[f]rom the point of view of the English Administration full ownership of land undoubtedly implied the grant of all the rights which accompanied the ownership of land according to English Law . . .'

agrarian society into one which was essentially urban and industrial. In the process, the role of land in the national economy changed. Previously valued for its fertility and conceived in terms of its physical nature as soil and water, it now came to be valued as a platform for industrial activities and a repository of the mineral and other resources required to fuel industrial processes. The changing function of land meant that landowners developed different claims and expectations in respect of their use of the land. The industrialist wanted to be able to dam and control flowing water to drive his machinery; to be able to excavate his land to the fullest extent in order to win its mineral resources; and to use the ambient air and flowing waters as dumping places for the wastes and residues of manufacturing processes. These demands and expectations received legal recognition in the form of the concept of 'natural rights' attached to land ownership. The maxim *cuius est solum eius est usque ad inferos et ad coelum*[111] postulated land as a three-dimensional unit. Legal rights extended not only over the surface of the land but also over the space above the surface and the soil below. The owner's right to exploit the land was now conceived in terms of these spatial dimensions. The owner owned all that was on the surface and under it, and could use the space above it for his own purposes.

The complexities of matching these uses with those of neighbouring owners were managed under the provisions of the doctrine of nuisance and its defining maxim *sic utere tuo ut alienum non laedas*.[112]

The process of developing and defining the concepts of natural rights of property and nuisance occurred through the course of the nineteenth century.[113] Inevitably, these new approaches to the nature of land ownership were familiar to the men who were the judges of the Cape Supreme Court; and they were reflected in their judgments on issues relating to land ownership at the Cape.

2. Water rights

The earliest manifestation of a new approach to the concept of land ownership at the Cape occurred in relation to the question of the rights of land owners in respect of flowing waters.

From the beginning of the settlement, the Council of Policy at the Cape acted upon the principle that water with a perennial flow was *res publica*, that the Government was *dominus fluminis*[114] in regard to flowing water, and that riparian land owners had no inherent right to the water arising

---

[111] (To whom the ground belongs, to him it belongs down to the underworld and up to the sky.) See below, n. 136.

[112] (Use what belongs to you so as not to injure anyone else.) Cf. J. R. L. Milton, *The Concept of Nuisance in English Law* (unpublished Ph.D. thesis, University of Natal, 1978), *passim*.

[113] Ibid. ch. 5.   [114] Hall (n. 109), 14.

on[115] or flowing to their land.[116] Rights in water were acquired only by award of the government. When grants were made, the Council of Policy was always at pains to point out that these rights were granted as a privilege which could be withdrawn at any time.[117] The notion of the Government as *dominus fluminis* seemed still to prevail in 1830.[118]

However, in mid-century the judges of the Cape Supreme Court began a process of 'depublicizing' water resources and reconstituting access to flowing waters as a natural right of land ownership.

The process began in 1855 with the case of *Retief v. Louw*.[119] The case involved a dispute between adjoining land owners regarding access to water flowing from the upper tenement of the defendant to the lower tenement of the plaintiff. In the course of his judgment Bell J observed:[120]

In a country such as this, where the value of land is greatly dependent upon the facilities for obtaining water, there are few questions which can be conceived of greater magnitude or importance to the inhabitants, yet, singular to say, after making inquiry, I am not able to discover that any case upon the subject has ever been decided by this Court, or by its predecessors, or that there is any judicial authority upon the subject . . .

Thus, disposing of the principle of the State as *dominus fluminis* by the simple expedient of ignoring the concept,[121] Bell J and his brother judge Cloete J proceeded to consider the law relating to flowing waters as if it were *res nova*. Bell J in his judgment sought to introduce the Anglo-American doctrine of riparian rights[122] to the natural flow of water.[123]

[115] See ibid. 17.   [116] Hall (n. 109), 13.   [117] Visagie (n. 30), 173; Hall (n. 109) 2.
[118] In the case of *De Wet v. Cloete* (1830) 1 Menz 403, some of the judges expressed the view that 'notwithstanding the *ex facie* absolute grant of any lands, once the property of the government, the Government remained *dominus fluvius*, and had the sole power, from time to time, to regulate the use of waters . . . ' (410). On this case see Hall (n. 109), 21 sqq.
[119] The judgment in this case was delivered on 12 Jan. 1856, but only published in a law report in 1874. See (1874) Buch 165, 166. On the historic significance of the case see J. C. de Wet, 'One Hundred Years of Water Law', 1959 *Acta Juridica* 31; Hall (n. 109), 32 sqq.
[120] 173.
[121] Hall (n. 109), 28, noting that in English law there was no such concept as the state being *dominus fluminis*, suggests that in the British era the concept disappeared at the Cape because it 'was probably incomprehensible to the English officials . . .'
[122] The doctrine that land ownership provides rights in the waters riparian to the land. The right is not one of exclusive title to the flowing water but rather a usufructuary right: the right of making reasonable use of the water as it flows past. See S. Weil, 'The Origin and Comparative Development of the Law of Watercourses in the Common Law and the Civil Law', (1918) 6 *California LR* 245.
[123] Noting that the law of Holland on the subject was 'very meagre' which was 'to be expected, water being in Holland rather a nuisance than an advantage', Bell J launched upon an examination of English, Scottish, and American law, and adopted a formulation of water law to the effect that in respect of perennial streams running over a number of adjoining land parcels, landowners 'have each a common right in the use of the water which use, at every stage of its exercise by any one of the proprietors, is limited by a consideration of the rights of other proprietors'. Discussing whether a proprietor may dam the stream, he observed that the 'maxim applies *sic utere [tuo] ut alienum non laedas*' (182).

Cloete J, who also delivered a judgment in this case, approached the matter on the basis of the landowner's right to waters arising on the land, ignoring the question of rights in perennially flowing rivers. Claiming to state the Roman-Dutch law, he held that in relation to streams of water upon his land the landowner 'has the right to treat as he would with any other part of his private property'.[124] In 1866 Cloete J reiterated this doctrine in *Dreyer v. Ireland,*[125] holding that as a general rule 'the upper proprietor may use water flowing through his land in any way he thinks proper'.[126] In *Silberbauer v. Van Breda and the Cape Town Municipality*[127] Hodges CJ asserted that the 'law of this colony is quite clear' that 'the right of the freeholder to water rising on springs from his land is undisputed and undisputable. He may use it for any purpose relating to irrigation or he may convey it away and use it as he pleases'.[128] Watermeyer J repeated that 'a man might do whatever he pleased with water that rose on his own property'.[129]

The somewhat confused picture as to the nature of a landowner's rights in waters[130] was clarified in the 1870s when the new Chief Justice, Sir J. H. de Villiers, steered the law towards the Anglo-American doctrine of riparian rights to water in perennial running streams.[131]

Broadly speaking, the water law regime introduced by De Villiers CJ posited a distinction between 'public' and 'private' streams. In relation to

[124] 189. He went on: 'In my opinion, therefore, he might construct ponds or reservoirs, irrigate his lands with any part thereof, erect mills for his own or the public's use or turn the same to any lawful or beneficial purpose . . .'
[125] (1866) 4 Buch 193 at 200.   [126] See also *Erasmus v. De Wet* (1866) 4 Buch 204.
[127] (1866) 5 Searle 231.
[128] The words quoted do not appear in the report of the judgment of Hodges CJ in Buchanan's Report. They are, however, cited by De Villiers CJ in *Vermaak v. Palmer* (1876) 6 Buch 25, 33.
[129] (1866) 5 Searle 231, 240.
[130] *Obiter dicta* in the Judicial Committee of the Privy Council in *Silberbauer v. Van Breda* (1869) 6 Moo PCCNS 319 (an appeal from the decision in *Silberbauer v. Van Breda and the Cape Town Municipality* (1866) 5 Searle 231) disputed the correctness of the doctrine of absolute ownership in water *erumpens in suo*.
[131] The seminal case is *Hough v. Van der Merwe* (1874) 4 Buch 148, where De Villiers CJ treated the question of the use of water for irrigation as *res nova* and proceeded to lay down the principle of common use by all riparian proprietors as being recognized in South African law. Hall (n. 109) points out that although the judgment contains no reference to American law, the principles were almost certainly derived from J. K. Angell, *A Treatise on the Law of Watercourses* (1840), and the decisions quoted in fns. 95, 120, 121, and 128 of that work, and it bears a remarkable similarity to the judgment of Bell J in *Retief v. Louw* (see above n. 119). In *Van Heerden v. Wiese* (1880) 1 Buch AC 5 De Villiers CJ laid down what were to become the basic principles of South African water law; they were accepted as such when the task of codification was first undertaken in 1906. The most important feature of the decision in *Van Heerden v. Wiese* was that a sharp distinction was drawn between public and private streams. Public streams were defined as perennial streams, having a defined channel, and being capable of common use by the riparian owners. While the owner of the land on which a private stream rose was accorded full ownership of the water, the principle of common use by all riparian owners was declared to obtain in the case of a public stream.

the latter, the doctrine of absolute ownership of the water in private streams was recognized subject only to any claims upon the water established by *vetustas* and provided that the stream was not the source of a public stream.[132] As regards 'public' streams, the doctrine was that riparian landowners enjoyed a co-ownership in the stream, subject to the common law rights of the public.[133]

The effect of these decisions of the Cape judges was that 'the waters of public rivers ceased to be *res publica* and became the common property of a limited category of persons, *viz.* owners of land riparian to the particular river'.[134] By mere judicial precedent the Court had 'in effect expropriated the rights of the state in the water of public rivers and handed these right over to the owners of riparian land as their private property'.[135]

3. Ownership in the space above and below the surface

The Accursian Gloss proclaimed *cuius est solum eius est usque ad coelum*. This precept seems not to have been applied in Roman-Dutch law.[136] It was, however, adopted by English law as early as the sixteenth century[137] and emerges as an important defining element in the transformation of the prevailing concept of ownership in late nineteenth-century South African law in the case of *London and SA Exploration Company v. Rouliot*,[138] where De Villiers CJ casually observed: 'The theory of the law is that the owner of land owns upwards to the skies and downwards to the centre of the earth . . .'

The proposition seems to have been accepted as self-evident and uncontroversial. Certainly when it was next articulated in 1911 in *Rocher v. Registrar of Deeds*[139] Mason J regarded it as trite law: 'As I understand our law, the owner of the surface of the land is the owner of the whole of the land . . . [H]e is the owner of what is above and what is below.'

The import of this principle for the natural rights of land ownership lay in the landowner's ability to use the space above his land for certain purposes and to excavate below the surface.

(a) Rights to use space above

The right to use land as the platform upon which to erect buildings and other structures is so elementary an incident of land ownership as to pre-

---

[132] See *Van Heerden v. Wiese* (1880) 1 Buch AC 5   [133] Ibid. 8 sq.
[134] De Wet, 1959 *Acta Juridica* 31, 33.
[135] Ibid. Generally on the later history of South African water law, see K. D. Nunes, 'Sources of Public Streams in Modern South African Law', 1975 *Acta Juridica* 298; Hall (n. 109), *passim*; J. C. de Wet, *Opuscula Miscellanea* (1979), 3 sqq.
[136] G. Pienaar, 'Die Ruimtelike Aspek van Eiensdomreg op Onroerende Goed: Die *Cuius Est Solum*-beginsel', (1989) 52 *THRHR* 216, 219 sq.
[137] Pienaar, (1989) 52 *THRHR* 216, 220.   [138] (1891) 8 SC 74, 90
[139] 1911 TPD 311, 315.

sent no obvious difficulty in recognition. One consequence of the erection of a structure is that it may interfere with the line of vision from a particular viewpoint, or exposure to the natural fall of sunlight. South African common law has, however, not regarded these kinds of interference as justifying any limitation upon the right of the owner to build upon his land[140]. However, as pointed out below,[141] planning and building legislation has made serious inroads upon common law rights to build on land.

An incidental consequence of the use of land for industrial processes is the production of effluents and wastes which are dispersed into the atmosphere. To the extent that the *ad coelum* principle purported to confer upon the landowner rights to the air-space above his land, it was in principle lawful to use the superadjacent space as a waste dump.

The ability to use the *coelum* as a dumping place for domestic and industrial effluents was regulated in English law by the tort of nuisance, and the South African judges quickly adopted a similar policy in regard to this facet of the *ad coelum* doctrine.[142]

(b) Rights to use space below

The principle significance of the right to exploit the space below the surface of the land concerns mining for precious and other minerals. Mining was an activity not prevalent in Holland and consequently the Roman-Dutch law had no significant body of principle regarding the landowner's rights to the minerals in his land.[143] Thus when, towards the end of the nineteenth century, deposits of gold and diamonds were discovered in South Africa, the South African courts were required to develop *de novo* principles relating to the law of mining for precious minerals.

In *Union Government v. Marais*[144] Innes CJ, clearly invoking the *cuius est solum eius debet esse usque ad coelum* precept, observed that the 'principle is fundamental that the owner of land is owner not only of the surface but of everything legally adherent thereto and also of everything contained in the soil below the surface'.

While this common law principle indicated that the owner of the land owned also the minerals below its surface, the economic realities of the nascent mining industry prompted a different approach to the situation. Intent upon facilitating the efficient exploitation of especially gold and

---

[140] In *Van der Heever v. Hanover Municipality* 1938 CPD 95 the Court refused to order the removal of a tree casting shadow on the sickroom of the wife of the owner of the adjoining land.

[141] IV. 1.

[142] The seminal case in South African law was *Holland v. Scott* (1882) 2 EDC 307. See also *Dell v. Town Council of Cape Town* (1879) 9 Buch 2. On nuisance in South African law see below, III. 6.

[143] H. P. Viljoen, *The Rights and Duties of the Holder of Mineral Rights* (1975), 11.

[144] 1920 AD 240, 246.

diamonds, government promoted the enactment of mining laws which did not accord with the principles of the common law.

The effect of the mining laws was to vest in government the power to 'proclaim' any land as a public 'digging' for either precious or base minerals. Upon proclamation of land as a digging, persons who were not owners of the land could acquire the right to mine minerals below the surface of the land. Such a dispensation inevitably created a conflict between the enjoyment of the right to mine and enjoyment of the landowner to use his land according to his own preference. When the courts were called upon to resolve disputes between the landowner and the person holding the right to excavate and mine the land, they adopted an approach which left the landowner's natural rights virtually devoid of substance. As Wessels J put it in *Neebe v. Registrar of Mining Rights*:[145]

By the Roman-Dutch law the ownership in the minerals lies in the *dominus* of the soil. The Gold Law has not entirely abrogated the common law but it has modified it to the extent of giving to the State the right of disposing of the precious metals. The Gold Law provides the machinery by which the State disposes of these metals. The farm is proclaimed and the owner's full rights of ownership are, during the proclamation, suspended.

In *Witwatersrand Gold Mining Co Ltd v. Municipality of Germiston*[146] Curlewis JP explained the effect of the mining laws in stark terms. The effect of the provisions of the Gold Law as to the ownership of ground which has been proclaimed is, he said:[147] 'to deprive the owner of the beneficial use or occupation of the surface of the ground; the beneficial ownership is suspended so far as the surface rights are concerned. All that the owner possesses are such rights as are conferred upon him by the Gold Law.'

4. Lateral support

The advent of the mining industry caused the courts to consider the matter of the landowner's right to have his land laterally supported by the land of his neighbour. The question first arose in the late nineteenth century, in the

---

[145] 1902 TS 65.   [146] 1926 TPD (reported in 1963 (1) SA 311).
[147] These residual rights were identified in the following terms: 'He has the right to share in claim licences, to peg off claims, and he has also the right under the Townships Act, taken together with the Gold Law, to apply to have a township laid out on the proclaimed ground. He has the right also to apply to the mining commissioner, as has any member of the public, for permission to occupy a portion of the proclaimed ground, and without such permission he has no right to occupy any portion of the proclaimed ground. He has also the right to lay out brickfields on the proclaimed ground and such like rights conferred on him by the Gold Law. In addition to that he has what apparently is regarded by the Local Rating Ordinance as a reversionary right and I take it by a reversionary right, under the Local Rating Ordinance, is meant the right which the owner has to recover and use the freehold property unrestricted when the ground is deproclaimed under the Law . . .'

unique context of the open cast system of mining for diamonds that prevailed on the newly discovered Diamond Fields.

The diamonds were found in 'pipes', the throats of long extinct volcanoes. Miners obtained a claim, a defined portion of the surface of the pipe, with the right to excavate downwards within the length and breadth allowed by the claim, in search of the diamonds contained in the pipe. In the event, some claims were excavated more rapidly than those adjoining. These rapidly deprived neighbouring parcels of lateral support, creating the possibility of the collapse of the unsupported column of earth. Inevitably loss and damage occurred and the courts were called upon to enunciate rules to deal with this situation.

Confronted by the peculiarities of this system of winning diamonds from the soil, the Chief Justice observed in *Murtha v. Von Beek:*[148]

I do not see how the principle of lateral support embodied in the English law can be made to apply to cases of this kind. Even if it be the law of the Colony that a man is entitled to lateral support, I do not see how it can apply to cases where a person takes a claim for the express purpose of digging. If this principle of lateral support were to be allowed, it might follow that a person having a claim surrounded by neighbours who were not as diligent as he was, might have to leave extensive lateral support to each of those neighbours, leaving very little ground for himself to work in.

However, it soon appeared that this denial of the right to lateral support was to be confined to the peculiar situation in the Diamond Fields. In *London and SA Exploration Co v. Rouliot*[149] the right of landowners generally to have their soil laterally supported by that of their neighbours was recognized as a natural incident of land ownership. Referring to the right of lateral support as recognized in other systems, De Villiers CJ noted that 'all important though the different mining industries are to the wealth and prosperity of the country, the rights of the owners of the surface to support from adjacent as well as sub-adjacent land have always been carefully guarded'. Smith J expressly acknowledged the existence of the right: 'the owner of land has the right of lateral support from his neighbour's land.'

The right of lateral support to land, established by *Rouliot's* case, has subsequently been accepted without any question by the courts. The owner of land:

is entitled absolutely as of right to the support afforded it by his neighbour's land, and it is an absolute right which he cannot be deprived of, merely because his neighbour takes what appears to be reasonable precautions in carrying out any particular operations . . . on his own land.[150]

---

[148] (1882) 1 Buch AC 121, 125. [149] (1891) 8 SC 74.
[150] *Grieves & Anderson v. Sherwood* (1901) 22 NLR 225, 227.

5. Right to enjoy

The English law had evolved, from the law of nuisance and as a natural right in respect of land, the right to personal welfare and physical comfort.[151] The tort provided a remedy for interferences with the enjoyment of land. Its effect was to provide compensatory damages in circumstances where a neighbour discharged smoke, odours, noise, or other annoying media onto the land of the complainant. The premise of the nuisance remedy was, however, the principle that an owner of land should be able to occupy the land without suffering sensory distress to his person arising from exposure to excessive volumes of sound, odour, or other noxious or annoying matter.

In the course of the nineteenth century the South African judges, taking over the English law of nuisance,[152] imported the right to personal welfare and comfort as an incident of land ownership.

6. *Sic utere tuo ut alienum non laedas*

Whatever the natural right attributed to land ownership by the South African judges, they accepted that natural rights in land cannot be considered as an absolute imperative but are liable to be limited by the interests of neighbouring landowners. This concept of the relative nature of the natural rights of property is derived from the English nuisance concept as expressed in the maxim *sic utere tuo ut alienum non laedas*. The application of this precept in South African law can be traced back to Bell J's formulation of water rights in *Retief v. Louw* (1855). Discussing whether a proprietor may dam the stream, he observed that the 'maxim applies *sic utere ut alienum non laedas*'.[153] So, too, in formulating the right to lateral support of land, Smith J in *London and SA Exploration Co v. Rouliot*[154] observed that 'one who has rights connected with land adjoining that of another cannot, in the exercise of those rights, do anything that will cause his neighbour's soil to fall down.'

Even after the repudiation of the English law of nuisance in *Regal v. African Superslate (Pty) Ltd*[155] the Appellate Division of the Supreme Court was at pains to maintain the principle that land ownership in South African law was not absolute in its nature. After stating the general principle that '*iedereen [kan] met sy eiendom doen wat hy wil*' (everybody can do with his property whatever he will), Steyn CJ went on to say:

---

[151] The history of nuisance and its relationship to the concept of natural rights of land ownership is traced in Milton (n. 112); cf. Ch. 21 below by D. van der Merwe.

[152] See immediately below. [153] 182. [154] (1891) 8 SC 74.

[155] 1963 (1) SA 102 (A) 107A.

*maar by aangrensende vasgoed spreek dit vanself dat daar minder ruimte is vir
onbeperkte regsuitoefening. Die reg moet 'n reëling voorsien vir die botsende eiendoms-
en genotsbelange van bure, en hy doen dit deur eiendomsregte te beperk en aan die eien-
aars teenoor mekaar verpligtings op te lê* . . . (but with regard to adjacent property it
is self-evident that there is less room for the unlimited exercise of one's right. The
law has to provide a regulation for the conflicting ownership and enjoyment interests of neighbours, and it does this by limiting the rights of ownership and by imposing obligations upon the owners *vis-à-vis* each other).

In *Gien v. Gien*,[156] the leading modern exposition of the South African
law of nuisance, Spoelstra AJ noted that the rights of ownership are not
absolute but qualified: '*Geen eienaar het dus altyd 'n onbeperkte bevoegdheid
om na vrye welbehae en goeddunke sy eiendomsbevoegdhede ten aansien van
sy eiendom uit te oefen nie*' (No owner therefore, always has the unlimited
power to exercise his rights of ownership with regard to his property in his
free discretion and at pleasure).

Regarding the conflict between owners arising from the exercise of rights
of ownership, the judge observed:

*Waar die onbeperkte bevoegdheid van een eienaar om 'n saak te gebruik en die
bevoegdheid van 'n ander eienaar om onbelemmerde genot van sy saak te hê, met
mekaar in botsing kom, word die regte beperk* . . . *deur wedersydse verpligtinge op te
lê. 'n Eienaar se eiendomsbevoegdhede strek dan* . . . *slegs sover as wat daar 'n verpligting op sy buurman rus om die uitoefening van daardie bevoegdheid te verduur. Dit bring
'n verpligting vir die een eienaar mee om sy reg so uit te oefen dat hy nie daardie perk
oorskry nie. Word dit oorskry, tree hy nie meer op ingevolge die bevoegdhede wat sy
reg aan hom verleen nie en maak hy inbreuk op die reg van sy buurman. Dit is onregmatige optrede wat die reg nie duld nie en wat die grondslag vir 'n interdik kan vorm*
(Where the unlimited power of an owner to use a thing clashes with the power of
another owner to unimpeded enjoyment, the rights are limited . . . by imposing
mutual obligations. The powers of ownership of an owner will then . . . only reach
so far as there is an obligation on his neighbour to put up with the exercise of that
power. This entails an obligation for the one owner to exercise his right in such a
way that he does not transgress this limit. If this limit is transgressed, he no longer
acts in terms of the powers granted to him by his right and encroaches upon the
right of his neighbour. This is an unlawful behaviour that the law cannot tolerate
and that can serve as the basis for an interdict).

IV. LAND OWNERSHIP, RESTRICTIONS (*CIRCA* 1930–1995)

1. Introduction

Soon after the mid-twentieth century a former chief Registrar of Deeds,
recalling that in the theory of South African law 'an owner of land could

---

[156] 1979 (2) SA 1113 (T).

do what he wished with it', pointed out that '[w]ithin the last three or four decades' this situation had been changed as a result of legislative provisions which conferred upon 'public bodies' and others 'the right by law to interfere with the private ownership of land'.[157] Birch added the perceptive observation: '[i]t will come perhaps as a surprise to realize what few rights of ownership a landowner can have to what was a precious possession until fairly recently, and how the controls, given by statute, may be exercised to restrict the use of land or interfere with the enjoyment thereof.'

The statutory instruments of this drastic change in the position of land ownership were provisions relating to the regulation of the establishment of townships, town planning schemes, control of the subdivision of land, building regulations, national monuments legislation, and provisions regulating the exploitation of natural resources.

The phenomenon to which Birch had drawn attention was the important shift in the perception of the role and status of land in a modern, industrialized state. The change in perception was expressed by MacDonald ACJ in these terms:[158]

The idea which prevailed in the past that ownership of land conferred the right on the owner to use his land as he pleased is rapidly giving way in the modern world to the more responsible conception that an owner must not use his land in a way which may prejudice his neighbours or the community in which he lives, and that he holds his land in trust for future generations. Legislation dealing with such matters as town and country planning, the conservation of natural resources, and the prevention of pollution, and regulations designed to ensure that proper farming practices are followed, all bear eloquent testimony of the existence of this more civilized and enlightened attitude towards the rights conferred by ownership of land.

Space does not permit a detailed examination of the relevant pieces of legislation which manifest this new era in the history of the ownership of land in South Africa. It must suffice to examine only some of the more prominent examples.

2. Mining law

South Africa is extraordinarily richly endowed with mineral resources. The determination of government that these resources be fully and efficiently exploited saw the enactment of mining laws which brutally brushed aside any rights which had traditionally been part of land ownership but which now seemed to impede this goal.[159]

In the Cape Colony, land granted under the Cradock Proclamation was

---

[157] W. H. Birch, 'Public Rights over the Private Ownership of Land', (1957) 74 *SALJ* 420.
[158] *King v. Dykes* 1971 (3) SA 540 (RA).
[159] Cf. C. Lewis, 'The Modern Concept of the Ownership of Land', 1985 *Acta Juridica* 241, 260.

subject to a reservation to the state of rights 'on mines of precious stones, gold and silver'.[160] Acting under this provision the Government set up statutory provisions for regulating the mining of diamonds.[161] The owner of land on which a diamond mine was established was entitled to a share of the mine, the other portions vesting in the Government and the discoverer of the diamonds.

In the South African Republic, where the principal deposits of gold were located, the Cradock system of land tenure did not apply[162] and thus there was no automatic reservation of mineral rights to the state. However, when gold was discovered the legislature enacted legislation (the Gold Laws[163]) which reserved to the state the right to *mine* all precious minerals. Mining licences were issued by the state. The owner of the land was granted a mining 'lease' (*mijnpacht*) and received a portion of the licence fees exacted by the State.

Given the expense of prospecting for and mining diamonds and gold, the likelihood of individual private landowners becoming the medium for the exploitation of these resources was remote. In order to facilitate the exploitation of minerals it was necessary somehow to confer upon an entrepreneur legal rights in the minerals which were separate from the ownership rights of the landowner. The common law did not allow for the separate ownership of layers of land;[164] it did, however, allow for the acquisition of the fruits of property by gathering. This principle allowed the invention of a right to the minerals in the soil which was separate from the ownership of the landowner.

The existence of a right to own the minerals in the soil separately from the ownership of the soil was recognized, as it were, by default: the courts simply accepted without question the assertion that such a right existed.[165]

The recognition of a separate right to win minerals from the soil created a conflict with the rights of the landowner. Faced with the choice of balancing the (usually) agrarian exploitation of the land over the industrial exploitation of the minerals in the land, the judges preferred the latter. The law as articulated in a line of cases was described in *Hudson v. Mann*[166] as follows:

Such a [mineral right] holder . . . is entitled to go upon the property, search for minerals and if he finds any to remove them. In the course of his operations he is entitled to exercise all such subsidiary or ancillary rights, without which he will not be able effectively to carry on his prospecting and/or mining operations. When the

---

[160] See above, text to n. 71.

[161] For an account of the early legislation regarding the diamond mining industry see M. Nathan, *The Diamond Laws of South Africa* (1920).

[162] See above, II 3.

[163] For an account of the early gold laws see S. H. Barber, *Transvaal Gold Law* (1896).

[164] *Coronation Collieries v. Malan* 1911 TPD 577, 591.

[165] Viljoen (n. 143), 14.   [166] 1950 (4) SA 485 (T).

owners are able reasonably to enjoy their respective rights without any clashing of interests no dispute is, as a rule, likely to arise. The difficulty arises, as has happened in the present case, when the respective claims enter into competition and there is no room for the exercise of the rights of both parties simultaneously. The principles underlying the decisions appear to be that the grantee of mineral rights may resist interference with a reasonable exercise of those rights either by the grantor or by those who derive title through him. In case of irreconcilable conflict the use of the surface rights must be subordinated to mineral exploration . . . [The holder of mineral rights] must exercise his rights in a manner least onerous or injurious to the owner of the surface rights, but he is not obliged to forego ordinary and reasonable enjoyment merely because his operations or activities are detrimental to the interests of the surface owner. The fact that the use to which the owner of the surface rights puts the property is earlier in point of time cannot derogate from the rights of the holder of the mineral rights.

The extent to which the landowner's rights in his land are diminished under this dispensation is illustrated by the stark *dictum* in *Transvaal Property & Investment Co Ltd & Reinhold & Co v. SA Townships Mining & Finance Corp Ltd and the Administrator*[167] that '[n]o use of the surface by the owner is defensible which has the effect of taking away the right of the holder of the mineral rights, when he decides to do so, to prospect for precious metals and if they are found to mine for them'.

3. Town planning legislation

Perhaps the most extensive inroads upon the traditional rights of land owners were made by town planning legislation.[168] First introduced in South Africa in 1931,[169] the town planning process evolved out of the massive health, welfare, and housing problems created by the urbanization and industrialization of society brought about by the Industrial Revolution.[170]

Town planning schemes are an institutionalized process for organizing the components of urbanized human settlement in such a way as to enhance welfare, prosperity, and progress to the highest feasible level.[171] In practice the process involved the development of a set of legally enforceable pre-

---

[167] 1938 TPD 512, 519.

[168] See generally, J. R. L. Milton, 'Property and Planning', 1985 *Acta Juridica* 267.

[169] On the history of town planning legislation in South Africa see T. B. Floyd, *Town Planning in South Africa* (1960); F. G. Price, J. W. M. Cameron, *The Evolution and Application of Town Planning Legislation in South Africa* (Technical Report RT/45/81 National Institute for Transport & Road Research CSIR (1982)); F. G. Price, *The Evolution of Town Planning Legislation in South Africa* (1982) (Report RT/40/81); Milton, 1985 *Acta Juridica* 267, 269 sq.

[170] Milton, 1985 *Acta Juridica* 268.

[171] The provincial town planning ordinances require every town planning scheme to have as its general purpose or objective a 'co-ordinated and harmonious development' of the area to which it relates in such way as will 'most effectively tend to promote health, safety, good order, amenity [beauty], convenience and general welfare, as well as efficiency and economy in the process of development.'

scriptions which direct, control, and regulate the existing and future uses that owners of immovable property may make of their property. In particular, zoning provisions determine the sort of activity (residential, commercial, industrial) which an owner may carry out on his land, while 'bulk and coverage' provisions regulate the manner and extent to which the owner may erect buildings and structures upon his property. The process allows a local authority to resolve to prepare a town planning scheme for the area under its jurisdiction. An immediate consequence of the decision is that the use and development of land within the affected area becomes subject to a system of official control. This 'interim control' prescribed that no new development of land or changes of the use of land within the area may occur except with the permission of the local authority. The scheme itself (in the form of a plan and accompanying manual) acquires the force of law. Typically[172] a scheme provides for 'zoning' of the land subject to the scheme as residential, industrial, commercial, educational, institutional, agricultural, or open. Tables contained in the manual specify the purposes for which land in each zone may or may not be used. This is elaborated by additional provisions indicating purposes for which the land may be used at the discretion of the local authority ('consent uses'). The provisions of the scheme are implemented by imposing penal sanctions on landowners for using their land other than in conformity with the scheme and, likewise, proscribing 'consent uses' for which the requisite permission has not been obtained.

The effect of these and other provisions of the schemes is that town planning legislation invades the realms of what used to be private decision-making concerning immovable property and restricts the freedom of choice of landowners in relation to the use and development of their immovable property.[173] These invasions, it may be noted, are not in the nature of compensatable expropriation of rights but rather restraints placed upon ownership in the interests of the public good.[174]

---

[172] See Milton (n. 170), 267, 270 sqq.

[173] See *Pretoria City Council v. SA Organ Builders (Pty) Ltd* 1953 (3) SA 400 (T) 409H ('limitation on the individual's right to use his property in any way he thinks fit is implicit in the notion of town planning'); *Broadway Mansions Ltd v. Pretoria City Council* 1955 (1) SA 517 (A) 523 ('A town planning scheme . . . has characteristics of legislation . . . making wide inroads into private rights'); *Klerksdorp Council v. Flamwood Estates (Pty) Ltd* 1959 (3) SA 715 (T) 723 ('It is not disputed that a town planning scheme, proclaimed, may have the effect of taking away rights from the owners of land . . .'); *Spathariotis v. Durban City Council* 1967 (3) SA 645 (D) 651C ('The effect of the relevant provisions of the town planning scheme . . . was . . . to deprive the applicant of one of his rights flowing from the *dominium* of his property').

[174] Milton (n. 170), 267, 274 sq.

4. Other

The restraints upon ownership imposed by town planning schemes were accepted without noticeable public complaint or resistance.[175] This no doubt emboldened government to impose other restraints upon land ownership in pursuit of other social, economic, and environmental goals. Subdivision of agricultural and urban land was prohibited or regulated so as to ensure that land units were of a suitable size or location in order to achieve proper usage for agricultural and residential development.[176] Other legislation restricted ownership in order to promote agriculture (the most important industry after mining) by ensuring the proper and efficient exploitation of land as an agricultural[177] resource, while provisions for the protection and conservation of natural resources and the natural[178] and man-made environment[179] likewise made inroads into the rights of owners. A less benign social policy, in the form of apartheid, saw invasions into the rights of landowners in order to achieve social segregation of the races.[180]

---

[175] Milton (n. 170), 267, 274.

[176] The Subdivision of Agricultural Land Act 70 of 1970 regulates the subdivision of agricultural land in order to prevent a kind of subdivision into units that are not economically viable. Subdivision control in urban areas is effected under the town planning legislation.

[177] Conservation of Agricultural Resources Act 43 of 1983. The Minister may prescribe control measures which should be complied with by land users to whom they apply. Such control measures may relate, *inter alia*, to (a) the cultivation of virgin soil; (b) the utilization and protection of land which is cultivated; (c) the utilization and protection of the vegetation; (d) the maximum number and the kind of animals which may be kept on *veld*; (e) the construction, maintenance, alteration, or removal of soil conservation works or other structures on land. Land users may be 'directed' to comply with particular control measures; failure to receive or comply with such a directive is an offence. See generally R. F. Fuggle, M. A. Rabie (eds.), *Environmental Management in South Africa* (1992), 197 sqq.

[178] Environment Conservation Act 73 of 1989. Under this Act the Minister of Environment Affairs may identify and prohibit land usage which in his opinion may have a substantial detrimental effect on the environment. These may include transformation, agricultural, and industrial processes. See generally A. Rabie, 'The Impact of Environmental Conservation on Landownership', 1984 *Acta Juridica* 289; A. J. van der Walt, 'The Effect of Environmental Conservation Measures on the Concept of Landownership', (1987) 104 *SALJ* 469; Fuggle/Rabie (n. 177), ch. 7.

[179] A. J. van der Walt, 'Possibilities for Conservation of the Built-up Environment in Current South African Statutory Law', (1987) 20 *CILSA* 209.

[180] Lewis, 1985 *Acta Juridica* 241, 261; D. G. Kleyn, A. Boraine, *Silberberg & Schoeman's The Law of Property* (3rd edn., 1992), 493 sqq. Happily, since 1991 this policy has been abandoned and most of the offending legislation repealed.

V. PROTECTION OF OWNERSHIP

1. The vindicatory action

The ability of an owner to recover the lost possession of what he owns by way of the *ius vindicandi* is 'the most signal quality'[181] of the Roman-Dutch law's concept of ownership.[182]

The sources reveal little or nothing about the recognition or application of the *ius vindicandi* in South African law during the Dutch era. It would seem, however, that the existence of the vindicatory action was an established feature of the administration of the law during this period. Certainly, the first law report published in South Africa in 1828 reveals counsel speaking in familiar terms about an owner's right to 'vindicate' property.[183] Furthermore, during the period of British influence there is hardly any indication of attempts to invoke analogous concepts of the English law[184] which may suggest that the process of vindication was sufficiently well established and understood[185] as not to induce practitioners to look to the English law for inspiration or guidance.[186]

An examination of judicial application of the vindicatory action is instructive for what it reveals about contemporary attitudes towards the

---

[181] R. W. Lee, *An Introduction to Roman-Dutch Law* (5th edn., 1953), 121.

[182] Cf. Grotius (n. 7), 2, 3, 1: 'Ownership is the property in a thing whereby a person who has not the possession may acquire the same by legal process' (trans. R. W. Lee).

[183] *Commissioner for the Sequestrator v. Vos* (1828) 1 Menz 286, 290.

[184] In *Escombe v. Henderson & Scott* 1872 NLR 117 a suggestion by Phillips J that the English action for trover applied in an action for recovery of stolen goods was sternly repudiated by Connor J.

[185] The earliest reported case devoted exclusively to the vindicatory remedy, *Escombe v. Henderson & Scott* 1872 NLR 124, concerned the question of whether the owner could recover stolen property, or its value, from a person who had *bona fide* possessed the property and parted with it in good faith. The Court, after considering only Roman and Roman-Dutch sources, concluded correctly that the vindicatory action did not lie. The essential averments required for success in the vindicatory action were set out in a judgment of De Villiers CJ in 1878 (*Phillips Brothers v. Wetzlar* (1878) 8 Buch 77). A number of early cases were devoted to clearing up the complication of vindication in respect of sales for cash where the price had not been paid. Again, the principles enunciated were derived entirely from Roman and Roman-Dutch law (*Commissioner for the Sequestrator v. Vos* (n. 183); *Keyter v. Barry's Executors* (1879) 9 Buch 175; *Daniels v. Cooper* (1880) 1 EDC 174).

[186] The only deviation occurred in the matter of actions for ejectment of possessors from immovable property. In the 1950s some judges treated the action as being analogous to the action for trespass, and borrowed rules from English law which were inappropriate for the South African legal system. Thus, in *Thomas v. Gurguis* 1953 (2) SA 36 (W) (followed in *Jasdwat & Moola v. Seedat* 1956 (4) SA 273 (N)) it was held that an owner who had parted with the right to possess the property could not vindicate it from a third party unless his 'reversionary right' to the possession was affected. This doctrine was repudiated by the Appellate Division in *Hefer v. Van Greuning* 1979 (4) SA 952 (A) on the ground that it constituted an inappropriate borrowing from the English law. On these cases see D. L. Carey Miller, *The Acquisition and Protection of Ownership* (1986), 258.

nature and role of ownership. The vindicatory action, as developed in Roman law, proceeded on the principle *ubi rem meam invenio, ibi eam vindico*.[187] Germanic law, by contrast, recognized the principle of *mobilia non habent sequelam, a* doctrine which precluded the vindication by owners of lost movable property. The latter principle evolved in the context of a mercantile community, anxious to encourage commerce and trade. By preventing the vindication of movable property acquired in the course of ordinary commercial transactions, the *mobilia* doctrine assured persons in the market that the title to goods acquired in commerce was assured, a principle that clearly encouraged trade.

In the late nineteenth century South African judges were called upon to determine which of these competing doctrines applied in South African law.

The leading case turned out to be *Van der Merwe v. Webb* (1883)[188] where the plaintiff sought to recover stolen oxen purchased by the defendant in good faith at a public market. The defendant invoked the *mobilia non habent sequelam* doctrine in the form of the institution of the market overt. Dutch customary law, of local application to specific markets, did not allow vindication of movables sold on a so-called *vrije mark* to a *bona fide* purchaser unless the owner refunded the purchase price.[189]

Barry JP, addressing the question of whether such a principle existed in South African law, and after noting that there 'are no direct decisions binding upon us', considered the question from a historical-philosophical point of view. His point of departure was 'the origin of ownership'.[190] From a discussion of the 'first title to property' arising from 'occupancy' and the 'feeble and precarious' rights attached to it, Barry JP described how:

the title to property, whether acquired by possession or otherwise, was gradually strengthened, and acquired great solidity and energy when it became to be understood that no man should be deprived of his property without his consent, and that even the honest purchaser was not safe under a defective title.

The learned Judge President then set out what was to become the prevailing position among the South African judiciary regarding the rights of owners to recover lost property:

The general principle applicable to the law of personal property throughout civilised Europe became therefore and now is, '*nemo plus juris ad alium transferre potest quam ipse haberet*' (Dig., 50, 17, 54), preceded by the other maxim, '*Id quod nostrum est sine facto nostro ad alium transferri non potest*', (Dig., 50, 17, 11). From the latter maxim, the owner cannot be deprived of his right of property by the wrongful act of any one who has taken it without title, or who, having it in his possession for

---

[187] Cf. e.g. Max Kaser, *Das römische Privatrecht*, vol. I (2nd edn., 1971), 432 sqq. As far as the history of modern European private law is concerned see, most recently, Werner Hinz, 'Die Entwicklung des gutgläubigen Fahrniserwerbs in der europäischen Rechtsgeschichte', (1995) 3 *Zeitschrift für Europäisches Privatrecht* 398 sqq.

[188] (1883) 3 EDC 97.				[189] Grotius (n. 7) 2, 3, 6.				[190] 101.

another purpose, sells it. From the latter maxim it follows that the thief or borrower cannot give title even to a bona fide purchaser. The original owner was entitled to reclaim his property, whether acquired *bona* or *mala fide* by the purchaser; and the reason that he is bound to give it up is this, not because he has done any wrong in buying it, but because it is the untransferred property of some one else who cannot be divested of it without his consent. The right of property does not go with the possession.

The Court decided that the Dutch institution of a sale in *vrije mark* was of only local and not general application and thus not a universal principle of Roman-Dutch law. Accordingly this instance of the *mobilia non habent sequelam* principle had no application in South African law. While this characterization of the application of sales in *vrije mark* was disputed in *Retief v. Hamerslach* (1884),[191] and although there is no authoritative decision on the point, the consensus is that *Van der Merwe v. Webb* expresses the preferable view.[192]

Other instances of the *mobilia non habent sequelam* principle likewise received short shrift at the hands of nineteenth-century South African judges. The exception, found in local legislation in Holland, by which public money-lenders (*tafel-houders*), dealers in old clothes, and gold and silversmiths were not obliged to hand back stolen goods which they had *bona fide* bought or received in pledge unless the owner was prepared to refund the purchase price,[193] was held in 1903 not to apply in South Africa.[194] Nor has the principle of Roman-Dutch law, which prevented an owner from vindicating from a *bona fide possessor* of an object obtained from the agent, or factor, for sale of the owner,[195] been adopted in South African law.[196]

If South African judges gave priority to the interests of the owner in these cases, there were other situations where they were willing to deny the owner the vindicatory action. An important consideration which weighed with the judges in this regard was the administration of the law, and particularly the processes for the execution of judgments of the civil courts. Thus, it was held that property sold in execution at judicial sales could not be vindicated from a *bona fide* purchaser.[197] Likewise, it was established that things sold

---

[191] (1884) 1 SAR 171. Followed in *Jantje v. Pretorious* (1889) 3 SAR 65.

[192] Cf. *Woodhead Plant & Co v. Gunn* (1894) 11 SC 4; *Kotze v. Prins* (1903) 20 SC 156; *Roberts & Letts v. Fynn* 1920 AD 23; Carey Miller (n. 186), 293.

[193] Grotius (n. 7), 2, 3, 6; Johannes Voet, *Commentarius ad Pandectas*, 4, 1, 7.

[194] *Muller v. Chadwick & Co* 1906 TS 30.

[195] Vindication was allowed if the owner paid the purchaser the price he had had to pay for the *res*.

[196] The rule was discussed in: *Adams v. Mocke* (1906) 23 SC 782; *Morum Brothers Ltd v. Nepgen* 1916 CPD 392; *Pretorius v. Loudon* 1985 (3) SA 845 (A), but not applied in any of these cases. For a critical review of the position see J. R. Harker, 'The Sale of Movable Property by a Factor or an Agent for Sale and the *Rei Vindicatio*', (1986) 49 *THRHR* 411.

[197] *Lange v. Liesching* 1880 Foord 55; *South African Assoc v. Van Staden* (1892) 9 SC 95; *Adams v. Mocke* (n. 196).

by trustees of insolvent estates and liquidators of companies could not be vindicated from *bona fide* purchasers.[198] (The ready denial of the vindicatory action may have been due to the belief that, in these cases, ownership passed at the sale and vindication was thus technically not possible.[199])

A certain sympathy for commercial interests was revealed in the case of stolen money or bearer-negotiable instruments. They were not, the judges said, ordinary forms of property and could therefore not be vindicated from a *bona fide* possessor.[200]

In considering the conflict between the owner and the *bona fide* possessor, the judges showed some sensitivity to considerations of equity or fairness, albeit in a tentative and ambiguous fashion. The issue arose in cases where the owner of property by his own conduct represented to others that ownership was capable of being lawfully transferred. Should the owner be allowed to vindicate, if another had relied upon the misrepresentation to his prejudice? Certainly, considerations of equity suggested that since the owner was the cause of the other person's misfortune the law should favour the innocent victim rather than the careless owner.

A remedy which met the demand of the prejudiced plaintiff presented itself in the form of the English doctrine of 'estoppel by representation'. Stating that it was no different in principle to the Roman *exceptio doli mali*,[201] South African judges adopted and imported the notion of estoppel[202] and relied principally upon the English law as authority for the application of the doctrine.[203] English law is no longer regarded as the source of the South African law of estoppel;[204] yet the courts apply the doctrine in a substantially similar form.[205]

The effect of the defence of estoppel is, of course, to allow into the South African law a version of the *mobilia non habent sequelam* principle.

---

[198] *Lange v. Liesching* (n. 197).   [199] Cf. *Conradie v. Jones* 1917 OPD 112.

[200] *Woodhead Plant & Co v. Gunn* (1894) 11 SC 4; *Adams v. Mocke* (n. 196), 787; *Leal & Co v. Williams* 1906 TS 554.

[201] In the case of *Waterval Estate and Gold Mining Co v. New Bullion Gold Mining Co* 1905 TS 717 it was observed that 'the application of the maxim of Roman Law *nemo contra suum factum venire debet*, would create the same legal consequences as estoppel in English law: it is practically the estoppel by conduct of the English law'. See further W. A. Joubert (ed.), *The Law of South Africa*, vol. 9 (1979), § 369. For a critique of the supposed connection between estoppel and the *exceptio doli* see J. C. de Wet, *Estoppel by Representation in die Suid-Afrikaanse Reg* (1939), 15.

[202] For a detailed account of this process of reception see P. J. Rabie, *The Law of Estoppel in South Africa* (1992), 21 sqq.; cf. Ch. 7 by Reinhard Zimmermann, above.

[203] The Appellate Division in the case of *Baumann v. Thomas* 1920 AD 428, 434–5 observed: 'The word estoppel is one which has been taken over by us from the English law, and which is now freely used in our daily practice. The doctrine, however, is as much a part of our law as it is of that of England . . . The subject . . . however, has been much more fully developed by the decisions of the English Courts than it has in our own authorities, so that in practice we usually look for guidance to the former rather than the latter.'

[204] *Trust Bank van Afrika Bpk v. Eksteen* 1964 (3) SA 402 (A); *Johaadien v. Stanley Porter (Paarl) (Pty) Ltd* 1970 (1) SA 394 (A).

[205] Cf. Carey Miller (n. 186), 308.

However, the South African law 'so jealously protects the right of owner-ship'[206] that this exception is only grudgingly extended. The courts have adopted the position that not only must the owner have caused the preju-dice, it must also be shown that he did so *negligently*.[207] The requirement of *culpa* on the part of the owner has shifted the focus away from the equi-table consideration that the innocent plaintiff has suffered prejudice as a result of the defendant's actions. There are, however, *indiciae* that it may be waived 'by compelling considerations of fairness'.[208]

2. Private defence

An incidental, though important form of protection of ownership in South African law is the right of an owner to resort to private defence of his prop-erty. In the case of *Ex parte Minister van Justisie: In re S v. Van Wyk*[209] it was decided by the Appellate Division of the Supreme Court that in appro-priate circumstances the owner may even kill in order to defend his prop-erty. Steyn CJ in formulating this principle observed:

If the use of necessary force is justified—as is the case—then it is not clear to me why deadly force must be excluded from that principle. The objection, arising from understandable humanitarian views, concerning the imbalance between life and property, does not in my view create a persuasive basis for a general exception . . . Proportionality will not do as a general basis for private defence . . . [W]hy should the defender, who is unquestionably entitled to protect his rights, be viewed as the one acting unlawfully if he uses deadly force rather than sacrifice his rights?

VI. NEW FORMS OF OWNERSHIP (1970–1995)

The concept of land ownership as understood in South Africa in the twen-tieth century precluded recognition of the ownership of space above the sur-face of the earth separately from the ownership of the surface. This followed from the Roman, Roman-Dutch, and South African principle of *superficies solo cedit*.[210] As a result, South African law did not recognize ownership in

---

[206] *Per* Holmes JA in *Oakland Nominees (Pty) Ltd v. Gelria Mining & Investment Co (Pty) Ltd* 1976 (1) SA 441 (A) 452A.

[207] *Grosvenor Motors (Potchefstroom) Ltd v. Douglas* 1956 (3) SA 420 (A) 427D; *Johaadien v. Stanley Porter (Paarl) (Pty) Ltd* (n. 204), 409E; *Oakland Nominees (Pty) Ltd v. Gelria Mining & Investment Co (Pty) Ltd* (n. 206). Cf. Rabie (n. 202), 83 sqq.

[208] *Per* Holmes JA in *Oakland Nominees (Pty) Ltd v. Gelria Mining & Investment Co (Pty) Ltd* (n. 206), 452B. Cf. *Johaadien v. Stanley Porter (Paarl) (Pty) Ltd* (n. 204), 409F. See Carey Miller (n. 186), 319.

[209] 1967 (1) SA 488 (A).

[210] Cf. Pienaar, (1989) 52 *THRHR* 216, 217 sqq.; C. G. van der Merwe, D. W. Butler, *Sectional Titles, Share Blocks and Time-sharing* (1985), 5.

a building or parts of a building separate from the ownership of the land on which the building was erected.[211]

In the 1950s the need for cheap, convenient housing saw the beginning of a campaign for the recognition of separate ownership of sections of buildings. A Commission of Inquiry, appointed in 1970 to investigate the matter, submitted a report which recommended the introduction of legislation to amend the common law so as to enable the acquisition of what was termed 'sectional titles' in immovable property. A bill was presented to Parliament and enacted as the Sectional Titles Act of 1971, which came into operation in 1973.[212]

The legal regime established under this Act created a new type of *res* in South African law, termed a 'unit' (essentially a section of a building) which could be acquired in ownership. The concept of ownership of a unit was, however, something significantly different from the traditional common law concept of ownership. It involved three essential components: individual ownership of a defined section of a building, joint ownership of the common parts of the immovable property subject to the sectional title scheme, and membership of a body corporate. When a unit is registered in the sectional title register in the name of a particular person, that person simultaneously becomes owner of the relevant section, joint owner with the other sectional owners of the common parts of the scheme, and a member of the body corporate consisting of all the persons in whose names units are registered.[213] These elements are immutably and inextricably linked, so that none of the elements can be disposed of separately.

By providing for the acquisition and regulation of separate ownership in a section or sections of a building, coupled with joint ownership of certain common property, the Act has in fact created a 'composite form of ownership', which differs in important respects from the traditional common law conceptions both of ownership and of joint ownership.

Individual ownership of the conventional kind is, in theory, the most far-reaching right in property known to our law, carrying with it the most extensive powers of control and disposition over a thing compatible with the social order. It normally involves ... extensive rights of enjoyment free from interference from others. However, the rights of the separate owners in respect of the statutory ownership of sections are in some measure subject to the wishes of specific majorities of other owners in the same complex. Ownership of a section also involves several contingent liabilities to which ordinary owners are not subject.[214] ... In regard to the joint

---

[211] Pienaar and Van der Merwe/Butler, *loc. cit.*

[212] Van der Merwe/Butler (n. 210), 5–7; C. G. van der Merwe, 'Sectional Titles', in: W. A. Joubert (ed.), *The Law of South Africa*, vol. 24 (1986), § 200.

[213] C. G. van der Merwe (n. 212), § 208.

[214] Under the Act, the section-owner has to allow authorized persons to enter his section at reasonable hours to inspect it and to perform necessary maintenance work on common

or co-ownership of the statutory common property, the Act has also introduced far-reaching modifications of the common law concept of co-ownership. In the typical case of co-ownership, at common law, the co-owners are, juridically speaking, strangers to each other and have full liberty to dispose of their undivided shares without reference to the wishes of the other co-owners. The position is different, however, in regard to the common property under the act. Dealings with the common property require a unanimous resolution of the owners. Again, in the ordinary case of co-ownership parties are able to bring the relationship to an end by the *actio communi dividundo*. This is not the case under the Act; statutory joint ownership is what Dutch lawyers aptly describe as *gebonde mede-eiendom*, and it can only be terminated in accordance the provisions of the act.[215]

Most South African authorities consider ownership in a sectional title scheme to be a form of 'true ownership', albeit of a unique and special character.[216] Its existence is seen as reflecting 'the less rigid state of our modern concept of ownership'.[217]

While South African law has modified its concept of ownership to enable ownership of space, it has not yet come to allow ownership of time. Time-sharing of immovable property is possible under South African law[218] but not as a type of ownership.[219]

---

installations; he is under an obligation to keep his section in a state of good repair; the owner may not use his section, or let it be used, in such a way as to cause a nuisance to any other occupant of the building, or to bring the good name of the building into disrepute, or to cause the insurance premium payable in respect of the building to be increased; the owner may not keep an animal in his section after notice to that effect by the trustees; and the section may not be utilized other than for the purpose which is expressly or tacitly indicated on the registered sectional plan. Apart from these restrictions contained in the Act and the schedules, further restrictions may be imposed on the sectional owner's right of use and enjoyment by unanimous, special, or ordinary resolutions of the body corporate, or by special rules of the developer registered with the sectional plan. In addition, the sectional owner's right to dispose of his section is restricted by various provisions of the Act: an owner may alienate his section only when all debts to the body corporate have been paid and if no other interdicts or caveats have been served on him; he must notify the body corporate forthwith of the alienation of, or any other juristic act in respect of, his section; and, in principle, no section may be disposed of independently of its accompanying share in the common property. See Van der Merwe/Butler (n. 210), 33.

[215] D. V. Cowen, 'South African Sectional Titles Act in Historical Perspective: An Analysis and Evaluation', (1973) 6 *CILSA* 1, 12.

[216] Ibid. 12; G. Pienaar 'Ontwikkelings in die Suid-Afrikaanse Eiendomsreg in Perspektief' 1986 *TSAR* 295; Van der Merwe/Butler (n. 210), 35.

[217] Van der Merwe/Butler (n. 210), 35. Cf. A. J. van der Walt, 'The South African Law of Ownership: A Historical and Philosophical Perspective', 1992 *De Jure* 446, 447, who sees the acceptance of sectional title ownership as characterizing the 'universal and timeless' qualities of the institution of ownership.

[218] Van der Merwe/Butler (n. 210), ch. 23.

[219] Cf. D. W. Butler, 'Time-Shares Conferring Ownership', 1985 *Acta Juridica* 315, at 319.

VII. CONCEPTUALIZING OWNERSHIP

In the period of almost three and a half centuries during which Roman-Dutch law has existed in South Africa the nature and character of ownership underwent a series of transformations in the European milieu from which it had originated: a phenomenon which, in turn, has influenced the nature and character of the concept of ownership in South African law.

1. The European background

When Roman-Dutch law first came to South Africa in the mid-seventeenth century, ownership in Europe was being freed from the social and political strictures of medieval feudalism.[220]

Bartolus of Saxoferato is said to have been the first person to attempt a definition of ownership, which he characterized as: the right perfectly to dispose over a corporeal object, unless this is prohibited by law.[221] The Roman-Dutch jurist Grotius largely adopted his definition,[222] but in so doing interpreted ownership as conferring upon the individual owner the freedom to use and exploit natural resources for his own advantage.[223]

In his *Inleidinge tot de Hollandsche Rechtsgeleertheyd*[224] Grotius distinguishes between two categories of patrimonial rights, namely creditors' rights and real rights, the distinction depending upon whether the right in question is directed at a corporeal thing as such, without reference to another person, or at another person in order to claim something from him.[225] Philosophically this classification is typical of post-medieval thinking in that it proceeds from the individual legal subject and his rights, and not from the world of objects and their characteristics.[226] Although this distinction relates back to the Roman distinction between personal and real actions, it contained a new element in juxtaposing the individual person and the world of physical objects and other people.

---

[220] See A. J. van der Walt, D. G. Kleyn, *'Duplex Dominium*: The History and Significance of the Concept of Divided Ownership', in: D. P. Visser (ed.), *Essays on the History of Law* (1989), 213.

[221] (*Ius de re corporali perfecte disponendi, nisi lege prohibeatur*): Bartolus on Digest 41, 2, 71, 1, n. 4. See A. J. van der Walt, 'Bartolus se Omskrywing van *Dominium* en die Interpretasies Daarvan Sedert die Vyftiende Eeu', (1986) 49 *THRHR* 305; *idem*, 'Gedagtes oor die Herkoms en Ontwikkeling van die Suid-Afrikaanse Eiendomsreg', 1988 *De Jure* 314.

[222] Grotius (n. 7) 2, 3, 10: '. . . that which entitles a man to do with a thing and for his advantage anything he pleases which is not forbidden by the law' (trans. R. W. Lee).

[223] I have relied heavily upon Van der Walt (n. 217), for the following account. Cf. esp. Van der Walt, 'Der Eigentumsbegriff', in: Feenstra/Zimmermann 485 sqq. and the contributions by R. Feenstra, cited by Van der Walt in fn. 3.

[224] Grotius (n. 7).   [225] Ibid. 2, 1, 57–9.

[226] Van der Walt (n. 217) 452; *idem*, in: Feenstra/Zimmermann (n. 7), 496 sqq.

According to Grotius' formulation only full ownership, with title and use in one hand, can provide humans with the necessary freedom to exercise the most complete right of disposal over property. Grotius reinterpreted both the definition and the classification of ownership in the light of the philosophical view of ownership as the right which provides the individual with the necessary space to exercise personal freedom.[227]

In the Grotian scheme of things the medieval plurality of property rights is replaced by the concept of only one form of ownership, which provides the owner with a fundamentally unlimited right of disposal fitting for an individual characterized by his moral freedom. Simultaneously, it constitutes the model against which all patrimonial rights are evaluated. This approach still forms the foundation of the modern perception of ownership and of patrimonial rights in general.[228]

Grotius' assumptions concerning the moral function of ownership as a guarantee of personal freedom were further substantiated by the German philosopher Immanuel Kant.[229] He defined law as the sum total of conditions under which the free will of one individual can be reconciled with the free will of all others in terms of a general law of freedom. Underlying this definition is the assumption that the function of the law and of legal principles and institutions is to enable human individuals to express and realize their own personal and individual freedom through, amongst other things, the use and exploitation of property.

These philosophical conceptions accorded with the economic liberalism which developed at the beginning of the nineteenth century. For the emerging middle classes of western Europe it was of the utmost importance that ownership be freed from its social and political limitations in order to facilitate the free accumulation and transfer of property in the market. The law of ownership thus came to be characterized by, and evaluated according to, its ability to allow individuals the maximum freedom of exploitation of property commensurate with the corresponding freedom of others to do the same. Basic to this view was the assumption that the freedom to exploit property with the minimum of interference is necessary for the full moral development of the individual.[230]

The nineteenth-century German school of jurisprudence known as pandectism transformed the theories of Grotius and Kant into a comprehensive and consistent scientific system of subjective rights.[231] The distinctions between creditors' rights and real rights, and between ownership and the

---

[227] Van der Walt (n. 217), 453. Based upon this point of departure, Grotius proceeds to introduce the well known contrast between full, or complete, ownership and limited real rights. For details see Van der Walt, in: Feenstra/Zimmermann (n. 7), 486 sqq.

[228] Van der Walt (n. 217), 453; G. C. J. J. van den Bergh, *Eigendom: Grepen Uit die Geschiedenis van Een Omstreden Begrip* (1979).

[229] Van der Walt (n. 217), 453.   [230] Ibid. 453 sq.

[231] Ibid. 454; *idem*, in: Feenstra/Zimmermann (n. 7), 516 sqq.

limited real rights, the relative value of ownership and limited real rights, and the characteristics ascribed to ownership (absoluteness, exclusivity, and abstractness) as they are known in modern Western European and South African law are all products of pandectist theory formulated by nineteenth-century lawyers such as Bernhard Windscheid.[232] The pandectists created and propagated the myth that they were merely returning to and expanding the work of the classical Roman lawyers, and that classical Roman doctrine and pandectist theory differed only in detail. By this device they created the impression that the principles discussed in their works were universal and timeless, while ignoring and disguising the significant differences between classical Roman law and their version of it.[233]

The pandectists cast their version of the law in the mould of a general, universal, and logically constructed scientific whole.[234] Ownership is presented as a universal, timeless, abstract, and logical concept which forms part of a larger whole, each part of which is determined by the neutral and abstract logic of its constituent concepts and their interrelationships. Ownership ceases to be a function of social power-relationships and becomes a function of mathematical calculation in terms of the strict and abstract logic of the theory of subjective rights. In this way the philosophical, social, and political perceptions and ideas that shaped the modern concept of ownership were hidden. This makes any discussion of these wider ramifications very difficult.[235]

2. Defining ownership in South Africa

Prior to the twentieth century South African legal literature consisted entirely of the writings of the Roman-Dutch authorities and contained no attempt to formulate the concept of ownership as it existed in South African law. It is, however, reasonable to assume that during the earlier period Grotius' definition of ownership ('that which entitles a man to do with a thing and for his advantage anything he pleases which is not forbidden by the law') would have been relied upon by the courts. Certainly, in the nineteenth century, when Grotius' *Inleiding* became an official law-book of the Orange Free State,[236] his definition would have been regarded, in that state at least, as the official version of the concept of ownership.

At the same time, a definition drafted in 1806 by Johannes van der Linden in his *Koopmans Handboek*[237] enjoyed wide circulation in South Africa due to both the work's early availability in English translation[238] and

---

[232] Van der Walt (n. 217), 454.   [233] Ibid.   [234] Ibid. 455.   [235] Ibid.
[236] See D. H. van Zyl, *Geskiedenis van die Romeins-Hollandse Reg* (1979), 468.
[237] Johannes van der Linden, *Regtsgeleerd, Practicaal, en Koopmans Handboek* (1806).
[238] By Jabez Henry, under the title *Institutes of the Laws of Holland* (1828), and by Henry Juta, also entitled *Institutes of the Laws of Holland* (1884).

its status, after 1859, as the official law-book of the South African (Transvaal) Republic.[239] The definition was as follows: 'Ownership is that right by which something belongs to a person to the exclusion of all others'.[240] It reflected the modernized version of ownership then prevalent in western European legal systems, which emphasized exclusivity as the characteristic quality of *dominium*.

Ownership, Van der Linden added, 'is especially known by its consequences'. These he listed as:

1st. The right of enjoying the fruits which result from such thing. 2nd. the right of making such proper use of such thing as the owner pleases. 3rd. The right of altering its shape or form at will. 4th. The right of entirely destroying it at will. 5th. The right of preventing others from making use of it. 6th. The right of alienating it or of transferring to others any other sort of right e.g. the use of it . . . All this must be understood, however, subject to this qualification viz. that neither the provisions of the law are transgressed nor the rights of third persons injuriously affected[241]

The earliest text book definition of ownership in South African legal literature adopts the notion of ownership as entailing exclusive rights: '*Eigendom is het recht om over eene zaak, by uitsluiting van alle anderen, op die volstrekste wijze te beschikken*' (Ownership is the right to dispose over a thing in the most perfect way, to the exclusion of all others).[242]

The earliest English language definition was that offered by the South African scholar and judge, A. F. S. Maasdorp, in his *Institutes of Cape Law*, first published in 1903. Maasdorp[243] defined ownership as 'the sum-total of all the real rights which a person can possibly have to and over a corporeal thing, subject only to the legal maxim *sic utere tuo ut alienum non laedas*'.

The modern scholarly definitions of ownership are almost identical: 'Ownership is potentially the most extensive private right which a person can have with regard to a corporeal thing'.[244]

Most modern judicial pronouncements define ownership in terms of its 'absolute' nature. In *Johannesburg Municipal Council v. Rand Townships Registrar*[245] Wessels J formulated a definition of ownership citing not Grotius or Van der Linden, but Friedrich Carl von Savigny:

---

[239] Sched. I, Constitution of the *Zuid-Afrikaansche Republiek*, of 19 Sept. 1859. See Van Zyl (n. 236), 396. Grotius was assigned the status of a subsidiary authority: ibid.

[240] Van der Linden (n. 237), 1, 7, 1.

[241] For this proposition he cites the French jurist Pothier, *Traité du droit de domaine de propriété*, § 14.

[242] Josson, *Schets van Het Recht van de Zuid-Afrikaanse Republiek* (1897) 15 (cited in Van der Walt, (1986) 49 *THRHR* 305, 323, fn. 150).

[243] A. F. S. Maasdorp, *The Institutes of Cape Law*, Book II, *The Law of Things* (1903), 31.

[244] C. G. van der Merwe, *The Law of Things* (1987), 104. A similar definition appears in the same author's *Sakereg* (n. 80), 109. For a review of definitions of ownership in the modern South African legal literature see Van der Walt, 1988 *De Jure* 17 sqq.

[245] 1910 TS 1314, 1319.

What . . . is the exact scope of *dominium* has been a matter of controversy for centuries . . . Savigny's definition may be accepted as of high authority. '*Dominium* is the unrestricted and exclusive control which a person has over a thing' (Savigny *System [des heutigen römischen Rechts]*, vol. 1, sec. 59, p. 367). Inasmuch as the owner has the full control, he also has the power to part with so much of his control as he pleases. Once the owner, however, he remains such until he has parted with all his rights of ownership over the thing.

In *Regal v. African Superslate (Pty) Ltd*[246] Steyn CJ stated that '*as algemene beginsel kan iedereen met sy eiendom doen wat hy wil, al strek dit tot nadeel of misnoeë van 'n ander, maar by aangrensende vasgoed spreek dit vanself dat daar minder ruimte is vir onbeperkte regsuitoefening*' (as a general principle, everybody can do with his property what he wants, even if it is to the disadvantage or displeasure of another, but with regard to adjacent property it is self-evident that there is less room for the unlimited exercise of rights). In *Gien v. Gien*[247] ownership is described by Spoelstra AJ as '*die mees volledige saaklike reg wat 'n persoon ten opsigte van 'n saak kan hê. Die uitgangspunt is dat 'n persoon, wat 'n onroerende saak aanbetref, met en op sy eiendom kan maak wat hy wil*' (the most complete real right a person can have with regard to a thing. The starting point is that, as far as immovable property is concerned, one can do with and on one's property what one wants).[248]

3. The pandectist influence

Although it is often said that the concept of ownership in South African law is derived from Roman law,[249] it has been convincingly demonstrated that since the beginning of the twentieth century the conceptual basis of ownership in South African law has been that provided by the pandectists.[250] Their influence became apparent as South African lawyers began to treat the German scholars as if they were institutional writers on Roman-Dutch law.[251] The extent of the adoption of the pandectist version of property

---

[246] 1963 (1) SA 102 (A) 106 sq.   [247] 1979 (2) SA 1113 (T)

[248] The following passage from Rudolph Sohm, *The Institutes* (3rd edn., 1907, trans. by Ledlie) is quoted as authority: 'Ownership is a right, unlimited in respect of its contents, to exercise control over a thing. The difference, in point of conception, between ownership in the *jura in re aliena* is this, that ownership, however susceptible of legal limitations (e.g. through rights of others in the same thing), is nevertheless absolutely unlimited as far as its own contents are concerned. As soon therefore as the legal limitations imposed upon ownership—whether by the rights of others or by rules of public law—disappear, ownership at once, and of its own accord, re-establishes itself as a plenary control. That is what is sometimes described as the "elasticity" of ownership'.

[249] Van der Merwe (n. 80), 110; Cowen (n. 215), 70.

[250] D. P. Visser, 'The "Absoluteness" of Ownership: The South African Common Law in Perspective', 1985 *Acta Juridica* 39; Van der Walt, (1986) 49 *THRHR* 307 sqq.

[251] Visser, 1985 *Acta Juridica* 47. Cf. *Johannesburg Municipal Council v. Rand Townships Registrar* (n. 245).

rights is illustrated by the authoritative and influential exposition of the South African law of property provided by C. G van der Merwe in his textbook *Sakereg*, first published in 1979. This work reflects, as Van der Walt has noted,[252] the spirit, framework, and content of pandectist terminology and methodology.[253]

It is due to the pervasive influence of pandectist scholarship that the concept of ownership is generally described and understood as 'absolute' in nature. This is supposed to indicate that ownership confers the most complete right that it is possible to acquire in a thing, and to convey the idea that the owner is free to use or dispose of his property at his own discretion.[254] As Van der Walt has pointed out,[255] this view prevails in the minds of South African lawyers, even though it is not borne out in the practice of South African law.

4. Redefining ownership

In 1984 the South African scholar D. V. Cowen delivered a lecture entitled 'New Patterns of Landownership, The Transformation of the Concept of Ownership as *Plena in Re Potestas*',[256] in which, for the first time in South Africa, it was suggested that the traditional view of land-ownership as full and uninhibited power over a thing can no longer be accepted in the modern socio-economic context. Cowen called for a radical transformation of the concept of land-ownership, arguing that new patterns of land-ownership, such as sectional title, group and cluster housing, property time-sharing, nature conservation areas, and ownership of airspace, can only be accommodated in a less rigidly absolute and individualistic framework of property rights. Thus, he called for the abandonment of the traditional notion of ownership as autonomous and individualistic.[257] The emerging new concept would instead have to provide for: (a) recognition that ownership carries a social responsibility and social obligations; (b) different attributes of ownership for different objects of ownership;[258] (c) fragmentation of ownership in order to comply with the needs of the day;[259] and (d) a more satisfactory jurisprudential formulation of ownership.[260]

---

[252] Van der Walt (n. 217), 455.

[253] Van der Merwe's work is much influenced by C. Asser, *Handleiding tot de Beoefening van het Nederlands Burgerlijk Recht Zakenrecht: Algemeen Deel* (1985), 4–45, and *idem Zakenrecht: Eigendom en Beperkte Zakelijke Genotsrechten* (1990), 13–28, a work based upon the pandectist version of property law.

[254] For this analysis of the nature of ownership in South African law see Van der Walt (n. 250), 305.

[255] Ibid.

[256] At the University of the Witwatersrand on 26 Apr. 1984 (page refs. are to the bound text of the paper available in the Law Library of the School of Law, University of the Witwatersrand).

[257] Cowen (n. 256) 67.   [258] Ibid. 70.   [259] Ibid. 71.   [260] Ibid. 72.

In a subsequent study, Carole Lewis[261] drew attention to the extent to which the traditional common law incidents of land-ownership had undergone extensive erosion at the hands of the legislatures. She concluded that the South African law of land-ownership had already been so far transformed by social, economic, and political forces that it was no longer consistent with the traditional Grotian-pandectist concept of ownership.[262]

In recent years A. J. van der Walt has provided a sustained analysis of the sources and nature of ownership in South African law. In his view, the traditional pandectist conceptual structure no longer has a place in twentieth-century South Africa; he forcefully urges a rethinking of ownership for contemporary South African law.

The need to rethink the nature of the concept of ownership in South Africa is not merely a matter of academic titillation but a task of some urgency in the changing constitutional and socio-economic circumstances of the country, following the new constitutional dispensation introduced in South Africa in 1993.[263] In this new dispensation the institution of private property,[264] especially in relation to land, will not escape the attention of the reformers.[265] Under the apartheid system black South Africans were dispossessed of and denied the right to own land; ownership in land was 'used as an instrument of oppression and racial discrimination'.[266] As a result, the issue of land rights in a new South Africa is fundamentally important in the process of redressing the wrongs of the past and and ensuring full human and civil rights for all citizens.[267]

According to Van der Walt, the rethinking of ownership is a necessary part of this wider process.[268] Particularly, he has pointed to the fact[269] that the traditional abstract concept of ownership has resulted in real rights

---

[261] 1985 *Acta Juridica* 241.

[262] Ibid. 262. Cf. Milton, 1985 *Acta Juridica* 267, drawing attention to the extent to which planning law has altered aspects of the common law of land-ownership.

[263] Brought about by the abandonment of apartheid and the negotiation of a new constitution. The interim constition (in the form of the Constitution of the Republic of South Africa Act 200 of 1993) which enabled the democratic election of legislatures and the implementation of a bill of human and civil rights, has already set the process of change and transformation in motion.

[264] Entrenched in the Bill of Rights. See s. 28, Constitution of the Republic of South Africa Act 200 of 1993. On s. 28 see D. Basson, *South Africa's Interim Constitution* (1994), 42; A. J. van der Walt, 'Property Rights, Land Rights and Environmental Rights', in: D. H. van Wyk, J. Dugard, B. de Villers, D. Davis, *Rights and Constitutionalism: The New South African Legal Order* (1994), 455; M. Chaskalson, 'The Property Clause: Section 28 of the Constitution', (1994) 10 *SAJHR* 131.

[265] See e.g. Geoff Budlender, 'The Right to Equitable Access to Land', (1993) 8 *SAJHR* 295; Carole Lewis, 'The Right to Private Property in a New Political Dispensation in South Africa', (1993) 8 *SAJHR* 389.

[266] Lewis (n. 261), 262.

[267] Cf. C. Cross, 'An Alternative Legality: The Property Rights Question in Relation to South African Land Reform', (1992) 8 *SAJHR* 305.

[268] A. J. van der Walt, 'The Fragmentation of Land Rights', (1992) 8 *SAJHR* 431.

[269] Ibid. 434.

being defined not according to their own characteristics, but in terms of what they are not, namely ownership. Ownership is regarded as the most comprehensive real right and simultaneously the source of all limited real rights. The limited real rights are, by definition, nothing more than temporary, and basically unnatural, rights, granted to non-owners by a temporary suspension of some aspect of another's full and unrestricted ownership. The content of a limited real right is thus determined by the various ways in which it falls short of (full) ownership: its limited character, its temporary existence, its ability to be reduced to specific entitlements, etc. In such a scheme of things, Van der Walt points out, 'land rights other than ownership are, in fact, mere shadows without essence: they are not-ownership'.[270] This being so:

[w]hen considering the actual distribution of land and the imbalance between landowners and land users in South Africa, it becomes apparent that this paradigm cannot provide answers for the restructuring of land rights in a future social order. In terms of the traditional ownership paradigm it is assumed that ownership is not only the most comprehensive but also the most natural and the most desirable land right, and all other land rights are regarded with a certain measure of disdain: they are temporary, limited and less valuable. However, realities regarding the availability of a limited resource such as land for an ever increasing population, coupled with people's need for access to secure land rights, dictate that greater importance should be accorded to land rights, and that they should not be evaluated purely negatively simply because they amount to less than full ownership. The abstract concept of ownership can no longer dominate the paradigm within which all land rights are formulated and evaluated.[271]

Thus, the traditional perception of ownership needs 'to be demythologised to allow for a more realistic perception of other land rights'.[272]

Whether, when, how and in what way this agenda will be carried out remain to be seen. It seems clear, however, that Hugo Grotius' *dominium plenum* will have to undergo yet another transformation in order to serve the needs of all people in the new South Africa.

---

[270] Ibid. 434.   [271] Ibid. 434.   [272] Ibid. 434.

21: *Original Acquisition of Ownership*

C. G. VAN DER MERWE

I. INTRODUCTION

The most important original modes of acquisition of ownership recognized in South African law are: occupation, treasure trove, accession, specification, mixing of liquids and mingling of solids, acquisition of fruits, prescription, expropriation, forfeiture to the state, and appropriation of minerals.[1] All these modes, except the last three, have their roots in Roman law and were further developed by the Roman-Dutch writers of the seventeenth and eighteenth centuries.[2] One of them, treasure trove, never received judicial recognition in a South African court,[3] while others, like mixing of liquids and mingling of solids,[4] and certain forms of accession, like alluvion and avulsion,[5] received only scant attention. The attachment of movables to land *(inaedificatio)*,[6] prescription,[7] and the occupation of wild animals,[8] on the other hand, have generated a substantial body of case-law.

Instead of examining the South African development of all these original modes of acquisition of ownership, this Chapter discusses only three of them in detail: prescription, the occupation of wild animals, and specification. These have been chosen because each was moulded by different

---

[1] See generally C. G. van der Merwe, M. J. de Waal, *The Law of Things and Servitudes* (1993), §§ 130–63; C. G. van der Merwe, *Sakereg* (2nd edn., 1989), 214–97; D. G. Kleyn, A. Boraine, *Silberberg & Schoeman's The Law of Property* (3rd edn., 1992), 195–241; D. L. Carey Miller, *The Acquisition and Protection of Ownership* (1986), 1–114.

[2] See, *inter alia*, Hugo Grotius, *Inleiding tot de Hollandsche Rechtsgeleertheyd*, 2, 4, 6–10 ; Johannes Voet, *Commentarius ad Pandectas*, 41, 1 and 3; Simon van Leeuwen, *Censura Forensis*, 1, 2, 1–6; *idem*, *Het Rooms-Hollands-Regt*, 2, 2–6; Dionysius Godefridus van der Keessel, *Praelectiones iuris hodierni ad Hugonis Grotii introductionem ad iurisprudentiam Hollandicam*, 2, 4, 6–10.

[3] Van der Merwe/De Waal (n. 1), § 134; Van der Merwe (n. 1), 228 sq.

[4] Only three reported cases could be found on mingling and mixing. See footnotes to Van der Merwe (n. 1), 263–5.

[5] Only one reported case, *Colonial Govt v. Town Council of Cape Town* (1902) 19 SC 87, deals directly with alluvion. The other cases concerned the description of an *ager limitatus* and a public river. There are no reported cases on avulsion.

[6] At least 50 decisions on *inaedificatio* have been reported in South African law reports, the latest being *Sumatie (Edms) Bpk v. Venter* 1990 (1) SA 173 (T) and *Mpisi v. Trebble* 1994 (2) SA 136 (A).

[7] More than 100 decisions on acquisitive prescription of ownership and servitudes have been reported.

[8] At least 30 decisions on occupation of wild animals and abandoned things (*res derelictae*) have been reported.

influences. The institution of prescription—especially the requirement of possession for acquisitive prescription—was initially profoundly influenced by English law.[9] Occupation of wild animals developed in fairly stereotypical fashion in accordance with Roman and Roman-Dutch principles until special legislation was introduced to protect the game-farm industry. The rules relating to specification proved so old-fashioned that academic writers and a judge of the Supreme Court, albeit only in an *obiter dictum*, have endeavoured to steer this institution in a new direction.

II. THE REQUIREMENT OF POSSESSION FOR ACQUISITIVE PRESCRIPTION

1. Introduction

It is generally accepted that the rules relating to the most important kind of acquisitive prescription of ownership in late Roman-Dutch law constituted an amalgamation of the Theodosian institution of *praescriptio longissimi temporis* and the early Dutch institution of *lange verjaring*.[10] The period for prescription was a third of a century in the case of immovables and thirty years for movables.[11] Neither a just title (*iustus titulus*) nor good faith (*bona fides*) were required.[12] The only prerequisite was peaceful and uninterrupted possession (*quieta et continuata possessio*) for the whole period of prescription.[13] Voet[14] indicated that possession involved not only a physical but also a mental element, namely the intention to hold the object of prescription for oneself and without acknowledgement of the rights of the true

[9] The same is true of *inaedificatio*. See Van der Merwe (n. 1), 256.

[10] See generally J. W. Wessels, *History of Roman-Dutch Law* (1908), 634–43; J. C. de Wet, 'Verjaring', in: J. J. Gauntlett (ed.), *Opuscula Miscellanea* (1979), 78–81; L. E. Krause, 'The History and Nature of Acquisitive Prescription and of Limitation of Actions in Roman Dutch Law', (1923) 40 *SALJ* 26; F. E. Marx, *Verkrygende Verjaring in die Suid-Afrikaanse Reg* (unpublished LL D thesis, University of Port Elizabeth, 1994), 47–65; Van der Merwe (n. 1), 271–3.

[11] Grotius (n. 2), 2, 7, 8; Simon van Groenewegen van der Made, *Tractatus de legibus abrogatis in Hollandia vicinisque regionibus*, ad C. 7, 39, 2; Van Leeuwen, *Rooms-Hollands-Regt* (n. 2), 2, 8, 5, 7; *idem*, *Censura Forensis* (n. 2), 1, 2, 10, 11; Van der Keessel (n. 2), 2, 7, 6.

[12] Voet (n. 2), 44, 3, 9; Van der Keessel (n. 2), 2, 7, 8; Antonius Matthaeus (II), *Paroemiae Belgarum jurisconsultis usitatissimae quibus praeter romanorum aliarumque gentium mores et Instituta Ultrajectinum exponitur et elucidatur ultrajecti* (1667), 9, 2, 3; *idem*, *De auctionibus libri duo, quorum prior venditiones, posterior locationes quae sub hasta fiunt, exequitur: Adjecto passim voluntariarum auctionum iure* (1680), 2, 7, 84, 85.

[13] Voet (n. 2), 44, 3, 9.

[14] 44, 3, 9: 'Rather is this single point regarded, whether a person has been for so long a space of time in peaceful and continued possession or quasi-possession. Thus for acquiring the ownership of corporeal things he must not have suffered any disturbance at the hands of the true owner during the whole of the period in which he possessed things of another with the intention of keeping them for himself, and he must not by any act have acknowledged him as the owner' (trans. Percival Gane, The Selective Voet, vol. VI, 1957).

owner. Concerning the acquisitive prescription of servitudes, the general view is that Justinian's *praescriptio longi temporis* was received into Roman-Dutch law and that a third of a century was accepted as the period for prescription. During this period there must have been continuous use of the object *nec vi, nec clam, nec precario*.[15]

In English law the notion of prescription is employed only in relation to the acquisition of easements (servitudes) and *profits à prendre* (civil fruits).[16] Under the influence of Roman law the requirements are continuous use for a period of twenty years *nec vi, nec clam, nec precario* and as of right.[17] The requirement that the use must be 'as of right' accords with the idea that the possession must have begun by way of a grant.[18] Acquisitive prescription of an easement is therefore in principle, not the acquisition of something belonging to another, but rather an *ex lege* confirmation of a right presumably already in existence. Thus, it is essentially similar to the Roman-Dutch (later South African) institution of *vetustas*, which implies that a valid title is presumed after time immemorial.[19]

Apart from the acquisition of easements by prescription, English law recognizes the institution of limitation of actions. The Limitation Acts of 1623, 1833, and 1874 limit the ability to enforce the right of ownership if legal proceedings against a person disputing this right are not instituted within a period of twelve years. This period only begins to run in the case of 'adverse user', that is, from the time the transgressor starts acting adversely to the rights of the owner. Thus, continuous adverse possession for the statutory period bars the owner from instituting an action to reclaim his property. As a result, the former owner loses his right and the adverse possessor becomes the new owner. The doctrine of limitation of actions, therefore, not only extinguishes the right of the original owner but also endows the adverse possessor with an unimpeachable title against him.[20]

---

[15] Voet (n. 2), 8, 4, 6; Grotius (n. 2), 2, 36, 4; Van Leeuwen, *Rooms-Hollands-Regt* (n. 2), 2, 19, 10; *idem, Censura Forensis* (n. 2), 1, 2, 14, 5; Van der Keessel (n. 2), 2, 36, 4. See generally Marx (n. 1), 65–8; Van der Merwe (n. 1), 530.

[16] See F. H. Lawson, W. W. Buckland, D. Arnold, *Roman Law and Common Law: A Comparison in Outline* (1965), 117.

[17] See E. H. Burn, *Cheshire and Burn's Modern Law of Real Property* (13th edn., 1982), 513. 'In technical language, it must be a *user as of right*, or, to use the expression taken by Coke from Bracton, *longus usus nec per vim, nec clam, nec precario*.' See Coke on Littleton, 113 b.

[18] The introduction of the presumption of *lost grant* played an important role in the development of the English law of prescription.

[19] See Burn (n. 17), 513; F. H. Lawson, B. Rudden, *The Law of Property* (2nd edn., 1982), 132; Marx (n. 10), 77–80.

[20] See generally J. A. Lightwood, *A Treatise on Possession of Land* (1894), 154–90; Burns (n. 17), 823 sqq.; Lawson/Buckland/Arnold (n. 16), 122; J. G. Riddall, *Introduction to Land Law* (2nd edn., 1979), 320 sqq.

2. South African case-law until 1910

Early South African case-law introduced the doctrine of adverse user, as applied under the English doctrine of limitation of actions, as well as English legal concepts concerning the acquisitive prescription of servitudes into South African law. Only a few cases applied unadulterated Roman-Dutch law principles of prescription as enunciated by Voet, *Commentarius ad Pandectas*, 44, 3, 9.

The English concept of 'adverse user' was first applied with regard to the acquisition of ownership in *Van Schalkwyk v. Hugo* in 1880.[21] The Cape Supreme Court had to decide whether the plaintiff had acquired a strip of land by prescription. It was alleged that the plaintiff, and his predecessors in title, had peaceably, openly, and as of right occupied the land until the year 1855. In 1853 it was discovered that, according to the original grant of the land, the boundary line passed through the plaintiff's vineyard. However, no action was, taken on the part of the defendant to put the matter in order. The Court found that there had been an 'adverse possession' of the strip of land in dispute from 1820 until 1853 and decided that as long as the adverse occupiers remained in actual possession, prescription could only be interrupted by means of a judicial interpellation. De Villiers CJ explained the matter as follows:

> Until the year 1855, therefore, the plaintiff and his predecessors in title had *peaceably, openly, and as of right* occupied the land in dispute. In 1853 or thereabouts it was discovered that the boundary line, according to the grant, passed through the vineyard, but no proceedings were taken against the occupiers, who remained in possession until after 1855. It does not even appear that any intimation of the discovery was made to them ... Can it then be said that there has been an interruption, or as the civilians would term it, an *usurpatio* of their *adverse enjoyment* (*usucapio*)? The occupation had begun in good faith, *without* force or fraud and even if afterwards they were informed that the land did not belong to them, there would be no such interruption, unless they were actually dispossessed, or unless, at all events, judicial proceedings were taken against them.[22]

The requirements 'peaceably, openly and as of right' as well as the reference to occupation 'without force or fraud' seem to latch on to the English law concerning prescription of easements. 'As of right', in the present context, may be taken to imply that the possessor must have exercised his possession *animo domini*, in spite of the English expression that the occupation was exercised in terms of a 'grant'. The fact that 'adverse enjoyment' is expressly used as a synonym for *usucapio* demonstrates that De Villiers CJ did not intend to introduce a separate requirement of 'adverse user' but

---

[21] 1880 Foord 89. It was introduced into South African law by the decision in *Farni v. Macdonald* (1876) 6 Buch 176 (on the acquisition of a servitude by prescription).
[22] 91, emphases added.

understood it as a collective phrase indicating the kind of possession required for prescription.[23]

The traditional requirements for the acquisitive prescription of servitudes (exercise of right *nec vi, nec clam, nec precario*) and their English equivalents for the acquisition of easements (peaceably, openly, and as of right) were employed for the first time in 1895 in *Jones v. Town Council of Cape Town*[24] with regard to acquisitive prescription of ownership. This case concerned an exception raised against the claim of the plaintiff that he had acquired ownership by prescription of a *stoep* built on the municipality's land. Although the exception was turned down, De Villiers CJ indicated that the right of the public to use the public way may be lost by 'adverse user'. De Villiers CJ explained: 'The occupation was peaceable, open and as of right—*nec vi, nec clam, nec precario*'.[25]

Without neither hesitation nor any explanation, the Chief Justice thus accepted the English requirements for the prescription of easements and their Roman-Dutch law equivalents for the prescription of servitudes as self-evident requirements for the acquisition of ownership by way of prescription. Unlike in Roman, Roman-Dutch, and English law, the acquisition of servitudes and the acquisition of ownership were treated alike, for the Roman-Dutch requirements for the acquisition of servitudes by prescription were simply transplanted to the acquisition of ownership by prescription.

In subsequent cases the courts either accepted the doctrine of 'adverse user' as the basis for deciding whether acquisitive prescription had taken place[26] or required that the exercise of the powers must have been *nec vi, nec clam, nec precario*: peaceably, openly, and as of right.[27] Usually, however, they mixed these two sets of requirements and stated that there had to have been 'an adverse user *nec vi nec clam nec precario*'.[28]

Several early decisions scrutinized the *nec clam* requirement of openness.[29] The *locus classicus* is the following remark by Lord De Villiers CJ in *Smith v. Martin's Executor Dative*:

---

[23] See also Marx (n. 10), 99. Several other early decisions followed *Van Schalkwyk v. Hugo* in equating adverse possession with the possession required for prescription. Almost invariably it was held that the 'adverse possession' must have been open and peaceful.

[24] (1895) 12 SC 19.   [25] 50.

[26] See, *inter alia, Lind v. Gibbs* (1895) 12 SC 287, 291; *Trustees of Kareiga Baptist Church v. Amos Charles Webber & Edward George Webber* (1903) 17 EDC 105, 108 (per Jones JP).

[27] See, *inter alia, Glass v. Palmer & Palmer* (1898) 13 EDC 83, 93; *Loest v. Lushington Board of Management* 1906 EDC 327, 334; *Lushington Village Board of Management v. Loest* 1907 EDC 168, 181.

[28] *Smith v. Martin's Executor Dative* (1899) 16 SC 148, 151; *Trustees of Kareiga Baptist Church v. Amos Charles Webber & Edward George Webber* (n. 26) (*per* Sheil J).

[29] See *Kohler v. Baartman* (1895) 12 SC 205; *De Klerk v. Niehaus* (1897) 14 SC 302; *Tarkastad Dutch Reformed Church v. Tarkastad Municipality* (1898) 15 SC 371; *Van Schalkwyk v. Du Plessis* (1900) 17 SC 454; *Cape Town Town Council v. Sassen* 1912 CPD 587, 600.

The occupation must have been not only peaceable and as of right, but open, that is to say, visible to others. The right to acquire by prescription is founded upon the negligence of the owner in not protecting his interests against strangers in possession, but this foundation fails where the adverse possession is not patent to him and others. It may not be necessary to prove that the whole of the land has been cultivated or fenced in, but there ought to be proof that the adverse possession was so patent that the owner, with the exercise of reasonable care, would have observed it.[30]

In the present case the petitioners had neither fenced in nor cultivated the land which they claimed to have acquired through prescription. Their cattle occasionally grazed on it, and on one or two occasions they impounded cattle trespassing on the land. On this evidence the Court found that there was insufficient visible proof of the petitioner's possession since the owner might have passed the land daily without realizing that it was in someone else's occupation. Lord De Villiers CJ therefore concluded that '[t]he doctrine of prescription would become an engine of injustice if, under such circumstances, the owner were to be deprived of his rights'.[31]

It should be noted that Lord De Villiers motivated the requirement of *openness* by accepting the negligence of the owner in not properly guarding his property as the ultimate rationale for acquisitive prescription.[32] It is shown below that this was not the only view supported by Roman-Dutch authority and that a different rationale is favoured by academics and modern South African case-law. Furthermore, the *nec clam* requirement corresponds closely to the mental element of possession required in Roman-Dutch law for prescription:[33] it must be apparent from the conduct of the possessor that he acts as if he were the owner of the object.

In spite of the English law influence, certain South African decisions still endeavoured to apply pure Roman-Dutch principles. An important case in point is *Paarl Municipality v. Colonial Government*[34] where the concept of 'adverse measures' was expressly equated with possession required in Roman-Dutch law by Voet.[35] The Paarl Municipality claimed to have acquired by prescription a certain *outspan* situated within the Municipality. It had been set apart as a public *outspan* in 1817 and the Colonial Government claimed to have resumed control over it under Act 41 of 1902. In 1840 the then village of Paarl was constituted a municipality and there

---

[30] (1899) 16 SC 148, 151. See also Jones JP in *Trustees of Kareiga Baptist Church v. Amos Charles Webber and Edward George Webber* (n. 26), 108: 'They fulfilled the requirement of prescriptive title, namely that their adverse possession should be such that the owner of the land would, with reasonable care, have observed it . . .'

[31] 151 sq.   [32] See the passage quoted above.   [33] See below.

[34] (1906) 23 SC 505. See *Trustees of Kareiga Baptist Church v. Amos Charles Webber and Edward George Webber* (n. 26), 108: 'I think it has been shown that from at least 1861 until the present time the church has exercised over this ground such rights as they would have exercised if they had complete ownership of it' (*per* Jones JP).

[35] Commentarius ad Pandectas (n. 2), 44, 3, 9. See above, n. 14.

was evidence that as from 1859 the municipal council had exercised control over the land, and had made certain profits therefrom by sales of manure, and of trees and timber, planted either by others or, in later years, by themselves. The court held that the Municipality acted within the terms of the by-laws promulgated in 1865 with regard to the use of the *outspan*. Consequently, it did not exercise control *animo domini* and therefore did not acquire the *outspan* by prescription.

Concerning the requirements for prescription, Hopley J remarked that the 'tests are succinctly and clearly stated by Voet (44, 3, 9) to be whether the claimant by prescription has been for the necessary period in continuous and quiet possession, and that during the whole of such time he has suffered no interference at the hands of the true owner and that he has not in any way acknowledged such a one as the owner'.[36] With reference to the case at hand he continued:

I am of the opinion that this by-law applies to the outspan and the wood upon it, and, if so, all the acts relied upon as showing the assumption of absolute ownership, and an *animus domini* would have been done under and by virtue of its provisions, and not in the mind and spirit which the plaintiffs contend must be attributed to them ... [T]he plaintiffs came upon the ground and took possession of it *ex mandato*, and in a fiduciary capacity, as managers and local governors thereof for municipal purposes and it is difficult to conceive that they could ever, in fact, have looked upon themselves as the possessors of the land in any other capacity or by any other title ...[37]

3. South African case-law 1910–43

Guided by earlier decisions, cases decided between 1910 and 1943 required possession *nec vi, nec clam, nec precario* sometimes with[38] and sometimes without[39] 'adverse user' for acquisitive prescription. During this period the concepts of *nec clam* and *nec precario* were more closely scrutinized.[40]

Concerning the *nec clam* requirement, the view taken by De Villiers CJ in *Smith v. Martins Executor Dative*[41] was confirmed in several cases,[42] most

---

[36] 527 sq.   [37] 519.   [38] See, *inter alia, Ex parte Skinner* 1926 EDL 291, 292.

[39] See, *inter alia, SA Hotels v. City of Cape Town* 1932 CPD 229, 236; *De Beer v. Van der Merwe* 1923 AD 378, 383.

[40] The *animus* requirement was only considered in one case (*Wilhelm v. Barkly East Divisional Council* 1914 EDL 519) in which it was stated at 527: 'It must be borne in mind that the Council never exercised its right of taking material from this farm with any idea of acquiring a servitude ... Prescription was an afterthought.' Marx (n. 10), 151 correctly remarks that the question was not whether the Council had the *animus* of acquiring a servitude but whether they exercised their rights as if they were entitled to a servitude.

[41] (Note 28), 151. See above, note 30.

[42] See, *inter alia, Smith v. Russouw* 1913 CPD 847; *Cape Town Town Council v. Sassen* 1912 CPD 587; *Wilderness (1921) Ltd v. Union Govt* 1927 CPD 455; *Head v. Du Toit* 1932 CPD 287; *Mocke v. Beaufort West Municipality* 1939 CPD 135, 142.

notably in *Wilhelm v. Barkly East Divisional Council*[43] where the following explanation provided by Lindley LJ in the English case of *Hollins v. Verney*[44] was quoted with approval by Ward J:

No user can be sufficient unless during the whole of the period the user is enough at any rate to carry to the mind of a reasonable person in possession of the servient tenement the fact that a continuous right of enjoyment is being asserted and ought to be resisted, if resistance to it is intended.[45]

The relationship of *nec clam* (openness) with the physical element of possession, adverse user, and uninterrupted possession was elucidated in two decisions of the Natal Supreme Court. In *Gifford v. Owen, Hopley, Arnold and Fagaza*[46] acquisition of property by prescription was claimed on the ground of cultivation and the grazing of cattle and because it had been let to natives and other tenants. Concerning the *nec clam* requirement, Dove Wilson JP referred to *Smith v. Martins Executors Dative*[47] and stated that 'there must be proof of such visible occupation, of some act or acts of appropriation so patent as to constitute reasonable notice to the owner and others, of the setting up of an adverse claim to the land'.[48] The Court found that the evidence in support of prescription was wholly lacking in these essentials and thus rejected the claim.

In *Mount Moreland Town Lands Board v. Guy* (1942),[49] a case which dealt with the acquisitive prescription of derelict land by a municipality, Selke J made the following remark:

I am justified in taking judicial cognisance of the fact that the cultivation of sugar cane on a piece of land is a very obvious thing, which could not escape the notice of anybody who chose to observe the land with any reasonable degree of attention. In this respect it differs from such a user as, say, running stock upon the land. It involves the land being ploughed and cultivated, and when the crop appears, its presence is very obvious. The crop is present at all times and everywhere on the land. That being so, it seems to me that it represents almost an ideal form of adverse user of derelict land for the purposes of prescription, and constitutes, as it were, perpetual notice of the fact of such user.[50]

From these and other cases on *nec clam* decided between 1910 and 1943 it is clear that acquisitive prescription was not held to have occurred unless the possession was sufficiently patent for a reasonable observer to become aware of the fact that the claimant possessed the object as if he were entitled thereto and that an owner exercising reasonable care could thus have noted acts conflicting with his rights. These decisions also emphasized the

---

[43] Above, n. 40.   [44] (1883) 13 QBD 304, 315.

[45] 527. *In casu* a servitude of digging for gravel was claimed to have been acquired by acquisitive prescription. In *Hollins v. Verney* (n. 44) a servitude was also claimed: hence the references to a 'servient tenement' and the 'right of enjoyment' (instead of ownership).

[46] (1916) 37 NLR 197.   [47] Above, n. 28.   [48] 209.

[49] 1942 NPD 402.   [50] 407.

relationship between openness and adverse user: adverse possession must be apparent from the patent occupation by the claimant. There must be a clear semblance of a right based on some conduct by the claimant. These cases also indicated that uninterrupted possession must be manifest to the outside world throughout the whole period of prescription.[51]

The most important decision concerning the requirement of *nec precario* between 1910 and 1943 is that of the Appellate Division in *De Beer v. Van der Merwe*.[52] Dealing with the acquisitive prescription of a servitude of discharge of water, Juta JA remarked:

... in order to establish prescription the exercise of the right must have been *non precario* or, as it is alleged in our modern pleadings, the right must have been exercised adversely and as of right. When the owner of the dominant tenement is also lessee of the servient tenement, the former has not, by diverting the water on to the latter tenement, done so adversely, and as of right, but *precario*.[53]

The judge then quoted Pardessus[54] as stating that 'the *precarium* exists whenever a person possesses by a title other than that of owner, so that if he owns a house and during the tenancy puts a window in the wall which separates the two houses, he cannot acquire a servitude thereto by prescription'.

From this statement it is clear that Juta JA treated *nec precario* and 'adversely and as of right' as synonymous. This interpretation is indeed supported by the case-law of the previous decades. Subsequently, however, *nec precario* was given a narrower meaning by certain provincial decisions. The Natal decision in *Union Government v. Parsons Executors*[55] is the most important in this regard. The defendants claimed to have acquired land by acquisitive prescription. It was alleged that Parsons occupied the land under a lease granted by the plaintiff. The Court, however, found no record of any lease between the Government and Parsons, nor of any rent of royalty having been paid by the latter. It therefore refused the plaintiff's claim for ejectment. In the course of his judgment Broome J had this to say:

It was argued ... that the effect of those negotiations was to make the occupation that of a mere licensee or tenancy at will and in short, *precario*. I cannot take this view and no authority was cited in support of it. In no sense can the occupation be said to have depended upon a precarious concession subject to the pleasure of the Government.[56]

This narrower interpretation of *nec precario* led to the introduction of 'adverse possession' as an additional requirement for acquisitive prescription, over and above *nec vi, nec clam,* and *nec precario*.

---

[51] See also Marx (n. 10), 159 sq.
[54] *Servitudes*, Part 3, Ch. 1, sec. 4, fn. 283.
[52] Above, n. 39.
[55] (1914) 35 NLR 496.
[53] 384.
[56] 155.

4. Case-law 1943–69

Section 2(1) of the Prescription Act of 1943 codified the requirements for acquisitive prescription as follows: 'Acquisitive prescription is the acquisition of ownership by the possession of another person's movable or immovable property ... continuously for thirty years *nec vi, nec clam, nec precario*.'[57]

Although the legislature chose to limit the requirements for acquisitive prescription to uninterrupted possession *nec vi, nec clam, nec precario*, subsequent court decisions were at pains to indicate that the legislation was never intended to abolish the common law concept of possession.[58] As a result, the Roman-Dutch concept of *possessio civilis* as a requirement for acquisitive prescription was still adhered to in a few cases, while the requirements of *nec clam* and *nec precario*, and especially the relationship between *nec precario* and 'adverse user', were further clarified.

In the well known case of *Welgemoed v. Coetzer*,[59] where a third of an adjoining farm was claimed on the ground of acquisitive prescription, Murray J observed:

The authorities appear to lay down that the possession required of the claimant in prescription is the full juristic possession—*possessio civilis*—the holding or detaining of the corporeal thing with the intention of keeping it for oneself (Voet 41.2.1). Both the physical act of detention and the mental state must concur . . .[60]

On the facts the Court decided[61] that the occupation by a predecessor of the claimant in title was 'not as a consequence of any intention on his part to occupy or exercise rights for himself or to hold that area for himself as owner'.[62]

In *Campbell v. Pietermaritzburg City Council*[63] the connection between the *animus domini* requirement for acquisitive prescription and 'adverse possession' was explained. *In casu* Campbell had possessed Council land for more than thirty years in the full knowledge that he was not its owner. Miller J remarked:

As I understand the authorities, property may be possessed 'adversely to the rights of the true owner' if it is held and possessed by one who, knowing that he is not the legal owner, nevertheless holds it as if he were i.e. without manifesting recognition of the true owner's rights as such . . . The inquiry is whether plaintiff possessed and used the property as if he were the owner or whether, by words or conduct, he

---

[57] Section 2(1).
[58] See, *inter alia, Welgemoed v. Coetzer* (n. 59), 710; *Stephenson v. Lamsley* 1948 (4) SA 794 (W); *Swanepoel v. Crown Mines* 1954 (4) SA 596 (A) 603.
[59] 1946 TPD 701.   [60] 712.   [61] 713.
[62] See also *Wicks v. Place* 1967 (1) SA 561 (E) on the *animus domini* required for *possessio civilis*.
[63] 1966 (2) SA 674 (N).

extended to the true owner recognition of his rights. If he in fact gave no recognition of the owner's rights but used the property as if he were the owner, then it seems to me from a practical point of view to make no difference whether one says that he had *possessio civilis* or that his possession was adverse to the owner. . . [I]f the Court is satisfied that there was *possessio civilis* . . . it is superfluous to inquire further whether there was adverse user and that if, on the other hand, the Court is satisfied that possession were *nec precario* and adverse to the owner's rights, it will also have been *possessio civilis.*[64]

It was confirmed in the case-law between 1943 and 1969 that the *nec clam* requirement is intimately connected with the *corpus* and *animus* elements needed for acquisitive prescription, as well as with the requirement of 'adverse possession'. Possession need not be continuous in the strict sense of the word as long as the right is exercised from time to time, as occasion requires, and with reasonable continuity.[65] With reference to the English decision in *Dalton v. Angus*[66] it was accepted in *Welgemoed v. Coetzer*[67] that the *nec clam* requirement would be complied with even 'without actual knowledge on the part of the true owner, provided it was open for all to see who wanted to see and could have been known to the true owner but for his carelessness in looking after his property'.[68]

The implication is that possession would still be considered *nec clam* if the owner could, with the exercise of reasonable care, have become aware of the adverse possession. This effectively rendered the *nec clam* requirement the same as before the enactment of the Prescription Act of 1943.[69]

The most important development effected by the courts during 1943 and 1969, however, concerned the *nec precario* requirement and its relationship with the concept of adverse user. If *nec precario* is interpreted as meaning 'without consent', adverse user is not needed as an additional requirement. If, however, *nec precario* is narrowly conceived as a 'revocable permission' then an additional requirement of 'adverse user' becomes necessary since possession *nec precario* in such a case would not always amount to unlawful possession.[70]

The *locus classicus* on *nec precario* is undoubtedly the decision of the Appellate Division in *Malan v. Nabygelegen Estates.*[71] In this case it had to be decided whether a servitude for drawing water could be acquired by way of prescription if it originated from an agreement which was never registered. Referring, *inter alia*, to the Digest,[72] the Court rejected the wider interpretation of *nec precario*: 'It will be seen from these references that *nec precario* does not mean without permission or without consent in the wide

---

[64] 690.
[65] See *Welgemoed v. Coetzer* (n. 59) 720; *Mocke v. Beaufort West Municipality* (n. 42).
[66] (1881) 6 App Cas 740, 815, 816, 828.   [67] Above, n. 59.   [68] 720.
[69] See also *Minister of Forestry v. Michaux* 1957 (2) SA 32 (N) 39.
[70] See Marx (n. 10), 183.   [71] 1946 AD 562.
[72] D. 43, 26, 1. References were also made to Savigny and Pothier.

sense . . . but "not by virtue of a precarious consent" or in other words "not by virtue of a revocable permission" or "not on sufferance" '.[73] The Court therefore decided that the contract relied upon for prescription did not constitute a revocable permission granted by the owner of the Farm *Nabygelegen*, but the purchase of a servitude in perpetuity. Thus, the plaintiff did not take the water by virtue of any consent in the sense of a revocable permission, but by virtue of the right under the contract.[74]

Although the narrow interpretation of *nec precario* was confirmed in several subsequent decisions,[75] it is questionable whether the legislature intended to deviate from the wider meaning given to the term by the Appellate Division in *De Beer v. Van der Merwe*.[76] As a result of the narrow interpretation now prevailing, adverse user had to be added as a requirement for prescription in order to prevent a tenant or usufructuary from acquiring ownership by prescription.[77] This had already been recognized in *Malan v. Nabygelegen Trustees*. Watermeyer CJ put the matter very clearly:

In order to avoid misunderstanding, it should be pointed out here that mere occupation of property '*nec vi nec clam nec precario*' for a period of thirty years does not necessarily vest in the occupier a prescriptive title to the ownership of that property. In order to create a prescriptive title, such occupation must be a user adverse to the true owner and not occupation by virtue of some contract or legal relationship such as a lease or usufruct which recognizes the ownership of another.[78]

The meaning of 'adverse user' corresponds with the Roman-Dutch requirement that the claimant must possess without acknowledging the rights of the owner. It has to be determined objectively whether the owner's rights are expressly or impliedly acknowledged in terms of the relationship between the claimant and the owner. However, since *precarium* is interpreted as a legal relationship which respects the ownership of another, a precarist can never be an adverse user and the requirement of *nec precario* accordingly becomes redundant.[79]

The acceptance of 'adverse user' as an additional requirement was put beyond doubt in *Pratt v. Lourens*.[80] As the result of a mutual mistake, a fence erected between two farms strayed from the true boundary line, so that a considerable part of the one farm was included on the other side of the fence. Had the plaintiff acquired this part of the land by prescription? Evidence was led that the plaintiff's husband had, some time before the period of prescription was completed, become aware of the fact that the fence was wrongly situated. He approached the owner who retorted that it

---

[73] 573.   [74] See esp. Watermeyer J, 576.
[75] See, *inter alia*, *City of Cape Town v. Abelsohn's Estate* 1947 (3) SA 315 (C); *Wynne v. Pope* 1960 (3) SA 37 (C); *Campbell v. Pietermaritzburg City Council* (n. 63).
[76] Above, n. 39.   [77] See also Marx (n. 10), 190 sq.   [78] 574.
[79] See also Marx (n. 10), 192 sq.   [80] 1954 (4) SA 281 (N).

'was an old thing and there was nothing to be done about it'. The Court refused to construe these words as a grant of permission (and thus a *precarium*). Instead it rejected the plantiff's claim on the ground that the occupier's acknowledgement of the owner's rights amounted to possession which was not adverse to the owner.

In the course of his judgment Broome JP introduced 'adverse user' as an additional requirement for prescription in the following words:

This, however, does not conclude the matter. Notwithstanding the wording of sec. 2(1) of Act 18 of 1943, it is a mistake to suppose that prescriptive title depends solely upon thirty years' continuous possession *nec vi nec clam nec precario*. In addition such possession must be adverse to the true owner . . . If the possessor acknowledges the rights of the owner, his ownership *ipso facto* ceases to be adverse to him. (See Voet 44.3.9; *Paarl Municipality v. Colonial Govt*, 23 SC 505 at p. 527). If therefore there has been any such acknowledgement, the plaintiff's case must fail, notwithstanding that such acknowledgement has not been followed by any permission, express or implied.[81]

If the reference to Voet was intended to equate 'adverse user' with the *animus domini* required for possession in Roman-Dutch law, it is submitted that the conduct of the plaintiff's husband did not amount to acquiescence in the ownership of the defendant: mere acknowledgement of the ownership of another does not necessarily imply that the claimant no longer has the *animus domini* to possess.[82]

The relationship between 'adverse user' and the *animus domini* requirement of Roman-Dutch law was highlighted in *Du Toit v. Furstenberg*.[83] A purchaser was unable to obtain transfer of property because the transfer of small subdivided portions of agricultural land was prohibited. However, he continued to possess the property as owner for more than thirty years. Considering whether the claimant's endeavour to obtain transfer of the property negatived adverse possession on his part, De Villiers J remarked: 'It seems to me possession which is adverse only ceases to be adverse where the true owner makes claim to the property, i.e. asserts his rights as owner and the person exercising possession acknowledges that other as the true owner';[84] and he concluded:

In the present case there is no evidence that D. S. du Toit ever possessed otherwise than as owner. All that he wanted was the assistance of M. C. Bosman, in whose name he knew the property to be registered, to help him to get transfer into his name, if that were possible, an act perfectly consistent with an intention to possess pro domino.[85]

---

[81] 282D–282F. See also *Du Toit v. Furstenberg* 1957 (1) SA 501 (O) 504; *Albert Falls Power Co (Pty) Ltd v. Goge* (n. 87), 48; *Vernon v. Bradley* 1965 (1) SA 422 (N) 426A; *Morkels Transport (Pty) Ltd v. Melrose Foods (Pty) Ltd* 1972 (2) SA 464 (W) 467, 479.
[82] See also Marx (n. 10), 197.   [83] 1957 (1) SA 501 (O).   [84] 505.
[85] 506.

The view that 'adverse possession' is equivalent to possession 'as of right' (as enunciated in Voet 44, 3, 9) was confirmed in several more recent cases,[86] notably in *Albert Falls Power Co Ltd v. Goge*[87] (per Jansen J) in the following terms: 'But I do not wish to be understood to hold that "possession adverse to the owner" is anything more or less than *possessio civilis*'.[88] Also significant is the following remark by Broome J in *Payn v. Estate Rennie*:

I may add that in my opinion 'recognition' or 'acknowledgement' of an owner's rights does not relate merely to the mental state of the claimant. To operate as a bar, such a state of mind must be accompanied by some overt act. Whether the 'recognition' or 'acknowledgement' must be to the owner or his representative is an interesting question . . .[89]

In English law *nec precario*, in the sense of 'possession as of right, not in accordance with an express grant', serves the same function in relation to prescription as 'adverse user' in the sense of 'unlawfully *vis-à-vis* the owner' does with regard to limitation of actions. Thus, it is not surprising that when the requirement of *nec precario* was restricted by the South African courts 'adverse user' came to be recognized as an additional requirement for the acquisition of both ownership and servitudes by prescription.

5. Case-law after the Prescription Act of 1969

The Prescription Act of 1969[90] draws a distinction between the acquisitive prescription of ownership and of servitudes.[91] With regard to the requirements for the acquisition of ownership, s. 2 of the Act provides that 'a person shall by prescription become the owner of a thing which he has possessed openly and as if he were the owner thereof for an uninterrupted period of thirty years . . .'. From this section it is clear that the requirements of *nec vi* and *nec precario* were discarded and that only the requirements of open possession (*nec clam*) and possession 'as if he were the owner' (*possessio civilis*) remained.[92]

Several decisions after 1969 have painstakingly shown that the erstwhile requirements of *nec precario* and 'adverse user' are comprised in the notion of *possessio civilis*. The following *dictum* by Van Heerden J in *Wood v. Baynesfield Board of Administration* is the culmination of this trend:

The concepts of civil possession, possession *nec precario* and possession adverse to the true owner's rights often merge into or overlap one another to some extent. In *Morkels Transport (Pty) Ltd v. Melrose Foods (Pty) Ltd & Another* . . . the view is

---

[86] *Campbell v. Pietermaritzburg City Council* (n. 63), 680E.   [87] 1960 (2) SA 46 (N).
[88] 48.   [89] 1960 (4) SA 261(N) at 262.   [90] Act 68 of 1969; effective from 1 Dec. 1970.
[91] Compare s. 2 (acquisition of ownership) with s. 6 (acquisition of servitudes).
[92] See De Wet (n. 10), 86 sqq.

expressed that the concept *non precario* is but a special case of the wider concept 'adverse'. It has also been said that 'possession adverse to the owner' is nothing more nor less than *possessio civilis*.[93]

The *animus* requirement was scrutinized in a few cases after 1969.[94] A special meaning was attached to *animus domini* by Rumpff CJ in *Minister van Landbou v. Sonnendecker*: '[H]oewel die besitter van grond geweet het dat die grond aan iemand anders behoort, hy die grond besit 'asof hy eienaar daarvan was' indien hy voortdurend besit het en eienaar wou word, hoewel hy bereid was om die grond terug te gee indien die eienaar sou opdaag en dit sou opeis'.[95] This passage has been subjected to severe criticism[96] and it is generally accepted that an 'intention to become owner' does not suffice for acquisitive prescription.

One case after 1969, *Pienaar v. Rabie*,[97] embarked on a close study of the rationale for prescription. Grosskopf AJA pointed out that several earlier decisions[98] had, on the basis of an inadequate analysis of the relevant Roman and Roman-Dutch sources, come to the conclusion that prescription penalized the owner who negligently failed to guard his property. Having noted that several types of prescription existed in Roman and Roman-Dutch law, Grosskopf AJA observed: '*Onder hierdie omstandighede kan daar skaars sprake wees van een enkele samehangende filosofiese grondslag wat onderliggend aan die regsfiguur van verkrygende verjaring in al sy gestaltes is. Wat 'n mens eerder vind by juriste is dat bepaalde regsreëls verduidelik of geregverdig word deur morele of filosofiese argumente*'.[99]

---

[93] 1975 (2) SA 692 (N) 698B-D. The Court refers in this respect to *Morkels Transport (Pty) Ltd v. Melrose Foods (Pty) Ltd* (n. 81); *Albert Falls Power Co (Pty) Ltd v. Goge* (n. 87), 48; *Campbell v. Pietermaritzburg City Council* (n. 63), 680; and J. E. Scholtens, '*Praescriptio: Ius Possidendi* and *Rei Vindicatio*', (1972) 89 *SALJ* 384. See also *Bisschop v. Stafford* 1974 (3) SA 1 (A) 8.

[94] See e.g. *Bisschop v. Stafford* (n. 93), 10C: 'With what state of mind? The probabilities are overwhelming that he did so as if of right, i.e. that he was a *quasi-possessor*, or, stated differently, that his user was adverse to the owner. There is not the slightest suggestion that he ever asked anyone's permission.'

[95] (Although the possessor knew that the land belonged to someone else he would still possess the land 'as if he were the owner' if he had uninterrupted possession and *wanted to become* the owner although he was prepared to give up the land if the owner would return and claim the land): 1979 (2) SA 944 (A) 947 (emphasis added).

[96] See Van der Merwe (n. 1), 281; *idem*, 1980 *TSAR* 183–8; Kleyn/Boraine (n. 1), 226; Carey Miller (n. 1), 75, fn. 71.

[97] 1983 (3) SA 126 (A) 135D–139A.

[98] *Smith v. Martin's Executor Dative* (n. 28), 151; *Van der Merwe v. Minister of Defence* 1916 OPD 47, 51; *Welgemoed v. Coetzer* (n. 59), 723; *City of Cape Town v. Abelsohn's Estate* 1947 (3) SA 315 (C) 325; *Van Wyk v. Louw* 1958 (2) SA 165 (C) 170; *Campbell v. Pietermaritzburg City Council* (n. 63), 468; *Morkels Transport (Pty) Ltd v. Melrose Foods (Pty) Ltd* (n. 81), 468; *Ex parte Puppli* 1975 (3) SA 461 (D) 463.

[99] (Under these circumstances it can hardly be argued that there is a single coherent philosophical basis for the legal phenomenon of acquisitive prescription in all its forms. One does, however, find that jurists tend to explain or justify certain legal rules with reference to moral or philosophical arguments): 135H.

The Court therefore reached the conclusion that the institution of acquisitive prescription may be justified in terms of at least three different considerations: legal certainty, the prevention of litigation resulting from such uncertainty, and (possibly) punishment of negligent owners.[100] However, the Court clearly stated that the rationale for prescription should not be regarded as a substantive requirement thereof.[101]

6. Conclusion

South Africa has developed a unique type of acquisitive prescription, based mainly on the Roman-Dutch *lange verjaring* and the Roman *praescriptio longissimi temporis*, but also strongly influenced by the English legal institution of limitation of actions. It is unique in that it differs fundamentally from the modern Dutch and English law of prescription. In Dutch law a presumption of ownership is created by a transfer which the parties thought to be valid. After continuous possession for three years this presumption is converted into ownership by the institution of prescription. In English law prescription is based on the fact that the owner, for a certain period, omitted to act against an 'adverse user' with the result that the owner's right is lost and simultaneously acquired by the adverse possessor.

The Prescription Act of 1943 codified the requirements for acquisitive prescription as developed in the early case-law and transplanted the requirements for the acquisition of servitudes to that of ownership. In addition to the traditional requirement of possession *nec vi, nec clam, nec precario* it was required that the possession be adverse to the owner. This additional requirement not only takes cognizance of the English notion of 'adverse user' but also reflects the Roman-Dutch mental element of *animus domini*, or overt conduct, on the part of the claimant, establishing his intention not to respect the right of the owner. This is strengthened by the *nec clam* requirement: an open manifestation of ownership which would induce a reasonable outsider to believe that the claimant was the (ostensible) owner of the thing.

The Prescription Act of 1969 discarded the requirements of *nec vi* and *nec precario*, which had become redundant as a result of the acceptance of 'adverse user', and confined itself to the true core requirement for prescription, i.e. open possession 'as if the claimant were the owner', which had finally been worked out in the development of case-law.[102] South African law has thus completed the full circle and realized that nothing more nor less is needed for prescription than *possessio civilis*, i.e. *corpus* and *animus domini*. If *animus domini* is construed objectively in the sense that overt con-

---

[100] 137H–138A.	[101] 138B.

[102] See also Carey Miller (n. 1), 76; Van der Merwe (n. 1), 281; Kleyn/Boraine (n. 1), 286; De Wet (n. 20), 86.

duct on the part of the claimant is necessary then the separate requirement of openness, or *nec clam*, is also rendered redundant. This tallies with the most acceptable rationale for acquisitive prescription, namely that the legal rules applicable to prescription aim at perpetuating the factual impression of ownership created by the long and uninterrupted possession enjoyed by the claimant.[103]

III. OCCUPATION OF WILD ANIMALS

1. Traditional legal position

The main requirement for the occupation of wild animals in South Africa is still that the acquirer must unilaterally take possession of a *res nullius*. This essentially reflects Roman law as received in the Netherlands.[104] South African law has added its own species of wild animals capable of being captured as, for instance, wild ostriches,[105] wildebeest,[106] blesbok,[107] kudu,[108] bees,[109] hippopotamuses,[110] fish,[111] snoek,[112] and whales.[113] The mere wounding or close pursuit of a wild animal is not sufficient for acquisition of ownership by occupation; actual capture is required.[114]

The animal need not be captured on the hunter's own land; if a hunter trespasses on the land of another he still becomes the owner of animals he captures there.[115] Earlier South African decisions[116] followed English precedents[117] and held that a hunter who is found trespassing can be held liable under the tort of trespass. This conflicts with the Roman Dutch position that a trespassing hunter can only be proceeded against with the *actio iniuriarum* if the owner's rights of personality have been infringed by the unlawful entry.[118]

---

[103] See Heinrich Dernburg, *Pandekten* (6th edn., 1900), vol. I, § 219: '*Der Grundgedanke der Ersitzung ist vielmehr, dass die Zeit den Besitz zum Rechte erhebt*' (The basic idea of acquisitive prescription is rather that time raises possession to a right). See also Grotius, *Inleiding* (n. 2), 2, *1*, 4; Van der Merwe (n. 1), 269 sq.; De Wet (n. 20), 78; F. E. Marx, 'Die Grondslag van Verkrygende Verjaring in Suid-Afrika', 1979 *Obiter* 11.

[104] Voet (n. 2), 41, 1, 3–7; Grotius, *Inleiding* (n. 2), 2, 4, 3–18; Van Leeuwen, *Censura Forensis* (n. 2), 1, 2, 3, 8 and 12; Van der Keessel (n. 2), 2, 4, 3–18.

[105] *De Villiers v. Van Zyl* 1880 Foord 77; *R v. Bekker* (1904) 18 EDC 128.

[106] *Richter v. Du Plooy* 1921 OPD 117.   [107] *Lamont v. Heyns* 1938 TPD 22.

[108] *R v. Mafohla* 1958 (2) SA 373 (SR).   [109] *S v. Mnomiya* 1970 (1) SA 66 (N).

[110] *Dunn v. Bowyer* 1926 NPD 516.

[111] *R v. Maritz* (1908) 25 SC 787; *Van Breda v. Jacobs* 1921 AD 330.

[112] *S v. Frost, S v. Noah* 1974 (3) SA 466 (C).   [113] *Langley v. Miller* (1848) 3 Menz 584.

[114] *R v. Mafohla* 1958 (2) SA 373 (SR).   [115] *R v. Maritz* (n. 111).

[116] *De Villiers v. Van Zyl* (n. 105); *Wright v. Ashton* (1905) 2 Buch AC 240, 243; *Gosani v. Kreusch* (1908) 25 SC 350; *Theron v. Steenkamp* 1928 CPD 429.

[117] See e.g. *Pritchard v. Long* (1842) 9 M & W 666; *Blades v. Higgs* 34 LJ (NS) CP 286.

[118] See Voet (n. 2), 41, 1, 4; Van Leeuwen, *Censura Forensis* (n. 2), 1, 2, 3, 8; *R v. Maritz* (n. 111).

Dunn v. Bowyer[119] relied on Roman-Dutch writers[120] for the proposition that whoever had captured animals in contravention of game laws, fishing ordinances,[121] or other statutory provisons did not become the owner of the captured animal. According to Roman-Dutch law an animal, captured in contravention of statutory provisions, had to be handed over to the gamekeeper (*houtvester*).[122] The opposite view was, however, expressed *obiter* in *R v. Mafohla*[123] and confirmed in *S v. Frost, S v. Noah.*[124] Following Roman law it was decided in these cases that the animals captured become the property of the captor unless the relevant legislation unequivocally states that the ownership in fish or game captured in contravention of the legislation will not vest in the captor.[125]

A captured animal remains the property of its captor until it regains its natural freedom, in which case it will be open to occupation again. Wild animals are deemed to have regained wildness when they disappear from sight or, if still in sight, are difficult to pursue.[126]

2. Game Theft Act of 1991

Most of the principles enunciated above have been radically affected by the Game Theft Act of 1991.[127] This Act was promulgated in order to protect the lucrative fledgling industry of game-farming as an adjunct to the growing South African tourist industry.[128] The Act regulates the ownership of a certain class of wild animals referred to as 'game'. It comprises all game kept or held for commercial or hunting purposes, including the meat, skin, carcass, or any portion of the carcass, of that game.[129]

The first part of s. 2 of the Act provides that if game escapes from a sufficiently enclosed camp, a pen, a kraal, or a vehicle then its owner shall, notwithstanding the provisions of any other law or the common law, retain ownership of the game. Land is deemed to fall under this provision if the

---

[119] (1926) 49 NLR 516.

[120] Grotius, *Inleiding* (n. 2), 2, 4, 5; Groenewegen (n. 11), ad Inst. 2, 1, n. 12; Voet (n. 2), 41, 1, 17.

[121] See, *inter alia*, ss. 30–7, Sea Fisheries Act 12 of 1988.

[122] The office of *houtvester* was abolished by the *Placaat van Jagt* of 1795. See Van der Keessel (n. 2), 2, 4, 7.

[123] 1958 (2) SA 373 (SR) at 374.   [124] Above, n. 112.

[125] See also C. G. van der Merwe, M. A. Rabie, 'Eiendom van Wilde Diere', (1974) 37 *THRHR* 38; A. F. S. Maasdorp, *Institutes of South African Law: The Law of Property* (10th edn., 1976), 29; Carey-Miller (n. 1), 3.

[126] Grotius, *Inleiding* (n. 2), 2, 4, 3 and 4; Van der Keessel (n. 2), 2, 4, 3; Arnoldus Vinnius, *In Quatuor Libros Institutionum Commentarius, J. G. Heineccius recensuit et praefationnem notulasque addidit* (1767), 2, 1, 12, n. 4.

[127] Act 105 of 1991.

[128] See generally C. G. van der Merwe, M. A. Rabie, 'Wildboerdery in Regsperspektief: Enkele Knelpunte', 1990 *Stellenbosch LR*, 112–28.

[129] Act 105 of 1991, s. 1 s.v. 'game'.

Administrator of the Province has issued a certificate stating that it is sufficiently enclosed to confine specified species of game to that land. A certificate is valid for three years and can then be renewed.

This section is in direct conflict with the traditional Roman-Dutch and South African view that a wild animal which regains its natural freedom becomes a *res nullius* and is thus capable, once again, of being acquired by occupation. Under the Game Theft Act the person capturing the animal does not acquire ownership, but may apparently be proceeded against by the owner of the enclosed land from which the animal had escaped by a vindicatory action. Proof of ownership may, however, cause grave practical difficulties in view of the fact that game-farmers are not required to brand their game in a distinctive manner.

The second part of s. 2 goes even further to protect the owners of game-farms which are not sufficiently enclosed. It provides that the ownership of game shall not vest in any person who catches, hunts, or takes possession of any game contrary to the provisions of any law or without the consent of the owner or lawful occupier of that land. Ownership, it is expressly stated, remains vested in the owner from whose land the game had escaped, or the owner of the land on which the game was hunted, caught, or taken into possession.

It appears from s. 2 that the *rei vindicatio*, and in appropriate circumstances also the *actio iniuriarum*, may be instituted against a hunter who has entered land without the consent of the landowner. Since the definition of 'game' also includes 'the meat, skin, carcass, or any portion of the carcass', the landowner remains the owner of these products, and can presumably claim them by *rei vindicatio* even if the game has been flayed.

The exact scope of the provision that a person who 'keeps or holds game . . . shall not lose ownership' if the game escapes from enclosed land is open to doubt. It is arguable that this provision has not altered the status of wild animals sufficiently for a mere certificate from the Administrator to transfer to the landowner ownership of all game inside an enclosure. First, it is not specifically stated that a person who keeps game in an enclosed camp becomes its owner. The Act does not directly deal with the acquisition of ownership but, in effect, presumes fictional ownership of the game. This facilitates the onus of proving ownership which is necessary for the conviction of poachers. Secondly, it is stated in the Preamble of the Act that its aim is to regulate the ownership of game '*in certain circumstances*'. The wording is sufficiently wide to justify the conclusion that the main purpose of regulating the ownership of game was to combat theft and wrongful hunting. Thirdly, the introductory phrase of s. 2 '[n]otwithstanding the provisions of any other law or the common law' implies that these provisions were adopted for the purpose of protecting game-farmers and of facilitating proof of theft. It was never the intention of the legislature to regulate all aspects of the ownership of game or to confer ownership on the landowner for all purposes. This view is supported by the *Memorandum on the Objects of the Game Theft Bill*[130] which states in its Preamble that the Bill is primarily aimed at amending the common law in respect of the acquisition and loss of ownership of game so as to protect the interests of game-farmers and to comply with prevailing requirements and circumstances as far as game is concerned.

Furthermore, the provisions of the Act are applicable only to game, i.e. animals kept or held for commercial or hunting purposes, and not to all wild animals. The *South African Pocket Oxford Dictionary* defines game as 'wild animals or birds hunted for sport or food'. It appears to be difficult to bring giraffes, monkeys, and baboons, which are not hunted for either sport or food, under this definition. In the terms of the Act, game must be kept in enclosed land, a pen, a kraal, or a vehicle; thus the Act appears to exclude fish kept in rivers or in the sea. Also, the fact that the game must be kept for hunting or commercial purposes seems to exclude game kept in a nature reserve for ecological reasons, unless the fact that visitors have to pay to watch the animals is taken to constitute a commercial purpose.

IV. SPECIFICATION

1. Introduction

There is a dearth of authority on specification in South African law. This mode of acquisition of ownership has only been discussed in three reported cases;[131] its requirements have never been found to have been met on the facts of any case.

2. Requirements for specification

The requirements for specification were summarized in the following *dictum* in *S v. Riekert*:[132] 'It would ... appear to be essential that a *nova species* (new thing) should have been manufactured, that the material used ceased to exist as such and cannot be restored to its original form and that, as a general rule, the maker *bona fide* thought that the material belonged to him.'

The first South African decision in which these requirements were dis-

---

[130] Game Theft Bill [B122–91(GA)] 8.

[131] *Aldine Timber Co (Pty) Ltd v. Hlatwayo* 1932 TPD 337; *S v. Riekert* 1977 (3) SA 180 (T); *Kahn v. Minister of Law and Order* 1991 (3) SA 439 (T). See generally on specification Van der Merwe (n. 1), 258–63; Kleyn/Boraine (n. 1), 218–21; Carey-Miller (n. 1), 40–5; H. G. Henckert, *Saakvorming as Wyse van Eiendomsverkryging* (unpublished LL M thesis, University of Stellenbosch, 1988).

[132] 1977 (3) SA 180 (T) 182F-G.

cussed is *Aldine Timber Co (Pty) Ltd v. Hlatwayo*.[133] A wood and iron shed had been donated to Hlatwayo's six-year-old son. Afterwards Hlatwayo bought materials from the plaintiff for £122. He then demolished the old building and erected another shed, measuring thirty feet square. In order to build the new shed he made use of the old as well as new materials. Hlatwayo failed to pay for the materials he had bought from the plaintiff. A summons was thereupon issued against him for an amount of money for goods sold and delivered. When Hlatwayo defaulted a writ was issued which eventually led to the attachment of the shed. An interpleader summons was instituted by the judgment debtor's minor son. After a magistrate had found that the building was movable and not available for execution an appeal was lodged, based, *inter alia*, on the ground that the hut had been acquired by Hlatwayo by way of *specificatio*. However, Barry J refused to accept that specification was applicable in this case. Citing a passage from Salkowski's *Roman Private Law* at 140 he argued as follows:

It seems to me that the circumstances in this case show that the work done on the old material was not in the nature of specification, because no new species has been created and the original article has not ceased to exist as such. The illustrations given, of turning grapes into wine and corn into bread, show clearly what specification means, and I think there can be no doubt that on the facts of this case, the material does not fall under that category.[134]

The Court held this to constitute a case of accession of movables.[135] Since the material purchased by Hlatwayo from the plaintiff was not only bigger in bulk but also more valuable, it was decided that the old material acceded to the new. Hlatwayo's son had, therefore, not discharged the onus of proving that he had become the owner of the new shed; the appeal succeeded.

This case, I think, should have been treated as an instance of specification. The new material had not been added to the old material for the purpose of enlarging the original shed. The shed had first been demolished, and thereafter the old material had skilfully been used with the new material to fashion a brand new hut. The creative skills employed to achieve the end result were not, to my mind, sufficiently taken into account by the Court. Had it done so, it could have come to the conclusion that Hlatwayo had acquired ownership in the new hut by way of specification.[136]

Another aspect of the case which deserves attention is that reference was made to the '*suo nomine* requirement' in the following passage of Salkowski[137] which was accepted by the Court as authoritative:[138] 'By so-called specification, that is, work . . . by which a new object . . . is created, ownership is acquired in such work by its maker, provided that . . . the

---

[133] Above, n. 131.   [134] 341.   [135] 341 sq.
[136] See also C. G. van der Merwe, M. J. de Waal, '*Accessio* deur die Verbinding van Roerende Sake in Historiese Perspektief', (1986) 49 *THRHR* 70; Henckert (n. 131), 85 sq.
[137] *Roman Private Law*, 140.   [138] 341.

maker has done it for himself.' *In casu* the father (Hlatwayo) had paid
workmen to erect the new building; thus the workmen acted as agents of
the father in fashioning the new hut. This means that the father, rather than
the son, could have acquired the hut by specification because material
belonging to his son and to the plaintiff were used to create a new thing on
behalf of the father.

The Court also emphasized the requirement of non-reducibility when it
held that the work done on the old material was not in the nature of specification 'because . . . the original material has not ceased to exist as
such'.[139] Obviously, therefore, specification was not found to be applicable
since the materials under discussion, wood and iron, still existed and could
be reduced to their original state.

Finally, it was also stated, though only in passing, that *bona fides* was a
requirement for specification: '[O]wnership is acquired in such work by its
maker, provided . . . that the maker has done it for himself and *bona fide*.'[140]

The next case concerning specification was *S v. Riekert*,[141] decided in
1977. While employed at a garage Riekert had fashioned a table from scrap
metal found in the garage and from pieces of iron which he had brought
from his home. Having been dismissed Riekert returned to the garage to
collect his belongings, and also took the table. He was sued and convicted
for the theft of the tabletop made from the scrap metal. In the appeal
against conviction it was argued that Riekert had acquired ownership of the
table by specification and could not therefore be convicted of theft.

After quoting from Salkowski's *Roman Private Law* and listing several
well known South African academic works,[142] Nestadt J provided the above
definition.[143]

He expressed doubts as to whether the first two requirements had been
complied with in the present case[144] but eventually found that the state had
failed to prove intention to steal on the part of the accused.

Arguably, however, the accused had indeed fashioned a *nova species*, for
the table consisted not only of the scrap metal which had been turned into
a tabletop but also of the pieces of iron which had been added as legs. At
least from an economic point of view the new object may be said to have
been totally different from the materials used to make it. It is also questionable whether the original materials could still have been reduced to their
original state.

The most recent case on specification is *Kahn v. Minister of Law and
Order*.[145] The applicant had purchased the wreck of a 1985 model BMW.

---

[139] *Loc. cit.*   [140] *Loc. cit.*   [141] Above, n. 132.
[142] H. R. Hahlo, Ellison Kahn, *The Union of South Africa: The Development of its Laws and
Constitution* (1960), 587; George Wille, *Principles of South African Law* (6th edn., 1970), 172;
Harry Silberberg, *The Law of Property* (1975), 108.
[143] 182F-G.   [144] *Loc. cit.*   [145] 1991 (3) SA 439 (T).

He then entered into an agreement with a panel-beater to rebuild the wreck to resemble, not a 1985 model, but rather a 1988 model BMW. Accordingly, the panel-beater cut the wreck just in front of the windscreen pillars and then joined the rear portion of a 1988 model to the front portion of the wreck. The latter was sprayed in the colour of the former. Finally, the applicant assembled the engine and other mechanical parts of the vehicle, fitted it with a gearbox supplied by the panel-beater, and registered the vehicle in his name as a built-up vehicle.

When the South African police seized the motor vehicle as stolen property the applicant sought an order directing the respondent, the Minister of Law and Order, to return the vehicle under s. 31(1) of the Criminal Procedure Act.[146] The case turned on whether he was allowed to possess the vehicle lawfully. In the course of the trial the rear portion, including the interior of the built-up vehicle, was identified as being stolen, whereas it was established that the engine and the inner front portion of the body of the car belonged to the applicant. The applicant contended that the rear portion had acceded to his vehicle, and that he, as owner, was therefore entitled to possession of the built-up car.

The Court accepted[147] that where one movable is joined to another in such a manner as to form an entity, the owner of the principal object becomes the owner also of the object joined to it. Du Plessis J accepted the guideline that the component of a composite thing, which gives the final product its character, form, and function, must be regarded as the principal thing.[148] Applying this test to the present facts, the Court concluded that the built-up vehicle could be said to be a 1988 model, to which a 1985 engine modified to conform to a 1988 engine was added together with small portions of a 1985 body. The vehicle was therefore not the applicant's 1985 wreck to which stolen parts had been added, but constituted in character, identity, form, and function the stolen 1988 model BMW to which a few accessories belonging to the applicant had been added. The applicant was thus held not to have been the lawful possessor of the vehicle.

In the course of his judgment Du Plessis J remarked *obiter* that the facts of *Aldine Timber Co (Pty) Ltd v. Hlatwayo*[149] might have been interpreted as a case of *specificatio* rather than of *accessio*. It is submitted that the facts in the *Aldine Timber* case, in which a completely new shed had been constructed, are very similar to the facts of *Kahn's* case in which a new BMW was constructed out of the undamaged parts of two BMW wrecks. Thus, this *obiter dictum* appears to invite a reconsideration of the traditional requirements of specification.

---

[146] Act 51 of 1977.   [147] 442G.   [148] 443D–E.   [149] Above, n. 131.

3. Evaluation

Starting from the premise that the *specificans* is rewarded with ownership on account of his creativity in fashioning a new and more valuable article, one should first consider whether the requirement of a *nova species* is interpreted too strictly. The concept of 'newness' has in the past been approached from an objective point of view, i.e. with reference to *indiciae* such as a new name, a new form, and irreducibility to the original form and material. Arguably, the issue of 'new name' has weighed too heavily in that the shed in the *Hlatwayo* case and the built-up BMW in the *Kahn* case were not considered *novae species*. The test should rather be whether the creative labour of the *specificans* considerably increased the economic or aesthetic value of the materials used to fashion the final product. Furthermore, irreducibility should no longer be required for specification, since it leads to odd distinctions: if a statue is made of stolen bronze the artist will not become the owner of the statue; if, however, he uses marble he becomes owner. The issue of irreducibility should serve only as one criterion which the courts take into consideration in determining the allocation of ownership. The requirement that the *specificans* be *bona fide* whilst manufacturing the thing is also questionable. Apart from the fact that the historical basis of this requirement is suspect,[150] it appears to be founded on a moral evaluation of the behaviour of the *specificans* which is not appropriate when dealing with the issue of allocating ownership. It should affect only the remedies available against the *specificans*.[151]

V. CONCLUSION

If any conclusions can be drawn from the foregoing discussion of the historical development of three original modes of acquisition of ownership in South African law, they are the following. First, the historical development of a particular legal institution depends largely on the legal education of, and the legal materials available to, legal practitioners and judges. Whenever an equivalent legal institution existed in English law, it stands to reason that colonial legal practitioners and judges drew heavily on English legal materials available at the Cape and in Natal during the last century. This explains why the institution of acquisitive prescription (and probably also *inaedificatio*) was originally strongly influenced by English legal concepts which academics and judges of a 'purist persuasion' later took pains to eradicate. Secondly, traditional legal institutions did not always meet the

---

[150] Grotius, *Inleiding* (n. 2), 2, 8, 2; Vinnius, *Institutiones* 2, 1, 25, § 2; and Van der Keessel (n. 2), 2, 8, 2 all require *bona fides*. *Contra*: Voet 41, 1, 4; Van der Merwe (n. 1), 262.

[151] For an exposition of the remedies available see Henckert (n. 131), 95.

requirements and aspirations of modern society. In the case of occupation of wild animals, the legislature has intervened and adapted the old common law regime to the new conditions. Specification has become practically irrelevant in modern law, and will remain so unless its requirements are reconsidered.

22: *Transfer of Ownership*

DAVID L. CAREY MILLER

I. INTRODUCTION

The Roman-Dutch common law which was brought to the Cape in the mid-seventeenth century was, as a matter of the basic requirements of the passing of ownership, a system of Roman law. Both the Roman and the Roman-Dutch law reflected the essential features of an owner, by voluntary act, transferring his right to an accepting party. Thus it was, firstly, a prerequisite that the transferor was owner and, secondly, essential that the requirement of a legal act of transfer, or 'conveyance', be met.

It is generally true, and especially clear in respect of property, that the Roman-Dutch common law prevailed in South Africa for about one hundred and fifty years without significant development.[1] When domestic development did commence it was primarily through the medium of an English form of case-law system which could have departed from the Roman-Dutch law. That this did not occur to any significant degree, as far as our topic is concerned, could be ascribed to the relative clarity of the law concerning the transfer of ownership, and probably to the strong element of universality inherent in the basics of derivative acquisition.

Certain general points can be made about the development of the law in South Africa. First, property—particularly that relating to corporeal movables—is an area in which the texts of the Roman-Dutch common law writers have continued to play an important role.[2] The strongly Romanist character of Roman-Dutch property law has largely survived in modern South African law; thus, one would wholly agree with the comment of Professor Wouter de Vos: '*Inderdaad is ons hedendaagse Sakereg die mees Romeinse deel van ons reg.*'[3] Secondly, in respect of corporeal movables the general development has been essentially through case-law, although insolvency legislation has had important implications. Thirdly, in respect of immovable property, although South African legislation has played a major role, the development has, on the whole, been in accordance with the basics of the Roman-Dutch common law system.

[1] An examination of the sources cited in Prof. C. G. van der Merwe's definitive work on property, *Sakereg* (2nd edn., 1989) shows this.

[2] The modern texts on property demonstrate this: see e.g. Van der Merwe (n. 1).

[3] (Our contemporary property law is, indeed, the most Roman part of our law.) Wouter de Vos, *Regsgeskiedenis* (1992), 262.

As indicated, the development of Roman-Dutch law in South Africa has not produced any radical departure from the property system of the Roman-Dutch writers; but the detailed implications of the principles concerned have been worked out and expounded upon by the courts so that most of the modern law is to be found in the reports of decisions by the South African courts. There has also been some innovation by the courts—especially in the area of constructive delivery—and, of course, this and any other original development is very much a matter for the present Chapter.

The subject is dealt with under the following general headings: the basis of derivative acquisition; modes of delivery of movable property; the transfer of ownership in land; and the requirement of payment in contracts of sale.

II. BASIS OF DERIVATIVE ACQUISITION

As already noted, derivative acquisition involves, first, the prerequisite of the transferor being in a position to convey title, and secondly, the requirement of a legal act of transfer involving an intention to pass ownership (*animus transferendi dominii*) on the part of the transferor, and an intention to acquire ownership (*animus accipiendi dominii*) on the part of the transferee. These two elements are dealt with seperately under the headings of the prerequisite of ownership and the act of transfer.

1. The prerequiste of ownership

The obvious prerequisite that the transferor is owner, or has the owner's authority to act, is reflected in *dicta* in a number of early South African cases. In *Van der Merwe v. Webb*,[4] for example, Barry JP observed:

The general principle applicable to the law of personal[5] property throughout civilised Europe became therefore and now is, '*nemo plus juris ad alium transferre potest quam ipse haberet*' (Dig., 50, 17, 54), preceded by the other maxim, '*Id quod nostrum est sine facto nostro ad alium transferri non potest*,' (Dig., 50, 17, 11). From the latter maxim, the owner cannot be deprived of his right of property by the wrongful act of any one who has taken it without title, or who, having it in his pos-

---

[4] (1883) 3 EDC 97, 102.

[5] This is a term of art of English law which distinguishes 'personal' and 'real' property; see M. G. Bridge, *Personal Property Law* (1993), 1: 'It is a commonplace observation that personal property (or personality) is all the property that is left once land, that is real property (or realty), has been subtracted.' In Roman-Dutch law the correct term would be 'movable'; although the maxim quoted necessarily applies to the transfer of ownership in any form of property, the Court was concerned with movable property which, of course, is peculiarly open to the purported transfer of ownership by a non-owner.

session for another purpose, sells it. From the former maxim it follows that a thief or borrower cannot give title even to a *bona fide* purchaser.

That the principle involved in the truncated maxim *nemo dat quod non habet* has been accepted by the South African courts as the basic position is unexceptionable. It is, however, interesting to note that despite the influence of English law in nineteenth-century South Africa[6] reference is made to the Digest texts rather than to the convenient shorthand *nemo dat quod non habet*. This abbreviation, probably attributable to the Commentators, was adopted by English property law and is still widely used in that system.[7]

Consistent with an emphasis upon the prerequisite of the transferor having title one finds, in earlier South African case-law, a clear rejection of any wide interpretation of the maxim *mobilia non habent sequelam*. Thus, in *Le Roux v. Mitchell & Rodkin*[8] Gregorowski CJ commented:

> The maxim *Mobilia sequelam non habent* was relied on . . . This principle has never been so far extended as to mean that one can transfer a greater right than he himself has, and never been so interpreted as to encroach on the maxim *Nemo plus juris transfere potest quam ipse habet*. I understand *Mobilia sequelam non habent* to mean that movable property is transferred to a purchaser free from all tacit hypothecs, and in this sense has this principle been applied in our law, but in no other sense.[9]

The significant point is that the maxim *mobilia non habent sequelam* has never been accepted in South African law to have any general role in limiting the right of a claimant to ownership to follow up movables as a matter of commercial policy. It did, of course, have such a wider role in certain limited local contexts in the Netherlands but without detracting from the general primacy of the owner's right in Roman-Dutch law.[10] A significant *dictum* on the question of the general scope of the maxim is that of De Villiers CJ in *Adams v. Mocke*: 'As applied, however, to the owner's right to follow up his goods into the hands of persons who have not acquired the same from him, the maxim is certainly more honoured in the breach than in the observance.'[11] Steyn CJ

---

[6] Sir Jacob Dirk Barry, in common with a number of 19th C. judges, including other South African born ones, had been called to the bar by one of the English Inns of Court, in his case the Inner Temple: see A. A. Roberts, *A South African Legal Bibliography* (1942), 348.

[7] See e.g. Bridge (n. 5), 88: 'The law has started from the policy of property protection, expressed in the Latin principle *nemo dat quod non habet*.' On the use of this maxim in English law see Ben Beinart, 'The English Legal Contribution in South Africa: The Interaction of Civil and Common Law', 1981 *Acta Juridica* 7, 30.   [8] (1898) 5 OR 157, 161.

[9] The following cases are also relevant to a restricted interpretation of *mobilia non habent sequelam*: *Hull v. McMaster* (1866) 5 Searle 220, 228; *Hare v. Trustee of Heath* (1884) 3 SC 32, 34; *Mangold Bros v. Eskell* (1884) 3 SC 48, 49; *Orson v. Reynolds* (1885) 2 Buch AC 102, 106; *Webster v. Ellison* (1911) 4 Buch AC 334, 345.

[10] See D. L. Carey Miller, *The Acquisition and Protection of Ownership* (1986), 263. Generally on *nemo dat quod non habet* and *mobilia non habent sequelam* in the history of European private law see Werner Hinz, 'Die Entwicklung des gutgläubigen Fahrniserwerbs in der europäischen Rechtsgeschichte', (1995) 3 *Zeitschrift für Europäisches Privatrecht* 398 sqq.

[11] (1906) 23 SC 782, 787.

commented to similar effect in a more recent case: '*Die beginsel dat roerende goed geen gevolg het nie . . . het wel in ons gemene reg 'n inslag gehad, maar behalwe vir sekere uitsonderings . . . is dit verdring deur die Romeinsregtelike gedagte:* ubi rem meam invenio, ibi vindico'.[12]

South African Roman-Dutch law has not developed any general limitation—based upon the perceived interests of commerce—of the owner's right to recover property. However, the law does recognize certain exceptions to the owner's right. Nonetheless, consistent with the approach of the courts in limiting the scope of the maxim *mobilia habent non sequelam*, the tendency has been towards limiting the scope of the acquisition of a good title by a purchaser buying on a 'free market' or from pawnbrokers or other dealers. Although certain Transvaal decisions gave effect to a doctrine of 'market overt'[13] the consensus of judicial opinion has been that acquisition on a free or public market does not protect the purchaser against a claimant who can establish a right of ownership. The decision in *Van der Merwe v. Webb*[14] rejects the notion of 'market overt' not only on the basis that it is not a part of the general Roman-Dutch law but also on its merits.[15] The consideration of the merits of the matter indicates that the Court assumed that it could have recognized the application of the doctrine of market overt. In the event, after noting its absence from the legal systems of the United States of America and Scotland, it declined to do so. As regards pawnbrokers in *Muller v. Chadwick & Co*[16] Mason J ruled that any exception which applied in Holland 'only existed in the special charters which were issued to pawnbrokers and were not granted by the general law'.

The recognition of other particular situations in which good title could be passed even though transfer was not by the owner has been in accordance with the Roman-Dutch common law. The principle behind the Roman-Dutch rules in respect of sales under judicial authority[17] has been given effect in some modern rules of court. In *Messenger of the Magistrate's Court, Durban v. Pillay*[18] Van den Heever JA—one of the most outstanding judicial exponents of the Roman-Dutch law in its South African history—commented as follows on the relevant provisions of the Magistrate's

---

[12] (The principle *mobilia non habent sequelam* . . . has had an impact in our common law, but apart from certain exceptions . . . it has been displaced by the Roman legal idea: *ubi rem invenio, ibi vindico*.) Johaadien v. Stanley Porter (Paarl) (Pty) Ltd 1970 (1) SA 394 (A) 406.

[13] *Retief v. Hamerslach* (1884) 1 SAR 171; *Jantje v. Pretorius* (1889) 3 SAR 65.

[14] Above, n. 4.

[15] It may be noted that market overt, an ancient institution of English law (but never part of Scots law; see s. 22(2), Sale of Goods Act 1979), was abolished on 3 Jan. 1995 by the Sale of Goods (Amendment) Act, c. 32, s. 1. See my comment in 'Stair's property: a Romanist system?', 1995 *Juridical Review* 70, 79.

[16] 1906 TS 30, 41.

[17] See Johannes Voet, *Commentarius ad Pandectas*, 6, 1, 13 and 23.

[18] 1952 (3) SA 678 (A) 683.

Courts Act 32 of 1944: 'These provisions are in harmony with the dispositions of the Common Law which regarded sales *sub hasta* as sacrosanct
. . . By reasoning *e contrario* the legislature did not intend proceedings to
that end prior to transfer of ownership to be unassailable.' Of course, what
is significant here is that the legislature limited the departure from the common law in a manner as far as possible consistent with it.[19] That there could
be no vindication of stolen money from an acquirer in good faith who had
spent it or mixed it with other money[20]—nor, on the same basis, of a bearer-
negotiable instrument—was accepted in the case of *Woodhead Plant & Co
v. Gunn*[21] on the basis of the notion of *confusio*. In a criminal matter[22] the
Court rejected the argument that this did not apply to the circumstances of
trust money—with the result that a trustee would become owner of trust
money mixed with his own—but of course, as Hoexter AJA noted, 'subject
to his trust duty to maintain a fund enabling him to apply an equivalent
amount to the trust purpose'. Here a decision on an aspect of the common
law has been made to accommodate the circumstances of trust. This,
arguably, is unexceptionable—indeed, consistent—given that in the South
African context the Roman-Dutch common law had been adapted to provide for a law of trusts essentially along the lines of an original institution
of English law.[23] Also in the 'trust' field, the sale by a fiduciary or trustee
is an example of a process of clarification of matters of common law
through the development of case-law; the decisions in *British SA Co v.
Bulawayo Municipality*[24] and *Ex parte Nell*[25] on the transfer of property
subject to a *fideicommissum* are relevant in this respect.

Estoppel is the most important exception to the principle behind the
maxim *nemo dat quod non habet* because, of all the exceptions, its scope is
the widest. With regard to the development of Roman-Dutch law in South
Africa estoppel represents a controversial topic: the issue being whether this
far-reaching device was purely and simply an import from English law (the
name 'estoppel' clearly was) or whether, perhaps like the evolution of trust
law, it was forged on the broad basis of an English model, but in a development which could be justified by reference to Roman-Dutch sources.
Professor J. C. de Wet, one of the most distinguished exponents of modern
Roman-Dutch law, seems in his Leiden doctoral thesis to have regarded it
as the former. '*Die gebruik van 'n vreemde woord lei maklik tot die oorname*

---

[19] Generally on the scope of the exception of sales under special authority see Carey Miller
(n. 10), 294 sqq.
[20] Voet (n. 17), 6, 1, 8 and 11.   [21] (1894) 11 SC 4.
[22] *S v. Gathercole* 1964 (1) SA 21 (A) 24 sq.
[23] See H. R. Hahlo, Ellison Kahn, *The Union of South Africa* (1960), 626; Tony Honoré,
Edwin Cameron, *Honoré's South African Law of Trusts* (4th edn., 1992), 15 sq. See also Ch.
26 by Tony Honoré, below.
[24] 1919 AD 84, 97.   [25] 1963 (1) SA 754 (A).

van vreemde beginsels wat daarmee in verband staan in die regstelsel, vanwaar dit oorgeneem word.'[26]

In the case of *Baumann v. Thomas*[27] Solomon JA justified the South African development in the following *dictum*:

The word estoppel is one which has been taken over by us from the English law, and which is now freely used in our daily practice. The doctrine, however, is as much a part of our law as it is of that of England. In the case of *Waterval G. M. Co v. New Bullion G. M. Co*[28] ... it was pointed out by Curlewis J that estoppel *in pais* of English law is analogous to what was known in Roman law as *exceptio doli mali*. In his judgement the learned judge says 'the application of the maxim of Roman Law *nemo contra suum factum venire debet*, would create the same legal consequences as estoppel in English law: it is practically the estoppel by conduct of the English law'.

On this *dictum* one may quote again from De Wet: '*Ons howe stel ons voor 'n voldonge feit. Die reels van estoppel deur wanvoorstelling is hier by ons ingeburger, en bestendig deur die Appelhof op gesag van 'n sogenaamde historiese ondersoek wat niks meer is as 'n lee generalisasie nie.*'[29]

The estoppel development should not be seen to reflect a failure on the part of the South African courts to remain faithful to the Roman-Dutch common law; rather it shows the vitality of a system capable of borrowing and adapting from foreign sources in a process of internal development. A comment of Trollip J, as he then was, is an apposite characterization of the development:

The English doctrine of estoppel by representation migrated to this country on the authority of a passport that it approximated the *exceptio doli mali* of Roman law. However doubtful the validity of this passport might originally have been ... the doctrine has now become naturalised and domiciled here as part of our law as Prof. de Wet's thesis (p. 15) and many authoritative decisions of our Courts show.[30]

An issue of some importance in the present context is whether estoppel, operating in favour of a possessor, amounts to a mode of acquisition of ownership because the effect of denying the title-holder's claim is to acknowledge the possessor's position as that of an owner. Steyn CJ recognized this as a general consequence of the maxim *mobilia non habent sequelam*: '*Die beginsel dat roerende goed geen gevolg het nie—wat ook daarop sou*

---

[26] (The use of a foreign word easily leads to the reception of foreign principles related to it within the legal system from which it is taken over.) '*Estoppel by Representation' in die Suid-Afrikaanse Reg* (1939), 10.

[27] 1920 AD 428, 434 sq.   [28] 1905 TS 722.

[29] (Our courts present us with a *fait accompli*. The rules concerning estoppel by representation have established themselves with us, and have been confirmed by the Appeal court on the basis of a so-called historical investigation which is nothing more than an empty generalization.) De Wet (n. 26), 15.

[30] *Connock's (SA) Motor Co Ltd v. Sentraal Westelike Ko-op Bpk* 1964 (2) SA 47 (T) 49.

uitloop dat besit as volkome titel geld . . .'[31] While estoppel clearly amounts to a far-reaching exception to the principle *nemo dat quod non habet*, it seems inappropriate to think of it as a mode of derivative acquisition. Although the consequence of proof of estoppel is that the right of ownership has passed, in contrast to derivative acquisition its actual operation is negative. Moreover, it operates in a context in which derivative acquisition has failed because an intention to pass ownership on the part of the owner cannot be established.[32] Estoppel has not been authoritatively identified as a mode of acquisition in South African law. Arguably, any move to do so would have blurred the distinction between ownership and possession which is marked in Roman-Dutch law, but of course weak in English law, the parent system of estoppel. Estoppel is concerned with 'a better right to possession', seemingly the guiding star of the English approach to property rights. '[I]n English law, at any rate in the law of moveables, there is hardly such a thing as ownership. All we have is successive possessions, accompanied by titles of varying efficacy'.[33] Although estoppel is concerned with the issue of the better right to possession, a denial of the right to vindicate means that the other party is secure against the claimant without any necessary implication of ownership. South African law would have departed from its basic property dogma by any acknowledgment that estoppel operated as derivative acquisition.[34]

An interesting aspect in the development of South African case-law concerned with estoppel is the requirement of the allegation and proof of negligence. Superseding earlier case-law, a trilogy of Appellate Division decisions[35] have emphasized that the owner's representation, which is of course at the root of the denial of his recourse to the principle *nemo dat quod non habet*, must be culpable. In a number of the applicable *dicta* one finds a specific requirement of *culpa* alluded to: thus Steyn JA defines

---

[31] (The principle of *mobilia non habent sequelam*—which also boils down to acknowledging possession as an absolute title . . .) *Johaadien v. Stanley Porter (Paarl) (Pty) Ltd* 1970 (1) SA 394 (A) 406.

[32] As De Wet (n. 26), 67 demonstrates, the problem of whether ownership has passed on the basis of a putative *causa* may be irrelevant where estoppel is relied upon: '*As die* causa *nie bestaan nie, kan die oordraer die saak terugvorder. Wat derdes betref word die vraag:* causa *of nie* causa *nie, uitgeskakel deur estoppel. Onverskillig of daar* causa *was of nie,* animus *of nie, die eienaar kan hom op die afwesigheid van* causa *of* animus *nie beroep nie wanneer hy derdes onder die indruk gebring het dat daar wel oorgang van eiendom plaasgevind het*' (If the *causa* does not exist, the transferor may claim the object back. As far as third parties are concerned, the question: *causa* or no *causa* is eliminated by estoppel. No matter whether or not there was *causa*, or whether or not there was *animus*, the owner cannot rely on the absence of *causa* or *animus* where he has induced the impression in third parties that transfer of ownership has in fact taken place.)

[33] See W. W. Buckland, A. D. McNair, *Roman Law and Common Law* (2nd edn. revised by F. H. Lawson 1952), 76.

[34] Carey Miller (n. 10), 309.

[35] *Grosvenor Motors (Potchefstroom) Ltd v. Douglas* 1956 (3) SA 420 (A) 427; *Johaadien v. Stanley Porter (Paarl) (Pty) Ltd* (n. 31), 409; *Oakland Nominees (Pty) Ltd v. Gelria Mining & Investment Co (Pty) Ltd* 1976 (1) SA 441 (A) 452.

estoppel as a principle in terms of which an owner 'forfeits his right to vindicate where the person who acquires his property does so because, by the *culpa* of the owner, he has been misled into the belief that the person from whom he acquires it, is entitled to dispose of it'.[36] Although the case-law indicates a reluctance to be absolutely final in limiting the basis to *culpa*[37] it would appear that the concept of *culpa* was introduced to strengthen the dogmatic basis of what was probably seen as a somewhat open-ended device; the importance of the concept of fault, as a consideration resorted to in a number of contexts in Roman-Dutch law, may have been a factor in its identification as a requirement of estoppel. Significantly, De Wet takes the view that from a domestic point of view there can be no basis for estoppel other than negligence.[38]

2. The act of transfer

Derivative acquisition necessarily involves an act of conveyance in which the transferor and the transferee participate. Moreover, in principle, as Grotius noted,[39] the coincidence of the requisite intentions should logically be sufficient to effect a change of ownership. However, in the interests of certainty the civil law required a physical act of delivery. Thence the essential principle of the parties' intention that ownership should pass plus the policy requirement of a completed act of delivery. In the development of South African law it has been recognized, as a matter of essential principle, that the intention element must always be present. The delivery element, however, recognized as being a matter of policy, has been departed from where other considerations of policy are taken to be more compelling. Although not articulated, this difference is implicit in the decision in *Groenewald v. Van der Merwe*[40] where, in a dispute concerning ownership of a threshing machine, Innes CJ pointed out that while delivery was possible without a physical handing over, the mental element was a prerequisite to the extent that the delivery of an item could be perfected, as a legal act, only 'if the mind of the transferee contemplates and desires so to deal with it'. The approach of the courts to the requirement of delivery will be considered in detail in Section 3, below.

The central role of the parties' intention that ownership should pass emerges clearly from the case-law. In *Greenshields v. Chisholm*[41] the decisive fact was that the purchaser of oat-hay did not accept what was tendered; it was acccordingly found that ownership had not passed because it could not

---

[36] *Grosvenor Motors (Potchefstroom) (Pty) Ltd v. Douglas* (n. 35), 427.
[37] See e.g. *Oakland Nominees (Pty) Ltd v. Gelvia Mining & Investment Co (Pty) Ltd* (n. 35).
[38] De Wet (n. 20), 96; but cf. P. J. Rabie, *The Law of Estoppel in South Africa* (1992), 86 sqq.
[39] *De jure belli ac pacis*, 2, 6, 1.   [40] 1917 AD 233, 239.
[41] (1884) 3 SC 220.

be said that this was mutually intended. In another case concerned with a refusal to accept the goods consigned, the critical role of the parties' intention was clearly spelled out by Juta AJA:

So that it is quite clear that he never accepted the goods, nor had he any intention of doing so. This being so, the law applicable is clear. Upon a contract of sale the ownership in the property sold does not pass to the purchaser, unless in addition to giving delivery the seller has the intention of transferring the property, and the purchaser has the intention of becoming owner.[42]

The natural tendency of a case-law system to feed upon itself and develop in a self-contained manner is seen in Schreiner JA's approving adoption of this statement of the law in a subsequent case.[43] As a consequence, the role of the basic common law sources tends to recede while what the sources represent becomes increasingly entrenched in the case-law. The result may be something of a paradox in that where the common law has been followed most closely it is likely that future reference will be primarily to its enunciation in case-law rather than to the original sources. This may be seen as characteristic of the 'mixed' South African system in so far as adherence to basic principles—a civilian feature—is achieved not by referring to the relevant text, but through the English form of legal development with authority and precedent provided by case-law.

A matter of considerable importance with regard to the passing of ownership concerns the relationship between the basis, or *causa*, upon which the act of transfer proceeds and the act itself. While it was well understood in Roman-Dutch common law that the act of transfer was necessarily driven by a concurrence of the respective intentions of the transferor and the transferee, it is not readily apparent from the sources whether the required intention was to be derived from the underlying *causa*, upon which the act of transfer proceeded, or whether it was independent in the sense of being the critical driving force in the self-standing act of transfer.[44] On this basis, and following the nineteenth-century work of Friedrich Carl von Savigny,[45] modern legal theory distinguishes 'causal' and 'abstract' systems of passing of ownership.

Early South African law appears to have required a causal basis for the passing of ownership. The first Chief Justice of the Union of South Africa, as Chief Justice of the Cape Supreme Court, stated in a decision of 1880 that a valid underlying *causa* was a prerequisite to the passing of ownership. The issue was whether ownership had passed in respect of horses sold on

---

[42] *Weeks v. Amalgamated Agencies Ltd* 1920 AD 218, 230.

[43] *R v. Markins Motors (Pty) Ltd* 1959 (3) SA 508 (A) 512.

[44] See D. L. Carey Miller, 'Tranfer of Ownership', in: Robert Feenstra, Reinhard Zimmermann (eds.), *Das römisch-holländische Recht: Fortschritte des Zivilrechts im 17. und 18. Jahrhundert* (1992), 537 sqq.

[45] See *Das Obligationenrecht*, vol. II (1853), 254 sqq.

by a party who had purchased on the fraudulent pretext that he was acting on behalf of the Government.

There must be some valid cause, such as donation, sale or other contract, to make the delivery an effective transfer of the property; and, in the present case, there being no such contract, the property never passed to Holmes, who could not therefore give a good title to the defendant.[46]

This is a characteristic dictum from Lord de Villiers whose judgments are notable for decisiveness, typically in a context of sparing recourse to the authorities of Roman-Dutch law.[47] Another factor in the early tendency in South African law towards a form of final legal rule determined through case-law, following the English pattern, was of course the scope available to judges to leave their own individual mark on legal development. The influence of Lord[48] De Villiers exemplifies this factor to a marked degree.[49]

Subsequent cases do not reflect the avowedly causal basis of the De Villiers *dictum*[50] and in 1913 another major figure in South African legal development, Sir James Rose Innes,[51] who in 1914 succeeded Lord de Villiers as Chief Justice of the Union, gave a judgment containing an *obiter dictum* which could only be identified with the abstract system. In essence, what Innes J said was that ownership of land could pass on the basis of registration of transfer regardless of a defective underlying *causa* in an underhand—and therefore invalid—agreement of sale. Emphasizing the importance of the parties' intentions relating to the act of transfer Innes J noted that '... the *traditio* duly made with the knowledge of all the facts and with the intent to pass the *dominium*, and the price duly paid with similar knowledge and with the object of acquiring *dominium* would bind the respective parties'.[52]

The issue of the basis of the passing of ownership was settled in definite terms in 1941 in the case of *Commissioner of Customs and Excise v. Randles, Brothers and Hudson Ltd.*[53] The issue was whether ownership had passed in a consignment of imported cloth on the basis of a purported sale to a clothing manufacturer by an importer under an agreement which provided for resale to the importer for the price paid plus the costs of manufacture. The arrangement was manifestly a device for the avoidance of duty. From the

---

[46] *Beyers v. McKenzie* 1880 Foord 125, 127. De Villiers CJ also refers to the *causa* requirement in *Kleudgen & Co v. Trustees in Insolvent Estate of Rabie* 1880 Foord 63, 65.

[47] See Roberts (n. 6), 356: ' ... not a profound scholar of Roman Dutch law'.

[48] South African-born Johan Hendrik de Villiers was created Baron de Villiers of Wynberg in 1910.

[49] See generally Roberts (n. 6), 356 sqq.

[50] See *Wolf v. Richards* (1884) 3 HCG 102, 116; *Lucas' Trustee v. Ismail and Amod* 1905 TS 239, 243; *Marcus v. Stamper and Zoutendijk* 1910 AD 58, 78.

[51] See Roberts (n. 6), 374: 'It is not easy to determine who is the greatest of all South African judges, but Sir James has strong claims to that distinction.'

[52] *Wilken v. Kohler* 1913 AD 135, 144.　　　　　　　　　　　　　[53] 1941 AD 369.

point of view of property law it was clear that the parties intended the passing of ownership but the simulated sale was probably not the true basis of the act of transfer. The Appellate Division decided that ownership had passed even though there was no valid underlying contractual basis for the act of transfer. Watermeyer JA explained the law on the basis of an abstract approach to the passing of ownership:

If the parties desire to transfer ownership and contemplate that ownership will pass as a result of delivery, then they in fact have the necessary intention and the ownership passes by delivery. It was contended, however, on behalf of the appellant that delivery accompanied by the necessary intention on the part of the parties to the delivery is not enough to pass ownership; that some recognized form of contract . . . is required in addition . . . I do not agree with this contention. The *habilis causa* referred to by Voet means merely an appropriate *causa*, that is, either an appropriate reason for the transfer or a serious and deliberate agreement showing an intention to transfer.[54]

The judgment of Centlivres JA in the same case also explains the law on the basis of the abstract approach:

From these passages it is clear, I think, that a wide meaning must be given to the words '*justa causa*' or '*causa habilis*' (Voet, 41.1.35), and that all that these words mean in the context I am at present considering is that the legal transaction preceding the *traditio* may be evidence of an intention to pass and acquire ownership. But there may be direct evidence of an intention to pass and acquire ownership and, if there is, there is no need to rely on a preceeding legal transaction in order to show that ownership has, as a fact, passed. To put it more briefly it seems to me that the question whether ownership passed depends on the intention of the parties and such intention may be proved in various ways.[55]

It is interesting to note that both the above *dicta* seek to explain the law on the basis of Voet's statement of the Roman-Dutch common law position. Two related points are relevant here: the tendency of the Appellate Division to develop the law by interpreting Roman-Dutch common law sources and the importance of Voet in this process. The approach of the two judges concerned, who both made significant contributions to the development of Roman-Dutch law in the first half of the twentieth century,[56] is very much representative of a school of thought that sought to achieve satisfactory legal development on the basis of the sources of Roman-Dutch law. Johannes Voet's *Commentarius ad Pandectas* lent itself to this approach. As a comprehensive and detailed treatise it proved, over many years, an

---

[54] Ibid. 398 sq.   [55] Ibid. 411.
[56] Roberts (n. 6), 382 describes Watermeyer as 'one of the most brilliant "all rounders" in our judicial history'. Both he and Centlivres had been called to the English Bar, Watermeyer after Cambridge and Centlivres after Oxford. The legal education of both included Roman and English law which very probably produced a healthy appreciation of the important differences between the systems.

invaluable source of Roman-Dutch material; indeed, two distinguished modern writers have commented: '[b]ut for the *Commentarius* Roman-Dutch law might well have disappeared from legal practice in South Africa.'[57] According to Roberts,[58] who published his bibliography in 1942, of the 4,833 sections in Voet's *Commentaries*, 3,670 had been translated into English or Dutch. The complete translation of Percival Gane, a judge of the Eastern Cape Division, published in seven volumes over the period 1955–8 soon replaced the Latin text and earlier translations as the everyday source of Voet.

Case-law subsequent to *Commissioner of Customs and Excise v. Randles, Brothers & Hudson Ltd*[59] continued to determine the passing of ownership by reference to the act of transfer rather than the underlying transaction. In *MCC Bazaar v. Harris & Jones (Pty) Ltd* Rumpff J explained *justa causa traditionis* as not necessarily requiring a legal basis because in the context in question *causa* referred to the circumstances from which the parties' intentions to convey ownership derived: '*Die omstandighede waaruit die bedoeling van die partye te voorskyn tree is die* causa.'[60] From the time of a seminal article published by Professor J. E. Scholtens[61] South African academic writers began to expound upon the abstract basis of the transfer of ownership. In relatively recent times the full implications of the abstract theory have been worked out in the periodical literature[62] and in textbooks.[63] This is an example of the strength of the contribution of juristic writers to the development of Roman-Dutch law in its more recent phase in South Africa.

A complete acceptance that the transfer of ownership proceeds on an abstract basis and an enhanced state of knowledge as to the workings of the system are reflected in more recent decisions of the courts. Thus, in *Air-Kel (Edms) Bpk h/a Merkel Motors v. Bodenstein*[64] Jansen JA followed the writings of modern jurists and identified the parties' mutual intentions as to the passing of ownership as an agreement to that effect—' *'n ooreenkoms*

---

[57] H. R. Hahlo, Ellison Kahn, *The South African Legal System and its Background* (1968), 556 sq. Roberts (n. 6), 317 quotes Sir John Kotzé—one of the most respected exponents of Roman-Dutch law who retired as an Appellate Division judge in 1927 and another South African who read for the English Bar—as stating that Voet 'is without a competitor as a comprehensive legal encyclopaedia, which will always justly remain a standard and authoritative work on Roman and Roman-Dutch Law'.

[58] Roberts (n. 6), 318.   [59] Above, n. 53.

[60] (The circumstances from which the intention of the parties appears is the *causa*) 1954 (3) SA 158 (T) 161.

[61] J. E. Scholtens, '*Iusta causa traditionis* and contracts induced by fraud', (1957) 74 *SALJ* 280.

[62] See e.g. Wouter de Vos, '*Solutio indebiti* en eiendomsoorgang', 1976 *TSAR* 79; D. S. P. Cronjé, 'Die saaklike ooreenkoms by die eiendomsoordrag van roerende sake', (1978) 41 *THRHR* 227.

[63] C. G. van der Merwe, *Sakereg* (n. 1) 305 sqq. is the primary example.

[64] 1980 (3) SA 917 (A).

tussen oorhandiger en ontvanger dat daarmee eiendomsreg gegee en geneem word,[65] amounting to ' *'n abstrakte stelsel van eiendomsoordrag'*.[66]

The development of a basis upon which to work out questions concerning the transfer of ownership has been achieved in modern law despite limited material in the sources.[67] As indicated, the courts, operating in the manner of the English courts, have led in the development of the law but have sought to do so on the basis of the classic writings of Roman-Dutch law. The modern juristic writers, in an important—but nonetheless secondary—role, have enhanced the development by explaining and expanding upon the decisions in a body of literature which has been selectively used in subsequent decisions.

III. MODES OF DELIVERY OF MOVABLE PROPERTY

1. General observations

The relationship between the parties' intention that ownership should pass and the act of delivery has been alluded to above. Although the act of delivery, as an integral part of the act of transfer of ownership, must necessarily operate in a context which meets the general requirements, considered above, there is scope for considerable difference between the actual forms of delivery, at least in respect of movable property.

In derivative acquisition the requirement that the parties intend the passing of ownership is a matter of principle which cannot be departed from. Although an intention to convey property may conveniently be inferred from an act of delivery, it is obvious that delivery is in no sense a prerequisite to the existence of the parties' intention that ownership should pass. Rather, delivery is required as a matter of policy, and so it is open to exception on the basis of what may be seen to be more compelling considerations of policy. In the evolution of the Roman-Dutch common law in South Africa the requirement of delivery has been shaped in accordance with perceived considerations of policy. The interests of commerce have been the most important; not infrequently, English commercial law developments have been influential. Even in the straightforward case of actual physical delivery an example can be found. Where, pursuant to a contract of sale, delivery is made by a carrier, English law was followed and the carrier was

---

[65] (An agreement between transferor and transferee that the right of ownership be given and taken.) 1980 (3) SA 917 (A), at 922.
[66] (An abstract system of transfer of property.) 1980 (3) SA 917 (A), 923.
[67] See generally Carey Miller (n. 44), 537 sqq.

treated as the purchaser's agent: with the consequence that ownership passed to the purchaser upon receipt of the goods by the carrier.[68]

In the area of constructive delivery South African law has adhered to the traditional forms of *clavium traditio, traditio longa manu, traditio brevi manu,* and *constitutum possessorium*[69] but there has been significant domestic development within that framework. Showing its capacity to move beyond the traditional civilian categories, English law has been influential in a form of delivery which facilitates the transfer of property held by a third party. This is sometimes referred to by the English term 'attornment'.[70] The forms of constructive delivery are considered individually below.

2. *Clavium traditio*

The Roman-Dutch common law sources are not altogether conclusive[71] on the question of whether the handing over of something other than the object concerned was a purely symbolic act or whether the item delivered—typically a key—had to provide the transferee with access to the object being conveyed. South African law appears to have resolved this problem by recognizing that the act of delivery serves two purposes. First, it demonstrates the parties' intention to transfer ownership and, secondly, it gives the transferee some degree of control over the object. On this basis delivery is symbolic in the sense that the parties' intention to pass ownership is symbolized by the act of handing over but property will only pass if the transferee obtains a sufficient degree of physical control. As De Villiers CJ noted in *Heydenrich v. Saber*: 'No doubt a mere symbol is not sufficient to effect delivery.'[72] The intention element being in any event indispensable, the essence of this form of delivery is in fact the substitute physical aspect, pertinently defined in an early example of the rich legal literature which South African law has produced[73] as the 'physical transference of some article which affords the means of possessing the article sold, or is the external *indicium* of the right to its control'.[74]

In *London and South Africa Bank v. Donald Currie & Co*[75] the Cape Supreme Court recognized the concept of symbolic delivery but, in treating the handing over of a key as analogous with the transfer of a bill of lading,

---

[68] See *London SA Bank v. Donald Curry & Co* (1875) 5 Buch 29. In *Stephen Fraser & Co v. Clydesdale Collieries* 1903 TH 121, 125, Solomon J placed reliance upon Benjamin's definitive text on the English law of sale.
[69] See e.g. Van der Merwe (n. 1), 298.
[70] In Professor Van der Merwe's treatment 'attornment' follows the 4 traditional forms.
[71] See Carey Miller (n. 44), 529.   [72] (1900) 17 SC 73, 76.
[73] Juta, the main domestic legal publisher, dates from 1853.
[74] H. G. Mackeurtan, *Sale of Goods in South Africa* (1921), 144.
[75] (1875) 5 Buch 29.

it seems that the Court regarded the key from the point of view of access to and control over the goods. A persistent tendency to see delivery by bill of lading as a primary form of symbolic delivery[76] has not been conducive to a clear appreciation of what is required for symbolic delivery. The handing over of a bill of lading is an effective form of constructive delivery *sui generis*: not so much symbolic delivery as the only appropriate means of dealing with goods in transit. The misconceived tendency to equate delivery by bill of lading and symbolical delivery,[77] following English case-law, may have been a factor leading to an excessive notion, expressed in certain *dicta*,[78] of what is required by way of physical element in case of symbolic delivery.

3. *Traditio longa manu*

The form of delivery not involving an actual handing over but where what is done may be construed as a handing over has been the subject of analysis in a number of South African decisions. In *Xapa v. Ntsoko*[79] Sampson J, having noted the prerequisite intention element, identified the physical aspects as a pointing out *in praesenti* by the transferor and the placing of the thing at the disposal of the transferee. This case followed the Appellate Division decision of *Groenewald v. Van der Merwe*[80] in which Innes CJ considered the underlying basis of the form of constructive delivery labelled *traditio longa manu*. The *dictum* concerned is a powerful instance of a phenomenon common in South Africa: the law being taken forward by a judge in a thoroughly abstract exposition which, from a civilian point of view, would be seen as representing a juristic rather than a judicial role.

But physical prehension is not essential if the subject-matter is placed in presence of the would-be possessor in such circumstances that he and he alone can deal with it at pleasure. In that way the physical element is sufficiently supplied; and if the mind of the transferee contemplates and desires so to deal with it, the transfer of possession,—that is the delivery—is in law complete . . . When this deposit of the subject-matter in the presence and at the disposition of the new possessor takes the place of physical prehension, the delivery is said to be made *longa manu*, and it constitutes one of the forms of fictitious as distinguished from actual delivery.

---

[76] See e.g. *Hochmetals Africa Ltd v. Otavi Mining Co* 1968 (1) SA 571 (A) 579, where Van Blerk JA quoted a *dictum* of English law describing a bill of lading as 'a key which in the hands of the rightful owner is intended to unlock the door of the warehouse floating or fixed, in which the goods may chance to be'.

[77] See Carey Miller (n. 10), 146 sqq.

[78] See e.g. *Erasmus v. M Rosenberg Ltd* 1910 TPD 1188, 1191: 'Delivery must be notorious' (*per* Wessels J).

[79] 1919 EDL 177, 182.   [80] 1917 AD 233, 239.

A consequence of the principles of the law being open to a process of active development through case-law—English style—is that statements of the law by judges are not always consistent, and as a result the law may well be retarded in its development. A degree of inconsistency in the outcome of similar cases is inevitable in any system but it is a demerit of a case-law system that differences in outcome may manifest themselves as changes in the law. An example of this can be found in a modern case concerning *traditio longa manu*. In *Botha v. Mazeka*[81] cattle were bought and paid for but left on the seller's premises while the purchaser sought permission to move the animals. The stock was stolen; the issue was whether ownership had passed to the buyer. In spite of the fact that the animals had been marked with the buyer's brand and placed in a separate enclosure on the seller's farm it was held that ownership had not passed and that the loss was the seller's. The Court referred with approval[82] to the 'physical prehension' *dictum* of Innes CJ quoted above, but took the view that the inference to be drawn from the branding was ambivalent because an intention merely to identify the stock as the subject of the parties' transaction was no less consistent with the act of branding than an intention that ownership should pass. That a contract had been concluded could hardly be in doubt in the circumstances and the finality of an act of branding would appear to demonstrate the parties' intention that ownership should pass.

Differences manifested in case-law are sometimes reconciled, or even corrected, by writers seeking to establish a systematic basis for the law.[83] Although contemporary writings have only persuasive authority, South African courts are more receptive to textbooks and periodical literature than those in England.[84]

4. *Traditio brevi manu*

Where the object concerned is held by the party to acquire ownership a transfer can be achieved on the basis of a transaction between the parties, as a consequence of which the holder's *detentio* may be taken to be possession as owner. Put another way, where the circumstances provide an event from which the requisite mutual intention that ownership should pass can be inferred, the transferee's pre-existing holding may be seen as sufficient as far as the physical element required for transfer of ownership is concerned. The critical feature of a changed contractual relationship between the parties was illustrated in *Marcus v. Stamper and Zoutendijk*[85] in which an

---

[81] 1981 (3) SA 191 (A).   [82] Ibid. 195.
[83] See e.g. M. Reinsma, C. G. van der Merwe, 'Die aard van *traditio longa manu*', (1969) 32 *THRHR* 302.
[84] See D. L. Carey Miller, 'Legal writings as a source in English law', 1975 *CILSA* 236.
[85] 1910 AD 58.

auctioneer had paid the owner but had not collected the sale price of goods which had been sold on by the buyer. The auctioneer's difficulty was that he could not claim to have acquired the goods because there was no event which could be taken to support a change in his status from that of a mandatory; as De Villiers CJ noted, 'if a mandatory has the goods of the *mandans* in his possession, and by a fresh contract the property is intended to be passed to the mandatory, it is not necessary to have a fresh delivery'.[86]

The concept of *traditio brevi manu* has been applied as a possible basis to explain the acquisition of ownership by one who holds property under a hire-purchase agreement when payment of the final instalment is made. In *Forsdick Motors Ltd v. Lauritzen*[87] James J analysed this situation in terms of constructive delivery:

But whatever the proper interpretation of the law should be it is clear that the mere physical handing over of the article sold to the potential purchaser does not make him the owner. He has its *detentio* but the mental element involved in every transfer of ownership is lacking because neither the seller nor the buyer intends that ownership shall pass. When the contract finally comes into operation a further act of delivery is necessary to effect transfer. As the purchaser already has the *detentio* of the property that further act relates to the intention of the parties towards it and requires that the parties should agree that the transferee who already has the physical detention of the property, although holding it on behalf of the transferor, would in future possess it as his own. Transfer is brought about by *traditio brevi manu*. For *traditio brevi manu* to take effect the potential transferee must be in physical possession of the article and must have the *animus* to hold it for himself.

This *dictum* reflects the inherent capacity of the common law forms of constructive delivery to meet new needs in the development of the law. A strong basis of principle, well articulated in the Roman-Dutch sources which judges and writers have been ready to exploit, is probably the single most important factor in the development of South African private law. However, the adaptation of the common law to novel situations has not always proceeded without controversy. Indeed, in the matter under consideration, a subsequent Court was critical of the approach adopted in *Forsdick Motors* case. In *Trust Bank van Afrika Bpk v. Van Jaarsveldt, Trust Bank van Afrika Bpk. v. Bitzer*[88] Viljoen AJ took the view that the analysis in question was inappropriate because it postulated the suspension of the whole agreement until payment of the final instalment.

5. *Constitutum possessorium*

The distinctive feature of this controversial form of delivery is that it involves a departure from the principle that an act of delivery is required

---

[86] Ibid. 73 sq.   [87] 1967 (3) SA 249 (N) 253.   [88] 1978 (4) SA 115 (O) 121.

for the transfer of ownership on a derivative basis. In allowing the transferor to give title simply by a legal act in terms of which the object is retained on a basis other than that of ownership *constitutum possessorium* may well be said to make 'nonsense of the rule *traditionibus non nudis pactis*'.[89]

The failure to meet—even on a minimal basis—the requirement of a physical element in the act of transfer caused the issue of the acceptability of *constitutum possessorium* to arise in South African case-law. In *Haupt's Trustees v. P J Haupt & Co*[90] recognition of the the controversial nature of the device is manifest in counsel's invitation to the Court to declare that it no longer applied. In *Orson v. Reynolds*[91] De Villiers CJ noted that he did not know of any case in which the Supreme Court had applied the doctrine. In *Woodhouse v. Odendaal*,[92] however, Maasdorp CJ stated the attitude to *constitutum possessorium* which was to prevail: '[T]he doctrine of *constitutum possessorium* still obtains with us and the only difficulty lies in its application.'

The position of the doctrine was made secure in an Appellate Division decision in which Innes CJ rejected the argument that it had become obsolete in South Africa. In *Goldinger's Trustee v. Whitelaw & Son*[93] Innes CJ noted that *constitutum possessorium* 'is only the converse of *traditio brevi manu*' and that 'both are examples of a transfer of possession and consequently of ownership due to a contractual change of intention on the part of the person who retains throughout the physical control'.[94] While noting that *constitutum possessorium* was open to possible abuse, the Appellate Division identified certain safeguards against 'the mischief resulting from an abuse of the facility for the transfer of *dominium* which our law allows'.[95] In the same case the Appellate Division, having settled the issue of the place of *constitutum possessorium*, went on to clarify the limitations which controlled its operation:

One is that a *constitutum* is never presumed: the party alleging it must establish facts from which its existence clearly and necessarily follows . . . Another is that a distinct *causa detentionis* is essential . . . If A, after selling a movable to B, were to determine to hold it on behalf of the latter, that change of mind would not effect a transfer of ownership. There must be a clearly proved contractual relationship under which he becomes the detentor for the purchaser. Only in such a case would the doctrine of *constitutum possessorium* operate to pass the property by a kind of fictitious delivery.[96]

---

[89] W. M. Gordon, *Studies in the Transfer of Property by Traditio* (1970), 15, puts this forward as a prevalent view of *constitutum possessorium*.

[90] (1852) 1 Searle 287, 294.   [91] (1885) 2 Buch AC 102, 105.

[92] 1914 OPD 48, 56.   [93] 1917 AD 66, 74.   [94] Ibid.

[95] Ibid. 75.   [96] Ibid.

6. Property held by a third party

An important form of delivery in any developed economy is that which operates on the basis of an agreement between transferor and transferee concerning property held by a third party, often an agent. Merchandise is frequently held in store and commerce requires a means by which ownership can be transferred without the need physically to move the goods. A form of delivery which would achieve this end was recognized in late nineteenth-century case-law.[97] Delivery was seen to take place upon the third party detentor receiving instructions to hold henceforth for the buyer, to whom possession then passed. In an early case the terminology of English law—that the holder would 'attorn to' the buyer, thus delivery by 'attornment'—was adopted by De Villiers CJ.[98] Two years later the Chief Justice set out to clarify his *dictum* in the earlier case: 'The phrase [attorn to] is not known to our law, but the undertaking itself would, in my opinion, be as binding under our law as it is under the law of England.'[99]

This is an early instance of what was to become a familiar theme: that it was permissible to adopt some aspects of English law on the basis that the concept or rule in question was in accordance with Roman-Dutch law. This approach persisted into modern times and, as Professors Hahlo and Kahn have recorded,[100] is evidenced as late as 1945 by a statement of Greenberg JA that '[w]here there is no difference in principle our courts have always sought and obtained guidance from the decisions of the English Courts'.[101] However, by the 1950s the tendency to develop aspects of South African law on the basis of an assumed correspondence between Roman-Dutch and English law had begun to be seriously questioned. A classic instance is the robust *dictum* of Van den Heever JA in *Preller v. Jordaan*:[102]

Hier het ons 'n verskynsel wat in ons jurisprudensie maar al te dikwels voorkom. 'n Romeins-Hollandse regsreël word met sy Engelse ewenknie vergelyk; met welgevalle, indien nie met vreugde nie, word gekonstateer dat daar geen verskil is nie en dan staan die deur wyd oop vir die resepsie van Engelse reg. Gewag is gemaak van die feit dat ons 'n lewende regsstelsel het wat vatbaar is vir ontwikkeling. Ek wil egter daarop attent maak dat geleidelike aanpassing aan nuwe omstandighede en probleme 'n soort van groei is wat tot krag lei; onbeheerde groei daarenteen lei tot boosaardige gewasse en ontbinding.[103]

---

[97] See *Standard Bank v. O'Connor* (1888) 6 SC 32, 44; *Standard Bank v. Union Boating Co* (1890) 7 SC 257, 268; *Court v. Mosenthal & Co* (1896) 13 SC 127, 153 sq.

[98] See *Standard Bank v. O'Connor* (n. 97), 44. See also Mackeurtan (n. 74), 145.

[99] See *Standard Bank v. Union Boating Co* (n. 97), 268.

[100] Hahlo/Kahn (n. 57), 587.   [101] *Feldman (Pty) Ltd v. Mall* 1945 AD 733, 776.

[102] 1956 (1) SA 483 (A) 504.

[103] (Here we have a phenomenon that occurs all too often in our law. A Roman-Dutch legal rule is compared with its English counterpart; it is established with pleasure, if not with joy, that there is no difference; and then the door is wide open for the reception of English law. It

Given the prominence of the word 'attorney' in South African law it could be seen as absurd that there should be any concern about the use of 'attornment' as a label for delivery on the basis of a tripartite agreement. However, expressions of this concern have continued into modern law; for example, in a 1972 Appellate Division case, Rumpff JA pointed out that 'attornment' is merely an epithet to describe a form of delivery '*wat voldoen aan die vereistes vir lewering van roerende goed in die Romeins-Hollandse reg*'.[104]

It would indeed seem that the civil law did accept delivery on the basis of according control to the transferee without any actual transfer of the object[105] and, of course, this is not surprising given how far *constitutum possessorium* went in terms of dispensing with a physical element. It may be noted that in Scots law the form of delivery based on an order to a third party to hold for the transferee rather than the transferor is well developed and its basis has been accepted as civilian by Professor W. M. Gordon who observed that '[t]his seems a development of the principle implicit in D.46.3.79, that there is delivery by giving instructions which put the thing out of the control of the present possessor and into the control of the acquirer'.[106]

In modern South African law there has been some development of the form of delivery applicable to the circumstances of property held by a third party. A rigorous analysis of the basis, in legal principle, of what is involved has characterized the development, as appears from the *dictum* of Jansen JA in *Air-Kel (Edms) Bpk h/a Merkel Motors v. Bodenstein*:[107]

*Die erkenning van die bestaan van die moontlikheid van middellike besit—nl. dat een persoon besitter (*possessor*) kan wees alhoewel hy selfs geen regstreekse daadwerklike beheer oor die saak voer nie, maar iemand anders (*detentor*) dit namens hom doen—skep egter die moontlikheid van besitsoordrag deur blote ooreenkoms ... Dit is ook in ooreenstemming hiermee duidelik dat waar A* possessor *is deur middel van B (*detentor*) dit deur ooreenkoms bewerkstellig sou kon word dat B voortaan as* detentor *namens C sal optree, wat dan voortaan* possessor *sal wees.*

has been mentioned that ours is a living legal system which is capable of development. However, I want to draw attention to the fact that gradual adaption to new circumstances and problems constitutes a kind of growth leading to strength: but uncontrolled growth leads to malignant excrescences and decay.) See also the *dictum* of Steyn CJ in *Trust Bank van Afrika Bpk v. Eksteen* 1964 (3) SA 402 (A) at 410 sq. Other authorities relevant to this issue are given by Hahlo/Kahn (n. 57), 585 sqq.

[104] (. . . that complies with the requirements for delivery of movables in Roman-Dutch law.) *Caledon & SWD Eksekuteurskamer Bpk v. Wentzel* 1972 (1) SA 270 (A), 272 sq.

[105] D. 46, 3, 79.   [106] Gordon (n. 89), 217.

[107] (Recognition that there is the possibility of indirect possession—viz. that one person may be possessor even though he himself does not exercise direct and effective control over the object but someone else (the *detentor*) exercises it in his name—does, however, create the possibility of transfer of possession by mere agreement ... Accordingly, it is also clear that where A is possessor by means of B (*detentor*) it can be effected by agreement that B shall, henceforth, conduct himself as *detentor* in the name of C, who will, henceforth, be possessor.) 1980 (3) SA 917 (A) 922 sq.

Although there has been some extension of the scope of this form of constructive delivery[108] the Appellate Division has sought to control the development on a basis seen to be rational in terms of principle.[109]

The area of delivery of property held by a third party could be taken as a microcosm of a not uncommon pattern of development of South African private law. The adoption as a matter of expediency of a concept or device of English law; the development over what may be a quite considerable period through the random incidence of case-law of a position likely to reflect the perspectives of Roman-Dutch law; and the eventual articulation of the position by a process of judicial analysis, possibly informed by modern juristic writing.[110] Of course, though, this pattern is not a common one in property law where the strong principles of Roman-Dutch law have tended to dominate. Nonetheless, the common process by which all aspects of South African private law develop is evolution through case-law and, to this extent, the law belongs to the Anglo-American rather than the civilian school. A significant aspect of the development of, at any rate, English and Scots law[111] is the extent to which *obiter dicta* plays a role in signalling future change: something which has to be done because overruling by subsequent decision operates retrospectively as well as prospectively. In the present context *obiter* remarks by Rumpff CJ in the *Caledon* case[112] moot the possibility of delivery on the basis of the cession of the transferor's interest to the transferee where the holder has agreed in advance that if and when a cession occurs he will henceforth hold on behalf of the transferee. Professor C. G. van der Merwe has pointed out[113] that this would amount to a 'cession of ownership', something South African law—unlike the modern Dutch law referred to by Rumpff CJ[114]—does not permit because '*[e]iendomsreg kan nie, soos in die Engelse reg, deur blote ooreenkoms oorgaan nie*'.[115] It remains to be seen whether this *obiter dictum* is in any sense a prognosis of a possible erosion of the delivery requirement.[116]

---

[108] See esp. *Caledon & SWD Eksekuteurskamer Bpk v. Wentzel* (n. 104). The implications of this decision are considered in my textbook: see Carey Miller (n. 10), 154 sqq. See also Van der Merwe (n. 1), 330 sqq.; Stefanus Rootman Rossouw, *Attornment en sessie van eiendomsreg as verskyningsvorme van fiktiewe lewering in die Suid-Afrikaanse reg* (unpublished LL M thesis, University of Stellenbosch, 1993).

[109] See the comments of Jansen JA in *Air-Kel (Edms) Bpk h/a Merkel Motors v. Bodenstein* 1980 (3) SA 917 (A) 923, 924 sq. regarding the *Caledon* case (n. 104).

[110] The development of the South African law of agency is a good example of the interplay between English and Roman-Dutch law; see the brilliant account of M. A. Millner in Hahlo/Kahn (n. 57), 694 sqq.

[111] For this purpose Scots law is also in the Anglo-American camp.

[112] Above, n. 104, 274 sqq.   [113] Van der Merwe (n. 1), 330 sq.

[114] *Caledon* (n. 112), 273 sqq.

[115] (Ownership cannot, as in English law, be transferred by mere agreement.) Van der Merwe (n. 1), 331.

[116] A negative sign for the future of Rumpff's radical *dictum* is that it was not considered in the Appellate Division case of *Barclays Western Bank Ltd v. Ernst* 1988 (1) SA 243 (A).

IV. THE TRANSFER OF OWNERSHIP IN LAND

1. Historical continuity

Long before the arrival of Roman-Dutch law in South Africa a systematic
approach to the transfer of ownership in land had emerged in the territories of the Netherlands as part of a general but, of course, uncoordinated
European pattern of development.[117] The development continued in the
Republic of the United Netherlands which had obtained its independence
from Spain only a short time before the settlement at the Cape. Roman law,
of course, originally required compliance with certain formalities to obtain
an effective transfer of the right of ownership in land and other important
forms of property, together designated *res mancipi*; but Roman-Dutch law
reflected the more modern position of certain prescribed formalities in
respect of land with relative flexibility within a framework of legal principle
in respect of movable property.[118]

The important basis of an official act of conveyance which had developed
in the Netherlands[119] was adopted in South Africa where, in the initial
Dutch East India Company period, transfers were executed before two
Commissioners of the Council of Policy and subscribed by the Secretary.[120]
Reflecting a shift from official control of the allocation of rights in land to
a system of official control of the act of transfer, an Ordinance of 1718
required execution before the Commissioners of the Court of Justice.[121] An
early judicial *dictum (per curiam)* notes that South African practice followed the Dutch system:

By the law of Holland, the *dominium* or *jus in re* of immovable property can only
be conveyed by transfer made *coram legi loci*, and this species of transfer is an essential to divest the seller of, and invest the buyer with, the *dominium* or *jus in re* of
immovable property as actual tradition is to convey the *dominium* of movables, and
that the delivery of the actual possession of immovable property has no force or
legal effect whatever in transferring its *dominium*. This rule of the law of Holland
was not a mere fiscal regulation. It was with the rest of the law of Holland introduced into this Colony on its first settlement, and has been acted on invariably ever
since, except that, by certain colonial laws, the Registrar of Deeds has been substituted for the magistrates before whom in Holland transfers were by law required to
be made.[122]

---

[117] See Van der Merwe (n. 1), 333 sqq.   [118] See Carey Miller (n. 44), 535.
[119] See e.g. the *Placaat* of Emperor Charles V of 1529 referred to in Carey Miller (n. 44),
535.
[120] See George Denoon, 'The Development of Methods of Land Registration in South
Africa', (1943) 60 *SALJ* 179, 181.
[121] Denoon (n. 120), 182.
[122] *Harris v. Trustee of Buissinne* (1840) 2 Menz 105, 107 sq.

An important development, and a first indication of a dominating feature of future land law, was the appointment in 1828 under the British administration of a Registrar of Deeds.[123] With regard to future restrictions on the acquisition of land on a racial basis it is interesting to note that an Ordinance passed in the same year accorded Hottentots, Bushmen, and free Coloured persons full civil rights including equality with Europeans for the purpose of the acquisition and occupation of land.[124] At the time there was still slavery, and it was originally envisaged that the office would be a joint one designated 'Registrar of Slaves and Deeds'[125] but this position was short-lived because slaves were emancipated in 1834.

Whether the acquisition of land takes place on the basis of original grant or act of transfer, the issue of title subsequently to deal with the property concerned will inevitably arise. While in respect of movable property the maxim *nemo dat quod non habet* could be taken to be satisfied by the transferor's possession, in the case of land the position of the transferor, as the party vested with the right to convey, could only be established in a sufficient manner by a document or some other record of title. The utility of a document of title and the benefit of some form of official recording of rights in land were recognized in the Cape long before the creation of the office of Registrar of Deeds. Efforts were made in the late seventeenth century, to consolidate the system of official recording of rights in land, the precursor of an important function of a deeds registry. Denoon records the Preamble of a *Placaat* which as early as 1685 noted the problem of the possession of land with insufficient proof of right or title.[126]

From the point of view of the transfer of ownership the pertinent questions are how this was achieved and to what extent, if any, the registration or recording of a transfer was a prerequisite to its effectiveness. It is clear that the essential feature was a formal act of transfer before an official. This, of course, was entirely consistent with the requirement of the common law that ownership did not pass by bare agreement but only on the basis of an act of delivery which could be identified as a separate legal act. However, the fundamental basis of the requirement of registration of transfer is frequently overlooked—or at least taken for granted—in statements concerning the rationale of registration. Thus, in a Transvaal case decided in 1905, *Houtpoort Mining and Estate Syndicate Ltd v. Jacobs*,[127] the emphasis appears to have been on the publicity which is a consequence of the act of delivery, even if a desired one, rather than the *raison d'être* for the requirement. As regards any requirement of recording, insofar as this can be separated from the actual act of transfer, the better view is that it is concerned not with the passing of ownership but with the security of rights in land: as

---

[123] Ord. 39 of 1828. See also Denoon (n. 120), 183. [124] Ord. 50 of 1828.
[125] Denoon (n. 120), 457. [126] Ibid. 184 sq.
[127] 1904 TS 105, 108 sq.; approved in *Frye's (Pty) Ltd v. Ries* 1957 (3) SA 575 (A) 582.

such, what is required by way of recording primarily reflects policy rather than principle.

Although many changes and local variations were reflected in the detailed requirements of the law prior to the consolidating Deeds Registries Act of 1937 the essential requirement of a separate act of conveyance remained a prerequisite throughout. In modern law there has been little, if any, change to the requirement of an act of registration of transfer based upon execution of a deed before a subscribing official. By far the greater part of the considerable body of legal development has been concerned with associated matters relating to rights in land and land tenure; in particular, the organization and improvement of a co-ordinated uniform system of the recording of information relating to real rights in land based upon the deeds registries in the four provinces. For present purposes the most important matter concerns the system of the transfer of ownership under the consolidating Deeds Registries Act 47 of 1937.

2. The Deeds Registries Act of 1937

A degree of consolidation was achieved in the immediate post-Union era by the Deeds Registries Act 13 of 1918 but this legislation allowed the existing systems of the pre-Union states to continue.[128] Although the modern system of conveyancing essentially derives from the new starting-point of the 1937 Act it is not the case that the legislation broke with the past. In respect of the transfer of ownership the 1937 Act was no more than a restatement of the established principles. This important point was recognized in a Transvaal Supreme Court *dictum* of the mid-1970s:

In hierdie verband moet onthou word dat die Akteswet geen nuwigheid in die reg inge-bring het nie en ook nie, breedweg gesproke, 'n verbetering van die gemenereg is nie. Dit is hoofsaaklik net modernisering van die Nederlandse registrasie metodes en prak-tyke om by huidige behoeftes aan te pas.[129]

That the system reflects continuity with the past is shown by s. 16 of the Deeds Registries Act providing for '[h]ow real rights shall be transferred'; the relevant part of this section being as follows: 'the ownership of land may be conveyed from one person to another only by means of a deed of transfer executed or attested by the registrar'. Although this principle is stated

---

[128] Section 3(k), Act 13 of 1918 provided for registration 'under any law' and 'according to the usage and practice'.

[129] (In this context it must be remembered that the Deeds Registries Act has not brought anything new into the law and that it is also, broadly speaking, not an improvement of the common law. Primarily, it merely modernizes the Dutch registration methods and practices in order to adjust to modern requirements.) *Barclays Nasionale Bank Bpk v. Registrateur van Aktes Tvl* 1975 (4) SA 936 (T) 942 *per* Coetzee J.

subject to the qualification of any other law, the mixed bag of 'exceptions'[130] show that it is essentially true that particular derivative acquisition of land can only be on the basis of registration as provided for in the Act. But although the modern law remains faithful to its roots it is also true that the external and internal history is of limited relevance to modern practice based on the Deeds Registries Act 47 of 1937. That the legislation did not introduce any major departure from the principles—or indeed the system—of registration[131] already developed is important but the fact remains that the Act and its concomitant regulations amounted to a comprehensive code, introduced with the aim that it should entirely govern the transfer of ownership in land. To this extent the Act represents an approach to law reform not unfamiliar in Britain[132]—the consolidating and clarifying statute which puts past law and practice into a form which is intended to be a new starting-point. Any modern text on conveyancing shows the extent to which the Act and Regulations control the field.[133]

3. Nature of registration

In one important aspect the South African system of tranfer of ownership in land by registration mirrors the Roman-Dutch common law position in general. The Act provides no positive guarantee of the validity of a registered deed. The better view is that the system is one of registration of deeds rather than title: the latter term of art being generally synonymous with a system which warrants the title of a registered owner.[134]

In principle, the transferee gets no better title than the transferor can give; this, of course, is consistent with the position in respect of movable property. A possible reason for not moving towards a system of guaranteed title as *per* the register is that conveyancing in South Africa has always been based on a public act involving official control. Because the development has not entailed the difficulty of a transition from a private to an official system of conveyancing, titles have been relatively secure from the start and, in the circumstances, there has been no need for a guarantee to protect against any inherent insecurity in the system.[135] The nature and require-

---

[130] See the list in van der Merwe (n. 1), 343. See also N. J. J. Olivier, G. J. Pienaar, A. J. van der Walt, *Law of Property* (2nd edn., 1992), 9.3.3.9.

[131] As Denoon (n. 120), 465 sqq. shows, the 1937 Act had to make choices from the distinctive systems of registration which had been developed in the different registries.

[132] A good example is the Sale of Goods Act 1893 (now 1979), a comprehensive codification reflecting the existing English legal development in the area. That this Act represented a departure from the developed Scottish common law is only relevant here in that the Deeds Registries Act had to opt for one of a number of different systems of registration; see n. 131.

[133] See e.g. R. J. M. Jones, *Conveyancing in South Africa* (4th edn., 1991). My brief treatment of Registration in 85 pp. contains approx. 250 references to the Act and Regulations: Carey Miller (n. 10), xxxviii sq.

[134] See Carey Miller (n. 10), 169.   [135] Ibid. 166.

ments of the system promote security and no need has apparently been perceived for a guarantee which would give an unempeachable title but have the potential to produce results contrary to two basics principles of derivative acquisition: *nemo dat* and the requirement that the transferor must intend to pass ownership. These principles would be disregarded if good title could follow on registation regardless of whether the transferor was in a position to pass ownership, and regardless of whether the person in the position of the transferor intended to pass ownership. On the question of intention Carlisle AJ in a Natal Provincial Division decision noted that 'a mere deed of transfer of land does not of itself pass the *dominium* unless there is an intention on the part of the transferor to divest himself of the ownership and an intention on the part of the transferee to acquire it'.[136] In a modern case the vindication of immovable property was allowed because the transferor, an executrix whose appointment was void, was held to have no power to effect transfer.[137] This is an illustration of the law operating, in respect of a registered deed of transfer, in accordance with the ordinary principles of derivative acquisition.

An aspect in which the registration of deeds does not altogether fit the general principles of derivative acquisition is the requirement of a *iusta causa traditionis*. In the early case-law relating to the acquisition of land the courts emphasized the *iusta causa* requirement[138] as they did in respect of movable property.[139] The departure from the requirement of a valid underlying *causa* in relation to the transfer of ownership in movable property by delivery has been considered above. The development of a theory of acquisition based on the notion a real (*saaklike*) agreement to tranfer ownership has not been accepted as applicable to the passing of ownership in land, although in principle registration of transfer is also intention-driven. While the abstract theory of acquisition serves the useful purpose, in respect of movable property, of clarifying the basis upon which ownership passes in a context which is otherwise lacking in form or structure, there is not the same need for clarification in the system of transfer by registration of a deed of transfer. This said the registrar (or conveyancer after 1983: see below) may well want to satisfy himself that the transferor in the draft deed of transfer does in fact intend that ownership should pass to the person named as transferee. The only way in which this can be established is by an examination of the *causa*, the underlying basis from which one might infer an intention to pass ownership by the act of registration involving a conveyancer appointed by the transferor. The *causa* is the only independent source of information from which the transferor's intention can be verified.

136 *Gounder v. Saunders* 1935 NPD 219, 224 sq.
137 *Mngadi v. Ntuli* 1981 (3) SA 478 (D).
138 *Kleudgen & Co v. Trustees in Insolvent Estate of Rabie* 1880 Foord 63, 65 sq.
139 *Beyers v. McKenzie* 1880 Foord 125, 127.

The power of attorney appointing a conveyancer to effect the transfer is required in any event for the obvious purpose of establishing that the conveyancer has been empowered to act. As it must always be lodged with the draft deed it will always support the inference that the transferor intends that ownership should pass. However, although the practice of registration requires that a *causa* be identified[140] a *iusta causa*—in the sense of an underlying transaction unimpeachable from the point of view of consent—is not necessarily required. To this extent the system of transfer of ownership is the same in respect of both movable and immovable property.[141] An Appellate Division decision of 1956 is authority for the proposition that ownership will pass by registration effected pursuant to a power of attorney obtained by duress or undue influence because, regardless of the interference with the transferor's volition in these cases, it remains the case that transfer was intended; on the other hand, ownership will not pass in the case of a power of attorney signed in error by a party who believed that it was some other document. In the case in question Fagan JA saw the appropriate enquiry as follows:

Wat ons dus moet vra, is of die eiser die beweerde regshandeling willens en wetens verrig het, met die doel om die regsgevolge wat dit inhou, tot staan te bring, of nie. Indien wel, dan is dit 'n geldige handeling solang dit nie ongeldig verklaar is nie, al is dit vernietigbaar op sy aandrang omdat hy opongeoorloofde wyse daartoe oorreed is. Indien egter sy wil nie met die handeling gepaard gegaan het nie . . . het die handeling (afgesien van die effek wat estoppel *mag hê) geen regsgevolg nie.*[142]

The registration of deeds seeks to promote security of title on the basis of the common law principles governing the transfer of ownership—essentially by a system which aims to establish that the transferor is in a position to convey a right of ownership in the property concerned and intends to convey it, and that the transferee is in a position to receive the right and intends to receive it. It should be noted, however, that whereas formerly the responsibility for ensuring that the principles of derivative acquisition were complied with rested, in any particular matter, with the Registrar of Deeds, a change in 1983 shifted responsibility to the conveyancer. The basic principle of the new s. 15A of the Deeds Registries Act is that the conveyancer who signs the 'preparation certificate' accepts responsibility for the accuracy of facts stated in the deed as well as those external facts relevant for the

---

[140] See Carey Miller (n. 10), 167 sqq.

[141] See D. G Kleyn and A. Boraine, *Silberberg and Schoeman's The Law of Property* (3rd edn., 1992), 109 sqq.

[142] (What we therefore have to ask is whether or not the plaintiff has carried out the alleged legal act knowingly and intentionally, with the aim to bring about the legal consequences implicit in it. If he has, then it is a valid act as long as it is not declared invalid, even if it is, at his request, voidable because he has been induced in an unlawful manner. If, however, his act has not been supported by his will . . . the act has no legal consequence (except for the possible effect of estoppel).) *Preller v. Jordaan* 1956 (1) SA 483 (A) 496.

purposes of registration. While this change did not remove the ultimate control of the registrar over what would be registered it probably reduced the inherent security of the system by increasing the likelihood of a registration which does not comply with the requirements of the law.

4. Units of land and land tenure

An important factor in promoting the security of transactions relating to immovable property was the relatively early requirement that parcels of land be surveyed.[143] For the greater part of its modern history the South African system of land-ownership has been subject to the prerequisite that only properly surveyed units represented by an officially approved diagram could be transferred.[144] A surveyor-general's office came to be established in each deeds registry centre, the matter being dealt with in the Land Survey Act of 1927 which provided for control over the surveying of land by provincial surveyors-general subject to overall national control by a director general. The general rule that every unit of land must be represented by a separate approved survey diagram came, in modern law, to be subject to the necessary exception that in the case of a township an approved general plan showing the entire development was sufficient.[145] The effectiveness of the system in providing for the defining of a unit of land as a prerequisite to transferring ownership can probably be ascribed partly to the fact that, for almost the entire history of the development, either on account of socio-economic factors or political discrimination, only a minority of the population has had access to the individual acquisition of rights in land. In addition, of course, by far the greater part of South Africa is comprised of rural land which, in general, is made up by a relatively small number of large separate units. The circumscribed notion of the definition of a unit of land and the extent to which this was a controlling factor in the acquisition of title to land has proved to be a handicap in South Africa's political and social development. What was once seen as a system excellent for its clarity and security has come, in modern times, to be regarded as conceptually outmoded[146] and in need of reform.[147]

The history of South Africa, including its legal history, may reflect relative stability during much of the twentieth century. However, the apartheid time-warp of a substantial part of the period has meant that matters which could have been dealt with gradually now have to be addressed as matters

---

[143] See Jones (n. 133), 1 sqq.   [144] Ibid.

[145] See the definitions of 'diagram' and 'general plan' in s. 102, Deeds Registries Act 47 of 1937.

[146] There is a strong hint of this in the posthumously published article of Ben Beinart (n. 7), 30 sqq.

[147] See generally A. J. van der Walt (ed.), *Land Reform and the Future of Landownership in South Africa* (1992).

of urgency. The discriminatory legislation which, *inter alia*, controlled the acquisition of land on a racial basis[148] was only relevant to the transfer of ownership insofar as it meant that certain land could not be acquired by persons who belonged to certain racial groups. Although the Group Areas Act 36 of 1966 'permeate[d] the law of property in South Africa by using the institutions of ownership and occupation to achieve racial segregation'[149] it did not *per se* have any implications for the technical operation of the system of the transfer of ownership; rather, it simply prevented the process from occuring in certain circumstances.[150] The racial legislation has now been repealed[151] but dealing with its socio-economic legacy is likely to require radical measures in the area of land-ownership, probably including the actual process of transfer of ownership.

It has for some time been recognized that it is necessary to find a more flexible means of providing for legal rights in units of immovable property than the traditional notion of an exactly defined unit of land acquired by the relatively expensive process of official registration of a deed prepared by a conveyancer.[152]

However, it would probably be inaccurate to suggest that the efficient and organized survey, transfer, and tenure package of South African land law up to the 1990s was the product of solely domestic factors. Transfer is so important an aspect of ownership that it must necessarily reflect the attitudes and values which surround the very concept. As Professor D. P. Visser has shown, Pandectist learning influenced the South African conception of ownership and 'in the process the notion of the fundamental unrestrictedness of ownership found its way into our law'.[153] In another valuable piece of research Professors A. J. van der Walt and D. G. Kleyn have examined the history of the concept of divided ownership with a view to the pressing problems which South African law is now facing in the property area.[154]

V. THE REQUIREMENT OF PAYMENT IN SALE

The Roman law rule requiring payment or security as a prerequisite to the passing of ownership in the case of a cash transaction was well established

[148] See J. T. Schoombee, 'Group Areas Legislation: The Political Control of Ownership and Occupation of Land', 1985 *Acta Juridica* 77.

[149] Carole Lewis, 'The Modern Concept of the Ownership of Land', 1985 *Acta Juridica* 241, 251.

[150] See Carey Miller (n. 10), 191 sqq.

[151] See the Abolition of Racially Based Land Measures Act No. 108 of 1991.

[152] See Gerrit Pienaar, 'Is 'n Eenvormige Registrasiestelsel van Saaklike Regte op Onroerende Goed Moontlik?', 1990 *TSAR* 29.

[153] 'The "Absoluteness" of Ownership: The South African Common Law in Perspective', 1985 *Acta Juridica* 39, 47.

[154] '*Duplex Dominium*: the History and Significance of the Concept of Divided Ownership', in: D. P. Visser (ed.), *Essays on the History of Law* (1989), 213.

in Roman-Dutch law.[155] Although local Dutch enactments which put time-limits on the seller's right to vindicate the thing sold were common, the notion of a *recht van reclame* prevailed in the development of the law.[156]

In South Africa, as in Holland, the rule stated by the Roman-Dutch writers had no application in the context of the transfer of immovable property by registration. In respect of movable property it applied without qualification, but this was consistent with the general position that departures from the common law, reflected in legislation, did not apply.[157] This meant that South African law, in a given case, could have denied itself the benefit of access to reforms based on commercial policy more up-to-date than the Romanist common law. A *dictum* of Shippard J in an early Eastern Districts Court decision indicating strong dissatisfaction with the unpaid seller's absolute right of recovery may be relevant: 'So far as I am aware our law is at variance with every well-considered modern system of mercantile law throughout the world.'[158] In the leading case of *Laing v. South African Milling Co Ltd*[159] Juta JA noted that where nothing is said about payment the fact of delivery to the buyer does not raise a presumption of credit: '[o]n the contrary the presumption is that the sale was for cash.' The learned judge went on to imply criticism of the position of the law in South Africa: 'The rigour of the law was modified in various parts of the Netherlands by local customs, by which the owner lost his right of vindicating his property and was presumed to have given credit if he allowed a certain time to elapse.'

That the law allowed a cash seller to withold delivery pending payment[160] could have led to a development along the lines of the English doctrine of stoppage *in transitu*,[161] but plainly this doctrine was irrelevant in the context of an unpaid seller's unrestricted right to recover. What is significant in this regard is that the well developed English commercial law relating to sale did not displace the more rudimentary law of the Roman-Dutch institutional writers. That this did not occur, in spite of the familiarity of contemporary South African judges with English law, was probably due to the fact that the relevant English rules were codified in the Sale of Goods Act (1893).[162] [163]

---

[155] See Carey Miller (n. 44), 531 sq. For the Roman rule see Reinhard Zimmermann, *The Law of Obligations: Roman Foundations of the Civilian Tradition* (1990, reprint 1993), 272 sqq.

[156] See Robert Feenstra, 'Eigendomsovergang bij koop en terugvorderingsrecht van de onbetaalde verkoper: Romeins recht en Middeleeuws handelsrecht', (1987) 50 *THRHR* 127, 128.

[157] See *R v. Harrison & Dryburgh* 1922 AD 320, 330.

[158] *Daniels v. Cooper* (1880) 1 EDC 174, 186. Shippard J, later Sir Sidney Shippard, the author of this comment, was well regarded as a judge: see Roberts (n. 6), 375.

[159] 1921 AD 387, 399.   [160] See Mackeurtan (n. 74), 252.

[161] See Feenstra (n. 156), 128.   [162] But cf. Beinart (n. 7), 50.

[163] This Act applies, with minor modifications, in Scotland, where it has affected the civilian orientation of Scottish private law. See D. L. Carey Miller, *Corporeal Moveables in Scots Law* (1991), 139.

One possible reason for retaining the rule of Roman-Dutch law which so favoured the cash seller was that an important aspect of the problem was dealt with in pre-Union insolvency legislation which placed a time-limit on the unpaid seller's right to vindicate where the buyer was insolvent.[164] The approach adopted in nineteenth-century insolvency legislation is reflected in modern law:

If a person, before the sequestration of his estate, by virtue of a contract of purchase and sale which provided for the payment of the purchase price upon delivery of the property in question to the purchaser, received any movable property without paying the purchase price in full, the seller may, after the sequestration of the purchaser's estate, reclaim that property if within ten days after delivery thereof he has given notice in writing to the purchaser or to the trustee of the purchaser's insolvent estate or to the Master, that he reclaims the property.[165]

The far-reaching importance of this provision lies in the fact that a seller's right to vindicate property delivered to the buyer is most likely to be resorted to where the latter is in parlous financial circumstances; limiting the right in this situation represents a major inroad.

In the case of *Laing* one finds a clear rejection of any notion that what could be taken to have been intended by the parties should govern regardless of whether they had actually contracted on a cash or credit basis.[166] Subsequent case-law appears to have turned this approach around in commencing from the parties' intentions to determine whether the contract was for cash or on credit. This, of course, is significant in that the greater the scope for interpreting the parties' contract as a credit one, the greater the potential for limiting the scope of the rule which allows an unpaid seller to vindicate. Holmes JA stated the position in a *dictum* which has the important effect of subsuming the rule under the general enquiry as to the parties' intention regarding the passing of ownership:

This, however, is not an irrefrangible principle of law. It is basically a question of fact in each case. It depends whether the totality of the circumstances shows, by inference or otherwise, that the parties intended ownership to pass or not to pass, as the case might be.[167]

The Roman-Dutch common law rule protecting the unpaid seller for cash has, in principle, remained in full force and effect in South African law. However, by dint of insolvency legislation, it has not been allowed to operate in a manner too generous to sellers at the possible expense of creditors. This seems to reflect a compromise achieved in a manner characteristic of English law: unsystematic but effective. The modern case-law which gives

---

[164] See e.g. the Cape Ord. referred to by Juta JA in *Laing's* case 1921 AD 387, 399.
[165] Section 36(1), Insolvency Act 1936. [166] See *Laing's* case, 1921 AD 387, 402.
[167] *Eriksen Motors (Welkom) Ltd v. Protea Motors, Warrenton* 1973 (3) SA 685 (A) 694. See also *Lendalease Finance (Pty) Ltd v. Corporation de Mercadeo Agricola* 1976 (4) SA 464 (A) 489 sq.

scope for limiting the doctrine on the basis of the theory of the passing of ownership, on the other hand, reflects an approach probably more in keeping with the tendency towards logical consistency demonstrated in modern civilian systems.

VI. CONCLUSION

The body of law governing the transfer of ownership is not an area in which one would emphasize the mixed nature of the South African legal system. On the contrary, the substantive law concerned is more or less purely civilian and the English legal system has had only a peripheral role in its general influence over the processes of legal development. As the Hon. O. D. Schreiner noted in his Hamlyn lectures: '[o]ur law of property owes little to English law.'[168] It is significant that in respect of insolvency—a self-contained subject but one of considerable importance to the problem cases of title to property—the foundation legislation in the Cape, while much influenced by English law, took its provisions concerning the vesting of ownership and preferences from Roman-Dutch law.[169] Of course, an answer to this, and indeed an answer to the general question of the absence of English legal influence, is the simple point that the English and Roman-Dutch systems of property are too far apart in matters of basic grammar for influence to occur.[170]

In South Africa the focus of the law has shifted and a new phase in the history of the Roman-Dutch system in the subcontinent has commenced. The regulation of the transfer of ownership is very likely to change to meet needs which have finally become priorities. In concluding his Hamlyn lectures, Schreiner depicted the law as a growing tree 'not losing its roots but ever throwing out fresh branches'.[171] It remains to be seen how the fresh branches of property will develop but the era of Roman-Dutch law in South Africa up to the late twentieth century appears to have given a sound and versatile basis for the necessary changes. The derivative acquisition of property, with which this essay has been concerned, is well established in South African law; future development, at least in respect of land, will be partly driven by the Constitution and concerned with the restitution, redistribution and upgrading of rights.[172]

[168] *The Contribution of English Law to South African Law; and the Rule of Law in South Africa* (1967), 40.

[169] See Hahlo/Kahn (n. 23), 20 referring to J. W. Wessels, *History of Roman-Dutch Law* (1908), 397, 669 sqq.

[170] See D. L. Carey Miller, 'Systems of Property; Worlds Apart: a Miscellany of Works', 1985 *Acta Juridica* 369; but cf. Beinart (n. 7), 30 where attention is drawn to some of the similarities.

[171] Schreiner (n. 168), 105.

[172] See D. P. Visser, 'Giving Back the Country: Thoughts on Restitution in a Public Law Environment'; paper presented to the Society of Public Teachers of Law (Restitution Group) at its 1994 annual conference held at the University of East Anglia, Norwich. See also A. J. van der Walt and G. J. Pienaar, *An Introduction to the Law of Property* (1996) 405 sqq.

23: *Neighbour Law*

DEREK VAN DER MERWE

I. INTRODUCTION

The South African law of neighbours has many peculiar features which render its study both fascinating and frustrating: it consists of common law principles which are a composite mix of the rich conceptual categories of the Roman-Dutch law and the equity-based discretionary style of adjudication which is the hallmark of the English law of nuisance; it occupies an intermediate position between the law of property and the law of delict; and it represents a jurisprudence of concepts strikingly adaptable to the social realities of neighbourly existence.

This Chapter focuses specifically on that branch of the law of neighbours known as 'nuisance', and aims to reflect upon, and to explain, the adaptations made to Roman-Dutch neighbour law as a result of its application (or otherwise) in the social and economic setting of South Africa.

'Nuisance' is a term of art unknown to Roman-Dutch law; it was introduced into South Africa from English law. The law of nuisance may be defined as that branch of the law which provides the conceptual apparatus needed to adjudicate upon a situation where the occupant of fixed property, in the course of using that property, conducts himself in such a way in or on such property, as to cause actual or potential damage (or injury or discomfort) to the occupant of neighbouring or nearby fixed property. Other topics that fall within the ambit of the law of neighbours, such as the rights and duties in respect of common boundaries, trespass, encroachments, and statutory and public nuisance, are excluded from this discussion as they concern issues of no immediate relevance to the evolution of the Roman-Dutch substratum of the South African common law.

The English law of nuisance was introduced into South African law by English-trained Cape lawyers in the late nineteenth century. Sporadic reference to the English tort of 'nuisance' can be found in the case-law of the Cape Colony in the 1860s and the 1870s.[1] The landmark decision, *Holland v. Scott*,[2] dates from 1882. In this case Barry JP expressed the opinion that 'the English Law upon this subject of nuisance seems to be in every respect

---

[1] See *Berry v. Blaine* 1867 (unreported; see the reference in *Holland v. Scott* (1882) 2 EDC 307, 315, 317) and *Redelinghuis v. Silberbauer* 1874 Buch 95.
[2] (1882) 2 EDC 307.

similar to that of the Roman and Roman-Dutch law'.[3] He regarded it as similar because the maxim *prohibitne ne quis faciat in suo quod nocere possit alieno* (which was said—incorrectly—to be of Roman origin,[4] and upon which Barry JP deemed the plaintiff's case—one of noise nuisance—to be based) was quoted[5] with approval by Lord Coke in *Aldred's* case.[6] Also in 1882, in the case of *Austen Bros v. Standard Diamond Mining Co Ltd*,[7] Jones J, having given a full exposition of the Roman-Dutch *actio aquae pluviae arcendae*, found that English law had developed similar principles on the basis of the maxim *sic utere tuo ut alienum non laedas*.[8] These principles had found expression in the so-called 'rule in *Rylands v. Fletcher*'[9] and therefore 'the result in these cases [i.e. English cases referred to in *Rylands v. Fletcher*] would have been the same whether tried under the English law or in the Court of Friesland'.[10]

These decisions paved the way for a comprehensive adoption of English judicial wisdom on the topic of nuisance into South African law, in many respects effectively replacing existing Roman-Dutch law. Perhaps this was not the intention of the judges, for their judgments create the impression that they merely attempted to show that the Roman-Dutch law of neighbours was as rich a source of rules and principles applicable to the resolution of disputes between neighbours as the English law of nuisance; and that therefore parties to nuisance disputes should rather couch their arguments in the language of the Roman-Dutch law and use English law as a comparative source only.[11] Nevertheless, these judgments had the contrary effect. Judicial definitions of nuisance in English law were adopted and applied by South African judges, and English case-law was a constant and

---

[3] 312 (*per* Barry JP). See *dicta* to the same effect in the judgments of Shippard J (317) and Buchanan J (331).

[4] It is, in fact, to be found in the writings of the medieval English jurist, Sir Henry Bracton, *De Legibus et Consuetudinibus Angliae*, fol. 232. To be fair, though, one has to concede that, although the maxim will not be found *expressis verbis* in the Roman sources, the principle contained in it can be readily extracted from certain parts of the *Digest*, notably from D. 8, 5, 8, 5. Bracton, of course, was much influenced by Roman law, most notably via the glossator Azo (cf. Reinhard Zimmermann, 'Der europäische Charakter des englischen Rechts', (1993) 1 *Zeitschrift für Europäisches Privatrecht* 13 sqq. with references). It is perhaps more correct, therefore, to ascribe the maxim to Romanist inspiration.

[5] *Holland v. Scott* (n. 2), 312.

[6] (1611) 9 Co Rep 57 b (77 ER 816).   [7] (1883) 1 HCG 363.

[8] 'The principles of the Roman and Dutch law may appear undeserving of their notice to some practitioners in this court, but upon referring to the English case-law we find very much the same legal principles have been evolved out of the maxim *sic utere tuo ut alienum non laedas*' (378).

[9] The rule was formulated by Blackburn J in *Rylands v. Fletcher* (1866) LR 1 Exch 265, 279 sq.

[10] 378 sq. See too *Victoria Diamond Mining Co v. De Beer's Mining Co* (1883) 1 Buch AC 300, 308.

[11] This is indeed the view taken by T. W. Price, 'Nuisance: The *Carnarvon Municipality* Case', (1949) 66 *SALJ* 377. See too J. R. L Milton, 'The Law of Neighbours in South Africa', 1969 *Acta Juridica* 123, 140.

comprehensive source of inspiration. The maxim *sic utere tuo ut alienum non laedas*, deemed by Lord Coke in *Aldred*'s case to be synonymous with that other maxim, *prohibitne ne quis faciat in suo quod nocere possit alieno*,[12] became a popular point of departure for judges called upon to adjudicate nuisance issues.

The adoption of the English law of nuisance was not questioned until the Appellate Division was confronted with a typical nuisance matter in *Regal v. African Superslate (Pty) Ltd*,[13] in 1963. Steyn CJ criticized the ease with which the judges in *Holland v. Scott* had found a total concordance between the Roman-Dutch law of neighbours and the English law of nuisance, on the basis merely of 'two general and insufficiently defined maxims' which articulated the point of departure in neighbour law disputes in both systems. He refused to accept 'that our law [the Roman-Dutch law] had been replaced by the English law of nuisance and that our common-law sources had lost their authority'. Thus, he maintained, it was necessary first to investigate 'our own sources', even though they provided little by way of definitive answers.[14] Van Blerk JA concurred in this view[15] and Rumpff JA held similarly that 'it cannot be said that the whole of the English law of nuisance had, on the basis of some or other magic formula, become part of South African law'; at best, it could serve as a rich comparative source.[16]

The purist stance adopted by these judges did not succeed in effecting a wholesale return to the original sources in subsequent nuisance disputes. The reasons (as formulated by Hoexter JA in the *Regal* case[17]) were 'that considerations of fairness and equity . . . are the basis of the law between neighbours'; that judges, in seeking to define the limits of reasonableness where an occupant exercises the right to the use and enjoyment of his property, are primarily guided by the need to give effect to '[t]he homely phrases "give and take" and "live and let live" '[18] and that 'between neighbours a measure of tolerance is expected in the exercise of their property rights'.[19] When such common-sense considerations are uppermost in the minds of the judges one would not expect to encounter much anxious deliberation of the true pedigree of the rules and principles guiding in the decision-making process.

What then remains of the Roman-Dutch law of neighbours in modern South African law? To answer this question it is necessary, first of all, to provide a brief description of the original Dutch version of Roman-Dutch neighbour law and thereafter to present its South African variant. In so doing, an attempt will be made to detail the influence that English law (as

---

[12] Cf. *Van der Merwe v. Carnarvon Municipality* 1948 (3) SA 613 (C) 619.
[13] 1963 (1) SA 102 (A).
[14] 106E-G of the report; my translation from the Afrikaans original.   [15] 115A.
[16] 120C; my translation from the Afrikaans original.   [17] 114G.
[18] *Per* Warner AJ in *Assagay Quarries v. Hobbs* 1960 (4) SA 237 (N) 240H.
[19] *Per* Hoexter JA in an earlier judgment: *Malherbe v. Ceres Municipality* 1951 (4) SA 510 (A) 518A; my translation from the Afrikaans original.

absorbed into South African law) has exerted on this part of Roman-Dutch law and to evaluate the results of this process of reception, both wholesome and deleterious.

II. THE 'PURE' ROMAN-DUTCH LAW OF NEIGHBOURS AS TRANSPLANTED TO THE CAPE OF GOOD HOPE[20]

A recognizably separate rubric, 'neighbour law', did not exist in Roman-Dutch law. Numerous Roman forms of action were received into the Dutch customs and local laws that provided remedies for certain types of conduct by occupants of fixed property, where such conduct was actually or potentially harmful to the occupants of neighbouring property. Some of these forms of action were designed to deal only with disputes between neighbours, while others had a wider function, but were capable, at least, of *also* being applied to such disputes. The most important of the Roman forms of action, designed to deal only with neighbour disputes, were the *actio negatoria* and the *actio aquae pluviae arcendae*.

The *actio negatoria* probably most closely resembles the English action based on the tort of nuisance. With the *actio negatoria* an owner of property sought an order denying the occupant of neighbouring property the right to cause deleterious matter to escape onto or into the applicant's property, thereby unlawfully inhibiting the applicant in the enjoyment of his property. The neighbour's conduct was deemed unlawful if the *immissio* so caused was abnormal or extraordinary. Typical emissions were smoke, damp, running water, and stone chips. The Romanist jurists of medieval Europe were willing to extend the scope of the action to include conduct that did not result in the escape of some or other physical substance, such as the causing of stench and noise. The action was a real action and therefore the successful applicant could, apart from receiving a declaratory order, also claim restitution and a guarantee from the neighbour against future intrusions into the applicant's property rights. It is not clear what the Roman lawyers meant by restitution, but for the Dutch jurists it meant repair costs and compensation for damage, actual and prospective, suffered by the applicant. A successful claim for damages did not require the offending neighbour to have conducted himself in a culpable fashion: proof of unlawfulness was sufficient to found liability. In Dutch practice the Roman guarantee was replaced by a prohibitory interdict.

The *actio aquae pluviae arcendae* would typically be instituted by an

---

[20] This section is a summary of my contribution, 'Grundlagen des Nachbarrechts', in: Robert Feenstra, Reinhard Zimmermann (eds.), *Das römisch-holländische Recht: Fortschritte des Zivilrechts im 17. und 18. Jahrhundert* (1992), 597 sqq. I have therefore dispensed with citations of authority for the statements contained in this section and refer the reader to that earlier contribution, where full citations of the primary sources are provided.

owner of lower-lying rural property, to compel the occupant of higher-lying property to remove (or allow the applicant to remove) any man-made constructions on the property that changed the natural flow of rain-water to the potential or actual detriment of the lower-lying property. Damages could not be claimed with this action. The action would fail if the construction was necessary for sound agricultural practice, or if it had stood since time immemorial. If the lower-lying property was urban, the proper remedy was the *actio negatoria*.

The *interdictum quod vi aut clam* was a remedy with many facets. The Roman texts are capable of interpretations that impute to the interdict functions ranging from an interlocutory order to a delictual action for damages. Later it was often used, especially in Dutch legal practice, in conjunction with the *actio aquae pluviae arcendae*. Provided the interdict was instituted within a year of the conduct complained of, it protected any person whose interest in fixed property was infringed as a result of the violent or secretive (*vi aut clam*) conduct of another, usually when such conduct occurred on the complainant's property, but also on the neighbouring property. The qualification *vi aut clam* was widely interpreted to refer to any conduct which was against the express wishes of the complainant or about which no notice had been given to the complainant. It was a restitutory interdict: the claimant sought to have his property restored to its condition prior to the conduct complained of. If restitution was no longer possible then damages were payable, in which case the interdict functioned as a delictual action. The Roman-Dutch jurists dealt with the interdict in the context of the possessory remedies, primarily designed to protect the possession of property against interference by others. Interestingly enough, though, it continued to function as a delictual action when used in conjunction with the *actio aquae pluviae arcendae*, and it was indeed in this capacity that the interdict was most often used.

Two other Roman remedies were available to the owner of fixed property who wished to protect himself against the possibility of future damage as a result of what was going on on the neighbouring property. In terms of the *cautio damni infecti* an owner who feared damage as a result of the defective condition of a building on neighbouring property, or as a result of the potentially damaging effect of excavations, could require from his neighbour security against future damage. Such security had to be given within a stipulated period of time and was valid for a specified duration. If the security was not forthcoming within that time the claimant was placed in possession of the defective property (the so-called *missio in possessionem*) as detentor, so that he could better protect his interests. The owner of the defective property was then granted another period of time within which to provide security. If he failed to do so, the claimant was granted bonitary ownership of the property, which in time turned into quiritary ownership. If the security was given and damage did ensue then the amount stipulated could be claimed by means of an *actio damni infecti*, provided no other remedy (such as the Aquilian action) was available.

Another procedure geared towards pre-empting possible future damage was the *operis novi nuntiatio*. This was a public notice given by the owner of fixed property to the possessor of neighbouring property, asking him to desist from conducting building operations already in progress or soon to be commenced, materially altering the character of the property, for a stipulated period of time, until the lawfulness of such building activity had been judicially determined. If the neighbour continued his building operations in spite of the notice the complainant could demand demolition by means of a restitutory interdict. If the neighbour wished to continue building, he had either to provide security that he would demolish any structures later found to have been unlawfully erected, or to obtain conditional remission of the notice pending later judicial investigation.

Both the *cautio damni infecti* and the *operis novi nuntiatio* underwent significant procedural changes in Roman-Dutch law in order to conform to Dutch legal practice. Together with the *interdictum quod vi aut clam* they were dealt with under the rubric *bouw-aankondigingen*. Instead of a claim for security for imminent damage, it was sufficient for the complainant to serve a notice of protest on the neighbour, which notice constituted the sole basis for a claim for damages if such damage did in fact materialize. It also provided the basis for forcing the neighbour to abandon the ruins by way of *noxae deditio*. However, it was more common for dilapidated houses simply to be confiscated by the local authority and then sold at a public auction. The Roman *nuntiatio* was replaced by an application to a public official to serve notice on the neighbour to discontinue his building operations. This official set a date for a judicial hearing to determine the lawfulness of the building operations. The builder could be interdicted from continuing his building operations in defiance of the notice and forced to effect restitution, the effect being much the same as a spoliation order.

Apart from these remedies, general remedies for unlawful conduct, such as the Aquilian action and the *actio iniuriarum*, as well as the possessory remedies of Roman and Roman-Dutch law, were available to the occupant of fixed property, the use and enjoyment of which were being either threatened or actually interfered with as a result of activities on neighbouring property. Special remedies also existed for nuisance occasioned by trees, whether by overhanging branches, intruding root systems, or falling fruit.

It remains briefly to sketch some of the general principles informing the remedies available in Roman and Roman-Dutch law in the event of infringements arising from the concurrent use and enjoyment of neighbouring properties. These may be stated as follows:

1. The legal relationship between occupants of neighbouring properties was deemed to be a reciprocal natural obligation not to harm each other's enjoy-

ment of their respective property rights. Such obligation was neither contractual nor delictual, but was usually regarded as quasi-contractual.

2. The occupant of fixed property was free, in principle, to use and enjoy his property as he deemed fit, the only condition being that he did not thereby cause a substance to escape onto or into neighbouring property.

3. The occupant of fixed property had no cause of action if the harm he suffered from activity on neighbouring property resulted from the loss of an advantage (*lucrum*) he had hitherto enjoyed, rather than from an infringement of his right to use and enjoy his property.

4. The underlying policy of the remedies commonly employed to conceptualize and resolve neighbour disputes is to prevent recourse to self-help.

5. An occupant of fixed property was not allowed to abuse his property rights by engaging in any conduct that amounted to an ostensible exercise of his rights to the use and enjoyment of his property, if his sole or primary purpose was to cause harm to his neighbour.

III. THE ROMAN-DUTCH LAW OF NEIGHBOURS IN SOUTH AFRICA

Little remains of the various remedies available in Roman-Dutch law to settle nuisance disputes between neighbours. The only remedy which may confidently be said to have retained its vitality in South African conditions is the *actio aquae pluviae arcendae*. The other remedies were initially used, but as time wore on not only references to them but also the application of their underlying principles became more and more sporadic. This was, of course, the natural result of these remedies being absorbed into, and replaced by, a conceptual apparatus derived from English law which was considered to be better adapted to the living conditions of modern society.

1. The *actio aquae pluviae arcendae*

Since the mid-nineteenth century the *actio pluviae arcendae*, or more properly the principles informing this action, have been consistently applied in disputes between neighbours involving changes to the natural flow of rainwater. Of all the remedies available in Roman-Dutch law for the resolution of neighbour disputes, the *actio aquae pluviae arcendae* has received far more judicial attention than any other. It was first employed in a case heard by the Cape Supreme Court in 1855[21] and received judicial recognition in the Swaziland Court of Appeal as late as 1981.[22]

---

[21] Not reported until 1874: *Retief v. Louw* 1874 Buch 165.

[22] The case was not reported: see my discussion 'The Fault of Nuisance or the Nuisance of Fault: A Discussion of the Judgment of the Swaziland Court of Appeal in *M. F. Johnson v. Commonwealth Development Corporation* 6 May 1981', (1983) 16 *CILSA* 65 sqq.

As mentioned above,[23] the English law of nuisance was introduced into South African law in 1882 in the case of *Holland v. Scott*.[24] In this case, where an occupant of property sought to prohibit his neighbour, who was creating excessive noise on his premises, from causing him discomfort in the enjoyment of his property, Barry JP took the view that the underlying principle governing the dispute was the same in both Roman-Dutch neighbour law and the English law of nuisance: *prohibitne ne quis faciat in suo quod nocere possit alieno*. Five years later Lord de Villiers, sitting in the Cape Supreme Court, was at pains to point out in *Ludolph v. Wegner*[25] that the *actio aquae pluviae arcendae* was founded on the same principle:

> The action *aquae pluviae arcendae* is as old as the laws of the twelve tables and rests upon the broad principle that no one has a right to do any acts for the improvement or benefit of his own land to the prejudice of his neighbour unless there is an obligation in the nature of a servitude upon his neighbour's land to submit to such acts.

The early application of the action in South African law was therefore facilitated by its identification with the generic notion of nuisance, and as a result it was viewed, not as an archaic relic from a bygone age, but rather as a developed conceptual apparatus, well suited to dealing with a kind of nuisance frequently found in South Africa.[26] The rules formulated by the Roman and Roman-Dutch jurists were applied in a great number of South African cases. Some extension of these rules did, however, take place, and it is primarily to these extensions that the rest of this Section is devoted.

One such extension was occasioned by the Kimberley diamond diggings. The *actio aquae pluviae arcendae*, as its name indicates, was confined to instances of (potential) damage caused by surface rain-water. In a number of decisions, however, the principles underlying the action were applied to situations where underground mining activities in diamond claims had caused subterranean water to flood adjacent claims.[27] In each case the claimant succeeded on the basis of the general principle that an occupant of property may not change the natural flow of water to the detriment of adjacent, lower-lying property. No explicit reference was made to English law, but in the first of these cases, *Bank of Africa v. Levin*, Jones J referred back to his judgment in *Austen Bros v. Standard Diamond Mining Co Ltd*,[28] in which he found no material difference between the principles underlying the *actio aquae pluviae arcendae* and the English law applicable to these situa-

---

[23] Section I, above.   [24] Note 2.   [25] (1888) 6 SC 193, 197.

[26] Jones J expressed an opinion similar to that held by Lord de Villiers in *Austen Bros v. Standard Diamond Mining Co Ltd* (1883) 1 HCG 363, 378, barely two years after the decision in *Holland v. Scott* (n. 2). In the early case of *Retief v. Louw* (n. 21), Bell J took the view that the rules of the *actio* were a formulation of 'what common sense enforces'.

[27] See *Bank of Africa v. Levin* (1885) 3 HCG 245; *Reed v. De Beer's Consolidated Mines* (1892) 9 SC 333.

[28] (1883) 1 HCG 363.

tions.[29] Since English law draws no distinction between different sources of water causing a nuisance,[30] one has to conclude that it was the influence of English law that brought about this extension of the *actio* to nuisance other than that caused by rain-water.

If the *actio aquae pluviae arcendae* was brought into line with English law in this manner, this also entailed that it was immaterial for the determination of the issue of unlawfulness[31] whether a statement of claim for relief, based on the alteration of the natural flow of water on higher-lying ground, was couched in the terms of the specific action or in general nuisance terms. This is especially true in respect of nuisance arising from a change in the quantity of the water reaching the lower-lying property. On more than one occasion such disputes were decided by reference to general nuisance principles rather than the specific rules of the *actio aquae pluviae arcendae*, which could as well have been made applicable to these disputes,[32] and were in fact applied in similar cases.[33]

The expansion of this action to cases of mining-related water nuisance necessitated a concomitant expansion of its rules. In Roman and Roman-Dutch law a change in the natural flow of surface water to the detriment of a neighbouring property did not lead to liability if the change had been brought about in the course of agricultural operations (*agri colendi causa*), provided these operations were not unreasonable in the sense of causing unnecessary harm. In the *Austen Brothers* case, decided in 1883,[34] Jones J introduced into South African law the notion that the 'natural and ordinary user' of land would not give rise to liability in terms of the *actio aquae pluviae arcendae* even if, as in the case of the working of mining claims, it were to cause an accumulation of subterranean water that could overflow into an adjoining mine with harmful consequences. Liability would arise only if a construction or excavation undertaken by the defendant had the effect of '[storing] up artificially a "wild beast" which may be injurious to his neighbours'.[35] This notion he borrowed from the English case[36] in which the 'rule in *Rylands v. Fletcher*' was formulated.[37] Jones J was of the opinion that the outcome in this case would have been the same if the principles governing the *actio aquae pluviae arcendae* had been applied. Therefore, if it is

---

[29] 379.

[30] See e.g. *Sadien v. Vosper*, Krummeck's Water Court Decisions 1.

[31] But not for the determination of liability for damages: see Section IV, below.

[32] See *Van der Merwe v. Van Dyk* (1899) 17 SC 538; *Salisbury Municipality v. Jooala* 1911 AD 178; *Sadien v. Vosper* Krummeck's Water Court Decisions 1.

[33] See *Bhayroo v. Van Aswegen* 1915 TPD 195, 196–7; *Prinsloo v. Luipaardsvlei Estates and Gold Mining Co Ltd* 1933 WLD 6, 15.

[34] Above, n. 26.   [35] 380.   [36] (1868) LR 3 HL 330.

[37] Blackburn J formulated the rule thus in the Court of Exchequer Chamber (279 sq.): 'the person who for his own purposes brings on his lands and collects and keeps there anything likely to do mischief if it escapes, must keep it in at his peril and, if he does not do so, is *prima facie* answerable for all the damage which is the natural consequence of its escape.'

accepted that the notion of 'natural and ordinary user' can be equated with the agricultural exception of Roman law, Jones J had in effect expanded that exception to include mining operations and had used English legal principles to do so.[38]

It is not surprising that the notion of 'natural and ordinary user' (or 'ordinary and reasonable user') became an acceptable alternative formulation of the *agri colendi causa* exception of Roman and Roman-Dutch law.[39] The courts experienced few conceptual problems in this regard. However, as so often happens, the wide scope of this formula and its roots in English legal principles led to yet another expansion of the rules concerning the *actio aquae pluviae arcendae*, which had become the vehicle for the continued application of this notion. The question arose whether a harmful run-off of rain-water onto urban land was to be excused if the defendant could satisfy the court that the run-off had been caused by the natural and ordinary user of the land. This question was answered in the affirmative by Wessels J in 1915 in *Bhayroo v. Van Aswegen*,[40] but judges were subsequently not inclined to extend this notion beyond the confines of agricultural operations, even where the construction complained of was obviously in line with good husbandry.[41]

However, although the notion of natural and ordinary user did not gain acceptance in respect of water nuisances on urban property, the general flexibility brought about by the application of this kind of broad standard to the determination of the unlawfulness of water nuisances made it inevitable that judicial attention be given to the applicability of the basic rules governing the *actio aquae pluviae arcendae* to harmful run-offs onto urban property. In Roman-Dutch law that action lay when rain-water caused damage to rural property; the *actio negatoria* was available when rain-water caused damage to urban property.[42] Voet[43] was at pains to point out, in the introduction to his discussion of the former remedy, that both of them

[38] Mr. Justice Jones's line of argument was subsequently adopted in other disputes concerning mining operations that cause water nuisances: see *Bank of Africa v. Levin* (n. 27), esp. 248; *Reed v. De Beer's Consolidated Mines* (n. 27), esp. 342; *Levin v. Vogelstruis Estates and Gold Mining Co Ltd* 1921 WLD 66, 69. It is interesting that an English judge had, in the 1859 case of *Chasemore v. Richards* (1859) 7 HL Cas 349 (11 ER 140), based his decision (excavation of minerals on land causing a spring on adjoining land to be cut off not unlawful, but legitimate improvement of land) on a passage in the *Digest* under the title *actio aquae pluviae arcendae* (D. 39, 3, 1, 9) stating that work done with a view to the recovery of 'fruges' was not actionable. He pointed out that Paul had in another *Digest* fragment defined 'fruges' so widely that it may well have included minerals (155).

[39] See e.g. *Ludolph v. Wegner* (1888) 6 SC 193, 203; *Sadien v. Vosper* (n. 30), 7 sq.; *Labuschagne v. Steyn* 1929 OPD 20, 23; *Barklie v. Bridle* 1956 (2) SA 103 (SR) 108.

[40] 1915 TPD 195, 196.

[41] See *Barklie v. Bridle* 1956 (2) SA 103 (SR) 108D-E; *Benoni Town Council v. Meyer* 1959 (3) SA 97 (W).

[42] D. 39, 3, 1, 17–20; see too Johannes Voet, *Commentarius ad Pandectas*, 39, 3, 4.

[43] Voet (n. 42), 39, 3, 2.

proceeded from the same basic principle, namely that in the absence of a servitudal right[44] no one was allowed to do anything on his property that caused an emission of water or a similar substance onto his neighbour's property.

In the *Austen Bros* case Jones J, citing Voet, expressed the opinion that, since the same general principle governed both actions, 'the distinction between the two species of action is not of much importance'.[45] In 1976, however, this point of view was explicitly rejected by Steyn J in *Redelinghuis v. Bazzoni*.[46] The difference between the remedies was now seen to lie in the 'more onerous duty' that rested on the defendant in proceedings under the *actio negatoria*; the reason being that the defendant, as the occupant of urban property, was obliged to ensure that rain-water falling on or reaching his property was channelled harmlessly away from neighbouring property. This was based on a rule formulated by Hugo Grotius in the following terms: *Want na't gemeen recht moet yder sijn water op't sijne leiden: ofte door't sijne ter straten uit.*[47] Under the *actio aquae pluviae arcendae* no such obligation rested on the occupant of rural property.

The abovementioned difference is, however, more apparent than real. Changes to the original topographical characteristics of urban land often ensure that rain-water does not—indeed cannot—flow naturally from higher- to lower-lying land. Therefore, the duty that rests on the occupant of urban land to divert rain-water away from neighbouring property is really no different from the duty of the occupant of rural property not to cause rainwater to reach neighbouring property in a harmful fashion. Arguably, therefore, the extended application of the rules governing the *actio aquae pluviae arcendae* to urban property is neither wrong in principle nor at odds with Roman-Dutch legal wisdom on the topic.

The *actio aquae pluviae arcendae* of the Roman and Roman-Dutch law was instituted with a view to preventing the owner of neighbouring property from interfering with the natural flow of rain-water to the detriment of

[44] In the case of the *actio aquae pluviae arcendae* the servitude to which Voet refers is a 'natural servitude', said to exist in favour of higher-lying property, by which the lower-lying property was obliged to receive rain-water that flowed naturally (i.e. without human interference) from higher- to lower-lying land: see D. 39, 3, 1, 22 and 23, 2, pr. Therefore, just as the claim based on the *actio negatoria* was a denial of the neighbour's (servitudal) right to deposit water onto the plaintiff's property, so the claim based on the *actio aquae pluviae arcendae* was a denial that the neighbour's natural servitude extended as far as entitling him to cause, by artificial means, a harmful run-off of rain-water onto the plaintiff's property.

[45] (1883) 1 HCG 363, 377 sq. Jones J's opinion was cited with approval by Kuper J in *Benoni Town Council v. Meyer* (n. 41), 101C-D, who also refers to other decisions where the rules of the *actio aquae pluviae arcendae* were discussed and applied in relation to water nuisances that occurred on urban land (although the distinction between urban and rural was not explicitly discussed in these cases).

[46] 1976 (1) SA 110 (T).

[47] (For by the common law every one must lead his water on his own land, or over his own land out to the street): *Inleiding tot de Hollandsche Rechtsgeleertheyd*, 2, 34, 16.

the adjoining property, whether he had caused the interference or not. Damages could only be claimed by the plaintiff if suffered after the joinder of issue *(litis contestatio)*. Thus, the remedy served the same function as an interdict: damages were claimable from the actual perpetrator (be it the owner or some other occupant) in terms of the *interdictum quod vi aut clam* that could be instituted concurrently.[48] Although the correct position in Roman-Dutch law in this regard was set out by Solomon JA in the Appellate Division as early as 1917,[49] and even though the principles of the *actio aquae pluviae arcendae* were often applied (either expressly or tacitly) in applications for an interdict only, judges frequently found the requirements of a claim for damages to have been satisfied even when the plaintiff was only able to prove that the requirements for the *actio aquae pluviae arcendae* had been met.[50] Whereas Solomon JA, in *Benning's* case, was adamant that 'the liability of an owner of land for diverting water onto the property of another arises quite independently of negligence',[51] Centlivres JA, in an Appellate Division decision of 1943,[52] seems to have been of the opinion that proof of harmful interference with the natural flow of rain-water was in itself sufficient to establish negligence. The question of the proper basis upon which to determine liability for damage caused by a water nuisance has thus been approached in a rather haphazard fashion by the South African courts. This is due as much to the direct link to the English law of nuisance, in which proof of negligence was not deemed an essential component of a successful claim for damages, as to the inability of South African judges to appreciate the true function of the *interdictum quod vi aut clam* in conjunction with the *actio aquae pluviae arcendae* in Roman-Dutch law.

2. The *interdictum quod vi aut clam*

This interdict was used in Roman-Dutch law most frequently to complement a claim based on the *actio aquae pluviae arcendae*. Ulrich Huber[53] informs us that the Roman remedies were no longer mentioned by name in Dutch legal practice and consequently no distinction was made between the *actio* and the *interdictum* in claims in the Dutch courts based on harmful interference with the natural flow of rain-water.

[48] See discussion in Section II, above.

[49] In *Cape Town Council v. Benning* 1917 AD 315. The true Roman-Dutch position was confirmed twice in the Appellate Division by Steyn CJ: *Thormahlen v. Gouws* 1956 (4) SA 430 (A); *Van Schalkwyk v. Van der Wath* 1963 (3) SA 636 (A).

[50] See *Austen Bros v. Standard Diamond Mining Co* (n. 26); *Bank of Africa v. Levin* (n. 27); *Sadien v. Vosper* (n. 30); *De Beer v. Van der Merwe* 1922 AD 378; *Gorgen v. Williams* 1946 CPD 10.

[51] *Cape Town Council v. Benning* (n. 49), 319. Solomon JA hereby answered in the affirmative a question left open by Searle J in *Van der Merwe v. Zak River Estates* 1913 CPD 1053, 1071.

[52] *De Villiers v. Galloway* 1943 AD 439, 446.   [53] *Praelectiones Iuris Civilis*, 39, 3, 4.

In South Africa, in spite of the frequent application of the *actio aquae pluviae arcendae*, the *interdictum* has only rarely been referred to or discussed.[54] Whereas the rare appearance of the *interdictum* in Dutch practice was the result of its assimilation with the *actio*, the same does not hold true of South Africa. If the interdict simply does not feature in twentieth-century case-law[55] then the reason must be sought in its complex character. It is exceedingly difficult to deal with a remedy which is partly a spoliation order, partly a restitutory remedy, and partly a delictual remedy, and to do so within the broad sweep of general principles (as adopted from English law[56]) that govern nuisance disputes in South African law.

Whenever the interdict was considered[57] it was always within the context of damage (potential or actual) to property, caused by interferences with the natural flow of surface water. This confirmed a trend already noticeable in Roman-Dutch law to narrow down the interdict's broad field of application to water nuisances only. The difficulty experienced by judges (and academic writers) in making sense of this remedy is apparent from the confusion surrounding two issues: the nature of the interdict (and therefore also of the relief it provided) and the proper meaning to be attached to the requirement that the activity complained of had to have been conducted *vi aut clam*.

Solomon JA, in his 1917 decision in *Cape Town Council v. Benning*,[58] described the interdict as 'an action differing only in name from an ordinary action', which in the context of his discussion means a delictual action for damages. This was also the view of Steyn JA in *Thormahlen v. Gouws*,[59] decided some forty years later.[60] Steyn J, too, defined the plaintiff's statement of claim in *Redelinghuis v. Bazzoni*[61] as 'a claim residing in delict and based on the concept of nuisance or the restoration of an injustice by means of the *interdictum quod vi aut clam*'.[62] This unanimity on the delictual nature of the interdict was, however, broken in 1980, when Kumleben J, in *Wassung v. Simmons*,[63] found the interdict to be a proprietary action to claim removal of, and reparation for, whatever had infringed the applicant's

---

[54] Cf., however, C. G. van der Merwe, in a case-note on the decision of *Wassung v. Simmons* 1980 (4) SA 753 (N), in (1982) 45 *THRHR* 214, 217 sq., according to whom the principles governing the *interdictum* were tacitly applied in a number of cases in which it was found that one co-owner may order restitution against another, if the latter engaged in building operations on the property held in co-ownership, and provided the construction took place without the permission of the other co-owner.

[55] However, nuisance disputes often featured in the decisions of the higher courts during the 19th century. All of the remedies of the Roman-Dutch law of neighbours were subjected to judicial scrutiny in this period, except the *interdictum quod vi aut clam*, which was discussed for the first time only in 1917, in *Cape Town Council v. Benning* (n. 49).

[56] See the discussion Section I, above.

[57] This happened on six occasions only, four of which were at Appellate level.

[58] Above, n. 49, at 320.   [59] 1956 (4) SA 430 (A) 436.

[60] See Ulrich Huber, *Heedendaegse Rechtsgeleertheyt*, 5, 9.

[61] 1976 (1) SA 110 (T) 112A.   [62] My translation from the Afrikaans original.

[63] Above, n. 54.

proprietary right (the term 'reparation' being used in the sense of 'restoration'). It was therefore neither a compensatory action *in personam* nor an interdict proper.[64] The judge deemed it important to make these distinctions, since the application *in casu* was for removal and restoration, which he maintained could not be demanded under a delictual action or an interdict. This reasoning has been criticized,[65] and rightly so. Yet one year later, in a decision of the Swaziland Court of Appeal,[66] Dendy Young JA held the interdict to be inappropriate in a claim for damages resulting from damage caused by an interference with the natural flow of surface water on higher-lying neighbouring property. In effect, therefore, he followed Kumleben J's line of argument that the interdict was a reparatory action *in rem*, not a compensatory action *in personam*.

Even greater confusion ensued when the requirement of conduct *vi aut clam* was subjected to judicial (and academic) scrutiny. Solomon JA was adamant in the *Benning* case that 'the liability of an owner of land for diverting water on to the property of another arises quite independently of negligence',[67] a conviction shared by Steyn JA in *Thormahlen's* case.[68] Steyn JA's judgment has been taken to mean that liability for damages in terms of the interdict is strict[69] and that the *vi aut clam* requirement is no more than a practical norm to determine the unlawfulness of the conduct.[70] Others, however, have equated the requirement with culpable conduct[71] and, more specifically, with intent.[72]

The *interdictum quod vi aut clam* has had a chequered career in South Africa, due largely to the ambivalent nature of the remedy. The true Roman-Dutch position seems to have been that it was a possessory remedy in terms of which the party interfering with the applicant's proprietary rights was bound to effect restitution. Being a possessory remedy, proof of unlawful conduct was unnecessary: the establishment of violent or clandestine conduct (whether actual or constructive) was sufficient.[73] However, in

---

[64] See the discussion at 760G–763D.

[65] By C. G. van der Merwe, (1982) 45 *THRHR* 214, 218–21, who correctly points out that the *interdictum* is partly delictual in nature, as well as being restitutory, and that no distinction in principle exists between the claim for restitution based on the *interdictum* and the relief sought in terms of a restitutory interdict.

[66] *Johnson v. Commonwealth Development Corp*; see my discussion of this unreported judgment in (1983) 16 *CILSA* 65 sqq.

[67] 1917 AD 315, 319.   [68] 1956 (4) SA 430 (A) 435D–E.

[69] See J. R. L. Milton, 1969 *Acta Juridica* 123, 193; J. C. van der Walt, *Delict: Principles and Cases* (1979), § 5, fn. 29.

[70] See J. C. van der Walt, *Risiko-Aanspreeklikheid uit Onregmatige Daad* (unpublished LL D thesis, University of South Africa, 1974), 373.

[71] See R. G. McKerron, *The Law of Delict* (7th edn., 1971), 237; W. J. Vos, *Principles of South African Water Law* (2nd edn., 1978), 82; C. G. van der Merwe, (1980) 45 *THRHR* 214, 219, 221.

[72] This would seem to be the view taken by Steyn J in *Redelinghuis v. Bazzoni* (n. 61), 118G.

[73] Cf. the *dictum* of a Dutch court (as quoted by O. Schrassert in a 1620 opinion published in *Cosultatien, Advysen en Advertissementen, Gegeven ende Geschreven by Verschyden*

claims based on the harmful interference with the natural flow of surface water, the interdict in due course became assimilated with the *actio aquae pluviae arcendae*. It thereby acquired a delictual character and the requirement of unlawfulness was added to the other elements of the *actio*. A close resemblance exists between the requirement of fault and that of conduct *vi aut clam*, but an equation had never been contemplated in Roman-Dutch law. This remedy, more than any other, reflects the *sui generis* nature of the relationship between neighbours and the flexible, chameleon-like qualities required of the conceptual apparatus for what is commonly known as the 'law of nuisance'. For the interdict (or at least its underlying principles) to continue to serve a useful purpose in South African law, this *sui generis* nature must be recognized and all attempts at rigid classification abandoned.[74]

3. The *cautio damni infecti*

The notion that a neighbour was able to lodge a formal protest against the potentially harmful condition of existing structures or excavations on neighbouring property, and that such protest, or failure to protest, has legally significant consequences was recognized at an early stage in South African law. Again (as in the case of the *actio aquae pluviae arcendae*) it was the mining of South Africa's mineral riches, and the fact that the remedy could be assimilated within the broad principles governing nuisances, that provided the impetus for its acceptance. In acknowledging the existence of the principles underlying the *cautio*, Gregorowski J, in his 1887 decision in *Hyul and Webell v. Jones and Lockhardt*,[75] found them to give expression to the rights and duties existing 'when persons are brought into closer relations than usual', as in the case of neighbours and golddiggers on adjoining claims. The *cautio*, he said, was based on the maxim *sic utere tuo ut alienum non laedas*.[76] Eight years later, in *Burnett and Taylor v. De Beers Consolidated Mines Ltd*,[77] Solomon J found the following rule of the Roman-Dutch law to be 'eminently fair and reasonable':[78] a person who did not raise a protest when excavations on a higher-lying adjoining claim entailed the danger of

---

Treffelijke Rechts-Geleerden in Holland, vol. III, Cons. 97) in a claim based on the *interdictum*, to the effect that '*volgens de Rechten alle clandestine wercken sive iure sive iniuria gedaen, moeten worden voor alles gedestrueert ende gerestitueert in haren ouden staet*' (according to the laws all clandestine constructions, whether lawfully or unlawfully made, must first of all be destroyed and restored to their previous state).

[74] Similar sentiments are expressed by C. G. van der Merwe (n. 71), 219, 221.

[75] As quoted in the anonymous note, 'Miner's Obligations', (1887) 4 *Cape LJ* 155, 158.

[76] In *East London Municipality v. South African Railways and Harbours* 1951 (4) SA 466 (E), 483C-F. Reynolds J also subsumed the *cautio* under the umbrella notion of *sic utere tuo*. See too *Regal v. African Superslate (Pty) Ltd* (n. 13), 121C.

[77] (1895) 8 HCG 5.

[78] 19. Hopley J (33–5) expressed a substantially similar point of view.

a landslide damaging his diamond claim could not claim damages, if these consequences did in fact materialize. Seventy years later, in *Regal v. African Superslate (Pty) Ltd*,[79] the continued availability of the *cautio* was acknowledged in the Appellate Division, although more with regard to the substantive principles it stood for than the detail of its application in Roman-Dutch law.[80] In the opinion of Rumpff JA the *cautio* represented a compromise between the absolute right of an owner to keep a dilapidated house on his property and the right of the adjoining owner to recover damages if such a building collapsed.

Although South African judges had no difficulty in accepting the principles underlying the *cautio*, considerably less clarity existed with regard to the procedure which the plaintiff was expected to follow to obtain relief in the event of the anticipated event materializing. The basis of the defendant's liability for damage was also far from clear.

Dutch legal practice had modified the Roman procedure to the extent that the Roman *cautio* was replaced by a notice of protest served on the offending owner, which obliged the latter, in the event of the threatened damage actually coming about, either to remove the rubble and pay damages or to abandon the derelict building. The building could be abandoned either to the plaintiff (in which case a form of *noxae deditio* took place) or, more frequently, to the local magistrate, who would then sell it with the proviso that the new owner effected the necessary repairs. If the owner of the neighbouring property served no notice of protest, although he could and should have, he forfeited his claim for damages.[81]

In *Burnett and Taylor v. De Beers Consolidated Mines Ltd*[82] the plaintiffs failed in their claim for damages because the requisite notice of protest had not been given. In *Central South African Railways v. Geldenhuis Main Reef Gold Mining Co Ltd*,[83] on the other hand, a claim for damages succeeded; the plaintiff had protested to the defendant against the potentially hazardous excavations on the neighbouring property. In spite of the judge's finding that the Roman procedure of *missio in possessionem* no longer existed, it was acknowledged that, in view of the fact that the defendant had denied the hazardous nature of the excavations, the plaintiff would have been entitled to enter upon the property of the latter in order to take steps to safeguard his property. This is what the Romans had in mind with the procedure of *missio in possessionem*.[84] In *Regal v. African Superslate (Pty) Ltd*[85] Steyn CJ, whilst recognizing that the Roman procedure had fallen

---

[79] Above, n. 13.   [80] See Steyn CJ's discussion, 109H–110C.

[81] On Dutch legal practice see, *inter alia*, Johannes Voet (n. 42), 39, 2, 15; Simon van Groenewegen van der Made, *Tractatus de Legibus Abrogatis et Inusitatis in Hollandia Vicinisque Regionibus*, ad D. 39, 2; Simon van Leeuwen, *Censura Forensis*, 1, 5, 31, nn. 5 and 6; cf. Huber (n. 53), 39, 2, 4.

[82] Above, n. 77.   [83] 1907 TH 270.   [84] See D. 41, 2, 3, 23.

[85] 1963 (1) SA 102 (A) 110C.

into desuetude and had been replaced by the notice of protest, was not prepared to dismiss the possibility that this kind of procedure might still feature in South African law,[86] especially in instances where the interdict was not an appropriate remedy.[87] This reflects the uncertainty surrounding the notice of protest. The critical question, from a theoretical point of view, is: what is required for a notice of protest to be deemed a legitimate protest, eliciting legal consequences?[88]

The fact that in Dutch practice it happened more frequently that a public—rather than a private—procedure was instituted (i.e. selling the property at a public auction) suggests that a notice of protest was regarded as an unsatisfactory instrument for creating such far-reaching legal obligations.[89] This also explains the uncertainty in South African law as to the basis of liability for damages. In Roman law, if a *cautio* had been given and the damage subsequently materialized, the *actio damni infecti* lay for the amount stipulated in the *cautio*. Thus, it was an action *ex stipulatu*, not *ex delicto*.[90] Conversely, if no *cautio* had been given and the damage subsequently eventuated, no action was available in order to recover damages. At most, a restitutory interdict could be instituted so as to oblige the neighbour to remove the rubble; or the rubble could be regarded as *pro derelicto*; or, if the neighbour sought to reclaim his rubble, a *ius retentionis* was available until he was willing to give a *cautio* for present and future damage.[91] Furthermore, the *actio damni infecti* was of a subsidiary nature, which meant that it could be instituted only if the damages were not claimable in terms of another action (such as the Aquilian action).[92] In Roman-Dutch law the *cautio*, on which the *actio damni infecti* was based, had become obsolete, so the basis of liability in terms of the notice of protest had to be redefined. Simon van Leeuwen[93] likened liability under the *cautio* to noxal

[86] On the strength of the fact that certain Dutch jurists (among which he reckoned the Frisian jurist Ulrich Huber) had acknowledged the existence of the Roman procedure in exceptional circumstances.

[87] The reference is obviously to the requirement that a 'clear right' be proven before an interdict can be successfully instituted: see *Setlogelo v. Setlogelo* 1914 AD 221, 227.

[88] Wessels J, in *Central South African Railways v. Geldenhuis Main Reef Gold Mining Co Ltd* (n. 83), 292, found that a notice of protest was legitimate if it concerned activity in respect of which 'there is a contingency that damage will accrue unless the property is restored to its former state'.

[89] The *cautio* of Roman law was given at the insistence of the *praetor* (or similar official) after having been officially petitioned by the complainant: see D. 39, 2, 7 pr.

[90] See D. 39, 2, 18, 6 and 11; D. 39, 2, 37; D. 39, 2, 40, 2. The person furnishing security could escape liability if he could prove that the damage was the result of *vis maior* or *casus fortuitus*, or that it had been otherwise beyond his capacity to prohibit a dangerous construction (see D. 39, 2, 24, 2–12): this does indeed smack of delictual liability. Perhaps a correct interpretation would be to regard such instances as defences based on contractual impossibility of performance.

[91] See D. 39, 2, 6 and 7; D. 39, 2, 9 pr.

[92] See D. 39, 2, 32; D. 39, 2, 18, 9. But cf. D. 9, 2, 27, 10; D. 39, 2, 13, 10; D. 43, 15, 1, 5.

[93] Van Leeuwen (n. 81), 1, 5, 31, nn. 5 and 6.

liability, arguing that both were based on an *obligatio quasi ex delicto*, as opposed to Aquilian liability.

This theme struck a responsive chord in South Africa. In *Hyul and Webell v. Jones and Lockhardt*[94] Gregorowski J referred to Van Leeuwen when he described the claim based on the principles of the *cautio damni infecti* as a noxal action. In *Regal v. African Superslate (Pty) Ltd*,[95] however, Rumpff JA lamented the 'quasi noxal element' exhibited in Voet's discussion of the *cautio*, since it hampered the modern application of that remedy. In its modern guise it was shorn of its noxal character (for in 1927 the Appellate Division had found that noxal liability no longer existed in South African law[96]) and was therefore a claim for damages only. Since the noxal element had been removed, liability was no longer strict, but based on Aquilian principles and the maxim of *sic utere tuo ut alienum non laedas*.[97]

However, Rumpff JA was not the first to shift the focus of the remedy based on the notice of protest to fault. In *East London Municipality v. South African Railways and Harbours*[98] Reynolds J had already used the *sic utere tuo* maxim in order to explain the principles of the *cautio*. Liability of the owner, he held, referring to the well known fragment D. 39, 2, 24, 12, was founded on his intentionally or negligently causing harm to neighbouring property, by virtue of engaging in activity on his property, the potentially harmful nature of which he knew or should have known.

The assimilation of the principles of the *cautio* within the framework of Aquilian liability does not reflect Roman law (nor for that matter Roman-Dutch law). This is apparent from the fact that in Roman and Roman-Dutch law it was generally recognized that if no *cautio* (or notice of protest) was required of the owner of property from which damage might emanate, the latter was not liable to his neighbour for any damage that did materialize, not even in terms of the Aquilian action.[99] The Roman texts did not explain the ratio underlying the denial of liability. Several suggestions have been made. Some authors have speculated that mere *omissiones* did not generate liability, while others have drawn attention to the fact that an owner, in exercising his property rights, was entitled to keep constructions on his property in a state of disrepair and that his conduct was not therefore unlawful. A third suggestion was that the neighbour's failure to protest amounted to a voluntary assumption of risk. Therefore an owner's failure to prevent foreseeable harm would not be deemed wrongful in the absence of an indication from his neighbour (who after all lives and works in close and continuous proximity to the danger) that he was not prepared to put up with such a risk. This latter line of argument seems to be the most

---

[94] See 'Miner's Obligations' (n. 75), 160 sq.
[95] Above, n. 13, 121B-C.
[96] See *O'Callaghan v. Chaplin* 1927 AD 310.
[97] *Regal v. African Superslate (Pty) Ltd* (n. 13), 121B-C.
[98] Above, n. 76, 483C-G.
[99] D. 39, 2, 6; D. 39, 2, 7, 1.

acceptable explanation and was (indirectly) approved in the early cases dealing with the *cautio*.[100]

One is forced to conclude that in Roman and Roman-Dutch law the principles underlying the *cautio* were designed to reflect the special relationship
between owners of fixed property who lived and worked in close and continuous proximity to one another. This relationship clearly demanded special treatment and provided the reason why liability under the *cautio* was of
a subsidiary nature. The neighbour who suffered harm as a result of activity on his neighbour's property first had to seek redress by availing himself
of general remedies, such as the Aquilian action or a possessory interdict.
Only if this failed could he base his claim on the special steps he had taken
to prevent harm within the confines of the neighbourly relationship. Early
South African cases still reflected this point of view and the subsidiary
nature of the principles underlying the *cautio* was acknowledged as late as
1943.[101] However, later judges were unwilling to accord the *cautio*—and by
implication the relationship between neighbours—*sui generis* status and
sought rather to subsume it under accepted and generally approved notions
of delictual liability for damages.

The true basis upon which the neighbour could escape liability for damages if no *cautio* had been required was not the only feature of this remedy that continued to exercise the minds of modern jurists. A well known
set of texts in the Digest title dealing with the *cautio*, namely D. 39, 2, 24,
12, D. 39, 2, 25, and D. 39, 2, 26, was for many centuries a rich source of
controversy.[102] In these texts three situations are sketched: someone digs a
well on his land, cutting off his neighbour's subterranean supply of water;
excavation works on one property lead to the collapse of a wall on a neighbouring property; the erection of a tall building on one property cuts off
the light from a neighbouring property. There is no liability in the first case
(in spite of a *cautio* having been given by him) because the person digging
the well did not act unlawfully. The second case is different in that he did
act unlawfully As to the third situation, opinion differed. In view of the
fact that the *cautio* was a *sui generis* remedy for a *sui generis* relationship,
it is likely that Roman lawyers approached the problems in a casuistic
rather than a dogmatic manner. Circumstances such as the directness and
extent of the damage and the extent to which the excavation reflected the
ordinary use of the property, rather than strict logic, apparently determined

---

[100] See *Hyul and Webell v. Jones and Lockhardt*, (1887) 4 *Cape LJ* 155, 159 sq.; *Burnett and Taylor v. De Beers Consolidated Mines Ltd* (1895) 8 HCG 5, 18 sq. and 34. See too J. C. Macintosh, C. Norman Scoble, *Negligence in Delict* (5th edn., 1970), 215 sq.

[101] *Queenstown Municipality v. Wiehahn* 1943 EDL 134, 142.

[102] An exhaustive treatment of these texts and the theories and commentaries they elicited from Romanist authors through the centuries is provided by L. Kadirgamar, 'Lateral Support for Land and Buildings: An Aspect of Strict Liability', (1956) 82 *SALJ* 210 sqq., 357 sqq., 495 sqq., esp. 362–74, 495–505.

the way in which the judicial discretion in granting or denying liability was exercised.

The notion that someone who excavates his property and thereby causes a structure on the neighbouring property to collapse is liable for damages on the basis of a *cautio* that had previously been given was acknowledged to form part of South African law. As with other Roman-Dutch remedies for disputes between neighbours, it was assimilated with English legal notions; in this instance that of a property-owner's right of lateral support from adjoining property.[103] Once again, mining operations played a major part in the process of conceptual conflation. The seed was sown in *Hyul and Webell v. Jones and Lockhardt*[104] by Gregorowski J, who deemed the right to lateral and subjacent support to be derived from the principles underlying the *cautio*. His remarks were *obiter*, but four years later, in *London and SA Exploration Co v. Rouliot*,[105] Lord de Villiers, in a detailed statement of the law and with reference to both English and civilian authorities,[106] stated categorically that a right to lateral support for land 'exists as a natural right incident to . . . land'.[107] No reference was made to the *cautio*, although other texts from the Digest were consulted. Three years later, in *Johannesburg Board of Executors and Trust Co Ltd v. Victoria Building Co*,[108] Morice J was prepared to grant an action in respect of damage to the plaintiff's adjoining building by excavations on the defendant's property. The damage was taken to have resulted from a breach of the adjoining property-owner's right to lateral support for his building. According to Morice J this right had existed in Roman-Dutch law, and he adduced D. 39, 2, 24, 12[109] in support of this proposition. Again, no mention was made of the context within which this statement of the law had been made. The result was that the right to lateral support of land and buildings, imported from English law, was in a somewhat backhanded fashion taken to have formed part of Roman-Dutch law.[110]

An effort was made by Reynolds J in *East London Municipality v. South African Railways and Harbours*[111] to divorce the notion of a right to lateral support from D. 39, 2, 24, 12 (a text which was part and parcel of the expo-

---

[103] The concept of a right to lateral support was accepted into South African law as a matter of course in *Murtha v. Von Beek* (1882) 1 Buch AC 121.

[104] Above, n. 100, 158.   [105] (1891) 8 SC 74, 93.

[106] His Lordship did, however, remark upon the paucity of references to such a right in the civil law.

[107] The other judges in the case, Smith and Buchanan JJ, both sought recognition for a right to lateral support in the umbrella notion of *sic utere tuo*.

[108] (1894) 1 OR 43.

[109] As well as Voet (n. 42), 39, 1, 1 who, however, offers no more than a paraphrase of the *Digest* fragment.

[110] Cf. e.g. the remark made by De Villiers AJ in *Phillips v. South African Independent Order of Mechanics and Fidelity Benefit Lodge and Brice* 1916 CPD 61, 64 sq., with reference to the *Victoria Building* case, that 'the Roman-Dutch law recognizes a right of lateral support for land and buildings as between adjoining tenements'.

[111] Above, n. 76. See too *Gordon v. Durban City Council* 1955 (1) SA 634 (D) 638B.

sition concerning the *cautio damni infecti*) on the grounds that a breach of the former right gave rise to strict liability, whereas a claim for damages on the basis of the *cautio* required intentional or negligent conduct. This attempt at purification, however, was misguided, for D. 39, 2, 24, 12 does not support the contention of a fault based liability in Roman law. Also, the notion that liability for breach of the right to lateral support is strict— a notion that gained general currency in later years[112]—was obviously influenced by the very fact that the existence or otherwise of fault is not in issue in the text under consideration.

Thus, one has to conclude that according to South African law the *cautio*, in its developed form, constitutes a type of liability based on fault, but that in its undeveloped form, i.e. when applied within the context of the right to lateral support, it entails strict liability. Neither of these approaches reflects a proper appreciation of the true nature of the *cautio damni infecti*. Yet it has to be admitted that the texts in the Digest concerning the *cautio damni infecti* also do not present a very clear picture on issues such as wrongfulness and fault.

4. The *operis novi nuntiatio*

The *interdictum quod vi aut clam* may not have been particularly popular among South African judges, and the *cautio damni infecti* may have become garbled in its application over the years, but at least they can be said to form part of South African law. The *operis novi nuntiatio*, on the other hand, has hardly featured in the South African judicial landscape at all. Only one reported judgment expressly applies the principles governing this remedy and only two others apply them by implication. The last reported judgment to take cognizance of these principles dates from 1906. Thus, one may safely conclude that the process (already apparent in Roman-Dutch law) of replacing the private notification of disapproval of the commencement of building operations (on the ground of an expected nuisance) with requests for intervention to public authorities is now complete, and that the *nuntiatio* is consequently obsolete in South African law. It has been replaced by the application for an interdict or a rule *nisi*,[113] while in developed areas its usefulness has been obviated by municipal building regulations.

---

[112] See, *inter alia*, *Demont v. Akals' Investments Ltd* 1955 (2) SA 312 (D) 316F; *Foentjies v. Beukes* 1977 (4) SA 964 (C) 966G.

[113] In a number of cases the English interdict *quia timet*, available to a complainant in circumstances where damage resulting from a nuisance was imminent or would be of an irreparable nature, was applied in circumstances where the principles underlying the *nuntiatio* could properly also have been applied: see *Herrington v. Johannesburg Municipality* 1909 TH 179, 195 sq.; *Simmer and Jack Proprietary Mines Ltd v. Union Govt (Minister of Railways and Harbours)*, *Union Govt (Minister of Railways and Harbours) v. Simmer and Jack Proprietary Mines Ltd* 1915 AD 368, 382 sq.; *Rivas v. Premier (Transvaal) Diamond Mining Co Ltd* 1928 WLD 1, 13 sq.

In his 1891 decision in *Durban Trolley Co v. Durban Corporation*[114] Gallwey CJ brought the *nuntiatio* home under the general consideration that according to 'all accepted laws in any civilized community one is not obliged to wait until the nuisance arises, but may prohibit any act or work which would cause a nuisance'. Arguments that an application for a rule *nisi* to be made absolute could not succeed because it was not possible to determine whether the construction complained of would create a nuisance until the building had actually been completed were consistently rejected.[115] From this one may gather that the spoliatory nature of the *nuntiatio*, to which Johannes Voet had made reference,[116] i.e. its use to prevent perceived future wrongful conduct, had by implication been absorbed into South African law, albeit by means of other legal instruments.

Confirmation of the fact that private notification expressing disapproval of the commencement of building operations no longer has any legal effect is provided by *Psillos v. Salisbury Municipality*.[117] The Municipality had rejected the applicant's building plans. When challenged on the basis that they had no statutory competence to do so, they relied on a common law right to prevent building operations that would cause a nuisance. The court rejected this argument and found that only a court had the competence to disallow building operations on the ground that they created a nuisance.

5. The *actio negatoria*

The *actio negatoria* is the Roman-Dutch neighbour remedy which most closely resembles the English tort of nuisance. It comes as no surprise, therefore, that once English nuisance principles had been absorbed into South African law[118] nuisance disputes were dominated by English concepts, rather than those derived from the *actio negatoria*. Nevertheless, the *actio negatoria* did receive honourable mention in South African case-law.

It was recognized that this Roman-Dutch action was a remedy by which an owner of fixed property could prevent interference with his property rights by prohibiting his neighbour from engaging in a kind of activity on the defendant's property which constituted the exercise of a servitude in respect of the plaintiff's property.[119] It was also acknowledged in *Wade v. Paruk*[120] to be an action for damages and it was held that an order could

---

[114] (1891) 12 NLR 104, 111.

[115] See, apart from the *Durban Trolley Co* decision (n. 114), *Municipality of Cape Town v. Levin* (1884) 3 SC 164; *Joseph Ellis Brown v. James Bennett McCord* (1906) 27 NLR 674.

[116] Voet (n. 42), 39, 1, 7.   [117] 1936 SR 236, 241 sq.

[118] Owing to their fundamental similarity to Roman-Dutch principles regarding neighbour disputes: see Section I, above.

[119] See *Wade v. Paruk* (below, n. 120), 223 sq.; *Setlogelo v. Setlogelo* 1921 OPD 161, 164; and *Botha v. Minister of Lands* 1965 (1) SA 728 (A), 740H–741A.

[120] (1904) 25 NLR 219, 223 sq.

be made in terms of the action to prohibit similar future conduct on the part of the defendant. However, a plaintiff who had allowed the activity to carry on for a year and a day could thereafter no longer claim damages but only restitution.

In two decisions in the 1960s the question whether the *actio negatoria* still formed part of South African law was left open,[121] although the later of these seemed to incline to the view that it had become part and parcel of the developed Aquilian action. Academic writers also doubt the continued relevance of the *actio negatoria* in modern South African law; they argue that it has been replaced by the interdict or by a request for a declaration of rights.[122]

As discussed above,[123] the *actio negatoria* was employed in cases concerning water nuisances, and in these cases the similarity of the principles underlying the *actiones aquae pluviae arcendae* and *negatoria* was scrutinized. For a long time no difference was seen to exist in principle in the determination of wrongful behaviour for the purposes of either action. However, this view has been rejected in a more recent decision where it was held that the *actio negatoria* placed 'a more onerous duty' on a property-owner with respect to his management of surface run-off than was the case with the other action.[124]

The *actio negatoria* shares the same fate as most other Roman-Dutch neighbour remedies, namely that its true nature has not been properly appreciated. It was a multi-purpose remedy, as befitting an action designed primarily to settle disputes between persons who lived and worked on fixed property in close and continuous proximity to one another and who therefore enjoyed a special relationship. It served prohibitory, restitutory, and compensatory functions. As far as its compensatory function is concerned, fault did not form part of the treatment of this action by the civilian lawyers. The conclusion may therefore be drawn that liability for damages was determined independently of fault. As is the case with the *interdictum quod vi aut clam*, such an all-purpose remedy seems to have no place in modern South African law, although I believe this to be a matter of regret.

What remains, therefore, is a set of principles governing nuisances, which are English in concept and structure, but might readily be taken to give expression to the developed principles of the *actio negatoria*. No difference exists, for example, between the basis of unlawful conduct in terms of the *actio negatoria* and the following statement by Stratford JA in *Bloemfontein Town Council v. Richter*: 'The counterpart to an English statement of claim

---

[121] See *Botha v. Minister of Lands* 1965 (1) SA 728 (A), 740H–741B; *Moller v. South African Railways and Harbours* 1969 (3) SA 374 (N), 381A-B.
[122] See C. G. van der Merwe, *Sakereg* (2nd edn., 1989), 360; N. J. J. van der Merwe, P. J. J. Olivier, *Die Onregmatige Daad in die Suid-Afrikaanse Reg* (5th edn., 1985), 227 sq. These views probably correctly reflect the Roman law, but not the Roman-Dutch law.
[123] Above, Section III 1.   [124] See text following n. 46.

founded on nuisance would, in our law, be a declaration by the plaintiff that he is the owner (or occupier[125]) of land and that his legal rights of enjoyment of it are being infringed by another'.

The standards applied by South African judges to determine wrongful conduct are similar to the civilian grounds of wrongfulness. The test of ordinary and natural user of land is, according to Hoexter JA in *Malherbe v. Ceres Municipality*,[126] an expression of the notion that property owners are expected to endure inconveniences from their neighbours in the exercise of their property rights. This notion is, furthermore, substantially similar to the Roman approach to determining wrongful conduct for purposes of the *actio negatoria*.[127]

It was a generally accepted rule of the civil law that an occupier of property, whose conduct on his property would ordinarily be deemed lawful, was liable for harm caused to his neighbour if his conduct had been *ad aemulationem*, i.e. spiteful. Spite could be proved by showing that the conduct complained of held little or no advantage for the defendant whilst bringing about substantial harm for the plaintiff. This is also the position in South African nuisance law.[128]

In both Roman and Roman-Dutch law a neighbour's conduct gave rise to an *actio negatoria* only if it constituted an *immissio* onto the plaintiff's property, whereas Warner AJ in *Assagay Quarries v. Hobbs*[129] held the 'escape of deleterious matter onto a neighbour's land' not to be a prerequisite for a successful claim based on nuisance. However, there is enough evidence in the civil law that, in relationships between neighbours, the Roman and later civilian lawyers were led by pragmatic considerations rather than doctrinal blinkers and, therefore, that conduct not entailing an *immissio* could on occasion give rise to liability.

Finally, fault was not a requirement for liability in terms of the *actio negatoria*. This action, like so many of the neighbour remedies of the Roman and Roman-Dutch law, was not subject to classification as either a real or a delictual action, but served more than one purpose. In *Van der Merwe v. Carnarvon Municipality*[130] De Villiers AJP found that 'the existence of a delict has been recognized of which neither *dolus* nor *culpa* is an

[125] 1938 AD 195, 229. It is, however, true that only an owner may institute the *actio negatoria*: *Setlogelo v. Setlogelo* (n. 119).
[126] Above, n. 19, 518A.
[127] See D. 8, 2, 19 pr.; D. 8, 2, 13 pr.; D. 8, 5, 8, 5 and 6. See too M. de Villiers, 'Nuisances in Roman Law', (1897) 13 *LQR* 387, 389.
[128] See e.g. *Kirsh v. Pincus* 1927 TPD 199; *Millward v. Glaser* 1949 (4) SA 931 (A) 942; *Regal v. African Superslate (Pty) Ltd* (n. 13), 107G–108C. In *Vanston v. Frost* 1930 NLR 121, however, the erection of a 'spite fence' was not deemed unlawful, since '[t]he respondent had a perfect right to erect the fence upon his land ... [and] the existence of a bad motive will not convert his legal act into a civil wrong for which reparation may be claimed', a point of view approved in the Appellate Division: see *Tsose v. Minister of Justice* 1951 (3) SA 10 (A) 17H.
[129] 1960 (4) SA 237 (N).   [130] Above, n. 12, 619.

element', a finding generally approved and followed in South African law.[131] Also expressive of the multi-purpose nature of the *actio negatoria* is the order by Young J in *Cosmos (Pvt) Ltd v. Phillipson*,[132] to the effect that a plaintiff whose drainage system had been damaged by the roots of trees growing on the defendant's property and who was unable to prove fault on the part of the defendant was responsible for the repair costs, but that the defendant had to contribute half of the costs of exposing the drain for inspection. This was based on the following consideration:[133]

A claim for compensation can arise from sources other than contract and delict. In order to secure fair dealing between persons brought into contact with one another, it is often necessary for the law to make a reparation ... In my judgement, modern conditions require the exercise of a wide discretion in the adjustment of neighbour relationships ...

Interestingly, this statement could have been made by a civilian describing the function of the *actio negatoria* in neighbour disputes.

IV. CONCLUSION

Only the *actio aquae pluviae arcendae* can truly be said not only to have survived the ravages of time, but to have undergone constructive adaptation. The other remedies discussed in this paper have to a larger or lesser degree become absorbed in a conceptual apparatus which has deprived them of much of their vitality. This development, however, was foreshadowed in certain instances by Dutch legal practice.

The question, posed at the outset, as to what remains of the Roman-Dutch law of neighbours can be answered on different levels. On one level the answer must surely be that (with the exception of the *actio aquae pluviae arcendae*) little remains of the forms of action moulded and discussed by generations of jurists in Rome and in Holland. This is indeed how it should be. The forms of action should not rule us from the grave, and modern concepts of substantive justice should provide guidance in the determination of the particular legal style in which a claim has to be couched.

However, on another level, much remains of the ancient remedies, although they have been filtered through a conceptual mould of English origin and have thus become distorted, and apparently largely useless. Yet they provide confirmation of a point often made in the course of this discussion: a special relationship exists between two persons who occupy premises adjacent to one another for an extended period of time and who are therefore

---

[131] In the most recent nuisance case, *Flax v. Murphy* 1991 (4) SA 58 (W) 64D-E, Marais J regarded liability for damages caused by a nuisance to be strict. Such recognition of strict liability for nuisance has been the subject of much controversy in academic writings.

[132] 1968 (3) SA 121 (R).   [133] 129C–130A.

forced into some intimacy in their living and working conditions. Such a relationship demands a special approach, inspired by pragmatic rather than dogmatic considerations. The Roman remedies provide just that: they are couched in very broad terms, providing in many instances for relief of a discretionary nature, of variable content, and of a multifunctional character. Notions of fault did not greatly exercise the minds of the civilian jurists, simply because it would be possible to construe culpable conduct on the basis of virtually any harmful interference with a neighbour's property rights. Of far greater importance for the civilian jurists was the need to forestall undue interference with property rights or, if such interference had already materialized, to provide the means of its removal. These concerns are not absent from the South African law of nuisance, yet the modern approach has tended to focus on achieving a form of conceptual purity which the civilian lawyers would have shunned. South African law would clearly benefit if it were to take guidance from the spirit rather than the letter of the civilian sources—or indeed from a conceptual superstructure imposed upon these sources.

24: *Servitudes*

M. J. DE WAAL*

I. INTRODUCTION

The author has demonstrated, in a previous publication; that the Roman-Dutch law of servitudes is firmly based on Roman law.[1] At the same time, however, it has been argued that this branch of the law shows some remarkably progressive features as a result of the work of the Roman-Dutch authors of the seventeenth and eighteenth centuries. The fruits of their work lie, on a theoretical level, in the establishment of a definition of the concept of a servitude and, on a more practical level, in matters such as the classification of tenements into rural and urban, the treatment of the requirements for the establishment of praedial servitudes, and in a pragmatic approach towards the creation of new types of personal servitudes.[2]

In this Chapter, as throughout the present volume, the focus should shift from the 'pure' Roman-Dutch law of servitudes to the development of this branch of the law after its importation into South Africa. In order to trace this development certain elements within the theoretical framework of the law of servitudes are used as examples; this necessarily involves selection. Due to restrictions of space, to attempt a comprehensive overview would inevitably result in superficiality. The elements chosen are those of which exegesis provides an insight into the historical development of the institution as a whole. In the analysis of each element one should remain mindful of the questions forming the focal point of this volume: how has this particular institution been preserved, changed, or elaborated upon since its origin in 'pure' Roman-Dutch law?

In this exercise the following core elements of the law of servitudes are analysed: the definition of the concept of a servitude and the classification of servitudes; the requirements for the establishment of praedial servitudes; the contents and the development of specific rural and urban praedial

* The author wishes to record, with gratitude, the financial assistance of the Alexander von Humboldt-Stiftung (Bonn) and the Centre for Science Development of the Human Sciences Research Council (Pretoria) which enabled him to undertake part of the research and writing of this Chapter while on sabbatical leave at the University of Regensburg, Germany, during 1994.

[1] M. J. de Waal, Servitudes, in: Robert Feenstra, Reinhard Zimmermann (eds.), *Das römisch-holländische Recht: Fortschritte des Zivilrechts im 17. und 18. Jahrhundert* (1992), 567 sqq.

[2] For a summary see De Waal (n. 1), 594–5.

servitudes; and lastly, certain aspects concerning personal servitudes (with the emphasis on usufruct, the most important personal servitude).

In the analysis of each of these core elements the Roman-Dutch law is, as a point of departure, briefly sketched. Against this background further development in South African law is then traced, with the emphasis on the specific questions posed above. The influence, if any, of English law on these elements is also monitored.

This Chapter will, in the broadest sense, be a development of the exposition in the author's previous work.[3] However, not all the themes touched upon in that volume are revisited, and new themes are introduced.

II. CONCEPT AND DEFINITION

In contrast to Roman law, where no formal attempt was made to define the concept of a servitude,[4] the Roman-Dutch authors did engage in such efforts.[5] Prominent in many of these definitions is the emphasis on the advantage derived by the holder of the servitude as opposed to the prejudice suffered by the servient owner. Voet,[6] for example, saw servitudes as '. . . rights established in favour of one person over the property of another, by which a property brings to someone other than the owner an advantage which is contrary to the nature of ownership'.[7] This echoes those texts in which servitudes are described as a *pars dominii*.[8] Another feature of the definition of a servitude in Roman-Dutch law is that the essential characteristic of a servitude as a limited real right *(ius in re aliena)* can only be deduced from it by implication (if at all).[9]

These two features are also found in the earliest attempts to define the concept of a servitude in South African law. Maasdorp, in one of the early works on servitudes, gives the following definition: 'A servitude may be defined as a detachment of some of the rights of ownership from the ownership of some particular property and the conferring of them upon a person other than the owner, or the attachment of them to the ownership of another property.'[10]

This way of defining a servitude in fact goes back to many of the older

---

[3] For a summary see De Waal (n. 1), 567 sqq.   [4] Ibid. 568 sq.

[5] Ibid. 569 sq.

[6] Johannes Voet, *Commentarius ad Pandectas*, 7, 1, 1.

[7] Trans. by Percival Gane, *The Selective Voet* (1955 sqq.). See also Hugo Grotius, *Inleiding tot de Hollandsche Rechtsgeleertheyd*, 2, 33, 4.

[8] De Waal (n. 1), 569.

[9] As pointed out elsewhere (De Waal (n. 1), 570, fn. 19), authors such as Gerard Noodt and Arnoldus Vinnius do, however, stress this aspect in their respective definitions.

[10] C. G. Hall (ed.), *Maasdorp's Institutes of South African Law*, vol. II (7th edn., 1948), 166. See also C. G. Hall, E. A. Kellaway, *Servitudes* (1942), 1; R. W. Lee, *An Introduction to Roman-Dutch Law* (3rd edn., 1931), 170.

court decisions. In *In re Bennett and Green and the Bank of Africa Ltd*[11] for example, it is stated, that 'whenever a servitude is created there is a parting with a share in the *dominium* or ownership of the servient tenement, the value of which is proportionately diminished'. The Roman-Dutch view of a servitude as a *pars dominii* is reflected in *Maclear Divisional Council v. Norton*[12] where a servitude is described as 'a carving out of a part of the dominium . . .'[13]

These early definitions, reflecting the still unsophisticated attempts of the Roman-Dutch authors, are unsatisfactory from a theoretical point of view. First, they approach the problem from the perspective that *dominium*, or ownership, is a 'bundle of rights', of which one is detached and transferred to the holder of the servitude.[14] The tendency in modern South African law is rather to view ownership as a single right from which a variety of powers (*bevoegdhede*) flow. The granting of a servitude should then, more correctly, be seen as resulting in a diminution of one or more of these powers of ownership.[15] Secondly, these definitions do not generally reflect the fact, essential for a clear theoretical understanding of the institution, that a servitude is a limited real right (*ius in re aliena*).

Later definitions of the concept of a servitude are more satisfying on both counts. An example of a definition which more accurately reflects current thinking can be found in *Lorentz v. Melle*:

A servitude is, of course, a right belonging to one person in the property of another entitling the former either to exercise some right or benefit in the property or to prohibit the latter from exercising one or other of his normal rights of ownership . . . It is an example of a *ius in re aliena*; it diminishes an owner's *dominium* in a thing.[16]

The definitions provided by modern authors more or less follow this pattern.[17]

III. CLASSIFICATION

Although there is considerable variation in the terminology employed by the Roman-Dutch authors to indicate both the important differences between, and the common characteristics of, praedial and personal servitudes, this is

---

[11] (1901) 22 NLR 404, 414.   [12] 1918 CPD 16, 23.

[13] See also *Consistory of Steytlerville v. Bosman* (1893) 10 SC 67, 69; *Willoughby's Consolidated Co Ltd v. Copthall Stores Ltd* 1913 AD 267, 281.

[14] C. G. van der Merwe, *Sakereg* (2nd edn., 1989), 458.   [15] Ibid.

[16] 1978 (3) SA 1044 (T) 1049. In my view, however, the phrase 'normal rights of ownership' should be replaced by 'normal powers of ownership'.

[17] See D. G. Kleyn, A. Boraine, *Silberg and Schoeman's The Law of Property* (3rd edn., 1992), 367; N. J. J. Olivier, G. J. Pienaar, A. J. van der Walt, *Sakereg: Studentehandboek*, 2nd edn., 1992, 245; Van der Merwe (n. 14), 458; C. G. van der Merwe, M. J. de Waal, 'Servitudes', in: W. A. Joubert (ed.), *The Law of South Africa*, vol. 25 (1991), § 36.

nevertheless a conceptual division which is fully accepted by these authors.[18] Notwithstanding these differences in terminology, there is no real disagreement as to the basic difference between praedial and personal servitudes. A praedial servitude is a right which a person holds in his capacity as owner of a particular piece of land (the dominant tenement or *praedium dominans*) over a piece of land belonging to another person (the servient tenement or *praedium serviens*).[19] The servitude links these two tenements and in principle is therefore perpetual. A personal servitude, on the other hand, is a right held by a particular person and by which a burden is imposed upon another's land or movable property.[20] The servitude is constituted in favour of the holder in his personal capacity and not, as is the case with a praedial servitude, in his capacity as owner of land.

This basic classification, and also the general terminology expressing it, has become firmly entrenched in South African law.[21] South African law also follows Roman-Dutch law as far as the essential subdivisions within each category are concerned. Thus, praedial servitudes are still subdivided into rural and urban praedial servitudes.[22] Concerning this subdivision, South African law follows the majority of Roman-Dutch authors in viewing the nature and exploitation of the dominant tenement as the determining factor.[23] According to this view, which is certainly the most satisfactory one, rural praedial servitudes are established in favour of tenements exploited for agricultural purposes. Urban praedial servitudes, on the other hand, are established in favour of tenements used for residential, commercial, or industrial purposes.

As regards personal servitudes, usufruct (*ususfructus*), use (*usus*), and habitation or dwelling (*habitatio*) are, as in Roman-Dutch law,[24] treated as the main types.[25] This does not mean, however, that South African law adheres to a *numerus clausus* of personal servitudes. As illustrated below,[26] South African law in this regard follows the progressive example set by the Roman-Dutch authors[27] in acknowledging that new types of personal servitudes may be created if the need arises.

---

[18] See De Waal (n. 1), 571 and the authorities cited there.   [19] Ibid.   [20] Ibid.

[21] See generally Kleyn/Boraine (n. 17), 368 sq.; Olivier/Pienaar/Van der Walt (n. 17), 245; Van der Merwe (n. 14), 459; Van der Merwe/De Waal (n. 17), § 37.

[22] Kleyn/Boraine (n. 17), 369; Olivier/Pienaar/Van der Walt (n. 17), 250; Van der Merwe (n. 14), 479 sq.; Van der Merwe/De Waal (n. 17), § 45.

[23] See the authorities cited above, n. 22. For a discussion of the position in Roman-Dutch law see De Waal (n. 1), 572 sq.

[24] De Waal (n. 1), 589 sq.

[25] See e.g. the discussions by Kleyn/Boraine (n. 17), 385–9; Olivier/Pienaar/Van der Walt (n. 17), 251–5; Van der Merwe (n. 14), 506–25 (who also discusses the personal servitude of service (*opera*)); Van der Merwe/De Waal (n. 17), §§ 64–88. By focusing on these main types of personal servitudes the modern authors follow the example of earlier authors such as Hall/Kellaway (n. 10), 147 sqq.; Lee (n. 10), 181–6; Maasdorp (n. 10), 207 sqq.

[26] Below, Section V. 1.   [27] De Waal (n. 1), 590.

The elements identified for discussion[28] are next analysed within the classification set out above.

IV. PRAEDIAL SERVITUDES

1. Requirements for the establishment of praedial servitudes

There is clear authority that, as in the case of personal servitudes,[29] there was no *numerus clausus* of praedial servitudes in Roman-Dutch law.[30] The fact that certain standard examples of praedial servitudes are discussed in the sources does not imply that new types could not be created. The only qualification was that certain basic requirements had to be met before a praedial servitude could be added to the list of those already recognized. These requirements were examined haphazardly by the Roman-Dutch authors, with no apparent attempt at systematization of any kind.

In the author's previous publication these requirements received special attention as a way of illustrating the Roman-Dutch jurists' treatment of an issue which has received extensive scrutiny throughout the ages of European legal history.[31] In the present Chapter the emphasis is on whether these requirements, as received into and modified in Roman-Dutch law, have been further developed and refined by the South African courts.

In the discussion which follows the fundamental *ratio* for these requirements should be kept in mind: to prevent ownership of land from becoming excessively encumbered by a proliferation of praedial servitudes. At the same time, the requirements should remain flexible enough to allow for the creation of new praedial servitudes when the needs of a developing society dictate.[32]

(a) Two tenements

A fundamental requirement for the establishment of a praedial servitude is the existence of both a dominant tenement (*praedium dominans*) and a servient tenement (*praedium serviens*) belonging to different owners. The importance of this requirement was clearly articulated in Roman-Dutch law.[33] In South African law it also appears as the constant element in cases where the establishment of praedial servitudes was in issue.[34] As it has

---

[28] Above, Section 1.   [29] Above, Section III and below, Section V. 1.
[30] Voet (n. 6), 8, 3, 12. See also De Waal (n. 1), 573 sq.   [31] De Waal (n. 1), 573–86.
[32] For a full discussion of these requirements and the considerations on which they are based see M. J. de Waal, *Die Vereistes vir die Vestiging van Grondserwitute in die Suid-Afrikaanse Reg* (unpublished LL D thesis, University of Stellenbosch, 1989).
[33] De Waal (n. 1), 574 and the authorities cited there.
[34] Many court decisions can be cited where the requirement of 2 tenements was mentioned directly or indirectly, e.g. *Saunders v. Executrix of Hunt* (1840) 2 Menz 295, 295 sq.; *Van*

posed no problems and was never doubted, it requires no further comment here.

(b) Vicinity or locality (vicinitas)

Inasmuch as *vicinitas* is an elastic concept with various possible nuances, its application as a requirement for the establishment of praedial servitudes is open to different interpretations.[35] *Stricto sensu* it could mean that the dominant and servient tenements must have a common border. Alternatively, it could merely imply that the two tenements have to be situated in the same neighbourhood or at least within a reasonable distance from each other.

As illustrated elsewhere,[36] traces of both the narrow and the more liberal interpretation can be found in (classical) Roman-Dutch law. Moreover, authors supporting the liberal interpretation apparently did not regard *vicinitas* as an independent requirement, but as a factor which had to be taken into consideration when the more fundamental issue of utility (*utilitas*)[37] was examined.[38] In other words, the distance between the dominant and servient tenements was merely one of the factors to be examined when the question was asked whether a particular servitude could be of benefit to the dominant tenement. The question arises whether this view, which was also advanced by the pandectists[39] and is today accepted in German law,[40] has been received into South African law.

Analysis of the relevant South African court decisions creates the distinct impression that the *vicinitas* requirement has never been given top priority in the establishment and exercise of praedial servitudes. This can be ascribed partly to the fact that the individual circumstances of many cases were such that the requirement was not in issue:[41] the dominant and servient tene-

Niekerk v. Wimble (1878) 5 Buch 190, 192; *Otto v. Pretorius* (1891) 4 SAR 42, 44; *Baehnisch v. Estate Odendaal* (1909) 26 SC 152, 159 sq.; *Federal Timber Co v. Celliers* 1909 TS 909, 911 sq.; *Hough v. Collett* 1911 CPD 389, 392 sq.; *Ex parte Geldenhuys* 1926 OPD 155, 163; *Van der Vlugt v. Salvation Army Property Co* 1932 CPD 56, 59; *Ex parte Jerrard* 1934 WLD 87, 93 sq.; *Rabie v. De Wit* 1946 CPD 346, 350; *Van den Berg v. Dart* 1949 (2) SA 884 (T) 885; *Molotlegi v. Brummerhoff* 1955 (1) SA 592 (T) 594; *Jonordon Investment (Pty) Ltd v. De Aar Drankwinkel (Edms) Bpk* 1969 (2) SA 117 (C) 123, 126; *Hollmann v. Estate Latre* 1970 (3) SA 638 (A) 644 sq.; *Lorentz v. Melle* 1978 (3) SA 1044 (T) 1049; *Penny v. Brentwood Gardens Body Corporate* 1983 (1) SA 487 (C) 489; *Brink v. Van Niekerk* 1986 (3) SA 428 (T) 431; *Malan v. Ardconnel Investments (Pty) Ltd* 1988 (2) SA 12 (A) 37; *Erlax Properties (Pty) Ltd v. Registrar of Deeds* 1992 (1) SA 879 (A) 885. As far as academic authors are concerned, see e.g. H. J. Delport, N. J. J. Olivier, *Sakereg: Vonnisbundel* (2nd edn., 1985), 546 sq.; Olivier/Pienaar/Van der Walt (n. 17), 249; Van der Merwe (n. 14), 468; Van der Merwe/De Waal (n. 17), § 42.

[35] De Waal (n. 1), 574.   [36] Ibid. 574–7.

[37] As to the requirement of utility see below, Section IV. 1. (d).

[38] Voet (n. 6), 8, 4, 19. See also Ulrich Huber, *Heedendaegse Rechtsgeleertheyt*, 2, 43, 17; Vinnius (n. 9), 2, 3.

[39] See De Waal (n. 1), 577 and authorities there cited.   [40] Ibid.

[41] See e.g. *Laubscher v. Reve* (1866) 1 Roscoe 408 (a servitude of watering cattle); *Wolvaardt v. Pienaar* (1884) 1 SAR 162 (a servitude to ensure a free flow of water); *De Klerk v. Niehaus* (1897) 14 SC 302 (a servitude of leading water); *City Deep v. McCalgan* 1924 WLD 276 (a servitude of way); *Mocke v. Beaufort West Municipality* 1939 CPD 135 (a servitude of

ments were in any event contiguous. Yet there are also several decisions where the requirement was not considered, even though the tenements did not in fact have a common border.[42] Unfortunately no useful deductions can be drawn from these cases.

However, several early court decisions indicate that the pragmatic approach of some Roman-Dutch authors, according to which the *vicinitas* requirement should be judged within the wider context of the *utilitas* requirement, did indeed acquire a foothold in South African law. The earliest of these decision is probably *Hawkins v. Munnik*.[43] The tenements of the plaintiff and the defendant were separated from each other by a narrow river. The plaintiff approached the Court for an order that a bridge be erected over the river, connecting the two tenements. The purpose of this bridge would have been to allow the plaintiff and his labourers to reach the defendant's tenement in order to exercise a servitude of drawing water (*servitus aquaehaustus*) from a fountain on the tenement. In the course of its judgment the Court declared: 'when the dominant and servient tenements are on different sides of a river forming the boundary between them, the said servitude implies a right to a footbridge over the river'.[44] The fact that the two tenements were not directly contiguous did not, therefore, prevent the establishment and exercise of a servitude. This decision is a modern example of a situation discussed in the Digest and solved in the same pragmatic manner.[45]

This line of reasoning was followed in several later decisions. In *Briers v. Wilson*,[46] for example, it was applied in a situation where the possible acquisition of a servitude of way by means of prescription was complicated by the presence of a piece of land between the 'dominant' and 'servient' tenements. The Court was referred, *inter alia*, to the flexible approach of Voet[47] in terms of which the mere presence of such a tenement does not prevent the establishment of a servitude, provided that a further servitude can also be established over the latter. As this was not possible *in casu*, the Court concluded that no servitude had been acquired through prescription. Of importance, however, is the fact that the Court ultimately based its decision on the *utilitas* rather than the *vicinitas* requirement: an indication that the crucial link between these two requirements, already evident in Roman-Dutch law, was also recognized by the Court.[48]

trekpath); *Penny v. Brentwood Gardens Body Corporate* 1983 (n. 34), (a servitude of way); *Brink v. Van Niekerk* (n. 34), (a servitude of way).

[42] Examples of cases in this category include *Heidelberg Municipality v. Uys* (1898) 15 SC 156; *Kempenaars v. Jonker, Van der Berg and Havenga* (1898) 5 OR 223; *Aberdeen Municipality v. Aberdeen Dutch Reformed Church* (1905) 22 SC 474; *Volschenk v. Van den Berg* 1917 TPD 321; *Badenhorst v. Joubert* 1920 TPD 100.

[43] (1830) 1 Menz 465.   [44] 466.   [45] Paul. D. 8, 3, 38.
[46] 1952 (3) SA 423 (C).   [47] Voet (n. 6), 8, 4, 19.
[48] For further examples of this approach see *Martins v. De Waal* 1963 (3) SA 787 (T); *Bisschop v. Stafford* 1974 (3) SA 1 (A).

The courts are apparently willing to go even further and to discard the *vicinitas* requirement where it serves no practical purpose. This is evident in the sphere of 'restrictive conditions', a new kind of servitudal right developed in South African law according to guidelines taken, *inter alia*, from English law.[49] Restrictive conditions are, basically, conditions registered against the title deeds of all tenements sold in terms of certain township development schemes. Their purpose is usually to preserve a specific character of that township, and they can be construed, depending on the facts of each specific case, as either personal or praedial servitudes.[50] Where the conditions are construed as praedial servitudes they operate as negative servitudes[51] in favour of, or against, all tenements in the particular scheme.

Except for the qualification that the tenements must form part of the same development scheme,[52] the *vicinitas* requirement plays no role in the establishment of restrictive conditions which are construed as praedial servitudes. A good illustration is provided by the decision in *Cannon v. Picadilly Mansions (Pty) Ltd.*[53] Under restrictive conditions registered against the title deeds of tenements in a specific township, only private residences could be erected on the tenements. An owner of one tenement, who wanted to erect a block of flats, argued that he was not bound by the conditions since that specific area of the township had already lost its residential character. The Court rejected this argument as being too narrow an interpretation of the concept of neighbourhood: 'the area governed by the . . . scheme is *ex hypothesi* one and indivisible and every purchaser within the area comes under the scheme . . . it is difficult to see upon what principles a judge can break up the area and release a portion of it'.[54]

The restrictive conditions could therefore be enforced against any owner in the township, regardless of the location of the respective tenements in relation to each other: 'But even if the applicant's lots were situated *at the other extremity* of [the township], he would in my judgment have none the less been entitled to urge an objection to any further departure from [the condition in question]'.[55]

The approach towards the *vicinitas* requirement in the sphere of restrictive conditions is illustrated even more clearly in the following *dictum* from the decision in *Gassner and Blumber v. Baker*: 'The lots need not be contiguous. They need not have anything to do with each other.'[56]

---

[49] See below, Section IV. 2. (b) for a discussion of restrictive conditions and of the role of English law concerning their reception into and their further development in South African law.

[50] See below, Section IV. 2. (b).

[51] In other words: the owner of each tenement is *prohibited* from performing a specific action: e.g. using certain building materials to erect more than one building, or trading in liquor: see below, Section IV. 1. (d).

[52] De Waal (n. 32), 60.

[53] 1934 WLD 187.

[54] 191 sq.

[55] 193. Emphasis added.

[56] 1931 WLD 23, 26.

(c) Permanent basis (perpetua causa)

This requirement, as originally conceived in Roman law,[57] implies that the servient tenement must be capable of continuously fulfilling the needs of the dominant tenement. If applied literally, this formulation of the requirement would severely restrict the establishment of praedial servitudes. This may explain why the German pandectists never adhered to such a strict interpretation of the *perpetua causa* requirement. They saw it, like *vicinitas*, as an inevitable corollary of the requirement of utility (*utilitas*).[58] In terms of the latter, a praedial servitude may not be aimed solely at the casual or temporary needs of a specific dominant owner, but must reflect the needs of all successive owners of the dominant tenement who use the tenement in accordance with its nature and characteristics.[59] This, according to the pandectists, necessarily implies that the nature and qualities of the servient tenement, from which the benefit is derived, cannot be merely transient or incidental.[60]

There are few traces of this sophisticated approach towards the *perpetua causa* requirement among those Roman-Dutch authors who deal with the issue in any detail. Thus, the treatments of Voet[61] and Huber[62] remain within the strict confines of the Roman texts. Also, the examples used by these authors go no further than the stereotyped problems concerning the servitudes of leading and drawing water (*aquaeductus* and *aquaehaustus*).[63] Authors such as Groenewegen[64] and Van der Keessel,[65] on the other hand, dealt with the requirement in a much more indirect way and advanced a less dogmatic approach than Voet and Huber. Yet it is evident that the important connection between the requirements of *perpetua causa* and *utilitas* was never fully appreciated, at least never articulated, by the Roman-Dutch jurists.[66]

As far as South African law is concerned, the *perpetua causa* requirement is referred to only in passing by academic writers[67] and not a single court decision could be found in which it was specifically analysed. Thus, it is not

---

[57] Paul. D. 8, 2, 28.   [58] De Waal (n. 1), 578 and authorities there cited.
[59] As to the requirement of utility see below, Section IV. 1. (d).
[60] De Waal (n. 1), 578.   [61] Voet (n. 6), 8, 4, 17.
[62] Huber (n. 38), 2, 43, 7 and 8. Huber's motivation is, however, more refined than that of Voet: an indication that he might have seen a connection between the requirements of *perpetua causa* and *utilitas*.
[63] De Waal (n. 1), 579.
[64] Simon van Groenewegen van der Made, *Tractatus de legibus abrogatis et inusitatis in Hollandia vicinisque regionibus* (ed. and trans. by Ben Beinart, 4 vols., 1974 sqq.), ad D. 8, 2, 28.
[65] Dionysius Godefridus van der Keessel, *Praelectiones iuris hodierni ad Hugonis Grotii introductionem ad iurisprudentiam Hollandicam* (ed. by P. van Warmelo, L. I. Coertze, H. L. Gonin, 1964), 2, 35, 14.
[66] De Waal (n. 1), 580.
[67] See e.g. Delport/Olivier (n. 34), 548 sq.; Van der Merwe (n. 14), 471.

easy to determine the exact place and status of this requirement in the establishment of praedial servitudes in South African law.

It is clear, however, that *perpetua causa* is indeed taken into consideration in the establishment of praedial servitudes.[68] What is more, it seems that the view held by the pandectists, namely that this requirement is only a manifestation or implication of the *utilitas* requirement, is echoed in some court decisions. This is borne out, first, by statements in a whole range of decisions which clearly indicate that the elements of *perpetua causa* and *utilitas* cannot, in the eyes of the court, be separated from each other. An illustration[69] of this is the following *dictum* from the decision in *Lorentz v. Melle*:[70] 'It is of the essence of a praedial servitude that it burdens the land to which it relates and that it provides *some permanent advantage to the dominant land* (as distinct from serving the personal benefit of the owner thereof).'[71]

A second indication of a more flexible and pragmatic interpretation of the *perpetua causa* requirement in South African law lies in several decisions on the servitudes of leading and drawing water (*aquaeductus* and *aquaehaustus*). In Roman law,[72] and also according to Roman-Dutch authors such as Voet,[73] these servitudes could only be established over a source of 'living water' (*aqua viva*). For example, fountains and springs qualified as *aqua viva*, but not lakes (*lacus*) or ponds (*stagnum*). This strict requirement appears to have been supported in an 1866 decision,[74] where the Court described a servitude of leading water as 'the right of leading *aqua viva*, flowing water, over the property of another'.[75] However, this statement was probably *obiter* as the Court concluded that the parties never intended to create a praedial servitude. Several other decisions lend indirect support to the more pragmatic view of Groenewegen[76] and Van der Keessel,[77] namely that a servitude of leading water (and probably also of drawing water) can be established over sources other than those with *aqua viva*. Thus it has on occasion been accepted (without discussion) that a servitude of leading water may be established over a dam in a river which runs dry at certain times of the year;[78] or over a dam fed by a *spruit* (creek).[79] It has also frequently been accepted, without discussion, that a dam is sufficient.[80] In one

---

[68] See the early decision in *Dreyer v. Ireland* (1874) 4 Buch 193.

[69] See *Venter v. Minister of Railways* 1949 (2) SA 178 (E) 185; *Hotel De Aar v. Jonordon Investment (Edms) Bpk* 1972 (2) SA 400 (A) 405; *Bisschop v. Stafford* (n. 48), 12.

[70] 1978 (3) SA 1044 (T) 1049.

[71] Emphasis added.

[72] See Paul. D. 8, 2, 28; Ulp. D. 8, 3, 9; Ulp. D. 43, 20, 1 and 5; Ulp. D. 43, 22, 1, 1 and 4. (D. 43 deals with interdicts and their application, not with praedial servitudes as such.)

[73] Above, n. 61.   [74] *Dreyer v. Ireland* (1866) 4 Buch 193.   [75] 199.

[76] Above, n. 64.   [77] Above, n. 65.

[78] *De Klerk v. Niehaus* (1897) 14 SC 302.   [79] *Van Heerden v. Coetzee* 1914 AD 167.

[80] *Judd v. Fourie* (1881) 2 EDC 41; *Smit v. Russouw* 1913 CPD 847; *Schwedhelm v. Hauman* 1947 (1) SA 127 (E); *Van den Berg v. Van Tonder* 1963 (3) SA 558 (T).

instance no attention at all was paid to the source over which the particular servitude had been established.[81]

(d) Utility (utilitas)

As argued so far, the requirements of *vicinitas* and *perpetua causa* can only be fully understood in the light of the more fundamental requirement of *utilitas*. Its interpretation is therefore of fundamental importance for the establishment of praedial servitudes. Generally speaking, the *utilitas* requirement can be interpreted in three ways.[82] The first interpretation is extremely narrow: the requirement is satisfied only if the particular servitude is of direct utility to the dominant tenement in accordance with the tenement's natural character and condition. The second interpretation is somewhat wider: the servitude has to increase the utility, or usefulness, of the dominant tenement in accordance with the tenement's economic, industrial or professional purpose; in other words, the tenement's economic exploitation is of importance and not only its natural character and condition. Thirdly, an extremely wide interpretation is possible: it is sufficient if the establishment of the servitude results in an increase in the financial value of the dominant tenement.

It has been argued elsewhere[83] that the second interpretation provides the most useful guideline for the establishment of praedial servitudes, the first interpretation being too restrictive and the third one being so arbitrary as not to provide any effective limitation at all. It has also been shown[84] that in Roman-Dutch law praedial servitudes had already shed their intimate link with agriculture. One finds several pointers in Roman-Dutch sources towards a wider interpretation of the *utilitas* requirement in which far more than the agricultural needs of tenements is stressed.[85] This approach, in essence, amounts to the adoption of the second interpretation sketched above.

Analysis of South African court decisions (particularly the older ones) concerning traditional praedial servitudes such as leading and drawing water, or pasturage, shows a marked tension between the first and second interpretation of the *utilitas* requirement. Even though it is clearly accepted that these servitudes should no longer be restricted to the agricultural sphere, no clear limits are set for their establishment. The use of water in pursuance of a servitude of leading or drawing water, for example, varies

---

[81] *Otto v. Pretorius* (n. 34).

[82] De Waal (n. 32), 101; J. L. Neels, 'Erfdiensbaarhede: Nut vir die Heersende Erf', 1988 *TSAR* 528 sq.; C. G. van der Merwe, 'Die Nutvereiste by Erfdiensbaarhede', in: D. J. Joubert (ed.), *Petere Fontes: L. C. Steyn-Gedenkbundel* (no publication date), 164 sqq.

[83] De Waal (n. 32), 99 sqq.   [84] De Waal (n. 1), 580–2.

[85] See esp. Voet (n. 6), 8, 4, 15; Huber (n. 38), 2, 43, 11; Dionysius Godefridus van der Keessel, *Dictata ad Justiniani Institutionum* (ed. by B. Beinart, B. L. Hijmans, P. van Warmelo, 1965), 2, 3, 8. See also De Waal (n. 1), 580–2.

from use for only 'beneficial' purposes[86] to use 'for all purposes of comfort and enjoyment'.[87] Concerning servitudes of pasturage the requirements of the dominant tenement were, as a rule, taken to provide the maximum limit for the contents of the servitude. Although this appears to be a useful guideline, its application is rendered difficult by the fact that the requirements of the dominant tenement have not been determined in a consistent fashion. In some instances the dominant tenement's size, nature, and characteristics are regarded as the determining factor,[88] whereas in others its exploitation or utilization is viewed as decisive.[89] The last-mentioned approach is obviously more consistent with a wider interpretation of the *utilitas* requirement than the first, for here the economic exploitation of the dominant tenement determines the establishment as well as the contents of the particular servitude. The former approach is reminiscent of the narrowest interpretation of the *utilitas* requirement—an interpretation already outgrown in Roman-Dutch law. The more liberal interpretation also underlies cases where servitudes of pasturage were established with regard to a fixed number of animals and were approved without first determining whether the needs of the dominant tenement warranted such servitudes.[90]

The establishment of praedial servitudes in South African law has moved outside the narrow range of agricultural activities.[91] Proof of this proposition can be found in a number of decisions where purely mercantile considerations provided the basis for the establishment of the respective servitudes. Thus, the courts have on occasion shown a distinct willingness to construe the right to trade on another tenement as a praedial servitude.[92] The basis on which a praedial servitude of this nature can be established does not, however, emerge from these decisions. The decisive consideration appears throughout, to be, the intention of the parties involved. The question was merely whether the parties intended the particular servitude to be

---

[86] *Landman v. Daverin* (1881) 2 EDC 1, 7 sq.   [87] *Dreyer v. Ireland* (n. 74), 199.

[88] *Badenhorst v. Joubert* 1920 TPD 100; *Minister of Forestry v. Michaux* 1957 (2) SA 32 (N).

[89] *Volschenk v. Van den Berg* 1917 TPD 321.

[90] See e.g. *Nolan v. Barnard* 1908 TS 142; *Hough v. Collett* 1911 CPD 389. See also Van der Merwe (n. 82), 163, 170. It is suggested that the wider interpretation is also supported by a line of decisions concerning general servitudes of pasturage over a commonage (*meent*). In these decisions the respective servitudes were granted without first determining whether the small tenements in favour of which they were established were really in need thereof: see e.g. *Municipality of Swellendam v. Surveyor-General* (1848) 3 Menz 578; *Heidelberg Municipality v. Uys* (1898) 15 SC 156; *Aberdeen Municipality v. Aberdeen Dutch Reformed Church* (n. 42); *Greyton Municipality v. Registrar of Deeds* 1911 CPD 472; *Marais v. Maartens* 1914 CPD 95; *Clack v. Morgan* 1922 EDL 55; *Wood v. Baynesfield Board of Administration* 1975 (2) SA 692 (N).

[91] This is, of course, apart from the traditional urban praedial servitudes where agricultural considerations play no role whatsoever. See below, Section IV. 2. (b).

[92] See e.g. *Stuart v. Grant* (1903) 24 NLR 416; *Willoughby's Consolidated Co Ltd v. Copthall Stores Ltd* (n. 13), 1918 AD 1. Cf. the comment by Steyn CJ in *Hollmann v. Estate Latre* (n. 34), 644. The view proposed in older textbooks such as Hall/Kellaway (n. 10), 165, that the right to trade on another tenement can only be established as a personal servitude, is therefore incorrect.

praedial or personal.[93] One is therefore left with the impression that the courts do not regard other considerations, such as whether the *utilitas* requirement has been satisfied, to be of any importance in cases of this nature. The same applies to praedial servitudes in terms of which a particular trade on the dominant tenement is protected from the competition of similar activities on the servient tenement.[94] This type of servitude, known as a *Wettbewerbsverbot* in German law,[95] has been recognized as a praedial servitude in several South African court decisions.[96] According to German[97] and modern Dutch law it has to be taken into account[98] whether the dominant tenement has been specifically prepared for a particular trade or activity. This factor does not appear to be decisive in South African law.[99,100] This demonstrates the lack of sensitivity by the South African courts towards the crucial role of the *utilitas* requirement in the establishment of praedial servitudes outside the traditional agricultural sphere.

In the discussion of the *vicinitas* requirement[101] it has been pointed out that restrictive conditions,[102] a new kind of servitudal right developed in South African law, provide an important research model with regard to the application of the traditional requirements for the establishment of praedial servitudes in a modern sphere. As demonstrated, the *vicinitas* requirement has essentially ceased to play any role in this context. We will now have to consider which role (if any) is attributed to the *utilitas* requirement when it comes to the establishment of restrictive conditions.

Restrictive conditions which have come to be construed as praedial servitudes are divergent in nature. Examples include conditions that tenements may only be utilized for residential purposes;[103] that business of a

---

[93] See esp. *Willoughby's Consolidated v. Copthall Stores* (n. 13), 1918 AD 1.

[94] Thus, the sole aim of such a servitude is the protection of a particular trade on the dominant tenement against competition from a similar trade on the servient tenement.

[95] De Waal (n. 32), 142–5.

[96] See e.g. *Tonkin v. Van Heerden* 1935 NPD 589; *Ex parte Steinberg* 1940 CPD 1; *Venter v. Minister of Railways* (n. 69); *Jonordon Investment v. De Aar Drankwinkel* (n. 34); *Hollmann v. Estate Latre* (n. 34); *Hotel De Aar v. Jonordon Investment* (n. 69).

[97] See De Waal (n. 32), 142–5 for discussion of this aspect of German law.

[98] Ibid. 159–62 for discussion of this aspect of the law of the Netherlands.

[99] Ibid. 185–95, based on an analysis of the cases cited above in n. 96.

[100] This consideration links the whole issue with the *utilitas* requirement. A benefit for all successive owners of the dominant tenement (a crucial consideration regarding the question whether the *utilitas* requirement has been satisfied) can only be realized if the dominant tenement has been specifically adapted for the particular trade or business that requires the protection. Examples include a dominant tenements adapted as a bakery, a brewery, a factory, or a hotel. The specific nature or condition of the dominant tenement must, therefore, objectively provide a justification for the establishment of the prohibition as a praedial servitude: see De Waal (n. 32), 206.   [101] Above, Section IV. 1. (b).

[102] Below, Section IV. 2. (b) for a discussion of restrictive conditions.

[103] *Cannon v. Picadilly Mansions (Pty) Ltd* 1934 WLD 187; *Ex parte Johannesburg Diocesan Trustees* 1936 TPD 21; *Siegfried v. Tidswell* 1952 (4) SA 319 (C); *Braham v. Wood* 1956 (1) SA 651 (D); *Pollard v. Friedlander* 1959 (4) SA 326 (C); *Ex parte Rovian Trust (Pty) Ltd* 1983 (3) SA 209 (D).

particular nature is prohibited on the tenements;[104] that tenements may not
be subdivided;[105] that only one residence may be erected on each tenement;[106] that certain building materials may not be used;[107] and that certain race groups may not own or occupy tenements.[108] In many of these
instances the courts had to face the question whether the conditions in issue
were of the nature of praedial or of personal servitudes. Use was often made
of guidelines worked out with reference to the English decision of *Elliston
v. Reacher*.[109] The only one of these that relates to the *utilitas* requirement
is that the conditions in question, in order to qualify as praedial servitudes,
have to benefit all the tenements in the particular development scheme.
However, the way in which the courts examine this requirement creates the
distinct impression that it is not viewed as an equivalent of, or a substitute
for, the *utilitas* requirement. Rather it seems to be but one of the aspects
taken into consideration in order to determine whether the particular
restrictive condition(s) can be construed as a contract for the benefit of a
third party (*stipulatio alteri*) so as to operate in favour of all the owners of
tenements in the development scheme.[110]

One of the results of this approach is that the establishment of restrictive
conditions still appears to be a relatively uncontrolled and subjective
process. The experience in German law with the *Annehmlichkeitsdienst-
barkeiten*, which display a striking similarity to restrictive conditions, has
demonstrated that the *utilitas* requirement can operate as an objective
guideline in this context.[111] In South Africa it has the potential of fulfilling
a similar function.

On balance one may conclude that South African law has shed the
strictest interpretations of the *utilitas* requirement. The widest interpretation
(i.e. the third possibility mentioned above) has been only tentatively
advanced in one decision.[112] As this interpretation would seriously undermine the regulatory function of the requirement, it is just as well that it has

---

[104] *Norwood Township Syndicate v. Dawson* 1910 TPD 235; *Gassner and Blumber v. Baker*
1931 WLD 23; *Dunbar v. Rossmaur Mansions (Pty) Ltd* 1946 WLD 235; *Norbreck (Pty) Ltd
v. Rand Townships Registrar* 1948 (1) SA 1037 (W); *Siegfried v. Tidswell* 1952 (4) SA 319 (C);
Ex parte Extension Investments (Pty) Ltd 1967 (4) SA 185 (W).
[105] *Ex parte Johannesburg Diocesan Trustees* (n. 103); *Norbreck v. Rand Townships Registrar*
(n. 104); *Kleyn v. Theron* 1966 (3) SA 264 (T); *BEF (Pty) Ltd v. Cape Town Municipality* 1983
(2) SA 387 (C); *Ex p Rovian Trust* (n. 103).
[106] *Wyndham v. Rubinstein* 1935 CPD 364; *Siegfried v. Tidswell* (n. 103); *Swiss Hotels (Pty)
Ltd v. Pedersen* 1966 (1) SA 197 (C); *Ex p Rovian Trust* (n. 103).
[107] *Norbreck v. Rand Townships Registrar* (n. 104); *Siegfried v. Tidswell* (n. 103).
[108] *Norwood Township Syndicate v. Dawson* (n. 104); *Alexander v. Johns* 1912 AD 393;
Epstein v. Arenstein 1942 WLD 52; *Norbreck v. Rand Townships Registrar* (n. 107); *Siegfried
v. Tidswell* (n. 103); *Braham v. Wood* (n. 103). See further below, Section IV. 2. (b).
[109] [1908] 2 Ch 374. See below, Section IV. 2. (b).
[110] See below, Section IV. 2. (b).   [111] De Waal (n. 32), 139–42.
[112] *Hollmann v. Estate Latre* (n. 34). The relevant part of the judgment is clearly *obiter*. Also,
the Court failed to advance convincing authority for this interpretation.

not acquired a firm foothold. All in all, it is the second (and most functional) interpretation of the *utilitas* requirement which is most often applied in South African law. South African courts and legal writers have thus followed the lead provided by some of the Roman-Dutch sources.[113] It is disappointing, under these circumstances, that the courts have not proved more creative in applying the requirement, in this more subtle and flexible cast, as a regulatory tool in the establishment of the more 'modern' categories of praedial servitudes mentioned above.

*(e) Passivity (*servitus in faciendo consistere nequit*)*

According to Pomp. D. 8, 1, 15, 1 the owner of a servient tenement can be obliged by a servitude to endure some act being performed on his tenement, or to refrain from performing an act himself. He cannot, however, be compelled to perform a positive duty. As a result of this text the requirement of passivity, as expressed in the maxim *servitus in faciendo consistere nequit*, has come to be accepted as a basic principle of the law of servitudes.

The principle of passivity became firmly entrenched in Roman-Dutch law.[114] In some works one even finds a tentative motivation for this requirement, namely that the imposition of positive duties on the servient owner was seen as irreconcilable with the nature of a servitude as a real right.[115] The true basis underlying the principle of passivity, i.e. the fundamental distinction between personal and real rights, is also implicit in these statements.

The only exception to the maxim *servitus in faciendo consistere nequit* acknowledged in Roman law was the servitude of support (*servitus oneris ferendi*).[116] The Roman-Dutch authors confirm that by this servitude the servient owner can be compelled to perform a positive duty: he has to maintain the building providing the support.[117] Only Voet[118] interpreted another praedial servitude, the *servitus altius tollendi*, as one by which a positive duty could be imposed on the servient owner. According to Voet, this servitude requires the servient owner to raise a building on his land in order to protect the dominant tenement against the sun or cold winds. As suggested elsewhere,[119] Voet probably interpreted the contents of this servitude

[113] See the authorities cited above, n. 85. See also De Waal (n. 1), 580–2.

[114] Voet (n. 6), 8, 2, 7; 8, 4, 17 and 8, 6, 4; Huber (n. 38), 2, 43, 4; Gerlach Scheltinga, *Dictata on De Groot's Inleiding tot de Hollandsche Rechtsgeleerdheid* (ed. by W. de Vos, G. G. Visagie, 1986), 2, 35, 13; Van der Keessel (n. 85), 2, 3, 15. See also Willem Pauw, *Observationes Tumultuariae Novae*, 236; Cornelis van Bynkershoek, *Observationes Tumultuariae*, 3313.

[115] See esp. Huber (n. 38), 2, 43, 4; Van der Keessel (n. 85), 2, 3, 15.

[116] Texts in which support for this exception can be found include Paul. D. 8, 2, 1, 1; Paul. D. 8, 2, 33; Ulp. D. 8, 5, 6, 2 and 3 and 5–7; Paul. D. 8, 5, 7; Ulp. D. 8, 5, 8.

[117] Voet (n. 6), 8, 2, 1; Huber (n. 38), 2, 43, 16; Van der Keessel (n. 65), 2, 34, 3; *idem* (n. 85), 2, 3, 14, 1; Simon van Leeuwen, *Het Rooms-Hollands-Regt*, 2, 20, 2; Vinnius (n. 114), 2, 3, 21.

[118] Voet (n. 6), 8, 2, 7; 8, 4, 17.   [119] De Waal (n. 1), 585 sq.

incorrectly. There is also no sign that Voet received support for this interpretation from any other Roman-Dutch author.[120]

From the above it is evident that the requirement of passivity has a firm
foundation in both Roman and Roman-Dutch law. One would therefore
expect it to have been received into South African law. The matter has not,
however, been as easy as that. When analysing the relevant pronouncements
of the South African courts we must keep in mind that, with the distinction
between personal and real rights, a more fundamental principle is at stake.

The most useful starting-point for our investigation is the line of cases in
which it had to be decided whether a condition could be registered against
the title-deed of land by which all successive owners of that land would be
bound to pay a sum of money to another person. Obviously, an affirmative
answer to this question would blur the distinction between personal and real
rights and would open the door to the recognition of other positive servitudal duties.

Analysis of this line of cases reveals conflicting approaches. In a few
instances the courts did accept that an obligation to pay a sum of money
could be registered as a real right. However, no clear *ratio* for this approach
emerged from these decisions. In some the question was not debated at
all,[121] in others registration was simply accepted on the basis of practical
considerations.[122] In *Registrar of Deeds (Transvaal) v. Ferreira Deep Ltd,*[123]
for example, the Court accepted the right to receive a percentage of 'claim
and stand licences' moneys as being real and registrable for, the Court said,
the registration of this type of right 'has been sanctioned by usage and practice in the Transvaal'.[124] In a number of decisions the 'subtraction from the
dominium' test[125] was used to explain why these rights could indeed be
regarded as real and registrable.[126] However, the way in which the test was
applied in these decisions, and consequently also the conclusions reached by
the courts, have been generally criticized.[127]

Moreover, in a number of decisions the classification of such rights as real
rights has been consistently refused. *Ex parte Geldenhuys,*[128] decided in the

---

[120] De Waal (n. 1), 585 sq.

[121] See e.g. *Barclays Western Bank Ltd v. Comfy Hotels* 1980 (4) SA 174 (E).

[122] See *Registrar of Deeds (Transvaal) v. Ferreira Deep Ltd* 1930 AD 169.

[123] Above, n. 122.   [124] 180.

[125] The 'subtraction from the *dominium*' test is sometimes used as a guideline to distinguish
between real and personal rights: see generally Van der Merwe (n. 14), 72–83.

[126] See e.g. *Ex parte Pierce* 1950 (3) SA 628 (O); *Odendaalsrus Gold, General Investments and
Extensions Ltd v. Registrar of Deeds* 1953 (1) SA 600 (O); *Pearly Beach Trust v. Registrar of
Deeds* 1990 (4) SA 614 (C).

[127] P. J. Badenhorst, P. P. J. Coetzer, 'The Subtraction from the *Dominium* Test Revisited',
(1991) 24 *De Jure* 375; De Waal (n. 32), 264–7; J. C. Sonnekus, 'Saaklike Regte of
Vorderingsregte?: Tradisionele Toetse en 'n *Petitio Principii*', 1991 *TSAR* 173; Van der Merwe
(n. 14), 72–83. See, however, A. J. van der Walt, 'Personal Rights and Limited Real Rights: an
Historical Overview and Analysis of Contemporary Problems Related to the Registrability of
Rights', (1992) 55 *THRHR* 170.   [128] 1926 OPD 155.

mid-1920s, is a classic example of such a decision. *Geldenhuys* concerned a stipulation in a will by which one of the testator's children was obliged, under certain circumstances, to pay a sum of money to all the other children. De Villiers JP held this to constitute a *ius in personam*; he said: 'the obligation to pay money cannot easily be held to form a *ius in re*, unless it takes the form of a duly constituted hypothec . . . This direction of the will therefore does not constitute a real right and it is not *per se* registrable.'[129]

Geldenhuys was followed in a number of decisions.[130] Of these decisions *Lorentz v. Melle*[131] perhaps provides the clearest and most persuasive authority against the acceptance of a claim to receive money as a real right. In the *Lorentz* case the Court was confronted with the question of whether the right to claim a percentage of the profit generated by a township development scheme could be classified as a real right. After a thorough investigation of the historical sources and of the relevant case-law the Court came to the conclusion that the particular condition was 'essentially a personal one sounding in money'.[132] In the course of the judgment the Court also specifically rejected the possibility that the condition in question could form the basis of a praedial servitude.[133]

It is evident that the courts are, at the very least, hesitant to encumber the successive owners of a piece of land with a positive obligation—even if this obligation is, as with the payment of a sum of money, 'neutral' in character. The crucial question, of course, is whether this general unwillingness has translated, in the context of praedial servitudes, into a confirmation of the maxim *servitus in faciendo consistere nequit*. The relevant case-law unfortunately does not provide a clear answer. In a number of old decisions it was apparently accepted, without discussion, that an owner of a servient tenement could indeed be burdened with a positive servitudal duty.[134] On the other hand, many more decisions can be cited in which it was held, again without discussion, that all positive duties have to be carried out by the owner of the dominant tenement.[135]

In the final analysis the question of whether the requirement of passivity has been received into the South African law of servitudes revolves around

[129] 165. Registration was allowed, however, on the basis that this condition was 'intimately connected' with another condition which was indeed registrable. But registration *per se* did not convert the personal right into a real right.

[130] See e.g. *Ex parte Van Vuuren* 1947 (2) SA 1142 (T); *Ex parte Gitelson* 1949 (2) SA 881 (O); *Lorentz v. Melle* (n. 34). The question was specifically left open by the Appellate Division in *Nel v. Commissioner for Inland Revenue* 1960 (1) SA 227 (A).

[131] 1978 (3) SA 1044 (T).   [132] 1052.   [133] 1049, 1051 sq.

[134] See e.g. *Landman v. Daverin* (1881) 2 EDC 1; *Louw v. De Villiers* (1893) 10 SC 324; *Hattingh v. Robertson* (1904) 21 SC 273.

[135] See e.g. *Hawkins v. Munnik* (1830) 1 Menz 465; *Judd v. Fourie* (1881) 2 EDC 41; *Wolvaardt v. Pienaar* (n. 41); *Steyn v. Zeeman* (1903) 20 SC 221; *Salmon v. Lamb's Executor and Naidoo* 1906 EDC 351; *Whitaker, Paterson and Brooks Ltd v. Hughes and Co* 1907 EDC 4; *Swart v. Trustees of Jeffreys Bay* (1907) 24 SC 447; *Du Plessis v. Philipstown Municipality* 1937 CPD 335; *Stuttaford v. Kruger* 1967 (2) SA 166 (C); *Du Plessis v. Pieterse* 1970 (3) SA 468 (C).

two conflicting judgments delivered in the late 1940s. In both these decisions, *Schwedhelm v. Hauman*[136] and *Van der Merwe v. Wiese*,[137] it had to
be decided whether the owner of a servient tenement could, by a servitude
of drawing water (*servitus aquaehaustus*), be obliged to perform positive
duties (essentially, the supply of water and the maintenance of the network
of pipes). In *Schwedhelm* the requirement of passivity was confirmed and
the Court refused to countenance the proposition that those duties could
form part of the servitude. In *Van der Merwe v. Wiese*, on the other hand,
the maxim *servitus in faciendo consistere nequit* was described as providing
no more than a useful guideline in the interpretation and application of
servitudes. The Court therefore concluded that the maxim did not prevent
the creation of the positive servitudal duties in question.

Van der Merwe v. Wiese has been exhaustively analysed elsewhere.[138]
Today there is general agreement that the case was wrongly decided. There
can be no doubt that Fagan J interpreted the Roman and Roman-Dutch
sources incorrectly. Moreover, commentators are also highly critical of the
scope and method of the comparative research upon which His Lordship
embarked.[139] Thus, it is not surprising that *Schwedhelm v. Hauman* has ever
since been regarded as correctly reflecting the position in South African law
concerning the maxim *servitus in faciendo consistere nequit*. South African
legal literature generally accepts the requirement of passivity for the establishment of praedial servitudes.[140] The *servitus oneris ferendi* is, however,
still regarded as an exception to this rule.[141]

The Deeds Registries Act[142] is the piece of South African legislation
which is concerned, generally, with the registration of real rights to land
and, more specifically, with the constitution of both praedial and personal
servitudes. Legislative encroachments, if any, upon the requirement of passivity must therefore be sought first within the framework of this act. The
only relevant provision appears to be section 63(1). Leaving aside its proviso, it reads: 'No deed, or condition in a deed, purporting to create or
embodying any personal right, and no condition which does not restrict the
exercise of any right of ownership in respect of immovable property, shall
be capable of registration'.

---

[136] 1947 (1) SA 127 (E).   [137] 1948 (4) SA 8 (C).
[138] See De Waal (n. 32), 278–84; R. J. P. Jordan, 'Praedial Servitudes: The Imposition of
Positive Duties upon the Servient Owner', (1958) 75 *SALJ* 181; Van der Merwe (n. 14), 474–6.
[139] Ibid.
[140] Delport/Olivier (n. 34), 549 sqq.; Hall/Kellaway (n. 10), 122; Kleyn/Boraine (n. 17), 378
sq.; Maasdorp (n. 10), 198; Olivier/Pienaar/Van der Walt (n. 17), 249 sq.; Van der Merwe (n.
14), 471 sqq.; Van der Merwe/De Waal (n. 17), § 42.
[141] See generally the authorities cited above, n. 140. Some of these authors mention the *servitus altius tollendi* as another exception to the requirement of passivity: see Hall/Kellaway (n.
10), 105, 122; Kleyn/Boraine (n. 17), 373, fn. 37; Maasdorp (n. 10), 167 sq., 201. As suggested
elsewhere, this view is probably incorrect: De Waal (n. 1), 585 sq.
[142] Act 47 of 1937.

Thus, section 63(1) first prohibits the registration of personal rights, and secondly confirms the 'subtraction from the *dominium*' test[143] as a guideline for distinguishing between personal and real rights. In the light of the above exposition one would have thought this constituted a bar to the registration of positive servitudal duties. However, section 63(1) was amended in 1973[144] by the addition of the following proviso: 'a deed containing such a condition as aforesaid may be registered if, in the opinion of the registrar, such condition is complementary or otherwise ancillary to a registrable condition or right contained or conferred in such deed.'

Under this proviso the Registrar of Deeds can allow the registration of personal rights, including one obliging another person to perform a positive duty, if he sees that right as 'complementary or otherwise ancillary' to a registrable condition. At first blush this provision would indeed appear to undermine the requirement of passivity for praedial servitudes. There is general agreement, however, that this could not have been the intention of the legislature.[145] The proviso to section 63(1) is merely regarded as providing a practical solution to the type of problem encountered in cases such as *Schwedhelm v. Hauman*[146] and *Van der Merwe v. Wiese*.[147] The Registrar of Deeds would now be allowed to register a deed of servitude in which positive duties for the owner of the servient tenement are contained: but—and this is of crucial importance—the mere act of registration would not convert these conditions from personal into real rights.[148] Only the party who initially undertakes to perform these positive duties will be contractually bound to do so and the duties will not, with the servitude itself, evolve upon all successive owners of the servient tenement.[149] The positive duties do not attain a servitudal character and consequently the proviso does not negate the requirement of passivity in South African law.

A clear balance of authority therefore favours the conclusion that the maxim *servitus in faciendo consistere nequit* has been received unscathed into South African law. Although it is based upon the fundamental distinction between personal and real rights, it is nevertheless convenient to regard it as a (negative) requirement for the establishment of praedial servitudes. It indicates what may not constitute the content of a praedial servitude. As such it fulfils the same function as the other requirements, namely to safeguard against a proliferation of servitudes and servitudal obligations.

---

[143] Above, n. 125.
[144] By Act 62 of 1973, s. 10.
[145] See generally the authorities cited below, n. 148.
[146] Above, n. 136.
[147] Above, n. 137.
[148] Delport/Olivier (n. 34), 8, 542, 544; De Waal (n. 32), 285 sqq.; Kleyn/Boraine (n. 17), 379; Olivier/Pienaar/Van der Walt (n. 17), 250; Van der Merwe (n. 14), 477.
[149] A subsequent purchaser of the servient tenement can, of course, be held to the *agreement* if he bought the tenement in full knowledge thereof. The fact that the undertaking to perform positive duties has been registered as part of the deed of servitude can make the proof of knowledge easier: see De Waal (n. 32), 289.

2. Principal rural and urban praedial servitudes

Even though there was no *numerus clausus* of praedial servitudes in Roman-Dutch law, the sources focus on the discussion of certain well established types of praedial servitudes: types which for the most part were already known in Roman law.[150] Most of these traditional praedial servitudes have been transplanted into South African law. They have, however, been adapted to suit local conditions. Also, new types have been developed to cater for new needs. This process of transplantation, adaptation, and growth is analysed in this Section. Of course, one must remain mindful of the important function fulfilled by the traditional requirements in the creation of new types of praedial servitudes.[151] These requirements have to guard against the uncontrolled growth of this area of the law; at the same time, they must be flexible enough to allow for the creation of praedial servitudes for which need has arisen as a result of agricultural, economic, social, and technological progress and development[152]. Attention focuses first on the principal rural praedial servitudes, after which a number of the more important urban praedial servitudes will be discussed. Finally, a number of praedial servitudes acknowledged in South African law but not falling strictly within either of these categories is briefly mentioned.

(a) Rural praedial servitudes

The old Roman servitudes of way, namely *iter, actus*, and *via*, all form part of modern South African law.[153] Following the terminology developed in Roman-Dutch law,[154] they are generally known today as footpath (*voetpad*), drive (*dreef*), and way (*weg*). In Roman-Dutch law 'footpath' entailed the right to cross another's tenement on foot or horseback; 'drive' constituted the right to drive animals over the servient tenement; 'way', as well as comprising both footpath and drive, allowed the holder of the servitude to drive wagons over the servient tenement.[155] All these have been adapted to suit the conditions of modern South Africa. For instance, a servitude of way would normally allow the holder of the servitude to drive with a motor vehicle over the servient tenement; and the width of the roads to be used in pursuance of the servitude would be interpreted so as to allow their proper use under modern conditions.[156]

[150] For a discussion of the principal praedial servitudes in Roman-Dutch law, and also the most important authorities in this regard, see De Waal (n. 1), 586–9.

[151] Above, Section IV. 1.					[152] Ibid.

[153] As to the servitudes of way, see generally Hall/Kellaway (n. 10), 41, 63–5; Kleyn/Boraine (n. 17), 369; Maasdorp (n. 10), 193; Olivier/Pienaar/Van der Walt (n. 17), 250; Van der Merwe (n. 14), 481–4; Van der Merwe/De Waal (n. 17), §§ 49 sq. See also A. B. de Villiers, 'Ter Beskerming van 'n Reg op 'n Voetpad', (1984) 47 *THRHR* 280 sqq.

[154] De Waal (n. 1), 586 sq.					[155] Ibid.

[156] Van der Merwe (n. 14), 482. As to the route over which a servitude of way may be exercised, see *Nach Investments (Pty) Ltd v. Yaldai Investments (Pty) Ltd* 1987 (2) SA 820 (A).

Trekpath is a peculiar South African servitude of way by which the holder of the servitude may drive cattle and sheep across a strip of a particular width of the servient land within the limits of which the animals may graze as they go.[157] Long distances and the lack of railway transport earlier this century were some of the conditions responsible for the creation of this servitude.[158] *Trekpath* differs from a servitude of drive (*actus*) in that a much greater area of land is required for it and sufficient grazing must be provided.[159] A servitude of *outspan* is another uniquely South African servitude. It is closely linked to *trekpath* in that it was also created in response to the long distances between towns and even farms in the same area. *Outspan* entails the right to unyoke or unharness draught animals in order to allow them to rest and graze on the servient tenement.[160] The importance of this type of servitude has, of course, gradually diminished as oxwagons and horsecarts have been replaced by motor vehicles and trains.[161]

With the reception of Roman law in Holland, the Roman-Dutch authors used the *iter ad sepulcrum* (way to a grave) in order to develop a special servitude of way, the 'way of necessity' (*via ex necessitate*).[162] A way of necessity was granted if a tenement was landlocked with no (or only a very inconvenient) access to a public road.[163] The concept of a way of necessity has been accepted in South African law; if the number of cases in which it has been raised is anything to go by it is obviously of great practical importance.[164] The treatment of this institution by the Roman-Dutch authors has generally been followed in South Africa. In *Van Rensburg v. Coetzee*[165] the Appellate Division has, however, questioned the traditional distinction[166] between a *ius viae plenum* (which operates like a normal servitude of way) and a *ius viae precario* (which can be used only in cases of necessity) in respect of land which is utilized on a regular basis. The Court expressed its doubts about the suitability of the *ius viae precario* under modern farming conditions.[167]

---

[157] *Van Heerden v. Pretorius* 1914 AD 69.

[158] Ibid.; Hall/Kellaway (n. 10), 46; Van der Merwe (n. 14), 483.

[159] Hall/Kellaway (n. 10), 46.

[160] See e.g. *Bok v. Allen* (1884) 1 SAR 119; *Divisional Council of Albany v. Lombard* (1895) 10 EDC 1; *Barkly East Divisional Council v. Greyling* (1909) 26 SC 603; *Schreve v. Minister of Agriculture* 1974 (3) SA 76 (E).

[161] Van der Merwe (n. 14), 496.

[162] Voet (n. 6), 8, 3, 4; Van der Keessel (n. 65), 2, 35, 7 and 8; Simon van Leeuwen, *Censura forensis theoretico-practica*, 1, 2, 14, 34; *idem* (n. 117), 2, 21, 7.

[163] See, in general, authorities cited in n. 162, above.

[164] See the following authorities and the court decisions cited by them: Hall/Kellaway (n. 10), 65–70; Kleyn/Boraine (n. 17), 369 sq.; Olivier/Pienaar/Van der Walt (n. 17), 260 sq.; Van der Merwe (n. 14), 484–92; Van der Merwe/De Waal (n. 17), § 51; C. G. van der Merwe, G. F. Lubbe, 'Noodweg', (1977) 40 *THRHR* 111 sqq.

[165] 1979 (4) SA 655 (A).   [166] Voet (n. 6), 8, 3, 4.

[167] 672. See also *Naudé v. Ecoman Investments* 1994 (2) SA 95 (T); Kleyn/Boraine (n. 17), 370.

South Africa is a country in which agriculture has always played a crucial role. It is therefore not surprising that praedial servitudes closely associated with agricultural activities have always proved to be of great practical
importance. This is true of the servitudes of way, but even more so of the
servitudes of water. The importance of the servitudes of water also has to
be appreciated in the light of the fact that South Africa is a country not
richly endowed with water resources. First and foremost in this category are
the servitudes of leading water (*aquaeductus*) and of drawing water (*aquaehaustus*).[168] The first entails the right to lead water from, or over, someone
else's land, whilst the second one concerns the right to draw water from a
source on someone else's land. The practical importance of these servitudes
can hardly be better illustrated than by referring, once again, to the pragmatic approach adopted by the South African courts towards the *perpetua
causa* requirement in this regard. As pointed out above,[169] South African
law no longer requires a source of 'living water' (*aqua viva*) for the establishment of these servitudes; sources such as a dam, creek, or borehole have
on occasion been regarded as sufficient.[170] A third example of a servitude
of water closely associated with agriculture, the servitude of watering animals on someone else's land (*pecoris ad aquam appulsus*), is less frequently
encountered in the case-law. Apart from these traditional servitudes, known
already in Roman and Roman-Dutch law,[171] attention must also be drawn
to a variety of servitudes of water which can be created in terms of the
Water Act.[172]

The servitude of pasturage, significant in the agricultural domain, has
already been discussed in the context of the *utilitas* requirement.[173] It entails
the right to pasture a defined or undefined number of cattle on someone
else's land. As it did not receive much attention in Roman or Roman-Dutch
law, South African courts tend to rely on old German and French sources
in order to work out the contents of this servitude for contemporary circumstances.[174]

(b) Urban praedial servitudes

The Roman-Dutch sources contain a detailed discussion of many of the traditional urban praedial servitudes.[175] They relate mainly to light and view
(for example the *servitus luminibus non officiendi*, the *servitus prospectus*, and

---

[168] As to the servitudes of water see generally Hall/Kellaway (n. 10), 79–90; Kleyn/Boraine
(n. 17), 371; Maasdorp (n. 10), 136–42; Van der Merwe (n. 14), 492–4; Van der Merwe/De
Waal (n. 17), §§ 52 sq.
[169] Above, Section IV. 1. (c).   [170] Ibid.   [171] De Waal (n. 1), 587 sq.
[172] Act 54 of 1956, ch. VIII.   [173] Above, Section IV. 1. (d).
[174] See e.g. *Volschenk v. Van den Berg* 1917 TPD 321, and esp. *Badenhorst v. Joubert* 1920
TPD 100; Van der Merwe (n. 14), 494–6. More recent decisions, in which this servitude was
discussed or referred to, include *Minister of Forestry v. Michaux* 1957 (2) SA 32 (N) and *Pillay
v. Marburg Immigration Settlement Board* 1978 (3) SA 566 (D).
[175] De Waal (n. 1), 588 sq.

the *servitus altius tollendi*), the construction of buildings (for example the *servitus oneris ferendi* and the *servitus tigni immittendi*), and lastly, the regulation of the flow of rain-water (for example the *servitus stillicidii immittendi* and the *servitus fluminis immittendi*). Even though these traditional servitudes are still discussed in modern textbooks,[176] they are in fact of minor significance in contemporary South African law. The reasons for this are obvious: building styles and methods have changed considerably and, more importantly, the relevant matters are nowadays governed by building and health regulations.[177] The law reports still contain the odd case concerning the one or other of these old servitudes,[178] but generally speaking they have become 'relics of the past'.[179]

By far the most important category of urban praedial servitudes in South African law are the restrictive conditions.[180] As indicated earlier,[181] this is a new kind of servitudal right developed in reaction to a then new phenomenon, namely township development. It gained its recognition at an early stage; South African court decisions in which restrictive conditions are discussed in fact go back to the late nineteenth century.[182] Restrictive conditions play an important role in the establishment and development of new townships and their aim is generally to preserve a specific township character.[183] Over the years the practice has developed to register these conditions against the title-deeds of the various tenements in the particular township without mentioning in whose favour they are supposed to operate. A particularly difficult question arising in these cases is whether the conditions have to be construed as personal servitudes (operating in favour of the orig-

[176] See e.g. Hall/Kellaway (n. 10), 92–4; Kleyn/Boraine (n. 17), 372 sq.; Maasdorp (n. 10), 197–206; Olivier/Pienaar/Van der Walt (n. 17), 250 sq.; Van der Merwe (n. 14), 497–501; Van der Merwe/De Waal (n. 17), §§ 56–60.

[177] Maasdorp (n. 10), 197; Van der Merwe (n. 14), 497 sq.

[178] E.g. *Salmon v. Lamb's Executor and Naidoo* 1906 EDC 351 (the *servitus tigni immittendi*); *Kruger v. Downer* 1976 (3) SA 172 (W) (the *servitus prospectus*); *NBS (Cape Town) (Pty) Ltd v. Citymark Investments (Pty) Ltd* 1986 (2) SA 290 (C) (the servitudes *altius non tollendi* and *ne luminibus officiatur*); *Provisional Trustees, Alan Doggett Family Trust v. Karukundis* 1992 (2) SA 33 (A) (the *servitus altius non tollendi*). See also M. J. de Waal, 'Onderverdelingsvoorwaardes, Beperkende Voorwaardes en die Toepassing van Tradisionele Serwituutreëls', (1992) 3 *Stellenbosch LR* 59 sqq.

[179] Maasdorp (n. 10), 197.

[180] As to restrictive conditions see generally Hall/Kellaway (n. 10), 94–102; C. P. Joubert, 'Beperkende Bepalings in die Titelaktes van Grond', (1960) 23 *THRHR* 174 sqq.; Kleyn/Boraine (n. 17), 391–403; Olivier/Pienaar/Van der Walt (n. 17), 264–7; J. M. Pienaar, 'Die Regsaard van Beperkende Voorwaardes', (1992) 55 *THRHR* 50 sqq.; Van der Merwe (n. 14), 501–5; Van der Merwe/De Waal (n. 17), § 61; J. van Wyk, 'The Nature and Classification of Restrictive Covenants and Conditions of Title', (1992) 25 *De Jure* 270 sqq.; *idem*, 'The Historical Development of Restrictive Conditions', 1992 *TSAR* 280 sqq.

[181] Above, Section IV. 1. (b), IV. 1. (d).

[182] See e.g. *Consistory of Steytlerville v. Bosman* (1893) 10 SC 67; *Tarkastad Dutch Reformed Church v. Tarkastad Municipality* (1898) 15 SC 371.

[183] For a variety of examples of the contents of restrictive conditions see above, Section IV. 1. (d) and the cases cited above in nn. 103–8

inal seller) or as praedial servitudes (operating in favour of, or against, all the tenements in the township). In order to answer this question the courts have employed an institution well known to them, the contract for the benefit of third parties (*stipulatio alteri*).[184] This contract had to be concluded between the original seller and the purchasers of the tenements in favour of all future purchasers of any of the tenements. Conditions of this nature are construed as praedial servitudes, operating as negative servitudes[185] in favour of, or against, all tenements in the particular scheme.

Whether or not, on this basis, a restrictive condition has been inserted in the title-deeds has to be decided on the facts of each case. The courts normally make use of a number of guidelines[186] formulated in the English case of *Elliston v. Reacher*.[187] These guidelines, approved as early as 1912 by the Appellate Division in the leading case of *Alexander v. Johns*,[188] do not constitute rigid requirements. They are no more than 'useful guides'[189] for determining the true nature of the restrictive conditions in question. Moreover, in a more recent decision the Appellate Division[190] cautioned that *Elliston v. Reacher* should always be seen in its proper context. After observing that 'our system of land registration is entirely unknown and foreign to English law',[191] the Court declared:

Unlike English law which on the establishing of the four points set out in *Elliston v. Reacher* . . . had recourse to 'equity' to make restrictive covenants run with the land in townships and to render them reciprocally binding on the owners of lots in townships, our law has the advantage of making restrictive title conditions run with the land in townships as registered servitudes. Moreover, in our law registration of servitudes as real rights dispenses with the necessity of proof of knowledge of their existence by third parties.[192]

Finally, it has to be pointed out that restrictive conditions have in the past occasionally been used to prohibit persons of specific race groups from owning or occupying tenements in certain township schemes.[193] It is likely that, apart from any other possible ground for immorality or illegality, conditions of this nature will in future be declared invalid by the Bill of Rights

[184] Kleyn/Boraine (n. 17), 395 sq. and the cases cited there; Van der Merwe (n. 14), 503 and the cases cited there.

[185] Above, n. 51.

[186] These guidelines are, briefly, the following: (a) all tenements should be derived from a common seller, usually the township developer; (b) all tenements must be subject to similar conditions; (c) the conditions must have been intended by the common seller, and must in fact be, for the benefit of all the tenements in the scheme; (d) all the owners of tenements, or their predecessors in title, should have bought from the common seller on the supposition that the conditions were to operate for the benefit of all the other tenements in the scheme. A positive response to these questions may be indicative of an intention to create praedial servitudes.

[187] [1908] 2 Ch 374.   [188] 1912 AD 431.

[189] *Swiss Hotels (Pty) Ltd v. Pedersen* (n. 106), 202.

[190] *Malan v. Ardconnel Investments (Pty) Ltd* 1988 (2) SA 12 (A).   [191] 33.

[192] 36 sq.   [193] See cases cited above, n. 108.

incorporated in South Africa's new Constitution. As well as the general anti-discrimination provision in s. 8(2), s. 19 specifically provides that '[e]very person shall have the right freely to choose his or her place of residence anywhere in the national territory.'

(c) General

There being no *numerus clausus* of praedial servitudes in South African law,[194] the courts have over the years given recognition to certain praedial servitudes not fitting easily into either of the categories discussed above. The recognition of these 'new' servitudes provides ample evidence of both the inherent flexibility of the traditional requirements for the establishment of praedial servitudes[195] and the way in which the contents of a legal institution can evolve as a consequence of changing conditions. Examples of these servitudes include the right to trade on another's tenement,[196] the right to protection against trade competition emanating from another's tenement,[197] the servitude of 'market square',[198] the servitude of 'submersion',[199] and the servitude of 'commonage'.[200]

V. PERSONAL SERVITUDES

1. Definition and types

A personal servitude was defined in Roman-Dutch law as a right held by a particular person which imposes a burden on a piece of land or movable object.[201] The servitude is constituted in favour of the holder in his personal capacity and not, as with a praedial servitude, in his capacity as owner of a piece of land.[202] This is still the core feature of a personal servitude in South African law. The Appellate Division, in an early decision, expressed it in the following terms:[203] 'a personal servitude is one in which *res non servit rei*, but *res servit personae*.'

Modern textbooks, while accepting this to be the essence of a personal servitude, also stress its character as a limited real right:[204] 'A personal

---

[194] See above, Section IV. 1. [195] Discussed above, Section IV.

[196] See above, Section IV. 1. (d) and esp. the cases cited in n. 92.

[197] Above, Section IV. 1. (d), esp. the cases cited in n. 96.

[198] *Stuart v. Grant* (1903) 24 NLR 416.

[199] *Stephens v. De Wet* 1920 OPD 78. It is not altogether clear, however, whether the Court was willing to recognize this as a praedial servitude. This type of servitude is now recognized by the Water Act 54 of 1956, s. 139.

[200] *Marais v. Maartens* 1914 CPD 95; *Wood v. Baynesfield Board of Administration* 1975 (2) SA 692 (N).

[201] Above, Section III.; De Waal (n. 1), 571 sq., 589 sq. [202] Ibid.

[203] *Willoughby's Consolidated v. Copthall Stores* (n. 13), 281.

[204] Van der Merwe/De Waal (n. 17), § 62. See also Olivier/Pienaar/Van der Walt (n. 17), 246; Van der Merwe (n. 14), 506.

servitude is a limited real right in terms of which a burden is imposed upon a servient tenement or a movable for the benefit of a particular person.'

There is no indication that, as in Roman law, only a *numerus clausus* of personal servitudes was recognized in Roman-Dutch law.[205] South African law follows Roman-Dutch law in this respect, and has in fact developed several new categories of personal servitudes. The most important ones of these are the 'irregular servitudes' (*servitutes irregulares*)[206] and restrictive conditions construed as personal servitudes.[207] The development of new personal servitudes is not, however, restricted to these categories. The Appellate Division has recently even suggested that the right of extension of a sectional title scheme in terms of the Sectional Title Act[208] could, in appropriate circumstances, be construed as a personal servitude in favour of the developer.[209]

Although personal servitudes of a great variety exist, South African authors, like their Roman-Dutch predecessors,[210] tend to restrict themselves to an exposition of usufruct (*ususfructus*), use (*usus*), and habitation or dwelling (*habitatio*). As in the contribution to the Feenstra/Zimmermann volume on classical Roman-Dutch law,[211] only the most important and comprehensive personal servitude, usufruct, is here outlined.

2. Usufruct (*ususfructus*)

(a) Nature and duration

Usufruct was defined by the Roman-Dutch authors as a servitude under which a person acquires the right to enjoy, for the duration of his life, the profits and the revenue of a thing belonging to another person.[212] Voet's[213] further subdivision into 'causal' and 'formal' usufruct received no support from other Roman-Dutch authors.[214]

The definition of usufruct found in South African sources corresponds with that of the Roman-Dutch law. Again, however, it is specifically

---

[205] See e.g. Voet (n. 6), 7, 1, 2.

[206] *Servitutes irregulares* are servitudes with the content of praedial servitudes which are, however, constituted in favour of a person as such and not in his capacity as the owner of a dominant tenement. E.g. a right of way which is granted to a specific person: see Van der Merwe/De Waal (n. 17), § 63 and the cases cited there.

[207] Above, Section IV. 2. (b).   [208] Act 95 of 1986.

[209] *Erlax Properties (Pty) Ltd v. Registrar of Deeds* 1992 (1) SA 879 (A). For other examples of personal servitudes acknowledged by the courts and not fitting into the 2 categories mentioned see Van der Merwe (n. 14), 507 sq.

[210] See De Waal (n. 1), 590 and the authorities cited there.

[211] De Waal (n. 1), 590–4.

[212] See generally Grotius (n. 7), 2, 38, 5; Huber (n. 38), 2, 39, 4; Scheltinga (n. 114), 2, 38, 5; Van der Keessel (n. 65), 2, 39, 1; Van Leeuwen (n. 162), 1, 2, 15, 3; *idem* (n. 117), 2, 9, 1.

[213] Voet (n. 6), 7, 1, 3.   [214] De Waal (n. 1), 590 sq.

stressed today that usufruct is a limited real right:[215] 'Usufruct is a highly personal limited real right which entitles a person to have the use and enjoyment of another's property and to take its fruits without impairing the substance.'

For the duration of the usufruct the owner's powers of ownership are severely diminished—so much so that he is often referred to as a 'nude' owner. At the expiry of the usufruct these restrictions disappear and the owner is restored to his original position. The fact that a usufruct is a limited real right of a 'highly personal' nature has led to occasional misinterpretation of this servitude. Thus, for instance, in a recent decision usufruct has been analyzed in the following terms:[216]

... [it] is a personal right, held by the usufructuary only, to the use of the property and its fruits. It does not diminish the rights of ownership such as a real or praedial servitude does, and which confers on the holder of the servitude a right in the property adverse to the *dominium* holder ... it does not diminish in any way any of the rights of ownership or *dominium*.[217]

This judicial pronouncement runs counter to the true nature of a usufruct as a limited real right, and it is therefore regarded as not correctly reflecting the position in either Roman-Dutch or South African law.[218]

Usufruct being a personal servitude, it is not surprising that many Roman-Dutch authors stress that it is so intimately linked to the person of the usufructuary that it cannot be ceded to another person.[219] However, this basic principle was qualified in a very subtle way: even though the right itself cannot be ceded, the usufructuary can allow someone else to exercise his usufructuary interest for the duration of the usufruct.[220] This implies, *inter alia*, that the usufructuary can sell, lease, or pledge his usufructuary interest.[221] Obviously, the interest conveyed in this fashion is terminated when the usufruct expires, for instance on the death of the usufructuary.[222] The distinction between, on one hand, the inalienability of the usufructuary

---

[215] Van der Merwe/De Waal (n. 17), § 64. See also Kleyn/Boraine (n. 17), 386; Olivier/Pienaar/Van der Walt (n. 17), 252; Van der Merwe (n. 14), 508.

[216] *Cowley v. Hahn* 1987 (1) SA 440 (E).   [217] 446.

[218] For critical comments on *Cowley* see P. F. Breed, 'Usufruct: a Personal or a Real Right? A Ground of Eviction or a Latent Defect?', (1987) 50 *THRHR* 352 sqq.; A. Domanski, 'How Personal is a Personal Servitude?', (1988) 105 *SALJ* 205 sqq.; Kleyn/Boraine (n. 17), 386, fn. 14; J. Scott, 'Koopkontrak van Grond: Aard van Vruggebruik oor Grond', (1987) 20 *De Jure* 181 sqq.; Van der Merwe/De Waal (n. 17), § 64; A. J. van der Walt, 'Saaklike Regte en Persoonlike Serwitute', (1987) 50 *THRHR* 343 sqq.

[219] Grotius (n. 7), 2, 39, 4; Willem Schorer, *Aanteekeningen over de Inleidinge tot de Hollandsche Rechts-Geleerdheid* (trans. J. E. Austen, 1784), 2, 39, 3; Van der Keessel (n. 65), 2, 39, 4; Van Leeuwen (n. 117), 2, 9, 8.

[220] Grotius (n. 7), 2, 39, 4; Van der Keessel (n. 65), 2, 39, 4; Van Leeuwen (n. 162), 1, 2, 15, 14; *idem* (n. 117), 2, 9, 8.

[221] Voet (n. 6), 7, 1, 32; Van der Keessel (n. 65), 2, 39, 4; Van Leeuwen (n. 162), 1, 2, 15, 14.

[222] Voet (n. 6), 7, 1, 32; Van der Keessel (n. 65), 2, 39, 4.

right itself and, on the other hand, the alienability of the usufructuary interest (i.e. right of enjoyment) has been accepted from quite early on in South
African law.[223] Thus, it has been decided that the usufructuary may
pledge,[224] mortgage,[225] rent,[226] or lend[227] his usufructuary interest, or it
may be sold in execution.[228] However, in South African law a further still
refinement has taken place. In *Durban City Council v. Woodhaven Ltd*[229] the
Appellate Division was concerned with a personal servitude which allowed
the Electricity Supply Commission (Escom) to erect electric power-lines
over land owned by the appellant. The land was later sold and transferred
to the respondent. The question then arose whether Escom could cede the
servitude to the appellant. Not surprisingly the Court decided, following
Roman-Dutch law, that the personal servitude itself was inalienable.[230] It
was then contended that the usufructuary interest (or right of enjoyment)
was capable of being ceded. The Court accepted the general distinction
mentioned above[231] but questioned whether *in casu* there was room 'for the
fine distinction drawn in the case of a usufruct between the right of enjoyment and the right to the usufruct itself'.[232] As it was in any event clear that
the appellant had claimed nothing less than the usufruct itself, the application for cession was refused.

The Court may have been influenced by the fact that the servitude in
question was one of the *servitutes irregulares*: a personal servitude with the
same content as a praedial servitude but constituted in favour of a particular person.[233] The fundamental difference between this type of personal
servitude and the traditional personal servitudes of usufruct, use, and habitation is that its primary function is not to provide support and sustenance
for a particular person.[234] The *Durban City* case raises the possibility that
the nature and purpose of a particular personal servitude should in future
be taken into consideration in determining whether the rights under that
servitude are alienable.[235]

Apart from the general agreement concerning the inalienability of the

---

[223] See generally Van der Merwe (n. 14), 513 sq.; Van der Merwe/De Waal (n. 17), § 74.
[224] *In re Wilson and Durno* (1884) 5 NLR 57; *Colonial Orphan Chamber v. Johnston,
Johnston v. High Sheriff* 1923 CPD 286.
[225] *Haupt v. Van den Heever's Executor* (1888) 6 SC 49; *Williams v. Williams* (1895) 12 SC
392; *Executors of Hitge v. Botha* (1904) 21 SC 289; *Ex parte Jacobs* 1927 OPD 205; *Ex parte
Koen* 1930 OPD 154. The Deeds Registries Act 47 of 1937, s. 69(3)–(4), provides that the owner
of the usufructuary property must consent to this.
[226] *Parkin v. Lippert* (1895) 12 SC 179; *Ex parte Estate Lategan* 1943 CPD 442.
[227] *Barnett v. Rudman* 1933 OPD 193.
[228] *Ex parte Barnardo's Trustees* 1910 CPD 77; *Ex parte Van der Walt* 1924 OPD 9.
[229] 1987 (3) SA 555 (A).   [230] 561 sq.   [231] 560 sq.   [232] 561.
[233] Above, Section V. 1, esp. n. 206
[234] C. G. van der Merwe, 'Law of Property (Including Mortgage and Pledge)', in: 1987
Annual Survey of South African Law 205.
[235] Ibid. For a discussion of the *Durban City Council* case, see J. C. Sonnekus, 'Oordraag-
baarheid en Abandonnering van Persoonlike Diensbaarhede', 1987 *TSAR* 370 sqq.

usufruct itself, the Roman-Dutch authors were also *ad idem* that a personal servitude such as a usufruct could not extend beyond the lifetime of the holder of the right.[236] The Deeds Registries Act[237] gives full effect to this principle, as well as to that of the non-alienability of the usufruct itself, when it provides as follows:

No personal servitude of usufruct, *usus* or *habitatio* purporting to extend beyond the lifetime of the person in whose favour it is created shall be registered, nor may a transfer or cession of such personal servitude to any person other than the owner of the land encumbered thereby, be registered.[238]

There is also clear Roman-Dutch authority for the proposition that a usufruct constituted in favour of a legal person (such as a corporation) lapses after 100 years at the latest.[239] However, in *Durban City Council v. Woodhaven Ltd*[240] the Appellate Division declined to express a view on whether this rule, which was thought to be well established, still applies in South African law.

(b) Object of usufruct

The Roman-Dutch authors did not adopt a dogmatic approach concerning the question as to the possible objects of a usufruct.[241] They included movables and immovables,[242] corporeals and incorporeals,[243] single objects and the whole of an estate.[244] South African law continues their tradition; examples similar to those given by the Roman-Dutch authors are therefore found in modern cases and textbooks.[245]

Although a usufruct of money and other consumable things is impossible, Roman-Dutch law nevertheless followed Roman law[246] in recognizing a 'quasi-usufruct' pertaining to these kinds of objects.[247] The usufructuary, under a quasi-usufruct, becomes the owner of the usufructuary object.[248] He can use and enjoy the object, and take all the income derived from it for himself. However, the usufructuary must give security that, at the expiry of the usufruct, objects of the same quantity and quality, or the same amount of money, will be handed to the ultimate beneficiary (the 'nude' owner in

---

[236] Grotius (n. 7), 2, 39, 1; Voet (n. 6), 7, 4, 11 sq.
[237] Act 47 of 1937. See generally *Bhamjee v. Mergold Beleggings (Edms) Bpk* 1983 (4) SA 555 (T).
[238] S. 66.   [239] Grotius (n. 7), 2, 39, 15; Voet (n. 6), 7, 4, 1.
[240] Above, n. 229.   [241] De Waal (n. 1), 591 sq.
[242] Grotius (n. 7), 2, 39, 2; Huber (n. 38), 2, 39, 28; Van der Keessel (n. 85), 2, 4, 1.
[243] Huber (n. 38), 2, 39, 28; Van der Keessel (n. 65), 2, 39, 2.
[244] Voet (n. 6), 7, 1, 14; Huber (n. 38), 2, 39, 28; Van der Keessel (n. 65), 2, 39, 2.
[245] See generally Kleyn/Boraine (n. 17), 386; Van der Merwe (n. 14), 509 sq.; Van der Merwe/De Waal (n. 17), § 66, and the cases cited by these authors.
[246] See e.g. Ulp. D. 7, 5, 1; Gai. D. 7, 5, 2 and 7.
[247] Grotius (n. 7), 2, 39, 20; Voet (n. 6), 7, 5, 1 sqq.; Scheltinga (n. 114), 2, 39, 2; Van der Keessel (n. 85), 2, 4, 4; Van Leeuwen (n. 117), 2, 9, 6.
[248] Voet (n. 6), 7, 5, 1.

terms of a normal usufruct).[249] The legal institution of quasi-usufruct is thus a pragmatic exception to the rules governing usufruct in general; it is therefore not surprising that it has become firmly entrenched in South African law.[250]

(c) Exercise of usufruct

The powers and the duties of a usufructuary are numerous and a detailed discussion of them falls outside the scope of this paper. Only a few of the more important aspects receive attention against the background of the usufructuary's overall legal position.[251]

As can be deduced from their definition of usufruct,[252] the Roman-Dutch authors saw the essence of the usufructuary's powers in the possession, use, and enjoyment of the usufructuary object and in the drawing of its fruits, if any. This is evidently also the view in South African law.[253] South African law also follows the wide definition of the term 'fruit' recognized in Roman-Dutch law.[254] 'Fruit' therefore includes not only the natural produce of land and animals but also the 'civil fruits', i.e. income such as rent or interest.[255]

The main duty of the usufructuary has always been to return the property *salva rei substantia*, i.e. without deterioration or impairment, to the owner at the termination of the usufruct.[256] This, coupled with the rule that a usufructuary may only claim the fruits of the property, has always caused particular difficulties in the sphere of mining activities. In Roman law[257] the view was held that metals such as gold, silver, and iron were self-renewing (*renascentia*) and they were therefore treated as natural fruits. The Roman usufructuary was consequently allowed to exploit mines and to sell the minerals. In Roman-Dutch law[258] a distinction was drawn between self-renewing metals

[249] Grotius (n. 7), 2, 39, 20; Voet (n. 6), 7, 5, 1; Huber (n. 38), 2, 39, 32.

[250] *Master v. African Mines Corp Ltd* 1907 TS 925; *Ex parte Stevenson's Executors* 1939 CPD 29; *Geldenhuys v. Commissioner for Inland Revenue* 1947 (3) SA 256 (C); *Ex parte Eloff* 1953 (1) SA 617 (T); Olivier/Pienaar/Van der Walt (n. 17), 252; Van der Merwe (n. 14), 509 sq.; Van der Merwe/De Waal (n. 17), § 67.

[251] As far as classical Roman-Dutch law is concerned, see De Waal (n. 1), 593 sq.

[252] Above, Section V. 1.

[253] Hall/Kellaway (n. 10), 151 sq.; Kleyn/Boraine (n. 17), 386; Maasdorp (n. 10), 212; Olivier/Pienaar/Van der Walt (n. 17), 253; Van der Merwe (n. 14), 510; Van der Merwe/De Waal (n. 17), § 68.

[254] See e.g. Grotius (n. 7), 2, 39, 7 and 8; Voet (n. 6), 7, 1, 28 and 30.

[255] See generally the authorities cited above, n. 253.

[256] For Roman-Dutch law see Grotius (n. 7), 2, 38, 9; Voet (n. 6), 7, 1, 41; Van der Keessel (n. 85), 2, 4, 2; Van Leeuwen (n. 162), 1, 2, 15, 5; *idem* (n. 117), 2, 9, 3. For South African law see Hall/Kellaway (n. 10), 153 sq.; Kleyn/Boraine (n. 17), 386; Maasdorp (n. 10), 212; Olivier/Pienaar/Van der Walt (n. 17), 253; Van der Merwe (n. 14), 516; Van der Merwe/De Waal (n. 17), § 76.

[257] Ulp. D. 7, 1, 9, 2 and 3; Ulp. D. 24, 3, 7, 14.

[258] Voet (n. 6), 7, 1, 24; Van der Keessel (n. 65), 2, 37, 8; Van Leeuwen (n. 162), 1, 2, 15, 5; *idem* (n. 117), 2, 9, 4 and 5.

and minerals and those that could not renew themselves (*non renascentia*). Only the former were treated as natural fruits. Metals or minerals that were *non renascentia* (for example stones or clay[259]) had to be sold and the usufructuary could claim only the interest on the yield as civil fruits.[260] This distinction has been accepted in South African law.[261] However, today only salt is seen as *renascens*; all other metals and minerals are treated as *non renascentia*.[262] The usufructuary therefore has no claim to the metals or minerals as such, only to the interest on the capital yielded by their sale.[263] It should finally be noted that, as South Africa is a country rich in metals and minerals, most matters relating to mining activities are nowadays regulated by legislation.[264]

To ensure the fulfilment of his obligation to return the property *salva rei substantia*, the usufructuary was in Roman-Dutch law required to render security[265] to the owner and to furnish him with an inventory[266] of the usufructuary property. The duties of rendering security and an inventory are still viewed as important in South African law.[267] It is also interesting to note that the exceptions to the duty to give security, as they were acknowledged in Roman-Dutch law, are still applied in South Africa today.[268]

VI. CONCLUSION

Few areas of the Roman-Dutch law of property are as firmly based on Roman law as the law of servitudes.[269] It has been argued elsewhere that, as a consequence of this far-reaching reception of Roman law, Roman-Dutch authors show less reliance on other continental authors than in other areas of private law.[270] The history of the transplantation of the Roman-Dutch

---

[259] Van der Merwe (n. 14), 513.　　　　[260] See the authorities cited above, n. 258.
[261] Hall/Kellaway (n. 10), 153; Olivier/Pienaar/Van der Walt (n. 17), 252; Van der Merwe (n. 14), 513.
[262] Ibid.
[263] See the authorities cited above, n. 261, and *Master v. African Mines Corp Ltd* (n. 250); *Ex parte Graphorn* 1948 (4) SA 276 (O); *Ex parte Pierce* (n. 126); *Ex parte Eloff* (n. 250). However, the usufructuary has a claim to prospecting moneys as part of the usufruct: *Ex parte Venter* 1934 TPD 69; *Ex parte Erasmus* 1950 (1) SA 359 (T); *Ex parte Eloff* (n. 250); *Ex Parte Swiegers* 1966 (4) SA 7 (GW).
[264] The most important statute is the Minerals Act 50 of 1991.
[265] Grotius (n. 7), 2, 39, 3; Voet (n. 6), 7, 9, 1 sqq.; Johan Schrassert, *Consultatien, Advysen ende Advertissementen* (1744), Cons. 110, 4; Van Leeuwen (n. 162), 1, 2, 15, 6; *idem* (n. 117), 2, 9, 10.
[266] Voet (n. 6), 7, 9, 2.
[267] Hall/Kellaway (n. 10), 154 sq.; Kleyn/Boraine (n. 17), 387; Olivier/Pienaar/Van der Walt (n. 17), 253; Van der Merwe (n. 14), 516 sq.; Van der Merwe/De Waal (n. 17), § 77.
[268] See Voet (n. 6), 7, 9, 7–9; Van der Merwe (n. 14), 517 sq.; Van der Merwe/De Waal (n. 17), § 77.
[269] De Waal (n. 1), 567 sqq.　　　　[270] Ibid.

law of servitudes to South Africa and of the subsequent development of this branch of the law is largely a repetition, in a modern context, of the reception of the Roman law of servitudes in Holland. Thus, in South Africa we find an almost complete acceptance of the Roman-Dutch law of servitudes.

The reception of the Roman law of servitudes in Holland was followed by a process of refinement and adjustment. The development of the law of servitudes in South Africa has continued along those lines. Thus, we observe an unequivocal acceptance of Roman-Dutch law coupled with a readiness further to refine and adjust those Roman-Dutch rules and principles in order to make them cater for new needs. This process has been illustrated in various respects. Examples include the development of a more sophisticated definition of the concept of a servitude; an even more pragmatic application of the traditional requirements for the establishment of praedial servitudes; the willingness and ability to develop new types of praedial and personal servitudes; and the refinement of the rules relating to usufruct in the context of mining activities.

By and large, this development has been brought about by the courts. The influence of legislation on the matters discussed in this paper has been minimal. Legislation has played a more important role in connection with the constitution and extinction of servitudes: a somewhat technical matter which cannot be considered in the present context.[271]

With a clearly worked out system of rules and principles received from the Romans, the Roman-Dutch lawyers did not find it necessary to make much use of the works of other continental authors writing on servitudes. This probably explains the limited reliance on English law by the South African courts in their endeavour to develop this branch of the law. A sophisticated system was available to the courts and there was therefore little need to fall back on outside sources. Wherever *lacunae* did appear they could easily be filled by imaginative interpretation and adjustment of the existing law. Moreover, South African courts have on occasion referred to the fact that the English law of property in general, and the law of servitudes or 'easements' in particular, are 'basically different'[272] from the principles of Roman-Dutch law. Thus, sporadic references apart,[273] it is only in

---

[271] On the constitution and extinction of servitudes see generally Kleyn/Boraine (n. 17), 373–5, 382–5; Olivier/Pienaar/Van der Walt (n. 17), 255–62; Van der Merwe (n. 14), 525–40; Van der Merwe/De Waal (n. 17), §§ 94–104.

[272] *Venter v. Duff* 1946 OPD 294, 299. See generally *Malan v. Ardconnel Investments (Pty) Ltd* 1988 (2) SA 12 (A).

[273] See e.g. *Landman v. Daverin* (1881) 2 EDC 1, 10; *Dickens v. Colonial Govt* (1882) 3 NLR 103, 108 sq.; *In re Bennett and Green and the Bank of Africa Ltd* (1901) 22 NLR 404, 408–412; *Schultz v. Somerset East Municipality* 1931 EDL 37, 43 sq.; *Lategan v. Union Govt* 1937 CPD 197, 200 sq.; *Cliffside Flats (Pty) Ltd v. Bantry Rocks (Pty) Ltd* 1944 AD 106, 111, 117 sq.; *Reid v. Rocher* 1946 WLD 294, 297; *Schwedhelm v. Hauman* 1947 (1) SA 127 (E). In *Van der Merwe v. Wiese* 1948 (4) SA 8 (C) 25 the Court relied on English law to support the proposition that the requirement of passivity is not rigidly applied in the South African law of servi-

the context of restrictive conditions that English law has had a major impact.

tudes. The way in which the court used the English law in this decision has been criticized; see Jordan, (1958) 75 *SALJ* 184: 'Investigation of the English law, if relevant at all, is not pursued far enough.' See also De Waal (n. 32), 282. As to the requirement of passivity in general, see above, Section IV. 1. (e).

25: *Possession*

DUARD KLEYN

I. INTRODUCTION

From a comparative perspective, South African law is usually classified as a 'mixed system', representing a symbiosis between English law (common law) and Roman-Dutch law (Romano-Germanic or civil law).[1] However, although English law had a considerable influence in certain areas of modern South African law, its influence in the area of property law, of which possession traditionally forms part, is slight. Roman law is generally considered to be the more important source, in fact the basis, of South African property law.[2]

In seventeenth- and eighteenth-century Roman-Dutch law, general possessory theory was based predominantly on Roman law. However, this was not true in regard to the protection of possession (the possessory remedies): instead of the possessory interdicts of Roman law the *mandament van complainte*, the *mandament van maintenue*, and the *mandament van spolie* were used. *Complainte* had its origin in Anglo-Norman law, *maintenue* in medieval Italian law, and *spolie* in canon law. These remedies were received in the Netherlands from France via the Courts of Flanders.[3]

South African law presents very much the same picture. As far as general possessory theory is concerned (for example the theory in regard to the acquisition, retention, and loss of possession) South African authors have always relied heavily on Roman law and its interpretation by Roman-Dutch and other Western European *ius commune* authorities.[4] On the other hand,

---

[1] Tielman Roos, Hjalmar Reitz, *Principles of Roman-Dutch Law* (1909), 2 sqq.; J. G. Sauveplanne, *Rechtsstelsels in Vogelvlucht* (2nd reprint, 1981), 213 sqq.; D. H. van Zyl, *Beginsels van Regsvergelyking* (1981), 284 sqq.; René David, John E. C. Brierly, *Major Legal Systems in the World Today* (3rd edn., 1985), 25; Konrad Zweigert, Hein Kötz, *Introduction to Comparative Law*, vol. I (2nd edn., 1987), 240 sqq.; Reinhard Zimmermann, 'Roman Law in a Mixed Legal System: The South African Experience', in: Robin Evans-Jones (ed.), *The Civil Law Tradition in Scotland* (1995), 41 sqq.

[2] C. G. van der Merwe, *Sakereg* (2nd edn., 1989), 7 sqq.; D. G. Kleyn, A. Boraine, *Silberberg and Schoeman's The Law of Property* (3rd edn., 1992), 8.

[3] Duard Kleyn, 'The Concept and the Protection of Possession', in: Robert Feenstra, Reinhard Zimmermann (eds.), *Das römisch-holländische Recht: Fortschritte des Zivilrechts im 17. und 18. Jahrhundert* (1992), 545, 558.

[4] Cf. A. F. S. Maasdorp, *The Institutes of Cape Law: Book II, The Law of Things* (1903), 18: 'As regards the modes of acquisition of possession, it may be laid down generally that the rules of the Roman law with respect to the acquisition, as well as the retention and loss of

the only true possessory remedy in force today is the *mandament van spolie* (or spoliation order). This canon law remedy was received in South Africa as part of Roman-Dutch law, although it has subsequently experienced a number of modifications.[5]

In this Chapter I attempt first, to highlight some aspects of the history of general possessory theory, and then to deal with the history of the protection of possession.

II. GENERAL POSSESSORY THEORY

1. The distinction between possession and ownership

A fundamental principle of Roman law is the sharp distinction drawn between possession and ownership. This is reflected in the well known observation of Ulpian that possession has nothing in common with ownership.[6] In the Germanic law in force in the Netherlands during the pre-reception period, on the other hand, no such distinction was made. After the reception, however, the Roman law doctrine was followed and still forms part of modern Roman-Dutch law in South Africa.

The distinction between possession and ownership is usually explained in very simplistic terms by contrasting (i) possession as the *de facto* control of a thing[7] with (ii) ownership as a real right in respect of a thing. This gives rise to the following differences between the two concepts: mere loss of possession does not entail loss of ownership; for instance, in the case of theft the owner loses possession but not his right of ownership; and ownership may be acquired for someone without his knowledge or even against his wishes, whereas possession must be acquired with the knowledge of the pos-

---

possession, are still in most respects preserved and recognised amongst us'; J. W. Wessels, *History of the Roman-Dutch Law* (1908), 481: 'The effects of possession are with us very much the same as they were with the Romans'. See also William Burge, *Commentaries on the Civil Law and the Law of Holland* (1887), 135 sqq., who in his general discussion on possession refers to the *Digest*, Voet, Vinnius, Perezius, Brissonius, and Pothier; Maurits Josson, *Schets van Het Recht van de Zuid-Afrikaansche Republiek* (1897), 453 sqq., who relies heavily on Van der Linden; Manfred Nathan, *The Common Law of South Africa*, vol. I, *Persons and Property* (2nd edn., 1913), 373 sqq., who bases his entire discussion concerning general possessory theory on D. 41, 2; Maasdorp (as above) 12 sqq., who mainly uses Voet as authority, but also refers to Gaius and texts from the *Digest*. This is also the case in more recent textbooks on property law; cf. e.g. Van der Merwe (n. 2), 112 sqq.; C. G. van der Merwe, in: Dale Hutchison (ed.), *Wille's Principles of South African Law* (8th edn., 1991), 262 sqq.; Kleyn/Boraine (n. 3), 111 sqq.

[5] Below, Section III. 1.
[6] D. 4, 2, 12, 1: '*Nihil commune habet proprietas cum possessione . . .*'
[7] It is important to know that in South Africa the term 'thing' is commonly used to denote *res*, i.e. the object possessed. Usually the object of possession is corporeal but, as shown below, incorporeals may also be possessed in South African law.

sessor.[8] The most important consequence of the distinction between possession and ownership is the procedural differentiation between the petitory suit (*iudicium petitorium*) and the possessory suit (*iudicium possessorium*). This dichotomy has its roots in Roman law, and was consistently applied in canon and Roman-Dutch law.[9]

The same approach is followed in South Africa, as is clear from the earliest reported case-law. It is based on the principle that in the event of a dispute with respect to a thing, the parties must approach the court in a petitory suit if they are unable to settle the disagreement themselves. A petitory suit is based on the merits of the case. The rights of the parties in relation to the thing are in issue and must be proved. An important principle, however, is that no one is allowed to resort to self-help by high-handedly depriving a possessor of his possession. If anyone were to do so, the court would first of all restore the possession in a possessory suit, without considering the merits of the case. Thus, during spoliation proceedings (i.e. a possessory suit) the court will have regard only to the *de facto* issues of possession and deprivation (spoliation). The rights of the parties with respect to the thing are not in issue and are thus irrelevant.[10] The possessory suit provides '*interim* relief' only, as it may be followed by a subsequent petitory suit. In the latter suit the successful party at possessory proceedings might lose his possession if the opposing party proves a stronger right with respect to the thing.[11]

It is clear from the above why *mala fide* possession, such as that of a thief, is protected in a possessory suit. Usually the court will not know the possession to be *mala fide*, and even if it were to be alleged the investigation of such an allegation would not fall within the scope of those proceedings. Indeed, South African courts have protected *mala fide* possession even in

---

[8] Burge (n. 4), 135; Roos/Reitz (n. 4), 38; Nathan (n. 4), 373 sq. Cf. Van der Merwe (n. 2), 95 sqq.

[9] Kleyn (n. 3), 543 sq.

[10] *Curatoren van 'Pioneer Lodge, No. 1' v. Champion* 1879 OFS 51, 53: '*zoo vermeen ik dat in dit geval dit Hof alvorens eenig oordeel te geven omtrent quaestien van eigendomsrecht of bezitrecht de geappelleerden gelasten moet om de gespolieerde goederen te restitueren*' (so I take the view that in such a case the court, before giving decisions on property or rights of possession, must order the respondent to give back the spoliated goods); *De Villiers v. Holloway* (1902) 12 CTR 566, 569: '[The respondent] will be bound to restore possession before the further question as to the real rights of the parties to the property can be considered'; *Blomson v. Boshoff* 1905 TS 429, 432: 'He [the applicant] has been violently ejected from the premises, and he is therefore, without entering into any question of the rights of the parties, entitled to be restored to his possession, and when he is restored to his possession then the rights of the parties can be determined in the courts'. See also *Crause v. Reyersbach* (1882) 1 SAR 50, 51; *Strydom v. Markotter* (1903) 13 CTR 842, 843; *Xoxwana v. Hattingh* (1903) 24 NLR 67, 70; *Gwavu v. Makunga* (1906) 20 EDC 97, 99; *Armitage v. Govendalal* (1906) 27 NLR 587, 588 sq. This longstanding tradition has been confirmed by the Appellate Division in *Nienaber v. Stuckey* 1946 AD 1049, 1053 and *Mankowitz v. Loewenthal* 1982 (3) SA 758 (A) 763A.

[11] See *Nino Bonino v. De Lange* 1906 TS 120, 122.

instances where they were fully aware of the *mala fides*.[12] The character of the possessory protection under discussion is usually expressed by the maxim *spoliatus ante omnia restituendus est*. The despoiled possessor must be reinstated in his possession forthwith, before the merits of the case may be adjudicated on.[13]

In spite of the fact that the distinction between the possessory and petitory suit is of a fundamental nature according to civil law tradition, some earlier possessory proceedings did in fact require the applicant to prove a right with respect to the thing.[14] In certain cases the courts adjudicated the possessory suit specifically on the basis of the right of ownership.[15] This approach was occasionally followed even after the Appellate Division confirmed that the distinction between the possessory and petitory suits formed part of South African law.[16] Often an unfortunate use of language contributed to this confusion. For instance, in some possessory cases in which the court did not require the parties to prove a right with respect to the thing in issue it was nevertheless remarked in passing that the applicant had a possessory right or that he was despoiled of such a right.[17] This usage may also be attributed, in some instances, to the erroneous equation of the *man-*

[12] See *Yeko v. Qana* 1973 (4) SA 735 (A); *Fredericks v. Stellenbosch Divisional Council* 1977 (3) SA 113 (C); *Naidoo v. Moodley* 1982 (4) SA 82 (T). Cf., however, *Parker v. Mobil Oil of Southern Africa (Pty) Ltd* 1979 (4) SA 250 (NC) 255D-E; *Coetzee v. Coetzee* 1982 (1) SA 933 (C) 935D.

[13] *Greyling v. Estate Pretorius* 1947 (3) SA 514 (W) 516: '*Spoliatus ante omnia restituendus est*. If this principle means anything it means that before the court will allow any enquiry into the ultimate rights of the parties the property which is the subject of the act of spoliation must be restored . . . irrespective of the question as to who is in law entitled to be in possession of such property.' See also *Curatoren van Pioneer Lodge, No. 1 v. Champion* (n. 10), 53.

[14] *Goldsmith v. Irwin* (1907) 17 CTR 44, 45: 'The only question the court has now to decide is who is entitled lawfully to the possession of these articles'; *Van Malsen v. Alderson and Flitton* 1931 TPD 38, 39: 'It is quite clear that in order to succeed in a spoliation application the person asking for relief must show that there has been an illicit deprivation of the *right* of possession' (emphasis added).

[15] *Chambers v. Nongausa* 1919 EDL 85, 88: 'It seems to me that the question of ownership is important, for this reason—that there cannot be possession, in law, except by valid title. The title that is relied on in this case is ownership'. See also *Burnham v. Neumeyer* 1917 TPD 630, 634 sqq. where the court emphasized the ownership of the respondent and used it as confirmation that the applicant had not succeeded in proving his possession. See also *Hall v. Pitsoane* 1911 TPD 853, 860.

[16] See *Nienaber v. Stuckey* 1946 AD 1049, 1053; *Mankowitz v. Loewenthal* 1982 (3) SA 758 (A) 763A; cf. *Runsin Properties (Pty) Ltd v. Ferreira* 1982 (1) SA 658 (SEC) 670A: 'In my view, however, once the applicant has proved that it was in possession or was *entitled* to possession and that the respondent moved into the premises, it is for the respondent to establish his right to be there' (emphasis added). Cf. J. C. Sonnekus, '[Case discussion of] *Mbuku v. Mdinwa* 1982 (1) SA 219 (Tk) and *Runsin Properties (Pty) Ltd v. Ferreira* 1982 (1) SA 658 (EC)', 1982 *TSAR* 182.

[17] See the remark of Gardiner JP in *Mans v. Marais* 1932 CPD 352, 355: 'There was, in my opinion, an illicit deprivation by Mans of Marais' right of possession'. See also *Petersen v. Petersen* 1974 (1) PH B5 (R): 'In a situation such as this where *stante matrimonio* neither spouse's right to possession was inferior to the other's . . .'

dament van spolie with an interdict,[18] in the case of which *prima facie* proof of a clear right is required. In recent times it has become settled that the *mandament* cannot be considered to be an interdict.[19] Consequently the cases mentioned above must be treated with circumspection, as they do not reflect the true nature and character of the possessory suit.

2. The elements and definition of possession

Analysis of the distinction between possession and ownership does not, however, explain what possession is. As was the case in Roman and Roman-Dutch law, it is accepted today that possession consists of a physical element (*corpus*) and a mental element (*animus*).[20] *Corpus* denotes physical control over the thing in question, but does not in itself constitute possession in the legal sense. The *corpus* must be accompanied by a certain mental attitude or intention with respect to the thing. Therefore persons who are incapable of forming the intention required by law, for example lunatics and infants, must be considered unable to possess.[21]

In Roman law these two elements (especially the *animus*) came into play mainly with regard to the acquisition, retention and loss of possession. Thus it is taught that possession was acquired *corpore et animo*; it was imperative for both elements to be present. The measure of physical control (*corpus*) required depended on the nature of the thing and the surrounding circumstances. Possession of a piece of land did not necessitate the occupation of every square metre of the area. Possession could be retained by *animus* alone, as where an owner exercised his possession through a lessee or a borrower, or (in the case of immovable property) where he was secretly deprived of the thing in his possession. Possession could be lost through loss of either *corpus*, or *animus*, or both (*aut corpore aut animo*); for example, someone who relinquished the intention to possess lost possession (*animo solo*), even though he may still have exercised physical control.[22] The law regarding the acquisition, retention, and loss of possession in current South African law remains strongly influenced by Roman doctrine.[23]

[18] See e.g. *Hillkloof Builders (Pty) Ltd v. Jacomelli* 1972 (4) SA 228 (D) 231H: '... but nevertheless there is sufficient [control], to my mind, to create a strong doubt as to the *prima facie* right to "possession" asserted by the applicant'.

[19] Below, Section III. 1.

[20] See e.g. *Groenewald v. Van der Merwe* 1917 AD 233, 238; Van der Merwe (n. 2), 97 sqq.; Kleyn/Boraine (n. 2), 114 sqq.

[21] Van der Merwe (n. 2), 103.

[22] D. 41, 2, and see generally R. Dekkers, 'Hoe juristen een leer opbouwen: het bezit', vol. III (1949), no. 4, *Mededelingen van de Koninklijke Vlaamse Academie voor Wetenschappen, Letteren en Schone Kunsten van België* 23 sqq.; K. Olivecrona, *Three Essays in Roman Law* (1949), 52 sqq.; G. MacCormack, 'The role of *animus* in the classical law of possession', (1969) 86 *Zeitschrift der Savigny-Stiftung für Rechtsgeschichte (Romanistische Abteilung)* 105 sqq.; Max Kaser, *Das römische Privatrecht*, vol. I (2nd edn. 1971), 390 sqq.

[23] See Van der Merwe (n. 2), 112 sqq.

In the development of legal thought subsequent to the enactment of Justinian's codification, different functions of possession came to be identified. In certain instances possession was required for the acquisition of ownership. Some kinds of possession were protected by law, others not.[24] In order to distinguish between the different functions and variations of possession, recourse was had to the *animus* element. Different forms of *animus* were identified, such as the *animus domini* (the intention to be the owner of the thing), the *animus sibi habendi* (the intention to hold for oneself), the *animus ex re commodum acquirendi* (the intention to secure some benefit for oneself), and the *animus possidendi* (the intention to possess). This subdivision provided greater clarity in regard to certain aspects of the law of possession, but as far as defining possession and classifying it into different types are concerned it led to considerable confusion.

No definition of possession is to be found in Roman law. Paul,[25] following Labeo, merely points out that '*[p]ossessio appellata est, . . . a sedibus quasi positio*'; in other words, the term *possessio* is derived from 'seat' or 'position'. The Roman-Dutch author Arnoldus Vinnius[26] acknowledged that the task of defining possession is difficult, since such a definition should embrace all the possible meanings contained in the concept.

Early authorities on South African law did, however, attempt to provide a general, all-embracing definition of possession. William Burge, Mauritz Josson, Tielman Roos and Hjalmar Reitz, Manfred Nathan, as well as A. F. S. Maasdorp defined possession as the physical control of a thing accompanied by the *animus domini*. The *animus domini* was expressed in terms such as 'the intention to hold for oneself', 'to hold for oneself as owner', and 'to hold as one's own'. By this definition borrowers, depositaries, agents, servants, lessees, and usufructuaries were not considered to have possession.[27]

The prominence of the *animus domini* in relation to the concept of possession is characteristic of Roman and Roman-Dutch law. The position is different in English law, as pointed out by George Morice, a contemporary of the authors just mentioned, who wrote a comparative work on the differences between English and Roman-Dutch law. In English law also possession is said to consist of a physical and a mental element, but it is the physical control that constitutes legal possession. The intention to possess is implied from the acts denoting physical control, and persons are regarded as possessors even where the *animus domini* does not exist at all.[28]

The problem inherent in a definition of possession that emphasizes the

---

[24] Below, Section II. 3.   [25] D. 41, 2, 1 pr.

[26] *Selectarum Juris Quaestionum*, 2, 36. See Kleyn (n. 3), 554.

[27] Burge (n. 4), 135; Josson (n. 4), 453; Roos/Reitz (n. 1), 34; Nathan (n. 4), 373; Maasdorp (n. 4), 13.

[28] George T. Morice, *English and Roman-Dutch Law* (1903), 64 sq.

animus domini is that it does not include all the instances of possession protected by the possessory remedy (the *mandament van spolie*).[29] Thus Maasdorp, who in 1903 also defined possession as physical control accompanied by the *animus domini*, experienced difficulties in explaining the position of the lessee. He considered it an open question whether, in the light of the maxim *huur gaat voor koop* (lease takes precedence over sale), a lessee should not be awarded possession similar to that of a pledgee.[30] In later editions of his work it is stated that a lessee has 'a measure of possession'.[31] Recently C. G. van der Merwe[32] introduced his discussion of possession with this general definition: 'Possession is the physical control by a person of a corporeal thing with the intention of keeping the control of it for his own benefit.' This implies *corpus* plus *animus ex re commodum acquirendi*, and could arguably be said to create the problem that the definition does not embrace the kind of possession required for the acquisition of ownership.[33] The latest approach in textbooks on property law is to refrain from giving a single comprehensive definition of possession since, it is argued, the content thereof depends on the particular consequence or function one has in mind.[34]

3. The traditional classifications of possession

The tradition of classifying *possessio* into *civilis* and *naturalis*, *iusta* and *iniusta*, as well as *bona fide* and *mala fide* has its roots in Roman law. Regarding the first classification, there is a certain degree of confusion as to the meaning of the term *naturalis possessio* in Roman sources.[35] This confusion is also found in Roman-Dutch[36] and South African law, where the authoritative sources have attached different meanings to the concepts of *possessio civilis* and *naturalis*. The classification by Johannes Voet is of

---

[29] Below, Section III. 2.   [30] Maasdorp (n. 4), 13, fn. 6.

[31] See e.g. C. G. Hall, *Maasdorp's Institutes of South African Law*, vol. II (10th edn., 1976), 12.

[32] Van der Merwe (n. 4), 262.   [33] Below, Section II. 3.

[34] See Van der Merwe (n. 2), 90; Kleyn/Boraine (n. 2), 118. J. C. Sonnekus, J. L. Neels, *Sakereg Vonnisbundel* (2nd edn., 1994), 132 acknowledge the fact that the distinction between different forms of *animus* is still of practical importance in South African law. Nevertheless they propose (122), it seems, a general definition of possession. They define it as the physical control accompanied by the intention to keep the thing for oneself. This definition is too vague. The intention to keep for oneself can easily be interpreted as the *animus domini*. If this interpretation is followed the definition would not embrace possession protected by the *mandament van spolie*, as they indeed acknowledge (132).

[35] See S. Riccobono, 'Zur Terminologie der Besitzverhältnisse', (1910) 27 *Zeitschrift der Savigny-Stiftung für Rechtsgeschichte* (*Romanistische Abteilung*) 321 sqq.; G. MacCormack, *Naturalis possessio*, (1967) 84 *Zeitschrift der Savigny-Stiftung für Rechtsgeschichte* (*Romanistische Abteilung*) 47 sqq.; A. W. F. Middelberg, *Bescherming van het Houderschap* (unpublished LL D thesis, University of Pretoria, 1953) 17 sqq.; Kaser (n. 22), 386.

[36] See Kleyn (n. 3), 554 sqq.; Van der Merwe (n. 2), 108 sq.

particular importance and has strongly influenced South African law. Voet[37] attaches two meanings to *possessio civilis* and *possessio naturalis* respectively. The latter term may indicate the situation where a person controls a thing with his body and his mind (*corpore et animo suo*), whereas the former may refer to one who controls a thing *animo solo* (through others), for instance through a depositary. On the other hand *possessio civilis* may mean *possessio animo seu opinio domini*, whereas *possessio naturalis* may indicate *possessio animo sibi habendi* without the *opinio domini*. The latter category includes persons such as lessees and borrowers. In South African law Voet was followed by Nathan, Maasdorp, and C. G. van der Merwe, amongst others.[38] The courts too have accepted this classification,[39] but not always with felicitous results. In *Welgemoed v. Coetzer*[40] reference was made to the possession to be proved by a plaintiff in prescription proceedings as *possessio civilis*. Relying on Voet, the Court defined it as 'the holding or detaining of the corporeal thing with the intention of keeping it for oneself'. Unfortunately, however, this definition corresponds to Voet's definition of *naturalis possessio* rather than his definition of *possessio civilis*.

Traditionally the distinction between *possessio civilis* and *naturalis* has been used to differentiate between possession which is protected by the possessory remedies and that which is not. Considering that in modern South African law virtually everyone in physical control of a thing is protected,[41] this distinction has lost its importance and is no longer considered to be crucial.[42]

The distinction between *iusta* and *iniusta possessio* has its origin in the protection of possession by means of interdicts in Roman law.[43] The possessory interdicts served to protect *possessio iusta*, which was interpreted to mean possession held *nec vi, nec clam,* and *nec precario* (without force or stealth and not on sufferance). Although South African authors[44] writing in the early part of this century mentioned the distinction in their treatises, it is no longer relevant to the protection of possession.[45] The distinction was used in South Africa also in connection with the acquisition of ownership by prescription. The old Prescription Act[46] required the acquirer to possess *nec vi, nec clam,* and *nec precario.* This requirement was abolished by the new Prescription Act:[47] nowadays even a possessor with *iniusta possessio*

---

[37] Johannes Voet, *Commentarius ad Pandectas*, 41, 2, 3. See Kleyn (n. 3), 555 sq.
[38] See Nathan (n. 4), 374; Maasdorp (n. 4), 15 sq.; J. T. R. Gibson, *Wille's Principles of South African Law* (6th edn., 1970), 194; Hutchison/Van der Merwe (n. 4), 264 sq.
[39] E.g. *Scholtz v. Faifer* 1910 TS 243, 246.
[40] 1946 TPD 701, 712.   [41] Below, Section III. 2.
[42] Cf. Maasdorp (n. 4), 17, who as early as 1903 remarked that the distinction is of no practical importance. See also Van der Merwe (n. 2), 110; Hutchison/Van der Merwe (n. 4), 264, fn. 32; Kleyn/Boraine (n. 2), 125.
[43] Kaser (n. 22), 396 sqq.
[44] Cf. Burge (n. 4), 136; Nathan (n. 4), 375; Roos/Reitz (n. 1), 34; Maasdorp (n. 4), 15 sq.
[45] Van der Merwe (n. 2), 112; Kleyn/Boraine (n. 2), 126.
[46] 18 of 1943.   [47] 68 of 1969.

may acquire ownership by prescription. The distinction is therefore no longer of any use and can do little more than create confusion.

The only distinction of any practical value today is the distinction between *bona fide* and *mala fide* possession. It is used to establish a possessor's right to compensation for improvements to the property of another, the right to claim delictual damages, and the acquisition of fruits.[48] Here too confusion has been caused by inaccurate definitions. The early authorities on South African law described *bona* and *mala fide* possession without reference to the lawfulness of the possession. In its simplest form, *bona fide* possession was defined as 'possession by a man who thinks he is the owner', and *mala fide* possession as 'possession by a man who knows that he is not the owner'.[49] The latter definition, according to which every possessor would be *mala fide* if he were aware of the fact that he is not the owner of the thing, led to the absurd perception that the possession of a lessee and an usufructuary was, like that of a thief, *mala fide*.[50] This view was also followed by the courts.[51] In 1970 J. D. van der Vyver commented on this absurdity and made it clear that the distinction between *mala fide* and *bona fide* possession is only relevant and valid with respect to unlawful possession.[52] This approach is now followed in at least some of the more recent textbooks.[53]

4. The functions, or effects, of possession

Johannes Voet[54] discussed some of the advantages (*commoda*) of possession and indicated that these include, for example, that a *bona fide* possessor acquires fruits, that every possessor enjoys a stronger position in law with regard to the thing in question than a non-possessor, and that possession is protected by the possessory remedies. At the start of this century Morice[55] explained that in South African law 'possession is an elementary conception in law which enters into many other legal notions'. Many of the other early

---

[48] See generally Van der Merwe (n. 2), 112, 152 sqq.; Kleyn/Boraine (n. 2), 149 sqq., 216 sqq.; G. L. Peiris, 'Possession and Policy in a Modern Civil Law System', (1983) 16 *CILSA* 318 sqq.

[49] Roos/Reitz (n. 1), 34.

[50] Cf. Maasdorp (n. 4), 17; Morice (n. 28), 67; R. W. Lee, A. M. Honoré, T. W. Price, *The South African Law of Property, Family Relations and Succession* (1954), 10 sq.; Gibson (n. 38), 194; C. G. van der Merwe, *Sakereg* (1979), 81 sq.; Hutchison/Van der Merwe (n. 4), 265.

[51] See *Brunsdon's Estate v. Brunsdon's Estate* 1920 CPD 172 where the possession of a usufructuary was considered to be *mala fide*. The same approach was taken with respect to a lessee in *Rubin v. Botha* 1911 AD 568.

[52] See J. D. van der Vyver, 'Die juridiese grondslag van besitsbeskerming', (1970) 33 *THRHR* 231, 237 sqq.

[53] See Van der Merwe (n. 2), 154; Kleyn/Boraine (n. 2), 149 sqq.; Sonnekus/Neels (n. 34), 243. See also M. Klopper, 'Die aard van die juridiese belang van houers by skadevergoeding', (1983) 16 *Obiter* 71, 76; A. J. van der Walt, 'Die funksies en omskrywing van besit', (1988) 51 *THRHR* 276, 278 sq.

[54] Voet (n. 37), 41, 2, 16. See Kleyn (n. 3), 547.   [55] Morice (n. 28), 64.

authorities too identified certain 'effects' and 'benefits' of possession, as well as 'rights' of a possessor. They pointed mainly to the fact that possession can lead to the acquisition of ownership and that it is protected against any unlawful deprivation.[56]

In later years a more sophisticated and jurisprudentially sound effort was made to identify the different functions or effects of possession.[57] The result of these labours was that most authors, as stated above, preferred not to provide a general definition of possession.[58] Following the lead of the academic writers, South African courts now also tend to accept the notion that possession has a number of different consequences, or functions.[59] The most important functions usually distinguished are the following:[60]

(a) Possession may lead to the acquisition of ownership by means, for example, of delivery, *occupatio*, and prescription. Apart from *corpus*, *animus domini* is required. This is usually referred to as the property-related function (*saaklike funksie*) of possession.

(b) Possession is protected by the *mandament van spolie* against unlawful deprivation. Here the courts presently require the *animus ex re commodum acquirendi*. This constitutes the policy function (*regspolitieke funksie*) of possession.

(c) Furthermore, possession has a security function (*sekuriteitsfunksie*), in that it is necessary for the inception and continued existence of a right of pledge and retention. For this function the *animus ex re commodum acquirendi*, in the sense of the intention to hold the thing as real security, suffices.

(d) Possession creates a rebuttable presumption that the possessor of a movable thing is its owner, which constitutes the probative function (*bewysregtelike funksie*) of possession. The courts have accepted the approach that in this regard the *animus domini* is required.

(e) Possession is an element of a number of statutory crimes, where the exact meaning of possession (especially regarding *animus*) depends on the intention of the legislator in the specific statute.

(f) A *bona fide* possessor is entitled, *inter alia*, to the fruits of the thing in

[56] See Josson (n. 4), 453 sq.; Nathan (n. 4), 377; Roos/Reitz (n. 1), 37; Maasdorp (n. 4), 18, 23 sq.

[57] Wouter de Vos, ''n Bespreking van sekere aspekte van die regsposisie van besitters', 1959 *Acta Juridica* 14 sqq.; A. D. J. van Rensburg, C. G. van der Merwe, 'Die aard van besit en die *animus*-element daarvan', (1978) 41 *THRHR* 113 sqq. See also H. R. Hahlo, Ellison Kahn, *The Union of South Africa: The Development of its Laws and Constitution* (1960), 574; Van der Merwe (n. 49), 63 sqq.; *idem* (n. 2), 92 sqq.; H. J. Delport, N. J. J. Olivier, *Sakereg Vonnisbundel* (2nd edn., 1981), 57; Kleyn/Boraine (n. 2), 118. Cf. Van der Walt, (1988) 51 *THRHR* 282 sqq.

[58] Above, Section II. 2.

[59] See e.g. *Erasmus v. Minister van Wet en Orde* 1991 (1) SA 453 (O) 459A-C.

[60] For a resumé see Van der Merwe (n. 2), 92 sqq.; Kleyn/Boraine (n. 2), 118; Van der Walt, (1988) 51 *THRHR* 282 sqq.

his possession, should such fruits become separated from it prior to *litis contestatio*. A *bona fide* possessor must believe that he is the owner of the thing (*opinio domini*).

In his 1988 inaugural address A. van der Walt[61] criticized the aforementioned approach. He pointed out correctly that the prevailing confusion surrounding the law of possession is mainly due to inconsistent and vague terminology. In particular he objected to the use of the term 'possession' in a general sense, whilst at the same time a more specific meaning is attached to it depending on the context. Instead, he suggested using the term 'control' (*beheer*) to indicate all forms of physical or actual control of a thing. 'Control' would also consist of a physical and a mental element. The mental element could take on different forms, such as the intention to be owner and the intention to possess the thing for one's own benefit, constituting different forms of 'control'. Different consequences could be attached to the existence, transfer, and disturbance of 'control'. Van der Walt distinguished between lawful and unlawful 'control', and between 'control' in good and bad faith. The term 'possession' could, however, be used to refer to unlawful 'control' with intent to be the owner in the light of the legislation in regard to prescription. Control without intent to be the owner could also be referred to as 'detention'.

It has subsequently been submitted that Van der Walt's new possessory doctrine does not seem to depart from the present approach in any fundamental way. Apart from discarding Latin terminology, it continues to enshrine the various familiar functions and formulations of possession.[62]

5. Possession of incorporeals

The function of incorporeals (i.e. rights) as objects within the realm of property law was recognized by the Romans,[63] and the possession of incorporeals was accordingly protected by the possessory interdicts. This applied in particular to the possession of the right of a usufructuary, known as *quasi possessio*.[64] In canon law the possessory protection of *quasi possessio* (also referred to as *possessio iuris*) was extended far beyond the scope of usufruct. Thus even the *quasi* possession of the matrimonial state was awarded possessory protection.[65] Roman-Dutch law was similarly acquainted with the

[61] (1988) 51 *THRHR* 276 sqq., 508 sqq.

[62] Duard Kleyn, 'Besitsbeskerming en die besitsleer: 'n reddingspoging', (1991) 54 *THRHR* 21 sqq.

[63] See, for a discussion, H. F. Jolowicz, B. Nicholas, *Historical Introduction to the Study of Roman Law* (3rd edn., 1972), 412 sqq.; Kaser (n. 22), 453 sq., 465; Duard Kleyn, 'Dogmatiese probleme rakende die rol van onstoflike sake in die sakereg', (1993) 26 *De Jure* 6 sqq.

[64] D. 43, 16, 3, 13 sq.; D. 43, 16, 3, 16 sq.; R. M. W. Dias, 'A reconsideration of *possessio*', 1956 *Cambridge LJ* 241; Max Kaser, *Das römische Privatrecht*, vol. II (2nd edn., 1975), 256.

[65] See Duard Kleyn, *Die Mandament van Spolie in die Suid-Afrikaanse Reg* (unpublished LL D thesis, University of Pretoria, 1986) 114 sq., 121.

notion of *quasi possessio*: to prevent a person from exercising a servitudal right was regarded as an instance of spoliation and in such a case the *mandament van spolie* could be instituted.[66]

Early South African authorities generally recognized *quasi* possession of rights, especially with respect to servitudal rights.[67] South African courts have a long tradition of protecting this kind of possession by means of the *mandament van spolie*.[68] Although it is not as easy to establish the possession of incorporeals as it is to establish that of corporeals, it has become accepted that the possession of incorporeals essentially consists of the exercise of the professed right. This means that to prevent the exercise of such a right amounts to an act of spoliation.[69]

Regarding the nature of rights protected by the *mandament*, it appears that South African law does not follow the broad approach of canon law. Usually only the possession of a real or personal right that would entitle its holder to some form of use of the thing is protected in this manner. The *mandament* is used, for instance, to protect different kinds of servitudes[70] as well as the right to the supply of electricity or water.[71] Consequently, not all rights lend themselves to *quasi* possession. This would imply that the *mandament van spolie* does not serve a catch-all function in the sense that it can be used to enforce any contractual, delictual, or real right.[72]

---

[66] Kleyn (n. 65), 239, 242.

[67] See Burge (n. 4), 136; Nathan (n. 4), 377; Roos/Reitz (n. 1), 34; Maasdorp (n 4), 14 sq.; R. W. Lee, *An Introduction to Roman-Dutch Law* (1915), 148.

[68] *Nienaber v. Stuckey* 1946 AD 1049, 1055 sq.: 'The fact that these authorities [Wassenaer and Voet] state generally, and without any limitation or exception, that the possession of incorporeal rights is protected against spoliation means that the holders of such servitudal rights as rights of way, where clearly the person who holds the servitude does not have exclusive possession of the land, are entitled to the relief against dispossession by spoliation.' See also *Nino Bonino v. De Lange* 1906 TS 120, 122; *Pretorius v. Pretorius* 1927 TPD 178, 180 sq.; *Shapiro v. South African Savings and Credit Bank* 1949 (4) SA 985 (W) 991; *Sebastian v. Malelane Irrigation Board* 1950 (2) SA 690 (T) 694; *Painter v. Strauss* 1951 (3) SA 307 (O) 318; *Stanhope Motors and Machinery Sales v. Pretoria Light Aircraft Co (Pty) Ltd* 1951 (2) PH F79 (T); *Rooibokoord Sitrus (Edms) Bpk v. Louw's Creek Sitrus Koöperatiewe Maatskappy Bpk* 1964 (3) SA 601 (T) 604; *Deljon v. Bloemloop Properties (Pty) Ltd* 1972 (2) PH A58 (C); *Adamson v. Boshoff* 1975 (3) SA 221 (C) 230; *Beukes v. Crous* 1975 (4) SA 215 (NC) 218; *Bennett Pringle (Pty) Ltd v. Adelaide Municipality* 1977 (1) SA 230 (E) 233; *Bank van die Oranje-Vrystaat v. Rossouw* 1984 (2) SA 644 (C) 648; *Ntshwaqela v. Chairman, Western Cape Regional Services Council* 1988 (3) SA 218 (C) 221; *Bon Quelle (Edms) Bpk v. Munisipaliteit van Otavi* 1989 (1) SA 508 (A).

[69] *Rooibokoord Sitrus v. Louw's Creek Sitrus Koöperatiewe Maatskappy Bpk* (n. 68); *Jansen v. Madden* 1968 (1) SA 81 (GW) 84.

[70] *Nienaber v. Stuckey* (n. 68); *Shapiro v. South African Savings and Credit Bank* (n. 68); *Buffelsfontein Gold Mining Co Ltd v. Bekker* 1961 (3) SA 381 (T); *Bon Quelle (Edms) Bpk v. Munisipaliteit van Otavi* 1989 (1) SA 508 (A); *Willowdale Estates CC v. Bryanmore Estates Ltd* 1990 (3) SA 954 (W).

[71] *Sebastian v. Malelane Irrigation Board* (n. 68), 494; *Painter v. Strauss* 1951 (n. 68); *Naidoo v. Moodley* 1982 (4) SA 82 (T) 84; *Froman v. Herbmore Timber & Hardware (Pty) Ltd* 1984 (3) SA 609 (W) 610.

[72] Cf. *Stanhope Motors and Machinery Sales v. Pretoria Light Aircraft* (n. 68); *Slabbert v. Theodoulou* 1952 (2) SA 667 (T). See Sonnekus/Neels (n. 34), 168.

In certain spoliation cases concerning the protection of *quasi* possession, the applicant was required to prove the existence of the professed right in order to succeed with the *mandament*.[73] This is in accordance with canon law[74] but contrary to general possessory theory, since it implies that the Court must adjudicate upon the merits of the case, i.e. upon the rights of the parties; these rights, as remarked above, should not be in issue during possessory proceedings.[75] This approach has, however, been rejected by the Appellate Division[76] and it is now clear that the applicant need prove only that he performed the actions normally associated with such a right.

In spite of the fact that the possession and the protection of incorporeals are part and parcel of the South African common law, they have attracted criticism from certain academic writers during the past fifteen years. Sonnekus maintains that it is totally unacceptable from both an historical and a theoretical point of view, since only corporeals can be possessed. He considers the protection of incorporeals by means of the *mandament* as an extraordinary application of the remedy, and is of the opinion that, in cases where the so-called 'possession of rights' has in fact been protected, the possession concerned actually amounted to the possession of a corporeal thing.[77] This view does not deserve to be supported: apart from the fact that it is historically incorrect, it is doubtful whether the possession of, for instance, the right of way over a piece of land could ever constitute possession of the road or land itself. Van der Walt also considers the protection of *quasi* possession as peculiar, but ascribes its continual use to the extended application of the *mandament* as a remedy to protect the public against self-help. He does not acknowledge the *mandament* to be a true possessory remedy.[78]

In general the aversion to the whole concept of *quasi* possession in South African law can be seen as part of the recent tendency among some academics to regard only corporeals as things. According to them, property law should concern itself only with material objects. The functioning of incorporeals in this sphere of private law must be seen as exceptional. This view

---

[73] *Pretorius v. Pretorius* (n. 68), 181; *Jansen v. Madden* 1968 (1) SA 81 (GW) 84; *Beukes v. Crous* 1975 (4) SA 215 (NC) 221.

[74] See Kleyn (n. 65), 114 sq.   [75] Above, Section II. 1.

[76] *Bon Quelle (Edms) Bpk v. Munisipaliteit van Otavi* (n. 68), 513 sq. See also *Van Wyk v. Kleynhans* 1969 (1) SA 221 (GW) 223; *Willowvale Estates CC v. Bryanmore Estates Ltd* (n. 70), 957. See further A. J. van der Walt, 'Three cases on the *mandament van spolie*', (1983) 100 *SALJ* 691; Van der Merwe (n. 2), 123. Sonnekus, however, maintains that the existence of a right must be proved, although his submission was rejected by the Appellate Division in the *Bon Quelle* case: See Sonnekus/Neels (n. 34), 169 sq.

[77] J. C. Sonnekus, *Sakereg Vonnisbundel* (1980), 54; Sonnekus/Neels (n. 34), 168 sqq.; J. C. Sonnekus, 'Mandament van spolie: kragtige remedie by kragonderbreking?', 1985 *TSAR* 333 sqq.; *idem*, 'Besit van serwituutbevoegdhede, mandament van spolie en logika', 1989 *TSAR* 429 sqq.

[78] A. J. van der Walt, 'Nog eens *Naidoo v. Moodley*: 'n repliek', (1984) 47 *THRHR* 689 sqq.

does not, however, correspond with the approach followed either in legislation or by the courts.[79]

6. Is possession a real right?

The question of whether possession is or may be regarded as a real right forms the basis of an age-old debate, which remains unresolved in South African law.

As Roman private law did not function against the backdrop of subjective rights, it is generally accepted that in Roman law possession was seen as a factual relationship, which gave rise to certain consequences.[80]

According to the doctrine of subjective rights, developed much later, property law concerns itself with real rights. As possession is usually treated as part of property law the question arises whether it should not also be classified as a real right. The Roman-Dutch authorities held divergent opinions on this issue, but the majority apparently regarded possession as a factual situation.[81] The nomenclature used by some of them did, however, cause a great deal of confusion in South African law, due to its inconsistency with modern terminolgy regarding subjective rights.[82] Two approaches are of specific importance in this regard.

First, authors such as Grotius, Ulrich Huber, and Van der Keessel refer to the functions or consequences of possession as 'rights'; for example, they describe the fact that possession is protected against any unlawful deprivation as *bezit-recht* or *ius possessionis*. Although these authors point out that the 'right' is that which flows from possession, their way of expressing themselves can none the less easily create the impression that they regarded possession itself as a right.[83]

Secondly, Voet was of the opinion that possession may be regarded as both a factual situation and a right. Possession, being physical control (*corpus*), accompanied by a certain mental attitude (*animus*), is a matter of fact. However, a person who receives a thing *ex iusta causa* (for example via a contract of sale) from a *non dominus* has a *ius possessionis*. Here Voet regards as a right what we would regard as an 'entitlement' flowing from a right, i.e. the content of the right.[84]

The works of earlier South African authors do not debate the question in any great detail, but they reveal the same divergence of opinion as prevailed in Roman-Dutch law. Thus some authors merely state that possession is a

---

[79] See, for discussion, Kleyn, (1993) 26 *De Jure* 1 sqq.; Kleyn/Boraine (n. 2), 9 sqq.

[80] D. 4, 6, 19; D. 41, 2, 1, 3; Wouter de Vos, 1959 *Acta Juridica* 190 sqq.

[81] See, for discussion, Kleyn (n. 3), 549 sqq.

[82] See, esp. with respect to the terms 'right' and 'entitlement', J. D. van der Vyver, 'The Doctrine of Private Law Rights', in: S. A. Strauss (ed.), *Huldigingsbundel vir W. A. Joubert* (1988), 209 sqq.

[83] Kleyn (n. 3), 541 sqq.   [84] Ibid. 552 sq.

matter of fact,[85] whereas others regard it as a real right.[86] Some, adhering to the latter view, describe possession as 'the simplest form of real right'[87] or as 'the least in extent of the rights *in rem*'.[88] The opinion of Wille is influenced by both the above-mentioned approaches in Roman-Dutch law: 'Possession is a real right because the rights of a possessor are legally protected against all other persons. The question, however, whether a particular person has possession of a particular thing is a question of fact.'[89] In some instances South African courts have also regarded possession as a real right.[90]

More finely nuanced arguments have recently been advanced, though it is generally acknowledged that the debate is of little practical importance.[91]

Van der Merwe,[92] like Voet, is of the opinion that possession can be regarded as both a fact and a real right. The point of view adopted, according to him, depends on the following considerations. First, it is necessary to distinguish between possession as a legal fact and the consequences thereof. Possession as a legal fact consists of the physical control (*corpus*) accompanied by the *animus*. The consequence of possession, namely that it is protected against unlawful deprivation, can, on the other hand, be regarded as a real right. (It is noteworthy that Van der Merwe uses the term *ius possessionis* to denote 'consequence of possession'.) Secondly, the nature, or character, ascribed to a real right is of importance. If a real right is defined as the direct control over a thing, possession can qualify as a real right. On the other hand, if a real right is seen as an absolute right, possession can be regarded only as a fact. Thirdly, Van der Merwe points out that it is vital to distinguish between the different consequences of possession. Possession leading to the acquisition of ownership (the property-related function of possession) and the protection thereof (the policy function) display many characteristics of a real right.

Silberberg and Schoeman[93] also distinguish between possession as a fact and the various consequences thereof, to which they refer as 'rights'. By and large they advocate the same view as Van der Merwe. In the light of the different consequences of possession they suggest that it might also be considered as a right *sui generis*.

---

[85] Burge (n. 4), 135; Nathan (n. 4), 374.

[86] Josson (n. 4), 403. See also Roos/Reitz (n. 1), 34: 'Some writers consider possession as a fact which gives rise to certain rights; others take all these rights together and call them the right of possession.'

[87] Maasdorp (n. 4), 12.   [88] Morice (n. 28), 64.

[89] See Gibson (n. 38), 192; Hutchison/Van der Merwe (n. 4), 262.

[90] *Matthee v. Schietekat* 1959 (1) SA 344 (C) 347E; *Buchholtz v. Buchholtz* 1980 (3) SA 424 (W) 425C-E; *Chiloane v. Maduenyane* 1980 (4) SA 19 (W) 22 sq.

[91] H. Silberberg, J. Schoeman, *The Law of Property* (2nd edn., 1983), 115; Van der Merwe (n. 2), 92.

[92] Van der Merwe (n. 49), 66 sq.; *idem* (n. 2), 92.

[93] Silberberg/Schoeman (n. 91), 114 sqq.

Some attempts have been made to classify possession as a (real) right only and not as a fact, but this approach is ambiguous and leads to difficulties in the protection of unlawful possession.

Van der Vyver[94] has argued that a possessor is always entitled to possession based upon some or other (subjective) right. An owner is entitled to possession on account of his right of ownership; a non-owner is likewise entitled in the light of a 'possessory right'. Lawful possessors have a right against all other legal subjects. An unlawful possessor's claim to the thing will, however, finally have to submit to the 'better right' of the owner. Therefore, unlawful possessors have a right against all third parties, but not against the owner.

Klopper[95] has also voiced concern about the possessory protection of unlawful possessors and has maintained that only lawful possessors have subjective rights against others.

None of these views are entirely satisfactory. Possession cannot always be seen as an entitlement flowing from a subjective right: unlawful possession, for instance, cannot be such an entitlement. To maintain that an unlawful possessor has a possessory right against other parties implies the existence of an 'unlawful right', which is a contradiction in terms. Regarding the protection of an unlawful possessor, it is incorrect to maintain that such a possessor is not protected against the owner. Van der Vyver's view amounts to a confusion of the petitory (vindicatory) and possessory suits. An unlawful possessor is always afforded possessory protection against the owner, although such protection is of a temporary nature. The fact that the owner can ultimately reclaim the thing by means of the vindicatory action has nothing to do with the protection of possession.[96]

To try and solve the many problems experienced in attempting to explain the protection of possession within the paradigm of subjective (real) rights, two new views have been put forward. The first maintains that possession can be regarded as an 'entitlement' (in the non-technical sense) bestowed by the law (in an objective sense) on any possessor, to remain in possession until lawfully ousted. This 'entitlement' does not imply any entitlement provided by a subjective right: rather, it may be compared to the 'entitlement' of a parent to to his child, which likewise cannot be regarded as emanating from a subjective right.[97] Van der Walt, on the other hand, suggests a whole restructuring of the doctrine of subjective rights in order to accommodate the protection of possession, irrespective of its lawfulness. According to him the doctrine of subjective rights should be replaced by a doctrine of subjective 'relationships'.[98]

---

[94] (1970) 33 *THRHR* 231 sqq.   [95] (1983) 16 *Obiter* 71 sqq.
[96] See Kleyn (n. 65), 386 sq.; Sonnekus, 1985 *TSAR* 334; Van der Walt, (1988) 51 *THRHR* 280 sqq.; Sonnekus/Neels (n. 34), 125 sq.
[97] Kleyn (n. 65), 388 sq. *Contra*: Van der Walt, (1988) 51 *THRHR* 290 sqq.
[98] A. J. Van der Walt, 'The doctrine of subjective rights: a critical reappraisal from the fringes of property law', (1990) 53 *THRHR* 316 sqq.

Lately there has been a tendency to return to the position in Roman law: simply to regard possession as a factual relationship which gives rise to certain consequences.[99] However, standard textbooks still distinguish between the *ius possidendi* and the *ius possessionis*, and it seems that the matter is destined to remain clouded in confusion.[100]

III. POSSESSORY PROTECTION

1. General

The *mandament van spolie* can be traced back to the *exceptio spolii* of canon law, created in the ninth century by the unknown author of the *Decretales Pseudo-Isidorianae*. This remedy provided a defence for someone who had been despoiled (i.e. unlawfully deprived of possession) and against whom criminal proceedings or a civil claim was subsequently instituted. Such a person could refuse to answer to the charge or claim until he had been reinstated in his possession. In the glosses to the *Decretum Gratiani* a spoliatory action was derived from the *exceptio*. This action was known as the *condictio ex canone redintegranda* and was received in French law as the remedy of *réintégrande*, in German law as the *actio spolii*, and in Roman-Dutch law as the *mandament van spolie*. The *exceptio spolii*, however, retained an independent existence in the aforementioned legal systems.[101]

In Roman-Dutch law the most important possessory remedies were the *mandamenten* of *complainte*, *maintenue*, and *spolie*. Some confusion reigned concerning the precise limitations of, and differences between, these possessory remedies. This was especially true with respect to the *mandamenten* of *complainte* and *spolie*, both of which could be instituted to regain lost possession. Important differences existed between these remedies. *Complainte* protected only possession that had lasted for less than a year and a day. Such a limited period of possession was not a prerequisite for the other remedies. The *mandamenten* of *complainte* and *maintenue* could be instituted in the case of a mere disturbance of possession, whereas a loss of possession was required for the *mandament van spolie*. *Complainte* and *maintenue* were mainly used for immovables, whereas *spolie* protected the possession of movables, immovables, and incorporeals.[102]

In a few early South African cases the *mandamenten* of *complainte* and *maintenue* were referred to or even applied, but in a very vague and confusing manner, and not always in accordance with Roman-Dutch law.

---

[99] Kleyn/Boraine (n. 2), 112 sq.; Sonnekus/Neels (n. 34), 125 sq.
[100] Kleyn/Boraine (n. 2), 113 sq.; Sonnekus/Neels (n. 34), 123 sq.
[101] Kleyn (n. 65), 73 sqq.; Duard Kleyn, 'Die *exceptio spolii*', 1987 *TSAR* 303 sqq.
[102] See generally Kleyn (n. 3), 561 sqq.

In *Curatoren van Pioneer Lodge, No. 1 v. Champion*[103] members of a lodge removed certain objects that allegedly belonged to them from a building owned by another lodge. Chief Justice Reitz regarded the removal of the objects as spoliation, but applied the *mandament van complainte*, with which he associated the maxim *spoliatus ante omnia restituendus est*. What is remarkable is that although the judge referred to Boey's *Woorden-Tolk*[104]— from which it is clear that the maxim is of canon law origin—he refrained from mentioning anywhere in his judgment the *mandament van spolie*. Furthermore, he applied the *mandament van complainte* to the spoliation of movable objects, whereas it was traditionally applied to immovables only.

In *De Villiers v. Holloway*[105] the respondents erected a fence, depriving the applicant of a part of his orchard. The respondents argued that the applicant had actually proceeded on the basis of the *mandament van complainte*, to which he was not entitled, seeing that he had not applied for it within one year of the deprivation as required. They argued further that the applicant could possibly have succeeded with a *mandament van maintenue*, but definitely not with the *mandament van spolie*, as the latter remedy was applicable only to deprivation of possession by means of force or stealth. The applicant insisted that possession should be restored and relied on the maxim *spoliatus ante omnia restituendus est*. Maasdorp J ordered the respondents to remove the fence and to reinstate the applicant in his possession, but it is unclear which remedy he granted. He found that the deprivation had been committed by means of stealth and also that the applicant's delay in approaching the Court did not amount to acquiescence in the deprivation.

In *Bester v. Grundling*[106] a person who had been despoiled of some donkeys asked the Court to be reinstated in his possession or to be granted damages. Wessels J decided that the applicable remedy was the possessory action and not the *mandament van spolie*, as damages cannot be claimed with the latter. He found the possessory action to be the equivalent of the *mandament van complainte*.

These instances apart, it was accepted as early as the first decade of this century that the *mandament van complainte* and the *mandament van maintenue* are obsolete and that the only possessory remedy known to South African law is the *mandament van spolie*.[107] The first reported case on this was *Executors of Haupt v. De Villiers* in 1848.[108] In this matter the *mandament van spolie* was linked directly to the principle of *spoliatus ante omnia restituendus est*, an approach which in modern South African practice is accepted as 'trite law'.[109]

---

[103] 1879 OFS 51.   [104] 53.   [105] (1902) 12 CTR 566.
[106] 1917 TPD 492.   [107] See Roos/Reitz (n. 1), 37; Maasdorp (n. 4), 24 sq.
[108] (1848) 3 Menz 341.
[109] *Magadi v. West Rand Administration Board* 1981 (2) SA 352 (T) 354C.

2. The *mandament van spolie*

The *mandament van spolie* is variously referred to as a 'writ of spoliation',[110] a 'spoliation order',[111] or an 'interdict of spoliation'.[112] However, the latter term should be avoided, since it contributes to a regrettable tendency to equate the *mandament* with an interdict.[113] The origin of this confusion probably lies in Van der Linden's discussion of the requirements of the old *mandament poenaal*, which is the Roman-Dutch counterpart of the modern interdict.[114] The mere fact that both remedies were *mandamenten* does not mean that they amounted to one and the same thing. The main basis for the distinction between the *mandament van spolie* and an interdict lies in the fact that, in the case of a final interdict, the applicant is required to prove the existence of a clear right. By contrast, as we have seen, the rights of the parties are never taken into consideration during spoliation proceedings.[115]

As in Roman-Dutch law, the *mandament van spolie* applies only to loss of possession. There is no true possessory remedy in South African law for a mere disturbance of possession. In such instances recourse must be had to a prohibitory interdict. This remedy is based on 'trespass' and has its roots in English law.[116]

It is not clear why, of the three possessory remedies of Roman-Dutch law, only the *mandament van spolie* survived in South African law. 'It is remarkable', Hahlo and Kahn observe,[117] 'that it is this remedy . . . which was not much used in Roman-Dutch law, that has become the basis of the protection of possession in modern law'.

Middelberg[118] has attempted to attribute the survival of the *mandament van spolie* to the influence of English law, but he concedes that there is no

---

[110] *Klipplaats Wool Washing Co v. John Benjamin Leads* (1893) 7 EDC 206; *Gwavu v. Makunga* (1906) 20 EDC 97, 99; *Pillay v. Naiker* (1917) 38 NLR 122, 123; *Mans v. Marais* 1932 CPD 352, 357.

[111] *Lunn v. Kretzmer* 1947 (3) SA 591 (W) 597; *Yeko v. Qana* 1973 (4) SA 735 (A) headnote.

[112] *Sillo v. Naude* 1929 AD 21, 25. See also Manfred Nathan, *The Common Law of South Africa*, vol. IV (1907), 2330.

[113] See headnote *Anderson v. Anderson* 1919 EDL 57; *Pretorius v. Pretorius* 1927 TPD 178, 179; *Nienaber v. Stuckey* (n. 68), 1053; *Van Rooyen v. Burger* 1960 (4) SA 356 (O) 362H; M. Nathan, *The Law and Practice relating to Interdicts including Mandamus and Spoliation Orders* (1939), 1 sqq.; C. F. Eckard, *Grondtrekke van die Siviele Prosesreg in die Landdroshowe* (2nd edn., 1990), 96.

[114] See Nathan (n. 113), 5 sqq., who extensively discusses Van der Linden's views.

[115] See, for the distinction between the *mandament* and an interdict, *Burnham v. Neumeyer* 1917 TPD 630, 633; *Mans v. Marais* (n. 110), 359; *Potgieter v. Davel* 1966 (3) SA 555 (O) 558B; T. W. Price, *The Possessory Remedies in Roman-Dutch Law* (1947), 111; Silberberg/Schoeman (n. 91), 146 sqq.; M. J. de Waal,'[Case discussion of] *Naidoo v. Moodley* 1982 (4) SA 82 (T)', (1984) 47 *THRHR* 118; A. J. van der Walt, 'Mandament van spolie 'n interdik?', 1984 *De Rebus* 477 sqq.; Kleyn (n. 65), 323 sqq.

[116] Lee/Honoré/Price (n. 49), 8 sq.; Van der Merwe (n. 2), 148 sqq.; Kleyn/Boraine (n. 2), 146 sqq.

[117] Hahlo/Kahn (n. 57), 376 sq.

[118] Middelberg (n. 35), 91 sq.

clear authority for his theory. He points to the existence of the assize of *novel disseisin* as a possessory remedy in old English law, which, according to Pollock, also had its origin in canon law and is comparable to the modern English 'writ of right'. It is certainly not impossible that under the influence of English law more emphasis may have been placed on the *mandament van spolie* in South African practice, so that the other two remedies eventually became obsolete. The fact that the *mandament van spolie* is sometimes referred to as the 'writ of spoliation' might indicate such influence, but as far as can be established South African courts have never applied English law with respect to the *mandament van spolie*.[119] This area of law is dominated by Roman-Dutch law, to which the courts often refer.

Can the *mandament van spolie*, as presently applied in South Africa, be regarded as a continuation of the Roman-Dutch *mandament*? In *Muller v. Muller*[120] Curlewis J answered this question in the affirmative:

Now it is quite clear that, though our spoliation order has its roots in the Roman law, it is really derived from the Canon law, and the Canon law did not require the same formality that the Roman-Dutch law required in regard to possessory interdicts. We have to do then with the Canon law and with a *mandament van spolie* as obtained in the old Dutch Courts, where recourse was to a spoliation order—the possessory mandate which lies upon every person who has the actual legal possession of a movable.

However, a different approach was followed in the later decision of *Meyer v. Glendinning*,[121] the only case in which a court attempted a thorough investigation into the origins of the modern *mandament van spolie*. The owner of a racehorse removed the horse from the stables of the racehorse trainer without the latter's permission. The question before the Court was whether a detentor (the trainer, whom the Court regarded as a depositary) is entitled to possessory protection under the *mandament van spolie*. In its search for authority that a depository is indeed entitled to possessory protection, the Court expressed its views on the roots of the *mandament* in three separate judgments.

Van Zyl JP held that the *mandament van spolie* should be granted not only to the traditional possessors but also to certain holders. Interestingly, however, the Court found the origin of the modern *mandament* to be the *possessorium summariissimum*, rather the *condictio ex canone redintegranda*.

---

[119] Cf. *Dönges v. Dadoo* 1950 (2) SA 321 (A) 332: 'The remedy invoked was one which the Roman-Dutch law provides and which is governed by Roman-Dutch principles. It would be futile to suggest that, since the prerogative is involved, those principles have been modified by rules of British constitutional law . . .'; *Ntai v. Vereeniging Town Council* 1953 (4) SA 579 (A) 592H: 'During argument we were referred to certain English authorities, but they cannot assist us, since English law differs radically from our own on this subject. In the first place English law would appear to be far more lenient than ours towards a landlord who resorts to self-help in order to regain possession to which he is entitled.'

[120] 1915 TPD 28, 30 sq.   [121] 1939 CPD 84.

Although Van Zyl JP found ample authority[122] that the *condictio ex canone redintegranda* should indeed be regarded as the basis of both the *actio spolii* and the *mandament van spolie*, and that this canon law remedy in its various forms had been extended to detentors (holders), he chose to rely on the view of Menochius.[123] That author considered the *condictio ex canone redintegranda* not to have been extended to holders: in his opinion another 'remedy of a summary and temporary character', namely the *possessorium summariissimum*, offered possessory protection to holders and consequently it formed the root of the present-day *mandament*:[124]

It seems clear that under the influence of the Canon law the summary possessory action employed for the protection of possessors who had been deprived of their property by acts amounting to spoliation was extended to Roman-Dutch law so as to apply also in favour of persons such as lessees and others who did not possess in their own right or in the strict legal sense . . . . This summary proceeding came to be known as *mandament van spolie* . . .

Davis J expressed himself as follows:[125]

I may remark in parenthesis that I am not satisfied that our spoliation orders may not well be direct successors of these old summary orders—yet I am satisfied that such orders have as a fact at least influenced the nature both of the remedy itself and of the procedure . . . This granting of a summary provisional order is dealt with in many of the text writers. It is called by Savigny . . . *Possessorium Summarissimum*, and by Menochius *Remedium ex judicis officio*. See also Wassenaar . . . who incidentally applies to this summary remedy the maxim *spoliatus sit ante omnia restituendus*.

Judge Howes observed as follows:[126]

In my opinion the modern form of *mandament van spolie* resembles most closely, and is based on, the remedy referred to by Menochius as *remedium ex judicis officio* and by Leyser and others as *summariissimum possessorium* in the passage cited. This remedy was allowed to the *commodatarius et alii similes qui non possidere sed detinere dicuntur*.

Some South African authors have concluded that this actually means that the origin of our *mandament van spolie* lies in the old *mandamenten* of *complainte* and *maintenue*.[127] Thus, after discussing the three judgments in *Meyer v. Glendinning*, Price[128] stated:

The effect of these judgments is interesting; they seem to imply that the modern spoliation order is to be considered a direct descendant of the remedies of *Complainte* and *Maintenue*, applied to present day needs and circumstances, and extended to embrace movables as well as immovables. This is a radical departure from the generally accepted theories held in the past but, it may be suggested, wrongly held.

---

[122] 89 sqq.   [123] 91.   [124] 91 sq.   [125] 95.   [126] 96.
[127] Van der Merwe (n. 49), 94; Price (n. 115), 104 sq.   [128] Price (n. 115), 104 sq.

However, neither the views expressed in the *Meyer* case nor Price's theory deserve support. It is surprising that Van Zyl JP attached so much value to the opinion of Menochius, a sixteenth-century Italian authority, notwithstanding the fact that other authors of the *ius commune* held the canon law remedy and the *mandament van spolie* to have protected holders. The *possessorium summariissimum* had its origin in medieval law (but not in canon law[129]). Its purpose was to afford temporary protection in a case where one party feared self-help from the other party, before the dispute with respect to the thing in question was finally settled. It was created because the procedure of the *interdictum uti possidetis*, according to which the dispute had to be settled, was time-consuming and therefore impractical. Indeed, Jacobus Menochius himself points out that many authorities do not share his views with respect to the possessory remedies of canon law.[130] Robertus Maranta, another sixteenth-century Italian author, for instance, was of the opinion that the *condictio ex canone redintegranda* was available for the protection of holders (*detentors*).[131]

Furthermore, the Judge President's reference to Leyser (who supports the views of Menochius) is quite meaningless. Leyser awards possessory protection to holders in general by means of the *actio spolii*.[132] What is more, he specifically distinguishes the *possessorium summariissimum* from the *actio spolii*, and points to the fact that the former remedy is not applicable to instances of loss of possession.[133]

Savigny, to whom Davis J refers, likewise differentiates between the *possessorium summariissimum* and the spoliation remedy.[134] The fact that Wassenaar applies the maxim *spoliatus ante omnia restituendus est* to the remedy of *possessorium summariissimum* also does not justify finding the origin of the *mandament* in that remedy. This maxim had been applied by the Italian commentators, the old French authorities, and the authorities on the *usus modernus pandectarum* to all possible possessory remedies.[135] The reason for this lies in the fact that the rule embodies the general principle of possessory protection. Lost possession must be returned before consideration of the merits of the case.

Apart from Roman-Dutch common law authority, according to which holders are indeed protected by the *mandament van spolie*,[136] enough

---

[129] See C. G. Bruns, *Das Recht des Besitzes im Mittelalter und in der Gegenwart* (1848), 260 sqq.; Kleyn (n. 65), 155 sq.

[130] Jacobus Menochius, *De Recuperanda Possessione*, in: *De Adipiscenda, Retinenda et Recuperanda Possessione, Doctissima Commentaria* (Venetiis, 1606), 15, 5–9.

[131] Robertus Maranta, *De Ordine Iudiciorum Tractatus, vulgo Speculum Aureum, et Lumen Advocatorum dictus* (Coloniae Agrippinae, 1650), 4, 7, 58.

[132] Augustinus Leyser, *Meditationes ad Pandectas*, specimen 451, 1.

[133] Leyser (n. 132), specimen 505, 4.

[134] Friedrich Carl von Savigny, *Das Recht des Besitzes* (1803, reprint 1967), 523 sqq.

[135] See Kleyn (n. 65), 154, 170, 185 sq.   [136] Cf. e.g. Kleyn (n. 3), 564 sq.

authority to the same effect could have been found in South African case-law at the time of the decision in *Meyer v. Glendinning*.[137]

Although the Court did not specifically refer to *complainte* and *maintenue* in the *Meyer* case, it is understandable that some authors are of the opinion that the judgment in effect traces the *mandament van spolie* specifically to the *mandament van complainte*. For some of the authorities on the *ius commune*, and on Roman-Dutch law in particular, equate the remedy of *complainte* with the *inderdictum uti possidetis*, from which the *possessorium summariissimum* developed, as well as with the latter remedy itself.[138] However, in the light of the differences between the three possessory remedies of Roman-Dutch law, as set out above, it is clearly incorrect to hold the origin of the modern *mandament van spolie* to lie in *complainte* and *maintenue*.

Fortunately, the approach in *Meyer v. Glendinning* was not followed in subsequent decisions, all of which adhere to the view expressed in the *Muller* case. In *Van Rooyen v. Burger*[139] the Court referred to the existence of the *mandamenten* (i.e. *spolie*, *complainte*, and *maintenue*) in Roman-Dutch law,[140] but distinguished the *mandament van spolie* from the *mandament van complainte*.[141] Furthermore, it maintained that Greenberg JA in *Nienaber v. Stuckey*[142] had incorrectly applied a statement by Wassenaar concerning *complainte* to the modern *mandament van spolie*. The Court relied on authors such as Van der Linden, Willem de Groot, and Wassenaar, writing on the old Roman-Dutch *mandament van spolie*, as well as on Leyser, writing on the *actio spolii*.[143] In *Malan v. Dippenaar*[144] it was accepted that the maxim *spoliatus ante omnia restituendus est* has its origins in canon law and that it forms the basis of the modern *mandament van spolie*. This approach is now followed by the majority of authors.[145]

3. Modifications and adaptations of the Roman-Dutch remedy

Such statements as: 'the remedy of a *mandament of spolie* . . . grew as a new and distinct concept . . . in South Africa'[146] and claims that it has 'a fundamentally modified form'[147] in South African law, should therefore be seen

---

[137] See *McCallum v. McCallum's Trustee* 1916 GWL 414, in which the *mandament* was in fact awarded to a *depositarius*; in *Abdul Azeez v. Abdul Rahiman* [1911] AC 746 it was awarded to a trustee; in *Swanepoel v. Van der Hoeven* (1887) 8 Buch 4, *Blomson v. Boshoff* 1905 TS 429, and *Nino Bonino v. De Lange* 1906 TS 120 it was awarded to a lessee; in *Muller v. Muller* 1915 TPD 28 it was awarded to an agent.

[138] See Kleyn (n. 65), 172, 176, 275 sq. [139] 1960 (4) SA 356 (O). [140] 361B.

[141] 363D-F. [142] Above, n. 68, 1059. [143] 361C-F.

[144] 1969 (2) SA 59 (O), 64G-H.

[145] See e.g. Hahlo/Kahn (n. 57), 577, fn. 39; Van der Merwe (n. 2), 118; Kleyn/Boraine (n. 2), 128 sq.; Sonnekus/Neels (n. 34), 168.

[146] *Per* Steyn J in *Jivan v. National Housing Commission* 1977 (3) SA 890 (W) 892H.

[147] Hahlo/Kahn (n. 57), 576.

in perspective. The only respect in which the mandament portrays an essentially 'modified form', compared to its Roman-Dutch counterpart, is that it is usually applied for by notice of motion, a procedure unknown in Roman-Dutch law. There is a divergence of opinion as to how far our modern procedure corresponds, in this respect, to that of Roman-Dutch law. Wessels[148] considered Roman-Dutch procedure to have been very formal and cumbersome. Price[149] criticized this statement as being untrue, whereas in his judicial capacity Wessels remarked in *Bester v. Grundling*:[150] 'We do not nowadays adopt the same form of pleading that they did in the old Courts of Holland, but in substance it is the same.' Be that as it may, in modern South African law the *mandament*, like all other remedies received from Roman and Roman-Dutch law, functions within a system of civil procedure, which is predominantly based on English law. This does not, however, detract from the canon and Roman-Dutch law characteristics inherent in this remedy.

Nevertheless, the *mandament van spolie* has in some respects experienced adaptations and developments in South African law that distinguish it from its Roman-Dutch and German predecessors. (It should always be borne in mind that the German *usus modernus pandectarum* also exerted a strong influence on the South African law of possessory protection. In this regard the views of Augustinus Leyser, as expressed in his *Meditationes ad Pandectas*, were of particular importance.[151]) In some cases these adaptations have amounted to attempts to reconcile differences of opinion in the Roman-Dutch common law.

First, it was held by some Roman-Dutch authorities that only a forceful removal of possession constituted spoliation. Others were of the opinion that any unlawful deprivation would suffice.[152] The authors of the German *usus modernus pandectarum*, such as Leyser, generally followed the wider approach.[153] Some earlier South African cases and authorities required a deprivation by means of 'force or stealth',[154] However, since the decision in *Nino Bonino v. De Lange*,[155] in which Leyser's definition of spoliation was accepted, it is generally agreed that spoliation implies any unlawful or wrongful deprivation of possession. Unlawfulness in this regard would mean that a person relying upon alleged or supposed rights deprives another of his possession against his will and without recourse to due legal process,

---

[148] Wessels (n. 4), 482. See also Van der Merwe (n. 2), 119.
[149] Price (n. 115), 71.   [150] 1917 TPD 492, 494.
[151] Cf. the key decision in *Nino Bonino v. De Lange* (n. 137), 122; see further *Meyer v. Glendinning* 1939 CPD 84, 91.
[152] See Kleyn (n. 65), 240 sq.   [153] Ibid. 198 sq.
[154] *Armitage v. Govendalal* (1906) 27 NLR 587, 589; *Pillay v. Naiker* (1917) 38 NLR 122, 123; *Jossen* (n. 4), 454; Nathan (n. 112), 2330; Maasdorp (n. 4), 25.
[155] 1906 TS 120, 122.

so that it can be said that such a person acted as his own judge by taking the law into his own hands.[156]

Secondly, in Roman-Dutch and German law it was possible to claim not only restoration of possession but also damages with the *mandament van spolie*[157] and the *actio spolii*.[158] This is not possible in the case of the modern *mandament*. Damages, or the money value of the thing, have to be claimed separately with a delictual action or with the possessory action.[159]

Thirdly, in Roman-Dutch law an applicant was barred from bringing an application for a *mandament van complainte* after one year had elapsed since the loss of possession, but the authorities are silent about any time-limit in regard to the bringing of the *mandament van spolie*.[160] In German law[161] no time limit was imposed on the *actio spolii*. In *Jivan v. National Housing Commission*[162] Steyn J suggested that, since little or no assistance can be derived from the Roman-Dutch authorities, the time-limit in the case of the *mandament van complainte* should serve as a guide to modern practice as regards the *mandament van spolie*. Consequently, if an applicant delays for more than a year before he brings the application special circumstances would have to be present to allow the application. On the other hand, if an application is brought within a year special circumstances would have to be pleaded before relief may be refused on grounds of delay. This position actually corresponds to that adopted by the exponents of the *usus modernus pandectarum*.

At the outset of this Section it was stated that the *exceptio spolii* is the source of the spoliation remedies of canon law and that this remedy was also received in Roman-Dutch and German law. In these two systems the application of the *exceptio spolii* was limited in that it could be raised only by a defendant in a civil suit against the alleged spoliator. The defendant could refuse to answer the plaintiff's claim until he was reinstated in his lost possession. The *exceptio* functioned as a dilatory defence that delayed the claim. If the spoliator did not return the thing at all, it functioned as a peremptory defence that quashed the claim.[163] As far as can be established, this defence was raised only once in South African law, in the case of *Bank*

---

[156] See *Goldsmith v. Irwin* (1907) 17 CTR 44, 45; *Mathiba v. Du Toit* 1926 TPD 126, 131; *Pretorius v. Pretorius* (n. 68), 180; *Adonis v. Sisele* 1931 CPD 274; *Mans v. Marais* (n. 110), 355; *Dalby v. Soffiantini* 1934 EDL 100, 105; *Meyer v. Sentraal Westelike Ko-operatiewe Maatskappy* 1934 OPD 93, 105; *Remley v. Lupton* 1946 WLD 353, 356; *Scoop Industries (Pty) Ltd v. Langlaagte Estate & GM Co Ltd* 1948 (1) SA 91 (W) 99; *Yeko v. Qana* 1973 (4) SA 735 (A) 739G; *Adamson v. Boshoff* 1975 (3) SA 221 (C) 230B; *Mankowitz v. Loewenthal* 1982 (3) SA 758 (A) 767A; *Ntshwaqela v. Chairman, Western Cape Regional Services Council* 1988 (3) SA 218 (C) 225E-F.

[157] Kleyn (n. 65), 245 sq.   [158] Ibid. 205.

[159] *Matthee v. Schietekat* 1959 (1) SA 344 (C) 347F–348B; *Ntai v. Vereeniging Town Council* 1953 (4) SA 579 (A); *Potgieter v. Davel* 1966 (3) SA 555 (O); De Vos, 1959 *Acta Juridica* 186 sqq. But see M. D. Blecher, 'Spoliation and the demolition of legal rights', (1978) 95 *SALJ* 13.

[160] Kleyn (n. 65), 257.   [161] Ibid. 205.   [162] 1977 (3) SA 890 (W) 891 sqq.

[163] See Kleyn, 1987 *TSAR* 311 sqq.; Kleyn (n. 65), 205 sq., 268 sqq.

van die Oranje-Vrystaat v. Rossouw.[164] However, it was held that spoliation was irrelevant, since the defendant was not in possession of the object in question. Thus, it was unnecessary to decide whether this remedy forms part of South African law.[165] Van der Walt[166] argues that the remedy has not been abrogated by disuse and that it can be compared to the modern special plea, concerning facts which do not form part of the claim.

4. Protected possession

The last matter requiring attention concerns the kind of possession that is protected by the *mandament van spolie*. This is a problematic issue which has its roots in Roman law and has still not been satisfactorily solved in South African law.

In Roman law[167] possessory protection was afforded only to a *numerus clausus* of possessors (such as the owner and the *bona fide* possessor), while others who were also in control of a thing (detentors or holders, such as the lessee) were not protected. Apart from the fact that the artificial distinction between possessors and detentors was the result of the casuistic development of Roman law, it was at the same time based on the principle *plures eandem rem in solidum possidere non possunt*.[168] This meant that co-possession of a thing *in solidum* by more than one person was impossible. It has been argued that the possessor (for example the *bona fide* possessor) exercised his possession through the detentor (for example the lessee) so that prescription could always run in favour of the possessor. If the detentor were to be protected, he would actually qualify as a possessor in the light of the rule against co-possession. This approach also implies that no clear distinction was drawn in Roman law between the different functions of possession (for example the property-related function and the policy function).[169]

Ever since the reception of the learned law there has been a clash between Roman law and the more liberal approach of canon law, according to which protection was generally afforded to detentors.[170] Different forms of *animus* were used to distinguish between protected possession and unprotected detention.[171] The majority of Roman-Dutch jurists required the *animus sibi habendi* to be present in order for possession to be protected by the possessory remedies.[172]

In South African law the principles of Roman law preventing the protection of detentors have been abandoned. First, different functions of pos-

---

[164] 1984 (2) SA 644 (C). [165] 647H.
[166] '[Case discussion of] *Bank van die Oranje-Vrystaat v. Rossouw* 1983–09–19 (C), case A 60/83 unreported', (1984) 47 *THRHR* 224 sqq.
[167] See Kleyn (n. 3), 547 sqq. [168] D. 41, 2, 3, 5.
[169] See generally Kleyn (n. 65), 16 sqq. [170] Ibid. 123 sqq.
[171] Above, Section II. 2. [172] Kleyn (n. 3), 557.

session are distinguished.[173] Secondly, co-possession of the same thing is accepted.[174] Possessory protection has been extended to most of the traditional detentors, such as a lessee,[175] a holder of a right of retention,[176] a borrower,[177] a credit purchaser,[178] an agent,[179] a servant,[180] a trustee,[181] a share cropper,[182] and a depositary.[183]

Some earlier authors[184] and cases[185] still required the holder to have the *animus sibi habendi* (the intention to hold for oneself), as had been the case in Roman-Dutch law, in order to qualify for possessory protection. This implies that a lessee and a depositary would not qualify, as they hold for others. Consequently the *animus* required is presently accepted to be the *animus ex re commodum acquirendi*: the intention to secure some benefit for oneself.[186] An employee or quasi-employee does not have this kind of *animus*, and is consequently not protected by the *mandament van spolie*.[187]

If it were accepted that the *mandament van spolie* protects possession in order to discourage self-help and disturbances of the peace, the question may arise whether protection should not be extended to any person who wittingly exercises control of a thing. There seems to be no justification for the fact that a lessee and an agent are protected but not an employee. For

---

[173] Above, Section II. 3.

[174] *Beetge v. Drenka Investments (Isando) (Pty) Ltd* 1964 (4) SA 62 (W) 67H; *Brighton v. Clift* 1970 (4) SA 247 (R) 249B-C; *Rosenbuch v. Rosenbuch* 1975 (1) SA 181 (W) 183D; *Oglodzinski v. Oglodzinski* 1976 (4) SA 273 (D) 275E-G; *Bennett Pringle (Pty) Ltd v. Adelaide Municipality* 1977 (1) SA 230 (E) 233A.

[175] *Diamond v. Solomon Gill* (1893) 7 EDC 194; *Blomson v. Boshoff* 1905 TS 429; *Nino Bonino v. De Lange* (n. 110); *African Ice Co v. Kalk Bay Fisheries* 1907 TH 268; *Adonis v. Sisele* 1931 CPD 274; *Mandelkoorn v. Strauss* 1942 CPD 493; *Nienaber v. Stuckey* (n. 68); *Bennett Pringle v. Adelaide Municipality* (n. 174); *Magadi v. West Rand Administration Board* 1981 (2) SA 352 (T).

[176] *Klipplaats Wool Washing Co v. John Benjamin Leach* (1893) 7 EDC 206; *Cooper & Hewson v. Johnstone & Co* (1899) 6 OR 130; *Sterner v. Morom* (1903) 20 SC 499; *Pretoria Racing Club v. Van Pietersen* 1907 TS 687; *Scholtz v. Faifer* 1910 TS 243; *Elastocrete (Pty) Ltd v. Dickens* 1953 (2) SA 644 (SR).

[177] *Meyer v. Glendinning* 1939 CPD 84, 94.

[178] *Herring v. Kimpton's* 1931 SR 84; *Dawood v. Robb & Co* 1933 CPD 178; *Wicomb v. Rosen* 1936 CPD 502; *Mahilall v. Singh* 1945 NPD 193; *Malan v. Dippenaar* 1969 (2) SA 59 (O).

[179] *Maritzburg Sawing & Yoke Co Ltd v. Piesold* (1915) 36 NLR 69; *Muller v. Muller* 1915 TPD 28; *Slabbert v. Theodoulou* 1952 (2) SA 667 (T).

[180] *Martin v. Ingle* (1920) 41 NLR 1.

[181] *Executors of Haupt v. De Villiers* (1848) 3 Menz 341; *Abdul Azeez v. Abdul Rahiman* 1911 AC 746.

[182] *Van Rooyen v. Burger* 1960 (4) SA 356 (O); *Burger v. Van Rooyen* 1961 (1) SA 159 (O).

[183] *McCallum v. McCallum's Trustee* 1916 GWL 414; *Meyer v. Glendinning* (n. 177), 94.

[184] Maasdorp (n. 4), 16.

[185] *Kemp v. Roper* (1886) 2 Buch AC 141, 143; *Stanhope Motors & Machinery Sales v. Pretoria Light Aircraft Co (Pty) Ltd* 1951 (1) 2 PH F79 (T).

[186] *Yeko v. Qana* (n. 156), 739D-E; *Magadi v. West Rand Administration Board* 1981 (2) SA 352 (T) 354F; *Dlamini v. Mavi* 1982 (2) SA 490 (W) 493B-C.

[187] *Mpunga v. Malaba* 1959 (1) SA 853 (W) 861F; *Mbuku v. Mdinwa* 1982 (1) SA 219 (Tk) 222E-F; *Dlamini v. Mavi* 1982 (2) SA 490 (W) 493B-C.

this reason Van Rensburg and Van der Merwe[188] suggest a more liberal interpretation of the *animus ex re commodum acquirendi*, so as to include the employee;[189] but the required *animus* does not then seem any different from the mere *animus possidendi* (the intention to possess).

As far as possessory protection is concerned, South African law has not yet fully freed itself from Roman law doctrine, since a distinction is still drawn between protected possessors and unprotected detentors. Perhaps this can be attributed to the fact that South African lawyers are by and large not so well acquainted with, or appreciative of, canon law as a part of South African common law.

---

[188] Van der Merwe, (1978) 41 *THRHR* 126. See also A. S. Mathews, 'The mental element in possession', (1962) 79 *SALJ* 186 sqq.; A. J. van der Walt, (1983) 100 *SALJ* 699.

[189] However, in this instance the required *animus* does not seem to be any different from the mere *animus possidendi* (the intention to possess). See Kleyn (n. 65), 367 sqq.

PART VII

Fiduciary Transactions

26: *Trust*

TONY HONORÉ

I. INTRODUCTION

The English trust is an institution by which a trustee has the title to property which he holds or administers for another, the beneficiary, or for an abstract purpose. The trustee may himself be one of the beneficiaries. If there is more than one trustee they hold jointly (as 'joint tenants'), so that, by the rule of survivorship, if one ceases to be trustee the title to the property automatically vests in the surviving trustees. The trust property is a fund separate from the private property of the trustee and is not available to the trustee's private creditors. The trust beneficiary has not only a claim *in personam* against the trustee that he should administer the trust properly but also a property interest in the trust assets, called an 'equitable interest', and which may amount to 'beneficial ownership'. The courts, originally the Court of Chancery, have extensive jurisdiction over trusts. They can appoint and remove trustees and when necessary rule how a trust is to be administered, even altering its terms to carry out the trust object. A trust can be incorporated but is not in itself a juristic person. Its personality is that of its trustees.

In essence the English trust in 1806 possessed the same features as it does today. However, the trust did not exist at the Cape before the British occupations of 1806 and 1815. The Roman-Dutch law of the Cape of course had its own trust-like institutions, as has every developed system of law.[1] These were designed to protect the weak and safeguard the interests of those who were absent or dead. The property of minors was administered by tutors (guardians); that of prodigals, bankrupts, insane persons, absentees, and others whose interests needed to be represented in court, by curators; deceased estates were increasingly administered not by the heirs but by executors or administrators. Like the English trustee they derived no personal benefit from the property they administered. Alongside them existed (and exists) the *fideicommissum*. Under this the fiduciary, who may be an heir or legatee under a will or a donee *inter vivos*, does not hold an office.

---

[1] L. I. Coertze, *Die Trust in die Romeins-Hollandse Reg* (1948) (the author thanks the 'Jan Marais trust' for making the completion and publication of the book possible); Herman Frederik W. D. Fischer, 'Trust, *Fiducia, Bewind* (administration), *Stichting* (foundation)', (1957) 20 *THRHR* 25–38.

He owns and manages the property for his own benefit but subject to some restrictions. He is entitled to the income from the property, but as fiduciary he is bound to keep it intact and pass it on later, generally on his death, to a second owner, the fideicommissary.

English trusteeship is an administrative device rather like the Roman-Dutch administrative offices (tutorship, curatorship etc.) but less closely controlled by the state. In this respect it is unlike the Roman-Dutch *fideicommissum*, since the trustee, unlike the fiduciary, has no right *as trustee* to any income from the trust property.[2] He will only have a right to income or capital if, as well as being a trustee, he is also a beneficiary of the trust. In this, again, he resembles an executor or administrator, who may also be a beneficiary under the will or on the intestacy of the deceased.

When the British, both English and Scots, arrived at the Cape in the early nineteenth century, they brought the trust with them as part of their legal and intellectual baggage. How would it be received? Would it be accepted by the local law, and if so in what form? There were several possibilities. The trust might be integrated into Roman-Dutch law as (i) an extra institution of the administrative type or (ii) a sort of *fideicommissum*. Or (iii) it might not be fitted into any Roman-Dutch scheme but might maintain an independent existence alongside the Roman-Dutch institutions. Finally, (iv) it might fail to take root at all. Over the last two centuries in South Africa there has been little support for the third and none for the fourth solution. Both the first and second possibilities have had their advocates, but in the end the first has prevailed. From a Roman-Dutch point of view, therefore, there has been a reception of the trust as an institution alongside tutorship, curatorship, executorship, and administratorship, especially close to administratorship. However, the trust is an all-purpose institution, more flexible and wide-ranging than any of the others. From an English point of view one could say that the trust has taken root in South Africa but not in its English form. It has a modified shape that serves most of its functions in Anglo-American law. However it is subject to closer state control than the English trust, and has been pruned of some peripheral features of English trust law that are ill-adapted to local conditions. It has never been seriously suggested that South Africa would wholly reject the trust. In the upshot the South African trust is an evolutionary hybrid,[3] but in the path it has followed it is unique among civil law systems.

---

[2] Coertze (n. 1), 116–38.   [3] *'n eie trustreg'* (a trust law of its own): Coertze (n. 1), 133.

II. BEFORE UNION: 1806–1910

1. The Cape

Legislation at the Cape after the occupation took the form of proclamations and ordinances.[4] These were enacted exclusively in English. The threat that court proceedings would also be exclusively in English was, however, averted in 1826.[5] The new administration and its courts retained the Roman-Dutch law but adapted it piecemeal to the use of trusts by its English-speaking subjects. It needed to do so, for the trust was spontaneously employed by private individuals for a wide array of purposes: to build churches, run mercantile establishments, set up joint-stock companies, administer club property, make marriage settlements, and dispose of property by will.

Thus in 1829 the Cape Town English Church Ordinance provided for trustees, elected by subscribing shareholders, to supervise the erection of a church.[6] This pattern, by which English churches were built by subscription under the aegis of elected trustees, persisted[7] but once the churches had been built it was more usual to vest the administration of the church or parish in a vestry and churchwardens,[8] though the title to the land sometimes remained in trustees.[9] Moslems placed the administration of mosques in the hands of trustees (*vakheels*).[10] An 1836 Ordinance vested land in trustees for a mercantile warehouse at Port Beaufort.[11] The Cape Town Public Library, at first managed by trustees, was in 1836 reorganized and the administration vested in a committee of management in trust for the community,[12] the ownership now vesting in the government.[13] In 1844 a police pension fund was created and vested in trustees.[14] Sometimes, as with the South African Museum in 1857,[15] and the Port Elizabeth Library in 1864,[16] the Board of

---

[4] Coertze (n. 1), 60–3.

[5] Ord. 27 of 1826 postponing the exclusive adoption of the English language in all courts of justice (required by a Proclamation of 5 July 1822) and providing that Dutch could continue to be used.

[6] Ord. 4 of 1829 (C).

[7] Bathurst English Church Ord. 5 of 1832 (C); English Church, Wynberg Ord. 6 of 1833 (C); Rondebosch English Church Ord. 5 of 1845 (C).

[8] Sidbury English Church Ord. 2 of 1842 (C); Graaff-Reinet English Church Ord. 8 of 1846 (C).

[9] *Stewart v. Mzimba* (1899) 9 CTR 96.

[10] *Hessen v. Daout* (1889) 6 SC 372; *Re Salie* (1900) 10 CTR 404, 552; *Minto v. Trustees, Malay Mosque* (1906) 16 CTR 12.

[11] Port Beaufort Mercantile Establishment Ord. 7 of 1836 (C).

[12] Cape Town Public Library Ord. 71 of 1830 (C); 8 of 1836 (C); cf. *Grey's Trustees v. SA Public Library* (1881) 1 SC 243; Coertze (n. 1), 59.

[13] Cf. Ord. 20 of 1895 (C), transferring the assets of the SA Fine Art Association from trustees to the Government but vesting the administration in a Board of Trustees.

[14] Ord. 1 of 1844.   [15] Ord. 17 of 1857.   [16] Port Elizabeth Library Act 20 of 1864.

Trustees was itself incorporated as a juristic person. In 1873 the books and records of the Board of Public Examiners were transferred to the University of the Cape of Good Hope in trust.[17] A will of 1877 84 used the trust instead of the *fideicommissum* to provide an asylum or home upon a certain farm for those of the testators' descendants who might unfortunately be in poor or indigent circumstances.[18] Clubs and associations often put their property in the hands of trustees.[19] However, the trust was not the only administrative device employed. When a school whose land had been held by trustees was incorporated the land was vested in the school Council which was to hold the assets on the same terms.[20]

The government also made grants of land in trust for charitable purposes. An early instance was the grant in 1817 of land to the Moravian Brothers 'in trust for the Missionary Institution of the United Brethren at Groenkloof'.[21] In this context the trust was an alternative to the Roman-Dutch *modus*, which had been used before the occupation[22] and continued in use after it.[23] The government took steps to facilitate the use of trusts in business. It legislated to make loans by trustees more easily enforceable and landholdings by trustees more easily registrable. An Ordinance of 1846 for facilitating loans on shares in joint-stock companies provided for loans under trust deeds which vested the assets of the companies in trustees.[24] This was before the introduction of limited liability in 1861, but the practice of vesting company assets in trustees continued after limited liability was introduced.[25] In 1873 the Companies and Associations Trustees Act[26] was passed to remove doubt about the ownership of immovables held in trust for unincorporated joint-stock companies and other bodies. The Act also provided for the appointment where necessary of trustees for these companies and for bodies such as religious congregations, schools,[27] hospitals, libraries, and museums.[28] No transfer in the land register from outgo-

---

[17] Act 16 of 1873 (C), s. 16.   [18] *Van Rensburg v. Van Rensburg* 1937 EDL 59.
[19] E.g. *Re Panmure Club* (1886) 5 EDC 170.
[20] Diocesan College, Rondebosch Act 11 of 1891 (C).
[21] *Moravian Church Missionary Society v. September* (1909) Buch AC 494, 502–3. The technique varied. From this case it emerges that a later grant of 1842 was absolute, not in trust, while a transfer of 1858 was in trust for the residents of the institution at Mamre (*Magerman v. Moravian Missionary Society* 1921 CPD unreported: Coertze (n. 1), 60); cf. *Moravian Mission v. Mona* (1901) 15 EDC 13 (grant of 1876 absolute); *Mzubelo v. Ndaba & Breakfast* (1905) 22 SC 562 (grant of 1904 in terms absolute but rectified since intended to be in trust).
[22] *Re Consistory of the Dutch Reformed Church, Cape Town* (1897) 14 SC 5, 7 CTR 4 (government grant of 1735).
[23] *De Wet v. Marais* 1911 CPD 361 (donation of 1843); *Re Dutch Reformed Church, Wynberg* (1896) 13 SC 5, 6 CTR 7.   [24] Ord. 13 of 1846 (C).
[25] Joint Stock Companies Limited Liability Act 23 of 1861 (C); Coertze (n. 1), 62–3.
[26] Act 3 of 1873 (C).
[27] E.g. *Ex parte Trustees Infant School Wynberg* (1895) 5 CTR 1; *Consistory of the Dutch Reformed Church, Cradock v. Superintendant General of Education* (1899) 16 SC 112.
[28] But these bodies could operate without trustees, e.g. with a managing council, as under the Stellenbosch College and Schools Act 9 of 1881 (C).

ing to incoming trustees was henceforth needed. This measure in effect introduced the English principle of survivorship into Cape trusts of immovables. It was an important step in the reception of a basic principle of trust law, one aspect of which is that trust property does not form part of a trustee's estate on his death.[29]

In parallel with this recognition and use of private trusts the government set about modernizing the Cape law concerning the administration of the estates of deceased and insolvent persons, and those subject to disability. This involved treating trustees as similar to curators and administrators. In 1822 a law provided that the wills of British subjects should be deposited in the Orphan Chamber to facilitate administration by executors or administrators.[30] In 1828 registration in the office of the newly created Registrar of Deeds replaced registration of deeds of land transfer and mortgages before the court (*coram lege loci*).[31] In the same year the administration of bankrupt and insolvent estates was reorganized.[32] The estate of a bankrupt or insolvent was to vest in the Master of the Supreme Court until the creditors chose one or more trustees to administer it, the 'trustees' responding to Roman-Dutch curators.[33] Hence many early decisions on trusts concern trustees in insolvency,[34] who are in effect statutory rather than private trustees. There was much litigation about their claims to be indemnified for the costs they incurred. Were they liable to pay costs from their own pockets when they were at fault in the administration of the insolvent estate?[35] Then in 1833 the Master of the Supreme Court replaced the Orphan Chamber. Wills were now to be registered by the Master and administered under letters of administration issued by him, as were the estates of minors, lunatics, and absentees.[36]

In 1833 comes the first reported case about trustees. It concerned an antenuptial contract, English marriage settlements being treated as a variety of ante-nuptial contract.[37] When a trust is created, Menzies J observed, any

---

[29] *Randfontein Estates v The Master* 1909 TS 978. There is a complication as regards a sole surviving trustee: Tony Honoré, Edwin Cameron, *Honoré's South African Law of Trusts* (4th edn., 1993), 488–90.

[30] Proclamation of 12 July 1822, replaced by Ord. 39 of 1828 (C) and then by Ord. 104 of 1833 (C).

[31] Ord. 33 of 1827 (C).

[32] Ord. 46 of 1828 (C) with further legislation in 1843 by Ord. 6 of that year which abolished *cessio bonorum*.

[33] Cf. *Insolvente Boedels Wet* (Insolvent Estate Act) 21 of 1880 (SAR).

[34] E.g. *Harris v. Trustee of Buissinne* (1840) 2 Menz 105.

[35] *Re Insolvent Estate Phillips* (1845) 1869 Buch 321; *Steytler v. Cannon's Trustee & Norden's Executor & Curators* (1853) 1869 Buch 322; *Wehmeyer v. Swemmer, Trustee of Heyns* 1874 Buch 46; *Mackie Dunn v. Reinach's Trustee* (1885) 2 Buch AC 30; *Slater's Trustee v. Smith* (1886) 4 SC 135; *Du Toit v. Jones* (1894) 9 EDC 51; *Standard Bank v. Currey* (1899) 16 *Cape LJ* 185.

[36] Ords. 103, 104, 105 of 1833 (C); cf. Weeskamer en Administratie van Boedels Wet (Orphan Chamber and Administration of Estates Act) 12 of 1870 (SAR).

[37] *Twentyman v. Hewitt* (1833) 1 Menz 156; Coertze (n. 1), 54–5. This did not stand in the way of legislation about the leasing of 'settled estates': Act 17 of 1876 (C).

party interested in it may come to court to have it put into effect.[38] Although the actual decision seemed to overlook the rule that trustees must act jointly unless the trust instrument provides otherwise,[39] this case shows that the validity of the trust was recognized in Cape law soon after the British occupation. In 1835 the Court decided that, like an ante-nuptial contract, a trust in a marriage settlement could not be revoked during the subsistence of the marriage,[40] Voet being cited in support.[41] An 1865 decision however allows a trust under an ante-nuptial contract to be revoked with the consent of all parties and criticizes the resort to the trust device as unnecessary; the wife could have chosen to manage her own property during the marriage.[42] However, there is no suggestion that the trust was invalid. In 1842 it was decided that when a trustee under an ante-nuptial contract had merged the trust funds with his own and become insolvent the beneficiary was not entitled to a preference in insolvency.[43] This decision would probably be upheld even today under the Trust Property Control Act of 1988, although that Act endorses the English principle that trust property does not form part of the personal estate of the trustee,[44] because once it is merged with the trustee's personal funds the trust property is no longer identifiable. Trusts were therefore received into the law of ante-nuptial contracts,[45] but they remained subject not only to the Roman-Dutch rules of revocation but to the *placaat* of 1540.[46] By this, contrary to English law, a wife who was a trust beneficiary was not entitled to a preference in her husband's insolvency.[47]

In 1842 the Cape Court upheld a testamentary trust, albeit an odd one.[48] An English-born testator by a Cape will of 1832 left his estate to his executors 'upon trust' but failed to specify the beneficiary or purpose. The Court held that by implication the beneficiary was the testator's wife. Trusts *inter vivos* for charitable purposes were also recognized.[49] In 1863 the Privy Council decided that a transfer of land at Mowbray in 1854 for ecclesiastical purposes created an implied trust in the transferee, the Bishop of Cape

---

[38] Act 17 of 1876 (C), 161.

[39] *Trustee of Dodds King v. Watson* (1848) 1 Menz 140; *Walker v. Beaton's Trustees* 1868 Buch 225 (where the lack of authority from a co-trustee is described as giving rise to the *exceptio inhabilis procuratoris*); *Parkin v. Parkin* 1869 Buch 136; *Muller Bros v. Lombard, Van Aardt* (1904) 21 SC 657.

[40] *Buissinne v. Mulder* (1835) 1 Menz 162; cf., on trusts in marriage settlements, *Devenish v. Peacock & Joseph* (1842) 3 Menz 503; Coertze (n. 1), 55–7.

[41] Johannes Voet, *Commentarius ad Pandectas*, 36, 1, 9.

[42] *Marshall v. Marshall's Trustees* (1865) 5 Searle 144; Coertze (n. 1), 60.

[43] *Re Wright* (1842) 1 Menz 166.   [44] Act 57 of 1988, s. 12.

[45] See also *Jamieson v. Board of Executors* (1859) 3 Searle 50.

[46] *Placaat* of Charles V of 4 Oct. 1540, repealed by Act 21 of 1875 (C).

[47] *Re Insolvent Estate of Chiappini* (1856) 1869 Buch 143; *Paterson's Marriage Settlement v. Paterson's Trustees in Insolvency* 1869 Buch 95.

[48] *Batt v. Batt's Widow* (1835) 2 Menz 408.

[49] *Darroll v. Tennant* 1932 CPR 406 concerns a donation in trust of 1849.

Town. (Would a Cape court have treated this as creating a *modus* rather than a trust?) The agreement and transfer did not, however, confer jurisdiction on the Bishop since jurisdiction cannot be created by contract.[50] This decision was an episode in a church war for which the law of trusts provided a battleground. The disputes concerned the trusts that governed the (English) Colonial Bishoprics Fund and the land on which various English churches in South Africa had been built. Courts cannot alter trust purposes that are capable of being carried out,[51] and the purposes of religious organizations are defined by religious beliefs. So an awkward situation arises when a church for which property is held on trust alters its beliefs. The crucial question in South Africa was whether the beliefs of the Church of England and its locally organized offshoot, the Church of the Province of South Africa (CPSA) were so radically different that the assets originally intended for the former could not be used for the support of the latter.[52] The alleged difference arose because the CPSA had declined to be bound by rulings of the English courts, including the Privy Council, on matters of faith and doctrine.[53] In the end an interim solution was found by applying the English cy-près doctrine on the basis that, while the Church of England did not exist in South Africa, the CPSA was closer to it than its South African rivals.[54]

The Cape courts assumed jurisdiction to appoint, remove, and release trustees[55] and to sell land and buy other land or investments[56] when necessary for the proper administration of the trust. The management of private trusts was often undertaken by trust companies, such as the South African Association for the Administration of Estates, founded in 1834 and regulated by an Ordinance of 1855.[57] Though there was an earlier example from Massachusetts in 1818 or 1822, this was one of the earliest trust companies in the world. It was followed by the Board of Executors in 1838. When the

[50] *Long v. Bishop of Cape Town* (1863) 1 Moo PCCNS 411.
[51] Philip H. Pettit, *Equity and the Law of Trusts* (6th edn., 1989), 414–6; Honoré/Cameron (n. 29), 413–68.
[52] *Bishop of Natal v. Gladstone* (1866) LR 3 Eq 1; *Bishop of Cape Town v. Bishop of Natal* (1869) 6 Moo PC 203.
[53] *Merriman v. Williams* 1880 Foord 135, 196 (PC); *Re Trinity Church Trust* (1886) 4 SC 174; cf. *Lindley v. Jones (Archbishop of Cape Town) & Rector & Churchwardens of St John's, Wynberg* (1906) 16 CTR 695. In the dispute between the Free Church of Scotland and the United Free Church of Scotland only the legislature was able to alter the trusts on which church land was held: *Re United Free Church of Scotland: Ex parte Henderson* (1907) 24 SC 749, 17 CTR 1139.
[54] *Mills v. Registrar of Deeds* 1936 CPD 417.
[55] *Marshall v. Marshall's Trustees* (1865) 5 Searle 144; *Sinclair v. Meintjes* 1874 Buch 40; *Re Estate McKenny* (1884) 4 EDC 41; *Re Estate Neethling* (1899) 16 SC 409; *Salie v. Connelly* 1908 EDC 97; *Re Estate Miller* (1891) 1 CTR 34.
[56] *Re Salie* (n. 10), 552; *Ex parte Trustees of Boys Mission School, Simonstown* (1902) 19 SC 305. Contrast *Ex parte Trustee Rhodes Recreation Ground* (1907) 17 CTR 240 and *Re Estate Crosbie* (1909) 27 SC 50, where leave to sell or vary investments was refused.
[57] Ord. 9 of 1855 (C).

court had to appoint a trustee it often chose one of these Boards,[58] though the South African Association was sharply criticized for failing to keep trust assets separate from its own company assets.[59] These innovative companies administered the estates of deceased persons and insolvents.

2. Natal

In Natal,[60] where Roman-Dutch law was introduced in 1845,[61] settlers also made use of trusts. The legislature and courts gave effect to them, but with less appreciation of the interaction between English and Roman-Dutch law.[62] An Ordinance of 1856 gave natural-born British subjects the right to dispose of real and personal property according to the law of England,[63] so there were for a time two different systems of succession governing British- and colonial-born subjects. Another Ordinance law of that year authorized the consistory of the *Hervormde Kerk* in Pietermaritzburg to hold certain property in trust.[64] In 1861 a law created the Durban Collegiate Institution and vested the property of the institution in the Council as trustees.[65] In 1864 the Natal Native trust was created by Letters Patent which conferred on it juristic personality.[66] The Indian Immigration Trust Board was constituted by an Act of 1874.[67] In the same year a law authorized the transfer of land by the Durban Town Council in trust for the Durban Mechanics Institution.[68]

The Natal reports begin in 1879. The first reported case on trust came in 1880. It held that an application to court to advance money for a beneficiary's business was unnecessary since the trustees had the necessary powers under the will.[69] Another case of that year dealt with the vesting of the beneficiaries' interests under what was in effect a testamentary trust administered by 'executors'.[70] It was, however, decided on the basis of Roman and Roman-Dutch texts dealing with *fideicommissa*[71] and in this respect fitted a general tendency of the South African courts not to allow the reception of trust law to alter the principles of the Roman-Dutch law of succession or

---

[58] E.g. *Sinclair v. Meintjes* (n. 55) (Graaff Reinet Board of Executors); *Ex parte Kingsmill & Anderson: Re Crockart's Will* (1894) 4 CTR 100; *Ex parte Schreiner & Silke: Re Reitz's Will* (1895) 5 CTR 367; *Re Fichardt v. Aldum* (1898) 15 *Cape LJ* 282; *Re Estate Neethling* (n. 55).

[59] *Hiddingh v. Denyssen* (1885) 3 SC 424; *Hiddingh v. De Villiers* (1887) 5 SC 298 (PC).

[60] Coertze (n. 1), 63–7.   [61] Ord. 12 of 1845 (N).

[62] E.g. *Agar v. Agar* (1899) 20 NLR 48 deals with a mistaken transfer of land to the trustees under an ante-nuptial contract, their heirs and executors, despite the fact that a trustee holds an office that ends on his death and is not transmitted to his successors. The trust was created in 1866.

[63] Ord. 1 of 1856 (N).   [64] Ord. 11 of 1856 (N).   [65] Law 19 of 1861 (N).
[66] Coertze (n. 1), 65.   [67] Law 20 of 1874 (N).   [68] Law 27 of 1874 (N).

[69] *Testate Estate Fradd* (1880) 1 NLR 125.

[70] *Estate of Milne* (1880) 1 NLR 88.

[71] D. 36, 1, 162; C. 6, 25, 6; Simon van Groenewegen van der Made, *Tractatus de legibus abrogatis et inusitatis in Hollandia vicinisque regionibus*, ad D. 28, 5, 85.

the interpretation of wills. In 1881 a trustee under an ante-nuptial contract brought a claim against the husband's trustee in insolvency.[72] Trustees were also recognized under post-nuptial contracts, a Natal speciality,[73] and on behalf of companies to be formed but not yet in existence,[74] which were said to be like trusts for children not yet born. The Natal Court assumed a jurisdiction like that of the Cape Court for the appointment and removal of trustees,[75] the variation of trusts when the original object became impossible to realize,[76] and the award of costs against trustees in insolvency.[77]

Legislation to modernize Roman-Dutch institutions followed lines similar to the Cape. An Ordinance of 1846 extended the Cape scheme for insolvent estates to Natal.[78] Deeds Registration along Cape lines was introduced in 1860.[79] In 1849 a Trust Company Ordinance incorporated the Board of Directors of the Natal Fire Assurance and Trust company and empowered it to sue and be sued in the name of its secretary.[80] In 1887 a Board of Trustees was incorporated to hold and manage land in Mount Moreland.[81]

3. The Orange Free State

In the Orange Free State (OFS)[82] and the South African Republic (SAR)[83] there were at first few English settlers, so that the legislature and courts were less concerned with trusts. Even here, however, the term gained some currency. An OFS law of 1891 revoked the Grey College 'trust deed' and its conditions. It vested the ownership of the college in the government and its administration in a commission of curators.[84] In 1892 a law was passed on the lines of the Cape law for ensuring that title to land held by unincorporated partnerships need not be retransferred each time the membership of the association changes.[85] The first reported case on trusts is not found until 1911, but it appears from the report that the Court had appointed a trustee to this trust in 1908.[86]

4. The South African Republic and the Transvaal

In the SAR legislation in 1870 provided for the administration of deceased estates under the aegis of the Orphan Chamber, by executors and

---

[72] *Re Insolvent Estate Fraser* (1881) 2 NLR 186.
[73] *Trustees of Sturrock v. Executors Estate Sturrock* (1897) 18 NLR 252.
[74] *Re Utrecht Collieries* (1909) 30 NLR 309, 311.
[75] *Estate King* (1891) 12 NLR 200; cf. *Re Ellis and Sutherland* (1891) 12 NLR 68; *Re Estate Thompson* (1894) 15 NLR 3.
[76] *Ex parte Trustees of Escourt Recreation Ground* (1899) 20 NLR 66.
[77] *McNeil v. Trustee of Bradley's Insolvent Estate* (1885) 6 NLR 295.
[78] Ord. 24 of 1846 (N), consolidated by Ord. 47 of 1887 (N).
[79] Law 5 of 1860 (N).   [80] Law 4 of 1849 (N).   [81] Law 6 of 1887 (N).
[82] Coertze (n. 1), 68–70.   [83] Ibid. 67–8.   [84] Law 16 of 1891 (O).
[85] Law 16 of 1892 (O) referring to *curatoren*, translated as 'trustees'; cf. n. 33, above.
[86] *Ex parte Kerr* 1911 OPD 12.

administrators.[87] The Insolvency Law of 1895 arranged for the liquidation of insolvent estates on similar lines to the Cape, but translated trustees as curators.[88]

There were also judicial decisions touching trusts. This is not surprising since trusts were created as early as 1887.[89] A case of 1894 dealt with the handling of 'trust money' by attorneys.[90] In 1895 when a debtor agreed to hand over promissory notes *ten genoegen* (translated as 'in trust') for his creditors Kotzé CJ held that the ownership of the notes passed to the trustee.[91] The same judge in 1897 tentatively held that certain entrepreneurs who had obtained a concession on behalf of a syndicate had 'called a constructive trust into being'.[92] This hinted at the reception of a part of English trust law which was hardly needed in South Africa in view of the scope of the Roman-Dutch law of unjust enrichment. Constructive and resulting trusts have not in fact taken root in South African soil.[93] In 1898 the SAR court had to decide whether trustees who were registered owners of land belonging to a library association could mortgage it.[94] The court decided that a bond secured on the land would be valid since the trustees represented either an association (*universitas*)[95] or a charitable foundation clothed with juristic personality.[96] Hence the trustees for the time being and their successors would be bound but would not be personally liable on the bond. The judgment presupposes that the trustees would be personally liable unless they held on behalf of a juristic person. The basis for this assumption vanished thirteen years later when in 1911 a key Transvaal decision held that, unless they are guilty of breach of trust, trustees, like executors and administrators, are liable for debts incurred in the administration of the trust only to the extent of the trust assets.[97] This limitation was

[87] Weeskamer en Administratie van Boedels Wet (Orphan Chamber and Administration of Estates Act) 12 of 1870 (SAR).

[88] Insolventiewet (Insolvency Law) 13 of 1895 (SAR).

[89] *Re Pretoria Theatre and Offices Co* 1905 TS 235 refers to a transfer of land to trustees for a syndicate in 1887.

[90] *Incorporated Law Soc v. Lofthouse* (1894) 1 OR 367.

[91] *Gordon Mitchell v. Goldsmith* (1895) 2 OR 246.

[92] *Matabele Syndicate v. Lippert* (1897) 4 OR 372.

[93] *Agar v. Agar* (n. 62), 51; *Estate Kemp v. McDonald's Trustee* 1914 CPD 1084, 1092; *Verseput v. De Gruchy* 1977 (4) SA 440 (W); Honoré/Cameron (n. 29), 104–10.

[94] *Committee of the Johannesburg Public Library v. Spence* (1898) 5 OR 84.

[95] E.g. *Webb v. Northern Rifles* 1908 TS 462.

[96] Whether such foundations (*stigtinge*) can be created by private initiative without statutory authority in South Africa, as Gregorowski J asserted (*Spence's* case, above n. 94, 88), remains uncertain: Christian Petrus Joubert, *Die Stigting in die Romeins-Hollandse Reg en die Suid-Afrikaanse Reg* (1951); idem, 'Die Fideicommiss, die Trust en die Stigting', (1951) 14 *THRHR* 175–91, (1952) 15 *THRHR* 181–247; idem, 'Die Gemeenregtelike Administrateur', in: *Huldigingsbundel Pont* (1970), 162 sqq.; H. L. Swanepoel, 'Oor Stigting, Trust, Fideicommissum, Modus en Beding ten behoewe van 'n Derde', (1956) 19 *THRHR* 102–16, 197–214, 273–85; (1957) 20 *THRHR* 40–5; Honoré/Cameron (n. 29), 49–57.

[97] *Ehrlich v. Rand Cold Storage & Supply Co Ltd* 1911 TPD 170. Cf. for earlier hints in this direction *Standard Bank v. Jacobson's Trustee* (1899) 16 SC 352; *Re Estate Potgieter* 1908 TS 982.

inevitable if the office of trustee was to be treated like that of curator, executor, and administrator, whose personal property is separate from the property they administer. However, the position in English law was and is different. There trustees are personally liable for trust debts,[98] but can indemnify themselves from the trust assets.[99]

After the 1899–1902 war the Transvaal court assumed jurisdiction to appoint,[100] release,[101] and remove trustees.[102] The trust device was now used, apart from wills and ante-nuptial contracts,[103] to circumvent restrictions on the ownership[104] and lease of land[105] by non-whites.

5. Summary of developments to 1910

From these pre-Union statutes and cases certain general trends emerge. British settlers used trusts for a wide spectrum of purposes, and South African courts fitted the arrangements they made into the Roman-Dutch law whenever no great tension was created by doing so. When English and Roman-Dutch law possessed similar trust-like institutions the courts overlooked minor differences and treated the former as variants of the latter. Marriage settlements creating trusts were a type of ante-nuptial contract. Entails or settlements were a form of *fideicommissum*.[106] The duties of the trustees of deceased estates were like those of Roman-Dutch executors and administrators[107] so that, for example, the same principles governed their removal from office. This the Privy Council, upholding the Cape Supreme Court, ruled in an important decision in 1884.[108] More narrowly, testamentary trustees were identified with administrators.[109] When a trust failed, trust money was applied cy-près,[110] as in English law, to a similar object. This was analogous to the rule by which a gift subject to a *modus* that proved impracticable could be applied for a like object.[111] The sale and

[98] *Farhall v. Farhall* (1871) 7 Ch App 123; *Owen v. Delamere* (1872) LR 15 Eq 134; *Re Johnson* (1880) 15 ChD 548; *Re Morgan* (1881) 18 ChD 93, 99 (CA).

[99] Pettit (n. 51), 408–10.

[100] *Ex parte Slack* 1909 TS 1118; *Ex parte Marks* 1907 TS 24.

[101] *Ex parte Van Blommestein* 1907 TH 2.   [102] *Sephton v. Coetzee* 1909 TS 637.

[103] *Ex parte Ross* 1909 TS 1132.   [104] *Lucas' Trustee v. Ismail & Amod* 1905 TS 239.

[105] *Ngubani v. Sheppard* 1909 TS 717.

[106] *Drew v. Drew's Executor* 1876 Buch 203; *Agar v. Agar* (n. 62), 50; Ord. 29 of 1893 (C).

[107] *Atmore v. Chaddock* (1896) 13 SC 205, 6 CTR 181 ('do not differ materially from the law of England'); *Black v. Executor of Black and Black* (1904) 21 SC 555 (ownership of deceased estate held by executors and administrators in trust for grandchildren ultimately entitled to it under will).

[108] *Letterstedt v. Broers* (1884) 9 AC 371.

[109] *Hiddingh v. Denyssen* (1885) 3 SC 424, 441; *Black v. Black's Executor* (n. 107); *Furnivale v. Cornwell's Executors* (1895) 12 SC 6.

[110] Pettit (n. 51), 266–74; and see Reinhard Zimmermann, 'Cy-près', in: *Iuris Professio: Festgabe für Max Kaser* (1986), 395 sqq.

[111] *Re Dutch Reformed Church, Wynberg* (1896) 13 SC 5, 6 CTR 7; cf. *Ex parte Trustees of the Diocese of Cape Town* (1896) 13 SC 312; *Re Taylor* (1909) 26 SC 315.

reinvestment of unsuitable property subject to a trust was like the exchange of fideicommissary property, which was sanctioned by Voet and other Roman-Dutch authors.[112] It is true that there were mutterings in both the Cape and Natal about the Roman-Dutch rule, said to be laxer than English practice, that a person like an executor in a position of trust could purchase estate property provided he did so *palam et bona fide*.[113] Here again, however, the Privy Council, firmly wedded to assimilation, denied that there was any difference between the two systems.[114]

There was some tendency in both Cape and Transvaal to accept elements of English trust law that added nothing to existing Roman-Dutch institutions.[115] In the Cape De Villiers CJ gave currency to the idea that a person who has not been properly appointed can become a trustee *de facto* by administering the trust property without authority and can be made liable in that capacity.[116] Though he did not say so, this idea derives from the English conception of a trustee *de son tort*,[117] a device needed in English law because that system, unlike Roman-Dutch law with its machinery (*negotiorum gestio*) for calling meddlers to account, does not in general impose liability on those who manage the affairs of another without authority.[118] This idea has not taken hold in South Africa.[119]

However, when there was a real conflict between the Dutch and English rules concerning trust-like institutions, for example as regards the legitimate portion,[120] the position of a wife on her husband's insolvency,[121] or the revocation of ante-nuptial contracts,[122] the courts upheld the Roman-Dutch law unless and until it was changed by legislation.[123] There were, however, some cases in which it was not clear whether the English and South African rules were in conflict. The most controversial issues concerned the relations between trust and *fideicommissum* and between trust and the registration of title to immovables.

As for the first, Bell J said in a 1867 case that he could see no substantial difference between trust and *fideicommissum*, both being institutions designed to defraud![124] The issue to be decided in the case before him was whether the trust device could be used to outflank the principle that on

---

[112] Voet (n. 41), 36, 1, 63.

[113] *Louw v. Hofmeyr* 1869 Buch 290 at 294 (purchase by co-executor of estate property permitted on the basis of Voet (n. 41), 18, 1, 19, despite disapproval of Bell CJ); *Nel v. Louw* 1877 Buch 133; *Baxter v. Beningfield* (1883) 4 NLR 143, 159 sq.; *Mayer & De Chazal v. Natal Central Sugar Co Ltd and Evans* (1884) 5 NLR 323; *Re Minors Cowling* (1896) 6 CTR 387.

[114] *Beningfield v. Baxter* (1886) 12 App Cas 167, 178.

[115] Above, nn. 92–3, 106–8.

[116] *Consistory of the Dutch Reformed Church v. Master & the SA Asssociation* (1891) 8 SC 181; *Re Best* (1892) 9 SC 488.

[117] *Mara v. Browne* 1986 1 Ch 199 (CA); Pettit (n. 51), 153–4.

[118] Honoré/Cameron (n. 29), 92–3.   [119] Ibid. 107–8.

[120] *Buyskes v. Russouw's Executors* 1875 Buch 19; Coertze (n. 1), 58.

[121] Above, nn. 46–7.   [122] Above, nn. 40–2.

[123] *Castleman v. Stride's Executor* (1885) 4 SC 28, 30 (English law 'not a safe guide').

insolvency a debtor's property is available to his creditors. This could not be done by a *fideicommissum* to take effect on insolvency and it was decided in the 1867 case that it could not be done by trust either. Rules of public policy cannot be nullified by employing an alternative technique. In an 1894 case it was hinted that the rules about the vesting of successive interests might depend on whether the disposition was by an ordinary *fideicommissum* or by what was in effect a trust.[125] This suggestion was later taken up in the Appellate Division in 1949[126] but was definitively rejected in 1955.[127] It made sense only if: (i) there was a difference between the English rules as to the vesting of interests under a trust instrument and the Roman-Dutch rules about vesting in the absence of a trust, and (ii) South African courts were prepared to adopt the English rules. However, it is doubtful whether there is any such difference. The time when an interest vests in a beneficiary must depend on the intention of the testator or donor,[128] not on the legal form adopted to effect that intention. An 1896 case held that a '*fideicommissum* or similar limited interest' might exist under the umbrella of a trust, and if the trustees had a power to sell the property subject to the *fideicommissum* this merely made the *fideicommissum* conditional.[129] However, the really important distinction between trust and *fideicommissum* was (and is) that the trust is an administrative device, while the *fideicommissum* is a technique for enabling beneficiaries to enjoy property successively.[130] This was brought out by the Privy Council as early as 1887[131] in a case which decided that when a will gave property to the testator's daughter subject to a *fideicommissum* and also appointed 'administrators' no trust was created. The fiduciary heir was entitled to administer the property herself without their interference. Despite this rather obvious difference, the question whether a trust was to be construed as a sort of *fideicommissum* was reopened, as we shall see, in 1915[132] and was not finally settled until 1984.[133]

Another important issue concerned the relation of trusts to the system by which the ownership of immovables is, with minor exceptions, conclusively settled by the register of title to land in the Deeds Registry. Suppose a debtor who is the registered owner of land holds it as trustee or in some other administrative capacity not recorded on the register of title. When he

---

[124] (1883) 2 SC 430. The judge's *bon mot* refers to the use of *fideicommissa* to evade restrictions on testamentary disposition and of the use, later the trust, to evade feudal dues and taxes.

[125] *Strydom v. Strydom's Trustee* (1894) 1 SC 425, 428–9.

[126] *Smith v. Estate Smith* 1949 (1) SA 534 (A) 543–4.

[127] *Greenberg v. Estate Greenberg* 1955 (3) SA 361 (A) 364–5.

[128] As stressed by De Villiers CJ in *Strydom's* case (n. 125).

[129] *Re Myburgh* (1896) 13 SC 218.

[130] The differences are well brought out by Coertze (n. 1), 116–38.

[131] *De Montmort v. Broers* (1887) 13 App Cas 149 (Coertze (n. 1), 59–60); cf. *Mackenzie v. Estate Mackenzie* (1906) 23 SC 453, 16 CTR 700.

[132] *Estate Kemp v. McDonald's Trustee* 1915 AD 491; below, n. 156.

[133] *Braun v. Blann & Botha* 1984 (2) SA 850 (A).

becomes insolvent his private creditors claim the land as part of his insolvent estate, while the trust beneficiary claims a preference over the land on the ground that it is trust property and forms no part of the trustee's insolvent estate. An 1840 decision in the Cape held that on these facts the trust beneficiary has no preference in insolvency;[134] he is an ordinary unsecured creditor. In 1884 this was reversed in the Cape Appeal Court by three judges to two (the majority including De Villiers CJ) on the ostensible ground that the transfer in trust, though registered, lacked a just cause.[135]

In 1905 the Transvaal court, under the aegis of Innes CJ, reaffirmed the 1840 decision.[136] Though De Villiers cited Voet[137] for his opinion, the argument was really about whether the trust beneficiary had an unregistered 'equitable interest' in the land which gave him a preference in insolvency, as it would have done at the time in England where title to land did not depend on registration. According to the 1905 decision it was dangerous to call the landowner a trustee if that implied that the beneficiary had an equitable interest in the property. As Innes CJ put it, '[i]f by trustee is meant a man occupying some capacity recognised by our law, and undertaking some obligation known to our law, to hold property for another and not for himself, then the expression is a convenient one and may be safely applied. But if the word trustee is employed as somehow vaguely introducing the English doctrine of trusts, whether express or constructive, and as implying the existence of some real right in the *cestui que trust* (beneficiary) which would not be conferred by our law, then it is a dangerous word and should be very strictly scrutinized'.[138] The difference in approach between De Villiers CJ and Innes CJ may reflect the fact that, unlike De Villiers CJ, Innes CJ did not undergo an English legal education. Although it has now been settled that trust property does not form part of the trustee's personal estate[139] it is not clear that this reinstates the De Villiers view when the trust is not registered against the title to the land.[140] The argument that this would subvert the system of land registration[141] remains a powerful one. If on the other hand the trust was registered against the title to the land,[142] nowadays

---

[134] *Harris v. Trustee of Buissinne* (1840) 2 Menz 105.

[135] *Preston & Dixon v. Biden's Trustee* (1884) 1 Buch AC 322. In retrospect it seems perverse to say that just cause was lacking, but at the time De Villiers CJ held that just cause for a contract required consideration in the English sense: *Mtembu v. Webster* (1904) 21 SC 323. This view was rejected in *Conradie v. Rossouw* 1919 AD 279. Cf. Ch. 5 by Dale Hutchison, above.

[136] *Lucas' Trustee v. Ismail and Amod* 1905 TS 239.

[137] Voet (n. 41), 46, 3, 7, which, however, does not support the decision.

[138] *Lucas' Trustee v. Ismail & Amod* (n. 136), 243–4.   [139] Act 57 of 1988, s. 12.

[140] Honoré/Cameron (n. 29), 473–80.

[141] *Lucas' Trustee v. Ismail & Amod* (n. 136), 247.

[142] Examples go back to such transfers as those referred to in *Bishop of Cape Town v. Bishop of Natal* (1869) 6 Moo PCCNS 203; *Ex parte Trustees of the Diocese of Cape Town* (1896) 13 SC 312; and *Moravian Mission v. Mona* (1901) 15 EDC 13.

in the name of the 'trustees for the time being of such-and-such a trust', the land did not form part of the personal property of the trustee.[143]

The elements of English trust law received in South Africa up to 1910 were generally those that were consistent with existing Roman-Dutch institutions while adding something to them. Trusteeship, as a more flexible and wide-ranging administrative device, could be accepted alongside tutorship, curatorship and executorship. Given the rule of survivorship, it offered a convenient way of administering property on an ongoing basis for beneficiaries or for an abstract purpose, and could be adapted to almost any context. Trusts were relatively free from state control, since trustees, though they could be removed by the court, had only to account to their beneficiaries for their administration, not to the court or any administrative authority. The supervisory jurisdiction of the court came into play only if it was called on to intervene.

However, South African courts, while accepting the validity of trusts, rejected the English notion that a trust beneficiary had a proprietary interest in the trust assets, a notion which would, if accepted, have subverted the system of land registration. Innes prevailed over De Villiers, though not without a fight. The beneficiary, like a contract creditor, was given only a right *in personam* against the trustee to have the trust properly administered and to claim damages if it was not. Yet a number of important issues remained unsettled. What degree of state control over trusts was appropriate? Apart from the special case of land registration, were trust assets separate from the personal assets of the trustee? Could the trust device be adapted to trusts for running businesses?

III. UNION AND REPUBLIC: 1910–94

When the four provinces united in 1910 the new legislature and courts had a chance to modernize and rationalize the law. This Section begins with a survey of the legislation imposing state control on trusts and goes on to consider developments in the attitude of the courts to the reception of English trust law during this century and the invention by private initiative of new functions for the trust.

1. Legislative control over trusts

In 1913 Parliament enacted a unitary law for the administration of deceased estates by executors under the aegis of the Master of the Supreme Court.[144]

---

[143] *Ex parte Milton* 1959 (3) SA 347 (SR); *Magnum Financial Holdings v. Summerly* 1984 (1) SA 1650 (W).
[144] Act 24 of 1913.

This was the first of four laws that have at intervals of twenty or thirty years defined the extent of state control over trusts. The others are the Trust Moneys Protection Act 1934,[145] the Administration of Estates Act 1965,[146] and the Trust Property Control Act 1988.[147] In broad terms the 1934 Act extended to trusts *inter vivos* the control that the 1913 Act had introduced for testamentary trusts. The 1965 Act, of which the part relating to trusts was never brought into force, would have tightened state control over both types of trust. The 1988 Act, more liberal than that of 1965, took over some ideas from the abortive 1965 Act but opted for a looser degree of control. At the same time it shifted the focus of supervisory power from the court to the Master.

The 1913 Act made provision for administrators to manage any trusts created by will after the executors had liquidated the estate and paid the estate debts. Whenever a will directed that property, instead of being distributed to the beneficiaries, should be administered on their behalf the executor had, after paying debts, to deliver it, if movable, to the administrator. If the property was immovable a reference to the terms of the will had to be endorsed against the title-deeds of the property. Thereupon the administrator had full power to deal with the deceased person's property in terms of the will.[148] Like an executor, an administrator had to give security for the due and faithful administration of the estate unless he was a close relative or was exempted by the will or the court.[149] This requirement imposed on trustees a degree of supervision that does not exist in English law, where the general law does not require security to be given and trust instruments do not normally impose it. However, the Master had less control over administrators than over executors. He could not appoint an administrator, as he could an executor, to fill a vacancy, and he did not issue letters of administration to administrators, as he did to executors. For administrators, unlike executors, there was no official scale of remuneration.

The 1913 Act assumed that testamentary trusts would be administered by administrators. It implicitly identified testamentary trustees with administrators, despite the fact that in Roman-Dutch law administrators did not own the property they administered, whilst English trustees normally did.[150] A Transvaal decision of 1910[151] had anticipated this fusion of the two offices. The case concerned an application to remove as administrators two brothers who had borrowed or attempted to borrow money from the

---

[145] Act 34 of 1934.   [146] Act 66 of 1965.   [147] Act 57 of 1988.
[148] Administration of Estates Act 24 of 1913, s. 61.   [149] Ibid. s. 61(3)
[150] There are exceptions. When trustees hold for a body that is incorporated the ownership is in the corporate body, not the trustees. This is important in South Africa, where an association can have juristic personality as a *universitas* without state authorization: e.g. *Morrison v. Standard Building Soc* 1932 AD 229, 238; Honoré/Cameron (n. 29), 343–5.
[151] *The Master v. Edgecombe's Executors* 1910 TS 263, 269.

deceased estate on flimsy security. It was argued that the brothers, to whom the will gave ownership of the estate assets, could not be administrators, since in Dutch law an administrator did not own the assets he administered, which remained vested in the heir.[152] The Court however pointed out that the Roman-Dutch administrator 'was really an executor of the trusts of the will'. His obligations were those that had been transferred from Roman-Dutch tutors (guardians) to executors.[153] The brothers were 'not fiduciary heirs but trustees'[154] and administrators 'would in English law be called trustees'.[155] Thus the two were in effect treated as identical. The administrators had the legal but not the beneficial ownership. When removed from office they ceased to own the trust assets.

In the context of the administration of estates administrators and trustees have since then consistently been identified by the courts whether appointed by will or *inter vivos* and whether or not they own the trust assets. As Innes CJ said in a leading 1915 case, the word trustee means 'persons entrusted, as owners or otherwise, with the control of property with which they are bound to deal for the benefit of others'.[156] Judicial practice therefore early on reached the point of view implicit[157] in the legislation that a trustee need not be the owner of the trust property. This point of view has since been consistently upheld by the Appellate Division.[158] The arrangement by which the trustee does not own the trust property is often described by the Dutch term *bewind*.[159] However, by contrast with the legislature and the courts, some writers were reluctant to accept that the same institution could include both owning and non-owning administrators/trustees.[160] They did not accept that institutions which were once separate can in the course of time merge, even if they serve the same function. Institutional apartheid, as it may be termed, overlooks the degree to which legal institutions can adapt to social needs.

It therefore does not matter where the ownership of trust assets is located, since the powers of those who administer them derive from the trust instrument and the general law, not from whether they happen technically to own the property they administer. The fashion in names has oscillated between 'administrators' and 'trustees'. The 1965 Administration of Estates Act proposed to call trustees, both testamentary and *inter vivos*, administrators.[161]

---

[152] Ibid. 274–5; Herman Frederik W. D. Fischer, *Kort Begrip van Het Oud-Vaderlandsch Burgerlijk Recht* (7th edn., 1967), 377; Joubert (n. 96), 162 sqq.

[153] Ibid. [154] Ibid. 267. [155] Ibid. 274.

[156] *Estate Kemp v. McDonald's Trustee* (n. 132), 499.

[157] Made explicit by Act 57 of 1988, s. 1.

[158] *Estate Cato v. Estate Cato* 1915 AD 290; *Estate Watkins-Pitchford v. CIR* 1955 (2) SA 437 (A); *Schaumberg v. Stark* 1956 (4) SA 462 (A).

[159] Honoré/Cameron (n. 29), 4–7, 222–6.

[160] Christan Petrus Joubert, 'Honoré se Opvattings oor die Trustreg', (1969) 31 *THRHR* 124–46, 262–81; *idem, Stigting* (n. 96), 162; N. J. van der Merwe, C. J. Rowland, *Die Suid-Afrikaanse Erfreg* (6th edn., 1989), 345, fn. 77.

[161] Act 66 of 1965, s. 40.

However, those provisions were not brought into force and have now been repealed.[162] The 1988 Act calls them all trustees,[163] whether the property is made over or bequeathed by will or *inter vivos* to the trustee or to a beneficiary to be administered by a trustee on his behalf.[164] In what follows, as a matter of convenience, the term 'trustee' is used for both trustees and administrators.

The Administration of Estates Act 1913 extended state control over testamentary trustees but left the position of trustees *inter vivos* unchanged. In 1934 the gap was filled by the Trust Moneys Protection Act.[165] The scheme of the Act was to require a trustee to lodge a copy of the trust instrument with the Master[166] and to require him to find security for the due administration of the trust unless dispensed either by the trust instrument with the concurrence of the Master or by the court. If the trustee was guilty of default in the administration of the trust the Master could enforce the security.[167] Although there were slight differences between the security requirements of the 1913 and the 1934 Acts, the thrust of the legislation was to subject both testamentary and *inter vivos* trustees to sufficient control to ensure a remedy for beneficiaries if the trustee failed to administer the trust properly but lacked the resources to make good his default. The Act also empowered the Master to call on the trustee to account to him for the administration of the trust and, if he failed to do so, gave the Master the same remedies against the trustee that he had against an executor who failed to lodge his administration account. In practice the Master only called for an account if he received a complaint about the trust administration. The 1934 Act therefore subjected testamentary and *inter vivos* trustees to some control, but less than that required of executors, who were in any case bound to submit a liquidation and distribution account to the Master. Moreover, though the Master had the right and duty to appoint an executor dative under certain circumstances, he had no power to appoint a trustee unless the trust instrument so provided.

Chapter 111 of the Administration of Estates Act 1965 proposed tighter controls over both testamentary and *inter vivos* trustees. A trustee, like an executor, would only have power to administer the trust when the Master granted him 'letters of administratorship'.[168] He would then have to lodge with the Master an annual account properly audited.[169] The Master would have power to appoint a trustee if there was no trustee or the trustee was absent or a vacancy occurred which ought to be filled in the interests of the trust.[170]

The Master would have needed extra staff to undertake these duties. The necessary funds were not forthcoming and by the eighties the climate of

---

[162] Act 57 of 1988, s. 26.   [163] Ibid. s. 1.   [164] Ibid.   [165] Act 34 of 1934.
[166] Ibid. s. 2.   [167] Ibid. s. 3.   [168] Act 65 of 1966, s. 57.
[169] Ibid. s. 65.   [170] Act 66 of 1965, ss. 18, 60, 61, 95.

opinion had become more hostile to state intervention. Some of the features of the 1965 legislation were indeed retained in 1988. Trusts were to be administered only on the written authority of the Master.[171] The Master was given authority to appoint trustees if there was a vacancy, after consultation with as many interested parties as he thought necessary. However, the complex procedure of appointment envisaged in 1965 was abandoned.[172] The Master could in certain cases remove a trustee from office.[173] A trustee, who could previously only resign if given the power to do so in the trust instrument or authorized by the court, could now shed his office by notifying the Master.[174] The Master could call on the trustee to account or could order his administration of the trust to be investigated.[175] However, the requirement that an audited annual account be presented to the Master was dropped. Overall the Master acquired a number of powers that had previously been reserved to the court, though it remained possible to apply to the court for relief against the Master's decisions.[176] At the same time the legislation sought to minimize expense and state control, and to avoid some of the bureaucratic overlay that the 1966 Act would have involved.

2. Judicial developments in the law of trusts

So much for the legislative framework. The new courts, in particular the Appellate Division, soon had to deal with cases involving trusts, the first of them in 1912,[177] 1913,[178] and 1914.[179] The validity of trusts in South African law was not in doubt, but the courts had to decide, among other matters, how far the types of beneficial interest that were accepted in English trust law should be received in South Africa, whether the English rules about the creation and revocation of trusts *inter vivos* should be accepted, and whether the separation of trust property from the personal property of the trustee in English law should be recognized where its recognition did not tend to subvert the system of land registration.

(a) Life interests

As regards beneficial interests, the most important issues concerned life interests and powers of appointment. In 1915 the new Appellate Division in *Estate Kemp v. McDonald's Trustee* gave its first important judgment on trust law.[180] The question was whether under the umbrella of a trust a beneficial interest in property could be created similar to that of a fiduciary

---

[171] Act 57 of 1988, s. 6.   [172] Ibid. s. 7.   [173] Ibid. s. 20.   [174] Ibid. s. 21.
[175] Ibid. s. 16.   [176] Ibid. s. 23.   [177] *Van der Plank v. Otto* 1912 AD 353.
[178] *Sherriff v. Greene* 1913 AD 240, an early example of a trust for investment in mortgages, later regulated by the Participation Bonds Acts 1964 and 1981.
[179] *Robertson v. Robertson's Executors* 1914 AD 503.   [180] Above, n. 132.

under a *fideicommissum*, or whether it was possible to create only a life interest similar to a *usufruct*, that could in no circumstance extend beyond a lifetime. The Court held that it was possible to create a fiduciary-type interest which would extend beyond a lifetime and carry with it the capital of the trust fund if the *fideicommissum* failed. It interpreted the will in question as conferring on one of the beneficiaries an interest of that type, so that when the *fideicommissum* failed she and her trustee in insolvency were entitled to the capital. The Court made no attempt to investigate the interests that could be created in English law under the umbrella of a trust. One could support this on the ground that the trust was mere machinery which did not affect the substantive Roman-Dutch interests created by the will. Or one could say that the sort of interests created by *fideicommissum* should be extended by analogy to trusts. Lastly one could argue that the trust was actually a type of *fideicommissum*.

Innes CJ chose the last option. According to him 'the English law of trusts forms, of course, no portion of our jurisprudence . . . but it does not follow that testamentary dispositions couched in the form of trusts cannot be given full effect in our own law'.[181] A trustee corresponded in many respects to the Roman-Dutch administrator, 'but a testamentary trust is in the phraseology of our law a *fideicommissum* and a testamentary trustee may be regarded as covered by the term fiduciary'.[182] In the same case Solomon JA pointed out that 'trusts are common in our law', and that it was impossible to eradicate the use of the expression 'trustee', but that it did not follow that the English law on the subject had been taken over.[183] The substantial point that both judges were making was that the interests conferred on beneficiaries under a trust in South Africa should not be construed as the equitable property rights of English law. It is generally thought that Innes CJ went too far in asserting that a trust *was* a sort of *fideicommissum* and was mistaken in thinking there had been *fideicommissa* in Roman and Roman-Dutch law in which the fiduciary's duty was merely to hold or administer the property for the fideicommissary. This was in fact rarely if ever the case.[184] The judge's treatment of the trust as a species of *fideicommissum* was criticized in two Appellate Division cases in 1955[185] and was finally disowned in 1984.[186] A fiduciary is, and a trustee is not, entitled as such to the income from the property he holds. What remains of the 1915 decision is that the interests which can be created under a trust are analogous to those which can be created by *fideicommissum*.

---

[181] Above, n. 132, at 499. [182] Ibid. [183] Ibid. 507.

[184] D. 36, 2, 36, 1 is cited as an example of an administrative *fideicommissum*. D. 36, 1, 48 (46) is a better one. But these texts are at best curiosities. The *fideicommissum* never developed a steady trust-like function.

[185] *Estate Watkins-Pitchford v. CIR* (n. 158), 460; *Greenberg v. Estate Greenberg* 1955 (3) SA 361 (A) 367–8.

[186] *Braun v. Blann & Botha* (n. 133), 866.

(b) Powers of appointment

In English law a right, called a power of appointment, is often given to a beneficiary or trustee (appointor) to select income or capital beneficiaries (appointees) and to decide in what proportions they are to be entitled. Even if the appointor is a beneficiary, this is generally done under the umbrella of a trust. However, it can be objected that to confer such a right by will is to delegate testamentary power, which is in general not permissible.[187] By way of exception, however, the Roman-Dutch law of *fideicommissa* allowed a fiduciary (say the testator's son) to be given power to select from a class of potential fideicommissaries (say the testators' grandchildren). In practice the Appellate Division has from 1914[188] onwards held that a right of disposal[189] or power of choosing[190] is consistent with Roman-Dutch law but the conditions in which such powers will be upheld have been progressively refined. In 1914 the Court said that there was 'no need to define the exact legal rights of the appointor or to say whether any single expression of our law would accurately describe them'.[191] In the next phase the courts, as in the case of life interests, interpreted powers of appointment as *fideicommissa*. As a 1938 case puts it, 'this so-called power of appointment can under our law only be created by way of *fideicommissum*'.[192] The power had therefore to be exercised expressly and the rule of English law by which a person may be given a power[193] to appoint himself beneficiary was rejected.[194] Moreover, if the appointor was given the ownership of the property or the capital of the fund the power was valid only if there was a gift over to another beneficiary in case the power of appointment was not exercised.[195] Otherwise the conferring of the power was superfluous (*nudum praeceptum*) because the beneficiary possessed it anyhow. This necessarily followed if a power of appointment could only take effect by way of *fideicommissum*, since a fiduciary is, in default of a fideicommissary, unrestricted owner of the property he holds.[196]

However, once it had been made clear that the rules of English law as such did not form part of South African law, the courts felt free to re-examine the identification of powers of appointment with *fideicommissa*. In 1955

---

[187] Voet (n. 41), 28, 5, 29; 36, 1, 29.

[188] *Robertson v. Robertson's Executors* (n. 179); *Westminster Bank v. Zinn* 1938 AD 57; *Estate Watkins-Pitchford v. CIR* (n. 158); *CIR v. Estate Sive* 1955 (1) SA 249 (A); *Estate Orpen v. Estate Atkinson* 1966 (4) SA 589 (A); *Braun v. Blann & Botha* (n. 133).

[189] *Estate Orpen v. Estate Atkinson* 1966 (4) SA 589 (A) 593.

[190] *Smit v. Du Toit* 1981 (3) SA 1249 (A) 1259.

[191] *Robertson v. Robertson's Executors* (n. 179).

[192] *Union Govt v. Olivier* 1916 AD 74, 89–90; *Westminster Bank v. Zinn* (n. 188), 65, 78.

[193] 'General power of appointment'.

[194] *Westminster Bank v. Zinn* (n. 188).

[195] *Castleman v. Stride's Executor* (1885) 4 SC 28; *Kock v. Estate Kock* 1946 CPD 27; *Re Estate Ansaldi* 1950 (4) SA 417 (C).

[196] Voet (n. 41), 36, 1, 29.

it was held that the appointor might have a usufructuary rather than a fiduciary interest in the trust property.[197] A 1988 case decided that, as for life interests, so for powers of appointment, the rules of *fideicommissa* could be extended by analogy to powers conferred on trustees to select from among beneficiaries. This decision was reached not because trustees are fiduciaries but because the extension seemed a salutary development of the law in modern conditions.[198] However, if the appointor is a trustee, the class from whom the selection is to be made or, in the case of a charitable trust, the object to be achieved must be clearly defined.[199]

(c) Inter vivos *trusts*

The courts had also to decide whether *inter vivos* trusts could be created according to the English rules, which allow them to be declared unilaterally and dispense with acceptance by the beneficiary, or by the Roman-Dutch principles of contracts which recognize that a contract can confer a right on third parties but, as was settled in 1911, require acceptance of the benefit by the third party to render it irrevocable.[200] The courts were not seriously tempted to uphold a unilateral declaration of trust,[201] but hesitated as to whether, if a trust was created by contract, the donor and the trustee together could (apart from the special case of an ante-nuptial contract[202]) revoke it before the beneficiary accepted the benefit conferred on him. In 1943 the Appellate Division inclined to the view that revocation was possible before acceptance[203] but the issue was not finally settled until 1956, when by a majority of three to two the contractual approach, which requires acceptance by the beneficiary, was adopted.[204] The minority feared that this approach would open the door to demands by the trustee for payment for giving his consent to revocation of the trust. However, demands of this sort can be made by any contracting party who is asked to agree to revocation.

(d) Separation of the trust estate

Another question confronting the courts was how far trust assets were to be treated as separate from the personal assets of the trustee (apart from the special case of unregistered trusts of land where it has been settled in 1908 that the trust beneficiary had only a concurrent claim in the trustee's insolvency.[205]) The courts did not give a clear answer but inclined to the

[197] *CIR v. Smollan's Estate* 1955 (3) SA 266 (A); *CIR v. Lukin's Estate* 1956 (1) SA 617 (A).
[198] *Braun v. Blann & Botha* (n. 133), 859, 866–7.
[199] *CIR v. Estate Sive* (n. 188); *Braun v. Blann & Botha* (n. 133).
[200] *Mutual Life Insurance Co of New York v. Hotz* 1911 AD 556.
[201] *Brebner v. Wessels* 1927 OPD 142; *Crookes v. Watson* 1956 (1) SA 277 (A) 298; Honoré/Cameron (n. 29), 49–50, 115–18.
[202] *Buissinne v. Mulder* (1835) 1 Menz 162.   [203] *CIR v. Estate Crewe* 1943 AD 656.
[204] *Crookes v. Watson* 1956 (1) SA 277 (A).
[205] *Lucas' Trustee v. Ismail and Amod* (n. 136); *Mahomed v. Estate Du Toit* 1957 (3) SA 555 (A); cf. *Lief v. Dettman* 1964 (2) SA 252 (A).

view, contrary to English law but more consistent with Roman-Dutch principles, that the trustee's personal and trust property formed a single unit and that the trust beneficiary had only a concurrent claim in the trustee's insolvency.[206] The legislature, however, intervened to separate various classes of trust property from the personal property of the trustees in question. In 1934 this was laid down for the trust accounts of legal practitioners[207] and in 1964 for trust property registered in the name of banks and other financial institutions in their capacity as trustee.[208] In 1988 the principle was extended to trusts generally, so that now trust property does 'not form part of the personal estate of the trustee except in so far as he as the trust beneficiary is entitled to the trust property'.[209]

The development by the legislature and the courts of trust law over eighty years has been remarkably consistent in its rejection of peripheral doctrines of English trust law unless satisfied that they are well adapted to South African conditions and fit conveniently into its legal structures.

3. New functions of trusts

In the second half of the twentieth century trusts have been put to new uses, particularly in connection with business[210] and investment. The advantage of running a business as a trust rather than a partnership is that the trust device ensures limited liability, since a trustee, unless guilty of a breach of trust, is liable only to the extent of the trust (i.e. business) assets.[211] This advantage does not exist in English law where the trustee's liability is unlimited.[212] The advantage of making the business a trust rather than a company under the Companies Act 1973[213] or a close corporation under the Close Corporations Act 1984 is that the degree of state control is less, for instance because annual accounts do not have to be submitted to public scrutiny. However, changes in the regulatory or tax legislation can easily erode these advantages.

The main development of the trust for investment purposes has been the unit trust, for which an Act of 1947[214] first provided a statutory framework, now replaced by an Act of 1981,[215] and to a lesser extent the participation bond, regulated by Acts of 1964 and 1981.[216] The object of the legislation

---

[206] *Ex parte Estate Kelly* 1942 OPD 265; *Incorporated Law Society, Transvaal v. Visse* 1958 (4) SA 115 (T); *Hansen v. CIR* 1956 (1) SA 398 (A) 405.

[207] Act 23 of 1934, s. 33(7).   [208] Act 56 of 1964, s. 4(7).

[209] Act 57 of 1988, s. 12.

[210] P. A. Olivier, *Trustreg en Praktyk* (1989), 119–35; Basil Wunsh, 'Trading and Business Trusts', (1986) 103 *SALJ* 561–82; Lynette Theron, *Die Besigheidstrust* (unpublished thesis, Rand Afrikaans University, 1990); *idem*, 'Regulering van die Besigheidstrust', (1991) 108 *SALJ* 277; Honoré/Cameron (n. 29), 10–11, 74–7, 140–1.

[211] Above, n. 97.   [212] Above, n. 98.   [213] Act 61 of 1973.

[214] Unit Trusts Control Act 18 of 1947.   [215] Unit Trusts Control Act 54 of 1981.

[216] Acts 48 of 1964 and 55 of 1981.

is to protect investors by ensuring that the assets in which they invest are held by financially sound undertakings. Trusts are indeed continually being employed for new purposes: to protect debenture holders; to manage pension funds, investments trusts, share purchase and management investment schemes; as elements in estate planning; and to sell off property in an orderly way (realization trusts). As new functions emerge the appropriate degree of state control over the new function has naturally to be thought out. Indeed the shifting balance between enterprise and supervision has given and continues to give the history of trust law a special dynamism.

Index

Index of Persons

South African lawyers

All lawyers who were born in, educated in, or who have worked in Southern Africa and who are referred to in the text of this book

Lawyers outside of South Africa

Only authorities that have been referred to on several occasions in the text